COMPUTER GRAPHICS

PROCEEDINGS

SIGGRAPH 2000
Conference Proceedings
July 23–28, 2000
Papers Chair: Kurt Akeley

A Publication of ACM SIGGRAPH

Sponsored by the ACM's Special
Interest Group on Computer
Graphics

Sample Citation Information
...Proceedings of SIGGRAPH 2000 (New Orleans, Louisiana, July 23–28, 2000). In *Computer Graphics* Proceedings, Annual Conference Series, 2000, ACM SIGGRAPH, pp. xx – yy.

Notice to Past Authors of ACM-Published Articles
ACM intends to create a complete electronic archive of all articles and/or other material previously published by ACM. If you have written a work that was previously published by ACM in any journal or conference proceedings prior to 1978, or any SIG newsletter at any time, and you do not want this work to appear in the ACM Digital Library, please inform us by e-mail at `"permissions@acm.org"`, stating the title of the work, the author(s), and where and when published. If you have any questions regarding this statement, please contact us by e-mail at `"permissions@acm.org"`.

Orders from members of ACM:

U.S.A. and Canada:
ACM Order Department
P.O. Box 12114
Church Street Station
New York, NY 10257
    Telephone: +1-800-342-6626
    Telephone: +1-212-626-0500
    Fax: +1-212-944-1318
    E-mail: `orders@acm.org`
    URL: `http://www.acm.org/`

All other countries:
ACM European Service Center
108 Cowley Road
Oxford OX4 1JF
United Kingdom
    Telephone: +44-1-865-382338
    Fax: +44-1-865-381338
    E-mail: `acm_europe@acm.org`

ACM Order Number: 428000
ACM ISBN: 1-58113-208-5
ACM ISSN: 1069-529X

Orders from nonmembers of ACM:

Addison-Wesley will pay postage and handling on orders accompanied by check. Credit card orders may be placed by mail or by calling the Addison-Wesley Order Department at the number above. Followup inquiries should be directed at the same number. Please include the Addison-Wesley ISBN with your order:
    A-W Softcover Proceedings and
    CD-ROM Package ISBN:
    0-201-48564-8

United States:
Addison-Wesley Publishing Company
Order Department
Jacob Way
Reading, MA 01867
    Telephone: +1-800-447-2226

Europe/Middle East:
Addison-Wesley Publishing Group
Concertgebouwplein 25
1071 LM Amsterdam
The Netherlands
    Telephone: +31-20-6717296
    Fax: +31-20-6645334

Germany/Austria/Switzerland:
Addison-Wesley Verlag Deutschland
GmbH
Hildachstraße 15d
Wachsbleiche 7-12
53111 Bonn
Germany
    Telephone: +49-228-98-515-0
    Fax: +49-228-98-515-99

United Kingdom/Africa:
Addison-Wesley Publishers Ltd.
Finchampstead Road
Wokingham, Berkshire RG11 2NZ
United Kingdom
    Telephone: +44-734-794000
    Fax: +44-734-794035

Asia:
Addison-Wesley Singapore Pte. Ltd.
15 Beach Road
#05-02/09/10 Beach Centre
Singapore 0718
    Telephone: +65-339-7503
    Fax: +65-339-9709

Japan:
Addison-Wesley Publishers Japan Ltd.
Nichibo Building
1-2-2 Sarugakucho
Chiyoda-ku, Tokyo 101
Japan
    Telephone: +81-33-2914581
    Fax: +81-33-2914592

Australia/New Zealand:
Addison-Wesley Publishers Pty. Ltd.
6 Byfield Street
North Ryde, N.S.W. 2113
Australia
    Telephone: +61-2-878-5411
    Fax: +61-2-878-5830

Latin America:
Addison-Wesley Iberoamericana S.A.
Boulevard de las Cataratas #3
Colonia Jardines del Pedregal
Delegacion Alvaro Obregon
01900 Mexico D.F.
    Telephone: +52-5-660-2695
    Fax: +52-5-660-4930

Canada:
Addison-Wesley Publishing (Canada) Ltd.
26 Prince Andrew Place
Don Mills, Ontario M3C 2T8 Canada
    Telephone: +1-416-447-5101
    Fax: +1-416-443-0948

Contents

Papers Sessions, Thursday, 27 July 2000

Papers Sessions, Friday, 28 July 2000

Papers Preface

These proceedings contain 59 papers, selected by peer review from 304 submissions from around the world. Their sequence matches the order of presentation at SIGGRAPH 2000, where papers with related themes were grouped into sessions of four papers each. These groupings and themes were determined after the paper selection process was completed, so the selected papers are simply those that were deemed to meet the high standards of SIGGRAPH publication. They represent much of the best work in the areas of graphics and interactive techniques for the calendar year 1999.

The SIGGRAPH papers selection process is the treasured heirloom of an entire community of graphics researchers. It is both rigorous and impartial, and its perception as such is central to the preeminence of SIGGRAPH in the fields of graphics and interactive techniques. It is a privilege to be trusted with the care of this process, and I have strived to deliver it intact to the SIGGRAPH 2001 papers chair. No process is perfect, though, so I, like my predecessors, have made a few small adjustments.

Most important among these was a renewed emphasis on as-is evaluation of submissions. Authors were strongly encouraged to submit in final format, and reviewers were instructed to accept only papers that could be published as submitted, with no changes required. (Authors of accepted papers were, however, instructed to respond to the criticisms of their reviewers.) Because the SIGGRAPH papers program is not refereed, and has always had only a single review cycle, unconditional acceptance is not new policy. But it is tempting to accept papers that, either incompletely or imperfectly, describe outstanding work. By eliminating this temptation, and by explicitly stating this in the Call for Participation, I hoped simultaneously to strengthen the perception of impartiality in the selection process and to discourage the submission of incomplete work. While metrics for evaluating this approach are imperfect, submissions for SIGGRAPH 2000 were down five percent from the previous year, after a long upward trend, and the fraction of submissions accepted returned to the long-term norm of one-in-five, after falling in recent years to one-in-six.

A less significant but related change was the dropping of all length limits on papers. Because papers were submitted in final format, the length of each paper was obvious to all concerned. Reviewers were instructed to evaluate the contributions of submissions in relation to their lengths, favoring shorter over longer. Papers were accepted at the lengths of their submissions, and additional pages were allowed in only a few cases, where response to reviewer suggestions demanded it. This approach may be seen as more impartial, and is in any event less stressful for the chair.

Thirty-four individuals, all selected as leaders in their respective disciplines, comprised this year's papers selection committee. Twelve members had no previous SIGGRAPH committee experience, and, in keeping with tradition, none of the remaining twenty-two was serving for a third consecutive term. Each committee member took primary responsibility for approximately nine submissions, and took secondary review responsibility for another nine. In addition to writing a full review of all eighteen papers, each member assigned each primary paper to at least three additional reviewers not on the committee. Thus over 1600 complete reviews were written by more than 500 reviewers, in addition to the committee members. While committee members knew the identities of the authors, these identities were hidden from the additional assigned reviewers.

The committee met for two full days on the first weekend in March in Colorado Springs, Colorado. One full day was spent identifying a few acceptances, many rejections, and approximately 100 submissions that required additional consideration. Subcommittees were formed for each such submission, and committee members worked into the night reviewing their newly-assigned papers. The second day was spent primarily in subcommittee, with regular full-committee sessions to consider subcommittee recommendations. All decisions were made by consensus in full committee, and no decision became final until the process was completed late on the second day. To insure open expression of opinion, committee members left the room during discussions that would present a conflict of interest, and subcommittees were provided private meeting areas during the second day. The identities of all reviewers were hidden from committee members with conflicts, with special attention paid to the privacy of the subcommittee meetings. Under these conditions, and with the understanding that no limit to the number of accepted papers was imposed, committee members reached consensus free of all considerations other than the merit of the papers in question.

The SIGGRAPH papers program is a huge effort, undertaken almost entirely by volunteers, and I am therefore in the debt of many people. Thanks first to the authors of the hundreds of submissions, the high quality of which is the foundation of the entire program. The efforts expended by the committee members were extraordinary, and I can't thank them enough for a job well done. And thanks also to the assigned reviewers, some of whom take on almost as many papers as the committee members, and all of whom contribute substantially to the quality of the result.

Following the lead of my predecessor, Alyn Rockwood, I convened an advisory board to assist me with day-to-day decisions and judgement calls. Eugene Fiume, Pat Hanrahan, Mark Segal, Alyn Rockwood, and Michael Cohen provided assistance and insight in this capacity. In addition, Eugene, Pat, and Alyn worked with me to make the primary and secondary assignments of papers to the committee members. Their broad and detailed knowledge of the strengths of the committee members was invaluable in this task. Again following Alyn's lead I selected Capstone, a contract organization with deep roots in the SIGGRAPH community, to support the papers program. Vicki Caulfield and Janet McAndless of Capstone promptly and accurately took care of details small and large, and always with a smile.

Stephen Spencer, SIGGRAPH Director for Publications, worked tirelessly with the authors of accepted papers to generate the complete proceedings that you hold in your hands. And Leona Caffey, of Smith Bucklin, provided additional guidance from the time that papers were accepted until the conference was over.

And finally my special thanks to my employer, Silicon Graphics, where I was fully supported throughout this process. During my 18 years at SGI it has been my privilege to work in an environment populated with extraordinarily bright, energetic, committed people. My impression of everyone involved with SIGGRAPH 2000, from conference committee members to contractors to those in the papers program, is the same. I could not give any higher praise.

Kurt Akeley
SIGGRAPH 2000 Papers Chair

2000 ACM SIGGRAPH Awards

Computer Graphics Achievement Award

David H. Salesin

ACM SIGGRAPH is pleased to present the first of this century's Computer Graphics Achievement Award to David Salesin for pioneering the field of non-photorealistic rendering and introducing it to the SIGGRAPH community. His work on computer generated pen and ink illustrations and subsequently computer-generated watercolors are considered landmarks in this emerging field. For the past six years his publications in this area have been extremely significant and influential.

David achieved this breadth and versatility with a broad educational background at institutions covering almost the entire field of computer graphics. As a computer science major, he graduated magna cum laude in 1983 from Brown University, having gotten his start in computer graphics by being an undergraduate researcher on projects such as electronic books and mathematical visualization. In 1991 he finished his Ph.D. in geometric modeling under the supervision of Leonidas Guibas at Stanford University. He then spent the year with photorealistic rendering at the Program of Computer Graphics at Cornell University. He has worked at the Digital Equipment Corporation Research Lab in Paris, at Pixar and Lucasfilm in the development of algorithms and film production, and has a wealth of experience far beyond his years.

This superb background has enabled him to be among the most prolific authors in the SIGGRAPH community. In the past decade he has already authored or co-authored twenty eight papers, including one year when he participated in a record number of eight papers (1996). This is a remarkable achievement considering the enormous competition for this prestigious conference. His breadth of interests are illustrated by his expertise in a wide range of topics from solid geometry modeling to physically-based simulations to cinematography, non-photorealistic rendering and his contributions to wavelets and other hierarchical methods, via his co-authored book.

His teaching and mentoring skills are also renowned. Recently he has received the University of Washington Distinguished Teaching Award and has received Young Investigator Awards from both the Office of Naval Research and the National Science Foundation. Because of his pioneering efforts in non-photorealistic re dering and his prolific contributions to the SIGGRAPH community, David is well suited to join the list of outstanding individuals who have received the Computer Graphics Achievement Award.

Previous Award Recipients

1999	Tony DeRose
1998	Michael F. Cohen
1997	Przemyslaw Prusinkiewicz
1996	Marc Levoy
1995	Kurt Akeley
1994	Kenneth E. Torrance
1993	Pat Hanrahan
1992	Henry Fuchs
1991	James T. Kajiya
1990	Richard Shoup and Alvy Ray Smith
1989	John Warnock
1988	Alan H. Barr
1987	Robert Cook
1986	Turner Whitted
1985	Loren Carpenter
1984	James H. Clark
1983	James F. Blinn

2000 ACM SIGGRAPH Awards

Outstanding Service Award

Tom DeFanti and Copper Giloth are each a recipient of this year's SIGGRAPH Outstanding Service Award. DeFanti has been an inspirational executive committee member and conference contributor, helping create many of the organizational activities and conference venues that we now take for granted. Giloth's dedication to her vocation, computer art, and to SIG-GRAPH, enabled her to launch the conference's first Art Show and grow it into an internationally acclaimed annual event. While DeFanti and Giloth are being honored separately, we acknowledge that they are also contemporaries. With enthusiasm and hard work, they supported and inspired one another over the years, and contributed to SIGGRAPH's international stature. We appreciate this opportunity to publicly thank them for their outstanding service to SIGGRAPH.

Thomas A. DeFanti

When asked what SIGGRAPH activities he was most proud of, DeFanti responded, in no particular order:
- The growth of SIGGRAPH conferences
- The quality of A/V at SIGGRAPH conferences
- The inclusion of women and artists
- The international stature of SIGGRAPH
- The SIGGRAPH Video Review
- The popularization of scientific visualization
- The proliferation of projection-based virtual reality
- Lifelong friendships

From SIGGRAPH's first conference in 1974, DeFanti championed video as a communications medium for science and art, started the annual Film and Video Show (which subsequently became the Electronic Theater and is now the Computer Animation Festival), helped architect the conference's outstanding audio/visual environment, and was founder (and still is editor-in-chief) of the SIG-GRAPH Video Review (SVR).

He served on the SIGGRAPH Executive Committee for 12 years. During his four-year tenure as Chair, DeFanti provided leadership as the organization and conference blossomed in quality and attendance. DeFanti built a sand

Copper Frances Giloth

When asked what SIGGRAPH activities she was most proud of, Giloth pointed to the design and implementation of the first SIGGRAPH 82 and 83 juried art shows and traveling art shows. Prior to 1982, there had been a few computer art exhibitions, some of international renown, but none that would match the size and scope of the shows that SIGGRAPH eventually launched. Art works from SIGGRAPH 83 traveled to France, Italy, Canada, Japan, and the US. The art show became more than a showcase for artists; it changed corporate culture. It showcased artists who could use technology, and use it in novel and unique ways that made them a vital force in the computer graphics industry.

Giloth contributed to the SIGGRAPH organization and conference in additional ways, volunteering for several years as a member of the A/V team and helping produce the SIGGRAPH Video Review (SVR). For several years she applied her conference A/V and organizational skills to SIGGRAPH's sister organization, SIGCHI, helping them achieve the same high standards people came to expect at SIGGRAPH's annual conference. She applied her knowledge of the SVR to co-produce the Interactive Index of all the SVR issues. Giloth also served as the

2000 ACM SIGGRAPH Awards

Outstanding Service Award

Thomas A. DeFanti

box and invited his scientific, engineering and art friends to play, providing encouragement and seed money for new, special projects. He elevated SIGGRAPH to international stature by cooperating with computer graphics organizations in Europe and Japan. In 1987 he co-edited the landmark Visualization in Scientific Computing publication. For SIGGRAPH 92, he co-created and introduced the projection-based CAVE™ automatic virtual environment to hordes of screaming fans. Most of all, DeFanti continues to inspire others, particularly the students of the Electronic Visualization Laboratory at the University of Illinois at Chicago, feeding new ideas and energy into the life blood that is SIGGRAPH.

DeFanti has a BA from Queens College and a PhD from The Ohio State University. He is co-director of the Electronic Visualization Laboratory at the University of Illinois at Chicago.

Copper Frances Giloth

organization's Special Projects chair for three years, evaluating proposals and providing seed money for worthwhile projects. And, for 10 years she was the Cover Editor of the SIGGRAPH newsletter, and worked with artists to select images that would reproduce well in black-and-white. Most of all, however, Giloth has been the Grande Dame of the art show, formally and informally helping to ensure its continued success over the years.

As with all volunteers, Giloth has found the time to be a participant as well as an organizer, and exhibited art, published videos in the SVR, and was a member of the winning team of the SIGGRAPH 94 College Bowl.

Giloth has a BFA from Boston University and an MFA in electronic visualization from the University of Illinois at Chicago. She is currently an Associate Professor of Art and the Director of Academic Computing at the University of Massachusetts at Amherst.

Previous Award Recipient

1998 Maxine D. Brown

Computer-Generated Pen-and-Ink Illustration of Trees

Oliver Deussen*   Thomas Strothotte

Faculty of Computer Science, University of Magdeburg, Germany

Abstract

We present a method for automatically rendering pen-and-ink illustrations of trees. A given 3-d tree model is illustrated by the tree skeleton and a visual representation of the foliage using abstract drawing primitives. Depth discontinuities are used to determine what parts of the primitives are to be drawn; a hybrid pixel-based and analytical algorithm allows us to deal efficiently with the complex geometric data. Using the proposed method we are able to generate illustrations with different drawing styles and levels of abstraction. The illustrations generated are spatial coherent, enabling us to create animations of sketched environments. Applications of our results are found in architecture, animation and landscaping.

CR Categories: I.3.3 [Picture/Image Generation]: Display algorithms— [I.3.7]: Three-Dimensional Graphics and Realism—Animation

Keywords: Biological Systems, Frame Buffer Tricks, Non-Realistic Rendering

1   Introduction

During the last years, a variety of techniques have been proposed to sketch and non-photorealistically render objects. Research in this area was driven by the realization that drawings are able to convey visual information in a different way than photorealistic images do [21]. This is one of the reasons why a large percentage of images in many books are drawings (cf. [22]).

While the proposed methods allow creating line drawings of many objects and in many different styles, the illustration of plants has so far been neglected. This is surprising because drawings of these objects are needed in areas like architecture and landscaping. In both cases early designs are preferentially visualized as abstract line drawings that often include many trees [18].

In this paper we propose a method for automatic pen-and-ink illustration of trees. The approach allows us to create a variety of illustration styles. The underlying models are realistic 3-d plant geometries generated with the xfrog modeling system proposed by Lintermann and Deussen [8], but any other surface-oriented plant model can also be used.

---

*Universitätsplatz 2, D-39106 Magdeburg, Germany, odeussen@acm.org
http://isgwww.cs.uni-magdeburg.de/~deussen

In comparison to the art-based illustration styles for trees invented by Kowalski et al. [7], we are more interested in visually representing specific plants than to create generic representations. Our aim is to provide the user with a transition from a tree illustration with a realistic plant-specific look to an abstract representation consisting of only a few strokes. This enables the user to select a global degree of abstraction while at the same time enabling the system to draw plants in the background with a higher abstraction level. In combination with different drawing styles, this helps to adapt the visual appearance of the plants to other objects and also, for instance, allows the user to focus the viewer's attention on a certain part of the scene.

Among the various plant types and their combinations, we focus on complex trees and bushes. Collections of these objects are most interesting in architecture and landscaping. Also both categories require abstract visual representations as it is impossible to draw all the geometry in detail.

1.1   Related Work

Related work in illustrating trees was done in the field of non-photorealistic rendering and also in botanical plant generation.

Probably the first article with illustrated plants was presented by Yessios [25]. In an architectural framework he used abstract plant symbols and combined them with stones and ground materials.

Alvy Ray Smith, one of the early authors dealing with fractals and formal plant descriptions created a "cartoon tree" with small disks representing bunches of leaves [19]. A similar representation with smaller disks was used by Reeves and Blau [14] to constitute their structured particle systems for rendering realistic trees. The idea of representing numerous botanical leaves by an abstract geometric primitive inspired us (like Kowalski et al. [7]) to work on pen-and-ink illustrations of trees.

A line drawing is usually created by combining a number of brush or pencil strokes. Researchers in non-photorealistic rendering resemble that process by using virtual brushes. Strassmann [20] proposed the "path-and-stroke" metaphor: a path is defined and a physically simulated brush is used to generate the stroke. Hsu et al. [6] extended the metaphor by using general objects like textures, images and recursively defined fractals that are drawn along a given path.

Salisbury et al. [16] described a method for directing the strokes in line drawings on the basis of vector fields. In their paper they also showed an interactively generated tree image. Winkenbach and Salesin [23, 24] presented a variety of methods for the automatic generation of pen-and-ink illustrations. In contrast to Strassmann and Hsu et al. they do not work with individual strokes but with artistically elaborate stroke textures.

Sasada [17] presented some tree sketches in an architectural environment. He used images of synthetic tree skeletons that were mapped onto view-facing polygons. The method of Aono and Kunii [1] was used to create the skeletons, the foliage was not visualized in their computer-generated trees.

Kowalski et al. [7] generated abstract sketches of trees by using geometric primitives like spheres for defining rough approximations of a tree's foliage. These primitives were rendered conventionally to achieve gray-scale images. In a second step the images were used to place graftals – small objects representing leaves or hair – on the surfaces by applying the "difference image algorithm" proposed earlier by Salisbury et at. [16]. Doing so it is possible to create sketched images of generic trees, bushes, and grass.

In our work we start from a different point. Our models are de-tailed tree models consisting of a tree skeleton and leaves. Our line drawings are the result of visually combining many drawing primitives instead of placing graftal objects on some large geometries. A drawback of our approach is that we potentially have to deal with more input data. The solution to this problem is to represent a tree at several levels of detail. This makes it possible to adapt the geometric representation to what should be presented on the screen: If a more detailed drawing is to be created, a more detailed geometric tree description is used.

The use of realistic tree models thus offers some major advantages: We can make use of existing tree libraries, our tree illustrations can be abstract but we are also able to draw a specific plant. If the scene is to be rendered photorealistically later, the visual representation does not differ much from its illustrated counterpart. Having access to the detailed 3-d data enables us also to animate the complex line drawings with sufficient spatial and temporal coherency. Another advantage is the correct, tree-like shadow generation of our models.

The main contribution of our work is an efficient way of generating the illustration of realistic plant models using abstract drawing primitives; furthermore, we present a "depth difference algorithm" to determine important silhouette lines, which allows us to generate different levels of visual abstraction.

The remainder of this paper is organized as follows: Section 2 reviews the artistic work on illustrating trees, in Section 3 our synthetic illustration algorithm is given. Section 4 shows results, and in Section 5 we give some conclusions.

2 Traditional Illustration of Trees

Among the various styles used by artists to render trees (for a large set of examples see [3]) one can distinguish between flat styles that solely represent the shape of a tree and others that also approximate natural light interaction (cf. [9]).

The tree skeleton is usually drawn up to the second branching level, primarily by silhouette lines and crosshatching on the stem surface. The shape of the foliage is either represented by an abstract outline or by a collection of many small objects which do not necessarily resemble natural leaves but instead represent the characteristics of the foliage. In addition, the outline is sometimes drawn by many small line segments or just a few strokes.

The visual appearance of the foliage can be divided into three areas. The top of the tree is usually in the direct light and is therefore visualized by only some details and its outline. In the half shadow, more details are drawn to achieve an appropriate gray level. In this area the outline of the leaves is often drawn in detail. The third area is the shaded part. The three areas are generally not found in a single illustration, often only the half shadow and the full shadow region is drawn. Sometimes the complete foliage is represented uniformly.

Artists use different methods to generate shadows on the foliage: in many styles more details are drawn and thick lines are used, sometimes with whole areas being drawn in black. Other styles add crosshatching to the foliage.

A method for the synthetic illustration of trees must propose solutions to several subproblems: First, the stem skeleton must be represented properly by silhouette lines and crosshatching. Second,

an abstract leaf representation must be found that enables the user to represent different types of leaves as well as different illustration styles. Third, drawing the leaves must be modulated by the three areas: the leaves in the light must be represented solely by the outline of the foliage, leaves in the half shadow should be drawn with detailed outline or additional crosshatching, and regions of deep shadow are to be added appropriately.

Tree I Tree II Tree III

Figure 1: Photorealistically rendered images of the synthetic sample trees: Tree I: complex tree; Tree II: young lime tree; Tree III: conifer.

3 Automated Illustration of Trees

The first step to create a tree illustration is to create a tree with a conventional tree modeling program. As mentioned above, we use the xfrog modeling system [5, 8] for that purpose. The final model – some of them are shown in Figure 1 – is preprocessed and two files are created.

In the first file, the geometry of the tree skeleton is stored. Like artists we only draw the trunk and branches up to the second order in most of our illustrations with higher order branches being removed.

The second file stores the leaves as particles each with a position and a normal vector. The normal vectors are obtained by using the normal vector of the original leaves. If too much data is generated for all the leaves – Tree I in Figure 1 has about 183,000 leaves – we reduce them in the modeling system by reducing the number of leaves at each twig. If this is still too much we position the particles at the branching positions of the highest-order twigs. In the case of Tree I we end up with 8,800 particles.

The illustrations are generated as follows: The trunk and branches are drawn by applying techniques known from non-photorealistic rendering. The foliage is rendered by representing each leaf by a drawing primitive – a disk or arbitrary polygon facing the viewer – and by applying the depth difference algorithm to determine which part of the primitive outlines are to be drawn. Shadows can be applied at this stage, vegetation on the ground can also be added and is processed the same way. The resulting drawings are then composed to constitute the final image.

3.1 Drawing the tree skeleton

The tree skeleton is an assembly of generalized cylinders each representing a branch. The surface is more or less smooth, which allows us to apply analytical silhouette algorithms such as the one proposed by Markosian et al. [10] or the hybrid solution of Rakar and Cohen[13] to generate the outline. The depth difference algorithm proposed below can also be applied (see Figure 2).

In addition, the skeleton is shaded conventionally to find dark regions. These regions are then crosshatched in the drawing. The "Difference Image Algorithm"[16] that places individual strokes according to the local gray tone of an image is one solution to this problem. For our purpose a simpler method is sufficient that works with a variant of the Floyd Steinberg method[4].

The algorithm places short strokes instead of pixels if the cumulated gray scale is above a given threshold. The area of the stroke is determined and the corresponding error value is subtracted from the neighboring pixel values. The direction of the strokes is either at random or affected by the normal vector of the stem geometry. A similar technique for directing strokes was already used in[10].

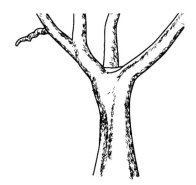

Figure 2: The trunk and main branches of Tree I are extracted and rendered by silhouette lines and cross hatching.

3.2 Drawing the foliage

The foliage of a tree differs by its very nature from all smooth surfaces and therefore must be handled separately. Several thousand individual surfaces must be combined visually into a shape or a set of strokes. In our first experiments, we placed special textures on the leaves of our realistic tree models that looked like strokes. This is a fast and simple method, but the generated images never appeared like drawings.

The observation that artists do not draw leaves correctly but try to represent their visual appearance led us to use abstract drawing primitives. Each leaf is represented by the outline of such a primitive, whereas its position is determined by the 3-d leaf position and the size is controlled by the user. A very simple drawing primitive is a view-facing disk. While other abstract drawing primitives are given below, we first describe the second ingredient of our approach, the depth difference algorithm, by using this primitive.

Depth differences

Depth differences are used to determine what part of each drawing primitive is to be drawn to constitute the foliage. Saito and Takahashi[15], two of the early authors in non-photorealistic rendering, used the depth-buffer to determine the outline of objects which were used to enhance photorealistic images. First and second order derivatives in the depth-buffer were additionally computed to find important lines on the surface of the objects.

While first and second order depth derivatives are helpful to find important lines on smooth surfaces, zero order derivatives are helpful for determining important lines in collections of isolated surfaces like assemblies of drawing primitives: The outline of a primitive is

drawn if the maximal depth difference of the surface to the neighboring surfaces is above a given threshold.

Instead of computing the differences analytically - which in the case of complex tree models is computationally expensive - we use the depth buffer for this purpose. The primitives are drawn as solids, the depth buffer is obtained, and for each pixel the depth difference is computed by comparing its depth value with all neighbor values. The maximal positive difference for each pixel is taken. This value indicates how far the pixel is in front of its neighboring pixels. It is stored in a separate buffer.

For interactive applications those pixels with a depth difference exeeding a given depth difference threshold are directly used to create a bitmap of the outlines. For printing purposes a vectorization is performed to obtain stroke paths (see Section 3.4).

It is well known that the values in the depth buffer have a non-linear characteristic. The depth z in the camera coordinate system or eye coordinates rsp. is determined from a depth value d ($d \in [0..1]$) by

$$z = \frac{\frac{z_1 z_0 (d_1 - d_0)}{z_1 - z_0}}{d - \frac{(z_1 + z_0)(d_1 - d_0)}{2(z_1 - z_0)} - \frac{(d_1 + d_0)}{2}} \qquad (1)$$

where d_0 and d_1 are minimal and maximal values represented in the depth buffer, and z_0 and z_1 the corresponding depth values of the near and far clipping plane in the camera projection (cf.[11]).

The depth differences can be computed for the depth values in eye coordinates to achieve linear differences or directly for the depth buffer values. In the second case depth differences for remote objects correspond to much larger differences in eye coordinates. In consequence the objects are represented by fewer lines.

To determine a depth difference threshold sufficient for the eye coordinates we compute the depth range of the tree and choose a percentage of this range, for example 10 percent. Analogously this is done with depth buffer values. The examples in this paper were rendered using depth buffer values directly by setting $d_0 = 0, d_1 = 65535, z_0 = 1$, and $z_1 = 11$. The depth difference in eye coordinates ($z_1 - z_0$) is approximately the one of real trees.

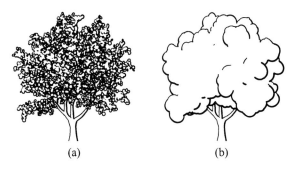

(a)   (b)

Figure 3: Tree I rendered with varying disk size and depth difference threshold: a) size=0.15, threshold=1000; b) size=0.7, threshold=2000.

Figure 3 shows two sketches of Tree I. In Figure 3(a) small disks are used and the threshold is low. This results in high detail and a good approximation of the real model. A more abstract rendering is achieved if disk size and threshold are enlarged (Figure 3(b)).

The threshold can be constant over the whole image or can be modulated by other buffers. In Figure 4(c) a shadow buffer was used to reduce the threshold in the shadow. The resulting image shows more detail in this area.

Abstract drawing primitives

Apart from disks, a number of drawing primitives can be used to represent the leaves. In Figure 4(a) a set of nine polygons was generated to represent leaves from different views. The normals of the given particles were used to interpolate the individual shapes of the leaves from the polygons. Using this interpolation scheme, a 3-d shape can be denoted without strictly adhering to perspective transformations.

If appropriate polygons are used, a representation similar to the graftals in [7] can be generated, but our interpolation method offers more freedom, allowing nearly all forms of leaves to be used.

The user is also able to decide to what extent the 3-d impression is generated: the leaves in Figure 4(b) are not drawn from the full range of views, instead a subset is used to generate a style between uniform shapes and the full 3-d impression. In Figure 4(c) the shape of the leaves is drawn only in the shadow region, additionally the linewidth is increased.

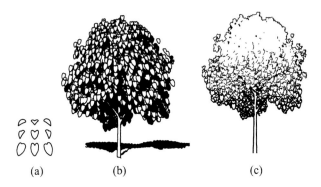

(a)   (b)   (c)

Figure 4: Two sketches of Tree II. a) The leaves are rendered using interpolated polygons from the nine given samples; b) Shadow is drawn in black, threshold=100. c) Threshold is set to 6,000, shadow is represented by detail.

3.3 Level-of-Abstraction

As mentioned above, the differences in the depth buffer have a non-linear characteristic. If they are used directly instead of re-projecting them into eye coordinates, the same tree that is drawn in the front with high detail will be sketched automatically by a few strokes if it is at the back.

The effect can be modulated by changing the z_1 to z_0 ratio of the perspective projection which is the basis for Equation (1). A small ratio causes a small non-linearity, a large ratio above 100:1 results in less depth resolution in the background and therefore in a small number of strokes.

This visual level-of-abstraction can be supported by scaling the primitive size for trees in the background. In [7] a formula for a scale factor r for the object size of graftals is suggested which uses a weighted average between a scaling d/s (d desired screen space, s current screen space of the object) that generates primitives of visual constant size and primitives that have a constant object size

$$r = w(d/s) + (1 - w) \qquad w \in [0..1].$$

In our case, we additionally allow w to be above one and in this case omit the second term. Now, the abstract drawing primitives appear larger in the background, which helps to achieve clear object shapes here.

In Figure 5 the process is shown. In the tree sequence of Figure 5(a) level-of-abstraction was done on the basis of depth differences only, in Figure 5(b) the size of the drawing primitives is doubled for the tree at the back.

3.4 Software Framework

The proposed method was designed to work in two environments. First, a fast method for interactive systems was needed. Second, high quality images should be produced for printouts, animations and architectural sketches. As a consequence the software works in stages that are partly omitted for the interactive process.

In the first step, depth differences have to be determined. In the interactive environment stem and foliage are rendered together, the depth buffer is obtained and all pixels above the given depth difference threshold are drawn in black. The resulting bitmap is directly used and blended with other geometries of the scene to constitute the final image.

For drawing purposes - and also for animations with high temporal coherency - the stem and the foliage are rendered separately, the images are combined by their depth buffer values to handle occlusion. For each image a separate depth difference threshold is used later.

For many styles shadows have to be introduced. We have to use a software implementation of shadows because volume shadows based on stencil buffering (cf. [11]) do not work for the huge number of isolated surfaces in the foliage. The result is stored in a separate shadow buffer. In the interactive case, shadows are omitted.

Now the threshold is applied and the pixels above the threshold are marked. As mentioned above, the threshold can be modulated by a shadow buffer, other G-buffers (cf. [15]) or by an arbitrary spatial function.

For generating high quality images, the bitmaps of the stem and the foliage are vectorized. We implemented two methods: The first algorithm determines vectors globally for the bitmaps by applying least square fitting [12]. The second algorithm adds an index buffer, a bitmap that stores at each pixel position the primitive identification as a color value.

For each depth value above the threshold, it is now possible to obtain the primitive number, therefore vectorization can be performed for each primitive separately. This results in a higher image quality, for instance closed primitive outlines can now easily be determined and represented by closed polygons. As a drawback, the method which is slow already needs even more time since the index buffer has to be rendered and processed additionally.

In both cases the polygons are drawn by spline interpolation, and line styles may be applied. As an example, line styles are responsible for the shading effect on the tree in Figure 3(b). Among varying the line width, which was done here, the styles may also affect the direction of the line or alter the endpoints.

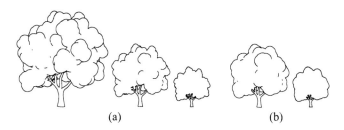

(a)   (b)

Figure 5: Tree I rendered for three different distances. a) Primitive sizes and threshold are constant for all distances. Visual abstraction is achieved automatically. b) Primitive sizes are enlarged up to the factor of two for the tree in the back.

4 Results

In Figure 6(a) and (b), Tree III is drawn using view-facing elliptic primitives of random orientation. After determining which part of each primitve has to be drawn, a small deformation was applied to each outline. This helps to achieve a more sketched drawing style.

In Figure 6(b) all visible outlines are drawn, and a threshold of 400 is used. The drawing of Figure 6(a) was created using a slight modification of the algorithm: Only the lower part of each ellipse is drawn when visible, the threshold having a value of 100. Rendering is performed in 10 seconds on our SGI Octane (Maximum Impact), the conifer consists of 13,200 particles.

The maple tree of Figure 6(c) consists of 16,200 particles which is far below the original model with 200,000 leaves. The parametrization of Figure 6(a) was used, threshold was set to 1,000.

Figure 6(d) was created similar to Figure 6(a). Only 2,300 particles are used, this causes nearly each ellipse to be visible, as a result a lot of semicircles appear. Figure 6(e) used drawing primitives in the form of real leaves, a very small threshold of 10 causes all visible outlines to be drawn.

The tree in Figure 6(f) consists of 90,000 particles, very small ellipses were used, shadow is added as black regions. The ground is represented by 23,000 elliptic primitives of larger size. Only the shadow is drawn, no primitive outlines are used. In this case rendering is performed in about one minute.

In the interactive version of the proposed algorithm it is possible to render three trees consisting of 20,000 primitives each and 25,000 ground particles with three frames per second on our SGI Onyx 2 at lower image quality. We hope to improve this in the future.

5 Conclusion and Future Work

We have presented a framework for rendering trees in pen-and-ink. The tree skeleton and the foliage are processed separately. The trunk and branches are represented by silhouette lines augmented by crosshatching in dark areas. The foliage is drawn by using abstract drawing primitives that represent leaves. Such primitives can be circles, ellipses or other polygons. An interpolation scheme allows us to adapt the form of the primitives to the normal vector of the particles that are used as input. Depth differences are used to determine what part of the primitives are drawn.

Our experiments reveal that it is possible to create various illustration styles with our approach, and they have opened several areas of future research:

- So far, shadows were introduced into the images by shadow buffers or by raising detail in shadow regions. As mentioned in Section 2 artists sometimes use crosshatching on the leaves to represent shadow. The hatching lines in this case must interact with the leaves. An intersection method as proposed in [2] can be applied here.

- To reduce the amount of geometric data, level-of-detail has to be applied to the tree models. Currently we work with some discrete representations that sometimes cause visual artifacts if representations are changed. A continuous level-of-detail algorithm for trees will improve performance while maintaining the visual quality.

- The primary goal of our paper was to provide pen-and-ink illustrations for architecture and landscaping. Another important application are cartoons. New styles and colored versions of our images need to be developed for that purpose.

References

[1] M. Aono and T. L. Kunii. Botanical tree image generation. *IEEE Computer Graphics and Applications*, 4(5):10–34, May 1984.

[2] O. Deussen, J. Hamel, A. Raab, S. Schlechtweg, and T. Strothotte. An illustration technique using hardware-based intersections and skeletons. In *Proceedings of Graphics Interface 99*, pages 175–182. Canadian Human-Computer Communications Society, 1999.

[3] L. Evans. *The New Complete Illustration Guide: The Ultimate Trace File for Architects, Designers, Artists, and Students*. Van Nostrand Reinhold Company, 1996.

[4] R. W. Floyd and L. Steinberg. An adaptive algorithm for spatial grey scale. *Proc. Soc. Inf. Display*, 17:75–77, 1976.

[5] Greenworks GbR. Home page of the xfrog modelling software. http://www.greenworks.de.

[6] S. Hsu and I. Lee. Drawing and animation using skeletal strokes. In *SIGGRAPH '94 Conference Proceedings*, pages 109–118. ACM SIGGRAPH, July 1994.

[7] M. Kowalski, L. Markosian, J. D. Northrup, L. Burdev, R. Barzel, L. Holden, and J. F. Hughes. Art-based rendering of fur, grass, and trees. In *SIGGRAPH '99 Conference Proceedings*. ACM SIGGRAPH, August 1999.

[8] B. Lintermann and O. Deussen. Interactive modeling of plants. *IEEE Computer Graphics and Applications*, 19(1):56–65, January/February 1999.

[9] F. Lohan. *The drawing handbook*. Contemporary Books, Chicago, 1993.

[10] L. Markosian, M. A. Kowalski, S. J. Trychin, L. D. Bourdev, D. Goldstein, and J. F. Hughes. Real-time nonphotorealistic rendering. In T. Whitted, editor, *SIGGRAPH '97 Conference Proceedings*, pages 415–420. ACM SIGGRAPH, 1997.

[11] T. McReynolds and D. Blyth. Advanced graphics programming techniques using OpenGL. SIGGRAPH '98 Course Notes, ACM SIGGRAPH, 1998.

[12] J. R. Parker. Extracting vectors from raster images. *Computers & Graphics*, 12(1):75–79, 1988.

[13] R. Raskar and M. Cohen. Image precision silhouette edges. In *1999 ACM Symposium on Interactive 3D Graphics*, pages 135–140. ACM SIGGRAPH, April 1999.

[14] W. T. Reeves and R. Blau. Approximate and probabilistic algorithms for shading and rendering structured particle systems. In *Computer Graphics (SIGGRAPH '85 Proceedings)*, volume 19, pages 313–322, July 1985.

[15] T. Saito and T. Takahashi. Comprehensive rendering of 3-d shapes. In *Computer Graphics (Proc. SIGGRAPH 90)*, volume 24(4), pages 197–206. ACM SIGGRAPH, 1990.

[16] M. Salisbury, M. Wong, J. F. Hughes, and D. Salesin. Orientable textures for image-based pen-and-ink illustration. In *SIGGRAPH '97 Conference Proceedings*. ACM SIGGRAPH, 1997.

[17] T. T. Sasada. Drawing natural scenery by computer graphics. *Computer Aided Design*, 19(4):212–218, 1987.

[18] J. Schumann, T. Strothotte, A. Raab, and S. Laser. Assessing the effect of non-photorealistic images in computer-aided design. In *ACM Human Factors in Computing Systems, SIGCHI '96*, pages 35–41, April 13-15 1996.

[19] A. R. Smith. Plants, fractals and formal languages. *Computer Graphics (SIGGRAPH '84 Proceedings)*, 18(3):1–10, July 1984.

[20] S. Strassmann. Hairy brushes. *Computer Graphics (SIGGRAPH '86 Proceedings)*, 20(3):225–232, 1986.

[21] C. Strothotte and T. Strothotte. *Seeing Between the Pixels: Pictures in Interactive Systems*. Springer-Verlag, Berlin-Heidelberg-New York, 1997.

[22] T. Strothotte, B. Preim, A. Raab, J. Schumann, and D. R. Forsey. How to render frames and influence people. *Computer Graphics Forum*, 13(3):455–466, 1994.

[23] G. Winkenbach and D. Salesin. Computer-generated pen-and-ink illustration. In *SIGGRAPH '94 Conference Proceedings*, pages 91–100. ACM SIGGRAPH, 1994.

[24] G. Winkenbach and D. Salesin. Rendering parametric surfaces in pen and ink. In *SIGGRAPH '96 Conference Proceedings*, pages 469–476. ACM SIGGRAPH, 1996.

[25] C. I. Yessios. Computer drafting of stones, wood, plant and ground materials. *Computer Graphics (Proceedings of SIGGRAPH 79)*, 13(3):190–198, 1979.

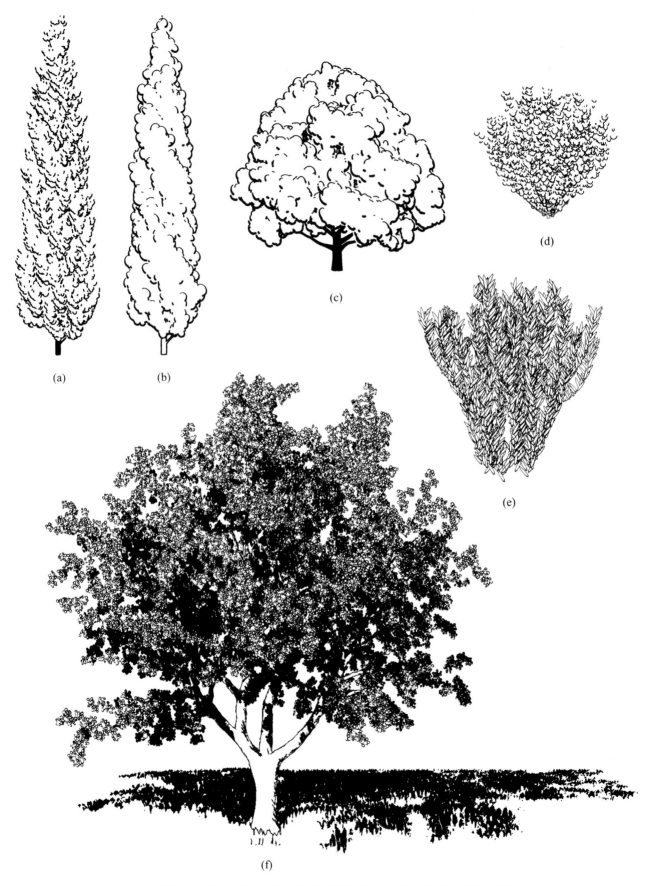

Figure 6: Several trees shaded with different styles. See Section 4 for details.

A Simple, Efficient Method
for Realistic Animation of Clouds

Yoshinori Dobashi[*]   Kazufumi Kaneda[**]   Hideo Yamashita[**]   Tsuyoshi Okita[*]   Tomoyuki Nishita[***]

[*]Hiroshima City University   [**]Hiroshima University   [***]University of Tokyo
[*]{doba, okita}@im.hiroshima-cu.ac.jp   [**]{kin, yama}@eml.hiroshima-u.ac.jp   [***]nis@is.s.u-tokyo.ac.jp

Abstract

This paper proposes a simple and computationally inexpensive method for animation of clouds. The cloud evolution is simulated using cellular automaton that simplifies the dynamics of cloud formation. The dynamics are expressed by several simple transition rules and their complex motion can be simulated with a small amount of computation. Realistic images are then created using one of the standard graphics APIs, OpenGL. This makes it possible to utilize graphics hardware, resulting in fast image generation. The proposed method can realize the realistic motion of clouds, shadows cast on the ground, and shafts of light through clouds.

CR Categories: I.3.1 [Computer Graphics]: Hardware Architecture; I.3.6 [Computer Graphics:] Methodology and Techniques; I.3.7 [Computer Graphics]: Three-Dimensional Graphics and Realism; I.6.3 [Simulation and Modeling]: Applications;

Additional Keywords: Animation, Atmospheric Effects, Rendering, Graphics Hardware, Volume Rendering.

1. INTRODUCTION

Clouds play an important role when making images for flight simulators or outdoor scenes. Their color and shapes change depending on the position of the sun and the observer. This means that the density distribution of clouds should be defined in three-dimensional space to create realistic images. Therefore, a lot of methods have been developed to display clouds [33, 10, 5, 14, 19, 30, 25]. Using these methods, extremely realistic images can be generated. Their main purpose is, however, to create images of static clouds. Fascinating animations of clouds with changing their shapes and color are often used, however, in movies,

commercial films and so on. They are often created by filming them in advance and replaying the film quickly. Since generating such realistic animations by computer graphics is useful, a lot of methods have been developed [13, 29, 6, 31, 7, 22, 9, 15, 8, 32].

This paper proposes a new method for realistic animation of clouds. Our aim is to develop a simple method that can create realistic animation as quickly as possible, preferably in real-time. We propose an efficient simulation method and a hardware-accelerated rendering method. In particular, the method is suitable for animation of cumulus-like clouds in landscape scale. Our method has the following features.

- Our simulation method creates realistic cloud motion with a small amount of computation. It uses cellular automaton that can simulate the motion just by simple Boolean operations.

- Our rendering method realizes a fast computation of photo-realistic images. It can quickly calculate shadows and shafts of light through clouds, as well as cloud color, by making the most of graphics hardware.

A straightforward approach to creating realistic cloud motion is to simulate the physical phenomena. That, however, is impractical since it is computationally expensive. Therefore, a simple and efficient method is required that maintains the visually convincing result. As one such methods, Nagel et al. extremely simplified the cloud dynamics using cellular automaton [21]. The method can simulate cloud formation by simple transition rules. Unfortunately, the method is not sufficient for our purpose since their aim is not to create realistic animation. So, we extend their work and propose a new method to realize realistic cloud evolution.

Furthermore, we propose a method for generating realistic images including cloud shadows and shafts of light using the standard graphics API, OpenGL. This results in fast image generation since we can make use of graphics hardware. Our rendering method can display the following three effects: 1) cloud color taking into account the single scattering of light, 2) shadows of clouds cast on the ground, 3) shafts of light through clouds. Most of the previous methods render these effects by using ray-tracing, one of the most time-consuming methods. To overcome this problem, we propose a hardware-accelerated rendering method based on OpenGL. Using the proposed method, a photo-realistic image can be generated within one minute on a standard PC.

Our method is not sufficient if the user needs physically exact cloud motion, since it is one of the numerical models that simplifies the physical phenomena. Our method is suitable for users who want a simple, easy-to-use, and computationally inexpensive method that can create visually convincing results. Furthermore, the proposed method makes as much use of graphics hardware as possible. Since graphics hardware is becoming faster and faster, we believe our method is one of the promising techniques that will realize real-time animation in the near future.

*3-4-1, Ozukahigashi, Asaminami-ku, Hiroshima, 731-3194 Japan
(Dobashi's current address: Hokkaido University, Faculty of Engineering, Kita 13, Nishi 8, Kita-ku, Sapporo 060-8628 Japan)
**1-4-1, Kagamiyama, Higashi-hiroshima, 739-8527 Japan
***7-3-1, Hongo, Bunkyo-ku, Tokyo, 113-0033 Japan

2. PREVIOUS WORK

In this section, previous works are briefly reviewed. Methods related to the simulation and methods to rendering are separately reviewed.

SIMULATION: In computer graphics, there are two categories to simulate the gaseous motion like clouds. One is to simulate the physical process of fluid dynamics [13, 29, 31, 9, 32]. The other is a heuristic approach [10, 6, 7, 22, 15, 8]. Most of the methods in the former category need a large amount of computation time. Stam, however, developed a fast simulation method by simplifying fluid dynamics [32]. He demonstrated a real-time animation of smoke on a high-end workstation. However, since our purpose is to simulate clouds covering a large area in the sky using a standard PC, it is sill time-consuming. Furthermore, the phase transition effects from vapor to water should be incorporated to simulate cloud formation. To our knowledge, the method developed by Kajiya et al. is the only one to include the phenomena [13]. It is, however, very complex and time-consuming. Controlling cloud shapes is also difficult by using the methods in this category.

On the other hand, the latter approaches, such as procedural modeling, are computationally inexpensive and much easier to implement. The disadvantage in these methods, however, is that the user has to search parameters by trial and error to create realistic animation. Creating realistic-looking motion using them does not seem to be an easy task.

Our method lies in an intermediate position between these two categories. The method reflects the physical formation process of clouds in part, and it is computationally more efficient and easier to implement than are the previous physical simulation methods. Our method can create more realistic cloudy scenes than the physical based methods do. Controlling the shapes and their motion to create realistic animation is an easy task using our method. Dobashi et al. tried to develop such a method using cellular automaton [3]. Unnatural animation is created by that, however, since the formation and extinction of clouds are frequently repeated. The method in this paper is an extension to their method.

RENDERING: One of the simplest ways to display clouds is to use mapping techniques, such as the method developed by Gardner [10]. In order to display photo-realistic images, however, it is desirable to use the physical model, taking into account scattering/absorption due to particles. Many such methods have therefore been developed [13,5, 14, 28, 29, 19, 31, 4, 32]. Some of them take into account multiple scattering of light [13, 19, 31, 25]. Additionally, Nishita et al. take into account the effect of skylight on the cloud color [25]. Multiple scattering and skylight are important for realistic image synthesis but is time-consuming. Our method approximates them as a constant ambient term. One of the major approaches to rendering the volume density similarly to clouds is to use 3D textures. Stam used 3D hardware texture mapping to display gases [32]. With the help of the high-end graphical workstation, the method can generate realistic images in real-time by combining 3D textures and advecting cloud textures developed by Max et al. [18]. Unfortunately, his method is not sufficient for our purpose since the method does not include the atmospheric effects such as shafts of light, one of the essential factors in generating realistic images of outdoor scenes. Our method can handle these effects. Although using 3D textures is simpler and efficient, the 3D texture mapping hardware is still expensive and not universally available as are 2D textures. Since one of our objectives is to create realistic animation on a standard

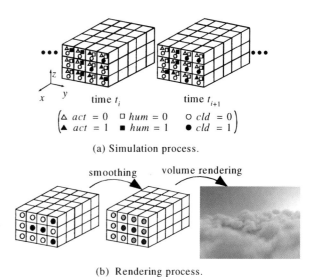

$$\begin{pmatrix} \triangle \ act = 0 & \square \ hum = 0 & \circ \ cld = 0 \\ \blacktriangle \ act = 1 & \blacksquare \ hum = 1 & \bullet \ cld = 1 \end{pmatrix}$$

(a) Simulation process.

(b) Rendering process.

Figure 1: Overview of our method.

PC, we propose a method using 2D textures. The idea of the method is of course applicable to 3D textures.

There are also a lot of methods for generating shafts of light [23, 11, 12, 16, 17, 27, 24]; most of them use the ray-tracing algorithm and require dozens of minutes. Although Nishita and Nakamae developed a faster method using a scanline accumulation buffer [24], it still requires several minutes. We propose a much faster method using hardware color blending and texture mapping functions. To our knowledge, no other methods are available making use of graphics hardware to render shafts of light.

3. BASIC IDEA

Fig. 1 shows an overview of our method. Our method consists of two processes, simulation and rendering. As shown in Fig. 1(a), the simulation space is divided into voxels. The voxels correspond to cells used in the cellular automaton. At each cell, three logical variables, vapor/humidity (*hum*), clouds (*cld*), and phase transition (or activation) factors (*act*) are assigned. The state of each variable is either 0 or 1. Cloud evolution is simulated by applying simple transition rules at each time step. The transition rules represent formation, extinction, and advection by winds. Since the state is either 0 or 1, the rules can be expressed by Boolean operations. Therefore, each variable can be stored in one bit to save the memory cost and the simulation process is accelerated by using bit field manipulation functions.

Images are generated in the rendering process by making use of the simulation results (Fig. 1(b)). As described above, what we can obtain from the simulation is no more than *there are clouds* (*cld* = 1) or, *there are not-clouds* (*cld* = 0) at each voxel. Therefore, a density at each point is calculated by smoothing the binary distribution as shown in Fig. 1(b). The clouds are then rendered using volume rendering techniques. The rendering process consists of two steps. The first step calculates the intensity of light reaching the center of each voxel. Cloud shadows are also calculated in this step. The shadows are obtained as a texture. Then, in the second step, images are generated. Clouds are rendered by using a splatting method [1]. To render shafts of light, we consider multi spherical shells with their center at the viewpoint (see Fig. 7). The shells are then drawn from back to front using the hardware alpha-blending function. Shafts of light are rendered by mapping the shadow texture on the shells (see section 5.2).

4. SIMULATION METHOD

We extend the following four points to Nagel's method [21]:

- Extinction of clouds
- Wind effects
- Speeding up of the simulation
- Controlling cloud motion

Details of the above extensions are explained in sections 4.2 through 4.5 after the brief description of Nagel's method in the next section.

4.1 Growth Simulation

In this section, Nagel's method to simulate the cloud formation process is described briefly. The physical processes of cloud formation are outlined as follows. Clouds are formed as a bubble of air is heated by underlying terrain heat, causing the bubble to become less dense, and to rise into regions of lower pressure in which the bubble expands. Expansion cools the bubble, increasing the relative humidity inside the bubble. The phenomenon called phase transition then occurs, that is, water vapor in the bubble becomes water droplets, or clouds. Nagel et al. used a cellular automaton [35] to simulate these processes in the following way.

For simplicity, the simulation space is aligned parallel to xyz axes and the number of cells is assumed to be $n_x \times n_y \times n_z$. As mentioned before, three logical variables, hum, act, and cld, are assigned at each cell (see Fig. 1(a)). Each represents vapor, phase transition factor, and clouds. The state of each variable is either 0 or 1. $hum=1$ means there is enough vapor to form clouds, $act=1$ means the phase transition from vapor to water (clouds) is ready to occur, and $cld=1$ means there are clouds. In the following, $A \wedge B$ and $A \vee B$ indicate conjunction and disjunctinon between A and B, respectively, and $\neg A$ indicates negation of A. Their transition rules are given as follows.

$$hum(i,j,k,t_{i+1}) = hum(i,j,k,t_i) \wedge \neg act(i,j,k,t_i) , \quad (1)$$

$$cld(i,j,k,t_{i+1}) = cld(i,j,k,t_i) \vee act(i,j,k,t_i) , \quad (2)$$

$$act(i,j,k,t_{i+1}) = \neg act(i,j,k,t_i) \wedge hum(i,j,k,t_i) \wedge f_{act}(i,j,k) , \quad (3)$$

where $f_{act}(i,j,k)$ is a Boolean function and its value is calculated by the status of act around the cell. The following function is used by taking into account the fact that clouds grow upward and horizontally.

$$
\begin{aligned}
f_{act}(i,j,k) = & \; act(i+1,j,k,t_i) \vee act(i,j+1,k,t_i) \\
& \vee act(i,j,k+1,t_i) \vee act(i-1,j,k,t_i) \vee act(i,j-1,k,t_i) \\
& \vee act(i,j,k-1,t_i) \vee act(i-2,j,k,t_i) \vee act(i+2,j,k,t_i) \\
& \vee act(i,j-2,k,t_i) \vee act(i,j+2,k,t_i) \vee act(i,j,k-2,t_i).
\end{aligned}
\quad (4)
$$

Of course, there are variations of the above function. We have tried some of them and we couldn't see significant differences of the simulation. So, we use the function in the original paper. The rules are summarized in Fig. 2. As shown in the top column of Fig. 2, act becomes 1 if hum is 1 and the state of act of one of the shaded cells around the center cell (i, j, k) is 1. Then, hum becomes 0 as shown in the middle. Finally, as shown in the bottom of Fig. 2, cld becomes 1. As a boundary condition, their states are assumed to be 0 outside the simulation space. Beginning from initial random status (all 3 status are set randomly), cloud growth is simulated by updating the state of each variable using Eqs. 1 through 4. As for the initialization, hum and act are

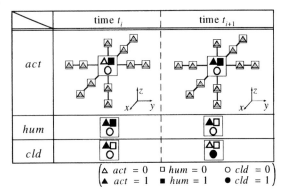

Figure 2: Basic transition rules.

determined randomly and cld is set to zero. For more details, please refer to [21].

4.2 Cloud Extinction

One of the disadvantages of Nagel's method is that cloud extinction never occurs since cld, after it has become 1, remains 1 forever. Dobashi et al. introduced a new state variable to solve this problem [3]. In that method, however, formation and extinction are repeated frequently, resulting in unnatural animation. In the real world, cloud extinction is caused by gradual transition of water droplets to vapor. Our method simulates the cloud extinction as follows. First, the animator specifies cloud extinction probability, p_{ext}. Next, at each cell whose cld is 1, a random number, rnd ($0 \leq rnd \leq 1$), is generated and cld is changed to 0 if $rnd < p_{ext}$. By changing the probability at each cell at different times, the animator can specify regions where cloud extinction occurs frequently. Although this realizes the cloud extinction, there remains another problem. Clouds are never generated after the extinction at the cell. To solve this, vapor (hum) and phase transition factors (act) are supplied at specified time intervals. Similar to extinction, vapor probability, p_{hum}, and phase transition probability, p_{act}, are used to set them randomly. That is, hum is changed to 1 if $rnd < p_{hum}$ and act is changed to 1 if $rnd < p_{act}$. Cloud motion can be controlled by controlling the probabilities, p_{hum}, p_{act}, and p_{ext} at each cell at each time step. The methods described in this section are summarized by the following three transition rules.

$$cld(i,j,k,t_{i+1}) = cld(i,j,k,t_i) \wedge IS(rnd > p_{ext}(i,j,k,t_i)), \quad (5)$$

$$hum(i,j,k,t_{i+1}) = hum(i,j,k,t_i) \vee IS(rnd < p_{hum}(i,j,k,t_i)), \quad (6)$$

$$act(i,j,k,t_{i+1}) = act(i,j,k,t_i) \vee IS(rnd < p_{act}(i,j,k,t_i)), \quad (7)$$

where rnd is a uniform random number, $IS(e)$ is a Boolean function that returns 1 if the expression e is true, otherwise returns 0.

4.3 Advection by Wind

We can observe clouds moving in one direction, blown by winds. New transition rules are introduced to include the wind effect. The idea is simply to shift all the variables toward the wind direction. We assume, for simplicity, the wind blows toward the direction of x-axis. Other cases can be handled by rotating the simulation space according to the wind direction. Furthermore, it is well known that the wind velocity is different depending on the height from the ground. The wind velocity, $v(z_k)$, is therefore specified as a function of z-coordinate of each cell (i,j,k). To implement the wind effect in the context of the cellular automaton, the function,

$v(z_k)$, is assumed to return integer values. The transition rules are as follows.

$$hum(i,j,k,t_{i+1}) = \begin{cases} hum(i-v(z_k),j,k,t_i), & i-v(z_k) > 0 \\ 0, & \text{otherwise} \end{cases}, \quad (8)$$

$$cld(i,j,k,t_{i+1}) = \begin{cases} cld(i-v(z_k),j,k,t_i), & i-v(z_k) > 0 \\ 0, & \text{otherwise} \end{cases}, \quad (9)$$

$$act(i,j,k,t_{i+1}) = \begin{cases} act(i-v(z_k),j,k,t_i), & i-v(z_k) > 0 \\ 0, & \text{otherwise} \end{cases}, \quad (10)$$

In this paper, the velocity function $v(z_k)$ is specified as a piecewise linear function.

4.4 Fast Simulation Using Bit Field Manipulation Functions

Each variable can be stored in one bit since its state is either 0 or 1. This means that simulations with large numbers of cells can be executed in a small amount of memory. The computation time is also reduced because of the following reasons. Let us assume all the variables are stored in an array of unsigned integers. Let m be the bit length of the unsigned integer variable. By making use of bit field manipulation functions of higher level language, such as C language, transitions of m cells can be computed at the same time. This realizes fast simulation. Most difficulties in implementing this idea lie in transition rules concerning cloud extinction, expressed by Eqs. 5 through 7, since random numbers have to be generated at each cell, i.e., each bit field. This may result in increasing the computation time. We used a look-up table that stores random bit sequences to save the computational cost. See Appendix A for more details.

4.5 Controlling Cloud Motion Using Ellipsoids

As mentioned in section 4.2, the animator can design the cloud motion by controlling vapor probability, phase transition probability, and cloud extinction probability. Ellipsoids are used to do this in this paper. When wet air parcels move upward and reach the height of the dew point, clouds are gradually formed. Ellipsoids are used to simulate the air parcels. The vapor probability and phase transition probability are assumed to be higher at their centers than at their edges. Inversely, the cloud extinction probability is assumed to be lower at the center since the extinction hardly ever occurs at the center of the air parcel. Ellipsoids also move in the direction of the wind. By controlling ellipsoid parameters, such as sizes and positions, different kinds of clouds can be simulated. The animator specifies the regions for ellipsoids to be generated. In our experiment, even the ellipsoids generated using uniform random numbers result in a realistic animation as shown in section 6.

5. RENDERIN METHOD

Methods for generating realistic images are proposed in this section. First, the density distribution of clouds is calculated by making use of the results of the simulation. Images are then rendered using OpenGL. Details of the methods are described in the following sections.

5.1 Continuous Density Distribution Calculation

The density distribution of clouds in the real world is continuous from 0 to 1. The distribution obtained from the simulation,

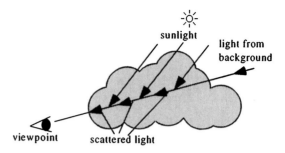

Figure 3: Calculation of cloud color.

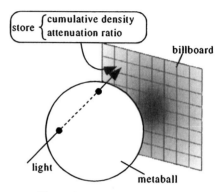

Figure 4: Billboard and its texture.

however, has only two values, that is, 0 or 1. Therefore, the proposed method calculates continuous distribution by smoothing the binary distribution, or two-valued distribution. First, the density, $q(i,j,k,t_i)$, is calculated at each cell (i,j,k) at each time step t_i using the following equation.

$$q(i,j,k,t_i) = \frac{1}{(2t_0+1)(2k_0+1)(2j_0+1)(2i_0+1)} \sum_{t'=-t_0}^{t_0}$$

$$\sum_{k'=-k_0}^{k_0} \sum_{j'=-j_0}^{j_0} \sum_{i'=-i_0}^{i_0} w(i',j',k',t')cld(i+i',j+j',k+k',t_i+t'), \quad (11)$$

where w is a weighting function and i_0, j_0, k_0, t_0 are sizes for the smoothing. As expressed by Eq. 11, we include time as well as space for the smoothing since the distribution is discrete in space and time. The density at an arbitrary point, $\mathbf{x}$, is then obtained as a weighted sum of a simple basis function, f. Gaussians are often used for the basis function [29, 31, 34]. In this paper, however, we use a field function of metaballs proposed by Wyvill et al [36]. The reason for this is as follows. A metaball has a parameter, an effective radius, which represents its size. This means that it is much easier to specify the domain of influence than Gaussians that have an infinite domain. Furthermore, the shape of Wyvill's field function is very similar to the Gaussians [36]. As a result, the density at point $\mathbf{x}$ is given by the following equation.

$$\rho(\mathbf{x},t_i) = \sum_{i,j,k \in \Omega(\mathbf{x},R)}^{N} q(i,j,k,t_i)f(|\mathbf{x}-\mathbf{x}_{i,j,k}|), \quad (12)$$

where R is the effective radius, $\Omega(\mathbf{x},R)$ is a set of cells those centers are within the distance R from the point $\mathbf{x}$, N is the number of elements of $\Omega(\mathbf{x},R)$, and $\mathbf{x}_{i,j,k}$ is the coordinate corresponding to the center of the cell (i,j,k). For the field function, f, see Appendix B. As shown in Eq. 12, the continuous density distribution is expressed by a set of metaballs. The user specifies the effective

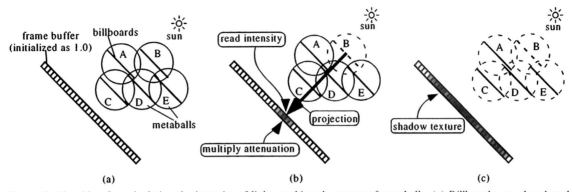

Figure 5: Algorithm for calculating the intensity of light reaching the center of metaballs. (a) Billboards are placed at the centers of metaballs and sorted based on their distances from the sun. The frame buffer is initialized as 1.0. (b) Billboards are projected onto the image plane. The colors in the frame buffer are multiplied by attenuation stored in billboard textures. (c) Shadow texture is obtained in the frame buffer. Each element stores the attenuation of light passing through clouds.

radius, R. The time step does not correspond to animation frames. Therefore, the density $\rho(\mathbf{x},t)$ at time t that corresponds to each animation frame is calculated by the linear interpolation of densities, $\rho(\mathbf{x},t_k)$ and $\rho(\mathbf{x},t_{k+1})$, where $t_k < t < t_{k+1}$.

5.2 Hardware-accelerated Rendering Using OpenGL

This section describes methods for displaying clouds as well as shafts of light using graphics hardware. Note that the algorithm is illustrated by a pseudo-code in appendix C.

5.2.1 Rendering Clouds

Rendering of clouds is based on the splatting algorithm using billboards. Details of the splatting method are well described in [34, 1, 20]. Therefore, let us omit the details. The basic idea for applying it to cloud display is described here.

Fig. 3 shows the idea of calculating the color of clouds taking into account the single scattering of light. First, the sum of the scattered light reaching from the sun on the viewing ray is calculated. The attenuated light reaching from behind the clouds is also calculated. The light reaching the viewpoint is the sum of those two. Therefore, the color of a voxel depends on the scattered color of the sun, the transmitted color of the sky, and the attenuation due to cloud particles. Calculation of cloud color using splatting is as follows. First, as shown in Fig. 4, textures for billboards are precalculated. Each element of the texture stores the attenuation ratio and cumulative density of the light passing through the metaball (see Fig. 4). Since the attenuation is not proportional to it, the texture has to be prepared for all meatballs when their center densities are different. However, this requires a large amount of memory. So, the density is discretized into n_q levels and n_q textures are prepared. In this paper, n_q is 64. The texture corresponding to the nearest density of each metaball is mapped onto the corresponding billboard. An image is calculated in two steps using the texture-mapped billboards. In the first step, the intensity of the light is calculated reaching from the sun at each metaball. The shadows of the clouds are also calculated in this step. In the second step, the image viewed from the viewpoint is generated. The two steps are as follows.

Fig. 5 shows the idea of the first step. The basic idea is to calculate an image viewed from the sun direction to obtain the intensity of light reaching each metaball. First, the viewpoint is placed at the sun position and the parallel projection is assumed. The frame buffer is initialized as 1.0. Then the billboards are placed at the center of each metaball with their normals oriented

to the sun direction as shown in Fig. 5(a). Next, attenuation ratio between the center of each metaball and the sun is calculated. For example, the attenuation ratio between the metaball C and the sun is obtained by multiplying the attenuation ratio of metaballs A, B, and D (see Fig. 5(a)). To do this for all metaballs, the billboards are sorted in ascending order using the distance from the sun (the order is B-E-A-D-C in Fig. 5). Then, beginning from metaball B, they are projected onto the image plane. The values in the frame buffer are multiplied by their attenuation ratios that are stored in the billboard texture (Fig. 5(b)). This can be easily done by using blending functions of OpenGL. Then the pixel value corresponding to the center of the metaball is read from the frame buffer. The value obtained is the attenuation ratio between the sun and the metaball. The color of the metaball is obtained by multiplying the pixel value by the sunlight color. These processes are repeated for all metaballs. After all the metaballs are processed, the image in the frame buffer stores the attenuation ratio of the sunlight passing through the clouds (Fig. 5(c)). The image is stored as a light map texture [1] to cast shadows on the ground.

In the second step, the image is generated by using the color of

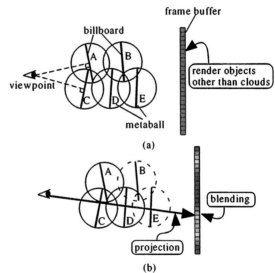

Figure 6: Algorithm for generating images. (a) Billboards are oriented to the viewpoint and sorted based on their distances from the viewpoint. (b) Billboards are projected onto the image plane. The colors in the frame buffer are attenuated and blended with the colors in the billborad textures.

the metaball obtained in the first step. First, all the objects except clouds are rendered. Next, as shown in Fig. 6(a), the billboards are faced perpendicularly to the viewpoint and sorted in descending order based on distances from the viewpoint (the order is E-B-D-A-C). Then they are projected onto the image plane in back-to-front order (Fig. 6(b)). The color in the frame buffer is blended with that of the billboard texture. The blending process is the same as the one used in the splatting method (see [1]). That is, the colors in the frame buffer are multiplied by the attenuation ratio of the billboard texture and then the colors in the texture are added. The process is repeated for all metaballs.

5.2.2 Rendering Shafts of Light

Fig. 7 shows the idea of calculating the shafts of light. Shafts of light are caused by particles in the atmosphere. The sunlight passing through gaps in clouds is scattered by the particles at P in Fig. 7. The scattered light, I_s, reaching the viewpoint is recognized as shafts of light. The scattering/absorption due to the atmospheric particles must therefore be taken into account. The intensity of light reaching the viewpoint is obtained by the following equation.

$$I = I_c \beta(T) + \int_0^T \gamma(s) I_s(s) \beta(s) ds , \qquad (13)$$

where I_c is the cloud color, $\beta(s)$ is the attenuation ratio from the viewpoint to P due to atmospheric particles, $\gamma(s)$ is the attenuation ratio due to cloud particles from the sun to P, and $I_s(s)$ is the intensity of the light scattered at P due to atmospheric particles. The first term in the right hand side of Eq. 13 indicates the attenuation ratio of the intensity of light from clouds. The second term is related directly to the shafts of light. Preetham et al. take into account the scattering of sky light as well as the sunlight to render the aerial perspective [26]. In this paper, however, we ignore the scattering of sky light since it has little effect on shafts of light. We also assume that the density of the atmospheric particles decreases exponentially to the height from the ground. Under these assumptions, the attenuation ratio, $\beta(s)$, and the scattered light, $I_s(s)$, can be calculated analytically based on the positions of the viewpoint and P [14]. Furthermore, we assume the shafts of light are only visible under the cloud bottom, z_c. That is, the attenuation due to clouds, $\gamma(s)$, is 1.0 if $z_p > z_c$, where z_p is the z coordinate of P. In this case, $\gamma(s)$ is the attenuation ratio of the sunlight passing through the clouds. This means it has been stored in the shadow texture obtained in the first step described in the previous section. The shafts of light are rendered by calculating Eq. 13 as follows.

Eq. 13 is discretized as the following equation.

$$I = I_c \beta(T) + \sum_{k=0}^{n_s} \gamma(k\Delta s) I_s(k\Delta s) \beta(k\Delta s) \Delta s , \qquad (14)$$

where n_s and Δs are the number of samples and the sampling interval for the integral in Eq. 13, respectively. The attenuation, $\beta(T)$, in the first term is calculated analytically by the positions of the viewpoint and each metaball. The color of each metaball is then attenuated by multiplying it. To calculate the second term, spherical shells are considered as shown in Fig. 7. Their centers are placed at viewpoint and their radii are determined so that the intervals of shells coincide to Δs. The shells are approximated by a set of polygons to render them using OpenGL. Polygons outside the viewing pyramid are discarded. Next, the intensity of the light scattered at each vertex and the attenuation ratio of the path between the viewpoint and the vertex are calculated. Then $I_s(k\Delta s)\beta(k\Delta s) \Delta s$ is stored as the colors of vertices of all the polygons in the viewing pyramid. Finally, the second term is

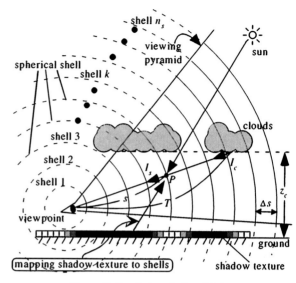

Figure 7: Rendering shafts of light.

computed by rendering the shells with OpenGL's additive blending function. To render the shafts of light, the colors of the polygons have to be multiplied by attenuation ratio due to clouds, $\gamma(s)$. This can be easily achieved just by mapping the shadow texture onto the polygons using OpenGL's texture mapping function (see Fig. 7). The function can map the texture, multiplying the polygon's color by the values stored in the shadow texture. Since we have assumed $\gamma(s)$ is 1 above the cloud bottom, z_c, only the polygons under the cloud bottom need this mapping process.

The second step in the previous section has to be modified to render the shafts of light together with clouds. Since both of the billboards and the shells are transparent objects, they have to be rendered in back-to-front order. The procedure is as follows.

1. Calculate the colors of vertices of the polygons of the shells in the viewing pyramid.

2. Repeat the following steps for $k = n_s, n_s -1, ..., 1$.

    2.1 Render the shell k with additive blending function. Map the shadow texture for polygons under the cloud bottom.

    2.2 Render billboards for displaying clouds between the shell k-1 and the shell k.

6. RESULTS

We have made an animation to demonstrate the usefulness of our method. Figs. 8 through 11 show sequences of images from the animation.

Figs. 8 and 9 show the simulation of cloud formation. The number of cells is 256x128x20. The memory for store the binary distribution is 80 KB. In Fig. 8, clouds are formed above the mountains. Ellipsoids described in section 4.5 are randomly generated. Probabilities for vapor, phase transition and extinction are set to 0.1, 0.001, and 0.1, respectively, at the centers of ellipsoids. Images at every 50 steps are shown. The viewpoint is placed above clouds. Fig. 9 shows clouds formed around the mountain. In this example, ellipsoids are manually placed around the top of the mountain as an initial state. Vapor probability, phase transition probability, and extinction probability are the same as those of Fig. 8 although they are forced to be 0 inside the mountain. These examples show the formation of clouds taking into account obstacles.

Figs. 10 and 11 show the effect of shafts of light. The cloud evolution is simulated on 256x256x20 cells. The memory for store the binary distribution is 160 KB. Fig. 10 shows examples in daytime, and Fig. 11 is in the evening. The color of the sky is calculated by using the method proposed by Dobashi et al. [2]. In Fig. 10, shadows on the ground and mountains are also visible. The number of the spherical shells to calculate shafts of light is 40. As shown in these examples, the shafts of light have a strong visual impact to enhance the reality. In particular, the cloud color turns red in the evening and this results in a fascinating animation when combined with their movement.

The calculation was done on Intergraph TDZ 2000 GX1 (PentiumIII 500MHz Dual). In Figs. 8 and 9, the computation time for the simulation takes 0.3 seconds per one time step on average. In Figs. 10 and 11, the simulation takes 0.5 seconds per one time step. Images are rendered using the same machine. The image sizes are 640x480. The computation time for each image in Fig. 8 was less than 10 seconds. For Fig. 9, it took about 20 seconds. For images in Figs. 10 and 11, the computation time ranged from 20 to 30 seconds. These results indicate that the proposed method realizes the interactive simulation and fast generation of realistic images.

7. CONCLUSION

In this paper, we have proposed a realistic animation method for clouds. The cloud motion is simulated using the cellular automation. Realistic images including the shadows and the shafts of light are generated using OpenGL. Our method has the following advantages.

(1) Simulation of the cloud evolution requires only a small amount of computation since it is executed by Boolean operations.

(2) The memory requirement of the simulation is also small.

(3) Images can be rendered quickly by making use of graphics hardware.

(4) Shadows of clouds and shafts of light can also be rendered.

There remain a few things to be done in the future. First, the simulation should take into account the effects of terrain under clouds. In this case, the wind no longer blows in one direction; hence, our simulation method must be capable of handling multiple wind directions, or velocity fields. For faster image generation, our rendering method should include the idea of the level of detail. One possible approach is to represent the voxels hierarchically and to use coarser voxels in the distant regions from the viewer. This could reduce the computation time of the splatting process since the number of metaballs could be decreased.

APPENDIX

A. Implementation of Transition Rules

Let us assume the simulation space is $n_x \times n_y \times n_z = (m \times n) \times n_y \times n_z$ for simplicity. n is the bit length and m is an integer value.

The necessary size of an array to store state variables is $m \times n_y \times n_z$. Let us denote the arrays for hum, act, cld at time step t_i as $h[m][n_y][n_z][t_i]$, $a[m][n_y][n_z][t_i]$, $c[m][n_y][n_z][t_i]$, respectively. Rules expressed by Eqs. 1 and 2 can be executed in a straightforward way:

$$h[i][j][k][t_{i+1}]=h[i][j][k][t_i] \wedge \neg a[i][j][k][t_i], \quad (A.1)$$

$$c[i][j][k][t_{i+1}] = c[i][j][k][t_i] \vee a[i][j][k][t_i], \quad (A.2)$$
$$(i=0, ..., m; j=0, ..., n_y; k=0, ..., n_z).$$

For the rule of Eq. 3, arrays that store bit patterns of act shifted in one and two bit are prepared. Let us denote them as a_right1, a_right2, a_left1, a_left2, respectively. Then Eq. 3 is calculated by the following equation.

$$a[i][j][k][t_{i+1}] = \neg a[i][j][k][t_i] \wedge h[i][j][k][t_i] \wedge$$

$$(a\_left1[i][j][k] \vee a\_left2[i][j][k] \vee a\_right1[i][j][k] \vee$$
$$a\_right2[i][j][k] \vee a[i][j+1][k][t_i] \vee a[i][j+2][k][t_i] \vee$$
$$a[i][j-1][k][t_i] \vee a[i][j-2][k][t_i] \vee a[i][j][k+1][t_i] \vee$$
$$a[i][j][k-1][t_i] \vee a[i][j][k-2][t_i]), \quad (A.3)$$
$$(i=0, ..., s; j=0, ..., n_y; k=0, ..., n_z).$$

To execute the rules of Eqs. 5 throught 7, n_t bit-sequences are prepared by setting each bit to 0 or 1 using random numbers that obey the probability i/n_p $(i=0,..,n_p)$. The sequences are stored in the look-up table, p[i][j] $(i=0,...,n_p; j=1,...,n_t)$. Using the table, the rules are executed as follows:

$$c[i][j][k][t_{i+1}]= c[i][j][k][t_i] \wedge p[int(p_{ext} \times n_p)][int(rnd \times n_t)], \quad (A.4)$$
$$h[i][j][k][t_{i+1}]= c[i][j][k][t_i] \wedge p[int(p_{hum} \times n_p)][int(rnd \times n_t)], (A.5)$$
$$a[i][j][k][t_{i+1}]= c[i][j][k][t_i] \wedge p[int(p_{act} \times n_p)][int(rnd \times n_t)], \quad (A.6)$$
where $int(x)$ indicates integer parts of x.

B. Field Function of Metaball as Basis Function

The field function proposed by Wyvill et al. is used [36]. The function is given by:

$$h(r) = \begin{cases} -\frac{4}{9}a^6 + \frac{17}{9}a^4 - \frac{22}{9}a^2 + 1, & (r \leq R) \\ 0, & (r > R) \end{cases}, \quad (B.1)$$

where $a = r/R$, r is the distance from the center of a metaball to a calculation point, and R the effective radius of the metaball. To use the function as basis function, we normalize it by its total density. That is, the basis function is given by $f = h(r)/c$, where c is the normalizing factor. c is given by the following equation.

$$c = 4\pi \int_0^R h(r)dr = \frac{748}{405}\pi R . \quad (B.2)$$

C. Rendering Algorithm

Pseudo-code for the rendering clouds including the shafts of light is given here. In each element of the billboard texture, RGB components store the cumulative density and A component stores the attenuation ratio of the light passing through the metaball.

PROCEDURE DisplayImage()
Place the camera at the sun position.
Set the parallel projection.
Clear screen with RGBA = (1.0, 1.0, 1.0, 1.0).
ShadeClouds()
Place the camera at the viewpoint.
Set the perspective projection.
Clear screen with background color.
RenderObject() /* Rendering objects except clouds */
RenderClouds()
END PROCEDURE

PROCEDURE ShadeClouds()
Sort metaballs in ascending order from the sun.
glDisable(GL_DEPTH_TEST)
glBlendFunc(GL_ZERO, GL_SRC_ALPHA)
glEnable(GL_BLEND)
FOR k = each metaball **DO**
  Place the billboard at the center of metaball k.

Rotate the billboard so that its normal is oriented to the sun.
Set the billboard color as RGBA = (1.0, 1.0, 1.0, 1.0).
Map the billboard texture with GL_MODULATE.
Render the billboard.
Read the pixel value corresponding to the center of metaball k.
Multiply the pixel value by the sunlight color.
Store the color into an array C[k] as the color of the billboard.
END FOR
Store the image (T) in the frame buffer as a light map texture.
END PROCEDURE

PROCEDURE RenderClouds()
Sort metaballs in descending order from the viewpoint.
Store distances between metaballls and the viewpoint in an array D.
glDisable(GL_DEPTH_TEST)
glEnable(GL_BLEND)
k = number of shells
WHILE D[0] < distance to shell k **DO**
RenderShell(k)
$k = k - 1$
END WHILE
glBlendFunc(GL_ONE, GL_SRC_ALPHA)
FOR n = each metaball **DO**
IF D[n] < distance to shell k **DO**
Render shell(k)
$k = k - 1$
glBlendFunc(GL_ONE, GL_SRC_ALPHA)
END IF
Place the billboard at the center of the corresponding metaball n.
Rotate the billboard so that its normal is oriented to the viewpoint.
Set the billboard color as C[n].
Map the billboard texture.
Render the billboard with the blending function.
END FOR
WHILE $k > 0$ **DO**
RenderShell(k)
$k = k - 1$
END WHILE
END PROCEDURE

PROCEDURE RenderShell(k)
Calculate colors of vertices of shell k.
Map the light map texture T with GL_MODULATE.
Render shell k.
glBlendFunc(GL_ONE, GL_ONE)
END PROCEDURE

REFERENCES

[1] D. Blythe, "Advanced Graphics Programming Techniques Using OpenGL," *Course Note #29 of SIGGRAPH 99*, 1999.

[2] Y. Dobashi, T. Nishita, K. Kaneda, H. Yamashita, "A Fast Display Method of Sky Color Using Basis Functions," *The Journal of Visualization and Computer Graphics*, Vol. 8, No. 2, 1997, pp. 115-127.

[1] Y. Dobashi, T. Nishita, T. Okita, "Animation of Clouds Using Cellular Automaton," *Proc. of Computer Graphics and Imaging'98*, 1998, pp. 251-256.

[2] Y. Dobashi, T. Nishita, H. Yamashita, T. Okita, "Using Metaballs to Modeling and Animate Clouds from Satellite Images," *The Visual Computer*, Vol. 15, No. 9, 1998, pp. 471-482.

[3] D. S. Ebert, R. E. Parent, "Rendering and Animation of Gaseous Phenomena by Combining Fast Volume and Scanline A-Buffer Techniques," *Computer Graphics*, Vol. 24 No. 4, 1990, pp. 357-366.

[4] D. S. Ebert, W. E. Carlson, R. E. Parent, "Solid Spaces and Inverse Particle Systems for Controlling the Animation of Gases and Fluids," *The Visual Computer*, 10, 1990, pp. 471-483.

[5] D. S. Ebert, "Volumetric Modeling with Implicit Functions: A Cloud is Born," *Visual Proc. of SIGGRAPH'97*, 1997, pp. 147.

[6] D. S. Ebert, "Simulating Nature: From Theory to Application," *Course Note #26 of SIGGRAPH 99*, 1999, pp. 5.1-5.52.

[7] N. Foster, D. Metaxas, "Modeling the Motion of a Hot, Turbulent Gas," *Proc. of SIGGRAPH'97*, 1997, pp. 181-188.

[8] G.Y. Gardner, "Visual Simulation of Clouds," *Computer Graphics*, Vol.19, No. 3, 1985, pp. 279-303.

[9] M. Inakage, "Volume Tracing of Atmospheric Environments," *The Visual Computer*, 7, 1991, pp. 104-113.

[10] H. W. Jansen, P. H. Christensen, "Efficient Simulation of Light Transport in Scenes with Participating Media using Photon-Maps," *Proc. of SIGGRAPH'98*, 1998, pp. 311-320.

[11] J. T. Kajiya, B. P. V. Herzen, "Ray Tracing Volume Densities," *Computer Graphics*, 1984, Vol. 18, No. 3, pp. 165-174.

[12] K. Kaneda, T. Okamoto, E. Nakamae, T. Nishita, "Photorealistic Image Synthesis for Outdoor Scenery under Various Atmospheric Conditions," *The Visual Computer*, 7(5&6), 1991, pp. 247-258.

[13] T. Kikuchi, K. Muraoka, and N. Chiba, "Visual Simulation of Cumulonimbus Clouds," *The Journal of The Institute of Image Electronics and Electronics Engineers of Japan*, Vol. 27, No. 4, 1998, pp. 317-326 (in Japanese).

[14] N. Max, "Light Diffusion through Clouds and Haze," *Graphics and Image Processing*, Vol. 13, No. 3, 1986, pp. 280-292.

[15] N. Max, "Atmospheric Illumination and Shadows," *Computer Graphics*, Vol. 20, No. 4, 1986, pp. 117-124.

[16] N. Max, R. Crawfis, D. Williams, "Visualizing Wind Velocities by Advecting Cloud Textures," *Proc. of Visualization'92*, 1992, pp. 179-183.

[17] N. Max, "Efficient Light Propagation for Multiple Anisotropic Volume Scattering," *Proc. of the Fifth Eurographics Workshop on Rendering*, 1994, pp. 87-104.

[18] K. Meuller, N. Shareef, J. Huang, R. Crawfis, "Hight-Quality Splatting on Rectilinear Grids with Efficient Culling of Occluded Voxels," *IEEE Trans. on Visualization and Computer Graphics*, Vol. 5, No. 2, 1999, pp. 116-134.

[19] K. Nagel, E. Raschke, "Self-Organizing Criticality in Cloud Formation?," *Phisica A*, 182, 1992, pp. 519-531.

[20] F. Neyret, "Qualitative Simulation of Convective Clouds Formation and Evolution," *Proc of Eurographics Computer Animation and Simulation Workshop'97*, 1997, pp. 113-124.

[21] T. Nishita, Y. Miyawaki, E. Nakamae, "A Shading Model for Atmospheric Scattering Considering Distribution of Light Sources," *Computer Graphics*, Vol. 21, No. 4, 1987, pp. 303-310.

[22] T. Nishita, E. Nakamae, "Method of Displaying Optical Effects within Water using Accumulation Buffer," *Proc. of SIGGRAPH'94*, 1994, pp. 373-379.

[23] T. Nishita, Y. Dobashi, E. Nakamae, "Display of Clouds Taking into Account Multiple Anisotropic Scattering and Sky Light," *Proc. of SIGGRAPH'96*, 1996, pp. 379-386.

[24] A. J. Preetham, P. Shirley, B. Smits, "A Practical Analytic Model for Daylight," *Proc. of SIGGRAPH'99*, 1999, pp. 91-100.

[25] H. E. Rushmeier, K. E. Torrance, "The Zonal Method for Calculating Light Intensities in The Presence of a Participating Medium," *Computer Graphics*, Vol. 21, No. 4, 1987, pp. 293-302.

[26] G. Sakas, M. Gerth, "Sampling and Anti-Aliasing of Discrete 3-D Volume Density Textures," *Proc. of EUROGRAPHICS'91*, 1991, pp. 87-102.

[27] J. Stam, E. Fiume, "Turbulent Wind Fields for Gaseous Phenomena," *Proc. of SIGGRAPH'93*, 1993, pp. 369-376.

[28] J. Stam, "Stochastic Rendering of Density Fields," *Proc. of Graphics Interface'94*, 1994, pp. 51-58.

[29] J. Stam, E. Fiume, "Dipicting Fire and Other Gaseous Phenomena Using Diffusion Processes," *Proc. of SIGGRAPH'95*, 1995, pp. 129-136.

[30] J. Stam, "Stable Fluids," *Proc. of SIGGRAPH'99*, 1999, pp. 121-128.

[31] R. Voss, "Fourier Synthesis of Gaussian Fractals: $1/f$ noises, landscapes, and flakes," *SIGGRAPH'83: Tutorial on State of the Art Image Synthesis*, 10, 1983.

[32] L. Westover, "Footprint Evaluation for Volume Rendering," *Computer Graphics*, Vol. 24, No. 4, 1990, pp. 367-376.

[33] S. Wolfram, "Cellular automata as models of complexity," *Nature*, Vol. 311, No. 4, 1984, pp. 419-424.

[34] G. Wyvill, A. Trotman, "Ray-Tracing Soft Objects," *Proc. of CG International*, 1990, pp. 439-475.

(a) $t_i = 0$ (b) $t_i = 50$ (c) $t_i = 100$ (d) $t_i = 200$

Figure 8: Simulation of cloud formation.

(a) $t_i = 0$ (b) $t_i = 200$

(c) $t_i = 400$ (d) $t_i = 600$

Figure 9: Cloud formation around mountains.

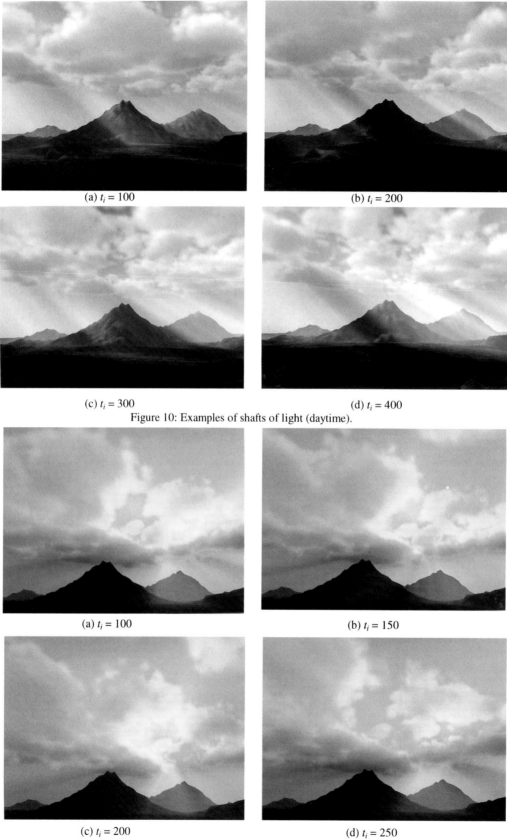

(a) $t_i = 100$

(b) $t_i = 200$

(c) $t_i = 300$

(d) $t_i = 400$

Figure 10: Examples of shafts of light (daytime).

(a) $t_i = 100$

(b) $t_i = 150$

(c) $t_i = 200$

(d) $t_i = 250$

Figure 11: Examples of shafts of light (evening).

Animating Explosions

Gary D. Yngve   James F. O'Brien   Jessica K. Hodgins

GVU Center and College of Computing
Georgia Institute of Technology

Abstract

In this paper, we introduce techniques for animating explosions and their effects. The primary effect of an explosion is a disturbance that causes a shock wave to propagate through the surrounding medium. This disturbance determines the behavior of nearly all other secondary effects seen in explosions. We simulate the propagation of an explosion through the surrounding air using a computational fluid dynamics model based on the equations for compressible, viscous flow. To model the numerically stable formation of shocks along blast wave fronts, we employ an integration method that can handle steep pressure gradients without introducing inappropriate damping. The system includes two-way coupling between solid objects and surrounding fluid. Using this technique, we can generate a variety of effects including shaped explosive charges, a projectile propelled from a chamber by an explosion, and objects damaged by a blast. With appropriate rendering techniques, our explosion model can be used to create such visual effects as fireballs, dust clouds, and the refraction of light caused by a blast wave.

CR Categories: I.3.5 [Computer Graphics]: Computational Geometry and Object Modeling—Physically based modeling; I.3.7 [Computer Graphics]: Three-Dimensional Graphics and Realism—Animation; I.6.8 [Simulation and Modeling]: Types of Simulation—Animation

Keywords: Animation, Atmospheric Effects, Computational Fluid Dynamics, Natural Phenomena, Physically Based Animation

1 Introduction

Explosions are among the most dramatic phenomena in nature. A sudden burst of energy from a mechanical, chemical, or nuclear source causes a pressure wave to propagate outward through the air. The blast wave "shocks up," creating a nearly discontinuous jump in pressure, density, and temperature along the wave front. The wave is substantially denser than the surrounding fluid, allowing it to travel supersonically and to cause a noticeable refraction of light. The air at the shock front compresses, turning mechanical energy into

College of Computing, Georgia Institute of Technology, Atlanta, GA 30332. gyngve@acm.org, job@acm.org, jkh@cc.gatech.edu.

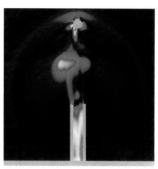

Figure 1: An image of a projectile propelled from a chamber by an explosion. On the right is a cross-section of the three-dimensional fluid volume using a colormap where hotter colors indicate higher densities.

heat. The waves reflect, diffract, and merge, allowing them to exhibit a wide range of behavior.

An explosion causes a variety of visual effects in addition to the light refraction by the blast wave. An initial chemical or nuclear reaction often causes a blinding flash of light. Dust clouds are created as the blast wave races across the ground, and massive objects are moved, deformed, or fractured. Hot gases and smoke form a rising fireball that can trigger further combustion or other explosions and scorch surrounding objects.

We present a physically based model of an explosion and show how it can be used to simulate many of these effects. We model the explosion post-detonation as compressible, viscous flow and solve the flow equations with an integration method that handles the extreme shocks and supersonic velocities inherent in explosions. We cannot capture many of the visual effects of an explosion in a complex setting if we rely only on an analytical model of the blast wave; a fluid dynamics model of the air is necessary to capture these effects. The system includes a two-way coupling between dynamic objects and fluid that allows the explosions to move objects. Figure 1 illustrates this phenomenon with a projectile propelled from a chamber. We also use the pressure wave generated by the explosion to fracture and deform objects. The user can simulate arbitrarily complex scenarios by positioning polygonal meshes to represent explosions and objects. The user controls the scale and visual qualities of the explosion with a few physically motivated parameters.

Our fluid model of an explosion simulates many phenomena of blast waves that existing graphics techniques do not capture. Figure 2 shows a cross-section of pressures for a three-dimensional explosion near a wall. The initial disturbance in the first image interacts with the surrounding fluid and causes a pressure wave to propagate through the medium. In the second image, the blast wave has "shocked up," as is evident by the large differences in pressure across the shock front. The blast wave reflects off the wall and the ground in the third image. In the fourth, the wave that reflected off the ground merges with the initial blast wave

Figure 2: Shown here is a cross-section of pressures for a three-dimensional explosion near an immovable wall. The timestep between frames is 10 ms. Many of the behaviors of the blast wave can be seen, specifically the Mach stem formed from the blast wave merging with the wave reflected off the ground plane, and the diffracted wave formed when the blast wave crests over the wall.

to form a Mach stem, which has pressure values twice that of the initial wave. In the final two images, the blast wave crests over the wall and forms a weaker diffracted wave.

In the entertainment industry, explosions are currently created at full scale in the real world, in miniature, or using heuristic graphics techniques[20, 9, 22]. Each of these methods has significant disadvantages, and we believe that in many scenarios, simulation may provide an easier solution. When explosions are generated and filmed at full scale in the real world, they often must be faked to appear dangerous and destructive by using multiple charges and chemicals with a low flashpoint. Because of the cost and danger of exploding full-size objects, many explosions are created using miniatures. With miniatures, the greatest challenge is often scaling the objects and the physics to create a realistic effect. Current graphics techniques for creating explosions are based on heuristics, analytical functions, or recorded data, and although they produce nice effects for spherical blast waves, they are not adequate for the complex effects required for many of the scenarios used in the entertainment industry.

Physically based simulations of explosions offer several potential advantages over these three techniques. In contrast to real physical explosions, simulations can be used in an iterative fashion, allowing the director many chances to modify or shape the effect. The rendering of the explosion is to a large extent decoupled from the simulation, allowing the visual characteristics of the dust clouds or fireball to be determined as a post-process. Unlike heuristic or analytical graphical methods, physically based simulations allow the computation of arbitrarily complex scenes with multiple interacting explosions and objects.

The next section discusses relevant previous work in explosions, fluids, flame, and fracture. The following section introduces the explosion model in the context of computational fluid dynamics. The next two sections discuss coupling between the fluid and solids and other secondary effects such as refraction and fireballs. We close with a discussion of our results.

2   Previous Work

Explosions used in the entertainment industry tend to be visually rich. Because of the inherent computational complexity of these explosions, researchers largely neglected this field after the publication of particle simulation techniques[16, 17]. Procedural methods can generate fiery, billowy clouds that could be used as explosions[3].

Recently two papers specifically addressed explosions. Mazarak and colleagues simulate the damage done by an explosion to voxelized objects[10]. They model the explosion as an ideal spherical blast wave with a pressure profile curve approximated by an analytic function based on the modified Friedlander equation and scaled according to empirical laws[2]. The spherical blast wave expands independent of existing obstacles, and forces are applied to objects in the direction of the blast radius. Objects are modeled as connected voxels and based on various heuristics, these radial forces may cause the voxels to disconnect.

Neff and Fiume use data from empirical blast curves to model an explosion[12]. The blast curves relate the pressure and velocity of the blast wave to time and are scalable. Unlike Mazarak and colleagues, they use a curve representing the reflection coefficient to apply forces to objects based on the angle of incidence of the blast wave. They assume quasi-static loading conditions where the blast wave encloses the entire object and effects due to reflected waves are ignored. They also model explosion-induced fracture in planar surfaces using a procedural pattern generator.

An alternative to these analytic and empirical models is a computational fluid dynamic simulation of the blast wave and the surrounding air. Foster and Metaxas presented a solution for incompressible, viscous flow and used it to animate liquids[5] and hot, turbulent gas[4]. They modeled fluid as a three-dimensional voxel volume with appropriate boundary conditions. The fluid obeys the Navier-Stokes equations; gas also follows an equation that represents thermal buoyancy. Using an explicit scheme, they update velocities and temperatures every timestep via Euler integration and readjust the values to guarantee conservation of mass. The fluid is rendered by tracing massless particles along the interpolated flow field. Their work with liquids included dynamic objects that were moved by the fluid, although they assumed that the objects were small enough not to influence the fluid. Recently Stam addressed the computational cost of guaranteeing stability by introducing extra damping to afford larger timesteps and using an implicit method to solve a sparse system of equations[18]. Stam's method is inappropriate for shocks and explosions because his integration scheme achieves stability by encouraging the fluid to dissipate.

In the dramatic effects produced by the entertainment industry, a fireball is often the most salient visible characteristic of an explosion. Stam and Fiume modeled flame and the corresponding fluid flow and rendered the results using a sophisticated global illumination method[19]. The gases behaved according to advection-diffusion equations; Stam and Fiume solve these equations efficiently by reformulating the problem from a grid to "warped blobs." Illumination from gas is affected by emission and anisotropic scattering and absorption. They only consider continuous emissions from blackbody radiation and ignore line emissions from electron excitation. They develop a heuristic for smoke emission due to the lack of a scientific analytic model.

Compressible flow has been studied for years in the computational fluid dynamics community[1, 2, 8]. We have built on this work by taking the governing equations and the donor-acceptor method of integration from this literature. However, the reasons for simulating explosions, combustion, detonation, and supersonic flow in engineering differ significantly from those in computer graphics. Engineering problems often require focusing on one element such as the boundary layer and simulating the other elements only to the extent that they affect the phenomenon under study. For example, engineering simulations are often two-dimensional and assume symmetry in the third dimension. Because they are focused on a specific event, their simulations may run for only a few microseconds. In computer graphics, on the other hand, we need to produce a visually appealing view of the behavior throughout the explosion. As a result, we need a more complete model with less quantitative accuracy.

3 Explosion Modeling

An explosion is a pressure wave caused by some initial disturbance, such as a detonation. In the results presented here, we assume that the detonation has occurred and that its properties are defined in the initial conditions of the simulation. This assumption is reasonable for most chemical explosions because the detonation is complete within microseconds. We animate explosions by modeling the pressure wave and the surrounding air as a fluid discretized over a three-dimensional rectilinear grid. The following two subsections describe the governing equations for fluid dynamics and the computational techniques used to solve them. The remaining two subsections describe the parameters available to the user for controlling the appearance of the explosion via the boundary conditions and initial conditions.

3.1 Fluid Dynamics

In nearly all engineering problems, including the analysis of explosions, fluids are modeled as a continuum. They are represented as a set of equations in terms of density $\rho\,(\mathrm{kg/m^3})$, pressure $P\,(\mathrm{N/m^2})$, velocity $\boldsymbol{v}\,(\mathrm{m/s})$, temperature $T\,(\mathrm{K})$, the internal energy per unit mass $N\,(\mathrm{J/kg})$, and the total energy per unit mass $E = N + \frac{1}{2}\boldsymbol{v}^2\,(\mathrm{J/kg})$. The equations that govern these quantities are defined in an Eulerian fashion, that is, they apply to a differential volume of space that is filled with fluid rather than to the fluid itself. In addition to the Navier-Stokes equations, which model the conservation of momentum, the equations for compressible, viscous flow include governing equations for the conservation of mass and energy and for the fluid's thermodynamic state[7].

We introduce several simplifying assumptions that make the equations easier to compute but nevertheless allow us to capture the effects of compressible, viscous flow. We discount changes in the vibrational energies of molecules and assume air to be at chemical equilibrium; we ignore the effects from dissociation or ionization. These assumptions, which are commonly used in the engineering literature[1], allow us to reduce to constants many of the coefficients that vary with temperature. The resulting deviation in the values of the coefficients is negligible at temperatures below $1000\,\mathrm{K}$; only minor deviations occur below $2500\,\mathrm{K}$. Our implementation produces aesthetic results with temperatures above $100000,\mathrm{K}$, although deviations in constants could be on the order of a magnitude or two.

The first governing equation of fluid dynamics arises from the conservation of mass. Because fluid mass is conserved, the change of fluid density in a differential volume must be equal to the net flux across the volume's boundary, giving

$$\frac{\partial \rho}{\partial t} = -\nabla \cdot (\rho \boldsymbol{v}). \qquad (1)$$

The second governing equation, commonly known as the Navier-Stokes equation, concerns the conservation of momentum. For a Stokes fluid, where the normal stress is independent of the rate of dilation, the equation for the x

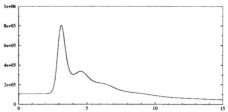

Figure 3: Pressure profile $(\mathrm{N/m^2})$ over time (ms) near an explosion.

component of the fluid velocity is given by

$$\rho\frac{\partial \boldsymbol{v}_x}{\partial t} = \rho \boldsymbol{f}_x - \nabla P + \frac{\mu}{3}\nabla \cdot \left(\frac{\partial \boldsymbol{v}}{\partial x}\right) + \mu \nabla^2 \boldsymbol{v}_x - \rho(\boldsymbol{v}\cdot\nabla)\boldsymbol{v}_x, \quad (2)$$

where $\boldsymbol{f}$ represents the body forces such as gravity and μ is the coefficient of viscosity. The equations for the y and z components are similar. The first two terms on the right-hand side of the equation model accelerations due to body forces and forces arising from the pressure gradient; the next two terms model accelerations due to viscous forces. The last term is not a force-related term; rather it is a convective term that models the transport of momentum as the fluid flows. This distinction between time derivative (force) terms and convective terms will be important for the integration scheme.

The final governing equation enforces the conservation of energy in the system. The First Law of Thermodynamics dictates that the change in energy is equal to the amount of heat added and the work done to the system. Accounting for the amount of work done from pressure and viscosity and the heat transferred from thermal conductivity yields

$$\rho\frac{\partial N}{\partial t} = k\nabla^2 T - P\nabla \cdot \boldsymbol{v} + \Phi - \rho(\boldsymbol{v}\cdot\nabla)N, \qquad (3)$$

where k is the thermal conductivity constant and Φ is the viscous dissipation given by

$$\Phi = -\frac{2\mu}{3}(\nabla \cdot \boldsymbol{v})^2 + \frac{\mu}{2}\sum_{i,j\in\{x,y,z\}}\left(\frac{\partial \boldsymbol{v}_i}{\partial j} + \frac{\partial \boldsymbol{v}_j}{\partial i}\right)^2. \qquad (4)$$

As with equation (2), the last term of equation (3) is a convective term and models the transport of energy as the fluid flows.

In addition to the three governing equations, we need equations of state that determine the relationship between energy, temperature, density, and pressure. They are

$$N = c_V T, \quad P = \rho R T, \qquad (5)$$

where the coefficient c_V is the specific heat at constant volume and R is the gas constant of air.

Figure 4: This figure illustrates the donor-acceptor method in which the amount of mass transferred is proportional to the mass of the donor. The voxels on the left show the transfer of mass and energy according to the flow, indicated by the blue arrow. The two voxels on the right represent the scenario with reversed flow of the same magnitude. Density is represented as height, and unit energy is represented as color. Corresponding amounts of energy are sent with the mass.

3.2 Discretization and Numerical Integration

The equations in the previous section describe the behavior of a fluid in a continuous fashion. However, implementing them in a form suitable for numerical computation requires that the space filled by the fluid be discretized in some manner and that a stable method for integrating the governing equations forward in time be devised.

Finite differences are used to discretize the space into a regular lattice of cubical cells. These finite voxels take the place of the differential volumes used to define the continuous equations, and the governing equations now hold for each voxel. Fluid properties such as pressure and velocity are associated with each voxel and these properties are assumed to be constant across the voxel. The spatial derivatives used in the governing equations are approximated on the lattice using central differences. For example, the x component of the pressure gradient, ∇P, at voxel $[i, j, k]$ is given by

$$\frac{\partial P}{\partial x} \approx \frac{P_{[i+1,j,k]} - P_{[i-1,j,k]}}{2h}, \qquad (6)$$

where subscripts in square brackets index voxel locations and h is the voxel width.

After the governing equations have been expressed in terms of discrete variables using finite differences, they may be used as the update rules for an explicit integration scheme. However, rapid pressure changes created by steep pressure gradients moving at supersonic speeds would cause such a scheme to diverge rapidly. (See Figure 3.) To deal with this problem, we improved the basic integration technique using two modifications described in the fluid dynamics literature[2, 8]. The first modification involves updating equations (2) and (3) in two steps, first using only the temporal portion of the derivatives and second using the convective derivatives. The second modification is called the *donor-acceptor method* and is described in detail below. It addresses problems that arise when mass, momentum, and energy are convected across steep pressure gradients.

The modified update scheme operates by applying the following algorithm to each voxel at every timestep:

1. Approximate the fluid acceleration at the current time, $\widetilde{\boldsymbol{a}}_t = (\partial \boldsymbol{v}/\partial t)_t$, using the non-convective (first four) terms of equation (2).

2. Compute the tentative velocity at the end of the timestep, $\widetilde{\boldsymbol{v}}_{t+\Delta t} = \boldsymbol{v}_t + \Delta t \widetilde{\boldsymbol{a}}_t$, and the approximate average velocity during the timestep $\bar{\boldsymbol{v}}_t = (\widetilde{\boldsymbol{v}}_{t+\Delta t} + \boldsymbol{v}_t)/2$.

3. Approximate change in internal energy, N, using the non-convective terms of equation (3) and substituting $\bar{\boldsymbol{v}}_t$ for the fluid velocity.

4. Using $\bar{\boldsymbol{v}}_t$ for the fluid velocity, compute the new density, $\rho_{t+\Delta t}$ with equation (1).

5. Calculate the complete $\boldsymbol{v}_{t+\Delta t}$ and $N_{t+\Delta t}$ with equations (2) and (3) using the convective terms and the new value of ρ.

6. Use state equations (5) to update secondary quantities such as temperature.

Although this update scheme is more stable than a simple Euler integration, sharp gradients in fluid density may still allow small flows from nearly empty voxels to generate negative fluid densities and cause inappropriately large changes to both velocity and internal energy. To prevent these problems, we use a donor-acceptor method when computing $-\nabla \rho \boldsymbol{v}$ of the convective terms in steps 4 and 5 above.

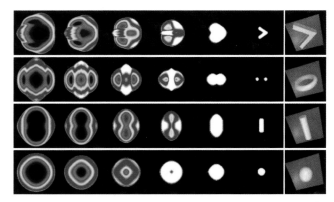

Figure 5: This figure shows cross-sections of pressure for three-dimensional explosions of equal-volume charges in the shape of a sphere, cylinder, torus, and wedge. The timestep between frames is 5 ms.

The donor-acceptor method transfers mass proportional to the mass of the voxel in the upstream direction, or donor voxel. Suppose we have voxel i and one of its six neighbors j in direction $\boldsymbol{d}$ from i. Let $v_{ij} = \frac{1}{2}(\boldsymbol{v}_i + \boldsymbol{v}_j) \cdot \boldsymbol{d}$. If $v_{ij} > 0$, then flow is going from i to j, i is the donor, and ρ_i is used in equation (1) to compute the change in voxel i's density. Likewise, if $v_{ij} < 0$, then j is the donor, and the density of j is used when computing the change in voxel i's density. These calculations are repeated for the six neighbors of i to obtain the new density for i, $\rho_{t+\Delta t}$. The velocity and energy convection are then scaled by $\rho_t/\rho_{t+\Delta t}$ to conserve momentum and energy. Figure 4 illustrates the donor-acceptor method. The left and right diagrams show flows in opposite directions of the same magnitude. The sent mass is proportional to the mass of the donor and carries with it corresponding amounts of energy.

3.3 Boundary Conditions

The system has several types of boundary conditions that allow the fluid to exhibit a wide range of behaviors. Free boundaries allow blast waves to travel beyond the voxel volume as if the voxel volume were arbitrarily large. This type of boundary allows us to model slow, long-term aspects of explosions, such as fireballs and dust clouds. Hard boundaries force fluid velocity normal to them to be zero while leaving all other fluid attributes unchanged. We treat these boundaries as smooth surfaces, so tangential flow is unaffected. We implement a third boundary condition to achieve faster execution. If a voxel and its neighbors have pressure differences less than a threshold, the voxel is treated as a free boundary and is never evaluated. This optimization prunes out the majority of the volume while the blast wave is expanding.

3.4 Initial Conditions

The user specifies the pressure and temperature of the air, and the initial values of other variables are determined from the state equations (5). The detonation is initialized by specifying a region of the volume with higher temperature or pressure. For example, a chemical explosion might have a temperature of 2900 K and a pressure of 1000 atm with the surrounding air at 290 K and 1 atm. The creation of the explosion may be time-delayed or may be triggered when the fluid around the charge reaches a threshold temperature.

The detonation may have an arbitrary geometry represented by a manifold polygonal mesh. The mesh is voxelized to initialize the appropriate voxels in the fluid simulation. By controlling the geometry, the user can produce a variety of effects that could not be achieved with a spherical model. In blast theory, planar, cylindrical, and spherical blast waves can be modeled by analytic functions[2]; however nonstandard shapes can create surprising and interesting effects. Figure 5 shows cross-sections of pressure for three-dimensional explosions from equal-volume charges in the shape of a sphere, cylinder, torus, and wedge. The inner blast wave of the torus merges to create a strong vertical blast wave. The wedge concentrates its force directly to the right, while leaving the surrounding area relatively untouched.

4 Interaction with Solids

People use explosions to impart forces on objects for both constructive and destructive purposes. The movements of these objects and the resulting displacement of air create many of the compelling visual effects of an explosion. In this section, we present methods to implement a two-way coupling between the fluid and solids. The coupling from fluid to solid allows us to model phenomena such as a projectile being propelled by an explosion. The coupling from solid to fluid can be used to model a piston compressing or the shock wave formed as a projectile moves through the air supersonically. We also extend previously published techniques for fracture to allow the pressure wave to shatter objects.

To allow the two-way coupling, objects have two representations: a polygonal mesh that is used to apply forces to the object from the fluid, and a volume representation in voxels that is used to displace fluid based on the motion of the object. We incorporate the coupling into the fluid dynamics code in the following way:

1. Apply forces on the objects from the fluid and compute the rigid body motion of the objects.

2. If the object has moved more than a fraction of a voxel, recompute the voxelization of the object.

3. Displace fluid based on object movement.

4. Update the fluid using the techniques described in Section 3.2.

We explain the first three of these items in greater detail in the following subsections.

4.1 Coupling from Fluid to Solid

An object embedded in a fluid experiences two separate sets of forces on its surface, those arising from hydrostatic pressure and those arising from dynamic forces due to fluid momentum. The forces due to hydrostatic pressure act normal to the surface and are generated by the incoherent motions of the fluid molecules against the surface. The dynamic forces are generated by the coherent motion of the continuous fluid and can be divided into a force normal to the surface of the object and a tangential shearing force. We neglect the tangential shearing force because in the context of explosions, it is negligible in comparison to the force due to hydrostatic pressure. We assume that the object is in equilibrium under ambient air pressure and the hydrostatic forces are computed using the overpressure $\bar{P}$, which is the difference between the hydrostatic pressure P and ambient pressure.

The magnitude of the normal force per unit area on the surface is given by the dynamic overpressure:

$$\bar{P}_{dyn} = \bar{P} + \frac{1}{2}\rho\left(\boldsymbol{v}_{rel}\cdot\hat{\boldsymbol{n}}\right)^2, \quad (7)$$

Figure 6: A glass window is shattered by a blast wave. The blast wave pressure is approximately 3 atm when it reaches the window. The images show the scene at 0 ms, 13 ms, 40 ms, 67 ms, 107 ms, and 160 ms.

where $\boldsymbol{v}_{rel}$ is the velocity of the fluid relative to the surface, and $\hat{\boldsymbol{n}}$ is the outward surface normal.

We assume that the triangles composing each object are small enough that the force is constant over each triangle. The force on a triangle with area A is then

$$\boldsymbol{f} = -\hat{\boldsymbol{n}}A\bar{P}_{dyn}, \quad (8)$$

where the fluid properties are measured at the centroid of the triangle. The forces are computed for all triangles of an object, and the translational and angular velocities of the object are updated accordingly.

In addition to acting on rigid objects, the forces can also be applied to flexible objects that deform and fracture[14]. The explosion simulation results in pressures, velocities, and densities for each voxel in the discretization of the fluid. The fracture simulation uses this information to compute the forces that should be applied to a finite element model of the objects in the scene. The force computation is similar to that for rigid objects. This method was used to simulate the breaking window shown in Figure 6 and the breaking wall shown in Figure 7. This coupling is one-way in that the fluid applies forces to the finite-element model, but the fluid is not moved by the fragments that pass through it.

4.2 Coupling from Solid to Fluid

To allow the solid to displace fluid, the triangular mesh representing the object is converted to voxels[13], which are then used to define the hard boundaries in the fluid volume dynamically. The objects move smoothly through the fluid, but because of the discrete nature of the voxelization, large changes in the amount of fluid displaced may occur on each timestep. To address this problem, the fluid displaced or the void created by the movement of the objects is handled over a period of time rather than instantaneously.

The voxelization returns a value between zero and one representing the proportion of the voxel that is not interior

Figure 7: A wall is knocked over by a blast wave from an explosion 3.5 m away. The images are spaced 250 ms apart.

to any object. This value is independent of geometric considerations about the exact shape of the occupied volume. If any dimension of an object is smaller than the size of a voxel, the appropriate voxels will have partial volumes, but because there are no fully occupied voxels, the fluid will appear to move through the object. Nonzero partial volumes below a certain threshold are set to zero to increase stability. The implementation of partial volumes requires slight modifications to the donor-acceptor method to conserve mass, momentum, and energy because two adjacent voxels could have different volumes.

When any part of an object moves more than a fraction of a voxel, the object is revoxelized, and the hard boundaries of the fluid are updated. When this process occurs, the partial volume in a voxel might change, resulting in fluid flow. We allow this flow to occur smoothly by sacrificing conservation of mass and energy in the short-term. The voxelization determines the partial volumes in an instantaneous fashion, but the fluid displacement routine maintains internal partial volumes that change more slowly and are used to compute the pressure, density, and temperature of the affected voxels. The internal partial volumes change proportionally to the velocities of the moving objects, and mass and energy are restored over time.

To compute a smooth change in the internal partial volume from V_1 to V_2, we model an object moving into a voxel as a piston compressing or decompressing fluid. We simplify the computation of the change in partial volume by assuming that the piston is acting along one of the axes of the voxelization. The appropriate axis is selected based on the largest axial component of the velocity of the object, $\boldsymbol{v}_p$. The displacement of the piston after t seconds and the corresponding change in partial volume of a voxel with width h are

$$\boldsymbol{l} = \boldsymbol{v}_p t, \quad \Delta V = V_2 - V_1 = h^2 \boldsymbol{v}_p t. \quad (9)$$

The displacement occurs linearly over

$$t = \frac{\Delta V}{h^2 \boldsymbol{v_p}} \quad (10)$$

at a velocity of $\boldsymbol{v}_p$.

Given this model of the change in internal partial volume, we know that $\rho_1 V_1 = \rho_2 V_2$ because mass is conserved. However, the fluid is compressible, so mechanical energy is not conserved (otherwise $P_1 V_1 = P_2 V_2$). To obtain the new pressures and densities of the fluid, we use a thermodynamic equation relating the work done to the system from changing the volume (or density),

$$\frac{P_2}{P_1} = \left(\frac{\rho_2}{\rho_1}\right)^{\gamma} = \left(\frac{T_2}{T_1}\right)^{\gamma/(\gamma-1)}, \quad (11)$$

where $\gamma = 1 + R/c_V$ (γ is about 1.4 for air and is closer to 1 the more incompressible the fluid)[1]. Internal unit energy and total unit energy are then updated by the state equations.

When the partial volume of a voxel changes from one nonzero value to another, the resulting pressure changes cause fluid to move to or from a neighbor based on the governing equations. However, when the partial volume of a voxel changes from zero to nonzero or vice versa, the situation must be handled as a special case by treating the affected voxel and one of its neighbors as a single larger voxel with a nonzero partial volume. The neighbor is selected based on the largest axial component of the object's velocity, $\boldsymbol{v}_p$. We calculate the internal partial volume for each of the involved voxels A and B as $\widetilde{V}_{A_1}$ and $\widetilde{V}_{B_1}$.

Figure 8: Refraction of light from a blast wave. Each frame is 10 ms apart. The index of refraction is exaggerated tenfold to enhance the effect.

When V_{A_1}, the original partial volume of A, is zero and V_{A_2}, the new partial volume of A, is nonzero, we use initial volumes $\widetilde{V}_{A_1}$ and $\widetilde{V}_{B_1}$ such that $\widetilde{V}_{A_1} + \widetilde{V}_{B_1} = V_{B_1}$ (the initial volume is conserved) and $\widetilde{V}_{A_1} V_{B_2} = \widetilde{V}_{B_1} V_{A_2}$ (the voxels are treated as a single larger voxel). The change in volume is

$$\Delta V_A = V_{A_2} - \widetilde{V}_{A_1} = V_{A_2} - V_{A_2}\frac{V_{B_1}}{V_{A_2} + V_{B_2}}, \quad (12)$$

$$\Delta V_B = V_{B_2} - \widetilde{V}_{B_1} = V_{B_2} - V_{B_2}\frac{V_{B_1}}{V_{A_2} + V_{B_2}}. \quad (13)$$

When the original partial volume of A, V_{A_1}, is nonzero and the new partial volume of A, V_{A_2}, is zero, we force $\widetilde{V}_{A_1}$ to be zero and treat $\widetilde{V}_{B_1}$ as a single larger voxel. To treat the two voxels as one, we first average the properties of A and its neighbor B, transferring any lost kinetic energy to internal energy. The change in volume is then

$$\Delta V_B = V_{B_2} - \widetilde{V}_{B_1} = V_{B_2} - \frac{\rho_A V_{A_1} + \rho_B V_{B_1}}{\rho_B} \quad (14)$$

by making sure that $\rho_B \widetilde{V}_{B_1} = \rho_A V_{A_1} + \rho_B V_{B_1}$ (mass is conserved).

5 Secondary Effects

An explosion creates a number of visual secondary effects including the refraction of light, fireballs, and dust clouds. These secondary effects do not significantly affect the simulation, so they can be generated and edited as a post-process.

One of the most stunning, but often ignored, effects of an explosion is the bending of light from the blast wave. Because the blast wave is substantially denser than the surrounding air, it has a higher index of refraction, η. Light travels at the same velocity between molecules, but near molecules it is slowed down from interactions with electrons. This concept is expressed numerically as $\eta - 1 = k\rho$, $k = 2.26 \times 10^{-4}$ m³/kg, by the Dale-Gladstone law[11]. We capture the refraction of light by ray tracing through the

Figure 9: A fireball after one second of simulation time. Tracer particles from the fluid simulation determine the position and coloration of the fireball.

fluid volume. (See Figure 8.) As the ray is traced through the volume, the index of refraction is continually updated based on the interpolated density of the current position. For simplicity, we compute the density of each point using a trilinear interpolation of the densities of the neighboring voxels. When the index of refraction changes by more than a threshold, the new direction of the ray is computed via Snell's law using the density gradient as the surface normal. The trilinear interpolation results in minor faceting effects that cause small errors in the reflected direction.

An advantage of using a full volumetric fluid representation for explosions is that the simulation can be used to model a fireball in addition to the blast wave. We assume that the fireball is composed of detonated material from inside the explosive. To track this material, the system initializes the fireball by placing particles inside the shape specified by the user for the explosion. The particles are massless and flow with the fluid, allowing the fluid dynamics model to capture effects critical for a fireball such as thermal conductivity and buoyancy. Some fluid simulations[4, 18] model thermal buoyancy explicitly; in our simulation, thermal buoyancy is a behavior derived from the governing equations. For rendering, each particle takes on a temperature that is interpolated based on its position in the volume. The particles are rendered as Gaussian blobs with values for red, green, blue, and opacity. The color values are based on blackbody radiation at appropriate wavelengths given the temperature of the particle[11]. Figure 9 shows a fireball and corresponding tracer particles after one second of simulation. Figure 10 shows a fireball coming around a corner; the hallway is illuminated by the flames.

The tracer particles couple the appearance of the fireball to the motion of the fluid, and although heat generated by the initial explosion is added to the fluid model, any additional heat generated by post-detonation combustion is ignored. Radiative energy released at detonation could also be modeled for rendering. Much like the difficulties encountered with rendering the sun[15], the high contrast of this effect may require contrast-reduction techniques such as LCIS[21].

The blast wave and other secondary waves create dust clouds by disturbing fine particles resting on surfaces. The creation of dust clouds is difficult to quantify either experimentally or analytically, so the rate at which the dust becomes airborne is left as a control for the animator. Once a dust particle is airborne, its behavior is dictated by its size. The smaller it is, the more it is influenced by drag forces and the less it is influenced by inertial forces. Smaller dust particles have lower terminal velocities and exhibit more Brownian motion. With the exception of coagulated particles, experiments reveal that most dust particles are approximately ellipsoidal with low eccentricity, and the particles do not orient themselves to the fluid flow[6]. The difference in dynamics between these particles and spherical particles is not that significant, so we assume dust particles to be spherical. We implement dust as metaparticles, each representing a Gaussian density of homogeneous dust particles. The dust size for each metaparticle is chosen according to size distributions from experimental data for blasted shale[6]. The metaparticles travel through the fluid as if single particles were located at their centers. Their variances grow according to the mean Brownian diffusion per unit time. Figure 11 shows dust clouds in a city scene.

6   Results and Discussion

We ran the system with several scenarios. The physical constants used in the simulation were constants for air that were

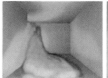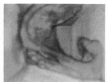

Figure 10:   A fireball coming around a corner. The images are spaced 333 ms apart.

Example (figure)	h (m)	Δt (ms)	t_{tot} (ms)	V_0 (m^3)	P_0 (atm)	T_0 (K)
projectile (1)	1.0	0.10	450	73.60	1000	2900
barrier (2)	0.2	0.01	25	0.52	1000	2900
shapes (5)	1.0	0.10	30	1000.00	1000	2900
fracture (6,7)	0.2	0.02	20	0.52	1000	2900
fireball (8,9)	1.0	0.10	1000	65.40	1000	2900
corner (10)	1.0	0.10	10000	268.08	1000	2900
city (11)	1.0	0.10	5000	65.40	1000	2900
nuclear (12)	50.0	0.50	30000	9.1×10^7	345	1×10^5

Table 1:   Parameters for simulations: voxel width, timestep, total simulation time, and initial volume, pressure, and temperature of detonation.

taken from an engineering handbook[7]. Table 6 shows the voxel width, timestep, total simulation time, initial volume of the explosion (proportional to yield), and initial pressure and temperature of the explosion. The timesteps Δt increase by a factor of five once the blast wave leaves the volume.

The simulations ran on a single 195 MHz R10K processor and used a $101 \times 101 \times 101$ volume. The running times per timestep varied considerably from several seconds to two minutes because of the pruning described in Section 3.3. For coupling with fracture, I/O became a major factor because in each iteration the entire volume was written to disk; however, using better compression would reduce this expense. Running times of the simulations varied from a few hours (Figure 5) to overnight (Figures 2, 6, 7, and 8) to a few days (Figures 1, 9, 10, and 12).

We use an explicit integration technique to compute the motion of the pressure wave caused by the detonation. Despite its magnitude, the wave does not transport fluid large distances. Previously, fluid dynamics has been used most often in computer graphics to capture the effects of macroscale fluid transport where the fluid does move a significant distance. Implicit integration techniques with large timesteps are appropriate for these situations because they achieve stability by damping high frequencies. The propagation of the pressure wave in our stiff equations, however, is characterized by these high frequencies and it is essential that they not be artificially damped. We chose, therefore, to use an explicit integration technique; however, an implicit integration technique could be used to simulate the fireball and dust clouds after the blast wave and the secondary waves have left the volume. Using an implicit integration technique in the slow flow regime could allow larger timesteps and faster execution times.

We assume that the voxels in the fluid volume are of a

Figure 11:   An explosion among buildings. The images are spaced 667 ms apart.

Figure 12: A large-scale high-temperature explosion resembling a nuclear explosion: after 3 s, 6 s, 12 s, 24 s.

size appropriate for the phenomena that we wish to capture. In particular, if solid objects have a dimension smaller than a voxel, then they will not create a hard boundary that prevents fluid flow. For example, a wall that is thinner than a voxel will permit the blast wave to travel through it because partial volumes do not maintain any geometric information about the sub-voxel shape of the object. The difficulty of a two-way coupling with fracturing objects stems from having to model subvoxel cracks, which should allow flow to go through. If small objects are required, the voxel size could be decreased or dynamic remeshing techniques could be used to create smaller voxels in the areas around boundaries.

There are effects from explosions that we have not investigated. Although smoke is often a visible feature of an explosion that includes a fireball, we do not have a physically based model for smoke creation. Incomplete combustion at lower temperatures results in smoke, and that observation could be used as a heuristic to determine where smoke should be created in the fireball and how densely. Stam and Fiume used a similar heuristic model[19]. Textures of objects could be modified to show soot accumulation and scorching over time. Dust clouds are created when an object fractures or pulverizes. Dust could be introduced into our system when the finite-element model produces small tetrahedra or when cracks form.

We made several assumptions in constructing our model of explosions. Most discounted effects that did not contribute noticeably to the final rendered images; however, some could produce a noticeable change in behavior in certain situations and may warrant further investigation. We only model the blast wave traveling through air. However, waves travel through other media, including solid objects, and complex interface effects occur when a wave travels between two different media. For large-scale explosions, meteorological conditions such as the change in pressure with respect to altitude or the interface between atmospheric layers (the tropopause) may need to be considered.

Our goal in this work has been to create a physically realistic model of explosions. However, this model should also lend itself to creating less realistic effects. Even though our model does not incorporate high-temperature effects such as ionization, we can still obtain interesting results on high-temperature explosions. The fireball in Figure 12 resulted from an initial detonation at $10^5 K$. Explosions used in feature films often include far more dramatic fireballs than would occur in the actual explosions that they purport to mimic. By using more tracer particles and adjusting the rendering parameters of the fireballs, we should be able to reproduce this effect. Noise could be added either to the velocity fields or particle positions post-process to make the explosion look more turbulent. Similarly, explosions in space are often portrayed as more colorful and violent than explosions that occurred outside of the atmosphere should be. Imparting an initial outward velocity to the explosion, turning off gravity, and increasing the thermal buoyancy by modifying the state equations might create a similar effect.

7 Acknowledgments

This project was supported in part by NSF NYI Grant No. IRI-9457621, Mitsubishi Electric Research Laboratory, and a Packard Fellowship. The second author was supported by a Fellowship from the Intel Foundation.

References

[1] J. D. Anderson Jr. *Modern compressible flow: with historical perspective.* McGraw-Hill, Inc., 1990.

[2] W. E. Baker. *Explosions in air.* University of Texas Press, 1973.

[3] D. Ebert, K. Musgrave, D. Peachy, K. Perlin, and S. Worley. *Texturing and Modeling: A Procedural Approach.* AP Professional, 1994.

[4] N. Foster and D. Metaxas. Modeling the motion of a hot, turbulent gas. *Proceedings of SIGGRAPH 97*, pages 181–188, August 1997.

[5] N. Foster and D. Metaxas. Realistic animation of liquids. *Graphics Interface '96*, pages 204–212, May 1996.

[6] H. L. Green and W. R. Lane. *Particulate Clouds: Dusts, Smokes and Mists.* D. Van Nostrand Company, Inc., 1964.

[7] A. M. Kuethe and C. Chow. *Foundations of aerodynamics: bases of aerodynamic design.* John Wiley and Sons, Inc., 1998.

[8] C. L. Madder. *Numerical modeling of detonations.* University of California Press, 1979.

[9] K. H. Martin. Godzilla: The sound and the fury. *Cinefex*, pages 82–107, July 1998.

[10] O. Mazarak, C. Martins, and J. Amanatides. Animating exploding objects. *Graphics Interface '99*, pages 211–218, June 1999.

[11] J. R. Meyer-Arendt. *Introduction to classical and modern optics.* Prentice-Hall, Inc., 1984.

[12] M. Neff and E. Fiume. A visual model for blast waves and fracture. *Graphics Interface '99*, pages 193–202, June 1999.

[13] F.S. Nooruddin and G. Turk. Simplification and repair of polygonal models using volumetric techniques. Technical Report GIT-GVU-99-37, Georgia Institute of Technology, 1999.

[14] J. F. O'Brien and J. K. Hodgins. Graphical modeling and animation of brittle fracture. *Proceedings of SIGGRAPH 99*, pages 137–146, August 1999.

[15] A. J. Preetham, P. Shirley, and B. E. Smits. A practical analytic model for daylight. *Proceedings of SIGGRAPH 99*, pages 91–100, August 1999.

[16] W. T. Reeves. Particle systems—a technique for modeling a class of fuzzy objects. *ACM Transactions on Graphics*, 2(2):91–108, April 1983.

[17] K. Sims. Particle animation and rendering using data parallel computation. *Computer Graphics (Proceedings of SIGGRAPH 90)*, 24(4):405–413, August 1990.

[18] J. Stam. Stable fluids. *Proceedings of SIGGRAPH 99*, pages 121–128, August 1999.

[19] J. Stam and E. Fiume. Depicting fire and other gaseous phenomena using diffusion processes. *Proceedings of SIGGRAPH 95*, pages 129–136, August 1995.

[20] R. Street. Volcano: Toasting the coast. *Cinefex*, pages 56–84, September 1997.

[21] J. Tumblin and G. Turk. LCIS: A boundary hierarchy for detail-preserving contrast reduction. *Proceedings of SIGGRAPH 99*, pages 83–90, August 1999.

[22] M. C. Vaz. Journey to Armageddon. *Cinefex*, pages 68–93, October 1998.

Computer Modelling Of Fallen Snow

Paul Fearing
University of British Columbia*

Figure 1: A sudden snowfall comes to the North Pole.

Abstract

In this paper, we present a new model of snow accumulation and stability for computer graphics. Our contribution is divided into two major components, each essential for modelling the appearance of a thick layer of snowfall on the ground.

Our *accumulation model* determines how much snow a particular surface receives, allowing for such phenomena as flake flutter, flake dusting and wind-blown snow. We compute snow accumulation by shooting particles upwards towards the sky, giving each source surface independent control over its own sampling density, accuracy and computation time. Importance ordering minimises sampling effort while maximising visual information, generating smoothly improving global results that can be interrupted at any point.

Once snow lands on the ground, our *stability model* moves material away from physically unstable areas in a series of small, simultaneous avalanches. We use a simple local stability test that handles very steep surfaces, obstacles, edges, and wind transit. Our stability algorithm also handles other materials, such as flour, sand, and flowing water.

CR Categories: I.3.5 [Computer Graphics]: Computational Geometry and Object Modelling—Physically based modelling; J.2 [Physical Sciences and Engineering]: Earth and atmospheric sciences;

Keywords: snow, avalanches, stability, natural phenomena

---

*email: fearing@cs.ubc.ca

1 Introduction

One of nature's greatest beauties is the way fresh snow covers the world in a perfect blanket of crystalline white. It replaces sharp angles with gentle curves, and clings to surfaces to form ghostly silhouettes.

In many countries, snow is a common fact of life during the winter months. For example, January snow coverage in the Northern Hemisphere has ranged between 41.7 - 49.8 million square kilometres [17], or nearly half of the hemisphere's total land mass. A phenomenon that is so common and pervasive is clearly of interest and importance.

Despite the ubiquitous nature of snow, the entire season of winter has been almost completely ignored by computer graphics research and applications, with the exception of distant snow-capped mountains, and falling snowflakes. Without an automatic model of fallen snow, animators have so far relied upon intuition to produce snow-covered surfaces - an extremely tedious, time-consuming and potentially inaccurate task. A single tree might have a hundred branches, each with a complex drapery of snow, and each avalanching onto branches below, producing subtle second-order accumulation effects.

Besides the practicalities of research and application, there is another reason for investigating snowfall. Snow transforms commonplace scenes into fantastic wonderlands, greatly changing the appearance and mood of the landscape, allowing us to see familiar sights in a fresh, exciting way.

This paper presents a new method of snow pack modelling for computer graphics. We are primarily concerned with creating and simulating fallen snow at a scale where the thickness is clearly evident to the viewer. Our main emphasis is on a framework for efficiently handling large scenes with limited resources, and to a much lesser extent on a physically correct model of the snow itself. Snow is arguably one of the world's most complex naturally occurring substances, and accurate simulation is still a significant challenge to snow hydrologists and researchers.[1]

---

[1] We refer the reader to [9] or [1] for a discussion of the real substance.

Figure 2: A snow-covered gazebo with a hole in the roof. All snow was generated automatically, including snow on the mountains.

In order to generate images of a snowy world, we need to solve two major problems. Snow accumulation requires us to determine how much snow falls upon a scene, and where it accumulates. We simulate this with an adaptive particle/surface hybrid that addresses the proper allocation and conservation of snow mass around and under obstacles, the random nature of snowflake motion, and simple in-transit wind effects.

As snow accumulates, we compute snow stability in order to determine how much mass any particular surface can support. If not blocked by an obstacle, unstable surfaces release avalanches onto lower surfaces, also potentially covered in snow. We compute snow stability using a set of sequential local equations providing us with good results at a reasonable computational cost. Our approach allows us to simulate varying properties of both snow and like materials, as well as provide a simple model of mass transport due to wind.

Finally, we transform our model of accumulated, stable snow pack into a set of smoothly joining 3D surfaces that can be included in scenes or animations. During this step we can include bridging effects between nearby surfaces, as well as wind cornices. We augment our "thick" snow surfaces with flake dusting textures to provide extra noise and visual complexity.

Because of the sheer size and complexity of snowy scenes, our method is also inherently concerned with the practical issues of speed and control. Our primary contribution to this area is the counter-intuitive idea that snowflakes are shot *upwards* from individual surfaces, rather than dropped *downwards* from the sky. Giv-

ing individual surfaces control over their own "snowy destiny" allows us to prioritise computational effort on any number of criteria, including surface slope, area, distance to the camera, likelihood of interesting occlusions, or other measures of visual interest. Our algorithm provides a continuous, ever-improving result that can be terminated at any time, and still display the full snow depth.

As shown in Figure 3, our snow-adding algorithms are part of a larger pipeline involving a popular commercial animation package. Since the underlying scene remains unchanged, we retain the original lighting and animation and can rely upon strong commercial support for shader libraries and rendering. This makes it quite easy to add snow to a wide range of existing models and animations.

2 Related Work

Despite snow's common presence in many parts of the world, there has been little previous research towards a comprehensive model of snow for computer graphics.

Premoze et al. [16] generate realistic mountainous terrains that are likely the most convincing snow-covered scenes so far. Starting with a digital elevation model enhanced with an aerial photo, they use a detailed model of snow pack evolution to add zero-thickness patches of seasonal snow cover. The nature of the incoming satellite data restricts the technique to a scale much larger than our primary area of interest.

Muraoka et al. [13] simulate thick snow pack by dropping volume elements on the landscape, with provisions for snow evolution

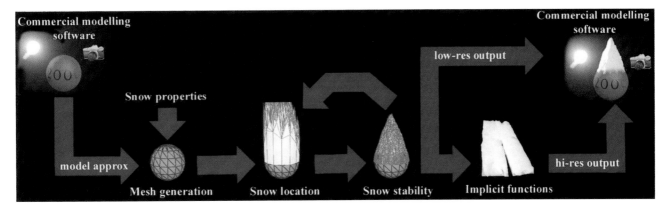

Figure 3: Overview of the snow pipeline. The underlying scene remains unchanged except for the inclusion of new snow surfaces.

[12]. Unfortunately, in order to cover the landscape with a computationally feasible number of particles, single-scale elements must be inflated to the point where they overwhelm underlying base surface detail.

Other work tangentially involving snow include Sims [20], and Shinya and Fournier [19], but both approaches are concerned only with falling and zero-thickness snow. Sumner et al. [21] simulate tracks in mud, sand, and snow using a regular height field and models of compression and erosion, but do not address snow accumulation. Nishita et. al [15] introduce a method of snow pack rendering based on multiple scattering of light within the snow volume. Snow surfaces were composed of individual metaballs placed by hand. Other work on snow illumination properties includes Hanrahan and Krueger [3] and Krueger [5].

Although not about snow, several other papers describe the motion of granular materials. Hsu and Wong [4] model zero-thickness dust accumulation with textures. Luciani et al. [8] introduce a multi-scale physical model for granular materials, designed to simulate such granular phenomena as piling, arching, and avalanching in the 2D plane. Li and Moshell [7] were responsible for a dynamic soil model on a constant regular grid, allowing for volume conservation, soil slippage, and manipulation of soil with a simulated bulldozer. Musgrave et al. [14] describe terrain generation, including an erosion and thermal weathering model that is quite applicable to snow stability.

3   Snow Accumulation

Peculiar to snow is the idea of "flake flutter", where falling ice crystals are affected by crystal shape and atmospheric micro-turbulence. These local disturbances can prevent falling snow from descending in a straight line, instead allowing flakes to sidestep blocking obstacles and land underneath on surfaces that have no direct exposure to the sky. Thus, simulating and modelling an accumulation pattern is akin to raytracing for light, except that we are interested in *path* (instead of straight-line) visibility.

Where an obstacle, such as a porch or a bush, blocks the ground underneath, the flake flutter effect eventually produces an occlusion boundary between completely blocked and unblocked areas. An example of this can be seen in Figure 4(a), where snow accumulates well underneath the overhang of the bush. Over billions of flakes, these occlusion boundaries exhibit a smooth drop-off, where the shape of the curve and amount of snow under an object depends on the size, shape, and number of blocking occlusions, the closeness of the occlusion to the ground, and the magnitude of the fluttering effect.

For objects with many occluding components (such as a pine tree) the occlusion boundaries are still present, but are much less pronounced. Most falling snow accumulates on the uppermost layer of branches, but some accumulates on the next layer, and most lower branches and the ground get at least a small dusting. This contributes to the visual impression that snow is everywhere in a scene, and not just sitting on the uppermost surfaces exposed to the sky.

3.1   Computing the Snowfall Accumulation Pattern

Our goal is to generate an accumulation pattern for every surface in the model, where the amount of snow each surface receives is proportional to the occlusion factors described above.

Our approach is to allow launch sites on each surface to emit a series of particles aimed upwards towards a sky bounding plane. As particles flutter upwards, they are checked for intersection with intervening surfaces, where a "hit" indicates that a particle is somehow blocked, and cannot contribute snow to its source surface. A "miss" means that the particle made it through or around all blocking obstacles and reached the sky.

As particles reach or are blocked from the sky they slowly build a picture of a given launch site's sky occlusion. Whenever a launch site has a sufficiently different sky occlusion from an adjacent neighbour, a new launch site is added at the perturbed midpoint to refine the transition. Likewise, launch sites can be merged whenever all surrounding neighbours have identical sky occlusions, usually in cases where sites are consistently confident that they are either completely exposed or completely occluded.

As soon as we have generated a mass accumulation picture that meets some resource criteria (compute time, number of samples, size of sample or some other importance-driven function) we can add an appropriate (and arbitrary) amount of snow. This generates a complete set of 3D snow surfaces that rise off the base model. Since the addition of a layer of blocking and obscuring snow changes the previously computed mass accumulation pattern, we can repeat the accumulation step as often desired, increasing accuracy at the cost of computation time.

3.2   Importance Ordering

The rationale for shooting upwards generally arises from the need for control: the idea that each individual surface can locally influence its resolution by deciding how many launch sites it needs, and how many particles each site should shoot. Since our sampling rate is orders of magnitude less complete than Nature's, prioritising the few samples we do have allows us to make better use of them. This ensures that even the tiniest surface is guaranteed at least a rough estimate of snow accumulation. This is a major advantage over potential approaches that drop blobby particles, since small surfaces are often missed at the expense of covering large ones. Figure 16 shows

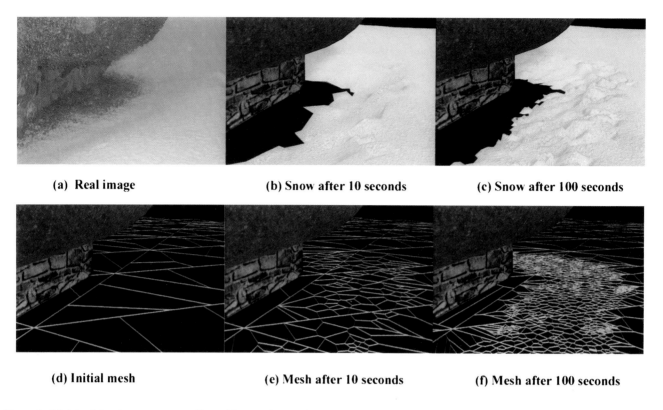

(a) Real image   **(b) Snow after 10 seconds**   **(c) Snow after 100 seconds**

(d) Initial mesh   **(e) Mesh after 10 seconds**   **(f) Mesh after 100 seconds**

Figure 4: **(a)** A bush leaning out over a wall provides a real example of the flake-flutter phenomena. **(b)** After 10 seconds, importance ordering has found the general shape of the boundary. **(c)** After 100 seconds, the boundary shape is essentially the same as (b), due to the importance ordering of launch areas. For illustration, neither (b) nor (c) have been smoothed. **(d)** Initial meshing of a crude bush model. No measurement of the real bush was done. **(e)** The denser mesh reflects the more interesting areas. A significant amount of refinement occurs behind the bush and is not visible from this viewpoint. **(f)** The denser mesh after 100 seconds.

how our multi-scale approach covers individual blades of hay in the middle of a very large snowy field.

Each launch site is given an importance ordering used to determine order of site testing, determine the number of particles to shoot per site, and decide if more sites are needed nearby to improve the resolution. As long as the allocated time has not expired, the most important launch site shoots a small batch of particles, gets a new importance based on the results, and is placed back in sorted order. The importance ordering is a heuristic weighting based on the following factors:

- Completeness. Launch sites with no previous chances to shoot are more important than sites that have had at least one chance, ensuring a crude global approximation exists before any further refinement begins.

- Area. As the area of a launch site increases, particles from a single site will pass through less of the volume immediately overhead. To prevent missing occlusions, large areas may need more particles per launch site and more initial sites. Occlusion boundaries in large areas are more visually obvious, and so gain preferential allocation of new refinement sites.

- Neighbourhoods. If the particle hit percentage of two neighbouring sites is sufficiently different, it implies that there is a nearby obstacle causing some kind of occlusion boundary. Both sites gain importance, asking for more particles to improve knowledge of the shape, orientation and magnitude of the boundary. If the neighbours are sufficiently different and important, a new refinement site may be added to the perturbed midpoint. Likewise, launch sites that are the same as all nearby neighbours become less important, and may be can-

didates for removal.

- Effort. If all other factors are equal, launch sites should use approximately the same number of particles, aiming for consistency of confidence.

- Limits. The user can set several parameters that limit the approximate scale of the finest allowable increase in resolution. This prevents launch sites from increasing indefinitely along very complex occlusion boundaries. If all sites have been resolved to this limit, the phase can terminate early.

- Steepness. Very steep launch sites are swept of what little snow they accumulate; in most scenes, these avalanches are negligible compared to accumulations on nearby stable sites.

- Camera. When optionally enabled, sites closer to the camera receive more particles, greater refinement, and improved accuracy at the cost of imposed view dependence.

- User. Importance ordering allows users to arbitrarily tag surfaces as being "boring" - useful for ignoring areas that will eventually be occluded or matted out.

We defer the reader to [1] for the actual parameterised importance weighting and further discussion of each factor. The important idea is that some launch sites get priority access to a limited sampling budget, based on criteria important to the user for a particular scene.

Figure 4(a) shows the occlusion boundary under a real snow-covered bush, illustrating the type of visual effects we want sampling to determine. After 10 seconds, the importance ordering has found the boundary, and generated an initial approximation. Spending an additional 90 seconds results in more subtle improvement, refining launch sites of less visual interest. Background unoccluded areas are of very low importance, and so undergo almost no improvement.

3.3 Launch Site Meshing

Launch site surfaces are represented as triangles, generated from the original (potentially non-polygonal) base models. Once snow has been generated, the polygonal approximation of the underlying model is discarded, allowing snow to accumulate on the original, unchanged base scene.

All upwards-facing triangles in the approximation of the underlying model are initially allocated at least one launch site. Additional launch sites are allocated based on the importance ordering of the surface, user-set resolution parameters, and the magnitude of the flake-flutter.

In order to properly allocate snow, each launch site must be responsible for some non-overlapping portion of the surface, ideally the area immediately surrounding the sample point. We have chosen a strategy based upon Voronoi diagrams, although there are numerous other valid meshing possibilities. Launch sites are connected in a constrained Delaunay triangulation, where each launch site is responsible for its own immediately surrounding Voronoi area, clipped to the edge of the triangle for maximal surface independence. Advantages of this approach include fast point-in-area tests and neighbour location, and the ability to quickly generate triangulations for intersection testing.

Figure 4 (d) shows an example of a sparse initial mesh undergoing the addition of more and more launch sites, shown in Figures 4 (e) and (f). Note how neighbouring constrained-Voronoi areas vary in size at the transition zones, and mostly minimise extreme angles. In practice, many surfaces are small and isolated (such as the brush and pine needles in Figure 1), and meshes are reduced to the trivial case of one or two samples in a triangle. Significant meshing occurs on large, connected surfaces, such as the ground.

Launch sites and their associated meshes are additionally divided into *edge groups*, which are isolated world objects, projected into the XY plane, bordered by the XY silhouette edges. Edge groups are used primarily for avalanche resolution, denoting sharp boundaries where snow may slide off from one edge group to another. Projecting into XY implies that launch sites can only be placed on surfaces with an angle of repose of $[0..90)°$. Since edge group silhouettes are not necessarily convex, we must do some additional processing to "break" constrained Delaunay neighbour links that cross a silhouette boundary or a hole in the mesh. A single edge group may also be arbitrarily broken into smaller edge groups, although this is inefficient since moving snow across group boundaries is more expensive than moving snow within the same edge group. Figure 5 shows how a sphere is converted into an edge group.

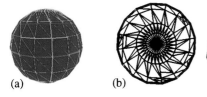

| (a) | (b) | (c) |

Figure 5: An isolated object (a), bordered by XY silhouette edges (in red) forms an edge group - top view (b), side view (c).

Our particular meshing strategy means that we have trouble with certain types of connected models that overlap in Z, such as a helix. However, this can be fixed by either splitting the model's natural object hierarchy, or increasing the number of edge groups, ultimately reaching the level of a group per polygon, if needed. Figure 6 shows an overlapping Z model that our meshing algorithm considers hard.

Note that although the knot was split into 200 edge groups, boundaries between the groups are not visible in the final result.

Figure 6: An object our meshing strategy considers "hard". Knot model courtesy of [18].

3.4 Locating Particles in the Sky

When a launch site reaches the head of the importance queue, it shoots a batch of particles towards the sky. Batch size is user definable, but generally within the order of 10-15 flakes. Particles originate from the launch site's snow surface, potentially reaching the sky plane unimpeded and contributing to the growth of the parent. We use a simple bucketing and filtering scheme to allocate the successful flakes to the total mass of the sky's available snow, while ensuring that small local areas of sky do not over-contribute. This is important, since the number of particles hitting any particular area of the sky may vary dramatically depending on the complexity of the underlying surfaces. We must ensure that a large concentration of flakes (say, directly above a tree), draws the same total snow as would the sky above a sparse flat surface. Furthermore, importance ordering implies that not all launch sites shoot the same number of particles.

We divide the sky into a grid of constant size buckets. When a flake reaches the sky successfully, we spread its representative area (defined as the launch site's projected area divided by the number of flakes in the current batch) across one or more buckets, as shown in Figure 7.

When the snow accumulation phase finishes, all sky buckets are allocated some mass based upon the arbitrary depth of snow desired. Each bucket b computes a mass per area value, based on available mass of b and the summation of all representative flake areas extending into b. An individual launch site l then receives new mass proportional to the summation of the representative area of all flakes belonging to l that hit b. A single launch site may receive snow from multiple buckets. Flake area filtering is done at the end of the accumulation phase, when a given launch site cannot change in area due to added or removed refinement sites.

Since a launch site's accumulation pattern may change with the addition of blocking snow, it is sometimes useful to split the desired snow depth up and run the accumulation phase more than once. Depending on the time allocated for each phase, lower-importance launch sites may not get a chance to shoot particles every pass. To

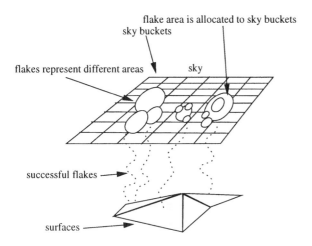

Figure 7: Allocating flake area to sky buckets.

allow fair mass allocation to those launch sites, we keep flake information in the sky until replaced by a "fresher" set of shot particles from a new pass.

The allocation of snow mass to sky buckets is usually constant, although interesting effects can be obtained by multiplying bucket mass by an input image. Figure 8 shows a scene where the sky generates very uneven amounts of snow.

Figure 8: Non-constant allocation of snow mass to sky bucketing can be used to "write" the SIGGRAPH 2000 logo with snow

3.5 Snowflake Motion

We simulate snowflake motion with a series of straight-line vectors approximating a curved path, where vector length and end position are determined with a random walk process based upon a circle of radius f_r, and Z step resolution is influenced by the importance ordering. At each step, the value of f_r is randomly chosen from a normal distribution. As f_r approaches zero, flakes duplicate vertical raycasting, producing no partial occlusion. As f_r increases, the "area of effect" of a flake widens, generally blurring occlusion boundaries and making it less obvious where bumps and depressions came from.

In practice, it is hard to match flake-flutter parameters with observed real scenes. We currently compare a grid of generated images to find the parameters that best match the shape of boundaries found in a real scene.

3.6 Determining Particle/Surface Intersection

In order to find particle/surface intersections, we allocate surfaces into a regular grid of XY buckets. Within each bucket, we compute the minimum and maximum Z values of the surface as it passes through the bucket bounding box. We then insert all Z ranges into a per-box range tree [23]. For a tree containing n ranges, it takes $O(log^2 n)$ per insert and delete, and $O(log^2 n + k)$ to return a list of the k elements that overlap the Z query range. During the accumulation phase, rebucketing is only needed upon completion, when

snow mass is added. During stability, rebucketing is done more often, although with a considerable lag for efficiency reasons.

3.7 Surface Construction

After snow allocation, each launch site is elevated by recently accumulated snow mass divided by the current launch site area. The polygonal top snow bounding surface is then the constrained-Delaunay triangulation of elevated launch sites, with corner vertices set to the minimum of adjacent neighbours. Additional vertical planes are included around edge group boundaries to close the surface down to the base plane.

3.8 Flake Dusting

In many instances, accumulated snow is not thick enough to completely obscure the underlying surface, appearing instead as a light "dusting"of flakes. This phenomena often occurs in areas of low snowfall, high instability, or on surfaces with microtexture bumps, such as tree bark. Since it is not practical to model dusting as thick 3D objects, we use already-computed snow occlusion percentages to generate procedural noise textures of the appropriate averaged dusting density. Dusting textures are semi-transparent, textured polygons oriented to float slightly in front of the original model. Figure 9 compares the texture dusting of a (slightly tilted) real and a computer generated sign. Figure 6 shows an example of the transition between thick surfaces and flake dusting textures.

In a view-dependent scene, flake dusting can be used to replace sufficiently thin and distant snow layers with a white texture, reducing the polygon count.

4 Snow Stability

The snow stability phase of the algorithm is responsible for redistributing recently accumulated snow mass into a configuration that is stable, according to some very simple surface and snow properties. It can be run at intermittent times as computational power and desired accuracy permit, usually immediately after snow accumulation.

All launch sites are initially sorted by absolute Z height plus accumulation, and placed in a list of unresolved sites u_1. The list is examined in decreasing Z order, immediately resolving unstable launch sites as they are discovered. The resolution of a single launch site s may affect a number of nearby neighbours: lower sites may receive new snow from s, while the loss of snow from s may create unstable angles with previously stable higher neighbours. Affected samples also include sites receiving edge-transit snow from s, or sites newly created to improve resolution.

If not there already, all launch sites affected by s, including s, are placed in a new sorted list u_2. At the completion of an entire pass through u_1, the list is destroyed and replaced with u_2, and the entire pass is repeated until termination.

The length of u_1 is not guaranteed to decrease on each pass, and in fact may increase, or undergo large fluctuations. Consider a large amount of very unstable snow on a wide flat surface. On the first pass, the vast majority of interior samples are considered stable, since they are at the same height as their neighbours. The band of instability exists only at the edges, where unsupported snow avalanches off into the void. As edge sites lose mass, adjacent interior neighbours are affected, and the area of instability widens. Fortunately, the erosion of snow from the edges towards the centre is very physically plausible.

Figure 9: (a) A real sign covered with real snow. (b) A computer generated sign covered with computer generated snow. Note how dusting density increases near the top and edges in both models.

4.1 Angle of Repose

Despite the wide range of physical factors influencing real snow, for simplicity we base our stability test mainly on the angle of repose (AOR) of a particular snow type. The AOR measures the static friction of a pile of granular material, and is one of the major parameters influencing our scene. It can range [6] [9] from near $90°$ in fresh dendritic snow to $15°$ in extreme slush conditions.

For a given type of snow, we use a transition curve that models the probability of stability over a range of angles around the AOR. Increasing the width of the transition curve gives a stability solution with bumpier surfaces and increased variation at snow boundary edges near the critical angle. A narrow curve generates smoother surfaces with less variation.

The AOR is based on the relative heights of accumulated snow, and not on the fixed angle of launch sites on the underlying surface. As snow drains from one launch site to another, the AOR changes continually. This means that launch sites on very steep surfaces may still support snow if the AOR of neighbouring sites is low enough, possibly because snow is blocked from moving away.

Figure 13 shows an example of this using water (AOR = $0°$) filling a fountain basin. The basin sides are too steep to support water, so mass avalanches towards the basin bottom. As the basin fills, this downward movement is blocked by the rising water level. Eventually, the basin fills to the brim, leaving a stable flat surface supported by the steep sides of the bowl.

4.2 Stability Test

The actual stability test for a single iteration on launch site s can be described as follows:

1. compute AOR between s and all neighbours n_i lower than s

2. for each i with an AOR too steep to support snow, perform an obstacle test between s and n_i

   i. if there is a non-snow obstacle in the way, the avalanche is blocked, and the neighbour n_i is ignored.

   ii. if there is a vertical snow surface (an edge group boundary) in the way, there an interpenetrating surface carrying snow between s and n_i, so the avalanche is also blocked.

   iii. if there is a non-vertical snow surface in the way, there is an interpenetrating surface B between s and n_i, where the interpenetrating surface could potentially receive the snow destined for n_i. Replace n_i with the closest launch site on B.

3. evenly shift snow from s to all neighbours n_i still in contention, until at least one neighbour becomes stable.

4. repeat steps 1 to 3 until all there are no unstable neighbours left, or s is bare of snow.

Figure 10 illustrates some of the obstacle cases.

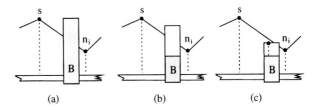

Figure 10: (a), (b), (c) illustrate stability test obstacle cases i, ii, and iii respectively

The obstacle test (step 2) checks to make sure that avalanche motion is not blocked by intervening surfaces or snow belonging to other objects. If an obstacle is found, snow is blocked and forced to pile up unless there is an alternative escape direction or snow rises above the intervening obstacle. Figure 13 shows how blocked water rises above the level of the basin sides, transferring to the top of the basin edge, eventually overflowing into the next basin.

Step 2 is expensive. Practically, we achieve large speedups by reducing the frequency of this step - from every test, to every pass, to once per stability phase, with corresponding decreases in accuracy. The most infrequent testing is usually sufficient for models where there is little inter-object penetration, although some blocking due to rising snow will be missed. Figure 1 was computed using the fastest method. Figure 16, containing thousands of interpenetrating and closely spaced grass blades, was computed using the slowest method.

Any time there is a non-snow obstacle between two adjacent neighbours, we can optionally improve the way snow builds up against the obstacle by adding refinement launch sites just before the intersection point.

4.3 Moving Snow over Edges

If an unstable launch site has no downhill neighbours, it is next to an edge. Before snow cascades over an edge into the air, we perform an intersection test with a very short vector oriented in the direction of avalanche motion. If an intersection is found, then some surface or nearby snow is sufficiently close to the avalanche origin to block movement. Blocked avalanches continue to accumulate until the origin launch site has enough snow to pass over the obstacle. If no intersection is found, the avalanche heads over the edge and is approximated as a few (usually < 5) avalanche particles moving on a simple projectile trajectory. Avalanche particles are tracked downwards, bouncing off surfaces until reaching a surface supporting launch sites. If the edge is on a shared boundary with an adjacent edge group, the particles end up "hopping" to the adjacent group via very short projectile motion.

When an avalanche particle comes to rest, it contributes its snow load to the nearest launch site on the destination surface. Depending on user-set parameters, new launch sites may be created if existing launch sites are not dense enough to capture the pattern of falling snow.

4.4 Stability Termination Criteria

A single pass of the stability algorithm reaches completion when it runs out of time, when the unresolved list u_1 becomes empty, or when all avalanches in the last pass moved only a very small amount of snow.

In most scenes, the first few passes through u_1 resolve a majority of the unstable snow, with subsequent passes handling smaller and smaller avalanches. Forced early termination may leave unstable areas, but all launch sites will usually have avalanched at least once. Our multi-pass approach avoids driving a large wave of snow downwards in a single pass, which leads to chaotic results on early termination.

If the stability phase completes before the alloted time expires, we re-run the entire phase to compensate for some speed-accuracy tradeoffs, such as missed obstacle testing, and lag in the rebucketing of changing snow surfaces. The extra phase usually fixes a few missed sites and completes immediately.

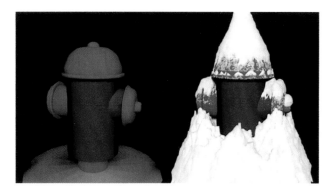

Figure 11: Covering a hydrant with low AOR snow.

5 Implicit Functions

Importance-ordering accumulation algorithms are surface-based, implying that snow can only accumulate on supporting objects. To allow for unsupported snow, such as gap bridging, edge bulges and wind cornices, we perform an additional (optional) conversion step using implicit functions. Figure 2 shows an example where snow on many closely-spaced pine needles has formed unsupported bridges and clumps.

Each snow volume is converted into one of several different implicit function types, as shown in Figure 12. Generator functions do not radiate uniformly. The one-sided "edge" function allows bulging and cornice formation, where size, bulging and direction are based upon wind velocity. The limited "top" function blends with snow directly above the generator surface, but does not blend much with adjacent neighbours. The resulting isosurface is polygonalized in $O(n^2)$ space [22].

In order to reduce blending discontinuities and apparent mass inflation at function boundaries, we use known adjacency information

to shrink and clip implicit functions so that the isosurface is coincident with the polygonal top surface. A small variable-radius line generator function blends cracks between adjacent functions, and smoothes over sharp creases in the snow. Our method is not entirely satisfactory, since surface cracks often remain visible - however, they are often minimised sufficiently to be destroyed during mesh reduction [2] after polygonization.

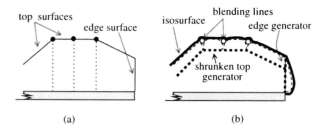

Figure 12: (a) Side view of adjacent snow volumes. (b) Side view of adjacent top and edge generator functions, with crack-filling blending lines.

Implicit functions potentially allow us to add animal tracks, wind ripples, and other patterns to snow surfaces by "stamping" the snow surface with appropriately scaled negative functions.

By interrupting the pipeline before the implicit function step in Section 5, we obtain polygonal results with no bridging or smoothing effects and a much lower polygon count. These compact intermediate results are appropriate for scene setup and real-time viewing, and may actually be sufficient for the final image. Figures 4, 13 and 16 were computed without the smoothing step. As well, intermediate polygonal results can be used as the underlying model for a completely new snow accumulation run, producing the effect of true snow layers.

6 Rain and Wind

By setting AOR = $0°$ and flake-flutter $f_r = 0$ the basic snow algorithm can also simulate the accumulation of water, from the sky or elsewhere. Figure 13 shows an example of an empty fountain slowly filling up with water. Only the patch of sky shown as a red square has any mass to contribute, approximating how water appears at a spout, fills the first basin, and overflows to lower basins.

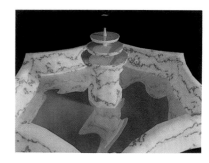

Figure 13: Snow stability algorithms can also be used to simulate water accumulation. Water from the red patch fills the first basin before overflowing into subsequent basins.

Wind is a major factor in the large-scale transport of snow, producing some very compelling and interesting effects. Although we cannot claim to duplicate these effects, we at least have a framework for simple wind phenomena in both snow accumulation and snow stability phases.

During snow accumulation, wind influence is easily included by modifying a flake's direction and distance by a velocity vector. Wind velocity vectors can be approximated with a constant direction, or much more accurately computed offline. The foreground haystack in Figure 16 shows the asymmetrical accumulation effects of a very slight breeze to the right, where the wind influence is globally constant.

During stability, we widen our single-site stability test to include neighbours that are within 90° of the downwind direction. Snow transport is then dependent on the neighbour's angle with respect to the local wind vector, the duration of the wind influence, and the carrying capacity of a given wind velocity, based on [10]. The instability vector is moved according to the rules of Section 4.2, including obstacle testing.

We use a simple heuristic to compensate for the different number of times each launch site may be stability tested. All launch sites compute a flux maximum that is reduced and moved over some small number of stability trials. Unfortunately, if the stability phase is terminated early, some areas may not get a chance to move all allowable wind transport snow. Figure 14 shows an example of wind and stability effects using a simple, globally constant wind vector.

Figure 14: (a) The initial scene without wind. (b) A globally constant wind blows the snow against the wall. Much of the snow has blown completely away.

7 Validation

Validation of snow-covered scenes is hard, in that snow observed outdoors is the result of uncontrollable and unknown environmental factors. Creating artificial snow is beyond our capabilities as a graphics lab, so instead we restrict validation to observation, asking the question: "does our algorithm produce phenomena and/or effects that are observable in nature?"

However, we were able to perform a few simple experiments to show that our snow stability algorithms are at least plausible. We substituted sifted flour for snow, to improve controllability and show that our algorithms work for materials other than snow. Figure 15 shows a side-by-side comparison of real and computer generated flour scenes. Figure 9 shows an additional side-by-side validation image of flake dusting.

8 Future Work

Our initial focus was on a framework for snow generation, and as a result we ignored, simplified, and actively avoided many extremely important physical properties and effects, including snow compression and packing, layers, slab avalanches, snow creep, snow pack metamorphosis, melting, and solar influence.

Other priorities include improving the overall smoothness of the final results. Our sampling method is very noisy, mainly due to the (relatively) tiny number of flakes used to extrapolate snow depth.

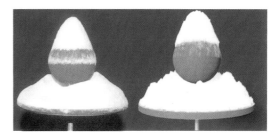

Figure 15: A real flour-covered scene (a) and a computer generated scene (b) compared to show that our stability algorithms are at least plausible. Our experimental setup was fairly ad-hoc: despite our best efforts, flour was distributed unevenly around the base of the real sphere.

Additionally, avalanching real snow distributes snow in a much wider and more complex cloud that we currently model with our few particles, leading to snow stalagmite artifacts, such as those near the foreground wall in Figure 1. Although we are able to artificially enforce surface smoothing, we have not done so in this paper.

Timing results are not fully applicable to our importance ordering scheme, as models are usually allocated a running time convenient to the user. However, the timing bottleneck of snow as a useful effect is the rendering phase, which is outside the scope of our current work. Large models such as Figures 1 and 2 were given overnight for snow accumulation, yet required weeks to raytrace animations of several hundred frames. Rendering is aggravated by aliasing in moving scenes - such as the distant, tiny, white snowpatches resting on distant, tiny, dark needles shown in Figure 1. We are interested in physically realistic, multi-resolution snow shaders or rendering models that are fast and accurate.

9 Conclusions

This paper describes a new algorithm for the creation of snow-covered models, using a novel particle location scheme that allows surfaces to independently control sampling effort needed to determine accumulation. Separability of surface accumulation produces many useful side effects, including importance ordering, adaptive refinement, smooth degradation upon early termination, and greater control of the final result. Our accumulation algorithm allows us simulate effects such as accumulation under obstacles, flake dusting, wind, falling rain, and "snow-writing".

We have also presented a simple model of snow stability that handles avalanches, edge-transit snow, obstacles supporting and blocking snow, materials other than snow, and mass transport due to wind. Additional features of the approach include support for snow bridges, cornices and various levels of model detail. Integration with commercial software allows us to snow upon existing models in a variety of formats, providing greater flexibility, power, and ease of use. Finally, we have shown that our approach is able to handle large, complex outdoor scenes consisting of hundreds of thousands of surfaces.

It is our hope that this work will open up an entire new season to computer graphics, and will stimulate other researchers to explore the natural, glorious beauties of winter.

10 Acknowledgements

Alain Fournier provided guidance and the haystack model, while colleagues and the anonymous reviewers provided many helpful suggestions. Most of base models were provided courtesy of Platinum Pictures.

Figure 16: A snowy scene inspired by Monet [11]. This model shows the results of omitting the final implicit smoothing phase. Haystack models courtesy of Alain Fournier.

References

[1] Paul Fearing. *The Computer Modelling of Fallen Snow*. PhD thesis, Dept. of Computer Science, University of British Columbia, July 2000.

[2] Michael Garland and Paul Heckbert. Surface Simplification Using Quadric Error Metrics. *SIGGRAPH 97 Conference Proceedings*, pages 209–216, August 1997.

[3] Pat Hanrahan and Wolfgang Krueger. Reflection From Layered Surfaces Due To Subsurface Scattering. *Computer Graphics (SIGGRAPH 93 Conference Proceedings)*, 27:165–174, August 1993.

[4] Siu-chi Hsu and Tien-tsin Wong. Simulating Dust Accumulation. *IEEE Computer Graphics and Applications*, 15(1):18–22, January 1995.

[5] Wolfgang Krueger. Intensity Fluctuations And Natural Texturing. *Computer Graphics (SIGGRAPH 88 Conference Proceedings)*, 22(4):213–220, August 1988.

[6] Daisuke Kuroiwa, Yukiko Mizuno, and Masao Takeuchi. Micrometrical Properties Of Snow. In *International Conference on Low Temperature Science (Physics of Snow and Ice)*, volume 1, Part II, pages 722–751. Institute for Low Temperature Science, Aug 1966.

[7] Xin Li and Michael Moshell. Modeling Soil: Realtime Dynamic Models For Soil Slippage And Manipulation. *SIGGRAPH 93 Conference Proceedings*, 27:361–368, August 1993.

[8] A. Luciani, A. Habibi, and E. Manzotti. A Multi-Scale Physical Model Of Granular Materials. In *Proceedings of Graphics Interface*, pages 136–137. Canadian Information Processing Society, 1995.

[9] David McClung and Peter Schaerer. *The Avalanche Handbook*. The Mountaineers, Seattle, Washington, 1993.

[10] Malcolm Mellor. Engineering Properties Of Snow. *Journal of Glaciology*, 19(81):15–66, 1977.

[11] Claude Monet. *Wheatstacks, Snow Effect, Morning*. Painting: oil on canvas, J. Paul Getty Museum, Los Angeles, 1891.

[12] K. Muraoka and N. Chiba. A Visual Simulation Of Melting Snow. *The Journal of the Institute of Image Electronics Engineers of Japan*, 27(4):327–338, 1998.

[13] K. Muraoka, N. Chiba, and I. Ohtawara. Snowfall Model For Simulating Close Views Of Snowy Landscapes. *The Journal of the Institute of Television Engineers of Japan*, 49(10):1252–1258, 1995.

[14] F.K. Musgrave, C.E Kolb, and R.S. Mace. The Synthesis And Rendering Of Eroded Fractal Terrains. *Computer Graphics (SIGGRAPH 89 Conference Proceedings)*, 23(3):41–50, July 1989.

[15] T. Nishita, H. Iwasaki, Y. Dobashi, and E. Nakamei. A Modeling And Rendering Method For Snow By Using Metaballs. In *Proc. EUROGRAPHICS*, volume 16. European Association for Computer Graphics, 1997.

[16] S. Premoze, W. Thompson, and P. Shirley. Geospecific Rendering Of Alpine Terrain. In *Eurographics Rendering Workshop*. European Association for Computer Graphics, June 1999.

[17] D.A Robinson. *Northern Hemisphere Snow Cover Charts*. National Snow and Ice Data Center, http://www-nsidc.colorado.edu/NSIDC/EDUCATION/SNOW/snow_Robinson.html, as of April 10, 2000.

[18] Robert G. Scharein. *Interactive Topological Drawing*. PhD thesis, Department of Computer Science, The University of British Columbia, 1998.

[19] Mikio Shinya and Alain Fournier. Stochastic Motion – Motion Under The Influence Of Wind. In *Proc. EUROGRAPHICS*, pages 119–128. European Association for Computer Graphics, 1992.

[20] Karl Sims. Particle Animation And Rendering Using Data Parallel Computation. *Computer Graphics (SIGGRAPH 90 Conference Proceedings)*, 24(4):405–413, August 1990.

[21] R. Sumner, J. O'Brien, and J. Hodgins. Animating Sand, Mud and Snow. In *Proceedings of Graphics Interface*, pages 125–132. Canadian Information Processing Society, 1998.

[22] Alan Watt and Mark Watt. *Advanced Animation and Rendering Techniques*. Addison-Wesley Publishing, Don Mills, Ontario, 1992.

[23] D.E. Willand. New Data Structures For Orthogonal Queries. *SIAM Journal of Computing*, 14(1):232–253, 1985.

Figure 17: Another view of Figure 1.

Figure 18: Snow covered brush.

Time-Dependent Visual Adaptation
For Fast Realistic Image Display

Sumanta N. Pattanaik, Jack Tumblin, Hector Yee, Donald P. Greenberg

Program of Computer Graphics, Cornell University

ABSTRACT

Human vision takes time to adapt to large changes in scene intensity, and these transient adjustments have a profound effect on visual appearance. This paper offers a new operator to include these appearance changes in animations or interactive real-time simulations, and to match a user's visual responses to those the user would experience in a real-world scene.

Large, abrupt changes in scene intensities can cause dramatic compression of visual responses, followed by a gradual recovery of normal vision. Asymmetric mechanisms govern these time-dependent adjustments, and offer adaptation to increased light that is much more rapid than adjustment to darkness. We derive a new tone reproduction operator that simulates these mechanisms. The operator accepts a stream of scene intensity frames and creates a stream of color display images.

All operator components are derived from published quantitative measurements from physiology, psychophysics, color science, and photography. Kept intentionally simple to allow fast computation, the operator is meant for use with real-time walk-through renderings, high dynamic range video cameras, and other interactive applications. We demonstrate its performance on both synthetically generated and acquired "real-world" scenes with large dynamic variations of illumination and contrast.

CR Categories: I.3.3 [**Computer Graphics**]: Picture/image generation – *Display algorithms;* I.4.3 [**Image Processing and Computer Vision**]: Enhancement – *Filtering.*

Keywords: Rendering, realistic image display, time course of adaptation, background intensity, adaptation model.

1. INTRODUCTION

The human visual system can accept a huge range of scene intensities (from about 10^{-6} to 10^{+8} cd/m^2, or 14 log$_{10}$ units), because it continually adjusts to the available light in any viewed scene. These adjustments for viewed intensity, known as visual adapta-

tion, occur almost entirely within the retina [4]. Surprisingly, the eye's iris diameter only mildly affects adaptation; its 2-8mm adjustment range varies retinal illumination by only about 1 log$_{10}$ unit [28].

Adaptation and its changes over time have profound effects on the visual appearance of any viewed scene. Continual adjustment helps keep the visual system acutely sensitive to scene content over a wide range of illumination, but adaptation also tends to hide or obscure any very slow changes in scene intensity or spectral content. For example, on an overcast late afternoon, an automobile driver may not notice the loss of daylight; adaptation can hide the gradual lighting reduction until another car's headlights reveal the darkness. Adaptation can also exaggerate large, rapid changes in scene intensity. For example, on a sunny day ($\sim 10^{+4}$ cd/m^2), people entering a dim motion picture theater ($\sim 10^{-1}$ cd/m^2) may see only blackness and the movie screen. Their vision is restored after tens of minutes of adaptation, and they may even see popcorn spilled under the seats ($\sim 10^{-3}$ cd/m^2). On leaving, people see only blinding whiteness, but in a few seconds their adaptation restores the normal appearance of a sunny day.

This paper offers a practical, accurate, and fully automatic way to reproduce similar visual experiences caused by time-dependent adaptation, even when scene intensity changes greatly exceed display device abilities. We present a new time-dependent *tone reproduction operator* that can rapidly create readily displayable color image sequences from any desired input scene, either static or dynamic, real or synthetic. The operator is simple, uses global rather than local adaptation models, and may be robust enough for real-time use with interactive renderings, with output from high dynamic range video cameras, or for rapid evaluations of lighting designs.

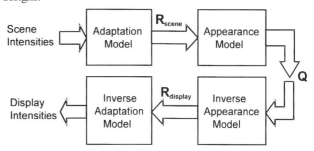

Figure 1: Tone Reproduction Operator Overview.

Our new operator follows the tone reproduction framework proposed by Tumblin and Rushmeier [19], and is built from a forward and inverse instance of a pair of perceptual models, as shown in Figure 1. The *adaptation model* transforms viewed

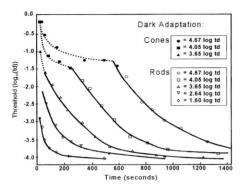

Figure 2: Increment Thresholds During Dark Adaptation. Ability to sense small illumination changes develops slowly in the dark. Test subjects were first adapted thoroughly to a uniform background intensity. Experimenters removed the background light and then periodically measured the test subject's thresholds in darkness. Five curves show results from five widely-spaced initial background intensities. Both rod and cone thresholds fall asymptotically, but cones (dashed lines, filled symbols) adapt to darkness more rapidly, and dominate threshold measurements until slower rod thresholds (solid lines, open symbols) can fall below them ([10], Table III).

scene intensities to retinal-response-like vectors $\mathbf{R}$, and the *appearance model* converts $\mathbf{R}$ to appearance vectors $\mathbf{Q}$ that express correlates of "whiteness/blackness" and "colorfulness." The upper model pair computes viewed scene appearance, and the lower pair of inverse models computes display intensities that match the scene appearance. Our forward adaptation model is an abbreviated version of an authoritative, sophisticated model of static color vision by R.W.G. Hunt and colleagues [15], augmented with exponential filters for time-dependent adaptation mechanisms. After reviewing related work in Sections 2 and 3, Section 4 presents detailed derivations of the entire operator, and Section 5 demonstrates its performance on time-varying scenes.

2. PREVIOUS WORK

There is a wealth of published psychophysical work measuring the performance of the human visual system as a function of steady background intensity [6, 8, 14, and 28]. These books and papers provide data about how thresholds increase, visual acuity improves, and motion, color, and contrast sensitivity increases with additional available light. During the last decade, computer graphics researchers [5, 17, 19, 20, 25, 26 and others] have used these data to construct more perceptually accurate scene-to-display mappings. Published mapping methods compute displayed images with improved appearance for a wide range of scene intensities as they might appear under static (steady-state) viewing conditions. These models capture many of the stationary light-dependent aspects of viewed scene appearance.

However, we found surprisingly little published work on time-dependent models of visual adaptation that is suitable for computer graphics. Though several authors, such as Graham & Hood [9], Sperling & Sondhi [18], Walraven & Valeton [23] and Wilson [27] have published extensive models of adaptation processes, the work primarily addressed psychophysical threshold experiments rather than the appearance of arbitrary image sequences. Accordingly, these models do not address appearance effects or consider the problems of displaying computed results. In the computer graphics literature, only Ferwerda [5] offers any time-dependent method, but his simple and clever model is not in accordance with psychophysical data on response compression, and the method is restricted to step-like scene intensity changes.

The work presented here is novel in three ways. First, the model is general: it accepts time sequences of arbitrary scene intensities. Next, it captures the appearance of widely varying amounts of adaptation, and includes both bleaching and network effects. Finally, the model is firmly grounded in published research results from psychophysics, physiology, and color science.

3. BACKGROUND

Almost all known adaptation mechanisms are found within the retina, and each mechanism has its own time course. In addition to the mild effect of pupil diameter adjustments, the combined effects of receptor types, photopigment bleaching and retinal connection networks explain the huge span of human vision [4].

The human retina holds two types of photoreceptor cells. Cones sense color and respond well in dim to bright light ($\sim10^{-1}$ to $\sim10^{+8}$ cd/m^2), and rods respond best between darkness and moderate light ($\sim10^{-6}$ to $\sim10^{+1}$ cd/m^2), but are blinded by saturation above $\sim10^{+2}$ cd/m^2[14]. Within their response ranges, receptors react when one of its "visual pigment" molecules captures a photon. The captured photon triggers a complex cascade of reactions known as "bleaching" that desensitizes the molecule. Bright light rapidly reduces a receptor's usable photopigment concentration, but slow retinal mechanisms restore it [4]. Photopigment concentration sets an upper limit on receptor sensitivity, and simple rate equations can predict reasonably well how these concentrations change with time and light [14].

Unlike film or television camera sensors, individual receptor cells share interdependent signals. Two more neural cell layers in the retina process these signals (see [4] Chapter 4 for a masterful summary) and their interactions strongly affect adaptation and its time course. Extensive psychophysical experiments (see [12] and [9]) have revealed rapid multiplicative and subtractive adaptation mechanisms, and more may exist within the retina ([24], pg. 76).

3.1 Adaptation Measurements and Models

Adaptation processes greatly complicate visual response function measurements because varying the test stimulus may cause adaptation that changes the response function as well. At least two very different approaches to this problem are common in the vision research literature. Psychophysicists often measure a test subject's ability to see test stimuli made so small, fast, or weak that adaptation does not change significantly, and physiologists measure the underlying biological mechanisms responsible for adaptation and light sensitivity. Both approaches offer only partial explanations of how adaptation affects visual appearance.

Increment threshold tests may offer the simplest measurements of adaptation. Test subjects first stare at a wide blank screen for enough time to adjust to its uniform "adapting intensity" I_a. Against this background, psychophysicists then show a small test spot of intensity $I_a+\Delta I$ and quickly find the smallest detectable ΔI. For moderate spot sizes and all I_a greater than about 10^{-4} cd/m^2, larger adapting backgrounds I_a cause larger increment thresholds ΔI. Over much of this range $(\Delta I/I_a)$ is nearly constant, a relation known for over 140 years as the Weber-Fechner fraction. This fraction suggests adaptation acts as a normalizer, scaling scene intensities to preserve our ability to sense contrasts within it.

A sudden change to background I_a temporarily disrupts the simple monotonic $(\Delta I$ vs. $I_a)$ function. Figure 2 shows how $\log_{10}(\Delta I)$ changes over time when test subjects are suddenly plunged into complete darkness after thoroughly adapting to one of five I_a intensities. Rods dominate retinal response while adapting from dim light (I_a=2.64 $\log_{10}$(td[1])) to darkness, and ΔI falls asymptotically to its dark-adapted value in just a few minutes. The time course of cone adaptation becomes important in the transition from bright light (4.67 $\log_{10}$(td)) to darkness. First ΔI drops quickly but pauses near the minimum cone threshold (about −1 log(td)), then as rod thresholds finally fall below cone thresholds, ΔI slowly approaches the rod dark-adapted value.

Direct cellular measurements on isolated and whole rat retinas by Dowling (1963), Weinstein, *et al.*, (1967) and others (see summary in [4], Chapter 7) offer further help. Their work showed dark adaptation in both rods and cones begins with a rapid decrease in threshold governed almost entirely by retinal network interconnections, but this fall is limited to a level directly predicted by photopigment concentrations. More recently, works by [1], [12] and [9] suggest these neural processes are complete in about 200mS for non-bleaching changes in adaptation.

Figure 3 shows increment threshold changes for a fully dark-adapted observer exposed to bright background light [2]. The entire light-adaptation process is much faster than dark adaptation, with a markedly different effect on thresholds. At the onset of the bright adapting light, ΔI jumps immediately to a very high value, then quickly settles back towards its static value. Light adaptation also includes both a fast neural component [1, 9] and a slower, pigment-limited process. Though initially puzzling, these threshold behaviors are reasonably well explained by examining retinal mechanisms.

Most retinal cells vary their response only within a range of intensities that is very narrow if compared against the entire range of vision. Adaptation processes dynamically adjust these narrow response functions to conform better to the available light. Direct cellular measurements of response functions for cone, rod, and bipolar cells [4] and firing rates for sustained ON-center retinal ganglia [24] closely follow:

$$R(I) = R_{max} \frac{I^n}{I^n + \sigma^n} \qquad (1)$$

an S-shaped curve (see multiple examples in Figure 5) where I is light intensity, R is neural response ($0 < R < R_{max}$), semi-saturation constant σ is the I value that causes the half-maximum response, and n is a sensitivity control similar to gamma for video, film, and CRTs. Introduced by Naka and Rushton in 1966 to describe fish S-potentials [14], this hyperbolic function appears repeatedly in both psychophysical experiments with flashed test stimuli [13, 1, 23, 27] and widely diverse, direct neural measurements [4, 7, 8, 22]. Psychophysical experiments modeling adaptation and saturation in rods [1] and cones [14] using Equation 1 show both R_{max} and σ depend on both I and time.

Equation 1 helps explain why threshold values differ so markedly during dark and light adaptation in Figure 2 and Figure 3. Suppose we choose values for R_{max} and σ to describe the visual response of a light-adapted observer, and make the simple assumption (as did [9],[14]) that thresholds measure some small fixed increment in response value R. Sudden darkness will not immediately change the viewer's response function, and though most scene intensities will fall well below σ in Equation 1, at first the threshold value ΔI is only weakly affected (for I near zero, $R \cong (I/\sigma)^n$; to change R by some small constant amount requires a ΔI value that is nearly unaffected by I). Over time, adaptation will

---

[1]Trolands (td) merge scene intensity with pupil area to estimate retinal illuminance: td = (Intensity in *cd/m²*)·(pupil area in *mm²*).

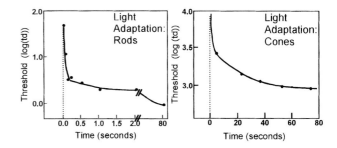

Figure 3: Increment Thresholds During Light Adaptation. Dark-adapted observers suddenly exposed to bright background light of 0.5 log Trolands for rods (left [1]) or to 3.7 log Trolands for cones (right [2]) initially experience very high thresholds, but these rapidly decay back to their static values.

gradually reduce the threshold by adjusting σ and R_{max} to their dark-adapted values as shown in Figure 2. However, once fully dark-adapted, suddenly large I values ($I \gg \sigma$) cause large response values near R_{max}, and any noticeable increase in this response requires a huge additional ΔI, a property known as "response compression" [23]. Only when adaptation brings σ nearer to the new, much brighter I values will the response and threshold fall to their static values.

Beginning in 1980, R. W. G. Hunt and colleagues have assembled and continually refined an intricate mathematical model of human color vision for use in printing, photography, and video [15]. His model is a masterful synthesis of published data from psychophysics, physiology and color science, and is suitable for critical evaluations of many forms of color image reproduction. Briefly, Hunt's model uses Equation 1 to estimate rod and cone responses to a viewed image, along with careful modeling of color response, to include numerous important subtleties. We will use parts of Hunt's model in Section 4.1.

3.2 Display Interpretation

Light-adapted response alone does not entirely explain the visual appearance of displayed images: humans easily accept and understand reduced-contrast image renditions printed in newspapers or seen on poorly adjusted CRTs under high ambient light levels. We prefer higher contrasts, as confirmed by both formal studies and advertisements for film, CRTs and printers, but do not require them. For example, bright office light has limited CRT display contrasts to only 18:1 at the computer used to write this text. Nevertheless, the displayed text and figures appear as dark, rich black against a clean, paper-white background.

Extensive studies of visual appearance and preference in photographic prints and transparencies by Jones, Nelson, Condit, Bartelson, Breneman and others (summary in [16]) offer some useful insights. Each surmised that viewers estimate scene intensities by comparing display intensities against mental estimates of *reference white* and possibly *reference black*. These values describe the display intensities needed to represent scene objects with very high and very low diffuse reflectances viewed under prevalent scene lighting. Hunt uses both reference white and reference black in his model, and we closely follow his work.

4. DERIVING THE OPERATOR

This section provides a complete description of all parts of our time-dependent tone reproduction operator. The operator makes a displayable sequence of RGB images from an input sequence of scene values expressed in cd/m² or similar units, even if the input values are not displayable. The operator creates one display image for each frame of input data, and keeps only a handful of

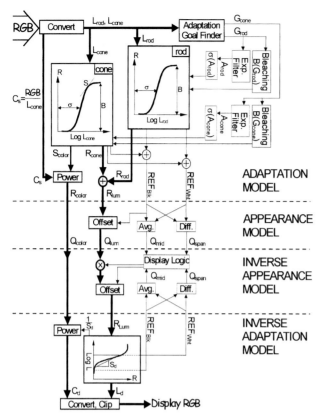

Figure 4: Detailed Tone Reproduction Block Diagram. The adaptation and appearance models of Equations 2-8 are diagrammed and assembled here according to the scheme shown in Figure 1. Thick lines carry pixel-by-pixel image data; thin lines convey scalars or vectors that apply to all pixels in an image but may vary over time. Dotted line divisions denote major sections shown in Figure 1.

time-dependent state variables from frame to frame; multiple frame buffers are not required. By following the outline given in Figure 1, we construct the complete operator as diagrammed in Figure 4. The next two subsections describe the operator's adaptation and appearance models.

4.1 Adaptation Model

The adaptation model acts as an idealized, film-like eye with uniform resolution and no localized differences in adaptation. At any instant, the same function governs response to light at all points in the scene. For each scene pixel, our model computes retina-like response signals R_{rod} and R_{cone} for rod and cone luminance and response vector R_{color} for color information.

Our adaptation model is a judicious simplification of Hunt's static model of color vision [15] that adds new, time-dependent adaptation components. These four components separately mimic the fast neural adaptation attributed to retinal interconnections (network) and the much slower process of photopigment bleaching and regeneration in both rods and cones.

4.1.1 Static Response

As shown in Figure 4, we begin by converting scene RGB values or radiances into luminance values for rods and cones (CIE standard Y', Y), labeled L_{rod} and L_{cone} respectively. We use only color-ratio components (red/L_{cone}, green/L_{cone}, blue/L_{cone}) for color.

As in Hunt's model (see [15], pg. 712, 721), we compute both rod and cone luminance responses using Equation 2, with the maximum response R_{max} given by a photopigment bleaching term B:

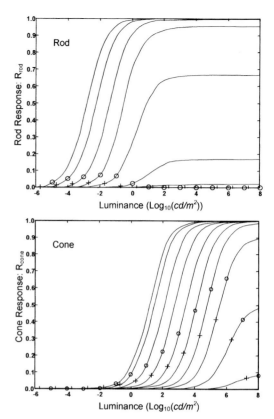

Figure 5: Model of Rod & Cone Response. These plots of R_{rod} and R_{cone} vs. luminances L_{rod} and L_{cone} were drawn with fixed adaptation luminance amounts $A_{cone} = A_{rod} = 2\cdot10^{-5}, 2\cdot10^{-4}, \ldots, 2\cdot10^{+6}, 2\cdot10^{+7} cd/m^2$. Crosses and circles mark response to adaptation luminance and "reference white" respectively. Note that rods adapted above about 10 cd/m^2 are saturated, with little or no response, as are cone above 10^{+5} cd/m^2.

$$R_{rod} = B_{rod}\frac{L_{rod}^n}{L_{rod}^n + \sigma_{rod}^n}, \quad R_{cone} = B_{cone}\frac{L_{cone}^n}{L_{cone}^n + \sigma_{cone}^n} \quad (2)$$

As before, R is the response to luminance L, and both B and σ are determined by adaptation to overall scene luminance. Our model is primarily concerned with variable responses to luminance, and discards the sophisticated color calculations performed by Hunt's model. Instead, we only approximate the amount of color compression caused by Equation 2 at L_{cone} and apply it to the color ratio vector C to make color response vector R_{color}:

$$R_{color} = \left((red, green, blue)/L_{cone}\right)^{S_{color}},$$

where:

$$S_{color} = \frac{dR_{cone}}{d\log(L_{cone})} = \frac{n\cdot B_{cone}L_{cone}^n\sigma_{cone}^n}{\left(L_{cone}^n + \sigma_{cone}^n\right)^2} \quad (3)$$

Hunt slightly modified the direct cellular measurements of Valeton and Van Norren [22] to restore pupil area effects removed from their data. He decreased n slightly to n = 0.73 and broadened the response range by about one $\log_{10}$ unit. Following Hunt's suggestion to define "reference white" as five times the adaptation luminance, the half-saturation parameters σ for rods and cones become:

$$\sigma_{rod} = \frac{2.5874 A_{rod}}{19000 j^2 A_{rod} + 0.2615(1 - j^2)^4 A_{rod}^{1/6}} \quad (4)$$

$$\sigma_{cone} = \frac{12.9223 \, A_{cone}}{k^4 A_{cone} + 0.171(1-k^4)^2 A_{cone}^{1/3}} \qquad (5)$$

where: $\quad j = \dfrac{1}{5 \times 10^5 A_{rod} + 1} \;$ and $\; k = \dfrac{1}{5 A_{cone} + 1}$.

Hunt's bleaching parameters for rods and cones are:

$$B_{cone} = \frac{2 \times 10^6}{2 \times 10^6 + A_{cone}} \;\; \text{and} \;\; B_{rod} = \frac{0.04}{0.04 + A_{rod}} \qquad (6)$$

Note B_{rod} shrinks rapidly towards zero for $A_{rod} \gg 1 \; cd/m^2$ to mimic rod saturation. The resulting static response model produces the curves for rods and cones shown in Figure 5. Our dynamic model will vary only the horizontal position (σ) and amplitude (B) of these curves.

Unlike Hunt's static values, we use separately computed, time-varying adaptation amounts (A_{rod}, A_{cone}) to compute σ, and bleaching and regeneration kinetics of pigments to compute B values for rods and cones. We rename Hunt's static (A_{rod}, A_{cone}) values as (G_{rod}, G_{cone}), the 'goal' adaptation values eventually reached if the current scene is held fixed. In the next section, the goal amounts computed for each frame drive calculations of time-varying adaptation effects.

4.1.2 Dynamic Response

Hunt's model assumes scene viewers have achieved a static, steady state of adaptation where $A_{rod} = G_{rod}$ and $A_{cone} = G_{cone}$. Typically, adaptation is measured by the amount of light required for a viewer to reach the same state while staring at a uniform blank background. Our new time-dependent or dynamic model will eventually reach this same state given enough time, but to model transient effects we use four separate time-dependent terms. 'A' terms describe fast, symmetric neural effects and are used to compute the σ values of Equations 4 and 5. 'B' terms model slower asymmetric effects from pigment bleaching, regeneration and saturation effects, and set response amplitudes as R_{max} did in Equation 1.

To compute 'A' and 'B' values, we first find the steady-state or goal adaptation values G_{rod} and G_{cone} for the current input frame of scene data. Several methods are plausible, and the best choice may depend on the application. In accordance with Hunt's 'reference white' values, we chose G values as one-fifth of the paper-white reflectance patch in the Macbeth chart for the image sequence on this paper's title page, but, in the movie sequence excerpted in Figure 7, we used the 1-degree foveal weighting method found in Ward-Larson et al.[26], and directed the foveal center to the roadway surface as a driver might. Users may also wish to aim this foveal weighting interactively as was done by Tumblin et al. [21]. Either method is a valid choice for the block labeled "Adaptation Goal Finder" in Figure 4.

Exponential decay functions are often used to model temporal processing of the visual system (see [18, 7, 1, 23, 12, 9]). Following this tradition, we chose to model the four adaptation signals A_{rod}, A_{cone}, B_{rod}, and B_{cone} with two forms of exponential smoothing filters applied to the adaptation goal signals G_{rod} or G_{cone} computed for every frame. The outputs of these filters are smoothed, delayed versions of their inputs, and Figure 6 illustrates our discrete implementation for both types.

We compute the fast, neurally-driven adaptation values A_{rod} and A_{cone} from goal values G_{rod} and G_{cone} respectively using simple fixed exponential filters where J and K functions are a fixed scale factor F: J(x)=K(x)=Fx. The response of these filters to a unit-

height step-like input as in Figure 6 is given by $\left(1 - e^{-t/t_0}\right)$, where t is time and t_0 is the "time constant." To find the constant F, just apply the discrete time-step size T to get $F = \left(1 - e^{-T/t_0}\right)$. We chose t_0 values by curve-fitting to the dark-adaptation time course data from [3] after discounting regeneration effects on measured thresholds, yielding $t_{0,rod} = 150\text{mS}$ and $t_{0,cone} = 80\text{mS}$. These data were measured on stimuli that caused significant bleaching, and our independent estimates agree reasonably well with non-bleaching measurements published by [1], [12] and [9]. We do not distinguish between multiplicative and subtractive adaptation in our model because the former is usually complete within one or two frame times.

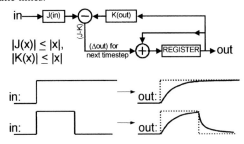

Figure 6: Discrete Exponential Smoothing Filter.

We compute time-dependent bleaching factors B_{rod}, B_{cone} by extending Hunt's static expressions in Equation 6 to include pigment kinetics (see [14], page 5-55, eqns. 10-17). The exponential filter of Figure 6 supplies the kinetics by its J and K functions. The J() functions describe the pigment depletion rate that depends on both the current amounts of light (G) and on the pigment concentration (B). The K() functions describe the competing process of pigment regeneration, which depends only on the pigment concentration (B). For rods, let $in = G_{rod}$ (current value) and $out = B_{rod}$, (previous result), then find B_{rod} for the next time-step using:

$$J_{rod}(in) = T \cdot \frac{out}{16} \cdot in; \quad K_{rod}(out) = T \cdot \frac{1-out}{\tau_{rod}}. \qquad (7a)$$

Similarly for cones, let $in = G_{cone}$ (current value) and $out = B_{cone}$ (previous result) then find B_{cone} for next timestep using:

$$J_{cone}(in) = T \cdot \frac{out}{2.2 \times 10^8} \cdot in; \quad K_{cone}(out) = T \cdot \frac{1-out}{\tau_{cone}}. \qquad (7b)$$

A published consensus on regeneration time constants is $\tau_{cone} = 110$ seconds for cones and $\tau_{rod} = 400$ seconds for rods [14]. Be sure to use cd/m^2 units in Equations 4-7 to agree with all constants.

4.2 Visual Appearance Model

Our visual appearance model is simple but extremely important to the behavior of the overall tone reproduction operator. As seen in Figure 5, even after adaptation, the response to a bright scene can be much stronger or weaker than any response achievable by a dim CRT display or a photographic print. Our appearance model assumes humans can assign equivalent appearance to dim displays and very bright or very dark scenes by a simple linear mapping of visual responses. The model determines "reference white" and "reference black" responses from among the current visual responses, and judges the appearance of any visual response against these reference standards. As shown Figure 4, our appearance model computes luminance appearance values Q_{Lum} by subtracting reference black response REF_{blk} from R_{lum}, where $R_{lum} = R_{rod} + R_{cone}$. We follow Hunt's suggestion and determine reference white as five times the current adaptation level and reference black as 1/32 the intensity of reference white. For our time-dependent adaptation model, we find the response to reference white and black as:

$$REF_{wht} = R_{rod}\Big|_{L_{rod}=5 \cdot A_{rod}} + R_{cone}\Big|_{L_{cone}=5 \cdot A_{cone}} \qquad (8)$$

$$REF_{blk} = R_{rod}\Big|_{L_{rod}=\frac{5}{32} \cdot A_{rod}} + R_{cone}\Big|_{L_{cone}=\frac{5}{32} \cdot A_{cone}}$$

(vertical line means "evaluated when"). We also compute the width and midrange of visual response as $Q_{span} = (REF_{wht}-REF_{blk})$ and $Q_{mid} = 0.5(REF_{wht} + REF_{blk})$. Color appearance values Q_{color} are set by R_{color} values of the scene.

4.3 The Tone Reproduction Operator

We can now assemble a new, time-dependent, tone reproduction operator by devising an inverse appearance and adaptation model to convert scene appearance values Q_{color}, Q_{Lum}, Q_{mid} and Q_{span} backwards into display intensity or RGB values as shown in Figure 4. We will explain these last models in reverse for clarity.

The inverse adaptation model finds display RGB values for a given set of visual response values R_{lum} and R_{color}. For simplicity, we assume the display device gamma is 1.0, forcing proportionality between RGB and display intensity values. Compared to the input range of the human visual system, the output range of most displays is quite small and usually cannot cause large changes in the visual adaptation values we compute for the display observer. (Some exceptions exist; brilliant video projectors viewed in an otherwise dark room can change viewer adaptation dramatically). For simplicity, we assume display observers have fixed, steady-state adaptation amounts. For the results shown in this paper, we assume a typical CRT display in ordinary office lighting, and set

$$A_{rod} = A_{cone} = L_{display} = 25 \; cd/m^2,$$

$$REF_{wht} = 125 \; cd/m^2, \; REF_{blk} = 4 \; cd/m^2,$$

$$\sigma_{rod} = 722 \; cd/m^2, \; \sigma_{cone} = 646 \; cd/m^2,$$

$$B_{cone} = 1, \; B_{rod} = 0.0016.$$

We compute display luminance using these constants and the inverse of Equation 2. For simplicity, we do not compute Equation 3 for color, but instead compute a constant display S_d value from a forward-difference estimate of the slope of Equation 2 measured between the display REF_{wht} and display REF_{blk}. For our typical CRT with a maximum contrast of 32:1, we set $S_d = 0.1383$. We raise color appearance value Q_{color} to the power $1/S_d$ to convert it to display color ratio C_d.

The inverse appearance model is only slightly more complicated. The model attempts to do the least harm to visual appearance in translation to the display. We assume display observers will accept minimal amounts of response offset and compression, but will object to any temporal discontinuities or response exaggerations. We also assume the display minimum and maximum values will evoke REF_{blk} and REF_{wht} responses in the viewer, and our inverse observer model attempts to map scene appearance values Q to a display observer's response values with as little distortion as possible using the following rules:

1. IF the display can directly reproduce scene visual responses, do so. Exactly cancel the offset to R_{Lum} that was applied by the forward appearance model. ELSE

2. IF scene Q_{span}>display Q_{span}, compress and offset scene Q_{Lum} to match scene REF_{wht} and REF_{blk} to display REF_{wht} and REF_{blk}. ELSE

3. IF scene Q_{mid}>display Q_{mid}, offset scene Q_L downwards only enough to ensure scene $REF_{wht} \leq$ display REF_{wht}. ELSE

4. Offset scene Q_{Lum} upwards only enough to ensure display $REF_{blk} \leq$ scene REF_{blk}.

5. RESULTS

We have constructed two examples to demonstrate the performance of our time-dependent tone reproduction operator on both real-world and synthetically generated scene intensity data. The strip of images across the top of the title page of this paper shows display images computed by our operator from two photographs of the same scene under widely different illumination conditions. The first frame in the sequence (t=0) shows predicted scene appearance for an observer statically adapted to the moonlight illumination from the side of the scene, where $A_{rod} = A_{cone} = 0.01$ cd/m^2. Immediately after this frame, the scene was suddenly lit by brilliant overhead illumination equivalent to mid-day sun: adaptation goal values are $G_{rod} = G_{cone} = 1000 cd/m^2$. In the next frame (T=30mS) the lighting has changed, but the scene viewer's adaptation state has not; a combination of clipping and response compression produces a displayed image that is almost entirely white. In subsequent frames, rapid retinal network adaptation increases rod and cone σ values to reduce response compression and restore the colorful appearance of daylight illumination.

In the second example, we simulate driving through a long highway tunnel on a sunny day, and Figure 7 shows frames from a videotape that accompanies this submission. As the daylight-adapted driver enters the tunnel, scene lighting falls quickly from about 5,000 cd/m^2 to 5 cd/m^2, and the driver is temporarily blinded while driving at highway speeds due to response compression. The driver's vision is again disrupted, though only very briefly, on leaving the tunnel.

Graphs below each video frame show the time-varying scene-to-display mapping applied by the tone reproduction operator. The effects of the exponential filters used to drive σ_{rod} and σ_{cone} are evident in slower adjustments on entering than on leaving the tunnel, and are demonstrated by the shift in the scene-to-display graph in response to large changes in scene lighting.

6. CONCLUSION AND FUTURE WORK

We have presented a simple time-dependent tone reproduction operator to reproduce the appearance of scenes that evoke changes to visual adaptation. Though the operator uses a broad range of published data, its global model of adaptation does not require extensive processing and is suitable for use in real-time applications. The operator is entirely automatic. We have demonstrated its effectiveness on both real-world and synthetic sources, and in both still and moving image sequences.

Though the results are simple to compute and have a pleasing and plausible appearance, tremendous opportunities for further improvements remain. An obvious refinement would include more of R. W. G. Hunt's model of static color vision and provide dynamic color adaptation. The operator could be improved by adding other secondary effects of adaptation, such as after-images, noise processes, and even loss of acuity under low-light conditions as already addressed by Ferwerda [5] and Ward [26]. More substantially, local adaptation effects are a vitally important part of visual appearance, and multiple instances of the tone reproduction function developed here might be applied to localized components of the scene if the proper scene decomposition could be found. Finally, a time-varying inverse adaptation model might further increase the accuracy of the displayed images.

ACKNOWLEDGEMENTS

We thank SuAnne Fu for designing the tunnel model used in our illustration, and Jonathan Corson-Rikert and Peggy Anderson for carefully proof-reading the paper.

This work was supported by the NSF Science and Technology Center for Computer Graphics and Scientific Visualization (ASC-8920219) and by the MRA parallel global illumination project ASC-9523483, and performed using equipment generously donated by Hewlett-Packard and Intel Corporation.

REFERENCES

[1] Adelson, E. H. (1982). Saturation and adaptation in the rod system. Vision Res., 22, 1299-1312.

[2] Baker, H. D. (1949). The course of foveal light adaptation measured by the threshold intensity increment. Journal of the Optical Society of America, 39, 172-179.

[3] Crawford, B.H. (1937). Change of visual sensitivity with time. Proc. of the Royal Soc., B123, 69-89.

[4] Dowling, J. E. (1987). The Retina: An approachable part of the brain. Cambridge: Belknap.

[5] Ferwerda, J. A., Pattanaik, S.N., Shirley, P. and Greenberg, D. P. (1996). A model of visual adaptation for realistic image synthesis, SIGGRAPH 96, 249-258.

[6] Finkelstein, M. A., Harrison, M., and Hood, D.C. (1990). Sites of sensitivity control within a long wavelength cone pathway. Vision Research, 30, 1145-1158.

[7] Geisler, W. S. (1981). Effects of bleaching and backgrounds on the flash response of the cone system. Journal of Physiology, 312, 413-434.

[8] Graham, N. (1989). Visual pattern analyzers, New York: Oxford University Press.

[9] Graham, N. and Hood, D. C. (1992). Modeling the dynamics of light adaptation: the merging of two traditions. Vision Research, 32, 1373-1393.

[10] Haig, C. (1941). The course of rod dark adaptation as influenced by the intensity and duration of pre-adaptation to light. Journal of General Physiology, 24, 735-751.

[11] Havard, J. (1991). New techniques and technology for tunnel lighting. Public works, November 1991, 122, 66-68.

[12] Hayhoe, M. M., Benimoff, N. I. and Hood, D. C. (1987). The time-course of multiplicative and subtractive adaptation process. Vision Research, 27, 1981-1996.

[13] Hood, D. C. and Finkelstein, M. A. (1979). Comparison of changes in sensitivity and sensation: implications for the response-intensity function of the human photopic system. Journal of Experimental Psychology: Human Perceptual Performance. 5, 391-405.

[14] Hood, D. C. and Finkelstein, M. A. (1986). Sensitivity to light. In Boff, K. R., Kaufman, L. R. and Thomas, J. P. (ed.), Handbook of Perception & Human Performance, Chapter 5, New York: Wiley.

[15] Hunt, R. W. G. (1995). The Reproduction of Colour, Chapter, Fountain Press, England.

[16] Nelson, C. N.(1966). The theory of tone reproduction, in James, T. H. (ed.), The Theory of the Photographic Process, 3rd ed. Chap. 22, 464-498, New York.

[17] Pattanaik, S. N., Ferwerda, J. A., Fairchild, M. and Greenberg D. P. (1998). A multiscale model of adaptation & spatial vision for realistic image display. Proceedings of SIGGRAPH 98, 287-298.

[18] Sperling, G. and Sondhi, M. M. (1968). Model for visual luminance discrimination and flicker detection. Journal of the Optical Society of America, 58, 1133-1145.

[19] Tumblin, J. and Rushmeier, H. (1993). Tone reproduction for realistic images, IEEE Computer Graphics and Applications, 13(6), 42-48.

[20] Tumblin, J. and Turk, G. (1999). LCIS: A boundary hierarchy for detail-preserving contrast reduction. Proceedings of SIGGRAPH 99, 83-90, Los Angeles.

[21] Tumblin, J. Hodgins, J., and Guenter, B. (1999) Two methods for display of high contrast images. ACM Transactions on Graphics, 18(1), 56-94.

[22] Valeton, J. M. and van Norren, D. (1983). Light adaptation of primate cones: An analysis based on extracellular data. Vision Research, 23, 1539-1547.

[23] Walraven, J. and Valeton, J. M. (1984). Visual adaptation and response saturation. In van Doorn, A. J., van de Grind W. A. and Koenderink J. J. (Ed.), Limits of Perception, The Netherlands:VNU Science Press.

[24] Walraven, J., Enroth-Cugell, C., Hood, D. C., MacLeod, D. I. A., and Schnapf, J.L. (1990) The Control of Visual Sensitivity. In Spillmann, L., and Werner, J. A. (ed.), Visual Perception: The Neurophysiological Foundations, Chapter 5, San Diego CA: Academic Press.

[25] Ward, G. (1994). A contrast-based scale-factor for luminance display. In Heckbert, P. S. (Ed.), Graphics Gems IV, Boston: Academic Press Professional.

[26] Ward-Larson, G., Rushmeier, H. and Piatko, C. (1997) A visibility matching tone reproduction operator for high dynamic range scenes. IEEE Transactions on Visualization and Computer Graphics, 3(4), 291-306.

[27] Wilson, R.H. and Kim, J. (1998). Dynamics of a divisive gain control in human vision, Vision Research, 38, 2735-2741.

[28] Wyszecki, G., and Stiles, W. S. (1982). Color Science. New York: Wiley.

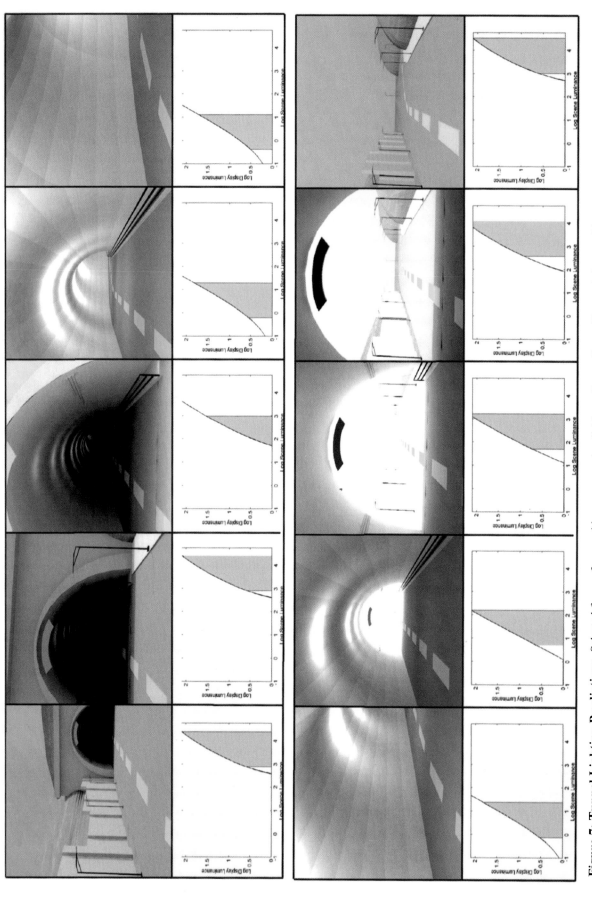

Figure 7: Tunnel Lighting Predictions Selected frames from a video sequence (available on Proceedings videotape) that combines our operator with global illumination solutions are used here to predict the appearance and safety of highway tunnel lighting. Roadway intensity varies between 5 and 5,000 cd/m². Tunnel designers ordinarily provide strong lighting just inside tunnel entrances to allow daytime drivers sufficient time to adapt to dim interior lighting [11], but excluding the lights here causes a dangerous momentary loss of vision while driving. Graphs below each frame show the time-varying, scene-to-display mapping curves computed by our tone reproduction operator; note the time-varying position and shape of the curves, and the pronounced but temporary response compression at the ends of the tunnel.

Toward a Psychophysically-Based
Light Reflection Model for Image Synthesis

Fabio Pellacini[*]   James A. Ferwerda[*]   Donald P. Greenberg[*]

Program of Computer Graphics
Cornell University

ABSTRACT

In this paper we introduce a new light reflection model for image synthesis based on experimental studies of surface gloss perception. To develop the model, we've conducted two experiments that explore the relationships between the physical parameters used to describe the reflectance properties of glossy surfaces and the perceptual dimensions of glossy appearance. In the first experiment we use multidimensional scaling techniques to reveal the dimensionality of gloss perception for simulated painted surfaces. In the second experiment we use magnitude estimation methods to place metrics on these dimensions that relate changes in apparent gloss to variations in surface reflectance properties. We use the results of these experiments to rewrite the parameters of a *physically-based* light reflection model in *perceptual* terms. The result is a new *psychophysically-based light reflection model* where the dimensions of the model are perceptually meaningful, and variations along the dimensions are perceptually uniform. We demonstrate that the model can facilitate describing surface gloss in graphics rendering applications. This work represents a new methodology for developing light reflection models for image synthesis.

Keywords

I.3.7 Three-Dimensional Graphics and Realism, Human Factors, Experimentation, Light Reflection Models, Gloss, Visual Perception.

1. INTRODUCTION

Color and *gloss* are two fundamental visual attributes used to describe the appearances of objects in synthetic images. In a typical graphics rendering application a user specifies an object's color as an RGB triple and describes its gloss in terms of the parameters of a light reflection model such as Phong [Phon75].

In addition to RGB, many rendering applications allow users to describe color in more perceptually meaningful color spaces such as HSV, Munsell, or CIELAB, that have grown out of the science of colorimetry [Wysz82]. Working in these spaces makes it easier to specify color, because the dimensions of the spaces are representative of our visual experience of color, and the scaling of the dimensions is perceptually uniform.

Unfortunately similar perceptually-based spaces for specifying

[*] 580 Rhodes Hall, Ithaca NY, 14853

http://www.graphics.cornell.edu/-{fabio,jaf,dpg}@graphics.cornell.edu

Figure 1: Coffee mugs with different gloss attributes.

surface gloss do not yet exist. At the present time the parameters used to describe gloss are either based on ad-hoc lighting models such as Phong, or are motivated by research into the physical aspects of light reflection [Blin77, Cook81, He91, Ward92, Schl93, LaFo97, Stam99]. In either case, the visual effects of the parameters are relatively unintuitive and interactions among different parameters make it difficult to specify and modify surface gloss properties. A light reflection model grounded in the visual psychophysics of gloss perception would greatly facilitate the process of describing surface gloss properties in computer graphics renderings, and could lead to more efficient and effective rendering methods.

In this paper we introduce a new light reflection model for image synthesis based on experimental studies of surface gloss perception. To develop the model, we have conducted two psychophysical studies to explore the relationships between the physical parameters used to describe the reflectance properties of glossy surfaces and the perceptual dimensions of glossy appearance. We use the results of these experiments to rewrite the parameters of a *physically-based* light reflection model in *perceptual* terms. The result is a new *psychophysically-based light reflection model* where the dimensions of the model are perceptually meaningful, and variations along the dimensions are perceptually uniform. We demonstrate that the model is useful for describing and modifying surface gloss properties in graphics rendering applications. However, the long-term impact of this work may be even more important because we present a new methodology for developing psychophysical models of the goniometric aspects of surface appearance to complement widely used colorimetric models.

2. BACKGROUND

To develop a psychophysically-based light reflection model for image synthesis we first need to understand the nature of gloss perception.

In his classic text, Hunter [Hunt87] observed that there are at least six different visual phenomena related to apparent gloss. He identified these as:

specular gloss – perceived brightness associated with the specular reflection from a surface

contrast gloss – perceived relative brightness of specularly and diffusely reflecting areas

distinctness-of-image (DOI) gloss – perceived sharpness of images reflected in a surface

haze – perceived cloudiness in reflections near the specular direction

sheen – perceived shininess at grazing angles in otherwise matte surfaces

absence-of-texture gloss – perceived surface smoothness and uniformity

Judd [Judd37] operationalized Hunter's definitions by writing expressions that related them to the physical features of surface reflectance distribution functions (BRDFs). Hunter and Judd's work is important, because it is the first to recognize the multidimensional nature of gloss perception.

In 1987 Billmeyer and O'Donnell [Bill87] published an important paper that tried to address the issue of gloss perception from first principles. Working with a set of black, gray, and white paints with varying gloss levels, O'Donnell collected ratings of the apparent difference in gloss between pairs of samples and then used multidimensional scaling techniques to discover the dimensionality of perceived gloss. He concluded that for his sample set and viewing conditions (flat samples, structured/direct illumination, black surround) the appearance of high gloss surfaces is best characterized by a measure similar to distinctness-of-image gloss, while the appearance of low gloss surfaces is better described by something like contrast gloss.

In the vision literature, studies of gloss have focused primarily on its effects on the perception of shape from shading. Todd and Mingolla [Todd83, Ming86] found that gloss generally enhances the perception of surface curvature. Blake [Blak90] found categorical changes in surface appearance and shape depending on the 3d location of the specular highlight. Braje [Braj94] found interactions between apparent shape and apparent gloss, showing that a directional reflectance pattern was perceived as more or less glossy depending on the shape of its bounding contour. More recently Nishida [Nisi98] also studied interactions between shape and gloss, and found that subjects are poor at matching the Phong parameters of bumpy surfaces with different frequency and amplitude components.

Finally, in computer graphics, while there has been extensive work on developing physically-based light reflection models, there has been relatively little effort to develop models whose dimensions are perceptually meaningful. One exception is Strauss's model [Stra90], a hybrid of Phong and Cook-Torrance, that describes surface properties with five parameters: color, smoothness, metalness, transparency, and refractive index. He reports that users find it much easier to specify surface gloss with this model than with others.

There is still much work to be done in this area. First, with the exception of Billmeyer and O'Donnell's work there has been little investigation of the multidimensional nature of glossy appearance from first principles. Hunter's observations about visual gloss phenomena are insightful but we need studies that quantify these different appearance dimensions and relate them to the physical properties of materials. Second, all previous gloss studies have looked exclusively at locally illuminated surfaces in uniform surrounds. This practice is understandable given the difficulty of controlling complex environments, but it's strange considering that one of the most salient things about glossy surfaces is their ability to reflect their surroundings. To really understand how we perceive surface gloss, we need to study three-dimensional objects in realistically rendered environments. Fortunately, image synthesis gives us a powerful tool to study the perception of surface gloss. Physically-based image synthesis methods let us make realistic images of three-dimensional objects in complex, globally-illuminated scenes, and gives us precise control over object properties. By using image synthesis techniques to conduct psychophysical experiments on gloss perception we should be able to make significant progress toward our goal of developing a psychophysically-based light reflection model that can describe the appearance of glossy materials.

3. EXPERIMENTS

3.1 Motivation

In many ways the experiments that follow are analogous to early research done to establish the science of colorimetry. In that work, researchers wanted to understand the relationships between the physical properties of light energy, and our perception of color. Many of the earliest experiments focused on determining the *dimensionality* of color perception, culminating with Young's trichromatic theory [Helm24]. Following this, further experiments were done to find *perceptually meaningful axes* in this three-dimensional color space. Hering's work [Heri64] on opponent color descriptions, falls into this category. Finally, many experiments have been done to scale these axes and create *perceptually uniform* color spaces. Munsell, Judd, and MacAdam's efforts to develop uniform color scales are good examples (see [Wysz82] for a review).

Although we recognize the great effort involved in the development of color science, our overall goals with respect to understanding gloss are similar: we are conducting experiments to understand gloss perception with the goal of building a psychophysical model of gloss that relates the visual appearance of glossy surfaces to the underlying physical properties of the surfaces.

- In Experiment 1 we will use multidimensional scaling techniques to reveal both the *dimensionality* of gloss perception, and to suggest *perceptually meaningful axes* in visual "gloss space"

- In Experiment 2 we will use magnitude estimation techniques to place quantitative metrics on these axes and create a *perceptually uniform* gloss space.

- Finally we will use these results to develop a psychophysically-based light reflection model for image synthesis.

Gloss is a visual attribute of a wide variety of materials including plastics, ceramics, metals, and other man-made and organic substances. Eventually we would like to develop a model that can explain the appearances of all these kinds of materials, but initially we need to restrict our studies to a manageable subclass. To start, we've chosen to study a set of achromatic glossy paints. We chose paints because they exhibit a wide variety of gloss levels from flat to high gloss; their reflectance properties have been measured extensively so there are good models to describe their physical characteristics, and they are widely used in art and industry, so hopefully our findings will be immediately useful.

3.2 Experiment 1: Finding the perceptual dimensions of gloss space

3.2.1 *Purpose*

The purpose of Experiment 1 is to determine the dimensionality of gloss perception for painted surfaces in synthetic images and to find perceptually meaningful axes in this visual gloss space. To do this we've designed an experiment based on multidimensional scaling techniques.

3.2.2 Methodology: Multidimensional scaling

Multidimensional scaling (MDS) is statistical method for finding the latent dimensions in a dataset [Borg97]. Multidimensional scaling takes a set of measures of the distances between pairs of objects in a dataset and reconstructs a space that explains the dataset's overall structure. This concept is best illustrated by example.

Table 1 shows a matrix of the distances between a number of U.S. cities. This matrix indicates how far one city is from another but gives no sense of their spatial relations. If this *proximity matrix* is used as input to the PROXSCAL MDS algorithm [Busi97], it attempts to reconstruct the spatial positions of the cities to best explain the proximity measures.

The two-dimensional MDS solution produced by the algorithm is shown in Figure 2, where you can see that MDS has recovered the true spatial layout of the cities (the outline of the U.S. map is overlaid for reference). Since distances in a space are unaffected by rotations or inversions, MDS solutions are only specific up to these transformations, and it is the experimenter's job to find meaningful axes in the solution.

Although a two-dimensional MDS solution is shown in Figure 2, MDS can produce solutions in any number of dimensions to try to achieve the best fit to the data. The goodness of the fit is known as the *stress* of the solution. The stress formula used in the example is:

$$stress = \sum_{i,j}\left[\delta_{i,j} - d(x_i, x_j)\right]^2 \quad (1)$$

where $\delta_{i,j}$ are the input proximities, x_i and x_j are the recovered locations in the nth dimensional solution, and d is a measure of the distance between them. The MDS algorithm attempts to minimize the stress for each of the solutions.

Figure 3 plots the stress values for solutions running from 1 to 5 dimensions. The stress curve will drop sharply as dimensions are added that explain more of the data and will decline more slowly as further superfluous dimensions are added. Standard practice is to choose the dimensionality indicated by this inflection point in the stress curve. The stress curve in Figure 3 indicates that a two-dimensional solution provides the best fit to the data, but this is to be expected since the dataset is inherently two dimensional, and error in the proximity measures is negligible, providing a perfect two-dimensional fit. In typical experimental datasets, noise in the data results in a stress curve that drops then asymptotes as greater-than-necessary dimensions are added.

MDS algorithms come in a variety of flavors that depend on the form of the stress function the algorithm uses. In our work we use a variant called *weighted Euclidean non-metric MDS* [Borg97] that allows us to combine data from multiple subjects, compensate for individual differences, and analyze datasets where the

Figure 2: MDS reconstruction of the U.S. map.

proximities may only reflect ordinal rather than interval relations in the data. We also use a second variant called *confirmatory* MDS [Borg97] which let us test hypotheses about the functional forms of the dimensions and their orthogonality.

3.2.3 Experimental Procedure

3.2.3.1 Stimuli

To apply MDS to the problem of finding the dimensionality of gloss perception, we first need to construct a stimulus set with objects that vary in gloss, and then collect measures of the apparent differences in gloss between pairs of objects in the set. These apparent gloss differences then serve as the proximities that the MDS algorithm uses to construct a representation of visual "gloss space".

A composite image of the stimulus set used in Experiment 1 is shown in Figure 4. The environment consisted of a sphere enclosed in a checkerboard box illuminated by an overhead area light source. Images were generated using a physically-based Monte Carlo path-tracer that used an isotropic version of Ward's [Ward92] light reflection model:

$$\rho(\theta_i,\phi_i,\theta_o,\phi_o) = \frac{\rho_d}{\pi} + \rho_s \cdot \frac{\exp[-\tan^2\delta/\alpha^2]}{4\pi\alpha^2\sqrt{\cos\theta_i\cos\theta_o}} \quad (2)$$

where $\rho(\theta_i,\phi_i,\theta_o,\phi_o)$ is the surface BRDF, θ_i,ϕ_i, and θ_o,ϕ_o are spherical coordinates for the incoming and outgoing directions, and δ is the half-angle between them. Ward's model uses three parameters to describe the BRDF: ρ_d – the object's diffuse reflectance; ρ_s – the energy of its specular component, and α – the spread of the specular lobe. Our reason for choosing Ward's model is that we wanted the objects in the stimulus set to be representative of the gloss properties of real materials, and Ward gives parameters that represent measured properties of a range of glossy paints. The parameters used in our stimulus set span this range. Each parameter was set to three levels. ρ_s values were (0.033, 0.066, 0.099), α values were (0.04, 0.07, 0.10), and ρ_d was set to (0.03, 0.193, 0.767) which are the diffuse reflectance factors corresponding to Munsell values (N2, N5, and N9). The

	Atl	Chi	Den	Hou	LA	Mia	NYC	SF	Sea	DC
Atlanta	0									
Chicago	587	0								
Denver	1212	920	0							
Houston	701	940	879	0						
LA	1936	1745	831	1374	0					
Miami	604	1188	1726	968	2339	0				
NYC	748	713	1631	1420	2451	1092	0			
SF	2139	1858	949	1645	347	2594	2571	0		
Seattle	2182	1737	1021	1891	959	2734	2406	678	0	
DC	543	597	1494	1220	2300	923	205	2442	2329	0

Table 1: Proximity matrix of distances between U.S. cities.

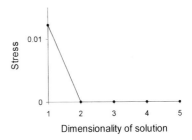

Figure 3: Stress vs. dimensionality graph for MDS solution.

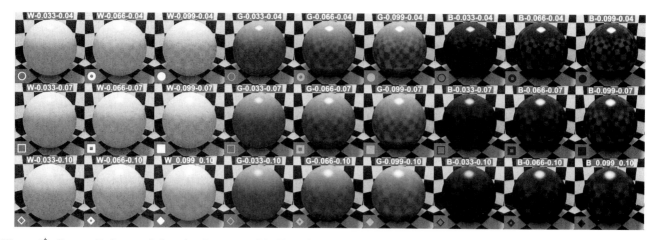

Figure 4[†]: Composite image of the stimulus set used in Experiment 1. Labels indicate the diffuse color (white, gray, black), and ρ_s and α values. Symbols are included as an aid for interpreting subsequent figures.

black and white checks in the checkerboard surround were completely diffuse and had ρ_d's of 0.03 and 0.767 respectively. By using all combinations of the ρ_d, ρ_s, and α parameters for the sphere objects, we produced the 27 images shown in Figure 4.

Choosing a tone reproduction operator to map from calculated image radiances to display values presented a challenge because the images had high dynamic ranges caused by the visible reflection of the light source. We experimented with a number of tone reproduction operators including simple clipping and gamma compression as well as Pattanaik [Patt98] and Ward-Larson's [Ward97] high dynamic range operators but we abandoned these methods because they produced objectionable artifacts such as halos and banding. We settled on Tumblin's [Tumb99] Rational Sigmoid function which compresses the light source highlight without abrupt clipping and allows all other scene values to be directly mapped to the display.

One of the consequences of the limited dynamic range of display devices is that any gloss attribute related to the absolute intensity of a highlight is not likely to play much of a role in how glossy surfaces appear in images. Given the amount of effort that has gone into developing physically accurate light reflection models for realistic image synthesis, addressing the particular dynamic range problems caused by trying to display images of glossy surfaces is certainly a subject that merits future work.

3.2.3.2 Procedure

Nine subjects participated in Experiment 1. The subjects were the first two authors and seven graduate and undergraduate Computer Science students. All had normal or corrected to normal vision. With the exception of the authors, all were naïve to the purpose and methods of the experiment.

In the experimental session, the subjects viewed pairs of images displayed on a calibrated SXGA monitor. Minimum and maximum monitor luminances were 0.7 and 108 cd/m^2 and the system gamma was 2.35. The images were presented on a black background in a darkened room. The monitor was viewed from a distance of 60 inches to ensure that the display raster was invisible. At this viewing distance each image subtended 3.2 degrees of visual angle.

Subjects were asked to judge the apparent difference in gloss between the pair of objects shown in the images. They entered their responses using a mouse to vary the position of a slider that

[†]Gloss appearance parameters are specified for the display conditions described in the experiments. Appearance in the printed images is subject to the limitations of the printing process.

was displayed below the images. The ends of the slider scale were labeled "0, small difference" and "100, large difference". A readout below the slider indicated the numeric position along the scale.

Subjects judged the apparent gloss differences of all 378 object pairs in the stimulus set. The pairs were presented in random order. For each subject, the apparent gloss differences measured in the experiment were used to fill out a 27 x 27 proximity matrix. All nine proximity matrices were used as input to the PROXSCAL MDS algorithm using the weighted Euclidean non-metric stress formulation.

3.2.4 Analysis/Discussion

Recall that our goal in this experiment is to discover the dimensionality of gloss perception for the painted surfaces and to find perceptually meaningful axes in this gloss space. To do this we observed how the stress varied with the dimensionality of the MDS solution. Figure 5 plots stress values for solutions running from 1 to 5 dimensions. The stress value drops significantly with the change from a 1-dimensional to a 2-dimensional solution, but declines more slowly with the addition of higher dimensions which are probably only accommodating noise in the dataset. *From this pattern of results we infer that under these conditions apparent gloss has two dimensions.*

The two-dimensional gloss space recovered by MDS is shown in Figure 6. In the Figure, MDS has placed the objects at locations that best reflect the differences in apparent gloss reported by the subjects.

As stated earlier, since distances in this space are invariant under rotation, inversion or scaling, it is our job to look for perceptually meaningful axes in the space. The cross in the lower right corner of the diagram indicates two important trends in the data that are related to properties of the reflected images formed

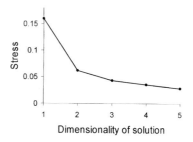

Figure 5: Dimensionality vs. stress graph for Experiment 1.

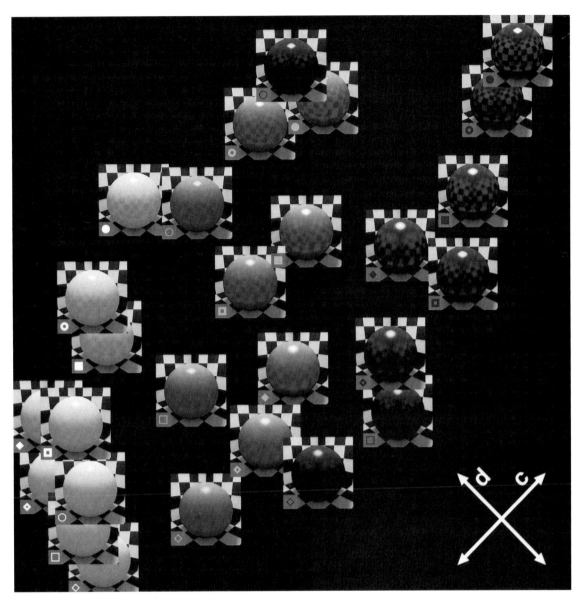

Figure 6[†]: Two-dimensional MDS solution for Experiment 1.

by the surfaces. First, the *apparent contrast of the reflected image* increases from the lower left to the upper right of the diagram. Second, the apparent sharpness or *distinctness of the reflected image* increases from lower right to upper left. We believe these dimensions are qualitatively similar to the *contrast gloss* and *distinctness-of-image (DOI) gloss* attributes Hunter observed and so we will name our dimensions c for contrast gloss and d for DOI gloss. However, to foreshadow the results of the next experiment, we will differ significantly from Hunter (and Judd) in the quantitative formulation of relationship between these perceptual dimensions and the physical dimensions used to describe surface BRDFs.

3.3 Experiment 2: Creating a perceptually uniform gloss space

3.3.1 Purpose

In Experiment 1 we discovered the dimensionality of gloss perception and identified perceptually meaningful axes in visual gloss space for painted surfaces in synthetic images. The purpose of Experiment 2 is to place psychophysical metrics on these axes

and rescale them to create a perceptually uniform gloss space. To do this we've designed an experiment based on magnitude estimation techniques.

3.3.2 Methodology: Magnitude estimation

Magnitude estimation is one of a family of psychophysical *scaling* techniques designed to reveal functional relationships between the physical properties of a stimulus and its perceptual attributes [Torg60]. In the basic magnitude estimation procedure, subjects are presented with a random sequence of stimuli that vary along some physical dimension, and they are asked to assign a number to each stimulus that indicates the apparent magnitude of the corresponding perceptual attribute. Magnitude estimates are then used to derive a psychophysical scale.

3.3.3 Experimental Procedure

3.3.3.1 Stimuli

Two magnitude estimation studies were performed in Experiment 2 to scale the perceptual gloss dimensions found in Experiment 1. In both cases the stimuli used were subsets of the stimuli used in Experiment 1, supplemented by new stimuli with

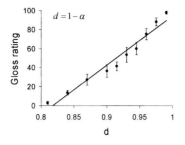

Figure 7: Magnitude estimates and fit for DOI gloss *d*.

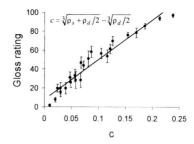

Figure 8: Magnitude estimates and fit for contrast gloss *c*.

parameters intermediate to those in the original set. In the *contrast gloss* scaling study 24 images were used, showing objects with combinations of ρ_d levels of (0.03, 0.087, 0.193, 0.420, 0.767) (black, dark/medium/light gray, white) and ρ_s levels of (0.017 0.033, 0.050, 0.066, 0.083 0.099) (low to high specular energy), the α parameter was fixed at 0.04 (small spread) to make variations along the contrast gloss dimension as salient as possible. In the *DOI gloss* scaling study, α was varied in 11 levels from 0.01 to 0.19 (small to large spread), and the ρ_d and ρ_s parameters were fixed at 0.03 (black) and 0.099 (high specular energy) to make variations along the DOI gloss dimension as salient as possible.

3.3.3.2 Procedure

The subjects in Experiment 2 were the same as those in Experiment 1, and the same display techniques, viewing conditions, and data gathering methods were used.

In each magnitude estimation study, subjects viewed single images from the new stimulus sets. Images were presented in a random sequence and each sequence was repeated three times. On each trial subjects were asked to judge the apparent glossiness of the object in the image on a scale from 0 to 100 by adjusting the on-screen slider.

3.3.4 Analysis/Discussion

Our goal in these experiments is to derive psychophysical scaling functions that relate changes in apparent gloss along the perceptual dimensions we discovered in Experiment 1 to variations in the parameters of the physical light reflection model. To achieve this goal we tested various hypotheses about functional relationships between the physical and perceptual dimensions, first with least squares fitting techniques on the magnitude estimation data and then with confirmatory MDS on the full dataset from Experiment 1. This approach allowed us to verify that the scaling functions are task independent and to determine whether the perceptual dimensions are orthogonal.

First we examined the *d* (DOI gloss) dimension. Our hypothesis was that *d* is inversely related to the α parameter. In Figure 7 subjects' gloss ratings are plotted versus the function $d = 1 - \alpha$. The line was obtained through linear regression and the r^2 value of the fit was 0.96. Polynomial fits only increased r^2 by less than 0.01 so we concluded that the relationship is linear.

Interpreting the *c* (contrast gloss) dimension was less straightforward. In the MDS solution from Experiment 1 (Figure 6) it is clear that *c* varies with diffuse reflectance, since the white, gray, and black objects form distinct clusters that occupy different ranges along the *c* dimension. Our first hypothesis was that *c* is a simple function of the physical contrast (luminance ratio) of the black and white patches in the reflected image but this provided a very poor fit to the data ($r^2 = 0.76$). Our second hypothesis was that "contrast" in this situation is a function of the *difference in*

apparent lightness of the two patches, where lightness is defined as in CIELAB [Fair98]. This second formulation provided a much better fit to the magnitude estimation data ($r^2 = 0.87$). However when we tested this second hypothesis on the full dataset from Experiment 1 using confirmatory MDS, we found that the fit was poor for surfaces with large α values where the physical contrast in the image plane drops as the reflected image gets blurrier. We then tested a third hypothesis that subjects' lightness judgments are based on inferred object-space reflectance values rather than image-space intensity values (i.e. subjects show lightness constancy [Fair98], compensating for blur-related image contrast losses). This hypothesis is formalized in Equation 4 which we derived using standard integration techniques under the assumption of small α values and high environmental contrast.

Figure 8 plots the data from the contrast gloss scaling study, which shows how subjects' gloss ratings relate to this final formulation for the *c* dimension. The line was obtained through linear regression and is a good fit to the data with an r^2 value of 0.94. This result shows that subjects appear to be compensating for the decrease in physical image contrast caused by blurring in making their judgments of the lightnesses of the reflected patches. Using this formulation also decreased the stress value in a subsequent confirmatory MDS test on the full dataset, which indicates that the *c* and *d* axes are independent, and therefore orthogonal in gloss space.

Equations 3 and 4 show the final formulas for the *c* and *d* axes. These formulas define psychophysical metrics that relate changes in apparent gloss along these two axes to variations in the physical parameters of the light reflection model.

$$d = 1 - \alpha \qquad (3)$$

$$c = \sqrt[3]{\rho_s + \rho_d/2} - \sqrt[3]{\rho_d/2} \qquad (4)$$

These axes are perceptually linear, but to make the space perceptually uniform, we need to find weighting factors for the axes so that distances in the space can be measured. These weights are given as a byproduct of the confirmatory MDS tests we ran which lets us write the distance as:

$$D_{ij} \propto \sqrt{[c_i - c_j]^2 + [1.78 \cdot (d_i - d_j)]^2} \qquad (5)$$

Figure 9 shows a visualization of the perceptually uniform gloss space with the stimuli from Experiment 1 placed at their predicted locations. The Figure shows the contrast gloss (*c*) and DOI gloss (*d*) dimensions form a two-dimensional space, (which is also shown in the inset), and surface lightness (*L*) (which we will incorporate in the following section) is an orthogonal third dimension.

Like perceptually uniform color spaces, this perceptually uniform gloss space has a number of important properties. For example, it allows us to:

- predict the visual appearance of a glossy paint from its physical reflectance parameters

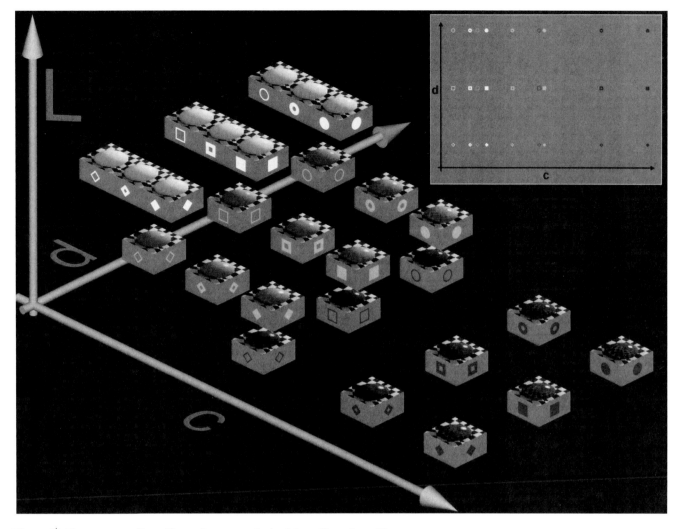

Figure 9[†]: The perceptually uniform gloss space derived from Experiment 2.

- compare two paints with respect to the two visual gloss dimensions
- produce paints with different physical reflectance values that match in terms of apparent gloss
- calculate isogloss contours that describe paints that differ equally in apparent gloss from a standard.

4. A PSYCHOPHYSICALLY-BASED LIGHT REFLECTION MODEL

To take full advantage of this new space, we are going to rewrite the parameters of the physically-based light reflection model (Equations 6,7,8) in perceptual terms to create a psychophysically-based light reflection model that can be used to describe both the physical and visual characteristics of the paints we studied. To do this, we need to introduce a perceptually linear parameter related to diffuse reflectance. For compatibility with perceptually uniform color spaces we chose CIELAB lightness (L). This final addition allows us to express the physical parameters in terms of the perceptual ones through the following equations:

$$\rho_d = f^{-1}(L) \quad (6)$$

$$\rho_s = \left(c + \sqrt[3]{f^{-1}(L)/2}\right)^3 - f^{-1}(L)/2 \quad (7)$$

$$\alpha = 1 - d \quad (8)$$

where f is the CIELAB lightness function normalized in [0,1].

Figure 10 illustrates the influence of the lightness of the diffuse component on perceived gloss. Here the solid curve plots the maximum contrast gloss c achievable for different lightness values (derived by enforcing energy conservation of the BRDF). This defines the envelope of gloss space with respect to lightness. We also plotted how contrast gloss varies with lightness for a fixed energy of the specular lobe. This curve shows that for the same specular energy, contrast gloss is smaller for lighter objects. That is to say, if two surfaces are painted with black and white paints having the same physical formulations, the black surface will appear glossier than the white one.

Strictly speaking, the model we've developed is only predictive

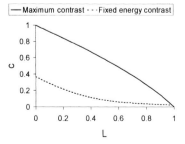

Figure 10: Effect of surface lightness on apparent gloss.

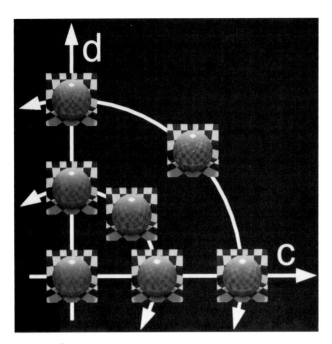

Figure 11[†]: **Isogloss difference contours.**

Figure 12[†]: **Matching apparent gloss: white, gray, and black objects having the same physical gloss parameters (top row) and perceptual gloss parameters (bottom row).**

within the range of our stimuli, which covers a substantial range of measured glossy paints. However we feel confident that the model can be applied outside this range to cover the space of physically plausible BRDFs expressible using the Ward model, but we believe that the physical parameters should be maintained in the range of the ones measured for real materials. In particular, the α value should not be much larger than 0.2 since the specular lobe of the BRDF is not normalized for larger values [Ward92].

5. APPLYING THE MODEL

In the previous section we used the results of our gloss perception studies to develop a psychophysically-based light reflection model for image synthesis where the dimensions of the model are perceptually meaningful and variations along these dimensions are perceptually uniform. In this section we demonstrate the power of the model by showing how it can be used to facilitate the process of describing surface appearance in graphics rendering applications.

5.1 Describing differences in apparent gloss

One of the benefits of working in a perceptually uniform description space is that steps along the dimensions produce equal changes in appearance. This is true of uniform color spaces such as CIELAB where equal numerical steps in lightness (L) or chroma (a,b) produce perceptually equal changes in color appearance.

The perceptually uniform gloss space our light reflection model is based on has similar properties. Figure 11 shows *isogloss difference contours* with respect to the object in the lower left corner of the diagram ($c = 0.087$, $d = 0.93$). According to the model, the objects falling on the circular contours are equally different in apparent gloss from the reference object. The concentric circles show two degrees of isogloss difference ($\Delta c = 0.04$, $\Delta d = 0.22 = 0.04/1.78$).

It's important to observe that because the gloss space is two-dimensional (c,d), objects equidistant from a reference object may have different reflectance properties even though they will be judged to be equally different in gloss from the reference. For example, the two objects at 12 and 3 o'clock in Figure 11 have

very different reflectance properties: the one at 12 o'clock produces a sharp but low contrast reflection, while the one at 3 o'clock makes a blurry but high contrast reflection, still the model predicts that they will be judged to be equally different in gloss from the reference object. This prediction was supported by an informal ranking study we ran using the stimulus set from Experiment 1. Objects whose parameters fell along isogloss contours with respect to a low gloss reference object received similar rank values implying that they appeared equally "glossy" but in different ways.

This demonstration shows that our model provides the ability to specify differences in apparent gloss. This should make it much easier to modify object gloss properties in controlled ways in graphics rendering applications.

5.2 Matching apparent gloss

Many studies of gloss perception [Hunt87, Bill87] have noted that apparent gloss is affected by the diffuse reflectance of a surface, with light colored surfaces appearing less glossy than dark ones having the same finish. This effect is illustrated in the top row of Figure 12 where the white, gray and black objects have the same physical gloss parameters ($\rho_s = 0.099$, $\alpha = 0.04$) but differ in apparent gloss with the white sphere appearing least glossy and the black sphere appearing most glossy. This phenomenon makes it difficult to create objects with different lightnesses that match in apparent gloss. The bottom row of Figure 12 shows the results produced with our psychophysically-based gloss model. When the objects are assigned the same perceptual gloss values ($c = 0.057$, $d = 0.96$) they appear to have similar gloss despite differences in their lightnesses. This property of the model should make it much easier to create objects that have the same apparent gloss, since the parameters that describe object lightness (L) and gloss (c,d) have been decoupled.

5.3 A new tool for modeling surface appearance in computer graphics

In the previous subsections we have demonstrated that our new model has two important features: it allows us to describe differences in apparent gloss, and it lets us make objects match in apparent gloss. These features should make it much easier to specify surface appearance in graphics rendering applications. To demonstrate how the model might be used, Figure 13 shows a prototype of a perceptually-based color/gloss picker for painted surfaces that could be incorporated into an application. We add color to the model by assuming (as suggested in [Astm89] and [Aida97]), that surface chromaticity and apparent gloss are

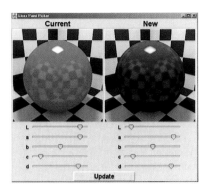

Figure 13[†]: Prototype of a perceptually-based color/gloss picker for painted surfaces. Surface appearance is specified by three color parameters CIELAB lightness (L) and chroma (a,b) and two gloss parameters (c) contrast gloss and (d) distinctness-of-image gloss.

relatively independent. For consistency with the lightness parameter *(L)* we use CIELAB chroma (*a,b*) to specify color. In the interface, surface appearance is specified by these three color parameters and by the two gloss parameters (c,d).

Figure 14 shows an image where this five parameter color/gloss description has been used to match the apparent gloss of the dark red and light blue mugs. Notice that the glossy appearance of the mugs is similar even though they differ significantly in lightness and color. This image suggests that psychophysically-based light reflection model we have developed through our experiments may be usefully applied under more general conditions, however further testing and validation are clearly necessary.

6. CONCLUSIONS/FUTURE WORK

In this paper we've introduced a new light reflection model for image synthesis based on experimental studies of surface gloss perception. To develop the model we conducted two experiments that explored the relationships between the physical parameters used to describe the reflectance properties of glossy surfaces and the perceptual dimensions of glossy appearance in synthetic images. We used the results of these experiments to develop a psychophysically-based light reflection model where the dimensions of the model are perceptually-meaningful and variations along the dimensions are perceptually uniform. We've demonstrated that the model can facilitate the process of describing surface appearance in graphics rendering applications. Although we feel that these results are promising, there is clearly much more work to be done.

First, we want to make clear that strictly speaking, the model we've developed only accurately predicts appearance within the range of glossy paints we studied, under the viewing conditions we used. Although we believe our results will generalize well, if the goal is to develop a comprehensive psychophysically-based light reflection model for image synthesis, many more studies need to be done: 1) to investigate different classes of materials like plastics, metals, and papers (possibly requiring different BRDF models); and 2) to determine how object properties like shape, pattern, texture, and color, and scene properties like illumination quality, spatial proximity, and environmental contrast and texture affect apparent gloss. Additionally, even though in our experiments we found that apparent gloss has two dimensions, we fully expect that for other materials and under other conditions different gloss attributes such as sheen and haze may play a greater role. Finally, we feel that a very important topic for future work is to develop better tone reproduction methods for

Figure 14[†]: Demonstration that the model can be used effectively in a typical rendering application (3D Studio MAX™). The model was used to make the dark red and light blue mugs match in apparent gloss.

accurately reproducing the appearance of high dynamic range glossy surfaces within the limited ranges of existing display devices.

By using physically-based image synthesis techniques to conduct psychophysical studies of surface appearance, we should be able to make significant progress in these areas. This will allow us to develop models of the goniometric aspects of surface appearance to complement widely used colorimetric models.

7. ACKNOWLEDGMENTS

Thanks to Steve Westin and our anonymous reviewers for their helpful comments on the preparation of this paper. Thanks to Will Alonso, Steve Berman, Reynald Dumont, Bill Feth, Suanne Fu, Clint Kelly, Rich Levy, and Corey Toler for serving as subjects in the experiments. Special thanks to James Cutting for his useful comments throughout this research project and for his help with the experimental design and data analysis.

8. REFERENCES

[Aida97]   Aida, T. (1997) Glossiness of colored papers and its application to specular glossiness measuring instruments. Systems and Computers in Japan, 28(1), 1106-1118.

[Astm89]   American Society for Testing and Materials. (1989) Standard practice for establishing color and gloss tolerances (Designation: D3134-89). Annual Book of ASTM Standards, 324-329.

[Bill87]   Billmeyer, F.W. and O'Donnell, F.X.D. (1987) Visual gloss scaling and multidimensional scaling analysis of painted specimens. Color Res. App. 12(6), 315-326.

[Blak90]   Blake, A. and Bulthoff, H. (1990) Does the brain know the physics of specular reflection? Nature, 343, 165-168.

[Blin77]   Blinn, J.F. (1977) Models of light reflection for computer synthesized pictures. Computer Graphics (SIGGRAPH 77 Conference Proceedings), 11(4), 192-198.

[Borg97]   Borg, I. and Groenen, P. (1997) *Modern Multidimensional Scaling: Theory and Applications.* Springer: New York.

[Braj94]   Braje, W. L. and Knill, D. C. (1994) Apparent surface shape affects perceived specular reflectance of curved surfaces. Invest. Ophth. Vis. Sci. Suppl. 35(4), 1628.

[Busi97]   Busing, F., Commandeur, J., and Heiser, W. (1997) PROXSCAL: a multidimensional scaling program for individual differences scaling with constraints. In W. Bandilla and Faulbaum (Eds.), *Advances in Statistical Software, 6*, Lucius & Lucius: Stuttgart, 67-73.

[Cook81]   Cook, R.L. and Torrance, K.E.. (1981) A reflectance model for computer graphics. Computer Graphics (SIGGRAPH 81 Conference Proceedings), 15(4), 187–196.

[Fair98]   Fairchild, M.D. (1998) *Color Appearance Models.* Addison-Wesley, Reading, MA.

[He91]   He, X.D., Torrance, K.E., Sillion, F.X., and Greenberg, D.P. (1991) A comprehensive physical model for light reflection. Computer Graphics (SIGGRAPH 91 Conference Proceedings), 25(4), 175–186.

[Helm24]   Helmholtz, H. von (1924) *Treatise on Physiological Optics* (vol. II), (Trans. by J.P. Southhall). Optical Society of America.

[Heri64]   Hering, E. (1964) *Outlines of a Theory of the Light Sense*, (Trans. by L. Hurvich and D. Jameson). Harvard University Press: Cambridge, MA.

[Hunt87]   Hunter, R.S. and Harold R.W. (1987) *The Measurement of Appearance* (2nd edition). Wiley, New York.

[Judd37]   Judd, D.B. (1937) Gloss and glossiness. Am. Dyest. Rep. 26, 234-235.

[Lafo97]   Lafortune, E.P., Foo, S.C., Torrance, K.E., and Greenberg, D.P. (1997) Non-linear approximation of reflectance functions. SIGGRAPH 97 Conference Proceedings, 117-126.

[Ming86]   Mingolla, E. and Todd, J.T. (1986) Perception of solid shape from shading. Bio. Cyber. 53(3), 137-151.

[Nish98]   Nishida, S. and Shinya, M. (1998) Use of image-based information in judgements of surface reflectance properties. J. Opt. Soc. Am., 15(12), 2951-2965.

[Patt98]   Pattanaik. S. Ferwerda, J.A., Fairchild, M.D. and Greenberg, D.P. (1998) A multiscale model of adaptation and spatial vision for realistic image display. SIGGRAPH 98 Conference Proceedings, 287-298.

[Phon75]   Phong B.T. (1975) Illumination for computer generated pictures. Comm. ACM 18(6), 311–317.

[Schl93]   Schlick, C. (1993) A customizable reflectance model for everyday rendering. Proc. 4th Eurographics Workshop on Rendering, 73–83.

[Stam99]   Stamm, J. (1999) Diffraction shaders. SIGGRAPH 99 Conference Proceedings, 101-110.

[Stra90]   Strauss, P. S. (1990) A realistic lighting model for computer animators. IEEE Comp. Graph. & Appl. 10(6), 56-64.

[Todd83]   Todd, J.T. and Mingolla, E. (1983) Perception of surface curvature and direction of illumination from patterns of shading. J. Exp. Psych.: Hum. Percept. and Perf. 9(4), 583-595.

[Torg60]   Torgerson, W.S. (1960) *Theory and Methods of Scaling.* Wiley: New York.

[Tumb99]   Tumblin, J., Hodgins J.K., and Guenter, B.K. (1999) Two methods for display of high contrast images. ACM Trans. on Graph., 18(1), 56-94

[Ward92]   Ward, G.J. (1992) Measuring and modeling anisotropic reflection. Computer Graphics (SIGGRAPH 92 Conference Proceedings), 26(2), 265–272.

[Ward97]   Ward-Larson, G., Rushmeier H., and Piatko, C. (1997) A visibility matching tone reproduction operator for high dynamic range scenes. IEEE Trans. on Vis. and Comp. Graph., 3(4):291-306.

[Wysz82]   Wyszecki, G. and Stiles, W.S. (1982) *Color Science: Concepts and Methods, Quantitative Data and Formulae* (2nd ed.), Wiley: New York.

A Microfacet-based BRDF Generator

Michael Ashikhmin   Simon Premože   Peter Shirley

University of Utah   www.cs.utah.edu

Abstract

A method is presented that takes as an input a 2D microfacet orientation distribution and produces a 4D bidirectional reflectance distribution function (BRDF). This method differs from previous microfacet-based BRDF models in that it uses a simple shadowing term which allows it to handle very general microfacet distributions while maintaining reciprocity and energy conservation. The generator is shown on a variety of material types.

CR Categories: I.3.7 [Computing Methodologies]: Computer Graphics—3D Graphics

Keywords: Reflectance & Shading Models, Rendering

1 Introduction

Physically-based rendering systems describe reflection behavior using the *bidirectional reflectance distribution function* (BRDF) [7]. At a given point on a surface the BRDF is a function of two directions, one toward the light and one toward the viewer. The characteristics of the BRDF will determine what "type" of material the viewer thinks the displayed object is composed of, so the choice of BRDF model and its parameters is important. There are a variety of basic strategies for modeling BRDFs that we categorize as follows.

Direct measurement. BRDFs can be measured directly using *gonioreflectometers* which mechanically vary the direction to a small light source and a spectral sensor and thus collect a large number of point samples for the BRDF [7]. Simpler and less accurate devices can also be constructed using CCD imaging devices [26]. More complex CCD devices can also be used which gather data quickly with accuracy almost that of full gonioreflectometry [12]. If enough is known about the microstructure of a material, a BRDF can be simulated by using a *virtual gonioreflectometer*, where statistical ray tracing followed by density estimation is used to create BRDF data [3, 5, 27].

Empirical methods. There exist a variety of purely empirical reflection models, the most familiar being the models introduced by Gouraud [6] and Phong [15]. These two initial models were meant to be used with hand-chosen parameters, and thus these parameters are intuitive. A variety of more complex methods have been introduced to improve characteristics of the Phong model for efficiency [19], to include anisotropy [26], and enforce physical constraints such as reciprocity [9]. Other models have been developed to fit measurement data as opposed to being intuitive [10].

 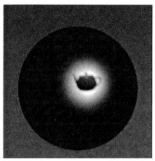

Figure 1: *Images generated using the new BRDF model with unusual microfacet distributions. The BRDFs used to create these images are both reciprocal and energy-conserving. The only illumination is a small distant source, and the highlights will stay unchanged if the spheres rotate about the axes through their north and south poles.*

Height correlation methods. In these methods a random rough surface is a realization of some Gaussian random process. Such a process can be described by its correlation function which is directly related to surface height correlations. This is the most complete surface representation used in computer graphics. Some of the most detailed descriptions of light scattering by a surface, including wave optics effects, were obtained using this approach [8, 22].

Microfacet methods. Somewhere between the height correlation methods and empirical methods lie models based on microfacet theory [2, 4]. Microfacet models assume the surface consists of a large number of small flat "micromirrors" (facets) each of which reflect light only in the specular direction. By computing the number of visible microfacets at the appropriate orientation to specularly reflect light from the source to the viewer, one can determine the BRDF.

All of these methods have their place. In applications where little is known about the low-level properties of the surface, measurement is essential. Where physical optics effects are important, height correlation methods should be used. Our interest is in visual computer graphics applications which do not have obvious physical optics effects (e.g. metal with relatively large scratches, fabric). The lesson from empirical models is that in many cases viewers are not particularly sensitive to the fine details of light scattering as long as the main character of the reflection is conveyed correctly. This paper uses this aspect of human sensitivity to suggest a new microfacet model specifically intended to capture the main character of reflection.

Microfacet models are able to capture the main character of reflection for surfaces whose appearance is dominated by surface scattering. Although microfacet models lack the precision of height correlation methods, they tend to be more intuitive with simpler expressions. However, to date there has been no microfacet model that is reasonably general in its assumptions, maintains a simple formulation, and conserves energy. In this paper we develop a model with all of these characteristics by introducing assumptions about surfaces that we believe are reasonable. These assumptions allow

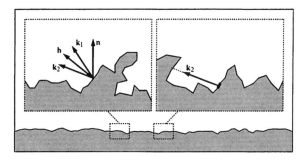

Figure 2: *Geometry of reflection. Note that* $\mathbf{k}_1$, $\mathbf{k}_2$, *and* $\mathbf{h}$ *share a plane, which usually does not include* $\mathbf{n}$. *On the left, the microfacet can "see" in directions* $\mathbf{k}_1$ *and* $\mathbf{k}_2$ *so it contributes to the BRDF. On the right, direction* $\mathbf{k}_2$ *is blocked and the microfacet does not contribute. Note that the microfacet distribution is not restricted to height fields.*

$(\mathbf{ab})$	scalar (dot) product of vectors $\mathbf{a}$ and $\mathbf{b}$
$\mathbf{k}_1$	normalized vector to light
$\mathbf{k}_2$	normalized vector to viewer
$\mathbf{n}$	surface normal to macroscopic surface
$\rho(\mathbf{k}_1, \mathbf{k}_2)$	BRDF
$\mathbf{h}$	normalized half-vector between $\mathbf{k}_1$ and $\mathbf{k}_2$
$p(\mathbf{h})$	probability density function of microfacet normals
$F(\cos\theta)$	Fresnel reflectance for incident angle θ
$P(\mathbf{k}_1, \mathbf{k}_2, \mathbf{h})$	Probability that light from $\mathbf{k}_1$ reflecting in direction $\mathbf{k}_2$ is *not* shadowed
$\langle f \rangle$	average of function f over distribution $p(\mathbf{h})$ (see Equation 9)
$\Omega_+(\mathbf{k})$	set of directions $\mathbf{h}$ where $(\mathbf{hk}) > 0$ (see Figure 4)
$g(\mathbf{k})$	average of positive $(\mathbf{hk})$ (see Equation 18)

Table 1: Important terms used in the paper

us to create a relatively simple formula for the probability that a microfacet at a certain orientation is visible to the light/viewer. The BRDF produced by this process is compact, reciprocal and energy-conserving with only mild restrictions on the distribution of microfacet orientation (e.g., the very general distributions in Figure 1).

Our assumptions and guiding principles in relation to microfacet theory are given in Section 2. Formalisms are developed in Section 3. The key development of the paper, a simplified shadowing term, is introduced in Section 4, and the resulting BRDF is derived. Section 5 shows that this BRDF model conserves energy, and derives a diffuse term to account for secondary and subsurface reflection. The model is applied to a variety of surfaces in Section 6. This last section serves as a set of case-studies which both show how the model can be applied, and that it is more general than previous microfacet approaches. We believe the only other method which is able to handle such a diverse set of surface microgeometries is the "virtual gonireflectometer" approach involving explicit modeling of the surface structure and statistical averaging the results of light scattering simulations.

2 Overview

The strategy behind our model is in balancing issues of practicality and accuracy to produce a simple formulation that is still expressive, reciprocal, and conserves energy. In this section we discuss the basic ideas of microfacet models, as well as our strategy for using this theory to produce BRDFs. Important symbols used in the paper are listed in Table 1.

Microfacet models assume that the surface consists of a large number of small flat "micromirrors" (facets) each of which reflects light only in the specular direction with respect to its own normal $\mathbf{h}$ (Figure 2) and the overall appearance of the surface is governed by two assumptions:

- the microfacet normals have an underlying probability density function $p(\mathbf{h})$.

- a microfacet contributes to BRDF for a given pair of directions if and only if it is visible (not shadowed) relative to the lighting direction $\mathbf{k}_1$ and the viewing direction $\mathbf{k}_2$.

The BRDF for a given direction pair $(\mathbf{k}_1, \mathbf{k}_2)$ is determined entirely by the Fresnel reflectance for that angle, the fraction of microfacets with normal vector $\mathbf{h}$ exactly between $\mathbf{k}_1$ and $\mathbf{k}_2$, and the *shadowing term*: the fraction of those microfacets which are visible to both eye and light (Figure 2). Microfacet theory's only knowledge of the

surface configuration is $p(\mathbf{h})$, and this alone does not uniquely determine the shadowing term. However, the shadowing term is still heavily constrained by energy conservation.

The shadowing term is the most complex part of most microfacet-based models, even if additional $p(\mathbf{h})$-specific information about the surface geometry is used. Because there are many possible surface geometries that are consistent with a given $p(\mathbf{h})$, it is the case that no specific shadowing function is "right". We believe that in most cases the shape of $p(\mathbf{h})$ function itself has a much greater impact on the appearance than the shadowing. This suggests the key idea in this paper: the shadowing term should be made as simple as possible while remaining physically plausible. Such a shadowing term is developed in Section 4. This key extension of the standard microfacet theories allows us to construct a general procedure to create a BRDF for a statistical surface starting from $p(\mathbf{h})$.

Note that surface description in the language of $p(\mathbf{h})$ is less detailed than that of using height correlation functions. Nevertheless, we believe that the microfacet normal distribution is more intuitive to deal with than the correlation functions. As we will emphasize in Section 6, enough useful information about $p(\mathbf{h})$ can be obtained from general notion of surface structure obtained through visual examination of the surface and the specular reflection highlight. Moreover, attempting to obtain more detailed information about the distribution might not be worth the effort. As in any other model, we make simplification in our approach which affect the final result, but what we are trying to do is generate a physically plausible BRDF having the general character of the surface reflection while restricting the range of allowed surface microstructures as little as possible. This is in contrast to most other physics-based approaches which concentrate on a particular type of surface, usually Gaussian height field, and emphasize the need for precise knowledge of surface characteristics.

Some care should be exercised when specifying $p(\mathbf{h})$. In particular, because we do not make the common assumption of a surface being a height field, in this general case $p(\mathbf{h})$ should refer only to the distribution of "visually important" or "surface" part of the microfacets. For example, a homogeneous porous substance thought of as a collection of microfacets will have an overall "volume" distribution of microfacets $p_v(\mathbf{h}) = const$ over the whole sphere of directions. However, that most of these microfacets will be completely hidden and will not be of any significance for the scattering process which occurs on the surface. In this case it is rather difficult to separate surface from the rest of the substance and judge the exact shape of $p(\mathbf{h})$. Fortunately, because we are not trying to reproduce all the details of the reflection function, a reasonable guess for $p(\mathbf{h})$

is all we need and for this surface; it might be $p(\mathbf{h}) = const$ in the upper hemisphere and $p(\mathbf{h}) = 0$ in the lower one. Note, that by making this particular choice for $p(\mathbf{h})$ the surface is restricted to be a height field. The initial choice can be refined later if necessary but in this particular case it the surface will be mostly diffuse and small refinements will not dramatically change the appearance.

We are concerned with single-bounce reflections from the microfacets and stay within the limits of geometric optics and Fresnel reflection. The result is a new form of the specular component of the BRDF which constitutes the main contribution of the paper. The complete BRDF can also have a diffuse term which accounts for multiple bounces and subsurface scattering. This issue along with other important properties of the BRDFs produced with the generator are briefly discussed in Section 5. Our framework is modular and allows the user to choose the form of the final BRDF most appropriate for the particular application.

3   Microfacet Theory

We now review the main results of microfacet theory as developed by Torrance and Sparrow [23] and later introduced to computer graphics by Cook and Torrance [4]. We follow their approach of considering a collection of microfacets of small but finite size, and we derive the basic formula for BRDF in terms of quantities convenient for our model.

The quantity we wish to derive an expression for is the BRDF $\rho(\mathbf{k}_1, \mathbf{k}_2)$ which gives the ratio of radiance observed by a viewer in the direction $\mathbf{k}_2$ to irradiance from infinitesimal solid angle about $\mathbf{k}_1$. Throughout the paper, all vectors are shown in **bold**. They are assumed to be normalized, and all quantities with subscript 1 refer to incident direction while those with subscript 2 belong to the outgoing direction. Both $\mathbf{k}_1$ and $\mathbf{k}_2$ and all normals point outward from the surface. If we expose the surface to a uniform radiance of L_1 coming from a small solid angle $\delta\omega_1$ around $\mathbf{k}_1$, the outgoing radiance in direction $\mathbf{k}_2$ will be

$$L_2 = \rho(\mathbf{k}_1, \mathbf{k}_2) \ L_1 \ (\mathbf{k}_1\mathbf{n})\delta\omega_1, \qquad (1)$$

where $\mathbf{n}$ is the surface geometric normal and two vectors written next to each other in parenthesis denotes their scalar product, i.e., the cosine of the angle between them. The use of δ is not standard notation, but is used to make the algebra less cluttered without losing the gist of the argument. By the definition of radiance, if $(\mathbf{k}_2\mathbf{n})A$ is the projected surface element area in the direction $\mathbf{k}_2$ and $\delta E(\mathbf{k}_1 \rightarrow \mathbf{k}_2)$ is the power reflected by the surface in the direction $\mathbf{k}_2$, then

$$L_2 = \frac{\delta E(\mathbf{k}_1 \rightarrow \mathbf{k}_2)}{A(\mathbf{k}_2\mathbf{n})\delta\omega_2}, \qquad (2)$$

and BRDF can be written as

$$\rho(\mathbf{k}_1, \mathbf{k}_2) = \frac{\delta E(\mathbf{k}_1 \rightarrow \mathbf{k}_2)}{A L_1 (\mathbf{k}_2\mathbf{n})(\mathbf{k}_1\mathbf{n})\delta\omega_1\delta\omega_2}. \qquad (3)$$

Only a fraction of all microfacets will participate in scattering the energy from $\mathbf{k}_1$ to $\mathbf{k}_2$. If the number of these active microfacets is N_{active} and all microfacets have the same area A_{mf}, their total projected area in the direction of $\mathbf{k}_1$ is $N_{active}A_{mf}(\mathbf{kh})$ and the total scattered power is

$$\delta E(\mathbf{k}_1 \rightarrow \mathbf{k}_2) = L_1\delta\omega_1 N_{active}A_{mf}(\mathbf{kh})F((\mathbf{kh})), \qquad (4)$$

where $\mathbf{h}$ is the normalized half-vector between $\mathbf{k}_1$ and $\mathbf{k}_2$ and $F((\mathbf{kh}))$ is Fresnel coefficient giving the fraction of incoming light which is specularly reflected by a microfacet. Note that we will drop subscripts in our notations if either of incoming and outgoing direction can be used in an expression (e.g., $(\mathbf{kh})$).

Out of the total of N surface microfacets, only $Np(\mathbf{h})\delta\omega_h$ will have their normals oriented in the appropriate direction. The density $p(\mathbf{h})$ does not specify all surface properties uniquely, but in our simplified approach this is the only characteristic of the surface we will use in our analysis. Note that this function operates in the domain of microfacet normals which is different from the space of incoming and outgoing light directions. In particular, for the case of specularly reflecting microfacets, the relationship between elementary solid angles [23] can be shown to be

$$\delta\omega_2 = 4(\mathbf{k}_1\mathbf{h})\delta\omega_h. \qquad (5)$$

Even if a microfacet has the required orientation, it might still not contribute to the single-bounce highlight if it is shadowed by other microfacets for either incoming or outgoing direction. Introducing the probability for a microfacet *not* to be shadowed in either incoming or outgoing directions as $0 \leq P(\mathbf{k}_1, \mathbf{k}_2, \mathbf{h}) \leq 1$ we will have $N_{active} = Np(\mathbf{h})P(\mathbf{k}_1, \mathbf{k}_2, \mathbf{h})\delta\omega_h$ and BRDF in the form

$$\rho(\mathbf{k}_1, \mathbf{k}_2) = \frac{N A_{mf}p(\mathbf{h})P(\mathbf{k}_1, \mathbf{k}_2, \mathbf{h})F((\mathbf{kh}))}{4A(\mathbf{k}_1\mathbf{n})(\mathbf{k}_2\mathbf{n})}. \qquad (6)$$

Equation 6 is a somewhat modified version of the original result of Torrance and Sparrow who present its more detailed derivation [23].

The area A of the surface element can be written as a sum of the projected areas of all microfacets:

$$A = \sum_{facets} A_{mf}(\mathbf{hn})P(\mathbf{n}, \mathbf{h}), \qquad (7)$$

where we introduce probability $P(\mathbf{n}, \mathbf{h})$ for a microfacet not to be "shadowed" in the surface normal direction $\mathbf{n}$ by other microfacets. If the surface is a height field, $P(\mathbf{n}, \mathbf{h}) = 1$ but in the general case some microfacets may not contribute to the area A of the projection. This question is related to the general shadowing term $P(\mathbf{k}_1, \mathbf{k}_2, \mathbf{h})$ and we postpone its discussion until the next section. The "P" is used with a variable number of arguments that depend on what assumptions are in play for that equation.

Given a large number of microfacets, Equation 7 can be rewritten using the average over the ensemble of microfacets as

$$A = N A_{mf}\langle(\mathbf{hn})P(\mathbf{n}, \mathbf{h})\rangle_{ens}, \qquad (8)$$

where $\langle...\rangle_{ens}$ denotes the averaging procedure. One of the most fundamental results in statistics states that as the size of the ensemble increases, for a certain function f of a random variable its average over ensemble $\langle f\rangle_{ens}$ converges with probability one to its average $\langle f\rangle$ over the distribution of the random variable. In our case we can write for any quantity $f(\mathbf{h})$:

$$\langle f(\mathbf{h})\rangle_{ens} = \langle f(\mathbf{h})\rangle = \int_\Omega f(\mathbf{h})p(\mathbf{h})d\omega_h, \qquad (9)$$

where the integration is done over the unit sphere Ω of microfacet normal directions (Gaussian sphere). So, for the BRDF we finally have

$$\rho(\mathbf{k}_1, \mathbf{k}_2) = \frac{p(\mathbf{h})P(\mathbf{k}_1, \mathbf{k}_2, \mathbf{h})F((\mathbf{kh}))}{4(\mathbf{k}_1\mathbf{n})(\mathbf{k}_2\mathbf{n})\langle(\mathbf{nh})P(\mathbf{n}, \mathbf{h})\rangle}, \qquad (10)$$

and in the important special case of surface being a height field,

$$\rho(\mathbf{k}_1, \mathbf{k}_2) = \frac{p(\mathbf{h})P(\mathbf{k}_1, \mathbf{k}_2, \mathbf{h})F((\mathbf{kh}))}{4(\mathbf{k}_1\mathbf{n})(\mathbf{k}_2\mathbf{n})\langle(\mathbf{nh})\rangle}. \qquad (11)$$

Although we have assumed that all microfacets have equal area A_{mf} the result does not change if there is an arbitrary distribution of microfacet areas so long as this distribution is not correlated with $p(\mathbf{h})$, the distribution of normals.

Given a density $p(\mathbf{h})$, all terms in Equation 11 are straightforward to compute except for the shadowing term $P(\mathbf{k}_1, \mathbf{k}_2, \mathbf{h})$. We now turn to the discussion of this shadowing term which is necessary to complete our formulation of the specular part of BRDF.

4 Shadowing Term

Most of the complexity of microfacet-based models arise from the shadowing function $P(\mathbf{k}_1, \mathbf{k}_2, \mathbf{h})$. In this section we describe how previous models deal with this term and introduce a new simplified shadowing term.

4.1 Previous Shadowing Terms

On any rough surface it is likely that some microfacets will either not receive light, or light reflected by them will be blocked by other microfacets. The first situation is referred to by many authors as *shadowing* and the second as *masking*. However, these events are symmetrical and for simplicity we will refer to both of them as *shadowing*. A rigorous derivation of the probability that a point on the surface is both visible and illuminated (also known as the bistatic shadowing function) leads to very complicated expressions and a set of approximations is made to make the problem tractable. Several forms of the shadowing term have been derived in different fields [1, 18, 21, 23, 25] and some of them (usually after further simplification) were later introduced to computer graphics reflection models [4, 8, 22].

The most popular shadowing functions currently used are modifications of those of Smith [21], Sancer [18] and the original Torrance and Sparrow shadowing term [23]. The first two formulations are rather complex and are designed only for Gaussian height fields. Smith, in addition, assumes an isotropic surface. The shadowing function by Torrance and Sparrow is simple, but assumes an inconsistent model of an isotropic surface exclusively made by very long V-cavities. None of the existing functions is flexible enough to accommodate a sufficiently general distribution of microfacets. Also, most of the formulations operate with height distributions, not the more intuitive normal distribution $p(\mathbf{h})$. In addition to space limitations, this is the reason we do not present the expressions of previously derived shadowing functions here.

The reason most authors deal with height distribution functions is that shadowing is clearly a non-local event intimately related to the height distribution of the surface and this information is necessary for rigorous treatment of shadowing. In the next subsection we will, however, make several assumptions which allows us to derive a very general form of the shadowing term $P(\mathbf{k}_1, \mathbf{k}_2, \mathbf{h})$ sufficient for our purposes.

4.2 New Shadowing Term

As indicated by the preceding discussion, we cannot treat shadowing rigorously if we assume a general form for the microfacet normal density function. Therefore, our generator is most appropriate in cases where the effects of shadowing are secondary compared with the influence of normal distribution shape. Even in these cases, however, we cannot ignore the shadowing term $P(\mathbf{k}_1, \mathbf{k}_2, \mathbf{h})$. As can be seen from Equation 10, at the very least shadowing should take care of the divergence at grazing angles where the denominator terms disappear: $(\mathbf{k}_1\mathbf{n})(\mathbf{k}_2\mathbf{n}) \to 0$.

The shadowing term can be written as

$$P(\mathbf{k}_1, \mathbf{k}_2, \mathbf{h}) = P(\mathbf{k}_1, \mathbf{h})P(\mathbf{k}_2, \mathbf{h} \,|\, \mathbf{k}_1), \qquad (12)$$

where $P(\mathbf{k}_1, \mathbf{h})$ is the probability of not being shadowed in the direction $\mathbf{k}_1$ and $P(\mathbf{k}_2, \mathbf{h} \,|\, \mathbf{k}_1)$ is conditional probability of not being shadowed in the direction $\mathbf{k}_2$ given that the facet is not shadowed in direction $\mathbf{k}_1$. In general, $P(\mathbf{k}_2, \mathbf{h} \,|\, \mathbf{k}_1) \neq P(\mathbf{k}_2, \mathbf{h})$. For example, it is easy to see that in the extreme case where $\mathbf{k}_1 = \mathbf{k}_2$ we have $P(\mathbf{k}_2, \mathbf{h} \,|\, \mathbf{k}_1) = 1$. This shows that visibilities in the incoming and outgoing directions are correlated. Most of shadowing functions, however, are derived under the assumption of uncorrelated

visibilities. Van Ginneken et al. [24] considered how this correlation affects Smith's shadowing function, and found that its effect can be accounted for by modifying the uncorrelated expression.

In most of this paper we will use the uncorrelated form of the shadowing term written as a product of the two independent factors for each of the two directions:

$$P(\mathbf{k}_1, \mathbf{k}_2, \mathbf{h}) = P(\mathbf{k}_1, \mathbf{h})P(\mathbf{k}_2, \mathbf{h}). \qquad (13)$$

This leads to some underestimation of the BRDF if directions $\mathbf{k}_1$ and $\mathbf{k}_2$ are close to each other. If the viewing conditions are such that this arrangement is of particular importance (in a night driving simulator, for example) or if retroreflection is one of the pronounced features of surface appearance (see Section 6.4) we propose using a different form of the shadowing term:

$$\begin{aligned} P(\mathbf{k}_1, \mathbf{k}_2, \mathbf{h}) = &(1 - t(\phi))P(\mathbf{k}_1, \mathbf{h})P(\mathbf{k}_2, \mathbf{h}) + \\ &t(\phi)min(P(\mathbf{k}_1, \mathbf{h}), P(\mathbf{k}_2, \mathbf{h})), \end{aligned} \qquad (14)$$

where $-\pi < \phi < \pi$ is the angle between the projections of vectors $\mathbf{k}_1$ and $\mathbf{k}_2$ onto the tangent plane and $t(\phi)$ is a correlation factor with values between 0 and 1. The case $t(\phi) = 0$ corresponds to the completely uncorrelated case. This form of correlated shadow term was chosen because it is simple and the resulting BRDF will still conserve energy with arbitrary $t(\phi)$, as will be shown in Section 5.3. We have not done extensive experimentation with the particular form of $t(\phi)$ but we do not believe it makes a large difference as long as $t(0) = 1$ and $t(\phi)$ monotonically decreases to almost zero as $|\phi|$ increases. The range of correlation effects was found in [24] to be on the order of 15-25 degrees, so we use a Gaussian in ϕ with the width of 15 degrees.

All we need now is an expression for $P(\mathbf{k}, \mathbf{h})$, the probability for a microfacet to be visible in a given direction $\mathbf{k}$. Note that $P(\mathbf{n}, \mathbf{h})$ in Equations 7, 8 and 10 of the previous section is just a special case of this probability with $\mathbf{k} = \mathbf{n}$. The key assumption we make is that probability for a microfacet to be visible in direction $\mathbf{k}$ does not depend on the microfacet's orientation $\mathbf{h}$ as long as it is not turned away from $\mathbf{k}$ (not self-shadowed), namely

$$P(\mathbf{k}, \mathbf{h}) = \begin{cases} P(\mathbf{k}) & \text{if } (\mathbf{k}\mathbf{h}) > 0 \\ 0 & \text{if } (\mathbf{k}\mathbf{h}) \leq 0 \end{cases} \qquad (15)$$

This assumption is equivalent to the absence of correlation between the microfacet orientation and its position. This "distant shadower" assumption has been invoked before to simplify complicated shadowing expressions obtained in other fields [1, 21, 25] but we will use it in a different way - as a basis for deriving a simple and general shadowing function. Intuitively, it corresponds to rather rough surfaces and does not hold if the microfacets with certain orientation are more likely to be found at a certain height. For example, a surface made of cylinders as shown in Figure 3a will not obey this assumption while a very similar surface in Figure 3b might. In general, the more correlated the surface microfacets are, the less likely $P(\mathbf{k}, \mathbf{h})$ is to obey Equation 15.

The two surfaces in Figure 3 may still have the same distribution $p(\mathbf{h})$ and there is no way for us to distinguish between the two cases. Similarly, we will not be able to distinguish, for example, between "positive" and "negative" cylinders of Poulin and Fournier [16] but from their images it is clear that the differences in appearance due to microfacet visibility issues and not to the distribution of microfacets are minor in this case. If finer details of microfacet arrangement not captured by $p(\mathbf{h})$ are expected to substantially affect the appearance, some different framework should be used (see also Section 6.4).

The total projected area of a surface element onto direction $\mathbf{k}$ is $A(\mathbf{k}\mathbf{n})$. It can also can be written in a way similar to Equation 7:

$$A(\mathbf{k}\mathbf{n}) = \sum_{facets} A_{mf}(\mathbf{h}\mathbf{k})_+ P(\mathbf{k}). \qquad (16)$$

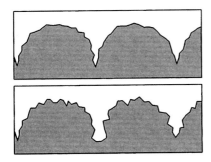

Figure 3: *Examples of surface microgeometry. Top: microfacets with almost vertical orientation are more likely to be found near the "bottom" of the surface and, therefore, are more likely to be shadowed. Bottom: orientation and height are largely uncorrelated.*

Here the subscript '+' refers to the fact that the summation is performed only over microfacets turned towards $\mathbf{k}$, namely the ones with $(\mathbf{hk}) > 0$. Introducing averaging over microfacets and, as before, replacing it by averaging over distribution, we get

$$A(\mathbf{kn}) = N A_{mf} P(\mathbf{k}) \langle (\mathbf{hk})_+ \rangle. \qquad (17)$$

We are able to take $P(\mathbf{k})$ out of the averaging integral because of our assumption that it does not depend on $\mathbf{h}$. Because of the great importance of quantity $\langle (\mathbf{hk})_+ \rangle$ we introduce a new notation

$$g(\mathbf{k}) = \langle (\mathbf{hk})_+ \rangle = \int_{\Omega_+(\mathbf{k})} (\mathbf{hk})_+ p(\mathbf{h}) d\omega_h, \qquad (18)$$

where the integration is done in $\mathbf{h}$-space over the hemisphere $\Omega_+(\mathbf{k})$ of directions $(\mathbf{hk}) > 0$ (Figure 4). Note that if the surface is a height field, $P(\mathbf{n}) = 1$ and Equations 8 and 17 immediately give a useful expression for $P(\mathbf{k})$:

$$P(\mathbf{k}) = \frac{(\mathbf{kn}) g(\mathbf{n})}{g(\mathbf{k})}. \qquad (19)$$

In this special case $p(\mathbf{h}) = 0$ in the lower hemisphere and the averaging in $g(\mathbf{n})$ is effectively done over the complete distribution.

To handle a more general case, we note that each microfacet turned away from the direction $\mathbf{k}$ will have a shadow with area $A_{mf}(\mathbf{hk})$. This area must be subtracted from the contribution of microfacets turned towards $\mathbf{k}$. Again replacing sums by averages over ensemble and then over distribution, we write the projected area on the right-hand side of Equation 17 as

$$N A_{mf} P(\mathbf{k}) \langle (\mathbf{hk})_+ \rangle =$$
$$N A_{mf} \langle (\mathbf{hk})_+ \rangle + N A_{mf} \langle (\mathbf{hk})_- \rangle, \qquad (20)$$

or

$$P(\mathbf{k}) = 1 + \frac{\langle (\mathbf{hk})_- \rangle}{g(\mathbf{k})}. \qquad (21)$$

The second term is negative and the integration in it is done over the part $\Omega_-(\mathbf{k})$ of distribution complimentary to $\Omega_+(\mathbf{k})$ (Figure 4). It is clear from this equation that $P(\mathbf{k}) \leq 1$ as it should be. For a distribution of microfacet normals $p(\mathbf{h})$ to represent a valid surface, at the very least the average normal vector over the entire distribution must lie in the direction of the geometric normal $\mathbf{n}$ of the surface:

$$\int_{\Omega_+(\mathbf{k})} \mathbf{h} p(\mathbf{h}) d\omega_h + \int_{\Omega_-(\mathbf{k})} \mathbf{h} p(\mathbf{h}) d\omega_h =$$
$$\int_{\Omega} \mathbf{h} p(\mathbf{h}) d\omega_h = \mathbf{n}(\langle \mathbf{h} \rangle \mathbf{n}) \qquad (22)$$

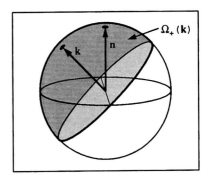

Figure 4: *Integration domain for $g(\mathbf{k})$*

Multiplying both sides of this equation by scalar $\mathbf{k}$ we have

$$\langle (\mathbf{hk})_+ \rangle + \langle (\mathbf{hk})_- \rangle = (\mathbf{kn}) \langle (\mathbf{hn}) \rangle, \qquad (23)$$

or

$$\langle (\mathbf{hk})_- \rangle = (\mathbf{kn}) \langle (\mathbf{hn}) \rangle - g(\mathbf{k}). \qquad (24)$$

Substituting this into Equation 21 we obtain an expression for $P(\mathbf{k})$:

$$P(\mathbf{k}) = \frac{(\mathbf{kn}) \langle (\mathbf{hn}) \rangle}{g(\mathbf{k})}. \qquad (25)$$

Averaging in the numerator is done over the complete sphere Ω of directions. Note that Equation 19 is now just a special case of Equation 25 and that Equations 21 and 25 show that for any physically valid distribution $p(\mathbf{h})$ our probability of being visible will indeed lie between 0 and 1.

The combination of Equations 10, 13 (or 14) and 25 completely describes the specular part of BRDF. Using the uncorrelated form of shadowing term of Equation 13, we get

$$\rho(\mathbf{k}_1, \mathbf{k}_2) = \frac{p(\mathbf{h}) \langle (\mathbf{hn}) \rangle F((\mathbf{kh}))}{4 g(\mathbf{k}_1) g(\mathbf{k}_2)}. \qquad (26)$$

Note the interesting fact that p.d.f. $p(\mathbf{h})$ does not even have to be normalized to be used in this equation. The above formula is well-suited to evaluation. Given $p(\mathbf{h})$, it is straightforward to evaluate the BRDF. Equation 26 is the main contribution of this paper. For the rest of the paper we will discuss implications and applications of this formula.

5 Extensions and Discussion

In this section we discuss several issues related to the specular-only single bounce BRDF model derived in the last section. In particular, we discuss an energy-conserving diffuse term, implementation issues, extension to non-Fresnel microfacets, and prove energy conservation.

5.1 Diffuse Term

Equation 26 describes the part of scattering process due to single-bounce reflections from microfacets. In addition to this specular part there will be other scattering events, such as multiple bounces and subsurface scattering. A complete description of these processes is rarely attempted in a general-purpose BRDF model and their combined contribution is usually represented by adding a diffuse component to the specular BRDF. The most common form of the diffuse term is Lambertian:

$$\rho(\mathbf{k}_1, \mathbf{k}_2) = \frac{k_d \rho_d}{\pi} + k_s \rho_s(\mathbf{k}_1, \mathbf{k}_2), \qquad (27)$$

where $0 \le \rho_d \le 1$ is diffuse albedo of the surface while k_d and k_s are user-specified constants controlling the relative importance of specular and diffuse reflections. This is a perfectly valid option in our case as well. We can simply use Equation 26 for ρ_s and ensure that $k_d + k_s \le 1$ to preserve the energy conservation achieved for the specular part (Section 5.3).

However, this simple form of diffuse term has problems. First of all, it is not obvious how to choose weights k_d and k_s. Second, it is clear that as more light is being reflected specularly, less of it is available for diffuse scattering, so the relative weights k_d and k_s of diffuse and specular reflections should not be constants. If Fresnel effects can cause k_s to approach one for grazing angles, k_d must be set to zero for all angles (since it is a constant). To take this effect into account in a way preserving reciprocity, we use a method of Shirley et al. [20] and write for k_d

$$k_d(\mathbf{k}_1, \mathbf{k}_2) = c(1 - R(\mathbf{k}_1))(1 - R(\mathbf{k}_2)), \qquad (28)$$

where

$$R(\mathbf{k}) = \int \rho_s(\mathbf{k}, \mathbf{k}')(\mathbf{k}'\mathbf{n})d\omega_{k'} \qquad (29)$$

is the directional hemispherical reflectance of the specular term, where $\mathbf{k}'$ is the mirrored direction of $\mathbf{k}$. We also completely dispose of k_s by allowing the specular reflection to "have its way" and adjust the diffuse term so that it consistently follows the specular reflection. The normalization constant c is computed such that for $\rho_d = 1$ the total incident and reflected energies are the same. A complete BRDF will have the form

$$\rho(\mathbf{k}_1, \mathbf{k}_2) = c(1 - R(\mathbf{k}_1))(1 - R(\mathbf{k}_2))\rho_d + \rho_s(\mathbf{k}_1, \mathbf{k}_2). \qquad (30)$$

This form of diffuse term implicitly assumes that there is no absorption on the surface and all the energy which is not reflected specularly is available for diffuse scattering. The situation is different in case of metals. First, if f_0 is the normal reflectance of the metal, only approximately f_0 fraction of incoming light is not absorbed by a flat metal surface. Second, diffuse scattering here is exclusively due to multiple bounces and thus the diffusely scattered light has a more saturated color of the metal than the primary reflection does. We attempt to take both of these effects into account by replacing ones in Equation 30 by f_0 and assigning ρ_d for a metal (which otherwise does not have any physical sense) to be f_0. Because the true fraction of non-absorbed light is greater than f_0, factor $(f_0 - R(\mathbf{k}))$ can become negative for some surfaces due to our approximation. We simply set the diffuse term to zero in such cases.

5.2 Implementation Issues

Implementation of our model in a rendering system is straightforward. For the Fresnel coefficient we use Schlick's approximate formula [19]

$$F((\mathbf{kn})) = f_0 + (1 - f_0)(1 - (\mathbf{kn}))^5 \qquad (31)$$

where again f_0 is the Fresnel factor at normal incidence. Note that we could also use the full Fresnel equations, but we use Schlick's formula only for convenience. This should not lead to significant accuracy problems as for the error introduced by Schlick's formula is smaller than one percent compared with the full Fresnel expression [19]. To generate a BRDF for a new distribution $p(\mathbf{h})$ all we

need, in addition to the implementation of $p(\mathbf{h})$ itself, are values for $g(\mathbf{k})$ and $R(\mathbf{k})$. Unfortunately, because of the non-standard integration domain of $g(\mathbf{k})$, analytical expressions for this function can be obtained only for the most trivial $p(\mathbf{h})$'s and we need to resort to numerical integration.

However, the integrals are well-behaved and the results are smooth functions for non-singular $p(\mathbf{h})$. This allows us to compute values of both $g(\mathbf{k})$ and $R(\mathbf{k})$ on a very coarse grid using available numerical packages, store the results in a table and use bilinear interpolation during the rendering process. We have used a total of 200 grid points (for many distributions an even coarser grid should be sufficient). Integration was done using both Matlab and a simple home-built Monte Carlo routine. Two sets of computed $R(\mathbf{k})$ (one with $f_0 = 1$ and one with $f_0 = 0$) are sufficient to compute $R(\mathbf{k})$ for a material with arbitrary f_0 for a given microfacet distribution.

In the BRDF generation phase we start from $p(\mathbf{h})$ and output a compact numerical representation of three two-dimensional functions: $g(\mathbf{k})$, $R(\mathbf{k})$ with $f_0 = 0$ and $R(\mathbf{k})$ with $f_0 = 1$. The last two functions are only used for the diffuse term and are not required for its simpler form in Equation 27. During rendering we use these data to compute the full four dimensional BRDF for arbitrary $\mathbf{k}_1$ and $\mathbf{k}_2$. At this stage we also use data for normal reflectance f_0 and diffuse albedo ρ_d. Wavelength dependence of these quantities controls the color of the surface. We have not done a careful performance analysis but from our experience for a non-trivial $p(\mathbf{h})$ most of the BRDF computation time is due to evaluating this normal distribution function.

Note that most distributions have some symmetry which can be exploited to further reduce the amount of data and/or generation time. Data for an anisotropic Gaussian distribution of normals, for example, need be computed only over a quarter of the hemisphere and for any isotropic distribution functions $g(\mathbf{k})$ and $R(\mathbf{k})$ become one dimensional.

Finally, if a particular type of parameterized distribution (Gaussian, for example) is used often it should be possible to approximate $g(\mathbf{k})$ with a simple function of $\mathbf{k}$ and distribution parameters as is commonly done to increase the efficiency of reflection models. The same is true for $R(\mathbf{k})$ but these functions usually have more complex shapes.

5.3 Energy Conservation

By inspection of the formulas, it is clear that generated BRDFs are reciprocal. We now prove now that they also conserve energy for any physically plausible $p(\mathbf{h})$. To do this, we assume the worst-case scenario of $F((\mathbf{kh})) = 1$ and shadowing term in Equation 14 with $t(\phi) = 1$ (because $P(\mathbf{k}) \le 1$ this corresponds to the largest possible shadowing term for our model). The BRDF in this case will be

$$\rho(\mathbf{k}_1, \mathbf{k}_2) = \frac{p(\mathbf{h})min(P(\mathbf{k}_1), P(\mathbf{k}_2))}{4\langle(\mathbf{hn})\rangle(\mathbf{k}_1\mathbf{n})(\mathbf{k}_2\mathbf{n})} \le$$
$$\frac{p(\mathbf{h})P(\mathbf{k}_1)}{4\langle(\mathbf{hn})\rangle(\mathbf{k}_1\mathbf{n})(\mathbf{k}_2\mathbf{n})}$$

Hemispherical reflectance for a given incoming direction is

$$R(\mathbf{k}_1) = \int \rho_s(\mathbf{k}_1, \mathbf{k}_2)(\mathbf{k}_2\mathbf{n})d\omega_2 \le$$
$$\frac{P(\mathbf{k}_1)}{4\langle(\mathbf{hn})\rangle(\mathbf{k}_1\mathbf{n})} \int p(\mathbf{h})d\omega_2 =$$
$$\frac{P(\mathbf{k}_1)}{4\langle(\mathbf{hn})\rangle(\mathbf{k}_1\mathbf{n})} \int p(\mathbf{h})4(\mathbf{k}_1\mathbf{h})d\omega_h$$

The last transition is done using Equation 5. The integration is done over a complex region of h-space which is in any case contained in the hemisphere $\Omega_+(\mathbf{k}_1)$. Extending the integral over the whole $\Omega_+(\mathbf{k}_1)$ and using definitions 18 of $g(\mathbf{k})$ and 25 of $P(\mathbf{k})$ we complete the proof:

$$R(\mathbf{k}_1) \le \frac{P(\mathbf{k}_1)}{\langle(\mathbf{hn})\rangle(\mathbf{k}_1\mathbf{n})} \int_{\Omega_+(\mathbf{k}_1)} (\mathbf{k}_1\mathbf{h})p(\mathbf{h})d\omega_h =$$

$$\frac{P(\mathbf{k}_1)g(\mathbf{k}_1)}{\langle(\mathbf{hn})\rangle(\mathbf{k}_1\mathbf{n})} = 1 \qquad (32)$$

The only fact we used in our proof is that $P(\mathbf{k}) \le 1$ for any $\mathbf{k}$. In Section 4, in turn, this was shown to be the case for any $p(\mathbf{h})$ whose average normal vector $\langle\mathbf{h}\rangle$ is parallel to the geometric normal of the surface. This is the only restriction on microfacet distribution $p(\mathbf{h})$. If it is satisfied, the generated BRDF will conserve energy.

5.4 Non-Fresnel Microfacets

Our model is not restricted to perfectly specular microfacets. In general, microfacets with many orientations will contribute to surface BRDF for given incoming and outgoing directions and integration of their contribution is necessary.

Let all microfacets have elementary BRDF β. Then we can repeat with some modifications the derivation from Sections 3 and 4 to arrive at the result

$$\rho(\mathbf{k}_1, \mathbf{k}_2) = \frac{P(\mathbf{k}_1, \mathbf{k}_2)}{(\mathbf{k}_1\mathbf{n})(\mathbf{k}_2\mathbf{n})\langle(\mathbf{nh})\rangle}$$

$$\int \beta(\mathbf{k}_1, \mathbf{k}_2)(\mathbf{k}_1\mathbf{h})_+(\mathbf{k}_2\mathbf{h})_+p(\mathbf{h})d\omega_h \qquad (33)$$

The integration is done over the sector where both $(\mathbf{k}_1\mathbf{h})$ and $(\mathbf{k}_2\mathbf{h})$ are positive and any of shadowing terms $P(\mathbf{k}_1, \mathbf{k}_2)$ from Section 4 can be used. Note that $\beta(\mathbf{k}_1, \mathbf{k}_2)$ is usually specified with respect to microfacet's local coordinate system and a coordinate transformation is necessary to obtain its value for the integral in Equation 33.

Although this extension considerably broadens the range of surfaces our model is applicable to, we also lose one of the main advantages of our approach: compactness. Before, we could represent a general four dimensional BRDF using only two dimensional functions. The integral in Equation 33, however, is a four dimensional function by itself and does not, in general, allow lower dimensional representation. For some special cases, such as Lambertian elementary BRDF coupled with isotropic $p(\mathbf{h})$ the integral becomes three dimensional and, therefore, feasible to compute, store and use in a way similar to that described in Section 5.2. For an isotropic Gaussian distribution of Lambertian microfacets the general behavior of the generated BRDF is similar to that of Oren-Nayar's model [14], namely, retroreflection is increased compared to a Lambertian surface (Figure 8).

6 Applications

In this section we apply our model to a variety of surface types. Although we have implemented our model in a Monte Carlo ray tracer capable of handling complex geometries and illumination effects, our images in this section intentionally show very simple objects and lighting conditions. In particular, illumination is coming from a single small light source far from the scene and indirect lighting is not included. This is done to emphasize effects due to BRDF of the material and to make the comparison with previous results easier.

Reflectance data of gold are used as f_0 (see Section 5.2) for all metal objects while for non-metals f_0 is set to 5% across the visible spectrum.

Figure 5: *Anisotropic Gaussian golden spheres with $\sigma_x = 0.1$, $\sigma_y = 1.0$. Left: Ward. Right: new model.*

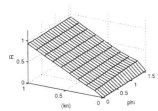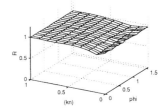

Figure 6: *Directional hemispherical reflectance as a function of incoming angle for perfectly reflecting microfacets with Gaussian distribution $\sigma_x = 0.1$, $\sigma_y = 0.2$. For an ideal flat surface R should be 1.0 everywhere. Left: Ward. Right: new model.*

Figure 7: *Anisotropic Gaussian golden painted plastic spheres with $\sigma_x = 0.1$, $\sigma_y = 0.2$. Left: Ward. Right: new model.*

Figure 8: *Gaussian spheres with Lambertian microfacets. Right: new model with $\sigma_x = \sigma_y = 1.0$. Left: Oren-Nayar with compatible parameters.*

6.1 Gaussian Surfaces

By far the most popular distribution used in BRDF research literature is Gaussian. This is due to both its practical importance and nice mathematical properties. Gaussians are used in all four major categories of BRDF models outlined in the introduction. While some of this work is closer to our approach in its theoretical foundations, we feel that from the practical point of view our model is closest to that of Ward [26]. Ward's BRDF is simple, handles anisotropic distributions and seeks to reproduce the main character of the material's reflectance behavior without attempting an overly detailed description. Other previous models do not simultaneously possess all these properties.

To create an anisotropic Gaussian BRDF, we use the distribution

$$p(\mathbf{h}) = c * \exp(-\tan^2\theta(\cos^2\phi/\sigma_x^2 + \sin^2\phi/\sigma_y^2)) \quad (34)$$

where θ is the angle between the half vector $\mathbf{h}$ and the surface normal, ϕ is the azimuth angle of $\mathbf{h}$ and c is a normalization constant.

Two side-by-side comparisons of our model with Ward's are shown in Figures 5 and 7. Note that the shape of highlight is nearly identical while there are some differences in the diffuse part of images which is due to Ward effectively using a simpler form (Equation 27) of the diffuse component. In particular, for our metal sphere on Figure 5 the diffuse component appears automatically when there is enough energy left after single-bounce scattering. To achieve the same effect in Ward's model (and any other using the popular Lambertian diffuse term) it would be necessary to manually adjust the diffuse reflectance parameter.

This figure also shows that the highlight is brighter for our BRDF. The general reason for this is clear from Figure 6 where the hemispherical reflectance R is plotted versus the incoming light direction. To make the plots directly comparable, we show data for most reflecting specular BRDF in both cases ($f_0 = 1$ for our model and $\rho_s = 1$ in Equation 5 of Ward's paper [26]) and do not include the diffuse term. For the values of parameters shown, the surface is quite close to being flat, so one would expect that R should be close to that of flat surface, 1.0 in this case. One can see from the plots that our model behaves as expected while Ward's does not. Note also that the true value for R at the grazing angle ($(\mathbf{k}\mathbf{n}) = 0$) is infinite for Ward's model [13] and we simply extrapolate previous behavior to get the data point at the grazing angle.

While our approach does require an extra generation step, computation time during the rendering process of our BRDF is close to that of Ward's and our model is a viable alternative where energy conservation is of great importance for a particular application.

Figure 8 compares a BRDF generated for an isotropic Gaussian distribution of Lambertian microfacets with an extension of our process (Section 5.4) and Oren-Nayar model with compatible parameters. Both BRDFs have the tendency to make objects appear "flatter" than the Lambertian BRDF due to increased retroreflection.

6.2 Grooved Surface

A surface consisting of ideal V-grooves all running in a given direction will have its $p(\mathbf{h})$ proportional to the sum of two delta functions, each accounting for microfacets forming one side of a groove. Replacing these delta functions with narrow Gaussians ($\sigma = 0.1$) to account for imperfections and going through our generation process, we create a BRDF which correctly shows the main feature of a grooved surface's reflectance, double reflections. Figure 9 shows a piece of grooved metal illuminated by a *single* light source. The orientation of the grooves on the left is perpendicular to the viewing direction while on the right they are parallel.

Figure 9: *Double highlights from a single light source for the same metallic grooved surface at two orientations of the grooves. Grooves are symmetrical with the angle of 40 degrees*

6.3 Satin

The microstructure of woven cloth is usually thought of as a symmetric pattern of interwoven cylindrical fibers running in perpendicular directions. While it would be possible to generate a BRDF corresponding to this structure with our approach, the surface of particular fabric we studied had a different microstructure shown in Figure 10. It is created almost exclusively by fibers running in one direction with about 70% of the fiber length lying in the relatively flat part of the fiber while the other 30% corresponding to the bent parts at the ends. We model the distribution of microfacets as a linear combination of two terms corresponding to these flat and bent parts of the cylindrical fiber: $p(\mathbf{h}) = 0.7 * p_{flats}(\mathbf{h}) + 0.3 * p_{ends}(\mathbf{h})$. The coefficients reflect mutual area contributions of the two parts to the complete distribution. Both $p_{flats}(\mathbf{h})$ and $p_{ends}(\mathbf{h})$ were chosen to be "cylindrical" Gaussian heightfields ($\sigma_y = \infty$, $p(\mathbf{h}) = 0$ for $(\mathbf{h}\mathbf{n}) < 0$) with different widths. Values $\sigma_x = 0.1$ for $p_{flats}(\mathbf{h})$ and $\sigma_x = 0.3$ for $p_{ends}(\mathbf{h})$ were used. Strictly speaking, the shape of real $p_{ends}(\mathbf{h})$ would probably be more accurately modeled by a distribution with flatter top and faster drop-offs than that of a Gaussian. This was attempted but the results were almost identical visually, so a simpler Gaussian distribution was used for the final image. This is consistent with our belief that the very precise characterization of the microfacet distribution is not needed for visual applications. Note that because $g(\mathbf{k})$ is linear in $p(\mathbf{h})$, no new integration is necessary to compute $g(\mathbf{k})$ if g's corresponding to $p_{flats}(\mathbf{h})$ and $p_{ends}(\mathbf{h})$ are already computed. This suggests an efficient way of creating new distributions as a linear combination of ones for which $g(\mathbf{k})$ has been previously computed. For example, small contribution due to perpendicular fibers can be added in this manner if necessary.

Because the appearance of real cloth is dramatically affected by the presence of characteristic wrinkles, we used a dynamic simulation method [17] to create cloth geometry. The left side of Figure 11 shows a satin tablecloth rendered with generated BRDF. It is interesting to contrast this image with the image on the right using the same geometric model with the BRDF described in the next section.

6.4 Velvet

Velvet is another example of a material with interesting reflectance properties not easily conveyed by conventional BRDFs. In their virtual gonioreflectometer, Westin et al. [27], model velvet microstructure as a forest of narrow cylinders (fibers) with the orientation of each cylinder perturbed randomly. While it is difficult to write an exact $p(\mathbf{h})$ corresponding to such "surface" for the reasons outlined in Section 2, a simple intuitive form of this function written as an "inverse Gaussian" heightfield is enough to capture the main char-

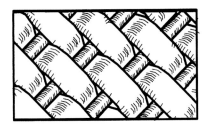

Figure 10: *Microgeometry of our sample of satin.*

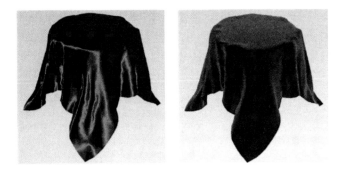

Figure 11: *Synthetic satin (left) and velvet (right) tablecloths. The geometries are identical.*

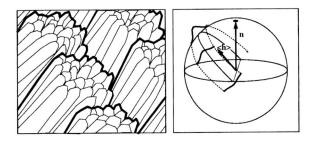

Figure 12: *Microgeometry of velvet (left) and p(**h**) used to model it (right).*

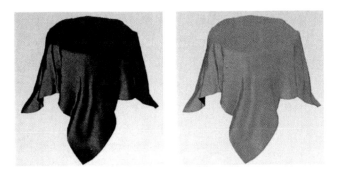

Figure 13: *A tablecloth made of two different colors of slanted fiber velvets.*

acter of the distribution:

$$p(\mathbf{h}) = c * \exp(-\cot^2 \theta / \sigma^2), \tag{35}$$

with $\sigma = 0.5$ for the image on the right of Figure 11 which shows a material with distinct velvet-like reflectance properties. Because retroreflection is one of the most pronounced reflection properties of velvet [11], we used the correlated form of shadowing term (Equation 14) to generate both this and slanted fiber (see below) velvet BRDFs. Contrary to Westin et al. we ignore the tips of the fibers due to their very small area. If there were any specular highlights due to the tips, their contribution can be easily added by forming a linear combination of an inverse Gaussian with a regular Gaussian distribution.

Although this approach produced good results, a symmetric forest of fibers was not what we saw when we examined a piece of real velvet. More realistic structure is shown on the left of Figure 12. The fabric consists of rows of tightly woven bundles of filament. Each bundle is slanted with the angle of about 40 degrees with respect to the geometric normal of the cloth surface. We can call this arrangement milliscale geometry in contrast with microgeometry formed by the thin fibers themselves. Similar geometry was credited as the major reason for velvet anisotropic reflection behavior by Lu et al. [11]. Strictly speaking, our model does not take into account visibility issues due to this higher-order arrangement of microfacets. The most consistent approach therefore would be to model this structure explicitly, for example as a collection of slanted cylinders applying two different BRDFs (both of which can be generated by our process) to the tops and to the sides of these cylinders. An easier alternative would be an attempt to create a simple distribution of microfacets $p(\mathbf{h})$ which, although potentially non-physical, can account for the milliscale visibility and produce a BRDF with necessary reflection properties.

Looking carefully at the velvet highlight structure we saw that it is the sides of the bundles and not the tops which contribute the most to the reflection. This suggests that we can try to reproduce most of the behavior with a specular BRDF based exclusively on the $p(\mathbf{h})$ accounting for the microfacets on the sides of the bundles. A "slanted" version of cylindrical Gaussian distribution ($\sigma_y = \infty$, $\sigma_x = 0.5$) schematically shown on the right of Figure 12 was used. The only place where we used the part of distribution due to the tops of the bundles is the computation of $\langle (\mathbf{hn}) \rangle$ when we double this value due to the tops contribution. Note two facts about this distribution: it is not a height field and its average vector $\langle \mathbf{h} \rangle$ does not point in the direction of geometric normal. While the first feature does not present any problem in our approach, the second one shows that this distribution is not physically realizable and, as a result, the energy conservation of the generated BRDF is not guaranteed. Computations of $R(\mathbf{k})$ show that this quantity indeed exceeds one for 14 out of our 200 directional data points in the hypothetical case of perfectly reflecting ($f_0 = 1.0$) fiber material but was never a problem for our $f_0 = 0.05$ synthetic fibers.

Figure 13 shows the results of this process. The illumination and viewing directions are almost parallel but due to the slant of the fibers the left side of the tablecloth is substantially brighter than the right one. This is in good agreement with the behavior of real velvet we observed. The right image of Figure 13 shows some limitations of our approach. Because we do not handle the details of multiple-bounce scattering and simply introduce a diffuse term to account for them, the right side of the red tablecloth does not look as it does for the real velvet. In the real material, light experiences multiple bounces among the red fibers for this viewing geometry acquiring a deep dark (almost black) color in the process. This is not captured by our simple diffuse term.

6.5 Unusual Distributions

We can take to extreme the use of the desired reflection properties as the only guidance in creating the distribution $p(\mathbf{h})$ regardless of whether a material described by this function exists or is even physically possible. For example, we can modulate a Gaussian $p(\mathbf{h})$ with an arbitrary function or even an image to create the unusual highlights shown in Figure 1. As long as the modulation is symmetric enough to keep the average vector $\langle \mathbf{h} \rangle$ in the normal direction (such as the distribution used for the image on the left of Figure 1), the BRDF will be energy conserving. A more general modulation may result in $\langle \mathbf{h} \rangle$ no longer parallel to $\mathbf{n}$ but in practice we notice that as long as this effect is not very strong, the energy conservation is not affected. For example, image on the right of Figure 1 was created with an energy conserving BRDF. While such unusual distributions are not of great value in realistic image synthesis, they clearly demonstrate the generality of our approach and can potentially find applications in the special effects industry.

7 Conclusion

The new BRDF model presented in this paper is well-suited to surfaces whose primary characteristic is the shape of the specular highlight. We have found it reasonably straightforward to design new BRDFs for surfaces because the diffuse term and energy conservation are handled in a natural manner that does not require substantial user intervention, and the parameters used in the model are intuitive. However, for surfaces whose appearance is not dominated by the specular highlight, our model is not well-suited.

We have found that using our model does not require much hand-tuning of parameters; the images in the last section were generated with very few iterations on parameter values. We speculate that a model for subsurface effects in a similar spirit to our model is possible. The user would specify some simple parameters analogous to $p(\mathbf{h})$ and a BRDF would be generated. We also believe that there should ultimately be separate terms for the components of the BRDF accounted for by primary specular reflection, multiple-bound specular reflection, and subsurface scattering.

Acknowledgements

This work was supported by NSF grants 96–23614, 97–96136, 97–31859, and 98–18344. Thanks to Robert McDermott for his help with production issues. The tablecloth models were done using Maya software generously donated by Alias/Wavefront.

References

[1] BECKMANN, P. Shadowing of random rough surfaces. *IEEE Transactions on Antennas and Propagation 13* (1965), 384–388.

[2] BLINN, J. F. Models of light reflection for computer synthesized pictures. *Computer Graphics (Proceedings of SIGGRAPH 77) 11*, 2 (July 1977), 192–198.

[3] CABRAL, B., MAX, N., AND SPRINGMEYER, R. Bidirectional reflectance functions from surface bump maps. *Computer Graphics 21*, 4 (July 1987), 273–282. ACM Siggraph '87 Conference Proceedings.

[4] COOK, R. L., AND TORRANCE, K. E. A reflectance model for computer graphics. *Computer Graphics 15*, 3 (August 1981), 307–316. ACM Siggraph '81 Conference Proceedings.

[5] GONDEK, J. S., MEYER, G. W., AND NEWMAN, J. G. Wavelength dependent reflectance functions. In *Proceedings of SIGGRAPH '94 (Orlando, Florida, July 24–29, 1994)* (July 1994), A. Glassner, Ed., Computer Graphics Proceedings, Annual Conference Series, ACM SIGGRAPH, ACM Press, pp. 213–220.

[6] GOURAUD, H. Continuous shading of curved surfaces. *Communications of the ACM 18*, 6 (June 1971), 623–629.

[7] GREENBERG, D. P., TORRANCE, K. E., SHIRLEY, P., ARVO, J., FERWERDA, J. A., PATTANAIK, S., LAFORTUNE, E. P. F., WALTER, B., FOO, S.-C., AND TRUMBORE, B. A framework for realistic image synthesis. *Proceedings of SIGGRAPH 97* (August 1997), 477–494.

[8] HE, X. D., TORRENCE, K. E., SILLION, F. X., AND GREENBERG, D. P. A comprehensive physical model for light reflection. *Computer Graphics 25*, 4 (July 1991), 175–186. ACM Siggraph '91 Conference Proceedings.

[9] LAFORTUNE, E. P., AND WILLEMS, Y. D. Using the modified phong BRDF for physically based rendering. Tech. Rep. CW197, Computer Science Department, K.U.Leuven, November 1994.

[10] LAFORTUNE, E. P. F., FOO, S.-C., TORRANCE, K. E., AND GREENBERG, D. P. Non-linear approximation of reflectance functions. *Proceedings of SIGGRAPH 97* (August 1997), 117–126.

[11] LU, R., KOENDERINK, J. J., AND KAPPERS, A. M. L. Optical properties (bidirectional reflection distribution functions) of velvet. *Applied Optics 37*, 25 (1998), 5974–5984.

[12] MARSCHNER, S. R., WESTIN, S. H., LAFORTUNE, E. P. F., TORRANCE, K. E., AND GREENBERG, D. P. Image-based BRDF measurement including human skin. *Eurographics Rendering Workshop 1999* (June 1999).

[13] NEUMANN, L., NEUMANN, A., AND SZIRMAY-KALOS, L. Compact metallic reflectance models. *Computer Graphics Forum 18*, 13 (1999).

[14] OREN, M., AND NAYAR, S. K. Generalization of lambert's reflectance model. In *Proceedings of SIGGRAPH '94 (Orlando, Florida, July 24–29, 1994)* (July 1994), A. Glassner, Ed., Computer Graphics Proceedings, Annual Conference Series, ACM SIGGRAPH, ACM Press, pp. 239–246.

[15] PHONG, B.-T. Illumination for computer generated images. *Communications of the ACM 18*, 6 (June 1975), 311–317.

[16] POULIN, P., AND FOURNIER, A. A model for anisotropic reflection. *Computer Graphics 24*, 3 (August 1990), 267–282. ACM Siggraph '90 Conference Proceedings.

[17] PROVOT, X. Deformation constraints in a mass-spring model to describe rigid cloth behavior. In *Proceedings of Graphics Interface '95* (1995), pp. 147–154.

[18] SANCER, M. I. Shadow corrected electromagnetic scattering from randomly rough surfaces. *IEEE Transactions on Antennas and Propagation AP-17*, 5 (September 1969), 577–585.

[19] SCHLICK, C. An inexpensive BRDF model for physically-based rendering. *Computer Graphics Forum 13*, 3 (1994), 233—246.

[20] SHIRLEY, P., HU, H., SMITS, B., AND LAFORTUNE, E. A practitioners' assessment of light reflection models. In *Pacific Graphics* (October 1997), pp. 40–49.

[21] SMITH, B. G. Geometrical shadowing of a random rough surface. *IEEE Transactions on Antennas and Propagation 15* (1967), 668–671.

[22] STAM, J. Diffraction shaders. *Proceedings of SIGGRAPH 99* (August 1999), 101–110.

[23] TORRANCE, K. E., AND SPARROW, E. M. Theory for off-specular reflection from roughened surfaces. *Journal of Optical Society of America 57*, 9 (1967).

[24] VAN GINNEKEN, B., STAVRIDI, M., AND KOENDERINK, J. J. Diffuse and specular reflectance from rough surfaces. *Applied Optics 37*, 1 (1998), 130–139.

[25] WAGNER, R. J. Shadowing of randomly rough surfaces. *Journal of Acoustic Society of America 41* (1967), 138–147.

[26] WARD, G. J. Measuring and modeling anisotropic reflection. *Computer Graphics 26*, 4 (July 1992), 265–272. ACM Siggraph '92 Conference Proceedings.

[27] WESTIN, S. H., ARVO, J. R., AND TORRANCE, K. E. Predicting reflectance functions from complex surfaces. *Computer Graphics 26*, 2 (July 1992), 255–264. ACM Siggraph '92 Conference Proceedings.

Monte Carlo Evaluation Of Non-Linear Scattering Equations For Subsurface Reflection

Matt Pharr   Pat Hanrahan

Stanford University

Abstract

We describe a new mathematical framework for solving a wide variety of rendering problems based on a non-linear integral scattering equation. This framework treats the scattering functions of complex aggregate objects as first-class rendering primitives; these scattering functions accurately account for all scattering events inside them. We also describe new techniques for computing scattering functions from the composition of scattering objects. We demonstrate that solution techniques based on this new approach can be more efficient than previous techniques based on radiance transport and the equation of transfer and we apply these techniques to a number of problems in rendering scattering from complex surfaces.

CR Categories: I.3.7 [Computer Graphics]: Three-Dimensional Graphics and Realism—Color, shading, shadowing, and texture; I.3.3 [Computer Graphics]: Picture/Image Generation

Keywords: Rendering, Illumination, Monte Carlo Techniques, Reflectance and Shading Models, Scattering Function, Invariant Imbedding, Principles of Invariance, Equation of Transfer, Adding Equations, Chandrasehkar's Equation

1 Introduction

In this paper we describe a new framework for solving a broad class of rendering problems. It consists of a non-linear integral *scattering equation* that describes the overall scattering behavior of an object or volume accounting for all of the scattering events that happen inside of it, and a set of *adding equations* that describe aggregate scattering functions from the composition of objects with known scattering functions.[1] In some situations, techniques based on these equations can be much more efficient than corresponding techniques based on the equation of transfer [Cha60] (*i.e.* the rendering equation [Kaj86]).

Unlike the equation of transfer, these equations describe the scattering from an object directly; thus they reflect a shift in focus from energy transport to scattering behavior independent of a particular illumination setting. This approach has been developed over the

---

[1]We will use the term *scattering function* to describe the generic light scattering behavior of a surface or object, and we will use the term *scattering equation* to describe our Equation 3.5, which is equal to the scattering function in the general three-dimensional case.

past fifty years, primarily in astrophysics, where these equations are often used to compute light scattering [Amb42, Cha60, van80]. In this paper, we will focus on their application to computing subsurface scattering.

The resulting scattering functions generalize the concept of the bidirectional reflectance distribution function (BRDF). The BRDF is based on the simplifying assumption that light exits the surface at the same point it enters, or equivalently that the surface is homogeneous and uniformly illuminated over a reasonably large area [NRH+77]. This reduces the reflection function to a four-dimensional function over pairs of angles. BRDFs are the one-dimensional case since the surface may be inhomogeneous in the z dimension (the direction along the surface normal), but not in x and y.

More generally, Nicodemus *et al.* have introduced the bidirectional subsurface reflectance distribution function (BSSRDF) which accounts for light entering the surface at a different place than it exits [NRH+77]. This is a three-dimensional scattering function that accounts for inhomogeneity in all dimensions underneath the surface; it gives reflectance along an outgoing ray due to illumination along an incoming ray. A minor generalization lifts the restriction to a planar surface, giving a scattering function of ten dimensions: five to specify the origin and direction of each ray. This setting lets us treat mathematically the scattering functions of general three-dimensional objects. The BRDF and BSSRDF are both important abstractions in that they describe scattering behavior phenomenologically such that lower-level scattering processes can be ignored.

Max *et al.* were the first graphics researchers to recognize the importance of the scattering equations [MMKW97]. They used the one-dimensional scattering equation to compute light scattering in tree canopies by deriving a system of ordinary differential equations. They solved this system with an adaptive Runge-Kutta method, using a clever application of the Fourier transform to avoid an $O(n^3)$ matrix multiplication. Because their solution technique discretizes the hemisphere into sets of angles, it becomes increasingly expensive for strongly peaked phase functions. More importantly, the viability of the extension of this solution method to 3D scattering problems has not been demonstrated. We develop the scattering equation in a more general setting that makes it possible to derive both one and three-dimensional scattering equations. We also derive and use the adding equations and apply a more general solution technique, Monte Carlo integration, that scales to the three-dimensional setting.

In this paper, we discuss the history of these scattering equations and previous work in graphics that has used different techniques to compute generalized scattering functions. We derive the scattering equations in integral form in a very general setting and describe the derivation of the adding equations. Given this basis, we describe the use of Monte Carlo techniques to compute solutions to these equations, demonstrate their efficiency, and apply them to a number of problems in rendering light reflection from complex surfaces. We conclude with discussion and directions for future work.

2 Background and previous work

2.1 History of the scattering and adding equations

In a classic paper from the nineteenth century, Stokes derived expressions for the amount of light reflected and transmitted from a stack of glass layers [Sto62]. He introduced the innovations that overall scattering could be computed directly in terms of the reflection and transmission functions of the individual layers, and that the reflection and transmission for two layers together could be computed based on the already-computed reflection and transmission functions of each one. This work was the intellectual basis for the development of general scattering equations over the last fifty years.

The scattering and adding equations were first derived as a new way to compute 1D scattering functions without using the equation of transfer. The first applications were to the *standard problem* in astrophysics: given a slab of thickness z with known optical properties that do not vary in x or y and assuming that parallel beams of radiation are incident from a direction ω', we wish to know how much radiation is reflected in the direction ω (Figure 1).

Building on the ideas that Stokes developed, Ambarzumian derived a non-linear integral equation that describes scattering from semi-infinite homogeneous isotropic atmospheres directly in terms of the low-level scattering properties of the layers of the atmosphere [Amb42, Amb58].[2] Chandrasekhar greatly extended Ambarzumian's results and derived a non-linear integro-differential scattering equation that describes scattering from finite anisotropic atmospheres [Cha60]. Bellman and Kalaba extended this work to include inhomogeneity in depth and were the first to derive the purely integral form of this equation for theoretical analysis of solutions to the scattering equation [BK56, BKP63]. These one-dimensional scattering equations have been applied to a variety of other areas, including neutron transport, radiative transfer, and hydrologic optics [Mob94].

Recently, Wang has derived a scattering equation in the three-dimensional case where incident illumination from a distant source is constant over the entire upper boundary of the region and where the phase function varies only in z [Wan90] [NUW98, Section 4.6]. Unfortunately, this form is not generally useful for problems encountered in graphics.

The adding equations were developed by van De Hulst and Twomey *et al.* in the 1960s [van80, TJH66], and were later generalized by Preisendorfer [Pre76]. They were first discovered in the field of neutron transport by Peebles and Plesset [PP51] and have since been applied to a wide variety of scattering problems.

2.2 One-dimensional scattering functions

Computing scattering functions that hide the complexity of light scattering from surfaces has long been a research problem in graphics and optics. Examples include the Torrance–Sparrow reflection model [TS67], an analytic approximation to light scattering from rough surfaces; Blinn's model for dusty surfaces, which uses a single-scattering approximation [Bli82]; Kajiya's discussion of replacing complex geometry with reflection functions [Kaj85]; and Westin *et al.*'s computation of BRDF samples by simulating light scattering from micro-geometry [WAT92].

When no closed-form expression or approximation for multiple scattering at a surface is available, previous work has either ignored multiple scattering (*e.g.* [Bli82]), or based solutions on the equation of transfer and the definition of the BRDF (*e.g.* [WAT92]), where reflected radiance in the outgoing direction is computed given differential irradiance from the incident direction.

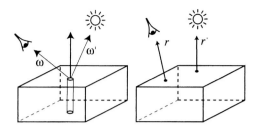

Figure 1: *Basic viewing geometry for the 1D (left) and 3D (right) scattering functions. All vectors and rays are specified in the outgoing direction.*

2.3 Three-dimensional scattering functions

In recent years, a number of researchers have worked on computing scattering functions that describe the aggregate scattering behavior of complex volumetric and geometric objects. Kajiya and Kay's volume texels were an early example [KK89], and Neyret extended their framework to include more general geometries and demonstrated applications to reducing aliasing due to level-of-detail changes [Ney98]. Rushmeier *et al.* approximated scattering from clusters of geometry by averaging the reflectance of surfaces hit by random rays [RPV93]. Sillion and Drettakis approximated occlusion due to complex objects as volume attenuation functions [SD95] and Sillion *et al.* approximated aggregate scattering functions from clusters of objects [SDS95]. However, none of these approaches accounts for multiple scattering inside the object or for light that enters the object at a different point than it exits.

Miller and Mondesir computed hypersprites that encoded specular reflection and refraction from objects [MM98], and Zongker *et al.* have described an apparatus for computing the scattering and transmission functions of glossy and specular real-world objects [ZWCS99]. Dorsey *et al.* have rendered rich images of stone and marble by computing BSSRDFs at rendering time [DEL⁺99]. Their solutions are based on the equation of transfer and photon mapping to accelerate multiple scattering computations, and they clearly showed the importance of this effect for some materials. This is the only previous application in graphics of rendering scattering from surfaces with BSSRDFs.

In general, scattering from an object can be described by the formal solution of the inverse of the light transport equation [Pre65, Section 22]. Veach and Guibas derived rendering algorithms based on recursive expansion of this solution operator [VG94, Vea97] and Lafortune used the Neumann expansion of the solution operator to derive recursively-defined integral equations that describe scattering from a collection of surfaces; he called this the global reflectance distribution function (GRDF) and also used it to derive new light transport algorithms [LW94, Laf96].

2.4 Composing scatterers

A variety of techniques have previously been used to compute aggregate reflection functions from a set of layers. The Kubelka-Munk model [KM31] is similar to a one-dimensional radiosity solution; it accounts for multiple scattering but not angular dependence. It was first introduced to graphics by Haase and Meyer [HM92] and has been widely used. However, due to assumptions built into the model, either glossy specular reflection has to be ignored or multiple reflection between the specular component and the added layer is lost. A different approach to layer composition is due to Hanrahan and Krueger [HK93]; they compose scattering layers considering only one level of inter-reflection. This misses the effect of multiple internal reflections before light leaves the layer, which is important except for objects with very low albedos.

---

[2]Homogeneity refers to whether or not the atmosphere has scattering properties that vary as a function of depth, and isotropy refers to the properties of the phase function inside the atmosphere; an isotropic phase function scatters light equally in all directions.

x	Generic point
ω	Generic direction
r	A ray through space, with origin $x(r)$ and direction $\omega(r)$
μ_r	Cosine of ray's direction with surface normal
$\delta(x)$	Delta function: Kronecker or Dirac, depending on context
$\mathcal{S}^2$	The sphere of all directions
Ω	The hemisphere around the $+z$ direction
$\mathcal{M}^2$	A 2D manifold
$\mathcal{R}$	Ray space: a set of rays going through a set of locations in a set of directions
$L(r)$	Radiance along the ray r
$p(x, \omega' \to \omega)$	Phase function at a point.
$k(r' \to r)$	Scattering kernel
$S(r' \to r)$	Scattering function for light reflected along ray r due to incident light along ray r'
$\sigma_a(x)$	Volume absorption coefficient at x
$\sigma_s(x)$	Volume scattering coefficient
$\sigma_t(x)$	Volume attenuation coefficient, $\sigma_s(x) + \sigma_a(x)$
$\alpha(x)$	Albedo $\sigma_s(x)/\sigma_t(x)$
z	Depth in one-dimensional medium
$R(z, \omega_i \to \omega_o)$	Reflection function from slab of depth z
$T(z, \omega_i \to \omega_o)$	Transmission function from slab of depth z

Figure 2: *Table of notation.*

3 Scattering Equations

In this section, we derive the integral scattering equation that describes how an object or volume scatters light. We also describe techniques for computing the scattering functions of composite objects directly from the scattering functions of their constituent parts. Our treatment is in terms of the scattering of a single wavelength of light; the extension to multiple wavelengths is straightforward.

We will consider scattering from objects in an axis-aligned rectangular region of space with height z. This does not require that the object be parallelepiped-shaped; it is just a convenient parameterization of space. This parameterization also makes it possible to ignore the issue of non-convex regions of space, where illumination may exit and later re-enter the space. That setting is tractable, though the notation is more complex.

3.1 Ray space and operator notation

Previous work in graphics has used a variety of parameterizations of surfaces and directions for the expression of the rendering equation (*e.g.* Kajiya used an integral over pairs of points on surfaces). Veach has recently introduced abstractions based on *ray space* that have a number of advantages: in addition to simplifying and clarifying formulas, ray space makes clear that any particular parameterization of surfaces and directions is an arbitrary choice, mathematically equivalent to any other [VG95, Vea97].

In this setting, ray space $\mathcal{R}$ is the set of rays given by the Cartesian product of points in three-space $\mathbb{R}^3$ and all directions $\mathcal{S}^2$: $\mathcal{R} = \mathbb{R}^3 \times \mathcal{S}^2$. We will define two specializations of $\mathcal{R}$. First is $\mathcal{R}_{\mathcal{M}^2}$, which is the subset of $\mathcal{R}$ where all rays start on a given two-dimensional manifold $\mathcal{M}^2$: $\mathcal{R}_{\mathcal{M}^2} = \mathcal{M}^2 \times \mathcal{S}^2$. A particular instance of $\mathcal{R}_{\mathcal{M}^2}$ that is often useful is $\mathcal{R}_{\mathcal{M}^2(z')}$, where the manifold is the plane at $z = z'$. Another useful specialization is to limit the directions of rays $\mathcal{R}$ to the hemisphere around the surface normal; we denote this by $\mathcal{R}_{\mathcal{M}^2}^+$. The negation of a ray $-r$ is defined as the ray with the same origin as r but going in the opposite direction.

The scattering kernel k describes light scattering at a point. In

ray space it is

$$ k(r' \to r) = \delta(x(r) - x(r')) \, \sigma_s(x(r)) \, p(x(r), \omega(r') \to \omega(r)), $$

where $p(x(r), \omega(r') \to \omega(r))$ is the phase function at the point $x(r)$ for scattering from $\omega(r')$ to $\omega(r)$ and we have included the scattering coefficient σ_s in k in order to simplify subsequent formulas (see Chandrasekhar for a summary of phase functions, scattering coefficients, *etc.* [Cha60]).

In contrast to the phase function, the scattering function $S(r' \to r)$ is potentially non-zero for any pair of rays because of multiple scattering; it is not necessary that the rays meet at a point for light along one ray to affect the response along another. Though the general scattering function is ten-dimensional, when we are considering scattering from a specific object, it is often more convenient to consider the eight-dimensional specialization where all rays originate on a parameterized two-dimensional manifold that bounds it. For the remainder of this paper, this is the only type of scattering function we will consider. In particular, we will just consider the scattering function from rays on a planar boundary of an object.

In order to be able to do integrals over $\mathcal{R}_{\mathcal{M}^2}$ and $\mathcal{R}_{\mathcal{M}^2(z)}$, we define a differential measure:

$$ dr = d\omega(\omega(r)) \, dA^\perp(x(r)) = \mu_r \, d\omega(\omega(r)) \, dA(x(r)) $$

where $x(r)$ is the origin of r, $\omega(r)$ is its direction, A is the area measure on $\mathcal{R}_{\mathcal{M}^2}$, and $d\omega$ is the differential solid angle measure.

Given an object's scattering function, outgoing radiance along a ray r is computed by integrating its product with incident radiance over the object's boundary.

$$ L_o(r) = \frac{1}{4\pi} \int_{\mathcal{R}_{\mathcal{M}^2}^+} \frac{S(r' \to r)}{\mu_r \mu_{r'}} L_i(r') \, dr' $$

This is the three-dimensional analogue to integrating the product of incident radiance and the BRDF at a point to compute outgoing radiance. Its added complexity stems from the fact that incident light scatters inside the object and may exit far from where it entered.

We will define operators **k** and **S**, where bold text signifies the operator and Roman text its kernel. Both operators are defined such that applying them to other functions gives:

$$ (\mathbf{S}f)(r) = \int_{\mathcal{R}_{\mathcal{M}^2}^+} \frac{S(r' \to r)}{\mu_r \mu_{r'}} f(r') \, dr' $$

We can define compositions like $\mathbf{kS}$, or $\mathbf{S}_a\mathbf{S}_b\mathbf{S}_c$, *etc.* These will be useful in computing new scattering functions that describe the scattering of multiple objects in terms of their individual scattering functions (see Section 3.3).

$$ (\mathbf{S}_1 \ldots \mathbf{S}_n)(r' \to r) = \int_{\mathcal{R}_{\mathcal{M}^2}^+} \cdots \int_{\mathcal{R}_{\mathcal{M}^2}^+} S_n(r' \to r_1) \cdots $$
$$ S_1(r_{n-1} \to r) \frac{dr_{n-1}}{\mu_{r_{n-1}}^2} \cdots \frac{dr_1}{\mu_{r_1}^2} \quad (3.1) $$

3.2 Derivation of the scattering equation

With operator notation in hand, we will derive a general integro-differential scattering equation in ray space. This equation describes how the scattering function of a complex object changes as layers with known scattering properties are added or removed from it. It can either be solved in integro-differential form or as a purely integral equation. Our derivation follows the *invariant imbedding* method [BK56, Pre58, BKP63, BW75].

We will consider the change in scattering behavior of this object as thin layers Δz are added on top of it. Because multiple scattering

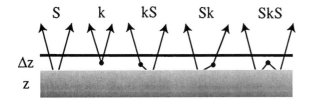

Figure 3: *The five types of scattering events to be considered in the invariant imbedding derivation of the scattering equation. The S events reflect the aggregate multiple scattering inside the z slab. All other scattering events, such as* kSk, *are gathered in an* $o(\Delta z^2)$ *term in Equation 3.2.*

in Δz occurs with probability $o(\Delta z^2)$, we just gather all multiple scattering in an $o(\Delta z^2)$ term. Later we will divide by Δz and take the limit as $\Delta z \to 0$, at which point all of the $o(\Delta z^2)$ terms disappear. As such, there are only five types of scattering events that need to be accounted for (see Figure 3):

1. $\mathbf{S}$: Light that is attenuated in Δz, scattered by the original object, and attenuated again in Δz.
2. $\mathbf{k}$: Light that is scattered in Δz so that it leaves the new layer without reaching the original object.
3. $\mathbf{kS}$: Light that is scattered in Δz so that it passes into the original object, is scattered, and then is attenuated in Δz as it exits.
4. $\mathbf{Sk}$: Light that is attenuated in Δz, scattered by the object, and is then scattered by Δz such that it leaves the object.
5. $\mathbf{SkS}$: Light that is attenuated in Δz, scattered by the object, scattered in Δz back into the object, scattered again by the object, and then attenuated again.

Accounting for each of the five modes of scattering in turn, a new scattering function for $z + \Delta z$ can be written

$$\mathbf{S}(z+\Delta z) = e^{-\sigma_t(\Delta z/\mu_i)} e^{-\sigma_t(\Delta z/\mu_o)} \bigg(\mathbf{S}(z) +$$
$$\mathbf{S}(z, z+\Delta z) + \mathbf{S}(z, z+\Delta z)\mathbf{S}(z) + \mathbf{S}(z)\mathbf{S}(z, z+\Delta z) +$$
$$\mathbf{S}(z)\mathbf{S}(z, z+\Delta z)\mathbf{S}(z) + o(\Delta z^2) \bigg), \quad (3.2)$$

where $\mathbf{S}(z)$ is the scattering operator for a slab of thickness z and $\mathbf{S}(a,b)$ is the scattering operator for the portion of the slab from depth a to b.

We can simplify this further by replacing the $e^{-c\Delta z}$ term with $1 - c\Delta z + o(\Delta z^2)$ and taking advantage of an approximation to $\mathbf{S}$ for a layer that is infinitesimally thin [GY89]:

$$\mathbf{S}(z, z+\Delta z) = \mathbf{k}\Delta z + o(\Delta z^2).$$

Making these simplifications and then taking the difference between the new scattering operator $\mathbf{S}(z+\Delta z)$ and the scattering operator of the original layer $\mathbf{S}(z)$, we have

$$\mathbf{S}(z+\Delta z) - \mathbf{S}(z) = o(\Delta z^2) + \bigg(-\sigma_t(\frac{1}{\mu_i} + \frac{1}{\mu_o})\mathbf{S}(z) +$$
$$\big(\mathbf{k}(z, z+\Delta z) + \mathbf{k}(z, z+\Delta z)\mathbf{S}(z) + \mathbf{S}(z)\mathbf{k}(z, z+\Delta z) +$$
$$\mathbf{S}(z)\mathbf{k}(z, z+\Delta z)\mathbf{S}(z)\big) \bigg) \Delta z$$

Now we divide by Δz and take the limit as $\Delta z \to 0$, which gives us the infinitesimal change in the scattering function due to the addition of the new layer.

$$\frac{\partial \mathbf{S}}{\partial z} = -\sigma_t \left(\frac{1}{\mu_i} + \frac{1}{\mu_o} \right) \mathbf{S} + (\mathbf{k} + \mathbf{kS} + \mathbf{Sk} + \mathbf{SkS}) \quad (3.3)$$

We now need a boundary condition in order to convert this non-linear integro-differential equation into an integral equation. If we assume that the object is bounded by a perfect absorber from below — *i.e.* $\mathbf{S}(0) = 0$ — then application of the Laplace transform gives Equation 3.4. General boundary conditions are most easily handled with the adding equations; see the next section.

$$\mathbf{S}(z) = \int_0^z e^{-\sigma_t(1/\mu_i + 1/\mu_o)(z-z')} \big(\mathbf{k}(z') + \mathbf{k}(z')\mathbf{S}(z') +$$
$$\mathbf{S}(z')\mathbf{k}(z') + \mathbf{S}(z')\mathbf{k}(z')\mathbf{S}(z') \big) dz'. \quad (3.4)$$

We have written this with the operators expanded out; see Figure 4. This is a formidable equation, but like the rendering equation, it expresses a simple fact about light scattering. With computers and numerical methods, it can be solved. We will discuss previous solution techniques and some new Monte Carlo approaches for solving it in Section 4.

3.3 Adding equations

An important advantage of treating scattering functions directly is that it is possible to compute the combined scattering functions of aggregate objects from their individual scattering functions. These new scattering functions can be written directly in terms of the original ones and account for all scattering between the objects.

Consider two non-overlapping objects a and b with scattering functions $\mathbf{S}_a$ and $\mathbf{S}_b$. The scattering functions of the two objects together can be derived by considering all of the possible interactions between them. For example, consider the new scattering function for a pair of rays r_a and r'_a, both of which originate on a's boundary. Light may enter at a, be scattered by $\mathbf{S}_a$, and then exit without interacting with b. This is the first term of Equation 3.6a. Or, it may be scattered in a so that it enters b, get scattered by b back into a, and then be scattered through a out to r_a; this gives the next term. By considering all such inter-reflections between a and b, we have the first adding equation [Pre65, Section 25].

$$\mathbf{S}_{a \to a} = \mathbf{S}_a + \mathbf{S}_a \mathbf{S}_b \mathbf{S}_a + \mathbf{S}_a \mathbf{S}_b \mathbf{S}_a \mathbf{S}_b \mathbf{S}_a + \cdots \quad (3.6a)$$
$$= \sum_{n=0}^{\infty} (\mathbf{S}_a \mathbf{S}_b)^n \mathbf{S}_a \quad (3.6b)$$
$$= (\mathbf{I} - \mathbf{S}_a \mathbf{S}_b)^{-1} \mathbf{S}_a \quad (3.6c)$$
$$= \mathbf{S}_a + \mathbf{S}_a \mathbf{S}_b \mathbf{S}_{a \to a}. \quad (3.6d)$$

Given a ray r_a that enters a and another ray r_b that exits from b, we can derive a similar equation:

$$\mathbf{S}_{a \to b} = \mathbf{S}_b \mathbf{S}_a + \mathbf{S}_b \mathbf{S}_a \mathbf{S}_b \mathbf{S}_a + \cdots \quad (3.7a)$$
$$= \mathbf{S}_b \sum_{n=0}^{\infty} (\mathbf{S}_a \mathbf{S}_b)^n \mathbf{S}_a \quad (3.7b)$$
$$= \mathbf{S}_b (\mathbf{I} - \mathbf{S}_a \mathbf{S}_b)^{-1} \mathbf{S}_a \quad (3.7c)$$
$$= \mathbf{S}_b \mathbf{S}_a + \mathbf{S}_b \mathbf{S}_a \mathbf{S}_{a \to b}. \quad (3.7d)$$

These equations are most easily understood by reading each term from right to left to see the order of scattering events.

Computing new scattering functions with the adding equations can be done much more efficiently than by recomputing the scattering functions of the aggregate object from scratch [van80]. This stems from the fact that $\mathbf{S}_a$ and $\mathbf{S}_b$ already incorporate all of the multiple scattering events inside a and b, so we need only to compute the effect of multiple scattering *between* the two objects. After a few terms, the series usually converges quickly, as long as not too much of the light is re-scattered at each step. Analysis based on the operator norm of each term could be used to describe the convergence more precisely. Since the results of this computation are new scattering functions, they can themselves be used in further computations of new scattering functions.

$$S(z, r_i \to r_o) = \int_0^z e^{-(\sigma_t(x_i)/\mu_i + \sigma_t(x_o)/\mu_o)(z-z')} \left(k(r_i(z') \to r_o(z')) + \frac{1}{4\pi} \int_{\mathcal{R}_{\mathcal{M}^2(z')}^+} k(r_o \to -r') S(z', r_i \to r') \frac{dr'}{\mu_{r'}^2} + \right.$$

$$\left. \frac{1}{4\pi} \int_{\mathcal{R}_{\mathcal{M}^2(z')}^+} S(z', r' \to r_o) k(r_i \to r') \frac{dr'}{\mu_{r'}^2} + \frac{1}{16\pi^2} \int_{\mathcal{R}_{\mathcal{M}^2(z')}^+} \int_{\mathcal{R}_{\mathcal{M}^2(z')}^+} S(z', r'' \to r_o) k(-r' \to -r'') S(z', r_i \to r') \frac{dr'}{\mu_{r'}^2} \frac{dr''}{\mu_{r''}^2} \right) dz' \quad (3.5)$$

Figure 4: *The three dimensional integral scattering equation, 3.4, with operators expanded out and where the ray $r(t)$ is a new ray along the same line as r, constructed by offsetting the origin by distance t along the z axis and $x_i = x(r_i(z - z'))$ and $x_o = x(r_o(z - z'))$.*

3.4 One-dimensional setting

There are useful special cases of the general scattering equation and the adding equations in the one-dimensional setting; this was where they were first derived. In one dimen-

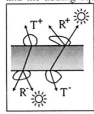

Figure 5: *The two reflection and transmission functions of a slab.*

sion, position in x and y is irrelevant, so the delta functions in the integral from the phase function disappear, leading to simpler formulas and easier implementation. A finite slab then has four scattering functions (see Figure 5): given illumination at the top, one gives the amount of light reflected at the top R^+ and another gives the amount of light transmitted at the bottom T^- [Cha60]. The other two, R^- and T^+, give reflection and transmission due to light incident at the bottom. R^+ and T^- are given in Equations 3.8 and 3.9, on the next page.

The application of the reflection and transmission operators to a function f is

$$(\mathbf{R} f)(\omega' \to \omega) = \frac{1}{4\pi} \frac{1}{\mu} \int_\Omega R(\omega' \to \omega) f(\omega') \, d\omega'$$

which gives us a nearly familiar equation for computing reflected radiance at a point:

$$L_o(\omega) = \frac{1}{4\pi} \frac{1}{\mu} \int_\Omega R(\omega' \to \omega) L_i(\omega') \, d\omega'$$

The reflection function of a surface is thus related to its BRDF f_r by $R(\omega' \to \omega) = 4\pi f_r(\omega' \to \omega)\mu'\mu$.

The adding equations are similarly simplified to integrals over just directions. In operator form, the scattering functions of two combined slabs a and b are

$$\begin{aligned}
\mathbf{R}_{a+b}^+ &= \mathbf{R}_a^+ + \mathbf{T}_a^+ \mathbf{R}_b^+ \mathbf{T}_a^- + \mathbf{T}_a^+ \mathbf{R}_b^+ \mathbf{R}_a^- \mathbf{R}_b^+ \mathbf{T}_a^- + \cdots \\
\mathbf{R}_{a+b}^- &= \mathbf{R}_b^- + \mathbf{T}_b^- \mathbf{R}_a^- \mathbf{T}_b^+ + \mathbf{T}_b^- \mathbf{R}_a^- \mathbf{R}_b^+ \mathbf{R}_a^- \mathbf{T}_b^+ + \cdots \\
\mathbf{T}_{a+b}^- &= \mathbf{T}_b^- \mathbf{T}_a^- + \mathbf{T}_b^- \mathbf{R}_a^- \mathbf{R}_b^+ \mathbf{T}_a^- + \cdots \\
\mathbf{T}_{a+b}^+ &= \mathbf{T}_a^+ \mathbf{T}_b^+ + \mathbf{T}_a^+ \mathbf{R}_b^+ \mathbf{R}_a^- \mathbf{T}_b^+ + \cdots
\end{aligned}$$

3.5 Discussion

The scattering equations thus bring us to a new framework for considering rendering problems. Note that there are no fundamentally new types of rendering problems that the scattering equations make accessible: as noted in Section 2.3, the formal inverse of the operator rendering equation can be used to solve the same kinds of scattering problems as well. For example, Hanrahan and Krueger effectively used a Neumman series expansion of the inverse to estimate four-dimensional scattering functions. This method could be easily extended to higher-dimensional scattering problems, and more sophisticated Monte Carlo techniques could be applied.

Conversely, the scattering equation can be used for more than just pre-computing scattering functions. Given knowledge of particular viewing conditions, particular lighting conditions, or both,

we can directly compute estimates of integrals such as $\mathbf{S} L_e$ (where L_e is emitted radiance), rather than first computing $\mathbf{S}$ and then passing emitted light through it. Since both approaches are based on formulae that directly describe the physics of light scattering, it is not surprising that the two approaches are connected in this way. In fact (and reassuringly), the scattering equation can be derived directly from the equation of transfer [Pre65].

In the next section, we will see that solving the scattering equation involves sampling chains of scattering events through a medium and evaluating their contribution—precisely how the equation of transfer is typically solved. Considered in light of its connections with the equation of transfer, we can use the scattering equation as a path to insights about how to solve the equation of transfer, and vice versa. This has the potential to lead to new ways of considering some classic rendering problems.

4 Monte Carlo Solution

A previously uninvestigated technique for solving the scattering and adding equations is Monte Carlo integration. Monte Carlo is a particularly effective technique for solving high dimensional integrals and integrals with discontinuities in the integrand. Its generality makes it possible to compute integrals where the functions in the integrand vary almost arbitrarily [KW86]; here, it allows wide variety in the possible phase functions, scattering and attenuation coefficients, and geometric shapes.

Techniques previously used to solve the scattering and adding equations have been based on the integro-differential form such as Equation 3.3. Typically, the set of angles is discretized and a system of non-linear differential equations is solved to compute scattering at the discrete angles (Max *et al.* took this approach). See van de Hulst [van80] for a survey and comparison of many of the variations of these techniques. These methods all break down in the face of complexity in the scattering medium: given highly anisotropic phase functions or non-homogeneous media, they are either not applicable due to the assumptions made in their derivations, or become increasingly inefficient because finer discretizations are required and the systems of equations become large. Furthermore, the generalization of these methods to higher-dimensional settings quickly becomes intractable, which has stymied the development of the more general theory.

4.1 Random walk solution

We will describe a simple recursive solution of the integral scattering equation. Because $\mathbf{S}(z)$ in Equation 3.4 is written recursively in terms of integrals of scattering functions of $\mathbf{S}(z')$, we can evaluate an estimate of $\mathbf{S}(z)$ based on a random walk. (The spirit of this algorithm is similar to Kajiya's path tracing solution to the rendering equation.) We follow a two step process:

1. First we sample the integral over depth by choosing z', where $0 < z' < z$. For constant attenuation functions, the exponential term can be importance sampled directly: to sample the integral $\int_0^z e^{az'} dz'$, where $a = -\sigma_t(1/\mu_i + 1/\mu_o)$, we first find the

$$\mathrm{R}^+(z,\omega_i \to \omega_o) = \int_0^z e^{-\sigma_t(z')(1/\mu_i+1/\mu_o)(z-z')} \, \sigma_s(z') \left(\mathrm{p}(z',\omega_i \to \omega_o) + \frac{1}{4\pi}\int_\Omega \mathrm{p}(z',-\omega' \to \omega_o)\mathrm{R}^+(z',\omega_i \to \omega')\frac{d\omega'}{\mu'} + \right.$$

$$\left. \frac{1}{4\pi}\int_\Omega \mathrm{R}^+(z',\omega' \to \omega_o)\,\mathrm{p}(z',\omega_i \to -\omega')\frac{d\omega'}{\mu'} + \frac{1}{16\pi^2}\int_\Omega\int_\Omega \mathrm{R}^+(z',\omega'' \to \omega_o)\mathrm{p}(z',-\omega' \to -\omega'')\mathrm{R}^+(z',\omega_i \to \omega')\frac{d\omega' d\omega''}{\mu'\mu''} \right) dz' \quad (3.8)$$

$$\mathrm{T}^-(z,\omega_i \to \omega_o) = \delta(\mu_i-\mu_o)e^{-\int_0^z \sigma_t(z')dz'/\mu_i} + \int_0^z e^{-\sigma_t(z)(z-z')/\mu_i}\,\sigma_s(z')\left(e^{-z'/\mu_o}\mathrm{p}(z',\omega_i \to -\omega_o) + \right.$$

$$e^{-z'/\mu_o}\frac{1}{4\pi}\int_\Omega \mathrm{p}(z',-\omega' \to \omega_o)\mathrm{R}^+(z,\omega_i \to \omega')\frac{d\omega'}{\mu'} + \frac{1}{4\pi}\int_\Omega \mathrm{T}^-(z',\omega' \to \omega_o)\,\mathrm{p}(z',\omega_i \to -\omega')\frac{d\omega'}{\mu'} +$$

$$\left. \frac{1}{16\pi^2}\int_\Omega\int_\Omega \mathrm{T}^-(z',\omega'' \to \omega_o)\mathrm{p}(z',-\omega' \to -\omega'')\mathrm{R}^+(z',\omega_i \to \omega')\frac{d\omega' d\omega''}{\mu'\mu''} \right) dz' \quad (3.9)$$

Figure 6: *The integral forms of the one-dimensional reflection and transmission equations. Since the medium is assumed to be homogeneous in x and y and that incident illumination is constant over a large area relative to σ_t, the equations are expressed in terms of depths and a pair of directions, rather than all of ray space. Note that an additional term is added to* T *to account for directly transmitted light.*

probability density function $\mathrm{pdf}(z') = \frac{ae^{az'}}{e^{az}-1}$. The cumulative distribution function $P(z)$ is $\int_0^z \mathrm{pdf}(z')dz'$. Given a random number ξ between 0 and 1, we set $\xi = P(z')$ and solve for z':

$$z' = \frac{\log(1+\xi(e^{az}-1))}{a}.$$

More generally, if the attenuation term varies with depth, the pdf cannot be computed analytically. In this case, we sample an optical thickness and march through the medium until that distance has been covered. In either case, the resulting sample is weighted by the exponential term at z' divided by the pdf.

2. We compute the product of the weight and estimates of the terms $\mathbf{k}(z') + \mathbf{k}(z')\mathbf{S}(z') + \mathbf{S}(z')\mathbf{k}(z') + \mathbf{S}(z')\mathbf{k}(z')\mathbf{S}(z')$. In computing the terms, we will come to have new estimates of the scattering equation $\mathbf{S}$ to compute; we proceed recursively.

This process is most easily understood in the one-dimensional case (Equation 3.8). Figure 7 gives pseudo-code for evaluating the 1D reflection function.

There is an important difference between this process and random walk solutions of the equation of transfer: as the recursion continues, the z' at which we are estimating $\mathbf{S}$ is monotonically decreasing. Once we have chosen a depth at which to estimate $\mathbf{S}$, all scattering above z' is irrelevant; it has already been accounted for. In effect, we are able to make a single pass through the medium from top to bottom, peeling off layers and solving scattering problems for thinner sub-objects. In comparison, standard approaches to solving the equation of transfer do not create a progressively simpler problem as they proceed.

4.2 Three-dimensional case

In the 3D case, this sampling process is less straightforward due to the delta function in the ray space phase function. Fortunately, delta functions generally fit easily into Monte Carlo sampling schemes. For example, given two rays r and r', the $\mathbf{k}(z')$ term of Equation 3.4 is zero unless both r and r' start at the same point *and* the z' depth sampled in step 1 above matches that point. In general two rays in 3D do not meet at all. Therefore, in the process of sampling the integrals, whenever we have a choice of rays to sample, sometimes we must carefully choose a ray and a depth such that this delta function is non-zero. To make this easier, we separate $\mathbf{S}$ into two components, $\mathbf{S}_s$, scattering due to a single scattering event, and $\mathbf{S}_m$, scattering due to multiple scattering events. This is analogous to distribution ray tracing with a mixed pure specular and diffuse surface where the two parts need to be sampled separately.

$\mathbf{S}_s(z) = \int_0^z e^{\cdots}\mathbf{k}\,dz'$ and $\mathbf{S}_m(z) = \int_0^z e^{\cdots}(\mathbf{kS}+\mathbf{Sk}+\mathbf{SkS})\,dz'$. Thus, $\mathbf{S} = \mathbf{S}_s + \mathbf{S}_m$.

Consider the specific case of estimating $\mathbf{L}_o = \mathbf{S}\mathbf{L}_e$ for a given outgoing ray r and a single point light source. Separating $\mathbf{S}$, we have two integrals, $\mathbf{S}_s\mathbf{L}_e + \mathbf{S}_m\mathbf{L}_e$. The first term is easily handled: it just represents single scattering of emitted light in the medium, so all scattering events are along r's path through the object. We choose positions for scattering events (*i.e.* x' in Figure 8a) by importance sampling points along r as above. Given these points, the incoming ray r' follows directly since the light is a point source; for an area light, a point can be chosen on the source and r then follows.

Moving on to $\mathbf{S}_m\mathbf{L}_e$, and in particular the term, $\mathbf{S}\mathbf{k}\mathbf{L}_e = \mathbf{S}_s\mathbf{k}\mathbf{L}_e + \mathbf{S}_m\mathbf{k}\mathbf{L}_e$ (treatment of $\mathbf{k}\mathbf{S}$ is analogous). We first randomly sample a point x' on the surface where the $\mathbf{k}$ scattering event happens, using an exponential distribution centered around $x(r)$ (Figure 8b). This strategy is based on the assumption that the longer the distance light travels under the surface, the more it will be attenuated and the less impact it will have. This defines a ray r' to the light due to the point light assumption (as above, area lights are a straightforward extension). The second single scattering event must be along r's path through the medium and must have a direction such that it passes through $x(r')$ in order for all of the respective delta functions to be non-zero. We therefore chose a depth along r with importance sampling.

There is more freedom in sampling from the $\mathbf{S}_m\mathbf{k}\mathbf{L}_e$ term (Figure 8c). We choose a ray r' as above, and still must have the $\mathbf{k}$ scattering event at $x(r')$ for the delta function in $\mathbf{k}$ to be non-zero. However, the direction of r'' can be chosen arbitrarily since $\mathbf{S}_m$ doesn't have the delta function along the path of r through the medium that $\mathbf{S}_s$ does. We simply importance sample the phase function based on $\omega(r')$ to get the ray direction for the r''.

Finally, the $\mathbf{S}\mathbf{k}\mathbf{S}\mathbf{L}_e$ term is slightly different: we also need to choose two rays that meet at a point where the $\mathbf{k}$ term will be evaluated (Figure 8d). We sample the shared ray origin from an exponential distribution centered around the midpoint between $x(r)$ and $x(r')$. Given this origin that the two new rays share, we again use importance sampling with the phase function to choose the two ray directions.

4.3 Solving the adding equations

Monte Carlo estimation of the adding equations introduces two issues: how many terms to evaluate of the infinite sum of products of scattering functions, and how to estimate individual terms of the sum. We solve the first problem and compute an unbiased estimate of the infinite sum by probabilistically terminating the series; after

```
Procedure R(z, ωᵢ, ω_o) ≡
    (z', pdf) := sampleDepth(σₜ, z)
    scale := e^(-(z-z')*σₜ*(1/μᵢ + 1/μ_o)) / pdf
    result := σₛ * p(ωᵢ, ω_o)
    if (not terminate()) then
        (ω', pdf') := sampleAngle(p, ω_o)
        result := result + σₛ * p(-ω', ω_o) * R(z', ωᵢ, ω') /
            (cos ω' * pdf')
        (ω'', pdf'') := sampleAngle(p, ωᵢ)
        result := result + R(z', ω'', ω_o) * σₛ * p(ωᵢ, -ω'') /
            (cos ω' * pdf'')
        result := result + R(z', ω', ω_o) * σₛ * p(-ω'', -ω') *
            R(z', ωᵢ, ω'') / (cos ω' * cos ω'' * pdf' * pdf'')
    endif
    return result * scale
```

Figure 7: Pseudo-code for evaluation of the one-dimensional reflection equation. The phase function p()*,* σ_s*, and* σ_t *are all potentially varying with depth. The* terminate() *function probabilistically stops the recursion using Russian roulette based on the weighted contribution that this estimate of* R *will make to the final solution. The* sampleAngle() *function uses importance sampling to choose an outgoing angle based on the phase function and the incoming angle; it returns the new direction and its probability density.*

computing estimates of the first few terms, we terminate with some probability after each successive term. When we continue on, subsequent terms until we do terminate are multiplied by a correction factor so that the final result is unbiased [AK90].

Given a particular term of the form of Equation 3.1, we have the multiple integral represented by the composition of a set of scattering functions to estimate. Given an incident and a reflected ray, we need to sample a set of rays r_i that connect the two of them together. These can be sampled in any order—the key is to find chains of rays where the scattering functions make a large contribution; this is the same problem faced in light transport problems [Vea97].

We have implemented routines that solve the 1D adding equations. We have implemented them in a modular fashion: they are given abstract data types describing the top and bottom layers as well as the incoming and outgoing directions. The layer objects provide a small number of operations to the adding routines. They are: evaluation given two angles, importance sampling one direction given the other (for layers where distributions for importance sampling are not easily computed, a default implementation uniformly samples the hemisphere), returning the probability density function of sampling one direction given the other direction (this is useful for multiple importance sampling), and a boolean function which tells if its scattering functions are delta functions (see below). These operations make it possible to implement a variety of representations for layers and easily add them together.[3]

Delta functions may be present in this series due to direct transmission (Equation 3.9) as well due to layers that specularly reflect or refract light (*e.g.* a mirror reflector at the bottom, or a Fresnel layer at the top). These are tricky because the delta functions cannot be evaluated, but only sampled—the evaluation routines always return zero. However, when such a layer samples a new direction given an incident or outgoing direction, it can pick the appropriate scattered direction. For example, when computing the term $T^+R^+T^-$ when the top layer is a Fresnel reflector, we compute both the incident and outgoing directions to the bottom layer by

[3]See Pharr and Veach for applications of similar abstractions to combining procedural shading with physically based rendering [PV00].

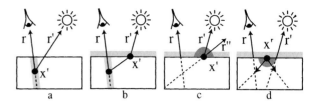

Figure 8: Sampling rays r' *in the 3D case; hilighted regions denote terms that are free to be sampled. From left to right: for direct lighting, all scattering events are along* r*'s path through the medium; for* S_s*, we sample a distance along* r *to find a scattering event—this gives a ray that connects through the point* x' *on the boundary; for* S_m*, we have more freedom to sample the direction of* r'' *and can use a variety of importance functions; finally, for* SkS*, we sample a point for the scattering event* **k** *and then sample the two outgoing directions.*

sampling T^+ and T^- given the outgoing and incident directions at the top, respectively; the reflection function R^+ has no choice in sampling its incident and outgoing directions, as it would never be able to randomly find an outgoing direction that is transmitted into the final outgoing direction.

5 Results

In this section, we start by demonstrating the efficiency of the scattering equations for solving rendering problems. We then demonstrate the use of the 1D scattering and adding equations to rendering complex surfaces and show applications of the 3D scattering equation to accurate rendering of surfaces, accounting for light that enters the surface some distance from where it exits.

5.1 Accuracy and efficiency

We tested our implementation's accuracy against a model that corresponds to the standard problem in astrophysics. This model is specified by the atmosphere's optical thickness, albedo, and phase function. The resulting scattering functions have been computed and tabularized by many authors. We compared our results to tables from Bellman *et al.* [BKP63], which have results computed by using Gaussian quadrature to generate a system of differential equations which were then solved via the Runge-Kutta method.

For a set of roughly forty randomly-selected albedos, thicknesses, and pairs of angles, we found excellent agreement with the scattering function values our routines computed. We have also verified our implementation of the adding equations by comparing the scattering function values computed by applying the adding equations to two halves of an object to those computed directly for the aggregate. Finally, we verified that our 3D implementation gave the same results as the 1D equation for uniformly illuminated planar objects that have homogeneous scattering properties in *xy*.

We then conducted a series of experiments to compare the efficiency of our solution method to a standard solution method that uses the equation of transfer. We implemented a Monte Carlo sampling routine that uses the equation of transfer to estimate the scattering function of a medium for a pair of angles based on a random walk. Our implementation is similar to the algorithm described by Hanrahan and Krueger [HK93]: a particle is injected into the medium from the incident direction and followed along a path through the medium. The walk is biased so that at each scattering event, the attenuation to the surface in the outgoing direction is computed and the result is accumulated to estimate the function's value. Russian roulette is used to terminate this process, based on the accumulated weight of the path.

After verifying that both methods converged to the same results, we compared their relative efficiency. For a variety of thicknesses, scattering coefficients, absorption coefficients, and phase functions, we computed accurate estimates of the scattering function for a pair of angles. We used a phase function due to Henyey and Greenstein [HG41]; it takes an asymmetry parameter, g that is the average value of the product of the phase function with the cosine of the angle between ω' and ω. The range of g is from -1 to 1, corresponding to total back-scattering to total forward scattering, respectively. We then applied both solution methods to computing estimates of the scattering functions for the pair of angles, giving each the same amount of processor time. The same Russian roulette termination parameters were used for each method and importance sampling was applied in analogous places (*e.g.* for sampling the outgoing direction of the phase function at scattering events for the equation of transfer). Our implementation generally computed five to ten estimates with the equation of transfer in the time it took to compute one estimate with the scattering equation.

The graphs in Figure 9 show some of the results. We computed the ratio of variance of the equation of transfer solution to the scattering equation solution, after giving each the same amount of processor time. The scattering equation solution often had 5 to 10 times less variance, though for some configurations (strongly anisotropic phase functions and very thick objects), it sometimes had over 100 times less variance. Although the scattering equation generally performed quite well, for cases with high albedos the

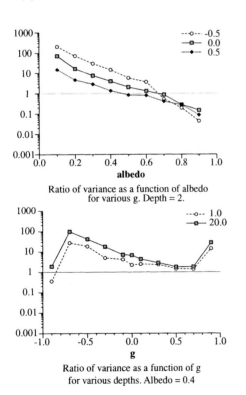

Ratio of variance as a function of albedo for various g. Depth = 2.

Ratio of variance as a function of g for various depths. Albedo = 0.4

Figure 9: Comparing our solutions of the "standard problem." After giving each method the same amount of processor time to compute the best possible solution, we have graphed the ratio of variance when the equation of transfer is sampled to the variance when the scattering equation is sampled. Points above 1 on the y axis indicate situations where the scattering equation is more efficient. Because both sampling methods converge at the same rate asymptotically, the ratio of running time to compute solutions of equivalent quality is proportional to the variance ratio.

equation of transfer was sometimes more efficient. We believe that this is due to our recursive sampling process: because we compute a geometrically-increasing number of recursive estimates of R^+ at each level of recursion, it is possible to end up computing a large number of estimates that have a relatively little influence on the final result. The scattering equation also did well for most phase function parameters, except for extreme backward scattering. In this case, although most of incident light is quickly scattered back out of the top, we still continue to work through the z depth of the medium, not allocating effort as well as we might.

5.2 Scattering from surfaces

To illustrate the use of the 1D adding and scattering equations for rendering, we took a dragon model with a standard specular and diffuse shading model and added scattering layers to it, using the adding equations to compute the new scattering function that describes the composition of the base surface layer with the new scattering layer. As such, the result is an accurate simulation of subsurface light transport. When the routines that compute the adding equations needed to evaluate the reflection or transmission functions of the added layer, a new Monte Carlo estimate for that pair of angles was computed. With a not-very-optimized implementation, the images each took a few minutes to render on a modern PC.

The series of images in Figure 10 shows the results. The first image shows the object shaded with the standard shading model. As the thickness of the new layer increases going from left to right, the shiny copper base surface is gradually overwhelmed by the grey and more diffuse added layer. Eventually just a shadow of the specular highlights is left and finally no trace of the base surface once the new layer is sufficiently thick. Notice that the silhouette edges are affected more strongly by the added layer; this is because the rays traveling at oblique angles go a longer distance through the new layer. The rightmost image shows the result of procedurally varying the thickness of the added layer based on the local surface normal in an effort to simulate scattering effects of dust (modeled in a manner similar to Hsu and Wong [HW95]).

5.3 Scattering from volumes

As a final example, we generated some images to demonstrate the use of the 3D scattering equation to compute reflection from complex surfaces and performed some experiments to understand the properties of subsurface light transport.

To determine how distance from the point of illumination affected the intensity of reflected light, we illuminated half of a slab from the direction along its normal and looked at the scattering function's magnitude in the normal direction at a series of points moving away from the illuminated area. Figure 11 shows the results. As one might expect, reflectance drops off roughly exponentially. Other experiments showed that as the object gets thinner, light entering from far away becomes less important, because more light scatters out of the object before traveling very far. These observations help validate some of the assumptions made in designing importance sampling techniques for 3D scattering equation.

Inspired by the images of Dorsey *et al.*, we rendered some images of marble, in the form of a marble block. Scattering properties were computed procedurally using noise functions [Per85]. Figure 12 shows a comparison of rendering a block with the 1D scattering equation (left) compared to a rendering with the 3D scattering equation (right). The right halves of the blocks were brightly illuminated by a directional light source, while the left halves were lit dimly. There are a number of significant differences between the two images. Most strikingly, when subsurface light transport is accounted for we can see the effect of light that entered in the illuminated half and then scattered into the unilluminated half. Furthermore, the veins of the marble, where the attenuation coefficient is high, cast shadows inside the volume; this effect is missing in the 1D case. A subtle difference between the two can be seen along

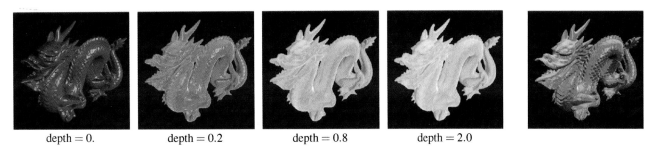

| depth = 0. | depth = 0.2 | depth = 0.8 | depth = 2.0 |

Figure 10: *Adding layers to a model; thicknesses are increasing from left to right. On the right, the thickness is determined procedurally to simulate dust. For all images, $\sigma_s = 0.5$, $\sigma_a = 0.5$, $g = -0.15$. Because the adding equations and scattering equations are used to compute the aggregate scattering function, the results accurately account for all inter-reflection inside the added layer as well as between the layer and the base surface.*

the edges: they are more transparent in the 3D version, since the geometry of the object is accounted for in computing subsurface scattering and rays leave the object after a short distance.

6 Summary and Conclusion

In this paper we have introduced a new theoretical framework for light scattering to computer graphics. This theory has scattering as its basic foundation, rather than light transport. We have applied the theory to rendering subsurface scattering from complex objects using Monte Carlo integration. For some rendering problems (and with the sampling algorithms we used), the scattering equation can be solved more efficiently than the equation of transfer. The adding equations exhibit efficiencies by providing a way to break rendering problems into smaller parts and then reassemble the partial solutions; this gives a theoretical basis to clustering algorithms and a new way to apply clustering to Monte Carlo rendering algorithms.

Part of the advantage from the scattering equation solution stems from the fact that its recursive expansion has a bidirectional effect— paths are constructed in both directions and meet in the middle. Our sampling of the **SkS** term reflects a *non-local* sampling strategy [Vea97], where a scattering event at **k** is chosen before either of its adjacent scattering events have been sampled. This is in contrast to previous bidirectional sampling strategies that incrementally build paths by finding new vertices directly from a previous vertex. As such, understanding the connections between the path sampling strategies that we have used and previous bidirectional path sampling strategies is important future work. In particular, techniques that ameliorate the exponential nature of the recursive sampling and more effectively re-use sub-paths should improve performance in cases where the albedo is high. Another area for further investigation is better importance sampling techniques for the 3D case and the application of multiple importance sampling to reduce variance.

Our example of subsurface scattering as a demonstration of the three-dimensional scattering equation reflects a choice in scale

rather than limitation of theory. The scattering and adding equations have applications to computing scattering from complex volumetric objects at larger scales, such as clouds, smoke, sunbeams, *etc.* As such, this approach has applications to the level-of-detail problem. The 3D scattering and adding equations provide the correct mathematical setting for two of the outstanding problems in level-of-detail identified by Kajiya and Kay [KK89]: automatic computation of texels from complex geometry, and computation of aggregate texels that represent two nearby texels. Furthermore, scattering functions are the correct abstraction to use to replace geometry; techniques based on BRDFs (*e.g.* [Kaj85, Ney98]) are inaccurate in that they do not correctly incorporate the effect of light that enters an object at a different place than it exits.

This theory has applications to many classic problems in rendering, including replacing geometry with scattering functions and efficiently re-rendering scenes with changes in illumination or as objects are added to or removed from them. Equally important, it has promise as a way to suggest new sampling strategies for solving the rendering equation more effectively. Understanding the connections between solution techniques that have previously been used for each of these approaches gives many directions for future work.

Acknowledgements

Discussions with Eric Veach about this work and about connections with bidirectional light transport algorithms in particular were very useful. Thanks also to the reviewers for insightful comments. The dragon model was provided by the Stanford 3D Scanning Repository. Matt Pharr was supported by a Pixar Animation Studios graduate fellowship, DARPA contract DABT63-95-C-0085 and NSF contract CCR-9508579.

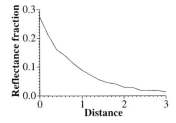

Figure 11: *Reflection function magnitude in the unilluminated part of an object as a function of distance from the boundary of illuminated region. $\sigma_a = 0.5$, $\sigma_s = 0.5$, $g = 0$.*

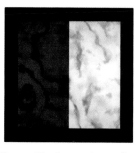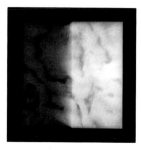

Figure 12: *Comparison of rendering subsurface scattering from a side-lit marble cube with the 1D scattering equation (left) and the 3D scattering equation (right). Since the 3D solution considers light that enters the surface away from where it exits, subsurface light transport is more accurately modeled.*

References

[AK90]   James Arvo and David Kirk, *Particle transport and image synthesis*, Computer Graphics **24** (1990), no. 4, 63–66.

[Amb42]   V. A. Ambarzumian, *A new method for computing light scattering in turbid media*, Izv. Akad. Nauk SSSR **3** (1942).

[Amb58]   V. A. Ambarzumian (ed.), *Theoretical astrophysics*, Pergamon Press, New York, New York, 1958.

[BK56]   Richard Bellman and Robert Kalaba, *On the principle of invairant imbedding and propagation through inhomoheneous media*, Proceedings of the National Academy of Sciences **42** (1956), 629–632.

[BKP63]   Richard E. Bellman, Robert E. Kalaba, and Marcia C. Prestrud, *Invariant imbedding and radiative transfer in slabs of finite thickness*, American Elsevier Publishing Company, New York, 1963.

[Bli82]   James F. Blinn, *Light reflection functions for simulation of clouds and dusty surfaces*, Computer Graphics **16** (1982), no. 3, 21–29.

[BW75]   Richard E. Bellman and G. M. Wing, *An introduction to invariant imbedding*, John Wiley & Sons, New York, 1975.

[Cha60]   S. Chandrasekar, *Radiative transfer*, Dover Publications, New York, 1960, Originally published by Oxford University Press, 1950.

[DEL+99]   Julie Dorsey, Alan Edelman, Justin Legakis, Henrik Wann Jensen, and Hans Køhling Pedersen, *Modeling and rendering of weathered stone*, Proceedings of SIGGRAPH 99 (August 1999), 225–234.

[GY89]   R. M. Goody and Y. L. Yung, *Atmospheric radiation*, Oxford University Press, 1989.

[HG41]   L. G. Henyey and J. L. Greenstein, *Diffuse radiation in the galaxy*, Astrophysical Journal **93** (1941), 70–83.

[HK93]   Pat Hanrahan and Wolfgang Krueger, *Reflection from layered surfaces due to subsurface scattering*, Computer Graphics Proceedings, August 1993, pp. 165–174.

[HM92]   Chet S. Haase and Gary W. Meyer, *Modeling pigmented materials for realistic image synthesis*, ACM Transactions on Graphics **11** (1992), no. 4, 305–335.

[HW95]   Siu-Chi Hsu and Tien-Tsin Wong, *Simulating dust accumulation*, IEEE Computer Graphics and Applications **15** (1995), no. 1, 18–25.

[Kaj85]   James T. Kajiya, *Anisotropic reflection models*, Computer Graphics (SIGGRAPH '85 Proceedings), vol. 19, July 1985, pp. 15–21.

[Kaj86]   James T. Kajiya, *The rendering equation*, Computer Graphics **20** (1986), no. 4, 143–150.

[KK89]   James T. Kajiya and Timothy L. Kay, *Rendering fur with three dimensional textures*, Computer Graphics **23** (1989), no. 3, 271–280.

[KM31]   P. Kubelka and F. Munk, *Ein Beitrag zur Optik der Farbanstriche*, Z. Tech. Physik. **12** (1931), 593.

[KW86]   Malvin H. Kalos and Paula A. Whitlock, *Monte Carlo methods: Volume I: Basics*, John Wiley & Sons, New York, 1986.

[Laf96]   Eric Lafortune, *Mathematical models and Monte Carlo algorithms for physically based rendering*, Ph.D. thesis, Katholieke Universiteit Leuven, February 1996.

[LW94]   Eric Lafortune and Yves Willems, *A theoretical framework for physically based rendering*, Computer Graphics Forum **13** (1994), no. 2, 97–107.

[MM98]   Gavin Miller and Marc Mondesir, *Rendering hyper-sprites in real time*, Eurographics Rendering Workshop 1998 (1998), 193–198.

[MMKW97]   Nelson Max, Curtis Mobley, Brett Keating, and En-Hua Wu, *Plane-parallel radiance transport for global illumination in vegetation*, Eurographics Rendering Workshop 1997, Eurographics, Springer Wien, June 1997, pp. 239–250.

[Mob94]   Curtis D. Mobley, *Light and water: Radiative transfer in natural waters*, Academic Press, 1994.

[Ney98]   Fabrice Neyret, *Modeling, animating, and rendering complex scenes using volumetric textures*, IEEE Transactions on Visualization and Computer Graphics **4** (1998), no. 1.

[NRH+77]   Fred E. Nicodemus, J. C. Richmond, J. J. Hisa, I. W. Ginsberg, and T. Limperis, *Geometrical considerations and nomenclature for reflectance*, Monograph number 160, National Bureau of Standards, Washington DC, 1977.

[NUW98]   H. H. Natsuyama, S. Ueno, and A. P. Wang, *Terrestial radiative transfer*, Springer-Verlag, Hong Kong, 1998.

[Per85]   Ken Perlin, *An image synthesizer*, Computer Graphics (SIGGRAPH '85 Proceedings), vol. 19, July 1985, pp. 287–296.

[PP51]   Glenn H. Peebles and Milton S. Plesset, *Transmission of gamma-rays through large thicknesses of heavy materials*, Physical Review **81** (1951), no. 3, 430–439.

[Pre58]   Rudolph W. Preisendorfer, *Invariant imbedding relation for the principles of invariance*, Proceedings of the National Academy of Sciences **44** (1958), 320–323.

[Pre65]   Rudolph W. Preisendorfer, *Radiative transfer on discrete spaces*, Pergamon Press, Oxford, 1965.

[Pre76]   R. W. Preisendorfer, *Hydrologic optics*, U.S. Department of Commerce, National Oceanic and Atmospheric Administration, Honolulu, Hawaii, 1976, Six volumes.

[PV00]   Matt Pharr and Eric Veach, *Shading with closures*, In preparation, 2000.

[RPV93]   Holly Rushmeier, Charles Patterson, and Aravindan Veerasamy, *Geometric simplification for indirect illumination calculations*, Proceedings of Graphics Interface '93, May 1993, pp. 227–236.

[SD95]   François Sillion and George Drettakis, *Feature-based control of visibility error: A multi-resolution clustering algorithm for global illumination*, SIGGRAPH 95 Conference Proceedings, Addison Wesley, August 1995, pp. 145–152.

[SDS95]   François Sillion, G. Drettakis, and Cyril Soler, *A clustering algorithm for radiance calculation in general environments*, Eurographics Rendering Workshop 1995, Eurographics, June 1995.

[Sto62]   George Stokes, *On the intensity of the light reflected from or transmitted through a pile of plates*, Proceedings of the Royal Society (1862), Reprinted in Mathematical and Physical Papers of Sir George Stokes, Volume IV, Cambridge, 1904.

[TJH66]   S. Twomey, H. Jacobowitz, and H. B. Howell, *Matrix methods for multiple-scattering problems*, Journal of the Atmospheric Sciences **23** (1966), 289–296.

[TS67]   K. E. Torrance and E. M. Sparrow, *Theory for off-specular reflection from roughened surfaces*, Journal of the Optical Society of America **57** (1967), no. 9.

[van80]   Hendrik Christoffel van de Hulst, *Multiple light scattering*, Academic Press, New York, 1980, Two volumes.

[Vea97]   Eric Veach, *Robust Monte Carlo methods for light transport simulation*, Ph.D. thesis, Stanford University, December 1997.

[VG94]   Eric Veach and Leonidas Guibas, *Bidirectional estimators for light transport*, Fifth Eurographics Workshop on Rendering (Darmstadt, Germany), June 1994, pp. 147–162.

[VG95]   Eric Veach and Leonidas J. Guibas, *Optimally combining sampling techniques for Monte Carlo rendering*, Computer Graphics Proceedings, August 1995, pp. 419–428.

[Wan90]   Alan P. Wang, *Basic equations of three-dimensional radiative transfer*, Journal of Mathematical Physics **31** (1990), no. 1, 175–181.

[WAT92]   Stephen Westin, James Arvo, and Kenneth Torrance, *Predicting reflectance functions from complex surfaces*, Computer Graphics **26** (1992), no. 2, 255–264.

[ZWCS99]   Douglas E. Zongker, Dawn M. Werner, Brian Curless, and David H. Salesin, *Environment matting and compositing*, SIGGRAPH 99 Conference Proceedings, Addison Wesley, August 1999, pp. 205–214.

Displaced Subdivision Surfaces

Aaron Lee
Department of Computer Science
Princeton University
http://www.aaron-lee.com/

Henry Moreton
NVIDIA Corporation
moreton@nvidia.com

Hugues Hoppe
Microsoft Research
http://research.microsoft.com/~hoppe

ABSTRACT

In this paper we introduce a new surface representation, the *displaced subdivision surface*. It represents a detailed surface model as a scalar-valued displacement over a smooth domain surface. Our representation defines both the domain surface and the displacement function using a unified subdivision framework, allowing for simple and efficient evaluation of analytic surface properties. We present a simple, automatic scheme for converting detailed geometric models into such a representation. The challenge in this conversion process is to find a simple subdivision surface that still faithfully expresses the detailed model as its offset. We demonstrate that displaced subdivision surfaces offer a number of benefits, including geometry compression, editing, animation, scalability, and adaptive rendering. In particular, the encoding of fine detail as a *scalar* function makes the representation extremely compact.

Additional Keywords: geometry compression, multiresolution geometry, displacement maps, bump maps, multiresolution editing, animation.

1. INTRODUCTION

Highly detailed surface models are becoming commonplace, in part due to 3D scanning technologies. Typically these models are represented as dense triangle meshes. However, the irregularity and huge size of such meshes present challenges in manipulation, animation, rendering, transmission, and storage. Meshes are an expensive representation because they store:

(1) the irregular connectivity of faces,

(2) the (x,y,z) coordinates of the vertices,

(3) possibly several sets of texture parameterization (u,v) coordinates at the vertices, and

(4) texture images referenced by these parameterizations, such as color images and bump maps.

An alternative is to express the detailed surface as a displacement from some simpler, smooth domain surface (see Figure 1). Compared to the above, this offers a number of advantages:

(1) the patch structure of the domain surface is defined by a control mesh whose connectivity is much simpler than that of the original detailed mesh;

(2) fine detail in the displacement field can be captured as a scalar-valued function which is more compact than traditional vector-valued geometry;

Permission to make digital or hard copies of all or part of this work for personal or classroom use is granted without fee provided that copies are not made or distributed for profit or commercial advantage, and that copies bear this notice and the full citation on the first page. To copy otherwise, to republish, to post on servers or to redistribute to lists, requires prior specific permission and/or a fee.

©2000 ACM 0-58113-208-5/00/0007 $5.00

(3) the parameterization of the displaced surface is inherited from the smooth domain surface and therefore does not need to be stored explicitly;

(4) the displacement field may be used to easily generate bump maps, obviating their storage.

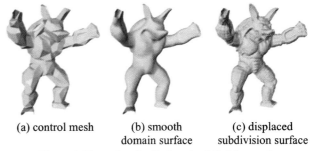

(a) control mesh   (b) smooth domain surface   (c) displaced subdivision surface

Figure 1: Example of a displaced subdivision surface.

A simple example of a displaced surface is terrain data expressed as a height field over a plane. The case of functions over the sphere has been considered by Schröder and Sweldens [33]. Another example is the 3D scan of a human head expressed as a radial function over a cylinder. However, even for this simple case of a head, artifacts are usually detectable at the ear lobes, where the surface is not a single-valued function over the cylindrical domain.

The challenge in generalizing this concept to arbitrary surfaces is that of finding a smooth underlying domain surface that can express the original surface as a scalar-valued offset function.

Krishnamurthy and Levoy [25] show that a detailed model can be represented as a displacement map over a network of B-spline patches. However, they resort to a vector-valued displacement map because the detailed model is not always an offset of their B-spline surface. Also, avoiding surface artifacts during animation requires that the domain surface be tangent-plane (C^1) continuous, which involves constraints on the B-spline control points.

We instead define the domain surface using subdivision surfaces, since these can represent smooth surfaces of arbitrary topological type without requiring control point constraints. Our representation, the *displaced subdivision surface*, consists of a control mesh and a scalar field that displaces the associated subdivision surface locally along its normal (see Figure 1). In this paper we use the Loop [27] subdivision surface scheme, although the representation is equally well defined using other schemes such as Catmull-Clark [5].

Both subdivision surfaces and displacement maps have been in use for about 20 years. One of our contributions is to unify these two ideas by defining the displacement function using the same subdivision machinery as the surface. The scalar displacements are stored on a piecewise regular mesh. We show that simple subdivision masks can then be used to compute analytic properties on the resulting displaced surface. Also, we make displaced subdivision surface practical by introducing a scheme for constructing them from arbitrary meshes.

We demonstrate several benefits of expressing a model as a displaced subdivision surface:

Compression: both the surface topology and parameterization are defined by the coarse control mesh, and fine geometric detail is captured using a scalar-valued function (Section 5.1).

Editing: the fine detail can be easily modified since it is a scalar field (Section 5.2).

Animation: the control mesh makes a convenient armature for animating the displaced subdivision surface, since geometric detail is carried along with the deformed smooth domain surface (Section 5.3).

Scalability: the scalar displacement function may be converted into geometry or a bump map. With proper multiresolution filtering (Section 5.4), we can also perform magnification and minification easily.

Rendering: the representation facilitates adaptive tessellation and hierarchical backface culling (Section 5.5).

2. PREVIOUS WORK

Subdivision surfaces: Subdivision schemes defining smooth surfaces have been introduced by Catmull and Clark [5], Doo and Sabin [13], and Loop [27]. More recently, these schemes have been extended to allow surfaces with sharp features [21] and fractionally sharp features [11]. In this paper we use the Loop subdivision scheme because it is designed for triangle meshes.

DeRose et al. [11] define scalar fields over subdivision surfaces using subdivision masks. Our scalar displacement field is defined similarly, but from a denser set of coefficients on a piecewise regular mesh (Figure 2).

Hoppe et al. [21] describe a method for approximating an original mesh with a much simpler subdivision surface. Unlike our conversion scheme of Section 4, their method does not consider whether the approximation residual is expressible as a scalar displacement map.

Displacement maps: The idea of displacing a surface by a function was introduced by Cook [9]. Displacement maps have become popular commercially as procedural *displacement shaders* in RenderMan [1]. The simplest displacement shaders interpolate values within an image, perhaps using standard bicubic filters. Though displacements may be in an arbitrary direction, they are almost always along the surface normal [1].

Typically, normals on the displaced surface are computed numerically using a dense tessellation. While simple, this approach requires adjacency information that may be unavailable or impractical with low-level APIs and in memory-constrained environments (e.g. game consoles). Strictly local evaluation requires that normals be computed from a continuous analytic surface representation. However, it is difficult to piece together multiple displacement maps while maintaining smoothness. One encounters the same vertex enclosure problem [32] as in the stitching of B-spline surfaces. While there are well-documented solutions to this problem, they require constructions with many more coefficients ($9\times$ in the best case), and may involve solving a global system of equations.

In contrast, our subdivision-based displacements are inherently smooth and have only quartic total degree (fewer DOF than bicubic). Since the displacement map uses the same parameterization as the domain surface, the surface representation is more compact and displaced surface normals may be computed

more efficiently. Finally, unifying the representation around subdivision simplifies implementation and makes operations such as magnification more natural.

Krishnamurthy and Levoy [25] describe a scheme for approximating an arbitrary mesh using a B-spline patch network together with a vector-valued displacement map. In their scheme, the patch network is constructed manually by drawing patch boundaries on the mesh. The recent work on surface pasting by Chan et al. [7] and Mann and Yeung [29] uses the similar idea of adding a vector-valued displacement map to a spline surface.

Gumhold and Hüttner [19] describe a hardware architecture for rendering scalar-valued displacement maps over planar triangles. To avoid cracks between adjacent triangles of a mesh, they interpolate the vertex normals across the triangle face, and use this interpolated normal to displace the surface. Their scheme permits adaptive tessellation in screen space. They discuss the importance of proper filtering when constructing mipmap levels in a displacement map. Unlike our representation, their domain surface is not smooth since it is a polyhedron. As shown in Section 5.3, animating a displaced surface using a polyhedral domain surface results in many surface artifacts.

Kobbelt et al. [23] use a similar framework to express the geometry of one mesh as a displacement from another mesh, for the purpose of multiresolution shape deformation.

Bump maps: Blinn [3] introduces the idea of perturbing the surface normal using a bump map. Peercy et al. [31] present recent work on efficient hardware implementation of bump maps. Cohen et al. [8] drastically simplify meshes by capturing detail in the related *normal maps*. Both Cabral et al. [4] and Apodaca and Gritz [1] discuss the close relationship of bump mapping and displacement mapping. They advocate combining them into a unified representation and resorting to true displacement mapping only when necessary.

Multiresolution subdivision: Lounsbery et al. [28] apply multiresolution analysis to arbitrary surfaces. Given a parameterization of the surface over a triangular domain, they compress this (vector-valued) parameterization using a wavelet basis, where the basis functions are defined using subdivision of the triangular domain. Zorin et al. [39] use a similar subdivision framework for multiresolution mesh editing. To make this multiresolution framework practical, several techniques have been developed for constructing a parameterization of an arbitrary surface over a triangular base domain. Eck et al. [14] use Voronoi/Delaunay diagrams and harmonic maps, while Lee et al. [26] track successive mappings during mesh simplification.

In contrast, displaced subdivision surfaces do not support an arbitrary parameterization of the surface, since the parameterization is given by that of a subdivision surface. The benefit is that we need only compress a *scalar*-valued function instead of *vector*-valued parameterization. In other words, we store only geometric detail, not a parameterization. The drawback is that the original surface must be expressible as an offset of a smooth domain surface. An extremely bad case would be a fractal "snowflake" surface, where the domain surface cannot be made much simpler than the original surface. Fortunately, fine detail in most practical surfaces is expressible as an offset surface.

Guskov et al. [20] represent a surface by successively applying a hierarchy of displacements to a mesh as it is subdivided. Their construction allows most of the vertices to be encoded using scalar displacements, but a small fraction of the vertices require vector displacements to prevent surface folding.

3. REPRESENTATION OVERVIEW

A displaced subdivision surface consists of a triangle control mesh and a piecewise regular mesh of scalar displacement coefficients (see Figure 2). The domain surface is generated from the control mesh using Loop subdivision. Likewise, the displacements applied to the domain surface are generated from the scalar displacement mesh using Loop subdivision.

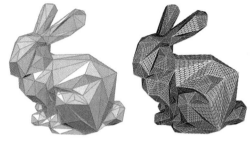

Figure 2: Control mesh (left) with its piecewise regular mesh of scalar displacement coefficients ($k = 3$).

Displacement map: The scalar displacement mesh is stored for each control mesh triangle as one half of the sample grid $(2^k +1) \times (2^k +1)$, where k depends on the sampling density required to achieve a desired level of accuracy or compression.

To define a *continuous* displacement function, these stored values are taken to be subdivision coefficients for the same (Loop) subdivision scheme that defines the domain surface. Thus, as the surface is magnified (i.e. subdivided beyond level k), both the domain surface geometry and the displacement field are subdivided using the same machinery. As a consequence, the displacement field is C^l even at extraordinary vertices, and the displaced subdivision surface is C^1 everywhere *except* at extraordinary vertices. The handling of extraordinary vertices is discussed below.

For surface minification, we first compute the limit displacements for the subdivision coefficients at level k, and we then construct a mipmap pyramid with levels $\{0,...,k-1\}$ by successive filtering of these limit values. We cover filtering possibilities in Section 4.5. As with ordinary texture maps, the content author may sometimes want more precise control of the filtered levels, so it may be useful to store the entire pyramid. (For our compression analysis in Section 5.1, we assume that the pyramid is built automatically.)

For many input meshes, it is inefficient to use the same value of k for all control mesh faces. For a given face, the choice of k may be guided by the number of original triangles associated it, which is easily estimated using MAPS [26]. Those regions with lower values of k are further subdivided *logically* to produce a mesh with uniform k.

Normal Calculation: We now derive the surface normal for a point $\bar{S}$ on the displaced subdivision surface. Let $\bar{S}$ be the displacement of the limit point $\bar{P}$ on the domain surface:

$$\bar{S} = \bar{P} + D\hat{n} ,$$

where D is the limit displacement and $\hat{n} = \bar{n} / \|\bar{n}\|$ is the unit normal on the domain surface. The normal $\bar{n}$ is obtained as $\bar{n} = \bar{P}_u \times \bar{P}_v$ where the tangent vectors $\bar{P}_u$ and $\bar{P}_v$ are computed using the first derivative masks in Figure 3.

The displaced subdivision surface normal at S is defined as $\bar{n}_s = \bar{S}_u \times \bar{S}_v$ where each tangent vector has the form

$$\bar{S}_u = \bar{P}_u + D_u \hat{n} + D \hat{n}_u .$$

If the displacements are relatively small, it is common to ignore the third term, which contains second-order derivatives [3].

However, if the surface is used as a modeling primitive, then the displacements may be quite large and the full expression must be evaluated. The difficult term $\hat{n}_u = \bar{n}_u / \|\bar{n}_u\|$ may be derived using the Weingarten equations [12]. Equivalently, it may be expressed as:

$$\hat{n}_u = \frac{\bar{n}_u - \hat{n}(\bar{n}_u \cdot \hat{n})}{\|\bar{n}\|} \quad \text{where} \quad \bar{n}_u = \bar{P}_{uu} \times \bar{P}_v + \bar{P}_u \times \bar{P}_{uv} .$$

At a regular (valence 6) vertex, the necessary partial derivatives are given by a simple set of masks (see Figure 3). At extraordinary vertices, the curvature of the domain surface vanishes and we omit the second-order term. In this case, the standard Loop tangent masks may be used to compute the first partial derivatives. Since there are few extraordinary vertices, this simplified normal calculation has not proven to be a problem.

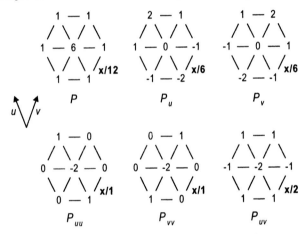

Figure 3: Loop masks for limit position P and first and second derivatives at a regular control vertex.

Bump map: The displacement map may also be used to generate a bump map during the rendering of coarser tessellations (see Figure 13). This improves rendering performance on graphics systems where geometry processing is a bottleneck. The construction of this bump map is presented in Section 5.4.

Other textures: The domain surface parameterization is used for storing the displacement map (which also serves to define a bump map). It is natural to re-use this same inherent parameterization to store additional appearance attributes for the surface, such as color. Section 4.4 describes how such attributes are re-sampled from the original surface.

Alternatively, one could define more traditional surface parameterizations by explicitly specifying (u,v) texture coordinates at the vertices of the control mesh, as in [11]. However, since the domain of a (u,v) parameterization is a planar region, this generally requires segmenting the surface into a set of charts.

4. CONVERSION PROCESS

To convert an arbitrary triangle mesh (Figure 5a) into a displaced subdivision surface (Figure 5b), our process performs the following steps:

- Obtain an initial control mesh (Figure 5c) by simplifying the original mesh. Simplification is done using a traditional sequence of edge collapse transformations, but with added heuristics to attempt to preserve a scalar offset function.

- Globally optimize the control mesh vertices (Figure 5d) such that the domain surface (Figure 5e) more accurately fits the original mesh.

- Sample the displacement map by shooting rays along the domain surface normals until they intersect the original mesh. At the ray intersection points, compute the signed displacement, and optionally sample other appearance attributes like surface color. (The black line segments visible in Figure 5f correspond to rays with positive displacements.)

4.1 Simplification to control mesh

We simplify the original mesh using a sequence of edge collapse transformations [22] prioritized according to the quadric error metric of Garland and Heckbert [16]. In order to produce a good domain surface, we restrict some of the candidate edge collapses.

The main objective is that the resulting domain surface should be able to express the original mesh using a scalar displacement map. Our approach is to ensure that the space of normals on the domain surface remains locally similar to the corresponding space of normals on the original mesh.

To maintain an efficient correspondence between the original mesh and the simplified mesh, we use the MAPS scheme [26] to track parameterizations of all original vertices on the mesh simplified so far. (When an edge is collapsed, the parametrizations of points in the neighborhood are updated using a local 1-to-1 map onto the resulting neighborhood.)

For each candidate edge collapse transformation, we examine the mesh neighborhood that would result. In Figure 4, the thickened 1-ring is the neighborhood of the unified vertex. For vertices on this ring, we compute the subdivision surface normals (using tangent masks that involve vertices in the 2-ring of the unified vertex). The highlighted points within the faces in the 1-ring represent original mesh vertices that are currently parameterized on the neighborhood using MAPS.

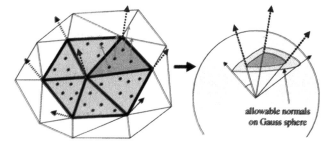

Figure 4: Neighborhood after candidate edge collapse and, for one face, the spherical triangle about its domain surface normals.

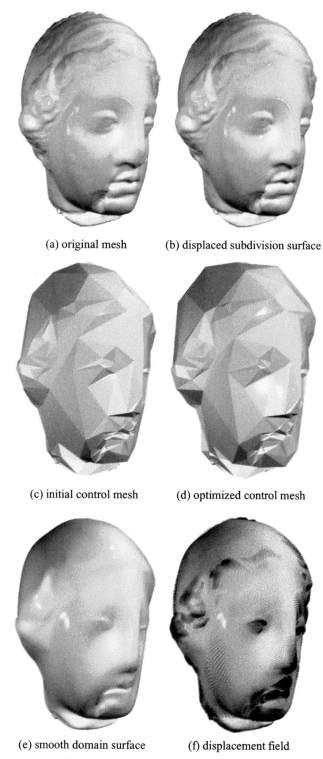

(a) original mesh   (b) displaced subdivision surface

(c) initial control mesh   (d) optimized control mesh

(e) smooth domain surface   (f) displacement field

Figure 5: Steps in the conversion process.

For each face in the 1-ring neighborhood, we gather the 3 subdivision surface normals at the vertices and form their spherical triangle on the Gauss sphere. Then, we test whether this spherical triangle encloses the normals of the original mesh vertices parameterized using MAPS. If this test fails on any face in the 1-ring, the edge collapse transformation is disallowed. To allow simplification to proceed further, we have found it useful to broaden each spherical triangle by pushing its three vertices an additional 45 degrees away from its inscribed center, as illustrated in Figure 4.

We observe that the domain surface sometimes has undesirable undulations when the control mesh has vertices of high valence. Therefore, during simplification we also disallow an edge collapse if the resulting unified vertex would have valence greater than 8.

4.2 Optimization of domain surface

Having formed the initial control mesh, we optimize the locations of its vertices such that the associated subdivision surface more accurately fits the original mesh. This step is performed using the method of Hoppe et al. [21]. We sample a dense set of points from the original mesh and minimize their squared distances to the subdivision surface. This nonlinear optimization problem is approximated by iteratively projecting the points onto the surface and solving for the most accurate surface while fixing those parameterizations. The result of this step is shown in Figure 5d-e.

Note that this geometric optimization modifies the control mesh and thus affects the space of normals over the domain surface. Although this invalidates the heuristic used to guide the simplification process, this has not been a problem in our experiments. A more robust solution would be to optimize the subdivision surface for each candidate edge collapse (as in [21]) prior to testing the neighborhood normals, but this would be much more costly.

4.3 Sampling of scalar displacement map

We apply k steps of Loop subdivision to the control mesh. At each of these subdivided vertices, we compute the limit position and normal of the domain surface. We seek to compute the signed distance from the limit point to the original surface along the normal (Figure 5f).

The directed line formed by the point and normal is intersected with the original surface, using a spatial hierarchy [17] for efficiency. We disregard any intersection point if the intersected surface is oriented in the wrong direction with respect to the directed line. If multiple intersection points remain, we pick the one closest to the domain surface. Figure 6 illustrates a possible failure case if the domain surface is too far from the original.

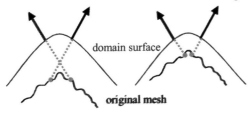

Figure 6: The displacement sampling may "fold over itself" if the domain surface is too distant from the original mesh.

Near surface boundaries, there is the problem that the domain surface may extend beyond the boundary of the original surface, in which case the ray does not intersect any useful part of the original surface. (We detect this using a maximum distance threshold based on the mesh size.) In this case, the surface should really be left undefined, i.e. trimmed to the detailed boundary of the original mesh. One approach would be to store a special illegal value into the displacement map. Instead, we find the closest original triangle to the subdivided vertex, and intersect the ray with the plane containing that triangle. Precise surface trimming can be achieved using an alpha mask in the surface color image, but we have not yet implemented this.

4.4 Resampling of appearance attributes

Besides sampling the scalar displacement function, we also sample other appearance attributes such as diffuse color. These attributes are stored, filtered, and compressed just like the scalar displacements. An example is shown in Figure 11.

4.5 Filtering of displacement map

Since our displacement field has the same structure as the domain surface, we can apply the same subdivision mask for magnification. This is particular useful when we try to zoom in a tiny region on our displaced subdivision surface. For sampling the displacements at minified levels of the displacement pyramid, we compute the samples at any level $l<k$ by filtering the limit displacements of level $l+1$. We considered several filtering operations and opted for the non-shrinking filter of Taubin [35].

Because the displacement magnitudes are kept small, their filtering is not extremely sensitive. In many rendering situations much of the visual detail is provided by bump mapping. As has been discussed elsewhere [2], careful filtering of bump maps is both important and difficult.

4.6 Conversion results

The following table shows execution times for the various steps of the conversion process. These times are obtained on a Pentium III 550 MHz PC.

Model	armadillo	venus	bunny	dinosaur
Conversion Statistics				
Original mesh #F	210,944	100,000	69,451	342,138
Control mesh #F	1,306	748	526	1,564
Maximum level k	4	4	4	4
Execution Times (minutes)				
Simplification	61	28	19	115
Domain surface optimiz.	25	11	11	43
Displacement sampling	2	2	1	5
Total	88	41	31	163

5. BENEFITS

5.1 Compression

Mesh compression has recently been an active area of research. Several clever schemes have been developed to concisely encode the combinatorial structure of the mesh connectivity, in as few as 1-2 bits per face (e.g. [18] [35]). As a result, the major portion of a compressed mesh goes to storing the mesh geometry. Vertex positions are typically compressed using quantization, local prediction, and variable-length delta encoding. Geometry can also be compressed within a multiresolution subdivision framework as a set of wavelet coefficients [28]. To our knowledge, all previous compression schemes for arbitrary surfaces treat geometry as a vector-valued function.

In contrast, displaced subdivision surfaces allow fine geometric detail to be compressed as a scalar-valued function. Moreover, the domain surface is constructed to be close to the original surface, so the magnitude of the displacements tends to be small.

To exploit spatial coherence in the scalar displacement map, we use linear prediction at each level of the displacement pyramid, and encode the difference between the predicted and actual values. For each level, we treat the difference coefficients over all faces as a subband. For each subband, we use the embedded quantizer and embedded entropy coder described in Taubman and Zakhor [37]. The subbands are merged using the bit allocation algorithm described by Shoham and Gersho [34], which is based on integer programming.

An alternative would be to use the compression scheme of Kolarov and Lynch [24], which is a generalization of the wavelet compression method in [33].

Figure 10 and Table 1 show results of our compression experiments. We compare storage costs for simplified triangle meshes and displaced subdivision surfaces, such that both compressed representations have the same approximation accuracy with respect to the original reference model. This accuracy is measured as L^2 geometric distance between the surfaces, computed using dense point sampling [16]. The simplified meshes are obtained using the scheme of Garland and Heckbert [16]. For mesh compression, we use the *VRML compressed binary format* inspired by the work of Taubin and Rossignac [36]. We vary the quantization level for the vertex coordinates to obtain different compressed meshes, and then adjust our displacement map compression parameters to obtain a displaced surface with matching L^2 geometric error.

For simplicity, we always compress the control meshes losslessly in the experiments (i.e. with 23-bits/coordinate quantization). Our compression results would likely be improved further by adapting the quantization of the control mesh as well. However, this would modify the domain surface geometry, and would therefore require re-computing the displacement field. Also, severe quantization of the control mesh would result in larger displacement magnitudes.

Table 1 shows that displaced subdivision surfaces consistently achieve better compression rates than mesh compression, even when the mesh is carefully simplified from detailed geometry.

5.2 Editing

The fine detail in the scalar displacement mesh can be edited conveniently, as shown in the example of Figure 7.

Figure 7: In this simple editing example, the embossing effect is produced by enhancing the scalar displacements according to a texture image of the character 'B' projected onto the displaced surface.

5.3 Animation

Displaced subdivision surfaces are a convenient representation for animation. Kinematic and dynamics computation are vastly more efficient when operating on the control mesh rather than the huge detailed mesh.

Because the domain surface is smooth, the surface detail deforms naturally without artifacts. Figure 8 shows that in contrast, the use of a polyhedron as a domain surface results in creases and folds even with a small deformation of a simple surface.

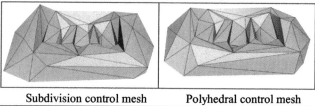

| Subdivision control mesh | Polyhedral control mesh |

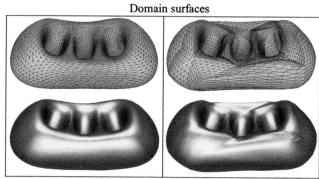

Domain surfaces

Displaced surfaces

Figure 8: Comparison showing the importance of using a smooth domain surface when deforming the control mesh. The domain surface is a subdivision surface on the left, and a polyhedron on the right.

Figure 12 shows two frames from the animation of a more complicated surface. For that example, we used 3D Studio MAX to construct a skeleton of bones inside the control mesh, and manipulated the skeleton to deform this mesh. (The complete animation is on the accompanying video.)

Another application of our representation is the fitting of 3D head scans [30]. For this application, it is desirable to re-use a common control mesh structure so that deformations can be conveniently transferred from one face model to another.

5.4 Scalability

Depending on the level-of-detail requirements and hardware capabilities, the scalar displacement function can either be:

- rendered as **explicit geometry**: Since it is a continuous representation, the tessellation is not limited to the resolution of the displacement mesh. A scheme for adaptive tessellation is presented in Section 5.5.

- converted to a **bump map**: This improves rendering performance on graphics systems where geometry processing is a bottleneck. As described in [31], the calculation necessary for tangent-space bump mapping involves computing the displaced subdivision surface normal relative to a coordinate frame on the domain surface. A convenient coordinate frame is formed by the domain surface unit normal $\hat{n}$ and a tangent vector such as $\vec{P}_u$. Given these vectors, the coordinate frame is:

$$\left\{\hat{b}, \hat{t}, \hat{n}\right\} \text{ where } \begin{aligned} \hat{t} &= \bar{P}_u / \left\|\bar{P}_u\right\| \\ \hat{b} &= \hat{n} \times \hat{t} \end{aligned} \quad.$$

Finally, the normal $\hat{n}_s$ to the displaced subdivision surface relative to this tangent space is computed using the transform:

$$\hat{n}_{\text{tangent space}} = \left\{\hat{b}, \hat{t}, \hat{n}\right\}^{\mathrm{T}} \cdot \hat{n}_s \quad.$$

The computations of $\hat{n}$, $\bar{P}_u$, and $\hat{n}_s$ are described in Section 3. Note that we use the precise analytic normal in the bump map calculation. As an example, Figure 13 shows renderings of the same model with different boundaries between explicit geometry and bump mapping. In the leftmost image, the displacements are all converted into geometry, and bump-mapping is turned off. In the rightmost image, the domain surface is sampled only at the control mesh vertices, but the entire displacement pyramid is converted into a bump map.

5.5 Rendering

Adaptive tessellation: In order to perform adaptive tessellation, we need to compute the approximation error of any intermediate tessellation level from the finely subdivided surface. This approximation error is obtained by computing the maximum distance between the dyadic points on the planar intermediate level and their corresponding surface points at the finest level (see Figure 9). Note that this error measurement corresponds to parametric error and is stricter than geometric error. Bounding parametric error is useful for preventing appearance fields (e.g. bump map, color map) from sliding over the rendered surface [8]. These precomputed error measurements are stored in a quadtree data structure. At runtime, adaptive tessellation prunes off the entire subtree beneath a node if its error measurement satisfies given level-of-detail parameters. By default, the displacements applied to the vertices of a face are taken from the corresponding level of the displacement pyramid.

Note that the pruning will make adjacent subtrees meet at different levels. To avoid cracks, if a vertex is shared among different levels, we choose the finest one from the pyramid. Also, we perform a retriangulation of the coarser face so that it conforms to the vertices along the common edges. Figure 14 shows some examples of adaptive tessellation.

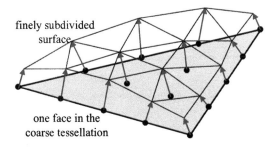

finely subdivided surface

one face in the coarse tessellation

Figure 9: Error computation for adaptive tessellation.

Backface patch culling: To improve rendering performance, we avoid rendering regions of the displaced subdivision surface that are entirely facing away from the viewpoint. We achieve this using the *normal masks* technique of Zhang and Hoff [38].

On the finely subdivided version of the domain surface, we compute the vertex normals of the displaced surface as described in Section 3. We convert these into a normal mask for each subdivided face. During a bottom-up traversal of the subdivision hierarchy, we propagate these masks to the parents using the logical *or* operation.

Given the view parameters, we then construct a viewing mask as in [38], and take its logical *and* with the stored masks in the hierarchy. Generally, we cull away 1/3 to 1/4 of the total number of triangles, thereby speeding up rendering time by 20% to 30%.

6. DISCUSSION

Remeshing creases: As in other remeshing methods [14] [26], the presence of creases in the original surface presents challenges to our conversion process. Lee et al. [26] demonstrate that the key is to associate such creases with edges in the control mesh. Our simplification process also achieves this since mesh simplification naturally preserves sharp features.

However, displaced subdivision surfaces have the further constraint that the displacements are strictly scalar. Therefore, the edges of the control mesh, when subdivided and displaced, do not generally follow original surface creases exactly. (A similar problem also arises at surface boundaries.) This problem can be resolved if displacements were instead vector-based, but then the representation would lose its simplicity and many of its benefits (compactness, ease of scalability, etc.).

Scaling of displacements: Currently, scalar displacements are simply multiplied by unit normals on the domain surface. With a "rubbery" surface, the displaced subdivision surface behaves as one would expect, since detail tends to smooth as the surface stretches. However, greater control over the magnitude of displacement is desirable in many situations. A simple extension of the current representation is to provide scale and bias factors (s, b) at control mesh vertices. These added controls enhance the basic displacement formula:

$$\bar{S} = \bar{P} + (sD + b)\hat{n}$$

Exploring such scaling controls is an interesting area of future work.

7. SUMMARY AND FUTURE WORK

Nearly all geometric representations capture geometric detail as a vector-valued function. We have shown that an arbitrary surface can be approximated by a displaced subdivision surface, in which geometric detail is encoded as a scalar-valued function over a domain surface. Our representation defines both the domain surface and the displacement function using a unified subdivision framework. This synergy allows simple and efficient evaluation of analytic surface properties.

We demonstrated that the representation offers significant savings in storage compared to traditional mesh compression schemes. It is also convenient for animation, editing, and runtime level-of-detail control.

Areas for future work include: a more rigorous scheme for constructing the domain surface, improved filtering of bump maps, hardware rendering, error measures for view-dependent adaptive tessellation, and use of detail textures for displacements.

ACKNOWLEDGEMENTS

Our thanks to Gene Sexton for his help in scanning the dinosaur.

REFERENCES

[1] Apodaca, A. and Gritz, L. Advanced RenderMan – Creating CGI for Motion Pictures, Morgan Kaufmann, San Francisco, CA, 1999.

[2] Becker, B. and Max, N. Smooth transitions between bump rendering algorithms. Proceedings of SIGGRAPH 93, Computer Graphics, Annual Conference Series, pp. 183-190.

[3] Blinn, J. F. Simulation of wrinkled surfaces. Proceedings of SIGGRAPH 78, Computer Graphics, pp. 286-292.

[4] Cabral, B., Max, N. and Springmeyer, R. Bidirectional reflection functions from surface bump maps. Proceedings of SIGGRAPH 87, Computer Graphics, Annual Conference Series, pp.273-281.

[5] Catmull, E., and Clark, J. Recursively generated B-spline surfaces on arbitrary topological meshes. Computer Aided Design 10, pp. 350-355 (1978).

[6] Certain, A., Popovic, J., DeRose, T., Duchamp, T., Salesin, D. and Stuetzle, W. Interactive multiresolution surface viewing. Proceedings of SIGGRAPH 96, Computer Graphics, Annual Conference Series, pp. 91-98.

[7] Chan, K., Mann, S., and Bartels, R. World space surface pasting. Graphics Interface '97, pp. 146-154.

[8] Cohen, J., Olano, M. and Manocha, D. Appearance preserving Simplification. Proceedings of SIGGRAPH 98, Computer Graphics, Annual Conference Series, pp. 115-122.

[9] Cook, R. Shade trees. Computer Graphics (Proceedings of SIGGRAPH 84), 18(3), pp. 223-231.

[10] Deering, M. Geometry compression. Proceedings of SIGGRAPH 95, Computer Graphics, Annual Conference Series, pp. 13-20.

[11] DeRose, T., Kass, M., and Truong, T. Subdivision surfaces in character animation. Proceedings of SIGGRAPH 98, Computer Graphics, Annual Conference Series, pp. 85-94.

[12] Do Carmo, M. P. Differential Geometry of Curves and Surfaces. Prentice-Hall, Inc., Englewood Cliffs, New Jersey, 1976.

[13] Doo, D., and Sabin, M. Behavior of recursive division surfaces near extraordinary points. Computer Aided Design 10, pp. 356-360 (1978).

[14] Eck, M., DeRose, T., Duchamp, T., Hoppe, H., Lounsbery, M., and Stuetzle, W. Multiresolution analysis of arbitrary meshes. Proceedings of SIGGRAPH 95, Computer Graphics, Annual Conference Series, pp. 173-182.

[15] Forsey, D., and Bartels, R. Surface fitting with hierarchical splines. ACM Transactions on Graphics, 14(2), pp. 134-161 (April 1995).

[16] Garland, M., and Heckbert, P. Surface simplification using quadric error metrics. Proceedings of SIGGRAPH 97, Computer Graphics, Annual Conference Series, pp. 209-216.

[17] Gottschalk, S., Lin, M., and Manocha, D. OBB-tree: a hierarchical structure for rapid interference detection. Proceedings of SIGGRAPH 96, Computer Graphics, Annual Conference Series, pp. 171-180.

[18] Gumhold, S., and Straßer, W. Real time compression of triangle mesh connectivity. Proceedings of SIGGRAPH 98, Computer Graphics, Annual Conference Series, pp. 133-140.

[19] Gumhold, S., and Hüttner, T. Multiresolution rendering with displacement mapping. SIGGRAPH workshop on Graphics hardware, Aug 8-9, 1999.

[20] Guskov, I., Vidimce, K., Sweldens, W., and Schröder, P. Normal meshes. Proceedings of SIGGRAPH 2000, Computer Graphics, Annual Conference Series.

[21] Hoppe, H., DeRose, T., Duchamp, T., Halstead, M., Jin, H., McDonald, J., Schweitzer, J., and Stuetzle, W. Piecewise smooth surface reconstruction. Proceedings of SIGGRAPH 94, Computer Graphics, Annual Conference Series, pp. 295-302.

[22] Hoppe, H. Progressive meshes. Proceedings of SIGGRAPH 96, Computer Graphics, Annual Conference Series, pp. 99-108.

[23] Kobbelt, L., Bareuther, T., and Seidel, H. P. Multi-resolution shape deformations for meshes with dynamic vertex connectivity. Proceedings of EUROGRAPHICS 2000, to appear.

[24] Kolarov, K. and Lynch, W. Compression of functions defined on surfaces of 3D objects. In J. Storer and M. Cohn, editors, Proc. of Data Compression Conference, IEEE, pp. 281-291, 1997.

[25] Krishnamurthy, V., and Levoy, M. Fitting smooth surfaces to dense polygon meshes. Proceedings of SIGGRAPH 96, Computer Graphics, Annual Conference Series, pp. 313-324.

[26] Lee, A., Sweldens, W., Schröder, P., Cowsar, L., and Dobkin, D. MAPS: Multiresolution adaptive parameterization of surfaces. Proceedings of SIGGRAPH 98, Computer Graphics, Annual Conference Series, pp. 95-104.

[27] Loop, C. Smooth subdivision surfaces based on triangles. Master's thesis, University of Utah, Department of Mathematics, 1987.

[28] Lounsbery, M., DeRose, T., and Warren, J. Multiresolution analysis for surfaces of arbitrary topological type. ACM Transactions on Graphics, 16(1), pp. 34-73 (January 1997).

[29] Mann, S. and Yeung, T. Cylindrical surface pasting. Technical Report, Computer Science Dept., University of Waterloo (June 1999).

[30] Marschner, S., Guenter, B., and Raghupathy, S. Modeling and rendering for realistic facial animation. Submitted for publication.

[31] Peercy, M., Airey, J. and Cabral, B. Efficient bump mapping hardware. Proceedings of SIGGRAPH 97, Computer Graphics, Annual Conference Series, pp. 303-306.

[32] Peters, J. Local smooth surface interpolation: a classification. Computer Aided Geometric Design, 7(1990), pp. 191-195.

[33] Schröder, P., and Sweldens, W. Spherical wavelets: efficiently representing functions on the sphere. Proceedings of SIGGRAPH 95, Computer Graphics, Annual Conference Series, pp. 161-172.

[34] Shoham, Y. and Gersho, A. Efficient bit allocation for an arbitrary set of quantizers. IEEE Transactions on Acoustics, Speech, and Signal Processing, Vol. 36, No. 9, pp. 1445-1453, Sept 1988.

[35] Taubin, G. A signal processing approach to fair surface design. Proceedings of SIGGRAPH 95, Computer Graphics, Annual Conference Series, pp. 351-358.

[36] Taubin, G. and Rossignac, J. Geometric compression through topological surgery. ACM Transactions on Graphics, 17(2), pp. 84-115 (April 1998).

[37] Taubman, D. and Zakhor, A. Multirate 3-D subband coding of video. IEEE Transactions on Image Processing, Vol. 3, No. 5, Sept, 1994.

[38] Zhang, H., and Hoff, K. Fast backface culling using normal masks. Symposium on Interactive 3D Graphics, pp. 103-106, 1997.

[39] Zorin, D., Schröder, P., and Sweldens, W. Interactive multiresolution mesh editing. Proceedings of SIGGRAPH 97, Computer Graphics, Annual Conference Series, pp. 259-268.

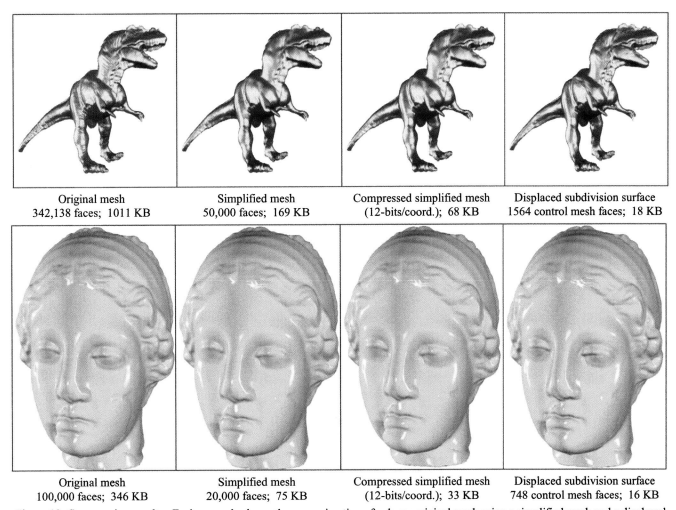

| | Original mesh
342,138 faces; 1011 KB | Simplified mesh
50,000 faces; 169 KB | Compressed simplified mesh
(12-bits/coord.); 68 KB | Displaced subdivision surface
1564 control mesh faces; 18 KB |

| | Original mesh
100,000 faces; 346 KB | Simplified mesh
20,000 faces; 75 KB | Compressed simplified mesh
(12-bits/coord.); 33 KB | Displaced subdivision surface
748 control mesh faces; 16 KB |

Figure 10: Compression results. Each example shows the approximation of a dense original mesh using a simplified mesh and a displaced subdivision surface, such that both have comparable L^2 approximation error (expressed as a percentage of object bounding box).

Dinosaur	Original mesh		Compressed simplified mesh		Displaced subdivision surface (k=4)		
	#V=171,074 #F=342,138		#V=25,005 #F=50,000		#V^0=787 #F^0=1564 ≡ 6.5KB		
Quantization (bits/coord.)	L^2 error	Size (KB)	L^2 error	Size (KB)	L^2 error	Size (KB)	Size ratio
23	0.002%	1011	0.024%	169	0.025%	22	7.7
12	0.014%	322	0.028%	68	0.028%	18	3.8
10	0.053%	217	0.059%	50	0.058%	10	5.0
8	0.197%	169	0.21%	35	0.153%	7	5.0

Venus	Original mesh		Compressed simplified mesh		Displaced subdivision surface (k=4)		
	#V=50,002 #F=100,000		#V=10,002 #F=20,000		#V^0=376 #F^0=748 ≡ 3.4KB		
Quantization (bits/coord.)	L^2 error	Size (KB)	L^2 error	Size (KB)	L^2 error	Size (KB)	Size ratio
23	0.001%	346	0.027%	75	0.027%	17	4.4
12	0.014%	140	0.030%	33	0.031%	16	2.0
10	0.054%	102	0.059%	26	0.053%	8	3.2
8	0.207%	69	0.210%	18	0.149%	4	4.5

Table 1: Quantitative compression results for the two examples in Figure 10. Numbers in red refer to figures above.

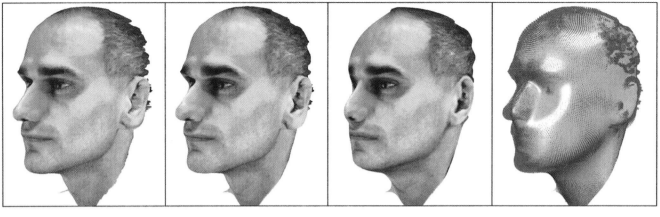

Original colored mesh	Displaced subdivision surface	Domain surface	Displacement samples *(k=4)*

Figure 11: Example of a displaced subdivision surface with resampled color.

Original mesh	Control mesh	Displaced subdiv. surface	Modified control mesh	Resulting deformed surface

Figure 12: The control mesh makes a convenient armature for animating the displaced subdivision surface.

Level 4 (134,656 faces)	Level 3 (33,664 faces)	Level 2 (8,416 faces)	Level 1 (2,104 faces)	Level 0 (526 faces)

Figure 13: Replacement of scalar displacements by bump-mapping at different levels.

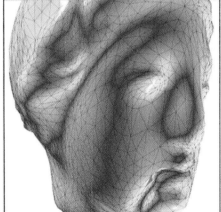 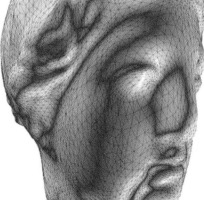 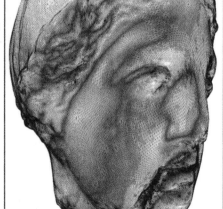

Threshold = 1.87% diameter	Threshold = 0.76% diameter	Threshold = 0.39% diameter
12,950 triangles; L^2 error = 0.104%	88,352 triangles; L^2 error = 0.035%	258,720 triangles; L^2 error = 0.016%

Figure 14: Example of adaptive tessellation, using the view-independent criterion of comparing residual error with a global threshold.

Normal Meshes

Igor Guskov	Kiril Vidimče	Wim Sweldens	Peter Schröder
Caltech	Mississippi State University	Bell Laboratories	Caltech

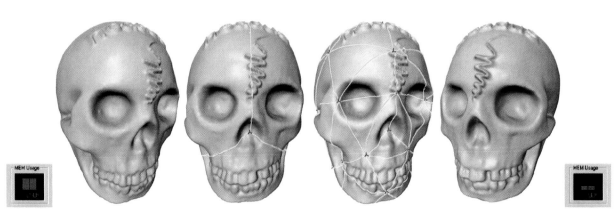

Figure 1: *Left: original mesh (3 floats/vertex). Middle: two stages of our algorithm. Right: normal mesh (1 float/vertex). (Skull dataset courtesy Headus, Inc.)*

Abstract

Normal meshes are new fundamental surface descriptions inspired by differential geometry. A normal mesh is a multiresolution mesh where each level can be written as a normal offset from a coarser version. Hence the mesh can be stored with a single float per vertex. We present an algorithm to approximate any surface arbitrarily closely with a normal semi-regular mesh. Normal meshes can be useful in numerous applications such as compression, filtering, rendering, texturing, and modeling.

CR Categories and Subject Descriptors: I.3.5 [**Computer Graphics**]: Computational Geometry and Object Modeling - *curve, surface, solid, and object representations; hierarchy and geometric transformations*; G.1.2 [**Numerical Analysis**]: Approximation - *approximation of surfaces and contours, wavelets and fractals*

Additional Keywords: Meshes, subdivision, irregular connectivity, surface parameterization, multiresolution, wavelets.

1 Introduction

The standard way to parameterize a surface involves *three* scalar functions $x(u,v)$, $y(u,v)$, $z(u,v)$. Yet differential geometry teaches us that smooth surfaces locally can be described by a *single* scalar height function over the tangent plane. Loosely speaking one can say that the geometric information of a surface can be contained

in only a single dimension, the height over this plane. This observation holds infinitesimally; only special cases such as terrains and star-shaped surfaces can globally be described with a single function.

In practice we often approximate surfaces using a triangle mesh. While describing meshes is relatively easy, they have lost much of the structure inherent in the original surface. For example, the above observation that locally a surface can be characterized by a scalar function is not reflected in the fact that we store 3 floats per vertex. In other words, the correlation between neighboring sample locations implied by the smoothness assumption is not reflected, leading to an inherently redundant representation.

While vertex locations come as 3-dimensional quantities, the above considerations tell us that locally two of those dimensions represent parametric information and only the third captures geometric, or shape, information. For a given smooth shape one may choose different parameterizations, yet the geometry remains the same. In the case of a mesh we can observe this by noticing that infinitesimal tangential motion of a vertex does not change the geometry, only the sampling pattern, or parameterization. Moving in the normal direction on the other hand changes the geometry and leaves parameter information undisturbed.

1.1 Goals and Contributions

Based on the above observations, the aim of the present paper is to compute mesh representations that only require a single scalar per vertex. We call such representations *normal meshes*. The main insight is that this can be done using multiresolution and local frames. A normal mesh has a hierarchical representation so that all detail coefficients when expressed in local frames are scalar, i.e., they only have a normal component. In the context of compression, for example, this implies that parameter information can be perfectly predicted and residual error is entirely constrained to the normal direction, i.e., contains only geometric information. Note that because of the local frames normal mesh representations are non-linear.

Of course we cannot expect a given arbitrary input mesh to possess a hierarchical representation which is normal. Instead we describe an algorithm which takes an arbitrary topology input mesh and produces a semi-regular normal mesh describing the same geometry. Aside from a small amount of base domain information, *our normal mesh transform converts an arbitrary mesh from a 3 parameter representation into a purely scalar representation.* We demonstrate our algorithm by applying it to a number of models and experimentally characterize some of the properties which make normal meshes so attractive for computations.

The study of normal meshes is of interest for a number of reasons: they

- bring our computational representations back towards the "first principles" of differential geometry;

- are very storage and bandwidth efficient, describing a surface as a succinctly specified base shape plus a hierarchical normal map;

- are an excellent representation for compression since all variance is "squeezed" into a single dimension.

1.2 Related Work

Efficient representations for irregular connectivity meshes have been pursued by a number of researchers. This research is motivated by our ability to acquire densely sampled, highly detailed scans of real world objects [19] and the need to manipulate these efficiently. Semi-regular—or subdivision connectivity—meshes offer many advantages over the irregular setting due of their well developed mathematical foundations and data structure simplicity [23]; many powerful algorithms require their input to be in semi-regular form [21, 22, 25, 1]. This has led to the development of a number of algorithms to convert existing irregular meshes to semi-regular form through remeshing. Eck et al. [9] use Voronoi tiling and harmonic maps to build a parameterization and remesh onto a semi-regular mesh. Krischnamurthy and Levoy [15] demonstrated user driven remeshing for the case of bi-cubic patches, while Lee et al. [18] proposed an algorithm based on feature driven mesh reduction to develop smooth parameterizations of meshes in an automatic fashion. These methods use the parameterization subsequently for semi-regular remeshing.

Our work is related to these approaches in that we also construct a semi-regular mesh from an arbitrary connectivity input mesh. However, in previous work prediction residuals, or detail vectors, were not optimized to have properties such as normality. The main focus was on the establishment of a smooth parameterization which was then semi-regularly sampled.

The discussion of parameter versus geometry information originates in the work done on irregular curve and surface subdivision [4] [13] and intrinsic curvature normal flow [5]. There it is shown that unless one has the correct parameter side information, it is not possible to build an irregular smooth subdivision scheme. While such schemes are useful for editing and texturing applications, they cannot be used for succinct representations because the parameter side-information needed is excessive. In the case of normal meshes these issues are entirely circumvented in that all parameter information vanishes and the mesh is reduced to purely geometric, i.e., scalar in the normal direction, information.

Finally, we mention the connection to displacement maps [3], and in particular normal displacement maps. These are popular for modeling purposes and used extensively in high end rendering systems such as RenderMan. In a sense we are solving here the associated inverse problem. Given some geometry, find a simpler geometry and a set of normal displacements which together are equivalent to the original geometry. Typically, normal displacement maps are single level, whereas we aim to build them in a fully hierarchical way. For example, single level displacements maps were used in [15] to capture the fine detail of a 3D photography model. Cohen et al. [2] sampled normal fields of geometry and maintained

these in texture maps during simplification. While these approaches all differ significantly from our interests here, it is clear that maps of this and related nature are of great interest in many contexts.

In independent work, Lee et al. pursue a goal similar to ours [17]. They introduce displaced subdivision surfaces which can be seen as a two level normal mesh. Because only two levels are used, the base domain typically contains more triangles than in our case. Also the normal offsets are oversampled while in our case, the normal offsets are critically sampled.

2 Normal Polylines

Before we look at surfaces and normal meshes, we introduce some of the concepts using curves and normal polylines. A curve in the plane is described by a pair of parametric functions $\mathbf{s}(t) = (x(t), y(t))$ with $t \in [0, 1]$. We would like to describe the points on the curve with a single scalar function. In practice one uses polylines to approximate the function. Let $\mathbf{l}(\mathbf{p}, \mathbf{p}')$ be the linear segment between the points $\mathbf{p}$ and $\mathbf{p}'$. A standard way to build a polyline multiresolution approximation is to sample the curve at points $\mathbf{s}_{j,k}$ where $\mathbf{s}_{j,k} = \mathbf{s}_{j+1,2k}$ and define the jth level approximation as

$$\mathbf{L}_j = \bigcup_{0 \leq k < 2^j} \mathbf{l}(\mathbf{s}_{j,k}, \mathbf{s}_{j,k+1}).$$

To move from $\mathbf{L}_j$ to $\mathbf{L}_{j+1}$ we need to insert the points $\mathbf{s}_{j+1,2k+1}$ (Figure 2, left). Clearly this requires two scalars: the two coordinates of $\mathbf{s}_{j+1,2k+1}$. Alternatively one could compute the difference $\mathbf{s}_{j+1,2k+1} - \mathbf{m}$ between the new point and some predicted point $\mathbf{m}$, say the midpoint of the neighboring points $\mathbf{s}_{j,k}$ and $\mathbf{s}_{j,k+1}$. This detail has a tangential component $\mathbf{m} - \mathbf{b}$ and a normal component $\mathbf{b} - \mathbf{s}_{j+1,2k+1}$. The normal component is the *geometric* information while the tangential component is the *parameter* information. The way to build polylines that can be described with one

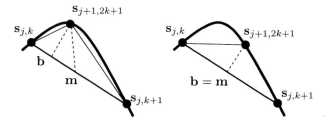

Figure 2: *Removing one point* $\mathbf{s}_{j+1,2k+1}$ *in a polyline multiresolution and recording the difference with the midpoint* $\mathbf{m}$. *On the left a general polyline where the detail has both a normal and a tangential component. On the right a normal polyline where the detail is purely normal.*

scalar per point, is to make sure that the parameter information is always zero, i.e., $\mathbf{b} = \mathbf{m}$, see Figure 2, right. If the triangle $\mathbf{s}_{j,k}$, $\mathbf{s}_{j+1,2k+1}$, $\mathbf{s}_{j,k+1}$ is Isosceles, there is no parameter information. Consequently we say that a polyline is normal if a multiresolution structure exists where every removed point forms an Isosceles triangle with its neighbors. Then there is zero parameter information and the polyline can be represented with one scalar per point, namely the normal component of the associated detail.

For a general polyline the removed triangles are hardly ever exactly Isosceles and hence the polyline is not normal. Below we describe a procedure to build a normal polyline approximation for any continuous curve. The easiest is to start building Isosceles triangles from the coarsest level. Start with the first base $\mathbf{l}(\mathbf{s}_{0,0}, \mathbf{s}_{0,1})$, see Figure 3. Next take its midpoint and check where the normal direction crosses the curve. Because the curve is continuous, there has to be at least one such point. If there are multiple pick any one.

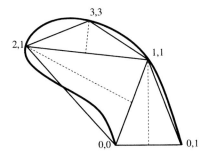

Figure 3: *Construction of a normal polyline. We start with the coarsest level and each time check where the normal to the midpoint crosses the curve. For simplicity only the indices of the $\mathbf{s}_{j,k}$ points are shown and only certain segments are subdivided. The polyline $(0,0)-(2,1)-(3,3)-(1,1)-(0,1)$ is determined by its endpoints and three scalars, the heights of the Isosceles triangles.*

Call this point $\mathbf{s}_{1,1}$ and define the first triangle. Now split the curve into two parts and repeat the procedure on each subcurve. Each time $\mathbf{s}_{j+1,2k+1}$ is found where the normal to the midpoint of $\mathbf{s}_{j,k}$ and $\mathbf{s}_{j,k+1}$ crosses the portion of the curve between $\mathbf{s}_{j,k}$ and $\mathbf{s}_{j,k+1}$. Thus any continuous curve can be approximated arbitrarily closely with a normal polyline. The result is a series of polylines $\mathbf{L}_j$ all of which are normal with respect to midpoint prediction. Effectively each level is parameterized with respect to the one coarser level. Because the polylines are normal, only a single scalar value, the normal component, needs to be recorded for each point. We have a polyline with no parameter information.

One can also consider normal polylines with respect to fancier predictors. For example one could compute a base point and normal estimate using the well known 4 point rule. Essentially any predictor which only depends on the coarser level is allowed. For example one can also use irregular schemes [4]. Also one does not need to follow the standard way of building levels by downsampling every other point, but instead could take any ordering. This leads to the following definition of a normal polyline:

Definition 1 *A polyline is normal if a removal order of the points exists such that each removed point lies in the normal direction from a base point, where the normal direction and base point only depend on the remaining points.*

Hence a normal polyline is completely determined by a scalar component per vertex.

Normal polylines are closely related to certain well known fractal curves such as the Koch Snowflake[1], see Figure 4. Here each time a line segment is divided into three subsegments. The left and right get a normal coefficient of zero, while the middle receives a normal coefficient such that the resulting triangle is equilateral. Hence the polylines leading to the snowflake are normal with respect to midpoint subdivision.

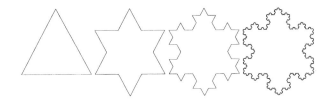

Figure 4: *Four normal polylines converging to the Koch snowflake.*

There is also a close connection with wavelets. The normal coefficients can be seen as a piecewise linear wavelet transform of the original curve. Because the tangential components are always zero there are half as many wavelet coefficients as there are original scalar coefficients. Thus one saves 50% memory right away. In addition of course the wavelets have their usual decorrelation properties. In the functional case the above transform corresponds to an unlifted interpolating piecewise linear wavelet transform as introduced by Donoho [6]. There it is shown that interpolating wavelets with no primal, but many dual moments are well suited for smooth functions. Unlike in the function setting, not all wavelets from the same level j have the same physical scale. Here the scale of each coefficient is essentially the length of the base of its Isosecles triangle.

3 Normal Meshes

We begin by establishing terminology. A triangle mesh $\mathcal{M}$ is a pair $(\mathcal{P}, \mathcal{K})$, where $\mathcal{P}$ is a set of N point positions $\mathcal{P} = \{\mathbf{p}_i = (x_i, y_i, z_i) \in \mathbf{R}^3 \mid 1 \le i \le N\}$, and $\mathcal{K}$ is an *abstract simplicial complex* which contains all the topological, i.e., adjacency information. The complex $\mathcal{K}$ is a set of subsets of $\{1, \ldots, N\}$. These subsets come in three types: vertices $\{i\}$, edges $\{i, j\}$, and faces $\{i, j, k\}$. Two vertices i and j are *neighbors* if $\{i, j\} \in \mathcal{E}$. The 1-ring neighbors of a vertex i form a set $\mathcal{V}(i) = \{j \mid \{i, j\} \in \mathcal{E}\}$.

We can derive a definition of normal triangle meshes inspired by the curve case. Consider a hierarchy of triangle meshes $\mathcal{M}_j$ built using mesh simplification with vertex removals. These meshes are nested in the sense that $\mathcal{P}_j \subset \mathcal{P}_{j+1}$. Take a removed vertex $\mathbf{p}_i \in \mathcal{P}_{j+1} \setminus \mathcal{P}_j$. For the mesh to be normal we need to be able to find a base point $\mathbf{b}$ and normal direction N that only depend on $\mathcal{P}_j$, so that $\mathbf{p}_i - \mathbf{b}$ lies in the direction N. This leads to the following definition.

Definition 2 *A mesh $\mathcal{M}$ is normal in case a sequence of vertex removals exists so that each removed vertex lies on a line defined by a base point and normal direction which only depends on the remaining vertices.*

Thus a normal mesh can be described by a small base domain and one scalar coefficient per vertex.

As in the curve case, a mesh is in general not normal. The chance that the difference between a removed point and a predicted base point lies exactly in a direction that only depends on the remaining vertices is essentially zero. Hence the only way to obtain a normal mesh is to change the triangulation. We decide to use semi-regular meshes, i.e., meshes whose connectivity is formed by successive quadrisection of coarse base domain faces.

As in the curve setting, the way to build a normal mesh is to start from the coarse level or base domain. For each new vertex we compute a base point as well as a normal direction and check where the line defined by the base point and normal intersects the surface. The situation, however, is much more complex than in the curve case for two reasons: (1) There could be no intersection point. (2) There could be many intersection points, but only one correct one.

In case there are no intersection points, strictly speaking no fully normal mesh can be built from this base domain. If that happens, we relax the definition of normal meshes some and allow a small number of cases where the new points do not lie in the normal direction. Thus the algorithm needs to find a suitable non-normal location for the new point. In case there are many intersection points the algorithm needs to figure out which one is the right one. If the wrong one is chosen the normal mesh will start folding over itself or leave creases. Any algorithm which blindly picks an intersection point is doomed.

Parameterization In order to find the right piercing point or suggest a good alternate, one needs to be able to easily navigate around the surface. The way to do this is to build a smooth parameterization of the surface region of interest. This is a basic building block of our algorithm. Several parameterization methods have been proposed and our method takes components from each of them: mesh simplification and polar maps from MAPS [18], patchwise relaxation from [9], and a specific smoothness functional similar to the one used in [10] and [20]. The algorithm will use local parameterizations which need to be computed fast and robustly. Most of them are temporary and are quickly discarded unless they can be used as a starting guess for another parameterization.

Consider a region $\mathcal{R}$ of the mesh homeomorphic to a disc that we want to parameterize onto a convex planar region $\mathcal{B}$, i.e., find a bijective map $u : \mathcal{R} \to \mathcal{B}$. The map u is fixed by a boundary condition $\partial\mathcal{R} \to \partial\mathcal{B}$ and minimizes a certain energy functional. Several functionals can be used leading to, e.g., conformal or harmonic mappings. We take an approach based on the work of Floater [10]. In short, the function u needs to satisfy the following equation in the interior:

$$u(\mathbf{p}_i) = \sum_{k \in \mathcal{V}(i)} \alpha_{ik} u(\mathbf{p}_k), \qquad (1)$$

where $\mathcal{V}(i)$ is the 1-ring neighborhood of the vertex i and the weights α_{ik} come from the shape-preserving parameterization scheme [10]. The main advantage of the Floater weights is that they are always positive, which, combined with the convexity of the parametric region, guarantees that no triangle flipping can occur within the parametric domain. This is crucial for our algorithm. Note that this is not true in general for harmonic maps which can have negative weights. We use the iterative biconjugate gradient method [12] to obtain the solution to the system (1). Given that we often have a good starting guess this converges quickly.

Algorithm Our algorithm consists of 7 stages which are described below, some of which are shown for the molecule model in Figure 5. The molecule is a highly detailed and curved model. Any naive procedure for finding normal meshes is very unlikely to succeed.

The first four stages of the algorithm prepare the ground for the piercing procedure and build the net of curves splitting the original mesh into triangular patches that are in one-to-one correspondence with the faces of the base mesh, i.e., the coarsest level of the semi-regular mesh we build.

1. Mesh simplification: We use the Garland-Heckbert [11] simplification based on half-edge collapses to create a mesh hierarchy $(\mathcal{P}_j, \mathcal{K}_j)$. We use the coarsest level $(\mathcal{P}_0, \mathcal{K}_0)$ as an initial guess for our base domain $(\mathcal{Q}_0, \mathcal{K}_0)$. The first image of Figure 5 shows the base domain for the molecule.

2. Building an initial net of curves: The purpose of this step is to connect the vertices of the base domain with a net of non intersecting curves on the different levels of the mesh simplification hierarchy. This can easily be done using the MAPS parameterization [18]. MAPS uses polar maps to build a bijection between a 1-ring and its retriangulation after the center vertex is removed. The concatenation of these maps is a bijective mapping between different levels $(\mathcal{P}_j, \mathcal{K}_j)$ in the hierarchy. The desired curves are simply the image of the base domain edges under this mapping. Because of the bijection no intersection can occur. Note that the curves start and finish at a vertex of the base domain, but need not follow the edges of the finer triangulation, i.e., they can cut across triangles. These curves define a network of triangular shaped patches corresponding to the base domain triangles. Later we will adjust these curves on some intermediate level and again use MAPS to propagate these changes to other levels. The top middle image of Figure 5 shows these curves for some intermediate level of the hierarchy.

3. Fixing the global vertices: A normal mesh is almost completely determined by the base domain. One has to choose the base domain vertices $\mathcal{Q}_0$ very carefully to reduce the number of non-normal vertices to a minimum. The coarsest level of the mesh simplification $\mathcal{P}_0$ is only a first guess. In this section we describe a procedure for repositioning the global vertices $\mathbf{q}_i$ with $\{i\} \in \mathcal{K}_0$. We impose the constraint that the $\mathbf{q}_i$ needs to coincide with some vertex $\mathbf{p}_k$ of the original mesh, but not necessarily $\mathbf{p}_i$.

The repositioning is typically done on some intermediate level j. Take a base domain vertex $\mathbf{q}_i$. We build a parameterization from the patches incident to vertex $\mathbf{q}_i$ to a disk in the plane, see Figure 6. Boundary conditions are assigned using arclength parameterization, and parameter coordinates are iteratively computed for each level j vertex inside the shaded region. It is now easy to replace the point $\mathbf{q}_i$ with any level point from $\mathcal{P}_j$ in the shaded region. In particular we let the new $\mathbf{q}_i'$ be the point of $\mathcal{P}_j$ that in the parameter domain is closest to the center of the disk. The exact center of the disk, in general, does not correspond to a vertex of the mesh.

Once a new position $\mathbf{q}_i'$ is chosen, the curves can be redrawn by taking the inverse mapping of straight lines from the new point in the parameter plane. One can keep iterating this procedure, but we found that if suffices to cycle once through all base domain vertices.

We also provide for a user controlled repositioning. Then the user can replace the center vertex with any $\mathcal{P}_j$ point in the shaded region. The algorithm again uses the parameterization to recompute the curves from that point.

The top right of Figure 5 shows the repositioned vertices. Notice how some of them like the rightmost one have moved considerably.

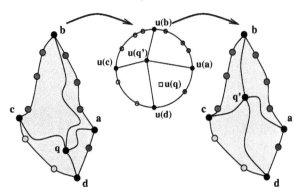

Figure 6: *Base domain vertex repositioning. Left: original patches around $\mathbf{q}_i$, middle: parameter domain, right: repositioned $\mathbf{q}_i$ and new patch boundaries. This is replaced with the vertex whose parameter coordinate are the closest to the center. The inverse mapping (right) is used to find the new position $\mathbf{q}_i'$ and the new curves.*

4. Fixing the global edges: The image of the global edges on the finest level will later be the patch boundaries of the normal mesh. For this reason we need to improve the smoothness of the associated curves at the finest level. We use a procedure similar to [9]. For each base domain edge $\{i, k\}$ we consider the region formed on the finest level mesh by its two incident patches. Let l and m be the opposing global vertices. We then compute a parameter function ρ within the diamond-shaped region of the surface. The boundary condition is set as $\rho(\mathbf{q}_i) = \rho(\mathbf{q}_k) = 0$, $\rho(\mathbf{q}_l) = 1$, $\rho(\mathbf{q}_m) = -1$, with linear variation along the edges. We then compute the parameterization and let its zero level set be our new curve. Again one could iterate this procedure till convergence but in practice one cycle suffices. The curves of the top right image in Figure 5 are the result of the curve smoothing on the finest level.

Note that a similar result can be achieved by allowing the user to position the global vertices and draw the boundaries of the patches manually. Indeed, the following steps of the algorithm do not depend on how the initial net of surface curves is produced.

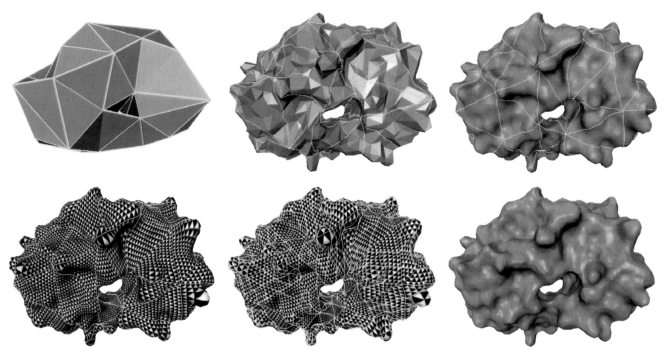

Figure 5: *The entire procedure shown for the molecule model. 1. Base domain. 2. Initial set of curves. 3. Global vertex repositioning 4. Initial Parameterization 5. Adjusting parameterization 6. Final normal mesh. (HIV protease surface model courtesy of Arthur Olson, The Scripps Research Institute)*

5. Initial parameterization: Once the global vertices and edges are fixed, one can start filling in the interior. This is done by computing the parameterization of each patch to a triangle while keeping the boundary fixed. The parameter coordinates from the last stage can serve as a good initial guess. We now have a smooth global parameterization. This parameterization is shown in the bottom left of Figure 5. Each triangle is given a triangular checkerboard texture to illustrate the parameterization.

6. Piercing: In this stage of the algorithm we start building the actual normal mesh. The canonical step is for a new vertex of the semi-regular mesh to find its position on the original mesh. In quadrisection every edge of level j generates a new vertex on level $j + 1$. We first compute a base point using interpolating Butterfly subdivision [8] [24] as well as an approximation of the normal. This defines a straight line. This line may have multiple intersection points in which case we need to find the right one, or it could have none, in which case we need to come up with a good alternate.

Suppose that we need to produce the new vertex $\mathbf{q}$ that lies halfway along the edge $\{\mathbf{a}, \mathbf{c}\}$ with incident triangles $\{\mathbf{a}, \mathbf{c}, \mathbf{b}\}$ and $\{\mathbf{c}, \mathbf{a}, \mathbf{d}\}$, see Figure 7. Let the two incident patches form the region $\mathcal{R}$.

Build the straight line L defined by the base point $\mathbf{s}$ predicted by the Butterfly subdivision rule [24] and the direction of the normal computed from the coarser level points. We find all the intersection points of L with the region $\mathcal{R}$ by checking all triangles inside.

If there is no intersection we take the point $\mathbf{v}$ that lies midway between the points $\mathbf{a}$ and $\mathbf{c}$ in the parameter domain: $u(\mathbf{v}) = (u(\mathbf{a}) + u(\mathbf{c}))/2$. This is the same point a standard parameterization based remesher would use. Note that in this case the detail vector is non-normal and its three components need to be stored.

In the case when there exist several intersections of the mesh region $\mathcal{R}$ with the piercing line L we choose the intersection point that is closest to the point $u(\mathbf{v})$ in the parameter domain. Let us denote by $u(\mathbf{q})$ the parametric coordinates of that piercing point.

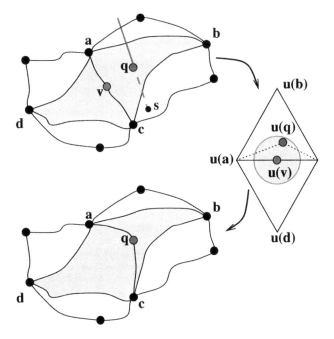

Figure 7: *Upper left: piercing, the Butterfly point is $\mathbf{s}$, the surface is pierced at the point $\mathbf{q}$, the parametrically suggested point $\mathbf{v}$ lies on the curve separating two regions of the mesh. Right: parameter domain, the pierced point falls inside the aperture and gets accepted. Lower left: the parameterization is adjusted to let the curve pass through q.*

We accept this point as a valid point of the semi-regular mesh if $\|u(\mathbf{q}) - u(\mathbf{v})\| < \kappa \|u(\mathbf{a}) - u(\mathbf{v})\|$, where κ is an "aperture" parameter that specifies how much the parameter value of a pierced point is allowed to deviate from the center of the diamond. Otherwise, the piercing point is rejected and the mesh takes the point with the parameter value $u(\mathbf{v})$, resulting in a non-normal detail.

7. Adjusting the parameterization: Once we have a new piercing point, we need to adjust the parameterization to reflect this. Essentially, the adjusted parameterization u should be such that the piercing point has the parameters $u(\mathbf{v}) =: u(\mathbf{q})$. When imposing such an isolated point constraint on the parameterization, there is no mathematical guarantee against flipping. Hence we draw a new piecewise linear curve through $u(\mathbf{q})$ in the parameter domain. This gives a new curve on the surface which passes through $\mathbf{q}$, see Figure 7. We then recompute the parameterization for each of the patches onto a triangle separately. We use a piecewise linear boundary condition with the half point at $\mathbf{q}$ on the common edge.

When all the new midpoints for the edges of a face of level j are computed, we can build the faces of level $j + 1$. This is done by drawing three new curves inside the corresponding region of the original mesh, see Figure 8. Before that operation happens we need to ensure that a valid parameterization is available within the patch. The patch is parameterized onto a triangle with three piecewise linear boundary conditions each time putting the new points at the midpoint. Then the new points are connected in the parameter domain which allows us to draw new finer level curves on the original mesh. This produces a metamesh similar to [16], so that the new net of curves replicates the structure of the semi-regular hierarchy on the surface of the original. The construction of the semi-regular mesh can be done adaptively with the error driven procedure from MAPS [18]. An example of parameterization adjustment after two levels of adaptive subdivision is shown in the bottom middle of Figure 5. Note that as the regions for which we compute parameterizations become smaller, the starting guesses are better and the solver convergence becomes faster and faster.

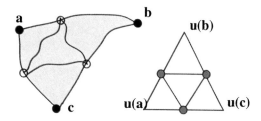

Figure 8: *Face split: Quadrisection in the parameter plane (left) leads to three new curves within the triangular patch (right).*

The aperture parameter κ of the piercing procedure provides control over how much of the original parameterization is preserved in the final mesh and consequently, how many non-normal details will appear. At $\kappa = 0$ we build a *non-normal* mesh entirely based on the original global parameterization. At $\kappa = 1$ we attempt to build a purely *normal* mesh independent of the parameterization. In our experience, the best results were achieved when the aperture was set low (0.2) at the coarsest levels, and then increased to 0.6 on finer levels. On the very fine levels of the hierarchy, where the geometry of the semi-regular meshes closely follows the original geometry, one can often simply use a naive piercing procedure without parameter adjustment.

One may wonder if the continuous readjustment of parameterizations is really necessary. We have tried the naive piercing procedure without parameterization from the base domain and found that it typically fails on all models. An example is Figure 9 which shows 4 levels of naive piercing for the torus starting from a 102 vertex base mesh. Clearly, there are several regions with flipped and self-intersecting triangles. The error is about 20 times larger than the true normal mesh.

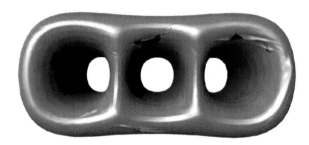

Figure 9: *Naive piercing procedure. Clearly, several regions have flipped triangles and are self-intersecting.*

Dataset	Size	Base	Normal mesh size	Not normal (%)	% L^2 error	Time (min)
Feline	49864	156	40346	729 (1.8%)	.015	4
Molecule	10028	37	9521	270 (2.8%)	.075	1.5
Rabbit	16760	33	8235	196 (2.4%)	.037	2
Torus3	5884	98	5294	421 (8.0%)	.03	3
Skull	20002	112	25376	817 (3.2%)	.02	2.5
Horse	48485	234	59319	644 (1.1%)	.004	6.8

Table 1: *Summary of normal meshing results for different models. The normal mesh is computed adaptively and contains roughly the same number of triangles as the original mesh. The relative L^2 errors are computed with the I.E.I.-CNR Metro tool. The times are reported on a 700MHz Pentium III machine.*

4 Results

We have implemented the algorithms described in the preceding section, and performed a series of experiments in which normal meshes for various models were built. The summary of the results is given in Table 1. As we can see from the table, the normal semi-regular meshes have very high accuracy and hardly any non normal details.

One interesting feature of our normal meshing procedure is the following: while the structure of patches comes from performing simplification there are far fewer restrictions on how coarse the base mesh can be. Note for example that the skull in Figure 1 was meshed with the tetrahedron as base mesh. This is largely due to the robust mesh parameterization techniques used in our approach.

Figure 10 shows normal meshes for rabbit, torus, feline, and skull, as well as close-up of feline (bottom left) normal mesh. Note how smooth the meshes are across global edges and global vertices. This smoothness mostly comes from the normality, not the parameterization. It is thus an intrinsic quantity.

One of the most interesting observations coming from this work is that locally the normal meshes do not differ much from the non-normal ones, while offering huge benefits in terms of efficiency of representation. For example, Table 2 shows how the "aperture parameter" κ that governs the construction of normal meshes affects the number of detail coefficients with non-trivial tangential components for the model of the three hole torus (these numbers are typical for other models as well). In particular, we see that already a very modest acceptance strategy ($\kappa = 0.2$) gets rid of more than 90% of the tangential components in the remeshed model, and the more aggressive strategies offer even more benefits without affecting the error of the representation.

5 Summary and Conclusion

In this paper we introduce the notion of *normal meshes*. Normal meshes are multiresolution meshes in which vertices can be found in the normal direction, starting from some coarse level. Hence only one scalar per vertex needs to be stored. We presented a robust

κ	normal	error (10^{-4})
0	0%	1.02
0.2	91.9%	1.05
0.4	92.4%	1.04
best	98.3%	1.02

Table 2: *The relation between the acceptance strategy during the piercing procedure and the percentage of perfectly normal details in the hierarchy. The original model has 5884 vertices, all the normal meshes have 26002 vertices (4 levels uniformly), and the base mesh contained 98 vertices. The best strategy in the last line used $\kappa = 0.2$ on the first three levels and afterward always accepted the piercing candidates.*

algorithm for computing normal semi-regular meshes of any input mesh and showed that it produces very smooth triangulations on a variety of input models.

It is clear that normal meshes have numerous applications. We briefly discuss a few.

Compression Usually a wavelet transform of a standard mesh has three components which need to be quantized and encoded. Information theory tells us that the more non uniform the distribution of the coefficients the lower the first order entropy. Having 2/3 of the coefficients exactly zero will further reduce the bit budget. From an implementation viewpoint, we can almost directly hook the normal mesh coefficients up to the best known scalar wavelet image compression code.

Filtering It has been shown that operations such as smoothing, enhancement, and denoising can be computed through a suitable scaling of wavelet coefficients [7]. In a normal mesh any such algorithm will require only 1/3 as many computations. Also large scaling coefficients in a standard mesh will introduce large tangential components leading to flipped triangles. In a normal mesh this is much less likely to happen.

Texturing Normal semi-regular meshes are very smooth inside patches, across global edges, and around global vertices even when the base domain is exceedingly coarse, cf. the skull model. The implied parameterizations are highly suitable for all types of mapping applications.

Rendering Normal maps are a very powerful tool for decoration and enhancement of otherwise smooth geometry. In particular in the context of bandwidth bottlenecks it is attractive to be able to download a normal map into hardware and only send smooth coefficient updates for the underlying geometry. The normal mesh transform effectively solves the associated inverse problem: construct a normal map for a given geometry.

The concept of normal meshes opens up many new areas of research.

- Our algorithm uses interpolating subdivision to find the base point. Building normal meshes with respect to approximating subdivision is not straightforward.

- The theoretical underpinnings of normal meshes need to be studied. Do continuous variable normal descriptions of surfaces exist? What about stability? What about connections with curvature normal flow which acts to reduce normal information?

- We only addressed semi-regular normal meshes here, while the definition allows for the more flexible setting of progressive irregular mesh hierarchies.

- Purely scalar compression schemes for geometry need to be compared with existing coders.

- Generalize normal meshes to higher dimensions. It should be possible to represent a M dimensional manifold in N dimensions with $N - M$ variables as opposed to the usual N.

- The current implementation only works for surfaces without boundaries and does not deal with feature curves. We will address these issues in our future research.

Acknowledgments This work was supported in part by NSF (ACI-9624957, ACI-9721349, DMS-9874082, DMS 9872890), Alias|Wavefront, a Packard Fellowship, and a Caltech Summer Undergraduate Research Fellowship (SURF). Special thanks to Nathan Litke for his subdivision library, to Andrei Khodakovsky, Mathieu Desbrun, Adi Levin, Arthur Olson, and Zoë Wood for helpful discussions, Chris Johnson for the use of the SGI-Utah Visual Supercomputing Center resources, and to Cici Koenig for production help. Datasets are courtesy Cyberware, Headus, The Scripps Research Institute, and University of Washington.

References

[1] CERTAIN, A., POPOVIC, J., DeROSE, T., DUCHAMP, T., SALESIN, D., AND STUETZLE, W. Interactive Multiresolution Surface Viewing. *Proceedings of SIGGRAPH 96* (1996), 91–98.

[2] COHEN, J., OLANO, M., AND MANOCHA, D. Appearance-Preserving Simplification. *Proceedings of SIGGRAPH 98* (1998), 115–122.

[3] COOK, R. L. Shade trees. *Computer Graphics (Proceedings of SIGGRAPH 84) 18*, 3 (1984), 223–231.

[4] DAUBECHIES, I., GUSKOV, I., AND SWELDENS, W. Regularity of Irregular Subdivision. *Constr. Approx. 15* (1999), 381–426.

[5] DESBRUN, M., MEYER, M., SCHRÖDER, P., AND BARR, A. H. Implicit Fairing of Irregular Meshes Using Diffusion and Curvature Flow. *Proceedings of SIGGRAPH 99* (1999), 317–324.

[6] DONOHO, D. L. Interpolating wavelet transforms. Preprint, Department of Statistics, Stanford University, 1992.

[7] DONOHO, D. L. Unconditional Bases are Optimal Bases for Data Compression and for Statistical Estimation. *Appl. Comput. Harmon. Anal. 1* (1993), 100–115.

[8] DYN, N., LEVIN, D., AND GREGORY, J. A. A Butterfly Subdivision Scheme for Surface Interpolation with Tension Control. *ACM Transactions on Graphics 9*, 2 (1990), 160–169.

[9] ECK, M., DeROSE, T., DUCHAMP, T., HOPPE, H., LOUNSBERY, M., AND STUETZLE, W. Multiresolution Analysis of Arbitrary Meshes. *Proceedings of SIGGRAPH 95* (1995), 173–182.

[10] FLOATER, M. S. Parameterization and Smooth Approximation of Surface Triangulations. *Computer Aided Geometric Design 14* (1997), 231–250.

[11] GARLAND, M., AND HECKBERT, P. S. Surface Simplification Using Quadric Error Metrics. In *Proceedings of SIGGRAPH 96*, 209–216, 1996.

[12] GOLUB, G. H., AND LOAN, C. F. V. *Matrix Computations*, 2nd ed. The John Hopkins University Press, Baltimore, 1983.

[13] GUSKOV, I., SWELDENS, W., AND SCHRÖDER, P. Multiresolution Signal Processing for Meshes. *Proceedings of SIGGRAPH 99* (1999), 325–334.

[14] KHODAKOVSKY, A., SCHRÖDER, P., SWELDENS, W. Progressive Geometry Compression. *Proceedings of SIGGRAPH 2000* (2000).

[15] KRISHNAMURTHY, V., AND LEVOY, M. Fitting Smooth Surfaces to Dense Polygon Meshes. *Proceedings of SIGGRAPH 96* (1996), 313–324.

[16] LEE, A. W. F., DOBKIN, D., SWELDENS, W., AND SCHRÖDER, P. Multiresolution Mesh Morphing. *Proceedings of SIGGRAPH 99* (1999), 343–350.

[17] LEE, A. W. F., MORETON, H., HOPPE, H. Displaced Subdivision Surfaces. *Proceedings of SIGGRAPH 00* (2000).

[18] LEE, A. W. F., SWELDENS, W., SCHRÖDER, P., COWSAR, L., AND DOBKIN, D. MAPS: Multiresolution Adaptive Parameterization of Surfaces. *Proceedings of SIGGRAPH 98* (1998), 95–104.

[19] LEVOY, M. The Digital Michelangelo Project. In *Proceedings of the 2nd International Conference on 3D Digital Imaging and Modeling*, October 1999.

[20] LÉVY, B., AND MALLET, J. Non-Distorted Texture Mapping for Sheared Triangulated Meshes. *Proceedings of SIGGRAPH 98* (1998), 343–352.

[21] LOUNSBERY, M., DeROSE, T. D., AND WARREN, J. Multiresolution Analysis for Surfaces of Arbitrary Topological Type. *ACM Transactions on Graphics 16*, 1 (1997), 34–73. Originally available as TR-93-10-05, October, 1993, Department of Computer Science and Engineering, University of Washington.

[22] SCHRÖDER, P., AND SWELDENS, W. Spherical Wavelets: Efficiently Representing Functions on the Sphere. *Proceedings of SIGGRAPH 95* (1995), 161–172.

[23] ZORIN, D., AND SCHRÖDER, P., Eds. *Subdivision for Modeling and Animation*. Course Notes. ACM SIGGRAPH, 1999.

[24] ZORIN, D., SCHRÖDER, P., AND SWELDENS, W. Interpolating Subdivision for Meshes with Arbitrary Topology. *Proceedings of SIGGRAPH 96* (1996), 189–192.

[25] ZORIN, D., SCHRÖDER, P., AND SWELDENS, W. Interactive Multiresolution Mesh Editing. *Proceedings of SIGGRAPH 97* (1997), 259–268.

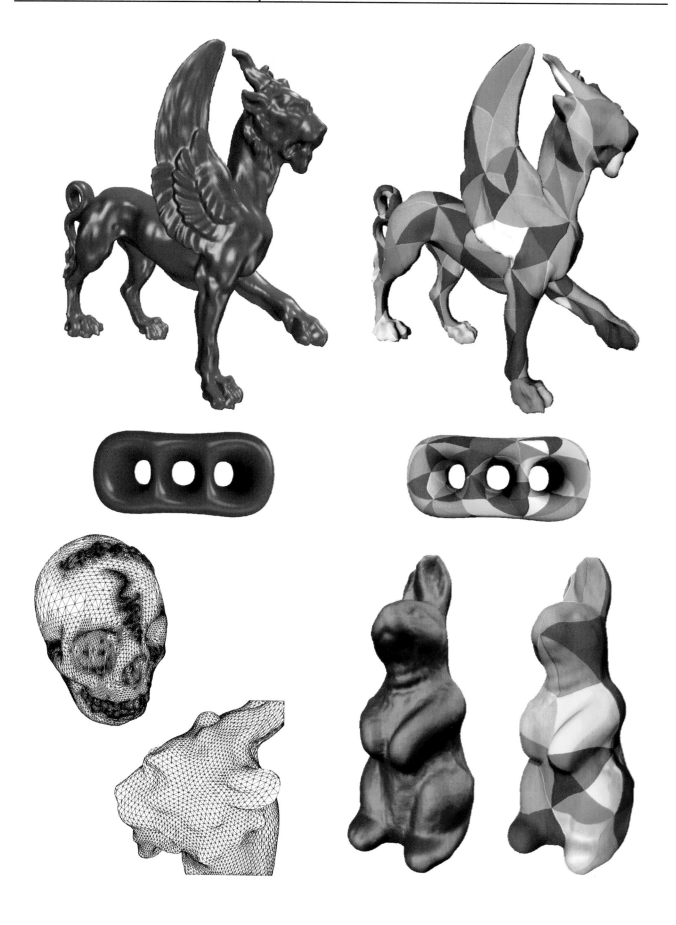

Figure 10: *Colorplate.*

$\sqrt{3}$-Subdivision

Leif Kobbelt*

Max-Planck Institute for Computer Sciences

Abstract

A new stationary subdivision scheme is presented which performs *slower* topological refinement than the usual dyadic split operation. The number of triangles increases in every step by a factor of 3 instead of 4. Applying the subdivision operator *twice* causes a uniform refinement with *tri*-section of every original edge (hence the name $\sqrt{3}$-subdivision) while two dyadic splits would *quad*-sect every original edge. Besides the finer gradation of the hierarchy levels, the new scheme has several important properties: The stencils for the subdivision rules have minimum size and maximum symmetry. The smoothness of the limit surface is C^2 everywhere except for the extraordinary points where it is C^1. The convergence analysis of the scheme is presented based on a new general technique which also applies to the analysis of other subdivision schemes. The new splitting operation enables locally adaptive refinement under built-in preservation of the mesh consistency without temporary crack-fixing between neighboring faces from different refinement levels. The size of the surrounding mesh area which is affected by selective refinement is smaller than for the dyadic split operation. We further present a simple extension of the new subdivision scheme which makes it applicable to meshes with boundary and allows us to generate sharp feature lines.

1 Introduction

The use of subdivision schemes for the efficient generation of freefrom surfaces has become commonplace in a variety of geometric modeling applications. Instead of defining a parameteric surface by a functional expression $F(u,v)$ to be evaluated over a planar parameter domain $\Omega \in \mathbf{R}^2$ we simply sketch the surface by a coarse control mesh $\mathcal{M}_0$ that may have arbitrary connectivity and (manifold) topology. By applying a set of refinement rules, we generate a sequence of finer and finer meshes $\mathcal{M}_1, \ldots, \mathcal{M}_k, \ldots$ which eventually converge to a smooth limit surface $\mathcal{M}_\infty$.

In the literature there have been proposed many subdivision schemes which are either generalized from tensor-products of curve generation schemes [DS78, CC78, Kob96] or from 2-scale relations in more general functional spaces being defined over the three-directional grid [Loo87, DGL90, ZSS96]. Due to the nature of the refinement operators, the generalized tensor-product schemes natu-

---

*Max-Planck Institute for Computer Sciences, Im Stadtwald, 66123 Saarbrücken, Germany, kobbelt@mpi-sb.mpg.de

Permission to make digital or hard copies of all or part of this work for personal or classroom use is granted without fee provided that copies are not made or distributed for profit or commercial advantage, and that copies bear this notice and the full citation on the first page. To copy otherwise, to republish, to post on servers or to redistribute to lists, requires prior specific permission and/or a fee.

©2000 ACM 0-58113-208-5/00/0007 $5.00

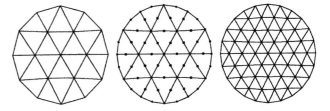

Figure 1: *Subdivision schemes on triangle meshes are usually based on the 1-to-4 split operation which inserts a new vertex for every edge of the given mesh and then connects the new vertices.*

rally lead to quadrilateral meshes while the others lead to triangle meshes.

A subdivision operator for polygonal meshes can be considered as being composed by a (topological) split operation followed by a (geometric) smoothing operation. The split operation performs the actual refinement by introducing new vertices and the smoothing operation changes the vertex positions by computing averages of neighboring vertices (generalized convolution operators, relaxation). In order to guarantee that the subdivision process will always generate a sequence of meshes $\mathcal{M}_k$ that converges to a smooth limit, the smoothing operator has to satisfy specific necessary and sufficient conditions [CDM91, Dyn91, Rei95, Zor97, Pra98]. This is why special attention has been paid by many authors to the design of optimal smoothing rules and their analysis.

While in the context of quad-meshes several different topological split operations (e.g. primal [CC78, Kob96] or dual [DS78]) have been investigated, all currently proposed stationary schemes for triangle meshes are based on the uniform 1-to-4 split [Loo87, DGL90, ZSS96] which is depicted in Fig 1. This split operation introduces a new vertex for each *edge* of the given mesh.

Recently, the concept of uniform refinement has been generalized to *irregular* refinement [GSS99, KCVS98, VG99] where new vertices can be inserted at arbitrary locations without necessarily generating semi-uniform meshes with so-called *subdivision connectivity*. However, the convergence analysis of such schemes is still an open question.

In this paper we will present a new subdivision scheme for triangle meshes which is based on an alternative uniform split operator that introduces a new vertex for every *triangle* of the given mesh (Section 2).

As we will see in the following sections, the new split operator enables us to define a natural stationary subdivision scheme which has stencils of minimum size and maximum symmetry (Section 3). The smoothing rules of the subdivision operator are derived from well-known necessary conditions for the convergence to smooth limit surfaces. Since the standard subdivision analysis machinery cannot be applied directly to the new scheme, we derive a modified technique and prove that the scheme generates C^2 surfaces for regular control meshes. For arbitrary control meshes we find the limit surface to be C^2 almost everywhere except for the extraordinary vertices (valence $\neq 6$) where the smoothness is at least C^1 (see the Appendix).

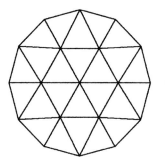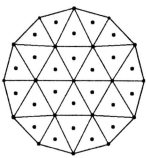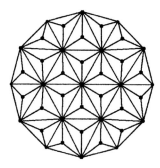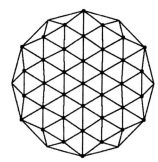

Figure 2: *The $\sqrt{3}$-subdivision scheme is based on a split operation which first inserts a new vertex for every face of the given mesh. Flipping the original edges then yields the final result which is a 30 degree rotated regular mesh. Applying the $\sqrt{3}$-subdivision scheme twice leads to a 1-to-9 refinement of the original mesh. As this corresponds to a tri-adic split (two new vertices are introduced for every original edge) we call our scheme $\sqrt{3}$-subdivision.*

Inserting a new vertex into a triangular face does only affect that single face which makes locally adaptive refinement very effective. The global consistency of the mesh is preserved automatically if $\sqrt{3}$-subdivision is performed selectively. In Section 4 we compare adaptively refined meshes generated by dyadic subdivision with our $\sqrt{3}$-subdivision meshes and find that $\sqrt{3}$-subdivision usually needs fewer triangles and less effort to achieve the same approximation tolerance. The reason for this effect is the better *localization*, i.e., only a relatively small region of the mesh is affected if more vertices are inserted locally.

For the generation of surfaces with smooth boundary curves, we need special smoothing rules at the boundary faces of the given mesh. In Section 5 we propose a boundary rule which reproduces cubic B-splines. The boundary rules can also be used to generate sharp feature lines in the interior of the surface.

2 $\sqrt{3}$-Subdivision

The most wide-spread way to uniformly refine a given triangle mesh $\mathcal{M}_0$ is the *dyadic split* which bi-sects all the edges by inserting a new vertex between every adjacent pair of old ones. Each triangular face is then split into four smaller triangles by mutually connecting the new vertices sitting on a face's edges (cf. Fig. 1). This type of splitting has the positive effect that all newly inserted vertices have valence six and the valences of the old vertices does not change. After applying the dyadic split several times, the refined meshes $\mathcal{M}_k$ have a semi-regular structure since the repeated 1-to-4 refinement replaces every triangle of the original mesh by a regular patch with 4^k triangles.

A straightforward generalization of the dyadic split is the n-adic split where every edge is subdivided into n segments and consequently every original face is split into n^2 sub-triangles. However, in the context of stationary subdivision schemes, the n-adic split operation requires a specific smoothing rule for every new vertex (modulo permutations of the barycentric coordinates). This is why subdivision schemes are mostly based on the dyadic split that only requires two smoothing rules: one for the old vertices and one for the new ones (plus rotations).

In this paper, we consider the following refinement operation for triangle meshes: Given a mesh $\mathcal{M}_0$ we perform a 1-to-3 split for every triangle by inserting a new vertex at its center. This introduces three new edges connecting the new vertex to the surrounding old ones. In order to re-balance the valence of the mesh vertices we then flip every original edge that connects two old vertices (cf. Fig 2).

This split operation is uniform in the sense that if it is applied to a uniform (three-directional) grid, a (rotated and refined) uniform grid is generated (cf. Fig. 2). If we apply the same refinement operator twice, the combined operator splits every original triangle into

nine subtriangles (*tri-adic split*). Hence one single refinement step can be considered as the "square root" of the tri-adic split. In a different context, this type of refinement operator has been considered independently in [Sab87] and [Gus98].

Analyzing the action of the $\sqrt{3}$-subdivision operator on arbitrary triangle meshes, we find that all newly inserted vertices have exactly valence six. The valences of the old vertices are not changed such that after a sufficient number of refinement steps, the mesh $\mathcal{M}_k$ has large regions with regular mesh structure which are disturbed only by a small number of isolated extraordinary vertices. These correspond to the vertices in $\mathcal{M}_0$ which had valence $\neq 6$ (cf. Fig. 3).

There are several arguments why it is interesting to investigate this particular refinement operator. First, it is very *natural* to subdivide triangular faces at their center rather than splitting all three edges since the coefficients of the subsequent smoothing operator can reflect the threefold symmetry of the three-directional grid.

Second, the $\sqrt{3}$-refinement is in some sense *slower* than the standard refinement since the number of vertices (and faces) increases by the factor of 3 instead of 4. As a consequence, we have more levels of uniform resolution if a prescribed target complexity of the mesh must not be exceeded. This is why similar uniform refinement operators for quad-meshes have been used in numerical applications such as multi-grid solvers for finite element analysis [Hac85, GZZ93].

From the computer graphics point of view the $\sqrt{3}$-refinement has the nice property that it enables a very simple implementation of adaptive refinement strategies with no inconsistent intermediate states as we will see in Section 4.

In the context of polygonal mesh based multiresolution representations [ZSS96, KCVS98, GSS99], the $\sqrt{3}$-hierarchies can provide an intuitive and robust way to encode the detail information since the detail coefficients are assigned to faces ($\approx$ tangent planes) instead of vertices.

3 Stationary smoothing rules

To complete the definition of our new subdivision scheme, we have to find the two smoothing rules, one for the placement of the newly inserted vertices and one for the relaxation of the old ones. For the sake of efficiency, our goal is to use the smallest possible stencils while still generating high quality meshes.

There are well-known necessary and sufficient criteria which tell whether a subdivision scheme S is convergent or not and what smoothness properties the limit surface has. Such criteria check if the eigenvalues of the *subdivision matrix* have a certain distribution and if a local regular parameterization exists in the vicinity of every vertex on the limit surface [CDM91, Dyn91, Rei95, Zor97, Pra98].

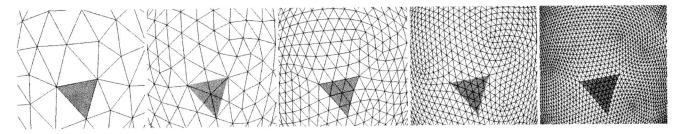

Figure 3: *The √3-subdivision generates semi-regular meshes since all new vertices have valence six. After an even number 2k of refinement steps, each original triangle is replaced by a regular patch with 9^k triangles.*

By definition, the subdivision matrix is a square matrix S which maps a certain sub-mesh $\mathbf{V} \in \mathcal{M}_k$ to a topologically equivalent sub-mesh $S(\mathbf{V}) \in \mathcal{M}_{k+1}$ of the refined mesh. Every row of this matrix is a rule to compute the position of a new vertex. Every column of this matrix tells how one old vertex contributes to the vertex positions in the refined mesh. Usually, $\mathbf{V}$ is chosen to be the neighborhood of a particular vertex, e.g., a vertex $\mathbf{p}$ and its neighbors up to the k-th order (k-ring neighborhood).

To derive the weight coefficients for the new subdivision scheme, we use these criteria for some kind of *reverse engineering* process, i.e., instead of analyzing a given scheme, we derive one which by construction satisifies the known necessary criteria. The justification for doing this is that if the necessary conditions uniquely determine a smoothing rule then the resulting subdivision scheme is the *only* scheme (with the given stencil) that is worth being considered. In the Appendix we will give the details of the sufficient part of the convergence analysis.

Since the √3-subdivision operator inserts a new vertex for every triangle of the given mesh, the minimum stencil for the corresponding smoothing rule has to include at least the three (old) corner vertices of that triangle. For symmetry reasons, the only reasonable choice for that smoothing rule is hence

$$\mathbf{q} := \frac{1}{3}\left(\mathbf{p}_i + \mathbf{p}_j + \mathbf{p}_k\right), \qquad (1)$$

i.e., the new vertex $\mathbf{q}$ is simply inserted at the center of the triangle $\triangle(\mathbf{p}_i, \mathbf{p}_j, \mathbf{p}_k)$.

The smallest non-trivial stencil for the relaxation of the old vertices is the 1-ring neighborhood containing the vertex itself and its direct neighbors. To establish symmetry, we assign the same weight to each neighbor. Let $\mathbf{p}$ be a vertex with valence n and $\mathbf{p}_0, \ldots, \mathbf{p}_{n-1}$ its directly adjacent neighbors in the unrefined mesh then we define

$$S(\mathbf{p}) := (1 - \alpha_n)\mathbf{p} + \alpha_n \frac{1}{n} \sum_{i=0}^{n-1} \mathbf{p}_i. \qquad (2)$$

The remaining question is what the optimal choice for the parameter α_n would be. Usually, the coefficient depends on the valence of $\mathbf{p}$ in order to make the subdivision scheme applicable to control meshes $\mathcal{M}_0$ with arbitrary connectivity.

The rules (1) and (2) imply that the 1-ring neighborhood of a vertex $S(\mathbf{p}) \in \mathcal{M}_{k+1}$ only depends on the 1-ring neighborhood of the corresponding vertex $\mathbf{p} \in \mathcal{M}_k$. Hence, we can set-up a $(n+1) \times (n+1)$ matrix which maps $\mathbf{p}$ and its n neighbors to the next refinement level. Arranging all the vertices in a vector

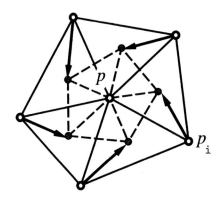

Figure 4: *The application of the subdivision matrix S causes a rotation around $\mathbf{p}$ since the neighboring vertices are replaced by the centers of the adjacent triangles.*

$[\mathbf{p}, \mathbf{p}_0, \ldots, \mathbf{p}_{n-1}]$ we derive the subdivision matrix

$$S = \frac{1}{3}\begin{pmatrix} u & v & v & v & \cdots & v \\ 1 & 1 & 1 & 0 & \cdots & 0 \\ 1 & 0 & \ddots & \ddots & \ddots & \vdots \\ \vdots & \vdots & \ddots & \ddots & \ddots & 0 \\ 1 & 0 & & \ddots & \ddots & 1 \\ 1 & 1 & 0 & \cdots & 0 & 1 \end{pmatrix} \qquad (3)$$

with $u = 3(1 - \alpha_n)$ and $v = 3\alpha_n/n$. However, when analysing the eigenstructure of this matrix, we find that it is not suitable for the construction of a convergent subdivision scheme. The reason for this defect is the rotation around $\mathbf{p}$ which is caused by the application of S and which makes all eigenvalues of S complex. Fig. 4 depicts the situation.

From the last section we know that applying the √3-subdivision operator two times corresponds to a tri-adic split. So instead of analysing one single subdivision step, we can combine two successive steps since after the second application of S, the neighborhood of $S^2(\mathbf{p})$ is again aligned to the original configuration around $\mathbf{p}$. Hence, the back-rotation can be written as a simple permutation matrix

$$R = \begin{pmatrix} 1 & 0 & \cdots & 0 & 0 \\ 0 & 0 & \cdots & 0 & 1 \\ 0 & 1 & \ddots & & 0 \\ \vdots & \ddots & \ddots & \ddots & \vdots \\ 0 & \cdots & 0 & 1 & 0 \end{pmatrix}.$$

The resulting matrix $\tilde{S} = RS^2$ now has the correct eigenstructure for the analysis. Its eigenvalues are:

$$\frac{1}{9}\left[9,(2-3\alpha_n)^2,2+2\cos(2\pi\frac{1}{n}),\ldots,2+2\cos(2\pi\frac{n-1}{n})\right] \quad (4)$$

From [Rei95, Zor97] it is known that for the leading eigenvalues, sorted by decreasing modulus, the following necessary conditions have to hold

$$\lambda_1 = 1 > \lambda_2 = \lambda_3 > \lambda_i, \quad i = 4,\ldots,n+1. \quad (5)$$

Additionally, according to [Pra98, Zor97], a natural choice for the eigenvalue λ_4 is $\lambda_4 = \lambda_2^2$ since the eigenstructure of the subdivision matrix can be interpreted as a generalized Taylor-expansion of the limit surface at the point $\mathbf{p}$. The eigenvalue λ_4 then corresponds to a quadratic term in that expansion. Consequently, we define the value for α_n by solving

$$\left(\frac{2}{3}-\alpha_n\right)^2 = \left(\frac{2+2\cos(2\pi\frac{1}{n})}{9}\right)^2$$

which leads to

$$\alpha_n = \frac{4-2\cos(\frac{2\pi}{n})}{9} \quad (6)$$

where we picked that solution of the quadratic equation for which the coefficient α_n always stays in the interval $[0,1]$ and (2) is a convex combination. The explanation for the existence of a second solution is that we actually analyse a double step $\widetilde{S} = RS^2$. The real eigenvalue $(\frac{2}{3}-\alpha_n)^2$ of $\widetilde{S}$ corresponds to the eigenvalue $\frac{2}{3}-\alpha_n$ of S both with the same eigenvector $[-3\alpha_n,1,\ldots,1]$ which is invariant under R. Obviously we have to choose α_n such that negative real eigenvalues of S are avoided [Rei95].

Equations (1), (2) and (6) together completely define the smoothing operator for our stationary subdivision scheme since they provide all the necessary information to implement the scheme. Notice that the spectral properties of the matrices S and $\widetilde{S}$ are not sufficient for the actual convergence analysis of the subdivision scheme. It is only used here to derive the smoothing rule from the necessary conditions! The sufficient part of the convergence analysis is presented in the Appendix.

4 Adaptive refinement strategies

Although the complexity of the refined meshes $\mathcal{M}_k$ grows slower under $\sqrt{3}$-subdivision than under dyadic subdivision (cf. Fig. 13), the number of triangles still increases exponentially. Hence, only relatively few refinement steps can be performed if the resulting meshes are to be processed on a standard PC. The common techniques to curb the mesh complexity under refinement are based on adaptive refinement strategies which insert new vertices only in those regions of the surface where more geometric detail is expected. Flat regions of the surface are sufficiently well approximated by large triangles.

The major difficulties that emerge from adaptive refinement are caused by the fact that triangles from different refinement levels have to be joined in a consistent manner (*conforming meshes*) which often requires additional redundancy in the underlying mesh data structure. To reduce the number of topological special cases and to guarantee a minimum quality of the resulting triangular faces, the adaptive refinement is usually restricted to *balanced meshes* where the refinement level of adjacent triangles must not differ by more than one generation. However, to maintain the mesh balance at any time, a local refinement step can trigger several additional split operations in its vicinity. This is the reason why adaptive refinement techniques are rated by their *localization* property, i.e.,

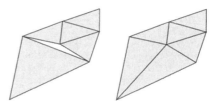

Figure 5: *The gap between triangles from different refinement levels can be fixed by temporarily replacing the larger face by a triangle fan.*

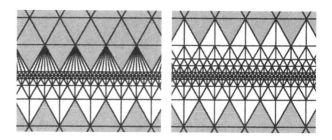

Figure 6: *The gap fixing by triangle fans tends to produce degenerate triangles if the refinement is not balanced (left). Balancing the refinement, however, causes a larger region of the mesh to be affected by local refinement (right).*

by the extend to which the side-effects of a local refinement step spread over the mesh.

For refinement schemes based on the dyadic split operation, the local splitting of one triangular face causes gaps if neighboring faces are not refined (cf. Fig. 5). These gaps have to be removed by replacing the adjacent (unrefined) faces with a triangle fan. As shown in Fig. 6 this simple strategy tends to generate very badly shaped triangles if no balance of the refinement is enforced.

If further split operations are applied to an already adaptively refined mesh, the triangle fans have to be removed first since the corresponding triangles are not part of the actual refinement hierarchy. The combination of dyadic refinement, mesh balancing and gap fixing by temporary triangle fans is well-known under the name *redgreen triangulation* in the finite element community [VT92, Ver96].

There are several reason why $\sqrt{3}$-subdivision seems better suited for adaptive refinement. First, the slower refinement reduces the expected average over-tesselation which occurs when a coarse triangle slightly fails the stopping criterion for the adaptive refinement but the result of the refinement falls significantly below the threshold.

The second reason is that the localization is better than for dyadic refinement and no temporary triangle fans are necessary to keep the mesh consistent. In fact, the consistency preserving adaptive refinement can be implemented by a simple recursive procedure. No refinement history has to be stored in the underlying data structure since no temporary triangles are generated which do not belong to the actual refinement hierarchy.

To implement the adaptive refinement, we have to assign a generation index to each triangle in the mesh. Initially all triangles of the given mesh $\mathcal{M}_0$ are generation 0. If a triangle with *even* generation index is split into three by inserting a new vertex at its center, the generation index increases by 1 (giving an odd index to the new triangles). Splitting a triangle with *odd* generation index requires to find its "mate", perform an edge flip, and assign even indices to the resulting triangles.

For an already adaptively refined mesh, further splits are performed by the following recursive procedure

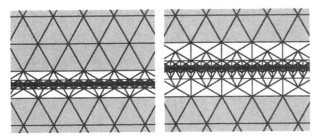

Figure 7: *Adaptive refinement based on $\sqrt{3}$-subdivision achieves an improved localization while automatically preventing degenerate triangles since all occuring triangles are a subset of the underlying hierarchy of uniformly refined meshes. Let us assume the horizontal coarse scale grid lines in the images have constant integer y coordinates then the two images result from adaptively refining all triangles that intersect a certain $y = const.$ line. In the left image y was chosen from $[\frac{1}{3}, \frac{2}{3}]$ and in the right image $y = 1 + \varepsilon$ which explains the different localization.*

```
split(T)

  if (T.index is even) then

    compute midpoint P
    split T(A,B,C) into T[1](P,A,B),T[2](P,B,C),T[3](P,C,A)
    for i = 1,2,3 do
      T[i].index = T.index + 1
      if (T[i].mate[1].index == T[i].index) then
        swap(T[i],T[i].mate[1])
  else

    if (T.mate[1].index == T.index - 2)
      split(T.mate[1])

    split(T.mate[1])    /* ... triggers edge swap */
```

which automatically preserves the mesh consistency and implicitly maintains some mild balancing condition for the refinement levels of adjacent triangles. Notice that the ordering of the vertices in the 1-to-3 split is chosen such that reference `mate[1]` always points to the correct neighboring triangle (outside the parent triangle T). The edge flipping procedure is implemented as

```
swap(T1,T2)

  change T1(A,B,C), T2(B,A,D) into T1(C,A,D), T2(D,B,C)
  T1.index++
  T2.index++
```

All the triangles that are generated during the adaptive $\sqrt{3}$-refinement form a proper subset of the uniform refinement hierarchy. This implies that the shape of the triangles does never degenerate. The worst triangles are those generated by an 1-to-3 split. Edge flipping then mostly re-improves the shape. Fig. 7 shows two adaptively refined example meshes. Another approach to adaptive mesh refinement with built-in consistency is suggested in [VG00].

When adaptive refinement is performed in the context of stationary subdivision, another difficulty arises from the fact that for the application of the smoothing rules a certain neighborhood of vertices from the same refinement level has to be present. This puts some additional constraints on the mesh balance. In [ZSS97] this is explained for Loop subdivision with dyadic refinement.

For $\sqrt{3}$-subdivision it is sufficient to slightly modify the recursive splitting procedure such that *before* splitting an even-indexed triangle by vertex insertion, all older odd-indexed neighbors have to be split (even-indexed neighbors remain untouched). This guarantees that enough information is available for later applications of the smoothing rule (2). The rule (1) is always applicable since it only uses the three vertices of the current triangle. Notice that the

1-to-3 split is the only way new vertices enter the mesh. Moreover, every new vertex eventually has valence six — although some of its neighbors might not yet be present.

The modification of the recursive procedure implies that when a new vertex $\mathbf{p}$ is inserted, its neighboring vertices $\mathbf{p}_1, \ldots, \mathbf{p}_6$ either exist already, or at least the triangles exist at whose centers these vertices are going to be inserted. In any case it is straightforward to compute the average $\frac{1}{n} \sum_i \mathbf{p}_i$ which is all we need for the application of (2).

The remaining technical problem is that in an adaptively refined mesh, the geometric location of a mesh vertex is not always well-defined. Ambiguities occur if triangles from different refinement levels share a common vertex since the smoothing rule (2) is non-interpolatory. We solved this problem by implementing a multi-step smoothing rule which enables direct access to the vertex positions at any refinement level. Accessing a `Vertex`-object by `Vertex::pos(k)` returns the vertex coordinates corresponding to the kth refinement level. `Vertex::pos(inf)` returns the corresponding point on the limit surface which is the location that is eventually used for display.

Multi-step rules are generalizations of the rule (2) which allow direct evaluation of arbitrary powers of S. As we already discussed in Section 3, the 1-ring neighborhood $[\mathbf{p}, \mathbf{p}_0, \ldots, \mathbf{p}_{n-1}]$ of a vertex $\mathbf{p}$ is mapped to (a scaled version of) itself under application of the subdivision scheme. This is reflected by the matrix S in (3). If we compute the mth power of the subdivision matrix in (3), we find in the first row a linear combination of $[\mathbf{p}, \mathbf{p}_0, \ldots, \mathbf{p}_{n-1}]$ which directly yields $S^m(\mathbf{p})$. For symmetry reason this multi-step rule can, again, be written as a linear combination of the original vertex $\mathbf{p}$ and the average of its neighbors $\frac{1}{n} \sum_i \mathbf{p}_i$.

By eigenanalysis of the matrix S it is fairly straightforward to derive a closed form solution for the multi-step rule [Sta98]:

$$S^m(\mathbf{p}) := (1 - \beta_n(m)) \, \mathbf{p} + \beta_n(m) \frac{1}{n} \sum_{i=0}^{n-1} \mathbf{p}_i \qquad (7)$$

with

$$\beta_n(m) = \frac{3\alpha_n - 3\alpha_n \left(\frac{2}{3} - \alpha_n\right)^m}{1 + 3\alpha_n}$$

especially

$$\beta_n(\infty) = \frac{3\alpha_n}{1 + 3\alpha_n}.$$

Since the point $\mathbf{p}^{(\infty)} = S^\infty(\mathbf{p})$ on the limit surface is particularly important, we rewrite (7) by eliminating the average of $\mathbf{p}$'s neighbors

$$S^m(\mathbf{p}) := \gamma_n(m) \, \mathbf{p} + (1 - \gamma_n(m)) \, \mathbf{p}^{(\infty)} \qquad (8)$$

with

$$\gamma_n(m) = \left(\frac{2}{3} - \alpha_n\right)^m.$$

In our implementation, every `Vertex`-object stores its original position $\mathbf{p}$ (at the time it was inserted into the mesh) and its limit position $\mathbf{p}^{(\infty)}$. The vertex position at arbitrary levels can then be computed by (8).

5 Boundaries

In practical and industrial applications it is usually necessary to be able to process control meshes with well-defined boundary polygons which should result in surfaces with smooth boundary curves. As the neighborhood of boundary vertices is not complete, we have to figure out special refinement and smoothing rules.

When topologically refining a given open control mesh $\mathcal{M}_0$ by the $\sqrt{3}$-operator we split all triangular faces 1-to-3 but flip only the

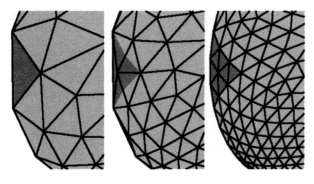

Figure 8: *The boundary is subdivided only in every other step such that a uniform 1-to-9 refinement of the triangular faces is achieved.*

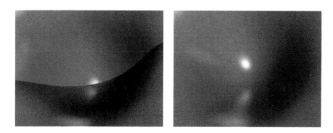

Figure 9: *The use of univariate smoothing rules at the boundaries enables the generation of sharp feature lines where two separate control meshes share an identical boundary polygon.*

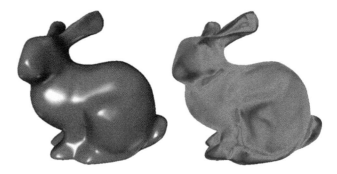

Figure 10: *A decimated Stanford bunny was used as a subdivision control mesh $\mathcal{M}_0$. We applied the $\sqrt{3}$-subdivision scheme 4 times (left). The right image shows the mean curvature distribution.*

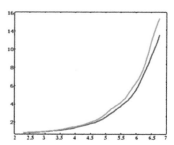

Figure 11: *This plot shows the triangle count (Y : in $K\triangle$) vs. approximation error (X : in $-\log(\varepsilon)$). The red curve is the complexity of the Loop-meshes, the blue curve the complexity of the $\sqrt{3}$-meshes. The ratio lies between 5% and 25%.*

interior edges. Edge flipping at the boundaries is not possible since the opposite triangle-mate is missing. Hence, the boundary polygon is not modified in the first $\sqrt{3}$-subdivision step.

As we already discussed in Section 2, the application of a second $\sqrt{3}$-step has the overall effect of a tri-adic split where each original triangle is replaced by 9 new ones. Consequently, we have to apply a univariate tri-section rule to the boundary polygon and connect the new vertices to the corresponding interior ones such that a uniform 1-to-9 split is established for each boundary triangle (cf. Fig. 8).

The smoothing rules at the boundaries should only use boundary vertices and no interior ones. This is the simplest way to enable the generation of C^0 creases in the interior of the surface (*feature lines*) since it guarantees that control meshes with identical boundary polygons will result in smooth surfaces with identical boundary curves [HDD+94] (cf. Fig. 9). More sophisticated techniques for the design of optimal boundary smoothing rules with normal control can be found in [BLZ99].

For our $\sqrt{3}$-subdivision scheme we choose, for simplicity, a univariate boundary subdivision scheme which reproduces cubic splines (maximum smoothness, minimum stencil). From the trivial tri-section mask for linear splines we can easily obtain the corresponding tri-section mask for cubic splines by convolution

$$\tfrac{1}{3}[1,2,3,2,1] * (\tfrac{1}{3}[1,1,1])^2$$
$$= \tfrac{1}{9}[1,3,6,7,6,3,1] * \tfrac{1}{3}[1,1,1]$$
$$= \tfrac{1}{27}[1,4,10,16,19,16,10,4,1]$$

Hence the resulting smoothing rules are

$$
\begin{aligned}
\mathbf{p}'_{3i-1} &= \tfrac{1}{27}\left(10\mathbf{p}_{i-1} + 16\mathbf{p}_i + \mathbf{p}_{i+1}\right)\\
\mathbf{p}'_{3i} &= \tfrac{1}{27}\left(4\mathbf{p}_{i-1} + 19\mathbf{p}_i + 4\mathbf{p}_{i+1}\right) \qquad (9)\\
\mathbf{p}'_{3i+1} &= \tfrac{1}{27}\left(\mathbf{p}_{i-1} + 16\mathbf{p}_i + 10\mathbf{p}_{i+1}\right).
\end{aligned}
$$

6 Examples

To demonstrate the quality of the $\sqrt{3}$-subdivision surfaces we show a mesh generated by uniformly refining a decimated version of the Stanford bunny (cf. Fig 10). The C^2 smoothness of the limit surface guarantees curvature continuity and the relaxing properties of the smoothing rules with only positive weights lead to a fair distribution of the curvature.

We made several numerical experiments to check the relative complexity of the adaptively refined meshes $\mathcal{M}_k$ generated either by $\sqrt{3}$-subdivision or by Loop-subdivision. For the stopping criterion in the adaptive refinement we used the local approximation error of the current mesh (with all vertices projected onto the limit surface) to the limit surface. A reliable estimation of the exact approximation error can be computed by constructing tight bounding envelopes as described in [KDS98].

After testing various models with different geometric complexities over the range $[10^{-2}, 10^{-7}]$ for the approximation tolerance, we found that adaptive $\sqrt{3}$-subdivision meshes usually need fewer triangles than adaptive Loop-subdivision surfaces to obtain the same approximation tolerance. The improvement is typically between 5% and 25% with an average at 10%. Fig. 11 shows the typical relation between approximation tolerance and mesh complexity.

Fig. 12 shows another example mesh generated by the adaptive $\sqrt{3}$-subdivision scheme in comparison to the corresponding Loop subdivision surface defined by the same control mesh. This time we use a *curvature* dependent adaptive refinement strategy: The subdivision level is determined by a discrete local curvature estimation.

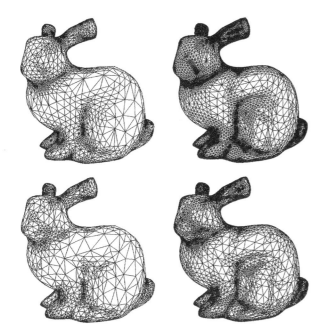

Figure 12: *Adaptive refinement based on red-green triangulation with Loop subdivision (top row) and based on the $\sqrt{3}$-refinement (bottom row). While the same stopping criterion is used (left and right respectively), the Loop meshes have 10072 and 28654 triangles while the $\sqrt{3}$-meshes only have 7174 and 20772 triangles.*

7 Conclusion

We presented a new stationary subdivision scheme which iteratively generates high quality C^2 surfaces with minimum computational effort. It shares the advantages of the well-known standard schemes but has important additional properties. Especially the slower increase of the mesh complexity and the suitability for adaptive refinement with automatic consistency preservation makes it a promising approach for practical and industrial applications.

The analysis technique we present in the Appendix provides a simple tool to analyse a very general class of subdivision schemes which are not necessarily based on some known polynomial spline basis function and not generated by taking the tensor-product of some univariate scheme.

Future modifications and extensions of the $\sqrt{3}$-subdivision scheme should aim at incorporating more sophisticated boundary rules [BLZ99] and interpolation constraints [Lev99]. Modifications of the smoothing rules with different stencils could lead to new subdivision schemes with interesting properties.

Acknowledgements

I would like to thank Stephan Bischoff and Ulf Labsik for implementing the $\sqrt{3}$-subdivision scheme and performing some of the experiments.

References

[BLZ99]   H. Biermann, A. Levin, D. Zorin, *Piecewise smooth subdivision surfaces with normal control*, Preprint

[CC78]   E. Catmull, J. Clark, *Recursively generated B-spline surfaces on arbitrary topological meshes*, CAD **10** (1978), 350–355

[CDM91]   A. Cavaretta, W. Dahmen, C. Micchelli, *Stationary Subdivision*, Memoirs of the AMS 93 (1991), pp. 1-186

[DS78]   D. Doo, M. Sabin, *Behaviour of recursive division surfaces near extraordinary points*, CAD **10** (1978), 356–360

[DGL90]   N. Dyn, J. Gregory, D. Levin, *A Butterfly Subdivision Scheme for Surface Interpolation with Tension Control*, ACM Trans. Graph. 9 (1990), pp. 160–169

[Dyn91]   N. Dyn, *Subdivision Schemes in Computer Aided Geometric Design*, Advances in Numerical Analysis II, Wavelets, Subdivisions and Radial Functions, W.A. Light ed., Oxford University Press, 1991, pp: 36-104.

[GSS99]   I. Guskov, W. Sweldens, P. Schröder, *Multiresolution signal processing for meshes*, SIGGRAPH 99 Proceedings, 1999, pp. 325 – 334

[GvL96]   G. Golub, C. van Loan, *Matrix Computations*, 3rd, Johns Hopkins Univ Press, 1996

[GZZ93]   M. Griebel, C. Zenger, S. Zimmer, *Multilevel Gauss-Seidel-Algorithms for Full and Sparse Grid Problems*, Computing 50, 1993, pp. 127–148

[Gus98]   I. Guskov, *Multivariate subdivision schemes and divided differences*, Preprint, Princeton University, 1998

[Hac85]   W. Hackbusch, *Multi-Grid Methods and Applications*, Springer, Berlin, 1985

[HDD+94] H. Hoppe, T. DeRose, T. Duchamp, M. Halstead, H. Jin, J. McDonald, J. Schweitzer, W. Stuetzle, *Piecewise smooth surface reconstruction*, SIGGRAPH 1994 Proceedings, 1994, pp. 295–302

[Kob96]   L. Kobbelt, *Interpolatory Subdivision on Open Quadrilateral Nets with Arbitrary Topology*, Computer Graphics Forum 15 (1996), Eurographics '96 Conference Issue, pp. 409–420

[KDS98]   L. Kobbelt, K. Daubert, H-P. Seidel, *Ray-tracing of subdivision surfaces*, 9th Eurographics Workshop on Rendering Proceedings, 1998, pp. 69 – 80

[KCVS98] L. Kobbelt, S. Campagna, J. Vorsatz, H-P. Seidel, *Interactive multiresolution modeling on arbitrary meshes*, SIGGRAPH 98 Proceedings, 1998, pp. 105–114

[Lev99]   A. Levin, *Interpolating nets of curves by smooth subdivision surfaces*, SIGGRAPH 99 Proceedings, 1999, pp. 57 – 64

[Loo87]   C. Loop, *Smooth subdivision surfaces based on triangles*, Master Thesis, Utah University, USA, 1987

[Pra98]   H. Prautzsch, *Smoothness of subdivision surfaces at extraordinary points*, Adv. Comp. Math. 14 (1998), pp. 377 – 390

[Rei95]   U. Reif, *A unified approach to subdivision algorithms near extraordinary vertices*, CAGD 12 (1995), pp. 153–174

[RP98]   U. Reif, J. Peters, *The simplest subdivision scheme for smoothing polyhedra*, ACM Trans. Graph. 16 (1998), pp. 420 – 431

[Sab87]   M. Sabin, *Recursive Division*, in The Mathematics of Surfaces, Clarendon Press, 1986, pp. 269 – 282

[Sta98]   J. Stam, *Exact evaluation of Catmull/Clark subdivision surfaces at arbitrary parameter values*, SIGGRAPH 98 Proceeding, 1998, pp. 395 – 404

[VG99]   L. Velho, J. Gomes, *Quasi-stationary subdivision using four directional meshes*, Preprint

[VG00]   L. Velho, J. Gomes, *Semi-regular 4-8 refinement and box spline surfaces*, Preprint

[VT92]   M. Vasilescu, D. Terzopoulos, *Adaptive meshes and shells: Irregular triangulation, discontinuities and hierarchical subdivision*, Proceedings of the Computer Vision and Pattern Recognition Conference, 1992, 829 – 832

[Ver96]   R. Verfürth, *A review of a posteriori error estimation and adaptive mesh refinement techniques*, Wiley-Teubner, 1996

[War00]   J. Warren, *Subdivision methods for geometric design*, unpublished manuscript

[ZSS96]   D. Zorin, P. Schröder, W. Sweldens, *Interpolating Subdivision for Meshes with Arbitrary Topology*, SIGGRAPH 96 Proceedings, 1996, pp. 189–192

[Zor97]   D.Zorin, C^k *Continuity of Subdivision Surfaces*, Thesis, California Institute of Technology, 1997

[ZSS97]   D. Zorin, P. Schröder, W. Sweldens, *Interactive multiresolution mesh editing*, SIGGRAPH 97 Proceedings, 1997, pp. 259–268

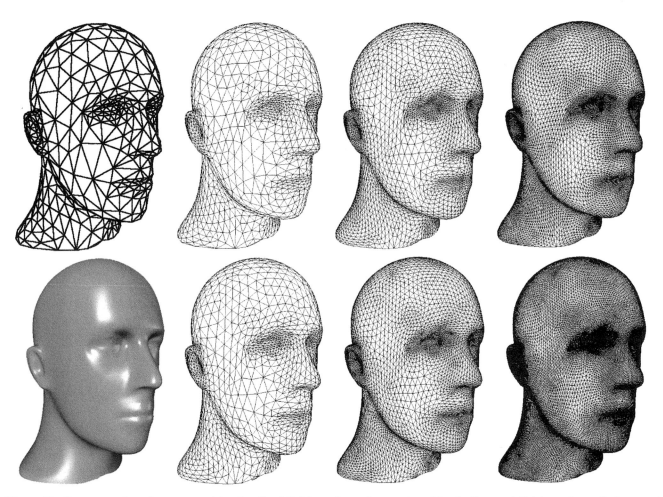

Figure 13: *Sequences of meshes generated by the $\sqrt{3}$-subdivision scheme (top row) and by the Loop subdivision scheme (bottom row). Although the quality of the limit surfaces is the same (C^2), $\sqrt{3}$-subdivision uses an alternative refinement operator that increases the number of triangles slower than Loop's. The relative complexity of the corresponding meshes from both rows is (from left to right) $\frac{3}{4} = 0.75$, $\frac{9}{16} = 0.56$, and $\frac{27}{64} = 0.42$. Hence the new subdivision scheme yields a much finer gradation of uniform hierarchy levels.*

Appendix: Convergence analysis

The convergence analysis of stationary subdivision schemes is generally done in two steps. In the first step, the smoothness of the limit surface is shown for *regular* meshes, i.e. for triangle meshes with all vertices having valence 6. Due to the nature of the topological refinement operator, subdivided meshes $\mathcal{M}_k$ are regular almost everywhere. Once the regular case is shown, the convergence in the vicinity of extraordinary vertices (with valence $\neq 6$) can be proven. For many existing subdivision schemes, the first part of the proof is trivial since a closed form representation of the limit surface in the regular case is known, e.g. B-splines for Catmull/Clark or Doo/Sabin surfaces, Box-splines for Loop-surfaces.

For the two steps in the proof different techniques have to be used. The smoothness of the limit surface for regular control meshes follows from the *contractivity* of certain difference schemes S_n. These are generalized subdivision schemes which map directional forward differences of control points directly to directional forward differences (instead of the original subdivision scheme S mapping control points to control points).

In the vicinity of the extraordinary vertices, the convergence analysis is based on the eigenstructure of the local subdivision matrix. It is important to notice that the criteria for the eigenstructure of the subdivision matrix do only apply if the convergence in the regular regions of the mesh is guaranteed [Rei95, Zor97].

In the following we present a general technique for the analysis of subdivision schemes on regular meshes which we will use to prove the smoothness of the $\sqrt{3}$-subdivision limit surface. Nevertheless, the technique also applies to a larger class of non-standard subdivision schemes. Another analysis technique that is also based on a matrix formulation is used in [War00].

Regular meshes

Instead of using the standard generating function notation for the handling of subdivision schemes [Dyn91], we propose a new matrix formulation which is much easier to handle due to the analogy with the treatment of the irregular case. In fact, rotational symmetries of the subdivision rules are reflected by a blockwise circulant structure of the respective matrices just like in the vicinity of extraordinary vertices. Our matrix based analysis requires only a few matrix computations which can easily be performed with the help of Maple or MatLab. In contrast, the manipulation of the corresponding generating functions would be quite involved if the subdivision scheme does not have a simple factorization (cf. [CDM91, Dyn91]).

To prove the contractivity of some difference scheme, it is sufficient to consider a local portion of a (virtually) infinite regular triangulation. This is due to the shift invariance of the subdivision scheme (*stationary* subdivision). Hence, similarly to the treatment of extraordinary vertices, we can pick an arbitrary vertex **p** and a

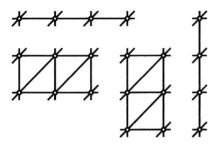

Figure 14: *The* support *of a directional difference includes the vertices that contribute to it. Here we show the supports of D_{10}^3, $D_{01}D_{10}^2$, $D_{01}^2 D_{10}$, and D_{01}^3.*

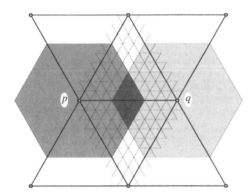

Figure 15: *The two refined neighborhoods $S^m(\mathbf{V_p})$ and $S^m(\mathbf{V_q})$ (grey areas) of the (formerly) adjacent vertices $\mathbf{p}$ and $\mathbf{q}$ have to overlap (dark area) such that every possible directional difference can be computed from either one.*

sufficiently large neighborhood $\mathbf{V}$ around it. The size of this neighborhood is determined by the order n of the differences that we want to consider and by the number m of subdivision steps we want to combine (the analysis of one single subdivision step often does not yield a sufficient estimate to prove contractivity). For a given subdivision scheme S the neighborhoods have to be chosen such that for two adjacent vertices $\mathbf{p}$ and $\mathbf{q}$ in $\mathcal{M}_k$ the corresponding sets $S^m(\mathbf{V_p})$ and $S^m(\mathbf{V_q})$ in the refined mesh $\mathcal{M}_{k+m}$ have enough overlap to guarantee that the support of each nth order directional difference is contained in either one (cf. Fig 14).

In our case we want to prove C^2 continuity and hence have to show contractivity of the 3rd directional difference scheme. For technical reasons we always combine an even number of $\sqrt{3}$-subdivision steps since this removes the 30 degree rotation of the grid directions (just like we did in Section 3). To guarantee the required overlap, we hence have to use a 3-ring neighborhood if we analyse one double $\sqrt{3}$-step and a 6-ring neighborhood if we analyse two double $\sqrt{3}$-steps. The corresponding subdivision matrices are 37×37 and 127×127 respectively (cf. Fig 15).

We start by introducing some notation: A regular triangulation is equivalent to the three directional grid which is spanned by the directions

$$\mathbf{v}_{01} = \begin{pmatrix} 1 \\ 0 \end{pmatrix}, \quad \mathbf{v}_{10} = \begin{pmatrix} 0 \\ 1 \end{pmatrix}, \quad \mathbf{v}_{11} = \begin{pmatrix} 1 \\ 1 \end{pmatrix}$$

in index space. Hence the two types of triangular faces in the mesh are given by $\triangle(\mathbf{p}_{i,j}, \mathbf{p}_{i+1,j}, \mathbf{p}_{i+1,j+1})$ and $\triangle(\mathbf{p}_{i,j}, \mathbf{p}_{i+1,j+1}, \mathbf{p}_{i,j+1})$. Accordingly, we define the three directional difference operators

$$D_{uv}: \quad \mathbf{p}_{i,j} \quad \mapsto \quad \mathbf{p}_{i+u,j+v} - \mathbf{p}_{i,j}$$

with $(u,v) \in \{(1,0),(0,1),(1,1)\}$. If we apply these difference operators D_{uv} to a finite neighborhood $\mathbf{V}$ we obtain all possible differ-

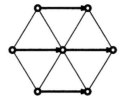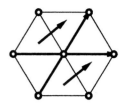

Figure 16: *Directional differences on a finite neighborhood $\mathbf{V}$. Left: the application of D_{10} yields four different vectors. Right: the application of J_2 yields four vectors, one for D_{10}^2, one for D_{01}^2 and two "twist" vectors for the mixed derivative $D_{10}D_{01}$.*

ences where both $\mathbf{p}_{i,j}$ and $\mathbf{p}_{i+u,j+v}$ are elements of $\mathbf{V}$. For a fixed neighborhood $\mathbf{V}$ the operator D_{uv} can be represented by a matrix that has two non-zero entries in every row, e.g.,

$$\mathbf{V} = \left\{ \begin{pmatrix} 0 \\ 0 \end{pmatrix}, \begin{pmatrix} 1 \\ 0 \end{pmatrix}, \begin{pmatrix} 1 \\ 1 \end{pmatrix}, \begin{pmatrix} 0 \\ 1 \end{pmatrix}, \begin{pmatrix} -1 \\ 0 \end{pmatrix}, \begin{pmatrix} -1 \\ -1 \end{pmatrix}, \begin{pmatrix} 0 \\ -1 \end{pmatrix} \right\}$$

implies

$$D_{10} = \begin{pmatrix} -1 & 1 & 0 & 0 & 0 & 0 & 0 \\ 0 & 0 & 1 & -1 & 0 & 0 & 0 \\ 1 & 0 & 0 & 0 & -1 & 0 & 0 \\ 0 & 0 & 0 & 0 & 0 & -1 & 1 \end{pmatrix}.$$

See Fig. 16 for a geometric interpretation. Based on the difference operators, we can build the *Jet-operators*

$$J_1 = \begin{pmatrix} D_{10} \\ D_{01} \end{pmatrix} \quad J_2 = \begin{pmatrix} D_{10}D_{10} \\ D_{10}D_{01} \\ D_{01}D_{01} \end{pmatrix} \quad J_3 = \begin{pmatrix} D_{10}D_{10}D_{10} \\ D_{10}D_{10}D_{01} \\ D_{10}D_{01}D_{01} \\ D_{01}D_{01}D_{01} \end{pmatrix} \quad (10)$$

which map the control vertices in $\mathbf{V}$ to the complete set of independent directional differences $J_n(\mathbf{V})$ of a given order n.

Let S be the subdivision scheme which maps control vertices $\mathbf{p}^{(k)}$ from the kth refinement level to the $(k+1)$st refinement level $\mathbf{p}^{(k+1)} = S(\mathbf{p}^{(k)})$. Again, if we consider the action of S on a local neighborhood $\mathbf{V}$ only, we can represent S by a matrix with each row containing an affine combination that defines the position of one new control vertex.

For the convergence analysis we need a so-called *difference scheme* S_n which maps the differences $J_n(\mathbf{V}^{(k)})$ directly to $J_n(\mathbf{V}^{(k+1)}) = J_n(S(\mathbf{V}^{(k)})) = S_n(J_n(\mathbf{V}^{(k)}))$. From [Dyn91] it is well-known that the subdivision scheme S generates C^n limit surfaces (for regular control meshes) if the scheme $h^n S_{n+1}$ is contractive, i.e., if $\|S_{n+1}\| \leq q < h^{-n}$ with respect to an appropriate matrix norm. Here, the factor h^n takes the implicit parameterization into account. For subdivision schemes which are based on the dyadic split operation, edges are bi-sected in every step and hence $h = 2$. This is true for all standard schemes. However, for our new $\sqrt{3}$-subdivision scheme we have to choose $h = 3$ since we are analysing the double application of the $\sqrt{3}$-operator which corresponds to an edge tri-section.

In the univariate case these difference schemes S_n can be obtained by simple factorization of the corresponding generating function representations. In the bivariate case the situation is much more difficult since *jets* are mapped to *jets*! In general we cannot find a simple scheme which maps, e.g., the differences $D_{10}(\mathbf{V})$ to $D_{10}(S(\mathbf{V}))$ because the directional differences are not independent from each other. Hence we have to find a more general matrix scheme

$$\begin{pmatrix} D_{10}(S(\mathbf{V})) \\ D_{01}(S(\mathbf{V})) \end{pmatrix} = S_1 \begin{pmatrix} D_{10}(\mathbf{V}) \\ D_{01}(\mathbf{V}) \end{pmatrix}$$

which maps $J_1(\mathbf{V})$ to $J_1(S(\mathbf{V}))$ by allowing $D_{10}(S(\mathbf{V}))$ to depend on both $D_{10}(\mathbf{V})$ and $D_{01}(\mathbf{V})$. As this construction requires quite

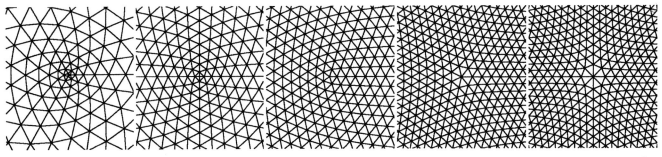

Figure 17: *The local regularity of the subdivision surface at extraordinary vertices requires the injectivity of the characterisitc map. We show the isoparameter lines for these maps in the vicinity of irregular vertices with valence $n = 3, 4, 5, 7,$ and 8 (form left to right).*

involved factorizations and other polynomial transformations, we now suggest a simpler approach where most of the computation can be done automatically.

Let J_n by the nth jet-operator restricted to $\mathbf{V}$ and J_n^{-1} its SVD pseudo-inverse. Because J_n has a non-trivial kernel (containing all configurations where the points in $\mathbf{V}$ are uniformly sampled from a degree $n - 1$ polynomial) its inverse cannot be well-defined. At least we know that

$$J_n J_n^{-1} J_n = J_n$$

which means that if J_n^{-1} is applied to a set of nth order differences $J_n(\mathbf{V})$ it reconstructs the original data up to an error $\mathbf{e}$ which lies in the kernel of J_n, i.e., $J_n^{-1}(J_n(\mathbf{V})) = \mathbf{V} + \mathbf{e}$ with $J_n(\mathbf{e}) = \mathbf{0}$.

If the subdivision scheme S has *polynomial precision* of order $n - 1$ this implies that S maps the kernel of J_n into itself:

$$S(\ker(J_n)) \subset \ker(J_n). \tag{11}$$

As a consequence $J_n(S(\mathbf{e})) = 0$ as well, and therefore

$$J_n S J_n^{-1} J_n = J_n S.$$

Since the operator on the right hand side of this equation maps the vertices of the control mesh $\mathbf{V}^{(k)}$ to the nth differences on the next refinement level $J_n(\mathbf{V}^{(k+1)})$, the operator

$$S_n := J_n S J_n^{-1} \tag{12}$$

does map the nth differences $J_n(\mathbf{V}^{(k)})$ directly to the nth differences on the next level $J_n(\mathbf{V}^{(k+1)})$. This is exactly the difference scheme that we have been looking for! In order to prove the convergence of the subdivision scheme, we have to show that the maximum norm of $h^{n-1}S_n$ is below 1. Alternatively, it is sufficient to show that the maximum singular value of the matrix $h^{n-1}S_n$ is smaller than 1 since this provides a monotonically decreasing upper bound for the maximum nth difference.

To verify the polynomial precision (11) for a given subdivision matrix S we first generate another matrix K whose columns span the kernel of J_n. Notice that the dimension of $\ker(J_n)$ is the dimension of the space of bivariate degree $n - 1$ polynomials which is $\dim \Pi_{n-1}^2 = \frac{1}{2}(n+1)n$. The matrix K can be read off from the SVD decomposition of J_n [GvL96]. The polynomial reproduction is then guaranteed if the equation

$$SK = KX \tag{13}$$

has a matrix solution $X = (K^T K)^{-1} K^T SK$. If this is satisfied, we find the nth difference scheme S_n by (12).

For the analysis of our $\sqrt{3}$-subdivision scheme we let $\mathbf{V}$ be the 6-ring neighborhood of a vertex which consists of 127 vertices. Let S be the single-step $\sqrt{3}$-subdivision matrix, R be the back-rotation-by-permutation matrix and D_{10} the directional difference matrix. Although these matrices are quite large, they are very sparse and can be constructed quite easily (by a few lines of MatLab-code) due to their block-circulant structure.

From these matrices we compute $\widetilde{S} = RS^2$ and a second directional difference operator $D_{01} = R^2 D_{10} R^{-2}$. The two directional differences are combined to build the 3rd order jet-operator J_3 (cf. (10)). Here we use the 3rd differences since we want to prove C^2 continuity. From the singular value decomposition of J_3 we obtain the matrix K whose columns span the kernel of J_3 and the pseudo-inverse J_3^{-1}. The matrix K is then used to prove the quadratic precision of S (cf. (13)) and the pseudo-inverse yields the difference scheme $\widetilde{S}_3 = J_3 \widetilde{S} J_3^{-1}$. The contractivity of the 3rd order difference scheme finally follows from the numerical estimation $\|\widetilde{S}_3^2\| = \|J_3 \widetilde{S}^2 J_3^{-1}\| \leq 0.78 \times 3^{-4}$ which proves that the $\sqrt{3}$-subdivision scheme S generates C^2 surfaces for regular control meshes.

Extraordinary vertices

In the vicinity of the extraordinary vertices with valence $\neq 6$ we have to apply a different analysis technique. After the convergence in the regular mesh regions (which for subdivision meshes means "almost everywhere") has been shown, it is sufficient to analyse the behavior of the limit surface at the remaining isolated extraordinary *points*.

The intuition behind the sufficient convergence criteria by [Rei95, Zor97, Pra98] is that the representation of the local neighborhood $\mathbf{V}$ with respect to the eigenvector basis of the local subdivision matrix S corresponds to a type of Taylor-expansion of the limit surface at that extraordinary point. Hence, the eigenvectors ("eigen-functions") have to satisfy some regularity criteria and the leading eigenvalues have to guarantee an appropriate scaling of the tangential and higher order components of the expansion. Especially the conditions (5) have to be satisfied for all valences $n = 3, \ldots, n_{max}$.

When checking the eigenstructure of the subdivision matrix S we have to use a sufficiently large r-ring neighborhood $\mathbf{V}$ of the center vertex $\mathbf{p}$. In fact the neighborhood has to be large enough such that the regular part of it defines a complete surface ring around $\mathbf{p}$ by itself [Rei95]. In the case of $\sqrt{3}$-subdivision we hence have to use $r = 4$ rings around $\mathbf{p}$ (since 4 is the diameter of the subdivision basis function's support). This means we have to analyse a $(10n+1) \times (10n+1)$ matrix where n is $\mathbf{p}$'s valence.

Luckily the subdivision matrix S has a block circulant structure and it turns out that the leading eigenvalues of S are exactly the eigenvalues we found in (4). Since those eigenvalues satisfy (5) we conclude that the matrix S has the appropriate structure for C^1 convergence.

The exact condition on the eigenvectors and the injectivity of the corresponding *characteristic map* are quite difficult to check strictly. We therefore restrict ourselves to the numerical verification by sketching the iso-parameter lines of the characterisitc map in Fig. 17.

Piecewise Smooth Subdivision Surfaces with Normal Control

Henning Biermann*
New York University

Adi Levin†
Tel Aviv University

Denis Zorin‡
New York University

Abstract

In this paper we introduce improved rules for Catmull-Clark and Loop subdivision that overcome several problems with the original schemes, namely, lack of smoothness at extraordinary boundary vertices and folds near concave corners. In addition, our approach to rule modification allows the generation of surfaces with prescribed normals, both on the boundary and in the interior, which considerably improves control of the shape of surfaces.

CR Categories and Subject Descriptors: I.3.5 [**Computer Graphics**]: Computational Geometry and Object Modeling – Curve, surface, solid, and object representations; Boundary representations.

Additional Keywords: Subdivision surfaces, boundary control.

1 Introduction

Subdivision surfaces are rapidly gaining popularity in computer graphics. A number of commercial systems use subdivision as a surface representation: Alias|Wavefront's Maya, Pixar's Renderman, Nichimen's Mirai, and Micropace' Lightwave 3D, to name just a few. The greatest advantage of subdivision algorithms is that they efficiently generate smooth surfaces from arbitrary initial meshes. Subdivision algorithms are also attractive because they are conceptually simple and can be easily modified to create surface features without making major changes to the algorithm.

At the same time, one of the drawbacks of subdivision is a lack of precise definition of the schemes with guaranteed behavior for a sufficiently general type of control meshes. Anyone who tries to implement a subdivision scheme can observe that more often than not it is unclear how rules should be specified in certain cases (most commonly on boundaries and creases). Ad hoc solutions have to be used, which often have unexpected undesirable behavior. The lack of precise and complete definition makes it more difficult to exchange data between applications, reuse control meshes, and design new algorithms based on subdivision.

The difficulty in defining a reasonably complete set of subdivision rules is related to the fact that subdivision algorithms allow a large variety of data as input: an arbitrary polygonal or triangular mesh, possibly with boundary, marked edges, and vertices. Subdivision rules for the interior of a control mesh are well understood, while the boundary rules have received less attention. Boundary rules are quite important for a variety of reasons. The boundary of the surface, together with the contour lines, forms the visual outline.

---

*biermann@mrl.nyu.edu
†adilev@math.tau.ac.il
‡dzorin@mrl.nyu.edu

Often, only an approximate definition is required for the interior of the surface, whereas the boundary conditions may be significantly more restrictive. For example, it is often necessary to join several surfaces along their boundaries. Boundary subdivision rules lead to rules for sharp creases [8] and soft creases [3]. In addition to specifying the boundary or crease curves, it is often desirable to be able to specify tangent planes on the boundary; existing subdivision schemes do not allow to control tangent plane behavior.

The goal of this paper is to present two complete sets of subdivision rules for generating piecewise-smooth, C^1-continuous, almost everywhere C^2 subdivision surfaces, with tangent plane control. Our rules extend the well-known subdivision schemes of Catmull-Clark [2] and Loop [10]. The properties of our schemes were rigorously verified. We use a uniform approach to derive a set of rules, including new rules for concave corners, improved smooth boundary rules, new rules for tangent plane modification, and C^2 rules. While our approach is based on a number of known ideas, its advantage is that all desired features are handled in a unified framework.

Our approach to building a complete set of rules can be applied to any stationary subdivision scheme. In this paper, we focus on the Loop and Catmull-Clark subdivision schemes as schemes having the greatest practical importance. The code implementing our algorithms is available on the Web[1].

2 Previous Work

A number of subdivision schemes have been proposed since Catmull and Clark introduced subdivision surfaces in 1978 [2]. A detailed survey of subdivision can be found in [1].

Theoretical analysis of subdivision rules was performed in [18, 15, 6, 19, 24, 23]. Most of this work has focused on closed surfaces; while the general theory does not impose symmetry restrictions on the subdivision rules, almost all theoretical analysis of specific schemes relies on the rotational symmetry of the subdivision rules and applies only to the interior rules.

Subdivision rules for Doo-Sabin dual surfaces for the boundary were discussed by Doo [4] and Nasri [12, 13, 11], but only partial theoretical analysis was performed. Our work builds on the work of Hoppe et al. [8] and partially on the ideas of Nasri [14].

To the best of our knowledge, the boundary subdivision rules proposed in work [8] are the only ones that result in provably C^1-continuous surfaces (the analysis can be found in Schweitzer [19]). However, these rules suffer from two problems:

• The shape of the boundary of the generated surface depends on the control points in the interior;

• Only one rule for corners is defined, which works well for convex corners but does not work well for concave corners.

Standard Catmull-Clark rules, when applied to the boundary, suffer from the same problems.

Sederberg et al. [20] proposed a generalization of Catmull-Clark and Doo-Sabin subdivision rules that contains NURBS as a subset. For some applications it is important to include NURBS patches, however, the complexity of the algorithms is increased and the behavior of the surface near the extraordinary points becomes difficult

---

[1]http://www.mrl.nyu.edu/biermann/sub

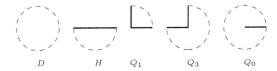

Figure 1: The charts for a surface with piecewise smooth boundary.

to analyze and predict. The smooth crease effects that are obtained by manipulating NURBS weights for subdivision surfaces can be achieved using an elegant technique proposed by DeRose et al. [3].

Our approach to C^2 subdivision is similar to the approach of [16].

Levin recently introduced a combined subdivision scheme which interpolates a network of curves [9]. There are two main distinctions between the present work and [9]. First, we are solving a different problem: rather than assuming that we are given a network of smooth curves that has to be interpolated, we assume only a discrete mesh with tags, which controls the behavior of our surface, but no interpolation is required. Second, Levin's combined subdivision schemes are an interesting new research direction; not much is known and understood about their behavior, especially on arbitrary meshes. In contrast, we focus on completing the subdivision toolbox with provably reliable tools.

Halstead et al. [7] describe a method of interpolating positions and normal direction on subdivision surfaces. However, this method involves the solution of a global system of equations, unlike our local subdivision rules.

3 Piecewise smooth surfaces

Piecewise smooth surfaces. Our goal is to design subdivision schemes for the class of *piecewise smooth surfaces*. This class includes common modeling primitives such as quadrilateral free-form patches with creases and corners. However, we exclude certain singularities (e.g., cone-like singularities and corners).

Here we give a somewhat informal description of piecewise-smooth surfaces, mathematical details will be presented elsewhere [25]. For simplicity, we consider only surfaces without self-intersection.

Recall that for a closed C^1-continuous surface in $\mathbf{R}^3$, each point has a neighborhood that can be smoothly deformed (that is, there is a C^1 map of maximal rank) into an open planar disk D. A surface with a *smooth boundary* can be described in a similar way, but neighborhoods of boundary points can be smoothly deformed into a half-disk H, with closed boundary (Figure 1). In order to allow *piecewise* smooth boundaries, we introduce two additional types of local charts: concave and convex corner charts, Q_3 and Q_1. We conclude that a C^1-continuous surface with piecewise smooth boundary looks locally like one of the domains D, H, Q_1, or Q_3. *Piecewise-smooth surfaces* are constructed out of surfaces with piecewise smooth boundaries joined together. If two surface patches have a common boundary, but different normal directions along the boundary, the resulting surface has a sharp crease.

We allow two adjacent smooth segments of a boundary to be joined, producing a crease ending in a *dart* (cf. [8]). For dart vertices an additional chart Q_0 is required; the surface near a dart can be deformed into this chart smoothly everywhere except at an open edge starting at the center of the disk.

It is important to observe that convex and concave corners, while being equivalent topologically, are not differentially equivalent. That is, there is no C^1 *nondegenerate* map from Q_1 to Q_3. Therefore, a single subdivision rule can not produce both types of corners [26]. In general, any complete set of subdivision rules should contain separate rules for all chart types. Most, if not all, known schemes miss some of the necessary rules.

4 Problems with common rules

In this section, we demonstrate some problems of existing subdivision rules. We will see that not all piecewise-smooth surfaces can be adequately represented in these schemes.

Concave corners. Concave corners often arise in modeling tasks (e.g., surfaces with holes). In an attempt to model such a corner with subdivision surfaces, one might arrange the control mesh in a concave configuration and expect the surface to approximate the configuration. However, the corner rules of popular subdivision schemes (e.g., [8]) can only generate convex corners. If the control mesh is in a concave configuration, the rules force the surface to approach the corner from the outer, convex, side, causing the surface to develop a fold (Figure 2).

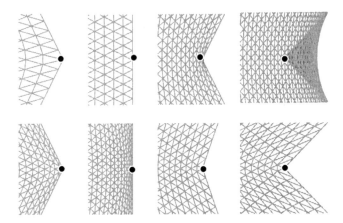

Figure 2: Upper row: behavior of a subdivision surface when rules of Hoppe et al. [8] are applied near a corner of the control mesh. As the corner of the control mesh is moved, the surface develops a fold. Lower row: our concave corner rules applied to the same mesh. The concave rules produce a small fold if applied to a convex control mesh configuration (not visible in the picture). For a concave configuration, our rule produces surfaces without folds.

Boundary rules. Hoppe et al. [8] observed that standard subdivision rules fail to produce smooth surfaces at extraordinary boundary vertices. They propose to change the subdivision scheme for the boundary curve in order to generate smooth surfaces. However, the boundary curve now depends on the interior of the control mesh. More specifically, the number of the interior vertices adjacent to each boundary vertex. This side effect is undesirable if one wants to join surfaces along their boundary curves: Two separate meshes might initially have the same boundary, but after subdivision a gap between the meshes can appear (Figure 6).

Moreover, even though the rules of [8] are formally smooth, they might produce undesirable sharp normal transitions if the control mesh is twisted (Figure 7).

5 Subdivision and eigenanalysis

In this section, we briefly state several facts of the theory of subdivision [1], which are helpful to understand the problems described above and our solutions.

Subdivision algorithms recursively refine a control mesh, recomputing vertex positions and inserting new vertices on edges (and possibly faces).

Our method of constructing subdivision rules is based on manipulating the eigenstructure of *subdivision matrices* associated with most common subdivision rules. This idea can be traced back to

[5]. Consider a vertex v, and let p be the vector of control points in a neighborhood of the vertex (Figure 3).

Let S be the matrix of subdivision coefficients relating the vector of control points p^m on subdivision level m to the vector of control points p^{m+1} on a similar neighborhood on the next subdivision level. Suppose the size of the matrix is N. Many properties of the subdivision scheme can be deduced from the eigenstructure of S. Let us decompose the vector of control points p with respect to the eigenbasis $\{x^i\}$, $i = 0..N-1$, of S, $p = \mathbf{a}_0 x^0 + \mathbf{a}_1 x^1 + \mathbf{a}_2 x^2 + \dots$ (it exists in the cases of importance to us).

Note that we decompose a vector of 3D points: the coefficients $\mathbf{a}_i$ are 3D vectors, which are componentwise multiplied with eigenvectors x^i.

We assume that the eigenvectors x^i are arranged in the order of non-increasing eigenvalues. For a convergent scheme, the first eigenvalue λ_0 is 1, and the eigenvector x_0 has all components equal to one; this is also required for invariance with respect to rigid and, more generally, arbitrary affine transformations.

Subdividing the surface m times means that the subdivision matrix is applied m times to the control point vector p.

$$S^m p = \lambda_0^m \mathbf{a}_0 x^0 + \lambda_1^m \mathbf{a}_1 x^1 + \lambda_2^m \mathbf{a}_2 x^2 + \cdots \quad \text{(Iterated Subdivision)}$$

If we further assume that λ_1 and λ_2 are real and equal, and $\lambda_1 = \lambda_2 = \lambda > |\lambda_3|$, we see from this formula that the vector of control points p^m can be approximated by $\mathbf{a}_0 x^0 + \lambda^m (\mathbf{a}_1 x^1 + \mathbf{a}_2 x^2)$; the rest of the terms decay to zero faster. If $\mathbf{a}_1 \times \mathbf{a}_2$ is not zero, then all of the control points p_i^m are close to the plane passing through $\mathbf{a}_0$ and spanned by vectors $\mathbf{a}_1$ and $\mathbf{a}_2$. As $m \to \infty$, the positions of all points converge to a_0.

This means that the limit position of the center vertex is $\mathbf{a}_0$; the tangent directions at this position are $\mathbf{a}_1$ and $\mathbf{a}_2$. We compute these values using the left eigenvectors of S (i.e., vectors l^i, satisfying $(l^i, x^i) = 1$ and $(l^i, x^j) = 0$ if $i \neq j$): $\mathbf{a}_i = (l^i, p)$.

These observations form the basis of our method: to ensure convergence to the tangent plane, we decrease the magnitudes of all eigenvalues except for those that correspond to the vectors $\mathbf{a}_1$, $\mathbf{a}_2$ spanning the desired tangent plane. We also modify the vectors $\mathbf{a}_1$ and $\mathbf{a}_2$ to change the direction of the normal. It should be noted that obtaining the correct spectrum of the subdivision matrix is not sufficient for smoothness analysis of subdivision; once our rules are formulated, we still have to prove that the resulting surfaces are C^1, using the characteristic map analysis [25].

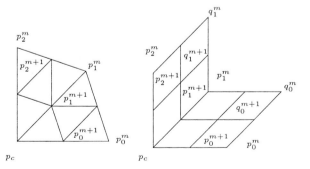

Figure 3: Neighborhoods of a vertex on different subdivision levels. The subdivision matrix relates the vector of control points p^m to the control points on the next level p^{m+1}. For a neighborhood of k triangles $p^m = \{p_c^m, p_0^m \dots p_{k-1}^m\}$, for k quadrilaterals $p^m = \{p_c^m, p_0^m \dots p_{k-1}^m, q_0^m \dots q_{k-1}^m\}$

6 Algorithm

6.1 Tagged meshes

Before describing our set of subdivision rules, we start with the description of the tagged meshes which our algorithms accept as input. We use these meshes to represent piecewise-smooth surfaces: edges and vertices of the mesh can be tagged to generate the singularities described in Section 3.

The complete list of tags is as follows. Edges can be tagged as *crease edges*. A vertex with incident crease edges receives one of the following tags:

- *crease vertex:* joins exactly two incident crease edges smoothly.
- *corner vertex:* connects two or more creases in a corner (convex or concave).
- *dart vertex:* causes the crease to blend smoothly into the surface.

We require that all edges on the boundary of the mesh are tagged as crease edges. Boundary vertices are tagged as corner or crease vertices.

Crease edges divide the mesh into separate patches, several of which can meet in a corner vertex. At a corner vertex, the creases meeting at that vertex separate the ring of triangles around the vertex into sectors. We label each sector of the mesh as *convex sector* or *concave sector* indicating how the surface should approach the corner.

The only restriction that we place on sector tags is that we require concave sectors to consist of at least two faces. An example of a tagged mesh is given in Figure 4.

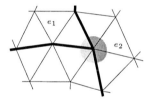

Figure 4: Crease edges meeting in a corner with two convex (light grey) and one concave (dark grey) sectors. Our subdivision scheme modifies the rules for edges incident to crease vertices (e.g., e_1) and corners (e.g. e_2).

In our implementation, the user applies the tags interactively, and the user interface prohibits an inconsistently tagged mesh (for example, there cannot be a corner vertex with some sector untagged). Also, the user can specify normal directions and *flatness parameters* for untagged vertices, crease vertices, and for each sector at a corner vertex. The flatness parameter determines how quickly the surface approaches the tangent plane in the neighborhood of a control point. This parameter is essential to our concave corner rules. Additionally, it improves the user control over the surface, for example, one can flatten a twist in the mesh (as shown in Figure 7). It is important to note however, that while manipulating these parameters is possible, it is not necessary: we provide default values reasonable for most situations (Section 6.2).

6.2 Subdivision rules

We describe our sets of rules for the triangular and quadrilateral schemes in parallel, as they are structurally very similar.

Our algorithm consists out of two stages, which, if desired, can be merged, but are conceptually easier to understand separately.

The first stage is a single iteration over the mesh during which we refine the position of existing vertices (vertex points) and insert new vertices on edges (edge points). For the quadrilateral scheme, we also need to insert vertices in the centers of faces (face points). The first stage is similar to one subdivision step of standard algorithms, but the weights that we use are somewhat different. In the following we refer to the rules of Loop and Catmull-Clark as standard rules.

Vertex points. We apply the standard vertex rules to reposition untagged vertices and dart vertices. The new control point at a vertex is the weighted average of the control points in its neighborhood.

If a vertex has k adjacent polygons, then its new position is a combination of the old position with weight $5/8$ and of the sum all surrounding control points with weight $3/8k$, for $k \neq 3$. In case $k = 3$ we use a special set of coefficients with the weight of the central vertex equal to $7/16$ [22]. For the quadrilateral scheme, the center vertex has weight $1 - \beta_1 - \beta_2$, while all adjacent vertices have weight β_1/k; the remaining vertices in the ring receive weight β_2/k with $\beta_1 = 3/(2k)$ and $\beta_2 = 1/(4k)$.

A crease vertex is refined as the average of its old position with weight $3/4$ and the two adjacent crease vertices with weight $1/8$ each. Corner vertices are interpolated.

Face points. For the quadrilateral scheme we insert a vertex at the centroid of each face; only one rule is necessary.

Edge points. This is the most complicated case. We choose the rule for an edge point depending on the tag of the edge and the tags of adjacent vertices and sectors. In the absence of tags, we apply the standard edge rules. The averaging masks are given in Figure 5.

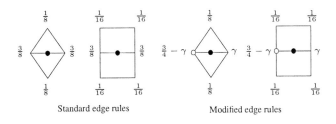

Standard edge rules   Modified edge rules

Figure 5: Edge rules for triangular and quadrilateral schemes. These rules apply to untagged edges. When both endpoints are untagged, we use standard rules. In case of a tagged endpoint we modify the rule such that the tagged endpoint (marked with a circle) receives coefficient $3/4 - \gamma$.

We insert a new vertex on a crease edge as the average of the two adjacent vertices.

The remaining case of an untagged edge e adjacent to a tagged vertex v is illustrated in Figure 4. We modify the standard edge rule in the following way: we parameterize the rule by θ_k, which depends on the adjacent vertex tag and sector tag. Let the vertices be labeled as in Figure 3, and let the position of the tagged endpoint be p_c^m, the other endpoint is p_i^m. We insert a vertex on the edge at position p_i^{m+1}. The edge rule for the triangular scheme is

$$p_i^{m+1} = (3/4 - \gamma) p_c^m + \gamma p_i^m + 1/8 \left(p_{i-1}^m + p_{i+1}^m \right).$$

We use a similar rule for the quadrilateral case:

$$p_i^{m+1} = (3/4 - \gamma) p_c^m + \gamma p_i^m + 1/16 \left(p_{i-1}^m + p_{i+1}^m + q_{i-1}^m + q_i^m \right).$$

The subdivision masks are illustrated in Figure 5. In each case γ is given in terms of parameter θ_k:

$$\gamma(\theta_k) = 1/2 - 1/4 \cos \theta_k \quad \text{(triangular scheme)}$$
$$\gamma(\theta_k) = 3/8 - 1/4 \cos \theta_k \quad \text{(quadrilateral scheme)}.$$

For a dart vertex v, we use $\theta_k = 2\pi/k$, where k is the total number of polygons adjacent to v. If v is a crease vertex, we use $\theta_k = \pi/k$, where k is the number of polygons adjacent to v in the sector of e.

At a corner vertex v we differentiate whether e is in a convex or concave sector. For a convex corner we use $\theta_k = \alpha/k$, where α is the angle between the two crease edges spanning the sector (k as above), for concave corners $\theta_k = (2\pi - \alpha)/k$.

6.3 Flatness and normal modification

The second stage of the algorithm is always applied at concave corner vertices and vertices with prescribed normals. It can be also applied at other boundary and interior vertices when it is desirable to increase flatness near a vertex or achieve C^2-continuity.

There are two slightly different types of position modifications performed at this stage: normal and flatness modification. Whenever we compute a vertex position in the neighborhood of a vertex subject to normal or flatness modification we compute the position using the rules above and modify it in a second step. The required eigenvectors for these modifications are listed in the appendix A.

Flatness modification. We observe that we can control how quickly the control points in a neighborhood converge towards the tangent plane. The equation for iterated subdivision suggests to accelerate the convergence by reducing eigenvalues λ_i, $i = 3 \ldots N - 1$. We introduce a *flatness parameter* s and modify the subdivision rule to scale all eigenvalues except λ_0 and $\lambda = \lambda_1 = \lambda_2$ by factor $1 - s$. The vector of control points p after subdivision in a neighborhood of a point is modified as follows:

$$p^{\text{new}} = (1 - s) p + s \left(\mathbf{a}_0 x^0 + \mathbf{a}_1 x^1 + \mathbf{a}_2 x^2 \right),$$

where $\mathbf{a}_i = (l^i, p)$, and $0 \leq s \leq 1$. Geometrically, the modified rule blends between control point positions before flatness modification and certain points in the tangent plane, which are typically close to the projection of the original control point. The limit position $\mathbf{a}_0$ of the center vertex remains unchanged.

The flatness modification is always applied at concave corner vertices; the default values for the parameter s is $s = 1 - 1/(2 + \cos \theta_k - \cos k\theta_k)$, which ensures that the surface is C^1 in this case. In other cases, s can be taken to be 0 by default.

C^2-**modification.** The flatness modification can be also used to make the subdivision scheme C^2, similar to the flat spot modifications [16]. It is known from the theory of subdivision that under certain conditions a scheme which is C^2 away from extraordinary vertices, generates surfaces which are C^2 at extraordinary vertices if all eigenvalues excluding 1 and λ are less than the squared subdominant eigenvalue. This can be easily achieved using flatness modification: s is taken to be less than $|\lambda|^2 / \max_{i>3} |\lambda_i|$. In general, values of s close to this quantity produce surfaces of better shape, but with greater curvature oscillations. It is worth noting that this approach has a fundamental problem: the resulting surface has zero curvature at the extraordinary vertex; the results of [17] indicate that for schemes with small support this is inevitable.

Normal modification. We introduce a similar modification, which allows one to interpolate given tangent and normal position at a vertex v. As above, we modify the control point positions in v's neighborhood after each subdivision step. In this case, the parameter t blends between the unmodified positions and positions in the prescribed tangent plane, while the limit position $\mathbf{a}_0$ of v remains unchanged.

For a prescribed tangent vector pair $\mathbf{a}_1'$ and $\mathbf{a}_2'$, we modify

$$p^{\text{new}} = p + t \left(\left(\mathbf{a}_1' - \mathbf{a}_1 \right) x^1 + \left(\mathbf{a}_2' - \mathbf{a}_2 \right) x^2 \right);$$

where $\mathbf{a}_i = (l^i, p)$ and $0 \leq t \leq 1$. In case of a prescribed normal direction n we compute the tangent vectors as $\mathbf{a}_i' = \mathbf{a}_i - (\mathbf{a}_i, n)n$.

We observe that the subdivision rules are no longer applied to each coordinate of the control points separately; rather, the whole 3D vector is required. We can think of this as a generalized form of subdivision, where the coefficients are matrices rather than scalars. Thus, a control point position p_i^{m+1} in a neighborhood with prescribed normal n on level $m + 1$ can be explicitly expressed as

$$p_i^{m+1} = \sum_j p_j^m \left(s_{ij}\mathbf{Id} - t \left(\sum_k x_i^1 l_k^1 s_{kj} + x_i^2 l_k^2 s_{kj} \right) n^T n \right)$$

where s_{ij} are entries of the original subdivision matrix S and $\mathbf{Id}$ the 3×3 identity matrix. It should be noted that our analysis in [25] applies only to the case $t = 1$, which we use as a default value; the analysis of the general case is still an open question.

7   Discussion

We have presented a number of simple extensions to the standard Catmull-Clark and Loop subdivision schemes that resolve some problems with existing rules.

Our rules are designed to coincide with cubic endpoint interpolating B-splines rules along a crease. As a consequence, the generated crease curves depend only on the crease control points. Therefore, it is possible to modify the interior of a surface patch without any effect on the bounding crease curves; moreover, one can join piecewise-smooth surfaces without gaps and combine them with other surface representations supporting B-spline boundaries.

A complete C^1-continuity analysis of our subdivision rules is outside of the scope of this paper, and will be given elsewhere [25]. Here we describe only the intuition behind our construction.

We can understand the behavior of the surface in a neighborhood of a corner or crease vertex from the eigenstructure of the corresponding subdivision matrix.

If we apply the standard rules in the neighborhood of a crease vertex, the eigenvalue $1/2$ corresponding to the tangent vector of the crease is not subdominant. As a result, the surface contracts at a different rate from the crease, leading to a degenerate configuration without tangent plane (Figure 2). The situation for corner vertices is similar as both tangent vectors are determined from crease curve segments with eigenvalue $1/2$.

Our subdivision rules ensure that $1/2$ is the subdominant eigenvalue in both cases. It it not difficult to see that $1/2$ is an eigenvalue: Consider a planar fan of k congruent polygons, where each polygon contributes an angle θ_k to the total angle $\theta = k\theta_k$. If we treat this configuration as a crease or corner neighborhood and apply our modified subdivision rules, then the center vertex does not change its position, and for each adjacent edge we insert a vertex at exactly the midpoint. Thus, the configuration is scaled down by a factor of $1/2$, i.e., $1/2$ is an eigenvalue.

It turns out that $\lambda = 1/2$ is indeed subdominant for crease vertices and convex corners. For concave corners we ensure subdominance by reducing all other eigenvalues (except $\lambda_0 = 1$) using the flatness modification with parameter s satisfying $(1 - s)(2 + \cos\theta_k - \cos k\theta_k) < 2$. Figure 10 demonstrates how the flatness modification pulls the neighborhood of a convex corner into its tangent plane.

Our implementation of the rules is available on the Web. We have also developed explicit evaluation rules for our schemes, extending [21].

8   Results and Conclusions

Surfaces with creases and corners of various types are illustrated in Figures 11 and 12(b). All the surfaces in Figure 11 are generated from the same control mesh by applying different tags. Note how convex and concave sectors meet along the crease of the torus.

Figures 8 and 9 demonstrate normal interpolation for boundary, corner and interior vertices; directions of normals are adjusted to obtain desired shapes without modifying the control mesh. Other applications are possible: we have applied normal modification to create certain surface characteristics: randomly perturbing the top-level normals produces a wavy doughnut from a torus-like control mesh; perturbing normals on the first subdivision levels creates a noisy doughnut (Figure 12(c) and (d)).

Conclusions and future work. We have presented a simple modification of the two most popular subdivision schemes that improves the behavior of the generated surfaces on boundary and creases and provides additional controls for surface modeling.

Even though the class of surfaces considered in this paper is quite general, we have excluded many types of surface singularities. Future work might explore which other singularities are useful for modeling purpose and how to construct subdivision rules to create such features.

9   Acknowledgments

We are greatly indebted to Peter Schröder for his support and suggestions, and for trying out the schemes and discovering numerous hard-to find typos in the formulas. This work has its origin in discussions with Tom Duchamp. We would like to thank the anonymous reviewers for their comments.

A portion of this work was supported by NSF award ACI-9978147.

References

[1] Subdivision for modeling and animation. SIGGRAPH 2000 Course Notes.

[2] Ed Catmull and James Clark. Recursively generated B-spline surfaces on arbitrary topological meshes. *Computer Aided Design*, 10(6):350–355, 1978.

[3] Tony DeRose, Michael Kass, and Tien Truong. Subdivision surfaces in character animation. In Michael Cohen, editor, *SIGGRAPH 98 Conference Proceedings*, Annual Conference Series, pages 85–94. ACM SIGGRAPH, Addison Wesley, July 1998. ISBN 0-89791-999-8.

[4] D. Doo. A subdivision algorithm for smoothing down irregularly shaped polyhedrons. In *Proceedings on Interactive Techniques in Computer Aided Design*, pages 157–165, Bologna, 1978.

[5] D. Doo and M. Sabin. Analysis of the behaviour of recursive division surfaces near extraordinary points. *Computer Aided Design*, 10(6):356–360, 1978.

[6] Ayman Habib and Joe Warren. Edge and vertex insertion for a class of C^1 subdivision surfaces. *Computer Aided Geometric Design*, 16(4):223–247, 1999.

[7] Mark Halstead, Michael Kass, and Tony DeRose. Efficient, fair interpolation using Catmull-Clark surfaces. In *Computer Graphics Proceedings*, Annual Conference Series, pages 35–44. ACM Siggraph, 1993.

[8] Hugues Hoppe, Tony DeRose, Tom Duchamp, Mark Halstead, Huber Jin, John McDonald, Jean Schweitzer, and Werner Stuetzle. Piecewise smooth surface reconsruction. In *Computer Graphics Proceedings*, Annual Conference Series, pages 295–302. ACM Siggraph, 1994.

[9] Adi Levin. Interpolating nets of curves by smooth subdivision surfaces. In Alyn Rockwood, editor, *SIGGRAPH 99 Conference Proceedings*, Annual Conference Series, pages 57–64. Addison Wesley, 1999.

[10] Charles Loop. Smooth subdivision surfaces based on triangles. Master's thesis, University of Utah, Department of Mathematics, 1987.

[11] A. Nasri. Interpolation of open B-spline curves by recursive subdivision surfaces. In Tim Goodman and Ralph Martin, editors, *Mathematics of Surfaces VII*, pages 173 –188. Institute of mathematics and its applications, Information Geometers, 1997.

[12] Ahmad H. Nasri. Polyhedral subdivision methods for free-form surfaces. *ACM Transactions on Graphics*, 6(1):29–73, January 1987.

[13] Ahmad H. Nasri. Boundary corner control in recursive subdivision surfaces. *Computer Aided Design*, 23(6):405–410, 1991.

[14] Ahmad H. Nasri. Surface interpolation on irregular networks with normal conditions. *Computer Aided Geometric Design*, 8:89–96, 1991.

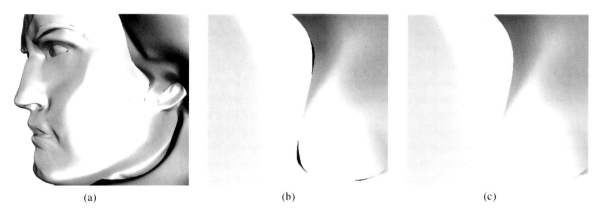

Figure 6: Subdivision on meshes with boundaries: Beethoven's face and hair are modeled as separate meshes with identical boundaries. (a) and (b): the rules of [8] result in a gap between the surfaces due to extraordinary vertices. (b) A close-up on the gaps at the ear. (c) With our rules no gap is created.

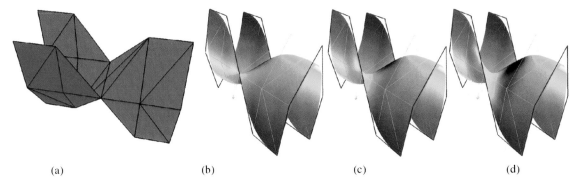

Figure 7: (a) Control mesh with a twist on the boundary. (b) Normal varies rapidly near the point although the surface is formally smooth: there is a single bright spot on the front-facing boundary. (c), (d) Our algorithm reduces the variation: the highlights become larger.

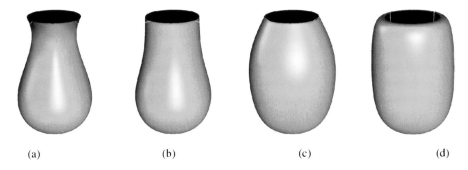

Figure 8: Normal interpolation for quadrilateral subdivision. Prescribed directions: (a) tilted downwards, (b) horizontal, (c) no modication, (d) vertical.

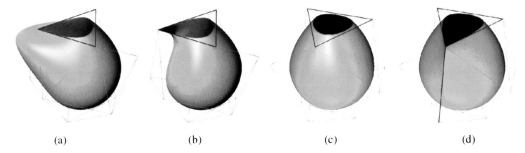

Figure 9: Features: (a) concave corner, (b) convex corner, (c) smooth crease, (d) corner with two convex sectors.

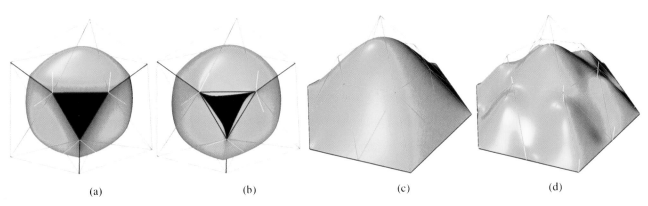

Figure 10: Normal interpolation. (a) Surface with convex corners. (b) Prescribed directions: at each corner we tilt the normal for one surface sector slightly inwards. (c) Smooth surface. (d) Same control mesh but all normals vertical.

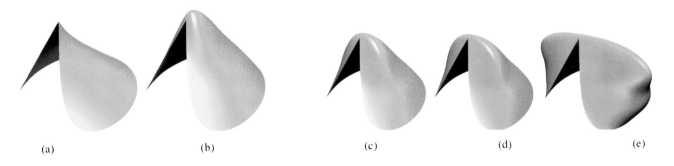

Figure 11: Concave corner rules. (a) A corner without flatness modication. (b) Flatness modication lifts the surface into its tangent plane. (c-e) The corner shape for different values of θ_k.

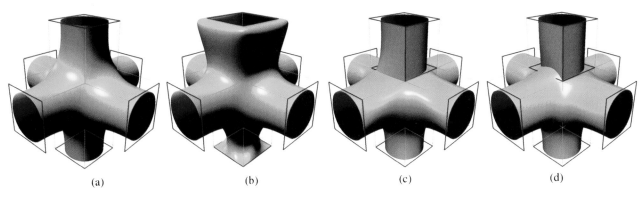

Figure 12: Surface manipulation with corners. (a) Smooth boundary curves. (b) Concave corners on top, convex corners on bottom. (c) Corners with convex and concave sectors. (d) Creases and corners as for (c) but with prescribed normal direction on concave sectors.

Figure 13: Manipulating a torus. (a) The original surface. (b) A surface with creases and convex/concave corners. (c) Wavy torus: we deform the torus by randomly perturbing normals of the control mesh. (d) Noisy torus: we perturb the normals on the first four subdivision levels.

[15] Jörg Peters and Ulrich Reif. Analysis of algorithms generalizing B-spline subdivision. *SIAM Journal on Numerical Analysis*, 35(2):728–748 (electronic), 1998.

[16] H. Prautzsch and G. Umlauf. A G^2-subdivision algorithm. In *Geometric modelling (Dagstuhl, 1996)*, pages 217–224. Springer, Vienna, 1998.

[17] Hartmut Prautzsch and Ulrich Reif. Degree estimates for C^k-piecewise polynomial subdivision surfaces. *Adv. Comput. Math.*, 10(2):209–217, 1999.

[18] Ulrich Reif. A unified approach to subdivision algorithms near extraordinary points. *Computer Aided Geometric Design*, 12:153–174, 1995.

[19] J. E. Schweitzer. *Analysis and Application of Subdivision Surfaces.* PhD thesis, University of Washington, Seattle, 1996.

[20] Thomas W. Sederberg, Jianmin Zheng, David Sewell, and Malcolm Sabin. Nonuniform recursive subdivision surfaces. In Michael Cohen, editor, *SIGGRAPH 98 Conference Proceedings*, Annual Conference Series, pages 387–394. ACM SIGGRAPH, Addison Wesley, July 1998. ISBN 0-89791-999-8.

[21] Jos Stam. Exact evaluation of Catmull-Clark subdivision surfaces at arbitrary parameter values. In *SIGGRAPH 98 Converence Proceedings*, Annual Conference Series, pages 395–404. Addison Wesley.

[22] Joe Warren. Subdivision methods for geometric design. Unpublished manuscript, November 1995.

[23] Denis Zorin. A method for analysis of C^1-continuity of subdivision surfaces. 1998. submitted to SIAM Jornal of Numerical Analysis.

[24] Denis Zorin. Smoothness of subdivision on irregular meshes. *Constructive Approximation*, 16(3), 2000.

[25] Denis Zorin, Tom Duchamp, and H. Biermann. Smoothness of subdivision surfaces on the boundary. Technical report, New York University, Dept. of Computer Scinece, 2000.

[26] Denis N. Zorin. *Subdivision and Multiresolution Surface Representations.* PhD thesis, Caltech, Pasadena, California, 1997.

A Coefficients for left and right subdominant eigenvectors

Here we list the left and right eigenvectors necessary for the subdivision rules described above. Recall that the eigenvector coefficients are applied to a control points of a polygon ring/fan. A subscript c denotes the coefficient corresponding to the center vertex. For the quadrilateral scheme, we mark edgepoint coefficients with subscript p and facepoint coefficients with q.

We define the *degree* of a vertex as the number of polygons asjacent to this vertex; note that this definition is different from the standard one (the number of incident edges) for boundary vertices. The *crease degree* is the number of polygons adjacent to a crease or corner vertex with respect to a specific sector.

Also, recall that dominant right eigenvector x^0 is the vector consisting of ones.

Loop scheme.

- Interior vertex of degree k. In all cases i is in the range $0 \ldots k-1$, and $\theta_k = 2\pi/k$.

$$l_c^0 = \frac{1}{1 + (8k/3)\beta}, \quad l_i^0 = \frac{(8/3)\beta}{1 + (8k/3)\beta}$$

$$x_c^1 = x_c^2 = l_c^1 = l_c^2 = 0$$

$$x_i^1 = \sin i\theta_k, \quad x_i^2 = \cos i\theta_k, \quad l_i^1 = \frac{2}{k}\sin i\theta_k, \quad l_i^2 = \frac{2}{k}\cos i\theta_k$$

- Smooth crease vertex of crease degree k. Let $\theta_k = \pi/k$; then

$$l_c^0 = 2/3, \quad l_1^0 = l_k^0 = 1/6, \quad l_i^0 = 0, \quad i = 1 \ldots k-1$$

For $k = 1$,

$$x_c^1 = -1/3,\ x_1^1 = 2/3,\ x_2^1 = 2/3, \quad x_c^2 = 0,\ x_1^2 = 1,\ x_2^2 = -1$$

$$l_c^1 = -1,\ l_1^1 = 1/2,\ l_2^1 = 1/2, \quad l_c^2 = 0,\ l_1^2 = 1/2,\ l_2^2 = -1/2;$$

otherwise $x_c^1 = x_c^2 = l_c^1 = 0$,

$$x_i^1 = \sin i\theta_k, \quad x_i^2 = \cos i\theta_k, \quad i = 0 \ldots k$$

$$l_0^1 = 1/2, \quad l_k^1 = -1/2, \quad l_i^1 = 0, \quad i = 1 \ldots k$$

$$l_c^2 = -\frac{2}{k}\left(\left(\frac{2}{3} - a\right)\sigma_1 - b\sigma_3\right)$$

$$l_0^2 = l_k^2 = -\frac{2}{k}\left(\left(\frac{a}{2} + \frac{1}{6}\right)\sigma_1 + \frac{1}{2}b\sigma_3\right)$$

$$l_i^2 = \frac{2}{k}\sin i\theta_k, \quad i = 1 \ldots k-1$$

where

$$a = \frac{\frac{1}{4}(1 + \cos\theta_k)}{3(\frac{1}{2} - \frac{1}{4}\cos\theta_k)} \qquad b = \frac{\frac{2}{3} - a}{\cos\frac{k\zeta}{2}}$$

$$\sigma_1 = \frac{\sin\theta_k}{1 - \cos\theta_k} \qquad \sigma_3 = \frac{\cos\frac{k\zeta}{2}\sin\theta_k}{\cos\zeta - \cos\theta_k}$$

$$\zeta = \arccos(\cos\theta_k - 1)$$

- Convex/concave corner vertex of crease degree k with parameter θ_k. Let $\theta = k\theta_k$.

$$l_c^0 = 1, \quad l_i^0 = 0, \quad i = 0 \ldots k$$

$$x_c^1 = x_c^2 = 0, \quad x_i^1 = \frac{\sin i\theta_k}{\sin\theta}, \quad x_i^2 = \frac{\sin(k-i)\theta_k}{\sin\theta}, \quad i = 0 \ldots k$$

$$l_c^1 = -1, \quad l_1^1 = 1, \quad l_i^1 = 0, \quad i = 0 \ldots k-1$$

$$l_c^2 = -1, \quad l_0^2 = 1, \quad l_i^2 = 0, \quad i = 1 \ldots k$$

Catmull-Clark scheme.

- Interior vertex of degree k. Let $\theta_k = 2\pi/k$ and i from 0 to $k-1$.

$$l_c^0 = \frac{k}{k+5}, \quad l_{pi}^0 = \frac{4}{k(k+5)}, \quad l_{qi}^0 = \frac{1}{k(k+5)}$$

$$x_c^1 = x_c^2 = l_c^1 = l_c^2 = 0$$

$$x_{pi}^1 = \frac{1}{\sigma}\sin i\theta_k \quad x_{pi}^2 = \frac{1}{\sigma}\cos i\theta_k$$

$$x_{qi}^1 = \frac{\sin i\theta_k + \sin(i+1)\theta_k}{\sigma(4\lambda - 1)}, \quad x_{qi}^2 = \frac{\cos i\theta_k + \cos(i+1)\theta_k}{\sigma(4\lambda - 1)}$$

$$l_{pi}^1 = 4\sin i\theta_k \quad l_{pi}^2 = 4\cos i\theta_k$$

$$l_{qi}^1 = \frac{\sin i\theta_k + \sin(i+1)\theta_k}{4\lambda - 1}, \quad l_{qi}^2 = \frac{\cos i\theta_k + \cos(i+1)\theta_k}{4\lambda - 1}$$

where $\lambda = 5/16 + 1/16\left(\cos\theta_k + \cos\theta_k/2\sqrt{9 + \cos 2\theta_k}\right)$, and $\sigma = k(2 + \frac{1 + \cos\theta_k}{(4\lambda - 1)^2})$.

- Smooth crease vertex of crease degree k. Let $\theta_k = \pi/k$.

$$l_c^0 = 2/3, \ l_{p1}^0 = l_{pk}^0 = 1/6, \ l_{q0}^0 = l_{qi}^0 = l_{pi}^0 = 0, \ i = 1 \ldots k-1$$

For $k = 1$,

$$x_c^1 = 1/18, \quad x_{p0}^1 = -2/18, \quad x_{p1}^1 = -2/18, \quad x_{q0}^1 = -5/18$$
$$x_c^2 = 0, \quad x_{p0}^2 = -1/2, \quad x_{p1}^2 = 1/2, \quad x_{q0}^2 = 0$$
$$l_c^1 = 6, \quad l_{p0}^1 = -3, \quad l_{p1}^1 = -3, \quad l_{q0}^1 = 0$$
$$l_c^2 = 0, \quad l_{p0}^2 = -1, \quad l_{p1}^2 = 1, \quad l_{q0}^2 = 0;$$

otherwise $l_c^2 = x_c^1 = x_c^2 = 0$, and

$$x_{pi}^1 = \sin i\theta_k, \quad x_{pi}^2 = \cos i\theta_k, \quad i = 0 \ldots k$$

$$x_{qi}^1 = \sin i\theta_k + \sin(i+1)\theta_k, \quad i = 0 \ldots k-1$$

$$x_{qi}^2 = \cos i\theta_k + \cos(i+1)\theta_k, \quad i = 0 \ldots k-1$$

$$l_{p0}^2 = 1/2, \quad l_{pk}^2 = -1/2, \quad l_{q0}^2 = l_{qi}^2 = l_{pi}^2 = 0, \quad i = 1 \ldots k-1$$

$$l_c^1 = 4R(\cos\theta_k - 1), \quad l_{p0}^1 = l_{pk}^1 = -R(1 + 2\cos\theta_k)$$

$$l_{pi}^1 = \frac{4\sin i\theta_k}{(3 + \cos\theta_k)k}, \quad i = 1 \ldots k-1$$

$$l_{qi}^1 = \frac{4(\sin i\theta_k + \sin(i+1)\theta_k)}{(3 + \cos\theta_k)k}, \quad i = 0 \ldots k-1$$

where $R = \frac{\cos\theta_k + 1}{k\sin\theta_k(3 + \cos\theta_k)}$.

- Convex/concave corner vertex of crease degree k with parameter θ_k. Let $\theta = k\theta_k$. Left eigenvectors are the same as for Loop with zeroes everywhere except l_c, l_{p0} and l_{pk}.

$$x_{pi}^1 = \frac{\sin i\theta_k}{\sin\theta}, \quad x_{pi}^2 = \frac{\sin(k-i)\theta_k}{\sin\theta}, \quad i = 0 \ldots k$$

$$x_{qi}^1 = \frac{\sin i\theta_k + \sin(i+1)\theta_k}{\sin\theta}, \quad i = 0 \ldots k-1$$

$$x_{qi}^2 = \frac{\sin(k-i)\theta_k + \sin(k-i-1)\theta_k}{\sin\theta}, \quad i = 0 \ldots k-1$$

Environment Matting Extensions:
Towards Higher Accuracy and Real-Time Capture

Yung-Yu Chuang[1]   Douglas E. Zongker[1]   Joel Hindorff[1]   Brian Curless[1]   David H. Salesin[1,2]   Richard Szeliski[2]

[1]University of Washington   [2]Microsoft Research

Abstract

Environment matting is a generalization of traditional bluescreen matting. By photographing an object in front of a sequence of structured light backdrops, a set of approximate light-transport paths through the object can be computed. The original environment matting research chose a middle ground—using a moderate number of photographs to produce results that were reasonably accurate for many objects. In this work, we extend the technique in two opposite directions: recovering a more accurate model at the expense of using additional structured light backdrops, and obtaining a simplified matte using just a single backdrop. The first extension allows for the capture of complex and subtle interactions of light with objects, while the second allows for video capture of colorless objects in motion.

CR Categories: I.2.10 [**Artificial Intelligence**]: Vision and Scene Understanding — modeling and recovery of physical attributes; I.3.3 [**Computer Graphics**]: Picture/Image Generation — display algorithms; I.3.7 [**Computer Graphics**]: Three-Dimensional Graphics and Realism — color, shading, shadowing, and texture

Keywords: Alpha channel, augmented reality, blue-screen matting, blue spill, clip art, colored transparency, environment map, environment matte, image-based rendering, real-time capture, reflection, refraction.

1 Introduction

Conventional *matting* consists of filming a foreground object against a known background and determining the foreground color and opacity at each image pixel. Conventional *image compositing* simply layers the foreground over an arbitrary background using the opacity to control the relative contributions at each pixel. *Environment matting* and *compositing* generalize the conventional methods by modeling arbitrary transport paths from the background through the foreground object to the camera. After making a set of approximations, Zongker *et al.* [19] demonstrate the ability to capture and render the effects of reflection, refraction, scatter, and colored filtering of light from a background. These effects, none of which are modeled with conventional matting and compositing, make a dramatic contribution to the visual realism of the final image.

The original environment matting method employs a sequence of structured backdrops to estimate mappings from the background through the foreground object. These backdrops consist of a hierarchy of finer and finer horizontal and vertical square-wave stripes from which the matte can be extracted with $O(\log k)$ images for

Figure 1 Sample composite images constructed with the techniques of this paper: slow but accurate on the left, and a more restricted example acquired at video rates on the right.

an $k \times k$ pixel grid. This choice of backdrops is inspired by a related technique developed for 3D range scanning [1]. In practice, however, this approach has a number of shortcomings.

The previous approach of Zongker *et al.* assumes, first of all, that each image pixel collects light from a single region of the background, augmented with an alpha component for straight-through partial coverage. This assumption fails when we consider the effects of simultaneous reflection and refraction at a dielectric. Second, the method is tuned to capturing highly specular interactions, but breaks down in the presence of surfaces that are even moderately rough. Third, the mappings that are captured assume axis-aligned filtering of background pixels. At pixels where this assumption does not hold, this axis alignment results in excessive blurring and degrades the quality of the final composite. Fourth, the original method accounts for colored filtering of light, but does not account for the effects of dispersion, which necessitate different mappings per color channel and give rise to prismatic rainbowing effects. Finally, the number of images required is typically about 20 per matte, and thus the technique does not lend itself to real-time acquisition.

In this paper, we address each of these limitations. Again taking inspiration from the 3D range-scanning literature, we follow two distinct paths. In the first approach, the background consists of a single stripe swept over time in the vertical, horizontal, and two diagonal directions. In each case, the stripe orientation is perpendicular to the sweeping direction. By combining sweeps with stripes of varying widths and intensity profiles, we demonstrate an efficient method for extracting the highest quality environment mattes to date. This method, however, requires $O(k)$ images and is even less suitable for real-time acquisition than the previous method.

Our second approach utilizes a *single* background image consisting of a color ramp. Through careful simplification of the governing equations, we demonstrate a method capable of extracting pure specular refractive and reflective mappings through a moving, deforming colorless object, such as water pouring into a glass. This technique is real-time in the sense that the data it requires can be collected in real-time, though the analysis and extraction of the matte must still be performed offline.

1.1 Related work

Environment matting [19] builds upon and substantially extends research and practice in blue screen matting. Pioneered by Vlahos [15], conventional (and commercial) blue screen matting relies on a single-color background sufficiently different from the foreground objects to extract an alpha and foreground color at each pixel. Smith and Blinn [15] use two backdrops to lift restrictions on the color of foreground objects. Neither of these techniques models transport paths beyond scalar (non-color) attenuation and partial pixel coverage. In addition, the Smith and Blinn technique does not easily extend to real-time capture, given the two-frame requirement. Our real-time method for capturing environment mattes is actually similar in spirit to the Vlahos work in that we must place constraints on the object and lighting in order to achieve our results.

The structured-light range-scanning literature suggests many possible ways to capture spatially varying properties of an object [1]. We should note that the end goals are substantially simpler in the range-scanning case. Range scanners attempt to recover just a handful of parameters per pixel: primarily, depth and reflectance. Environment-matting procedures, on the other hand, generally need to recover a continuous, wavelength-dependent mapping from a background to the image plane. Even with the approximations described in Section 3, we must estimate at least 21 parameters per pixel, and sometimes many more.

Despite the dissimilarities, the range-scanning *illumination patterns* do inspire a number of techniques for environment matting.

The most "brute force" range-scanning method is to sweep a beam of light over an object in a raster pattern. Such an approach, while $O(k^2)$ in time since each range-image pixel is acquired sequentially, is actually practical for triangulation and imaging radar systems [1], since the reflected light seen by the sensor is known to have followed a straight line from the object. As a result, objects can be imaged with fast 1D (triangulation) or 0D (imaging radar) sensors. These faster sensors make the acquisition speeds comparable to, and in some cases better than, the $O(k)$ swept-stripe techniques described below. By contrast, typical objects used in environment matting will cause light from the background to bend through or reflect off of the object in unpredictable ways, thus requiring a full 2D sensor array to capture the light. In this case, the $O(k^2)$ penalty is prohibitive.

Using a swept plane of light, $O(k)$ images can provide shape information through optical triangulation [1]. The first environment matting technique described in Section 3 uses such a pattern, though multiple oriented sweeps are required to capture all the parameters. Note that this particular environment matting technique bears some resemblance to the space-time analysis described by Kanade *et al.* [9] and Curless and Levoy [4], in which the authors study the time evolution of reflected light and triangulate over space and time.

By projecting a hierarchy of progressively finer stripe patterns, the required number of images for optical triangulation can be reduced to $O(\log k)$ [13]. Zongker *et al.* [19] use such a stripe hierarchy with some accompanying compromises over the swept-stripe technique.

Finally, using a color ramp, researchers have demonstrated single-frame triangulation, that is, an acquisition with time complexity $O(1)$, albeit with increased susceptibility to noise [6, 14]. In Section 4, we apply a similar pattern to extract environment mattes in real time. To combat the effects of noise, we apply a non-linear, discontinuity-preserving filter [10] to the resulting matte sequence.

Hybrid stripe-ramp methods have been proposed to manage the trade-off between number of images and susceptibility to noise [3, 8]. We have not explored such methods for environment matting,

as they will likely yield results of lower quality than the swept-stripe method we describe here, and will still require multiple frames, making them unsuitable for real-time capture.

Our work also has some connection to BRDF acquisition. Though we do not explicitly solve for the BRDF, one could certainly imagine using environment matting to capture reflection functions over a uniformly coated surface of known geometry, such as a sphere. A more direct connection lies in the BRDF fitting work of Ward [16]. Using an elliptical Gaussian model for rough specular reflection, he achieves excellent matches to goniometric samples. This model is the motivation for our choice of oriented, elliptical, Gaussian weighting functions described in Section 3.

1.2 Overview

In Section 2 we describe the general environment matting model. The two following sections describe the two extensions we have developed—higher accuracy mattes in Section 3 and real-time-capture mattes in Section 4. Each of Sections 3 and 4 describes the assumptions made to reduce the general matting equation to something that can be captured, then describes the experimental procedure used and shows results. We conclude in Section 5 with a summary and ideas for future work.

2 The environment matting equation

We begin by developing a general expression for the environment matting equation and showing how it reduces to the traditional compositing equation, as well as the equation developed by Zongker *et al.* [19].

An imaging system, such as a CCD camera, records a discrete set of samples over an image plane. Let's assume for the moment that we have a camera that measures the irradiance at each wavelength separately. Then, for a given pixel, the camera records a value C for each wavelength.[1] Following the environment mapping work of Blinn and Newell [2], we can express this color in terms of an infinitely distant environment illumination $E(\omega)$:

$$C = \int W(\omega)\, E(\omega)\, d\omega \,. \tag{1}$$

The weighting function W comprises all means of transport of environment lighting from all directions ω through a foreground object to the camera, including any blurring due to the camera optics and area integration at a sensor cell. This equation holds under the assumption that none of the materials that are scattering light from the environment exhibit any wavelength coupling (e.g., fluorescence).

Next, we rewrite this equation as a spatial integral over a bounding surface (e.g., an environment map). Further, we augment the equation to include an additive foreground color F. This foreground color is typically due to some additional lighting that is separate from the environment map, though it could encompass object emissivity as well. Under these assumptions, our equation becomes

$$C = F + \int W(x)\, T(x)\, dx \,. \tag{2}$$

From this equation, we can develop a series of approximations that allow us to embed a foreground object in a new environment with varying degrees of quality.

---

[1]Throughout this paper, we use ordinary italics for scalar quantities (e.g., a position x); bold-italics for functions of more than one spatial parameter (e.g., an area A); colored italics for functions of wavelength (e.g., a color C); and colored bold-italics for functions of both wavelength and more than one spatial parameter (e.g., a texture map T).

To arrive at the traditional image compositing equation [11], we assume that the straight-through background pixel is the only environment sample that affects the camera pixel. Let P be the rectangular-area support of the pixel p on the background. Then we describe the (in this case, monochromatic) weighting function as

$$W(x) = (1 - \alpha) \, \Pi(x; P) \,, \qquad (3)$$

where α represents the foreground's transparency or partial pixel coverage, and $\Pi(x; A)$ is the box function of unit volume supported over an arbitrary axis-aligned area A. Next we define $\mathcal{M}(T, A)$ as the "texture-mapping operator" that performs the area integral and returns the average value of the texture T over region A:

$$\mathcal{M}(T, A) \equiv \int \Pi(x; A) \, T(x) \, dx \,. \qquad (4)$$

Finally, defining the filtered background B to be the integral over the pixel's support

$$B \equiv \mathcal{M}(T, P) \,, \qquad (5)$$

and substituting the previous three equations into Equation 2, gives the traditional compositing equation:

$$C = F + (1 - \alpha) \, B \,. \qquad (6)$$

Note that α does not have any wavelength dependence and thus cannot model color-filtered transparency. In addition, F is a measured quantity that is added directly to the attenuated background—in effect, it is pre-multiplied by α.

Zongker *et al.* model more complex lighting effects by approximating the environment as a set of m texture maps $T_i(x)$ (the six sides of a bounding cube for instance), and by using more general light transport paths. Their weighting function is

$$W(x) = (1 - \alpha) \, \Pi(x; P) + \sum_{i=1}^{m} R_i \, \Pi(x; A_i) \,. \qquad (7)$$

In their formulation, the A_i represent various axis-aligned regions, each lying on a different texture map (corresponding, typically, to a different face of the environment cube). The R_i are reflectance coefficients describing the amount of light from the designated area of texture map i that is reflected or transmitted by the object at a given wavelength. In this formulation, R_i captures color-filtered transparency, and α represents only partial pixel coverage of the object. Substituting this weighting function into Equation 2 gives the environment matting equation used by Zongker *et al.*:

$$C = F + (1 - \alpha) \, B + \sum_{i=1}^{m} R_i \, \mathcal{M}(T_i, A_i) \,. \qquad (8)$$

Note that this approach not only permits colored filtering of light, but also enables effects such as reflection and refraction since the light contributing to a pixel can be scattered from parts of the environment other than just the pixel directly behind the object. This approach, however, does have several distinct limitations. First, the components of the weighting function are assumed to be separable products of wavelength functions R_i and spatial functions $\Pi(x; A_i)$. Thus, phenomena such as dispersion are not handled, since these require the weighting functions to shift spatially with wavelength. Second, the axis-aligned rectangle weighting functions do not simulate the effects of, for example, smooth BRDF's, which when mapped onto a background have a smooth, oriented footprint. Finally, other than the straight-through α-component, the approach models only a single mapping from a texture face to the camera. In reality, multiple mappings to the same face can and do happen and must be modeled, for example, when reflection and refraction at an

interface cause view rays to split into distinct groups that strike the same backdrop.

Our first objective, then, is to choose a different model for the weighting function that is more physically motivated and whose parameters are still easy to acquire using a simple apparatus.

3 Towards higher accuracy

To address the limitations of the weighting function described in Zongker *et al.*, we generalize it to a sum of Gaussians:

$$W(x) = \sum_{i=1}^{n} R_i \, G_i(x) \,. \qquad (9)$$

In our formulation, we allow any number of contributions from a single texture map. Here, R_i is an attenuation factor, and each G_i is the unit-area, elliptical, oriented $2D$ Gaussian:

$$G_i(x) \equiv G_{2\text{D}}(x; c_i, \sigma_i, \theta_i) \,, \qquad (10)$$

where $G_{2\text{D}}$ is defined as

$$G_{2\text{D}}(x; c, \sigma, \theta) \equiv \frac{1}{2\pi\sigma_u\sigma_v} \exp\left[-\frac{u^2}{2\sigma_u{}^2} - \frac{v^2}{2\sigma_v{}^2} \right] \qquad (11)$$

with

$$u = (x - c_x)\cos\theta - (y - c_y)\sin\theta$$
$$v = (x - c_x)\sin\theta + (y - c_y)\cos\theta \,.$$

Here, $x = (x, y)$ are the pixel coordinates, $c = (c_x, c_y)$ is the center of each Gaussian, $\sigma = (\sigma_u, \sigma_v)$ are the "unrotated" widths (a.k.a. standard deviations) in a local uv-coordinate system, and θ is the orientation. Figure 2 illustrates these parameters. Thus, our weighting function is some n-modal Gaussian with each term contributing a reflective or refractive effect from the object. Substituting into Equation 2, we arrive at a new form of the matting equation:

$$C = F + \sum_{i=1}^{n} R_i \int G_{2\text{D}}(x; c_i, \sigma_i, \theta_i) \, T(x) \, dx \,. \qquad (12)$$

(In this equation, we use $T(x)$ to represent the set of all texture maps. The n modes of the weighting function are distributed over m textures, where n may be larger than m in general. The choice of the particular texture map used in computing a given Gaussian contribution i should be assumed to be implicitly controlled by the position c_i of the Gaussian weighting function.)

The key advantages of this weighting function over the one used by Zongker *et al.* are that: (1) the spatial variation can be coupled with wavelength to permit modeling of dispersion; (2) it supports multiple mappings to a single texture; and (3) it approximates the behavior of BRDF's more closely (by using oriented Gaussian weighting functions rather than box functions).

In practice, each of the "colored" values $C, F, R_i, c_i, \sigma_i, \theta_i$ and T in Equation 12 is implemented as an *rgb* vector. So, in practice, this equation actually represents three independent equations, one for each of the color components. Our unknowns are $F, R_i, c_i, \sigma_i, \theta_i$, which means that each pixel encodes $3 + 18n$ parameters.

3.1 Swept Gaussians for environment matting

Recovering the environment matte requires taking a set of images of an object in front of a sequence of backdrops. Our method consists of three steps: (1) identifying pixels outside the object silhouette, (2) recovering the foreground color, and (3) applying a set of novel

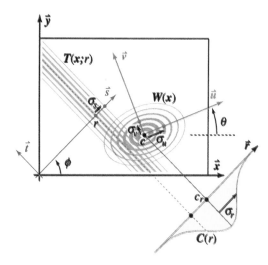

Figure 2 Illustration of the variables used in recovering an unknown elliptical, oriented Gaussian by sweeping out convolutions with known Gaussian stripes. As a tilted stripe $T(\boldsymbol{x}; r)$ of width σ_s and position r sweeps across the background in direction s, it passes "under" the elliptical Gaussian weighting function $W(\boldsymbol{x})$ associated with a single camera pixel. The camera records the integral of the product of the stripe and the weighting function, which describes a new, observed function $C(r)$ as the stripe sweeps. The center c_r and width σ_r of this observed function are related to the center c and width $\sigma = (\sigma_u, \sigma_v)$ of the weighting function and the width of the stripe through Equations 20 and 21.

background *stimulus functions* to estimate the remaining parameters in the matte.

In the first step of our high-accuracy matting method, we identify pixels that are outside the silhouette of the object. This step is desirable for two reasons: it saves us the computational effort of estimating the matte parameters at these pixels, and it prevents us from making potentially noisy estimates of how straight-through background pixels map to the image, which would result in shimmering artifacts when rendering. To identify these pixels, we use the method of Zongker *et al.* In particular, we display a coarse-to-fine sequence of horizontal and vertical square-wave background patterns with and without the object. If we measure the same color (within a user-specified tolerance) at a pixel both with and without the object for each background, then we consider the pixel to map straight through. The overhead of taking these additional images is small compared to the total acquisition time.

To recover the foreground color, we photograph the object against two solid backgrounds. Replacing $T(\boldsymbol{x})$ in Equation 12 with a single backdrop of constant color T and integrating, we get

$$C = F + RT \qquad (13)$$

where $R \equiv \sum_{i=1}^{n} R_i$. Given the two images, we have two equations in two unknowns for each color channel, i.e., the foreground color F and the aggregate attenuation factor R. Solving the system of equations yields the foreground color.

Once we have the silhouette mask and the foreground color, we can solve for the remaining parameters of Equation 12 using a large set of controlled backdrops (i.e., stimulus functions). Zongker *et al.* use a hierarchical set of square-wave stripe patterns in both the vertical and horizontal directions. They encounter difficulties with this method for two reasons: (1) the square waves are not good stimuli for recovering smooth functions, and (2) there is no obvious way to recover multiple mappings to the backdrop using these stimuli. To combat the first problem, we choose a smooth set of stimulus functions. To address the second, we constrain the stimuli to be narrow in one dimension, sweeping over time to reveal multiple mappings

to the same background. Our choice of stimulus function, then, is a set of swept Gaussian stripes.

Let's see how we can use sweeping stripes to recover some of the parameters of our weighting functions. To begin, let us assume that the weighting function is unimodal and axis-aligned ($n = 1$ and $\theta = 0$). Under these assumptions, we can omit the summation and the subscript i in Equations 9 and 10 and then decompose the 2D Gaussian weighting function into two 1D components:

$$W(\boldsymbol{x}) = R\, G_{1D}(x; c_x, \sigma_u)\, G_{1D}(y; c_y, \sigma_v), \qquad (14)$$

where

$$G_{1D}(x; c, \sigma) = \frac{1}{\sqrt{2\pi}\sigma} \exp\left[-\frac{(x-c)^2}{2\sigma^2} \right]. \qquad (15)$$

Our first stimulus function will be a vertical stripe that is constant in y and has a 1D Gaussian intensity profile in x with width σ_s:

$$T(\boldsymbol{x}) = G_{1D}(x; 0, \sigma_s). \qquad (16)$$

Now consider sweeping the stripe horizontally, displacing it at each step by some offset r:

$$T(\boldsymbol{x}; r) = G_{1D}(x - r; 0, \sigma_s) = G_{1D}(r - x; 0, \sigma_s). \qquad (17)$$

The camera observation at a pixel is then given by:

$$\begin{aligned}
C(r) &= \int W(\boldsymbol{x})\, T(\boldsymbol{x}; r)\, d\boldsymbol{x} \\
&= \iint R\, G_{1D}(x; c_x, \sigma_u)\, G_{1D}(y; c_y, \sigma_v)\, G_{1D}(r-x, 0, \sigma_s)\, dx\, dy \\
&= \int R\, G_{1D}(x; c_x, \sigma_u)\, G_{1D}(r-x; 0, \sigma_s)\, dx \cdot \int G_{1D}(y; c_y, \sigma_v)\, dy \\
&= R\, G_{1D}(r; c_x, \sigma_u) * G_{1D}(r; 0, \sigma_s) \cdot 1 \\
&= R\, G_{1D}(r; c_x, \sqrt{\sigma_u^2 + \sigma_s^2}). \qquad (18)
\end{aligned}$$

Thus, at each pixel, we expect to record a Gaussian evolving over time. Given an illumination stripe of known width, we can now estimate the *rgb* parameters c_x and σ_u using the procedure described below in Section 3.2. By symmetry, we can recover the vertical center coordinate and width by sweeping a horizontal Gaussian stripe in the vertical direction behind the foreground object. Thus, for the case of a single, unoriented Gaussian weighting function, a horizontal and a vertical swept Gaussian stripe are enough to estimate all the remaining parameters of the environment matte.

Figure 2 illustrates the more general case of a sweeping stripe that is constant in the t-direction and has Gaussian profile in the s-direction. This stripe is oriented at an angle ϕ with respect to the xy-coordinate system and travels in the s-direction. Under these circumstances, it is straightforward to show that the observation at a pixel will be:

$$C(r) = R\, G_{1D}(r; c_r, \sigma_r), \qquad (19)$$

where

$$c_r = c_x \cos\phi + c_y \sin\phi \qquad (20)$$

$$\sigma_r = \sqrt{\sigma_u^2 \cos^2(\phi - \theta) + \sigma_v^2 \sin^2(\phi - \theta) + \sigma_s^2} \qquad (21)$$

Here, c_r is the center of the weighting function projected onto the r-axis, and σ_r is the projected, convolved standard deviation of the observed Gaussian.

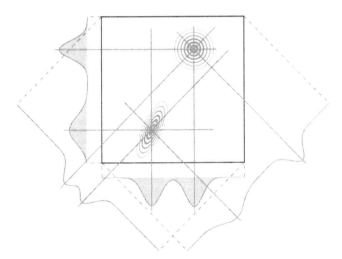

Figure 3 The green concentric rings depict a possible bimodal weighting function. The curves around the image indicate the convolved projections resulting from sweeping horizontal, vertical, and left and right diagonal Gaussian stripes across the screen independently. The horizontal and vertical sweeps alone (purple) are insufficient to determine the mode positions, but by adding additional diagonal sweeps (yellow) the correct modes can be determined.

Figure 4 A photograph of our experimental setup. In this instance an accurate environment matte is being acquired.

Horizontally and vertically swept stripes alone ($\phi = 0°$ and $90°$, respectively) are not enough to determine the weighting function, so we introduce two diagonal passes at $\phi = 45°$ and $-45°$. The additional oriented stripes serve another purpose: disambiguating multiple mappings to the backdrop. As shown in Figure 3, a bimodal weighting function results in two Gaussian images over time at a pixel as the stripe sweeps across. If we use just the horizontal and vertical stripes, the two modes recorded in each sweep yield multiple indistinguishable interpretations of the bimodal weighting function. The oriented stripes can be used to disambiguate these choices, as described below.

3.2 Estimating the matte parameters

In practice, our acquisition process entails stepping each Gaussian stripe across a computer screen and recording a set of samples for each sweep and for each color channel. Given this data, we seek the best set of parameters that explain the measurements. We estimate these parameters (separately for each color channel) in four steps: (1) identifying the number of Gaussians modes in the response, (2) solving for the projected centers and widths associated with each Gaussian mode, (3) intersecting the centers to localize the Gaussian modes, and (4) computing the parameters for each Gaussian mode.

To identify the number of Gaussians for the response to a given stripe sweep, we search for a series of peaks above the noise floor of the sensor. To make this process more robust, we first filter the 1D response function, and then identify the peaks. The locations of the peaks are the starting points for the projected centers of the projected modes. If the projected modes are clearly separated, we also estimate the projected widths by examining the extent of the signal that is above the noise floor. For two overlapping modes, we compute the distances from the left mode to the left extent and the right mode to the right extent and then estimate widths accordingly. For more overlapping modes, we compute the total width and divide by the number of modes. In any case, these center and width estimates are simply starting points for a Levenburg-Marquardt optimization procedure [12] that takes the original data, the number of Gaussians, and the initial center and width estimates in order to find the best centers and widths that explain the data.

Next, we use the sets of projected centers to choose the most likely locations of the Gaussian modes G_i (from Equation 10). The cen-

ters computed in the previous step should each correspond to the center of a Gaussian mode as projected onto the axis defined by the stripe. We then construct a line passing through each projected center point running parallel to the stripe's t direction. We consider all 4-tuples of horizontal, vertical, and two diagonal lines, and hypothesize their intersections by computing the point closest to each set of four lines. We measure the distance of that point to each of the lines, and apply a user-specified tolerance to reject or accept the purported intersection.

Finally, given the set of Gaussian modes selected by the intersection process, we determine the parameters of each Gaussian mode. For each identified mode, we have estimates of the convolved, projected parameters according to Equations 20 and 21. We compute R as the average of individually computed R's. The center c_i of G_i is simply the closest point to the lines as described in the previous step. Finally, we have four equations that relate the width and orientation of each Gaussian mode to the four measured widths. We solve this over-constrained, non-linear system of equations by finely sampling the space of possible orientations, solving for the linear-least-squares-best width parameters, and then choosing the orientation and widths that yield the lowest overall error.

The result of this sequence of steps is a reasonable estimate for the number of Gaussian modes and their parameters. As a final step, we apply a full Levenburg-Marquardt optimization to find the best c_i, σ_i, and θ_i that explain all of the measurements.

3.3 Results of accurate matting

Figure 4 shows our experimental setup. A Sony DCR-TRV900 digital video camera records images of an object as one of three monitors presents a sequence of stimulus functions. We correct for non-linearities in the video camera using Debevec and Malik's method [5]. To calibrate each monitor's brightness settings, we display a sequence of solid gray images and record them with the radiometrically corrected camera. After averaging the gray values within each image, we have a mapping between gray values on the computer and displayed radiance. Each stripe image is adjusted so that the profile is Gaussian in radiance space.

After calibration, we begin imaging the object by extracting the foreground color and silhouette mask as described in the previous section. Next, we display the sequence of background patterns. We translate each Gaussian stripe across the screen in steps of $\sigma_s/2$ to ensure enough samples for the estimation procedure. We typically use $\sigma_s = 2$ or 4 (measured in camera pixels) requiring about 300 or 150 stripe positions, respectively, per horizontal, vertical, or diagonal sweep. Due to the lack of synchronization between the monitor refresh and the camera, we are unable to capture at video rates; instead, a typical capture plus digital video transfer requires roughly 30 minutes. (With a synchronized system and real-time transfer to PC memory, we expect acquisition could take less than a minute.) Processing time for an environment matte is typically about 20 minutes on a 400 MHz Pentium II PC with 128 MB of RAM.

We demonstrate the accuracy of our new environment matting algorithm on three objects. For each example, we render the matte by explicitly integrating the oriented Gaussian filters over the background. The results are shown in Figures 5 and 6.

The first object is a crystal in the shape of a regularly triangulated sphere, shown in Figure 5(a). The planar facets give rise to prismatic rainbowing effects due to dispersion. This effect is captured by our new matting algorithm because we estimate a different Gaussian weighting function (with a different center) for each color channel. This effect is not modeled by the old matting algorithm, which breaks down even further due to the multiple mappings at pixels that straddle crystal facets.

The multiple mapping problem is more clearly demonstrated by our next object, a beer glass laid on its side (Figure 5(b)). Due to the grazing angle, simultaneous reflection and refraction at the top of the glass results in bimodal mappings to the background. The old method simply cannot handle this phenomenon, whereas the new method captures the effect realistically.

Finally, we captured an environment matte for a pie tin with a rough surface, oriented to cause tilted reflections from the backdrop. Figure 5(c) demonstrates the failure of the old method to capture the large, smooth weighting function indicative of surface roughness, in contrast to the new method's success.

Figure 6 demonstrates the importance of capturing the orientation of the weighting function. When we apply the new method without estimating orientation (i.e., by simply using the widths determined by the horizontal and vertical sweeps), the texture lines running at 25° off of vertical are significantly blurred. After estimating the orientation, we obtain a matte that faithfully preserves these details.

4 Towards real-time capture

In the previous section, we considered ways to increase the accuracy of composites produced with the environment matting technique, at the expense of increasing the number of input images required. Now we will attempt to go the other way—to see how much realism can be maintained when we restrict the input to just a single image of the object.

The single-image case is interesting for two reasons. First, it represents a definite, extreme end of the image-count-versus-accuracy spectrum—a sort of lower bound on the quality of the whole environment matting technique. Secondly, unlike a solution that requires even two or three images of the object, a single-image solution makes it straightforward to capture video environment mattes of *moving* objects in front of a still, structured background. The original environment matting work [19] produced video using a sort of stop-motion technique, where a rigid object was placed on a motion platform, allowing multiple photographs to be taken of each pose. This severely limited the kinds of motions that could be captured. In contrast, a method utilizing just a single background image could be used to capture breaking glass, sloshing liquids, and other kinds of non-repeatable, uninterruptible motions. Although the data capture itself is real-time, the matte extraction process is performed off-line at a slower speed. The matte extraction process analyzes the frames of a captured video and constructs a matte for each frame.

4.1 Simplifying the matting equation

Using the high-accuracy matting process, we enjoy the luxury of having many samples per pixel. In the current process, we only have three samples per pixel: red, green, and blue. Our first objective, then, is to simplify the problem just enough to be solvable—that is, so that there will be only three unknowns remaining. We choose these simplifications to maximize the visual impact of the final matte. Then, using some carefully designed heuristics, we attempt to recover more variables in order to significantly improve visual appearance.

We begin by examining the original environment matting equation [19], written here as Equation 8. Assuming a single backdrop texture, we drop the summation and the subscript i:

$$C = F + (1 - \alpha) B + R \underline{\mathcal{M}}(\boldsymbol{T}, \boldsymbol{A}). \qquad (22)$$

We can now count variables, keeping in mind that where we see a wavelength dependence, we can assume an *rgb* vector in practice. The unknowns are then F and R (*rgb* vectors), α, and $\boldsymbol{A}$. The $\boldsymbol{A}$ term can be broken into $\{\boldsymbol{c}, \boldsymbol{w}\}$, where $\boldsymbol{c} = (c_x, c_y)$ is the center of the area and $\boldsymbol{w} = (w_x, w_y)$ is the width in x and y. Thus, we have eleven variables.

The properties of the matte that we would most like to preserve are, in order: (1) the capacity to refract, reflect, and attenuate the background ($\boldsymbol{A}, R$); (2) smooth blending with the background on silhouettes (α); and (3) specular highlights due to foreground lighting (F).

Let's focus on preserving the first property, which still has seven unknowns. We can simplify this set to three unknowns under the assumption that the object is both colorless and specularly reflective and refractive (i.e., has no roughness or translucency). If the object is colorless, then R becomes a scalar ρ, with no wavelength dependence. In addition, pure specularity implies that neighboring pixels do not have overlapping support in their weighting functions. Thus, $\boldsymbol{c}$ is now an image warping function, and $\boldsymbol{w}$, derived from the warping function, indicates the size of the filter support for proper antialiasing [17]. We have found the following approximation for $\boldsymbol{w}$ to work well in practice:

$$w_x \equiv \frac{\partial}{\partial x} c_x \approx \frac{1}{2} [c_x(x+1, y) - c_x(x-1, y)] \qquad (23)$$

$$w_y \equiv \frac{\partial}{\partial y} c_y \approx \frac{1}{2} [c_y(x, y+1) - c_y(x, y-1)]. \qquad (24)$$

Thus, our *rgb* environment matting equation becomes

$$C = \rho \mathcal{M}(\boldsymbol{T}, \boldsymbol{A}) \qquad (25)$$

4.2 Single image matte recovery

What kind of stimulus function could we use to recover all the parameters in this problem? A logical choice would be a smooth function, where we define smoothness as

$$\mathcal{M}(\boldsymbol{T}, \boldsymbol{A}) \approx \boldsymbol{T}(\boldsymbol{c}) \qquad (26)$$

for any area A. Such a function would have the property under our simplified model that

$$C \approx \rho \boldsymbol{T}(\boldsymbol{c}). \qquad (27)$$

Treating this equation as three equations in r, g, and b, we can easily solve for the three unknowns ρ, c_x, c_y. Backgrounds that are smooth according to the definition in Equation 26 include constant color functions and linear color ramps. However, our function must

SIGGRAPH 99 technique   higher accuracy EM   reference photo

Figure 5 Comparisons between the composite results of the previously published algorithm, the higher accuracy environment matting technique described here, and reference photographs of the matted objects in front of background images. Lighting in the room contributed a yellowish foreground color F that appears, e.g., around the rim of the pie tin in the bottom row. (a) A faceted crystal ball causes rainbowing due to prismatic dispersion, an effect successfully captured by the higher accuracy technique since shifted Gaussian weighting functions are determined for each color channel. (b) Light both reflects off and refracts through the sides of a glass. This bimodal contribution from the background causes catastrophic failure with the previous unimodal method, but is faithfully captured with the new multi-modal method. (c) The weighting functions due to reflections from a roughly-textured pie tin are smooth and fairly broad. The new technique with Gaussian illumination and weighting functions handles such smooth mappings successfully, while the previous technique based on square-wave illumination patterns and rectangular weighting functions yields blocky artifacts.

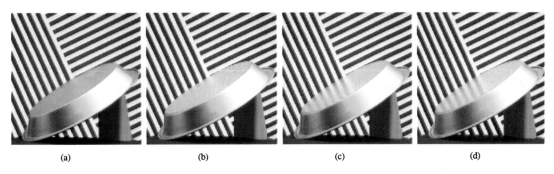

(a)   (b)   (c)   (d)

Figure 6 Oriented weighting functions reflected from a pie tin. (a) As in Figure 5, the previous method yields blocky artifacts for smooth weighting functions. (b) Using the higher accuracy method with unoriented Gaussians ($\theta = 0$) produces a smoother result. (c) Results improve significantly when we orient the Gaussians and solve for θ. In this case, $\theta \approx 25^\circ$ over most of the bottom surface (facing up) of the pie tin. (d) Reference photograph.

also be invertible, so that we can identify which pixel we are seeing from its color. Obviously, a constant color function does not fill this requirement. Instead, we display a color ramp background which is a slice through the *rgb* cube.

Before extracting the environment matte against a ramp background, we add a step that will allow us to recover an estimate of α, the second desirable property on our list. In Section 3, we described a method for classifying pixels as to whether they belong to the object. We can think of this classification as choosing between either $\alpha = 1$ (i.e., the pixel belongs to a foreground object) or $\alpha = \rho = 0$ (i.e., the pixel belongs to the background).

To classify pixels, we first take a series of pictures of the background without the object and average them together to give us a low noise estimate of the ramp background. Once we begin recording video of the object, we apply a simple difference threshold to each frame, comparing the image of the object to the image of the background alone. This step separates foreground and background pixels. We then use some morphology operations (dilation followed by hole-filling followed by erosion) to clean up this binary map, giving us a reasonably accurate mask of the pixels covered by the object. To avoid a sharp discontinuity, we slightly feather the alpha at the boundaries of the object as a post-processing step. Thus, we arrive at the improved matting equation:

$$C = (1 - \alpha)B + \rho\,\mathcal{M}(T, A) \qquad (28)$$

which, for a smooth background, reduces to

$$C = (1 - \alpha)\,B + \rho\,T(c)\,. \qquad (29)$$

We can now begin to recover an environment matte. Because we assume that $F = 0$ everywhere, we photograph the object in a dark room, lit only by the structured backdrop. The structured background is a smoothly-varying wash of color, in particular, a planar slice through the *rgb* cube. Due to non-linearities in the system, including crosstalk between the spectra of the monitor phosphors and the CCD elements, the gamma of the backdrop display, and processing in the camera's electronics, this plane in color space will be distorted, becoming a curved 2D manifold lying within the *rgb* cube, as in Figure 7(b).

To extract matte parameters at each pixel, we consider the line joining the observed color and the black point in *rgb* space. The point where this line intersects the background-color manifold gives us the point c, and the fractional distance of the observed color to the manifold gives us ρ, as illustrated in Figure 7(a). The manifold is difficult to characterize algebraically, so rather than projecting the observed color onto it, we do a multiresolution search to find the point on the manifold closest to the construction line.

A single frame of video captured with a CCD camera will have considerable noise. While we can capture several seconds of the empty background and average frames to create a nearly noise-free reference, we get only one frame of the object in front of the backdrop. This leads to grainy composite images, as seen in Figure 8(a). One way to combat this effect is to filter the input images to smooth out noise before matte extraction. However, our extraction process is so sensitive to noise that we have not been successful in obtaining smooth mappings without also significantly smoothing away detail in the images. Instead, we find that directly smoothing the extracted warping function, c, is most effective. To this end, we apply the edge-preserving smoothing operator of Perona and Malik [11] to the c_x and c_y channels. This operator averages each pixel with its neighborhood, with unequal contributions from neighboring pixels. The relative contributions are determined by the difference of the pixels' values, so that similarly-valued pixels affect each other more. This filter smoothes out regions with low-to-moderate noise levels while preventing significant energy

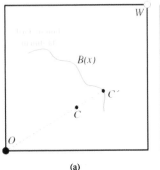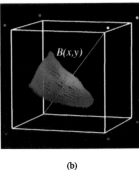

(a)   (b)

Figure 7 (a) 2D version of the algorithm for constructing environment mattes from a single image, assuming that $F = 0$. The observed color C is projected from black onto the background manifold. The position of point C' on the manifold gives the position x, and $\rho = \overline{OC}/\overline{OC'}$. (b) In reality, the background colors lie on a 2D manifold within the *rgb* cube, and we recover an (x, y) position.

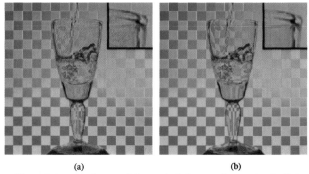

(a)   (b)

Figure 8 A composite created from a single-frame environment matte. Part (a) shows the results when no filtering is applied. Filtering the matte both spatially and temporally reduces noise in the composite considerably, as seen in part (b).

transfer across sharp edges. For video, the best results are obtained when this operator is applied temporally as well as spatially, giving frame-to-frame coherence, which is especially important in areas of the object that are not moving.

4.3 Heuristics for specular highlights

The most noticeable visual effect of this restricted model is the loss of specular highlights. The objects we capture are typically curved glass, and highlights are both important for communicating the shape of the object and for making it visually appealing. In this section, we develop a method for recovering the intensity of the foreground color F, under the restriction that it is white. Thus, $F = fW$ where $W = (1, 1, 1)$, so that only one additional parameter, f is added to the matting equation. This new single-image environment matting equation then becomes

$$C = f\,W + (1 - \alpha)\,B + \rho\,\mathcal{M}(T, A) \qquad (30)$$

or, for a smooth background:

$$C = f\,W + (1 - \alpha)\,B + \rho\,T(c)\,. \qquad (31)$$

We extend our simple model by allowing the objects to be photographed with bright, near-point light sources. Because the surfaces of our objects are curved, such light sources primarily create bright spots and highlight contours where the normal is equal to the halfway vector between the viewing and lighting rays.

When applied to images taken with lighting other than the backdrop, the recovery algorithm of the last section will discover some points where $\rho > 1$, i.e., where the observed color point lies on the side of the background manifold closer to white. The theory

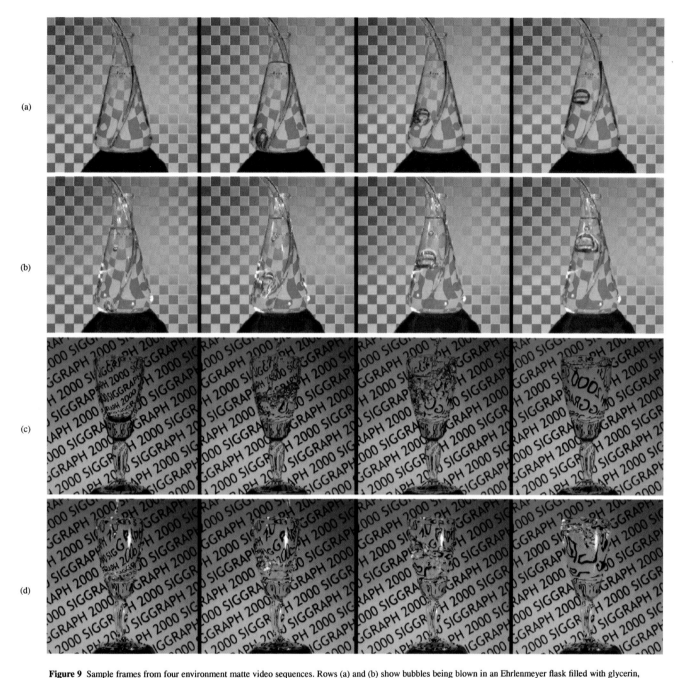

Figure 9 Sample frames from four environment matte video sequences. Rows (a) and (b) show bubbles being blown in an Ehrlenmeyer flask filled with glycerin, while rows (c) and (d) show a glass being filled with water. Sequences (a) and (c) were captured with no lighting other than the backdrop, so that the foreground color is zero. Sequences (b) and (d) were captured separately, shot with the lights on, and the foreground estimation technique is used to recover the highlights.

light transport [18] tells us that this should not happen when the object is lit only by the backdrop, so we assume that wherever ρ exceeds unity there must be some F-term contribution to the pixel. (In practice, sensor noise means that ρ can occasionally exceed unity even where there is no highlight. Our algorithm actually looks for highlights only in regions where $\rho > 1 + \delta$, and clamps smaller ρ values to the range $[0, 1]$. For our (fairly noisy) video camera, a δ in the range 0.03–0.10 is typically used.)

Since the highlights we observe will be small or narrow, we make the assumption that the refraction direction and transparency will be smoothly varying in the area of the highlight. We estimate the parameters ρ, c_x, and c_y for the neighborhood around the highlight by interpolating from the values at nearby pixels outside the highlight area and then applying Gaussian smoothing. Once we have esti-

mates for these parameters, we can use Equation 31 to compute f independently for each color channel, e.g.:

$$f_g = C_g - (1 - \alpha) B_g - \rho T_g(\mathbf{c}), \qquad (32)$$

where the g subscript on each variable represents the green color component. Similarly, we compute f_r and f_b for the red and blue color components, respectively, and then combine them to estimate f:

$$f = \max\{f_r, f_g, f_b\}. \qquad (33)$$

In principle, f_r, f_g, and f_b should all be the same, but in practice some or all channels of the observed color C can be clipped, resulting in an artificially low f value. We compute f using each channel separately and take the maximum to counter the effects of such clipping. In practice, the resulting f values may still appear too dim,

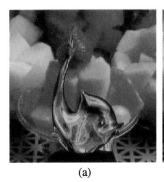 

(a)   (b)

Figure 10 Image (a) is an image of a glass fish sculpture captured in front of a photograph displayed on a computer monitor. Image (b) shows a single frame environment matte composite—the same fish photographed in front of a color wash and digitally composited onto the fruit image. The background image was darkened using the color histogram matching technique of Heeger and Bergen [7] to approximate the darkening produced by photographing the image on a monitor.

so we scale them up when compositing to produce a more vivid highlight. In addition, we currently solve for f before feathering α, though it would be straightforward to solve for f after feathering.

Figure 9 shows some still images taken from an environment matte video captured with this method. While this technique is most effective for video, still images can also be used for gauging the quality of the extracted mattes. The first four rows all show examples of liquids in motion, which could not be captured by a technique requiring multiple images of the same object pose. Figure 10 compares the results of video environment matting to a photograph. Some details, such as the ridges on the fish's dorsal fin, which are clearly visible in the photograph, have become indistinct with the environment matte, but the environment matte has done a reasonable job of capturing the gross refraction pattern of the object.

5 Conclusion

Environment matting involves an inherent tradeoff: the amount of input data required versus the quality of the resulting matte. The original environment matting and compositing paper by Zongker *et al.* [19] provided one data point in this space—a reasonably accurate model obtained using a reasonably small (logarithmic) number of photographs. In this work, we have presented two additional data points in the environment matting design space. The first captures a higher quality model in which each pixel can see one or more different Gaussian regions of the environment on a per-channel basis. This approach allows for accurate capture of objects with multimodal refraction and reflection qualities, or with prismatic color dispersion. In the second approach, we limited ourselves to a single input image to see how much quality could be retained. While the range of modeled effects must be severely pared down, in many interesting situations the composite images created are still quite convincing. The effect is greatly enhanced by matting an object in motion, an effect made possible with a single-frame solution.

One general area of future work is to develop more sophisticated mathematical tools for extracting environment mattes from our input data. For the higher accuracy method, we are developing a sensitivity analysis of our parameter estimation process in hopes of selecting a new, smaller set of basis functions that exhibit greater noise immunity. For the fast, lower accuracy method, we are researching a more principled Bayesian approach to fitting matte parameters given noisy image streams.

Finally, our accurate environment matting methods should enable us to capture the behaviors of surfaces with bimodal BRDF's, e.g.,

having specular and diffuse components. Our initial experiments in this direction have yielded promising results. However, we have found that monitor illumination is too weak when reflected off of a diffuse surface. By acquiring high dynamic range radiance maps [5], we hope to solve this problem and demonstrate interactive lighting of these more complex environment mattes. We also expect that Gaussian weighting functions will not accurately model diffuse reflection. Choosing new sets of weighting functions to handle such cases is another area for future work.

Acknowledgements

We would like to thank Eric Veach for his insights on light transport. This work was supported by NSF grants 9803226 and 9875365, and by industrial gifts from Intel, Microsoft, and Pixar, and by the Intel Fellowship program.

References

[1] Paul Besl. Active optical range imaging sensors. In Jorge L.C. Sanz, editor, *Advances in Machine Vision*, chapter 1, pages 1–63. Springer-Verlag, 1989.

[2] J. F. Blinn and M. E. Newell. Texture and reflection in computer generated images. *Communications of the ACM*, 19:542–546, 1976.

[3] G. Chazan and N. Kiryati. Pyramidal intensity ratio depth sensor. Technical Report 121, Center for Communication and Information Technologies, Department of Electrical Engineering, Technion, Haifa, Israel, October 1995.

[4] B. Curless and M. Levoy. Better optical triangulation through spacetime analysis. In *Proceedings of IEEE International Conference on Computer Vision*, pages 987–994, June 1995.

[5] Paul E. Debevec and Jitendra Malik. Recovering high dynamic range radiance maps from photographs. In *Proceedings of SIGGRAPH 97*, pages 369–378, August 1997.

[6] Gerd Häusler and Dieter Ritter. Parallel three-dimensional sensing by color-coded triangulation. *Applied Optics*, 32(35):7164–7169, December 1993.

[7] David J. Heeger and James R. Bergen. Pyramid-based texture analysis/synthesis. *Proceedings of SIGGRAPH 95*, pages 229–238, August 1995.

[8] Eli Horn and Nahum Kiryati. Toward optimal structured light patterns. In *Proceedings of the International Conference on Recent Advances in Three-Dimensional Digital Imaging and Modeling*, pages 28–35, 1997.

[9] T. Kanade, A. Gruss, and L. Carley. A very fast VLSI rangefinder. In *1991 IEEE International Conference on Robotics and Automation*, volume 39, pages 1322–1329, April 1991.

[10] P. Perona and J. Malik. Scale space and edge detection using anisotropic diffusion. *IEEE Trans. on Pattern Analysis and Machine Intelligence*, 12(7):629–639, July 1990.

[11] Thomas Porter and Tom Duff. Compositing digital images. In *Proceedings of SIGGRAPH 84*, volume 18, pages 253–259, July 1984.

[12] William H. Press, Saul A. Teukolsky, William T. Vetterling, and Brian P. Flannery. *Numerical Recipes in C: The Art of Scientific Computing (2nd ed.)*. Cambridge University Press, 1992.

[13] K. Sato and S. Inokuchi. Three-dimensional surface measurement by space encoding range imaging. *Journal of Robotic Systems*, 2:27–39, 1985.

[14] Erhard Schubert. Fast 3d object recognition using multiple color coded illumination. In *Proc. IEEE Conference on Acoustics, Speech, and Signal Processing*, pages 3057–3060, 1997.

[15] Alvy Ray Smith and James F. Blinn. Blue screen matting. In *Proceedings of SIGGRAPH 96*, pages 259–268, August 1996.

[16] Gregory J. Ward. Measuring and modeling anisotropic reflection. In Edwin E. Catmull, editor, *Computer Graphics (SIGGRAPH '92 Proceedings)*, volume 26, pages 265–272, July 1992.

[17] G. Wolberg. *Digital Image Warping*. IEEE Computer Society Press, 1990.

[18] Yung Yu Chuang, Douglas E. Zongker, Joel Hindorff, Brian Curless, David H. Salesin, and Richard Szeliski. Environment matting extensions: Towards higher accuracy and real-time capture. Technical Report 2000-05-01, University of Washington, 2000.

[19] Douglas E. Zongker, Dawn M. Werner, Brian Curless, and David H. Salesin. Environment matting and compositing. In *Proceedings of SIGGRAPH 99*, pages 205–214, August 1999.

The Digital Michelangelo Project: 3D Scanning of Large Statues

Marc Levoy [1] *   Kari Pulli [1]   Brian Curless [2]

Szymon Rusinkiewicz [1]   David Koller [1]   Lucas Pereira [1]

Matt Ginzton [1]   Sean Anderson [1]   James Davis [1]

Jeremy Ginsberg [1]   Jonathan Shade [2]   Duane Fulk [3]

[1] Computer Science Department   [2] Department of Computer Science and Engineering   [3] Cyberware Inc.
Stanford University   University of Washington

Figure 1: Renderings of the statues we scanned (except the David). Our raw database (including the David) contains 10 billion polygons and 40,000 color images, occupying 250 gigabytes. From left to right: St. Matthew, Bearded Slave, Slave called Atlas, Awakening Slave, Youthful Slave, Night, Day, Dusk, and Dawn.

Abstract

We describe a hardware and software system for digitizing the shape and color of large fragile objects under non-laboratory conditions. Our system employs laser triangulation rangefinders, laser time-of-flight rangefinders, digital still cameras, and a suite of software for acquiring, aligning, merging, and viewing scanned data. As a demonstration of this system, we digitized 10 statues by Michelangelo, including the well-known figure of David, two building interiors, and all 1,163 extant fragments of the Forma Urbis Romae, a giant marble map of ancient Rome. Our largest single dataset is of the David - 2 billion polygons and 7,000 color images. In this paper, we discuss the challenges we faced in building this system, the solutions we employed, and the lessons we learned. We focus in particular on the unusual design of our laser triangulation scanner and on the algorithms and software we developed for handling very large scanned models.

CR Categories: I.2.10 [Artificial Intelligence]: Vision and Scene Understanding — modeling and recovery of physical attributes; I.3.3 [Computer Graphics]: Picture/Image Generation — digitizing and scanning; I.3.7 [Computer Graphics]: Three-Dimensional Graphics and Realism — color, shading, shadowing, and texture; I.4.8 [Image Processing]: Scene Analysis — range data

Additional keywords: 3D scanning, rangefinding, sensor fusion, range images, mesh generation, reflectance and shading models, graphics systems, cultural heritage

---

* Email: levoy@cs.stanford.edu   Web: http://graphics.stanford.edu/projects/mich/

1. Introduction

Recent improvements in laser rangefinder technology, together with algorithms for combining multiple range and color images, allow us to accurately digitize the shape and surface characteristics of many physical objects. As an application of this technology, a team of 30 faculty, staff, and students from Stanford University and the University of Washington spent the 1998-99 academic year in Italy digitizing sculptures and architecture by Michelangelo.

The technical goal of this project was to make a 3D archive of as many of his statues as we could scan in a year, and to make that archive as detailed as scanning and computer technology would permit. In particular, we wanted to capture the geometry of his chisel marks, which we found to require a resolution of 1/4 mm, and we wanted to scan the David, which stands 5 meters tall without its pedestal. This implies a dynamic range of 20,000:1. While not large for a computer model, it is very large for a scanned model.

Why did we want to capture Michelangelo's chisel marks? On his finished or nearly finished statues, especially those in the Medici Chapel (first through fourth from the right in figure 1), Michelangelo often left the surface deliberately bumpy. The tiny shadows cast by these bumps deepen the shading of curved surfaces. If we wanted our computer models to look realistic under arbitrary lighting, we had to capture these bumps geometrically. On his unfinished statues, for example St. Matthew and the Slaves (first through fifth from the left), his chisel marks tell us how he worked. Starting from a computer model, it might be possible to segment the statue surface according to the chisels used to carve each region (figure 2).

In addition to capturing shape, we also wanted to capture color. More specifically, we wanted to compute the surface reflectance of each point on the statues we scanned. Although extracting reflectance is more difficult than merely recording color, it permits us to relight the statue when rendering it. It also constitutes a unique and useful channel of scientific information. Old statues like the David are covered with a complex brew of marble veining, dirt, waxes and other materials used in prior restorations, and, since it sat outside for 400 years, discoloration and other effects of weathering [Dorsey99]. These tell us a story about the history of the statue. To help uncover this story, we scanned the David under white light and, separately, under ultraviolet light (figure 14). Unfinished statues, like St. Matthew (figure 9), have different stories to tell. The bottoms of its chisel marks are whiter than the surrounding marble due to the crushing of marble crystals under the impact of the chisel. The characteristics of these whitened areas might tell us how Michelangelo held his chisel and how hard he struck it.

Although digitization of 2D artwork is a mature field and is widely deployed in the museum and library communities, relatively few groups have tackled the problem of digitizing large 3D artworks. Two notable exceptions are the National Research Council of Canada (NRC) and IBM. The NRC efforts are interesting because they focus on building robust, field-deployable systems, and consequently their papers echo some of the same concerns raised in this paper [Beraldin99]. The IBM efforts are interesting first because they scanned a statue under field conditions, and second because they used a structured-light scanner in conjunction with photometric stereo, producing geometry at 2.0 mm and a normal vector field at sub-millimeter resolution [Rushmeier97]. Although their resulting models are not as detailed as ours, their equipment is lighter-weight and therefore more portable.

In the remaining sections, we describe the scanner we built (section 2), the procedure we followed when scanning a statue (section 3), and our post-processing pipeline (section 4). In section 5, we discuss some of the strategies we developed for dealing with the large datasets produced by our scanning system. In addition to scanning the statues of Michelangelo, we acquired a light field of one statue, we scanned two building interiors using a time-of-flight scanner, and we scanned the fragments of an archeological artifact central to the study of ancient Roman topography. These side projects are described briefly in figures 12, 15, and 16, respectively.

2. Scanner design

The main hardware component of our system was a laser triangulation scanner and motorized gantry customized for digitizing large statues. Our requirements for this scanner were demanding; we wanted to capture chisel marks smaller than a millimeter, we wanted to capture them from a safe distance, and we wanted to reach the top of Michelangelo's David, which is 23 feet tall on its pedestal. In the sections that follow, we describe the range and color acquisition systems of this scanner, its supporting mechanical gantry, and our procedure for calibrating it.

2.1. Range acquisition

To a first approximation, marble statues present an optically cooperative surface: light-colored, diffuse (mostly), and with a consistent minimum feature size imposed by the strength of the material. As such, their shape can be digitized using a variety of non-contact rangefinding technologies including photogrammetry, structured-light triangulation, time-of-flight, and interferometry. Among these, we chose laser-stripe triangulation because it offered the best combination of accuracy, working volume, robustness, and portability. Our design, built to our specifications by Cyberware Inc., employed a 5 mW 660-nanometer laser diode, a 512 x 480 pixel CCD sensor, and a fixed triangulation angle. Although based on

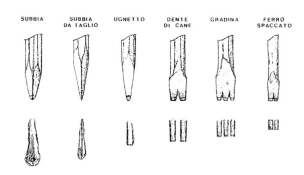

Figure 2: Some of the chisels that Michelangelo may have used when carving St. Matthew (figure 9). At top are the tools themselves, labeled with their Italian names. At bottom are sketches of the characteristic trace left by each tool. The traces are 2-10 mm wide and 1-5 mm deep [Giovannini99].

Cyberware's commercial systems, it differed in two important respects: we used a triangulation angle of 20° rather than 30°, and our sensor viewed the laser sheet from only one side rather than combining views from both sides using a beam splitter. These changes were made to reduce our baseline, which in turn reduced the size and weight of our scan head.

Resolution and field of view. One of our goals was to capture Michelangelo's chisel marks. It is not known exactly what tools Michelangelo used, but they almost certainly included the single-point and multi-point chisels shown in Figure 2. We wished not only to resolve the traces left by these chisels, but to record their shape as well, since this gives us valuable clues about how Michelangelo held and applied his chisels. After testing several resolutions, we decided on a Y sample spacing (along the laser stripe) of 1/4 mm and a Z (depth) resolution at least twice this fine [1]. This gave us a field of view 14 cm wide (along the laser stripe) by 14 cm deep. In retrospect, we were satisfied with the resolution we chose; anything lower would have significantly blurred Michelangelo's chisel marks, and anything higher would have made our datasets unmanageably large.

Standoff and baseline. The ability of lasers to maintain a narrow beam over long distances gave us great latitude in choosing the distance between the camera and the target surface. A longer standoff permits access to deeper recesses, and it permits the scanner to stay further from the statue. However, a longer standoff also implies a longer baseline, making the scan head more cumbersome, and it magnifies the effects of miscalibration and vibration. Keeping these tradeoffs in mind, we chose a standoff of 112 cm - slightly more than half the width of Michelangelo's David. This made our baseline 41 cm. In retrospect, our standoff was sometimes too long and other times not long enough. For an inward-facing surface near the convex hull of a statue, the only unoccluded and reasonably perpendicular view may be from the other side of the statue, requiring a standoff equal to the diameter of the convex hull. In other cases, the only suitable view may be from near the surface itself. For example, to scan the fingertips of David's upraised and curled left hand, we were forced to place the scan head uncomfortably close to his chest. A scanner with a variable standoff would have helped; unfortunately, such devices are difficult to design and calibrate.

---

[1] As built, our Y sample spacing was 0.29 mm. Our CCD was interlaced, so samples were acquired in a zigzag pattern and deinterlaced by interpolation. Our Z (depth) resolution was 50 microns.

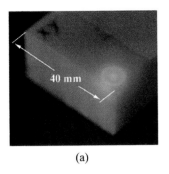 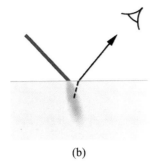

(a)   (b)

Figure 3: *Subsurface scattering of laser light in marble. (a) Photograph of a focused 633-nanometer laser beam 120 microns in diameter striking an unpolished sample of Carrara Statuario marble. (Photo courtesy of National Research Council of Canada.) (b) The scattered light forms a volume below the marble surface, leading to noise and a systematic bias in derived depth.*

2.2. How optically cooperative is marble?

Although marble is light-colored and usually diffuse, it is composed of densely packed transparent crystals, causing it to exhibit subsurface scattering. The characteristics of this scattering greatly depend on the type of marble. Most of Michelangelo's statues were carved from Carrara Statuario, a highly uniform, non-directional, fine-grain stone. Figure 3(a) shows the interaction of a laser beam with a sample of this marble. We observe that the material is very translucent. Fortunately, the statues we scanned were, with the exception of Night, unpolished, which increased surface scattering and thus reduced subsurface scattering. Moreover, several of them, including the David, were coated with dirt, reducing it more.

In the context of our project, subsurface scattering had three implications: it invalidated our assumption that the surface was ideal Lambertian (see section 4.2), it changed the way we should render our models if we wish to be photorealistic, and it degraded the quality of our range data. Given the goals of our project, the latter effect was important, so working in collaboration with the Visual Information Technology lab of the National Research Council of Canada (NRC), we have been analyzing the effect of subsurface scattering on 3D laser scanning.

When a laser beam enters a marble block, it creates a volume of scattered light whose apparent centroid is below the marble surface, as shown in figure 3(b). This has two effects. First, the reflected spot seen by the range camera is shifted away from the laser source. Since most laser triangulation scanners operate by detecting the center of this spot, the shift causes a systematic bias in derived depth. The magnitude of this bias depends on angle of incidence and angle of view. On this marble sample, we measured a bias of 40 microns at roughly normal incidence and 20° viewing obliquity. Second, the spot varies in shape across surface of the block due to random variations in the crystalline structure of the marble, leading to noise in the depth values. Our scanner exhibited a 1-sigma noise of 50 microns on an optically cooperative surface. However, this noise was 2-3 times higher on Michelangelo's statues, more on polished statues, and even more if the laser struck the surface obliquely. The latter effect made view planning harder.

For a statue of reasonably homogeneous composition, it should be possible to correct for the bias we describe here. However, we know of no way to completely eliminate the noise. These effects are still under investigation.

2.3. Color acquisition

Some Cyberware laser-stripe scanners acquire range and color in a single pass using a broadband luminaire and a 1D color sensor. Simultaneous acquisition makes sense for moving objects such as faces, but avoiding cross-talk between the laser and luminaire is difficult, and consequently the color fidelity is poor. Other scanners employ RGB lasers, acquiring color and shape at once and avoiding cross-talk by sensing color in three narrow bands. However, green and blue lasers, or tunable lasers, are large and complex; at the time we designed our system no portable solution existed. We therefore chose to acquire color using a broadband luminaire, a separate sensor, and a separate pass across the object. The camera we chose was a Sony DKC-5000 - a programmable 3-CCD digital still camera with a nominal resolution of 1520 x 1144 pixels [1].

Standoff. Having decided to acquire color in a separate pass across the object, we were no longer tied to the standoff of our range camera. However, to eliminate the necessity of repositioning the scanner between range and color scans, and to avoid losing color-to-range calibration, we decided to match the two standoffs. This was accomplished by locking off the camera's focus at 112 cm.

Resolution and field of view. Our color processing pipeline (section 4.2) uses the surface normals of our merged mesh to convert color into reflectance. Since the accuracy of this conversion is limited by the accuracy of these normals, we decided to acquire color at the same resolution as range data. To achieve this we employed a 25 mm lens, which at 112 cm gave a 25 cm x 19 cm field of view on the statue surface. The spacing between physical CCD pixels was thus 0.31 mm. By contrast, the IBM group acquired color at a higher resolution than range data, then applied photometric stereo to the color imagery to compute high-resolution normals [Rushmeier97]. Our decision to match the two resolutions also simplified our 3D representation; rather than storing color as a texture over parameterized mesh triangles [Sato97, Pulli97, Rocchini99], we simply stored one color per vertex.

Lighting and depth of field. When acquiring color, it is important to control the spatial and spectral characteristics of the illumination. We employed a 250-watt quartz halogen lamp focused to produce as uniform a disk as possible on the statue surface. Since we planned to acquire color and range data from the same standoff, it would be convenient if the color camera's depth of field matched or exceeded the Z-component of the field of view of our range camera. For our lighting, we achieved this by employing an aperture of f/8. This gave us a circle of confusion 0.3 mm in diameter at 10 cm in front of and behind the focused plane.

2.4. Gantry: geometric design

Although our scan head was customized for scanning large statues, its design did not differ greatly from that of other commercial laser-stripe triangulation systems. Our mechanical gantry, on the other hand, was unusual in size, mobility, and reconfigurability.

Scanning motions. Most laser-stripe scanners sweep the laser sheet across the target surface by either translating or rotating the scan head. Rotational tables are easy to build, but curved working volumes don't work well for scanning flat or convex surfaces, and motion errors are magnified by the lever arm of the standoff

---

[1] The 3 CCDs actually have a physical resolution of only 795 x 598 pixels; the camera's nominal resolution is achieved by offsetting the CCDs diagonally and interpolating.

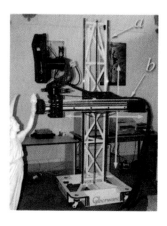

Figure 4: Our laser triangulation scanner and motorized gantry. The scanner, built to our specifications by Cyberware Inc., consisted of an 8-foot vertical truss (*a*), a 3-foot horizontal arm (*b*) that translated vertically on the truss, a pan (*c*) and tilt (*d*) assembly that translated horizontally on the arm, and a scan head (*e*) that mounted on the pan-tilt assembly, The scan head contained a laser, range camera, white spotlight, and digital color camera. The four degrees of freedom are shown with orange arrows.

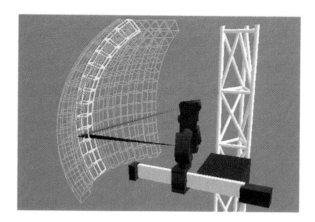

Figure 5: The working volume of our scanner. The volume scannable using our tilt motion was a curved shell 14 cm wide, 14 cm thick, and 195 cm long (yellow). Our pan axis increased the width of this shell to 195 cm (blue). Our horizontal translation table increased its thickness to 97 cm (not shown), assuming the scan head was looking parallel to the table. Including vertical motion, all truss extensions, and all scan head reconfigurations, our working volume was 2 meters x 4 meters x 8.5 meters high.

distance. Translational tables avoid these problems, but they are harder to build and hold steady at great heights. Also, a translating scan head poses a greater risk of collision with the statue than a rotating scan head. Mainly for this reason, we chose a rotating scanner. Our implementation, shown in figure 4, permits 100° of tilting motion, producing the working volume shown in yellow in figure 5. To increase this volume, we mounted the scan head and tilt mechanism on a second rotational table providing 100° of panning motion, producing the working volume shown in blue in the figure. This was in turn mounted on horizontal and vertical translation tables providing 83 cm and 200 cm of linear motion, respectively.

Extensions and bases. To reach the tops of tall statues, the 8-foot truss supporting our vertical translation table could be mounted above a 2-foot or 4-foot non-motorized truss (or both), and the horizontal table could be boosted above the vertical table by an 8-foot non-motorized truss (see figure 6). The entire assembly rested on a 3-foot x 3-foot base supported by pads when scanning or by wheels when rolling. To maintain a 20° tipover angle in its tallest configuration, up to 600 pounds of weights could be fitted into receptacles in the base. To surmount the curbs that surround many statues, the base could be placed atop a second, larger platform with adjustable pads, as shown in the figure. Combining all these pieces placed our range camera 759 cm above the floor, and 45 cm higher than the top of David's head, allowing us to scan it.

Scan head reconfigurations. Statues have surfaces that point in all directions, and laser-stripe scanning works well only if the laser strikes the surface nearly perpendicularly. We therefore designed our pan-tilt assembly to be mountable above or below the horizontal arm, and facing in any of the four cardinal directions. This enabled us to scan in any direction, including straight up and down. To facilitate scanning horizontal crevices, e.g. folds in carved drapery, the scan head could also be rolled 90° relative to the pan-tilt assembly, thereby converting the laser stripe from horizontal to vertical.

Discussion. The flexibility of our gantry permitted us to scan surfaces of any orientation anywhere within a large volume, and it gave us several ways of doing so. We were glad to have this flexibility, because we were often constrained during scanning by various obstructions. On the other hand, taking advantage of this flexibility was arduous due to the weight of the components, dangerous since some reconfigurations had to be performed while standing on a scaffolding or by tilting the gantry down onto the ground, and time-consuming since cables had to be rerouted each time. In retrospect, we should probably have mechanized these reconfigurations using motorized joints and telescoping sections. Alternatively, we might have designed a lighter scan head and mounted it atop a photographic tripod or movie crane. However, both of these solutions sacrifice rigidity, an issue we consider in the next section.

2.5. Gantry: structural design

The target accuracy for our range data was 0.25 mm. Given our choice of a rotating scanner with a standoff of 112 cm, this implied knowing the position and orientation of our scan head within 0.25 mm and 0.013°, respectively. Providing this level of accuracy in a laboratory setting is not hard; providing it atop a mobile, reconfigurable, field-deployable gantry 7.6 meters high is hard.

Deflections. Our scan head and pan-tilt assembly together weighed 15.5 kg. To eliminate deflection of the gantry when panning or tilting, the center of gravity of each rotating part was made coincident with its axis of rotation. To eliminate deflection during horizontal motion, any translation of the scan head / pan-tilt assembly in one direction was counterbalanced by translation in the opposite direction of a lead counterweight that slid inside the horizontal arm. No attempt was made to eliminate deflections during vertical motion, other than by making the gantry stiff.

Vibrations. Our solutions to this problem included using high-grade ball-screw drives for the two scanning motions (pan and tilt), operating these screws at low velocities and accelerations, and keeping them well greased. One worry that proved unfounded was the stability of the museum floors. We were fortunate to be operating on marble floors supported below by massive masonry vaults.

Repeatability. In order for a mechanical system to be calibratable, it must be repeatable. Toward this end, we employed high-quality drive mechanisms with vernier homing switches, we always scanned in the same direction, and we made the gantry stiff. Ultimately, we succeeded in producing repeatable panning, tilting, and horizontal translation of the scan head, even at maximum height. Repeatability under vertical translation, including the insertion of extension trusses, was never assumed. However, reconfiguring the pan-tilt assembly proved more problematic. In retrospect, this should not have surprised us; 11 microns of play - 1/10 the diameter of a human hair - in a pin and socket joint located 5 cm from the pan axis will cause an error of 0.25 mm at our standoff distance of 112 cm. In general, we greatly underestimated the difficulty of reconfiguring our scanner accurately under field conditions.

2.6. Calibration

The goal of calibrating our gantry was to find a mapping from 2D coordinates in its range and color images to 3D coordinates in a global frame of reference. Ideally, this frame of reference should be the (stationary) statue. However, we did not track the position of the gantry, so it became our frame of reference, not the statue. The final mapping from gantry to statue was performed in our system by aligning new scans with existing scans as described in section 4.1.

Calibration of the range and motion systems. To calibrate any system, one must first choose a mathematical model that approximates the system behavior, then estimate the parameters of that model by measuring the behavior of the system. In our case, the natural mathematical model was a parameterized 3D geometric model of the scan head and gantry. If the components of the system are sufficiently independent, then calibration can be partitioned into stages corresponding to each component. For us, independent meant rigid - yet another reason to build a stiff gantry. Partitioning calibration into stages reduces the degrees of freedom in each stage and therefore the number of measurements that must be made to calibrate that stage. For a mechanical system, it also reduces the physical volume over which these measurements must be taken, a distinct advantage since our gantry was large. Finally, multi-stage calibration is more resistant to the replacement of individual components; if our laser had failed in the field, only one part of our calibration would have been invalidated. We had six calibration stages:

(1) a 2D mapping from pixel coordinates in the range camera image to physical locations on the laser sheet

(2) a 2D -> 3D rigid transformation from the laser sheet coordinate system to steel tooling balls attached to the scan head

(3) a 3D rigid transformation to accommodate rolling the scan head 90° (by remounting it) relative to the pan-tilt assembly

(4) the location of the tilting rotation axis and the nonlinear mapping from motion commands to physical rotation angles

(5) the location of the panning rotation axis and the mapping from its motion commands to physical rotation angles

(6) the location of the translation axis, which also depended how the pan-tilt assembly was mounted on the horizontal arm

We chose not to calibrate our vertical translation axis, since its motion induced deflections in the gantry that exceeded our error budget. The results of our calibration procedure can be visualized as the concatenation of six 4 x 4 transformation matrices:

$$\begin{bmatrix} \text{horizontal} \\ \text{translation} \end{bmatrix} \begin{bmatrix} \text{panning} \\ \text{rotation} \end{bmatrix} \begin{bmatrix} \text{tilting} \\ \text{rotation} \end{bmatrix} \begin{bmatrix} \text{rolling} \\ \text{rotation} \end{bmatrix} \begin{bmatrix} \text{laser to} \\ \text{scan head} \end{bmatrix} \begin{bmatrix} \text{image} \\ \text{to laser} \end{bmatrix}$$

Calibration of the color system.

- To correct for geometric distortion in our color camera, we photographed a planar calibration target, located a number of feature points on it, and used these to calculate the camera's intrinsic parameters. Our model included two radial and two tangential distortion terms, off-center perspective projection, and a possibly non-uniform (in X and Y) scale [Heikkilä97].

- To obtain a mapping from the color camera to the scan head, we scanned the target using our laser and range camera. Since our scanner returned reflected laser intensity as well as depth, we were able to calculate the 3D coordinates of each feature point.

- To correct for spatial radiometric effects, including lens vignetting, angular non-uniformity and inverse-square-law falloff of our spotlight, and spatial non-uniformity in the response of our sensor, we photographed a white card under the spotlight and built a per-pixel intensity correction table.

Discussion. How well did our calibration procedures work? Only moderately well; in fact, this was the weakest part of our system. The fault appears to lie not in our geometric model, but in the repeatability of our system. Comparing scans taken under different conditions (different scan axes, translational positions, etc.), we have observed discrepancies larger than a millimeter, enough to destroy Michelangelo's chisel marks if they cannot be eliminated. Fortunately, we have been able to use our software alignment process to partially compensate for the shortcomings of our calibration process, as discussed in section 4.1. An alternative solution we are now investigating is self-calibration - using scans taken under different conditions to better estimate the parameters of our geometric model [Jokinen99]. We also learned a few rules of thumb about designing for calibration: store data in the rawest format possible (e.g. motion commands instead of derived rotation angles) so that if the calibration is later improved, it can be applied to the old data (we did this), check the calibration regularly in the field (we didn't do this), and be wary of designing a reconfigurable scanner. Finally, we found that partitioning calibration into stages, and our particular choice of stages, forced us to measure scan head motions to very fine tolerances. We are currently exploring alternative partitionings.

3. Scanning procedure

Figure 6 shows our typical working environment in a museum. The basic unit of work was a "scan"; an efficient team could complete 10-15 scans in an 8-hour shift. Here are the steps in a typical scan:

Scan initiation. An operator interactively moved the scan head through a sequence of motions, setting the limits of the volume to be scanned. The volume that could be covered in a single scan was constrained by four factors:

- the field of view and limits of motion of the scanner
- the falloff in scan quality with increasing laser obliquity
- occlusions of either the laser or the line of sight to the camera
- physical obstructions such as walls, the statue, or the gantry

Once a scan was planned, a scanning script ran automatically, taking from a few minutes to an hour or more to complete, depending on how large an area was to be covered.

135

Figure 6: Our Cyberware gantry standing next to Michelangelo's David. In this photograph the gantry is sitting atop its curb-hopping platform (*a*) and is extended to its maximum height, thus placing the scan head (*b*) 25 feet above the floor. The truss section at (*c*) was added at the last minute when we discovered that the David was taller than we thought [1]. The scanner was tethered to a mobile workbench (*d*), which contained the scanner electronics, a Silicon Graphics Octane, and 72 GB of disk storage.

Range scanning. A typical range scan consisted of several concentric curved shells separated by translational motion of the scan head along the horizontal table. Each shell in turn consisted of several horizontally adjacent vertical sweeps of the laser, as shown in figure 5. If the laser line was turned vertically, then the sweeps were horizontal instead. We decided to overlap adjacent sweeps and shells by 40% and 15%, respectively - enough to align them in software in the absence of precisely calibrated motion. Since scanning was slow (1 cm per second), we preceded each sweep with a high-speed (10 cm per second), low-resolution pre-scan that conservatively determined which part of the sweep actually contained data.

Color scanning. To maintain color-to-range calibration, we interspersed color and range scanning. Since the field of view and depth of field of the color camera were greater than the field of view of the range camera, we acquired color images more sparsely than range sweeps. To compensate for ambient lighting (we often scanned during the day), we shot each image twice, once with and once without our spotlight. By subtracting these two images, we obtained an image as if illuminated only by the spotlight.

[1] We designed our gantry according to the height given in Charles De Tolnay's 5-volume study of Michelangelo [Tolnay45] and echoed in every other book we checked, including the official guidebook sold at the museum. However, the David is not 434cm without his pedestal, as given by these sources; he is 517cm, an error of nearly 3 feet! We do not know the original source of this error.

```
for horizontal = min to max by 12 cm
  for pan = min to max by 4.3°
    for tilt = min to max continuously
      perform fast pre-scan (5°/sec)
    search pre-scan for range data
    for tilt = all occupied intervals
      perform slow scan (0.5°/sec)
on every other horizontal position,
for pan = min to max by 7°
  for tilt = min to max by 7°
    take color image without spotlight
warm up spotlight
for pan = min to max by 7°
  for tilt = min to max by 7°
    take color image with spotlight
```

Figure 7: The sequence of events executed by a typical scanning script. For this script, the scan head is assumed to be mounted above the horizontal arm, looking parallel to it, and the laser stripe is assumed to be horizontal.

Discussion. Figure 7 summarizes the sequence of events executed by a typical scanning script. In general, our scanning procedure worked smoothly. Figure 8(a) and 8(b) show our scanner acquiring range and color data on St. Matthew.

Our biggest failure was the lack of an automated method for planning scans. View planning is a well-known computational geometry problem. Recent papers covering the special case of 3D scanning include [Maver93, Pito96]. Most of these methods focus on what might be called the "midgame": given a partially complete 3D model, what are the next best *n* scans to acquire? However, our experience suggests that the "endgame" is more important: given a 3D model that contains a few holes, how can these holes be filled? Since we did not have an automated view planning system, we planned scans by eye - a slow and error-prone process. We often spent hours positioning the gantry in fruitless attempts to fill holes in our model of the David. A view planner might have saved 25% of the man-hours we spent in the museum.

A mixed success was our attempt to use a commercial handheld laser triangulation scanner for hard-to-reach places. (Ours was a 3D Scanners ModelMaker mounted on a Faro Silver Series digitizing arm.) Although its Y-resolution (along the laser stripe) matched that of our Cyberware scanner, its X-resolution depended on how slowly the user swept the stripe across the surface. In practice, hand tremors made it difficult to obtain smooth and monotonic motion. The latter introduced folds into the range data, complicating our post-processing pipeline. Moreover, it was fatiguing to hold the scanner for long periods of time. We used it on St. Matthew and the Slaves, but not on the David or the Medici Chapel statues.

3.1. Safety for the statues

An overriding concern throughout our project was to avoid harming the statues we were digitizing. Laser triangulation is fundamentally a non-contact digitization method; only light touches the artwork. Nevertheless, light and heat can potentially damage art, so their levels must be controlled. Our scanning beam was a 5 mW red semiconductor laser, but its power was spread into a line 20 cm wide at the statue surface, and it moved nearly continuously during scanning. Our white light source was a 250 W incandescent bulb,

(a) Acquiring range data. The laser line sweeps downward at 1 cm per second, acquiring 14,400 points per second. After a sweep, the head pans to the right and performs another sweep.

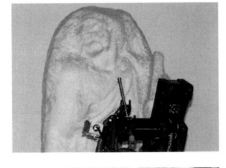

(b) Acquiring color data. One 1520 x 1144 pixel image is acquired every 3 seconds. Our white spotlight can be seen illuminating the statue. Figures (c) and (d) are taken from the upper neck.

(c) Computer rendering, with artificial lighting and reflectance, of the scan from (a). The spacing between samples is 0.29 mm, and the depth resolution is 50 microns. This area was carved with a gradina (see figure 2).

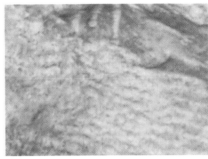

(d) Typical color image acquired in (b). The nominal X,Y pixel spacing is 0.15 mm; the physical spacing is 0.31 mm. The image seems flat because the spotlight is nearly co-axial with the camera.

(e) Closeup of (c). This is a single sweep, so it is a regular 2D array (note that the triangles are in rows). The gaps are missing data due to occlusions.

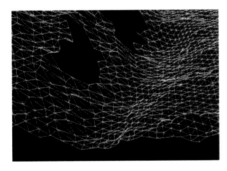

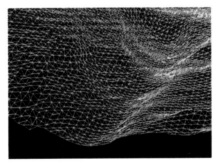

(f) Closeup of a merged mesh combining (c) and other scans. It is irregular since it is the isosurface of a volume. It is made finer than the raw scans to avoid aliasing.

(g) Rendering of merged mesh. It is slightly blurrier than (c), due to miscalibration and misalignment of the scans, but the chisel marks are still clearly visible. Not all of our scans were used here, so some holes remain.

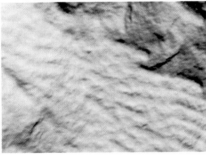

(h) Merged mesh from (g) with per-vertex reflectances blended from (d) and other color images. This view is not lit, so the whitening at the bottom of chisel marks is easy to see, e.g. at the extreme right and top.

(i) Mesh from (h), but lit and rendered like (c) and (g). The whitening, which is easy to see in (h), is masked here by lighting effects. However, it becomes obvious if the light is moved interactively.

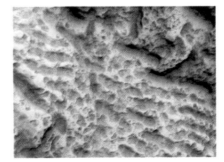

(j) A non-photorealistic visualization of the chisel marks. The geometry is the same as (g), but per-vertex colors are computed using accessibility shading [Miller94].

Figure 8: Our scanning procedure and post-processing pipeline. The statue is Michelangelo's unfinished apostle St. Matthew, in the Accademia gallery in Florence. It took us 6 days to scan this statue and another week to post-process it. The full model is shown in figure 9.

but its power was conducted to the scan head through a fiber-optic cable, which effectively blocked heat, and its light was spread into a disk 50cm wide at the statue surface. In both cases, energy deposition on the statue was negligible compared to ambient lighting.

A more serious danger was posed by accidental collisions between the scanner and the statue. Our primary defense against such accidents was our long standoff, but as discussed earlier, we often ended up working closer to the statue than we expected. To reduce the chance of collisions in these situations, we used manual rather than software motor controls to plan scan head motions, we mounted pressure-sensitive motion cutoff switches on the rails of the horizontal and vertical translation tables, and we assigned one member of each scanning team to operate as a spotter. To reduce the chance of damage in case of inadvertent contact, our scan head was encased in foam rubber. Finally, we established rigid operating protocols, we tried (mostly unsuccessfully) to avoid putting ourselves under time pressure, and we tried to get enough sleep.

In the end, we succeeded in scanning nearly around-the-clock for five months without damaging anything. However, we consider ourselves lucky. There is no silver bullet for these safety issues. Scanners employing longer standoffs can reduce the risks during certain phases, but most statues cannot be scanned entirely from outside their convex hull. Eventually, either a scanner or a mirror must be positioned close to the statue.

4. Post-processing

As soon as a scan was acquired, it entered a lengthy post-processing pipeline, whose eventual goal was to produce a polygon mesh with a reflectance value at each mesh vertex.

4.1. Range processing pipeline

Our range processing pipeline consisted of aligning the scans taken from different gantry positions, first interactively, then automatically, merging these scans using a volumetric algorithm, and filling holes using space carving. The output of this pipeline was a watertight irregular triangle mesh.

Aligning scans. The first step was to bring the hundreds of scans for a statue, which were acquired with the gantry in different (untracked) locations, into a common coordinate system. Alignment was done in four steps, as follows:

(1) As each scan completed, an operator interactively aligned it to the existing model by translating and rotating it until it lay in roughly the correct position. Alternatively, the operator could identify three corresponding points on the new scan and any existing scan. This sounds easy, but it's not, especially if the scans are smooth or the overlap with existing scans is slight.

(2) Once the new scan was approximately positioned, the operator chose one existing scan that substantially overlapped the new scan and invoked a modified iterated-closest-points (ICP) algorithm [Besl92, ChenMed92] to refine their alignment. ICP algorithms operate by finding matching points on two meshes, computing the rigid transformation that minimizes the sum of squared distances between these point pairs, and iterating until some convergence criterion is met.

(3) After the statue was completely scanned and the data brought back to the laboratory, a script was run to find every pair of substantially overlapping scans, isolate them from the rest of the data, and run ICP on them to find their mutual alignment.

For every such alignment we stored the rigid transformation between the two scans and a list of matching point pairs.

(4) Finally, these lists of matching point pairs were used as constraints in an iterative relaxation algorithm designed to bring the scans into global alignment while evenly spreading out the error among the pairwise alignments [Pulli99].

Previous solutions to the global alignment problem typically generalize pairwise ICP [Bergevin96], that is, each scan is aligned in turn with all other nearby scans, and the process is iterated until it converges. However, this approach requires all scans to be resident in memory, and the repeated use of ICP makes it slow. Our algorithm produces comparable results, and it is more efficient in space and time. However, it is not infinitely scalable; we must at least fit our lists of matching points into memory. Our justification for separating pairwise alignment from the relaxation step is that pairwise alignment of scans finds the best local matching of points that can be found; repeating this step can only make these matches worse.

Merging scans. To reconstruct a surface from a set of aligned range scans, we employed the method described in [Curless96]. Beginning with a dense volumetric grid, we visit each voxel near one or more range surfaces and store a weighted sum of the signed distances from that voxel to each range surface, where distances are taken along lines of sight from the voxel to the range camera. Voxels in front of the surface but on a line of sight are marked as empty, a process known as space carving. All remaining voxels are marked as unseen. We can extract from the volume either an accurate isosurface that corresponds to the observed surface, or we can extend the isosurface to include the boundaries between empty and unseen regions, resulting in a watertight (hole-free) surface. The triangles added in this way can be flagged as "reconstructed" rather than "observed", to differentiate them for scientific purposes. To enable this algorithm to handle large datasets, we broke large volumes into blocks and processed them independently Each block yielded a piece of reconstructed surface, which we stitched together by identifying and merging common vertices between neighboring blocks.

Discussion. How well did our pipeline work? In most cases, it worked well. However, it was time-consuming, occupying about 25% of our man-hours in the museum and several man-days per statue in the laboratory afterwards. Some time could have been saved if we had tracked our gantry; even a rough estimate of the position and orientation of the scan head would have permitted us to bypass step 1 of our alignment procedure. To eliminate step 2 we would have had to track the scan head with 25 micron accuracy from a distance of up to 10 meters [1]. We know of no field-deployable technology with this accuracy. Alternatively, we could have replaced step 1, possibly combined with step 2, with searching globally for an alignment to the existing model using heuristics such as in [Besl92, Hebert95, Johnson97, Zhang99]. The problem with global search methods is that they require more surface overlap than local methods. This is an area for further research.

To our surprise, our software alignment process proved sufficiently robust that we could use it to partially compensate for our calibration problems. Miscalibration manifested itself in our system as misalignments between sweeps and as warpage of individual sweeps. The first effect could be reduced by treating sweeps as

---

[1] An error of 25 microns in the position of a tooling ball located on the scan head 11 cm from the tilt axis would produce an angular error of 0.013° (see section 2.5) in the tilt of the scan head, leading in turn to an error of 0.25 mm in the position of digitized objects located 112 cm from this axis.

separate scans in steps 3 and 4 of our alignment procedure. This strategy works only if a sweep contains enough fine detail for the ICP algorithm to lock on to. So far, we have used it successfully to align St. Matthew, which contains 104 scans and 2285 sweeps (see figure 9). Aligning this data took 20 hours on one processor of an SGI Onyx2, and volumetric merging took 50 hours. Note that Michelangelo's chisel marks are preserved. For statues without fine geometric detail, like some portions of the David, it might be possible to use color imagery to guide alignment [Pulli97, Bernardini00]. In the future, we envision breaking sweeps into smaller pieces and aligning them separately in order to distribute the warp more uniformly across the statue. We also plan to experiment with non-rigid alignment. Finally, we plan to use theodolite data as constraints, to ensure that the additional degrees of freedom introduced by using these techniques do not cause distortion of the entire model [Beraldin97] [1].

Although our merging process worked well, we were disappointed by the number of holes, some several centimeters in size, that remained after we had done our best job scanning a statue. A sculptor can, using chisels and a drill, carve recesses too deep to scan using any triangulation rangefinder. The David has many such recesses, especially around his hands, hair, and scrotum. We can bridge these gaps using space carving as described earlier, but the bridge surfaces sometimes look objectionable. We believe they can be ameliorated by relaxing their shape, subject to maintaining tangency where they meet observed surfaces, but we have not tried this.

4.2. Color processing pipeline

Our color processing pipeline consisted of correcting our color images geometrically and radiometrically, discarding pixels that were occluded with respect to the camera or light, projecting the remaining pixels onto our merged mesh, and converting color to reflectance. The output of this pipeline was an RGB reflectance triplet for each vertex of the mesh.

For this last step we needed a model of the bidirectional reflectance distribution function (BRDF) at each point on the surface. Clean marble is a dielectric material with varying color (due to veining) and a roughness that depends on the level of polish. For surfaces of this type, Sato and Ikeuchi have used range and color measurements to estimate diffuse, specular, and roughness parameters [Sato97]. Our pipeline is similar to theirs, except that so far we have only attempted to extract diffuse reflectances. To eliminate specular contributions, we discarded observations close to the mirror direction. This approach is robust, and since under a diffuse assumption we have redundant color observations for each point on the surface, the loss of data is inconsequential. Discarding pixels near the mirror direction also circumvents the problem of sensor saturation, although this could be solved using high dynamic range methods [Debevec97] at the cost of acquiring more images.

Mapping color onto the mesh. The first step in our pipeline was to subtract the images acquired with and without the spotlight as described in section 3, thereby compensating for ambient illumination. Next, the difference image was corrected for geometric distortion, chromatic aberration, and radiometric effects using the

---

[1] A theodolite is a surveying tool that locates points in 3-space by optically sighting them from two calibrated locations on the ground and measuring their direction angles from those locations. Using an optical theodolite with an accuracy of 0.5 mm, we measured several points on most of the statues we scanned.

Figure 9: A rendering of our full-resolution, merged model of Michelangelo's St. Matthew. The original dataset contained 104 scans, 800,000,000 polygons, and 4,000 color images. The model shown here contains 386,488,573 polygons. It still contains some holes, and we have not yet mapped our color data onto it. See figure 8 for closeup views.

calibration data described in section 2.6. We then needed to decide which vertices of our merged mesh saw the color camera and light source. For this purpose we used a hardware-accelerated polygon renderer. We rendered the mesh from both points of view, read back the depth buffers, and for each mesh vertex compared its distance from the camera and light source with the contents of the depth buffers at the appropriate pixel. If the vertex was occluded from the camera or light source, we discarded it. Although it is possible to miss thin occluders using this approach, marble statues generally do not contain any. If a vertex saw both the camera and the light, we projected it to the camera image and sampled the color found there.

Computing reflectance. Once we associated a color with a vertex, we performed an inverse lighting calculation to convert color to reflectance. This calculation is sometimes called "de-shading." Since the exit pupil of our fiber-optic cable's focusing assembly was small relative to its distance from the statue, we treated it as a point source. In this case, the irradiance E on the surface is

$$E = \frac{1}{r^2} I \cos\theta$$

where I is the radiant intensity of the point source, θ is the obliquity of the surface relative to the light, and r is the distance between them. Knowing the irradiance and the reflected radiance $L(\omega_r)$ in the direction ω_r towards the camera, and assuming ideal Lambertian reflection, the reflectance R is

$$R = \frac{L(\omega_r)}{E} = \frac{L(\omega_r)\, r^2}{I \cos\theta}$$

In our case, we did not know the radiant intensity of our light source, and, because we did not measure the absolute sensitivity of our camera, we knew reflected radiance only up to an unknown constant k. However, we knew from our calibration procedure the radiance (up to this same constant) reflected from a white card placed at the standoff distance. Assuming that the card is also ideal Lambertian, its reflectance R_c is

$$R_c = \frac{L_c(\omega_r)\, r^2}{I \cos\theta_c}$$

where $\theta_c = 0$ and $r = 112$ cm. The ratio of the reflectance of the statue surface to the reflectance of the white card is

$$\frac{R}{R_c} = \frac{L(\omega_r)}{L_c(\omega_r) \cos\theta}$$

where r and the unknowns I and k have canceled out. By separately determining the reflectance R_c of our white card relative to a reflectance standard such as Spectralon®, we could estimate the absolute reflectance of the statue surface.

Blending multiple observations. Each mesh vertex usually saw many color images. If the surface were ideal Lambertian, the computed reflectances would agree. However, our surfaces were not, and our observations included noise, miscalibration, and other errors. We therefore needed a rule for blending reflectances together. For this purpose, we computed a confidence for each reflectance based on the following factors:

- obliquity of the surface with respect to the light
- projected area of the surface with respect to the camera
- proximity to the mirror direction, to suppress highlights
- proximity to a silhouette edge with respect to the camera
- proximity to a silhouette edge with respect to the light
- proximity to the edge of the color image

Confidence was made lower near silhouettes to account for blur in the camera lens and penumbrae due to the non-zero extent of the light source. To prevent rapid changes in confidence from triggering sudden switches from one color image to another, we smoothed confidences among neighbors on the mesh. However, to remain conservative we never increased confidence, only decreased it. The last step was to sum the weighted reflectances at each mesh vertex.

Discussion. Although our color processing pipeline produced visually satisfactory results (see figure 10), there are several factors we did not consider. We treated the diffuse reflectance as ideal Lambertian, although it is not [Oren94]. We also ignored inter-reflections, which may be significant since our statues are light-colored [Yu99]. By modeling the effect of these interreflections, it may be possible to improve our estimate of surface shape [Nayar90]. Similarly, we ignored subsurface scattering [Dorsey99]. However, its contribution is probably minor on dirty, unpolished statues like the David, especially relative to its size.

Finally, in calculating irradiance at each point, we are employing an aggregate surface normal obtained from a 3D scan of the surface. Such de-shading calculations suffer from two problems. First, they are sensitive to noise in the surface normals; however, our use of redundant range images and a volumetric range merging algorithm reduces this noise somewhat. Second, geometric details too fine to scan will not be present in the normal field and will not enter the irradiance calculation. These details consequently manifest themselves as changes to the diffuse reflectance. As a result, care must be taken when using our reflectances for scientific analyses, for example to estimate marble properties. Interestingly, we may have acquired enough redundant color imagery to calculate a view-dependent reflectance texture [Dana99], permitting correct renderings from all viewpoints. This is a topic for future research.

5. Handling large datasets

One significant challenge we faced in this project was the size of our datasets, the largest of which was the David (see table 1). In our post-processing pipeline, we addressed this problem by using an efficient global alignment algorithm and a blocked range image merging algorithm. However, our scanning procedure posed additional challenges. In order to plan scans for a statue, we had to load its 3D model into memory. As each scan completed, we needed to add it quickly to the model. At the time of the project we knew of no modeling package into which we could load a 2-billion polygon model, nor any simplification algorithm that could be reasonably run on a mesh of this size (and we tried several). Therefore, we spent a lot of time writing code for handling large scanned models.

Range images versus polygon meshes. Our first technique was to store our data as range images instead of as polygon meshes. A range image is a 2D array $r(u, v)$ of range values r, some of which might be invalid due to occlusions of the laser or range camera. A range image is, of course, only a special case of a displacement map, a well-known object in computer graphics. Range images are efficient because the u and v coordinates are implicit and the r values have limited precision. To take advantage of this natural compression, we designed a file format containing an array of 16-bit range values and a header with enough information to map these range values to 3D points. To efficiently skip over missing range samples, we run-length encoded this array. If stored as uncompressed 3D vertex coordinates and index lists, the geometry of the David would occupy 36 gigabytes. Stored as run-length encoded

Figure 10: On the left is a photograph of Michelangelo's David. On the right is a rendering made from our model. Constructed at a resolution of 1.0 mm, the model is watertight and contains 4 million polygons. Its surface reflectance was computed from digitized color images as described in section 4.2. The photograph was taken under uncalibrated conditions, so its viewpoint and illumination differ slightly from those of the rendering. The raw data for this part of the statue was acquired at a resolution of 0.29 mm and contained 480 million polygons and 2,000 color images. Using one processor of an SGI Onyx2, it took 12 hours to align merge, and map color onto this model.

range images, it occupies only 2 gigabytes, a savings of 18:1 with no loss in information. More lossless compression could be obtained by using entropy coding, but decoding would be slower.

Range image pyramids. No matter how efficient our storage mechanism is, no current workstation can display 2 billion polygons in real time, so we needed strategies for working at reduced resolution. Fortunately, as long as we stored our models as range images, we could simplify them quickly by subsampling them, thereby creating range image pyramids. Depending on the task, we had several ways of constructing these pyramids, as shown in figure 11.

Lazy evaluation. To save space and time, we constructed range image pyramids from range images on demand, never storing them, and we constructed only those levels requested by the user. To display a range image, or to merge multiple range images as described in section 4.1, it must be converted to 3D points, then to a triangle mesh. We did this lazily as well. Fortunately, the conversion from range samples to 3D points can be done quickly using incremental arithmetic, and since the points appear in scanline order, they can be triangulated quickly by connecting adjacent points. Of course, care must be taken to avoid bridging depth discontinuities.

Viewer based on point rendering. If one only wants to view a 3D model, and not perform geometric operations on it, then it need not be represented polygonally. With this in mind we developed a viewer that combines a multiresolution hierarchy based on bounding spheres with a rendering system based on points [Rusinkiewicz00]. Our viewer preprocesses new meshes in seconds, launches quickly, maintains a constant frame rate regardless of object complexity, yields reasonable image quality during motion, and refines progressively if idle to a high final image quality. With modest hardware acceleration, our viewer permits real-time navigation of scanned models containing hundreds of millions of polygons.

The statue	
height without pedestal	517 cm
surface area	19 m^2
volume	2.2 m^3
weight	5,800 kg
Our raw dataset	
number of polygons	2 billion
number of color images	7,000
losslessly compressed size	32 GB
Other statistics	
total size of scanning team	22 people
staffing in the museum	3 people (on average)
time spent scanning	360 hours over 30 days
man-hours scanning	1,080
man-hours post-processing	1,500 (so far)

Table 1: Some statistics about our scan of Michelangelo's statue of David. The area, volume, and weight of the statue are estimated from our data.

6. Conclusions

We have described a system for digitizing the shape and color of large statues, and a demonstration of this system on the statues of Michelangelo. As computer scientists and technologists, our principal goal in pursuing this project was to push the state-of-the-art in 3D scanning. Our model of Michelangelo's David is two orders of magnitude larger than any existing scanned model. In trying to acquire and post-process this data, we were forced to invent new methods for representing, viewing, aligning, merging, and viewing large 3D models, methods that we have presented here and in related papers [Pulli99, Rusinkiewicz00].

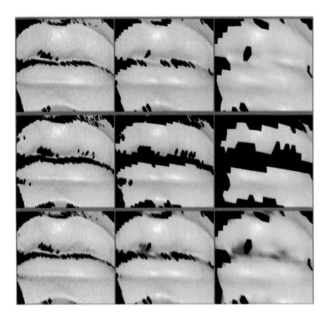

Figure 11: Range image pyramids of David's lips. The fastest way to construct a pyramid is to subsample the range image, without filtering, by successive factors of 2x in u and v (top row, left to right). To help us find holes, we can also delete any range sample if any of its 4 children at the next finer pyramid level is missing (middle row), making holes visible even at the coarsest resolution. Alternatively, we can redden the parents of missing children in proportion to the fraction of its children that are missing (bottom).

Although it is not the purpose of this paper to tell the story of the Digital Michelangelo Project, we faced many logistical problems that future digitizing projects may encounter, so it is worthwhile briefly enumerating them.

First and foremost, getting permission to scan Michelangelo's statues was a long, delicate, and occasionally painful process. Part of the pain was developing meaningful, equitable, and enforceable intellectual property agreements with the cultural institutions whose artistic patrimony we were digitizing. Since the goals of our project were scientific, our arrangement with the museums was simple and flexible: we are allowed to use and distribute our models and computer renderings for scientific use only. In the event we, or they, desire to use the models commercially, there will be further negotiations and probably the payment of royalties.

Second, we underestimated the difficulty of digitizing under field (non-laboratory) conditions. Shipping 4 tons of equipment to a foreign country, trucking it through narrow streets, and carrying it into historic buildings, was nerve-wracking and expensive. As soon as we moved our equipment into a museum, we became a liability to them - physically, logistically, and legally. During 5 months of scanning, we spent $50,000 hiring museum guards to watch over us, the statues, and the tourists. In the Accademia gallery, we found it necessary to remove the glass security barricades surrounding every statue, including the David. To minimize the time these statues were left unprotected, shifts were long and days off were few. Scanning during museum hours posed additional problems: bumped scanners, color images ruined by tourist flashbulbs, and a constant stream of questions (which we always answered).

Lastly, although most of our plans worked out, there were several disappointments. In particular, we were unable to scan the

Pietà (in St. Peter's Basilica) because it was under restoration in preparation for the Year 2000 Jubilee. Scanning this statue may be impractical in any case; it is mounted high on a pedestal, it is sandwiched between an immovable altar in front and a niche behind, and it is highly polished. It may also be too geometrically complicated to scan using laser triangulation technology.

One of the tangible results of the Digital Michelangelo Project is a set of 3D geometric models, one per statue, architectural setting, or map fragment that we scanned. In the months (and maybe years) ahead we will process the data we have collected, and in the case of the Forma Urbis Romae (see figure 16) we will try to assemble the map. Our plan is to make these models freely available to the research community.

7. Acknowledgements

More people helped us than we can possibly acknowledge in this space. Scanning alongside us in the museums were Alana Chan, Kathryn Chinn, Jelena Curless, Unnur Gretarsdottir, Rahul Gupta, Wallace Huang, Dana Katter, Dan Perkel, Domi Piturro, Semira Rahemtulla, Alex Roetter, Marco Tarini, Maisie Tsui, and Daniel Wood. Backing us up in the Stanford Computer Graphics Laboratory à Firenze were John Gerth and Lisa Pacelle. Key contributors to the scanner design were Everett Reed, Jim Meek, Lloyd Addleman, and David Addleman of Cyberware. Our Italian collaborators (and occasional political brushfire fighters) included Cristina Acidini Luchinat, Licia Bertani, Barbara Caputo, Franca Falletti, Laura Ferrea, Eugenio La Rocca, Susanna Le Pera, Roberto Scopigno, and Anna Mura Somella. Our collaborators at the National Research Council of Canada included Marc Rioux, Guy Godin, Angelo Beraldin, and Luc Cournoyer. We received invaluable technical advice throughout the project from Paul Debevec and Matti Auvinen. Figure 13 was rendered by Henrik Wann Jensen. Our sponsors were Stanford University, Interval Research Corporation, and the Paul Allen Foundation for the Arts.

8. References

[Beraldin97] Beraldin, J.-A., Cournoyer, L., Rioux, M., Blais, F., El-Hakim, S.F., Godin, G., "Object model creation from multiple range images: acquisition, calibration, model building and verification," *Proc. 1st Int'l Conf. on 3-D Digital Imaging and Modeling*, IEEE, 1997, pp. 326-333.

[Beraldin99] Beraldin, J.-A., Blais, F., Cournoyer, L., Rioux, M., El-Hakim, S.F., Rodell, R., Bernier, F., Harrison, N., "Digital 3D imaging system for rapid response on remote sites," *Proc. 2nd Int'l Conf. on 3-D Digital Imaging and Modeling*, IEEE, 1999, pp. 34-43.

[Bergevin96] Bergevin, R., Soucy, M., Gagnon, H., Laurendeau, D., "Towards a general multi-view registration technique," *IEEE Trans. PAMI*, Vol. 18, No. 5, May, 1996, pp. 540-547.

[Bernardini00] Bernardini, F., Martin, I., Rushmeier, H., "High-Quality Texture Synthesis from Multiple Scans," IBM Research Report RC 21656(97598), February, 2000, IBM Research, Yorktown Heights, NY.

[Besl92] Besl, P., McKay, N., "A Method for Registration of 3-D Shapes," *IEEE Trans. PAMI*, Vol. 14, No. 2, February, 1992, pp. 239-256.

[ChenMed92] Chen, Y., Medioni, G., "Object modeling by registration of multiple range images," *Image and Vision Computing*, Vol. 10, No. 3, April, 1992, pp. 145-155.

[Rocchini99] Rocchini, C., Cignoni, P., Montani, C., Scopigno, R., "Multiple textures stitching and blending on 3D objects," *Proc. 10th Eurographics Rendering Workshop*, Springer-Verlag, 1999, pp. 119-130.

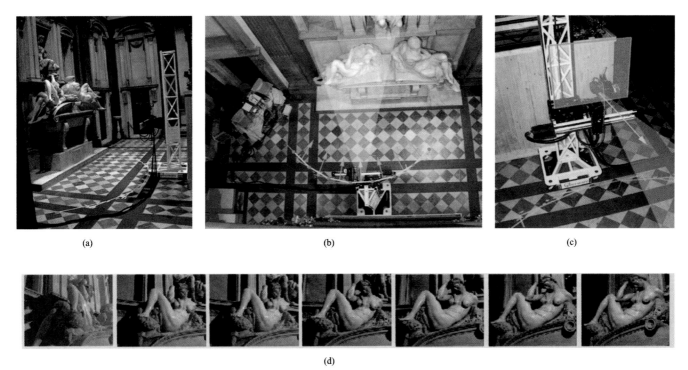

(a)   (b)   (c)

(d)

Figure 12: In addition to scanning Michelangelo's statue of Night, we also acquired a dense light field of it [Levoy96]. This particular statue is highly polished and thus optically interesting. (a) Our camera "swath" followed a 90° eye-level arc around the statue (taped out on the floor). (b) A plan view of the camera path. It consisted of 7 "light field slabs," shown here by yellow line segments. (c) Each slab was a planar array of 62 x 56 images, with images spaced 12.5mm apart on the plane. The total number of images was thus 24,304. (d) A representative image from each slab. Acquisition was performed using a Sony DKC-ST5 ultra-high resolution 3-CCD digital still camera mounted in place of our scan head. Shooting the light field took 35 hours over 4 consecutive nights. Keeping the illumination constant throughout the shoot was hard. Having a 3D model and dense light field of the same object will provide a unique opportunity for exploring hybrid image-based representations in which these two kinds of data are combined [Wood00].

[Curless96] Curless, B., Levoy, M., "A Volumetric Method for Building Complex Models from Range Images," Proc. SIGGRAPH '96, ACM, 1996, pp. 303-312.

[Dana99] Dana, K.J., Nayer, S.K., Ginneken, B.V, Koenderink, J.J., "Reflectance and Texture of Real-World Surfaces," *ACM Trans. on Graphics*, Vol. 18, No. 1, January 1999, pp. 1-34.

[Debevec97] Debevec, P.E., Malik, J., "Recovering high dynamic range radiance maps from photographs," Proc. SIGGRAPH '97, ACM, 1997, pp. 369-378.

[Dorsey99] Dorsey, J., Edelman, A., Jensen, H.-W., Legakis, J., Pedersen, H.-K., "Modeling and rendering of weathered stone," Proc. SIGGRAPH '99, ACM, 1999, pp. 225-234.

[Giovannini99] Giovannini, P., "Il 'San Matteo' di Michelangelo: analisi delle tracce di lavorazione, studio degli strumenti e osservazioni sulla tecnica di scultura," *Rivista dell'Opificio delle Pietre Dure*, Vol. 10, 1998, pp. 205-228.

[Hebert95] Hebert, M., Ikeuchi, K., Delingette, H., "A Spherical Representation for Recognition of Free-Form Surfaces," *IEEE Trans. PAMI*, Vol. 17, No. 7, July, 1995, pp. 681-690.

[Heikkilä97] Heikkilä J., Silvén O., "A four-step camera calibration procedure with implicit image correction," *Proc. CVPR '97*, IEEE, 1997, pp. 1106-1112.

[Johnson97] Johnson, A.E., Hebert, M., "Surface Registration by Matching Oriented Points," *Proc. 1st Int'l Conf. on 3D Digital Imaging and Modeling*, IEEE, 1997, pp. 121-128.

[Jokinen99] Jokinen, O., "Self-calibration of a light striping system by matching multiple 3-D profile maps," *Proc. 2nd Int'l Conf. on 3-D Digital Imaging and Modeling*, IEEE, 1999, pp. 180-190.

[Levoy96] Levoy, M., Hanrahan, P., "Light Field Rendering," Proc. SIGGRAPH '96, ACM, 1996, pp. 31-42.

[Miller94] Miller, G., "Efficient Algorithms for Local and Global Accessibility Shading," Proc. SIGGRAPH '94, ACM, 1994, *Computer Graphics* pp. 319-326.

[Nayar90] Nayar, S. K., Ikeuchi, K., Kanade, T., "Shape from Interreflections," *Proc. ICCV '90*, IEEE, 1990, pp. 2-11.

[Oren94] Oren, M., Nayar, S.K., "Generalization of Lambert's reflectance model," Proc. SIGGRAPH '94, ACM, 1994, pp. 239-246.

[Maver93] Maver, J., Bajcsy, R., "Occlusions as a Guide for Planning the Next View," *IEEE Trans. PAMI*, Vol. 15, No. 5, May, 1993, pp. 417-433.

[Pito96] Pito, R., "A sensor-based solution to the next best view problem," *Proc. ICPR '96*, 1996, pp. 941-945.

[Pulli97] Pulli, K., *Surface Reconstruction and Display from Range and Color Data*, Ph.D. dissertation, University of Washington, 1997.

[Pulli99] Pulli, K., "Multiview registration for large data sets," *Proc. 2nd Int'l Conf. on 3-D Digital Imaging and Modeling*, IEEE, 1999, pp. 160-168.

[Rushmeier97] Rushmeier, H., Taubin, G., Guéziec, A., "Applying shape from lighting variation to bump map capture," *Proc. 8th Eurographics Rendering Workshop*, Springer-Verlag, 1997, pp. 35-44.

[Rushmeier98] Rushmeier, H., Bernardini, F., Mittleman, J., Taubin, G., "Acquiring input for rendering at appropriate levels of detail: digitizing a Pietà," *Proc. 9th Eurographics Rendering Workshop*, Springer-Verlag, 1998, pp. 81-92.

[Rusinkiewicz00] Rusinkiewicz, S., Levoy, M., "Qsplat: a multiresolution point rendering system for large meshes," Proc. SIGGRAPH 2000 (these proceedings).

[Sato97] Sato, Y., Wheeler, M.D., Ikeuchi, K., "Object shape and reflectance modeling from observation," Proc. SIGGRAPH '97, ACM, 1997, pp. 379-387.

[Tolnay45] De Tolnay, C., "Michelangelo," Princeton University Press, 1945.

[Wood00] Wood, D., Azuma, D., Aldinger, K., Curless, B., Duchamp, T., Salesin, D., Stuetzle, W., "Surface Light Fields for 3D Photography," Proc. SIGGRAPH 2000 (these proceedings).

[Yu99] Yu, Y., Debevec, P., Malik, J., Hawkins, T., "Inverse global illumination: recovering reflectance models of real scenes from photographs," Proc. SIGGRAPH '99, ACM, 1999, pp. 215-224.

[Zhang99] Zhang, D., Hebert, M., "Harmonic maps and their applications in surface matching," *Proc. Computer Vision and Pattern Recognition (CVPR) '99*, IEEE, 1999, pp. 525-530.

Figure 14: A photograph of David's head taken under ultraviolet light. Once mapped onto our 3D model, this data will show the location of waxes and other organic materials. This may help conservators plan future cleanings of the statue.

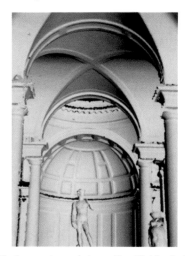

Figure 15: A computer rendering, with artificial reflectance, of a 15-million polygon model of the Accademia gallery in Florence. The data for this model was acquired using a Cyra time-of-flight laser scanner with a Z resolution of about 5 mm. We also acquired a model of the Medici Chapel, and we acquired color data at both sites.

Figure 13: A computer rendering made from a 2.0 mm, 8-million polygon model of Michelangelo's David. The raw 0.29 mm dataset contains 2 billion polygons. The veining and reflectance are artificial. The rendering includes physically correct subsurface scattering [Dorsey99], but with arbitrary parameters. The model contains some slightly misaligned scans and is not watertight. Improving this model, and computing correct reflectances for it, is an ongoing project.

Figure 16: A fragment of the Forma Urbis Romae. During our year in Italy, we scanned all 1,163 fragments of this ancient marble map. This fragment is 68 cm long. Our goal is to piece the map back together by developing compact digital signatures for the geometry of the fragments and searching among these signatures for matches.

Acquiring the Reflectance Field of a Human Face

Paul Debevec[†]   Tim Hawkins[†]   Chris Tchou[†]   Haarm-Pieter Duiker[†]   Westley Sarokin[†]

and Mark Sagar[‡]

[†]University of California at Berkeley[1]   [‡]LifeF/X, Inc.

ABSTRACT

We present a method to acquire the reflectance field of a human face and use these measurements to render the face under arbitrary changes in lighting and viewpoint. We first acquire images of the face from a small set of viewpoints under a dense sampling of incident illumination directions using a light stage. We then construct a reflectance function image for each observed image pixel from its values over the space of illumination directions. From the reflectance functions, we can directly generate images of the face from the original viewpoints in any form of sampled or computed illumination. To change the viewpoint, we use a model of skin reflectance to estimate the appearance of the reflectance functions for novel viewpoints. We demonstrate the technique with synthetic renderings of a person's face under novel illumination and viewpoints.

Categories and subject descriptors: I.2.10 [**Artificial Intelligence**]: Vision and Scene Understanding - *intensity, color, photometry and thresholding*; I.3.7 [**Computer Graphics**]: Three-Dimensional Graphics and Realism - *color, shading, shadowing, and texture*; I.3.7 [**Computer Graphics**]: Three-Dimensional Graphics and Realism - *radiosity*; I.4.1 [**Image Processing and Computer Vision**]: Digitization and Image Capture - *radiometry, reflectance, scanning*; I.4.8 [**Image Processing**]: Scene Analysis - *photometry, range data, sensor fusion*. **Additional Key Words and Phrases:** facial animation; image-based modeling, rendering, and lighting.

1 Introduction

Creating realistic renderings of human faces has been an endeavor in computer graphics for nearly three decades [28] and remains a subject of current interest. It is a challenging problem due to the complex and individual shape of the face, the subtle and spatially varying reflectance properties of skin, and the complex deformations of the face during movement. Compounding the problem, viewers are extremely sensitive to the appearance of other people's faces.

Recent work has provided solutions to the problems of geometrically modeling and animating faces. 3D photography techniques, such as the Cyberware scanner, can acquire accurate geometric

[1]Computer Science Division, University of California at Berkeley. Email: {debevec,tsh,ctchou,duiker,wsarokin}@cs.berkeley.edu, msagar@lifefx.com. For more information see http://www.debevec.org/

models of individual faces. Work to animate facial expressions through morphing [2, 4, 29], performance-driven animation [38], motion capture [14], and physics-based simulation [34, 20, 30] has produced examples of realistic facial motion.

An outstanding problem is the lack of a method for capturing the spatially varying reflectance characteristics of the human face. The traditional approach of texture-mapping a photograph of a face onto a geometric model usually fails to appear realistic under changes in lighting, viewpoint, and expression. The problem is that the reflectance properties of the face are complex: skin reflects light both diffusely and specularly, and both of these reflection components are spatially varying. Recently, skin reflectance has been modeled using Monte Carlo simulation [16], and several aggregate reflectance descriptions have been recorded from real people [22], but there has not yet been a method of accurately rendering the complexities of an individual's facial reflectance under arbitrary changes of lighting and viewpoint.

In this paper we develop a method to render faces under arbitrary changes in lighting and viewing direction based on recorded imagery. The central device in our technique is a *light stage* (Fig. 2) which illuminates the subject from a dense sampling of directions of incident illumination. During this time the subject's appearance is recorded from different angles by stationary video cameras.

From this illumination data, we can immediately render the subject's face from the original viewpoints under any incident field of illumination by computing linear combinations of the original images. Because of the additive nature of light [5], this correctly reproduces all of the effects of diffuse and specular reflection as well as interreflections between parts of the face. We demonstrate this technique by rendering faces in various forms of natural illumination captured in real-world environments, and discuss how this process can be performed directly from compressed images.

In the second part of this paper we present a technique to extrapolate a complete reflectance field from the acquired data which allows us to render the face from novel viewpoints. For this acquire a geometric model of the face through structured lighting, which allows us to project the appearance from the original viewpoints onto the geometry to render from novel viewpoints. However, rerendering directly from such projected images does not reproduce view-dependent reflection from the face; most notably, the specular components need to shift position according to the rendered viewpoint.

To reproduce these view-dependent effects, we use a skin reflectance model to extrapolate the reflectance observed by the cameras to that which would be observed from novel viewpoints. The model is motivated by a set of in-plane reflectance measurements of a patch of skin using polarizers on the light and the camera to separate the reflection components. This model allows us to separate the specular and sub-surface reflection components of the light stage data using chromaticity analysis, and then to transform each reflectance component into how it would appear from a novel viewpoint. Using this technique, we can realistically render the face from arbitrary viewpoints and in arbitrary lighting.

The rest of this paper is organized as follows. In the next section we review related work and discuss the reflectance field. In Section 3 we describe the light stage and how we synthesize physically correct images of the subject under arbitrary illumination. In Section 4 we develop a model of skin reflectance and use it to render the face from novel viewpoints under arbitrary illumination. We discuss future work in Section 5 and conclude in Section 6.

2 Background and Related Work

In this section we give an overview of related work in the areas of facial modeling and animation, reflectometry, and image-based modeling and rendering. We conclude with a description of the reflectance field.

Facial Modeling and Animation Since the earliest work in facial modeling and animation [28], generating realistic faces has been a central goal. 3D photography techniques for acquiring facial geometry, such as the laser-triangulation based scanners made by Cyberware, have been a helpful development. Such techniques often also photograph a texture map for the face at the time of the scan, which can be projected onto the face to produce renderings. However, using such texture maps usually falls short of producing photorealistic renderings since the map is illumination-dependent and does not capture directionally varying reflectance properties. Other work estimates facial models directly from images: [11, 29, 3] recover geometry by fitting morphable facial models; [11, 3] use the models to estimate albedo maps but do not consider specular properties. [29] produces view-dependent reflectance under the original illumination conditions through view-dependent texture mapping [10].

Several techniques have been used to animate facial models; [2, 4, 29] blend between images in different expressions to produce intermediate expressions. [38, 14] use the captured facial motion of a real actor to drive the performance of a synthetic one. Physics-based simulation techniques [34, 30, 40, 20] have helped animate the complex deformations of a face in its different expressions.

Reflectometry Reflectometry is the measurement of how materials reflect light, or, more specifically, how they transform incident illumination into radiant illumination. This transformation can be described by the four-dimensional bi-directional reflectance distribution function, or BRDF, of the material measured [25]. Several efforts have been made to represent common BRDFs as parameterized functions called *reflectance models* [35, 6, 37, 27, 19].

Hanrahan and Krueger [16] developed a parameterized model for reflection from layered surfaces due to subsurface scattering, with human skin as a specific case of their model. Their model of skin reflectance was motivated by the optical properties of its surface, epidermal, and dermal layers [36]. Each layer was given several parameters according to its scattering properties and pigmentation, and a Monte Carlo simulation of the paths light might take through the skin surfaces produced renderings exhibiting a variety of qualitatively skin-like reflectance properties. The authors selected the reflectance properties manually, rather than acquiring them from a particular individual. The authors also simulated a uniform layer of oil over the face to produce specular reflection; in our work we acquire a reflectance model that reproduces the varying diffuse and specular properties over the skin.

Much work has been done to estimate reflectance properties of surfaces based on images taken under known lighting. [37] and [17] presented techniques and apparatus for measuring anisotropic reflectance of material samples; [7] applied reflectometry techniques to the domain of textured objects. In our work, we leverage being able to separate reflection into diffuse and specular components. This separation can be done through colorspace analysis [31] as well as a combined analysis of the color and polarization of the reflected light [24]; in our work we make use of both color and polarization. [32] used object geometry and varying light directions to derive diffuse and specular parameters for a coffee mug; [41]

used an inverse radiosity method to account for mutual illumination in estimating spatially varying diffuse and piecewise constant specular properties within a room.

Marschner, Westin, Lafortune, Torrance, and Greenberg [22] recently acquired the first experimental measurements of living human facial reflectance in the visible spectrum. The authors photographed the forehead of their subjects under constant point-source illumination and twenty viewing directions, and used the curvature of the forehead to obtain a dense set of BRDF samples. From these measurements, they derived a non-parametric isotropic BRDF representing the average reflectance properties of the surface of the forehead. In our work, we have chosen the goal of reproducing the spatially varying reflectance properties across the surface of the face; as a result, we sacrifice the generality of measuring a full BRDF at each surface point and use models of specular and diffuse reflectance to extrapolate the appearance to novel viewpoints.

Image-Based Modeling and Rendering In our work we leverage several principles explored in recent work in image-based modeling and rendering. [26, 15] showed how correct views of a scene under different lighting conditions can be created by summing images of the scene under a set of basis lighting conditions; [39] applied such a technique to create light fields [21, 13] with controllable illumination. [42] showed that by illuminating a shiny or refractive object with a set of coded lighting patterns, it could be correctly composited over an arbitrary background by determining the direction and spread of the reflected and refracted rays. [8] presented a technique for capturing images of real-world illumination and using this lighting to illuminate synthetic objects; in this paper we use such image-based lighting to illuminate real faces.

2.1 Definition of the Reflectance Field

The light field [12, 21], plenoptic function [1], and lumigraph [13] all describe the presence of light within space. Ignoring wavelength and fixing time, this is a five dimensional function of the form $P = P(x, y, z, \theta, \phi)$. The function represents the radiance leaving point (x, y, z) in the direction (θ, ϕ).

[21, 13] observed that when the viewer is moving within unoccluded space, the light field can be described by a four-dimensional function. We can characterize this function as $P' = P'(u, v, \theta, \phi)$, where (u, v) is a point on a closed surface A and (θ, ϕ) is a direction as before. A light field parameterized in this form induces a five-dimensional light field in the space outside of A: if we follow the ray beginning at (x, y, z) in the direction of (θ, ϕ) until it intersects A at (u, v), we have $P(x, y, z, \theta, \phi) = P'(u, v, \theta, \phi)$. In an example from [21] A was chosen to be a cube surrounding the object; in an example from [13] A was chosen to be the visual hull of the object. We can also consider the viewer to be inside of A observing illumination arriving from outside of A as shown in [21].

Images generated from a light field can have any viewing position and direction, but they always show the scene under the same lighting. In general, each field of incident illumination on A will induce a different field of radiant illumination from A. We can represent the radiant light field from A under every possible incident field of illumination as an eight-dimensional *reflectance field*:

$$R = R(R_i; R_r) = R(u_i, v_i, \theta_i, \phi_i; u_r, v_r, \theta_r, \phi_r) \qquad (1)$$

Here, $R_i(u_i, v_i, \theta_i, \phi_i)$ represents the incident light field arriving at A and $R_r(u_r, v_r, \theta_r, \phi_r)$ represents the radiant light field leaving A (see Figure 1(a)). Except that we do not presume A to be coincident with a physical surface, the reflectance field is equivalent to the bidirectional scattering-surface reflectance distribution function S, or BSSRDF, described in Nicodemus et al. [25]. Paraphrasing [25], this function "provides a way of quantitatively expressing the connection between reflected flux leaving (u_r, v_r) in a given direction and the flux incident at (u_i, v_i) in another given direction."

In this work we are interested in acquiring reflectance fields of real objects, in particular human faces. A direct method to acquire the reflectance field of a real object would be to acquire a set of light fields of an object $R_r(u_r, v_r, \theta_r, \phi_r)$ for a dense sampling of incident beams of illumination from direction (θ_i, ϕ_i) arriving at the surface A at (u_i, v_i). However, recording a four dimensional light field for every possible incident ray of light would require a ponderous amount of acquisition time and storage. Instead, in this work we acquire only *non-local reflectance fields* where the incident illumination field originates far away from A so that $R_i(u_i, v_i, \theta_i, \phi_i) = R_i(u_i', v_i', \theta_i, \phi_i)$ for all u_i, v_i, u_i', v_i'. Thus a non-local reflectance field can be represented as $R' = R'(\theta_i, \phi_i; u_r, v_r, \theta_r, \phi_r)$. This reduces the representation to six dimensions, and is useful for representing objects which are some distance from the rest of the scene. In Section 3.4 we discuss using a non-local reflectance field to produce local illumination effects.

In this work we extrapolate the complete field of radiant illumination from data acquired from a sparse set of camera positions (Section 3) and choose the surface A to be a scanned model of the face (Figure 1(b)), yielding a surface reflectance field analogous to a surface light field [23]. A model of skin reflectance properties is used to synthesize views from arbitrary viewpoints (Section 4).

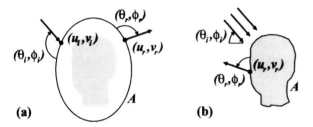

(a)   **(b)**

Figure 1: **The Reflectance Field** *(a) describes how a volume of space enclosed by a surface A transforms an incident field of illumination $R_i(u_i, v_i, \theta_i, \phi_i)$ into a radiant field of illumination $R_r(u_r, v_r, \theta_r, \phi_r)$. In this paper, we acquire a non-local reflectance field (b) in which the incident illumination consists solely of directional illumination (θ_i, ϕ_i). We choose A to be coincident with the surface of the face, yielding a surface reflectance field which allows us to extrapolate the radiant light field $R_r(u_r, v_r, \theta_r, \phi_r)$ from a sparse set of viewpoints.*

3 Re-illuminating Faces

The goal of our work is to capture models of faces that can be rendered realistically under any illumination, from any angle, and, eventually, with any sort of animated expression. The data that we use to derive our models is a sparse set of viewpoints taken under a dense set of lighting directions. In this section, we describe the acquisition process, how we transform each facial pixel location into a reflectance function, and how we use this representation to render the face from the original viewpoints under any novel form of illumination. In the following section we will describe how to render the face from new viewpoints.

3.1 The Light Stage

The light stage used to acquire the set of images is shown in Fig. 2. The subject sits in a chair which has a headrest to help keep his or her head still during the capture process. Two digital video cameras view the head from a distance of approximately three meters; each captures a view of the left or right side of the face. A spotlight, calibrated to produce an even field of illumination across the

Figure 2: **The Light Stage** *consists of a two-axis rotation system and a directional light source. The outer black bar θ is rotated about the central vertical axis and the inner bar ϕ is lowered one step for each θ rotation. Video cameras placed outside the stage record the face's appearance from the left and right under this complete set of illumination directions, taking slightly over a minute to record. The axes are operated manually by cords and an electronic audio signal triggered by the θ axis registers the video to the illumination directions. The inset shows a long-exposure photograph of the light stage in operation.*

subject's head, is affixed at a radius of 1.5 meters on a two-axis rotation mechanism that positions the light at any azimuth θ and any inclination ϕ. In operation, the light is spun about the θ axis continuously at approximately 25 rpm and lowered along the ϕ axis by $\frac{180}{32}$ degrees per revolution of θ (the cord controlling the ϕ axis is marked at these increments). The cameras, which are calibrated for their flat-field response and intensity response curve, capture frames continuously at 30 frames per second which yields 64 divisions of θ and 32 divisions of ϕ in approximately one minute, during which our subjects are usually capable of remaining still. A future version could employ high-speed cameras running at 250 to 1000 frames per second to lower the capture time to a few seconds. Some source images acquired with the apparatus are shown in Fig. 5.

3.2 Constructing reflectance functions

For each pixel location (x, y) in each camera, we observe that location on the face illuminated from 64×32 directions of θ and ϕ. From each pixel we form a slice of the reflectance field called

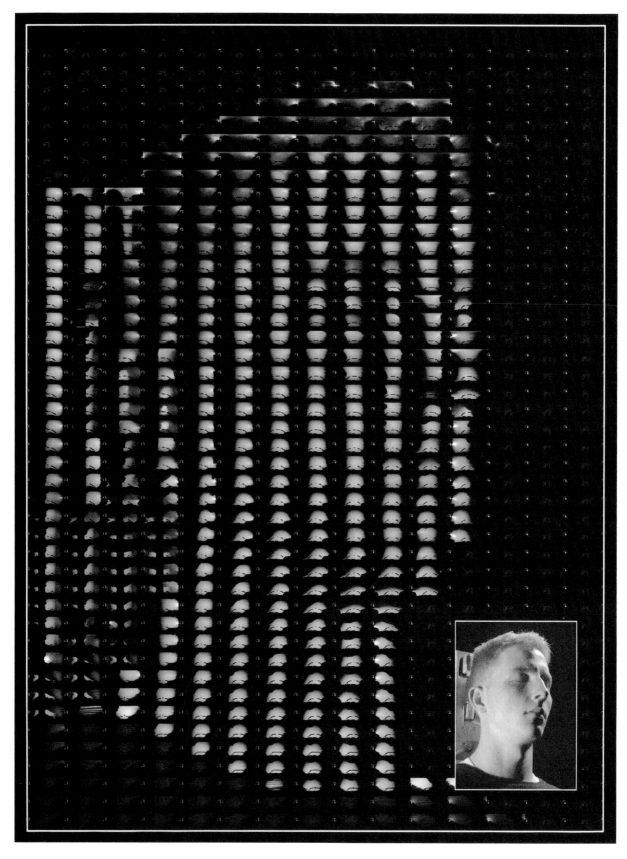

Figure 3: **Reflectance Functions for a Face** *This mosaic is formed from the reflectance functions of a* 15×44 *sampling of pixels from the original* 480×720 *image data. Each* 64×32 *reflectance function consists of the corresponding pixel location's appearance under two thousand lighting directions distributed throughout the sphere. The inset shows the same view of the face under a combination of three lighting directions. The functions have been brightened by a factor of four from the original data.*

a *reflectance function* $R_{xy}(\theta, \phi)$ corresponding to the ray through that pixel. Note that we are using the term "reflectance" loosely as true reflectance divides out the effect of the foreshortening of incident light. However, since the surface normal is unknown, we do not make this correction. If we let the pixel value at location (x, y) in the image with illumination direction (θ, ϕ) be represented as $L_{\theta, \phi}(x, y)$, then we have simply:

$$R_{xy}(\theta, \phi) = L_{\theta, \phi}(x, y) \qquad (2)$$

Fig. 3 shows a mosaic of reflectance functions for a particular viewpoint of the face. Four of these mosaics are examined in detail in Fig. 4. The reflectance functions exhibit and encode the effects of diffuse reflection, specular reflection, self-shadowing, translucency, mutual illumination, and subsurface scattering.

3.3   Re-illuminating the face

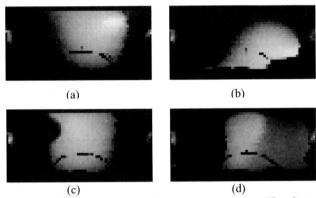

(a)   (b)

(c)   (d)

Figure 4: **A Sampling of Facial Reflectance Functions** *The above reflectance functions appear in the mosaic of Fig. 3. The middle of each function corresponds to the pixel being illuminated from the direction of the camera; as one moves within the reflectance function the light direction moves in the same manner. Reflectance function* **(a)** *is taken from the forehead toward the right of the image, and exhibits a noticeable specular lobe as well as an unoccluded diffuse lobe.* **(b)** *from the right of the underside of the jaw exhibits a weaker specular component and some self-shadowing at lower lighting angles caused by the shoulder blocking the light source.* **(c)** *from the subject's cheek to the right and below the nose exhibits a mild specular reflection and shadowing due to the nose in the upper left.* **(d)** *sampled from a pixel inside the pinna of the ear exhibits illumination from diffuse reflection and from light scattering through the tissue when illuminated from behind. Each function exhibits a thin black curve in its lower half where the phi axis bar occasionally obscures the view of the face, and a bright spot due to lens flare where the light points into the camera. These regions appear in the same places across images and are ignored in the lighting analysis.*

Suppose that we wish to generate an image of the face in a novel form of illumination. Since each $R_{xy}(\theta, \phi)$ represents how much light is reflected toward the camera by pixel (x, y) as a result of illumination from direction (θ, ϕ), and since light is additive, we can compute an image of the face $\hat{L}(x, y)$ under any combination of the original light sources $L_i(\theta, \phi)$ as follows:

$$\hat{L}(x, y) = \sum_{\theta, \phi} R_{xy}(\theta, \phi) L_i(\theta, \phi) \qquad (3)$$

Each color channel is computed separately using the above equation. Since the light sources densely sample the viewing sphere, we can represent any form of sampled incident illumination using this basis. In this case, it is necessary to consider the solid angle δA covered by each of the original illumination directions:

$$\hat{L}(x, y) = \sum_{\theta, \phi} R_{xy}(\theta, \phi) L_i(\theta, \phi) \delta A(\theta, \phi) \qquad (4)$$

For our data, $\delta A(\theta, \phi) = \sin \phi$; the light stage records more samples per solid angle near the poles than at the equator. Equation 5 shows the computation of Equation 4 graphically. First, the map of incident illumination (filtered down to the 64×32 (θ, ϕ) space) is normalized by the map of $\delta A(\theta, \phi)$. Then, the resulting map is multiplied by the pixel's reflectance function. Finally, the pixel values of this product are summed to compute the re-illuminated pixel value. These equations assume the light stage's light source is white and has unit radiance; in practice we normalize the reflectance functions based on the light source color. Figure 6 shows a face synthetically illuminated with several forms of sampled and synthetic illumination using this technique.

light map × δA = normalized light map

normalized light map × reflectance function = lighting product   (5)

‖ lighting product ‖₁ = rendered pixel

Writing the re-illumination equation of Equation 4 as the sum of the product of two 64×32 images allows us to gain efficiency in both storage and computation using the techniques presented by Smith and Rowe [33] by computing the product directly on JPEG-compressed versions of the images. This can reduce both storage and computation by a factor of twenty while maintaining good image quality.

3.4   Discussion

Since each rendered image can also be represented as a linear combination of the original images, all of the proper effects of non-diffuse reflection, mutual illumination, translucence, and subsurface scattering are preserved, as noted in [26]. The 64×32 set of illumination directions used is somewhat coarse; however, the reflectance functions are generally not aliased at this resolution, which implies that when the light maps are also properly filtered down to 64×32 there will be no aliasing in the resulting renderings. The place where the reflectance functions do become aliased is where there is self-shadowing; the expected result of this is that one would see somewhat stairstepped shadows in harsh lighting situations. Such effects could be smoothed by using an area light source to illuminate the subject.

Since this technique captures slices of a non-local reflectance field, it does not tell us how to render a person under dappled light or in partial shadow. A technique that will in many cases produce reasonable results is to illuminate different pixels of the face using different models of incident illumination; however, this will no longer produce physically valid images because changes to the indirect illumination are not considered. As an example, consider rendering a face with a shaft of light hitting just below the eye. In reality, the light below the eye would throw indirect illumination on the underside of the brow and the side of the nose; this technique would not capture this effect.

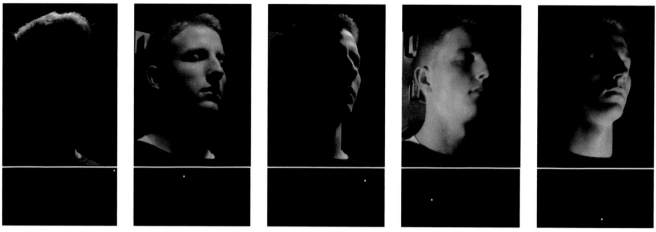

Figure 5: **Light Stage Images**   *Above are five of the 2048 images taken by one camera during a run of the light stage. The pixel values of each location on the face under the 2048 illumination directions are combined to produce the mosaic images in Fig. 3. Below each image is the impulse light map that would generate it.*

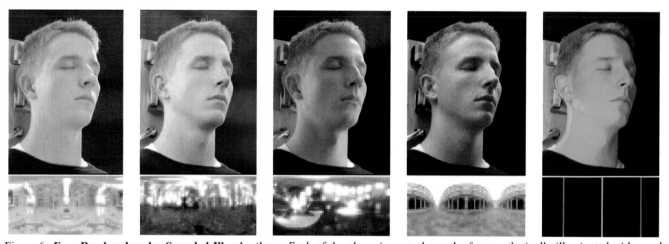

Figure 6: **Face Rendered under Sampled Illumination**   *Each of the above images shows the face synthetically illuminated with novel lighting, with the corresponding light map shown below. Each image is created by taking the dot product of each pixel's reflectance function with the light map. The first four illumination environments are light probe measurements acquired from real-world illumination (see [8]) recorded as omnidirectional high dynamic range images; the rightmost lighting environment is a synthetic test case.*

A person's clothing reflects indirect light back onto the face, and our capture technique reproduces the person's appearance in whatever clothing they were wearing during the capture session. If we need to change the color of the person's clothing (for example, to place a costume on a virtual actor), we can record the subject twice, once wearing white clothing and once with black clothing. Subtracting the second image from the first yields an image of the indirect illumination from the clothing, which can then be tinted to any desired color and added back in to the image taken with the black clothing; this process is illustrated in Figure 7.

By recording the light stage images in high dynamic range [9] and using the process of environment matting [42], we can apply this technique to translucent and refractive objects and reproduce the appearance of the environment in the background; this process is described in the Appendix.

4   Changing the Viewpoint

In this section we describe our technique to extrapolate complete reflectance fields from the reflectance field slices acquired in Section 3, allowing us to render the face from arbitrary viewpoints as well as under arbitrary illumination. In our capture technique, we

observe the face under a dense set of illumination conditions but from only a small set of viewpoints. To render the face from a novel viewpoint, we must resynthesize the reflectance functions to appear as they would from the new viewpoint.

To accomplish this, we make use of a skin reflectance model which we introduce in Section 4.1. This model is used to guide the shifting and scaling of measured reflectance function values as the viewpoint changes. As such, our technique guarantees that the resynthesized reflectance function will agree exactly with the measured data if the novel viewpoint is the same as the viewpoint for data capture.

The resynthesis technique requires that our reflectance functions be decomposed into specular and diffuse (subsurface) components. Section 4.2 describes this separation process. Section 4.3 describes the re-synthesis of a reflectance function for a new viewpoint. Section 4.4 discusses the technique in the context of shadowing and mutual illumination effects. Section 4.5 explains the method used to produce renderings of the entire face using resynthesized reflectance functions.

(a)   (b)   (c)

Figure 7: **Modeling indirect light from clothing** *Indirect reflectance from the subject's clothing can be modeled by recording the subject wearing both white (a) and black (b) clothing (we drape the white clothing on the subject and pull it away to reveal the black clothing.) (a) exhibits indirect lighting on the neck and beneath the chin and nose. Correct renderings of the person wearing any color clothing can be created by adding a tinted version of (a) minus (b) to (b). Using this method, (c) shows the subject with the indirect light she would receive from green clothing.*

4.1 Investigating skin reflectance

In this section we consider the reflectance properties of skin, and describe our data-driven skin reflectance model. The model is intended to capture the behavior of skin, but could be useful for a wider class of surfaces.

Following [16], we note that the light reflected from the skin can be decomposed into two components: a specular component consisting of light immediately reflected at the index of refraction transition at the air-oil interface (see Figure 8), and a non-Lambertian diffuse component consisting of light transmitted through the air-oil interface that, after some number of subsurface scattering interactions, is transmitted from the oil layer to air.

We first investigated the general behavior of these two components. As shown in Figure 8, light which reflects specularly off the skin will maintain the polarization of the incident light; however, light which emerges from below the surface will have been depolarized by scattering interactions. Taking advantage of this fact, we can separate the reflection components by placing linear polarizers on both the light source and the camera[1]. Figure 9 shows separated specular and diffuse reflection components of a face using this technique.

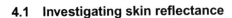

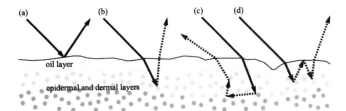

Figure 8: **Skin Reflectance** *Light reflecting from skin must have reflected specularly off the surface (a) or at some point entered one or more of the scattering layers (b, c, d). If the incident light is polarized, the specularly reflected light will maintain this polarization; however, light which scatters within the surface becomes depolarized. This allows reflection components to be separated as in Figures 9 and 10.*

Using this effect, we carried out an in-plane experiment to measure the specular and diffuse reflectance properties of a small patch

[1] In these tests we polarize the light source vertically with respect to the plane of incidence so that the specular reflection does not become attenuated near the Brewster angle.

(a)   (b)   (c)   (d)

Figure 9: **Separating diffuse and specular components** *can be performed by placing a linear polarizer on both the light source and the camera. (a) Normal image under point-source illumination. (b) Image of diffuse reflectance obtained by placing a vertical polarizer on the light source and a horizontal polarizer on the camera, blocking specularly reflected light. (c) Image of accentuated specular reflectance obtained by placing both polarizers vertically (half the diffusely reflected light is blocked relative to the specularly reflected light). (d) Difference of (c) and (b) yielding the specular component. The images have been scaled to appear consistent in brightness.*

of skin on a person's forehead. Figure 10 shows how we adapted the light stage of Figure 2 for this purpose by placing the ϕ axis in the horizontal position and placing a vertical polarizer on the light source. We rotated the horizontal θ axis continuously while we placed a video camera aimed at our subject's vertically aligned forehead at a sampling of reflected illumination angles. The camera angles we used were $\pm(0, 22.5, 45, 60, 75, 82.5, 86.25, 89)$ degrees relative to the forehead's surface normal in order to more densely sample the illumination at grazing angles. At 89 degrees the skin area was very foreshortened so we were not able to say with certainty that the measurement we took originated only from the target area. We performed the experiment twice: once with the camera polarizer placed horizontally to block specular reflection, and once with the camera polarizer placed vertically to accentuate it. The average intensity and color of the reflected light from a 2×5 pixel area on the forehead was recorded in this set of configurations.

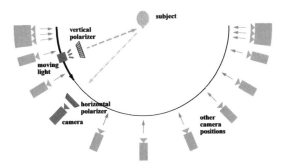

Figure 10: **Reflectometry Experiment** *In this experiment, the diffuse and specular reflectance of an area of skin on the subject's forehead was recorded from sixty-four illumination directions for each of fifteen camera positions. Polarizers on the light and camera were used to separate the reflection components.*

We noted two trends in the acquired reflectance data (Figure 11). First, the specular component becomes much stronger for large values of θ_i or θ_r and exhibits off-specular reflection. To accommodate this behavior in our model, we use the microfacet-based framework introduced by Torrance and Sparrow [35]. This framework assumes geometric optics and models specular lobes as surface (Fresnel) reflection from microfacets having a Gaussian distribution of surface normals. Shadowing and masking effects between the microfacets are computed under the assumption that the microfacets form V-shaped grooves. Our model differs only in that we do not

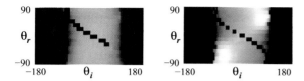

Figure 11: **Reflectometry Results** *The left image shows the measured diffuse (sub-surface) component of the skin patch obtained from the experiment in Fig. 10 for incident illumination angle θ_i and viewing direction θ_r. θ_r is nonuniformly spaced at angles of $\pm(0, 22.5, 45, 60, 75, 82.5, 86.25, 89)$ degrees. Invalid measurements from the light source blocking the camera's view are set to black. The right image shows the corresponding data for accentuated specular reflectance.*

assume that the microfacet normal distribution is Gaussian; since we have measurements of the specular component for dense incident directions, we simply take the microfacet normal distribution directly from the observed data. This allows the measured specular lobe to be reproduced exactly if the viewpoint is unchanged.

The second trend in the data is a desaturation of the diffuse component for large values of θ_i and θ_r. To accommodate this, we make a minor deviation from pure Lambertian behavior, allowing the saturation of the diffuse chromaticity to ramp between two values as θ_i and θ_r vary.

Representing chromaticities as unit RGB vectors, we model the diffuse chromaticity as:

$$normalize(\vec{d_0} + f(\theta_i, \theta_r)(\vec{d_0} - \vec{s})) \qquad (6)$$

where $\vec{d_0}$ is a representative diffuse chromaticity, $\vec{s}$ is the light source chromaticity, and $f(\theta_i, \theta_r)$ is given by:

$$f(\theta_i, \theta_r) = \alpha_0(\cos\theta_i \cos\theta_r) + \alpha_1(1 - \cos\theta_i \cos\theta_r) \qquad (7)$$

We recover the parameters α_0 and α_1 directly from our data for each reflectance function. This correction to the diffuse chromaticity is used for the color space separation of diffuse and specular components described in Section 4.2, and also in our reflectance function resynthesis technique described in Section 4.3.

In addition to this experiment, we also performed Monte Carlo simulations of subsurface scattering similar to those in [16]. We used two scattering layers, both with strong forward scattering, and with the lower layer having significant absorption of shorter wavelengths to simulate the presence of blood in the dermis. These simulations yielded a variation in the chromaticity of the diffuse component similar to that observed in our data.

4.2 Separating specular and subsurface components

We begin by separating the specular and subsurface (diffuse) components for each pixel's reflectance function. While we could perform this step using the polarization approach of Section 4.1, this would require two passes of the lighting rig (one for diffuse only and one that includes specular) or additional cameras. Furthermore, one of the polarizers would have to rotate in a non-trivial pattern to maintain the proper relative orientations of the polarizers when ϕ is non-horizontal. Instead, we use a color space analysis technique related to [31].

For a reflectance function RGB value $R_{xy}(\theta, \phi)$, we can write R as a linear combination of its diffuse color $\vec{d}$ and its specular color $\vec{s}$. In reality, due to noise, interreflections, and translucency, there will also be an error component $\vec{e}$:

$$R = \mu_d\vec{d} + \mu_s\vec{s} + \mu_e\vec{e}$$

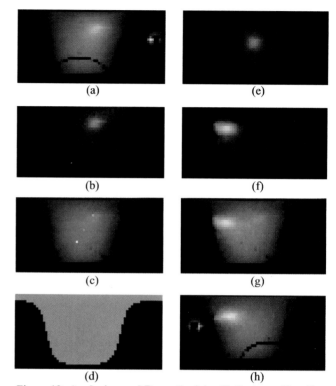

Figure 12: **Analyzing and Resynthesizing Reflectance Functions** *Reflectance functions (a) can be decomposed into specular (b) and diffuse (c) components using colorspace analysis based on a model of the variation in diffuse chromaticity (d). We compute a surface normal $\vec{n}$ based on the diffuse component (magenta dot in (c)), and a normal $\vec{n}_s$ (coincident with $\vec{n}$ in this case) based on the maximum (green dot) of the specular component and the known viewing direction (yellow dot). We demonstrate the resynthesis of reflectance functions for new viewpoints by resynthesizing (a), which was captured by the left camera, from the viewpoint of the right camera. We first transform the specular component to a representation independent of the original viewpoint (essentially a microfacet normal distribution) as shown in (e), then transform (e) in accordance with the new viewpoint to produce (f). The diffuse component is chrominance-shifted for the new viewpoint and added to the transformed specular component to produce the new reflectance function (g). For comparison, (h) shows the actual reflectance function (with lens flare spot and ϕ-bar shadow) from the second camera.*

We choose $\vec{e} = \vec{d} \times \vec{s}$ and determine values for μ_d, μ_s, and μ_e by inverting the resulting 3×3 matrix. To form the final separation, we compute $S = max(\mu_s, 0)\vec{s}$ and $D = R - S$ so that the sum of D and S yields the original reflectance function R.

This analysis assumes that the specular and diffuse colors are known. While we can assume that the specular component is the same color as the incident light, the diffuse color presents a more difficult problem, because it changes not only from pixel to pixel, but also within each reflectance function, as described in Section 4.1. To achieve an accurate separation, we must first estimate the diffuse chromaticity ramp.

Since we assume the diffuse chromaticity is a function f of θ_i and θ_r, we must first estimate the surface normal. For this we perform an initial rough color space separation based on a uniform diffuse chromaticity d_0. We derive this diffuse chromaticity by computing the median of the red-green and green-blue ratios over reflectance function values falling in a certain brightness range. We then perform a diffuse-specular separation and fit a Lambertian lobe to the diffuse component, using a coarse-to-fine direct search. This fitting yields an estimate of the surface normal.

We then find the parameters α_0 and α_1 which give the best fit to the observed chromaticities in the original unseparated reflectance function, again using a coarse-to-fine direct search. Knowing the viewpoint and the surface normal, we downweight values near the mirror angle to prevent the color ramp from being biased by strong specularities. The final separation into diffuse and specular components is computed using the fitted model of diffuse chromaticity as shown in Fig. 12.

We use the final separated diffuse component to recompute the surface normal $\vec{n}$, as seen in Fig. 14(b). For visualization purposes, we can also compute an estimate of the diffuse albedo $\vec{\rho_d}$ and total specular energy ρ_s, which are shown in Fig. 14(c) and (d).

4.3 Transforming Reflectance Functions to Novel Viewpoints

The process of resynthesizing a reflectance function for a novel viewpoint is illustrated in Fig. 12. The resynthesis algorithm takes the following input:

1. The diffuse reflectance function $D(\theta, \phi)$
2. The specular reflectance function $S(\theta, \phi)$
3. The surface normal $\vec{n}$
4. The index of refraction for surface (specular) reflection
5. The diffuse chromaticity ramp parameters α_0 and α_1
6. The original and novel view direction vectors $\vec{v}_0$ and $\vec{v}_n$

The diffuse and specular reflectance functions may optionally be transformed to a representation that does not depend on the original viewing direction, for example by transforming the functions to the form they would have if $\vec{v} = \vec{n}$. In this case, the resynthesis no longer requires the original view direction. An example of this for the specular component is shown in Fig. 12(e).

To synthesize a reflectance function from a novel viewpoint, we separately synthesize the diffuse and specular components. A sample in a specular reflectance function represents a specular response to a light source in the corresponding direction. If the view direction is known, we may consider this specular response to be a measure of the proportion of microfacets with normals oriented within some solid angle of the halfway vector between the view direction and the sample's light source direction sample. To compute a specular reflectance function from a new view direction $\vec{v}_n$, we compute for each light source direction $\vec{l}_p$ the halfway vector:

$$\vec{H} = normalize(\vec{v}_n + \vec{l}_p)$$

We then find the light source direction $\vec{l}_q$ that would have responded to microfacets near $\vec{H}$ from the original view direction $\vec{v}_0$:

$$\vec{l}_q = 2(\vec{H} \cdot \vec{v}_0)\vec{H} - \vec{v}_0$$

Letting ω_i specify a direction of incoming radiance, the Torrance-Sparrow model relates the observed radiance L to the microfacet normal distribution P as follows:

$$L_{\vec{v}} = \int \frac{PL_{\omega_i}GF}{4\cos\theta_r}d\omega_i \qquad (8)$$

where G is a geometric attenuation factor and F is the Fresnel reflectivity. G depends on $\vec{v}$, $\vec{l}$, and $\vec{n}$. The expression for G is somewhat complicated, and we refer the interested reader to [35]. F is given by the Fresnel equation for unpolarized light, which can be computed from $\vec{v}$ and $\vec{l}$.

Considering all quantities in (8) to be constant over the small solid angle Ω subtended by our light source, we have:

$$L_{\vec{v}} = \frac{PL_{\vec{l}}\Omega GF}{4(\vec{v} \cdot \vec{n})}$$

Assuming the light source presents a constant $L_{\vec{l}}\,\Omega$ as it moves, and recalling that the light direction $\vec{l}_q$ is chosen to sample the same point in the microfacet normal distribution as $\vec{l}_p$, we can compute the new sample radiance $L_{\vec{v}_n}$ due to a light at $\vec{l}_p$ as a function of the original radiance sample $L_{\vec{v}_0}$ due to a light at $\vec{l}_q$:

$$L_{\vec{v}_n} = L_{\vec{v}_0}\frac{G(\vec{v}_n,\vec{l}_p,\vec{n})F(\vec{v}_n,\vec{l}_p)\ (\vec{v}_0 \cdot \vec{n})}{G(\vec{v}_0,\vec{l}_q,\vec{n})F(\vec{v}_0,\vec{l}_q)\ (\vec{v}_n \cdot \vec{n})} \qquad (9)$$

Fig. 12(f) shows a specular reflectance function synthesized using (9) for a view direction 80 degrees from the original view.

For the diffuse component we apply our diffuse chrominance ramp correction to each value in the diffuse reflectance function, first inverting the chrominance shift due to the original view direction and then applying the chrominance shift for the new view direction. The chrominance shift is computed with the recovered parameters α_0 and α_1 as in (6), using the actual sample chromaticity in place of $\vec{d}_0$.

A final resynthesized reflectance function consisting of the resynthesized diffuse and specular components is shown in Fig. 12(g), and is consistent with an actual reflectance function acquired from the novel viewpoint in Fig. 12(h).

4.4 Considering Shadowing and Interreflection

Since our geometry is presumed to be non-convex, we expect reflectance functions in areas not on the convex hull to exhibit global illumination effects such as shadows and interreflections. To deal with such areas, we compute a shadow map for each reflectance function. This could be done using our geometric model, but since the geometry is incomplete we instead compute the shadow map using brightness thresholding on the original reflectance function. This is demonstrated in Figure 13. We then do the analysis of Section 4.2 on the reflectance function modulated by the shadow map. This will give good results when the direct light dominates the indirect light over the non-shadowed portion of the reflectance function, a good assumption for most areas of the face.

When synthesizing a new specular reflectance function, the shadow map is used to prevent a specular lobe from appearing in shadowed directions. The converse of this effect is that when a specularity is shadowed in our original data, we are unable to recover the specular lobe. This problem could be reduced by using more cameras.

An advantage of our synthesis technique is that diffuse interreflections, and in fact all light paths terminating with a diffuse reflection, are left intact in the diffuse reflectance function and are thus reproduced without the necessity of performing the difficult steps of inverse and forward global illumination.

4.5 Creating renderings

With the ability to resynthesize reflectance functions for new view directions, it is straightforward to render the face in arbitrary illumination from arbitrary viewpoints. We first use the technique of Section 3 to render a view of the face in the novel lighting using the modified reflectance functions. Although geometrically from the original point of view, the face is shaded as if it were viewed from the novel point of view. We then project this image onto a geometric model of the face (see Fig. 14(e)) and view the model from the novel viewpoint, yielding a rendering in which the illumination and viewpoint are consistent. In our work we use two original viewpoints, one for the left and one for the right of the face, and blend the results over the narrow region of overlap (with more cameras, view-dependent texture mapping could be used to blend between viewpoints as in [10, 29]). Renderings made with this technique are shown in Figs. 14(f),(g) and (h), and comparisons with actual photographs are shown in Fig. 15.

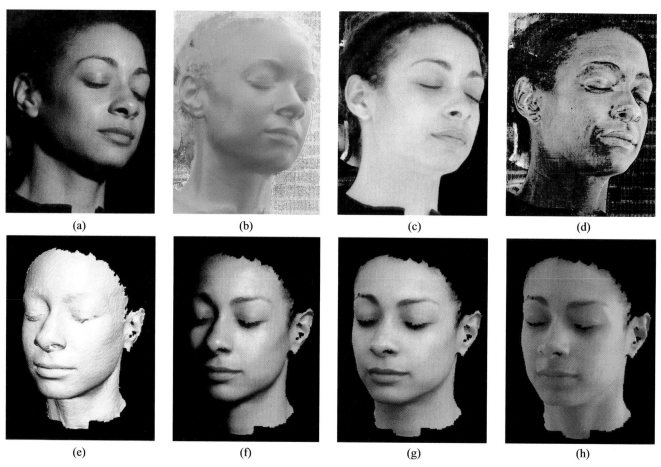

(a) (b) (c) (d)

(e) (f) (g) (h)

Figure 14: **Analyzing Reflectance and Changing the Viewpoint** (a) An original light stage image taken by the left camera. (b) Recovered surface normals n_d derived from the fitted diffuse reflectance lobe for each pixel; the RGB value for each pixel encodes the X, Y, and Z direction of each normal. (c) Estimated diffuse albedo ρ_d. Although not used by our rendering algorithm, such data could be used in a traditional rendering system. (d) Estimated specular energy ρ_s, also of potential use in a traditional rendering system. (e) Face geometry recovered using structured lighting. (f) Face rendered from a novel viewpoint under synthetic directional illumination. (g,h) Face rendered from a novel viewpoint under the two sampled lighting environments used in the second two renderings of Fig. 6.

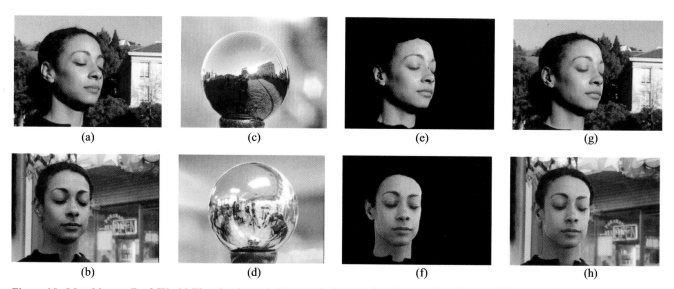

(a) (c) (e) (g)

(b) (d) (f) (h)

Figure 15: **Matching to Real-World Illumination** (a,b) Actual photographs of the subject in two different environments. (c,d) Images of a light probe placed in the position of the subject's head in the same environments. (e,f) Synthetic renderings of the face matched to the photographed viewpoints and illuminated by the captured lighting. (g,h) Renderings of the synthetic faces (e,f) composited over the original faces (a,b); the hair and shoulders come from the orginal photographs and are not produced using our techniques. The first environment is outdoors in sunlight; the second is indoors with mixed lighting coming from windows, incandescent lamps, and fluorescent ceiling fixtures.

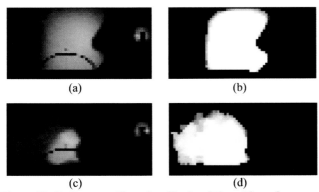

(a) (b)

(c) (d)

Figure 13: **Reflectance Function Shadow Maps** *The reflectance function of a point near the nose (a) and the corresponding shadow map (b) computed using brightness thresholding. (c) shows a point in the ear which receives strong indirect illumination, causing the non-shadowed region in (d) to be overestimated. This causes some error in the diffuse-specular separation and the diffuse albedo to be underestimated in the ear as seen in Fig. 14(c).*

5 Discussion and Future work

The work we have done suggests a number of avenues for improvements and extensions. First, we currently extrapolate reflectance functions using data from single viewpoints. Employing additional cameras to record reflectance functions for each location on the face would improve the results since less extrapolation of the data would be required. Using the polarization technique of Fig. 9 to directly record specular and subsurface reflectance functions could also improve the renderings, especially for subjects with pale skin.

A second avenue of future work is to animate our recovered facial models. For this, there already exist effective methods for animating geometrically detailed facial models such as [29], [14], and [34]. For these purposes, it will also be necessary to model and animate the eyes, hair, and inner mouth; reflectometry methods for obtaining models of such structures would need to be substantially different from our current techniques.

We would also like to investigate real-time rendering methods for our facial models. While the fixed-viewpoint re-illumination presented in Section 3 can be done interactively, synthesizing new viewpoints takes several minutes on current workstations. Some recent work has presented methods of using graphics hardware to render complex reflectance properties [18]; we would like to investigate employing such methods to create renderings at interactive rates. We also note that the storage required for a reflectance field could be substantially reduced by compressing the source data both in (u, v) space as well as (θ, ϕ) space to exploit similarities amongst neighboring reflectance functions.

Real skin has temporally varying reflectance properties depending on temperature, humidity, mood, health, and age. The surface blood content can change significantly as the face contorts and contracts, which alters its coloration. Future work could characterize these effects and integrate them into a facial animation system; part the acquisition process could be to capture the reflectance field of a person in a variety different expressions.

Lastly, the data capture techniques could be improved in a number of ways. High-definition television cameras would acquire nearly eight times as many pixels of the face, allowing the pixel size to be small enough to detect illumination variations from individual skin pores, which would increase the skin-like quality of the renderings. One could also pursue faster capture by using high-speed video cameras running at 250 or 1000 frames per second, allowing full reflectance capture in just a few seconds and perhaps, with more advanced techniques, in real time.

6 Conclusion

In this paper we have presented a practical technique for acquiring the reflectance field of a human face using standard video equipment and a relatively simple lighting apparatus. The method allows the the face to be rendered under arbitrary illumination conditions including image-based illumination. The general technique of modeling facial reflectance from dense illumination directions, sparse viewpoints, and recovered geometry suggests several areas for future work, such as fitting to more general reflectance models and combining this work with facial animation techniques. It is our hope that the work we have presented in this paper will help encourage continued investigations into realistic facial rendering.

Acknowledgements

We would like to thank Shawn Brixey and UC Berkeley's Digital Media/New Genre program for use of their laboratory space, as well as Bill Buxton and Alias Wavefront for use of the Maya modeling software, and Larry Rowe, Jessica Vallot (seen in Fig. 14), Patrick Wilson, Melanie Levine, Eric Paulos, Christine Waggoner, Holly Cim, Eliza Ra, Bryan Musson, David Altenau, Marc Levoy, Maryann Simmons, Henrik Wann Jensen, Don Greenberg, Pat Hanrahan, Chris Bregler, Michael Naimark, Steve Marschner, Kevin Binkert, and the Berkeley Millennium Project for helping make this work possible. We would also like to acknowledge the Cornell's 1999 Workshop on Rendering, Perception, and Measurement for helping encourage this line of research. Thanks also to the anonymous reviewers for their insightful suggestions for this work. This work was sponsored by grants from Interactive Pictures Corporation, the Digital Media Innovation Program, and ONR/BMDO 3DDI MURI grant FDN00014-96-1-1200.

References

[1] ADELSON, E. H., AND BERGEN, J. R. *Computational Models of Visual Processing.* MIT Press, Cambridge, Mass., 1991, ch. 1. The Plenoptic Function and the Elements of Early Vision.

[2] BEIER, T., AND NEELY, S. Feature-based image metamorphosis. *Computer Graphics (Proceedings of SIGGRAPH 92) 26*, 2 (July 1992), 35–42.

[3] BLANZ, V., AND VETTER, T. A morphable model for the synthesis of 3d faces. *Proceedings of SIGGRAPH 99* (August 1999), 187–194.

[4] BREGLER, C., COVELL, M., AND SLANEY, M. Video rewrite: Driving visual speech with audio. *Proceedings of SIGGRAPH 97* (August 1997), 353–360.

[5] BUSBRIDGE, I. W. *The Mathematics of Radiative Transfer.* Cambridge University Press, Bristol, UK, 1960.

[6] COOK, R. L., AND TORRANCE, K. E. A reflectance model for computer graphics. *Computer Graphics (Proceedings of SIGGRAPH 81) 15*, 3 (August 1981), 307–316.

[7] DANA, K. J., GINNEKEN, B., NAYAR, S. K., AND KOENDERINK, J. J. Reflectance and texture of real-world surfaces. In *Proc. IEEE Conf. on Comp. Vision and Patt. Recog.* (1997), pp. 151–157.

[8] DEBEVEC, P. Rendering synthetic objects into real scenes: Bridging traditional and image-based graphics with global illumination and high dynamic range photography. In *SIGGRAPH 98* (July 1998).

[9] DEBEVEC, P. E., AND MALIK, J. Recovering high dynamic range radiance maps from photographs. In *SIGGRAPH 97* (August 1997), pp. 369–378.

[10] DEBEVEC, P. E., YU, Y., AND BORSHUKOV, G. D. Efficient view-dependent image-based rendering with projective texture-mapping. In *9th Eurographics workshop on Rendering* (June 1998), pp. 105–116.

[11] FUA, P., AND MICCIO, C. From regular images to animated heads: A least squares approach. In *ECCV98* (1998).

[12] GERSHUN, A. Svetovoe Pole (the Light Field, in English). *Journal of Mathematics and Physics XVIII* (1939), 51—151.

[13] GORTLER, S. J., GRZESZCZUK, R., SZELISKI, R., AND COHEN, M. F. The Lumigraph. In *SIGGRAPH 96* (1996), pp. 43–54.

[14] GUENTER, B., GRIMM, C., WOOD, D., MALVAR, H., AND PIGHIN, F. Making faces. *Proceedings of SIGGRAPH 98* (July 1998), 55–66.

[15] HAEBERLI, P. Synthetic lighting for photography. Available at http://www.sgi.com/grafica/synth/index.html, January 1992.

[16] HANRAHAN, P., AND KRUEGER, W. Reflection from layered surfaces due to subsurface scattering. *Proceedings of SIGGRAPH 93* (August 1993), 165–174.

[17] KARNER, K. F., MAYER, H., AND GERVAUTZ, M. An image based measurement system for anisotropic reflection. In *EUROGRAPHICS Annual Conference Proceedings* (1996).

[18] KAUTZ, J., AND MCCOOL, M. D. Interactive rendering with arbitrary BRDFs using separable approximations. *Eurographics Rendering Workshop 1999* (June 1999).

[19] LAFORTUNE, E. P. F., FOO, S.-C., TORRANCE, K. E., AND GREENBERG, D. P. Non-linear approximation of reflectance functions. *Proceedings of SIGGRAPH 97* (August 1997), 117–126.

[20] LEE, Y., TERZOPOULOS, D., AND WATERS, K. Realistic modeling for facial animation. *Proceedings of SIGGRAPH 95* (August 1995), 55–62.

[21] LEVOY, M., AND HANRAHAN, P. Light field rendering. In *SIGGRAPH 96* (1996), pp. 31–42.

[22] MARSCHNER, S. R., WESTIN, S. H., LAFORTUNE, E. P. F., TORRANCE, K. E., AND GREENBERG, D. P. Image-based BRDF measurement including human skin. *Eurographics Rendering Workshop 1999* (June 1999).

[23] MILLER, G. S. P., RUBIN, S., AND PONCELEON, D. Lazy decompression of surface light fields for precomputed global illumination. *Eurographics Rendering Workshop 1998* (June 1998), 281–292.

[24] NAYAR, S., FANG, X., AND BOULT, T. Separation of reflection components using color and polarization. *IJCV 21*, 3 (February 1997), 163–186.

[25] NICODEMUS, F. E., RICHMOND, J. C., HSIA, J. J., GINSBERG, I. W., AND LIMPERIS, T. Geometric considerations and nomenclature for reflectance.

[26] NIMEROFF, J. S., SIMONCELLI, E., AND DORSEY, J. Efficient re-rendering of naturally illuminated environments. *Fifth Eurographics Workshop on Rendering* (June 1994), 359–373.

[27] OREN, M., AND NAYAR, S. K. Generalization of Lambert's reflectance model. *Proceedings of SIGGRAPH 94* (July 1994), 239–246.

[28] PARKE, F. I. Computer generated animation of faces. *Proc. ACM annual conf.* (August 1972).

[29] PIGHIN, F., HECKER, J., LISCHINSKI, D., SZELISKI, R., AND SALESIN, D. H. Synthesizing realistic facial expressions from photographs. *Proceedings of SIGGRAPH 98* (July 1998), 75–84.

[30] SAGAR, M. A., BULLIVANT, D., MALLINSON, G. D., HUNTER, P. J., AND HUNTER, I. W. A virtual environment and model of the eye for surgical simulation. *Proceedings of SIGGRAPH 94* (July 1994), 205–213.

[31] SATO, Y., AND IKEUCHI, K. Temporal-color space analysis of reflection. *JOSA-A 11*, 11 (November 1994), 2990–3002.

[32] SATO, Y., WHEELER, M. D., AND IKEUCHI, K. Object shape and reflectance modeling from observation. In *SIGGRAPH 97* (1997), pp. 379–387.

[33] SMITH, B., AND ROWE, L. Compressed domain processing of JPEG-encoded images. *Real-Time Imaging 2*, 2 (1996), 3–17.

[34] TERZOPOULOS, D., AND WATERS, K. Physically-based facial modelling, analysis, and animation. *Journal of Visualization and Computer Animation 1*, 2 (August 1990), 73–80.

[35] TORRANCE, K. E., AND SPARROW, E. M. Theory for off-specular reflection from roughened surfaces. *Journal of Optical Society of America 57*, 9 (1967).

[36] VAN GEMERT, M. F. C., JACQUES, S. L., STERENBERG, H. J. C. M., AND STAR, W. M. Skin optics. *IEEE Transactions on Biomedical Engineering 36*, 12 (December 1989), 1146–1154.

[37] WARD, G. J. Measuring and modeling anisotropic reflection. In *SIGGRAPH 92* (July 1992), pp. 265–272.

[38] WILLIAMS, L. Performance-driven facial animation. *Computer Graphics (Proceedings of SIGGRAPH 90) 24*, 4 (August 1990), 235–242.

[39] WONG, T.-T., HENG, P.-A., OR, S.-H., AND NG, W.-Y. Image-based rendering with controllable illumination. *Eurographics Rendering Workshop 1997* (June 1997), 13–22.

[40] WU, Y., THALMANN, N. M., AND THALMANN, D. A dynamic wrinkle model in facial animation and skin aging. *Journal of Visualization and Computer Animation 6*, 4 (October 1995), 195–206.

[41] YU, Y., DEBEVEC, P., MALIK, J., AND HAWKINS, T. Inverse global illumination: Recovering reflectance models of real scenes from photographs. *Proceedings of SIGGRAPH 99* (August 1999), 215–224.

[42] ZONGKER, D. E., WERNER, D. M., CURLESS, B., AND SALESIN, D. H. Environment matting and compositing. *Proceedings of SIGGRAPH 99* (August 1999), 205–214.

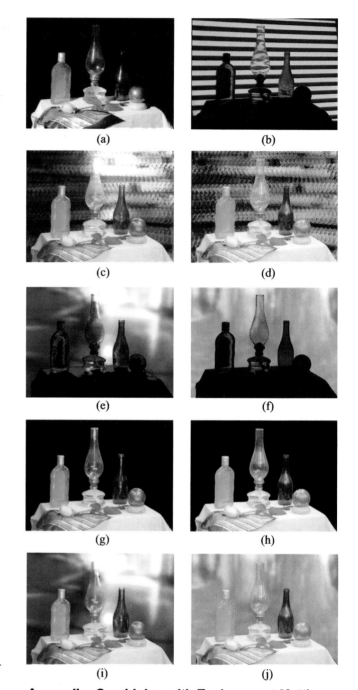

(a)　　　　　　　　(b)

(c)　　　　　　　　(d)

(e)　　　　　　　　(f)

(g)　　　　　　　　(h)

(i)　　　　　　　　(j)

Appendix: Combining with Environment Matting

The light stage can be used to relight objects as well as faces. In this experiment we created a scene with diffuse, shiny, refractive, and transmissive objects seen in (a). Because of the sharp specularities, we recorded the scene with a finer angular resolution of 128×64 directions of θ and ϕ and in high dynamic range [9] using five passes of the light stage at different exposure settings. Renderings of the scene in two environments are shown in (c,d). Because high dynamic range imagery was used, the direct appearance of the light source was captured properly, which allows the renderings to reproduce a low-resolution version of the lighting environment in the background. To replace this with a high resolution version of the environment, we captured an environment matte [42] of the scene (b) and computed the contribution of the reflected, refracted, and transmitted light from the background (e,f). We then summed all but the contribution from the background lighting directions to produce (g,h) and added in the light from the environment matte (e,f) to produce a complete rendering of the scene and background (i,j).

As-Rigid-As-Possible Shape Interpolation

Marc Alexa
Darmstadt University of Technology

Daniel Cohen-Or
Tel Aviv University

David Levin
Tel Aviv University

Figure 1: The Statue of Liberty becomes the Christ statue on the Corcovado.

Abstract

We present an object-space morphing technique that blends the interiors of given two- or three-dimensional shapes rather than their boundaries. The morph is rigid in the sense that local volumes are least-distorting as they vary from their source to target configurations. Given a boundary vertex correspondence, the source and target shapes are decomposed into isomorphic simplicial complexes. For the simplicial complexes, we find a closed-form expression allocating the paths of both boundary and interior vertices from source to target locations as a function of time. Key points are the identification of the optimal simplex morphing and the appropriate definition of an error functional whose minimization defines the paths of the vertices. Each pair of corresponding simplices defines an affine transformation, which is factored into a rotation and a stretching transformation. These local transformations are naturally interpolated over time and serve as the basis for composing a global coherent least-distorting transformation.

CR Categories: I.3.3 [Computer Graphics]: Picture/Image Generation—Display algorithms; I.3.5 [Computer Graphics]: Computational Geometry and Object Modeling—Curve, surface, solid, and object representations; I.3.7 [Computer Graphics]: Three-Dimensional Graphics and Realism—Animation; I.4.7 [Image Processing]: Feature Measurement—Size and shape

Keywords: shape blending, vertex path problem, compatible triangulation

1 Introduction

Techniques that transform one graphical object into another have gained widespread use in recent years. These techniques, known as *morphing* or *blending* techniques, involve the creation of a smooth transition from an initial object to a target object. They have proven to be powerful for visual effects, and there are now many breathtaking examples in film and television. In most cases, these morphing effects are generated using image-based techniques [3, 21, 30] where the geometry of the source and target object are somewhat similar, or the process requires extensive user labor. A primary challenge in this area is to devise algorithms to blend two given objects of significantly different shape, with minimal user interaction, so that the in-between objects retain their original appearance and properties as much as possible. The morph example in Figure 1 is difficult to achieve with an image-based technique, because foreground and background behave differently.

Object-space morphing treats explicit representations of the objects [14, 20] instead of discretizations of space (images, volumes). Assuming the objects are either polygons (in 2D) or polyhedra (in 3D), the morphing process consists of generating a correspondence between the geometric features of the representation, known as the *vertex correspondence* problem [23, 19, 6, 18, 14, 1, 20], and then interpolating the positions of the boundary representations along predetermined paths, known as the *vertex path* problem [24, 25, 13, 8].

Most of the cited object-space morphing techniques are concerned with the correspondence problem while simply linearly interpolating the corresponding vertices, not taking into account that the blended shapes are implicitly representing meta-physical entities. Generally speaking, aesthetic and intuitive shape blending should aim at treating the objects as rigidly as possible and avoid superfluous global or local deformations. In [24], Sederberg intro-

Figure 2: Morph sequence of Haring-like figures showing their homeomorphic dissections

157

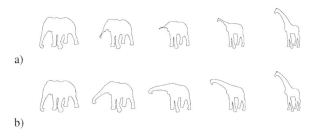

a)

b)

Figure 3: Contour blends of the elephant-giraffe example. Simple linear vertex interpolation in (a) vs. as-rigid-as-possible shape interpolation in (b).

Figure 4: The homeomorphic dissections of the shapes in the elephant-giraffe example

duced techniques that minimize the deformation of the boundaries. Shapira and Rappaport [25] suggested that a proper morph cannot be expressed merely as a boundary interpolation, but as a smooth blend of the interior of the objects. To achieve such an interior interpolation, they represented the interior of the 2D shapes by compatible skeletons and applied the blend to the parametric description of the skeletons. The automatic creation of corresponding equivalent skeletons of two shapes is involved, and though theoretically possible for all shapes, it seems natural for similar shapes, but ambiguous for rather different shapes like the letters **U** and **T**.

In this paper, we present an object-space morphing technique that blends the interior of the shapes rather than their boundaries to achieve a sequence of in-between shapes which is locally least-distorting. Assuming that a boundary vertex correspondence of the source and target shapes is given, we apply an algorithm for dissecting the source and target shapes into isomorphic simplicial complexes, i.e. triangles or tetrahedra. Then, we develop a method for interpolating the locations of corresponding vertices, both boundary and interior, along their paths from the source to the target object.

Simplicial complexes allow the local deformation of the shapes to be analyzed and controled. Floater and Gotsman have used barycentric coordinates to morph compatible triangulations with convex boundary so that no triangles flip on their way from the source to the target configuration [10]. However, interpolation of barycentric coordinates is not motivated by or related to physical or esthetical principles.

We start by determining an optimal least-distorting morphing between a source simplex and a target simplex (triangles in the 2D case and tetrahedra in the 3D case). Then, the general idea is to find a transformation which is locally as similar as possible to the optimal transformation between each pair of corresponding simplices.

2 Transforming Shapes

Given two objects together with a set of point-to-point correspondences between user-defined control (anchor) points, one can define an elastic transformation between the objects that exactly satisfies the correspondences. However, to reduce the distortion of the in-between shapes, it is advisable to determine the *rigid* part of the transformation and interpolate it separately from the *elastic* part [8, 31]. The rotational component of the rigid part should be interpolated so that the object is non-deforming, e.g. using quaternion interpolation [27]. The rigid-elastic decomposition of the warp function and its particular interpolation are so chosen to minimize the distortion of the intermediate shapes. The rigid part performs the general positional changes, while the fine details are gradually changed by the elastic part.

In many applications, this decomposition does improve the morphing results, though it cannot prevent local distortions in cases of body movements which are more involved as may be found in articulated objects. The underlying assumption in [6, 8, 31] is that the movement can roughly be approximated by rotation, stretching and translation. If we consider objects such as animals' bodies or sophisticated mechanical objects, such as industrial robots, it is clear that even the simplest movements cannot be well approximated by a single rotation and translation. To reduce distortions in transformations of bodies comprising local rotations, the decomposition should be more elaborate. The idea is to determine local non-distorting motions rather than a global one. The composed shape morphing should behave locally as close as possible to the ideal local ones. Figure 3 shows a blend between an elephant and a giraffe. The two shapes are aligned and a single rotation cannot prevent the distortions of a linear interpolation, whereas the locally least-distorting interpolation yields a pleasing blend of such articulated objects.

Based on a compatible dissection of the interiors of the shapes (see Figures 2 and 4), we first define local affine transformations. Each of the local linear maps can be separately decomposed into a rotation and a stretch. Thus, locally, we know how to achieve a non-distorting morph. Then, these local transformations are composed into a global coherent non-distorting transformation, which minimizes the overall local deformation. It should be noted that our transformation is (globally) rigidly reducible; that is, if there is a single rigid transformation that aligns the objects, the morph follows such a path.

We only consider simplicial complexes as dissections of shapes. Specifically, a two-dimensional shape is a *polygon* and its dissection a *triangulation*, and a three-dimensional shape is a *polyhedron* and its dissection a *tetrahedralization*. In the following, we introduce an interpolation technique for determining vertex paths in shape blending, given a source and a target shape represented by homeomorphic (compatible) triangulations. In Section 3, we show how to compute such homeomorphic dissections from boundary representations. Note that we describe the concept of determining the vertex paths in two dimensions for clarity; the extension to three or more dimensions is straightforward.

2.1 Least-Distorting Triangle-to-Triangle Morphing

Suppose the triangulation of the source and target shapes consists of only one triangle each. Let the source vertices be $P = (\vec{p_1}, \vec{p_2}, \vec{p_3})$ and the target vertices be $Q = (\vec{q_1}, \vec{q_2}, \vec{q_3})$, where vertices with the same index correspond. An affine mapping represented by matrix A transforms P into Q:

$$A\vec{p_i} + \vec{l} = \begin{pmatrix} a_1 & a_2 \\ a_3 & a_4 \end{pmatrix} \vec{p_i} + \begin{pmatrix} l_x \\ l_y \end{pmatrix} = \vec{q_i}, \quad i \in \{1, 2, 3\} \quad (1)$$

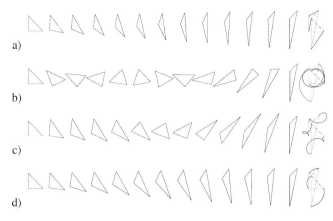

a)

b)

c)

d)

Figure 5: Transformations of a single triangle. (a) Linear vertex interpolation. (b-d) An affine map from the source to the target triangle is computed and factored into rotational and scale-shear parts. Intermediate triangles are constructed by linearly interpolating the angle(s) of rotation, the scaling factors, and the shear parameter. (b) corresponds to Equation 4; (c) shows the results of reducing the overall angle of (b) by subtracting 2π from one of the angles; (d) corresponds to Equation 5 and represents the method of our choice. The last column in all rows shows plots of the vertex paths.

We do not take the translation $\vec{l}$ into account for shape interpolation since it does not describe any property of the shape itself except for its placing in the scene. Rather, we want to describe intermediate shapes by varying the rotational and scaling parts comprising A, over time. Note that the coefficients of $A(t)$ are linear in the coordinates of the target shape.

Intermediate shapes $V(t) = (\vec{v_1}(t), \vec{v_2}(t), \vec{v_3}(t))$ are described as $V(t) = A(t)P$. The question is how to define $A(t)$ reasonably? The simplest solution would be: $A(t) = (1-t)I + tA$. However, some properties of $A(t)$ seem to be desirable, calling for a more elaborate approach:

- The transformation should be symmetric with respect to t.

- The rotational angle(s) and scale should change linearly.

- The triangle should keep its orientation, i.e. should not be reflected.

- The resulting vertices' paths should be simple.

The basic idea is to factor A into rotations (orthogonal matrices) and scale-shear parts with positive scaling components. We have examined several decompositions. A natural candidate is the singular value decomposition (SVD) [12], since the resulting decomposition is symmetric and well-defined for arbitrary dimensions:

$$A = R_\alpha D R_\beta = R_\alpha \begin{pmatrix} s_x & 0 \\ 0 & s_y \end{pmatrix} R_\beta, \quad s_x, s_y > 0 \quad (2)$$

However, through experimentation, we have found a decomposition into a single rotation and a symmetric matrix, to yield the visually-best transformations. This result is supported by Shoemake in [27] for mathematical, as well as psychological, reasons. The decomposition can be deduced from the SVD as follows:

$$
\begin{aligned}
A &= R_\alpha D R_\beta = R_\alpha (R_\beta R_\beta^T) D R_\beta = \\
&= (R_\alpha R_\beta)(R_\beta^T D R_\beta) = R_\gamma S = R_\gamma \begin{pmatrix} s_x & s_h \\ s_h & s_y \end{pmatrix} \quad (3)
\end{aligned}
$$

with $s_x, s_y > 0$. Based on the decomposition, $A(t)$ is computed by linearly interpolating the free parameters in the factorizations in (2) and (3), i.e.

$$A_{\alpha,\beta}(t) = R_{t\alpha}((1-t)I + tD)R_{t\beta} \quad (4)$$

and respectively,

$$A_\gamma(t) = R_{t\gamma}((1-t)I + tS) \quad (5)$$

Figure 5 illustrates the resulting transformations from a source to a target triangle. For comparison, 5(a) shows linear interpolation of vertex coordinates. The transformation resulting from a singular value decomposition and linear interpolation $A_{\alpha,\beta}(t)$ is depicted in 5(b). Note that the result is symmetric and linear in the rotation angle but still unsatisfactory, since a rotation of more than π is unnecessary. However, if we subtract 2π from one of the angles (depicted in 1(c)) the result is even more displeasing. We have found that decomposing A into one rotation and a symmetric matrix and using $A_\gamma(t)$ yields the best results (Figure 5(d)). It avoids unnecessary rotation or shear compared to the SVD and is usually more symmetric than a QR decomposition-based approach. Note that the rotation of the triangle does not contribute to its shape. However, this is no longer true for more than a single triangle, as we shall see in the next section, which discusses the generalization to more than one triangle.

2.2 Closed-Form Vertex Paths for a Triangulation

We now consider a triangulation $\mathcal{T} = \{T_{\{i,j,k\}}\}$ rather than a single triangle. Each of the source triangles $P_{\{i,j,k\}} = (\vec{p_i}, \vec{p_j}, \vec{p_k})$ corresponds to a target triangle $Q_{\{i,j,k\}} = (\vec{q_i}, \vec{q_j}, \vec{q_k})$. For each pair of triangles, we compute a mapping $A_{\{i,j,k\}}$, which can be factored by Eq. 5 to determine $A_{\{i,j,k\}}(t)$. Since most of the vertices correspond to more than one triangle, a mapping of all vertices could not (in general) be conforming with all the individual ideal transformations $A_{\{i,j,k\}}(t)$.

Let

$$V(t) = (\vec{v_1}(t), \ldots, \vec{v_n}(t)), t \in [0,1] \quad (6)$$

be the desired paths of the vertices, satisfying

$$
\begin{aligned}
V(0) &= (\vec{p_1}, \ldots, \vec{p_n}) \\
V(1) &= (\vec{q_1}, \ldots, \vec{q_n}).
\end{aligned}
$$

We define $B_{\{i,j,k\}}(t)$ to be the matrix in the affine transformation from $P_{\{i,j,k\}}$ to $\vec{v_i}(t), \vec{v_j}(t), \vec{v_k}(t)$, i.e.

$$B_{\{i,j,k\}}(t)\vec{p_f} + \vec{l} = \vec{v_f}(t), \quad f \in \{i,j,k\} \quad (7)$$

Note that the coefficients of $B_{\{i,j,k\}}(t)$ are linear in $\vec{v_i}(t), \vec{v_j}(t), \vec{v_k}(t)$. We define an intermediate shape $V(t)$ as the vertex configuration which minimizes the quadratic error between the actual matrices $B_{\{i,j,k\}}(t)$ and the desired ones $A_{\{i,j,k\}}(t)$. This quadratic error functional is expressed as

$$E_{V(t)} = \sum_{\{i,j,k\} \in \mathcal{T}} \left\| A_{\{i,j,k\}}(t) - B_{\{i,j,k\}}(t) \right\|^2, \quad (8)$$

where $\|\cdot\|$ is the Frobenius norm. In this expression, the $A_{\{i,j,k\}}(t)$ are known for a fixed time t and each $B_{\{i,j,k\}}$ is linear in the $\vec{v_i}(t), \vec{v_j}(t), \vec{v_k}(t)$. Thus, $E_{V(t)}$ is a positive quadratic form in the elements of $V(t)$. In order to have a unique minimizer to $E_{V(t)}$, we should predetermine the location of one vertex, say $v_{1_x}(t), v_{1_y}(t)$, for example, by linear interpolation.

Figure 6: Transformations of different shapes representing solid objects. Note that parts of the shapes transform rigidly whenever possible. The lowest row shows an example where the shapes have no obvious common skeleton.

The functional $E_{V(t)}$ can be expressed in matrix form, setting $u^T = (1, v_{2_x}(t), v_{2_y}(t), \ldots, v_{n_x}(t), v_{n_y}(t))$ as

$$E_{V(t)} = u^T \begin{pmatrix} c & G^T \\ G & H \end{pmatrix} u, \qquad (9)$$

where $c \in \mathbb{R}$ represents the constant, $G \in \mathbb{R}^{2n \times 1}$ the linear, and $H \in \mathbb{R}^{2n \times 2n}$ the mixed and pure quadratic coefficients of the quadratic form $E_{V(t)}$. The minimization problem is solved by setting the gradient $\nabla E_{V(t)}$ over the free variables to zero:

$$H \begin{pmatrix} v_{2_x}(t) \\ v_{2_y}(t) \\ \vdots \end{pmatrix} = -G \qquad (10)$$

Note that H is independent of t. This means we can invert H and find solutions for time t by computing the corresponding $G(t)$ and a single matrix multiplication:

$$V(t) = -H^{-1}G(t) \qquad (11)$$

In practice, we compute the LU decomposition of H and find $V(t)$ by back substitution. Furthermore, the computations are separable and are performed independently for the two coordinates. Note that only G depends on the dimension, while H is the same for the x and y components. Thus, H is effectively of size $n - 1 \times n - 1$, which means the dominating factor of the computation is independent of the dimension.

The above definition has the following notable properties:

- For a given t, the solution is unique.

- The solution requires only one matrix inversion for a specific source and target shape. Every intermediate shape is found by multiplying the inverted matrix by a vector.

- The vertex path is infinitely smooth, starts exactly in the source shape, and ends exactly in the target shape. These are properties typically difficult to achieve in physically-based simulations.

Figure 6 shows transformations of some simple shapes produced with the described method.

2.3 Symmetric Solutions

While we were satisfied with the degree of symmetry the previosly explained approach exhibited in most of our test cases, a symmetric solution can be advantageous – in particular, if the corresponding triangles in the source and target shapes have largely differing area. We can make the solution symmetric by simply blending the optimization problems from both directions. Let $A_f^{\rightarrow}(t)$ be the affine transformation of triangle f from source to intermediate shape at time t, and $A_f^{\leftarrow}(t)$ the respective transformation coming from the target shape. Similarly, we define $B_f^{\rightarrow}(t)$ and $B_f^{\leftarrow}(t)$. We define intermediate $E_{V(t)}$, the vertex configuration at time t, by

$$E_{V(t)} = (1 - t)E_{V(t)}^{\rightarrow} + tE_{V(t)}^{\leftarrow} \qquad (12)$$

where

$$E_{V(t)}^{\rightarrow} = \sum_{f \in \text{Tri}} \left\| A_f^{\rightarrow}(t) - B_f^{\rightarrow}(t) \right\|^2 \qquad (13)$$

$$E_{V(t)}^{\leftarrow} = \sum_{f \in \text{Tri}} \left\| A_f^{\leftarrow}(1 - t) - B_f^{\leftarrow}(1 - t) \right\|^2 \qquad (14)$$

With this definition, we lose the advantage of only one matrix inversion for given source and target shapes. Instead, every time t requires the solution of a linear system of equations. Whether the computation times are acceptable depends on the shapes and the desired application.

3   Isomorphic Dissections of Shapes

In this section, we construct isomorphic dissections given two shapes in boundary representation. We assume that the correspondence of the boundaries has been established, i.e. a bijective map between boundary vertices is given. For polygons, reasonable correspondence can be found automatically [23, 7]. In difficult cases, few correspondences could be specified manually and the remaining vertices are matched automatically. For polyhedral objects, several techniques exist, which are based on topological merging introduced by Kent et al. [19]. Recent work [14, 20] also allows the specification of corresponding features which seems sufficient to produce acceptable results for a variety of polyhedral models.

3.1   Polygons

The problem of constructing a common triangulation for two given polygons is discussed in the literature as *compatible triangulation* [2]. Triangulating a single polygon π is possible using only the vertices of the polygon (e.g. [5]). However, this is usually not possible for two different polygons. Aronov et al. [2] show how to triangulate two polygons in a compatible way if at most $O(n^2)$ additional vertices (so-called Steiner points) are allowed. The general scheme [2] is to first triangulate each polygon independently. Then, both polygons are mapped to a regular n-gon so that corresponding boundary vertices coincide. The compatible triangulation is established by overlaying the two edge sets in the convex n-gon. The resulting new interior vertices are then mapped back into the original polygons, yielding compatible triangulations of the source and target shapes.

We would like to stress that the quality of the blend, in terms of the quality of the in-between shapes, strongly depends on the shape of the simplices. In particular, skinny triangles (or tetrahedra in 3D) cause numerical problems. Thus, in the following, we describe how this scheme can be enhanced to yield compatible triangulations with a significantly better triangle shape.

First, we apply Delaunay triangulations (see any textbook on Computational Geometry, e.g. [4]) as the initial triangulation since

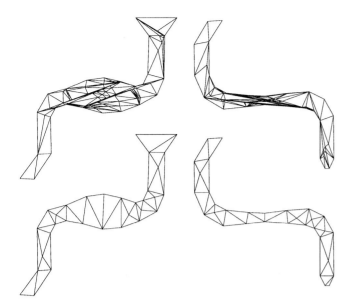

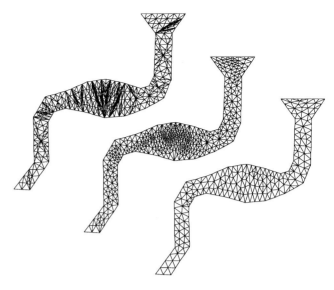

Figure 7: A comparison of compatible triangulations. The upper row shows triangulations generated from using ear-capping for the initial triangulation step. Initial triangulations are overlaid on a convex domain to produce compatible triangulations. The triangulations in the lower row were generated with the same general procedure, but using initial Delaunay triangulations. Far fewer triangles are induced, since Delaunay triangulations yield similar partitioning for similar regions.

Delaunay triangulations maximize the minimum interior angle and, thus, avoid skinny triangles. Of course, any skinny triangle in the independent triangulations is inherited by the merged triangulation. Moreover, Delaunay triangulations are unique, and similar regions in the shapes will result in similar triangulations. Thus, skinny triangles resulting from the overlay process can be avoided.

Nevertheless, the merged triangulations still have skinny triangles, and further enhancement is required to avoid numerical problems. We optimize the triangulations by further maximizing the minimum interior angle, which is known to be a reasonable triangulation quality criterion (see e.g. [4]). We use two independent operations:

1. Moving interior vertices. Freitag et al. [11] show how to find vertex positions which maximize the minimum angle for a given triangulation.

2. Flipping interior edges simultaneously in both triangulations. This procedure follows the edge flip criteria used in Delaunay triangulation. Given that an edge flip is legal in both triangulations, it is performed if the operation increases the overall minimum angle.

The above two operations are applied in turn until no valid flips are necessary. Convergence is assured since each step can only increase the minimum angle. We call this procedure *compatible mesh smoothing*. The smoothing step optimizes the compatible triangulations without changing the vertex count.

However, we also consider changing the vertex count by means of splitting edges. The split operation is well-defined in terms of topology, if it is applied to both triangulations simultaneously, the isomorphy remains. The idea is to split long edges to avoid long skinny triangles. Splitting edges according to their lengths does not guarantee an increase in triangle quality. In practice, smaller triangles are more likely to be improved by the smoothing step. After each edge split, the triangulations are smoothed. This avoids the

Figure 8: The mesh refinement process. In the first row, the merged Delaunay triangulations from Figure 7 are refined by edge splits until all edge lengths are bounded. The second row shows the result of compatible mesh smoothing on this triangulation. The third row shows the actual technique, where splitting and smoothing is performed concurrently. Note that the edge length bound is the same in the first and third row.

generation of edges in regions where the smoothing operation would produce nicely-shaped triangles. Figure 8 illustrates the results of splitting edges, as well as of the smoothing process.

3.2 Polyhedra

To the best of our knowledge, the three-dimensional analog to compatible triangulations has not been discussed in the literature. Work has been done to dissect polyhedra into simplicial complexes, a process referred to as tetrahedralization. However, the work of Aronov et al. [2] can be extended to genus 0 polyhedra. First, the source and target polyhedra are tetrahedralized independently using common techniques, e.g. Barry Joe's Geompack [17]. Then, the tetrahedralizations are mapped to a corresponding convex shape. Alexa [1] as well as Shapiro and Tal [26] describe methods to map an arbitrary genus 0 polyhedron to a convex shape. Since the source and target polyhedra are assumed to have the same vertex-edge topology and the convexification process is deterministic, the polyhedra are mapped to the same convex shape. The interior vertices of their tetrahedralizations are mapped using barycentric coordinates. The fact that vertices are mapped to a convex shape using barycentric coordinates for interior vertices assures that no tetrahedra will be flipped. Then, an overlay of the two tetrahedralizations is computed, where faces are cut against faces, resulting in new edges. Note that the intersection of two tetrahedra results in four-, five-, or six-sided convex shapes, which are easy to tetrahedralize. The resulting structure is mapped back into original polyhedra. In case the source and target shapes are not genus 0, they have to be cut into genus 0 pieces which are independently treated as explained above.

4 Results and Conclusion

We have applied the techniques explained above to various inputs. The two-dimensional shapes are generated by extracting a contour out of an image. For the correspondence of contours, we defined manually several vertex-to-vertex correspondences, while the re-

Figure 9: The contour of a maple leaf blended with a plane using as-rigid-as-possible shape interpolation. Note that the features of the plane grow out of contour according to the current direction of wings and not their final position.

maining vertices were automatically aligned. The resulting polygons were dissected as described above. In Figures 10, 11, 12, and 15, the triangulations were used to map a texture to the shape (as was suggested by Tal and Elber in [28]). Textures were extracted with the contours from the source images. More elaborate techniques for space-time control (e.g. [21]) could be easily integrated in our work to give the user more control as to what is transformed and when. Also note that the techniques are not restricted to simple polygons.

Since our technique interpolates shapes "naturally" in the sense that it preserves parts that just change relative position or orientation, it could be also used to extrapolate beyond the source and target shapes. Figure 13 demonstrates this with the example of Leonardo DaVinci's studies on proportions (see Figure 15 for the interpolation). We can generate shapes for time values -0.5 and 1.5 while preserving the proportions of the human figure.

We have also applied the interpolation technique to three-dimensional models. The examples in Figure 14 were generated by using deformed versions of a polyhedral model. Note the difference between linear vertex interpolation (upper row) and as-rigid-as-possible interpolation (lower row). In Figure 16, morphable polyhedral models were generated using topological merging. As in the two-dimensional case, the vertex paths result from defining transformations for each pair of corresponding tetrahedra by factoring the affine transform into rotational and stretching components and, then, minimizing the deviation from these ideal transformations.

The current implementation seems to be robust and fast. The most time-consuming step is optimizing triangle shape. Without optimizing triangle shape numerical problems are likely to occur. In all our examples no simplex changed orientation (i.e. flipped), however, we have not been able to prove this to be a property of our approach.

The examples clearly demonstrate the superior quality of our approach compared to plain linear vertex interpolation. Additionally, it offers the possibility to texture the shapes, so that shape blending becomes applicable to images. In turn, traditional image morphing techniques could serve to generate the homeomorphic dissections of the shapes and, thus, make use of more advanced vertex/pixel interpolation technique(s). However, the quality of a morph lies in the eye of the beholder. Nevertheless, there is a clear consensus that - lacking other information - the geometry along the morph sequence should change monotonically with no superfluous distortions. The idea of as-rigid-as-possible shape interpolation is to avoid distortions as much as possible and let angles and scales change linearly. We believe that this captures the notion of the above-mentioned consensus.

Despite this, shape blending is always an aesthetic problem and no automatic method will meet the needs that arise in different applications. Consequently, user interaction will always be necessary to produce the desired results. Nevertheless, we believe that more elaborate methods for shape blending simplify and minimize the involvement of the designer.

Finally, we want to mention that dissections of shapes seem to extend the concept of skeletons while fully capturing their information. Dissections are more powerful in representing the mechanics

Figure 10: Morphs between Egyptian art pieces using textures from the original images. Contours are blended using as-rigid-as-possible shape interpolation and texture colors are linearly interpolated.

Figure 11: Contour blend of a penguin and a dolphin using only the texture of the penguin.

of shapes as they allow fine grained analysis of local behaviour. In many cases, shapes naturally have no skeleton or their metamorphoses could not be described in terms of a skeleton. These benefits come along with easier and less ambiguous computation of dissections as compared to skeletons.

Acknowledgements

We thank Kai Kreuzer for helping with the implementation and many examples. Craig Gotsman, George Wolberg, Thomas Sederberg, Herbert Edelsbrunner, and the anonymous reviewers provided useful advice and suggestions. Thanks to Wolfgang Müller and Jose Encarnaçaõ for their support. Work on this paper has been partially supported by the Hermann Minkowski – Minerva Center for Geometry at Tel Aviv University and by The Israel Academy of Sciences.

References

[1] M. Alexa. Merging Polyhedral Shapes with Scattered Features. The Visual Computer, 16, 1, 2000

[2] B. Aronov, R. Seidel, and D. Souvaine. On compatible triangulations of simple polygons. Computational Geometry: Theory and Applications 3, pp. 27-35, 1993

[3] T. Beier and S. Neely. Feature-based Image Metamorphosis. SIGGRAPH '92 Proceedings, pp. 35-42, 1992

[4] M. de Berg, M. van Krefeld, M. Overmars, and O. Schwarzkopf. Computational Geometry - Algorithms and Applications. Springer, Berlin, 1997

[5] B. Chazelle. Triangulating a simple polygon in linear time. Proc/ 31st Symp. on Foundations of Computer Science (FOCS), pp. 220-230, 1990

[6] E. Carmel, D. Cohen-Or. Warp-guided Object Space Morphing. The Visual Computer, 13, 1997

[7] S. Cohen, G. Elber, R. Bar Yehuda. Matching of freeform curves. CAD, 19, 5, pp. 369-378, 1997

Figure 12: Morph between photographs of an elephant and a giraffe.

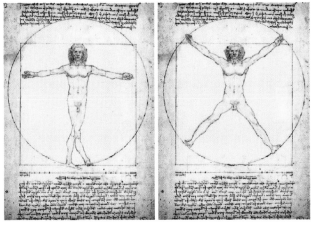

Figure 13: Shape extrapolation. Using as-rigid-as-possible shape interpolation, shapes can be naturally extrapolated beyond the source and target shapes. The images show the human figure of Leonardo DaVinci's proportions at time values -0.5 and 1.5.

Figure 14: A simple example of three-dimensional objects. The difference of linear and as-rigid-as-possible vertex interpolation is demonstrated on a bent cigar-like shape.

[8] D. Cohen-Or, D. Levin, and A. Solomovici. Three dimensional distance field metamorphosis. ACM Transactions on Graphics, 1998

[9] M. Etzion and A. Rappoprt. On Compatible Star Decompositions of Simple Polygons. IEEE Transactions on Visualization and Computer Graphics, 3, 1, pp. 87-95, 1997

[10] M. S. Floater and C. Gotsman. How to Morph Tilings Injectively. J. Comp. Appl. Math., 101, pp. 117-129, 1999

[11] L.A. Freitag, M.T. Jones, and P.E. Plassmann. An efficient parallel algorithm for mesh smoothing. 4th Int. Meshing Roundtable, pp. 47-58, 1995

[12] G.H. Golub and C.F. van Loan. Matrix Computations. The Johns Hopkins University Press, Baltimore, 1983

[13] E. Goldstein and C. Gotsman. Polygon Morphing using a Multiresolution Representation. Graphics Interface '95, pp. 247-254, 1995

[14] A. Gregory, A. State, M. Lin, D. Manocha, and M. Livingston. Feature-based surface decomposition for correspondence and morphing between polyhedra. Proceedings of Computer Animation '98, pp. 64-71, 1998

[15] T. He, S. Wang, and A. Kaufman. Wavelet-based Volume Morphing. Proceedings of Visualization, IEEE Computer Society, pp. 85-91, 1994

[16] J.F. Hughes. Scheduled Fourier Volume Morphing. Computer Graphics (SIGGRAPH '92 Proceedings), 26, 2, pp. 43-46, 1992

[17] B. Joe. Geompack. ftp://ftp.cs.ualberta.ca/pub/geompack

[18] T. Kanai, H Suzuki, and F. Kimura. 3D geometric metamorphosis based on harmonic maps. Proceedings of Pacific Graphics '97, pp. 97-104, 1997

[19] J.R. Kent, W.E. Carlson, and R.E. Parent. Shape Transformation for polyhedral objects. Computer Graphics, 26, pp. 47-54, 1992

[20] A.W.F. Lee, D. Dobkin, W. Sweldens, and P. Schröder. Multiresolution Mesh Morphing. SIGGRAPH '99 Proceedings, pp. 343-350, 1999

[21] S.Y. Lee, K.Y. Chwa, S.Y. Shin, and G. Wolberg. Image Metamorphosis Using Snakes and Free-Form Deformations. SIGGRAPH '95 Proceedings, pp. 439-448, 1995

[22] A. Lerios, C.D. Garfinkle, and M. Levoy. Feature-Based Volume Metamorphis. SIGGRAPH '95 Proceedings, pp. 449-456, 1995

[23] T.W. Sederberg and E. Greenwood. A physically based approach to 2D shape blending. Computer Graphics, 26, pp. 25-34, 1992

[24] T.W. Sederberg, P. Gao, G. Wang, and H. Mu. 2-D shape blending: An intrinsic solution to the vertex-path problem. Computer Graphics, 27, pp. 15-18, 1993

[25] M. Shapira and A. Rappoport. Shape blending using the star-skeleton representation. IEEE CG&A, 15, pp. 44-51, 1993

[26] A. Shapiro and A. Tal. Polyhedron realization for shape transformation. The Visual Computer, 14, 8/9, 1998

[27] K. Shoemake and T. Duff. Matrix Animation and Polar Decomposition. Proceedings of Graphics Interface '92, pp. 258-264, 1992

[28] A. Tal and G. Elber. Image Morphing with Feature Preserving Texture. Computer Graphics Forum (Eurographics '99 Proceedings), 18, 3, pp. 339-348, 1999

[29] G. Wolberg. Digital Image Morphing. IEEE Computer Society Press, 1990

[30] G. Wolberg. Image Morphing Survey. The Visual Computer, 14, 8/9, 1998

[31] Y. Zhang. A Fuzzy Approach to Digital Image Warping. IEEE Computer Graphics and Applications, pp. 33-41, 1996

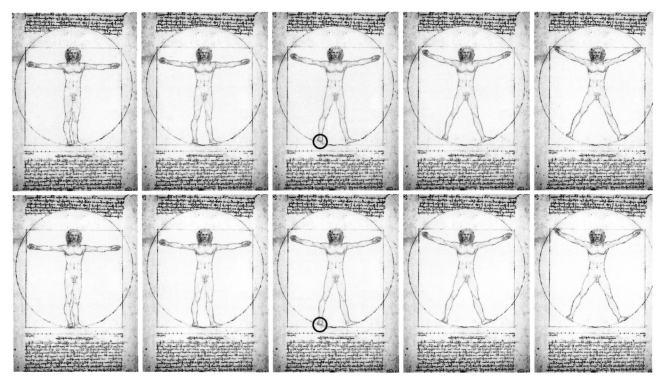

Figure 15: Leonardo DaVinci's studies on proportions. The two rows contrast linear and as-rigid-as-possible interpolation of the figure. The difference is subtle, but Leonardo proves our method right (see the feet leaving the circle in the linear interpolation).

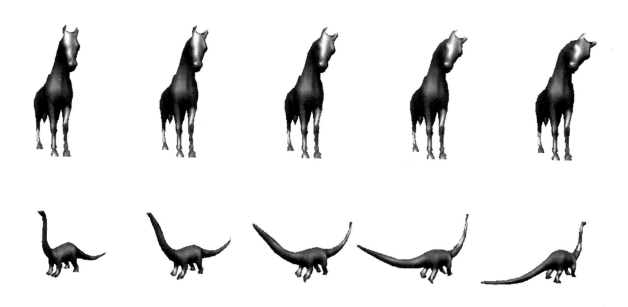

Figure 16: Our technique is also useful to mimic motions of articulated three-dimensional objects in case the underlying skeleton is missing, as demonstrated for a horse turning its head. The example in the lower row was produced using a polyhedral morphing technique (facilitating topological merging). Note that the lengths of the tails/necks are preserved.

Pose Space Deformation: A Unified Approach to Shape Interpolation and Skeleton-Driven Deformation

J. P. Lewis,* Matt Cordner, Nickson Fong

Centropolis

Abstract

Pose space deformation generalizes and improves upon both shape interpolation and common skeleton-driven deformation techniques. This deformation approach proceeds from the observation that several types of deformation can be uniformly represented as mappings from a *pose space*, defined by either an underlying skeleton or a more abstract system of parameters, to displacements in the object local coordinate frames. Once this uniform representation is identified, previously disparate deformation types can be accomplished within a single unified approach. The advantages of this algorithm include improved expressive power and direct manipulation of the desired shapes yet the performance associated with traditional shape interpolation is achievable. Appropriate applications include animation of facial and body deformation for entertainment, telepresence, computer gaming, and other applications where direct sculpting of deformations is desired or where real-time synthesis of a deforming model is required.

CR Categories: I.3.5 [Computer Graphics]: Computational Geometry and Object Modeling—Curve, surface, solid and object modeling I.3.6 [Computer Graphics]: Methodology and Techniques—Interaction techniques I.3.7 [Computer Graphics]: Three-Dimensional Graphics and Realism—Animation

Keywords: Animation, Deformation, Facial Animation, Morphing, Applications.

1 Introduction

Free form deformation has been approached from several distinct perspectives. As an abstract and general problem, good methods have been obtained both using the well known technique that bears this name [32, 12, 17] and other kinematic surface deformation techniques, and with physical models that simulate the time evolution of a membrane or solid.

The animation of human and creature skin deformation is arguably the most common and important application of free form deformation in computer graphics. While such creature animation can be considered a special case of general free form deformation, its importance and difficulty have lead researchers to propose a number of domain-specific algorithms that will be reviewed in Section 2.

The problem of realistic facial animation is being actively and successfully addressed by image-based and hybrid techniques. These techniques are not yet suitable for all applications, however:

---

*zilla@computer.org

Permission to make digital or hard copies of all or part of this work for personal or classroom use is granted without fee provided that copies are not made or distributed for profit or commercial advantage, and that copies bear this notice and the full citation on the first page. To copy otherwise, to republish, to post on servers or to redistribute to lists, requires prior specific permission and/or a fee.

©2000 ACM 0-58113-208-5/00/0007 $5.00

while a purely image-based approach can achieve very realistic images, this advantage may be lost if one needs to introduce geometry and surface reflectance in order to re-light characters to match preexisting or dynamically computed environments. Film and entertainment applications require fanciful creatures that fall outside the scope of image-based approaches.

Some of the most impressive examples of geometry-based (as opposed to image-based) human and creature animation have been obtained in the entertainment industry. These efforts traditionally use shape interpolation for facial animation and a standard but variously-named algorithm that we will term skeleton subspace deformation (SSD) for basic body deformation [25, 9]. While shape interpolation is well-liked by production animators, it is not suitable for skeleton-driven deformation. On the other hand SSD produces characteristic defects and is notoriously difficult to control.

These issues, which will be detailed in the next section, lead us to look for a more general approach to surface deformation. We consider the following to be desirable characteristics of a skeleton-based surface deformation algorithm:

- The algorithm should handle the general problem of skeleton-influenced deformation rather than treating each area of anatomy as a special case. New creature topologies should be accommodated without programming or considerable setup efforts.

- It should be possible to specify arbitrary desired deformations at arbitrary points in the parameter space, with smooth interpolation of the deformation between these points.

- The system should allow *direct manipulation* of the desired deformations [33].

- The locality of deformation should be controllable, both spatially and in the skeleton's configuration space (pose space).

- In addition, we target a conventional animator-controlled work process rather than an approach based on automatic simulation. As such we require that animators be able to visualize the interaction of a reasonably high-resolution model with an environment in real time (with 'high resolution' defined in accord with current expectations). Real time synthesis is also required for applications such as avatars and computer games.

Our solution, termed *pose space deformation*, provides a uniform and expressive approach to both facial skin deformation and skeleton-driven deformation. It addresses the previously mentioned drawbacks of shape interpolation and SSD while retaining the simplicity and performance associated with these techniques.

The next section reviews various approaches to free form deformation and describes shape interpolation and skeleton subspace deformation algorithms. The pose space deformation algorithm requires well behaved and efficient scattered data interpolation in high dimensional spaces; Section 3 considers this issue. The pose-space deformation algorithm itself is described in Section 4; examples and applications are shown in the last section.

2   Background

Recent research has delivered significant improvements in many areas of character animation, including surface representation, model capture, performance capture, and hybrid (partially image-based) rendering approaches. In this literature review we focus specifically on milestones in the surface deformation models and necessarily omit other important contributions.

2.1   Surface Deformation Models

Continuous deformation of a character skin was first addressed in Parke's pioneering facial animation work [26]. In this work, control vertices were deformed by custom algorithmic implementation of carefully selected high-level parameters ('raise-upper-lip', etc.).

Komatsu [13] and Magnenat-Thalmann et. al. [23] demonstrated human body deformation driven by an underlying skeleton. The region and shape of deformation is algorithmically defined in each of these approaches. Magnenat-Thalmann et. al. developed algorithms for each of the various joints in the hand. The discussion in Komatsu focuses on the elbow and shows how the skin crease on the acute side can be obtained by a suitable algorithmic manipulation of the surface control vertices. The algorithms in this early work do not suffer the 'collapsing elbow' characteristic of the SSD algorithm (below). On the other hand, the algorithms are specific to particular types of joints and are perhaps too simple to portray the complexity and individual variability of real anatomy.

The short film *Tony de Peltrie* [3] popularized the use of shape interpolation for facial animation. Forsey [11] describes a character-oriented deformation scheme in which the bending of a smooth surface can be controlled by anchoring levels of a multi-resolution spline surface to the underlying skeleton. These efforts are distinguished from the previous purely algorithmic approaches in giving the modeler control of and responsibility for the deformation.

The specification and animation of surface deformation remains an active area of investigation [17, 10]. The Wires technique [22] is one interesting recent contribution; this approach is notable in providing a direct manipulation interface in a form immediately familiar to sculptors (armatures).

2.2   Multi-Layered and Physically Inspired Models

Chadwick, Haumann, and Parent [7] introduced a multi-layered and physically inspired approach to skin deformation. In their model a free-form deformation abstractly represents underlying body tissues and mediates skin movement. Chadwick et. al. demonstrated expressive three-dimensional cartoon characters but deformation of a realistic character was not shown.

Other researchers have investigated modeling the underlying body tissues in greater depth [27, 24, 8, 35]. Most recently, several groups have undertaken ambitious efforts to produce anatomically inspired multi-layered models of animals and humans with considerable verisimilitude. Nedel and Thalmann [19] simulate the surface deformation of muscles using spring mesh dynamics; a modeled skin cross section is reshaped by a ray-casting procedure that finds the maximum displacement of the underlying tissue. Several papers by Wilhelms and coworkers have shown anatomically representative human and animal models. In Wilhelms and Van Gelder [36] several classes of muscles are algorithmically modeled with attention to volume conservation; skin is a spring mesh anchored to underlying tissue or bone in appropriate areas. Scheepers et. al. [31] produced convincing representations of muscles as well as preliminary but promising skin deformation.

2.3   Common Practice

In recent years character animation has moved beyond being a research topic and sophisticated deforming characters routinely appear in films and on television. Various techniques are employed,

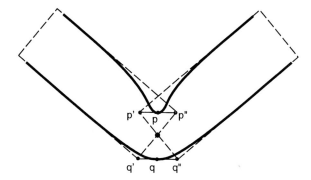

Figure 1: The skeleton subspace deformation algorithm. The deformed position of a point p lies on the line $p'p''$ defined by the images of that point rigidly transformed by the neighboring skeletal coordinate frames, resulting in the characteristic 'collapsing elbow' problem (solid line).

including manually animated FFDs and custom procedural approaches in the spirit of [26, 23, 13]. Arguably the most common practice in character animation (as reflected in commercial software, animation books and courses, and some custom software) is founded on the twin techniques of shape interpolation and SSD [18, 9].

2.3.1   Shape Interpolation

Shape interpolation (also called shape blending and multi-target morphing) is probably the most widely used approach to skin deformation for facial animation [3, 18, 9]. Surface control vertices are simply an animated linear combination (not necessarily convex, i.e., individual weights can be greater than one or less than zero) of the corresponding vertices on a number of key shapes S_k: $\sum_{k=0} w_k S_k$. A variation of this technique uses a single base shape S_0 and a number of delta shapes, $S_0 + \sum_{k=1} w_k(S_k - S_0)$. By writing the delta shape form as $(1 - \sum_1 w_k)S_0 + \sum_1 w_k S_k$ it is clear that the space of achievable shapes is identical in both variations.[1] An attractive feature of shape interpolation is that the desired expressions can be directly specified by sculpting.

The limitations of shape interpolation. Given the popularity and effectiveness of this simple approach, it would be desirable to employ it on regions of the body other than the face. The blending of rigid shapes is inconsistent with regions of the body that are bending under the action of an underlying skeleton, however. Of course the key shapes could be deformed to the moving articulated figure using some other algorithm, but this defeats the purpose of proposing shape interpolation as the means of obtaining the deformation in question.

Shape interpolation also has some drawbacks for its intended role of facial animation. For one, the interpolation is not always smooth. Consider interpolating from a smile (shape A) to a neutral pose (B) and then to a frown (C). An individual vertex travels in a straight line between A and B and again in a line between B and C. Selecting smoothly changing weights with $dw/dt = 0$ at the key shapes merely causes the deformation to "ease in" and stop at each key pose before continuing on – the time derivative of control point motion is smooth, but the motion path itself is only piecewise linear (parametric versus geometric continuity). In practice animators object to the linear nature of the interpolation [34] and have sometimes compensated by sculpting new key shapes as often as every three to five frames [38]. These comments will be revisited in the discussion of the pose space approach later in the paper.

---

[1]Provided that the weights sum to one. This is enforced in the delta shape formulation. It is not enforced in the (non-delta) shape interpolation formulation as written, but weights that do not sum to one are a separate effect – they cause the face to change overall scale.

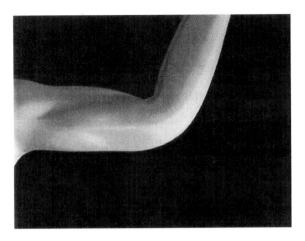

Figure 2: The 'collapsing elbow' in action, c.f. Figure 1.

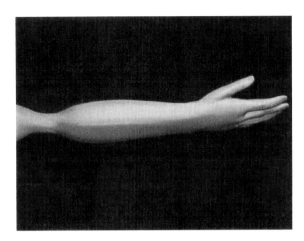

Figure 3: The forearm in the 'twist' pose, as in turning a door handle, computed by SSD. As the twist approaches $180°$ the arm collapses.

2.3.2 Skeleton-Subspace Deformation

This simple algorithm has been repeatedly conceived and appears in commercial software packages under several rather uninformative names such as skinning, enveloping, etc. The algorithm is unpublished but is subsumed by more general published schemes such as [23]. The position of a control vertex $\mathbf{p}$ on the deforming surface of an articulated object lies in the subspace defined by the rigid transformations of that point by some number of relevant skeletal coordinate frames (Figure 1). This may be notated

$$\bar{\mathbf{p}} = \sum w_k L_k(\mathbf{p})\,\mathbf{p}$$

(in more detail)

$$\bar{\mathbf{p}} = \sum w_k L_k^\delta L_k^{0\,-1} L_\mathbf{p}^0\,\mathbf{p}$$

where L_p^0 is the transform from the surface containing $\mathbf{p}$ to the world coordinate system, L_k^0 is the transform from the stationary skeletal frame k to the world system ($L_k^{0\,-1}L_p^0$ together represent $\mathbf{p}$ in the coordinate system of skeletal frame k), and L_k^δ expresses the moving skeletal frame k in the world system. The deformation is controlled by the user through the weights w_k.

SSD is fairly versatile. For example, secondary animation effects such as muscle bulging and swelling of the chest can be achieved by variably weighting the surface to an abstract "bone" whose translation or scale is manually animated.

The limitations of SSD. The first major shortcoming of SSD results directly from the fact that the deformation is restricted to the indicated subspace. In common situations such as shoulders and elbows the *desired* deformation does not lie in this subspace, hence no amount of adjusting the algorithm weights will produce good results. This fact leads to considerable frustration by users of the algorithm – the character of the deformation changes as the weights are changed, sometimes sustaining the incorrect assumption that *some* combination of weights will produce good results. In fact, the SSD algorithm can be easily identified in animations by its characteristic 'collapsing joint' defect (Figures 1, 2).

This problem is extreme in the case of simulating the twist of a human forearm (the pose taken in turning a door handle, Figure 3). In this case the subspace basis consists of surface points rigidly transformed by the forearm frame (no axis rotation) and the wrist frame (axis rotation). With a rotation of 180 degrees this line crosses the axis of the arm, i.e., the forearm collapses entirely as the SSD weights transition at some point from the forearm to wrist frames.

A second difficulty with SSD is that, unlike shape interpolation, it does not permit direct manipulation; artists instead directly or indirectly edit the meshes of weights w_k (for each control vertex on a surface there is one weight per skeletal frame that affects the vertex). SSD algorithms consequently have the reputation for being tedious and difficult to control. Artists with a poor understanding of the underlying algorithm have difficulty distinguishing between results that can be further improved by adjusting weights and results that cannot be improved since the desired result lies outside the achievable subspace, resulting in the impression of unpredictability ("sometimes adjusting the weights helps, sometimes it doesn't").

In some cases the SSD defects can be manually corrected using FFDs and other techniques, and one could consider a scheme whereby these fixes are procedurally invoked as the skeleton articulates. But although FFDs work well (and have a direct manipulation algorithm [12]) the layered FFDs do not reduce the difficulty in adjusting the underlying SSD. The algorithm introduced in the subsequent sections removes the need for such layered fix-it approaches and permits direct specification of the desired deformations.

2.3.3 Unified Approaches

Several published algorithms and commercial packages combine aspects of skeleton-driven deformation and shape interpolation in ways that anticipate our approach. In the pioneering work of Burtnyk and Wein, two dimensional characters were animated using a polygonal rubber sheet that afforded both skeletal and local deformation control [6]. Van Overveld described a two-dimensional animation system in which animation is controlled by a skeleton and character deformation is driven from this skeleton through a scattered interpolation [20]. This work is similar in spirit to ours but differs in that it used the image plane as a global interpolation domain rather than introducing a pose space. Litwinowicz and Williams's system [16] is also a precedent and introduced sophisticated scattered interpolation (again in the image domain). Several papers consider animation (and indeed image synthesis in general) as a special case of neural net learning and interpolation/extrapolation [14, 15, 21]. While this viewpoint is valid, in practice it is perhaps excessively general, for example, a skeleton is merely learned rather than being an intrinsic part of the model. While employed at Industrial Light and Magic the first author of the present paper developed a system that attempted to blend shape interpolation and SSD algorithms; a small portion of it remains in use in their well known *Caricature* animation system. Drawbacks of this work included both a complicated dependence on the details of SSD and its overall conception as a "correction" to SSD. Some commercial

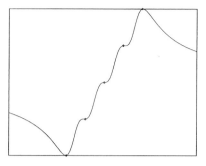

Figure 4: Shepard's interpolant operating on a set of colinear points. The derivative is zero at the data points, and the curve extrapolates to the average of the data values.

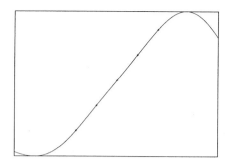

Figure 5: Radial basis functions $\phi(x) = \exp(-x^2/2\sigma^2)$, $\sigma = 10$ interpolating the same set of colinear points as in Figure 4. A different y scale is used to fit the curve. The curve extrapolates to zero.

packages allow blending between two sculpted deformations as a function of a single-joint rotation, thereby combining shape interpolation and skeleton-driven deformation in a limited but useful setting.

2.4 Kinematic or Physical Simulation?

The *depth of simulation* is a prevalent issue in computer graphics, albeit one that is not always consciously considered. Early approaches to animation were purely kinematic; an emphasis on physically based modeling appeared in the literature later. Recent sophisticated approaches allow a hybrid of animator-controlled and physically governed animation as needed. In rendering we perhaps see the opposite trend – much of the literature a decade ago focused on ever deeper simulations of reality, whereas 'shallower' image-based approaches are attracting attention at present.

Similarly, in character deformation both deep and shallow approaches have their place. Deep models promise universally accurate simulation, and the importance of representing humans justifies the needed effort. The authors of these approaches acknowledge that producing anatomically plausible models is a daunting task, however.

Pose space deformation is a shallow, purely kinematic approach to deformation (i.e. without reference to underlying forces, mass, volume), and it has consequent disadvantages. In particular, accuracy is reliant on the modeler/animator rather than being guaranteed by the simulation. On the other hand, our algorithm has clear advantages with respect to simplicity and generality, direct manipulation, real-time synthesis, and other criteria listed in the introduction.

3 Deformation as Scattered Interpolation

In abstract, we wish to express the deformation of a surface as a function of either the pose of an underlying skeleton, or equivalently as a function of some other set of parameters such as the {*smile, raise-eyebrow,...*} controls desirable in facial animation. We also wish to directly sculpt the desired deformation at various points in the parameter space, rather than working in a more abstract space such as the coefficients on various coordinate frames as required by the SSD algorithm.

A scattered data interpolation method is required because deformations will be sculpted at arbitrary (rather than regularly spaced) poses. Since this interpolation is central to our application (the results of the interpolation will be directly visible in the animating deformation), we will consider the available scattered interpolation approaches before settling on a candidate.

3.1 Shepard's Method

Shepard's method [1, 2] is a frequently employed scattered data interpolation scheme in computer graphics. In this method the interpolated value is a weighted sum of the surrounding data points

normalized by the sum of the weights,

$$\hat{d}(\mathbf{x}) = \frac{\sum w_k(\mathbf{x}) d_k}{\sum w_k(\mathbf{x})}$$

with weights set to an inverse power of the distance: $w_k(\mathbf{x}) = \|\mathbf{x} - \mathbf{x}_k\|^{-p}$. (This is singular at the data points $\mathbf{x}_k$ and should computed as $(\|\mathbf{x} - \mathbf{x}_k\| + \epsilon)^{-p}$). With $p > 1$ the interpolation surface is once differentiable. Unfortunately this simple scheme has some potentially undesirable properties. Far from the data the weights will be approximately the same, $\hat{d}(\infty) = w_\infty \sum d_k/w_\infty \sum 1 = \sum d_k/N$, i.e. the interpolated surface converges to the average of the data values. A serious drawback for some applications is that the derivative of the surface is zero at the data points (Figure 4).

3.2 Radial Basis Functions

Radial basis functions [28, 29] have become a popular choice for scattered interpolation. The interpolant is a linear combination of nonlinear functions of distance from the data points:

$$\hat{d}(\mathbf{x}) = \sum_k^N w_k \phi(\|\mathbf{x} - \mathbf{x}_k\|) \qquad (1)$$

If N values of d are available then the weights can be easily solved by a linear system; this can be derived either by least squares fit or by subspace projection. Taking the latter approach, we reconsider the available data points as a single point $\mathbf{d}$ in an N dimensional space, and consider $\phi_k() = \phi(\|\mathbf{x}_j - \mathbf{x}_k\|)$ as the kth basis vector. The best approximation to $\mathbf{d}$ in the space spanned by $\phi_k()$ occurs (in direct analogy with the three-dimensional case) when the weights are such that the error $\mathbf{d} - \mathbf{\Phi}\mathbf{w}$ (with $\phi_k()$ comprising the columns of $\mathbf{\Phi}$) is orthogonal to each of the $\phi_k()$:

$$\mathbf{\Phi}^T(\mathbf{\Phi}\mathbf{w} - \mathbf{d}) = \mathbf{0}$$

so (the so-called "normal equation")

$$\mathbf{\Phi}^T\mathbf{\Phi}\mathbf{w} = \mathbf{\Phi}^T\mathbf{d}$$

can be solved for the familiar

$$\mathbf{w} = (\mathbf{\Phi}^T\mathbf{\Phi})^{-1}\mathbf{\Phi}^T\mathbf{d}$$

A least squares approach leads to the identical result.

Any nonlinear function $\phi()$ will interpolate the data, including odd choices such as $\phi(x) = x$ (which is nonlinear since $x = \|\mathbf{x} - \mathbf{x}_k\|$ is the argument), provided that the columns of $\mathbf{\Phi}$ are independent. On the other hand a smooth $\phi()$ will result in a smooth interpolant (a weighted sum of continuous functions is continuous). In fact radial basis functions have a universal convergence property similar to Fourier series, though the convergence definition is different.

The preceding description maps a k-dimensional input space (arbitrary k) to a one dimensional range, i.e., it is the k-dimensional version of a height field. Surfaces can of course be interpolated by allowing different combinations of the same basis functions in different dimensions, i.e., vector valued w_k. The distance $\| \|$ can be generalized to Mahalanobis distance (effectively rotating and stretching the basis function) [4].

3.3 Energy Functionals and Non-Convex Methods

Various visual reconstruction schemes can be adapted for scattered data interpolation. In these schemes the interpolated or approximated surface is found as the minimum of a functional such as

$$\int |\hat{d}(\mathbf{x}) - d(\mathbf{x})|^2 d\mathbf{x} + \lambda P(\hat{d})$$

where the first term penalizes deviation of the surface $\hat{d}$ from the available data d and the second regularizing term votes for surface smoothness e.g. by integrating the squared second derivative of the surface. With small λ many of these schemes can serve as scattered data interpolants; reference [5] is a good introduction to these approaches.

In some of the most powerful formulations of scattered interpolation the regularizer is considered to hold everywhere except at an unknown set of edges – this is the piecewise-smooth prior desirable in image reconstruction. Since the unknown edges may exist (or not exist) at any location in the domain, all combinations of possible edge locations must be considered and the interpolation cost is prima facie exponential in the surface resolution.

4 Pose Space Deformation

The crux of our approach is the identification of an appropriate space for defining deformations. As discussed above, the interpolation domain is (a subset of) the pose space of an articulated character, or equivalently the space defined by some set of parameters such as facial controls.

In concept the range of the interpolation function could simply be the desired movement of the surface control vertices. To make the job easier for the interpolation we instead interpolate the desired *deviation* of a surface vertex (expressed in the local frame) from its initially computed position (the rigidly transformed position in the case of an articulated model). Several reasons for this choice will be mentioned shortly.

Thus the deforming surface is defined by $\mathbf{p} + \vec{\delta}$ with $\mathbf{p}$ moved rigidly by the skeleton or other underlying system, and

$$\vec{\delta} = f_{\text{interp}}(\text{configuration})$$

where *configuration* is the configuration of the set of joints or parameters controlled by the animator.

Our scheme can be bootstrapped on top of an existing software system: the model is posed as desired and the desired surface at that pose is sculpted. Our algorithm computes the difference between the initial and resculpted model at that pose. This 'deformation' is associated with the joints or other parameters that have moved from their default positions to create the particular pose. One or more deformations will then be interpolated in this subspace using a scattered data approach.

We now have enough criteria to select a particular interpolation scheme. Although it would be desirable to allow deformations to change both continuously and discontinuously with respect to the pose space, creature deformations that are discontinuous with respect to pose seem unlikely. As such the expensive energy functional and non-convex schemes are not necessary. In addition we want $\vec{\delta}$ to approach zero away from the data, and the width of this falloff should be selectable.

Together these comments support $\phi_k(\mathbf{x}) = \exp\left(\frac{-(\|\mathbf{x}-\mathbf{x}_k\|)^2}{2\sigma^2}\right)$ as one possible choice of radial basis (Figure 5). Gaussian radial basis functions are reputed to be well behaved and our experience supports this judgement. Gaussian radial basis functions with adjustable placement and σ are discussed in the neural net literature and optimizing over these parameters is possible. This issue does not arise in our application, however, since the animator decides where in the parameter space to sculpt a pose (effectively deciding the basis function placement). The falloff σ is also specified explicitly by the animator, as described below.

4.1 Algorithm Summary

The steps in a pose space deformation (PSD) algorithm will now be described consecutively.

Definitions. A pose is defined as the configuration of any *pose controls* (joints or abstract manipulators) that have changed from their default values. An abstract manipulator is a UI control or arbitrary piece of geometry whose movement will control the interpolation of some deformation, such as a muscle bulge or a desired facial attribute such as "happiness." A self-relative configuration of the controls is actually considered, for example, an elbow involves two skeletal frames but only one joint angle.

The *pose space* is the space spanned by the variations of these controls. If $n = 2$ pose controls are active and each has three degrees of freedom then a $3(n - 1)$ pose space is defined, and the particular position of the controls defines a point in that space.

Sculpt. The artist first positions some set of pose controls and then sculpts a deformation for that pose. The artist also assigns a falloff (Gaussian σ), either as a symmetric radius across all controls or to each control individually (axis stretched falloff).

Define $\vec{\delta}(\text{pose})$. Any control vertices that have moved from their rest position are found. This is done in the local coordinate frame, i.e., rigid body articulated motion results in zero $\vec{\delta}$. The $\vec{\delta}$ values for the deformed vertices are computed (again in the local coordinate system) and they are saved in a database together with their corresponding location in a pose space. (At the boundary of several surface patches there may be shared vertices that need to be coincident to maintain surface continuity. Unlike some SSD implementations interpolation in pose space by definition cannot separate such vertices).

Solve. When several such deformations have been saved (or when the artist is ready to try animating) it is necessary to solve the interpolation problem. For each control vertex that was moved during sculpting there are now one or more $\vec{\delta}$ values at points in the pose space. Note that the dimension of the pose space can vary across vertices, for example, a particular vertex might be modified in three sculpted deformations but a neighboring vertex might have been modified in only two deformations. The interpolation is done independently for each control vertex (but see additional details below); in our experience using patch surfaces this has not been problematic. Singular $\mathbf{\Phi}^T \mathbf{\Phi}$ is interpreted as a user error; in practice this has turned out to be the result of saving new deformations without moving any pose controls rather than a result of actual numerical problems.

Synthesis. The model is now moved to an arbitrary pose. The location in pose space is determined from the concatenated relative degrees of freedom of the pose controls (simply interpreted as independent dimensions). For each deforming control vertex a $\vec{\delta}$ is interpolated from the delta values at the stored poses using Eq. (1).

Evaluate and Repeat. At this point the model interpolates through the previously defined deformation(s). The most recently defined deformation may extend too far (or not far enough) in pose space, however. There is a rich literature of schemes for optimizing radial basis parameters including σ [4]. On the other hand, animators consider detailed control of the animation to be part of their craft and are quite happy to have interpolation parameters exposed to them. We have found that this potentially abstract parameter is comprehensible so long as it is possible to explore the effect of different values. At a minimum axis-aligned scaling of the falloff should be available; we have not experimented with Mahalanobis rotation of the basis. Based on the evaluation the artist may decide to sculpt additional poses as needed to achieve the desired motion.

A detail that was omitted previously will now be mentioned: when a deformed vertex is found the associated pose space is determined as described above. If there are previous deformations of this vertex in the same pose space then the new deformation is simply another point to interpolate. The new deformation's pose space may, however, be different from the previous spaces associated with the vertex! In such a case a new pose space is started, and the $\vec{\delta}$ is computed as a delta from the previous layered PSD synthesis rather than from the base model. This ensures that the previous deformations are interpolated while allowing the artist complete freedom in determining the extent of the deformation and the associated pose controls. While there is an issue of commutativity, in our experience artists consider this *iterative layered refinement* to be a natural process.

In the preceeding discussion we have not described the representation of rotations and other transformations. This is a well known issue; well behaved transformations are fundamental and are hopefully addressed early in the development of any character animation system.

4.2 Cost

With n poses three matrices of size n must be inverted for each surface control vertex. Typically n will be between 1 and 10, say, so this cost is small. Also it is incurred at a convenient time – during setup (as a pose is saved) rather than during synthesis.

For synthesis, the basis function $\phi(x)$ can be implemented by interpolated table lookup and the `sqrt` required in the Euclidean distance can be composed with $\phi(x)$ in the table. The cost of Eq. (1) is then not much greater than the cost of traditional shape interpolation, i.e., real time synthesis is possible with significant models on current machines.

5 Applications and Discussion

5.1 PSD for Skeleton-Driven Deformation

An articulated model such as a human will typically have a number of different deformation subspaces, each with one or several deformations; the deformations in different subspaces may overlap spatially e.g. to simulate the influence of different muscles. The deformations needed for an elbow, for example, will be interpolated in the one-dimensional subspace defined by the elbow joint angle. Deformations in a shoulder area will need to consider two or more degrees of freedom. The neck/chest/leg blend area of many quadrupeds is a more complex case – the motion of the skin surface in these regions may depend on the relative configuration of several leg bones as well as the rib cage and possibly the neck region of the spine. PSD handles all these cases simply and uniformly.

Figures 8 and 9 are a simple comparison of PSD and SSD algorithms in action on human elbow and shoulder regions.

5.2 PSD for Facial Animation

The application of PSD to facial animation is best described by comparison with shape interpolation (SI).

- In both approaches a set of key shapes (or delta shapes) are sculpted. The same set of shapes can be used in both approaches.

- Whereas shape interpolation is (despite the name) a *superposition* of a set of shapes, PSD *interpolates* among these shapes.

- The animator's task in PSD is to choose the interpolation path (and adjust interpolation parameters such as falloff if desired). With SI the animator's task is to choose the interpolation path but also solve the problem of representing this path by using a set of (non-orthogonal!) basis shapes. In practice this has been considered the major difficulty in applying SI when high quality animation demands large numbers of basis shapes [38].

- In shape interpolation the key shapes and the animation parameter space are one and the same – the keys define the axes of the animation parameter space. In PSD the key shapes are positioned as desired in a space of desired dimensionality.

    One can assign each shape in PSD to a separate dimension, exactly as with SI. On the other hand, PSD allows one to sculpt intermediate expressions (half-smile) and situate them half-way along the relevant (full-smile) axis. Similarly a sculpted pose that represents the simultaneous activation of several parameters (e.g. *happy but surprised,* or *smiling with a wink*) can simply be saved at the appropriate location in the pose space. Psychological research has shown that human facial expressions are largely described by two "emotional" axes [30] (Figure 6); this two-dimensional space would be a convenient high-level pose space for controlling facial animation.

- The PSD interpolation is smooth if so desired.

To illustrate these comments consider Figure 7, which abstractly represents both SI and PSD with an identical set of expressions (*neutral, half-smile, full-smile, frown*). In the SI side of the diagram expressions are arranged as independent (but not orthogonal) dimensions as required by SI. In the PSD diagram the expressions are situated in an expression space having a happy-unhappy axis; a second axis (arousal) and an expression (*delighted*) on that axis are added to show a multidimensional space.

As illustrated, a PSD path from *neutral* to *half-smile* to *full-smile* is monotonic, as might be expected; the motion of a surface point over this interpolation is also smooth. To interpolate these emotions using SI requires a zig-zag pattern of weights: the *half-smile* weight goes from zero to one, and then back to zero as the *full-smile* weight goes from zero to one. The motion of a surface point would also be piecewise linear using SI in this scenario.

5.3 PSD for Secondary Animation

Switches and dials. Additional "dimensions" of deformation can be added at any time by adding a new parameter and associating additional poses with the movement of this parameter. For example, a limb can be modeled in a particular pose both in an unloaded state and with muscles sculpted to express carrying a heavy load. The 'heavy' pose can be associated with the 'on' state of an abstract parameter (e.g. an isolated bone moved into the vertical position); light and heavy loads can then be controlled by flipping this switch. Similarly one can imagine setting up a dial that causes the character to morph; this would of course require a significant set of additional deformation poses.

6 Conclusions

Pose space deformation is not the last word in surface deformation for character animation; high quality anatomically based models are certainly preferable. Nevertheless both anatomically based and

Figure 6: Schematic diagram of emotion space obtained by multi-dimensional scaling from pairwise similarity ratings, simplified from [30].

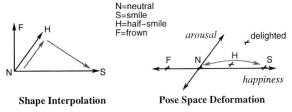

Figure 7: Abstract comparison of shape interpolation versus pose space deformation using the same set of facial expressions.

purely kinematic models have their place. In the current computer animation culture animators generally practice their craft by direct and exhaustive specification of the desired motion combined with quick evaluation using real-time playback. Deeper simulation approaches intrinsically take away some of this control, and animators often argue (rightly or not) that automated processes are inferior or will not produce a human feel. The performance of current anatomically based models prohibits animation preview and other real-time applications such as telepresence and gaming (one published result is several orders of magnitude slower than real time), and the effort needed to produce an anatomically accurate model is not always justified, nor even appropriate if the model is of a fanciful creature whose surface appearance may be inconsistent with any plausible internal anatomy in any case.

PSD unifies and improves upon two techniques that have been common graphics practice for more than a decade. This relatively simple algorithm uniformly handles a variety of deformation situations ranging from a simple elbow to secondary animation. The setup cost of the algorithm is insignificant, and the synthesis cost is only slightly more than that of shape interpolation, so real-time synthesis is possible at effective resolutions on current hardware. We expect that this algorithm will be a useful complement to current techniques.

Acknowledgements

The authors wish to thank Sean Jenkins, David Miya, Amir Nasrabadi, Steven Puri, Kosta Saric, Steffen Wild, Lance Williams, Raymond Yeung, and the anonymous reviewers.

References

[1] R. Barnhill, R. Dube, and F. Little, Properties of Shepard's Surfaces. *Rocky Mountain J. Math.*, vol.13, 1983, pp. 365-382.

[2] T. Beier and S. Neely, Feature-Based Image Metamorphosis. *Computer Graphics* vol. 26, no. 2 (Proc. SIGGRAPH 92), pp 35-42.

[3] P. Bergeron and P. Lachapelle, Controlling Facial Expression and Body Movements in the Computer Generated Short 'Tony de Peltrie'. *SIGGRAPH 85 Tutorial Notes*, ACM, 1985.

[4] C. Bishop, *Neural Networks for Pattern Recognition*, Oxford: Clarendon, 1995.

[5] A. Blake and A. Zisserman, *Visual Reconstruction*, MIT Press, Cambridge, 1988.

[6] N. Burtnyk and M. Wein, Interactive Skeleton Techniques for Enhancing Motion Dynamics in Key Frame Animation, *Comm. ACM*, vol. 19, no. 10 (October 1976), pp. 564-569.

[7] J. Chadwick, D. Haumann, and R. Parent, Layered Construction for Deformable Animated Characters. *Computer Graphics* vol. 23 no. 3 (Proc. SIGGRAPH 89), pp. 243-252.

[8] D. T. Chen and D. Zeltzer, Pump It Up: Computer Animation Based Model of Muscle Using the Finite Element Method. *Computer Graphics* vol. 26, (Proc. SIGGRAPH 92), pp. 89-98.

[9] *Cinefex*, Riverside, CA, various issues, e.g. vol. 66 (June 1996), p. 52 (*Dragonheart*); vol. 64 (Dec 1995), p. 62 (*Jumanji*).

[10] T. DeRose, M. Kass, and T. Truong, Subdivision Surfaces in Character Animation. *Proc. SIGGRAPH 98*, ACM, pp. 85-94.

[11] D. Forsey, A Surface Model for Skeleton-Based Character Animation. In *Second Eurographics Workshop on Animation and Simulation*, Vienna, Austria, 1991, pp. 55-73.

[12] W. M. Hsu, J. F. Hughes, and H. Kaufman, Direct Manipulation of Free-Form Deformations, *Computer Graphics* vol. 26 (Proc. SIGGRAPH 92), pp. 177-184.

[13] K. Komatsu, "Human Skin Model Capable of Natural Shape Variation," *The Visual Computer*, vol. 4, no. 3, 1988, pp. 265-271.

[14] J. P. Lewis, Creation by Refinement: A Creativity Paradigm for Gradient Descent Learning Networks. *International Conf. on Neural Networks*. San Diego, 1988, II: 229-233.

[15] J. P. Lewis, Probing the Critic: Approaches to Connectionist Pattern Synthesis. *IEEE International Joint Conference on Neural Networks* Seattle, July 1991.

[16] P. Litwinowicz and L. Williams, Animating Images with Drawings, *Proc. SIGGRAPH 94*, pp. 409-412.

[17] R. MacCracken and K. Joy, Free-Form Deformations with Lattices of Arbitrary Topology. *Proc. SIGGRAPH 96*, pp. 181-180.

[18] G. Maestri, *Digital Character Animation 2*, Vol 1. New Rider, Indianapolis, 1999. ISBN 1056205-930-0.

[19] L. Nedel and D. Thalmann, Modeling and Deformation of the Human Body Using an Anatomically-Based Approach, *www preprint*.

[20] C. W. A. M. van Overveld, A Technique for Motion Specification in Computer Animation, *Visual Computer*, vol. 6 (1990), p. 106-116.

[21] T. Poggio and R. Brunelli. A novel approach to graphics. AI Memo 1354, C.B.I.P Paper 71, MIT, 1992.

[22] K. Singh and E. Fiume, Wires: A Geometric Deformation Technique. *Proc. SIGGRAPH 98*, ACM, pp. 405-414.

[23] N. Magnenat-Thalmann, R. Laperriere, and D. Thalmann. Joint-Dependent Local Deformations for Hand Animation and Object Grasping. *Proc. Graphics Interface,* 1988, pp. 26-33.

[24] N. Magnenat-Thalmann and D. Thalmann. Human Body Deformations using Joint-Dependent Local Operators and Finite Element Theory. In N. Badler, B. Barsky, and D. Zeltzer, eds., *Making Them Move: Mechanics, Control, and Animation of Articulated Figures* San Mateo, CA: Morgan Kaufmann, 1991, pp. 243-262.

[25] *Maya* Alias/Wavefront, Santa Barbara, CA, 1998.

[26] F. I. Parke, Parameterized Models for Facial Animation. *IEEE Computer Graphics and Applications,* vol. 2, no. 9, November 1982, pp. 61-68.

[27] S. Pieper, Physically-Based Animation of Facial Tissue for Surgical Simulation, *SIGGRAPH 89 Tutorial Notes: State of the Art in Facial Animation*, ACM, 1989.

[28] J. D. Powell, The Theory of Radial Basis Function Approximation. Cambridge University Numerical Analysis Report, 1990.

[29] M. J. D. Powell, Radial Basis Functions for Multivariable Interpolation: A Review. In J. Mason and M. Cox, Eds., *Algorithms for Approximation,* Oxford: Clarendon, pp. 143-167.

[30] J. A. Russel, A Circomplex Model of Affect. *J. Personality and Social Psychology*, vol. 39, p. 1161-1178, 1980.

[31] F. Scheepers, R. Parent, W. Carlson, and S. May, Anatomy-Based Modeling of the Human Musculature. *Proc. SIGGRAPH 97*, ACM, pp. 163-172.

[32] T. Sederberg and S. Parry, Free Form Deformations of Solid Geometric Models. *Computer Graphics,* vol. 20 no. 4, (Proc. SIGGRAPH 86), pp. 150-161.

[33] B. Shneiderman, The Future of Interactive Systems and the Emergence of Direct Manipulation. *Behaviour and Information Technology,* 1, pp. 237-356.

[34] Pat Taylor, Disney/Dream Quest *Mighty Joe Young* facial animation, *personal communication.*

[35] R. Turner and D. Thalmann, The Elastic Surface Layer Model for Animated Character Construction. in N. M. Thalmann and D. Thalmann, eds., *Proc. Computer Graphis International*, New York: Springer Verlag, 1993, pp. 399-412.

[36] J. Wilhelms and A. Van Gelder, Anatomically Based Modeling. *Proc. SIGGRAPH 97*, pp. 173-180.

[37] G. Wyvill, C. McPheeters, and B. Wyvill, Animating Soft Objects. *Visual Computer,* 2, 235-242, 1986.

[38] Xinmin Zhao, Disney *Dinosaur* project, *personal communication.*

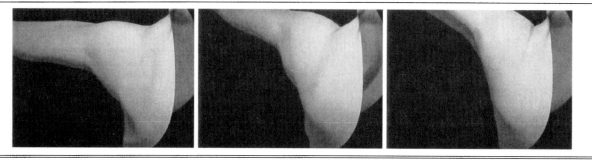

Figure 8a. Comparison of PSD and SSD on an animating shoulder – PSD using only two sculpted poses.

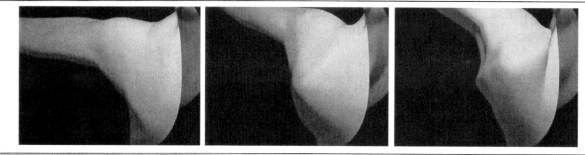

Figure 8b. SSD on an animating shoulder. The shoulder area is especially problematic for SSD due to the large range of rotational movement.

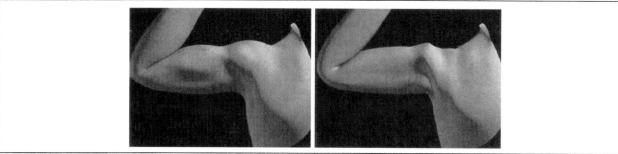

Figure 9. Comparison of PSD (at left) and SSD on the extreme pose of an elbow.

Figure 10. Smooth interpolation of four expressions (frown, neutral, smirk, smile) arranged along a single axis in a pose space, c.f. the discussion of Figure 7.

The EMOTE Model for Effort and Shape

Diane Chi, Monica Costa, Liwei Zhao, Norman Badler

Center for Human Modeling and Simulation

University of Pennsylvania

{chi | monicac | lwzhao | badler}@graphics.cis.upenn.edu

ABSTRACT

Human movements include limb gestures and postural attitude. Although many computer animation researchers have studied these classes of movements, procedurally generated movements still lack naturalness. We argue that looking only at the psychological notion of gesture is insufficient to capture movement qualities needed by animated characters. We advocate that the domain of movement observation science, specifically Laban Movement Analysis (LMA) and its Effort and Shape components, provides us with valuable parameters for the form and execution of qualitative aspects of movements. Inspired by some tenets shared among LMA proponents, we also point out that Effort and Shape phrasing across movements and the engagement of the whole body are essential aspects to be considered in the search for naturalness in procedurally generated gestures. Finally, we present EMOTE (Expressive MOTion Engine), a 3D character animation system that applies Effort and Shape qualities to independently defined underlying movements and thereby generates more natural synthetic gestures.

Keywords

Animation systems, human body simulation, gestures, procedural modeling, expression

1. INTRODUCTION

Human movement ranges from voluntary, goal-oriented movements to involuntary, subconscious movements. Voluntary movements include task-driven actions, such as walking to get somewhere or speaking. Involuntary movements occur for physiological or biological purposes; for instance, blinking, balancing, and breathing. A wide class of movement falls in between these two. In general, this class is characterized as consisting of movements which occur in concert and perhaps unconsciously with other activities. We note two interesting subclasses of this class of movements. One subclass consists of low-level motor controls that assist the accomplishment of a larger coordinated task. For instance, unconscious finger controls form grasps, leg and foot coordination enable walking or running, and lip movements generate speech. Another interesting subclass is the set of movements that accompany communicative acts: facial expressions, limb gestures, and postural attitude. While computer animation researchers have actively studied all these classes of human movements, it remains difficult to procedurally generate convincing, "natural" limb and postural movements .

We pose the problem as follows: What parameters characterize body or limb motions in real people performing communicative acts? The foremost computational approach to this issue has been through the gesture models proposed by McNeil [27], and elaborated with computer implementations primarily by groups led by Cassell [14,39,13], Badler [2,3], and Thalmann [8,12].

McNeil's approach is to characterize communicative arm gestures into several categories:

- **Iconics** represent some feature of the subject matter, such as the shape or spatial extent of an object.
- **Metaphorics** represent an abstract feature of the subject matter, such as exchange, emergence, or use.
- **Deictics** indicate a point in space that may refer to people or spatializable things.
- **Beats** are hand movements that occur with accented spoken words and speaker turn-taking.
- **Emblems** are stereotypical patterns with understood semantics, such as a good-bye wave, the OK-sign, or thumbs-up.

Such an approach has served to make conversational characters appear to gesture more-or-less appropriately while they speak and interact with each other or actual people. The impression that one gets when watching even the most recent efforts in making convincing conversational characters is that the synthetic movements still lack some qualities that make them look "right". Indeed, the characters seem to be doing the right things, but with a kind of robotic awkwardness that quickly marks the performance as synthetic. It is not a computer animation problem *per se* — conventional but skilled key-pose animators are able to produce excellent gestures in 3D characters. So there is some gap between what such an animator intuits in a character (and is therefore able to animate) and what happens in a procedurally synthesized movement. Key pose animators have managed to bridge the technology gap by careful application of classic rules for conventional animation [35,25].

The McNeil/Cassell approach to gesture is rooted in psychology and experimental procedures that use human observers to manually note and characterize a subject's gestures during a story-telling or conversational situation. The difficulty in this approach is *hidden within the decision to call something a gesture*. That is, the observer notes the occurrence of a gesture and then records its type. This kind of recording fails to capture the parameters of movement that makes one particular gesture appear over another, as well as what makes the gesture appear at all. This issue is crucial in the studies of Kendon [19], who tries to understand the deeper question: What makes a movement a gesture or not? In his work, a gesture is a particular act that appears in the arms or body during discourse. *There may be movements that are not gestures and there may be movements that are perceived as gestures in some cultures but not in others.* So clearly, the notion of "gesture" as a driver for computer-generated characters cannot be − in itself − the primary motivator of natural movements. Further, we note that these approaches are limited by their basis in linguistics.

To address this, we look toward movement representations outside the constraints of communicative acts. We find that the

Effort and Shape components of Laban Movement Analysis (LMA) [22,23,17,7,28] provide us with a more comprehensive set of parameters for describing the form and execution of the qualitative aspects of movements. Our approach to gesture augments the McNeil/Cassell approach by addressing a missing dimension: movement exists not just because it has underlying linguistic relationships *but also because it has some distinctiveness in its Effort and Shape parameters.* Effort and Shape provide a means to describe the aspect of human movement that relates to individual character, cultural norms and distinctions. Our approach meshes perfectly with the perspective offered by the LMA proponents: "Gesture ... is any movement of any body part in which Effort or Shape elements or combinations can be observed" [7].

Our approach to gesture also complies with two other important LMA concepts. The first one is synthesized by Bartenieff when she observes that it is not just the main movement actions that let us identify behavior but it is the sequence and phrasing of Effort and Shape components that express and reinforce content [7]. The other concept is best expressed by Lamb: a gesture localized in the limbs alone lacks impact, but when its Effort and Shape characteristics spread to the whole body, a person appears to project full involvement, conviction, and sincerity [24].

We present EMOTE (Expressive MOTion Engine), a 3D character animation system that allows the specification of Effort and Shape parameters to modify independently defined arm and torso movements. The underlying movements of the arms and torso are specified through key time and pose information much like conventional computer animation. However, rather than performing a simple linear interpolation, we apply Effort and Shape parameters to these motion templates to create expressive movements. Our approach allows users to specify separate parameter values for different body parts, as well as phrasing parameter values across the key poses. We note that the key pose values may be generated synthetically, by inverse kinematics, motion capture, or otherwise pre-stored movement patterns.

In the next section, we present related work, followed by a brief overview of the Effort and Shape components of LMA. Then, we present the EMOTE model for Effort and Shape. Next, we discuss several animations that were created to demonstrate the power of our approach. Finally, we point to some directions that guide our future investigations and conclude with the main contributions of our work.

2. RELATED WORK

In addition to the use of computational implementations of gesture models to animate synthetic humans during communicative acts [14,39,13,3,8,12], many researchers have addressed the issue of generating more natural movements in broader contexts. Several researchers have suggested methods of adding expressiveness to animated motions using such methods as stochastic noise functions [31], Fourier function models [38], or emotional transforms [1]. Such methods require an off-line modeling process for each different type of expression. Others have implemented tools that modify or interpolate existing motions to display different expressions or fit other constraints [10,40,33]. Various researchers have developed behavioral animation systems to generate animations of multiple creatures with varying personalities and/or goals [32,36,5,8]. Although creatures in behavioral animation systems display different high-level behaviors, their low-level movements are often very simple, non-expressive, or drawn from a small library of movements. A task-level animation system that generates arm motions of a human figure moving an object to a goal location has been developed using an inverse kinematics algorithm based on neurophysiological studies [21]. The focus of this system is on the "intention" of moving an object from one location to another and not on the underlying movement qualities of the character. The use of secondary motions has been proposed as a way to enliven computer generated animations. One approach adds secondary movements to walking characters based on user-specified personality and mood [29]. Another approach focuses on passive motions like the movement of clothing and hair, generated in response to environmental forces or the movements of characters and other objects [30].

Badler originally proposed (but did not implement) the use of Effort to provide users with expressive movement control of articulated figures [2]. Bishko suggested analogies between the "Twelve Principles of Animation" [35] and Laban Movement Analysis [8]. She shows that there is an abstract relationship between LMA and traditional animation techniques, but does not provide a computational means of exploiting this relationship. Others have done work with computerizing Labanotation (a notation, primarily used for recording dance, based on Laban's work that focuses on the structural aspects of movement) [4,11], but are only beginning to address the more qualitative aspects of movement provided by the Effort and Shape components.

3. BACKGROUND

Rudolf Laban (1879-1958) made significant contributions to the study of movement, bringing together his experiences as a dancer, choreographer, architect, painter, scientist, notator, philosopher, and educator. He observed the movement of people performing all types of tasks: from dancers to factory workers, fencers to people performing cultural ceremonies, mental patients to managers and company executives. His theories on movement, which were significantly extended and applied by his students and colleagues have resulted in a rich vocabulary for describing and analyzing movement, leading to the development of Laban Movement Analysis[1] [7,28,17,26]. LMA has evolved into a comprehensive system that has been used in dance, drama, nonverbal research, psychology, anthropology, ergonomics, physical therapy, and many other movement-related fields [6,15].

Laban Movement Analysis has five major components: Body, Space, Shape, Effort, and Relationship. Together these components constitute a textual and symbolic language for describing movement. Body deals with the parts of the body that are used and the initiation and sequencing of a motion. Space describes the locale, directions, and paths of a movement. Shape involves the changing forms that the body makes in space. Effort describes how the body concentrates its exertion while performing movements. Effort is often compared to dynamic musical terms such as legato, forte, dolce, etc., which give information on how a piece of music should be performed. Relationship describes modes of interaction with oneself, others, and the environment.

---

[1] LMA is promoted by the Laban/Bartenieff Institute of Movement Studies (LIMS), 234 Fifth Avenue, Room 203, New York, NY 10001; (212)477-4299; www.limsonline.org.

Relationship examples include facings, contact, and group forms. As part of our approach to gesture, we developed a computational model of the Effort and Shape components of LMA.

Effort comprises four motion factors: Space, Weight, Time, and Flow. Each motion factor is a continuum between two extremes: (1) *indulging* in the quality and (2) *fighting* against the quality. In LMA these extreme Effort Elements are seen as basic, "irreducible" qualities, meaning they are the smallest units needed in describing an observed movement. The eight Effort Elements are: Indirect/Direct, Light/Strong, Sustained/Sudden, and Free/Bound. The eight Elements can be combined and sequenced for innumerable variations of phrasings and expressions. Table 1 illustrates the motion factors, listing their opposing Effort Elements with textual descriptions and examples.

Space: attention to the surroundings	
Indirect:	flexible, meandering, wandering, multi-focus
Examples:	waving away bugs, slashing through plant growth
Direct:	single focus, channeled, undeviating
Examples:	pointing to a particular spot, threading a needle
Weight: sense of the impact of one's movement	
Light:	buoyant, delicate, easily overcoming gravity, marked by decreasing pressure
Examples:	dabbing paint on a canvas, describing the movement of a feather
Strong:	powerful, having an impact, increasing pressure into the movement
Examples:	punching, pushing a heavy object, expressing a firmly held opinion
Time: lack or sense of urgency	
Sustained:	lingering, leisurely, indulging in time
Examples:	stretching to yawn, stroking a pet
Sudden:	hurried, urgent
Examples:	swatting a fly, grabbing a child from the path of danger
Flow: attitude towards bodily tension and control	
Free:	uncontrolled, abandoned, unable to stop in the course of the movement
Examples:	waving wildly, shaking off water
Bound:	controlled, restrained, able to stop
Examples:	moving in slow motion, tai chi, carefully carrying a cup of hot liquid

Table 1: Motion Factors and Effort Elements

The Shape component involves three distinct qualities of change in the form of movement: Shape Flow, Directional Movement, and Shaping. A Shape Flow attitude primarily reflects the mover's concern with the changing relationship among body parts. These changes can be sensed as the increasing or decreasing volume of the body's form or a moving toward or away from the body center. Shape Flow can be seen from these two different perspectives. The first one emphasizes the torso, which can be said to Grow or Shrink. A continuous breathing pattern reveals changes in Shape Flow as seen from the torso perspective. The other perspective emphasizes the limbs, which are said to be Opening or Closing with respect to the longitudinal axis. Shrinking from the cold or stretching to wake up would be characterized as having a Shape Flow quality.

While Shape Flow is mainly concerned with sensing the body's shape changes within itself, Directional Movement describes the

mover's intent to bridge the action to a point in the environment. These movements can be simple spoke-like or arc-like actions to reach a direction or object, such as a reach to shake a hand or to touch an object or to move to a specific location.

Shaping Movement depicts the changes in movement form that demonstrate a carving or molding attitude as the body interacts with the environment. This form can be dictated by objects in space or simply created by the mover. An active adapting of the body shape in order to move through a crowd, or a gesture describing an elaborately carved sculpture might illustrate a Shaping mode.

Shape changes in movement can be described in terms of three dimensions: Horizontal, Vertical and Sagittal. Each one of these dimensions is in fact associated with one of the three main dimensions (Width, Length, and Depth) as well as one of the three planes (Horizontal, Vertical, and Sagittal) related to the human body. Changes in Shape in the Horizontal dimension occur mainly in the side-open and side-across directions; as the movement becomes planar there would be more of a forward-backward component added to the primary side component. Changes in the Vertical dimension are manifested primarily in the upward-downward directions; the plane would add more sideward component to the up-down. Finally, changes in the Sagittal dimension are more evident in the body's depth or the forward-backward direction; planar movement would add an upward-downward component.

We note that while there is distinct vocabulary for each quality – Shape Flow, Directional Movement, and Shaping – in the various dimensions, we have merged these three concepts (using them interchangeably) and chosen to use the Shaping terminology. The terms we are using to describe the opposing changes in these dimensions are Spreading and Enclosing, Rising and Sinking, Advancing and Retreating. It is important to point out that limbs and torso movements are not required to involve the same Shape qualities at a given time. In this way, Shape Flow functions as a breathing baseline to support Directional and Shaping movement of the limbs. In another example, a traffic officer might hold up one arm with a Directional reach, while the other arm gestures in a circular Shaping mode, and the head does small tilting Shape Flow actions to accompany the Shaping arm.

Horizontal	
Spreading:	affinity with Indirect
Examples:	opening arms to embrace, sprawling in a chair
Enclosing:	affinity with Direct
Examples:	clasping someone in a hug, huddling in the cold
Vertical	
Rising:	affinity with Light
Examples:	reaching for something in a high shelf
Sinking:	affinity with Strong
Examples:	stamping the floor with indignation
Sagittal	
Advancing:	affinity with Sustained
Examples:	reaching out to shake hands
Retreating:	affinity with Sudden
Examples:	avoiding a punch

Table 2: Shaping Dimensions and Affinities

Another LMA concept is Reach Space in the Kinesphere (near, middle, and far). Our current approach regards Reach Space only from the perspective of the limbs in relation to the distance from the body center. Though this is a simplified view, it adds an important feature to the limb range of movement.

Shape changes can occur in affinity with corresponding Effort Elements. Table 2 shows the opposing attitudes towards Shape, some examples, and their affinities with Effort Elements.

4. THE EMOTE APPROACH TO GESTURE

Our current implementation of EMOTE uses a commercially available, fully articulated, human model [18]. At this point, we focus on expressive gestures involving arm and torso movements.

EMOTE has four features which we believe are essential for creating gestures that convey naturalness and expressiveness:

1. A given movement may have Effort and Shape parameters applied to it independent of its geometrical definition.
2. A movement's Effort and Shape parameters may be varied along distinct numerical scales.
3. Different Effort and Shape parameters may be specified for different parts of the body involved in the same movement.
4. The Effort and Shape parameters may be phrased (coordinated) across a set of movements.

The underlying movements of a gesture are specified through key time and pose information defined for the arms and the torso. An external process, such as using a specific gesture stored in a motion library, a procedurally generated motion, or motion captured from live performance, could be used to generate these underlying movements. Key pose information could be extracted from these movements and used as input into EMOTE. With the key pose information, the EMOTE parameters could then be applied to vary the original performance (property 1).

Effort and Shape qualities are expressed using numeric parameters that can vary along distinct scales (property 2). Each Effort and Shape factor is associated with a scale ranging from -1 to +1. The extreme values in these scales correspond to the extreme attitudes of the corresponding factors. For example: a +1 value in Effort's Weight factor corresponds to a very Strong movement; a -1 value in Shape's Vertical dimension corresponds to a Rising movement. Effort parameters are translated into low-level movement parameters, while Shape parameters are used to modify key pose information. By interactively using one or many of the Effort and Shape dimensions, we can search for the desired quality of a particular movement. During procedural synthesis, EMOTE parameters can be applied directly based on parameter values dependent on a character's particular utterance, reactions, or personality.

EMOTE permits independent specification of Effort and Shape parameters for each part of the body (property 3). In its current implementation however, Effort parameters do not apply to torso movements. Although Shape parameters have proven to be effective in the specification of expressive torso movements, further investigation should be carried out to identify how Effort qualities are manifested in the torso. Moreover, the Shape parameters are mainly applied to torso movement. The general Space concept of Kinespheric Reach Space is used in the arms. Table 3 summarizes which dimensions of Effort and Shape can be used to modify the movements of the different parts of the human body.

Allowing the definition of expressive gestures that include the legs can be similarly done, however, additional constraints need to be carefully considered in order to provide static and dynamic balance and stability. Moreover, using Effort and Shape parameters to modify locomotion is a more complex task and involves the identification of a different set of low-level movement parameters, including an exploration of the pelvic-femoral movement rhythm. Furthermore, including the legs may also affect the movement of the torso and arms, because changing the qualities in the legs may result in a reworking of the posture. For instance, the additional effort in the legs is reflected and reinforced by the exertion of the torso and placement of the arms.

		Right Arm	Left Arm	Torso
Effort	Space	yes	yes	no
	Weight	yes	yes	no
	Time	yes	yes	no
	Flow	yes	yes	no
Shape	Horizontal	yes	yes	yes
	Vertical	yes	yes	yes
	Sagittal	yes	yes	yes
	Reach Spc	yes	yes	no

Table 3: Body Parts and Effort and Shape Dimensions

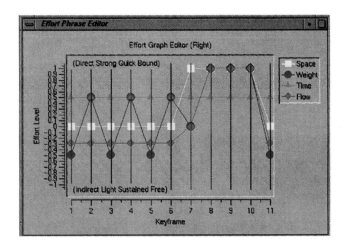

Figure 1: Effort Phrase Editor

Finally, our approach allows the specification of different sets of values for the Effort and Shape parameters across any series of keys that define the underlying motions (property 4). By property (3), this can be done separately for each part of the body.

Figure 1 depicts a graph editor used to specify Effort parameters across a series of keyframes defined for the arms.

4.1 Expressive Arms

The underlying key poses of the arms are defined as end-effector positions (keypoints). Keypoints can be defined as being global or local. Local keypoints are defined relative to the human's shoulders. Global keypoints, on the other hand, establish a constraint relative to the environment. Keypoints can also be classified into *Goal* or *Via* points. *Goal* points define a general movement path; the hand follows this path, stopping at each *Goal* point. *Via* points direct the motion between keyframes without pausing. For instance, a *Via* point might be used to generate a semi-circular path between two *Goal* points.

EMOTE uses an arm model with a 1 degree-of-freedom (DOF) elbow joint and spherical (3 DOF) shoulder and wrist joints. An analytical inverse kinematics algorithm (IKAN) computes the shoulder and elbow rotations, given a goal specified by three-dimensional position coordinates and an elbow swivel angle [36]. Wrist rotations are determined according to Effort settings (as described below).

Reflecting Effort and Shape definitions provided by the LMA system, Shape parameters are used to modify the keypoints that specify arm movements, while Effort parameters affect the execution of those movements resulting from the modified keypoints.

4.1.1 Applying Shape to Arm Movements

Let us first consider the Horizontal, Vertical and Sagittal dimensions of Shape and show how the parameters associated with them are used to modify the keypoints. Because we are striving to simulate volume-like changes in the movement we are associating the Shape changes more with planar action than with strictly dimensional movement.

For a particular keypoint, let the variables *hor*, *ver* and *sag* in the interval [-1, +1] represent the parameters corresponding to the Horizontal, Vertical and Sagittal dimensions, respectively. We define two constants $abratio > 1$ and $maxd\theta$. For each one of the above dimensions, we find an ellipse containing the keypoint and lying in a plane parallel to the plane associated with that dimension (as described in Section 3). The center of the ellipse is the projection of the shoulder joint position on that plane. The major axis of the ellipse is parallel to the direction mostly affected by changes in that dimension and its minor axis is parallel to the other direction affected by such changes. The quotient between its major radius *a* and its minor radius *b* is *abratio*. We calculate the angle $\theta \in [0, 2\pi)$ formed by the major axis of the ellipse and the segment whose endpoints are the center of the ellipse and the keypoint. We find the contributions of that dimension to the modified keypoint by rotating the keypoint by $d\theta$, a fraction of $maxd\theta$ determined by the numeric parameter associated with the dimension being considered. Figure 2 illustrates how we calculate *vdy* and *vdz*, the contributions of the Vertical parameter *ver* to a particular keypoint.

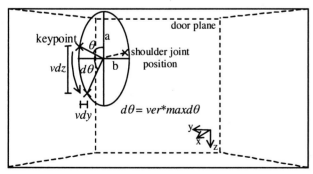

Figure 2: A Keypoint Modified by theVertical Parameter

Let *x*, *y* and *z* be the coordinates of the keypoint in Figure 2. We find θ such that

$$\begin{cases} \theta = atan(\dfrac{y}{-z} * abratio) \\ 0 \le \theta < 2\pi \end{cases} \qquad (1)$$

The major radius *a* of the ellipse is calculated by the following equation:

$$a = \frac{-z}{cos(\theta)} \qquad (2)$$

The angle formed by the rotated keypoint and the major axis of the ellipse is given by the function *rot* defined as follows:

$$rot(\theta) = \begin{cases} 0 & ver = 0 \\ min(\theta - ver * maxd\theta, 2\pi) & ver < 0, \theta \ge \pi \\ max(\theta + ver * maxd\theta, 0) & ver < 0, \theta < \pi \\ max(\theta - ver * maxd\theta, \pi) & ver > 0, \theta \ge \pi \\ min(\theta + ver * maxd\theta, \pi) & ver > 0, \theta < \pi \end{cases} \qquad (3)$$

Finally, the contributions *vdy* and *vdz* are calculated as follows:

$$vdz = -(a * cos(rot(\theta))) - z \qquad (4)$$

$$vdy = (a * \frac{1}{abratio} * sin(rot(\theta))) - y \qquad (5)$$

We use the same model as described above to determine the contributions of the Horizontal (*hdy*, *hdx*) and Sagittal (*sdx*, *sdz*) parameters to the modified keypoint. We find the *x'*, *y'* and *z'* coordinates of the modified keypoint by adding the appropriate contributions to the coordinates of the original keypoint. Then,

$$x' = x + hdx + sdx \qquad (6)$$
$$y' = y + hdy + vdy \qquad (7)$$
$$z' = z + vdz + sdz \qquad (8)$$

Let us now consider how the Kinespheric Reach Space parameter affects a particular keypoint. When considered from the perspective of the arms, Reach Space design describes the limb relationship with the body as it moves toward or away from the body center. Therefore, our Shape model modifies a particular keypoint by moving it along the direction that passes through the keypoint and the center of mass of the human figure. We use the Reach Space parameter *rs* to calculate the amount by which the keypoint is moved toward or away from the center of mass. This Reach Space modifier is considered after the keypoint has been modified according to its Horizontal, Vertical and Sagittal parameters. When the achievement of the modified keypoint requires shoulder angles outside the human body limits, stored joint limits avoid unattainable configurations of the body. As they establish a constraint relative to the environment, *Global* keypoints are not affected by the Shape parameters.

4.1.2 Applying Effort to Arm Movements

The translation of the qualitative Effort Elements into quantitative, low-level movement parameters was the key task in defining a computational model of the Effort component of LMA. Initially, we tried to deduce movement characteristics from motion capture data. We collected 3D motion capture data of a Certified Movement Analyst (CMA) trained in LMA performing numerous examples of combinations of Effort Elements. Analysis of the motion capture data led to only the most obvious conclusions; i.e.: Sudden is short in duration, Sustained is longer in duration, and Strong tends to have large accelerations. The inability to deduce the more subtle characteristic qualities of Effort arose from several factors. First, Effort reflects complex inner physiological processes that are related to a being's inner drive to respond to the physical forces in nature. Thus, Effort is embodied in the whole person and manifested in *all* body parts, whereas we were interested solely in the physical embodiment and visual result of inner attitudes on *movement*, particularly that of the arms. Furthermore, numerous other movements such as visual attention, changes in muscular tension, facial expressions, and breath patterns are not adequately captured by current motion capture technology. As a result, we turned to other methods for deducing the low-level movement parameters and corresponding settings for Effort. We defined underlying quantitative structures that model each Effort Element. Visual analysis of the motion capture data played an important role in extracting other manifestations of Effort and focusing our attention solely on the influence of Effort on arm movements. Other methods we used to derive an empirical model of Effort included descriptions of Effort from the literature [7,17,26,28], application of traditional animation principles [25,35], and much experimentation with feedback from a CMA.

First, we describe the set of low-level, quantitative movement parameters. Then, we show how these parameters are set based on the settings for the Effort parameters.

There are three types of low-level movement parameters: those that affect the arm trajectory, those that affect timing, and flourishes that add to the expressiveness of the movement.

4.1.2.1 Trajectory Definition

We define the arm trajectory for a given animation with two parameters:

- **Path curvature**: determines the straightness or roundness of the path segments between keypoints. We control the path curvature using the tension parameter introduced by Kochanek and Bartels for interpolating splines [20]. The tension parameter *Tval* ranges from -1 to +1.
- The **interpolation space**: defines the space in which the interpolation is performed: end-effector position, joint angle, or elbow position.

For end-effector interpolation, we use the end-effector position and swivel angle stored for each keypoint. We define an interpolating spline between the positions at keypoints using the tension parameter to determine the curvature of the path. We also interpolate between swivel angle values with an interpolating spline. For joint angle interpolation, we compute and store the shoulder and elbow rotations at keypoints. We then generate an interpolating spline between the elbow angle values at keypoints and perform spherical linear interpolation to determine the shoulder rotations. For interpolation in elbow position space, we compute and store the elbow position at keypoints using the posture defined by the end-effector position and swivel angle. We then define an interpolating spline between these positions, which are later used to set the shoulder rotations. The elbow rotations for elbow position interpolation are the same as those for end-effector interpolation. Interpolation in elbow position space gives smooth elbow motions, but a less path-driven movement than interpolation in end-effector position space.

The Effort settings determine which interpolation space is used. The default interpolation space uses end-effector position. Free movements use angular interpolation to achieve a less path-driven and less controlled movement. Our empirical studies show that Indirect movements tend to be driven by the elbow, and thus use interpolation in elbow position space.

4.1.2.2 Parameterized Timing Control

We separate timing control from trajectory definition by using a variation of the double interpolant method introduced by Steketee and Badler [34]. The interpolating splines that define the trajectory (described in the preceding section) compute values between keypoints using an interpolation parameter s that varies from 0 to 1 over the interval from keypoint i to keypoint $i+1$ [20]. Let the trajectory be defined by some function $P(s,i)$. We now need a method of translating frame numbers into s and i. At the ith keypoint, $s = 0$. For in-between frames, we define a variable $t' \in [0,1]$, a frame's relative time between the previous and following keypoints. Let *prev* equal the frame number of the previous keypoint, *next* equal the frame number of the next keypoint, and *curr* equal the current frame number. Then,

$$t' = \frac{curr - prev}{next - prev} \qquad (9)$$

We define a frame number-to-time function $Q(t', I) = s$, parameterized by a set of variables I to achieve various timing effects (described further below). For each in-between frame, we normalize the frame number to produce t', use function Q to compute s, and then input s and the corresponding keypoint number i into function P to compute the position values (or joint angle values for angular interpolation) for the given frame.

We provide several parameters for timing control:

- The **number of frames between keypoints** is initially set according to the user's specified key times, but these values get adjusted according to the Effort settings.
- **Input variables to the keyframe-to-time function** (I) include inflection time t_i, time exponent *texp*, start velocity v_0, and end velocity v_1.

Our parameterized frame number-to-time function Q assumes every movement (from one *Goal* keypoint to the next) starts and ends at rest. Also, every movement has a constant acceleration a until time t_i, followed by a constant deceleration. We introduce velocities v_0 at time t_0 and v_1 at time t_1 to achieve the traditional animation effects of anticipation and overshoot [25].

This model gives us the following velocity function (Figure 3):

$$v(t'') = \begin{cases} \dfrac{-v_0}{t_0} t'' & [0, t_0) \\[2mm] \dfrac{-(v_0 + t_i)t'' + v_0 t_i + t_0 t_i}{t_0 - t_i} & [t_0, t_i) \\[2mm] \dfrac{-(v_0 + t_i)t'' + v_1 t_i + t_1 t_i}{t_1 - t_i} & [t_i, t_1) \\[2mm] \dfrac{-v_1 t'' + v_1}{t_1 - 1} & [t_1, 1] \end{cases} \qquad (10)$$

where

$$t'' = (t')^{t\,\exp} . \qquad (11)$$

The function Q is the integral of Equation (10).

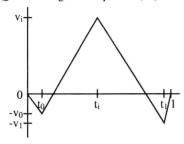

Figure 3: Velocity Function

The set of input variables I to the frame number-to-time function Q provides control to the acceleration/deceleration pattern of the movement, as well as allowing for anticipation and overshoot. The inflection point t_i represents the point (between 0 and 1) where the movement changes from accelerating to decelerating. A value of 0.5 gives a basic ease-in/ease-out curve. A value greater than 0.5 corresponds to a primarily accelerating motion, while a value less than 0.5 gives a decelerating motion. The default time exponent (*texp*) value of 1.0 does not affect the velocity curve; however, values greater than 1.0 magnify an acceleration, while values less than 1.0 exaggerate a deceleration. The start (v_0) and end (v_1) velocities[2] default to 0. Increasing v_0 generates movements with anticipation, where the hand pulls back before extending in preparation for a Strong movement. Decreasing v_1 generates movements with overshoot, such as in Free movements where an indulgence in flow causes one to swing out past a target before hitting it. We set t_0 to 0.01 and t_1 to 0.99, which gives us natural-looking anticipation and overshoot effects; however, these values can easily be included in I as variable low-level movement parameters.

4.1.2.3 Flourishes

Flourishes are miscellaneous parameters that add to the expressiveness of the movements. These are listed below:

- Wrist bend is determined by the wrist bend multiplier *wbmag* and the wrist extension magnitude *wxmag*. The *wbmag* parameter is a multiplier that represents the magnitude of the wrist bend. If the *wbmag* is set for a flexed wrist, the wrist bend is set to 0.6 radians about the x-axis. Otherwise, the wrist bend is set using

$$wrist\_bend = wbmag * sin(2\pi(t'+0.75)) + 1 - wxmag) \quad (12)$$

where $t' \in [0,1]$ and represents the normalized time between two keypoints. This results in a wrist that gradually bends inwards and back out. The value of *wxmag* shifts the sinusoidal graph, setting the beginning wrist extension to be positive (outward) or negative (inward).

---

[2] As mentioned, each movement begins and ends at rest. The start and end velocities represent shortly after the beginning or shortly before the end of a movement, respectively. They are so named to emphasize that they are not initial and final velocities, which remain 0.

- Arm twist is parameterized by wrist twist magnitude *wtmag*, wrist frequency *wfmag*, elbow twist magnitude *etmag*, and elbow frequency *efmag*. The wrist twist is measured in radians about the z-axis and is determined by:

$$wrist\_twist = wtmag * sin(wfmag * \pi t') . \quad (13)$$

Elbow twist is set using a similar equation, replacing *wtmag* and *wfmag* with *etmag* and *efmag*, respectively.

- Displacement magnitude is a multiplier *dmag* that adds a sinusoidal displacement to the elbow angle

$$elbow\_angle = elbow\_angle * (1 + dmag * sin(2\pi t')) \quad (14)$$

where t' is the normalized time between two keypoints.

4.1.2.4 Parameter Settings

To determine the mapping of the four Effort Elements into our low-level movement parameters, we first determined the default settings for each of the eight Effort Elements by trial and error using visual analysis and testing by a CMA. For example, the default interpolation space is set to elbow position for Indirect, joint angle for Free, and end-effector for the other Effort Elements. The default tension of the path curvature *Tval* is set to -1 for Indirect, +1 for Direct, and 0 for the other Effort Elements.

Once we had the default settings for the individual Effort Elements, we generated the range between opposing Effort Elements by interpolating continuous variables and using the nearest value for discrete variables such as the interpolation space. We note that these may lead to discontinuities in the animation if Space, Weight, or Flow cross zero when they are phrased across the keyframes. In [15], we show that such discontinuities occur only if the zero crossings occur at points that are *not Goal* keypoints, which is fairly uncommon in real human movements. In general, combinations of Effort Elements are achieved in a straightforward manner. The magnitude of an Effort Element is used to weight its contribution for a parameter setting. If more than one Effort Element contributes to a parameter setting, we take the maximum value of the weighted contributions. Several parameters undergo minor adjustments when combining Effort Elements from different motion factors.

Finally, we express our Effort model as a set of equations. Let the variables *ind*, *dir*, *lgt*, *str*, *sus*, *sud*, *fre*, and *bnd* represent the magnitudes for Indirect, Direct, Light, Strong, Sustained, Sudden, Free, and Bound, respectively. Each of these variables is in [0,1]. Variables within the same motion factor are related as such: if one Effort Element variable is positive, then its opposing Effort Element variable is zero. To adjust parameters for combined Effort settings, we use the function *f*:

$$f(a,b) = \begin{cases} a & a \le b \\ b & otherwise \end{cases} \quad (15)$$

Our model for translating Effort into low-level movement parameters is given by the following equations:

$$Tval = (-1 * ind + 1 * f(ind, fre)) + dir \quad (16)$$

$$wbmag = max(0.6 * ind, 0.5 * lgt, 0.4 * fre) \quad (17)$$

$$wxmag = -0.3 * lgt + (0.3 * fre - 0.9 * f(str, fre)) \quad (18)$$

$$dmag = etmag = wtmag = 0.4 * ind \quad (19)$$

$$efmag = wfmag = 2 * ind \quad (20)$$

$$t_i = 0.5 + 0.4 * max(str, sud)$$
$$- 0.4 * max(lgt, sus) + 0.8 * f(bnd, lgt) \quad (21)$$

$$v_0 = 0.1 * str - max(0.06 * f(sus, str), 0.1 * f(fre, str)) \quad (22)$$

$$v_1 = max(0.03 * max(lgt, sus), 0.2 * fre - 0.1 * f(ind, fre)) \quad (23)$$

$$texp = 1 + 2 * sud + (0.2 * f(str, sud) - f(fre, sud))$$
$$- 0.2 * max(str, f(dir, sus))$$
$$- 0.4 * fre - 0.5 * f(ind, fre) \quad (24)$$

4.2 Expressive Torso

The underlying key poses of the torso involve, in fact, the neck joint, the spine, the pelvis and the two clavicle joints. The neck has 3 DOF, the spine has 17 joints with 3 DOF each, the pelvis has 3 DOF and each clavicle has 2 DOF. A key pose consists of angles for the neck, the pelvis, and the clavicles, in addition to the configuration of the spine [18]. When, for a particular keyframe, no pose information is provided, the system assumes a neutral posture, where all the angles are 0. We use an ease-in/ease-out curve to interpolate the angles in the keyframes and hence calculate the angles in the in-between frames. In summary, Shape changes essentially provide "squash and stretch" within the limits of a fixed segment length articulated skeleton.

4.2.1 Applying Shape to Torso Movements

As seen before, EMOTE allows the definition of Shape parameters for the torso corresponding to the Horizontal, Vertical and Sagittal dimensions, which are used to modify the key poses. Each parameter lies in a scale ranging from -1 to +1.

Our Shape model for the torso associates each main body dimension (upward/downward, sideward-open/sideward-across, and forward/backward) with specific parts of the body. We note that our Shape model was designed considering the available controls in our selected articulated figure model [18]. In particular, the torso could not be expanded and contracted for breath and other volume-changing movements. We based our Shape to body part associations on the suitability of each body part in producing changes in the form of the body in given directions. Thus, we associate the upward-downward direction with the neck and the spine; the sideward direction with the clavicles, and the forward-backward direction with the pelvis. Therefore, changes in the Horizontal dimension, which occur mainly in the sideward direction but also have a forward-backward component as the movement becomes planar, affect mostly the angles of the clavicles but also slightly alter pelvis rotations. Changes in the Vertical dimension, which are manifested primarily in the upward-downward direction but also have a sideward component in planar movement, affect mostly the angles of the neck and the spine but also change clavicle angles. Finally, changes in the Sagittal dimension, which are more evident in the forward-backward direction but also involve an upward-downward component in planar movement, mainly affect pelvis rotations but also change the angles of the neck and spine.

For each opposing attitude associated with the above dimensions (Spreading, Enclosing, Rising, Sinking, Advancing, and Retreating), we define maximum displacement angles for all the body parts that are affected by changes in that dimension. For instance, for the opposing attitudes in the Horizontal dimension, we define the following constants: *spreading_clavicle_angle*, *enclosing_clavicle_angle*, *spreading_pelvis_angle*, and

enclosing_pelvis_angle. The first two angles represent clavicle rotations about the z-axis and the latter represent pelvis rotations about the y-axis.

For a particular keyframe, let the variables *spr*, *enc*, *ris*, *sin*, *adv*, and *ret* represent the magnitudes for Spreading, Enclosing, Rising, Sinking, Advancing, and Retreating, respectively. Each of these variables is in [0,1]. Variables referencing the same dimension are related such that if one variable is positive, then its opposing variable is zero. We modify the angles in the key pose by adding the weighted contribution of all the dimensions that affect the particular body part being considered. For instance, if the clavicle rotation about the z-axis is represented by the variable *clavicle_angle* and the pelvis rotation about the y-axis is represented by the variable *pelvis_angle*, then we modify those angles as follows:

$$
\begin{aligned}
clavicle\_angle \ = \ & clavicle\_angle \\
& + ris*rising\_clavicle\_angle \\
& + sin*sinking\_clavicle\_angle \\
& + spr*spreading\_clavicle\_angle \\
& + enc*enclosing\_clavicle\_angle
\end{aligned}
\quad (25)
$$

$$
\begin{aligned}
pelvis\_angle \ = \ & pelvis\_angle \\
& + spr*spreading\_pelvis\_angle \\
& + enc*enclosing\_pelvis\_angle \\
& + adv*advancing\_pelvis\_angle \\
& + ret*retreating\_pelvis\_angle
\end{aligned}
\quad (26)
$$

where *rising_clavicle_angle* and *sinking_clavicle_angle* are the maximum displacement angles of the clavicles corresponding to the opposing attitudes towards the Vertical dimension, and *advancing_pelvis_angle* and *retreating_pelvis_angle* are the maximum displacement rotations of the pelvis corresponding to the opposing attitudes towards the Sagittal dimension.

5. EXAMPLES

To demonstrate the power of our approach to gesture we have created a series of animations shown on the accompanying video. All the examples were generated in real-time. The first series of animations are all generated from the same set of key poses and try to mimic an actor during an actual performance. We vary the values of the Effort and Shape parameters across the animations and show how these variations can completely alter the meaning of the dramatization enacted by the synthetic actor. By suppressing its Shape parameters, we also show the important role that the torso plays in gesture and in the depiction of a convincing character.

The second video series emphasizes the slight differences in dynamic qualities of movements superimposed on American Sign Language phrases (from an ASL sign library) and tries to capture the nuances of meaning represented by these differences.

The movement of the hands in the video is implemented using forward kinematics and linear interpolations.

6. DISCUSSION

Our EMOTE computational model of Effort and Shape components allows the animation of characters with natural-looking gestures through the usage of high-level parameters that represent qualitative aspects of movements. By using EMOTE interactively we hope to avoid the hassle that the animator goes through while working with a large number of low-level parameters. In order to further assess the advantages of using Effort and Shape parameters from the perspective of user interaction, formal methods of evaluation of our approach should be devised.

We did a preliminary evaluation of the Effort Elements of EMOTE [15]. Using a stylized character with head, arms, and hands, we created a 16-minute video of randomly selected Effort Elements. In the first part of the tape, Effort gestures with 16 two-keypoint and 16 five-keypoints were paired with a neutral (no Effort Element) animation. The second part of the tape consisted of 30 long (5 keypoint) animations with various Effort combinations. The tape was given to 3 CMAs and the project consultant CMA. They were asked to view it once to get a feeling for the presentation and then a second time while marking a coding sheet. They were asked to mark the primary overall Effort Element(s) they observed as present (-1 or 1) or neutral (0).

The results are presented in Table 4. The first row indicates the percentage of correct responses – where the CMA either marked the Effort that we were trying to display in the animation or marked neutral when we were trying to display neutrality along a given motion factor. The second row indicates the percentage of neutral responses – where the CMA marked neutral when we were trying to display an Effort or where the CMA marked an Effort when we were trying to display neutral along a give motion factor range. The third row indicates the percentage of opposite responses – where the CMA marked the Effort opposite from the one we were trying to portray. The low but significant percentage of neutral responses is partially attributed to the fact that most of the animation segments on our video showed *combinations* of the Effort Elements – thus, a more prominent Effort may have masked other displayed Effort Elements.

One consequence of this experiment for us was to increase the maximum movement rate for the limbs. For example, the Sudden movements did not appear fast enough to trained observers. Also, the Shape elements were not included in this experiment. Note that the normal CMA observer situation is to watch motions repeatedly; by limiting their samples to two we were forcing them to pick distinctive Effort features in a slightly unnatural setting. The results were encouraging enough, however, for us to proceed with refinements to the Effort Elements and the incorporation of the torso and Shape components.

	Consultant	CMA 1	CMA 2	CMA 3
Correct	76.6	55.6	53.2	60.1
Neutral	22.6	38.7	39.1	37.1
Opposite	0.81	5.6	7.7	2.8

Table 4: Overall Percentages for Effort Element Evaluation

Our attempt to bridge the gap between characters manually animated and characters animated by procedures establishes a new layer in the motion control process in which expressiveness is represented by a small number of parameters. We expect that this layer of control will give rise to yet another layer, where characters controlled by natural language commands show different performances according to adverbs that convey manner. These adverbs should be automatically mapped into Effort and Shape parameters. For example, "carefully" might translate into Light and slightly Sustained Effort portrayed during arm movements and a little Retreating Shape displayed by the torso; "proudly" might translate into a Rising posture. Furthermore, we

expect to find connections between emotions and personality and our high-level parameters and so be able to synthesize movements that reflect these inner states.

7. CONCLUSIONS

We have introduced a new approach to procedural human animation that tries to close the gap between characters animated by the use of manual techniques and characters animated procedurally. This approach goes beyond the realm of psychology of gestures and linguistic-based approaches by exploring the domain of movement observation. This approach uncovers the movement qualities, which can be combined together to reveal different manners, inner states, personalities and emotions. The EMOTE approach to gesture proposes a computational model of the Effort and Shape components of Laban Movement Analysis and associates with each one of their dimensions numerical parameters that modify pre-defined movements.

Two other important aspects of EMOTE are inspired by the tenets of movement observation. The first is the ability to phrase Effort and Shape parameters across a set of movements. We believe that a character's gestures should be phrased similarly to communicative phrasing with an expressive content consonant with the principal utterance; for example, a strong accent in speech should be correlated by a strong Effort in gesture. Since Effort plays a key role in the interpretation of a character's action, a gesture must display Effort qualities that match his/her intentions, motivations, and mood. Otherwise, the character's message appears conflicted and confused. Furthermore, EMOTE reflects our belief that, even if a character moves its arms with appropriate gestures, it will lack conviction and naturalness if the rest of the body is not appropriately engaged. If the empirical principles of movement science hold up when transformed into computer code implementations, we should be able to animate engaging, committed, expressive, and believable characters consistently and automatically.

8. ACKNOWLEDGEMENTS

Janis Pforsich (courante@juno.com) was our LMA consultant for EMOTE. She played a key role in the development of our Effort and Shape model, was an enthusiastic teacher of movement observation, ensured the accuracy of the project and its documentation with LMA theory, and acted as a devoted proponent of our work. We are very grateful for her generous contributions. This research is partially supported by U.S. Air Force F41624-97-D-5002, Office of Naval Research K-5-55043/3916-1552793, and AASERTs N00014-97-1-0603 and N0014-97-1-0605, NSF EIA98-09209, SBR-8900230, and IIS-9900297, NASA NRA NAG 5-3990, and Engineering Animation Inc. (EAI). Support for Monica Costa by the National Scientific and Technological Development Council (CNpq) of Brazil is also gratefully acknowledged.

9. REFERENCES

[1] Amaya, K., Bruderlin, A., Calvert, T. Emotion from motion. In Davis, W.A., Bartels, R., editors, *Graphics Interface'96*, pp. 222-229. Canadian Information Processing Society, Canadian Human-Computer Comm. Society, May 1996.

[2] Badler, N. A computational alternative to effort notation. In Gray, J.A., editor, *Dance Technology: Current Applications and Future Trends*. National Dance Association, VA, 1989.

[3] Badler, N., Chi, D., Chopra S. Virtual human animation based on movement observation and cognitive behavior models. In *Computer Animation Conf.*, Geneva, Switzerland, May 1999. IEEE Computer Society Press.

[4] Badler, N., Smoliar, S. Digital representations of human movement. *ACM Computing Surveys*, 11(1):19-38, March 1979.

[5] Badler, N., Webber, B., Becket, W., Geib, C., Moore, M., Pelachaud, C., Reich, B., and Stone, M. Planning for animation. In N. Magnenat-Thalmann and D. Thalmann (eds), *Interactive Computer Animation*, Prentice-Hall, pp. 235-262, 1996.

[6] Bartenieff, I., Davis, M. Effort-Shape analysis of movement: The unity of expression and function. In Davis, M., editor, *Research Approaches to Movement and Personality*. Arno Press Inc., New York, 1972.

[7] Bartenieff, I., Lewis, D. *Body Movement: Coping with the Environment*. Gordon and Breach Science Publishers, New York, 1980.

[8] Becheiraz, P., Thalmann, D. A model of nonverbal communication and interpersonal relationship between virtual actors. *Pro. Computer Animation 1996*, IEEE Computer Society Press, pp.58-67, 1996.

[9] Bishko, L. Relationships between Laban Movement Analysis and computer animation. In *Dance and Technology I: Moving Toward The Future*, pp. 1-9, 1992.

[10] Bruderlin, A., Williams, L. Motion signal processing. In *Proc. of SIGGRAPH'95*, pp. 97-104, August 1995.

[11] Calvert, T.W., Chapman, J., Patla, A. Aspects of the kinematic simulation of human movement. *IEEE Computer Graphics & Applications*, 2:41-48, November 1982.

[12] Capin, T., Pandzic, I., Magnenat-Thalmann, N., Thalmann, D. *Avatars in Networked Virtual Environments*. Wiley, Chichester, England, 1999.

[13] Cassell, J. Not just another pretty face: Embodied conversational interface agents. *Comm. of the ACM*, 2000. (to appear).

[14] Cassell, J., Pelachaud, C., Badler, N., Steedman, M., Achorn, B., Becket, W., Douville, B., Prevost, S., Stone, M. Animated conversation: Rule-based generation of facial expression, gesture and spoken intonation for multiple conversational agents. In *Computer Graphics, Annual Conf. Series*, pp. 413-420. ACM, 1994.

[15] Chi, Diane. *A Motion Control Scheme for Animating Expressive Arm Movements*. PhD thesis, University of Pennsylvania, 1999.

[16] Davis, M. Effort-Shape analysis: Evaluation of its logic and consistency and its systematic use in research. In Bartenieff, I., Davis, M. and Paula, F., editors, *Four Adaptations of Effort Theory in Research and Teaching*. Dance Notation Bureau, Inc., New York, 1970.

[17] Dell, C. *A Primer for Movement Description: Using Effort-Shape and Supplementary Concepts*. Dance Notation Bureau, Inc., New York, 1970.

[18] Jack 2.2 Toolkit Reference Guide, Engineering Animation, Inc., 1999.

[19] Kendon, A. Gesticulation and speech: Two aspects of the process of utterance. In Key, M.R., editor, *The Relation between Verbal and Nonverbal Communication*, pp. 207-227. Mouton, 1980.

[20] Kochanek, D.H.U., Bartels, R.H. Interpolating splines with local tension, continuity, and bias control. In *Proc. of SIGGRAPH'84*, volume 18, pp. 33-41, July 1984.

[21] Koga, Y., Kondo, K., Kuffner, J., Latombe, J. Planning motions with intentions. In *Proc. of SIGGRAPH'94*, pp. 395-408, July 1994.

[22] Laban, R. *The Mastery of Movement*. Plays, Inc., Boston, 1971.

[23] Laban, R., Lawrence, F. C. *Effort: Economy in Body Movement*. Plays, Inc., Boston, 1974.

[24] Lamb, W. *Posture and Gesture: An Introduction to the Study of Physical Behavior*. Duckworth & Co., London, 1965.

[25] Lasseter, J. Principles of traditional animation applied to 3D computer animation. In *Proc. of SIGGRAPH'87*, volume 21, pp. 35-44, July 1987.

[26] Maletic, V. *Body, Space, Expression: The Development of Rudolf Laban's Movement and Dance Concepts*. Mouton de Gruyte, New York, 1987.

[27] McNeil, D. *Hand and Mind: What Gestures Reveal about Thought*. University of Chicago, 1992.

[28] Moore, C.-L., Yamamoto, K. *Beyond Words: Movement Observation and Analysis*. Gordon and Breach Science Publishers, New York, 1988.

[29] Morawetz, C., Calvert, T. Goal-directed human animation of multiple movements. In *Proceedings of Graphics Interface '90*, pp. 60-67, May 1990.

[30] O'Brien, J. F., Zordan, V. B., Hodgins, J. K. Combining Active and Passive Simulations for Secondary Motion. *IEEE Computer Graphics & Applications*. In Press.

[31] Perlin, K. Real time responsive animation with personality. *IEEE Transactions on Visualization and Computer Graphics*, 1(1):5-15, March 1995.

[32] Reynolds, C.W. Flocks, herds, and schools: A distributed behavioral model. In *Proc. of SIGGRAPH'87*, volume 21, pp. 25-34, July 1987.

[33] Rose, C., Cohen, M.F. and Bodenheimer, B. Verbs and adverbs: Multidimensional motion interpolation. *IEEE Computer Graphics & Applications*, 18(5), September-October 1998.

[34] Steketee, S., Badler, N. Parametric keyframe interpolation incorporating kinetic adjustment and phasing control. In *Proc. of SIGGRAPH'85*, volume 19, pp. 225-262, July 1985.

[35] Thomas, F., Johnston, O. *Illusion of Life: Disney Animation*. Hyperion, New York, 1995.

[36] Tolani, D. *Inverse Kinematics Methods for Human Modeling and Simulation*. PhD thesis, University of Pennsylvania, 1998.

[37] Tu, X., Terzopoulos, D. Artificial fishes: Physics, locomotion, perception, behavior. In *Proc. of SIGGRAPH'94*, pp. 43-50, July 1994.

[38] Unuma, M., Anjyo, K., Takeuchi, R. Fourier principles for emotion-based human figure animation. In *Proc. of SIGGRAPH'95*, pp. 91-96, August 1995.

[39] Vilhjalmsson, H.H., Cassell J. Bodychat: Autonomous communicative behaviors in avatars. In *Proc. of the Second International Conference on Autonomous Agents*, pp. 269-277. ACM, May 1998.

[40] Witkin, A., Popovic, Z. Motion warping. *Proceedings of SIGGRAPH '95*, pp. 105-108, Los Angeles, CA, August, 1995.

Style machines

Matthew Brand
Mitsubishi Electric Research Laboratory

Aaron Hertzmann
NYU Media Research Laboratory

A pirouette and promenade in five synthetic styles drawn from a space that contains ballet, modern dance, and different body types. The choreography is also synthetic. Streamers show the trajectory of the left hand and foot.

Abstract

We approach the problem of stylistic motion synthesis by learning motion patterns from a highly varied set of motion capture sequences. Each sequence may have a distinct choreography, performed in a distinct style. Learning identifies common choreographic elements across sequences, the different styles in which each element is performed, and a small number of stylistic degrees of freedom which span the many variations in the dataset. The learned model can synthesize novel motion data in any interpolation or extrapolation of styles. For example, it can convert novice ballet motions into the more graceful modern dance of an expert. The model can also be driven by video, by scripts, or even by noise to generate new choreography and synthesize virtual motion-capture in many styles.

CR Categories: I.3.7 [Computer Graphics]: Three-Dimensional Graphics and Realism—Animation; I.2.9 [Artificial Intelligence]: Robotics—Kinematics and Dynamics; G.3 [Mathematics of Computing]: Probability and Statistics—Time series analysis; E.4 [Data]: Coding and Information Theory—Data compaction and compression; J.5 [Computer Applications]: Arts and Humanities—Performing Arts

Keywords: animation, behavior simulation, character behavior.

1 Introduction

It is natural to think of walking, running, strutting, trudging, sashaying, etc., as stylistic variations on a basic motor theme. From a directorial point of view, the style of a motion often conveys more meaning than the underlying motion itself. Yet existing animation tools provide little or no high-level control over the style of an animation.

In this paper we introduce the style machine—a statistical model that can generate new motion sequences in a broad range of styles, just by adjusting a small number of stylistic knobs (parameters). Style machines support synthesis and resynthesis in new styles, as well as style identification of existing data. They can be driven by many kinds of inputs, including computer vision, scripts, and noise. Our key result is a method for learning a style machine, including the number and nature of its stylistic knobs, from data. We use style machines to model highly nonlinear and nontrivial behaviors such as ballet and modern dance, working with very long unsegmented motion-capture sequences and using the learned model to generate new choreography and to improve a novice's dancing.

Style machines make it easy to generate long motion sequences containing many different actions and transitions. They can offer a broad range of stylistic degrees of freedom; in this paper we show early results manipulating gender, weight distribution, grace, energy, and formal dance styles. Moreover, style machines can be learned from relatively modest collections of existing motion-capture; as such they present a highly generative and flexible alternative to motion libraries.

Potential uses include: **Generation:** Beginning with a modest amount of motion capture, an animator can train and use the resulting style machine to generate large amounts of motion data with new orderings of actions. **Casts of thousands:** Random walks in the machine can produce thousands of unique, plausible motion choreographies, each of which can be synthesized as motion data in a unique style. **Improvement:** Motion capture from unskilled performers can be resynthesized in the style of an expert athlete or dancer. **Retargetting:** Motion capture data can be resynthesized in a new mood, gender, energy level, body type, etc. **Acquisition:** Style machines can be driven by computer vision, data-gloves, even impoverished sensors such as the computer mouse, and thus offer a low-cost, low-expertise alternative to motion-capture.

2 Related work

Much recent effort has addressed the problem of editing and reuse of existing animation. A common approach is to provide interactive animation tools for motion editing, with the goal of capturing the style of the existing motion, while editing the content. Gleicher [11] provides a low-level interactive motion editing tool that searches for a new motion that meets some new constraints while minimizing the distance to the old motion. A related optimization method method is also used to adapt a motion to new characters [12]. Lee et al. [15] provide an interactive multiresolution motion editor for fast, fine-scale control of the motion. Most editing

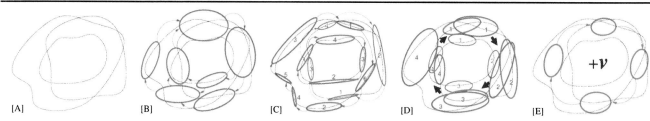

Figure 1: Schematic illustrating the effects of cross-entropy minimization. [A]. Three simple walk cycles projected onto 2-space. Each data point represents the body pose observed at a given time. [B]. In conventional learning, one fits a single model to all the data (ellipses indicate state-specific isoprobability contours; arcs indicate allowable transitions). But here learning is overwhelmed by variation among the sequences, and fails to discover the essential structure of the walk cycle. [C]. Individually estimated models are hopelessly overfit to their individual sequences, and will not generalize to new data. In addition, they divide up the cycle differently, and thus cannot be blended or compared. [D]. Cross-entropy minimized models are constrained to have similar qualitative structure and to identify similar phases of the cycle. [E]. The generic model abstracts all the information in the style-specific models; various settings of the style variable v will recover all the specific models plus any interpolation or extrapolation of them.

systems produce results that may violate the laws of mechanics; Popović and Witkin [16] describe a method for editing motion in a reduced-dimensionality space in order to edit motions while maintaining physical validity. Such a method would be a useful complement to the techniques presented here.

An alternative approach is to provide more global animation controls. Signal processing systems, such as described by Bruderlin and Williams [7] and Unuma et al. [20], provide frequency-domain controls for editing the style of a motion. Witkin and Popović [22] blend between existing motions to provide a combination of motion styles. Rose et al. [18] use radial basis functions to interpolate between and extrapolate around a set of aligned and labeled example motions (e.g., happy/sad and young/old walk cycles), then use kinematic solvers to smoothly string together these motions. Similar functionality falls out of our framework.

Although such interactive systems provide fine control, they rely on the labors of skilled animators to produce compelling and convincing results. Furthermore, it is generally difficult to produce a new motion that is substantially different from the existing motions, in style or in content (e.g., to convert by hand a ponderous walk to a jaunty dance, etc.)

The above signal-processing methods also require that the example motions be time-warped; in other words, that sequential correspondences can be found between each component of each motion. Unfortunately, it is rarely the case that any set of complex motions will have this property. Style machines automatically compute flexible many-to-many correspondences between sequences using fast dynamic programming algorithms.

Our work unites two themes that have separate research histories in motion analysis: estimation of dynamical (in the sense of time-evolving) models from examples, and style and content separation. Howe et al. [14] analyze motion from video using a mixture-of-Gaussians model. Grzeszczuk et al. [13] learn control and physical systems from physical simulation. Several authors have used hidden Markov Models to analyze and synthesize motion. Bregler [6] and Brand [5] use HMMs to recognize and analyze motion from video sequences. Brand [4] analyzes and resynthesizes animation of human speech from example audio and video. With regard to styles, Wilson and Bobick [21] use parametric HMMs, in which motion recognition models are learned from user-labeled styles. Tenenbaum and Freeman [19, 10] separate style from content in general domains under a bilinear model, thereby modeling factors that have individually linear but cooperatively multiplicative effects on the output, e.g., the effects of lighting and pose in images of faces.

These style/content models depend on large sets of hand-labeled and hand-aligned samples (often exponential in the number of stylistic degrees of freedom DOFs) plus an explicit statement of what

the stylistic DOFs are. We now introduce methods for extracting this information directly and automatically from modest amounts of data.

3 Learning stylistic state-space models

We seek a model of human motion from which we can generate novel choreography in a variety of styles. Rather than attempt to engineer such a model, we will attempt to learn it—to extract from data a function that approximates the data-generating mechanism.

We cast this as an unsupervised learning problem, in which the goal is to acquire a generative model that captures the data's essential structure (traces of the data-generating mechanism) and discards its accidental properties (particulars of the specific sample). Accidental properties include noise and the bias of the sample. Essential structure can also be divided into two components, which we will call structure and style. For example, walking, running, strutting, etc., are all stylistic variations on bipedal locomotion, a dynamical system with particularly simple temporal structure—a deterministic loop.

It is up to the modeler to make the structure/style distinction. State-space representations are very useful here: We take the *structure* of bipedal locomotion to be a small set of dynamically-significant qualitative states along with the rules that govern changes of state. We take *style* to be variations in the mapping from qualitative states to quantitative observations. For example, shifting one's weight load onto the right leg is a dynamically-significant state common to all forms of bipedal locomotion, but it will look quite different in running, trudging, etc.

An appropriate state-space model for time-series data is the hidden Markov model (HMM). An HMM is a probabilistic finite-state machine consisting of a set of discrete states, state-to-state transition probabilities, and state-to-signal emission probabilities—in this paper, each state has a Gaussian distribution over a small space of full-body poses and motions. (See §A for a concise HMM tutorial; see [17] for a detailed tutorial.) We will add to the HMM a multidimensional style variable v that can be used to vary its parameters, and call the result a *stylistic* HMM (SHMM), or time-series **style machine**. (See §B for formal definitions.) The SHMM defines a space of HMMs; fixing the parameter v yields a unique HMM.

Here we show how to separate structure, style, and accidental properties in a dataset by minimizing entropies in the SHMM. The main advantages of separating style from structure is that we wind up with simpler, more generative models for both, and we can do so with significantly less data than required for the general learning setting. Our framework is fully unsupervised and automatically identifies the number and nature of the stylistic degrees of freedom (often much fewer than the number of variations in the dataset).

The discovered degrees of freedom lend themselves to some intuitive operations that are very useful for synthesis: style mixtures, exaggerations, extrapolations, and even analogies.

3.1 Generic and style-specific models

We begin with a family of training samples. By "family" we mean that all the samples have some generic data-generating mechanism in common, e.g., the motor program for dancing. Each sample may instantiate a different variation. The samples need not be aligned, e.g., the ordering, timing, and appearance of actions may vary from sample to sample. Our modeling goal is to extract a single parameterized model which covers the generic behavior in the entire family of training samples, and which can easily be made to model an individual style, combination of styles, or extrapolation of styles, just by choosing an appropriate setting of the style variable v.

Learning involves the simultaneous estimation of a generic model and a set of style-specific models with three objectives: (1) each model should fit its sample(s) well; (2) each specific model should be close to the generic model; and (3) the generic model should be as simple as possible, thereby maximizing probability of correct generalization to new data. These constraints have an information-theoretic expression in eqn. 1. In the next section we will explain how the last two constraints interact to produce a third desirable property: The style-specific models can be expressed as small variations on the generic model, and the space of such variations can be captured with just a few parameters.

We first describe the use of style machines as applied to pure signal data. Details specific to working with motion-capture data are described in §4.

3.2 Estimation by entropy minimization

In learning we minimize a sum of entropies—which measure the ambiguity in a probability distribution—and cross-entropies—which measure the divergence between distributions. The principle of minimum entropy, advocated in various forms by [23, 2, 8], seeks the simplest model that explains the data, or, equivalently, the most complex model whose parameter estimates are fully supported by the data. This maximizes the information extracted from the training data and boosts the odds of generalizing correctly beyond it.

The learning objective has three components, corresponding to the constraints listed above:

1. The cross-entropy between the model distribution and statistics extracted from the data measures the model's misfit of the data.

2. The cross-entropy between the generic and a specific model measures inconsistencies in their analysis of the data.

3. The entropy of the generic model measures ambiguity and lack of structure in its analysis of the data.

Minimizing #1 makes the model faithful to the data. Minimizing #2 essentially maximizes the overlap between the generic and specific models and congruence (similarity of support) between their hidden states. This means that the models "behave" similarly and their hidden states have similar "meanings." For example, in a dataset of bipedal motion sequences, all the style-specific HMMs should converge to similar finite-state machine models of the locomotion cycle, and corresponding states in each HMM to refer to qualitatively similar poses and motions in the locomotion cycle. E.g., the nth state in each model is tuned to the poses in which the body's weight shifts onto the right leg, regardless of the style of motion (see figure 1). Minimizing #3 optimizes the predictiveness of the model by making sure that it gives the clearest and most concise picture of the data, with each hidden state explaining a clearly delineated phenomenon in the data.

Figure 2: Flattening and alignment of Gaussians by minimization of entropy and cross-entropy, respectively. Gaussian distributions are visualized as ellipsoid iso-probability contours.

Putting this all together gives the following learning objective function

$$\theta^* = \arg\min_{\theta} \overbrace{\underbrace{H(\omega)}_{\text{data entropy}} + \underbrace{D(\omega\|\theta)}_{\text{misfit}}}^{1:\text{-log likelihood}} + \overbrace{\underbrace{H(\theta)}_{\text{model entropy}} + \underbrace{D(\theta^\bullet\|\theta)}_{\text{incongruence}}}^{\text{-log prior}} + \cdots$$

(1)

where θ is a vector of model parameters; ω is a vector of expected sufficient statistics describing the data X; $\theta^\bullet$ parameterizes a reference model (e.g., the generic); $H(\cdot)$ is an entropy measure; and $D(\cdot)$ is a cross entropy measure.

Eqn. 1 can also be formulated as a Bayesian posterior $P(\theta|\omega) \propto P(\omega|\theta)P(\theta)$ with likelihood function $P(X|\theta) \propto e^{-H(\omega)-D(\omega\|\theta)}$ and a prior $P(\theta) \propto e^{-H(\theta)-D(\theta^\bullet\|\theta)}$. The data entropy term, not mentioned above, arises in the normalization of the likelihood function; it measures ambiguity in the data-descriptive statistics that are calculated *vis-à vis* the model.

3.3 Effects of the prior

It is worth examining the prior because this is what will give the final model θ^* its special style-spanning and generative properties.

The prior term $e^{-H(\theta)}$ expresses our belief in the parsimony principle—a model should give a maximally concise and minimally uncertain explanation of the structure in its training set. This is an optimal bias for extracting as much information as possible from the data [3]. We apply this prior to the generic model. The prior has an interesting effect on the SHMM's emission distributions over pose and velocity: It gradually removes dimensions of variation, because flattening a distribution is the most effective way to reduce its volume and therefore its entropy (see figure 2).

The prior term $e^{-D(\theta^\bullet\|\theta)}$ keeps style models close and congruent to the generic model, so that corresponding hidden states in two models have similar behavior. In practice we assess this prior only on the emission distributions of the specific models, where it has the effect of keeping the variation-dependent emission distributions clustered tightly around the generic emission distribution. Consequently it minimizes distance between corresponding states in the models, not between the entire models. We also add a term $-T' \cdot D(\theta^\bullet\|\theta)$ that allows us to vary the strength of the cross-entropy prior in the course of optimization.

By constraining generic and style-specific Gaussians to overlap, and constraining both to be narrow, we cause the distribution of state-specific Gaussians across styles to have a small number of degrees of freedom. Intuitively, if two Gaussians are narrow and overlap, then they must be aligned in the directions of their narrowness (e.g., two overlapping disks in 3-space must be co-planar). Figure 2 illustrates. The more dimensions in which the overlapping Gaussians are flat, the fewer degrees of freedom they have relative to each other. Consequently, as style-specific models are drawn toward the generic model during training, all the models settle into a parameter subspace (see figure 3). Within this subspace, all the variation between the style-specific models can be described with just a few parameters. We can then identify those degrees of freedom by solving for a smooth low-dimensional manifold that contains the parameterizations of all the style-specific models. Our

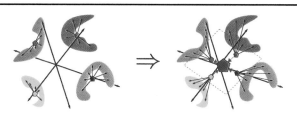

Figure 3: Schematic of style DOF discovery. LEFT: Without cross-entropy constraints, style-specific models (pentagons) are drawn to their data (clouds), and typically span all dimensions of parameter space. RIGHT: When also drawn to a generic model, they settle into a parameter subspace (indicated by the dashed plane).

experiments showed that a linear subspace usually provides a good low-dimensional parameterization of the dataset's stylistic degrees of freedom. The subspace is easily obtained from a principal components analysis (PCA) of a set of vectors, each representing one model's parameters.

It is often useful to extend the prior with additional functions of $\boldsymbol{\theta}$. For example, adding $-T \cdot H(\boldsymbol{\theta})$ and varying T gives deterministic annealing, an optimization strategy that forces the system to explore the error surface at many scales as $T \downarrow 0$ instead of myopically converging to the nearest local optimum (see §C for equations).

3.4 Optimization

In learning we hope to simultaneously segment the data into motion primitives, match similar primitives executed in different styles, and estimate the structure and parameters for minimally ambiguous, maximally generative models. Entropic estimation [2] gives us a framework for solving this partially discrete optimization problem by embedding it in a high-dimensional continuous space via entropies. It also gives us numerical methods in the form of maximum a posteriori (MAP) entropy-optimizing parameter estimators. These attempt to find a best data-generating model, by gradually extinguishing excess model parameters that are not well-supported by the data. This solves the discrete optimization problem by causing a diffuse distribution over all possible segmentations to collapse onto a single segmentation.

Optimization proceeds via Expectation-Maximization (EM) [1, 17], a fast and powerful fixpoint algorithm that guarantees convergence to a local likelihood optimum from any initialization. The estimators we give in §D modify EM to do cross-entropy optimization and annealing. Annealing strengthens EM's guarantee to quasi-global optimality—global MAP optimality with probability approaching 1 as the annealing shedule lengthens—a necessary assurance due to the number of combinatorial optimization problems that are being solved simultaneously: segmentation, labeling, alignment, model selection, and parameter estimation.

The full algorithm is:

1. Initialize a generic model and one style-specific model for each motion sequence.

2. EM loop until convergence:

    (a) E step: Compute expected sufficient statistics $\boldsymbol{\omega}$ of each motion sequence relative to its model.
    (b) M step: (generic): Calculate maximum *a posteriori* parameter values $\hat{\boldsymbol{\theta}}^{\bullet}$ with the minimum-entropy prior, using E-step statistics from the entire training set.
    (c) M step: (specific): Calculate maximum *a posteriori* parameter values $\hat{\boldsymbol{\theta}}$ with the minimum-cross-entropy prior, only using E-step statistics from the current sequence.

    (d) Adjust the temperature (see below for schedules).

3. Find a subspace that spans the parameter variations between models. E.g., calculate a PCA of the differences between the generic and each style-specific model.

Initialization can be random because full annealing will obliterate initial conditions. If one can encode useful hints in the initial model, then the EM loop should use partial annealing by starting at a lower temperature.

HMMs have a useful property that saves us the trouble of hand-segmenting and/or labelling the training data: The actions in any particular training sequence may be squashed and stretched in time, oddly ordered, and repeated; in the course of learning, the basic HMM dynamic programming algorithms will find an optimal segmentation and labelling of each sequence. Our cross-entropy prior simply adds the constraint that similarly-labeled frames exhibit similar behavior (but not necessarily appearance) across sequences. Figure 4 illustrates with the induced state machine and labelling of four similar but incongruent sequences, and an induced state machine that captures all their choreographic elements and transitions.

4 Working with Motion Capture

As in any machine-learning application, one can make the problem harder or easier depending on how the data is represented to the algorithm. Learning algorithms look for the most *statistically* salient patterns of variation the data. For motion capture, these may not be the patterns that humans find *perceptually* and *expressively* salient. Thus we want to preprocess the data to highlight sources of variation that "tell the story" of a dance, such as leg-motions and compensatory body motions, and suppress irrelevant sources of variation, such as inconsistent marker placements and world coordinates between sequences (which would otherwise be modeled as stylistic variations). Other sources of variation, such as inter-sequence variations in body shapes, need to be scaled down so that they do not dominate style space. We now describe methods for converting raw marker data into a suitable representation for learning motion.

4.1 Data Gathering and Preprocessing

We first gathered human motion capture data from a variety of sources (see acknowledgements in §8). The data consists of the 3D positions of physical markers placed on human actors, acquired over short intervals in motion capture studios. Each data source provided data with a different arrangement of markers over the body. We defined a reduced 20 marker arrangement, such that all of the markers in the input sequences could be converted by combining and deleting extra markers. (Note that the missing markers can be recovered from synthesized data later by remapping the style machines to the original input marker data.) We also doubled the size of the data set by mirroring, and resampled all sequences to 60Hz.

Captured and synthetic motion capture data in the figures and animations show the motions of markers connected by a fake skeleton. The "bones" of this skeleton have no algorithmic value; they are added for illustration purposes only to make the markers easier to follow.

The next step is to convert marker data into joint angles plus limb lengths, global position and global orientation. The coccyx (near the base of the back) is used as the root of the kinematic tree. Joint angles alone are used for training. Joint angles are by nature periodic (for example, ranging from 0 to 2π); because training assumes that the input signal lies in the infinite domain of $\mathbf{R}^{\mathbf{n}}$, we took some pain to choose a joint angle parameterization without discontinuities (such as a jump from 2π to 0) in the training data.[1] However, we were not able to fully eliminate all discontinuities. (This is partially due to some perversities in the input data such as inverted knee bends.)

Conversion to joint angles removes information about which articulations cause greatest changes in body pose. To restore this information, we scale joint angle variables to make statistically salient those articulations that most vary the pose, measured in the data set by a procedure similar to that described by Gleicher [11]. To reduce the dependence on individual body shape, the mean pose is subtracted from each sequence, Finally, noise and dimensionality are reduced via PCA; we typically use ten or fewer significant dimensions of data variation for training.

4.2 Training

Models are initialized with a state transition matrix $P_{j\to i}$ that has probabilities declining exponentially off the diagonal; the Gaussians are initialized randomly or centered on every nth frame of the sequence. These initial conditions save the learning algorithm the gratuitous trouble of selecting from among a factorial number of permutationally equivalent models, differing only in the ordering of their states.

We train with annealing, setting the temperature T high and making it decay exponentially toward zero. This forces the estimators to explore the error surface at many scales before committing to a particular region of parameter space. In the high-temperature phase, we set the cross-entropy temperature T' to zero, to force the variation models to stay near the generic model. At high temperatures, any accidental commitments made in the initialization are largely obliterated. As the generic temperature declines, we briefly heat up the cross-entropy temperature, allowing the style-specific models to venture off to find datapoints not well explained by the generic model. We then drive both temperatures to zero and let the estimators converge on an entropy minimum.

These temperature schedules are hints that guide the optimization: (1) Find global structure; (2) offload local variation to the specific models; (3) then simplify (compress) all models as much as possible.

The result of training is a collection of models and for each model, a distribution γ over its hidden states, where $\gamma_{t,i}(\boldsymbol{y}) = p(\text{state } i \text{ explains frame } t, \text{ given all the information in the sequence } \boldsymbol{y})$. Typically this distribution has zero or near-zero entropy, meaning that γ has collapsed to a single state sequence that explains the data. γ (or the sequence of most probable states) encodes the *content* of the data; as we show below, applying either one to a different style-specific model causes that content to be resynthesized in a different style.

We use γ to remap each model's emission distributions to joint angles and angular velocities, scaled according to the importance of each joint. This information is needed for synthesis. Remapping means re-estimating emission parameters to observe a time-series that is synchronous with the training data.

4.3 Making New Styles

We encode a style-specific HMM in a vector by concatenating its state means $\boldsymbol{\mu}_i$, square-root covariances ($\mathbf{K}_{ij}/\sqrt{|\mathbf{K}_{ij}|}$, for $i \leq j$), and state dwell times (on average, how long a model stays in one state before transitioning out). New styles can be created by interpolation and extrapolation within this space. The dimensionality of the space is reduced by PCA, treating each HMM as a single observation and the generic HMM as the origin. The PCA gives us a

subspace of models whose axes are intrinsic degrees of variation across the styles in the training set. Typically, only a few stylistic DOFs are needed to span the many variations in a training set, and these become the dimensions of the style variable $\boldsymbol{v}$. One interpolates between any styles in the training set by varying $\boldsymbol{v}$ between the coordinates of their models in the style subspace, then reconstituting a style-specific HMM from the resulting parameter vector. Of course, it is more interesting to extrapolate, by going outside the convex hull of the training styles, a theme that is explored below in §5.

4.4 Analyzing New Data

To obtain the style coordinates of a novel motion sequence $\boldsymbol{y}$, we begin with a copy of the generic model (or of a style-specific model which assigns $\boldsymbol{y}$ high likelihood), then retrain that model on $\boldsymbol{y}$, using cross-entropy constraints with respect to the original generic model. Projection of the resulting parameters onto the style manifold gives the style coordinates. We also obtain the sample's state occupancy matrix γ. As mentioned before, this summarizes the content of the motion sequence $\boldsymbol{y}$ and is the key to synthesis, described below.

4.5 Synthesizing Virtual Motion Data

Given a new value of the style variable $\boldsymbol{v}$ and a state sequence $S(\boldsymbol{y}) \in \gamma(\boldsymbol{y})$ encoding the content of $\boldsymbol{y}$, one may resynthesize $\boldsymbol{y}$ in the new style $\boldsymbol{y}'$ by calculating the maximum-likelihood path $\arg\max_{\boldsymbol{y}'} p(\boldsymbol{y}'|\boldsymbol{v}, S(\boldsymbol{y}))$. Brand [4] describes a method for calculating the maximum-likelihood sample in $O(T)$ time for T time-steps. §F generalizes and improves on this result, so that all the information in γ is used.

This resulting path is an inherently smooth curve that varies even if the system dwells in the same hidden state for several frames, because of the velocity constraints on each frame. Motion discontinuities in the synthesized samples are possible if the difference in velocities between successive states is large relative to the frame (sampling) rate. The preprocessing steps are then reversed to produce virtual motion-capture data as the final output.

Some actions take longer in different styles; as we move from style to style, this is accommodated by scaling dwell times of the state sequence to match those of the new style. This is one of many ways of making time flexible; another is to incorporate dwell times directly into the emission distributions and then synthesize a list of varying-sized time-steps by which to clock the synthsized motion-capture frames.

In addition to resynthesizing existing motion-capture in new styles, it is possible to generate entirely new motion data directly from the model itself. Learning automatically extracts motion primitives and motion cycles from the data (see figure 4), which take the form of state sub-sequences. By cutting and pasting these state sequences, we can sequence new choreography. If a model's state machine has an arc between states in two consecutively scheduled motion primitives, the model will automatically modify the end and beginning of the two primitives to transition smoothly. Otherwise, we must find a path through the state machine between the two primitives and insert all the states on that path. An interesting effect can also be achieved by doing a random walk on the state machine, which generates random but plausible choreography.

5 Examples

We collected a set of **bipedal locomotion time-series** from a variety of sources. These motion-capture sequences feature a variety of different kinds of motion, body types, postures, and marker placements. We converted all motion data to use a common set of markers on a prototypical body. (If we do not normalize the body,

---

[1] For cyclic domains, one would ideally use von Mises' distribution, essentially a Gaussian wrapped around a circle, but we cannot because no analytic variance estimator is known.

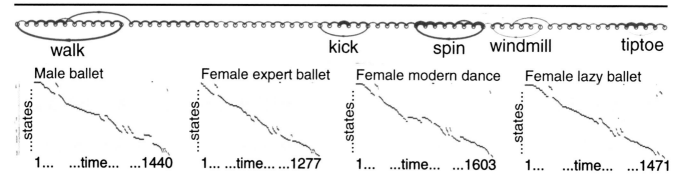

Figure 4: TOP: State machine learned from four dance sequences totalling 6000+ frames. Very low-probability arcs have been removed for clarity. Motion cycles have been labeled; other primitives are contained in linear sequences. BOTTOM: Occupancy matrices (constructed while learning) indicate how each sequence was segmented and labeled. Note the variations in timing, ordering, and cycles between sequences.

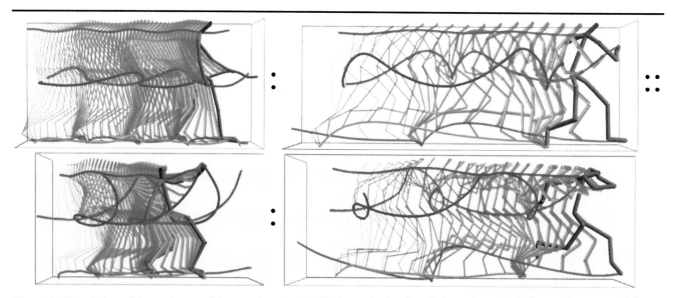

Figure 5: Completion of the analogy walking:running::strutting:X via synthesis of stylistic motion. Stick figures show every 5 frames; streamers show the trajectories of the extremities. X extrapolates both the energetic arm swing of strutting and the power stride of running.

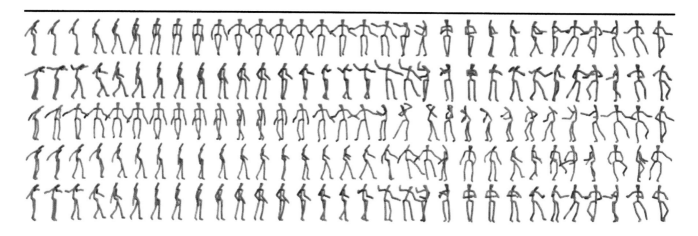

Figure 6: Five motion sequences synthesized from the same choreography, but in different styles (one per row). The actions, aligned vertically, are tiptoeing, turning, kicking, and spinning. The odd body geometry reflects marker placements in the training motion-capture.

the algorithm typically identifies variations in body geometry as the principal stylistic DOFs.)

As a hint to the algorithm, we first trained an HMM on a very low-dimensional representation of the data. Entropic estimation yielded a model which was essentially a phase-diagram of the locomotive cycle. This was used as an initialization for the full SHMM training. The SHMM was lightly annealed, so it was not constrained to use this hint, but the final generic model did retain some of the information in the initialization.

The PCA of the resulting style-specific models revealed that 3 stylistic degrees of freedom explained 93% of the variation between the 10 models. The most significant stylistic DOF appears to be global pose, e.g., one tilts forward for running, back for funny-walking. It also contains information about the speed of motion. Style DOF #2 controls balance and gender; varying it modifies the hips, the distance of the footfall to the midline, and the compensating swing of the arms. Finally, style DOF #3 can be characterized as the amount of swagger and energy in the motion; increasing it yields sequences that look more and more high-spirited. Extrapolating beyond the hull of specific models yields well-behaved motion with the expected properties. E.g., we can double the amount of swagger, or tilt a walk forward into a slouch. We demonstrate with analogies.

Analogies are a particularly interesting form of extrapolation. Given the analogical problem walking:running::strutting:X, we can solve for X in terms of the style coordinates $X=strutting+(running-walking)$, which is equivalent to completing the parallelogram having the style coordinates for walking, running, and strutting as three of its corners.

run.   .?

walk•   •strut

The resulting synthesized sequence (figure 5) looks like a fast-advancing form of skanking (a rather high-energy pop dance style). Similarly, the analogy walking:running::cat-walking:X gives something that looks like how a model might skip/run down a catwalk in a fashion show.

Now we turn to examples that cannot be handled by existing time-warping and signal processing methods.

In a more complicated example, the system was trained on four **performances by classically trained dancers** (man, woman-ballet, woman-modern-dance, woman-lazy-ballet) of 50-70 seconds duration each, with roughly 20 different moves. The performances all have similar choreographies but vary in the timing, ordering, and style of moves. A 75-state model took roughly 20 minutes to train on 6000+ frames, using interpreted Matlab code on a single CPU of a 400MHz AlphaServer. Parameter extinction left a 69-state SHMM with roughly 3500 parameters. Figure 4 shows that the system has discovered roughly equivalent qualitative structure in all the dances. The figure also shows a flowchart of the "choreography" discovered in learning.

We then took a 1600-frame sequence of a novice dancer attempting similar choreography, but with little success, getting moves wrong and wrongly ordered, losing the beat, and occasionally stumbling. We resynthesized this in a masculine-modern style, obtaining notable improvements in the grace and recognizability of the dance. This is shown in the accompanying video.

We then **generated new choreography** by doing a random walk on the state machine. We used the resulting state sequence to synthesize new motion-capture in a variety of styles: $\frac{3}{2}$ ballet-$\frac{1}{2}$ languid; modern+male, etc. These are shown in the video. Figure 6 illustrates how different the results are by showing poses from aligned time-slices in the different synthesized performances.

Finally, we demonstrate **driving style machines from video**. The essence of our technique is the generation of stylistically var-

ied motion capture from HMM state sequences (or distributions over states). In the examples above, we obtained state sequences from existing motion capture or random walks on the HMM state machine. In fact, such state sequences can be calculated from arbitrary signals: We can use Brand's shadow puppetry technique [5] to infer state sequences and/or 3D body pose and velocity from video image sequences. This means that one can create animations by acting out a motion in front of a camera, then use style machines to map someone else's (e.g. an expert's) style onto one's choreography. In the accompanying video we show some vision-driven motion-capture and stylistic variations thereon.

6 Discussion

Our unsupervised framework automates many of the dreariest tasks in motion-capture editing and analysis: The data needn't be segmented, annotated, or aligned, nor must it contain any explicit statement of the theme or the stylistic degrees of freedom (DOFs). All these things are discovered in learning. In addition, the algorithms automatically segment the data, identify primitive motion cycles, learn transitions between primitives, and identify the stylistic DOFs that make primitives look quite different in different motion-capture sequences.

This approach treats animation as a pure data-modeling and inference task: There is no prior kinematic or dynamic model; no representation of bones, masses, or gravity; no prior annotation or segmentation of the motion-capture data into primitives or styles. Everything needed for generating animation is learned directly from the data.

However, the user isn't forced to stay "data-pure." We expect that our methods can be easily coupled with other constraints; the quadratic synthesis objective function and/or its linear gradient (eqn. 21) can be used as penalty terms in larger optimizations that incorporate user-specified constraints on kinematics, dynamics, foot placement, etc. That we have *not* done so in this paper and video should make clear the potential of raw inference.

Our method generalizes reasonably well off of its small training set, but like all data-driven approaches, it will fail (gracefully) if given problems that look like nothing in the training set. We are currently exploring a variety of strategies for incrementally learning new motions as more data comes in.

An important open question is the choice of temperature schedules, in which we see a trade-off between learning time and quality of the model. The results can be sensitive to the time-courses of T and T' and we have no theoretical results about how to choose optimal schedules.

Although we have concentrated on motion-capture time-series, the style machine framework is quite general and could be applied to a variety of data types and underlying models. For example, one could model a variety of textures with mixture models, learn the stylistic DOFs, then synthesize extrapolated textures.

7 Summary

Style machines are generative probabilistic models that can synthesize data in a broad variety of styles, interpolating and extrapolating stylistic variations learned from a training set. We have introduced a cross-entropy optimization framework that makes it possible learn style machines from a sparse sampling of unlabeled style examples. We then showed how to apply style machines to full-body motion-capture data, and demonstrated three kinds of applications: resynthesizing existing motion-capture in new styles; synthesizing new choreographies and stylized motion data therefrom; and synthesizing stylized motion from video. Finally, we showed style machines doing something that every dance student has wished for: Superimposing the motor skills of an expert dancer on the choreography of a novice.

8 Acknowledgments

The datasets used to train these models were made available by Bill Freeman, Michael Gleicher, Zoran Popovic, Adaptive Optics, Biovision, Kinetix, and some anonymous sources. Special thanks to Bill Freeman, who choreographed and collected several dance sequences especially for the purpose of style/content analysis. Egon Pasztor assisted with converting motion capture file formats, and Jonathan Yedidia helped to define the joint angle parameterization.

References

[1] L. Baum. An inequality and associated maximization technique in statistical estimation of probabilistic functions of Markov processes. *Inequalities*, 3:1–8, 1972.

[2] M. Brand. Pattern discovery via entropy minimization. In D. Heckerman and C. Whittaker, editors, *Artificial Intelligence and Statistics #7*. Morgan Kaufmann., January 1999.

[3] M. Brand. Exploring variational structure by cross-entropy optimization. In P. Langley, editor, *Proceedings, International Conference on Machine Learning*, 2000.

[4] M. Brand. Voice puppetry. *Proceedings of SIGGRAPH 99*, pages 21–28, August 1999.

[5] M. Brand. Shadow puppetry. *Proceedings of ICCV 99*, September 1999.

[6] C. Bregler. Learning and recognizing human dynamics in video sequences. *Proceedings of CVPR 97*, 1997.

[7] A. Bruderlin and L. Williams. Motion signal processing. *Proceedings of SIGGRAPH 95*, pages 97–104, August 1995.

[8] J. Buhmann. Empirical risk approximation: An induction principle for unsupervised learning. Technical Report IAI-TR-98-3, Institut für Informatik III, Universität Bonn. 1998., 1998.

[9] R. M. Corless, G. H. Gonnet, D. E. G. Hare, D. J. Jeffrey, and D. E. Knuth. On the Lambert W function. *Advances in Computational Mathematics*, 5:329–359, 1996.

[10] W. T. Freeman and J. B. Tenenbaum. Learning bilinear models for two-factor problems in vision. In *Proceedings, Conf. on Computer Vision and Pattern Recognition*, pages 554–560, San Juan, PR, 1997.

[11] M. Gleicher. Motion editing with spacetime constraints. *1997 Symposium on Interactive 3D Graphics*, pages 139–148, April 1997.

[12] M. Gleicher. Retargeting motion to new characters. *Proceedings of SIGGRAPH 98*, pages 33–42, July 1998.

[13] R. Grzeszczuk, D. Terzopoulos, and G. Hinton. Neuroanimator: Fast neural network emulation and control of physics-based models. *Proceedings of SIGGRAPH 98*, pages 9–20, July 1998.

[14] N. R. Howe, M. E. Leventon, and W. T. Freeman. Bayesian reconstruction of 3d human motion from single-camera video. In S. Solla, T. Leend, and K. Muller, editors, *Advances in Neural Information Processing Systems*, volume 10. MIT Press, 2000.

[15] J. Lee and S. Y. Shin. A hierarchical approach to interactive motion editing for human-like figures. *Proceedings of SIGGRAPH 99*, pages 39–48, August 1999.

[16] Z. Popović and A. Witkin. Physically based motion transformation. *Proceedings of SIGGRAPH 99*, pages 11–20, August 1999.

[17] L. R. Rabiner. A tutorial on hidden Markov models and selected applications in speech recognition. *Proceedings of the IEEE*, 77(2):257–286, Feb. 1989.

[18] C. Rose, M. F. Cohen, and B. Bodenheimer. Verbs and adverbs: Multidimensional motion interpolation. *IEEE Computer Graphics & Applications*, 18(5):32–40, September - October 1998.

[19] J. B. Tenenbaum and W. T. Freeman. Separating style and content. In M. Mozer, M. Jordan, and T. Petsche, editors, *Advances in Neural Information Processing Systems*, volume 9, pages 662–668. MIT Press, 1997.

[20] M. Unuma, K. Anjyo, and R. Takeuchi. Fourier principles for emotion-based human figure animation. *Proceedings of SIGGRAPH 95*, pages 91–96, August 1995.

[21] A. Wilson and A. Bobick. Parametric hidden markov models for gesture recognition. *IEEE Trans. Pattern Analysis and Machine Intelligence*, 21(9), 1999.

[22] A. Witkin and Z. Popović. Motion warping. *Proceedings of SIGGRAPH 95*, pages 105–108, August 1995.

[23] S. C. Zhu, Y. Wu, and D. Mumford. Minimax entropy principle and its applications to texture modeling. *Neural Computation*, 9(8), 1997.

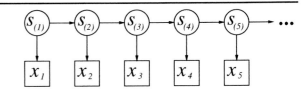

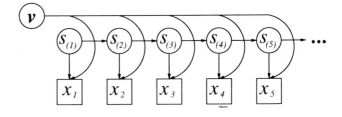

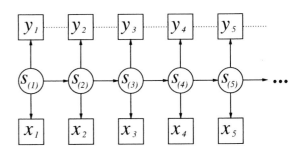

time

Figure 7: Graphical models of an HMM (top), SHMM (middle), and path map (bottom). The observed signal x_t is explained by a discrete-valued *hidden state* variable $s_{(t)}$ which changes over time, and in the case of SHMMs, a vector-valued *style* variable v. Both v and $s_{(t)}$ are hidden and must be inferred probabilistically. Arcs indicate conditional dependencies between the variables, which take the form of parameterized compatibility functions. In this paper we give rules for learning (inferring all the parameters associated with the arcs), analysis (inferring v and $s_{(t)}$), and synthesis of novel but consistent behaviors (inferring a most likely y_t for arbitrary settings of v and $s_{(t)}$).

A Hidden Markov models

An HMM is a probability distribution over time-series. Its dependency structure is diagrammed in figure 7. It is specified by $\theta = \{\mathcal{S}, P_i, P_{j \to i}, p_i(\boldsymbol{x})\}$ where

- $\mathcal{S} = \{s_1, ..., s_N\}$ is the set of discrete states;

- stochastic matrix $P_{j \to i}$ gives the probability of transitioning from state j to state i;

- stochastic vector P_i is the probability of a sequence beginning in state i;

- emission probability $p_i(\boldsymbol{x})$ is the probability of observing $\boldsymbol{x}$ while in state i, typically a Gaussian $p_i(\boldsymbol{x}) = \mathcal{N}(\boldsymbol{x}; \boldsymbol{\mu}_i, \boldsymbol{K}_i) = e^{-(\boldsymbol{x}-\boldsymbol{\mu}_i)^\top \boldsymbol{K}_i^{-1}(\boldsymbol{x}-\boldsymbol{\mu}_i)/2} \big/ \sqrt{(2\pi)^d |\boldsymbol{K}_i|}$ with mean $\boldsymbol{\mu}_i$ and covariance $\boldsymbol{K}_i$.

We cover HMM essentials here; see [17] for a more detailed tutorial. It is useful to think of a (continuous-valued) time-series $\boldsymbol{X}$ as a path through configuration space. An HMM is a state-space model, meaning that it divides this configuration space into regions, each of which is more or less "owned" by a particular hidden state, according to its emission probability distribution. The likelihood of a path $X = \{x_1, x_2, \ldots, x_T\}$ with respect to particular sequence of hidden states $S = \{s_{(1)}, s_{(2)}, \ldots, s_{(T)}\}$ is the probability of each point on the path with respect to the current hidden state ($\prod_{t=1}^{T} p_{s_{(t)}}(x_t)$), times the probability of the state sequence itself, which is the product of all its state transitions ($P_{s_{(1)}} \prod_{t=2}^{T} P_{s_{(t-1)} \to s_{(t)}}$). When this is summed over all possible hidden state sequences, one obtains the likelihood of the path with respect to the entire HMM:

$$p(X|\theta) = \sum_{S \in \mathcal{S}^T} \left[P_{s_{(1)}} p_{s_{(1)}}(x_1) \prod_{t=2}^{T} P_{s_{(t-1)} \to s_{(t)}} p_{s_{(t)}}(x_t) \right] \tag{2}$$

A maximum-likelihood HMM may be estimated from data X via alternating steps of Expectation—computing a distribution over the hidden states—and maximization—computing locally optimal parameter values with respect to that distribution. The E-step contains a dynamic programming recursion for eqn. 2 that saves the trouble of summing over the exponential number of state sequences in $\mathcal{S}^T$:

$$p(X|\theta) = \sum_i \alpha_{T,i} \tag{3}$$

$$\alpha_{t,i} = p_i(x_t) \sum_j \alpha_{t-1,j} P_{j \to i}; \quad \alpha_{1,i} = P_i \, P_i(x_1) \tag{4}$$

α is called the forward variable; a similar recursion gives the backward variable β:

$$\beta_{t,i} = \sum_j \beta_{t+1,j} p_j(x_{t+1}) P_{i \to j}; \quad \beta_{T,i} = 1 \tag{5}$$

In the E-step the variables α, β are used to calculate the expected sufficient statistics $\omega = \{C, \gamma\}$ that form the basis of new parameter estimates. These statistics tally the *expected* number of times the HMM transitioned from one state to another

$$C_{j \to i} = \sum_{t=2}^{T} \alpha_{t-1,j} P_{j \to i} p_i(x_t) \beta_{t,i} / P(X|\theta), \tag{6}$$

and the probability that the HMM was in hidden state s_i when observing datapoint x_t

$$\gamma_{t,i} = \alpha_{t,i} \beta_{t,i} \bigg/ \sum_i \alpha_{t,i} \beta_{t,i}. \tag{7}$$

These statistics are optimal with respect to all the information in the entire sequence and in the model, due to the forward and backward recursions. In the M-step, one calculates maximum likelihood parameter estimates which are are simply normalizations of ω:

$$\hat{P}_{i \to j} = C_{i \to j} \bigg/ \sum_i C_{i \to j} \tag{8}$$

$$\hat{\mu}_i = \sum_t \gamma_{t,i} x_t \bigg/ \sum_t \gamma_{t,i} \tag{9}$$

$$\hat{K}_i = \sum_t \gamma_{t,i} (x_t - \hat{\mu}_i)(x_t - \hat{\mu}_i)^\top \bigg/ \sum_t \gamma_{t,i} \tag{10}$$

After training, eqns. 9 and 10 can be used to remap the model to any synchronized time-series.

In §D we replace these with more powerful entropy-optimizing estimates.

B Stylistic hidden Markov models

A stylistic hidden Markov model (SHMM) is an HMM whose parameters are functionally dependent on a style variable v (see figure 7). For simplicity of exposition, here we will only develop the case where the emission probability functions $p_i(x_t)$ are Gaussians whose means and covariances are varied by v. In that case the SHMM is specified by $\theta = \{\mathcal{S}, P_i, P_{j \to i}, \mu_i, K_i, U_i, W_i, v\}$ where

- mean vector μ_i, covariance matrix K_i, variation matrices U_i, W_i and style vector v parameterize the multivariate Gaussian probability $p_i(x_t)$ of observing a datapoint x_t while in state i:

$$p(x_t|s_i) = \mathcal{N}(x_t; \mu_i + U_i v, K_i + W_i v).$$

  where the stylized covariance matrix $K_i + W_i v$ is kept positive definite by mapping its eigenvalues to their absolute values (if necesary).

The parameters $\{P_i, P_{j \to i}, \mu_i, K_i\}$ are obtained from data via entropic estimation; $\{U_i, W_i\}$ are the dominant eigenvectors obtained in the post-training PCA of the style-specific models; and v can be estimated from data and/or varied by the user. If we fix the value of v, then the model becomes a standard discrete-state, Gaussian-output HMM. We call the $v = 0$ case the *generic HMM*.

A simpler version of this model has been treated before in a supervised context by [21]; in their work, only the means vary, and one must specify by hand the structure of the model's transition function $P_{j \to i}$, the number of dimensions of stylistic variation $\dim(v)$, and the value of v for every training sequence. Our framework learns all of this automatically without supervision, and generalizes to a wide variety of graphical models.

C Entropies and cross-entropies

The first two terms of our objective function (eqn. 1) are essentially the likelihood function, which measures the fit of the model to the data:

$$H(\omega) + D(\omega\|\theta) = -\mathcal{L}(X|\theta) = -\log P(X|\theta) \tag{11}$$

The remaining terms measure the fit of the model to our beliefs. Their precise forms are derived from the likelihood function. For multinomials with parameters $\theta = \{\theta_1, \cdots, \theta_d\}$,

$$H(\theta) = -\sum_i \theta_i \log \theta_i, \tag{12}$$

$$D(\theta^\bullet\|\theta) = \sum_i \theta_i^\bullet \log (\theta_i^\bullet/\theta_i). \tag{13}$$

For d-dimensional Gaussians of mean μ, and covariance K,

$$H(\theta) = \frac{1}{2} \left[d \log 2\pi e + \log |K| \right], \tag{14}$$

$$D(\theta^\bullet\|\theta) = \frac{1}{2} \left[\log |K| - \log |K^\bullet| + \sum_{ij} (K^{-1})_{ij}((K^\bullet)^{-1})_{ij} \right.$$
$$\left. + (\mu - \mu^\bullet)^\top K^{-1}(\mu - \mu^\bullet) - d \right]. \tag{15}$$

The SHMM likelihood function is composed of multinomials and Gaussians by multiplication (for any particular setting of the hidden states). When working with such composite distributions, we optimize the sum of the components' entropies, which gives us a measure of model coding length, and typically bounds the (usually uncalculable) entropy of the composite model. As entropy declines the bounds become tight.

191

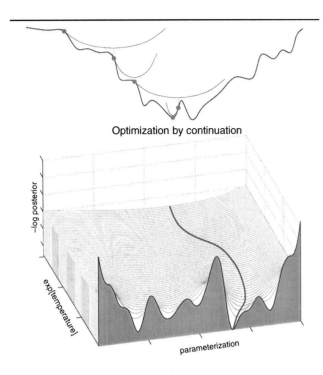

Optimization by continuation

Figure 8: TOP: Expectation maximization finds a local optimum by repeatedly constructing a convex bound that touches the objective function at the current parameter estimate (E-step; blue), then calculating optimal parameter settings in the bound (M-step; red). In this figure the objective function is shown as energy = -log posterior probability; the optimum is the lowest point on the curve. BOTTOM: Annealing adds a probabilistic guarantee of finding a global optimum, by defining a smooth blend between model-fitting—the hard optimization problem symbolized by the foremost curve—and maximizing entropy—an easy problem represented by the hindmost curve—then tracking the optimum across the blend.

D Estimators

The optimal Gaussian parameter settings for minimizing cross-entropy *vis-à-vis* datapoints x_i and a reference Gaussian parameterized by mean $\mu^\bullet$ and covariance $K^\bullet$ are

$$\hat{\mu} = \frac{\sum_i^N x_i + Z'\mu^\bullet}{N + Z'}, \qquad (16)$$

$$\hat{K} = \frac{\sum_i^N (x_i - \hat{\mu})(x_i - \hat{\mu})^\top + Z'((\hat{\mu} - \mu^\bullet)(\hat{\mu} - \mu^\bullet)^\top + \hat{K}^\bullet)}{N + Z + Z'} \qquad (17)$$

The optimal multinomial parameter settings *vis-à-vis* event counts ω and reference multinomial distribution parameterized by probabilities $\kappa^\bullet$ are given by the fixpoint

$$\hat{P}_{j \to i} = \exp\left[W\left(\frac{-(\omega_{j \to i} + Z'\kappa_{j \to i}^\bullet)}{Ze^{\lambda/Z - 1}} \right) + \lambda/Z - 1 \right], \quad (18)$$

$$\hat{\lambda} = \frac{1}{M} \sum_i^M \left(\frac{(\omega_{j \to i} + Z'\kappa_{j \to i}^\bullet)}{P_{j \to i}} + Z \log P_{j \to i} + Z \right) \quad (19)$$

where W is defined $W(x)e^{W(x)} = x$ [9]. The factors Z, Z' vary the strength of the entropy and cross-entropy priors in annealing. Derivations will appear in a technical report available from http://www.merl.com.

These estimators comprise the maximization step illustrated in figure 8.

E Path maps

A path map is a statistical model that supports predictions about the time-series behavior of a target system from observations of a cue system. A path map is essentially two HMMs that share a backbone of hidden states whose transition function is derived from the target system (see figure 7). The output HMM is characterized by per-state Gaussian emission distributions over both target configurations and velocities. Given a path through cue configuration space, one calculates a distribution γ over the hidden states as in §A, eqn. 7. From this distribution one calculates an optimal path through target configuration space using the equations in §F.

F Synthesis

Here we reprise and improve on Brand's [4] solution for likeliest motion sequence given a matrix of state occupancy probabilities γ. As the entropy of γ declines, the distribution over all possible motion sequences becomes

$$\lim_{H(\gamma)\downarrow 0} p_\theta(Y|\gamma) = e^{-\frac{1}{2}\sum_t \sum_i \gamma_{t,i} \tilde{y}_{t,i}^\top K_i^{-1} \tilde{y}_{t,i} + c}, \qquad (20)$$

where the vector $\tilde{y}_{i,t} \doteq [y_t - \mu_i, (y_t - y_{t-1}) - \dot{\mu}_i]^\top$ is the target position and velocity at time t minus the mean of state i, and c is a constant. The means μ_i and covariances K_i are from the synthesizing model's set of Gaussian emission probabilities $p_{s(t)}(y_t, \dot{y}_t) \doteq \mathcal{N}([y_t, y_t - y_{t-1}]; [\mu_{s(t)}, \dot{\mu}_{s(t)}], K_{s(t)})$. Breaking each inverse covariance into four submatrices $K_j^{-1} \doteq \begin{bmatrix} A_j & B_j \\ C_j & D_j \end{bmatrix}$, we can obtain the maximum likelihood trajectory Y^* (most likely motion sequence) by solving the weighted system of linear equations

$$\forall_{t=2}^{T-1} \forall_{j,i} \begin{bmatrix} -\gamma_{t-1,j}(B_j + D_j) \\ \gamma_{t-1,j}(A_j + B_j + C_j + D_j) + \gamma_{t,i}D_i \\ -\gamma_{t,i}(C_i + D_i) \end{bmatrix}^\top \begin{bmatrix} y_{t-1} \\ y_t \\ y_{t+1} \end{bmatrix} = \gamma_{t-1,j}F_j - \gamma_{t,i}E_i, \quad (21)$$

where $E_j \doteq [C_j\ D_j][\mu_j\ \dot{\mu}_j]^\top$, $F_j \doteq [A_j\ B_j][\mu_j\ \dot{\mu}_j]^\top + E_j$ and the endpoints are obtained by dropping the appropriate terms from equation 21:

$$\forall_j \gamma_{j,1} \begin{bmatrix} D_j \\ -C_j - D_j \end{bmatrix}^\top \begin{bmatrix} y_0 \\ y_1 \end{bmatrix} = -\gamma_{j,1}E_j \quad (22)$$

$$\forall_j \gamma_{j,T} \begin{bmatrix} -B_j - D_j \\ A_j + B_j + C_j + D_j \end{bmatrix}^\top \begin{bmatrix} y_{T-1} \\ y_T \end{bmatrix} = \gamma_{j,T}F_j \quad (23)$$

This generalizes Brand's geodesic [4] to use all the information in the occupancy matrix γ, rather than just a state sequence.

The least-squares solution of this $LY = R$ system can be calculated in $O(T)$ time because L is block-tridiagonal.

We introduce a further improvement in synthesis: If we set Y to the training data in eqn. 21, then we can solve for the set of Gaussian means $M = \{\mu_1, \mu_2, \ldots\}$ that minimizes the weighted squared-error in reconstructing that data from its state sequence. To do so, we factor the r.h.s. of eqn. 21 into $LY = R = GM$ where G is an indicator matrix built from the sequence of most probable states. The solution for M via the calculation $M = LYG^{-1}$ tends to be of enormous dimension and ill-conditioned, so we precondition to make the problem well-behaved: $M = (Q^\top Y)(Q^\top Q)^{-1}$, where $Q = LG^{-1}$. One caution: There is a tension between perfectly fitting the training data and generalizing well to new problems; unless we have a very large amount of data, the minimum-entropy setting of the means will do better than the minimum squared error setting.

Timewarp Rigid Body Simulation

Brian Mirtich*

MERL - A Mitsubishi Electric Research Lab

Figure 1: *Avalanche:* 300 rocks tumble down a mountainside.

Abstract

The traditional high-level algorithms for rigid body simulation work well for moderate numbers of bodies but scale poorly to systems of hundreds or more moving, interacting bodies. The problem is unnecessary synchronization implicit in these methods. Jefferson's *timewarp* algorithm [22] is a technique for alleviating this problem in parallel discrete event simulation. Rigid body dynamics, though a continuous process, exhibits many aspects of a discrete one. With modification, the timewarp algorithm can be used in a uniprocessor rigid body simulator to give substantial performance improvements for simulations with large numbers of bodies. This paper describes the limitations of the traditional high-level simulation algorithms, introduces Jefferson's algorithm, and extends and optimizes it for the rigid body case. It addresses issues particular to rigid body simulation, such as collision detection and contact group management, and describes how to incorporate these into the timewarp framework. Quantitative experimental results indicate that the timewarp algorithm offers significant performance improvements over traditional high-level rigid body simulation algorithms, when applied to systems with hundreds of bodies. It also helps pave the way to parallel implementations, as the paper discusses.

CR Categories: I.3.7 [Computer Graphics]: Three-Dimensional Graphics and Realism—Animation; I.6.8 [Simulation and Modeling]: Types of Simulation—Continuous, Discrete Event, Animation
Keywords: Physics Based Modeling, Animation.

1 Introduction

Today rigid body simulation is a mature technology. The major components have been well studied and made practical: fast, ro-

* mirtich@merl.com

©2000 ACM 0-58113-208-5/00/0007 $5.00

bust collision detection algorithms [10, 17, 21, 27]; impact models of varying accuracy [8, 12, 31]; methods to enforce general motion constraints [6, 37], especially the ubiquitous non-penetration constraints [3, 4, 35, 36]; and control strategies for articulated bodies [19, 20, 28, 32]. Thus rigid body simulation is available in many animation and CAD packages and used in computer games. Yet areas for significant improvement remain. An important one is increasing the number of moving, interacting bodies that can be simulated.

We are concerned with *general* rigid body simulation, meaning that the bodies have nontrivial geometries, all pairs can potentially collide, and second-order physics governs the motion. There are numerous techniques to simulate large numbers of rigid bodies by relaxing some of these assumptions. Milenkovic efficiently simulates vast numbers of interacting spheres and non-rotating polyhedra using linear programming techniques and zeroeth-order physics [25]. Carlson and Hodgins use different motion levels of detail, from fully dynamic to fully kinematic, to obtain an order of magnitude increase in the number of legged creatures that can be simulated in real time [11]. Chenney *et. al.* cull dynamics computations for off-screen objects; when they enter the field of view initial states are computed by sampling a probability distribution over their state space [13]. Brogan *et. al.* simulate large herds of fully dynamic agents in distributed virtual environments, but without full collision detection [9]. Despite these excellent techniques, the general case is worth pursuing because of its wide applicability; sometimes full collision detection and dynamics cannot be avoided.

Traditional techniques for the general problem become inefficient and even intractable with many-bodied systems for one of two reasons. Either the integration steps[1] become very small, or the amount of work that is wasted because of unpredictable events (like collisions) becomes very large. The problems are not in the component algorithms but in the glue holding them together—the high-level simulation loop. It imposes a synchronization between bodies that is usually unnecessary and wasteful. These problems are explored in depth in Section 2. Jefferson's *timewarp* algorithm [22], discussed in Section 3, is an elegant paradigm designed to alleviate similar problems in parallel discrete event simulation by running processes as asynchronously as possible. An optimistic, non-interaction assumption prevails, and when it is violated only the computation that is provably invalid is undone. Although rigid

---

[1] Throughout this paper, *integration step* means the time interval passed to the integrator, not the smaller steps it may take internally.

body dynamics is a continuous process, it exhibits many traits of a discrete process. With some modification, the timewarp algorithm can be used in rigid body simulators, improving both their speed and scalability. The method is described in Section 4, and Section 5 presents results from an actual implementation.

Timewarp rigid body simulation also supports the long-range goal of a highly parallel implementation. Rigid body simulation offers unlimited potential for modeling the complex and unanticipated interactions of rich virtual environments, but current technology cannot support this. Meeting this challenge will certainly require a multiprocessor approach, with perhaps hundreds of processors computing motion throughout the environment. Such a *simulation farm* is akin to the rendering farms that generate today's high quality computer animation. Section 6 touches on these issues.

2 Simulation Discontinuities

The dominating computation in a rigid body simulator is that of numerically integrating the dynamic states of bodies forward in time. The differential equations of motion have been known for centuries; the true difficulty lies in processing simulation *discontinuities,* here defined as events that change the dynamic states or the equations of motion of some subset of the bodies. Examples include collisions, new contacts, transitions between rolling and sliding, and control law changes. Integrators cannot blithely pass through discontinuities. Instead the integration must be stopped, the states or equations of motion updated, and then the integrator restarted from that point. Compounding this complication is the fact that the times of most discontinuities are impossible to predict. Thus the integration must be interrupted even more frequently than the rate at which discontinuities occur, just to *check* if they have occurred. There are two common approaches for coping with discontinuities, both of which have been shown practical for moderate numbers of bodies.

2.1 Retroactive Detection

Retroactive detection (**RD**) is the most common approach to handling discontinuities. The simulator takes small steps forward and checks for discontinuities after each step [2, 23]. For example, inter-body penetration indicates that a collision occurred at some time during the most recent integration step. A root finding method localizes the exact moment of the discontinuity. After resolution, the integration is restarted from that point. All of the bodies must be backed up to their states at the time of the discontinuity because (1) the discontinuity may have affected their motion, and (2) the bodies directly involved in the discontinuity must certainly be backed up to this time, and there is no framework for maintaining bodies at different times—the bodies must be kept synchronized. The first problem is avoidable by bounding a discontinuity's influence. A certain collision may provably have no influence on the motion of a distant body over the current integration step. However, the second problem is fundamental to **RD**. It does not suffice to maintain states at two different times, the time of the discontinuity and the time at the end of the step, because multiple discontinuities can occur at different times in a single step. Also, earlier discontinuities may cause or prevent later ones, and it is hard to determine which one occurred first without localizing the times of each. In practice, all bodies are backed up to the point of each discontinuity. This method is correct since it eventually processes all real discontinuities and no spurious ones, and Baraff has shown it to be efficient and eminently practical for moderate numbers of interacting bodies [5]. As the number of bodies increases, so does the the rate of discontinuities, and the wasted work per discontinuity increases since more bodies must be backed up. Shrinking the step size to reduce the amount of backup is not a good solution as we shall see. Eventually **RD** becomes intractable due to the amount of wasted work.

2.2 Conservative Advancement

Conservative advancement (**CA**) is an alternative to **RD** based on the idea of never integrating over a discontinuity. Conservative lower bounds on the times of discontinuities are maintained in a priority queue sorted by time, and the simulator repeatedly advances all simulated bodies to the bound at the front of the queue. The simulator tends to creep up to each discontinuity, taking smaller steps as it gets closer. Von Herzen *et. al.* use this approach to detect collisions between time-dependent parametric surfaces [18], and Mirtich uses it to support impulse-based simulation [26]. Snyder *et. al.* use a related approach to locate multi-point collisions by using interval inclusions to bound surfaces in time and space [33]. Finally, **CA** forms the basis for kinetic data structures pioneered by Basche *et. al.* [7]. These are used to solve a host of problems from dynamic computational geometry, such as maintaining the convex hull of a moving point set, by maintaining bounds on when the combinatorial structure may change. For rigid body simulation the advantage of **CA** is that it does not waste work by integrating bodies beyond a discontinuity. Unfortunately, as the number of bodies increases the average time to the next discontinuity check decreases, and the problem is exacerbated since it is difficult to compute tight bounds on times of collisions and contact changes. Stopping the integration of all bodies at each check is very inefficient, and **CA** becomes intractable with many bodies.

2.3 Step Sizes and Efficiency

Figure 2 graphically demonstrates the problem with small integration steps. It shows the computational cost of computing the 10-second trajectory of a ballistic, tumbling brick using a fifth order adaptive Runge-Kutta integrator [30] under various step sizes. The two qualitatively similar curves correspond to different integrator error tolerances. At small step sizes the integrator does not need to subdivide the integration step into smaller pieces to meet the error tolerance. Thus computation is proportional to the number of invocations: halving the step size doubles the work. At large step sizes the integrator breaks the requested step into smaller pieces to meet the error tolerance, so computation is insensitive to step size. Unfortunately, even with a moderate number of bodies, a simulator's operating point is to the left of the elbow in these curves. Thus, reducing the step size significantly increases computational cost.

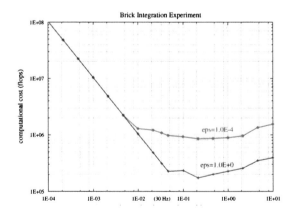

Figure 2: Cost of computing the trajectory of a brick versus integration step size (*eps* is the integrator error tolerance).

3 The Timewarp Algorithm

The problems of **RD** and **CA** result from unnecessary synchronization. Each discontinuity affects only a small fraction of the bodies, yet under **RD** every body must be backed up when a discontinuity occurs, and under **CA** integration of every body must stop for a discontinuity check. The inefficiencies are tolerable as long as there are not too many bodies. Similar issues arise in discrete event simulation (DES) , which is often applied to very large models such as cars on a freeway system. These simulations are often done in parallel or distributed settings. The simulated agents are partitioned among a number of processors, each of which advances its agents forward in time. There are causality relationships that must be preserved (e.g. a car suddenly braking causes the car behind it to brake), and the crux of the problem is that one agent may trigger an action of another agent on a different processor. Obviously communication by message passing or other means is needed.

Conservative DES protocols guarantee correctness by requiring that each processor advance its agents forward to a certain time only when it has provably received all relevant events from other processors occurring before that time. Optimistic protocols were a key breakthrough in distributed DES. These allow each processor to advance its agents forward in time by *assuming* all relevant events have been received, thereby avoiding idle time. The catch is that when an agent receives an event in its "past," the agent needs to be returned to the state it was in when the event occurred, its own actions since that time must be undone, and the intervening computation is wasted. Jefferson was among the first to define a provably correct, optimistic synchronization protocol along with a simple, elegant implementation called the *timewarp* mechanism [22]. We now give a brief, simplified description of this seminal algorithm.

Each process maintains the state of some portion of the modeled system. Each process also has a local clock measuring *local virtual time (LVT)* at that process. The local clocks are not synchronized, and processes communicate only by sending messages. Every message is time stamped[2] with a time not earlier than the sender's *LVT* but possibly earlier than the receiver's *LVT* when the message is received. Processes must process events in time order to maintain causality constraints. When a received message has a timestamp later than the receiver's *LVT*, it is inserted into an input queue sorted by timestamp. A process's basic execution loop is to advance *LVT* to the time of the first event in its input queue, remove the event, and process it. Advancing to a new time means creating a new state, and these are queued in time order in a state queue.

If the first event in a process's input queue has a receive time earlier than *LVT*, the process performs a *rollback* by returning to the latest state in its state queue before the exceptional event's time. This becomes the new current state, its time becomes the new *LVT*, and all subsequent states in the queue are deleted. Already processed events occurring after the new *LVT* are placed back in the input queue. Messages the processor sent to other processes at times after the new *LVT* are "unsent" via *antimessages*. When a process sends a message, it adds a corresponding antimessage to its output queue. This is a negative copy of the sent message, identical to it except for a flipped sign bit. When a process is rolled back to a new *LVT*, all antimessages in the output queue later than this time are sent. When a message and antimessage are united in a process's input queue, they annihilate one another, and the net effect is as if a message were never sent. Rollback is recursive: antimessages may trigger rollbacks that generate new antimessages.

Global virtual time (GVT) is the minimum of all *LVTs* among the processes and all times of unprocessed messages. It represents a line of commitment during the simulation: states earlier than *GVT* are provably valid while states beyond *GVT* are subject to rollback. Individual *LVTs* occasionally jump backwards, but *GVT* monotonically increases. Since rollback never goes to a point before *GVT*, each state queue needs only to maintain one state before *GVT*. Earlier states as well as saved messages prior to *GVT* may be deleted.

---

[2]Each message actually has two timestamps, a send and receive time, but one suffices for our purposes.

4 Timewarp Rigid Body Simulation

Rigid body simulation computes a continuous process but exhibits traits of DES. Bodies "communicate" through collisions and persistent contact. Collisions are in fact usually modeled as discrete events. Contact is a continuous phenomenon, but it can be viewed as occurring *within* a collection of bodies rather than between individual bodies. This view facilitates the adaptation of the timewarp algorithm to uniprocessor rigid body simulation. The result is a high-level simulation algorithm that does not suffer from the wasted work problem of **RD** nor the small timestep problem of **CA**.

4.1 Overview

First consider a simulation without connected or contacting bodies. Each body is a separate timewarp process with a state queue containing the dynamic state (position and velocity) of the body at the end of each integration step. The times of these states are different for different bodies. A global event queue contains events for all simulated bodies; this corresponds to a union of all the individual input queues in Jefferson's algorithm. Each event has a timestamp and a list of the bodies that receive it. One iteration of the main simulation loop consists of removing the event from the front of the event queue, integrating the receiving body or bodies to the event time, and then processing the event. Most events are rescheduled after they are processed. Our system supports four types of events:

1. *Collision check events* are received by pairs of bodies, causing a collision check to be performed between them at the given time. Processing these events may lead to collision resolution.

2. *Group check events* trigger collision checking between contacting bodies and also checking for when groups of such bodies should be split. They can also lead to collision resolution.

3. *Redraw events* exist for every rendered body. Processing one involves writing the current position of the body to a recording buffer. Rescheduling occurs at fixed frame intervals.

4. *Callback events* are received by arbitrary sets of bodies and invoke user functions written in *Scheme* that, for example, drive control systems. Rescheduling is user-specified.

4.2 Collisions and Rollback

If penetration is discovered in processing a collision check or group check event, then a collision has occurred at a time preceding the time of the event. This may be a normal collision or a soft collision producing a new persistent contact. Either way, the colliding bodies must be rolled back to the collision time. This behavior differs from that of standard timewarp events which only cause rollback up to the time of the event; it occurs in rigid body simulation because exact collision times cannot be predicted. To implement collision rollback each collision check and group check event has an additional timestamp, a *safe time*, which is the time when the pair or group of bodies was last verified to be disjoint. When a collision check or group check event is processed, and there is no penetration, the safe time is updated to the time of the check. When penetration is detected, the safe time forms a lower bound on the search for the collision time. Since rollback never proceeds to a point before the safe time, *GVT* can be computed as the minimum of all *LVTs* and all event safe times. This insures there are always states to back up to when a collision occurs.

The antimessage mechanism is more general than what is needed for uniprocessor rigid body simulation. Still considering only isolated bodies, the only inter-body communication is through collisions; a suitable record of these drives the rollback. Pairs of corresponding post-collision states are linked together, turning the individual state queues into a dynamic *state graph* as shown at the top of Figure 3. The figure depicts the actions taken when bodies A and B collide. Body A is rolled back by deleting all of its states after the post-collision state. (If B also had such states, a twin rollback operation would begin in its own state queue). Some of the deleted states are linked via collisions to states in other bodies. These inter-body communications are now suspect due to the A-B collision, thus rollback proceeds across the collision links and then recursively forward through other bodies' state queues. Upon completion of rollback, all states that were possibly affected by the A-B collision—and no others—are deleted. In this example the rollback invalidates a substantial amount of work. It is an unusual case but one the simulator must be prepared for.

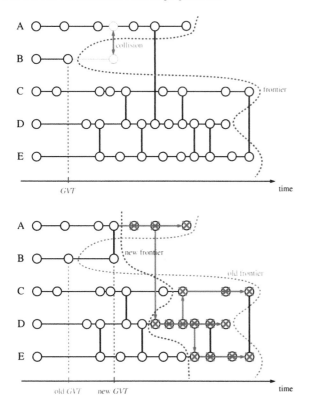

Figure 3: *Top:* State graph of a five body simulation. The vertical connections link post-collision states. The gray states are new post-collision states found while processing an A-B collision check event. *Bottom:* The rollback operation triggered by the collision. Crossed states are deleted and represent wasted work, but forward progress is indicated by the advancement of *GVT*.

Events must also be rolled back. This corresponds to placing messages back in a process's input queue in Jefferson's original algorithm. An event needs to be rolled back only if it involves a body whose state queue was rolled back to a time earlier than the scheduled time of the event. Event rollback is type-specific. Redraw events are simply rescheduled to the first frame time following the rollback time. Fixed-rate callback events are handled similarly. If the rollback time is earlier than the safe time of a collision check or group check event, the event is rescheduled to the rollback time. If the rollback time is between the safe time and the scheduled event time, the system optimistically assumes no action is necessary. This is a gamble since a collision may make the previously computed collision check time inaccurate, but the timewarp algorithm can recover gracefully from poorly predicted collision times.

In total the timewarp algorithm requires little overhead and few additional data structures when compared to a conventional simulator. Any simulator computes sequences of body states; the main change is that these are kept in queues and linked together at the collision points. Rollback is implemented with a simple recursive traversal of the state graph.

4.3 Multibodies

Multibodies (or articulated bodies) are collections of rigid bodies connected by joints, as in a human figure. The trajectory of a single multibody link cannot be determined in isolation; the motion of all links must be computed together. Little change is needed to incorporate multibodies into the timewarp framework. A single state queue serves for the entire multibody; it is advanced as a unit. Most events are still handled on a per rigid body (per link) basis. When, for example, a particular multibody link must be integrated to a certain time for a collision check, the whole multibody is integrated to that time. As a result, states are more densely distributed along multibody state queues than along rigid body state queues, especially for multibodies with many links. A collision involving a single link causes the whole multibody to be rolled back. Clearly timewarp does not offer much improvement if all of the bodies are connected into only a few multibodies.

4.4 Contact Groups

Contact groups are collections of rigid bodies and multibodies in persistent contact; the component bodies exert continuous forces on each other. The components must again be integrated as a unit, but unlike multibodies contact groups are fluid: bodies may join or leave groups, and groups are created and destroyed during a simulation. Contact groups have no analog in the classical timewarp algorithm, which is designed for a static set of processes. Most of the added work in implementing timewarp rigid body simulation is in managing contact groups. To impart some order we require that groups comprise a fixed set of bodies; when the set must change a new group is created. Groups are created by fusions and fissions. A fusion is a suitably soft collision between two bodies, after which they are considered to remain in contact. Either body may be part of a multibody or another group. A fission is a splitting of a group into two or more isolated bodies or separate (non-contacting) groups.

The complexities of contact group evolution are best explained by example. The top of Figure 4 shows the state graph for five rigid bodies labeled A-E and the various contact groups that exist over the time interval $[t_0, t_2]$ (body F does not have a state queue since it is fixed). The bottom of the figure depicts the physical configuration at three distinct times. At time t_0, only bodies B and E are isolated; the others are members of two contact groups, AF and CDF. Only kinematically controlled bodies, of which fixed bodies are a special case, may be members of multiple groups at a given time; such bodies do not link groups together since their motion and the forces they exert on other bodies are independent of the forces exerted on them. Dotted horizontal lines indicate intervals without isolated states since the body is part of a group. The first change after t_0 is a fusion collision between A and B, creating a new group, ABF. D and E then collide, but this is a standard (non-fusion) collision so E remains isolated and CDF intact. The D-E collision does set D in motion, eventually leading to an A-D fusion collision. This latter collision causes two previously separate groups to fuse into a single one, which is the situation at time t_1. Next D breaks contact with C, triggering the fission of $ABCDF$ into $ABDF$ and CF. No collision occurred here; fissions can be caused simply by breaking contacts. Still sliding, D pushes B off of A, causing B to leave the contact group and return to an isolated state. Finally, E lands and settles onto D, fusing into a new group $ADEF$.

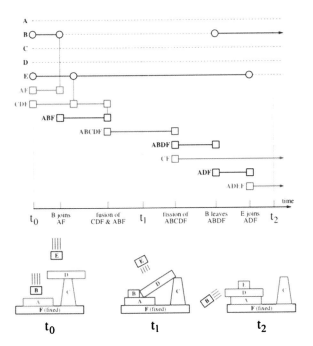

Figure 4: *Top:* The state graph for a portion of a six body simulation. Circles are isolated body states and squares are contact group states. *Bottom:* The physical configuration of the bodies at three distinct times. Moving bodies in contact groups are colored to match the top part of the figure. See text for details.

The state graph in the figure only shows states relevant to the discussion. There would actually be many more states along all of the state queues generated by other events and discontinuities. For example there are usually many non-fusion collisions leading up to a fusion collision as bodies settle. At any time coordinate each non-kinematic body is isolated or a member of exactly one group. Thus there is never ambiguity about what the state of a body is at a given time, or from which state to integrate when computing a new state of a body. To compute the state of body B at time t_2, integration proceeds from the latest isolated state of B prior to t_2. To compute the state of B at time t_1, integration proceeds from the latest state of group $ABCDF$ prior to t_1. To facilitate this, the state graph has additional pointers not shown in the figure. A fusion collision points to the new group it creates, if any. Also, the last state of every fissured group points to the newly isolated bodies and subgroups that succeed it. These pointers make it possible to find for any body B and time t the latest state of B, possibly in a group, prior to t. The search begins within B's own (isolated) state queue and extends into contact groups if necessary by following pointers. Sometimes several pointers and contact groups must be traversed to find the proper prior state. The pointers also facilitate rollback. When a fusion collision state is deleted, the rollback proceeds to the new group formed by the collision, if any. When the last state of a fissured group is deleted, rollback proceeds to the isolated body and subgroup states that succeeded it.

Over the interval shown in Figure 4, six new contact groups are created in addition to the two that existed at t_0. At t_2 only two remain. Groups are terminated when they fuse into new groups or when they fissure into pieces. Termination does not mean the group can be deleted since rollback can cause event processing in non-temporal order. For example it may be necessary to determine the state of body B at time t_1 *after* the group $ABCDF$ is terminated. Once GVT passes the last state in a terminated group, however, the group is obsolete and the storage can be reclaimed. A group is also deleted when a rollback operation annihilates all of its states.

Intra-group collision detection is handled in one of two ways. If bodies A and B are in the same group but not currently in contact, the standard A-B collision check event triggers collision detection between them. Each group has a group check event that performs all of the collision detection between already contacting bodies. The distinction is needed since most collision time predictors do not compute meaningful results when the separation distance is near zero. Instead, group check events are scheduled at a fixed, user-specified rate. While collision detection between A and B is being handled by a group check event, the ordinary A-B collision detection event is disabled.

Group check events are also responsible for detecting fissions. A graph is constructed in which the group's non-kinematic bodies are vertices and contacts are edges. A standard connected component algorithm is performed on this graph. Multiple components indicate that the group can be split. There is flexibility in the time to split a group. Integrating a group with multiple connected components does not give a wrong answer; it is simply inefficient since smaller groups can be integrated faster than a single combined one.

4.5 Collision Checks

At any given point in a simulation, collision checking is enabled between certain *active pairs* of bodies, which are hopefully small in number compared to the total number of pairs [21]. Every non-contacting active pair requires a collision check event. The bodies' state queues provide a simple way to keep the number of active pairs small. An axis-aligned bounding box is maintained around the set of states currently computed for each rigid body (hence there are multiple boxes for multibodies and groups). This swept volume grows as new states are computed; it shrinks when states are deleted as GVT moves past them. Using six heaps to maintain the minimum and maximum x, y, and z coordinates of the rigid body at each state, the swept volume over n states is updated in $O(\log n)$ time.

The pairs of swept volumes that overlap can be maintained using a hierarchical hash table [29] or by sorting coordinates along the three coordinate axes [3, 14]. If the swept volumes of bodies A and B do not overlap, then A and B are known to be collision free over the interval $[GVT, t_{\min}(A, B)]$, where $t_{\min}(A, B)$ is the time of A's or B's latest state, whichever is earlier. As long as the swept volumes remain disjoint, A and B are not an active pair. Now suppose integration of B causes its swept volume to overlap the previously disjoint swept volume of A. To avoid missing collisions, a new collision check event for A and B is scheduled for the time given by the value of $t_{\min}(A, B)$ *before* B was integrated (Figure 5). The bodies are known to be collision free before this point. This new event is in B's past, but the timewarp algorithm can accommodate it; if a collision did occur then rollback will rectify the situation. The collision check event for A and B remains active as long as their swept volumes overlap. This method works even though the swept volumes exist over different time intervals and may have no states at common times. Inactive pairs do not need to be synchronized in order to remain inactive, which avoids costly integration interruptions for the vast majority of body pairs.

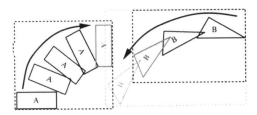

Figure 5: When B is integrated to the state shown in gray, swept volume overlap occurs. A and B become an active pair, and a collision check is scheduled at the earlier time of the two red states.

simulation	simu- lation duration (s)	# of rigid bodies moving/total	# of discont- inuities (thousands)	avg time between disconts (ms)	avg integr'n step (ms)	# of integr'ns (millions)	total integr'n / moving body (s)	total rollback / moving body (s)	comp time / frame (s)
atoms	120	302 / 308	51.9	2.31	6.25	6.04	125 (+4.2%)	0.278 (0.23%)	0.767
cars	60	428 / 524	17.8	3.38	14.9	1.98	69.2 (+15%)	1.57 (2.6%)	0.904
robots	120	240 / 430	26.8	4.48	9.88	3.00	124 (+3.3%)	1.45 (1.2%)	0.707
avalanche	45	300 / 824	217	0.208	3.39	5.84	66.0 (+47%)	7.15 (16%)	97.0

Table 1: Data collected over the four simulations.

4.6 Callback Functions

It is difficult to completely hide the underlying timewarp nature of the system from user callback functions. Because the bodies' *LVTs* are not synchronized, callback functions involving different bodies are not invoked in strict temporal order. In fact, a callback for a single body may not be invoked at monotonically increasing times due to rollback. Thus, a collision callback that counts a body's collisions by incrementing a global counter is flawed since it may get called with the same collision multiple times. One convention that guarantees correct behavior is to forbid callback functions from accessing global data. The function should only use the data passed in: the time of the event and the states of the relevant bodies at that time. Data that must persist across callback invocations are supported by adjoining new slots to the states of bodies. Unlike position and velocity values, the values in these slots are simply copied from state to state since there is no need to integrate them, but callback functions can access and modify these values. Changes are appropriately undone when the state queues are rolled back. The collision counter is implemented correctly by attaching an integer slot to the body state. The callback function increments the counter, and rollback may cause the counter to decrease.

5 Results

We now describe the results of simulating four different systems with a timewarp rigid body simulator (Figures 1 and 7). Our implementation draws from a myriad of component algorithms and techniques described in the literature; Appendix A describes the major ones. Robustness—always an issue in rigid body simulation—is paramount for the kinds of simulations studied here. Anything that can go wrong certainly will when simulating large systems over long times. Our implementation favors robustness over efficiency. The issues are not the underlying components nor the absolute efficiency of this particular implementation but the degree to which timewarp improves any implementation's performance.

Atoms simulates 200 spheres and 100 water-like molecules bouncing in a divided box. During the simulation the divider compresses one compartment and lifts to allow the gasses to mix. *Cars* simulates four multibody vehicles with active wheel velocity and steering angle controllers. These drive over a course with speed bumps and an array of 400 spherical pendulums. *Robots* simulates 20 eight-link manipulators that repeatedly pick up boxes and throw them. The robots are fully dynamic objects, controlled via joint torques commanded by callback functions. Callbacks also use an inverse kinematic model for motion planning. Finally *avalanche* simulates 300 rigid bodies tumbling down a mountainside, creating a vast number of interactions. With the exception of *atoms*, all simulations use realistic values for length, mass, time and earth gravity. Each was generated from a single run.

5.1 Full Timewarp Simulation Data

Table 1 shows data collected over the course of performing the full simulations. The percentages in the total integration and rollback columns are with respect to the simulation duration. Computation times were measured on an SGI Onyx (200MHz R10000 CPU). Integration and rollback intervals of multibodies and groups were weighted by the number of individual rigid bodies involved. The reason that total integration minus rollback exceeds duration is because of the added integration involved in localizing discontinuities. When a discontinuity is detected over an interval, the simulator must compute new states of the relevant bodies in order to localize it. This means re-integrating over certain time intervals, increasing the total integration time.[3]

Worth noting is the amount by which the average integration step exceeds the average interval between discontinuities. This of course is a key advantage of the timewarp algorithm: integration of a body does not halt at every discontinuity but only at the ones which are relevant to it. The fact that the actual integration steps are 2–16 times larger than the average interval between discontinuities is especially noteworthy since any simulation strategy (**RD**, **CA**, or timewarp) must *check* for discontinuities at a much higher rate than they actually occur. In our experiments, checks outnumbered actual discontinuities by two orders of magnitude. Under **RD** or **CA**, all bodies are halted at every check, although the problem is less severe under **RD** since collision checks are synchronized. Table 1 also shows that rollback is a modest cost. Through judicious undoing, timewarp avoids the large amount of wasted work inherent in **RD** as the number of bodies increases.

In several performance measures, the *avalanche* simulation is an outlier. The slow simulation speed is not because timewarp is not working. The ratio of average integration step to average time between discontinuities is quite good, and the total integration per body, while high, is not prohibitive. The main difficulty is the complexity of the contact groups: over 16,000 groups are formed, some having as many as 64 moving bodies and 217 simultaneous contacts. Simulating an avalanche using particle or position-based physics may be more practical, but the example shows that timewarp can handle even extreme cases well.

5.2 Comparative Simulation Data

Table 1 suggests the timewarp algorithm is a good idea. Further experiments give a more quantitative measure of the improvement it brings. We added alternate main loops to the simulator to let it use **RD** and **CA** policies instead of timewarp (**TW**). The **RD** algorithm is parameterized by the basic timestep to attempt on each iteration; we used values of 0.001, 0.01, and 1/30 second. All five algorithms were run on a two-second segment of an *atoms* simulation, with the divider stationary in the middle of the box and with the number of bodies varying from 25 to 200. The upper part of Figure 6 shows the average integration step taken by the simulator under the various algorithms. The results confirm the key problem with **CA**: as the number of bodies increases the average time to the next discontinuity check decreases. As Figure 2 shows, the small steps

---

[3]Baraff cleverly avoids this waste by using internal values of the Runge-Kutta integrator to obtain a polynomial approximation of the state over an integration step for free [5].

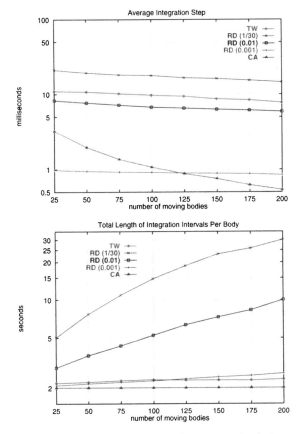

Figure 6: Integration statistics for various *atoms* simulations.

have a drastic effect on computational cost. **RD**'s average timestep is not as sensitive to the number of bodies since it always tries to take a fixed size step forward. **TW** is also not sensitive to it since the bodies are decoupled. The lower portion of the figure exposes the problem with **RD**: wasted work. For a two-second, 200-body simulation and a frame rate timestep, **RD** integrates each body an average of 30 seconds. This is to be compared with **TW**'s value of 2.3 seconds and the modest percentages in the *total integration* column of Table 1. **CA** never integrates more than two seconds per body since it uses a one-sided approach to each discontinuity.

Actual execution times shed further light. For 100 atoms, **RD-1/30** is the narrow winner at 0.142 s/frame, while **TW** was 0.147 s/frame and **CA** was 1.15 s/frame. By 200 atoms, **TW** is clearly superior at 0.388 s/frame, while **RD-0.01**, the fastest **RD** algorithm, was 2.61 s/frame, and **CA** was 4.74 s/frame.

6   Conclusion

Timewarp rigid body simulation is clearly able to simulate larger systems with more interactions than traditional synchronized simulation algorithms. The most obvious avenues for future research involve parallel rigid body simulation. Timewarp simulation helps pave the way to this goal since the individual bodies are evolved asynchronously. If the algorithm runs on multiple processors, delays due to communication latencies are handled in the same way as bad predictions of discontinuity times: with minimal rollback.

The simplest way to structure a parallel simulator would be to have one master processor that repeatedly sends integration tasks to a bevy of slave processors. All of the global data structures could be kept on the master processor, requiring little change in the algorithms presented here. This could significantly boost performance over the uniprocessor case but suffers from a bottleneck at the mas-

ter. An egalitarian approach in which bodies are distributed among processors is ultimately more scalable. Important open questions are how to parcel the bodies among processors and how to balance workloads. At odds are the goals of minimizing inter-processor communication by keeping bodies in the same spatial region on a common processor and minimizing idle time by shifting bodies to idle processors. At any rate some method and strategy for migrating the bodies between processors seems appropriate. Rollback probably requires a full antimessage mechanism since the state graph is likely to be distributed. Other questions surround how and where to store data structures like the spatial hash table, which is frequently accessed by all bodies. Events involving multiple bodies might be redundantly stored and processed on multiple processors or on only one of the relevant processors. Finally, there are various protocol choices for passing state information between processors. Clearly there are many challenges to building a large simulation farm. Yet the prospect of rich virtual environments built on a physics-based substrate is adequate motivation to pursue them.

A   Implementation Details

Our system is implemented in C++. All geometries are modeled as convex polyhedra or unions thereof. The *v-clip* algorithm [27] is used for narrow-phase collision detection; a hierarchical spatial hash table [26, 29] containing axes-aligned bounding boxes is used for the broad phase. For nearby bodies not in contact, times to impact are estimated from current positions and velocities as in [26], but the predictions are not conservative. Persistent contact is modeled using a penalty force method; spring and damper constants are specified per body pair. Inspired by [1] we use an implicit integrator (4th order Rosenbrock [30]) with a sparse solver [15] to handle stiffness induced by the penalty method. This is only necessary for contact groups; isolated bodies are integrated with a 5th order Runge-Kutta integrator [30]. We use a smooth nonlinear friction law, $f_t/f_n = \tanh(v_t/\varepsilon)$ [34]; static friction is not modeled. Reduced coordinates are used for multibodies, with dynamics computed by a generalized Featherstone algorithm [16] in the isolated case and by the spatial composite-rigid-body algorithm [24] within contact groups. The latter is more suited to generating the acceleration Jacobian required by the implicit integrator.

References

[1] D. Baraff and A. Witkin. Large Steps in Cloth Simulation. In Michael Cohen, editor, *SIGGRAPH 98 Conference Proceedings*, Annual Conference Series, pages 43–54. ACM SIGGRAPH, Addison Wesley, July 1998.

[2] David Baraff. Curved Surfaces and Coherence for Non-Penetrating Rigid Body Simulation. In *Computer Graphics (SIGGRAPH 90 Conference Proceedings)*, volume 24, pages 19–28. August 1990.

[3] David Baraff. *Dynamic Simulation of Non-Penetrating Rigid Bodies*. Ph.D. thesis, Department of Computer Science, Cornell University, March 1992.

[4] David Baraff. Fast Contact Force Computation for Nonpenetrating Rigid Bodies. In *SIGGRAPH 94 Conference Proceedings*, Annual Conference Series, pages 23–34. ACM SIGGRAPH, Addison Wesley, 1994.

[5] David Baraff. Interactive Simulation of Solid Rigid Bodies. *IEEE Computer Graphics and Applications*, 15(3):63–75, May 1995.

[6] Ronen Barzel and Alan H. Barr. A Modeling System Based on Dynamic Constraints. In *Computer Graphics (SIGGRAPH 88 Conference Proceedings)*, volume 22, pages 179–188. August 1988.

[7] J. Basch, L.J. Guibas, and J. Hershberger. Data Structures for Mobile Data. In *Proceedings of 8th Symposium on Discrete Algorithms*. 1997. To appear in J. of Algorithms.

[8] Raymond M. Brach. *Mechanical Impact Dynamics; Rigid Body Collisions*. John Wiley & Sons, Inc., 1991.

[9] David C. Brogan, Ronald A. Metoyer, and Jessica K. Hodgins. Dynamically Simulated Characters in Virtual Environments. *IEEE Computer Graphics and Applications*, 18(5):58–69, September 1998.

[10] Stephen Cameron. Enhancing GJK: Computing Minimum Penetration Distances between Convex Polyhedra. In *Proceedings of International Conference on Robotics and Automation*. IEEE, April 1997.

[11] Deborah A. Carlson and Jessica K. Hodgins. Simulation Levels of Detail for Real-time Animation. In *Proc. of Graphics Interface '97*, pages 1–8. 1997.

Figure 7: *Left* to *Right*: snapshots from the *atoms*, *cars* and *robots* simulations (thanks to Larry Gritz for *Blue Moon Rendering Tools*).

[12] Anindya Chatterjee and Andy Ruina. A New Algebraic Rigid Body Collision Law Based on Impulse Space Considerations. *Journal of Applied Mechanics*, 65:939–951, December 1998.

[13] Stephen Chenney, Jeffrey Ichnowski, and David Forsyth. Dynamics Modeling and Culling. *IEEE Computer Graphics and Applications*, 19(2):79–87, March/April 1999.

[14] Jonathan D. Cohen, Ming C. Lin, Dinesh Manocha, and Madhav K. Ponamgi. I-COLLIDE: An Interactive and Exact Collision Detection System for Large-Scaled Environments. In *Symposium on Interactive 3D Graphics*, pages 189–196. ACM SIGGRAPH, April 1995.

[15] J. Dongarra, A. Lumsdaine, R. Pozo, and K. Remington. A Sparse Matrix Library in C++ for High Performance Architectures. In *Proceedings of the Second Object Oriented Numerics Conference*, pages 214–218. 1992. www.math.nist.gov/iml++.

[16] R. Featherstone. The Calculation of Robot Dynamics Using Articulated-Body Inertias. *International Journal of Robotics Research*, 2(1):13–30, 1983.

[17] S. Gottschalk, M. C. Lin, and D. Manocha. OBB-Tree: A Hierarchical Structure for Rapid Interference Detection. In Holly Rushmeier, editor, *SIGGRAPH 96 Conference Proceedings*, Annual Conference Series. ACM SIGGRAPH, Addison Wesley, August 1996.

[18] Brian Von Herzen, Alan H. Barr, and Harold R. Zatz. Geometric Collisions for Time-Dependent Parametric Surfaces. In *Computer Graphics (SIGGRAPH 90 Conference Proceedings)*, pages 39–48. 1990.

[19] Jessica K. Hodgins and Nancy S. Pollard. Adapting Simulated Behaviors for New Characters. In Turner Whitted, editor, *SIGGRAPH 97 Conference Proceedings*, Annual Conference Series, pages 153–162. ACM SIGGRAPH, Addison Wesley, August 1997.

[20] Jessica K. Hodgins, Wayne L. Wooten, David C. Brogan, and James F. O'Brien. Animating Human Athletics. In *SIGGRAPH 95 Conference Proceedings*, Annual Conference Series, pages 71–78. ACM SIGGRAPH, Addison Wesley, 1956.

[21] Philip M. Hubbard. Approximating Polyhedra with Spheres for Time-Critical Collision Detection. *ACM Transactions on Graphics*, 15(3), July 1996.

[22] David R. Jefferson. Virtual Time. *ACM Transactions on Programming Languages and Systems*, 7(3):404–425, July 1985.

[23] V. V. Kamat. A Survey of Techniques for simulation of Dynamic Dynamic Collision Detection and Response. *Computer Graphics in India*, 17(4):379–385, 1993.

[24] Kathryn W. Lilly. *Efficient Dynamic Simulation of Robotic Mechanisms*. Kluwer Academic Publishers, Norwell, 1993.

[25] Victor J. Milenkovic. Position-Based Physics: Simulating the Motion of Many Highly Interacting Spheres and Polyhedra. In Holly Rushmeier, editor, *SIGGRAPH 96 Conference Proceedings*, Annual Conference Series, pages 129–136. ACM SIGGRAPH, Addison Wesley, August 1996.

[26] Brian Mirtich. *Impulse-based Dynamic Simulation of Rigid Body Systems*. Ph.D. thesis, University of California, Berkeley, December 1996.

[27] Brian Mirtich. *V-Clip*: Fast and Robust Polyhedral Collision Detection. *ACM Transactions on Graphics*, 17(3):177–208, July 1998. Mitsubishi Electric Research Lab Technical Report TR97–05.

[28] J. Thomas Ngo and Joe Marks. Spacetime Constraints Revisited. In *SIGGRAPH 93 Conference Proceedings*, Annual Conference Series, pages 343–350. ACM SIGGRAPH, Addison Wesley, 1993.

[29] M. Overmars. Point Location in Fat Subdivisions. *Information Processing Letters*, 44:261–265, 1992.

[30] William H. Press, Saul A. Teukolsky, William T. Vetterling, and Brian R. Flannery. *Numerical Recipes in C: The Art of Scientific Computing*. Cambridge University Press, Cambridge, second edition, 1992.

[31] Edward J. Routh. *Elementary Rigid Dynamics*. Macmillan, London, 1905.

[32] Karl Sims. Evolving Virtual Creatures. In *SIGGRAPH 94 Conference Proceedings*, Annual Conference Series, pages 15–22. ACM SIGGRAPH, 1994.

[33] John M. Snyder, Adam R. Woodbury, Kurt Fleischer, Bena Currin, and Alan H. Barr. Interval Methods for Multi-Point Collisions between Time-Dependent Curved Surfaces. In *SIGGRAPH 93 Conference Proceedings*, Annual Conference Series, pages 321–333. ACM SIGGRAPH, Addison Wesley, 1993.

[34] Peng Song, Peter R. Kraus, Vijay Kumar, and Pierre Dupont. Analysis of Rigid Body Dynamic Models for Simulation of Systems with Frictional Contacts, June 1999. Submitted to ASME Journal of Applied Mechanics.

[35] D.E. Stewart and J.C. Trinkle. An Implicit Time-Stepping Scheme for Rigid Body Dynamics with Inelastic Collisions and Coulomb Friction. *International Journal of Numerical Methods in Engineering*, 39:2673–2691, 1996.

[36] J.C. Trinkle, J.S. Pang, S. Sudarsky, and G. Lo. On Dynamic Multi-Rigid-Body Contact Problems with Coulomb Friction. *Zeitschrift fur Angewandte Mathematik und Mechanik*, 77(4):267–279, 1997.

[37] Andrew Witkin, Michael Gleicher, and William Welch. Interactive Dynamics. *Computer Graphics*, 24(2):11–22, March 1990.

Interactive Control For Physically-Based Animation

Joseph Laszlo   Michiel van de Panne   Eugene Fiume

Department of Computer Science
University of Toronto[1]

Abstract

We propose the use of interactive, user-in-the-loop techniques for controlling physically-based animated characters. With a suitably designed interface, the continuous and discrete input actions afforded by a standard mouse and keyboard allow for the creation of a broad range of motions. We apply our techniques to interactively control planar dynamic simulations of a bounding cat, a gymnastic desk lamp, and a human character capable of walking, running, climbing, and various gymnastic behaviors. The interactive control techniques allows a performer's intuition and knowledge about motion planning to be readily exploited. Video games are the current target application of this work.

CR Categories: I.3.6 [Computer Graphics]: Methodology and Techniques— Interaction Techniques; I.3.7 [Computer Graphics]: Three-Dimensional Graphics and Realism—Animation; I.6.8 [Simulation and Modeling]: Types of Simulation—Animation

Keywords: physically based animation, user interfaces

1 Introduction

Interactive simulation has a long history in computer graphics, most notably in flight simulators and driving simulators. More recently, it has become possible to simulate the motion of articulated human models at rates approaching real-time. This creates new opportunities for experimenting with simulated character motions and behaviors, much as flight simulators have facilitated an unencumbered exploration of flying behaviors.

Unfortunately, while the controls of an airplane or an automobile are well known, the same cannot be said of controlling human or animal motions where the interface between our intentions and muscle actions is unobservable, complex, and ill-defined. Thus, in order to create a tool which allows us to interactively experiment with the dynamics of human and animal motions, we are faced with the task of designing an appropriate interface for animators. Such an interface needs to be sufficiently expressive to allow the creation of a large variety of motions while still being tractable to learn.

Performance animation and puppetry techniques demonstrate how well performers can manage the simultaneous control of a

[1] {jflaszlo|van|elf}@dgp.utoronto.ca
http://www.dgp.utoronto.ca/~jflaszlo/interactive-control.html

large number of degrees of freedom. However, they are fundamentally kinematic techniques; if considerations of physics are to be added, this is typically done as a post-process. As a result, they do not lend themselves well to giving a performer a sense of embodiment for animated figures whose dynamics may differ significantly from that of the performer. In contrast, the physics of our simulated characters constrains the evolution of their motions in significant ways.

We propose techniques for building appropriate interfaces for interactively-controlled physically-based animated characters. A variety of characters, motions, and interfaces are used to demonstrate the utility of this type of technique. Figure 1 shows an example interface for a simple articulated figure which serves as a starting point for our work and is illustrative of how a simple interface can provide effective motion control.

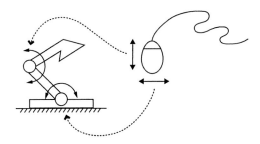

Figure 1: Interactive control for Luxo, the hopping lamp.

This planar model of an animated desk lamp has a total of 5 degrees of freedom (DOF) and 2 actuated joints, capable of exerting joint torques. The motion is governed by the Newtonian laws of physics, the internal joint torques, the external ground forces, and gravity. The joint torques are computed using a proportional-derivative (PD) controller, namely $\tau = k_p(\theta_d - \theta) - k_d\dot{\theta}$. The motions of the two joints are controlled by linearly mapping the mouse position, (m_x, m_y), to the two desired joint angles, θ_d.

Using this interface, coordinated motions of the two joints correspond to tracing particular time-dependent curves with the mouse. A rapid mouse motion produces a correspondingly rapid joint motion. With this interface one can quickly learn how to perform a variety of interactively controlled jumps, shuffles, flips, and kips, as well as locomotion across variable terrain. With sufficient practice, the mouse actions become gestures rather than carefully-traced trajectories. The interface thus exploits both an animator's motor learning skills and their ability to reason about motion planning.

Figure 2 shows an example of a gymnastic tumbling motion created using the interface. This particular motion was created using several motion *checkpoints*. As will be detailed later, these facilitate correcting mistakes in executing particularly unstable or sensitive motions, allowing the simultion to be rolled back to previous points in time. Figure 3 shows a user-controlled motion over variable terrain and then a slide over a ski jump, in this case performed without

Figure 2: Example of an interactively controlled back head-springs and back-flip for Luxo.

Figure 3: Example of an interactively controlled animation, consisting of hops across variable terrain and a carefully timed push off the ski jump.

the use of any checkpoints. The sliding on the ski hill is modelled by reducing the ground friction coefficient associated with the simulation, while the jump is a combined result of momentum coming off the lip of the jump and a user-controlled jump action.

This initial example necessarily provokes questions about scalability, given that for more complex characters such as a horse or a cat, one cannot hope to independently control as many input DOF as there are controllable DOF in the model. One possible solution is to carefully design appropriate one-to-many mappings from input DOF to output DOF. These mappings can take advantage of frequently occuring synergetic joint motions as well as known symmetry and phase relationships.

We shall also explore the use of discrete keystrokes to complement and/or replace continuous input DOF such as that provided by the mouse. These enrich the input space in two significant ways. First, keys can each be assigned their own action semantics, thereby allowing immediate access to a large selection of actions. This action repertoire can easily be further expanded if actions are selected based upon both the current choice of keystroke and the motion context of the keystroke. Second, each keystroke also defines *when* to perform an action as well as the selection of *what* action. The timing of keystrokes plays an important role in many of our prototype interfaces.

In its simplest form, our approach can be thought of as sitting squarely between existing virtual puppetry systems and physically-based animation. It brings physics to virtual puppetry, while bringing interactive interfaces to physically-based animation. The system allows for rapid, free-form exploration of the dynamic capabilities of a given physical character design.

The remainder of this paper is structured as follows. Section 2 reviews previous related work. Section 3 describes the motion primitives used in our prototype system. Section 4 illustrates a variety of results. Finally, section 5 provides conclusions and future work.

2   Previous Work

Building kinematic or dynamic motion models capable of reproducing the complex and graceful movements of humans and animals has long been recognized as a challenging problem. The book *Making Them Move*[3] provides a good interdisciplinary

primer on some of the issues involved. Using physical simulation techniques to animate human figures was proposed as early as 1985[2]. Since then, many efforts have focussed on methods of computing appropriate control functions for the simulated actuators which will result in a desired motion being produced. Among the more popular methods have been iterative optimization techniques [8, 13, 19, 23, 29, 30], methods based on following kinematically-specified reference trajectories [15, 16], suitably-designed state machines [9], machine learning techniques[14], and hybrids[5, 12].

A number of efforts have examined the interactive control of dynamically-simulated articulated figures[10, 11] or procedurally-driven articulated figures[6]. The mode of user interaction used in these systems typically involves three steps: (1) setting or changing specific parameters (2) running the simulation, and (3) observing the result. This type of observe and edit tools is well suited to producing highly specific motions. However, the interaction is less immediate than we desire, and it does not lend a performer a sense of embodiment in a character.

Motion capture and virtual puppetry both allow for user-in-the-loop kinematic control over motions[17, 21, 24], and have proven effective for specific applications demanding real-time animation. The use of 2d user gestures to specify object motion[4] is in an interesting early example of interactive computer mediated animation. Physical animatronic puppets are another interesting precedent, but they cannot typically move in an uncontrained and dynamic fashion in their environment. The system described in [7] is a novel application of using a haptic feedback device for animation control using a mapping which interactively interpolates between a set of existing animations. Our work aims to expand the scope of interactive real-time interfaces by using physically-based simulations, as well as exploring interfaces which allow various degrees of motion abstraction. Such interfaces could then perhaps also be applied to the control of animatronic systems.

The work of Troy[25, 26, 27] proposes the use of manual manipulation of several input devices to perform low-level control of the movement of bipedal characters. The work documents experiments with a variety of input devices and input mappings as having been performed, although detailed methods and results are unfortunately not provided for the manual control method. Nevertheless, this work is among the first we know of that points out the potential of user-in-the-loop control methods for controlling unstable, dynamic motions such as walking.

Computer and video games offer a wide variety of interfaces based both on continuous-input devices (mice, joysticks, etc.) and button-presses and/or keystrokes. However, the current generation of games do not typically use physically-based character animation, nor do they allow much in the way of fine-grained motion control. Exceptions to the rule include fighting games such as *Die by the Sword*[20] and Tekken[18]. The former allows mouse and keyboard control of a physically-based model, limited to the motion of the sword arm. The latter, while kinematic in nature, affords relatively low-level control over character motions. Telerobotics systems[22] are a further suitable example of interactive control of dynamical systems, although the robots involved are typically anchored or highly stable, and are in general used in constrained settings not representative of many animation scenarios.

3   Motion Primitives

The motion primitives used to animate a character can be characterized along various dimensions, including their purpose and their implementation. In this section we provide a classification based largely on the various interface methods employed in our example scenarios.

The joints of our simulated articulated figures are all controlled by the use of PD controllers. Motion primitives thus control mo-

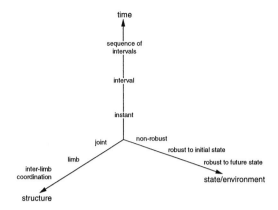

Figure 4: Three dimensions of control abstraction.

tions by varying the desired joint angles used by the PD controllers, as well as the associated stiffness and damping parameters.

PD controllers provide a simple, low-level control mechanism which allows the direct specification of desired joint angles. Coping with more complex characters and motions necessitates some form of abstraction. Figure 4 shows three dimensions along which such motion abstraction can take place. The interfaces explored in this paper primarily explore abstractions in time and structure by using stored control sequences and coordinated joint motions, respectively. The remaining axis of abstraction indicates the desirability of motion primitives which perform correctly irrespective of variations in the initial state or variations in the environment. This third axis of abstraction is particularly challenging to address in an automated fashion and thus our examples rely on the user-in-the-loop to perform this kind of abstraction.

3.1 Continuous Control Actions

The most obvious way to control a set of desired joint angles is using an input device having an equivalent number of degrees of freedom. The mouse-based interface for the hopping lamp (Figure 1) is an illustration of this. It is interesting to note for this particular example that although cursor coordinates are linearly mapped to desired joint angles, a nonlinearity is introduced by the acceleration features present in most mouse-drivers. This does not seem to adversely impact the continuous control. In general, continuous control actions are any mappings which make use of continuously varying control parameters, and are thus not limited to direct mappings of input DOF to output DOF.

The availability of high DOF input devices such as data-gloves and 6 DOF tracking devices means that the continuous control of input DOF can potentially scale to control upwards of 20 degrees of freedom. However, it is perhaps unreasonable to assume that a performer can learn to simultaneously manipulate such a large number of DOF independently, given that precedents for interfaces in classical puppetry and virtual puppetry are typically not this ambitious.

3.2 Discrete Control Actions

Discrete actions, as implemented by keystrokes in our interfaces, allow for an arbitrary range of action semantics. Action games have long made extensive use of keystrokes for motion specification, although not at the level of detail that our interfaces strive to provide. The following list describes the various action semantics used in prototype interfaces, either alone or in various combinations. Some of the actions in this list refer directly to control actions, while others serve as meta-actions in that they modify parameters related to the simulation and the interface itself.

set joint position (absolute) Sets desired position of joint or a set of joints to a prespecified value(s). If all joints are set simultaneously in order to achieve a desired pose for the figure, this becomes a form of interactive dynamic keyframing.

adjust joint position (relative) Changes the desired position of a joint or set of joints, computed relative to current desired joint positions.

grasp, release Causes a hand or foot to grasp or release a nearby point (e.g., ladder rung) or to release a grasped point.

select IK target Selects the target point for a hand or foot to reach toward using a fixed-time duration IK trajectory, modelled with a Hermite curve. The IK solution is recomputed at every time step.

initiate pose sequence Initiate a prespecified sequence of full or partial desired poses.

select next control state Allows transitions between the states of a finite-state machine; useful for modelling many cyclical or otherwise well-structured motions, leaving the timing of the transitions to the performer.

rewind, reset state Restarts the simulation from a previous state checkpoint.

set joint stiffness and damping Sets the stiffness and damping parameters of the PD joint controllers to desired values.

select control mode Chooses a particular mapping for a continuous input device, such as which joints the mouse controls.

set simulation rate Speeds up or slows down the current rate of simulation; helps avoid a motion happening 'too fast' or 'too slow' to properly interact with it.

set state checkpoint Stores the system state (optionally during replay/review of a motion) so that simulation may be reset to the same state later if desired.

modify physical parameters Effects changes to simulation parameters such as gravity and friction.

toggle randomized motion Begins or halts the injection of small randomized movements, which are useful for introducing motion variation.

Our default model for arbitration among multiple actions which come into conflict is to allow the most recent action to pre-empt any ongoing actions. Ongoing actions such as IK-based trajectories or pose sequences are respectively preempted only by new IK-based trajectories or pose sequences.

3.3 State Machines

Given the cyclic or strongly structured nature of many motions, state machine models are useful in helping to simplify the complexities of interactive control. For example, they allow separate actions such as 'take left step' and 'take right step' to be merged into a single action 'take next step', where a state machine provides the necessary context to disambiguate the action. As with many other animations systems, state machines serve as the means to provide apriori knowledge about the sequencing of actions for particular classes of motion.

4 Implementation and Results

Our prototype system is based on a number of planar articulated figures. The planar dynamics for these figures can easily be computed at rates suitable for interaction (many in real-time) on most current PCs and offer the additional advantage of having all aspects of their motion visible in a single view, thereby providing unobstructed visual feedback for the performer. Our tests have been conducted primarily on a 450 Mhz Mac and a 366 Mhz PII PC. While hard-coded interfaces were used with the original prototyping system behind many of our results, our more recent system uses Tcl as a scripting language for specifying the details of any given interface. This facilitates rapid iteration on the design of any given interface, even potentially allowing changes during the course of a simulation.

4.1 Luxo Revisited

Using the continuous-mode mouse-based interface shown in Figure 1, the desklamp is capable of executing a large variety of hops, back-flips, a kip manoevre, head-stands, and motion across variable terrain. This particular interface has been tested on a large number of users, most of whom are capable of performing a number of the simpler movements within 10–15 minutes, given some instruction on using the interface. Increasing the stiffness of the joints or scaling up the mapping used for translating mouse position into desired joint angles results in the ability to perform more powerful, dynamic movements, although this also makes the character seem rather too strong during other motions.

We have additionally experimented with a keystroke-based interface using 14 keys, each key invoking a short sequence of pre-specified desired poses of fixed duration. The various key actions result in a variety of hops and somersaults if executed from the appropriate initial conditions. The repertoire of action sequences and associated keystrokes are given in the Appendix. The animator or performer must choose when to execute keystrokes and by doing so selects the initial conditions. The initiation of a new action overrides any ongoing action.

The keystroke-based interface was created after gaining some experience with the continuous-mode interface. It provides an increased level of abstraction for creating motions and is easier to learn, while at the same time trading away some of the flexibility offered by the continuous-mode interface. Lastly, user-executed continuous motions can be recorded and then bound to a keystroke.

4.2 Animating a Cat

Experiments with a planar bounding cat and a planar trotting cat are a useful test of scalability for our interactive interface techniques. Figure 5 illustrates the planar cat as well as sets of desired angles assumed by the legs for particular keystrokes. In one control mode, the front and back legs each have 6 keys assigned to them, each of which drives the respective leg to one of the 6 positions illustrated in the figure. The keys chosen for each pose are assigned a spatial layout on the keyboard which reflects the layouts of the desired poses shown in the figure. An additional pose is provided which allows each leg to exert a larger pushing force than is otherwise available with the standard set of 6 poses. This can be achieved by temporarily increasing the stiffness of the associated leg joints, or by using a set of hyperextended joint angles as the desired joint positions. We use the latter implementation. This seventh overextended pose is invoked by holding the control key down when hitting the key associated with the backwards extended leg pose.

The animation sequence shown in Figure 6 was accomplished using 12 *checkpoints*. A checkpoint lets the performer restart the

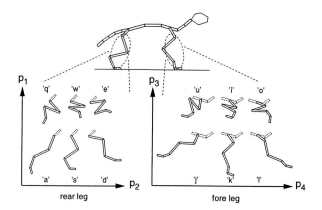

Figure 5: Parameterization of limb movements for cat.

simulation from a given point in time, allowing the piecewise interactive construction of sequences that would be too long or too error-prone to perform successfully in one uninterrupted attempt. Checkpoints can be created at fixed time intervals or at will by the performer using a keystroke. Some of the sequences between checkpoints required only 2 or 3 trials, while particularly difficult aspects of the motion required 10–20 trials, such as jumping the large gap and immediately climbing a set of steps (second-last row of Figure 6).

The cat weighs 5 kg and is approximately 50 cm long, as measured from the tip of the nose to the tip of the tail. Its small size leads to a short stride time and requires the simulation to be slowed down considerably from real-time in order to allow sufficient reaction time to properly control its motions. The cat motions shown in Figure 6 were controlled using a slowdown factor of up to 40×, which allows for 10–15 seconds to control each bound.

It is important to note that there is a 'sweet spot' in choosing the speed at which to interact with a character. Important features of the dynamics become unintuitive and uncontrollable if the interaction rate is either too slow or too fast. When the simulation rate is too fast, the user is unable to react quickly enough to correct errors before the motion becomes unsavable. When the motion is too slow, the user tends to lose a sense of the necessary rhythm and timing required to perform the motion successfully and lacks sufficient immediate feedback on the effects of the applied control actions. For basic bounding, a slowdown factor around 10, giving a bound time of 2-3 seconds is sufficient. For more complex motions such as leaping over obstacles, a factor of up to 40+ is required.

Figure 7 shows a trotting motion for a planar 4-legged cat model. The trotting was interactively controlled using only the mouse. The x, y mouse coordinates are used to linearly interpolate between predefined poses corresponding to the six leg poses shown in Figure 5. The poses are laid out in a virtual 2 × 3 grid and bilinear interpolation is applied between the nearest 4 poses according to the mouse position. The simplest control method assumes a fixed phase relationship among the 4-legs, allowing the mouse to simultaneously effect coordinated control of all legs. A more complex method uses the same mapping to control one leg at a time. This latter method met with less success, although was not pursued at length. The cat model is comprised of 30 articulated links, which makes it somewhat slow to simulate, given that we currently do not employ $O(n)$ forward dynamics methods.

4.3 Bipedal Locomotion

We have experimented with a number of bipedal systems which are capable of more human-like movements and behaviors such as walking and running. For these models, we make extensive use

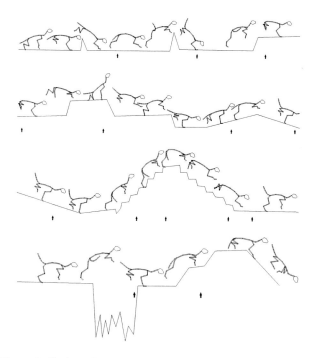

Figure 6: Cat bounding on variable terrain using piecewise interactive key-based control. The frames shown are manually selected for visual clarity and thus do not represent equal samples in time. The arrows indicate when the various checkpoints were used, denoting the position of the shoulders at the time of the checkpoint.

Figure 7: Cat trot using continuous mouse control. The animation reads from top-to-bottom, left-to-right. The first seven frames represent a complete motion cycle. The frames are equally spaced in time.

of a hybrid control technique which mixes continuous and discrete input actions in addition to purely discrete methods similar to those used with the cat and Luxo models. We have also experimented with a wide variety of other bipedal motions in addition to walking and running, including a number of motions such as a long jump attempt and a fall-recovery sequence that are readily explored using interactive control techniques.

Figure 8 shows the interface for an interactive walking control experiment. The mouse is used to control the desired angles for the hip and knee joints of the swing leg. A keypress is used to control when the exchange of stance and swing legs occurs and therefore changes the leg currently under mouse control. The stance leg assumes a straight position throughout the motion. The bipedal figure has human-like mass and dimensions, although it does not have a separate ankle joint. In our current implementation, joint limits are not enforced, although such constraints can easily be added to the simulation as desired.

An example of the resulting motion is shown in Figure 9. With some practice, a walk cycle can be sustained indefinitely. With significant practice, the walk can be controlled in real-time, although a simulation speed of 2–3 times slower than real-time provides a

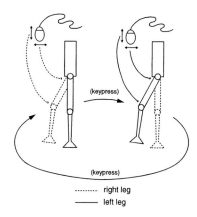

Figure 8: Interface for interactive control of bipdal walking.

sweet-spot for consistent interactive control. It is also possible to choose a particular (good) location for the mouse, thus fixing the desired joint angles for the swing leg, and achieve a marching gait by specifying only the the time to exchange swing and stance legs by pressing a key. This marching motion is quite robust and is able to traverse rugged terrain with reasonable reliability. Yet another mode of operation can be achieved by automatically triggering the swing-stance exchange when the forward lean of the torso exceeds a fixed threshold with respect to the vertical. With this automatic mechanism in place, it is then possible to transition from a marching walk to a run and back again by slowly moving only the mouse through an appropriate trajectory.

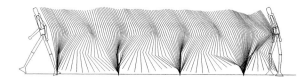

Figure 9: Bipedal walking motion

Figure 10 shows the results of a biped performing a long-jump after such an automatic run. This particular biped dates from earlier experiments and is smaller in size and mass than the more anthropomorphic biped used for the walking experiments. This motion makes use of the same interface as for the bipedal walking motion, shown in in Figure 8. A slowdown factor of up to 80 was necessary because of the small size of the character, as well as the precision required to achieve a final landing position having the legs extended and the correct body pitch. Approximately 20 trials are required to achieve a recognizable long jump, each beginning from a motion checkpoint one step before the final leap. However, we anticipate that the interface can be also be improved upon significantly by using a more reasonable default behavior for the uncontrolled leg.

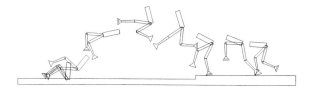

Figure 10: A long jump attempt.

4.4 Bipedal Gymnastics

Several other experiments were carried out using the bipedal figures with continuous-mode mouse control and one or more keys to select the mapping of the continuous input onto the model's desired joint angles. The basic types of motion investigated include a variety of climbing modes both with the bipedal model "facing" the view plane and in profile in the view plane, and swinging modes both with arms together and separated. Nearly every mapping for these control modes uses the mouse y coordinate to simultaneously drive the motion of all limb joints (hips, knees, shoulders and elbows) in a coordinated fashion and the mouse x coordinate to drive the bending of the waist joint to alter the direction of the motion.

The control modes differ from each other primarily in the particular symmetries shared between the joints. Figure 11 illustrates two forms of symmetry used for climbing "gaits" similar in pattern to those of a quadruped trotting and bounding. The mapping of the mouse x coordinate onto the waist joint is also shown. The control modes can produce interactive climbing when coupled with a state machine that grasps and releases the appropriate hands and feet each time a key is pressed (assuming that the hands and feet are touching a graspable surface). Swinging modes perform in a similar manner but use the mouse x or y coordinate to swing the arms either back-and-forth at the shoulder or in unison and can make use of either graspable surfaces or ropes that the user can extend and retract from each hand on demand. When used on the ground without grasping, these same modes of interaction can produce a range of gymnastic motions including handstands and different types of flips and summersaults, in addition to a continuously controlled running motion. Among the various interesting motions that are possible is a backflip done by running off a wall, a gymnastic kip from a supine position to a standing position and a series of giant swings as might be performed on a high bar. While not illustrated here, these motions are demonstrated in the video segments and CD-ROM animations associated with this paper.

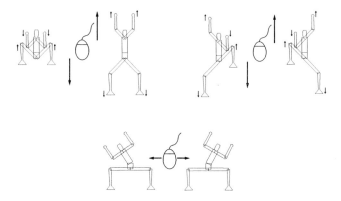

Figure 11: Control modes useful for climbing and gymnastics. Left-to-right, top-to-bottom: "bound" pattern climbing; "trot" pattern climbing; directional control.

4.5 Using IK Primitives

Figures 12 and 13 illustrate interactively-controlled movements on a set of irregularly-spaced monkeybars and a ladder, respectively. These are movements which require more precise interactions of the hands and feet with the environment than most of the other motions discussed to date. To deal with this, we introduce motion primitives which use inverse kinematics (IK) to establish desired joint angles.

In general, IK provides a rich, abstract motion primitive that can appropriately hide the control complexity inherent in many semantically-simple goal-directed actions that an interactive character might want to perform. This reduces the associated learning curve the user faces in trying to discover how to perform the action(s) from first principles while still taking good advantage of the user's intuition about the motion.

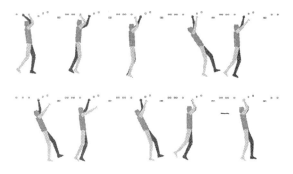

Figure 12: Traversing a set of irregularly-spaced monkeybars.

The interface for monkey-bar traversal consists of keystrokes and a state machine. IK-based trajectories for the hands and feet are invoked on keystrokes. The hand-over-hand motion across the monkeybars is controlled by keys which specify one of three actions for the next release-and-regrasp motion. The actions causes the hand to release its grasp on the bar and move towards the previous bar, the current bar, or the following bar. These actions can also be invoked even when the associated hand is not currently grasping a bar, which allows the figure to recover when a grasp manoevre fails due to bad timing. The interface does not currently safeguard against the premature execution of a regrasp motion with one hand while the other has not yet grasped a bar. The character will thus fall in such situations. A grasp on a new bar is enacted if the hand passes close to the target bar during the reaching action, where 'close' is defined to be a fixed tolerance of 4 cm in our example. Controlling the motion thus involves carefully choosing the time in a swing at which a new reach-and-grasp action should be initiated, as well as when to pull up with the current support arm. More information about the particulars of the interface is given in the Appendix.

The ladder climbing example is made up of a number of keys which serve to position the body using the hands and feet which are in contact with the ladder, as well as a key to initiate the next limb movement as determined by the state machine. The details of the interface are given in the appendix, as well as the specific keystroke sequence used to create Figure 13. Note, however, that the keystroke sequence by itself is insufficient to precisely recreate the given motion, as the timing of each keystroke is also important in all the motions discussed.

Figure 13: Climbing a ladder.

Finally, Figure 14 illustrates a standing up motion, followed by a few steps, a forward fall, crouching, standing up, and, lastly, a backwards fall. A set of 18 keys serves as the interface for this scenario, as documented in the appendix.

Figure 14: Fall recovery example.

5 Conclusions and Future Work

We have presented prototype interfaces for the interactive control of physically-based character animation. The techniques illustrate the feasibility of adding physics to virtual puppetry, or, alternatively, adding interactive interfaces to physically-based animation. They allow human intuition about motions to be exploited in the interactive creation of novel motions.

The results illustrate that dynamic motions of non-trivial articulated figure models can be reasonably controlled with user-in-the-loop techniques. Our experiments to date have focussed on first achieving a large action repertoire for planar figures, with the goal of using this experience as a suitable stepping stone towards 3D motion control. While it is not clear that the interaction techniques will scale to the type of nuanced 3D motion control need for foreground character animation in production animation, the interfaces could be readily applied to a new generation of physically-based interactive video games. The interfaces provide a compelling user experience — in fact, we found the interactive control experiments to be quite addictive.

One of the drawbacks of using interactive control is the effort required in both designing an appropriate interface and then learning to effectively use the interface. These two nested levels of experimentation necessitate a degree of expertise and patience. We are optimistic that tractable interfaces can be designed to control sylistic variations of complex motions and that animators or game players can learn these interfaces with appropriate training and practice.

Our work has many directions which require further investigation. We are still far from being able to reproduce nuanced dynamic motions for 3D human or animal characters[1, 28]. The large variety of high-DOF input devices currently available offers a possible avenue of exploration. Haptic devices may also play a useful role in constructing effective interfaces[7]. Nuanced performance may potentially require years of training, as it does for other arts (key-frame animation, dancing, music) and sports. We can perhaps expect that the instruments and interfaces required for composing motion to undergo continual evolution and improvement. A large community of users would offer the potential for a rapidly evolving set of interfaces for particular motions or characters.

Many dynamic motions would benefit from additional sensory feedback, such as an animated update of the location of the center of mass[25]. Going in the opposite direction, one could use an interactive environment like ours to conduct experiments as to the minimal subset of sensory variables required to successfully control a given motion. Questions regarding the transfer of skills between interfaces and between character designs are also important to ad-

dress if broad adoption of interactive control techniques is to be feasible.

The derivation of high-level abstractions of motion control is of interest in biomechanics, animation, and robotics. The training data and insight gained from having a user-in-the-loop can potentially help in the design of autonomous controllers or high-level motion abstractions. A variety of hybrid manual/automatic control methods are also likely to be useful in animation scenarios.

Beyond its application to animation, we believe the system also has potential uses in exploring deeper issues involved in controlling motions for biomechanics, robotics, or animation. What constitutes a suitable motor primitive or 'motor program'? How can these primitives be sequenced or overlaid in order to synthesize more complex motions? In what situations is a particular motion primitive useful? Our experimental system can serve as a tool towards exploring these questions by allowing interactive control over the execution and sequencing of user-designed motion-control primitives.

Acknowlededements: We would like to thank all of the following for their help: the anonymous reviewers for their comments; the Imager lab at UBC for hosting the second author during much of the work on this paper; and David Mould for suggestions and assistance investigating the automatic bipedal marching and running motions. This work was supported by grants from NSERC and CITO.

A Appendix

Details of keystrokes interface for Luxo:

k	small hop
l	medium hop
o	large hop
i	high backward hop
u	medium backward hop
j	small backward hop
y	back somersault
s	sitting to upright (slow)
d	standing to sitting / LB to sitting
f	LB to standing (small height) / standing to sitting
e	LB to standing (medium height) / standing to LB
w	standing to sitting / sitting to LB / LB to standing
q	big jump from base to LB / fwd somersault from LB
a	LB to standing with small jump
	A/B = a single action that performs either A or B depending on initial state
	LB = lying on back

Interface and keystrokes for monkeybar example:

a	grasp rung previous to CR
s	grasp CR
d	grasp rung following CR
f	grasp rung two rungs following CR
q	release with both hands, relax arms
e	pull up using support arm
R	reset to initial state
t	toggle defn of support/grasp arm
	CR = closest rung

Interface and keystrokes for ladder climbing example:

q	release both hands, fall from ladder
f	grasp two rungs higher with next grasp arm
h	shift body up
b	lower body down
n	pull body in with arms
g	push body out with arms
j	push body out with legs
m	pull body in with legs
R	reset to initial state

Interface and keystrokes for the fall recovery example:

p	ST, prepare for forwards fall
o	ST, prepare for backwards fall
t	HK, step back with left arm
y	HK, step back with right arm
q	HK, shift body back
w	HK, bend elbows, prepare for push up
W	HK, straighten elbows, push up
1	CR, straighten hips, knees, ankles
2	CR, assume intermediate pose towards being upright
3	CR, assume final upright pose
c	ST, step backwards with left leg
v	ST, step forwards with left leg
b	ST, step backwards with right leg
n	ST, step forwards with right leg
j	ST, lean back at hips
R	reset to initial state
M	checkpoint current state
L	restart at checkpoint state
ST = standing	
HK = on hands and knees	
CR = crouched	

References

[1] K. Amaya, A. Bruderlin, and T. Calvert. Emotion from motion. In *Graphics Interface '96*, pages 222–229, May 1996.

[2] W. W. Armstrong and M. Green. The dynamics of articulated rigid bodies for purposes of animation. *Proceedings of Graphics Interface '85*, pages 407–415, 1985.

[3] N. I. Badler, B. Barsky, and D. Zeltzer. *Making Them Move*. Morgan Kaufmann Publishers Inc., 1991.

[4] R. M. Baecker. *Interactive computer-mediated animation*. PhD thesis, Massachusetts Institute of Technology, 1969.

[5] A. Bruderlin and T. W. Calvert. Goal-directed animation of human walking. *Proceedings of ACM SIGGRAPH*, 23(4):233–242, 1989.

[6] A. Bruderlin and T. W. Calvert. Interactive animation of personalized human locomotion. *Proceedings of Graphics Interface*, pages 17–23, 1993.

[7] B. R. Donald and F. Henle. Using Haptic Vector Fields for Animation Motion Control. Technical Report PCS-TR99-353, Dartmouth College, Computer Science, Hanover, NH, May 1999.

[8] J. Auslander et al. Further experience with controller-based automatic motion synthesis for articulated figures. *ACM Transactions on Graphics*, October 1995.

[9] J. K. Hodgins et al. Animating human athletics. *Proceedings of SIGGRAPH 95, ACM Computer Graphics*, pages 71–78, 1995.

[10] T. Ertl et al. Interactive control of biomechanical animation. *The Visual Computer*, pages 459–465, 1993.

[11] D. Forsey and J. Wilhelms. Techniques for interactive manipulation of articulated bodies using dynamic analysis. In *Proceedings of Graphics Interface '88*, pages 8–15, 1988.

[12] M. Girard. Interactive design of computer-animated legged animal motion. *IEEE Comptuer Graphics and Applications*, 7(6):39–51, June 1987.

[13] R. Grzeszczuk and D. Terzopoulos. Automated learning of muscle-actuated locomotion through control abstraction. *Proceedings of SIGGRAPH 95, ACM Computer Graphics*, pages 63–70, 1995.

[14] R. Grzeszczuk, D. Terzopoulos, and G. Hinton. Neuroanimator: Fast neural network emulation and control of physics-based models. *Proceedings of SIGGRAPH 98*, pages 9–20, July 1998. ISBN 0-89791-999-8. Held in Orlando, Florida.

[15] H. Ko and N. Badler. Animating human locomotion with inverse dynamics. *IEEE Computer Graphics and Applications*, pages 50–59, 1996.

[16] E. Kokkevis, D. Metaxas, and N. Badler. User-controlled physics-based animation for articulated figures. In *Proceedings of Computer Animation '96*, 1996.

[17] A. Menache. *Understanding Motion Capture for Computer Animation and Video Games*. Morgan Kaufmann, 1999.

[18] Namco. Tekken, tekken2, and tekken3. computer game, 1998, 1999.

[19] J. T. Ngo and J. Marks. Spacetime constraints revisited. *Proceedings of SIGGRAPH 93*, pages 343–350, 1993.

[20] Interplay Productions. Die by the sword. computer game, 1998.

[21] M. Rosenthal. Dynamic digital hosts. *Computer Graphics World's Digital Magic*, pages 39–42, August 1998.

[22] T. B. Sheridan. *Telerobotics, Automation, and Human Supervisory Control*. MIT Press, 1992.

[23] K. Sims. Evolving virtual creatures. *Proceedings of SIGGRAPH 94, ACM Computer Graphics*, pages 15–22, 1994.

[24] D. J. Sturman. Computer puppetry. *IEEE Computer Graphics and Applications*, 18(1):38–45, January/February 1998.

[25] J. Troy. *Dynamic Balance and Walking Control of Biped Mechanisms*. PhD thesis, Iowa State University, 1995.

[26] J. Troy. Real-time dynamic balancing and walking control of a 7-link planar biped. In *Proceedings of ASME Design Engineering Technical Conferences*, 1998.

[27] J. Troy and M. Vanderploeg. Interactive simulation and control of planar biped walking devices. In *Workshop on Simulation and Interaction in Virtual Environments*, pages 220–224, July 1995.

[28] M. Unuma, K. Anjyo, and R. Takeuchi. Fourier principles for emotion-based human figure animation. *Proceedings of SIGGRAPH 95, ACM Computer Graphics*, pages 91–96, 1995.

[29] M. van de Panne and E. Fiume. Sensor-actuator networks. *Proceedings of SIGGRAPH 93*, pages 335–342, 1993.

[30] M. van de Panne, R. Kim, and E. Fiume. Virtual wind-up toys for animation. *Proceedings of Graphics Interface '94*, pages 208–215, 1994.

Interactive Manipulation of Rigid Body Simulations

Jovan Popović*   Steven M. Seitz   Michael Erdmann   Zoran Popović†   Andrew Witkin‡

Carnegie Mellon University
†University of Washington
‡Pixar Animation Studios

Abstract

Physical simulation of dynamic objects has become commonplace in computer graphics because it produces highly realistic animations. In this paradigm the animator provides few physical parameters such as the objects' initial positions and velocities, and the simulator automatically generates realistic motions. The resulting motion, however, is difficult to control because even a small adjustment of the input parameters cant drastically affect the subsequent motion. Furthermore, the animator often wishes to change the end-result of the motion instead of the initial physical parameters.

We describe a novel interactive technique for intuitive manipulation of rigid multi-body simulations. Using our system, the animator can select bodies at any time and simply drag them to desired locations. In response, the system computes the required physical parameters and simulates the resulting motion. Surface characteristics such as normals and elasticity coefficients can also be automatically adjusted to provide a greater range of feasible motions, if the animator so desires. Because the entire simulation editing process runs at interactive speeds, the animator can rapidly design complex physical animations that would be difficult to achieve with existing rigid body simulators.

CR Categories: I.3.7 [Computer Graphics]: Three-Dimensional Graphics and Realism—Animation; I.3.6 [Computer Graphics]: Methodology and Techniques—Interaction techniques; G.1.7 [Numerical Analysis]: Ordinary Differential Equations—Boundary value problems

Keywords: Physically Based Animation, Animation with Constraints

1 Introduction

Physical simulation programs provide powerful tools for creating realistic motion in animated shorts and feature films. These methods enable quick and easy generation of complex physical behaviors such as a ball bouncing, window breaking [22], cloth folding [2], and water flowing [10, 24]. An attractive feature of physical simulation is that the animation is generated automatically—the an-

---
*Carnegie Mellon University, 5000 Forbes Avenue, Pittsburgh, PA 15213–3891. http://www.cs.cmu.edu/~jovan

Figure 1: The animator manipulates the simulation by first fixing the hat's landing position on the coatrack with a "nail" constraint. While the animator rotates the hat at an earlier time to achieve the desired spin, the constraint maintains the desired landing location.

imator only needs to specify a few physical parameters such as initial positions and velocities.

Despite the appeal of simulation techniques, their primary drawback is lack of intuitive control over the resulting motion. The animator often wishes to adjust the motion to achieve a desired effect such as a new end-position or a more pleasing look. However, directly altering the underlying physical parameters to try to achieve the desired effect is often cumbersome and nonintuitive. In many cases, the animator would prefer to edit the animation itself, by direct manipulation of positions and velocities.

We introduce a novel interactive technique for manipulating rigid body simulations. Throughout the interaction, our system displays the entire trajectory of all objects in the scene. The animator is free to manipulate the *entire* motion by grabbing and changing the state of the object (position, velocity, etc.) at any location on its trajectory. For example, suppose the animator wants to design a scene in which an actor successfully tosses his hat onto a nearby coatrack, but instead has an animation of the hat falling to the floor. In our paradigm, the animator first selects the hat at its landing position and simply drags it onto the coatrack. There are many ways in which the hat can land on the coatrack and the current motion may not have the desired style. The animator can adjust the style by first fixing the landing position on the coatrack to ensure the desired landing location and then rotating the hat at an earlier time until the hat motion achieves the desired spin (Figure 1).

This hat example illustrates the use of position constraints to control rigid body animations. More generally, our system provides the ability to set arbitrary position, orientation, and velocity constraints on multiple objects at multiple points in time. Furthermore, we also provide floating time constraints that may be satisfied at any point in time. For example, an animator can adjust where a mug hits the ground on its third bounce, without fixing the time when that bounce occurs.

A key problem in controlling dynamic simulations is obtaining sufficient degrees of freedom to avoid over-constrained problems. In our system the animator may add degrees of freedom by varying physical parameters that specify the internal properties of the environment, including shapes, masses, surface normals, elasticity coefficients, and moments of inertia. Often the best choice for these parameters is not at all obvious to the animator but yet can have a very dramatic effect on the resulting animation. Our system automatically adjusts these physical parameters according to the animator's desired effect. We have found this capability to be useful even in under-constrained problems. In particular, motion in chaotic systems is highly sensitive to small perturbations in the initial conditions. Adding control variables near desired manipulation times (i.e. variation of surface normals at the previous collision) improves the conditioning without affecting the perceived realism of the animation [4]. Furthermore, the additional parameters increase the range of feasible motions, enhancing the animator's ability to create interesting effects.

Interaction is an integral component of our approach. The animator is able to directly control the motion without manipulating the underlying physical parameters, and immediately sees the results of her adjustments. As a result, she can quickly explore the space of possible motions to achieve the desired behavior. Unlike previous motion-construction tools [29, 8, 21, 19, 23], our system does not evaluate the quality of motion with an objective criterion such as time-optimal motion. Instead, the animator imparts her aesthetic or other subjective criteria and interactively guides the system towards the desired motion.

Internally, our system represents the entire motion of bodies by the physical parameters that control the simulation (i.e., initial positions and velocities, surface normal variations and other parameters included by the animator). As the animator interactively manipulates the motion, the system computes the new physical parameters that achieve the desired motion update. This is achieved in real time using a fast differential update procedure in concert with a rigid body simulator. Motion discontinuities pose an additional challenge (e.g. when a point of collision changes to a different facet on a body's polyhedral mesh) because the motion changes abruptly. When this happens, our system performs a local discrete search in physical parameter space to compute the motion that most closely complies with the desired adjustments.

The remainder of the paper is divided into six sections. In Section 2, we discuss related work. We outline the basic algorithm in Section 3, and discuss further details in Section 4 and Section 5. In Section 6, we outline the specifics of our prototype implementation and report on the experimental results, and in Section 7, we conclude and describe directions for future work.

2 Related Work

Dynamics and motion of mechanical systems are important to many fields. Optimal control theory provides the groundwork for maximizing the performance of evolving dynamic systems [25]. In robot path planning, kinodynamic planning refers to the problem of computing robot paths that satisfy both dynamic and kinematic constraints [9]. In computer graphics, the spacetime constraints technique for animation of characters computes optimal motion subject to constraints [29, 8, 21, 19, 23]. Other techniques [3, 6, 16] also rely on gradient information to compute the motion that satisfies certain constraints. All of the above techniques solve for the actuating forces which produce a motion. Because of this, they do not directly apply to our problem of controlling the rigid body simulations because we wish to control passive objects (i.e. objects without any self-propelling forces).

Several researchers have addressed the inverse problem of constructing a dynamic rigid body motion given the desired body configurations. Tang et al. [27] formulated this inverse problem as an optimization task and extended the genetic algorithm technique to compute solutions for a class of 2-D N-body problems. For a 2-D billiards simulation, Barzel and colleagues [4] computed successful shots using a backward search from the desired final locations of billiard balls. Chenney et al. [7] applied the Markov Chain Monte Carlo (MCMC) method to construct 3-D motions that achieve de-

sired body configurations. The MCMC technique excels at constructing motions for systems with chaotic behavior such as the motion of pins after collision with a bowling ball. The main drawback of these approaches is lack of interactivity: these systems may require several hours to construct a solution. If the animator does not like the resulting motion, she must adjust the desired body configurations and start again. We argue that interactivity is essential when aesthetics is a primary concern.

Our interactive technique is related to the method for geometric modeling described by Witkin et al. [28]. Similar techniques have also been devised for drawing applications [13], interactive camera control [14] and others. In its treatment of motion discontinuities, our approach most closely resembles that of Harada et al. [17], which combines continuous and discrete optimization for applications in architectural design. In this approach, when the imposed architectural constraints can no longer be enforced with the continuous parameters, the solver performs a local discrete search to find a new room arrangement in which the constraints are satisfied.

3 Interactive Manipulation

Our algorithm computes the required physical parameters so that the resulting motion satisfies desired constraints. In this section, we define some basic concepts and give a top-level description of our algorithm.

3.1 Simulation Function

Following the Lagrangian approach, we describe mechanical systems in terms of their generalized coordinates and velocities [26]. A system of one or more rigid bodies is described by a *generalized state* vector $\mathbf{q}$ whose components are the generalized coordinates and velocities of the bodies in the system. The behavior of a system is described by a set of ordinary second order differential equations [26], which we write in vector form as a coupled first order differential equation,

$$\frac{d}{dt}\mathbf{q}(t) = \mathbf{F}(t, \mathbf{q}(t)), \tag{1}$$

where $\mathbf{F}(t, \mathbf{q}(t))$ is derived from the Newton's law (e.g. see Equation 8). As mentioned in Section 1, our technique varies several physical parameters—in addition to the initial position and velocity $\mathbf{q}_0$—to modify the simulation. We encode all of these parameters in the *control vector* $\mathbf{u}$, and extend the differential equation appropriately:

$$\frac{d}{dt}\mathbf{q}(t) = \mathbf{F}(t, \mathbf{q}(t), \mathbf{u}). \tag{2}$$

This equation of motion completely describes the system in free flight (i.e. when there are no collisions): integrating Equation 2 yields

$$\mathbf{q}(t) = \mathbf{q}_0(\mathbf{u}) + \int_{t_0}^{t} \mathbf{F}(t, \mathbf{q}(t), \mathbf{u}) \, dt. \tag{3}$$

Collisions can be handled in a number of ways, but for computer animations the simple Poisson collision model suffices [20]. This model can represent elastic and inelastic impacts by applying instantaneous impulses to the colliding bodies. The system simulates the motion during free flight by numerically solving Equation 2. At collision times additional impulses are applied to the system. Because the control vector $\mathbf{u}$ includes physical parameters such as surface normals at collisions and elasticity coefficients, the impulse $\mathbf{I}(\mathbf{q}^-, \mathbf{u})$ directly depends on the control vector $\mathbf{u}$. At collisions the simulator maps the generalized state an instant before the collision $\mathbf{q}^-$ into the state an instant after the collision $\mathbf{q}^+$ (e.g. see Equation 10):

$$\mathbf{q}^+ = \mathbf{q}^- + \mathbf{I}(\mathbf{q}^-, \mathbf{u}). \tag{4}$$

More abstractly, given the control vector $\mathbf{u}$ the rigid body simulator computes the *simulation function* $\mathcal{S}$, which specifies the state of the bodies in the world at every point in time:

$$\mathbf{q}(t) = \mathcal{S}(t, \mathbf{u}). \tag{5}$$

In principle, the animator could manipulate the motion $\mathbf{q}(t)$ by adjusting the control vector $\mathbf{u}$. However, such a form of control would be tedious because the relation between $\mathbf{u}$ and $\mathbf{q}(t)$ is complex and nonintuitive. Instead, we would like to allow the animator to specify the state of bodies $\mathbf{q}(t_i)$ at specific times $t_i = t_0, \ldots, t_n$, and let the algorithm compute the control vector $\mathbf{u}$ that produces the desired motion. This is a difficult problem [27, 7] for three reasons. First, the domain of the simulation function $\mathcal{S}$ is high-dimensional: for a *single* 3-D body, the components of the generalized state $\mathbf{q}$ are the body's position, orientation, linear, and angular velocity (i.e. $\mathbf{q} \in \mathbf{R}^3 \times \mathrm{SO}(3) \times \mathbf{R}^3 \times \mathbf{R}^3$). Second the simulation function is highly nonlinear. A consequence of the integral nature of the simulation function is that small changes in the initial conditions can result in drastic modifications of the motion. Third, the simulation function is not continuous. Each collision event (e.g., different vertices of an object colliding with the ground) bifurcates the simulation function.

We adopt a differential approach for manipulating the simulation function. The animator adjusts the motion by specifying a differential change of motion $\delta\mathbf{q}_i$ in the generalized state $\mathbf{q}(t_i)$ at time t_i. The system responds by reshaping the current motion to comply with the adjustments. Continuing the interactive manipulation, the animator gradually guides the system toward the desired solution. To compute a new control vector that reshapes the motion in compliance with the differential changes $\delta\mathbf{q}_i$, we locally linearize Equation 5,

$$\delta\mathbf{q}_i = \frac{\partial \mathcal{S}(t_i, \mathbf{u})}{\partial \mathbf{u}} \delta\mathbf{u}. \tag{6}$$

We combine all animator-specified constraints into a linear system which we solve for $\delta\mathbf{u}$ by conjugate gradient technique. The differential vector $\delta\mathbf{u}$ describes the direction in which to change the current control vector $\mathbf{u}$ to obtain the desired motion change $\delta\mathbf{q}_i$. The differential update is simply a small step in the computed direction,

$$\mathbf{u}' = \mathbf{u} + \epsilon\, \delta\mathbf{u}. \tag{7}$$

Given the new, updated control vector $\mathbf{u}'$, a rigid body simulator computes the new motion and displays the result. At this point the entire process repeats.

3.2   2-D Particle Example

To help provide an intuition for the issues underlying our approach, we begin with an illustrative example. Suppose that a single 2-D particle moves under the action of gravity. The generalized state $\mathbf{q} \in \mathbf{R}^4$ encodes the particle's position $\mathbf{x} \in \mathbf{R}^2$ and velocity $\mathbf{v} \in \mathbf{R}^2$. If g is the acceleration of gravity, the equations of motion,

$$\frac{d}{dt} \begin{pmatrix} \mathbf{x}(t) \\ \mathbf{v}(t) \end{pmatrix} = \begin{pmatrix} \mathbf{v}(t) \\ \begin{pmatrix} 0 \\ -g \end{pmatrix} \end{pmatrix}, \tag{8}$$

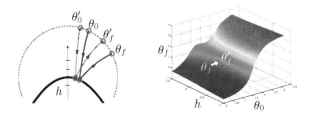

Figure 2: The simulation function for the motion of a particle bounce.

describe the particle's path in free flight. The solution to this differential equation yields the simulation function:

$$\mathcal{S}(t, \mathbf{q}_0) = \begin{pmatrix} \mathbf{x}(t) \\ \mathbf{v}(t) \end{pmatrix} = \begin{pmatrix} \mathbf{x}(0) + \mathbf{v}(0)t + \begin{pmatrix} 0 \\ -\frac{1}{2}gt^2 \end{pmatrix} \\ \mathbf{v}(0) + \begin{pmatrix} 0 \\ -gt \end{pmatrix} \end{pmatrix}. \tag{9}$$

If the particle collides with an immovable obstacle, the Poisson collision model applies an impulse to change the particle's velocity. For frictionless collisions, the impulse acts in the direction of the surface normal $\mathbf{n}$ at the point of collision. The equation,

$$\mathbf{v}^+ = \mathbf{v}^- - 2(\mathbf{n} \cdot \mathbf{v}^-)\mathbf{n}, \tag{10}$$

applies an impulse to instantaneously change the particle's velocity before the collision $\mathbf{v}^-$ into its velocity after the collision $\mathbf{v}^+$.

Given these analytical expressions for the particle's motion, we can plot the space of all possible trajectories for the particle as a function of the initial conditions and the environment. For concreteness, suppose the particle collides with a single parabolic obstacle. For notational convenience, we introduce a unit circle around the obstacle: the particle enters the circle at some angle θ_0 with unit velocity vector directed towards a point at height h above the tip, bounces off the obstacle, and exits the circle at another angle θ_f (Figure 2). Our objective is to determine θ_f as a function of θ_0 and h.

In this example, the simulation function $\mathcal{S} : \mathbf{R}^2 \to \mathbf{R}$ maps the control vector $\mathbf{u} = (\theta_0, h)$ into the particle's final, exit position θ_f. Given an initial entering θ_0 and exiting θ_f state, our gradient-based interactive technique can smoothly transform this solution to one which satisfies one or more constraints, for example to achieve a different exiting state θ_f'. Our technique converges easily because the simulation function is smooth over the domain of control parameters (Figure 2).

The general motion of many rigid bodies is much like this simple particle example. To describe the state of a single 3-D rigid body, we increase the dimensions of the generalized state, adding the components of orientation, angular velocity, and extending the position and linear velocity to 3-D. Two or more rigid bodies are modeled by adding additional components to the generalized state. Surface parameters such as normals and elasticity coefficients may also be added, if desired. Note that the number of rigid objects is not explicitly represented, we are merely expressing the cumulative degrees of freedom of the system. Our implementation makes use of this representation to enable complex multi-object simulations with the same computation techniques and data structures used to implement particle simulations.

4   Manipulation without Discontinuities

The algorithm outlined in Section 3 relies on the efficient computation of the Jacobian matrix $\partial \mathcal{S}(t_i, \mathbf{u})/\partial \mathbf{u}$. Computing the Jacobian matrix with finite differences is expensive because of the need to perform multiple simulations. In addition, the inaccuracies of the finite differences approach would be prohibitive for our approach.

Instead we use a specialized automatic differentiation technique. We decompose the simulation function $\mathcal{S}$ into analytically differentiable functions and numerically compose the Jacobian matrix using the chain rule. For example, suppose that a single collision occurs at time t_c and the simulation function $\mathcal{S}(t_f, \mathbf{u})$ describes the body's state at some time after the collision $t_f > t_c$. We decompose $\mathcal{S}(t_f, \mathbf{u})$ into three functions:

$\mathcal{F}_{t_c}$: pre-collision free-flight function, which maps the initial conditions and perhaps additional elements of the control vector $\mathbf{u}$ into the body's state at t_c, an instant before collision (e.g. Equation 9 for 2-D particles);

$\mathcal{C}_{t_c}$: collision function, which applies the impulse and maps the body's state an instant before collision into the body's state at t_c, an instant after collision (e.g. Equation 10 for 2-D particles);

$\mathcal{F}_{t_f}$: post-collision free-flight function, which maps the body's state an instant after the collision into the body's state at t_f.

The functional composition expressing $\mathcal{S}(t_f, \mathbf{u})$ becomes:[1]

$$\mathcal{S}(t_f, \mathbf{u}) = \mathcal{F}_{t_f}(\mathbf{u}) \circ \mathcal{C}_{t_c}(\mathbf{u}) \circ \mathcal{F}_{t_c}(\mathbf{u}). \qquad (11)$$

Although the free-flight motion of the particle in Section 3.2 has a closed-form and is analytically differentiable, this is generally not the case for 3-D rigid body motion.[2] To compute the derivatives of $\partial \mathcal{F}_{t_c}(\mathbf{u})/\partial \mathbf{u}$, we first integrate the equations of motion (Equation 1) until time t_c,

$$\mathcal{F}_{t_c}(\mathbf{u}) = \mathbf{q}_0(\mathbf{u}) + \int_{t_0}^{t_c(\mathbf{u})} \mathbf{F}(t, \mathbf{q}, \mathbf{u})\, dt,$$

and take the derivative of both sides with respect to $\mathbf{u}$

$$\frac{\partial \mathcal{F}_{t_c}(\mathbf{u})}{\partial \mathbf{u}} = \frac{\partial}{\partial \mathbf{u}} \left(\mathbf{q}_0(\mathbf{u}) + \int_{t_0}^{t_c(\mathbf{u})} \mathbf{F}(t, \mathbf{q}, \mathbf{u})\, dt \right).$$

To evaluate this expression we apply the Leibnitz rule [18] to interchange the integral and the derivative:[3]

$$\frac{\partial \mathcal{F}_{t_c}(\mathbf{u})}{\partial \mathbf{u}} = \mathbf{F}(t_c(\mathbf{u}), \mathbf{q}, \mathbf{u}) \frac{dt_c(\mathbf{u})}{d\mathbf{u}} +$$
$$\frac{\partial \mathbf{q}_0(\mathbf{u})}{\partial \mathbf{u}} + \int_{t_0}^{t_c(\mathbf{u})} \frac{\partial \mathbf{F}(t, \mathbf{q}, \mathbf{u})}{\partial \mathbf{u}}\, dt. \qquad (12)$$

The simulator computes the value of $\mathbf{F}(t_c(\mathbf{u}), \mathbf{q}, \mathbf{u})$ at the collision. To compute the collision time derivative $dt_c(\mathbf{u})/d\mathbf{u}$ we define a smooth collision event function $E(t, \mathbf{q})$ such that at the collision time $t_c(\mathbf{u})$,

$$E(t_c(\mathbf{u}), \mathbf{q}) = 0. \qquad (13)$$

For the 2-D particle, for example, the collision event function E can be defined as the signed distance function between the particle and the obstacle.

---

[1]The Equation 11 is written in this form for notational convenience. More precisely, this equation is $\mathcal{S}(t_f, \mathbf{u}) = \mathcal{F}_{t_f}(\mathbf{u}, \mathcal{C}_{t_c}(\mathbf{u}, \mathcal{F}_{t_c}(\mathbf{u})))$.

[2]For the special case of freely rotating 3-D rigid body (no torques), there is an analytic Poinsot's solution [26].

[3]The conditions for applying the Leibnitz rule require that $\mathbf{F}$ is continuous and has a continuous derivative $\partial \mathbf{F}/\partial \mathbf{u}$. These conditions are met under reasonable assumptions about external forces.

Differentiating Equation 13 and solving for the collision time derivative we obtain

$$\frac{dt_c(\mathbf{u})}{d\mathbf{u}} = -\frac{(\partial E/\partial \mathbf{q}) \cdot (\partial \mathbf{q}/\partial \mathbf{u})}{\partial E/\partial t}. \qquad (14)$$

The derivatives on the right-hand side of Equation 14 are computed analytically, with the exception of $\partial \mathbf{q}/\partial \mathbf{u}$, which is defined by the integral expression (second and third term in the sum) in Equation 12. We compute this integral expression by numerically integrating differential equation

$$\frac{d}{dt} \frac{\partial \mathbf{q}(t)}{\partial \mathbf{u}} = \frac{\partial \mathbf{F}(t, \mathbf{q}, \mathbf{u})}{\partial \mathbf{u}},$$

until time t_c with the initial condition $\partial \mathbf{q}_0(\mathbf{u})/\partial \mathbf{u}$.

The computation of $\partial \mathcal{F}_{t_f}(\mathbf{u})/\partial \mathbf{u}$ is similar: we apply the Leibnitz rule to obtain

$$\frac{\partial \mathcal{F}_{t_f}(\mathbf{u})}{\partial \mathbf{u}} = -\mathbf{F}(t_c(\mathbf{u}), \mathbf{q}, \mathbf{u}) \frac{dt_c(\mathbf{u})}{d\mathbf{u}} +$$
$$\frac{\partial \mathcal{C}_{t_c}(\mathbf{u})}{\partial \mathbf{u}} + \int_{t_c(\mathbf{u})}^{t_f} \frac{\partial \mathbf{F}(t, \mathbf{q}, \mathbf{u})}{\partial \mathbf{u}}\, dt$$

and evaluate the right-hand terms as before.

To compute the derivatives of $\partial \mathcal{C}_{t_c}(\mathbf{u})/\partial \mathbf{u}$ we differentiate the Equation 4:

$$\frac{\partial \mathcal{C}_{t_c}(\mathbf{u})}{\partial \mathbf{u}} = \frac{\partial \mathcal{F}_{t_c}(\mathbf{u})}{\partial \mathbf{u}} + \frac{\partial \mathbf{I}(\mathbf{q}^-, \mathbf{u})}{\partial \mathbf{u}}.$$

Once all derivatives of the sub-functions have been computed we find the simulation function derivatives by applying the chain rule:

$$\frac{\partial \mathcal{S}(t_f, \mathbf{u})}{\partial \mathbf{u}} = \frac{\partial \mathcal{F}_{t_f}}{\partial \mathcal{C}_{t_c}} \left(\frac{\partial \mathcal{C}_{t_c}}{\partial \mathcal{F}_{t_c}} \frac{\partial \mathcal{F}_{t_c}}{\partial \mathbf{u}} + \frac{\partial \mathcal{C}_{t_c}}{\partial \mathbf{u}} \right) + \frac{\partial \mathcal{F}_{t_f}}{\partial \mathbf{u}}$$

Although we have shown the derivative computations for the composition of three phases, an arbitrary number of such phases can be composed in an analogous manner.

4.1 Differential Update

Having computed the Jacobians, we can formulate the constraint equations (Equation 6). Given n such equations, we solve for the differential vector $\delta \mathbf{u}$. Because this system is often underconstrained (Section 1), we solve the following minimization instead:

$$\min_{\delta \mathbf{u}} \left(\delta \mathbf{u}^T \mathbf{M} \delta \mathbf{u} + \mathbf{d}^T \delta \mathbf{u} \right) \qquad (15)$$

$$\text{subject to} \quad \delta \mathbf{q}_1 = \frac{\partial \mathcal{S}(t_1, \mathbf{u})}{\partial \mathbf{u}} \delta \mathbf{u}$$

$$\vdots$$

$$\delta \mathbf{q}_n = \frac{\partial \mathcal{S}(t_n, \mathbf{u})}{\partial \mathbf{u}} \delta \mathbf{u}.$$

The minimized objective function has a dual purpose: it seeks the smallest change from the current state of the simulation and the smallest deviation from the desired values of the simulation parameters such as surface normals at the collision. The diagonal matrix $\mathbf{M}$ describes the relative scale between parameters in the control vector $\mathbf{u}$. The animator can describe the desired scaling to specify how the system should change the parameters. For example, the animator may instruct the system to favor changing the initial position rather than the initial velocity of a body. The vector $\mathbf{d}$ defines desired values for physical parameters. For example, if the system varies the surface normal at a collision we can specify the true geometric normal as the desired value and the system will attempt to stay as close as possible—once all constraints are satisfied—to the true surface normal. Specifically, if $\delta \mathbf{u}_d$ is the desired change in the control vector $\mathbf{u}$ then setting $\mathbf{d} = -\delta \mathbf{u}_d$ and optimizing Equation 15 will minimize $(\delta \mathbf{u} - \delta \mathbf{u}_d)^T (\delta \mathbf{u} - \delta \mathbf{u}_d)$. Because the objective is quadratic and all constraints are linear, we use the Lagrangian multipliers to reformulate the minimization as a linear system and solve for $\delta \mathbf{u}$ [12].

Our technique is a form of gradient descent: we continuously linearize the problem and move in the gradient direction $\delta \mathbf{u}$. For a large gradient stepsize ϵ, the gradient descent method may diverge. Line minimization is the preferred method for choosing the stepsize in a gradient method, but it requires considerable computation. In practice, a small fixed stepsize has good convergence properties while also enabling interactive update rates.

The gradient descent converges only to a local optimum [5]. Local convergence is sufficient and effective for our interactive setting: the animator drags a body towards the intended position—guiding the system out of undesirable local minima—and the system quickly reshapes the motion to comply with the change.

4.2 Manipulation Constraints

When the animator specifies the constraints, the system maps these constraints to the appropriate differential changes of motion $\delta \mathbf{q}_i$. We distinguish three types of constraints: state constraints, expression constraints, and floating constraints.

State constraints occur when the animator "nails down" objects (e.g., fixing position, orientation, linear velocity or angular velocity to specific values). Suppose that the animator wants the body A at time t_i to have the state $\mathbf{q}'_A$, and that $\mathbf{q}_A$ is a subset of the generalized state of the whole system $\mathbf{q}$ which describes the state of the body A. We write the desired differential change as $\mathbf{q}'_A - \mathbf{q}_A(t_i)$. In this case the nail constraint is enforced at a specific time instant t_i.

Expression constraints are generalizations of the state constraints. Any differentiable expression of the generalized state $\mathbf{q}$ can represent a constraint. For example, the animator can equate the speed of two bodies with the constraint $|\mathbf{v}(\mathbf{q}_A(t_i))| - |\mathbf{v}(\mathbf{q}_B(t_i))|$.

Both state and expression constraints can be specified without fixing the time of evaluation t_i. The animator can express a constraint at a particular event—say, the fifth collision in the simulation. Time of collision $t_c(\mathbf{u})$ is not fixed and thus the time of the constraint can "float." For example, we can reduce the angular velocity ω of body A with the constraint $-\omega(\mathbf{q}_A(t_i)) \cdot \omega(\mathbf{q}_A(t_i))$. Subsequent modification of various simulation parameters will change the time at which the collision occurs, but the floating constraint will still be enforced.

5 Manipulation with Discontinuities

When the simulation function is continuous, the interactive manipulation technique described in Section 4 effectively converges to the desired motion. In general, however, the simulation function contains discontinuities that may cause this technique to diverge. In this section we describe a method for improving the convergence for piecewise continuous simulation functions.

The simulation function is discontinuous whenever polygonal (piecewise linear) meshes are involved in collisions. For example, suppose we modify the particle example from Section 4 and replace the smooth, curved obstacle with a piecewise linear polygonal curve (Figure 3). As long as the particle collides with the same edge, the simulation function remains continuous. On the other hand, when the particle collides with a different edge, the surface normal on the

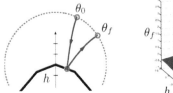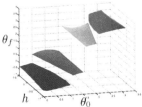

Figure 3: Sample particle bounce motions with polygonal obstacle and the corresponding piecewise smooth simulation function

obstacle changes abruptly and thus the collision impulse applied in Equation 10 is discontinuous. This abrupt change carries over to the subsequent particle motion and corresponds to a discontinuity in the simulation function. We cannot disregard piecewise linear approximations because the interactive rigid body simulators often approximate smooth geometric models with polygonal (piecewise linear) meshes—mostly because meshes facilitate faster and easier collision detection.

In general, the simulation function is piecewise continuous. A connected set of control vectors for which the simulation function is continuous defines a connected component in the control space. We call these connected components *smooth components* because on a smooth component the simulation function is continuously differentiable. For example, a set of control vectors for which the particle collides with the same edge of the obstacle defines a smooth component (Figure 3). In this example, the four smooth components correspond to motions of the particle colliding with each of the four edges. The figure emphasizes two main problems caused by discontinuities: the loss of physical feasibility and degradation of convergence. We describe these problems and our solutions in the remainder of this section.

5.1 Physical Feasibility

As shown in Figure 3, the polygonal approximation of the obstacle restricts the physically feasible exit points for the particle. Note that some values of θ_f are unattainable because the surface normal near the origin is discontinuous: the particle cannot exit at the section of the circle directly above the origin (θ_f near $\pi/2$). This restriction of feasible results becomes especially evident when the animator over-constrains the system with many desired body configurations. Finer polygonal approximations reduce the gaps in the piecewise smooth function, but overly fine approximations increase the collision detection time and reduce interactivity.

Our approach to this problem is twofold. First, we introduce additional control parameters to vary the surface normals on a polygonal mesh and to simulate a collision with a smooth obstacle. If the mesh approximates a smooth surface the desired normal can be computed from a smooth local interpolant or, if available, from the true surface. The normal can then be adjusted dynamically by including the normal deviation within the control vector $\mathbf{u}$. As Figure 4 illustrates varying surface normals extends the range of smooth components to increase the physically feasible regions.

Second, we use curvature-dependent polygonal approximations in our simulations because they keep the facet count low for fast collision detection and simulation, but also provide good first-order approximations to the original surface [11]. For discontinuities due to polygonal approximations of smooth surfaces, the computed differential change $\delta \mathbf{u}$ continues to contain valuable information. Approximating smooth surfaces with polygonal meshes is well studied in computer graphics. In general, good approximations allocate many facets to areas of high surface curvature and fewer facets to near-planar surface regions. For these polygonal meshes, despite the discontinuity in the surface normals, the currently collid-

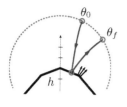
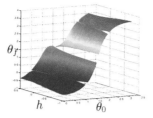

Figure 4: Varying surface normals reduces the gaps to increase physically feasible regions.

ing facet is also a good first-order approximation to the underlying surface. In this case the differential change $\delta\mathbf{u}$ continues to be a good predictor for the differential update because the first-order approximation is sufficiently accurate for linear Equation 6.

5.2 Convergence

The interactive technique of Section 4 converges to the desired motion if there exists a path from the initial to the desired control vector within a single smooth component. With discontinuities, such a path may not exist. The discrete search must guide the control vector between the appropriate components, piecing together a path that crosses discontinuities. Especially in higher dimensions, this is a daunting task for an interactive system. In general, the search must take into account physically feasible regions and jump to smooth components in possibly distant regions of a high-dimensional control space. The most important criterion for selecting smooth components is that they facilitate convergence to the desired motion. In addition, unless instructed otherwise, the components should preserve the "style" of the current motion, as that may be of primary importance. For example, if an animator desires a successful "off-the-backboard" basketball shot, it is undesirable to jump to a smooth component corresponding to a direct, "nothing-but-net" motion. Lastly, the discrete search must complete quickly to maintain interactivity. Our solution relies on two concepts: sampling and interaction.

Sampling In the presence of discontinuities our technique becomes more sensitive to the stepsize ϵ and the direction $\delta\mathbf{u}$ in the differential update (Equation 7). With a large stepsize ϵ, the gradient-descent method may diverge. The approximation errors in $\delta\mathbf{u}$ also adversely affect convergence. To improve convergence, we use sampling to find the best values for these parameters. To find a good stepsize ϵ we use a form of the successive stepsize reduction technique:[4] our discrete search chooses an initial stepsize ϵ and reduces it a few times to select the motion that most closely matches the desired result. Convergence results for gradient methods with non-random errors, such as approximation errors in $\delta\mathbf{u}$, exist [5], but there are no standard techniques for improving the convergence. Recall from Section 5.1 that for discontinuities due to polygonal approximations, the update vector $\delta\mathbf{u}$ is a good heuristic for the new samples. Thus, when the simulation is directed off the edge of the smooth component, our system samples the control space from the normal distribution centered around the suggested update $\delta\mathbf{u}$. Each such sample may produce a point on a new smooth component. We evaluate how well the corresponding motions comply with the constraints and jump to the most promising component. The animator perceives the jump as a minor "pop" in the resulting motion and typically, following the jump, the continuous manipulation continues. The sampling procedure also causes

---

[4]Successive stepsize reduction is not theoretically sound because the improvement at each iteration is not enough to guarantee convergence. Nevertheless, it often works in practice [5].

a momentary lag. While the lag could be reduced with a faster implementation, the visual pop is unavoidable in situations where the underlying motion is discontinuous. If sampling does not produce any reasonable smooth component, the system remains within the current smooth component. The animator is thus blocked from adjusting the motion in a particular way, but can continue to guide the system in a different way.

Interaction Of course, to guarantee convergence we would have to search through the entire control space. Our system does not address this more general problem—the high dimension of the control space makes the search especially difficult. Instead, our technique relies on the animator to guide the system to a motion that satisfies given constraints. For example, a body that initially flies over a wall may have to bounce off the wall and fly in the opposite direction to accomplish the desired constraint. Our technique will not make these transformations automatically. For a large class of motion design tasks, this behavior is desirable and sufficient. The interaction allows the animator to quickly experiment and guide the system toward the desired collision sequence. For example, to transform the motion of a basketball during a successful free throw, the animator may want to bounce the ball off the backboard before it goes through the hoop. In this case, the animator first guides the ball into a backboard collision, and then guides it through the hoop. We emphasize that the single constraint specifying a successful shot does not uniquely determine the desired collision configurations: the ball may bounce off the backboard, off the floor or even off the scoreboard. An automatic system would have to choose the desired motion (or keep track of a possibly exponential number of motions) according to some objective criteria. Instead, our system provides the animator with interactive, direct control over the motion and allows her to guide the system to the appropriate solution.

6 Implementation and Results

Implementation The implementation of our system is decomposed into three parts: (1) a differential control module, (2) a rigid body dynamics simulator, and (3) a user interface for motion display and editing. The control of the system is animator-driven. In response to an edit (a mouse event), the control module recomputes the control parameters $\mathbf{u}$ needed to accomplish the desired motion adjustments. These parameters are then provided to the physical simulator, which recomputes the motion and updates the display.

We use the general-purpose rigid body simulator developed by Baraff [1]. Alternatively, specialized simulators could be used that provide tighter integration with the differential control module. Our manipulation tool controls the simulator at two points: (1) it provides the control vector $\mathbf{u}$ for the simulation and (2) it modifies the impulses at collisions using the modified surface normals and elasticity coefficients. The simulator, in turn, computes the new motion and returns the new collision events. The computed motion is used to update the display and the collisions are used to define a new expression for the equations of motion (Equation 11).

For example, a single-bounce motion has a decomposition corresponding to Equation 11. A change in the control parameters may cause another bounce to occur. In this case, the simulator detects the additional collision. In response, our system automatically updates the equations of motion by adding an additional collision function and two more flight phases to expression in Equation 11.

We use the exponential map parameterization of orientations [15] in the control vector $\mathbf{u}$, finding that it yields better results than the normalized quaternions.

Examples This section demonstrates the use of our system to construct several physically based animations. All of these examples were created by direct manipulation in real-time, and each required between two and ten minutes of editing to achieve the desired animation. For each of these examples, Figure 5 shows the animations before interaction, at an intermediate point, and after the desired motion is obtained. Each image in the figure displays the entire simulation by tracing out the trajectories of one or two points on the moving objects (shown in black). After experimenting with a variety of different interfaces, we have found that this display minimizes clutter yet provides the animator with a sense of the cumulative motion that is sufficient for most interaction tasks. Of course the animator can choose to view the complete motion as a traditional frame sequence at any time during the interaction.

The objective of the first example is to have two eggs collide in the air and land successfully into two buckets on the ground (Figure 5(a)). Creating such a motion by simply adjusting initial positions and velocities of the objects would be extremely difficult due to the complexity of the motion and the constraint that the buckets themselves cannot be moved. In contrast, the desired animation is easily created from scratch using our interactive manipulation technique. First, the starting positions of the eggs are fixed, and the velocities and orientations are assigned arbitrarily. By clicking at a point on its flight path, the animator then interactively drags the first egg's trajectory towards the second egg so that the two objects collide in the air. Running at roughly 20 frames per second, the system computes the required changes in the initial orientation and velocity of *both* eggs to achieve the desired motion updates. Once one egg is in the bucket, the animator applies a nail constraint to fix its ending state and then drags the second egg into the other bucket.

In the second example, the animator's goal is to drop a plank onto two supports to form a table. The problem is made more difficult by requiring the plank to collide with a pyramid object in the air, prior to landing centered on the supports. This example requires the system to solve for the initial plank position, orientation, and velocity (both linear and angular) in order to achieve the desired configuration after the collision. Like the previous example, this is achieved by allowing the animator to directly manipulate the plank's desired position and orientation while the system interactively computes the corresponding physical parameters. This manipulation occurs in two steps: first the animator selects the plank after it collides with the pyramid, and positions it above the supports. Second, the plank's orientation is interactively aligned so that it lands squarely on the supports (Figure 5(b)).

The third example demonstrates the use of normal and elasticity parameters to aid editing operations, and the use of floating time constraints. Suppose the animator wishes to keep a falling mug from tipping over without changing its initial position, orientation, or velocity. This is accomplished by adding new control parameters to control the surface normal and elasticity parameters of the floor at the points where the mug hits the floor. To keep the mug from tipping over, the animator first straightens the mug so that it is upright at the fourth bounce. The system accommodates this change by modifying the floor normal at the third bounce. Note that this change in the normal will typically alter the time at which the fourth bounce occurs, requiring a floating time constraint (Section 4.2).

Due to its angular velocity, however, the mug still tips over (Figure 5(c), center). This is prevented by constraining its angular velocity to be zero after the fourth bounce, resulting in a motion where the mug does not tip over (right). The changes in surface normals are perceived as changes in the surface texture of the floor.

The final example illustrates the ability to edit the style of an animation by modifying a previously constructed motion. In this example, a scissors is thrown into the air and lands on a coatrack (Figure 5(d)). This initial animation is constructed by starting with a motion in which the scissors falls on the floor and then interactively dragging it to the coatrack. By selecting and manipulating the scissors at different points in its trajectory, this motion is trans-

formed into one in which the scissors first bounces off the ground, performs a somersault in the air, and still successfully lands on the coatrack. This example demonstrates how progressively more interesting and complex motions may be created from simpler motions using our interactive editing approach.

7 Conclusion

In this paper, we have described a new interactive technique for manipulating rigid multi-body simulations. Instead of changing the simulation parameters directly, we provide an intuitive interface through which the animator can manipulate the position and velocity of objects directly. Using our system, the animator can rapidly design difficult physical animations that would be difficult to achieve with existing rigid body simulators.

For some design tasks, the interactive paradigm is not the most effective. For example, the animator may be hard pressed to chart out the sequence of collisions that will lead *all* billiard balls into pockets. In general, this is a difficult problem that, in some cases, may not even have a solution. Other motion-construction techniques [7, 27] address these problems and, in some scenarios, construct appropriate motions after extensive computation. We envision a hybrid system that integrates a motion-construction technique with our interactive manipulation tool to improve the effectiveness of the interactive paradigm.

For the Jacobian evaluation (Section 4), our technique assumes that the collision function is analytically differentiable. This is not always the case with the rigid body simulator we use in our prototype implementation. During a resting (i.e. sustained) contact or for multiple simultaneous collisions the applied impulses are solutions to a linear complementarity problem (LCP) [1]. In general, LCP problems do not have closed-form, analytically differentiable solutions. There are many alternative formulations which may facilitate analytic differentiation. Further, the interactive manipulation technique would benefit from a specialized rigid body simulator. For example, the simulator could simultaneously integrate both body states and their derivatives.

Lastly, the interactive manipulation is not possible for all rigid multi-body systems: in some scenarios simulation alone requires considerable computational time. In these cases the animators will have to resort to an off-line motion-construction technique.

Acknowledgements

We would like to thank the members of the CMU graphics lab for helping us shape our ideas. Sebastian Grassia and Paul Heckbert provided valuable suggestions and insights. We especially thank David Baraff for kindly providing the rigid body simulator. We also thank Elly Winner and Ivan Sokić for helping us in the final stages of our paper submission. The support of the Microsoft Corporation is gratefully acknowledged.

References

[1] David Baraff. Fast Contact Force Computation for Nonpenetrating Rigid Bodies. In *Computer Graphics (Proceedings of SIGGRAPH 94)*, Annual Conference Series, pages 23–34. ACM SIGGRAPH, July 1994.

[2] David Baraff and Andrew Witkin. Large Steps in Cloth Simulation. In *Computer Graphics (Proceedings of SIGGRAPH 98)*, Annual Conference Series, pages 43–54. ACM SIGGRAPH, July 1998.

[3] Ronen Barzel and Alan H. Barr. A Modeling System Based On Dynamic Constraints. In *Computer Graphics (Proceedings of SIGGRAPH 87)*, Annual Conference Series, pages 179–188. ACM SIGGRAPH, August 1988.

[4] Ronen Barzel, John F. Hughes, and Daniel N. Wood. Plausible Motion Simulation for Computer Graphics Animation. In *Computer Animation and Simulation '96*, Proceedings of the Eurographics Workshop, pages 184–197, Poitiers, France, September 1996.

[5] Dimitri P. Bertsekas. *Nonlinear Programming*. Athena Scientific, Belmont, Massachusetts, 1995.

[6] Lynne Shapiro Brotman and Arun N. Netravali. Motion Interpolation by Optimal Control. In *Computer Graphics (Proceedings of SIGGRAPH 88)*, volume 26 of *Annual Conference Series*, pages 309–315. ACM SIGGRAPH, August 1988.

[7] Stephen Chenney and D. A. Forsyth. Sampling Plausible Solutions to Multi-body Constraint Problems. In *Computer Graphics (Proceedings of SIGGRAPH 2000)*, Annual Conference Series. ACM SIGGRAPH, July 2000.

[8] Michael F. Cohen. Interactive Spacetime Control for Animation. In *Computer Graphics (Proceedings of SIGGRAPH 92)*, Annual Conference Series, pages 293–302. ACM SIGGRAPH, July 1992.

[9] Bruce Donald, Patrick Xavier, John Canny, and John Reif. Kinodynamic Motion Planning. *Journal of the ACM*, 40(5):1048–1066, November 1993.

[10] Nick Foster and Dimitri Metaxas. Realistic Animation of Liquids. *Graphical Models and Image Processing*, 5(58):471–483, 1996.

[11] Michael Garland and Paul S. Heckbert. Surface Simplification Using Quadric Error Metrics. In *Computer Graphics (Proceedings of SIGGRAPH 97)*, Annual Conference Series, pages 209–216. ACM SIGGRAPH, August 1997.

[12] Philip E Gill, Walter Murray, and Margaret H. Wright. *Practical Optimization*. Academic Press, London, 1989.

[13] Michael Gleicher and Andrew Witkin. Differential Manipulation. In *Graphics Interface*, pages 61–67, June 1991.

[14] Michael Gleicher and Andrew Witkin. Through-the-Lens Camera Control. In *Computer Graphics (Proceedings of SIGGRAPH 92)*, Annual Conference Series, pages 331–340. ACM SIGGRAPH, July 1992.

[15] F. Sebastian Grassia. Practical Parameterization of Rotation Using the Exponential Map. *Journal of Graphics Tools*, 3(3):29–48, 1998.

[16] Radek Grzeszczuk, Demetri Terzopoulos, and Geoffrey Hinton. NeuroAnimator: Fast Neural Network Emulation and Control of Physics-Based Models. In *Computer Graphics (Proceedings of SIGGRAPH 98)*, Annual Conference Series, pages 9–20. ACM SIGGRAPH, July 1998.

[17] Mikako Harada, Andrew Witkin, and David Baraff. Interactive Physically-Based Manipulation of Discrete/Continuous Models. In *Computer Graphics (Proceedings of SIGGRAPH 95)*, Annual Conference Series, pages 199–208. ACM SIGGRAPH, August 1995.

[18] Wilfred Kaplan. *Advanced Calculus*. Addison-Wesley Publishing Company, Reading, Massachusetts, 1984.

[19] Zicheng Liu, Steven J. Gortler, and Michael F. Cohen. Hierarchical Spacetime Control. In *Computer Graphics (Proceedings of SIGGRAPH 94)*, Annual Conference Series, pages 35–42. ACM SIGGRAPH, July 1994.

[20] Matthew Moore and Jane Wilhelms. Collision Detection and Response for Computer Animation. In *Computer Graphics (Proceedings of SIGGRAPH 88)*, Annual Conference Series, pages 289–298. ACM SIGGRAPH, August 1988.

[21] J. Thomas Ngo and Joe Marks. Spacetime Constraints Revisited. In *Computer Graphics (Proceedings of SIGGRAPH 93)*, Annual Conference Series, pages 343–350. ACM SIGGRAPH, August 1993.

[22] James F. O'Brien and Jessica K. Hodgins. Graphical Modeling and Animation of Brittle Fracture. In *Computer Graphics (Proceedings of SIGGRAPH 99)*, Annual Conference Series, pages 111–120. ACM SIGGRAPH, August 1999.

[23] Zoran Popović and Andrew Witkin. Physically Based Motion Transformation. In *Computer Graphics (Proceedings of SIGGRAPH 99)*, Annual Conference Series, pages 11–20. ACM SIGGRAPH, August 1999.

[24] Jos Stam. Stable Fluids. In *Computer Graphics (Proceedings of SIGGRAPH 99)*, Annual Conference Series, pages 121–128. ACM SIGGRAPH, August 1999.

[25] Robert F. Stengel. *Optimal Control and Estimation*. Dover Books on Advanced Mathematics, New York, 1994.

[26] Keith R. Symon. *Mechanics, Third Edition*. Addison-Wesley Publishing Company, Reading, Massachussetts, 1971.

[27] Diane Tang, J. Thomas Ngo, and Joe Marks. N-Body Spacetime Constraints. *Journal of Visualization and Computer Animation*, 6:143–154, 1995.

[28] Andrew Witkin, Michael Gleicher, and William Welch. Interactive Dynamics. In *Proceedings of the 1990 symposium on Interactive 3D graphics*, pages 11–21, March 1990.

[29] Andrew Witkin and Michael Kass. Spacetime Constraints. In *Computer Graphics (Proceedings of SIGGRAPH 88)*, Annual Conference Series, pages 159–168. ACM SIGGRAPH, August 1988.

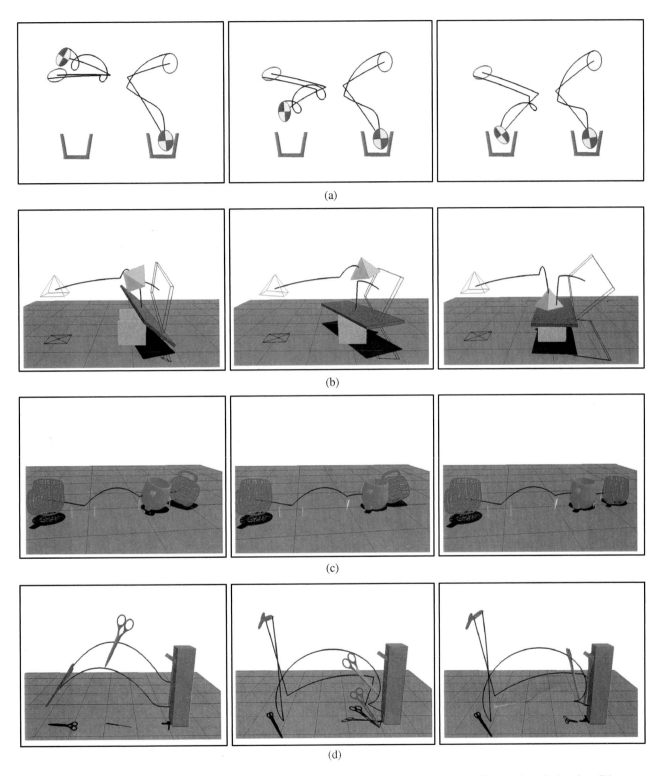

Figure 5: Physical motions (left) are interactively edited to satisfy desired constraints (right). Intermediate motions during the editing process are shown at center. (a) An egg is dragged into a bucket after collision with a second egg. The second egg is required to fall into a second bucket with a nail constraint. (b) A table top is made to land on its legs after collision with a pyramid. (c) A tumbling mug is kept from tipping over by editing its orientation and angular velocity at the fourth collision with the ground. (d) A bounce and a flip is added to an animation where a scissors lands on a coatrack. All interaction occurs in real time.

Sampling Plausible Solutions to Multi-body Constraint Problems

Stephen Chenney   D. A. Forsyth*

University of California at Berkeley

Abstract

Traditional collision intensive multi-body simulations are difficult to control due to extreme sensitivity to initial conditions or model parameters. Furthermore, there may be multiple ways to achieve any one goal, and it may be difficult to codify a user's preferences before they have seen the available solutions. In this paper we extend simulation models to include plausible sources of uncertainty, and then use a Markov chain Monte Carlo algorithm to sample multiple animations that satisfy constraints. A user can choose the animation they prefer, or applications can take direct advantage of the multiple solutions. Our technique is applicable when a probability can be attached to each animation, with "good" animations having high probability, and for such cases we provide a definition of physical plausibility for animations. We demonstrate our approach with examples of multi-body rigid-body simulations that satisfy constraints of various kinds, for each case presenting animations that are true to a physical model, are significantly different from each other, and yet still satisfy the constraints.

CR Descriptors: I.3.7 [**Computer Graphics**]: Three-Dimensional Graphics and Realism - *Animation*; I.3.5 [**Computer Graphics**]: Computational Geometry and Object Modeling - *Physically based modeling*; I.6.5 [**Simulation and Modeling**]: Model Development - *Modeling methodologies* G.3 [**Probability and Statistics**]: Probabilistic algorithms;

Keywords: plausible motion, Markov chain Monte Carlo, motion synthesis, spacetime constraints

1   INTRODUCTION

Collision intensive multi-body simulations are difficult to constrain because they exhibit extreme sensitivity to initial conditions or other simulation parameters. Adding uncertainty to a model helps when looking for animations that satisfy constraints [3], because it adds physically motivated degrees of freedom in useful places. For example, we can control tumbling dice by placing random bumps in specific places on the table, rather than by adjusting the initial conditions of the throw. The bumps are more effective because a small change to a bump part-way through the animation has

a limited effect on where the dice land, but a small change in the initial conditions generally has an unpredictable effect. It is difficult to design efficient control algorithms for the latter case.

As discussed by Barzel, Hughes and Wood [3], adding randomness to a simulation gives additional benefits:

- The real world contains fine scale variation that traditional simulation models generally ignore. We can use randomness to model this variation by, for instance, replacing a perfectly flat surface with one speckled with random bumps (the same random bumps used for control above). Animations generated with the new model can more accurately reflect the behavior of the world. In training environments, this results in the subject developing skills more compatible with the real world: a driver trained on simulations of bumpy roads will be better prepared for real world road surfaces.

- Visually, procedural animations can be more believable when uncertainty is added. Without uncertainty, a perfectly round ball dropped vertically onto a perfectly flat table moves strangely, a situation that may be improved by slightly perturbing the collisions to make the ball deviate from the vertical.

In a world with uncertainty, we generally expect a constrained problem to have multiple solutions. It is difficult to know beforehand what solutions are available, which compounds any difficulties a user may have in codifying their preferences. Hence, it is perverse to use a solution strategy that seeks a single answer, rather, we prefer a technique that produces many solutions that reflect the range of possible outcomes. While for feature animation a user is expected to choose the one animation they prefer, other applications benefit directly from multiple solutions:

- Computer game designers can use different animations each time a game is played, making it less predictable and potentially more entertaining.

- Training environments can present trainees with multiple physically consistent scenarios that reflect the physics and variety of the real world.

We generate multiple animations that satisfy constraints by applying a Markov chain Monte Carlo (MCMC) algorithm to sample from a randomized model. A user supplies the model of the world, including the sources of uncertainty and the simulator that will generate an animation in the world. The user also supplies a function that gives higher values for "good" animations — those that are likely in the world and satisfy the constraints. Finally, a user must provide a means of proposing a new animation given an existing one. The algorithm we describe in this paper generates an arbitrarily long sequence of animations in which "good" animations are likely to appear.

In this paper, along with the algorithm, we describe the sorts of models we use and how we sample from them, discussing examples from the domain of collision intensive rigid-body simulation. No previous algorithm has been shown for

*email: {schenney,daf}@cs.berkeley.edu

the range and complexity of the multi-body simulations we present.

2 RELATED WORK

The idea of *plausible motion simulation*, including the exploitation of randomness to satisfy constraints, was introduced by Barzel, Hughes and Wood [3]. They show solutions to constrained problems where, for instance, a billiard ball is controlled by randomly varying the collision normal each time it hits a rail. We extend their work by introducing the idea of sampling (instead of searching), giving a precise definition of plausibility, and by demonstrating MCMC's effectiveness on a wide range of difficult examples.

Motion synthesis algorithms aim to achieve a goal by finding an optimal set of control parameters and (sometimes) initial conditions. The goals described in the literature include finding good locomotion parameters [1, 8, 14, 16, 23, 26] and finding trajectories that satisfy constraints [2, 5, 9, 13, 15, 20, 32]. Some techniques [2, 5, 9, 13, 15, 20, 32] exploit explicit gradient information, but fail if the problem is too large (Popović discusses ways to reduce the problem size [25]) or the constraints are highly sensitive to, or discontinuous in, the control parameters. Randomized algorithms, such as simulated annealing [14, 16] (not a panacea [10, 11]), stochastic hill climbing [8], or evolutionary computing [1, 23, 26, 29], do not require gradients and may be suitable for collision intensive systems — Tang, Ngo and Marks [29] describe an example. Most of these methods return a single "best" animation, and hence may ignore other equally good, or even preferable solutions. The evolutionary computing solutions can exhibit variations within a population, which Auslander et. al. [1] refer to as different styles, but the number of examples is limited by the population size.

Multi-body constraint problems are good candidates for a *Design Galleries* [21] interface, in which a user browses through sample solutions to locate the one they prefer. Our work addresses the sampling aspect of a Design Galleries interface for multi-body constrained animations, but we do not consider other aspects of the interface.

3 ANIMATION DISTRIBUTIONS

The MCMC algorithm distinguishes itself from motion synthesis approaches by generating multiple, different, "good" animations that satisfy a set of constraints, but no "best" animation. To generate multiple plausible constrained animations, we must provide a model of the world defining:

- The objects in the world and their properties, including the sources of uncertainty.
- The simulator for generating animations in the world.
- The constraints to be satisfied by the animations.

For example, in a 2D animation of a ball bouncing on the table, we might have uncertainty in the normal vectors at the collision points, a constraint on the resting place of the ball, and a simulator that determines what happens when a 2D ball bounces on a table with arbitrary surface normals. We will use this example, from [3], throughout the next two sections.

A simulator used with our approach need not be physically accurate, or even physically based. Our 2D ball simulator is obviously non-physical, and the simulator we use in other examples has some problems with complex frictional behavior (section 5.2.3). In any case, we assume that if the simulator is given a plausible world as input it will produce a plausible

animation, according to some definition of plausibility (see section 3.3).

3.1 Incorporating Uncertainty

We define a function, $p_w(A)$, representing the probability of any possible animation A that might arise in the world model. Intuitively, $p_w(A)$ should be large for animations that are likely in the world, and low for unlikely animations. For the 2D ball example, $p_{w,ball}(A)$ should be high if all the normal vectors used to generate the animation were close to vertical, and low if most of them were far from vertical. Let us further insist that $p_w(A)$ be non-negative and have finite integral over the domain implied by the random variables in the model, so that we can view $p_w(A)$ as an unnormalized probability density function defined on the space of animations.

Expanding on the 2D ball example, let us describe the direction of the normal vector for each collision i as an independent random variable, θ_i, distributed according to the (bell-shaped) Gaussian distribution with standard deviation of, say, 10.0 degrees. In that case we get:

$$p_{w,ball}(A) \propto \prod_i e^{-\frac{1}{2}\left(\frac{\theta_i}{10.0}\right)^2}$$

which is the product of density functions for each collision normal. Note that we are ignoring normalization constants, an omission we justify in section 4. Also, we could in principle measure a real table to infer the true distribution of surface normals, and use that instead.

3.2 Constraints

If we restrict our attention to animations that satisfy constraints, we are concerned with the distribution function $p_w(A|C)$, which is the conditional distribution of A given that it satisfies the constraints C. For the 2D ball example, if we want the ball to land in a particular place, we could generate samples from $p_{w,ball}(A|C)$ using an inverse approach: join the ball's start point to its end point using a sequence of parabolic hops and then infer which normal vectors were required to generate such a trajectory. However, using this approach we cannot directly ensure that the animation we generate is likely in the world, because it is difficult to know which hops to use to get a set of likely normal vectors.

Unfortunately, it is frequently impractical to sample directly from $p_w(A|C)$, because there is no way to find, without considerable effort, any reasonable animation in which the constraints are satisfied. For example, in multi-body simulations a forward simulation approach doesn't work because no published algorithm can directly specify a set of control parameters leading to satisfaction of multi-body constraints, without doing some form of iterative, expensive search. The inverse approach also looks intractable: it is not clear how to set trajectories for all the participants such that, for instance, objects do not pass through each other.

In such cases (like all the examples in this paper), we expand $p_w(A)$ to include a term for the constraints, resulting in a function $p(A)$. The new intuition is that $p(A)$ will be large for animations that are likely in the world *and* satisfy the constraints, and small for animations that are either implausible in the world or don't satisfy the constraints. We will refer to $p(A)$ as the *probability* of an animation. Note that now even animations that don't satisfy the constraints have non-zero probability, so if we sample from $p(A)$ we may get an animation that doesn't satisfy the constraints, which we must discard.

For the examples in this paper, we define:

$$p(A) \propto p_w(A)p_c(A)$$

where $p_c(A)$ depends only on how well the animation satisfies the constraints. If we want our 2D ball to land at a point whose distance, d, from the origin is small, we can define

$$p_{c,ball}(A) \propto e^{-\frac{1}{2}\left(\frac{d}{\sigma_d}\right)^2}$$

which is the Gaussian density function with standard deviation σ_d, which we discuss in section 5.1. This function gives higher values for distances near zero, and lower values as distances increase. Hence, for the 2D ball example:

$$p_{ball}(A) \propto e^{-\frac{1}{2}\left(\frac{d}{\sigma_d}\right)^2} \prod_i e^{-\frac{1}{2}\left(\frac{\theta_i}{10.0}\right)^2}$$

This paper describes a technique for generating animations such that those with high probability will appear more frequently than those with lower probability, but even some low probability events will occur — as in the real world, unlikely things sometimes happen. In other words, we will sample according to the distribution defined by $p(A)$.

3.3 What does "Plausible" mean?

The restrictions on $p(A)$ are quite weak, so we can describe many types of uncertainty and a wide variety of constraints. By phrasing the problem as one involving probabilities, we can leverage a wide range of mathematical tools for talking about plausible motion, and make strong statements about the properties of the animations we generate (see section 4). We can also outline what it means to be physically plausible:

> A model, including its simulator, is plausible if the important statistics gathered from samples distributed according to $p(A)$ are sufficiently close to the real world statistics we care about.

This is a very general definition of plausibility, because we say nothing about which statistics we might care about, or what it means to be sufficiently close. For example, to validate a pool table model we could run simulations of virtual balls on a table, and analyze video of real balls on a real table, then compare statistics such as how long a ball rolls before coming to rest. For entertainment applications, we would care less about the quality of the match than if we were trying to build a training simulator for budding young pool sharks.

Our measure extends the traditional graphics idea of plausibility — "if it looks right it is right" — by allowing for definitions of statistical similarity other than a user's ability to detect a fake. However, for many applications, particularly involving motion, a viewer's ability to distinguish real from artificial remains the primary concern [17].

4 MCMC FOR ANIMATIONS

We use the Markov chain Monte Carlo (MCMC) method [12, 19] to sample animations from the distribution defined by $p(A)$. MCMC has several advantages for this task:

- MCMC generates a sequence, or *chain*, of samples, $A_0, A_1, A_2, \ldots$, that are distributed according to a given distribution, in this case $p(A)$.
- Apart from the initial sample, each sample is derived from the previous sample, which allows the algorithm to find and move among animations that satisfy constraints.

- If available, domain specific information can be incorporated into the algorithm, making it more efficient for special cases. On the other hand, the algorithm does not rely on any specific features of a model or simulator, allowing its application in a variety of situations.

Our MCMC algorithm for generating animations begins with an initial animation then repeatedly proposes changes, which may be accepted or rejected. Explicitly:

```
1     initialize(A_0)
2     simulate(A_0)
3     repeat
4         propose(A_c, A_i)
5         simulate(A_c)
6         u ← random(0, 1)
7         if u < min (1, p(A_c)q(A_i|A_c)/p(A_i)q(A_c|A_i))
8             A_{i+1} ← A_c
9         else
10            A_{i+1} ← A_i
```

Line 1 gives initial values to all the random variables in the world model. On line 4, a new animation, A_c, is proposed by making a random change to the previous animation, A_i. The details of this change are application specific. For example, in the 2D ball model of section 3 it might involve, for each normal, choosing to change it with probability one half and, if it is to be changed, adding a random offset uniformly distributed on $(-5, 5)$ degrees (for reasons discussed in section 5.1). The probability of making changes is defined by the *transition probability*, $q(X|Y)$, which is the probability of proposing animation X if the current animation is Y. For the 2D ball, the transition probability is:

$$q_{ball}(X|Y) \propto \left(\frac{1}{2}\right)^n \cdot \left(\frac{1}{5-(-5)}\right)^k$$

where n is the total number of collisions (assumed fixed) and k is the number of collisions that were changed. The first factor is the probability of choosing the particular set of normals to change, and the second factor codes the probability of choosing a particular offset for each normal that is changed.

The transition probabilities, along with the probabilities of the animations, are used in computing the *acceptance probability*, which is the probability of accepting the proposed candidate (line 7):

$$P_{accept} = \min\left(1, \frac{p(A_c)q(A_i|A_c)}{p(A_i)q(A_c|A_i)}\right)$$

Often, as in the 2D ball example, the transition probabilities are symmetric — $q(X|Y) = q(Y|X)$ — and will cancel. Note also that only the ratios of probabilities appear, so we can use functions that are only proportional to true probability density functions (section 3.1).

The proposal mechanism is one of the key factors in how well the algorithm will perform in a particular application. In practice, proposals are designed through intuitive reasoning and experimentation, using past experience as a guide. In section 5 we describe the motivation for our proposal mechanisms.

The MCMC algorithm guarantees that the samples in the chain will be distributed according to $p(A)$, as the number of samples approaches infinity and provided certain technical conditions are met [12]. Hence we can be certain that the samples our algorithm generates truly reflect the underlying model, and if this model is plausible (section 3.3), the collection of samples will be plausible. It is also the case that the samples in the chain will never satisfy the constraints if the underlying model says they cannot be satisfied. For instance, if a bowling simulator cannot capture complex frictional effects, animations that bowl the seven-ten split can never be found (see section 5.2.3).

MCMC has been used in graphics to generate fractal terrain that satisfies point constraints [28, 31]. The samples generated by an MCMC algorithm may also be used to estimate expectations, as in Veach's Metropolis algorithm for computing global illumination solutions [30]. In this paper we are not concerned with expectations, so we can use short chains, just long enough to satisfy a user with several different animations

5 EXAMPLES

We are interested in four things when designing an MCMC algorithm for generating animations:

- Is the motion plausible? We assume that the simulator produces plausible motion, so we are left to ensure that the distributions we use for the model are reasonable.

- How long does it take to find a sample that satisfies the constraints?

- How rapidly does the chain move among significantly different samples, or *mix*? Chains that mix faster are desirable because they produce many different animations quickly.

- How many of the samples satisfy the constraints well enough to be useful?

The following examples discuss issues in building models, defining constraints and selecting proposal strategies, all of which influence the behavior of the algorithm.

5.1 A 2D Ball

In the 2D ball example of section 3 a ball bounces on a table, starting in a fixed location and undergoing, for simplicity, a fixed number of collisions. For each collision we specify a random normal vector. The aim is to sample these normal vectors such that the ball comes to rest close to a particular location. As a specific case, we will drop the ball from above the origin at a height of $4.5D$, where D is the diameter of the ball, use five collisions, and specify that it come to rest near $x = D$ on the sixth collision.

The simulation model is: the ball moves ballistically between each collision, when the velocity of the ball is reflected about the corresponding normal vector and the normal component of velocity is scaled by $\frac{1}{\sqrt{2}}$. This model is not physically plausible (for instance, we are ignoring rotation effects), but for this example we value simplicity.

5.1.1 Uncertainty and Constraints

The probability of an animation is described in section 3.1, but probabilities (the values of density functions) can be very large numbers, so in practice we work with their logarithm. In this case, with x the horizontal position of the sixth collision:

$$\log(p(A)) = -\frac{1}{2}\left(\frac{x-D}{\sigma_d}\right)^2 - \frac{1}{2}\sum_{1 \le i \le 5}\left(\frac{\theta_i}{10.0}\right)^2 + C$$

for some constant C, which will cancel out when computing the acceptance probability.

The value of the constraint standard deviation, σ_d, has a major effect on the samples generated by the chain. Say we choose a small value for σ_d, corresponding to a very tight constraint because only values of x very close to D give high values for $p(A)$ and all other landing points have very low probability. From the initial animation, the chain will move to some high probability animation close to the constraint. But, once there, almost no new proposals are accepted (most candidates will be far from the constraint and have very low probability) and the user sees few different animations — an undesirable situation.

Alternatively, say we choose a large value for the standard deviation, corresponding to a weak constraint. Then $p(A)$ is relatively high for a wide range of landing positions. The result is undesirable: the chain will contain many high probability animations that are far from the constraints.

Hence we must choose a value for σ_d that is high enough to promote different samples but low enough to enforce the constraint. In this example we use a value of $0.1D$, where D is the diameter of the ball, which, as figure 2 shows, leads to the generation of very different samples that generally are close to the constraint. In this case, the algorithm is not very sensitive to the exact value for σ_d (anything within a factor of five works fine) and it is possible to experimentally evaluate a few values on short chains and choose the best, which in this case took only a few minutes.

In other applications there is no guarantee that we can achieve both good constraints and good mixing. In such cases the algorithm must run for many iterations to generate different samples, which may take prohibitively long. The tumbling dice example of section 5.4 is a borderline example in which we can satisfy constraints but mixing is poor. In such cases it is possible to run multiple chains in parallel.

5.1.2 Proposals

The proposal mechanism, which specifies normal vectors for a candidate animation, A_c, given those for the current animation, A_i, provides a means of moving around the space of possible normal vectors:

```
for j = 1 to 5
    A_c.normal[j] ← A_i.normal[j]
    if random(0, 1) < 0.5
        A_c.normal[j] ← A_c.normal[j] + random(−5, 5)
```

This proposal changes some of the normals by an amount between minus one half and half their standard deviation of 10.0 degrees. For good mixing it is important to allow more than one normal to be changed at once, because the effect of each change on the landing position (and hence the constraint) can then cancel. The alternative, changing only one normal, makes it very difficult to change the first collision normal, because any but the smallest change will move the ball far from the desired landing position, and hence be rejected. The size of the offset we add is chosen to allow both small changes and relatively large changes, but not so large as to shift the normals too far from their mean in one step, which would reduce their probabilities and result in rejection of the candidate animation.

5.1.3 An Example Chain

We ran the MCMC algorithm and generated a chain containing one thousand samples (many of these are repeats, arising when a candidate is rejected). Figure 2 plots the horizontal resting position of each sample. The first sample was initialized with randomly chosen normals, and came to rest a long way from the constraint. But within twenty iterations the chain moved toward a good location. The bumpiness of

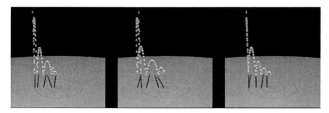

Figure 1: *Three sample paths from the 2D ball example, plotting the trajectory of the center of the ball (although the plot is 3D, the ball moves only in 2D). The green target is centered on the constraint. Each red arrow is located at a collision point and indicates the direction of the normal vector used at that point. Note that in each example one of the earlier normals pushes the ball toward the constraint, and later normals refine the final position. One ball bounces slightly away from the constraint before moving toward it, which is not implausible.*

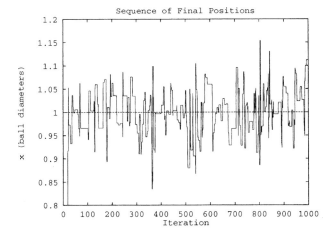

Figure 2: *The resting position of the first one thousand samples in a chain for the 2D ball example. The roughness of this graph indicates good mixing, and most samples are close to the constraint (the majority within $0.1D$). The position of the first few samples are far from the constraint (off the graph), but the chain moves to samples within twenty iterations.*

the graph indicates good mixing, because flat spots would indicate many repetitions of one sample as candidates were rejected. The majority of animations have the ball coming to rest within $0.1D$ of the desired position, indicating that σ_d is sufficiently small to enforce the constraint.

Three (randomly chosen) samples from the chain are shown in figure 1. They do not differ greatly from what one would expect: the ball tends to take an early bounce toward the constraint and keep moving in that direction, with later collisions adjusting it's final position.

5.2 Bowling

In this scenario the aim is to animate any particular ten-pin bowling shot (a goal suggested by Tang, Ngo and Marks [29]). The physical model is implemented by an impulse-based rigid-body simulator [6]. We model the bowling ball, the lane with simplified gutters and side walls, and the pins. All the models are roughly based on the rules of bowling, including variations allowed by those rules (details may be found in the CDROM version of this paper):

- The ball is simulated as a sphere, with variable radius, density, initial position, initial velocity and initial angular velocity.
- The lane is fixed with regulation length and width, and includes rectangular gutters and side walls starting in line with the front pin.
- Each pin, of fixed shape and mass, has its initial position on the lane perturbed by a small random amount.

The coefficients of friction and restitution between all the components are fixed. The probability $p_w(A)$ is proportional to the product of the distribution functions for each of the random variables in the model.

5.2.1 Constraints

The simulation begins with a subset of pins specified by the user, so we can specify the initial conditions for bowling spares. The user also sets the constraint by stating which pins should be knocked down and which should remain standing. We are unable to propose candidates for the MCMC algorithm that are certain to satisfy the constraints (section 3.2), so we assign non-zero probability to every possible outcome, but assign higher probability to those outcomes that are closer to the target, and the highest probability to outcomes matching the target. This is achieved with the Gibbs distribution function:

$$p_c(A) \propto \lambda^{k+m}$$

for some constant $\lambda > 1$ with k the number of pins that end up correctly standing or knocked down, and m the number of standing pins that have not moved far beyond their initial position. Animations that do not meet the goals will sometimes appear in the chain (they have non-zero probability), but these would not be shown to a user. The samples that remain are correctly distributed according to the conditional probability $p(A|C)$, the distribution of animations in which the constraints are fully satisfied. The constraint involves a term derived from the pins' final position because some simulations result in the pins being pushed but not knocked down — behavior we wish to discourage.

The value of λ affects the proportion of animations in the chain that must be discarded for not satisfying the constraints. High values for λ give animations satisfying the constraints much higher probability, making them more likely to appear in the chain. But the chain mixes better if some "bad" animations appear. Say only perfect animations appear, then getting to a significantly different animation requires making a big change that also happens to get all the pins correct, which is unlikely. If some pins are not correct, a big change only has to get the same number of pins correct, and they can be different pins. A low value for λ makes it easier to accept an animation with some incorrect pins, make big changes, and then move toward a different, fully correct state.

For this example, we used $\lambda = e^{2.5}$, which gives a wide variety of animations that satisfy the constraints. Animations that improve the constraints are favored enough to ensure that good animations come up often, but not so much as to inhibit mixing.

Our use of the Gibbs distribution was motivated by other applications of the MCMC algorithm, such as counting the number of perfect matchings in a graph. It is known [18] that there is an optimal λ that balances the concerns outlined above, but that the algorithm is relatively insensitive to its exact value. Experience suggests that many applications may exhibit similar behavior [27]: there exists a range of

Strike –

Six-seven Split $\longrightarrow$

Spare $\longrightarrow$

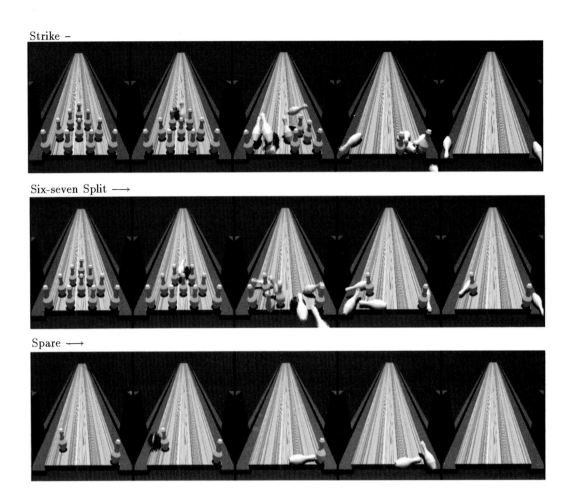

Figure 3: *Frames from three bowling examples. The initial conditions for the ball and the pin locations are random variables. Given an initial and final pin configuration, the MCMC algorithm samples particular values for the random variables that lead to the desired shot. In this case, we demanded a strike, a six-seven split and the corresponding spare.*

values for λ that give the chain good properties, and one such value may be found through experiment. Our results are consistent with this (also see section 5.3).

5.2.2 Proposals

Our proposal mechanism for bowling randomly chooses to do one of several things:

- Sample new values for all the random variables.
- Change the radius, density or initial conditions of the ball.
- Change the initial position of some pins.

The details are given in the CDROM version of this paper.

The first proposal strategy, which changes every random variable in the simulation, serves to make very large changes in the simulation. These are desirable as a means of escaping low probability regions, which we discuss in more detail in the next example (section 5.3). The other transitions are based on ideas similar to those in section 5.1: we must move around among possible values for the random variables, and we wish to do so with both large and small steps, but not so large as to make the new value highly unlikely under the model.

5.2.3 Sample Animations

We tested this model with three sets of constraints:

- Bowl a strike.

- Bowl a ball that leaves a six-seven split.
- Bowl the spare that knocks down the six-seven split.

Frames from example animations appear in figure 3. The strike example is the easiest, because strikes are quite likely given our simulator. Bowling the six-seven spare is not difficult either, because the various solutions probably form a connected set in state space, so once a single solution is found, the others can be explored efficiently. Bowling the ball that leaves a six-seven split is the hardest example, intuitively because it is hard to knock down the pins behind the six pin while leaving it in place.

We also attempted to bowl the seven-ten split (figure 4). This shot depends on the precise frictional properties of the ball and lane. Our simulator's friction model could not capture the required effect (we are not aware of any that can), so we could not make the shot. This demonstrates that the MCMC algorithm will only generate samples that are plausible according to our model (section 4). Our simulation model says that balls never take really big hooks, so we never see animations involving big hooks, regardless of the constraints.

5.3 Balls that Spell

In these experiments we drop a stream of balls into a box partitioned into bins so that, when everything has come to rest, the balls form letters or symbols (figure 5). We don't care which ball ends up in which designated bin. We use

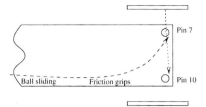

Figure 4: *The seven-ten split, in which the aim is to knock down both the seven and ten pins in one shot. The technique used by bowlers relies on the fact that a bowling ball will slide while spinning about an inclined axis, then, at some point, friction will cause the ball to grip, converting the angular momentum of the spin into linear momentum across the lane (dashed line). The seven pin must be struck behind its center of mass, so that it initially moves away from the ten pin (dotted line), bounces off the wall and moves back across the lane to hit the ten pin. Our simulator cannot model friction well enough to simulate this shot (we are not aware of any that can).*

Figure 5: *Two examples of the spelling balls model, in this case spelling "HI" in a seven by five grid. The shape of the boxes is allowed to vary slightly, as are the initial conditions of each ball. Our algorithm chooses box shapes and ball initial conditions that lead to the formation of a specific word.*

an impulse-based rigid-body simulator, as in the bowling example.

The uncertainty in this world arises from the shape of the partitions and the location from which each ball is dropped. The top surface of the partitions depends on a set of *partition vertices*, each of which is randomly perturbed about a default position. Each ball is dropped from a random location.

The constraint we impose is that, when all the balls have come to rest, each ball is in a designated bin. We fix the maximum number of balls, so if each ball falls into a designated bin there can be no ball in an undesignated bin. We face a situation in which we cannot propose animations that are certain to completely satisfy the constraints, so, as for the bowling example, we use the Gibbs distribution for the constraint probability $p_c(A) \propto \lambda^k$, where k is the number of balls in designated bins at the end of the animation.

To facilitate mixing we allow the number of balls in the simulation to vary between zero and the minimum number required to form the word, by flipping each ball between active and inactive states: inactive balls do not take part in the simulation. If all the designated bins are filled, removing a ball frees up a bin for another ball to move into, making a significant change to the animation. Removing the ball entirely, rather than just having it go into an undesignated bin, reduces the amount of interaction between the balls, possibly making it easier to make acceptable proposals. It also speeds the simulation when balls that aren't contributing anything are removed. Our initial experiments used a fixed number of balls, and the chain failed to mix well.

The probability of an animation depends on how many balls are participating, the initial locations of the balls and the offsets of each partition vertex.

5.3.1 Proposals

The proposal algorithm we use performs one of five actions:

- The *change-all* strategy: change all the partition vertices and change all the balls.
- Change a subset of partition vertices.
- Change an active ball.
- Activate some balls (possibly none).
- Deactivate some balls (possibly none).

The change-all strategy appears as a means of escaping from low probability regions (figure 7). When an animation is

found that satisfies the constraints, subsequent animations tend to also satisfy the constraints, but their probabilities degrade. This occurs because the reduction in probability for a partition vertex change may be quite small, and such proposals are likely to be accepted. The downward trend can continue, moving the chain into a region of low probability. Then, a change-all proposal can reset all the partition vertices to much higher probability values, and even though the constraints are no longer satisfied, the net change in probability will be positive and the proposal will be accepted. This *change-all effect* is good for mixing, because the next fully correct sample will generally be very different from the last.

The second and third proposals are designed to move around the state space by modifying balls or partitions, similar to proposals in previous examples. The proposals to activate or deactivate some balls let us change the number of balls in the simulation. The proposal strategy we use makes the probability of adding or deleting any given ball independent of the maximum number of balls. We first tried a proposal that chose a single ball and flipped its status, but if the maximum number of balls in the scenario is large, the probability of removing a ball goes up as more balls are activated while the probability of adding a ball goes down, making it difficult to get all the balls into the simulation.

The considerations in choosing a value for λ in this example are identical to those in the bowling example (a balance between good animations and good mixing), with an additional requirement due to the change-all effect: the constraint probability should be balanced against the model probability (in this case the probabilities of the partition vertices). If the constraint probability is too high, almost no change in partition vertices can overcome a well satisfied constraint. Good balance is achieved when a much better set of model values can overcome a constraint that is satisfied but uses poor model parameters.

As a specific example, we chose a bin designation that spells "HI" on a seven by five grid (figure 5). We used $\lambda = e^5$ for this word. A plot of k, the number of designated bins that are filled, for each iteration of an example chain is shown in figure 6. The important feature of this graph is that the chain tends to rapidly reach correct spellings, stays there for a short period, then drops back to incomplete spellings. The

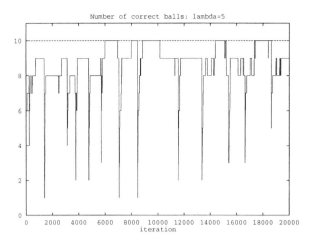

Figure 6: *The number of correctly positioned balls for each of twenty thousand iterations of the "HI" model, with* $\lambda = e^5$. *The maximum number of correct balls is ten. The chain finds its first good animation after around six thousand iterations (we have seen chains that find good animations within one thousand samples). This graph indicates good mixing because the chain spends only a short period of time near similar solutions, then makes significant changes before rapidly moving to a new good solution.*

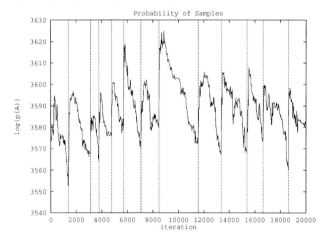

Figure 7: *The value of* $\log(p(A))$ *at each iteration of the chain in figure 6. The graph is quite bumpy, indicating good mixing. The dashed vertical lines correspond to all the iterations where the number of correct balls drops sharply (figure 6), yet all those iterations show a sharp rise in probability. This effect, due to the change-all proposal strategy, is discussed in the text.*

twenty thousand iterations shown here took a few hours to compute on a 200MHz Pentium Pro PC.

The change-all effect is evident in this chain. Figure 7 plots the probability of the sample for each iteration. Places are marked where there is a sharp reduction in the number of correct balls, and these correspond to sharp increases in probability. At each of these sharp changes, a change-all proposal has been accepted that replaces a poor set of partition vertex offsets with a much more likely set, even though this breaks the constraint.

We experimented with different values of λ, both higher and lower, but they lead to less satisfactory chains. Values of λ that are too low result in chains that have trouble finding

correct animations, because the chance of accepting a poor proposal (from the point of view of the constraints) is too high. Values of λ that are too high make it less likely that a change-all proposal will be accepted, and also make it hard for the chain to abandon poor near-solutions. It takes only a few thousand iterations to see enough of the chain to know how lambda should be changed, and the range of acceptable values is reasonably large (our experiments show that chains with $\lambda = e^{5\pm1}$ are not much worse than those for $\lambda = e^5$) so little time must be spent in tuning parameters.

We also performed a larger experiment, with 30 of the 105 bins on a fifteen by seven grid to be filled (figure 8). In this example we used a value of $\lambda = e^{7.25}$ after experimenting with other values of λ between six and eight. The higher value for λ is required because there are more partition vertices and more balls. The greater number of partition vertices allow the change-all proposal to remain effective at higher λ values, so we still see adequate mixing. In fact, higher λ values are required to make it harder for a change-all proposal to succeed, so that the chain has enough time between major changes to converge to good animations.

5.4 Random Tables with Dice

This summarized example demonstrates objects bouncing on a random table, coming to rest in constrained configurations. Dice are used as random number generators in the real world because they are exceptionally hard to control [3], yet our technique is capable of finding animations in which dice come to rest near a particular place with a particular face showing.

The 2D ball example (section 5.1) used a very simple table model, with two main drawbacks due to the use of independent normals at each collision:

- An object bouncing in place will appear to have the table change underneath it as a different normal vector is chosen for each collision.

- Nearby points on the table are not correlated, as points on a real, bumpy table would be, which reduces the plausibility of the animations.

In this example we use a continuous, bumpy surface for the table. Rather than describe random normals directly, we specify a random b-spline surface via control points on a grid with fixed spacing but random vertical offsets. We can also specify random restitution and friction values at the control points, to be interpolated by the spline, thus extending the model to include the concept of springy or sticky regions on the table (such as spilt beer). The b-splines defining the table shape and properties define random fields over the surface. In principle, we could measure real tables, model their particular random fields, and use those in our simulation.

The simulator used in this example simulates only one object at a time bouncing on the random b-spline surface. It uses special techniques to manage the large number of control points required for a table with fine bumps.

In this example, constraints can be defined for any aspect of the object's 3D state at any point in time. Initial conditions for the object are specified by constraining its state at the start of the simulation ($t = 0$). The probability of an animation in this world contains components for the control vertices defining the table's shape, friction and restitution, and a component for each constraint on the object.

An animation generated from this type of scenario is shown in figure 9. Each of six dice is dropped and told to land in a specific place showing a specific side up. The dice are treated individually and do not interact — the table is not the same for each die. It took an hour or so of processing

Example 1 $\longrightarrow$

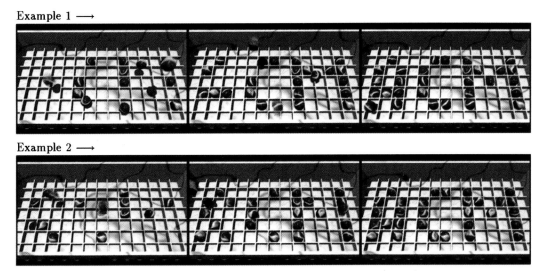

Example 2 $\longrightarrow$

Figure 8: *Balls that spell ACM. The box contains 105 bins, of which 30 are designated to contain balls. We show two animations, one on each row, generated from a single chain. Each has the bins being filled in a different order, evidence that the chain produces a good mix of samples.*

Figure 9: *A composite of six sample animations showing the control of a single bouncing die. Each die in the image was animated separately. Each had a different target location and desired side-up, but started with the same distribution on initial conditions.*

time to find a good animation for each die (a few hours for the complete animation). However, the chain does not mix well, so it takes many hours to find significantly different animations.

Proposals were made by changing one control point at a time, or one initial condition component at a time, or everything at once, the choice being made according to user supplied relative probabilities. Changes were made by adding a random offset to the current value, resulting in symmetric transition probabilities.

The ability to make changes at any point in the simulation, through the surface control points, makes it easier to find good animations in this world. Control points near the first few collisions get the die somewhere close to the target, and later collisions refine the location. This is not an explicitly coded strategy, rather it emerges naturally from the chain. However, a better proposal strategy might make

explicit use of the behavior.

6 FUTURE WORK

The models we use arise naturally in the real world, and we provide a means of verifying the plausibility of simulations. With further work it should be possible to experimentally obtain more accurate models, and test simulation algorithms on such models, to obtain results like those of Mirtich et. al. [22].

It is an open problem to determine the difficulty of a particular example without experimentation. Computation time can be adversely affected because the simulation itself is slower, or more iterations are required to find good animations, or both. For example, our bowling and spelling ball examples take comparable times to compute, the former due to slow simulation and the latter due to difficult constraints. Simulation time dominates the cost of each iteration, so it is reasonable to spend more time making better proposals to improve mixing and hence reduce the total number of iterations. For example, in the bowling simulation we might bias changes in the ball's initial conditions according to which pins were knocked down.

Constraints in our approach are specified as probability density functions, which allows almost any type of constraint. In particular, it might be possible to constrain collisions or other events to occur at specific times (or frames). This would allow physically-based animations to be choreographed to music, or collisions to occur at frame boundaries.

Popović et. al. [24] describe an interactive algorithm for manipulating colliding bodies. As they suggest, a system might be designed to take as input animations generated by our MCMC approach and allow users to fine tune the outcome as desired using local, interactive operations.

We have only touched on the possibilities of plausible motion with constraints, focusing entirely on rigid body dynamics. Our techniques may also work in other domains that are hard to constrain, including group behaviors [4] and deformable objects [8]. Another goal is to develop real time systems in which specific events are forced to occur in a plausible manner. For example, in a computer game we might like the monster to surprise the player in a particular way, with a plausibility model that takes into account the viewer's knowledge of the monster's state and how it moves [7].

Acknowledgements

We thank Ronen Barzel, John Hughes and Joe Marks for their very extensive and helpful comments on this work in general and on earlier drafts of this paper. This work was funded by ONR grant N00014-96-11200.

References

[1] Joel Auslander, Alex Fukunaga, Hadi Partovi, Jon Christensen, Lloyd Hsu, Peter Reiss, Andrew Shuman, Joe Marks, and J. Thomas Ngo. Further Experience with Controller-Based Automatic Motion Synthesis for Articulated Figures. *ACM Transactions on Graphics*, 14(4):311–336, October 1995.

[2] Ronan Barzel and Alan H. Barr. A Modeling System Based on Dynamic Constraints. In *Computer Graphics (SIGGRAPH 88 Conf. Proc.)*, volume 22, pages 179–188, August 1988.

[3] Ronan Barzel, John F. Hughes, and Daniel N. Wood. Plausible Motion Simulation for Computer Graphics Animation. In *Computer Animation and Simulation '96*, pages 184–197, 1996. Proceedings of the Eurographics Workshop in Poitiers, France, August 31-September 1, 1996.

[4] David Brogan and Jessica Hodgins. Group Behaviors for Systems with Significant Dynamics. In *Proceedings of the 1995 IEEE/RSJ International Conference on Intelligent Robots and Systems*, volume 3, pages 528–534, 1995.

[5] Lynne Shapiro Brotman and Arun N. Netravali. Motion Interpolation by Optimal Control. In *Computer Graphics (SIGGRAPH 88 Conf. Proc.)*, volume 22, pages 309–315, August 1988.

[6] Stephen Chenney. Asynchronous, Adaptive, Rigid-Body Simulation. SIGGRAPH 99 Technical Sketch. In Conference Abstracts and Applications, page 233, August 1999.

[7] Stephen Chenney, Jeffrey Ichnowski, and David Forsyth. Dynamics Modeling and Culling. *IEEE Computer Graphics and Applications*, 19(2):79–87, March/April 1999.

[8] Jon Christensen, Joe Marks, and J. Thomas Ngo. Automatic Motion Synthesis for 3D Mass-Spring Models. *The Visual Computer*, 13(3):20–28, January 1997.

[9] Michael F. Cohen. Interactive Spacetime Control for Animation. In *Computer Graphics (SIGGRAPH 92 Conf. Proc.)*, volume 26, pages 293–302, July 1992.

[10] Afonso G. Ferreira and Janez Zerovnik. Bounding the Probability of Success of Stochastic Methods for Global Optimization. *Computers and Mathematics with Applications*, 25(10):1–8, 1993.

[11] George S. Fishman. *Monte Carlo : concepts, algorithms, and applications*. Springer-Verlag, 1996.

[12] Walter R Gilks, Sylvia Richardson, and David J Spiegelhalter. *Markov Chain Monte Carlo in Practice*. Chapman & Hall, 1996.

[13] Michael Gleicher. Motion Editing with Spacetime Constraints. In *Proceedings 1997 Symposium on Interactive 3D Graphics*, pages 139–148, April 1997. Providence, RI, April 27-30.

[14] Radek Grzeszczuk and Demetri Terzopoulos. Automated Learning of Muscle-Actuated Locomotion Through Control Abstraction. In *SIGGRAPH 95 Conference Proceedings*, pages 63–70. ACM SIGGRAPH, August 1995.

[15] Radek Grzeszczuk, Demetri Terzopoulos, and Geoffrey Hinton. NeuroAnimator: Fast Neural Network Emulation and Control of Physics-Based Models. In *SIGGRAPH 98 Conference Proceedings*, pages 9–20. ACM SIGGRAPH, July 1998.

[16] Jessica Hodgins and Nancy Pollard. Adapting Simulated Behaviors for New Creatures. In *SIGGRAPH 97 Conference Proceedings*, pages 153–162. ACM SIGGRAPH, August 1997.

[17] Jessica K. Hodgins, James F. O'Brien, and Jack Tumblin. Perception of Human Motion With Different Geometric Models. *IEEE Transactions on Visualization and Computer Graphics*, 4(4):307–316, 1998.

[18] Mark Jerrum and Alistair Sinclair. Approximating the Permanent. *SIAM Journal of Computing*, 18:1149–1178, 1989.

[19] Mark Jerrum and Alistair Sinclair. The Markov Chain Monte Carlo Method: an approach to approximate counting and integration. In D.S.Hochbaum, editor, *Approximation Algorithms for NP-hard Problems*. PWS Publishing, Boston, 1996.

[20] Zicheng Liu, Steven J. Gortler, and Michael F. Cohen. Hierarchical Spacetime Control. In *SIGGRAPH 94 Conference Proceedings*, pages 35–42. ACM SIGGRAPH, July 1994.

[21] J. Marks, B. Andalman, P.A. Beardsley, W. Freeman, S. Gibson, J. Hodgins, T. Kang, B. Mirtich, H. Pfister, W. Ruml, K. Ryall, J. Seims, and S. Shieber. Design Galleries: A General Approach to Setting Parameters for Computer Graphics and Animation. In *SIGGRAPH 97 Conference Proceedings*, pages 389–400. ACM SIGGRAPH, August 1997.

[22] Brian Mirtich, Yan Zhuang, Ken Goldberg, John Craig, Rob Zanutta, Brian Carlisle, and John Canny. Estimating Pose Statistics for Robotic Part Feeders. In *Proceedings 1996 IEEE International Conference on Robotics and Automation*, volume 2, pages 1140–1146, 1996.

[23] J. Thomas Ngo and Joe Marks. Spacetime Constraints Revisited. In *SIGGRAPH 93 Conference Proceedings*, pages 343–350. ACM SIGGRAPH, August 1993.

[24] Jovan Popović, Steven Seitz, Michael Erdmann, Zoran Popović, and Andrew Witkin. Interactive Manipulation of Rigid Body Simulations. In *SIGGRAPH 2000 Conference Proceedings*. ACM SIGGRAPH, July 2000.

[25] Zoran Popović and Andrew Witkin. Physically Based Motion Transformation. In *SIGGRAPH 99 Conference Proceedings*, pages 11–20. ACM SIGGRAPH, August 1999.

[26] Karl Sims. Evolving Virtual Creatures. In *SIGGRAPH 94 Conference Proceedings*, pages 15–22. ACM SIGGRAPH, July 1994.

[27] Alistair Sinclair, 1999. Personal communication.

[28] Richard Szeliski and Demetri Terzopoulos. From Splines to Fractals. In *Computer Graphics (SIGGRAPH 89 Conf. Proc.)*, volume 23, pages 51–60, July 1989.

[29] Diane Tang, J. Thomas Ngo, and Joe Marks. N-Body Spacetime Constraints. *The Journal of Visualization and Computer Animation*, 6:143–154, 1995.

[30] Eric Veach and Leonidas J. Guibas. Metropolis Light Transport. In *SIGGRAPH 97 Conference Proceedings*, pages 65–76. ACM SIGGRAPH, August 1997.

[31] Baba C Vemuri, Chhandomay Mandal, and Shang-Hong Lai. A Fast Gibbs Sampler for Synthesizing Constrained Fractals. *IEEE Transactions on Visualization and Computer Graphics*, 3(4):337–351, 1997.

[32] Andrew Witkin and Michael Kass. Spacetime Constraints. In *Computer Graphics (SIGGRAPH 88 Conf. Proc.)*, volume 22, pages 159–168, August 1988.

Conservative Volumetric Visibility with Occluder Fusion

Gernot Schaufler   Julie Dorsey

Xavier Decoret   François X. Sillion

Laboratory for Computer Science
Massachusetts Institute of Technology

iMAGIS
GRAVIR/IMAG — INRIA

Abstract

Visibility determination is a key requirement in a wide range of graphics algorithms. This paper introduces a new approach to the computation of *volume visibility*, the detection of occluded portions of space as seen from a given region. The method is conservative and classifies regions as occluded only when they are guaranteed to be invisible. It operates on a discrete representation of space and uses the opaque interior of objects as occluders. This choice of occluders facilitates their extension into adjacent opaque regions of space, in essence maximizing their size and impact. Our method efficiently detects and represents the regions of space hidden by such occluders. It is the first one to use the property that occluders can also be extended into empty space provided this space is itself occluded from the viewing volume. This proves extremely effective for computing the occlusion by a set of occluders, effectively realizing *occluder fusion*. An auxiliary data structure represents occlusion in the scene and can then be queried to answer volume visibility questions. We demonstrate the applicability to visibility preprocessing for real-time walkthroughs and to shadow-ray acceleration for extended light sources in ray tracing, with significant acceleration in both cases.

1   Introduction

Determining visibility is central in many computer graphics algorithms. If visibility information were available in advance, scan-line renderers would not need to rasterize hidden geometry, and ray-tracers could avoid tracing shadow rays from points in shadow and testing objects that could not be hit. However, computing and storing all possible view configurations for a scene — the aspect graph [20] — is impractical for complex scenes. Even calculating all the visual events in a scene has very high complexity [9] and poses numerical stability problems.

It is generally easier to conservatively overestimate the set of potentially visible objects (PVS [1, 26]) for a certain region of space (referred to as a "viewcell" throughout this paper). While effective methods exist to detect occlusions in indoor scenes [1, 26] and terrain models [24], in more general types of complex scenes previous approaches [4, 6, 21] consider single convex occluders only to determine objects, or portions of space, that are completely hidden from the viewcell. This is known as volume visibility.

In many cases, objects are hidden due to the combination of many, not necessarily convex, occluders. This situation is exacerbated by the lack of large polygons in today's finely tessellated models. Figure 7 in Section 4.3 compares the number of occlusions detected using single convex occluders to the number detected with our method. Combining the effect of multiple, arbitrary occluders is complicated by the many different kinds of visual events that occur between a set of objects [9] and by various geometric degeneracies.

As a new solution to these problems, this paper proposes to calculate volume visibility on a conservative discretization of space. Occlusion is explicitly represented in this discretization and can be queried to retrieve visibility information for arbitrary scene objects — either static, dynamic or newly added.

We use opaque regions of space as blockers and automatically derive them from the scene description instead of expecting large convex occluders to be present in the scene. Our representation decouples the scene complexity from the accuracy and computational complexity at which visibility is resolved.

We show that hidden regions of space are valid blockers and that any opaque blocker can be extended into such regions of space. This effectively combines — *fuses* [32] — one blocker with all the other blockers that have caused this region to be occluded and results in a dramatic improvement in the occlusions detected. Collections of occluders need not be connected or convex.

The rest of the paper is organized as follows. In the next section, we review previous approaches to visibility computation with special emphasis on volume visibility methods. Next, we describe our approach in 2D and then extend it to 3D and 2 1/2 D. We present results for PVS computation and reducing the number of shadow rays in ray-tracing. We conclude with a discussion of our results and suggestions for future work.

2   Previous Work

The central role of visibility has resulted in many previously published approaches. We classify them into the following three categories: exact, point-sampled and conservative visibility computations and focus the discussion on volume visibility approaches. Examples of exact visibility representations are the aspect graph [20] or the visibility skeleton [9] and exact shadow boundaries [3, 8, 23, 27]. As mentioned above, they are impractical for complex scenes.

Point-sampling algorithms calculate visibility up to the accuracy of the display resolution [5, 7, 13]. One sample ray is sent into the scene and the obtained visible surface is reused over an area (e.g. a pixel or solid angle on the hemisphere). Today's most widely used approach is a hardware-accelerated z-buffer [2] or its variants, the hierarchical z-buffer [14] and hierarchical occlusion maps [32]. Visibility results obtained from these algorithms cannot be extended to volume visibility without introducing error. For volume visibility, projections are not feasible, as no single center of projection is appropriate.

To cope with the complexity of today's models, researchers have investigated conservative subsets of the hidden scene portion. Airey et al. [1] and Teller et al. [26, 28] propose visibility preprocessing for indoor scenes. They identify objects that are visible through sequences of portals. Yagel et al. [31] apply similar ideas in 2D for visibility in caves. Stewart [24] provides a solution for the case of terrain. Unfortunately, these algorithms do not generalize to volume visibility for more general types of complex scenes.

Conservative, but accurate, volume visibility computations for general scenes are limited to considering one convex occluder at a time for identifying hidden objects. Cohen-Or et al. [6] find hidden buildings in cities. Saona-Vazquez et al. [21] apply a similar strategy to the nodes in an octree. They intersect the PVS as seen from the eight corners of each voxel to obtain the PVS for the voxel. Coorg et al. [4] use supporting planes between the blocker and an occludee to determine occlusion. These planes also allow them to determine when the occluder will no longer hide the occludee. All these single occluder approaches share the difficulties of identifying good occluders, and none performs occluder fusion. Unfortunately, in practice many scenes do not contain any large polygons or convex objects. Durand [11] calculates volume visibility by projecting potential occluders onto planes. He modifies point-sampled projections and convolution to obtain a conservative algorithm.

In volume visibility it seems to be inherently difficult to combine the effects of multiple occluders in a provably accurate and efficient way. We believe that this is due to the nature of the occluders considered — convex polygons or objects — and because the portions of occluded space have not been explicitly represented or used in the computations.

Our visibility algorithm works entirely on a volumetric scene representation. We propose to abandon considering polygons as occluders, and instead let the volumetric nature of opaque objects occlude the space behind them. Several authors [4, 6, 10, 21] have required convex decompositions of arbitrary objects in order for their algorithms, operating on convex blockers, to work. Indeed, volumetric representations, such as octrees, provide such a convex decomposition. They also represent space itself so that efficient blockers can be found using occluded regions as described below. In our approach, we construct shafts around blockers as seen from the viewcell similar to Haines et al.'s shaft culling [16] and Teller et al.'s inter-cell visibility algorithm [28]. The difference is that Haines' shafts lie between the viewcell and the occludee, whereas ours lie behind the occluder as seen from the viewcell.

3 Definitions and Overview

Our goal is to determine occlusion from within a viewcell on a conservative discretization of space employing these definitions:

- A *viewcell* is an axis-aligned box that is either identical to or known to bound a volume of viewpoints of interest.

- An *occluder* (or *blocker*) is an axially-aligned box causing occlusion by opacity or other properties established by the algorithm (see Sections 4.2 and 4.3).

- A *shaft* is the convex intersection of half-spaces constructed from the visual events between the viewcell and the occluder. If the viewcell is considered as an extended light source, the volume inside the shaft is identical to the umbra of the occluder.

- A leaf voxel in the spatial subdivision is labeled *opaque* if it is completely inside an object, *empty* if it is completely outside all objects, or *boundary* [22] if it contains a portion of any object's surface. For this classification we require the blockers of the scene to be water-tight solids.

We seek a tight overestimate of the PVS as seen from a viewcell so that quick visibility queries with respect to any viewpoint in the viewcell are possible. Given a viewcell, these are the necessary steps:

Scene discretization. Rasterize the boundary of scene objects into the discretization of space and determine which voxels of space are completely inside an object and therefore opaque.

Blocker extension. Traverse the discretization of space and find an opaque voxel that is not already hidden. Group this blocker with neighboring opaque voxels to obtain an effective blocker.

Shaft construction. Construct a shaft that encompasses the region of space hidden by this blocker as seen from the viewcell.

Occlusion tracking. Use the shaft to classify the voxels into partially or completely outside the shaft and fully inside and thus occluded. Take note of occluded voxels.

The major contributions of this approach are a conservative scene discretization that decouples the effectiveness of visibility calculations from how the scene was modeled (i.e. presence of large polygons or convex objects, or number of polygons), and the introduction of blocker extension as a means of both finding efficient blockers and performing effective occluder fusion. Finally, we improve on shafts by observing that 3D shafts can be treated entirely in 2D.

We begin by describing our algorithm in the simple setting of two dimensions and note that this case is already suited to solve visibility queries on scenes such as a 2D floor plan or the map of a city.

4 2D Case

Our subdivisions of space are a quadtree in 2D and 2 1/2D, and an octree in 3D. In anticipation of the extension to 2 1/2D and 3D we will uniformly call a node in the tree a voxel. Its shape is always a (2D or 3D) axis-aligned box.

4.1 Scene Discretization

Our method requires that the interiors of objects can be distinguished from their exteriors. Objects need to have a solid volume. The discretization represents a cube of space containing the scene. All voxels containing a surface are marked as boundary voxels[1]. After this step, boundary voxels completely separate empty regions of space from opaque regions. Next we classify the non-boundary voxels into empty and opaque voxels using the odd-parity rule [12] for point-in-polygon or point-in-closed-shape testing.

We accelerate voxel classification by propagating the voxel status with depth-first seed-filling [22] up to the boundary voxels. Figure 1 shows an example taken from a simple test scene used throughout Section 4. Note that the blockers are not axis-aligned. Such an arrangement would improve the efficiency of the spatial discretization, but is not a requirement of the algorithm.

Our algorithm deals with scenes containing non-solid objects in several ways. If a voxel size is known, such that after marking boundary voxels the empty regions of space form a connected set of voxels, a single call to seed-filling will determine all empty voxels. The opaque voxels are the remaining non-boundary voxels. If some objects have holes or interior faces, the algorithm can still run and use the opaque interior of other objects. Objects with holes

---

[1]Near the surfaces, the spatial hierarchy is subdivided down to a maximum level. This maximizes the number of opaque voxels inside the objects.

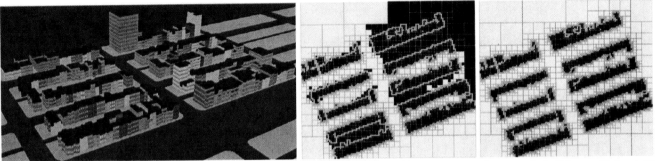

Figure 1: Left: ten blocks of buildings to be projected onto the ground. Right: Marking empty space between the buildings with flood-fill.

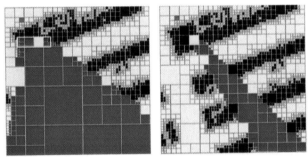

Figure 2: Left: a viewcell in red and a blocker with its extension outlined in yellow. The blocker hides the voxels in blue. Right: occlusion without blocker extension. (Opaque voxels are shown in black.)

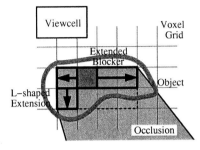

Figure 3: Example of L-shaped blocker extension. First the blocker is extended laterally. If after this step more than one side of the blocker is visible from the viewcell, the blocker is extended along this side away from the viewcell. The resulting occlusion is larger. Only the regions enclosed by the thick lines need to be opaque.

have no defined interior and therefore are not used as occluders. Interior faces are ignored by flood-filling only the empty space around objects. Alternatively, degenerate input data can be cleaned up and interior faces can be removed using a method such as the one given by Murali et al. [19].

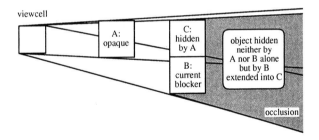

Figure 4: Because C is hidden by A, blocker B can be extended into C to create a much bigger region of occlusion, which hides the object on the right. Neither A nor B alone would occlude this object as seen from the viewcell.

4.2 Blocker Extension

We recursively traverse the tree until we find an opaque voxel. This is the blocker used with the viewcell to construct the region of occluded space. To maximize occlusion we first *extend* the blocker. This extension must not hinder the ease of constructing the hidden region, so we require the extension to keep the box-shape of the blocker (see left side of Figure 2). Other opaque voxels are shown in black and will be considered as blockers next.

We extend the blocker along the coordinate axis, which maximizes the angle subtended by the blocker. Extension proceeds on both sides in this direction until there is a non-opaque voxel within the width of the blocker. In the cases where two sides of the blocker are visible from the viewcell, the blocker can additionally be extended into an L-shape as shown in Figure 3. From the viewcell, this L-shape appears exactly the same as the big dashed box enclosing the L-shape that is the blocker's final extension.

We use two optimizations to quickly find large hidden regions of space. First, we use the blockers in the order from the viewcell outwards; hence, blockers that subtend a wide solid angle compared to their size get used first. Second, we use large blockers in high levels of our spatial data structure first, as these can be expected to occlude large regions of space quickly. Hidden regions are not considered further for blocker selection.

4.3 Blocker Extension into Hidden Space

Despite its simplicity, the idea of extending blockers into adjacent opaque space has not been used in previous approaches. In addition, we make an even stronger point with blocker extension into *hidden* space, regardless of whether this space is empty or opaque. Extending blockers into hidden regions of space is based on the following observation (see Figure 4).

An observer inside the viewcell is unable to distinguish whether a hidden voxel is opaque or empty. For the sake of finding large occluders for this viewcell, we can assume that the voxel is opaque, and blocker extension can proceed into hidden voxels just as into opaque voxels.

In fact, one can construct different scenes that look exactly the same from within the viewcell by arbitrarily changing hidden parts of the model. One well-known application of this property is the PVS, where all polygons in hidden areas of the scene are removed.

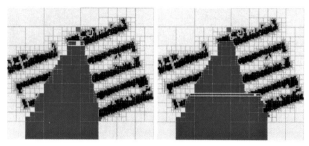

Figure 5: Left: marking the occlusion for one occluder. Right: extending a second occluder through the region hidden by the first one.

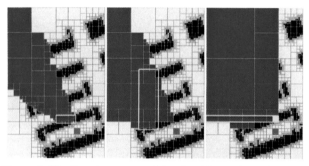

Figure 6: The first three steps of the algorithm as it marks occlusions for the red viewcell. Note how blockers are extended across the streets between the buildings.

It is therefore licit to change hidden voxels into opaque ones, with the benefit that larger blockers can be constructed.

The blocker on the right side of Figure 5 is extended across blocks through empty space connecting one block of buildings to another. Nonetheless, by the argument introduced above, extending the blocker this far is valid. It effectively fuses the current blocker with the blocker shown on the left side of Figure 5. It was this blocker that caused all the voxels between buildings to be hidden.

As shown in Figure 4, occluder fusion occurs if the second blocker overlaps the umbra of the first blocker. In general, any blocker can be arbitrarily extended inside the umbra of another blocker as the umbra is the region of space completely hidden from the viewcell.

Figure 6 shows the progress of the algorithm after using only three extended blockers. In general, especially with scenes containing no major large polygons, occluder fusion is essential as is obvious from the comparison given in Figure 7. It shows the occlusions detected after all blockers have been used for three different approaches from left to right: triangles as single convex occluders, opaque voxels without blocker extension, and opaque voxels with blocker extension. A few large polygons have caused some occlusion to be detected in the upper left of the triangle-based approach. If large polygons are present in the scene database, they can be used to bootstrap our approach to occlusion detection.

4.4 Shaft Construction and Occlusion Tracking

We construct a shaft around the occluded region from the supporting planes[2] between the viewcell and the blocker. Details are given in the appendix. Our implementation differs from the one by Haines et al. [16] in that we replace set manipulations on box corners with table lookups.

---

[2]A supporting plane contains an edge from one object and a vertex from another object, such that both objects lie on the same side of the plane [4].

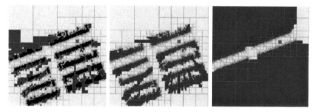

Figure 7: The blocks of buildings from above. Left: occlusions detected using triangles from the database as convex occluders. Middle: occlusions detected without blocker extension. Right: occlusions detected with blocker extension.

Once the shaft has been constructed, a recursive traversal of the spatial data structure flags hidden voxels as occluded in the highest tree node possible. Subtrees outside or inside the shaft are not traversed.

If all the children of a voxel in the spatial data structure are found to be hidden, the parent can be marked as being hidden as well. An exception occurs in the 2 1/2 D case, which will be discussed in Section 6. Propagating visibility up the tree is useful for accelerating traversal of the tree for blocker extension, for marking occluded regions, and for querying occlusion of original objects.

4.5 Querying Occlusion of Scene Objects

Occlusion of the original objects is determined by inserting their bounding boxes into the tree and checking that all the voxels they overlap are hidden. When a bounding hierarchy exists on the input scene — say on the block-, house-, and triangle-level — occlusion queries can be further accelerated by interleaving the traversal of the bounding box hierarchy with the traversal of the tree.

Note that we can also determine the visibility of objects that were not initially inserted into the tree. This allows objects unlikely to cause a lot of occlusion to be ignored when constructing the tree. Also, the visibility status can be determined for moving objects or objects that have been added to the scene.

5 3D Case

Usually visibility algorithms for 2D are difficult to extend to 3D because the number of occlusion boundaries grows from $O(n^2)$ to $O(n^4)$ [10], and because the occlusion boundaries are no longer planar in general. In our case, however, the shaft construction extends to 3D in a straightforward fashion. This is due to our choice of viewcells and blockers as axis-aligned boxes in which case occlusion boundaries remain planar.

5.1 Shafts in 3D

Haines et al. [16] simplify the construction of a shaft's plane equations by noting that a shaft around axis-aligned boxes consists entirely of planes, the normals of which have at least one zero coordinate. In addition, a 3D shaft can be more efficiently treated as the intersection of three 2D shafts, namely the shaft's projections onto the three coordinate planes as shown in Figure 8. A bounding box is then inside the shaft if it is inside each of the three 2D shafts. We ensure that planes orthogonal to the coordinate axes are included only in one 2D shaft.

5.2 Blocker Extension in 3D

In 3D, a blocker must be extended along more than one dimension to subtend a large solid angle. We first extend the blocker along one

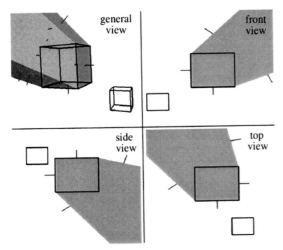

Figure 8: A 3D shaft can be treated as the intersection of three 2D shafts (the shaft's orthographic projection along the coordinate axes).

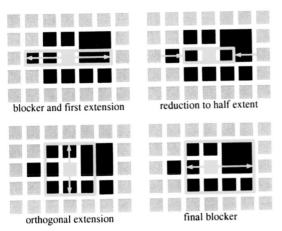

Figure 9: Blocker extension in 3D.

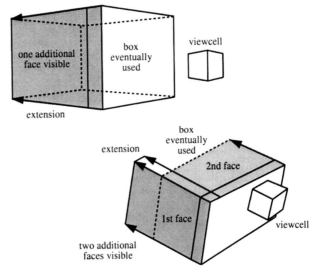

Figure 10: Additional step of blocker extension in the direction orthogonal to the extensions shown in Figure 9. If two additional faces are visible, their minimum extension must be used.

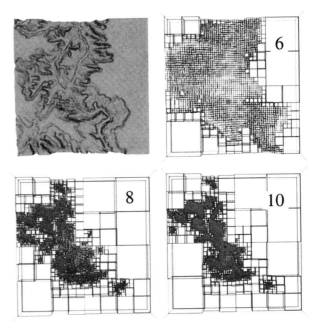

Figure 11: An example of occlusion culling in terrain: Grand Canyon. Top left: geometric model. In the other images the number indicates the maximum quadtree subdivision level down to which the quadtree has been built. Hidden nodes are shown in blue; potentially visible nodes are shown in grey as seen from the red viewcell.

axis, then reduce its size to half its length, then extend it orthogonally to the first extension, and finally, extend again along the first axis as shown in Figure 9.

We have tried to maximize the solid angle subtended by the blocker over different reduction fractions (see second step of Figure 9). We did not observe any noticeable increase in the occlusions identified, but CPU time increased considerably. It is our experience that occluder fusion more than compensates for any suboptimal blocker extension.

Similar to the L-shaped blocker extension in 2D, the blocker is also extended along additionally visible faces as shown in Figure 10. Other than that, occlusion detection in 3D works exactly the same as in 2D: voxels in the tree that are completely inside the shaft of the blocker are marked as occluded.

6 2 1/2D Case

Memory requirements for a 3D octree are sometimes a concern. However, scenes such as terrains or cities can often be dealt with in 2 1/2D. The 2 1/2D quadtree is constructed by recording the height of the highest and lowest points of every primitive falling within a certain voxel (i.e. a square on the ground plane). No ray-casting or seed-filling is necessary. Our tree construction algorithm strictly enforces the 2 1/2D characteristic of the input data set and filters

out multiple triangles above a single location on the ground plane. Voxels are occluded if they are inside the shaft up to their maximum height and can be used as an occluder up to their minimum height.

We perform occluder extension the same way as in the 2D case including L-shaped extension; shaft construction is the same as in the 3D case — three 2D shafts are generated. The shaft plane coincident with the ground is ignored. Even though only one shaft in the ground plane and one plane connecting the highest point on the viewcell with the lowest point on the blocker could be used, we found the three 2D shafts to be more effective as they allow easy tracking of occluded height in the 2D projections. We store this height per hidden voxel.

An important difference to the previous two cases of 2D and 3D occlusion detection occurs with the propagation of visibility up the tree. Even if all the children are hidden, the parent is not necessarily hidden everywhere up to its maximum height. Calculating and storing the height up to which a voxel is hidden helps both with visibility propagation up the tree and also with occluder extension, because higher occluders can be extended into a certain voxel.

Figure 11 shows examples of detected occlusion in a terrain model with the maximum tree subdivision of 6, 8 and 10.

7 Applications and Results

We apply occlusion detection to the following rendering algorithms: visibility preprocessing for real-time walkthroughs and shadow-ray culling in ray-tracing. We use the 2 1/2D quadtree to find both viewcells and their PVS in an outdoor city environment. The 3D version is then applied to find the surfaces not receiving direct light from extended light sources in a ray-tracer.

7.1 Visibility Preprocessing for Walkthroughs

Since cities and other outdoor scenes are predominantly 2 1/2D, we use the 2 1/2D quadtree described in Section 6 for occlusion calculations. The model shown in Figure 12 consists of 316,944 triangles that are organized into 665 buildings and 125 blocks complete with streets and sidewalks. Table 1 shows statistics on how long the quadtree takes to build based on the maximum subdivision level in the tree (e.g. subdivision 8 stands for a 256^2 maximum subdivision). Figure 12 shows the tree portions in blue found to be occluded for one viewcell.

Using a moderate tree subdivision level (up to 8 levels) visibility queries are possible at interactive rates (a few tenths of a second). This includes querying objects in the tree. To avoid this expense of computation at runtime, we pre-compute PVSs for those regions of our model reachable during visual navigation.

Our walkthrough system accepts the navigable space as a set of triangles describing the streets or paths. We first determine the PVS for every triangle in the street mesh by constructing a 3D bounding box around it and marking occluded sections of the model in the quadtree. Then we look up the objects such as buildings, terrain and street portions, trees, cars and people in the quadtree and only add those to the triangle's PVS that are not fully occluded.

A total of 2,538 triangles in the streets have been automatically grouped into 700 street sections for database paging as shown in Figure 13. By imposing an upper limit on the difference between the size of the triangles' PVSs in one street section, our greedy merge algorithm limits the amount of overdraw within one section. The walkthrough system pre-fetches the geometry for adjacent street sections as the user moves around so that exploration is possible without interruption. Such predictive database paging is impossible with online point-visibility methods.

Preprocessing this scene took 55 minutes, the vast majority of which was spent to find the PVS for every viewcell. The remaining time is used for building the tree and grouping viewcells into street sections. The average time for finding the PVS of a triangle is less than a second.

tree levels	nodes	memory (kB)	time to build (sec)
7	11,949	574	2.669
8	39,625	1,902	3.704
9	133,577	6,412	6.381
10	472,561	22,683	10.197

Table 1: 2 1/2 D quadtree generation statistics: number of nodes, memory, and build time as a function of the maximum subdivision level in the tree on a MIPS R10k processor running at 250 MHz.

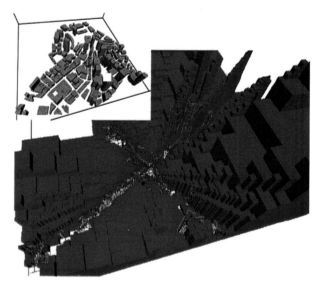

Figure 12: Top: a financial district from above (316,944 triangles). Bottom: occluded tree portion shown as blue boxes in the same overhead view as above. Box heights reflect the hidden height of voxels.

viewcell

Figure 13: Street triangles for the financial district grouped into sections. For one of them the PVS is shown, the rest of the buildings are shown in wire-frame.

We have retrieved the PVS for every triangle with two different granularities from the tree for comparison: blocks and buildings. For block-based PVS, an average of 33.96 blocks were found potentially visible out of 125 blocks, the minimum count of visible blocks was eight, the maximum 82. It is apparent that querying the bounding box of a whole block in the quadtree results in a rather high over-estimation of the PVS.

For building-based PVS, the average building count was 54 out of a total of 665 buildings, sidewalks, and road segments. The minimum and maximum numbers were 12 and 156. In this case, we queried the smallest bounding boxes available in the bounding-box hierarchy of our model.

We are unaware of a method that could compute an accurate reference solution to this problem. Instead we have tried to compute a good approximation to the true solution using point sampling. From every triangle in the street mesh we took twenty 360 degree

block-based PVS size	total: 125 blocks (about 2,500 tris on avg)		
	our method	point samples	difference
min	8	6	0
max	82	48	47
avg	33.96	20.3	13.64
building-based PVS size	total: 665 buildings (about 475 tris on avg)		
	our method	point samples	difference
min	12	8	0
max	156	90	81
avg	53.87	33.99	19.88

Table 2: Comparison of PVS sizes for block-based (125 blocks) and building-based (665 buildings) PVS computation. Going from block-based to building-based PVSs reduced the average difference between the two methods from 10.91% to 2.98% of the complete model.

256^2 pixel images recording the visible object per pixel into an item buffer. The set union of the objects visible in these images was saved as the PVS for that triangle.

We noted a couple of difficulties in this point-sampled reference solution: narrow gaps between buildings can still be missed and the blocks or buildings visible through these gaps are not reported as visible. Also, in views looking down long straight streets, the sidewalks and streets project to very small areas in screen space and can be missed as well. This supports the need for methods such as the one presented in this paper.

We give the comparison between our PVS and the point-sampled solution in Table 2. Note that the difference is always positive or zero, which demonstrates that our method is conservative.

Finally, Figure 14 shows the difference in drawing time measured on an SGI Infinite Reality system. The left shows results for block-based PVS, the right shows results for building-based PVS compared to IRIS Performer view-frustum culling.

7.2 Shadow Ray Acceleration

When ray-tracing complex scenes with many lights, tracing shadow rays and computing object intersections can account for 95% of the rendering time [15]. It is therefore desirable to minimize the number of rays traced. Methods have been developed to accelerate shadow rays for point sources [15, 30], but the work published for extended lights is either approximate [17] or not directly applicable to a ray tracer [25]. Extended lights are preferable, as they cast soft shadows rather than the unnaturally looking sharp shadows caused by point lights.

Our shadow ray acceleration is a generalization of the method of Woo and Amanatides [30] from point light sources to extended light sources. Figure 15 shows an example of the artifacts to be expected if one tries to apply a point-light acceleration technique to an extended light source. The point light causes a sharp shadow which is contained in the region of penumbra of an area light source at the same position. A point-light acceleration algorithm falsely identifies regions of the penumbra as in shadow and pronounced boundaries appear in the umbra where there should be a continuous light-intensity variation.

The acceleration technique uses the full 3D version of our algorithm with space represented as an octree, as described in Section 5. We find the bounding box for every light source in the model and use it as a viewcell. For every light source we copy and keep the visible portion of the octree[3]. In the case of many light sources, memory consumption is a concern, and only a specific number of top levels in the tree are copied with only a small increase in the

---

[3]Figure 19 shows that these copies require memory comparable to the initial octree

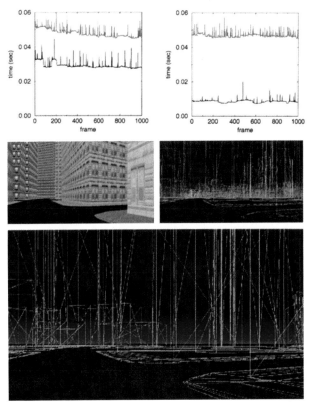

Figure 14: Drawing time without (red) and with (black) occlusion culling in our walkthrough system. Left: block-based PVS. Right: building-based PVS. Below: a frame from the walkthrough and a comparison of the amount of geometry drawn in wireframe.

Figure 15: An example of artifacts in the area of soft shadows introduced by an acceleration technique which was not designed for extended light sources (middle: correct shadow, right: artifacts. Geometric model and octree on the left).

number of occlusions that are not detected (as shown in the results below). Our representation of the octree uses eight bytes per node.

As the ray-tracer renders the scene, every light's octree is queried to determine whether the current sample point is potentially visible to the light. Shadow rays need only to be cast for potentially visible points. The top of Figure 16 shows a view of a city block at night with ten street lights around it. Below is a false-color image of the same block from above where every pixel is given a color based on which light sources would be queried with shadow rays. All

Figure 16: Top: accelerated rendering of a block of houses illuminated by ten street lamps. Bottom: false-color image from above encoding which lamps are queried with shadow rays at each surface point. Note how the corners of the building cause "occlusion boundaries."

Figure 17: Top: gallery: 17,701 triangles, 23 lights. Bottom: residential area, 616,509 triangles, 459 light sources.

images in this section are rendered with one sample per pixel, and global illumination taken into account using stochastic sampling optimized with irradiance gradient caching [29]. The ray tracer uses hierarchical grids as the general acceleration data structure.

Preprocessing took 53.3 seconds on a Pentium II 400MHz processor, and the time to render this image was reduced from about 250 seconds to 100 seconds (a 60% saving). This is particularly advantageous for animation sequences with static lighting, where the preprocessing is amortized over the full set of frames.

Figure 17 shows more complex scenes: a gallery with paintings and people (17,701 triangles and 23 light sources) and a residential area (616,509 triangles, 459 light sources). The bars on the left of Figures 18 and 19 give tree construction time and initial tree memory usage respectively as a function of the maximum octree subdivision level. The right graph in Figure 18 plots rendering time as a function of the number of levels kept in the octree per light. The right graph in Figure 19 gives the memory requirements for the octree copies. The original tree is no longer needed during rendering.

By considering both charts together, one observes that seven levels in the octree are not sufficient to accurately capture the occluders in the gallery scene (eight in the residential area scene). However, there is no longer a substantial difference between the rendering times using a 256^3 octree or a 512^3 octree (512^3 or 1024^3 for the residential area scene). It is surprising that three or more levels can be discarded from the light source octree without paying a significant price in the number of occlusions missed. However, the savings in memory are quite substantial.

Finally, Figure 20 shows the effectiveness of the method by giving the percentage of shadow rays successfully culled and the percentage of traced shadow rays, which were found to intersect geometry. This is the percentage of rays that was not reported as occluded even though the sample point is hidden from the light source. Note

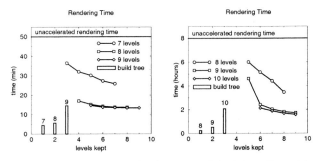

Figure 18: Rendering times for the two models: left: gallery, right: residential area. Different octree depths are shown, the number of levels kept per light varies along the x-axis.

how this number decreases as the octree resolution increases. In the case of the residential area, the percentage of rays blocked although not reported as such remains quite high, because the lamp geometry was not inserted into the octree and, therefore, sample points on the facades at a height above the light could not be found to be in shadow. The results can be summarized as follows: with a doubled memory consumption rendering is accelerated by a factor of three for the gallery scene and by a factor of four for the residential area scene.

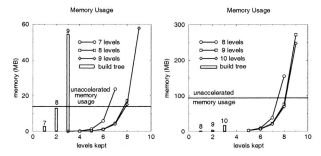

Figure 19: Memory requirements for building the octree (bars on the left) and during rendering: left: gallery, right: residential area as a function of octree levels kept per light. The bars on the left show tree build time as a function of the maximum octree subdivision level allowed.

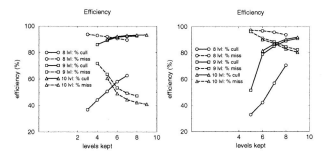

Figure 20: Effectiveness of the octree for eliminating shadow rays: left: gallery, right: residential area. The percent of shadow rays eliminated is shown as a solid line, the number of shadow rays that resulted in an intersection, but were not reported as occluded is shown as a dashed line. The number of levels kept per light varies along the x-axis.

8   Conclusions and Future Work

We have presented a method to compute a conservative approximation of the space hidden as seen from a viewcell. Voxels from a discretization of space are classified into empty, opaque, and boundary. Opaque voxels are used as blockers, and a shaft is constructed to determine the portion of space hidden behind them. We apply blocker extension both into adjacent opaque voxels and hidden voxels to maximize the size of blockers.

Blocker extension into hidden regions of space is motivated by the fact that arbitrary assumptions can be made about scene portions hidden to the viewer. For the sake of blocker extension, we assume them to be opaque and extend blockers into them, thereby fusing blockers with any blocker or group of blockers that caused this region to be hidden.

We have applied the method to visibility preprocessing and have obtained a tight superset of the actual PVS as seen from a region of space. Such information is also useful for subdividing the space of reachable viewpoints into sections for managing on-the-fly paging of geometry.

In the context of ray-tracing, we have successfully eliminated a major fraction of shadow rays cast toward extended lights. These rays are usually necessary to calculate the regions of shadow as cast by the light. Despite the memory requirements for a fine discretization of space during preprocessing, a moderate amount of memory is sufficient during rendering to capture occlusions with high fidelity even for a large number of light sources.

In the future we would like to investigate further applications of the available visibility information, automatic ways of choosing a sufficient octree subdivision level, and other subdivision schemes

such as kd-trees or more sophisticated boundary nodes to improve the effectiveness of the method. We also want to investigate the success of blocker extension in other previously proposed visibility methods. Moreover, by rasterizing freeform patches or constructive solid geometry our visibility algorithm could be extended to these modeling approaches.

Acknowledgments

We would like to thank Henrik Wann Jensen for allowing us to build on his *Dali* ray tracer for the results presented in Section 7.2. Max Chen built the city model that appears in Figure 17; Byong Mok Oh contributed shaders to render it.

This work was supported by an NSF Postdoctoral Research Associates award (EIA-9806139), an NSF CISE Research Infrastructure award (EIA-9892229), an NSF-INRIA Cooperative Research award (INT-9724005), and a grant from Intel Corporation. iMAGIS is a joint research project of CNRS, INRIA, INPG and the Joseph Fournier University of Grenoble.

References

[1] Airey, John M., John H. Rohlf and Frederick P. Brooks, Jr., *"Towards Image Realism with Interactive Update Rates in Complex Virtual Building Environments,"* Symposium on Interactive 3D Graphics 1990, pp 41-50.

[2] Catmull, Edwin, E., *"Computer Display of Curved Surface,"* IEEE Conference on Computer Graphics, Pattern Recognition and Data Structures, May 1975, pp 11-17.

[3] Chin, Norman and Steven Feiner, *"Fast Object-Precision Shadow Generation for Area Light Sources Using BSP Trees,"* Symposium on Interactive Graphics (1992), pp 21-30.

[4] Coorg, Satyan and Seth Teller, *"Temporally Coherent Conservative Visibility,"* Proc. Twelfth Annual ACM Symposium on Computational Geometry, Philadelphia, PA, May 24-26, 1996, pp 78-87.

[5] Cohen-Or, Daniel and Amit Shaked, *"Visibility and Dead-Zones in Digital Terrain Maps,"* EUROGRAPHICS '95 14 3 (1995) pp 171-180.

[6] Cohen-Or, D., G. Fibich, D. Halperin and E. Zadicario, *"Conservative Visibility and Strong Occlusion for Viewspace Partitioning of Densely Occluded Scenes,"* Computer Graphics Forum, 17 (3) 1998, pp 243-253.

[7] Chrysanthou, Y., D. Cohen-Or, and D. Lischinski, *"Fast Approximate Quantitative Visibility for Complex Scenes,"* Computer Graphics International '98, June 1998, pp 220-229.

[8] Drettakis George, Fiume Eugene L., *"A Fast Shadow Algorithm for Area Light Sources Using Backprojection,"* SIGGRAPH 94, pp 223-230.

[9] Durand, Fredo, George Drettakis and Claude Puech, *"The Visibility Skeleton: A Powerful and Efficient Multi-Purpose Global Visibility Tool,"* SIGGRAPH 97, pp 89-100.

[10] Durand, Fredo, *"3D Visibility: Analytical Study and Applications,"* PhD Dissertation, Universite Joseph Fournier, Grenoble, France.

[11] Durand, Fredo, George Drettakis, Joelle Thollot and Claude Puech, *"Conservative Visibility Preprocessing using Extended Projections,"* SIGGRAPH 2000.

[12] Foley, James, Andries van Dam, Steven Feiner and John Hughes, *"Computer Graphics: Principles and Practice,"* Addison-Wesley Publishing Co., ISBN 0-201-12110-7, 1990.

[13] Greene, Ned *"Approximating Visibility with Environment Maps,"* Graphics Interface '86, pp 108-114.

[14] Greene, Ned, Michael Kass and Gavin Miller, *"Hierarchical Z-Buffer Visibility,"* SIGGRAPH 93, pp 231-238.

[15] Haines, A. Eric and Donald P. Greenberg, *"The Light Buffer: A Ray Tracer Shadow Testing Accelerator,"* IEEE Computer Graphics and Applications, 6 9, 1986, pp 6-16.

[16] Haines, A. Eric and John R. Wallace, *"Shaft Culling for Efficient Ray Cast Radiosity,"* Photorealistic Rendering in Computer Graphics (Proceedings of the Second Eurographics Workshop on Rendering), Springer-Verlag, New York, 1994, pp 122-138.

[17] Hart, David, Philip Dutre and Donald P. Greenberg, *"Direct Illumination with Lazy Visibility Evaluation,"* SIGGRAPH 99, pp 147-154.

[18] Hudson, Tom, Dinesh Manocha, Jonathan Cohen, Ming Lin, Kenneth E. Hoff III, Hansong Zhang, *"Occlusion Culling using Shadow Volumes,"* Proceedings of 13th Symposium on Computational Geometry, Nice, France, June 4-6 1997, pp 1-10.

[19] Murali T.M., and Thomas A. Funkhouser, *"Consistent Solid and Boundary Representations from Arbitrary Polygonal Data,"* Symposium on Interactive 3D Graphics), 1997, pp 155-162.

[20] Plantinga, Harry. and Charles Dyer, *"Visibility, Occlusion and the Aspect Graph,"* International Journal of Computer Vision, 5(2) 1990, pp 137-160.

[21] Saona-Vazquez, Carlos, Isabel Navazo and Pere Brunet, *"The Visibility Octree. A Data Structure for 3D Navigation,"* TR LSI-99-22-R, Universitat Politecnica de Catalunya, Spain.

[22] Samet, Hanan, *"Applications of Spatial Data Structures,"* Addison-Wesley, Reading, MA, ISBN 0-201-50300-X, 1990.

[23] Stewart, James and S. Ghali, *"Fast computation of shadow boundaries using spatial coherence and backprojections,"* SIGGRAPH 94, pp 231-238.

[24] Stewart, James, *"Hierarchical Visibility in Terrains,"* Eurographics Rendering Workshop, June 1997, pp 217-228.

[25] Tanaka, Toshimitsu, and Tokiichiro Takahashi, *"Fast Analytic Shading and Shadowing for Area Light Sources,"* Computer Graphics Forum, Vol. 16, 3, 1997, pp 231-240.

[26] Teller, Seth J. and Carlo H. Sequin, *"Visibility Preprocessing For Interactive Walkthroughs"*, SIGGRAPH 91, pp 61-69.

[27] Teller, Seth, *"Computing the Antipenumbra of an Area Light Source*, SIGGRAPH 92, pp 139-148.

[28] Teller, Seth, and Pat Hanrahan, *"Global Visibility Algorithms for Illumination Computation,"* SIGGRAPH 94, pp 443-450.

[29] Ward, Gregory J. and Paul Heckbert, *"Irradiance Gradients,"* Third Eurographics Workshop on Rendering, May 1992, pp 85-98.

[30] Woo, Andrew and John Amanatides, *"Voxel Occlusion Testing: A Shadow Determination Accelerator for Ray Tracing,"* Graphics Interface '90, pp 213-219.

[31] Yagel, Roni, and William Ray, *"Visibility Computation for Efficient Walkthrough of Complex Environments,"* PRESENCE, Vol.5, No. 1, Winter 1996, pp 1-16.

[32] Zhang, Hansong, Dinesh Manocha, Tom Hudson and Kenneth E. Hoff, *"Visibility Culling using Hierarchical Occlusion Maps,"* SIGGRAPH 97, pp 77-88.

Appendix

In 2D the shaft between two boxes is delimited by lines through the corners of the boxes and a subset of the blocker faces. Table 3 lists the box corners that need to be connected. Figure 21 gives a pictorial overview of the cases.

Case	X: 0	X: 1	X: 2	X: 3
Y: 0	1,2	3,2	3,0	1,0
Y: 1	1,3	-	2,0	all
Y: 2	0,3	0,1	2,1	2,3
Y: 3	0,2	all	3,1	-

Table 3: Box corners to be connected based on the relative position of the boxes. Cases where four connections must be made are marked "all", but are only relevant for the 2 1/2D and 3D extensions if viewcells are limited to empty space.

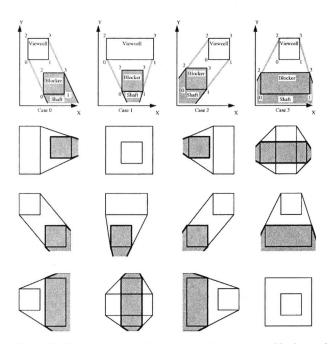

Figure 21: First row: cases of mutual positions between blocker and viewcell along the X-axis. The shafts are shown in grey. The rest of the figure gives a pictorial impression of the contents of Table 3.

Conservative Visibility Preprocessing using Extended Projections

Frédo Durand†‡, George Drettakis†, Joëlle Thollot†and Claude Puech †

†iMAGIS*- GRAVIR/IMAG - INRIA   ‡Laboratory for Computer Science - MIT

Abstract

Visualization of very complex scenes can be significantly accelerated using *occlusion culling*. In this paper we present a visibility preprocessing method which efficiently computes potentially visible geometry for volumetric viewing cells. We introduce novel *extended projection* operators, which permits efficient and conservative occlusion culling with respect to all viewpoints within a cell, and takes into account the combined occlusion effect of multiple occluders. We use extended projection of occluders onto a set of projection planes to create extended occlusion maps; we show how to efficiently test occludees against these occlusion maps to determine occlusion with respect to the entire cell. We also present an improved projection operator for certain specific but important configurations. An important advantage of our approach is that we can re-project extended projections onto a series of projection planes (via an *occlusion sweep*), and accumulate occlusion information from multiple blockers. This new approach allows the creation of effective occlusion maps for previously hard-to-treat scenes such as leaves of trees in a forest. Graphics hardware is used to accelerate both the extended projection and reprojection operations. We present a complete implementation demonstrating significant speedup with respect to view-frustum culling only, without the computational overhead of on-line occlusion culling.

KEYWORDS: Occlusion culling, visibility determination, PVS

1   Introduction

Visualization of very complex geometric environments (millions of polygons) is now a common requirement in many applications, such as games, virtual reality for urban planning and landscaping etc. Efficient algorithms for determining visible geometry are a key to achieving interactive or real-time display of such complex scenes; much research in computer graphics is dedicated to this domain. Object simplification using different levels of detail (LOD) (*e.g.*, [Cla76, FS93]) or image-based approaches (*e.g.*, [SLSD96]) have also been used to accelerate display, either as an alternative or in tandem with visibility algorithms.

Visibility *culling* algorithms try to reduce the number of primitives sent to the graphics pipeline based on occlusion with respect to the current view. In *view frustum culling* only the objects contained in the current view frustum are sent to the graphics pipeline.

---

*iMAGIS is a joint research project of CNRS/INRIA/UJF/INPG.
E-mail: {Fredo.Durand|George.Drettakis|Joelle.Thollot|
Claude.Puech}@imag.fr http://www-imagis.imag.fr/

Occlusion culling attempts to identify the visible parts of a scene, thus reducing the number of primitives rendered. We can distinguish two classes of occlusion culling: *point-based* methods which perform occlusion culling on-the-fly for the current viewpoint, and *preprocessing* approaches which perform this calculation beforehand, typically for given regions (volumetric cells).

Point-based methods are very effective, and in particular can treat the case of occluder fusion, *i.e.* the compound effect of multiple occluders. This is important, for example in a forest: each individual leaf hides very little, but all the trees together obscure everything behind them. However, point-based methods have significant computational overhead during display, and cannot be simply adapted for use with pre-fetching if the model cannot fit in memory.

No previous preprocessing method exists which can handle occluder fusion. In addition, the success of such preprocessing methods is often tied to the particular type of scene they treat (*e.g.*, architectural environments [TS91, Tel92]).

In this paper we present a visibility preprocessing algorithm based on a novel *extended projection* operator, which generalizes the idea of occlusion maps to volumetric viewing cells. These operators take occluder fusion into account, and result in an occlusion culling algorithm which is efficient both in memory and computation time. Our algorithm results in a speedup of up to 18 compared to optimized view-frustum culling only. In addition, using repeated re-projection onto several projection planes, we can treat particularly difficult scenes (*e.g.*, forests), for which we obtain speedups of 24, again compared to view-frustum culling. An example is shown in Fig. 1.

1.1   Previous work

It is beyond the scope of this paper to review all previous work on visibility. Comprehensive surveys can be found in *e.g.*, [Dur99]. In particular we do not review analytical 3D visibility methods (*e.g.*, [PD90, Dur99]) because their algorithmic complexity and their robustness problems currently prevent their practical use for large scenes. In what follows, we first briefly overview preprocessing occlusion culling algorithms and then discuss point-based approaches.

Occlusion culling techniques were first proposed by Jones [Jon71] and Clark [Cla76]. Airey *et al.* [ARB90] and Teller *et al.* [TS91, Tel92] were the first to actually perform visibility preprocessing in architectural environments. They exploit the fact that other rooms are visible only through sequences of *portals* (doors, windows). These methods have proven very efficient in the context of walkthroughs where they can be used in conjunction with LOD [FS93] for faster frame-rates. The problem of data size and the consequent treatment of disk pre-fetching and network bandwidth has been addressed, notably by Funkhouser (*e.g.*, [Fun95, Fun96]). Applications to global lighting simulation have also been demonstrated, *e.g.*, [TH93]. Unfortunately these methods rely heavily on the properties of indoor scenes, and no direct generalization has been presented. Visibility for terrain models has also been treated (*e.g.*, [Ste97]).

Preprocessing algorithms capable of treating more general scenes have recently begun to emerge (*e.g.*, [COFHZ98, COZ98, WBP98]). Nonetheless, they are currently restricted to occlusions caused by a single convex occluder at a time. Since they cannot

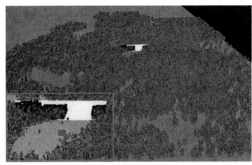

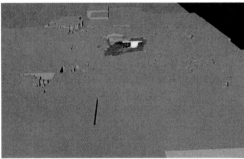

Figure 1: Top: A 7.8 M poly forest scene (only a tenth of the leaves are rendered here). The inset shows a close-up on the viewing cell (in red) and one of the projection planes. Bottom: Visibility computation from the view cell. In yellow we show the nodes of the hierarchy of bounding boxes culled by our method. We also show one of the projection planes used.

handle the general case of occluder fusion they compute potentially visible sets which are often very large. However, the technique by Schaufler *et al.* [SDDS00] in this volume can also handle occluder fusion for volumetric visibility.

A novel approach using conservative occluder simplification has also recently been proposed [LT99] to decrease the cost of occlusion preprocessing.

On the other hand, point-based methods have been proposed which perform an occlusion culling operation for each frame on-the-fly. Greene *et al.* [GKM93] create a 2D hierarchical z-buffer, used in conjunction with a 3D octree hierarchy to accelerate the occlusion of hidden objects. A related algorithm using hierarchical occlusion maps was introduced by Zhang *et al.* [ZMHH97], which uses existing graphics hardware. This approach includes "important" blocker selection and approximate culling for regions almost occluded. It is important to note that these approaches only work for a single given viewpoint and are thus unsuitable for precomputing visibility information; In a different vein, Luebke and George [LG95] presented an algorithm which extends view-frustum culling by restricting views through convex portals. Wonka and Schmalstieg [WS99] use a z-buffer from above the scene to perform occlusion culling in terrains.

Other point-based methods include the work by Coorg and Teller [CT96, CT97] which use spatial subdivision and the maintenance of separating planes with the viewpoint to achieve rapid culling of hidden surfaces. A similar technique is presented by Hudson *et al.* [HMC+97].

1.2 Overview

Our visibility preprocessing algorithm adaptively subdivides the scene into *viewing cells*, which are the regions of observer movement. For each such cell, we compute the set of objects which are potentially visible from all the points inside the cell. This set is called the *PVS* or potentially visible set [ARB90, Tel92, TS91].

To compute these sets efficiently, we introduce a novel *extended projection* operator. If we consider each individual viewpoint in a

cell, the extended projections are an *underestimate* of the projection of occluders, and an *overestimate* for the occludees. By defining these operators carefully, we can check if an occludee is hidden with respect to the *entire* cell by simply comparing the extended projections of the occludee to the extended projections of the occluder. Extended projections can handle occluder fusion and are efficient in the general case. We also present an improved extended projection for occludees for specific, but not uncommon configurations. Once occluders have been projected into a given projection plane, we can *re-project* them onto other planes, aggregating the effect of many small occluding objects. This *occlusion sweep* allows us to create occlusion maps for difficult cases such as the leaves in a forest.

The rest of this paper is organized as follows. In the next section we define the *extended projection* operators, and show how to compute them (section 3). An improvement for specific cases is presented in section 4. We then introduce a reprojection operator and the occlusion sweep in section 5. In section 6 we describe the preprocess to compute PVS's and discuss the interactive viewing algorithms which use the result of the preprocess. In section 7 we present the results of our implementation, together with a discussion and future work. The interested reader will find more details in the extended version present in the proceedings CD-ROM or on the authors' web page, as well as in the first author's thesis [Dur99].

2 Extended projections

To compute the potentially visible geometry in every direction for a given viewing cell, we perform a conservative occlusion test for each object (occludee) of the scene, with respect to every viewpoint in the cell. To do this efficiently, we use a representation of occlusion caused by occluders which is based on *extended projections* onto a plane.

2.1 Principle

In point-based occlusion culling algorithms [GKM93, ZMHH97], occluders and occludees are projected onto the image plane. Occlusion is detected by testing if the projection of an occludee is contained in the projection of the occluders (overlap test) and if this occludee is behind (depth test) for the given viewpoint.

Our approach can be seen as an extension of these single viewpoint methods to volumetric viewing cells. This requires the definition of *extended projection operators* for occludees and occluders. To determine whether an occludee is hidden with respect to all viewpoints within the viewing cell the new projection operators need to satisfy the following conditions: (i) the extended projection of the occludee must be contained in the extended projection of the occluders and (ii) the occludee must be behind the occluders.

Even though we describe our method for a single plane, six planes will actually be necessary to test occlusion in all directions. The position of the projection plane is an important issue and will be discussed in section 6.1.

We define a *view* as the perspective projection from a point onto a projection plane. However, in what follows, the projection plane will be shared by all viewpoints inside a given cell, resulting in sheared viewing frusta.

2.2 Extended projections

We next define extended projection operators for both occluders and occludees using *views* as defined above.

Definition 1 *We define the extended projection (or Projection) of an* **occluder** *onto a plane with respect to a cell to be the* **intersection** *of the views from any point within the cell.*

Definition 2 *The extended projection (or Projection) of an* **occludee** *is defined as the* **union** *of all views from any point of the cell.*

In what follows, we will simply use *Projection* to refer to an extended projection. The standard projection from a point will still be named *view*.

Fig. 2 illustrates the principle of our extended projection. The *Projection* of the occluder is the intersection of all views onto the projection plane (dark gray), while the *Projection* of the triangular occludee is the union of views, shown in light green.

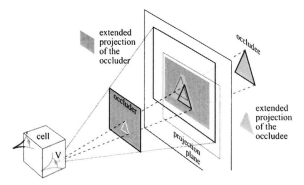

Figure 2: Extended projection of an occluder and an occludee. The view from point V is shown in bold on the projection plane. A view from another viewpoint is also shown with thinner lines. The extended projection of an occluder on a plane is the *intersection* of its views. For an occludee, it is the *union* of the views.

This definition of *Projection* yields conservative occlusion tests. To show this consider the case of a single occluder (Fig. 2). Assume (for the purposes of this example) that an occludee is behind the occluder. It is declared hidden if its *Projection* is contained in the *Projection* of the occluder. This means that the union of the occludee views is contained in the intersection of the views of the occluder. From any viewpoint V inside the cell, the view of the occludee is contained in the view of the occluder.

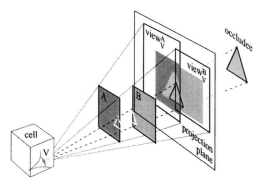

Figure 3: *Projections* handle *occluder fusion* of two occluders A and B. We show the example of a view from point V. The view of the occludee is contained in the cumulative view of the two occluders, as determined by the *Projection* occlusion test.

Consider now the case of an occludee whose *Projection* is contained in the cumulative *Projection* of two (or more) occluders. This means that from any viewpoint V in the cell, the view of the occludee is contained in the cumulative view of the occluders. To summarize, we have:

$$view_V(occludee) \subset \bigcup_{V \in cell} view_V(occludee)$$

$$\subset \bigcup_{occluders} \bigcap_{V \in cell} view_V(occluder)$$

$$\subset \bigcup_{occluders} view_V(occluder)$$

The occludee is thus also hidden in this case (see Fig. 3). Our *Projection* operators handle *occluder fusion*. We do not however claim that they always find *all* occluder fusions; as will be discussed in section 7.3, the position of the projection plane is central.

Note that convexity is not required in any of our definitions, just as for point-based occlusion-culling.

2.3 Depth

Unfortunately there is no one-to-one correspondence between a point in a *Projection* and a projected point of an object, as with a standard perspective view (see Fig. 4(a)). We can see that many depth values correspond to a single point in the *Projection*, depending on which point of the viewing cell is considered.

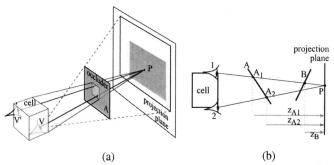

(a)   (b)

Figure 4: (a) We show the points of the occluder corresponding to P in the view from V and V'. The light blue region of the occluder corresponds to the set of points which project on P. (b) The *Depth* of a point P in the *Projection* of an occluder A is the maximum of the depth of the corresponding points (z_{A2} here). In the case of multiple occluders, the occluder closest to the cell is considered (occluder A here). Note that *Depths* are negative here.

Depth comparison is more involved than in the single viewpoint case since a simple distance between the viewpoint and a projected point cannot be defined (see Fig 4(a)). Our definition of depth must be consistent with the properties of occlusion; For each ray emanating from a viewpoint inside the cell and going through the projection plane, depth must be a monotonic function of the distance to the viewpoint. We define depth along the direction orthogonal to the projection plane. We chose the positive direction leaving the cell and placed zero at the projection plane.

Definition 3 *We define the extended depth (or Depth) of a point in the Projection of an* **occluder** *as the* **maximum** *of the depth of all the corresponding projected points.*
Similarly, the extended depth (Depth) of a point in the Projection of an **occludee** *is the* **minimum** *depth of its projected points.*

See Fig. 4(b) for an illustration where for point P and occluder A, depth z_{A2} is maximum and is thus used as *Depth*.

If the *Depth* of a point in the *Projection* of an occluder is smaller than the *Depth* of the point in the *Projection* of an occludee, all the corresponding points of the occludee are *behind* the occluder from any viewpoint inside the cell. As a result, this definition of *Depth* satisfies our conservative depth test requirement and yields valid occlusion computation.

We construct a *Depth Map* as follows: For each point of the projection plane, we define the value of the *Depth Map* as the *Depth* of the occluder closest to the cell which projects onto it (that is the occluder with the *minimum Depth*). In the example of Fig. 4(b), occluder A is closest to the cell, and thus chosen.

2.4 Implementation choices

Until now, our definitions have been quite general, and do not depend on the cell, plane, occludee nor on the way that we test for containment of an occludee *Projection* in an occluder *Projection*, or the way that *Depths* are compared. We now present the choices we have made for our implementation.

The viewing cells are non-axis-aligned bounding boxes. The projection planes will be restricted to the three directions of the cell (note that these three directions depend on the cell). The occludees are organized in a hierarchy of axis-aligned bounding boxes.

The projection planes we use are actually not infinite but are finite rectangles. We use a pixel-map representation of the *Depth* Map. This may at first seem like a concession to conservatism, but we will see in section 3.2 that a conservative rasterization is used. This allows the use of the graphics hardware simplifying most of the computation, and it avoids the robustness issues inherent to geometrical computations.

We store a *Depth* value for each pixel of the *Depth* Map. As described above, for each pixel we consider the closest occluder, *i.e.* the minimum *Depth*. Occluder fusion is handled by the natural aggregation in the *Depth* Map. Following [GKM93] we organize the *Depth* Map into a pyramid for efficient testing. We call it the Hierarchical *Depth* Map.

3   Computation of extended projections

Using the extended projections we defined, we can efficiently test occludee *Projections* against occluder *Projections* in a preprocess to find the potentially visible geometry for viewing cells. We next describe how to compute *Projections* for occludees and then for occluders (both convex and concave).

3.1   Occludee *Projection*

Recall that the *Projection* of an occludee is the union of its views. Our cells are convex as is the bounding box of an occludee. The *Projection* of such a box reduces by convexity to the 2D convex hull of its views from the vertices of the cell.

To simplify computation, we use the bounding rectangle of the *Projection* on the projection plane as an *overestimate* of the *Projection* (see Fig. 5). We then split the problem into two simpler 2D cases. We project the cell and the occludee bounding box onto two planes orthogonal to the projection plane and parallel to the sides of the cell. The 2D projection of the cell is a rectangle, while the 2D projection of the occludee bounding box is a hexagon in general (Fig. 5 shows a special case of a quadrilateral for simplicity).

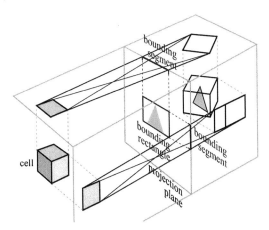

Figure 5: Occludee *Projection* is reduced to two 2D problems.

We then compute the separating and supporting lines [CT97] of the rectangle and hexagon. The intersections of these lines with the projection plane define a 2D bounding segment. A bounding rectangle on the projection plane is defined by the Cartesian product of the two 2D segments as illustrated in Fig. 5. Separating lines are used when the occludee is between the cell and the projection plane, while supporting lines are used if the occludee lies behind the plane.

This method to compute an occludee *Projection* is general and always valid, but can be overly conservative in certain cases. In

section 4 we will present an improvement of this *Projection* for some particular, but not uncommon, configurations.

3.2   *Projection* of convex occluders using intersections

By convexity of the cell and occluder, the intersection of all possible views from inside the cell is the intersection of the views from the vertices of the cell. This *Projection* can be computed using standard geometric intersection computation.

We have nevertheless developed an efficient method which takes advantage of the graphics hardware. It is a multipass method using the *stencil buffer*. The stencil buffer can be written, and compared to a test value for conditional rendering.

The basic idea is to project the occluder from each vertex of the cell, and increment the stencil buffer of the projected pixels without writing to the frame-buffer. The pixels in the intersection are then those with a stencil value equal to the number of vertices.

The consistent treatment of *Depth* values (as described in section 2.3) in the context of such an approach requires some care. More details on the hardware implementation are given in appendix A.

If standard OpenGL rasterization is used, the *Projections* computed are not conservative since partially covered pixels on the edges may be drawn. We use a technique proposed by Wonka *et al.* [WS99] which "shrinks" polygons to ensure that only completely covered pixels will be drawn. Each edge of a displayed polygon is translated in the 2D projection plane by a vector of (+/-1 pixel, +/-1 pixel) towards the interior of the polygon (the sign is determined by the normal). The 2D lines corresponding to the edges are translated and the vertices are computed by intersection. Note that only silhouette edges need be translated. If the polygons to be displayed are too small, the shrinking results in a void *Projection*.

3.3   Concave occluder slicing

Concave polygonal meshes can be treated in our method, by computing the *Projection* of each individual triangle of the mesh. However, some gaps will appear between the *Projections*, resulting in the loss of the connectivity of occluders. To overcome this problem, we use the following simple observation: the *Projection* of a closed manifold lying in the projection plane is the object itself. We thus consider the intersection of concave objects with the projection plane, which we call a *slice* of the object.

If the projection plane cuts the object, we compute the intersection and a 2D contour found. The normals of the faces are used to accurately treat contours with holes. The contour is then conservatively scan-converted with the value of the *Depth* Map set to zero (*i.e.* the *Depth* value of the projection plane).

4   Improved *Projection* of occludees

In this section we present an improvement to the extended projection calculation for the case of *convex* or *planar* occluders for configurations in which our initial *Projection* yields results which are too conservative. In what follows, we discuss only the case where the occludee is between the projection plane and the cell. If the occludee is behind the plane, the *Projection* which we have presented in section 2.2 yields satisfying results.

In Fig. 6(a) we show a 2D situation in which our *Projection* is too restrictive. The *Projection* of the occludee is not contained in the *Projection* of the occluder, even though the occludee is evidently hidden from any viewpoint in the cell. As illustrated in Fig. 8(a), we will show that in this case we can use the supporting lines instead of the separating lines in the computation of the occludee *Projection*.

To improve our occlusion test, we will first discuss conditions required to prove that an occludee is hidden by an occluder. We will then deduce a sufficient condition on the occludee *Projection* to yield valid tests. In 2D, this condition can be simply translated into the definition of an *improved Projection*. Based on this 2D construction, we develop an improved 3D occludee *Projection*, using a projection approach similar to that of section 3.1.

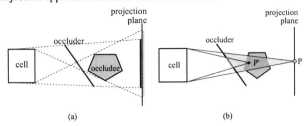

Figure 6: (a) Configuration where the initial *Projection* is too restrictive. The *Projection* of the occludee is not contained in the *Projection* of the occluder, even though it is obviously hidden. (b) Any point P' inside the cone defined by P and the cell and behind the occluder is hidden.

Property 1 *For a given point P in the occluder umbra region with respect to a cell, all points P' in space behind the occluder, which are also contained in the cone defined by P and the cell, are hidden with respect to the cell.*

The *occluder umbra region* with respect to a cell is the umbra (totally hidden) volume which results if the cell is considered as an area light source. This property is illustrated in Fig. 7. The proof is evident for convex occluders since the cone defined by P' and the cell is contained in the cone defined by P. The section of the occluder which occludes P is a superset of the section which occludes P'.

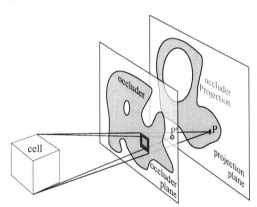

Figure 7: The intersection of the occluder and cone (defined by point P and the cell) is shown in dark blue.

The 3D case of concave planar occluders is similar to the convex case. Consider a point P in the umbra of a concave occluder (Fig. 7). Since P is in the umbra, the cone defined by P and the cell is "occluded": the intersection of this cone and the occluder is equal to the intersection of the cone and the plane of the occluder. The intersection of the cone defined by P' (the light blue inner square in Fig. 7) is a subset of this intersection. P' is thus also hidden.

Planarity of the occluder is required to ensure that the intersection of the cone and the occluder is convex. The planar occluder can be concave and have a hole (as in Fig. 7), but if P is in the umbra, the intersection is convex.

To yield valid occlusion tests, our *improved Projection* must have the following property:

Property 2 *The union of cones defined by each point of the improved Projection of the occludee and the visibility cell must contain the occludee.*

To see why this property is important, consider the cone defined by P and the cell in Fig 6(b). The points of the occludee contained in this cone are occluded by Property 1. Consider the union of cones defined by all the points of a hypothetical improved *Projection* and the cell. If the occludee is contained in this union of cones, any point of the occludee is in one of these cones, and is thus hidden by Property 1. Note that occluder fusion is still taken into account: all points P defining the cones need not be hidden by the same convex or planar occluder.

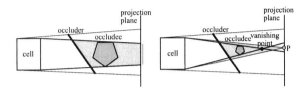

Figure 8: Improved *Projection* in 2D.

An improved *Projection* respecting property 2 is defined in 2D by considering the supporting lines of the cell and the occludee as illustrated in Fig. 8(a). However, if the occludee is too small, the two supporting lines intersect in front of the projection plane at the *vanishing point*. In this case, any point P between the intersections of the two supporting lines and the projection plane satisfies property 2, (Fig. 8(b)). In practice, we use the mid-point in our calculations.

Unfortunately, supporting planes cannot be used in 3D as simply as supporting lines, and the vanishing point is ill-defined. We thus project onto two planes orthogonal to the projection plane and parallel to faces of the cell, as illustrated in Fig. 9(a). On each plane we use our 2D improved *Projection*. The Cartesian product of these two 2D improved *Projections* defines our 3D improved *Projection*.

The 3D improved *Projection* is the Cartesian product of 2D improved *Projections* which are points or segments. It is a rectangle (segment × segment), a segment (segment × point) or a point (point × point).

5 Occluder reprojection and occlusion sweep

In the previous sections, we have limited the discussion to a single projection plane for a given cell. However, it can be desirable to use multiple parallel projection planes to take into account the occlusion due to multiple groups of occluders (Fig. 9(b)).

An important property of our method is that we can *re-project* occluders onto subsequent planes. The aggregated *Projections* are reprojected to compute a *Depth* Map on new projection planes (Fig. 9(b)). Occluder fusion occurring on the initial plane is thus also taken into account on the new planes. We next describe how we perform reprojection and its generalization which we call the *occlusion sweep*.

5.1 Reprojection

The *Projections* of occluders can be reprojected only if the initial projection plane is behind them. In this case, the initial *Projections* are inside the umbra of the occluders and can thus be used as a single conservative equivalent occluder (see appendix B for a proof).

The *Projections* onto the initial projection plane (and the conservative bit-map encoding) define a new planar occluder. The reprojection scheme we are about to present is in fact an extended projection operator for the special case of planar blockers parallel to the projection plane.

We base our reprojection technique on the work by Soler and Sillion [Max91, SS98] on soft shadow computation, even though we are interested only in the umbra region. They show that in the

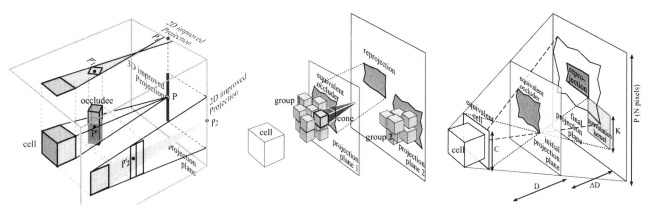

Figure 9: (a) The 3D improved *Projection* is the Cartesian product of two 2D improved *Projections*. Any point P' of the occludee is contained in a cone defined by one point P of the 3D improved *Projection* and the cell. This cone can be constructed by considering the two corresponding 2D projections. (b) If projection plane 2 is used for re-projection, the occlusion of group 1 of occluders is not taken into account. The shadow cone of one cube shows that its *Projection* would be void since it vanishes in front of plane 2. The same constraints apply for group 2 and plane 1. It is thus desirable to project group 1 onto plane 1, and *re-project* the aggregate equivalent occluder onto plane 2. (c) Occluder reprojection. The extended occlusion map of plane 1 is re-projected onto plane 2 from the center of the equivalent "cell". It is then convolved with the inverse image of the equivalent "cell" (dark region on plane 2).

case of planar blockers parallel to the source and to the receiver, the computation of soft shadows is equivalent to the convolution of the projection of the blockers with the inverse image of the source. Their method is an approximation in the general case, but we will use it in the particular case of parallel source, blockers and receiver, where it is exact.

We are nearly in this ideal case: our blocker (the *Projections* on the initial projection plane) and the receiver (the new projection plane) are parallel. However our light source (the cell) is a volume. We define an equivalent "cell" which is parallel to the projection planes and which yields conservative *Projection* on the new projection plane. Its construction is simple and illustrated in Fig. 9(c). We use the fact that our projection planes are actually finite rectangles. Our equivalent "cell" is the planar rectangle defined by the face of the cell closest to the plane, the supporting planes of the cell and the final projection rectangle.

Any ray going through the cell and the projection plane also intersects our equivalent "cell". Thus if an object is hidden from the equivalent "cell", it is also hidden from the cell.

To obtain a conservative umbra region, the inverse image of our equivalent cell (*i.e.* the convolution kernel) is conservatively rasterized (overestimated as opposed to the occluder underestimated conservative rasterization), which is straightforward since it is a 2D rectangle.

The convolution method computes continuous grey levels. To obtain a binary Occlusion Map, we only keep the black pixels (*i.e.* the umbra region). A *Depth* map can be used on the final plane. The *Depth* of the re-projected equivalent occluder is the depth of the initial plane.

5.2 Occlusion sweep

To handle the case where multiple concave or small occluders have to be considered, we generalize re-*Projection* to the *occlusion sweep*. This is a sweep of the scene by parallel projection planes leaving the cell. Occlusion is aggregated on these planes using re-*Projection*.

We project the occluders which lie in front of the current projection plane P onto P and also compute the slices of the concave objects which intersect the plane. We then advance to the following projection plane, by re-projecting the *Projections* of the previous plane. We compute the new slices of concave objects, and project the occluders which lie between the two planes. This defines the *Depth* Map of the new projection plane.

The distance ΔD between two projection planes is chosen to make optimal use of the discrete convolution. The size of the convolution kernel (the inverted image of the equivalent cell) must be an integer number K of pixels (there is then no loss in the conservative rasterization). Let D be the distance between the initial plane and the equivalent "cell", and C the size of the equivalent "cell". N is the resolution of the *Depth* Map, and P is the size of the projection plane. Applying Thales theorem gives: $\Delta D = \frac{D(K-1)P}{CN}$.

In practice we use $K = 5$ pixels. Note that this formula results in planes which are not equidistant. This naturally translates the fact that occlusion varies more quickly near the viewing cell.

6 Occlusion culling algorithm

The elements presented so far (*Projection* and re-*Projection* of occluders and occludees) can now be put together to form a complete occlusion culling algorithm. The algorithm has two main steps: pre-processing and interactive viewing.

6.1 Preprocess

The preprocess creates the viewing cells and the PVS's corresponding to the original input scene. Viewing cells are organized in a spatial hierarchical data-structure, potentially related to the specific application (*e.g.*, the streets of a city). The geometry of the scene itself is organized into a separate spatial hierarchy (*e.g.*, a hierarchy of bounding boxes).

Two versions of the preprocess have been implemented, one which simply uses the *Projection* onto 6 planes for each view cell (used in the city example) and one which uses the occlusion sweep (used for the forest scene).

Adaptive preprocess

We start by performing an occlusion computation for each viewing cell. First, we choose the appropriate occluders and projection planes (see the following two sections). We then *Project* the occluders and build a *Hierarchical Depth Map*. Finally, the occludees are tested recursively. If a node is identified as hidden or fully visible, the recursion stops. By fully visible, we mean that its *Projection* intersects no occluder *Projection*, in which case no child of this node can be identified as hidden. The occludees declared visible are inserted in the PVS of the cell.

If we are satisfied with the size of the PVS, we proceed to the next cell. Otherwise, the cell is subdivided and we recurse on the sub-cells. Nonetheless, occlusion culling is only performed on the remaining visible objects, *i.e.* those contained in the PVS of the parent.

Performing computation on smaller viewing cells improves occlusion detection because the viewpoints are closer to each other. The views from all these viewpoints are thus more similar, resulting in larger occluder *Projections*, and smaller occludee *Projections*.

The termination criterion we use is a polygon budget: if the PVS has more than a certain number of polygons, we subdivide the cell (up to a minimum size threshold). A more elaborate criterion would be to compare the PVS to sample views from within the cell. Note that our adaptive process naturally subdivides cells more in zones of larger visibility changes. However, more elaborate discontinuity-meshing-like strategies could be explored.

PVS data can become overwhelmingly large in the memory required. To avoid this we use a *delta-PVS* storage mechanism. We store the entire PVS for a single arbitrary initial cell (or for a small number of seed or "key" cells). Adjacencies are stored with each cell; a cell simply contains the *difference* with respect to the PVS of the neighboring cells. Our storage scheme is thus not very sensitive to the number of viewing cells, but to the actual complexity of the visibility changes. Other compression schemes could also be implemented [vdPS99].

Occluder selection

For each viewing cell we choose the set of relevant occluders using a solid angle heuristic similar to those presented previously [CT97, ZMHH97, HMC+97]. To improve the efficiency of occlusion tests, we have also implemented an adaptive scheme which selects more occluders in the direction where many occludees are still identified as visible, in a manner similar to Zhang [ZMHH97].

Since our preprocess is recursive, we also use the PVS of the parent cell to cull hidden occluders. Since, as we shall see, the *Projection* of the occluders is the bottleneck of the method, this results in large savings.

Choice of the projection plane

The heuristic we use is simple, based on the optimization of the number of pixels filled in our *Depth* Map. We place a candidate plane just behind each occluder. We evaluate the size of the *Projection* on each such plane for each occluder. This method is brute force, but remains very fast.

Moreover, since we discard occluders which are hidden from the parent cell, the heuristic is not biased towards regions where many redundant occluders are present.

Six projection planes are used to cover all directions. Unlike *e.g.*, the hemicube [CG85] methods, our six planes do not define a box. The planes are extended (*e.g.*, by 1.5 used in our tests) to improve occlusion detection in the corner directions, as shown in Fig. 13(c).

6.2 Interactive Viewing

For on-line rendering we use the SGI Performer library, which maintains a standard scene-graph structure [RH94]. A simple flag for each node determines whether it is active for display. Each time the observer enters a new cell, the visibility status of the nodes of the scene-graph are updated. This is very efficient thanks to our delta-PVS encoding. Nodes which where previously hidden are restored as visible, while newly hidden ones are marked as inactive. The viewer process adds very low CPU overhead, since it only performs simple scene-graph flag updates.

Dynamic objects with static occluders can be treated using our extended projection approach. However, dynamic occluders cannot be handled. A hierarchy of bounding boxes is constructed in the regions of space for which dynamic objects can move [SC96]. During preprocess, these bounding boxes are also tested for occlusion. In the viewing process the dynamic object is displayed, if the

bounding box containing the dynamic object is in the current PVS (see the moving cars in the video).

One of the advantages of our preprocess is that it could be used for scenes which are too big to fit into main memory, or to be completely loaded on-the-fly from the network. The techniques developed by Funkhouser *et al.* [Fun96] can easily be adapted. A separate process is in charge of the database management. Using the PVS of the neighboring viewing cells, the priority of the objects which are not yet loaded is evaluated. Similarly, a priority order is computed to delete invisible objects from memory. The prediction offered by our method cannot be achieved by previous online occlusion culling methods.

7 Implementation and results

We have implemented two independent systems for the preprocessor and the viewer. The preprocessor uses graphics hardware acceleration wherever possible, notably for the *Projection* and convolution. The *Depth* Maps are read from graphics memory, and the occludee test is performed in software. The delta-PVS's computed are stored to disk and made available to the interactive viewer.

Our current implementation of the viewer is based on SGI Performer [RH94]. Performer implements a powerful scene-graph and view-frustum culling, providing a fair basis for comparison. All timings presented are on an SGI Onyx2 Infinite Reality 200Mhz R10K using one processor for the preprocess and two processors for the viewer.

7.1 *Projection* onto a single projection plane

The test scenes we have used for the single plane method consist of a model of a city district which contains a total number of about 150,000 polygons replicated a variable number of times. The improved *Projection* was used to cull occludees lying between the projection plane and occluders more efficiently.

We first present statistics on the influence of the resolution of the *Depth* maps on running time of the preprocess in Fig. 10. Surprisingly, the curve is not monotonic. If the resolution is below 256x256, the occlusion efficiency (*i.e.* the percentage of geometry declared hidden) of the method is low because of the conservative rasterization. More recursion is thus needed, where more occluders are used because they have not been culled from the parent cell. If the resolution is higher than 256x256, occlusion efficiency is not really improved but the time required to build the Hierarchical *Depth* Map becomes a bottleneck (the huge increase for a resolution of 1,024x1,024 may be explained by cache failure). This part of the algorithm could have been optimized using the graphics hardware, but the very low occlusion efficiency gain made us use a resolution of 256x256 for the rest of our computations. Since we use pyramids, only resolutions which are powers of 2 were used.

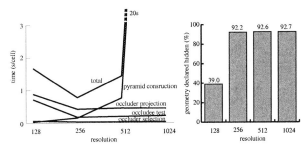

Figure 10: (left) Preprocess running time (sec./cell) versus *Depth* map resolution. (right) Geometry declared hidden vs. resolution of the *Depth* map. All timings for a scene consisting of 600,000 polygons.

We varied the complexity of the input scene by replicating the district. The average preprocessing time per cell is presented in

Fig. 11. The projection of the occluder is the most time-consuming task. A log-log linear fit reveals that the observed growth of the total running time is in $\sqrt{n}$ where n is the number of input polygons. If the total volume of all viewing cells varies proportionally to the number of input polygons, the growth is then $n^{1.5}$.

The improved *Projection* presented in section 4 results in PVS 5 to 10% smaller. This is not dramatic, but recall that it comes at no cost. In addition the implementation is simpler, since only supporting lines are considered.

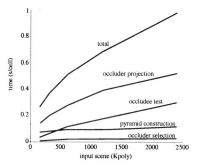

Figure 11: Preprocess running time versus input scene size.

We used a scene consisting of the city district replicated 12 times (1.8M polygons) and 3,000 moving cars of 1.4K polygons each, resulting in a total of 6M polygons. We performed the preprocess for the streets of only one district. The 1,500 initial visibility cells were subdivided into 6,845 leaf cells by our adaptive method (12,166 cells were evaluated, where parent cells are included). The average occlusion efficiency was 96% and the delta-PVS required 60 MBytes of storage. The total preprocess took 165 minutes (0.81s/cell), of which 101 minutes for the occluder *Projection*. We can extrapolate that the preprocess would take 33 hours for the streets of the 12 districts. For an 800 frame walkthrough, an average speed-up of 18 was obtained over SGI Performer view frustum culling (Fig. 12). This is lower than the average geometry ratio of 24 (*i.e.* $\frac{\text{\# polys after frustum cull}}{\text{\# polys after occlusion cull}}$) because of constant costs in the walkthrough loop of Performer. Fig. 13 illustrates our results.

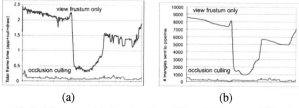

Figure 12: Statistics gathered during interactive walkthrough for a scene of 6M polygons on an Onyx2. (a) Total frame time (app+cull+draw) in seconds. (b) Number of triangles sent to the graphics pipeline.

As an informal comparison, we have implemented the algorithm of Cohen-Or *et al.* [COFHZ98, COZ98]. For the city model, their algorithm declares four times more visible objects on average and the computation time in our implementation is 150 times higher than for extended projection.

7.2 Occlusion sweep

To test the occlusion sweep, we used a model of a forest containing around 7,750 trees with 1,000 leaves each (7.8M triangles). The *Projection* of the leaves close to the projection plane were computed using the convex occluder *Projection* using the stencil buffer. The size of the convolution kernel was fixed to 5 pixels, and we used 15 planes for the sweep. The occlusion sweep took around 23 seconds per cell, 59 minutes for all 158 cells (no adaptive recursion was performed). This is slower than for the city because

15 successive planes are used for the occlusion sweep. 95.5% of the geometry was culled. Fig. 15 shows our sweeping process (we show only one quadrant of the forest for clarity). Observe how the leaves aggregate on the Occlusion Map.

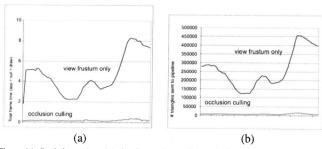

Figure 14: Statistics gathered during interactive walkthrough for a forest scene scene of 7.8M polygons on an Onyx2. (a) total frame time (app+cull+draw) in seconds. (b) Number of triangles sent to the graphics pipeline.

For a walkthrough of 30 sec, we obtained an average speed up of 24 for the interactive display, achieving a framerate between 8.6 and 15 fr/s (Fig. 14).

7.3 Discussion

We first have to note that the occlusions our method identifies are a subset of those detected by a point-based method [GKM93, ZMHH97]. Advantages of those methods also include their ability to treat dynamic occluders and the absence of preprocess or PVS storage. However, our method incurs no cost at display time, while in the massive rendering framework implemented at UNC [ACW+99] two processors are sometimes used just to perform occlusion culling. Moreover, for some applications (games, network-based virtual tourism, etc.), the preprocessing time is not really a problem since it is performed once by the designer of the application. Our PVS data then permits an efficient predictive approach to database pre-fetching which is crucial when displaying scenes over a network or which cannot fit into main memory.

We now discuss the conditions in which our method succeeds or fails to detect occlusion (infinite resolution of the *Depth* Map is here assumed). In Fig. 16 we represent in grey the volume corresponding to all the possible *Projections* of the occluders. The actual *Projections* corresponds to the intersection of these *Projection volumes* with the projection plane. The occlusion due to a single occluder is completely encoded if the occluder is in front of the plane and if its *Projection* volume intersects the plane (16(a)). If the plane is farther away, the *Projection* of the occluder becomes smaller, but so do the improved *Projections* of the occludees (however, if resolution is taken into account, more distant planes are worse because of our conservative rasterization).

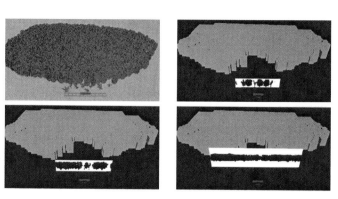

Figure 15: The sweeping process: (a) Part of our 7.8M polygon forest model, (b)-(d) three positions for the sweep projection planes. The yellow bounding boxes are the culled occludees.

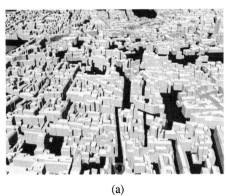
(a)

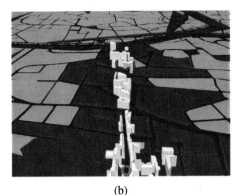
(b)

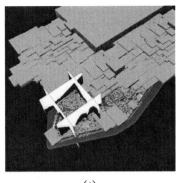
(c)

Figure 13: Results of our algorithm. (a) The scene from a bird's-eye view with no culling; the scene contains 600,000 building polygons and 2,000 moving cars containing 1,000 polygons each. (b) The same view using the result of our visibility culling algorithm (the terrain and street are poorly culled because of a poor hierarchical organization of our input scene). (c) Visualization of the occlusion culling approach, where yellow boxes represent the elements of the scene-graph hierarchy which have been occluded.

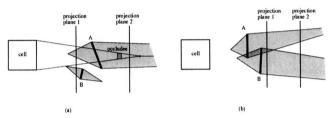

Figure 16: *Projection volumes* are represented in grey (supporting and separating lines are not represented for clarity). (a) Plane 1 does not completely capture the occlusion due to A (*e.g.*, for the occludee). Plane 2 does, but it does not capture the occlusion due to B. (b) Plane 1 capture occlusion fusion between A and B while plane 2 does not.

On the other hand, occluder fusion occurs between two occluders when their *Projection* volumes intersect in the region of the plane (Fig. 16(b)). In this case, the position of the plane is crucial, hence our heuristic which tries to maximize the projected surface on the plane. More elaborate heuristics could search for intersecting *Projection* volumes.

There are situations in which even a perfect occlusion culling method (*i.e.* an exact hidden-part removal) cannot cull enough geometry to achieve real-time rendering. For example, if the observer is at the top of a hill or on the roof of a building, the entire city may be visible. Other display acceleration techniques should thus be used together with our occlusion culling.

The trees used in the forest scene are coarse and made of large triangles. A typical high quality 3D model of tree may require around 50,000 triangles, and leaves are often smaller than our triangles. However, we consider that our results are obtained on a scene which is at least half-way between previous simple architectural examples with large occluders and a high quality forest scene.

8   Conclusions and future work

We have presented *extended projection* operators which permit conservative occlusion tests with respect to volumetric viewing cells. Our operators yield conservative occlusion tests and can handle *occluder fusion*. We have presented an efficient implementation of both operators, as well as an improvement in the case of convex or planar blockers.

We have defined a reprojection operator which allows us to reproject the *Projections* computed on a given projection plane onto another one, allowing us to define an *occlusion sweep*. The results we obtain show a significant speed-up of 15 times compared to a high-end interactive rendering library with view frustum culling only on a 6 million polygon city model.

Results have also been presented showing that our occlusion sweep makes it possible to compute occlusion caused by the cumulative effect of many small objects, such as leaves in a forest, with respect to a volumetric viewing cell.

Future work

Future work includes the computation of *Projections* for portals in architectural environments and the use of unions of convex shapes for the *Projection* of concave occluders. Concave polygonal meshes could also be projected from the center point of the cell, then "shrunk" to compute the *Projection*.

The speed of our method could make its use possible in an on-demand fashion, computing only visibility information for the neighbourhood of the observer. The extended projection concepts can also be used to allow some prediction with on-line occlusion culling methods [GKM93, ZMHH97]. Instead of only testing the bounding box of the objects, their extended projection with respect to a volume centered around the observer could also be tested.

Our method could also be applied to global illumination computation [TH93], LOD for animation, *e.g.,* [CH97], etc. The occlusion sweep could be extended to compute soft shadows.

To be really efficient for complex and cluttered scenes such as forest, our method should be extended to compute semi-quantitative occlusion to drive Level of Detail or image-based acceleration: the more hidden the object, the coarser its display. Human perception and masking effects should then be taken into account.

Acknowledgments

The ideas of this paper were initially developed when the first author was invited to the University of Stanford by Leo Guibas. The discussions with Leo and Mark de Berg have been invaluable for exploring and refining our ideas. Many thanks to Seth Teller, Pierre Poulin, Fabrice Neyret and Cyril Soler. This work was supported in part by a research grant of NSF and INRIA (INT-9724005).

References

[ACW+99]   D. Aliaga, J. Cohen, A. Wilson, Eric Baker, H. Zhang, C. Erikson, K. Hoff, T. Hudson, W. Stuerzlinger, R. Bastos, M. Whitton, F. Brooks, and D. Manocha. MMR: An interactive massive model rendering system using geometric and image-based acceleration. In *ACM Symp. on Interactive 3D Graphics*, 1999.

[ARB90]   J. Airey, J. Rohlf, and F. Brooks, Jr. Towards image realism with interactive update rates in complex virtual building environments. In *ACM Symp. on Interactive 3D Graphics*, 1990.

[CG85]   M. Cohen and D. Greenberg. The hemicube: A radiosity solution for complex environments. In *Computer Graphics (Proc. Siggraph)*, 1985.

[CH97]   D. A. Carlson and J. K. Hodgins. Simulation levels of detail for real-time animation. In *Graphics Interface*, 1997.

[Cla76]   J. H. Clark. Hierarchical geometric models for visible surface algorithms. *Communications of the ACM*, October 1976.

[COFHZ98] D. Cohen-Or, G. Fibich, D. Halperin, and E. Zadicario. Conservative visibility and strong occlusion for visibility partitionning of densely occluded scenes. In *Eurographics*, 1998.

[COZ98] D. Cohen-Or and E. Zadicario. Visibility streaming for network-based walkthroughs. In *Graphics Interface*, 1998.

[CT96] S. Coorg and S. Teller. Temporally coherent conservative visibility. In *ACM Symp. On Computational Geometry*, 1996.

[CT97] S. Coorg and S. Teller. Real-time occlusion culling for models with large occluders. In *ACM Symp. on Interactive 3D Graphics*, 1997.

[Dur99] Frédo Durand. *3D Visibility, analysis and applications*. PhD thesis, U. Joseph Fourier, Grenoble, 1999. http://www-imagis.imag.fr.

[FS93] T. Funkhouser and C. Séquin. Adaptive display algorithm for interactive frame rates during visualization of complex virtual environments. In *Computer Graphics (Proc. Siggraph)*, 1993.

[Fun95] T. Funkhouser. RING - A client-server system for multi-user virtual environments. *ACM Symp. on Interactive 3D Graphics*, 1995.

[Fun96] T. Funkhouser. Database management for interactive display of large architectural models. In *Graphics Interface*, 1996.

[GKM93] N. Greene, M. Kass, and G. Miller. Hierarchical Z-buffer visibility. In *Computer Graphics, (Proc. Siggraph)*, 1993.

[HMC+97] T. Hudson, D. Manocha, J. Cohen, M. Lin, K. Hoff, and H. Zhang. Accelerated occlusion culling using shadow frusta. In *ACM Symp. on Computational Geometry*, 1997.

[Jon71] C. B. Jones. A new approach to the 'hidden line' problem. *The Computer Journal*, 14(3):232–237, August 1971.

[LG95] D. Luebke and C. Georges. Portals and mirrors: Simple, fast evaluation of potentially visible sets. In *ACM Symp. on Interactive 3D Graphics*, 1995.

[LT99] F. Law and T. Tan. Preprocessing occlusion for real-time selective refinement. In *ACM Symp. on Interactive 3D Graphics*, 1999.

[Max91] Max. Unified sun and sky illumination for shadows under trees. *Comp. Vision, Graphics, and Image Processing. Graphical Models and Image Processing*, 53(3):223–230, May 1991.

[PD90] H. Plantinga and C. R. Dyer. Visibility, occlusion, and the aspect graph. *Int. J. of Computer Vision*, 5(2), 1990.

[RH94] J. Rohlf and J. Helman. IRIS performer: A high performance multiprocessing toolkit for real–Time 3D graphics. In *Computer Graphics (Proc. Siggraph)*, 1994.

[SC96] O. Sudarsky and C.Gotsman. Output-sensitive visibility algorithms for dynamic scenes with applications to virtual reality. In *Proc. Eurographics Conf.*, 1996.

[SDDS00] G. Schaufler, J. Dorsey, X. Decoret, and F. Sillion. Conservative volumetric visibility with occluder fusion. In *Computer Graphics (Proc. Siggraph)*, 2000.

[SLSD96] J. Shade, D. Lischinski, D. Salesin, and T. DeRose. Hierarchical image caching for accelerated walkthroughs of complex environments. In *Computer Graphics (Proc. Siggraph)*, 1996.

[SS98] C. Soler and F. Sillion. Fast calculation of soft shadow textures using convolution. In *Computer Graphics, (Proc. Siggraph)*, 1998.

[Ste97] A. James Stewart. Hierarchical visibility in terrains. *Eurographics Workshop on Rendering 1997*, June 1997.

[Tel92] S. J. Teller. *Visibility Computations in Densely Occluded Polyhedral Environments*. PhD thesis, UC Berkeley, 1992.

[TH93] S. Teller and P. Hanrahan. Global visibility algorithms for illumination computations. In *Computer Graphics (Proc. Siggraph)*, 1993.

[TS91] S. Teller and C. Séquin. Visibility preprocessing for interactive walkthroughs. In *Computer Graphics (Proc. Siggraph)*, 1991.

[vdPS99] M. van de Panne and J. Stewart. Effective compression techniques for precomputed visibility. In *Eurographics Workshop on Rendering*, 1999.

[WBP98] Y. Wang, H. Bao, and Q. Peng. Accelerated walkthroughs of virtual environments based on visibility processing and simplification. In *Proc. Eurographics Conf.*, 1998.

[WS99] P. Wonka and D. Schmalstieg. Occluder shadows for fast walkthroughs of urban environments. In *Proc. Eurographics Conf.*, 1999.

[ZMHH97] H. Zhang, D. Manocha, T. Hudson, and K. E. Hoff III. Visibility culling using hierarchical occlusion maps. In *Computer Graphics (proc. Siggraph)*, 1997.

A Extended projection using OpenGL

Recall that in Section 3.2 we described how to project convex occluders onto a projection plane as the intersection of the views from the vertices of the viewing cell. Here we present the details of an efficient OpenGL implementation. One of the problems is that during the projection of convex occluders we need to write consistent z-values and also treat the case of multiple blockers. An efficient way to do this in OpenGL is to use the stencil buffer, and a slightly involved z-buffer.

For a perspective projection, depth is considered from the viewpoint. Mapping the z value to our definition of depth requires an addition to set the zero on the projection plane. Unfortunately, OpenGL stores $\frac{1}{z}$ in the z-buffer, preventing a simple addition.

For a given occluder and a given cell, we project (in software) the blocker onto the projection plane, including the calculation of z values. The resulting 2D polygons are then rendered orthographically using a stencil buffer. Z-testing is performed with respect to z-values potentially written by a previously projected blocker, but depth values are not written. The stencil buffer is incremented by one. After all the polygons corresponding to each cell vertex have been rendered, the umbra region is defined by the region of the stencil buffer with the value 8 (*i.e.* blocked with respect to all cell vertices).

The eight 2D polygons are rendered again, using the stencil buffer to restrict writing to the umbra region only. The first polygon is rendered and z-values are written to the z-buffer. The 7 other polygons are then rendered but the z-test is inverted. This results in the *maximum* z-value being written to the z-buffer.

B Validity of the reprojection

We now show that the *Projection* of several occluders can be used as a single conservative equivalent occluder, *i.e.* an occludee hidden by this *Projection* is also hidden by the occluders. We prove the following more general property.

Property 3 *Consider an extended light source, any object A (convex or concave) and U the umbra region of A. Then the shadow of any subset U' of U lies inside U.*

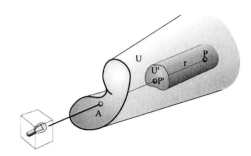

Figure 17: Umbra of the subset of an umbra. Point P is in the umbra of U' which is a subset of the umbra U of A. It is thus also in the umbra of A.

To prove this, consider a point P in the umbra of U' (Fig. 17). Any ray r going through P and the source intersects U'. Consider an intersection point P'. Since $P' \in U' \subset U$, P' is in the umbra of A. Thus any ray (r for example) going through P' and the source intersects A. We have shown that any ray going through P and the source intersects A. P is thus in the umbra of A. Note that property 3 presupposes neither convexity nor planarity of the object A.

If the cell is considered as a light source, this proves that any subset of the umbra of a set of occluders is a conservative version of these occluders. As we have seen, the *Projection* of an occluder which lies in front of the projection plane is its umbra on the plane. This *Projection* can thus be re-Projected as a new occluder. If the occluder lies behind the projection plane, its *Projection* does not lie inside its umbra because the projection plane is closer to the viewing cell than the occluder. Thus property 3 does not apply.

This proof together with property 1 is also an alternative proof of the validity of *Projection* when occluders are in front of the plane.

Adaptively Sampled Distance Fields: A General Representation of Shape for Computer Graphics

Sarah F. Frisken, Ronald N. Perry, Alyn P. Rockwood, and Thouis R. Jones

MERL – Mitsubishi Electric Research Laboratory

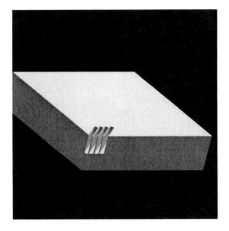

Figure 1. An ADF showing fine detail carved on a rectangular slab with a flat-edged chisel.

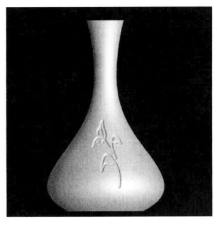

Figure 2. Artistic carving of a high order surface with a rounded chisel.

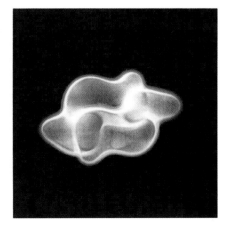

Figure 3. A semi-transparent electron probability distribution of a cyclohexane molecule.

ABSTRACT

Adaptively Sampled Distance Fields (ADFs) are a unifying representation of shape that integrate numerous concepts in computer graphics including the representation of geometry and volume data and a broad range of processing operations such as rendering, sculpting, level-of-detail management, surface offsetting, collision detection, and color gamut correction. Its structure is uncomplicated and direct, but is especially effective for quality reconstruction of complex shapes, e.g., artistic and organic forms, precision parts, volumes, high order functions, and fractals. We characterize one implementation of ADFs, illustrating its utility on two diverse applications: 1) artistic carving of fine detail, and 2) representing and rendering volume data and volumetric effects. Other applications are briefly presented.

CR Categories: I.3.6 [Computer Graphics]: Methodology and techniques – Graphics data structures; I.3.5 Computational Geometry and Object Modeling – Object modeling

Keywords: distance fields, carving, implicit surfaces, rendering, volume rendering, volume modeling, level of detail, graphics.

{frisken,perry,rockwood,jones}@merl.com

1. INTRODUCTION

In this paper we propose adaptively sampled distance fields (ADFs) as a fundamental graphical data structure. A distance field is a scalar field that specifies the minimum distance to a shape, where the distance may be signed to distinguish between the inside and outside of the shape. In ADFs, distance fields are adaptively sampled according to local detail and stored in a spatial hierarchy for efficient processing. We recommend ADFs as a simple, yet consolidating form that supports an extensive variety of graphical shapes and a diverse set of processing operations. Figures 1, 2, and 3 illustrate the quality of object representation and rendering that can be achieved with ADFs as well as the diversity of processing they permit. Figures 1 and 2 show fine detail carved on a slab and an artistic carving on a high order curved surface. Figure 3 depicts an electron probability distribution of a molecule that has been volume rendered with a glowing aura that was computed using a 3D noise function.

ADFs have advantages over several standard shape representations because as well as representing a broad class of forms, they can also be used for a number of important operations such as locating surface points, performing inside/outside and proximity tests, Boolean operations, blending and filleting, determining the closest points on a surface, creating offset surfaces, and morphing between shapes.

It is important to note that by *shape* we mean more than just the 3D geometry of physical objects. We use it in a broad context for any locus defined in a metric space. Shape can have arbitrary dimension and can be derived from measured scientific data, computer simulation, or object trajectories through time and space. It may even be non-Euclidean.

2. BACKGROUND

Commonly used shape representations for geometric design include parametric surfaces, subdivision surfaces, and implicit surfaces. Parametric representations include polygons, spline patches, and trimmed NURBs. Localizing (or generating) surface points on parametric surfaces is generally simpler than with other representations and hence they are easier to draw, tessellate, subdivide, and bound [3]. Parametric surfaces typically need associated data structures such as B-reps or space partitioning structures for representing connectivity and for more efficient localization of primitives in rendering, collision detection, and other processing. Creating and maintaining such structures adds to the computational and memory requirements of the representation. Parametric surfaces also do not directly represent object interiors or exteriors and are subsequently more difficult to blend and use in Boolean operations. While subdivision surfaces provide an enhanced design interface, e.g., shapes are topologically unrestricted, they still suffer from many of the same limitations as parametric representations, e.g., the need for auxiliary data structures [8], the need to handle extraordinary points, and the difficulty in controlling fine edits.

Implicit surfaces are defined by an implicit function $f(\mathbf{x} \in \mathbf{R}^n)$ = c, where c is the constant value of the iso-surface. Implicit functions naturally distinguish between interior and exterior and can be used to blend objects together and to morph between objects. Boolean operations defined for implicit functions provide a natural sculpting interface for implicit surfaces [3, 18]; however, when many operations are combined to generate a shape the computational requirements for interactive rendering or other processing become prohibitive. Furthermore, it is difficult to define an implicit function for an arbitrary object, or to chart points on its surface for rendering and other processing.

Volumetric data consists of a regular or irregular grid of sampled data, frequently generated from 3D image data or numerical simulation. Object surfaces can be represented as iso-surfaces of the sampled values and data between sample points can be reconstructed from local values for rendering or other processing. Several systems have been developed for sculpting volumetric data using Boolean operations on sample density values [1, 2]. However, in these systems, iso-surfaces lack sharp corners and edges because the density values are low-pass filtered near object surfaces to avoid aliasing artifacts in rendering. In addition, the need to pre-select volume size and the use of regular sampling force these systems to limit the amount of detail achievable. Sensable Devices™ has recently introduced a commercial volume sculpting system [21]. To create detailed models, very large volumes are required (a minimum of 512 Mbytes of RAM) and the system is advertised for modeling only "organic" forms, i.e. shapes with rounded edges and corners.

Additional representations of shape for computer graphics include look-up tables, Fourier expansions, particle systems, grammar-based models, and fractals (iterated function systems), all of which tend to have focused applications [10].

The ADF representation, its applications, and the implementation details presented in this paper are new. Sampled distance fields have, however, been used previously in a number of specific applications. They have been used in robotics for path planning [12, 13] and to generate swept volumes [20]. In computer graphics, sampled distance fields were proposed for volume rendering [11], to generate offset surfaces [4, 17], and to morph between surface models [7, 17]. Level sets can either be generated from distance fields or they can be used to generate sampled distance fields [15, 22]. As with regularly sampled volumes, regularly sampled distance fields suffer from large volume sizes and a resolution limited by the sampling rate. These limitations are addressed by ADFs.

3. ADAPTIVE DISTANCE FIELDS

A *distance field* is a scalar field that specifies the minimum distance to a shape, where the distance may be signed to distinguish between the inside and outside of the shape. As simple examples, consider the distance field of the unit sphere S in $\mathbf{R}^3$ given by $h(\mathbf{x}) = 1 - (x^2 + y^2 + z^2)^{\frac{1}{2}}$, in which h is the Euclidean signed distance from S, or $h(\mathbf{x}) = 1 - (x^2 + y^2 + z^2)$, in which h is the algebraic signed distance from S, or $h(\mathbf{x}) = (1 - (x^2 + y^2 + z^2))^2$, in which h is an unsigned distance from S.

The distance field is an effective representation of shape. However, regularly sampled distance fields have drawbacks because of their size and limited resolution. Because fine detail requires dense sampling, immense volumes are needed to accurately represent classical distance fields with regular sampling when *any* fine detail is present, even when the fine detail occupies only a small fraction of the volume. To overcome this limitation, ADFs use adaptive, detail-directed sampling, with high sampling rates in regions where the distance field contains fine detail and low sampling rates where the field varies smoothly. Adaptive sampling permits arbitrary accuracy in the reconstructed field together with efficient memory usage. In order to process the adaptively sampled data more efficiently, ADFs store the sampled data in a hierarchy for fast localization. The combination of detail-directed sampling and the use of a spatial hierarchy for data storage allows ADFs to represent complex shapes to arbitrary precision while permitting efficient processing.

In summary, ADFs consist of adaptively sampled distance values organized in a spatial data structure together with a method for reconstructing the underlying distance field from the sampled values. One can imagine a number of different instantiations of ADFs using a variety of distance functions, reconstruction methods, and spatial data structures. To provide a clear elucidation of ADFs, we focus on one specific instance for the remainder of this paper. This instance is simple, but results in efficient rendering, editing, and other processing used by applications developed in this paper. Specifically, we demonstrate an ADF which stores distance values at cell vertices of an octree data structure and uses trilinear interpolation for reconstruction and gradient estimation. The wide range of research in adaptive representations suggest several other ADF instantiations based on, for example, wavelets [5] or multi-resolution Delaunay tetrahedralizations [6].

3.1 Octree-based ADFs

Octree data structures are well known and we assume familiarity (see [19]). For purposes of instruction, we demonstrate the concepts in 2D (with quadtrees), which are easily generalized to higher dimensions. In a quadtree-based ADF, each quadtree cell contains the sampled distance values of the cell's 4 corners and pointers to parent and child cells.

Given a shape as in Figure 4a, subdivision of a cell in the quadtree depends on the variation of the distance field (shown in Figure 4c) over the parent cell. This differs from 3-color quadtrees [19] which represent object boundaries by assigning one of three types to each cell in the quadtree: interior, exterior, and boundary. In 3-color quadtrees, all boundary cells are subdivided to a predetermined highest resolution level. In contrast, boundary cells of ADFs are only subdivided when the distance field within a cell is not well approximated by bilinear interpolation of its corner values. Hence, large cells can be used to represent edges in regions where the shape is relatively smooth, resulting in significantly more compression than 3-color quadtrees. This is illustrated in Figures 4b and 4d where the ADF of 4d requires only 1713 cells while the 3-color quadtree of 4b requires 23,573 cells. In the ADF quadtree, straight edges of the "R" are represented by large cells; only corners provoke repeated

 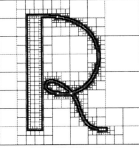

Figures 4a "R" and **4b** 3-color quadtree containing 23,573 cells.

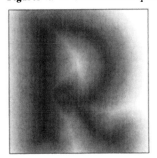 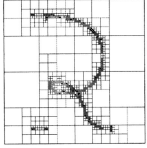

Figures 4c Distance field of "R" and **4d** ADF containing 1713 cells.

Error Tolerance	Triangle Count	ADF Cell Count	ADF Sample Count
6.25×10^{-5}	32,768	16,201	24,809
3.13×10^{-5}	131,072	44,681	67,405
1.56×10^{-6}	2,097,152	131,913	164,847

Table 1. Comparison of triangle count for a sphere (r = 0.4) to ADF size.

subdivision.

Figure 4d also shows that even highly curved edges can be efficiently represented by ADFs. Because bilinear interpolation represents curvature reasonably well, cells with smoothly curved edges do not require many levels in the ADF hierarchy. Cells that do require many levels in the hierarchy are concentrated at corners and cusps.

These are typical statistics for 2D objects. As another indication of ADF size, Table 1 compares the number of triangles required to represent a sphere of radius 0.4 to the number of cells and distance (sample) values of the corresponding ADF when both the triangles and the interpolated distance values are within a given error tolerance from the true sphere.

Higher order reconstruction methods and better predicates for subdivision might be employed to further increase compression, but the numbers already suggest a point of diminishing returns for the extra effort.

3.2 Generating ADFs

The generation of an ADF requires a procedure or function to produce the distance function, $h(\mathbf{x})$ at $\mathbf{x} \in \mathbf{R}^n$, where distance is interpreted very broadly as in Section 3. Continuity, differentiability, and bounded growth of the distance function can be used to advantage in rendering or other processing, but are not required. Some of the images in this paper utilize distance functions that are non-differentiable (Figure 8) and highly non-Euclidean with rapid polynomial growth (Figures 2 and 3).

One example of a distance function is the implicit form of an object, for which the distance function can correspond directly to the implicit function. A second example includes procedures that determine the Euclidean distance to a parametric surface. For

Figure 5. A thin walled version of the Utah Teapot rendered using sampled ray casting and Phong lighting from an ADF computed from a 32 bicubic Bezier patch model.

example, Figure 5 was rendered from the distance field computed for a 32 bicubic Bezier patch model of the Utah Teapot. Distances to Bezier patches were determined by solving 7th order Bezier equations using the Bezier clipping algorithm described in [14]. To define an inside and outside for the teapot, the unsigned distance from the Bezier surface is biased to produce the signed distance field of an offset surface, resulting in a thin-walled teapot. Other distance functions include Euclidean distances for a triangle model that can be computed as the minimum of the signed distances to each of the triangles in the model and distance fields computed by applying Boolean operations to the distance fields of primitive elements in a CSG representation.

Given a distance function, there are a number of ways to generate an ADF. Two simple examples include a bottom-up and a top-down approach which are described briefly here. The bottom-up approach starts with a regularly sampled distance field of finite resolution and constructs a fully populated octree for the 3D data. Starting with the smallest cells in the octree, a group of 8 neighboring cells is coalesced if and only if none of the cells have any child cells and the sampled distances of all of the 8 cells can be reconstructed from the sample values of their parent to a specified error tolerance. After all cells are considered for coalescing at a given level in the hierarchy, groups of cells at the next level are considered. When no cells are coalesced at a given level or the root node is reached, the ADF generation is complete.

In the top-down approach, first the distance values for the root node of the ADF hierarchy are computed. ADF cells are then recursively subdivided according to a subdivision rule. For example, if the primary interest is the iso-surface represented in the field, the recursive subdivision would stop if the given cell is guaranteed not to contain the surface, if the cell contains the surface but passes some predicate, or if a specified maximum level in the hierarchy is reached. One can imagine many predicates to control the subdivision. In examples presented in this paper, we use a simple predicate that compares distances within a cell computed using the distance function to distances reconstructed from the cell's sampled values. In this predicate, the absolute differences between the computed and reconstructed distances are determined at the center of the cell and the centers of each of the cell's faces and edges (i.e. 19 differences per cell). If any of the differences are greater than a specified error tolerance, the cell is subdivided.

3.3 Reconstructing ADFs

Each ADF cell has an associated method for reconstructing distance values between sampled points. In the case of the 3D octree, distance values within a cell are reconstructed from the 8 corner distance values stored per cell using standard trilinear interpolation. In addition to distance values, many operations such as rendering, collision detection, or closest point localization require surface normals and hence, processing an ADF may also require a method for estimating surface normals from the sampled data. For distance fields, the surface normal is equal to the normalized gradient of the distance field at the surface. There are several methods for estimating the gradient of sampled data. We use the analytic gradient of the trilinear reconstruction within each cell: $grad(x,y,z) = (h(x_r,y,z) - h(x_l,y,z), h(x,y_u,z) - h(x,y_d,z), h(x,y,z_f) - h(x,y,z_b))$, where (x_r,y,z), (x_l,y,z), (x,y_u,z), etc. are projections of (x,y,z) onto the right, left, up, down, front, and back faces of the cell, respectively. In theory, this cell-localized gradient estimation can result in C^1 discontinuities at cell boundaries but as can be seen from the figures, these artifacts are not noticeable with sufficient subdivision.

4. APPLICATIONS AND IMPLEMENTATION DETAILS

ADFs have application in a broad range of computer graphics problems. We present two examples below to illustrate the utility of ADFs and to provide some useful implementation details on processing methods such as rendering and sculpting ADF models. This section ends with short descriptions of several other applications to give the reader an idea of the diverse utility of ADFs.

4.1 Precise carving

Figures 1, 2, and 6 show examples of objects represented and carved as ADFs. Because objects are represented as distance fields, the ADF can represent and reconstruct smooth surfaces from sampled data. Because the ADF efficiently samples distance fields with high local curvature, it can represent sharp surface corners without requiring excessive memory. Carving is intuitive; the object is edited simply by moving a tool across the surface. It does not require control point manipulation, remeshing the surface, or trimming. By storing sample points in an octree, both localizing the surface for editing and determining ray-surface intersections for rendering are efficient.

Like implicit surfaces, ADFs can be sculpted using simple Boolean operations applied to the object and tool distance fields. Figures 1, 2, and 6 show carving using the difference operator, $h_{carved}(\mathbf{x}) = min(h_{object}(\mathbf{x}), -h_{tool}(\mathbf{x}))$. Other operators include addition, $h_{carved}(\mathbf{x}) = max(h_{object}(\mathbf{x}), h_{tool}(\mathbf{x}))$, and intersection, $h_{carved}(\mathbf{x}) = min(h_{object}(\mathbf{x}), h_{tool}(\mathbf{x}))$. Blending or filleting can also be defined for shaping or combining objects (as was done for the molecules of Figures 3 and 7). While these Boolean operations apply to the entire distance field, for systems where only surfaces are important, application of the operations can be limited in practice to a region within a slightly extended bounding box of the tool.

The basic edit operation is much like a localized ADF generation. The first step in the editing process is to determine the smallest ADF cell, or set of cells, entirely containing the tool's extended bounding box (obvious consideration of the ADF boundaries apply). The containing cell is then recursively subdivided, applying the difference operator to the object and tool values to obtain new values for the carved ADF. During the recursive subdivision, cell values from the object are obtained either from existing sampled values or by reconstruction if an edited cell is subdivided beyond its original level. Subdivision rules similar to those of top-down generation are applied, with the exception that the containing cell must be subdivided to some minimum level related to the tool size.

The carving examples were rendered using ray casting with analytic surface intersection. In this method, a surface point is determined by finding the intersection between a ray cast into the ADF octree from the eye and the zero-value iso-surface of the ADF. Local gradients are computed at surface points using the

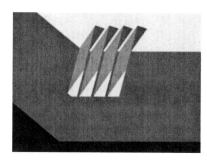

Figure 6. A close up of the carved slab in Figure 1.

gradient estimation described above (the figures were rendered with simple Phong lighting). When the traversing ray passes through a leaf node of the octree, intersection between the ray and the surface reconstructed from the 8 cell sample values is tested. We have used two different methods to find the ray-surface intersection; a cubic root solver that finds the exact intersection of the ray with the trilinear surface defined by the distance values at the cell corners (as in [16]), and a linear approximation which determines the distance values where the ray enters and exits the cell and computes the linear zero-crossing if the two values have a different sign. Both methods work well but the linear approximation has proven to be faster and its rendered images are not visibly different from those rendered with the cubic solver. When solving for intersections, we set the distance at the entry point of a cell to be equal to the distance at the exit from the previous cell. This avoids the crack problem discussed in [24] for rendering hierarchical volume data, preventing C^0 discontinuities in the surface where ADF cells of different size abut. Most of the images shown in this paper were rendered using a supersampling of 16 rays per pixel followed by the application of a Mitchell filter of radius 2.0.

The octree promotes efficient ray traversal even for very complicated scenes. Rendering the Menger Sponge (Figure 8) takes approximately the same amount of time as rendering less complex ADF models. As in most rendering methods based on spatial decomposition, rendering time is determined more by screen coverage than by model complexity. Current rendering rates are fast enough for interactive updating of the carving region during editing. Preliminary tests indicate that an order of magnitude improvement in the rendering speed of the entire image can be achieved by adaptive supersampling.

4.2 Volume data

ADFs are also amenable to volume rendering and can be used to produce interesting effects. For example, offset surfaces can be used to render thick, translucent surfaces. Adding volume texture within the thick surface in the form of variations in color or transparency is relatively easy. In addition, distance values farther away from the zero-valued iso-surface can be used for special effects. Figure 7 shows a cocaine molecule volume rendered in a haze of turbulent mist. The mist was generated using a color function based on distance from the molecule surface. To achieve the turbulence the distance value input to the color function is modulated by a noise function based on position [9].

We use a ray casting volume renderer to demonstrate some of these effects. Colors and opacities are accumulated at equally spaced samples along each ray using a back-to-front rendering algorithm. Sample points that lie near the zero-value iso-surface are shaded with Phong lighting.

Our sampled ray caster is not optimized for speed. However, properties of the ADF data structure can be used to greatly increase the rendering rate. For example, the octree allows us to quickly skip regions of the volume that are far from the surface. In

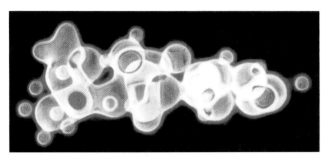

Figure 7. An ADF cocaine molecule volume rendered in a haze of turbulent mist. The mist was generated using a color function dependent on distance from the molecule surface.

addition, because distances to the closest surface are available at each sample point, space-leaping methods can be used to speed up rendering [26].

4.3 Other application areas

4.3.1 Representing complexity

Complexity may be considered from several viewpoints. Firstly, the *visual complexity* of an object might include factors such as surface variation and topology. Secondly, the *representation complexity* is determined by the size and intricacy of the data structure needed to represent the object. The third measure of complexity considers the *algebraic complexity* of the object, which includes such factors as polynomial degree, transcendental functions, and numerical routines required to define the object's shape. Such routines are pertinent especially when algebraic distance is employed for the distance field.

Figure 8 shows a good example of the first two types of complexity, the Menger Sponge, which is a fractal created recursively by subtracting smaller and smaller crossing cuboids from an initial cube. In the limit there is no neighborhood of the surface that is not punctured regardless of how small the neighborhood is chosen. It is an infinite perforation, a 3D version of the famous Cantor set.

After each level of subtraction there are 20 self-similar subcuboids generated. An artless approach to maintaining the data structure would generate order $O(20^n)$ faces for n iterations. Even if shared faces were combined and interior faces culled, an approach that keeps a boundary representation (B-rep) without troublesome T-junctions would have $O(12^n)$ faces. To be more exact, after seven iterations there would be 26 million+ faces in a B-rep data structure. Consider the difficulty of performing proximity tests, collision detection, or inside/outside tests with such a representation. In contrast, these tests are much simpler using ADFs. Far from being a contrived case, the complexity of the distance field of the Menger Sponge is representative of the distance fields of many naturally occurring shapes which would present similar problems for traditional methods.

Figures 2 and 7 both demonstrate ADFs' ability to handle algebraic complexity. While Figure 7 reconstructs an approximate probability density field for a molecule of 43 atoms ($C_{17}H_{21}NO_4$), the vase in Figure 2 is defined first as a rotation of a quintic Bezier curve. Mathematically, it is posed as a rational implicit function with a square root of a (total) degree 16 over 2. Cubic Bezier curves are then mapped onto the surface as paths for the carving tool. In this case, the carver is a curved chisel, resulting in a very high degree tubular surface on the vase. This carving path and vase create an algebraically very complex distance field, which is nevertheless cleanly reconstructed and rendered.

Figure 8. An ADF of the Menger Sponge, a fractal created recursively by subtracting smaller and smaller crossing cuboids from an initial cube. Four levels of recursion are shown.

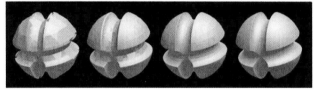

Figure 9. Four LOD models with varying amounts of error rendered from an ADF octree.

4.3.2 Level-of-detail models

There are at least two approaches for representing ADF models at different levels of detail for rendering and progressive transmission of models. The simplest approach is to truncate the ADF at fixed levels in the octree. The truncation can either be done during rendering or transmission, during generation, or to an existing high resolution ADF. A second method uses the error generated in the test for cell subdivision during top-down generation of the ADF. By storing this error within the cell, an LOD model can be generated by truncating ADF cells with errors less than that specified for the given LOD. This provides a more continuously varying parameter for selecting the LOD and provides degradation of the object shape that is consistent for both smooth and highly curved portions of the surface as the level of the LOD model decreases. This second method is illustrated in Figure 9 where four LOD models with varying amounts of error are rendered from an ADF octree.

4.3.3 Collision detection

Distance fields have been used for collision avoidance in robotics and for detecting collisions and computing penetration forces in haptics [12, 13]. Octrees or other hierarchies of bounding boxes have also been used successfully to accelerate collision detection algorithms. The combination of these two representations in the ADF as well as the ability to represent offset surfaces and surfaces at different levels of detail suggest that ADFs have significant potential for applications that require collision detection.

4.3.4 Color gamut representation

Devices such as color printers and monitors have unique color characteristics. Each can represent colors within their own particular color gamut, which is restricted, for example, by the types of dyes used by the printer. When an image is acquired or designed on one system and then displayed or printed on another, it is often important to match colors as closely as possible. This involves correcting colors that fall outside of the device's gamut and sometimes requires a complicated mapping to warp the gamut of one system onto that of another [23].

Most color devices represent their color gamuts in large look-up-tables (LUTs). Usually, a binary table is used to test colors against the device's gamut to see if they fall in or out of gamut. If a color falls out of gamut, a set of model coefficients and look-up tables are used to map the color onto the 'closest' device color. Using ADFs to represent a device's gamut has several advantages over the LUT approach. First, out-of-gamut tests are easily performed with ADFs and edge-sampling errors that occur with the use of binary tables are avoided. Second, an ADF out-of-gamut test provides more information than is available with binary tables; the distance indicates how far out of gamut a color lies and the gradient indicates the direction to the nearest in-gamut color. Third, since ADFs use adaptive sampling, they should provide significant compression over LUT representations. Finally, since distance fields can be used to warp between shapes, ADFs may prove to be a useful representation for mapping between device gamuts.

4.3.5 Machining

ADFs provide powerful tools for computer aided machining. The use of a distance function for representing surfaces allows the representation of the surface, the interior of the object, and the material that must be removed. Knowledge of the object interior can be used for part testing (e.g., part thickness tests [25]). A representation of the volume outside of the surface as well as distances to the closest surface can be used for planning tool paths and tool sizes for the machining process. Offset surfaces can be used to plan rough cutting for coarse-to-fine machining or for designing part molds for casting. The size of cells at the surface and the object normal near the surface can be used to select tool size and orientation. Finally, as illustrated in Figure 6, ADFs can represent fine surfaces and sharp corners efficiently, making it possible to represent machining precision in the ADF model.

5. CONCLUSIONS

Although distance fields have been used in certain specific applications as mentioned above, the breadth and flexibility of their application to problems in computer graphics has not been appreciated, in part due to their large memory requirements. ADFs address this issue by adaptively sampling the distance field and storing sampled values in a spatial hierarchy. For 2D shapes, we typically achieve better than 20:1 reductions over straightforward boundary (3-color) quadtrees. Nevertheless, ADFs maintain the reconstruction quality of the original distance field as seen in the examples presented; shapes, even those with high frequency components such as edges or corners, are reconstructed accurately.

Distance fields can embody considerable information about a shape, not just the critical zero-valued iso-surface, but also information about the volume in which it sits, an indication of inside vs. outside, and gradient and proximity information.

Operations on a shape can often be achieved by operations on its distance field. For example, Boolean set operations become simple max/min operations on the field; edges and corners can be rounded by low-pass filtering; and so forth.

ADFs tend to separate generation of shapes into a preprocess step that may require complex and time-consuming methods, and a process for graphical operations that is fast and tolerant of various types of complexity. Indeed, fractals and mathematically sophisticated or carved shapes can be processed as quickly as much simpler shapes. The wide diversity of such manipulations include, for example, proximity testing (for collision detection, haptics, color gamut correction, milling), efficient ray-surface intersection for rendering, localized reconstruction, surface and volume texturing, blending, filleting, offset surfaces, and shape warping.

6. FUTURE WORK

The introduction of ADFs opens up a wide range of future directions. Considerable research is left to investigate the possible transformations between shape and its distance field. Different hierarchical structures and reconstruction methods await testing and experience. For example, wavelets show particular promise [5], and Delaunay tetrahedralizations have been successfully used for multiresolution representation of volume data [6]. The relative compactness for very complex shapes has implications for level of detail management and progressive transmission. Efficient conversion between ADFs and standard (e.g. triangle and NURB) models is a valuable undertaking. Finally, we look forward to combining ADFs with more powerful rendering methods; for example, we envision hierarchical radiosity using form factors based on the ADF cells.

7. ACKNOWLEDGEMENTS

We gratefully acknowledge the help of Mars Brimhall, John Ford, and Stephan Roth in generating some of the images in this paper.

8. REFERENCES

[1] R. Avila and L. Sobierajski, "A haptic interaction method for volume visualization", Proc. IEEE Visualization'96, pp. 197-204, 1996.

[2] J. Baerentzen, "Octree-based volume sculpting", Proc. Late Breaking Hot Topics, IEEE Visualization'98, pp. 9-12, 1998.

[3] J. Bloomenthal, Introduction to Implicit Surfaces, Morgan Kaufman Publishers, 1997.

[4] D. Breen, S. Mauch and R. Whitaker, "3D scan conversion of CSG models into distance volumes", Proc. 1998 IEEE Symposium on Volume Visualization, pp. 7-14, 1998.

[5] M. Chow and M. Teichmann, "A Wavelet-Based Multiresolution Polyhedral Object Representation", Visual Proc. SIGGRAPH '97, p. 175, 1997.

[6] P. Cignoni, L. De Floriani, C. Montani, E. Puppo, R. Scopigno, "Multiresolution Modeling and Rendering of Volume Data based on Simplicial Complexes", 1994 ACM Volume Visualization Conference Proceedings, 1994, pp.19-26.

[7] D. Cohen-Or, D. Levin, and A. Solomovici, "Three-dimensional distance field metamorphosis", ACM Transactions on Graphics, 1997.

[8] T. DeRose, M. Kass, T. Truong, "Subdivision surfaces in character animation", Proc. SIGGRAPH '98, pp. 85-94, 1998.

[9] D. Ebert, F.K. Musgrave, D. Peachy, K. Perlin, S. Worley, Texturing and Modeling a Procedural Approach, Academic Press, 1998.

[10] J. Foley, A. van Dam, S. Feiner, and J. Hughes, Computer Graphics: Principles and Practice, Addison-Wesley, 1992.

[11] S. Gibson, "Using DistanceMaps for smooth surface representation in sampled volumes", Proc. 1998 IEEE Volume Visualization Symposium, pp. 23-30, 1998.

[12] R. Kimmel, N. Kiryati and A. Bruckstein, "Multi-valued distance maps for motion planning on surfaces with moving obstacles", IEEE Trans. on Robotics & Automation, 14, pp. 427-436, 1998.

[13] J. Lengyel, M. Reichert, B. Donald and D. Greenberg, "Real-time robot motion planning using rasterizing computer graphics hardware", Proc. SIGGRAPH '90, pp. 327-335, 1990.

[14] T. Nishita, T.W. Sederberg and M. Kakimoto, "Ray tracing trimmed rational surface patches", Proc. SIGGRAPH '90, pp. 337-345, 1990.

[15] S. Osher and J. Sethian, "Fronts propagating with curvature-dependent speed: algorithms based on Hamilton-Jacobi formulation", J. Computational Physics, 79, pp. 12-49, 1988.

[16] S. Parker, M. Parker, Y. Livnat, P. Sloan, C. Hansen, and P. Shirley, "Interactive ray tracing for volume visualization" IEEE Transactions On Visualization and Computer Graphics, Vol. 5 (3), pp. 238-250, 1999.

[17] B. Payne and A. Toga, "Distance field manipulation of surface models", IEEE Computer Graphics and Applications, pp. 65-71, 1992.

[18] A. Ricci, "A constructive geometry for computer graphics", Computer Journal, Vol. 16, No. 2, pp. 157-160, 1973.

[19] H. Samet, The Design and Analysis of Spatial Data Structures, Addison-Wesley, 1989.

[20] W. Schroeder, W. Lorensen, and S. Linthicum, "Implicit modeling of swept surfaces and volumes," Proc. Visualization '94, pp. 40-45, 1994.

[21] Sensable Devices' FreeForm modeling software. http://www.sensable.com/freeform.

[22] J. Sethian, Level Set Methods: Evolving Interfaces in Geometry, Fluid Mechanics, Computer Vision, and Material Science, Cambridge University Press, 1996.

[23] M. Stone, W. Cowan, J. Beatty, "Color gamut mappings and the printing of digital color images", ACM Transaction on Graphics, Vol. 7, pp. 249-292, 1988.

[24] R. Westermann, O. Sommer, T. Ertl, "Decoupling polygon rendering from geometry using rasterization hardware", in Proc. Eurographics Rendering Workshop '99, pp. 45-56, 1999.

[25] R. Yagel, S. Lu, A. Rubello, R. Miller, "Volume-based reasoning and visualization of dicastability" In Proc. IEEE Visualization '95, pp. 359-362, 1995.

[26] K. Zuiderveld, A. Koning, and M. Viergever, "Acceleration of ray-casting using 3D distance transforms", in Proc. Visualization in Biomedical Computing '92, pp. 324-335, 1992.

Patching Catmull-Clark Meshes

Jörg Peters*

University of Florida

NurbsSurface()

Figure 1: Catmull-Clark subdivision sequence completed as a collection of large Nurbs patches (top five patches are shown).

Abstract

Named after the title, the PCCM transformation is a simple, explicit algorithm that creates large, smoothly joining bicubic Nurbs patches from a refined Catmull-Clark subdivision mesh. The resulting patches are maximally large in the sense that one patch corresponds to one quadrilateral facet of the initial, coarsest quadrilateral mesh before subdivision. The patches join parametrically C^2 and agree with the Catmull-Clark limit surface except in the immediate neighborhood of extraordinary mesh nodes; in such a neighborhood they join at least with tangent continuity and interpolate the limit of the extraordinary mesh node. The PCCM transformation integrates naturally with array-based implementations of subdivision surfaces.

CR Categories: I.3.5 [surface representation, splines]: I.3.6—graphics data structures

Keywords: CAD, Curves & Surfaces, Geometric Modeling

1 Motivation

Catmull-Clark subdivision meshes [2] are an increasingly popular surface representation that comes equipped with tools for adapting shape locally and globally [3, 6]. The limit surfaces can be directly evaluated [13] and an ample body of analysis assures tangent continuity [1, 11, 14]. It would be nice though if we could stop the subdivision process at any point, apply a simple transformation and get a compact, explicit surface representation in the form of a small collection of maximally large, standard spline (Nurbs) patches that join just as smoothly and largely agree with the Catmull-Clark limit surface. The PCCM (Patching Catmull-Clark Meshes) algorithm is such a transformation.

*NSF NYI CCR-9457806

The paper has three parts: a review of basics and literature, the specification of the algorithm and the discussion of the properties of its output:

- Each Nurbs patch covers a maximally large region of the mesh corresponding to the coarsest level quadrilateral mesh facets.

- The patches join C^2 almost everywhere and are at least tangent continuous near the extraordinary mesh nodes. Transitions between patches are almost all parametric.

- The Nurbs patches are polynomial, of order 4 (degree 3) and in interpolating form with 4-fold knots.

- The Nurbs patches differ from the limit surface of the Catmull-Clark subdivision only near the extraordinary mesh nodes. (The patches have generically finite curvature whereas the generic curvature of the Catmull-Clark limit surface at extraordinary mesh nodes is infinite.)

- Nurbs patches, Catmull-Clark subdivision and the PCCM algorithm can use the same array-based data structures.

2 Nurbs, Catmull-Clark and Prior Work

A Nurbs patch $Q(u, v) \in \mathbf{R}^3$ of order 4 (bicubic tensor-product spline) is defined by two nondecreasing sequences of scalars (called *knots*) of length $k+4$, one for the u and one for the v parameter and k^2 control points $Q_{uv} \in \mathbf{R}^3$. If we connect control points whose indices differ by 1 in exactly one slot, we obtain a *control net* that outlines the patch. A concrete interface for Nurbs patches is the `gluNurbsSurface` specification in OpenGL [4]. By definition, Nurbs do not change geometrically under *knot insertion*. (Repeated insertion of the same knot just transforms to Bézier a.k.a. `glMap` form.) Inserting numbers into the knot sequence subdivides the parameter domain into more pieces between knots. Correspondingly, the control net must be refined or [sic] subdivided by specific rules. For example, if we start with a uniform (evenly spaced) knot sequence consisting of even integers and insert new knots at odd integers we can classify the new control points as (a) facet points, F, corresponding to odd knots, (b) edge points, E, corresponding to one odd and one even knot, and (c) vertex points, V, corresponding to even knots. The weights for new F, E and V type points as averages of the old points are displayed as averaging masks:

$$4F \leftarrow \begin{matrix} 1 & 1 \\ 1 & 1 \end{matrix} \qquad 16E \leftarrow \begin{matrix} 1 & 1 \\ 6 & 6 \\ 1 & 1 \end{matrix} \qquad 64V \leftarrow \begin{matrix} 1 & 6 & 1 \\ 6 & 36 & 6 \\ 1 & 6 & 1 \end{matrix} \qquad (1)$$

For example, a new F point is the average of four surrounding old points. A central contribution of [2] was the addition of a rule for extraordinary mesh nodes V with $n \neq 4$ neighbors:

$$4n^2 V \leftarrow \qquad A = 4n^2 - 7n. \qquad (2)$$

The idea of converting from the subdivision mesh back to a spline representation for rendering dates back at least to DeRose, Kass and Truong [3], before the availability of the full Pixar subdivision pipeline. Compared to the large patches derived below, these patches are smaller and more numerous and the conversion is not well-defined in the neighborhood of extraordinary mesh nodes. Nasri and Peters [9] use an approximation to the limit surface of the Doo-Sabin subdivision to get a quickly convergent series of approximations to the volume of the enclosed subdivision object. The approximation surface, however, is only position continuous. Prautzsch [12] gives an elegant solution to the difficult problem of filling n-sided holes. G^2 completion of a Catmull-Clark mesh requires order 7 patches and at least nine times as many as the large patches derived below. Grimm and Hughes [5] use subdivision as a preprocessing step to generating smooth manifolds with which they associate an interesting class of rationally blended spline surfaces. Their approach would generate at least nine times as many rational spline patches either over nonstandard domains or of high degree.

3 From Mesh to Surface

As Figure 1 illustrates, all mesh facets are four-sided either on input or after at most one subdivision step. We refer to each facet of this coarsest quad-mesh as the level 0 of a *quad* and think of ℓth step of Catmull-Clark subdivision as subdividing the level $\ell - 1$ of each quad into 4 times as many subfacets for a total of 4^ℓ subfacets at level ℓ.

Indexing. Since the goal is to transform a repeatedly subdivided mesh we can treat each corner of a quad in isolation as shown in Figures 2 and 3. The quads surrounding the corner point are arranged in counterclockwise order indexed by i. The nodes $P_{uv}(i)$ of the ith quad lie on a uv grid of mesh lines. The double subscripts uv are the Greville abscissae, scaled by 3, of the output Nurbs surface. $P_{00}(i)$ is the corner node for all i and $P_{l0}(i+1) = P_{0l}(i)$. The same indexing is used for the output control points $Q_{uv}(i)$. If a quad does not have a neighbor due to a manifold boundary, we use the same rule as the Catmull-Clark subdivision, say [8, 15], to provide an additional outside layer of mesh nodes.

The PCCM(ℓ) Algorithm: The *input* is a mesh of a ℓ times subdivided quads with nodes $P_{uv}(i) \in \mathbf{R}^3$. (If all vertices have 4 or an odd number of neighbors then $\ell > 0$ suffices otherwise $\ell > 1$ should hold.) The *output* is one bicubic (order 4) Nurbs surface (patch) for every quad. The patches are in standard *interpolating form*. That is, the u and the v knot sequence start and end with a 4-fold knot (at 0 and at $k = 2^\ell$ where ℓ is the subdivision level). Each sequence can have up to two double knots (at 1 and $2^\ell - 1$) and has single knots otherwise, e.g. 0, 0, 0, 0, 1, 1, 2, 3, 4, 5, 6, 7, 7, 8, 8, 8, 8. Systems that do not allow internal double knots but do allow uneven knot spacing with minimal distance ϵ can be accommodated by perturbing one inner

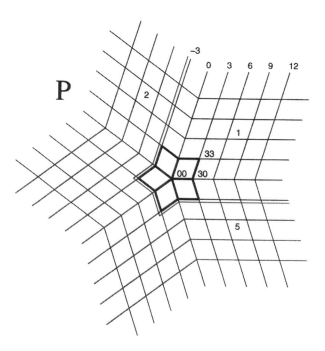

Figure 2: Catmull-Clark mesh in the neighborhood of an extraordinary mesh node of degree 5. Quads are labeled in counterclockwise order from 1 to n around the extraordinary mesh node so that all indices i are interpreted $(i + n - 1) \mod n + 1$. The double subscripts 00,30 and 33 in quad 1 belong to the extraordinary mesh node $P_{00}(1)$, its direct neighbor $P_{30}(1)$ and its diagonal facet neighbor $P_{33}(1)$. The double line delineates (one of the four corners of) a submesh used to define one quad level.

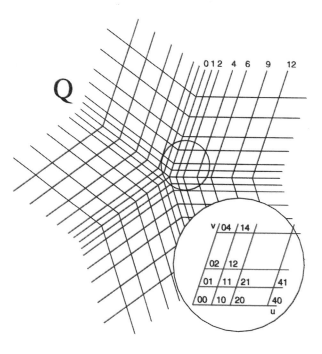

Figure 3: After Knot Insertion the Nurbs patches abut sharing the nodes $Q_{l0}(i+1) = Q_{0l}(i)$. The enlargement shows the indices of the control points relevant for Corner Smoothing.

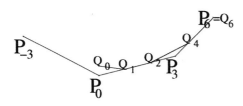

Figure 4: Knot insertion at $\mathbf{u} = 0$; P_{-3} is a mesh node borrowed from the neighboring quad.

double knot by ϵ. PCCM surfaces of level ℓ preserve the blend ratios (or smoothed creases) of the Catmull-Clark mesh [10, 3] up to level ℓ. The surface can additionally be pinched (flattened) at the extraordinary mesh node by decreasing the multiplier a of A_n to less than 1 (more than 1). The control points $Q_{\mathrm{uv}}(i)$ of the Nurbs patches are derived from the input mesh points $P_{\mathrm{uv}}(i)$ in two steps.

1. [Knot Insertion]
   For each quad, we define a submesh of the Catmull-Clark mesh that includes all subfacets of the quad and those sharing at least one node with the quad: we borrow one layer of nodes from all direct and diagonal neighbor quads to arrive at the submesh delineated by the double line in Fig. 2.
   We interpret the two perpendicular families of grid lines of quad i (without $P_{30}(j)$ for $j \notin \{i-1, i, i+1, i+2\}$) as the control net of an order 4 Nurbs patch with uniform u and v knot sequences $-4, -3, -2, -1, 0, 1, 2, \ldots$. To bring this Nurbs patch into standard interpolating form, we insert three knots first at $u = 0$ and $u = k$ then at $v = 0$ and $v = k$. Figure 4 illustrates the (standard) knot insertion procedure at $u = 0$ for a grid line indexed by $\mathbf{u}$. The new points $Q_{\mathbf{u}}$ are obtained from the old points $P_{\mathbf{u}}$ via

$$Q_0 = (P_{-3} + 4P_0 + P_3)/6, \quad Q_1 = (2P_0 + P_3)/3.$$

   For every edge with at least one extraordinary mesh node we insert a second knot, at 1 for $u = 0$ (at $k-1$ for $u = k$):

$$Q_2 = (P_0 + 2P_3)/3, \quad Q_4 = (2P_3 + P_6)/3.$$

   All remaining $Q_{3i,3j} = P_{3i,3j}$, except for the corner point $Q_{00}(1) = Q_{00}(2) = \ldots = Q_{00}(n)$ which we place directly on the Catmull-Clark limit surface [6]:

$$Q_{00}(1) = \ldots = Q_{00}(n) = \frac{\sum n P_{00}(i) + 4P_{30}(i) + P_{33}(i)}{n(n+5)}.$$

2. [Corner Smoothing]
   If we were to stop at this point, the Nurbs patches would only meet with position continuity close to extraordinary mesh nodes – although with C^2 continuity everywhere else. To obtain tangent continuity, we modify the control points near each extraordinary mesh node. The enlargement of Figure 3 shows the relevant double subscripts. We define, for every n, two n by n matrices A_n and B_n with rows $i = 1, \ldots, n$ and columns $j = 1, \ldots, n$ and entries

$$A_n(i,j) = \frac{2a}{n} \cos\left(\frac{2\pi}{n}(i-j)\right) \qquad a = 1 \text{(default) and}$$

$$B_n(i,j) = \begin{cases} (-1)^{n_{i-j}} & \text{if } n \text{ is odd,} \\ (-1)^j - 2n_{i-j}(-1)^{j-i}/n & \text{if } n \text{ is even,} \end{cases}$$

$$n_{i-j} = \mod(n+i-j, n).$$

For example, $B_6(3,3) = -1$. We collect the points $Q_{\mathrm{uv}}(i) \in \mathbf{R}^3$ generated by Knot Insertion for $i = 1, \ldots, n$ and $\mathrm{uv} \in \{00, 10, 20, 40\}$ into $\bar{Q}_{\mathrm{uv}} \in \mathbf{R}^{n \times 3}$. Only if n is even and greater than 4, do we compute $r = \sum_{i=1}^{n} (-1)^i \bar{Q}_{40}(i)/n$ and if $r \neq 0$ we add, for each i, $h_i = -(-1)^i r$ to $Q_{40}(i) = Q_{04}(i-1)$, $Q_{41}(i)$ and $Q_{14}(i-1)$ so that $\sum_{i=1}^{n} (-1)^i Q_{40}(i) = 0$ and $Q_{40}(i) = (Q_{41}(i) + Q_{14}(i-1))/2$. Otherwise all coefficients remain unchanged except

$$Q_{10} = Q_{00} + A_n \bar{Q}_{10},$$
$$Q_{20} = (Q_{40} + 6Q_{10} - 2Q_{00})/5,$$
$$Q_{11} = B_n \left(Q_{10} + \frac{\cos(2\pi/n)}{6}(Q_{40} - Q_{20}) \right).$$

For $i = 1, \ldots, n$, we copy $Q_{\mathrm{v}0}(i+1) = Q_{0\mathrm{v}}(i)$ for $\mathrm{v} \in \{1, 2, 4\}$ and add $Q_{20}(i) - \bar{Q}_{20}(i)$ to $Q_{21}(i)$ and $Q_{12}(i-1)$.

4   Smoothness and Approximation

We *claim*: the output Nurbs patches are internally parametrically C^2 and join the neighbors parametrically C^2 except possibly at extraordinary mesh nodes, across edges $u \in \{0, 1\}, v \in [0, 1]$ respectively $v \in \{0, 1\}, u \in [0, 1]$ shown in bold in Figure 2. Across these edges the surface is at least tangent continuous.

Before the Knot Insertion step, submeshes of adjacent patches overlap in three layers of cubic spline control points with a single knot associated with the center control point. Standard spline theory then guarantees that the patches join parametrically C^2 across the boundary edges $u \in \{0, k\}, v \in [1, k-1]$ and $v \in \{0, k\}, u \in [1, k-1]$. Knot insertion does not change the Nurbs surface and the smoothness of the transition. Therefore each patch is also internally C^2 before the Corner Smoothing step.

Corner Smoothing enforces tangent continuity for the remaining parameter interval at the corner from 0 to 1: with u_i, v_i the parameters of patch i and $v_i = u_{i+1} = t \in [0, 1]$ the parameter along the boundary between patch q_i and patch q_{i+1}, and $c = \cos(\frac{2\pi}{n})$, Corner Smoothing enforces the polynomial equation

$$2c(1-t)^2 \frac{\partial}{\partial v_i} q_i(0, t) = \frac{\partial}{\partial u_i} q_i(0, t) + \frac{\partial}{\partial v_{i+1}} q_{i+1}(t, 0).$$

The equation is easily verified by inserting two more knots at 1 and equating the four resulting Bézier coefficients in the variables Q. For example, at a corner point ($t = 0$) with $n = 3$ neighbors $c = -0.5$ and $-\partial q_i/\partial t = \partial q_i/\partial u_i + \partial q_{i+1}/\partial v_{i+1}$. This relation is enforced by applying A_n. The double root of $(1-t)^2$ at $t = 1$ is equivalent to the collinearity of $Q_{l1}(i)$, $Q_{l0}(i)$ and $Q_{1l}(i-1)$ for $l = 2$ and $l = 4$. The one remaining equation, for the mixed derivatives at $t = 0$, holds due to the choice of B_n and, if n even and greater than 4, the perturbation by h_i. The matrix B_n is derived following [10] but has slightly different entries in the even case.

The continuity across the knot line $u_i = 1$ and $v_i \in [0, 1]$ is that of an order 4 spline with a double knot and therefore is at least C^1. If $r \neq 0$ the joint movement of the nodes $Q_{41}(i)$, $Q_{40}(i)$ and $Q_{14}(i-1)$ preserves collinearity and thereby C^1-ness of the transition between adjacent Nurbs patches.

Unless $r \neq 0$, the Nurbs patches differ from the Catmull-Clark limit surface only near the corners for $(u, v) \in (0, 1]^2$. The difference increases with oscillation of the Catmull-Clark mesh at the extraordinary mesh node since application of A_n and B_n average the data and the choice of Q_{20} removes inflections. Each step of subdivision halves the extent of the region.

5 Conclusion

The strengths of the PCCM algorithm are that it (a) converts Catmull-Clark meshes to closed-form, smoothly-connected, standard Nurbs patches, (b) does so with simple, explicit formulas, (c) integrates seamlessly with the array-based view of subdivision (see the Appendix) and (d) remains local so that almost all patch transitions across patch boundaries are parametrically C^2.

Acknowledgement: I thank the referees, David Lutterkort, Malcolm Sabin, Andy Shiue and Georg Umlauf at SurfLab for their constructive comments.

References

[1] A. A. Ball and D. J. T. Storry. Conditions for tangent plane continuity over recursively generated B-spline surfaces. *ACM Trans. on Graphics*, 7:83–102, July 1988.

[2] E. Catmull and J. Clark. Recursively generated B-spline surfaces on arbitrary topological meshes. *Computer Aided Design*, 10:350–355, Oct 1978.

[3] Tony DeRose, Michael Kass, and Tien Truong. Subdivision surfaces in character animation. *Proceedings of SIGGRAPH 98*, pages 85–94, July 1998.

[4] OpenGL Foundation. http://trant.sgi.com/opengl/docs/man_pages/hardcopy/GL/html/glu/nurbssurface.html.

[5] Cindy M. Grimm and John F. Hughes. Modeling surfaces of arbitrary topology using manifolds. *Proceedings of SIGGRAPH 95*, pages 359–368, August 1995.

[6] Mark Halstead, Michael Kass, and Tony DeRose. Efficient, fair interpolation using Catmull-Clark surfaces. *Proceedings of SIGGRAPH 93*, pages 35–44, August 1993.

[7] Adi Levin. Interpolating nets of curves by smooth subdivision surfaces. *Computer Graphics*, 33:57–64, 1999. Appendix.

[8] A. H. Nasri. Boundary-corner control in recusive subdivision surfaces. *CAD*, 23(6):405–410, 1991.

[9] A. H. Nasri and J. Peters. Computing volumes of solids enclosed by recursive subdivision surfaces. *Comp. Gr. Forum*, 16(3), September 1997.

[10] J. Peters. C^1-surface splines. *SIAM J. Numer. Anal.*, 32(2):645–666, 1995.

[11] J. Peters and U. Reif. Analysis of generalized B-spline subdivision algorithms. *SIAM J. on Numer. Anal.*, 35(2):728–748, April 1998.

[12] H. Prautzsch. Freeform splines. *CAGD*, 14(3):201–206, 1997.

[13] Jos Stam. Exact evaluation of Catmull-Clark subdivision surfaces at arbitrary parameter values. *Proceedings of SIGGRAPH 98*, pages 395–404, July 1998.

[14] D. Zorin. *Subdivision and multiresolution surface representation*. PhD thesis, Caltech, 1997.

[15] D. Zorin. Implementing subdivision and multiresolution meshes. *Chapter 6 of Course notes 37 of SIGGRAPH 99*, Aug 1999.

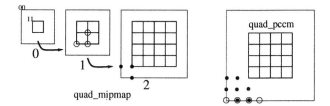

Figure 5: Collection ○ and distribution ● of points; *(left)* the Catmull-Clark mipmap at levels $\ell = 0, 1, 2$, *(right)* PCCM at level $\ell = 2$.

6 Appendix: array-based data structures

Catmull-Clark subdivision and PCCM can be implemented using only the connectivity information of the quads and a mipmap of control point arrays as would be input to `gluNurbsSurface` [4].

- For each quad, store a *mipmap* of arrays. The array at level ℓ is of size $k + 2$ by $k + 2$ by 3, $k = 2^\ell + 1$ and contains the x, y, z node positions of subdivision ℓ. Entry [1][1], short 11 (and symmetrically $1k$, $k1$ and kk), holds the position of a corner node (cf. Figs. 2, 5,*left*). If the corner node is an extraordinary mesh node then 00 is undefined. If $n = 3$ then the entries in 01 and 10 agree. PCCM outputs into an array of size $k + 4$ by $k + 4$ by 3. Entry 00 is the position of a corner coefficient.

- For each extraordinary mesh node, a *connectivity list* stores for each incident quad the global index and the corner of the quad corresponding to the extraordinary mesh node.

Catmull-Clark subdivision with this data structure consists of two parallelizable steps:

a. For each quad, create the mipmap level $\ell + 1$ from level ℓ by the regular subdivision rules (1).

b. For each extraordinary mesh node, use the connectivity list to
– *collect* at level ℓ, $P_{00} = P_{00}(1)$ and $P_{30}(i)$, $P_{33}(i)$ for all i (c.f. Figures 2, 5*left*: if P_{00} is entry 11 then $P_{30}(i)$ and $P_{33}(i)$ are entry 21 and 22).
– *Compute* new locations for $P_{30}(i)$ and $P_{33}(i)$ at level $\ell + 1$ from rules (1) and P_{00} from rule (2) (or use Sabin's curvature bounded rule [7], Appendix).
– *Distribute* the new locations to level $\ell + 1$ (Entry 01 receives $P_{30}(i + 2)$ and entry 10 receives $P_{30}(i - 1)$)).

PCCM with this structure consists of two parallelizable steps:

a. For each quad, apply Knot Insertion.

b. For each extraordinary mesh node, use the connectivity list to
– *collect* $Q_{00}(1)$ and $\tilde{Q}_{uv}(i)$, $uv \in \{10, 20, 40\}$.
– *Compute* $Q_{uv}(i)$, $uv \in \{10, 20, 11\}$, $Q_{20} - \tilde{Q}_{20}$ and possibly $Q_{40} - \tilde{Q}_{40}$.
– *Distribute* $Q_{uv}(i)$, $uv \in \{10, 01, 20, 02, 11\}$ and add to $\{21, 12\}$ and possibly $\{04, 40, 14, 41\}$.

All space for subdivision level ℓ can be allocated at the outset, and the connectivity list remains unchanged throughout. The quad-arrays can be input directly to `gluNurbsSurface` or displayed as quad-meshes.

Out-of-Core Simplification of Large Polygonal Models

Peter Lindstrom

Georgia Institute of Technology

Abstract

We present an algorithm for *out-of-core simplification* of large polygonal datasets that are too complex to fit in main memory. The algorithm extends the vertex clustering scheme of Rossignac and Borrel [13] by using error quadric information for the placement of each cluster's representative vertex, which better preserves fine details and results in a low mean geometric error. The use of quadrics instead of the vertex grading approach in [13] has the additional benefits of requiring less disk space and only a single pass over the model rather than two. The resulting linear time algorithm allows simplification of datasets of arbitrary complexity.

In order to handle degenerate quadrics associated with (near) flat regions and regions with zero Gaussian curvature, we present a robust method for solving the corresponding underconstrained least-squares problem. The algorithm is able to detect these degeneracies and handle them gracefully. Key features of the simplification method include a bounded Hausdorff error, low mean geometric error, high simplification speed (up to 100,000 triangles/second reduction), output (but not input) sensitive memory requirements, no disk space overhead, and a running time that is independent of the order in which vertices and triangles occur in the mesh.

1 INTRODUCTION

Polygonal simplification has been a hot topic of research over the last decade, with a vast number of published algorithms. Many of the early simplification algorithms were designed to handle modest size datasets of a few tens of thousands of triangles. As is common in most areas of computing, improvements in processor speed and memory capacity have served merely to promote the production of increasingly larger datasets, and a number of methods, particularly for out-of-core visualization, have been proposed for coping with models that are too large to fit in main memory, e.g. [3, 4, 10]. Following this trend, some of the more recent simplification algorithms have been designed to be memory efficient, and typically handle models with as many as several million triangles. In the last few years, however, there has been an explosion in model size, in part due to improvements in resolution and accuracy of data acquisition devices, such as laser range and CT/MRI scanners. Indeed, submillimeter resolution datasets such as the *Visible Human* [1], which consists of well over 10 billion voxels, and the range scans of Michelangelo's sculptures made independently by research groups at IBM [2] and Stanford University [7] contain up to two billion triangles. These enormous datasets pose great challenges not only for mesh processing tools such as rendering, editing, compression, and surface analysis, but paradoxically also for simplification methods that seek to alleviate these problems. In addition to their large

memory consumption, these algorithms also suffer from insufficient simplification speed to be practically useful for simplifying very large meshes. As an example, the "memoryless" simplification scheme proposed by Lindstrom and Turk [8]—one of the fastest and most memory efficient algorithms available—requires a minimum of $160n$ bytes of internal storage to represent an n-vertex model and the necessary edge collapse priority queue. Simplifying a one billion vertex model to a few million triangles using their algorithm would require 160 gigabytes of RAM and, disregarding memory thrashing, would take weeks to complete on a high end workstation!

One might argue that high resolution datasets such as the ones described above are greatly oversampled, and that this problem should be solved more directly during the data acquisition or synthesis stage, e.g. by using adaptive sampling and tessellation during range scanning and isosurface extraction. At best, this simply shifts the problem to an earlier stage of the modeling pipeline, and results not only in a need for specialized tools for each acquisition method, but often raises a number of practical issues. In particular, it places an additional burden on the data acquisitor in terms of deciding how to sample the model and dealing with the difficult issues of registering and integrating different resolution surface patches. In some cases, such a head-on approach is not even practical; one might not know in advance what parts of a surface should be sampled densely, or one might simply wish to retain the model at its full resolution and allow the end-user to resample the model in a manner that suits the given application.

Currently, few algorithms exist for performing high quality out-of-core simplification. One reason for this is that existing in-core methods are difficult to adapt to perform out-of-core simplification, because the majority of them are based on performing simple local operations that rely on having direct access to the connectivity of the mesh. For example, the quality measures associated with the *vertex removal* and *edge collapse* operations typically depend on the triangles surrounding the vertex or edge. Consequently, such methods use large in-core data structures to allow efficient queries of the local connectivity for any given mesh vertex. As mentioned above, such data structures may require hundreds of bytes per vertex, which might even be too large to off-load to disk. Instead, developers of out-of-core simplification algorithms are faced with two alternatives: segmenting the model into multiple pieces and simplifying them individually, or simplifying models using only limited connectivity information, which is the approach taken in this paper.

We propose an efficient and easy to implement surface simplification algorithm that accepts models of arbitrary complexity, and outputs a model that is small enough for in-core mesh processing tools to handle and store internally. The algorithm is based on uniform sampling via vertex clustering, and is enhanced by a novel use of error quadrics, which were originally developed for edge collapse methods (cf. [5, 8]). To our knowledge, our algorithm is one of very few, if not the only one, for doing fast, high quality simplification of arbitrarily large models.

2 PREVIOUS WORK

Polygonal models have grown rapidly in complexity over recent years, yet surprisingly little work has been done on out-of-core simplification. Because most conventional simplification algorithms are not relevant in the context of out-of-core simplification, we will restrict our discussion of related work to methods that are directly related to our algorithm, as well as the few methods that either

e-mail: *lindstro@cc.gatech.edu*   web: *http://www.cc.gatech.edu/~lindstro*

perform out-of-core simplification or can be adapted for that purpose. For a comparison of several well-known in-core simplification methods, we refer the reader to [8].

Rossignac and Borrel proposed one of the earliest simplification algorithms [13]. Their algorithm divides the model into cells from a uniform rectilinear grid, and replaces all vertices in a grid cell by a single representative vertex. When clustering vertices together, the majority of triangles degenerate into edges or points and can be discarded, thereby reducing the complexity of the model. Representative vertices are computed by first estimating the impact each vertex has on the visual appearance of the model using a number of ad hoc heuristics. This vertex grading is then used either to compute a weighted average or to select the most important of the original vertices in each cluster as the representative. As alluded to, but not explicitly stated, their algorithm can easily be adapted to work as an out-of-core method. The appeal of this method lies in its simplicity and speed, although the low quality models it produces, due in part to existing vertex positioning schemes, has lead to the use of more sophisticated simplification methods.

Recognizing that Rossignac and Borrel's method is sensitive to translation of the underlying grid, Low and Tan devised a method that uses "floating cells" constructed by sorting the vertices on their importance, and then iteratively letting the most important vertex be the center of a new cluster that absorbs all vertices within an arbitrarily shaped cell volume [9]. While providing higher quality results, one drawback of this approach is that it requires sorting the vertices, which is generally an $O(n \log n)$ procedure, compared to the $O(n)$ running time for Rossignac and Borrel's original scheme.

The *edge collapse* operator has been used extensively in simplification, and is generally considered to produce the highest quality results. Ronfard and Rossignac use edge collapse to coarsen a model while maintaining a list of supporting planes with each vertex [12]. Initially, each vertex is assigned the planes associated with its incident triangles. As two vertices are merged into one by an edge collapse, the new vertex inherits the planes of the merged vertices, and the maximum distance from the new vertex to its supporting planes is used to measure the cost of collapsing the edge. The edges of the model are ordered by increasing cost in a priority queue, and a greedy selection strategy is employed in which the cheapest edge is always collapsed. Inspired by this technique, Garland and Heckbert proposed using quadrics—a succinct encoding of the local surface geometry as a 4×4 symmetric matrix—that allow an efficient computation of the sum of squared distances from a vertex to its supporting planes [5]. Lindstrom and Turk [8] later showed that recomputing the quadrics from scratch in each iteration from the partially simplified surface, and weighting each quadric by the squared triangle area (thus measuring squared displacements in volume) improve the model quality. We use these area-weighted quadrics in our out-of-core simplification algorithm.

Bernardini et al. describe an algorithm that has been specifically designed to perform out-of-core simplification [2]. Their method splits the model up into separate patches that are small enough to be simplified separately in-core using a conventional simplification algorithm. The patch boundaries are left intact to allow the different pieces to be stitched together without cracks after simplification. A new set of patch boundaries is then used as another iteration of simplification is performed, allowing the seams between the previous set of patches to be coarsened. A similar technique was proposed by Hoppe for creating hierarchical levels of detail for height fields [6]. While conceptually simple, the time and space overhead of partitioning the model and later stitching it together adds to an already expensive in-core simplification process, rendering such a method less suitable for simplifying very large meshes.

3 SIMPLIFICATION ALGORITHM

The simplification algorithm presented here is a hybrid of several schemes, including [5, 8, 13]. At a high level, it resembles Rossignac and Borrel's vertex clustering algorithm, but is improved both in execution time and quality by using the quadric error metric

introduced by Garland and Heckbert, and later improved by Lindstrom and Turk, for positioning vertices. In particular, our linear time algorithm improves upon [13] by requiring only a single pass over the input model, compared to two or more, and does not use any disk space beyond the input mesh, whereas their algorithm requires an importance value to be stored with each vertex of the input model. In describing our algorithm, we will focus on its novel aspects and assume that the reader is familiar with vertex clustering and quadrics for simplification. We will first describe how the quadrics and representative vertices are computed, and follow with a description of the actual simplification algorithm.

3.1 Quadrics

In order to integrate quadrics with the general vertex clustering scheme, we first make the observation that vertex clustering is a special case of *vertex pair contraction*—a generalization of edge collapse to arbitrary pairs of vertices [5]. That is, merging n vertices within a cluster cell is equivalent to performing any sequence of $n - 1$ contractions of pairs of vertices within the cluster until a single vertex remains. As a consequence, we can extend Garland and Heckbert's original scheme from individual vertex contractions to a predefined sequence of such operations. In fact, our algorithm is equivalent to theirs, with the exception that our priority queue is determined by the cluster grid rather than by the local geometry. We use the quadrics from [8], which have proven to give better results in the mean error sense.

Based on [8], we compute for each triangle $t = (\mathbf{x}_1, \mathbf{x}_2, \mathbf{x}_3)$ its associated quadric matrix $\mathbf{Q}$ as follows:

$$\mathbf{Q} = \begin{pmatrix} \mathbf{A} & -\mathbf{b} \\ -\mathbf{b}^{\mathrm{T}} & c \end{pmatrix} = \mathbf{n}\mathbf{n}^{\mathrm{T}} \qquad (1)$$

$$\mathbf{n} = \begin{pmatrix} \mathbf{x}_1 \times \mathbf{x}_2 + \mathbf{x}_2 \times \mathbf{x}_3 + \mathbf{x}_3 \times \mathbf{x}_1 \\ -[\mathbf{x}_1, \mathbf{x}_2, \mathbf{x}_3] \end{pmatrix} \qquad (2)$$

where $\mathbf{n}$ is a 4-vector made up of the area-weighted triangle normal and the scalar triple product of its three vertices. We then distribute $\mathbf{Q}$ to the clusters associated with each of t's three vertices by adding $\mathbf{Q}$ to their quadric matrices. Since $\mathbf{Q}$ is symmetric, and since the scalar c is not used, only 9 scalar values need to be stored with each cluster. After adding up the quadrics of all the triangles in a cluster, we use the block decomposition of $\mathbf{Q}$ above and solve the linear system $\mathbf{A}\mathbf{x} = \mathbf{b}$ for the "optimal" representative vertex position $\mathbf{x}$. That is, $\mathbf{x}$ is the position that minimizes the sum of squared volumes of the tetrahedra formed by $\mathbf{x}$ and the triangles in the cell.

If a cell contains two nearly parallel surface sheets, the quadrics will sometimes suggest a solution $\mathbf{x}$ that is close to the intersection of the extension of these two surfaces. The solution may in such cases lie far outside the cell itself. We handle these degeneracies by restricting the position of $\mathbf{x}$, either by independently clamping its three coordinates to the cell bounds, or by "pulling" the vertex towards the cell center until it is sufficiently close.

3.1.1 Robust Inversion of Quadric Matrices

In the discussion above, we assumed that the matrix $\mathbf{A}$ is invertible and well-conditioned. In practice, this is often not the case, e.g. if the surface is locally flat or has zero Gaussian curvature. Lindstrom and Turk [8] proposed a partial solution to this problem by ensuring that the problem is overconstrained, and then combining linear constraints that yield a sufficiently large value for the determinant of $\mathbf{A}$. In our case, however, the quadrics yield at most three constraints, and we use a slightly different approach that is able to both diagnose potential problems and also robustly produce the "best" vertex in the sense that $\mathbf{x}$ is chosen such that its distance to the cell center is minimized. That is, $\mathbf{x}$ is the orthogonal projection of the cell center onto the space of all solutions to $\mathbf{A}\mathbf{x} = \mathbf{b}$. We accomplish this by performing a *singular value decomposition* $\mathbf{A} = \mathbf{U}\boldsymbol{\Sigma}\mathbf{V}^{\mathrm{T}}$, which for a real symmetric positive semidefinite matrix $\mathbf{A}$ is equivalent to doing an eigenvalue decomposition. This can be done quickly using a small number of Jacobi rotations [11]. For robustness, we set a lower limit on the singular values and discard (zero) the ones that are negligible:

$$\sigma_i^+ = \begin{cases} 1/\sigma_i & \text{if } \sigma_i/\sigma_1 > \epsilon \\ 0 & \text{otherwise} \end{cases} \qquad (3)$$

where σ_1 is the largest singular value and ϵ is a threshold parameter currently set to 10^{-3}. The vertex $\mathbf{x}$ closest to the cell center $\hat{\mathbf{x}}$ that satisfies $\mathbf{A}\mathbf{x} = \mathbf{b}$ is then

$$\mathbf{x} = \hat{\mathbf{x}} + \mathbf{V}\Sigma^+\mathbf{U}^\mathrm{T}(\mathbf{b} - \mathbf{A}\hat{\mathbf{x}}) \qquad (4)$$

which simplifies to $\mathbf{A}^{-1}\mathbf{b}$ whenever $\Sigma^+ = \Sigma^{-1}$, i.e. the above equation is used whether $\mathbf{A}$ is ill-conditioned or not, and always yields a numerically robust solution.

3.2 Vertex Clustering

For performance reasons, it is important that the external mesh representation is conducive to the types of mesh queries needed for the given simplification operator. Fortunately, the combination of vertex clustering and quadrics allows commonly used off-line data structures to represent the mesh, such as an *indexed mesh* in which each triangle is a triplet of indices associated with an ordered list of vertex coordinates. By storing the mesh in binary form as fixed-length records, the vertices of a triangle can be fetched from disk indirectly via random access. While such a format is compact, our algorithm requires no connectivity information, and is thus able to operate on a *triangle soup* in which each triangle is represented directly as a triplet of vertex coordinates. The triangle soup representation requires roughly twice as much disk space as the indexed mesh, but typically increases the simplification speed by a factor of 15–20, while also accommodating text file representations. In addition, since our algorithm makes a single pass over the mesh triangles, the triangle soup can be compressed externally and then uncompressed on-the-fly during simplification. The model can even be split up into several files if, for example, it is too large to store on a single disk. We used the triangle soup representation for the results presented in this paper. Similar to Rossignac and Borrel's original clustering algorithm, our algorithm also requires a bounding box for the model, which is divided into a user-specified number of rectilinear grid cells. We anticipate that most data acquisition methods are able to provide such bounds and store the mesh in either of these two formats.

Once the cluster grid has been determined, we proceed by reading the mesh one triangle at a time and incrementally construct an in-core representation of the simplified mesh. It is generally fair to assume that enough memory exists for this simplified mesh since our goal is to produce a mesh coarse enough for in-core tools to process it. Given a triangle $t \in T_{in}$ from the original mesh, we fetch its vertex coordinates. For each vertex v_{in} of t, we construct a hash key from the grid cell that the vertex falls in and do a hash table lookup. This dynamic hash table maps grid cells, or clusters, to the vertices V_{out} in the simplified mesh. If this cell has not been visited, a new vertex identifier v_{out} is created (e.g. using consecutive integers) and the quadric matrix associated with v_{out} is initialized to zero. If two or more of the triangle's vertices belong to the same cluster, then t reduces to an edge or a point, and is discarded. Otherwise, we add it, as a triplet of indices into V_{out}, to the set of simplified triangles T_{out}.

Before proceeding with the next triangle, we compute the quadric matrix $\mathbf{Q}$ associated with t. For each vertex of t, we add $\mathbf{Q}$ to the matrix of the cluster that the vertex belongs to. After the input has been exhausted, we are left with a list of quadrics and a list of triangles. Each quadric corresponds to a cluster of vertices and triangles that share a grid cell, and from the quadric matrix we compute the coordinates for the cluster's representative vertex v_{out} using the procedure described above. The simplification then ends by outputting the simplified mesh (V_{out}, T_{out}) in an appropriate format.

model	$|T_{in}|$	$|T_{out}|$	RAM (MB)			time (h:m:s)		
			[5]	[8]	OoCS	[5]	[8]	OoCS
dragon	871,306	244,562	213	134	28	5:31	11:59	0:16
dragon	871,306	113,090	214	134	11	5:55	14:12	0:12
dragon	871,306	47,228	214	134	7	6:06	15:21	0:10
buddha	1,087,716	204,750	250	166	26	7:13	16:58	0:17
buddha	1,087,716	62,354	251	166	8	7:35	19:19	0:12
blade	28,246,208	507,104	-	3,185	63	-	12:37:25	5:02
statue	386,488,573	3,122,226	-	-	366	-	-	1:59:20

Table 1: Simplification results of running QSlim [5], Memoryless Simplification [8], and the out-of-core method (OoCS). All results were gathered on a 195 MHz R10000 SGI Origin with 4 GB of RAM and a standard SCSI disk drive.

4 RESULTS AND DISCUSSION

To evaluate the performance of our algorithm, we include results of simplifying four large polygonal datasets: a buddha, a dragon, and a model of Michelangelo's St. Matthew statue created by researchers at Stanford using a range scanner, as well as a turbine blade model which was extracted from volume data as an isosurface. We applied two levels of Loop subdivision to the blade model to increase its triangle count by a factor of 16, thus making it more challenging to simplify. Table 1 includes the triangles counts, memory usage, and timing results of simplifying these models using our method as well as the in-core methods presented in [5, 8]. While being much more memory efficient than these two methods, our new algorithm is also orders of magnitude faster. Note that the reported memory usage is consistently higher than our implementation's theoretical usage of 63 to 72 $|T_{out}|$ bytes,[1] as the former includes freed memory not reclaimed by the operating system.

Figures 1a–c show the original buddha model and two out-of-core simplified models. Notice how the models in 1a and 1b are virtually indistinguishable, while some blocking artifacts appear in 1c, yet most details are still present. Figures 2b–d show several simplifications of the dragon model. We here compare our vertex positioning scheme based on quadrics against 1) using the mean of a cluster's vertices and 2) the vertex grading scheme of Rossignac and Borrel that chooses the most important vertex, and which has been improved using the technique in [9]. Fine details near the jaws, neck, and hind leg are washed out by the vertex averaging scheme, and the ridge along the back has lost its sharpness. The model produced by vertex grading has a more choppy appearance with loss of detail in the face. Finally, Figures 3a and 3b show close-ups of the face of the St. Matthew statue covering less than 15% of its overall height. This complex model consists of nearly 400 million triangles, and could only be simplified using our out-of-core method. Even after a reduction by a factor of 100, many fine details such as the chisel marks are still preserved.

While the quality of our method is high in comparison with other vertex clustering schemes, it does not perform adaptive sampling of the model, and often produces models that can be further coarsened in areas of low curvature with little loss in quality. For applications that require extreme reduction and very high visual quality, our algorithm can be used as a fast preprocessing step that produces a model with a few hundred thousand triangles, which can then be further simplified by a slower in-core simplification algorithm.

We envision several avenues for future research. As suggested in [13], adaptive sampling can be handled using hierarchical simplification, in which cells are recursively merged in less detailed regions. The idea is to allow quadrics to be merged wherever they "agree" on the local surface characterization. We also believe that the quadric information can be used to improve the connectivity of the mesh, for example by swapping edges in a manner that would reduce the associated quadratic function. Finally, it would be possible to directly integrate our algorithm with the popular *marching cubes* algorithm for isosurface extraction, thereby combining isosurfacing and simplification into a single step, and eliminating the need to output an overly complex intermediate isosurface.

---

[1]The theoretical memory usage varies with the size and load of the dynamic hash table.

Acknowledgements

I would like to thank Marc Levoy and the people working on the Digital Michelangelo Project for providing the St. Matthew dataset, and Greg Turk, Jarek Rossignac, F. S. Nooruddin, and Gabriel Taubin for valuable comments and suggestions.

References

[1] ACKERMAN, M. J. The Visible Human Project. In *Proceedings of the IEEE*, 86(3), March 1998, pp. 504–511. Project URL: *http://www.nlm.nih.gov/research/visible*.

[2] BERNARDINI, F., MITTLEMAN, J., and RUSHMEIER, H. Case Study: Scanning Michelangelo's Florentine Pietà. In *ACM SIGGRAPH 99* Course Notes, Course 8, August 1999. Project URL: *http://www.research.ibm.com/pieta*.

[3] BERNARDINI, F., MITTLEMAN, J., RUSHMEIER, H., SILVA, C., and TAUBIN, G. The Ball-Pivoting Algorithm for Surface Reconstruction. In *IEEE Transactions on Visualization and Computer Graphics*, 5(4), October–December 1999, pp. 349–359.

[4] CHIANG, Y.-J., SILVA, C. T., and SCHROEDER, W. J. Interactive Out-of-Core Isosurface Extraction. In *IEEE Visualization '98* Proceedings, October 1998, pp. 167–174.

[5] GARLAND, M. and HECKBERT, P. S. Surface Simplification using Quadric Error Metrics. Proceedings of SIGGRAPH 97. In *Computer Graphics* Proceedings, Annual Conference Series, 1997, ACM SIGGRAPH, pp. 209–216.

[6] HOPPE, H. Smooth View-Dependent Level-of-Detail Control and its Application to Terrain Rendering. In *IEEE Visualization '98* Proceedings, October 1998, pp. 35–42.

[7] LEVOY, M. The Digital Michelangelo Project. In proceedings of the *Second International Conference on 3D Digital Imaging and Modeling*, October 1999, pp. 2–11. Project URL: *http://graphics.stanford.edu/projects/mich*.

[8] LINDSTROM, P. and TURK, G. Fast and Memory Efficient Polygonal Simplification. In *IEEE Visualization '98* Proceedings, October 1998, pp. 279–286.

[9] LOW, K.-L. and TAN, T.-S. Model Simplification using Vertex-Clustering. In *Proceedings of 1997 Symposium on Interactive 3D Graphics*, April 1997, pp. 75–82.

[10] PHARR, M., KOLB, C., GERSHBEIN, R., and HANRAHAN, P. Rendering Complex Scenes with Memory-Coherent Ray Tracing. Proceedings of SIGGRAPH 97. In *Computer Graphics* Proceedings, Annual Conference Series, 1997, ACM SIGGRAPH, pp. 101–108.

[11] PRESS, W. H., TEUKOLSKY, S. A., VETTERLING, W. T., and FLANNERY, B. P. Numerical Recipes in C: The Art of Scientific Computing, Second Edition. Cambridge University Press, 1992, pp. 408–412.

[12] RONFARD, R. and ROSSIGNAC, J. Full-Range Approximation of Triangulated Polyhedra. Proceedings of Eurographics 96. In *Computer Graphics Forum*, 15(3), August 1996, pp. 67–76.

[13] ROSSIGNAC, J. and BORREL, P. Multi-Resolution 3D Approximations for Rendering Complex Scenes. In *Modeling in Computer Graphics*, edited by B. Falcidieno and T. L. Kunii, Springer-Verlag, 1993, pp. 455–465.

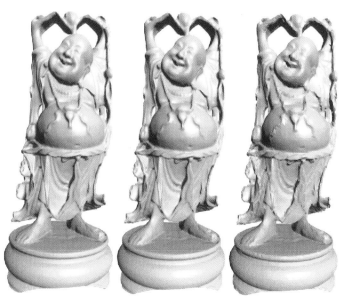

1a. Original buddha. 1,087,716 triangles.   1b. OoCS 204,750 triangles.   1c. OoCS 62,354 triangles.

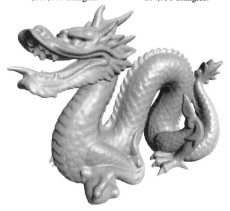

2a. Original dragon. 871,306 triangles.

2b. OoCS/Quadrics. 47,228 triangles.

3a. Original statue. 386,488,573 triangles.

2c. OoCS/Vertex mean. 47,228 triangles.

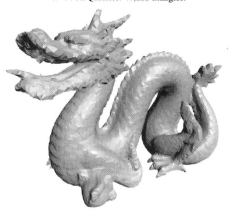

2d. OoCS/Vertex grading. 47,228 triangles.

3b. OoCS. 3,122,226 triangles.

Face Fixer: Compressing Polygon Meshes with Properties

Martin Isenburg*   Jack Snoeyink[†]

University of North Carolina at Chapel Hill

Abstract

Most schemes to compress the topology of a surface mesh have been developed for the lowest common denominator: triangulated meshes. We propose a scheme that handles the topology of arbitrary polygon meshes. It encodes meshes directly in their polygonal representation and extends to capture face groupings in a natural way. Avoiding the triangulation step we reduce the storage costs for typical polygon models that have group structures and property data.

CR Categories: I.3.5 [Computer Graphics]: Computational Geometry and Object Modeling—surface, solid, and object representations;

Additional Keywords: Mesh compression, connectivity encoding

1 INTRODUCTION

Because bandwidth to the graphics pipeline is a limiting factor in a number of graphics applications, compression schemes for geometric data sets have recently been the subject of intense study. In particular, many efficient techniques have been proposed for encoding polygonal meshes [3, 24, 25, 7, 16, 18, 13, 15]; we survey these in the next section. Generally mesh compression techniques focus on encoding fully triangulated data sets—a natural candidate for the lowest common denominator. Triangle meshes are easily derived from other surface representations and are widely supported by today's graphics hardware. Especially for data sets whose only destination is the trip down the rendering pipeline, a compact triangle-based representation is a good choice.

However, many models are represented by polygonal meshes that contain a surprisingly small percentage of triangles. Two examples are the standard 'triceratops' and 'galleon' models shown in Figure 1, which are initially not triangulated. The 'Premier Collection' from Viewpoint Datalabs [28]—a well-known source of high quality 3D models—consists mostly of meshes with very low triangle counts. Likewise, few triangles are found in the output formats of many computer aided design (CAD) packages. The dominating element of these models is the quadrangle or quadrilateral, but pentagons, hexagons and higher degree faces are also common.

Especially for storage purposes it is beneficial to keep a mesh in its native polygonal representation and delay the conversion to triangles until this becomes necessary. King et al. [13] have shown that the connectivity information of meshes mostly composed of quadrangles can be represented with fewer bits than that of their triangulated counterparts. Furthermore, most meshes have associated prop-

*isenburg@cs.unc.edu http://www.cs.unc.edu/~isenburg/facefixer
[†] snoeyink@cs.unc.edu

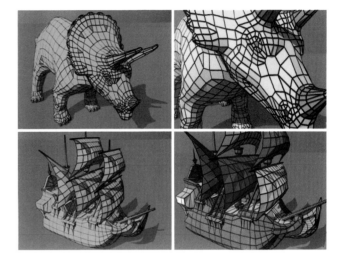

Figure 1: The triceratops and the galleon model contain only a small number of triangles shown in red (left). The group structures on these meshes are illustrated with arbitrary colours (right).

erties such as normal, colour or texture information that account for a large portion of the storage costs. Triangulating a polygon mesh not only adds an extra processing step, but also increases the number of faces and corners—replicating their associated properties.

Reconstructing the original polygon mesh rather than a triangulated version can also lead to better results for subsequent triangle strip generation. Stripification algorithms, such as STRIPE [5], exploit the freedom to triangulate polygons on demand to generate triangle strips that use a minimal number of swaps and restarts.

Often polygon models also contain structural information that classifies groups of faces into logical units. The triceratops and the galleon model in Figure 1 both contain such group information. Such a structure can establish a mapping between meaningful parts of the real-world object and the faces in the model that represent them. This information can also be used to attach material properties to groups of faces. Encoding such group structures has not been addressed by previously reported compression schemes.

We propose a simple scheme for encoding the connectivity of a polygon mesh that is based on assigning a code to each mesh edge. Section 3 describes our scheme as it applies to polygon meshes with holes and handles, and extends it in Section 4 to efficiently associate property data and encode group structures. We report compression rates for a number of meshes that have been used in the literature.

2 PREVIOUS WORK

After reviewing the problem of encoding polygon meshes and the approaches typically taken, we give a detailed survey of the recent literature on connectivity compression. However, we limit this description to the case of simple meshes. For details on how these schemes encode meshes with boundary, with holes, or with handles, we refer the reader to the original reference.

2.1 Preliminaries

A *polygon mesh* is a collection of polygonal *faces* that intersect only along shared edges and vertices. Any edge is shared by at most two faces; unshared edges are *boundary edges*. Around each face we find a cycle of vertices and edges; around each vertex we find a cycle of edges and faces. Each appearance of a face in a vertex list or of a vertex in a face list is called a *corner*. In the mesh compression literature, a distinction is often made between three things: mesh *geometry*, which includes vertex coordinates, mesh *properties* such as normals, colours, and texture coordinates that are attached to vertices, faces, or corners, and mesh *connectivity*, which describes the incidences between vertices, edges, and faces. The mesh connectivity information is also referred to as mesh topology.

Topologically, a mesh is a graph embedded in a 2-manifold surface in which each point has a neighborhood that is homeomorphic to a disk or a half-disk. Points with half-disk neighborhoods are on the boundary. A mesh has genus g if one can remove up to g closed loops without disconnecting the underlying surface; such a surface is topologically equivalent to a sphere with g handles. A mesh is *simple* if it has no handles ($g = 0$) and no boundary edges. Euler's relation says that a graph embedded on a sphere having f faces, e edges, and v vertices satisfies $f - e + v = 2$. When all faces have at least three sides, we know that $f \leq 2v - 4$ and $e \leq 3v - 6$, with equality if an only if all faces are triangles. For a mesh with g handles (genus g) the relation becomes $f - e + v = 2 - 2g$ and the bounds on faces and edges increase correspondingly.

The standard representation for uncompressed polygon meshes uses a list of vertex coordinates to store geometry and a list of vertex indices for each face to store mesh connectivity. For triangle meshes of v vertices, this requires approximately $6v \log_2 v$ bits for the mesh connectivity. Note that this representation does not directly store face adjacency, which must be recovered by sorting around vertices if the mesh is to be checked for cracks or turned into triangle strips.

However, mesh connectivity can be encoded in a constant number of bits per vertex, while geometry and property data can be efficiently compressed with schemes that predict a position or a feature from previously decoded neighbours. Researchers in mesh compression have aimed for three different objectives: efficient rendering, progressive transmission, and maximum compression.

Efficient rendering: Encodings for rendering use partial information about mesh connectivity to reduce the work in the graphics pipeline. In the standard representation, each triangle of the mesh must be rendered individually by sending its three vertices to the graphics hardware. On average, every mesh vertex is processed six times. Processing a vertex involves passing its coordinates from the memory to and through the graphics pipeline. Typically, this also includes normal, colour, and texture information. The most common technique to reduce the number of times this data needs to be transmitted is to send long runs of adjacent triangles. Such *triangle strips* [5, 30] are widely supported by today's graphics hardware. Two vertices from a previous triangle are re-used for all but the first triangle of every strip. Depending on the quality of the strips, this can reduce the number of vertex repetitions by a factor of three.

In addition to specifying quantizations and codings for coordinates, normals, colors, and other mesh properties, Deering's pioneering paper [3] introduced a technique to further reduce the number of vertex repetitions. His *generalized triangle mesh* is designed for a geometry engine that can cache up to sixteen of the vertices that have previously passed through the transformation pipeline.

Progressive transmission: Encodings for progressive transmission use incremental refinements of mesh connectivity and geometry so that partial data already represents the entire mesh at a lower resolution. Hoppe's Progressive Mesh scheme [8] encodes a mesh by collapsing edges one by one. Decoding starts with a small base mesh and expands the collapsed edges in reverse order.

While the first progressive schemes were not designed for compression and used a large number of bits per vertex, recent schemes [22, 17, 1, 2] group the refinement operations into large batches and achieve bit-rates that come close to those of non-progressive methods. Even though more bits are used for the connectivity information, the progressive nature of the decoding allows more accurate geometry and property prediction.

For the special case of terrains models based on Delaunay triangulations, Snoeyink and van Kreveld [20] used ideas from Kirkpatrick's point location scheme [14] to encode all topology information in a permutation of the vertices. Denny and Sohler's work [4] extended this scheme to arbitrary *planar* triangulations. Although the cost of storing the topology is zero, the unstructured order in which the vertices are received and the absence of adjacency information during their decompression prohibits predictive geometry encoding. This makes these schemes overall more expensive. Moreover, it is not clear that it is possible to extend this idea to general surface meshes.

Maximum compression: Most schemes for maximum mesh compression encode mesh connectivity through a compact and often interwoven representation of two dual spanning trees: one tree spans the vertices, and its dual spans the triangles. Neither the triangle nor the vertex tree is sufficient by itself to capture the connectivity information. Typically such compression schemes [24, 25, 7, 16, 9, 18] use a pair of spanning trees obtained by traversing the vertices and the triangles of the mesh with a deterministic strategy (e.g. breadth or depth first search). The geometry data and the property data of the mesh are usually compressed using predictive encoding based on local neighbourhood information [24, 25].

2.2 Connectivity Compression Techniques

One of the nicest proofs of Euler's relation for planar graphs partitions the edges into two spanning trees [21]. One tree, spanning the vertices, has $v - 1$ edges and the other, spanning the faces, has $f - 1$ edges, so $e = (v - 1) + (f - 1)$. Turan [26] was the first to observe that this partition into two spanning trees could be used to encode planar graphs. He gave an encoding that used 12 bits per vertex (bpv). Keeler and Westbrook [11] improved Turan's method to guarantee 9 bpv for encoding planar graphs and 4.6 bpv for simple triangle meshes, but reported no extension for general meshes.

Taubin and Rossignac proposed a scheme that explicitly encodes both spanning trees. Their Topological Surgery method [24] cuts a mesh along a set of edges that corresponds to a spanning tree of vertices. This produces a simple mesh without internal vertices that can be represented by the dual triangle spanning tree. Run-length encoding both trees results in practice in bit-rates of around 4 bpv.

Touma and Gotsman's Triangle Mesh Compression [25] encodes the degree of each vertex along a spiraling vertex tree with an "add <degree>" code. For each branch in the tree they need an additional "split <offset>" code that specifies the start and the length of the branch. This technique implicitly encodes the triangle spanning tree. They compress the resulting sequence of "add" and "split" commands using a combination of run-length and entropy encoding. Especially for regular meshes they achieve lower bit-rates than other schemes. Results on standard meshes range from 0.2 to 3.0 bpv.

Gumhold and Strasser [7] introduce a compressed representation for triangle meshes that is similar to the Edgebreaker method [18]. Starting with the three edges of an arbitrary triangle as what they call the initial "cut-border," they traverse the triangles of the mesh and include them into this boundary loop using three connect and one split operation. The offset value associated with the split operation is used to re-play the split operation during decoding. This makes it possible to decode the mesh connectivity in a single forward traversal of all operations, which allows encoding and decoding to run in parallel—with a minimal delay of one operation.

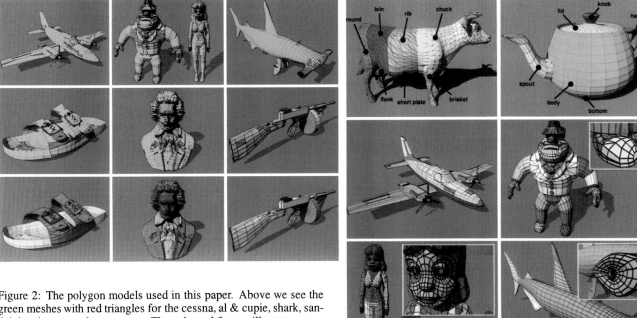

Figure 2: The polygon models used in this paper. Above we see the green meshes with red triangles for the cessna, al & cupie, shark, sandal, beethoven, and tommygun. The coloured figures illustrate group structures in these meshes, plus the cow with meat-cuts and the teapot.

name	groups	parts	vertices	faces		corners		△	▭	⬠	⬡	⋈	holes	hndls	name	bpv
triceratops	6	1	2832	2834	(5660)	11328	(16980)	346	2266	140	63	19	–	–	triceratops	**2.115**
galleon	17	12	2372	2384	(4698)	9466	(14094)	336	1947	40	18	43	–	–	galleon	**2.595**
cessna	38	11	3745	3927	(7446)	15300	(22338)	900	2797	180	27	23	–	–	cessna	**2.841**
beethoven	10	8	2655	2812	(5030)	10654	(15090)	680	2078	44	4	6	10	–	beethoven	**2.890**
sandal	5	9	2636	2953	(4952)	10858	(14856)	961	1985	7	–	–	14	12	sandal	**2.602**
shark	7	1	2560	2562	(5116)	10240	(15348)	188	2253	83	29	9	–	–	shark	**1.670**
al	35	21	3618	4175	(7152)	15502	(21456)	1579	2505	44	11	36	–	–	al	**2.926**
cupie	15	6	2984	3032	(5944)	12008	(17832)	384	2506	114	10	18	–	–	cupie	**2.307**
tommygun	15	39	4171	3980	(8210)	16170	(24630)	992	2785	84	21	98	–	6	tommygun	**2.611**
cow	8	1	2904	5804	(5804)	17412	(17412)	5804	–	–	–	–	–	–	cow	**2.213**
teapot	6	1	1189	1290	(2378)	4958	(7134)	215	1070	3	1	1	–	1	teapot	**1.669**

Table 1: The statistics of mesh topology and polygon types for all example models together with the achieved connectivity compression in bits per vertex (bpv). The numbers in brackets give the face and corner counts for the triangulated version of each model.

Rossignac's Edgebreaker scheme [18] gives the best guaranteed bit-rates for triangle mesh connectivity. The compression algorithm uses five operations, C, L, E, R and S, to include triangles into a boundary, which is initially defined around an arbitrary triangle. The operations S and E replace the split operation used by the "cut-border machine" [7], thereby eliminating the need for explicitly encoding the associated offset value. Improvements on the original paper give linear decoding time [19, 10] and tighten the guaranteed bit-rate to 3.67 bpv [12]. This is currently the lowest worst-case bound and lies within 13% of the theoretical lower limit by Tutte [27].

All of the above schemes have been designed to compress the connectivity of purely triangular meshes. However, several authors have reported extensions to their schemes in order to handle polygonal input. A naive approach arbitrarily triangulates the polygon mesh and then uses one bit per edge to distinguish the original edges from those added during the triangulation process. Marking every edge can be avoided by triangulating the polygons systematically.

For the Topological Surgery method [23] the extension to polygonal meshes first cuts the mesh along a vertex spanning tree and then triangulates the dual polygon spanning tree. Only the edges interior to the resulting triangle spanning tree need to be marked. Similarly

King et al. [13] describe how to let the Edgebreaker method guide the triangulation process. For simple polygon meshes without vertices of degree two they give an encoding that guarantees 5 bpv.

In fact, King et al. [13] are first to prove that quadrangular meshes can be compressed more efficient than their triangulated counterparts by avoiding the triangulation step. They give compact encodings for pure quadrangular meshes and for meshes containing mostly quadrangles and a few triangles. Similar results are reported by Kronrod and Gotsman [15]. Both papers suggest extensions to arbitrary polygons, but no experimental results are given.

We recently learned about the Dual Graph approach by Li et al. [16], which has similarities to the method presented here. Their scheme traverses the edges of the dual and records a stream of symbols and integer values, which is compressed with a carefully designed context based entropy coder. Decoding uses the recorded information to re-play this traversal, thereby reconstructing the mesh connectivity. Their use of split offsets resembles that of the "cut-border machine" [7], which is avoided by our method.

Inspired by Edgebreaker [18], we propose an edge-based compression scheme that encodes the connectivity of 2-manifold polygon meshes and extends to capture structural information as well.

3 FACE FIXER

The connectivity of the polygon mesh is encoded as a sequence of labels F_n, R, L, S, E, H_n, and $M_{i,k,l}$. The total number of labels equals the number of mesh edges. The sequence of labels represents an interwoven description of a polygon spanning tree and its complementary vertex spanning tree. For every face of n sides there is a label F_n and for every hole of size n there is a label H_n. Together they label the edges of the polygon spanning tree. For every handle there is a label $M_{i,k,l}$ that has three integer values associated. These specify the two edges of the polygon spanning tree that need to be 'fixed' together to re-create the handle. The remaining labels R, L, S, and E label the edges of the corresponding vertex spanning tree and describe how to 'fix' faces and holes together. Subsequently an entropy coder compresses the label sequence into a bit-stream.

3.1 Encoding and Decoding

Starting with a polygon mesh of v vertices, e edges, f faces, h holes, and g handles, the encoding process produces a sequence of e labels. This sequence contains f labels of type F_n, h labels of type H_n, g labels of type $M_{i,k,l}$, and $v - 2 + g$ labels of type R, L, S, or E. The connectivity of the polygon mesh can be reconstructed with a single reverse traversal of the label sequence.

The algorithm maintains one or more loops of edges that separate a single processed region of the mesh from the rest. Each of these *boundary loops* has a distinguished *gate* edge. The focus of the algorithm is on the *active boundary*; all others are temporarily buffered in a stack. The initial active boundary, defined clockwise around an arbitrary edge of the mesh, has two *boundary edges*. The gate of the active boundary is the *active gate*.

In every step of the encoding process the active gate is labeled with either F_n, R, L, S, E, H_n, or $M_{i,k,l}$. Which label the active gate is given depends on its adjacency relation to the boundary. After recording the label, the boundary is updated and a new active gate is selected. Depending on the label, the boundary expands (F_n and H_n), shrinks (R and L), splits (S), ends (E), or merges ($M_{i,k,l}$). Table 2 summarizes the changes to the processed region and its boundaries for each operation. The encoding process terminates after exactly e iterations, where e is the number of mesh edges.

| | change to # of processed | | | | | # of boundary | |
label	faces	holes	vertices	edges	handles	loops	edges
F_n	+1	$\cdots$	$\cdots$	+1	$\cdots$	$\cdots$	$+(n-2)$
H_n	$\cdots$	+1	$\cdots$	+1	$\cdots$	$\cdots$	$+(n-2)$
R, L	$\cdots$	$\cdots$	+1	+1	$\cdots$	$\cdots$	-2
S	$\cdots$	$\cdots$	$\cdots$	+1	$\cdots$	+1	-2
E	$\cdots$	$\cdots$	+2	+1	$\cdots$	-1	-2
$M_{i,k,l}$	$\cdots$	$\cdots$	$\cdots$	+1	+1	-1	-2
init	$= 0$	$= 0$	$= 0$	$= 0$	$= 0$	$= 1$	$= 2$
final	$= f$	$= h$	$= v$	$= e$	$= g$	$= 0$	$= 0$

Table 2: The changes for each label in number of processed faces, holes, vertices, edges, handles, boundary components, and boundary edges. Initial and final counts are listed at the bottom.

In Figure 3 we illustrate for each label the situation in which it applies and the respective updates for gate and boundary. Both encoding and decoding are shown. The details for encoding are:

label F_n The active gate is not adjacent to any other boundary edge, but to an unprocessed face of degree n. The active boundary is extended around this face. The new active gate is the rightmost edge of the included face.

label R The active gate is adjacent to the next edge along the active boundary. The gate is 'fixed' together with this edge. The new active gate is the previous edge along the active boundary.

label L The active gate is adjacent to the previous edge along the active boundary. The gate is 'fixed' together with this edge. The new active gate is the next edge along the active boundary.

label S The active gate is adjacent to an edge of the active boundary which is neither the next nor the previous. The gate is 'fixed' together with this edge, which splits the active boundary. The previous edge and the next edge along the active boundary become gates for the two resulting boundaries. One is pushed on the stack and encoding continues on the other.

label E The active gate is adjacent to an edge of the active boundary which is both the next and the previous. Then the active boundary consists of only two edges which are 'fixed' together. The encoding process terminates if the boundary stack is empty. Otherwise it continues on the boundary popped from this stack.

label H_n The active gate is not adjacent to any other boundary edge, but to an unprocessed hole of size n. The active boundary is extended around this hole. The new active gate is the rightmost edge of the included hole.

label $M_{i,l,k}$ The active gate is adjacent to a boundary edge which is not from the active boundary, but from a boundary in the stack. 'Fixing' the two edges together merges the two boundaries. Consequently this boundary is removed from the stack. Its former position i in the stack and two offset values l and k (see Figure 3) are stored together with the label. The new active gate is the previous edge along the boundary from the stack.

We use a simple half-edge structure [6] during encoding and decoding to store the mesh connectivity and to maintain the boundaries. Besides pointers to the origin, to the next half-edge around the origin, and to the inverse half-edge, we have two pointers to reference a next and a previous boundary edge. This way we organize all edges of the same boundary into a cyclic doubly-linked list.

The decoding process reconstructs the connectivity of the polygon mesh with a single reverse traversal of the label sequence. Each label has a unique inverse operation (see Figure 3) that undoes the gate and boundary updates that happened during encoding. The time complexity for decoding is linear in the number of mesh edges. An exception is the inverse operation for label $M_{i,k,l}$ which requires the traversal of $k + l$ edges. However, labels of this type correspond to handles in the mesh, which are of rare occurence.

3.2 Compression

The label sequence produced by the encoding process is subsequently mapped into a bit-stream. The frequencies with which the different labels occur are highly non-uniform, which invites some kind of entropy encoding. There is also a strong correlation among subsequent labels, which can be exploited using a memory-sensitive encoding scheme. With a simple order-3 adaptive arithmetic coder [29] we achieve excellent compression ratios.

For an adaptive arithmetic encoder with three label memory the space requirement for the probability table grows as the cube of the number of symbols. Therefore we limit the number of labels in the input sequence to eight: F_3, F_4, F_5, F_c, R, L, S, and E. This allows the implementation of the arithmetic order-3 entropy coder to be both space and time efficient. The probability tables need only 4 KB of memory and we can use fast bit operations to manage them. Labels F_n with $n > 5$ are expressed through the combination of a label F_5 and $n - 5$ subsequent labels of type F_c. We observe that labels of type F_n are never followed by label L or label E. We exploit this to express the typically infrequent appearing labels H_n and $M_{i,k,l}$ using the combinations $F_4 L$ and $F_4 E$. The integer values associated with these labels are stored using a standard technique for encoding variable sized integers into bit-streams.

The compression scheme described above is extremely fast and produces very compact encodings for the label sequence. In Table 1 we give connectivity compression results in bits per vertex (bpv) for a set of popular example meshes.

Simple triangle or quadrangle meshes. A simple triangle (quadrangle) mesh is a polygon mesh without holes and handles whose faces are all triangles (quadrangles). In this case we can give encodings with guaranteed bit-rates that are theoretically interesting. A simple triangle mesh with v vertices has $3v - 6$ edges and $2v - 4$ triangles. Thus, $2v - 4$ labels are F_3 while the remaining $v - 2$

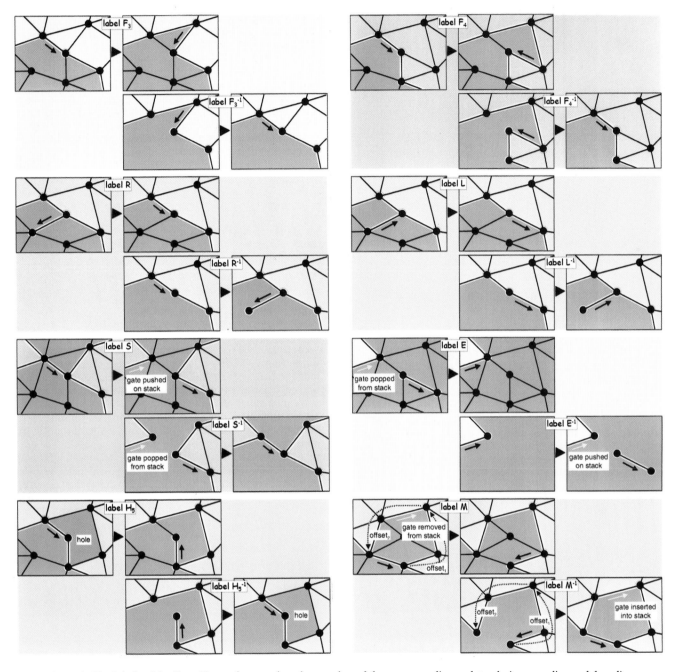

Figure 3: The labels of the Face Fixer scheme: when they apply and the corresponding updates during encoding and decoding.

labels are R, L, S, or E. An encoding that uses 1 bit for label F_3 and 3 bits each for the other labels guarantees a $5v - 10$ bit encoding.

Similarly, a simple quadrangle mesh with v vertices has $2v - 4$ edges and $v - 2$ quadrangles. Here $v - 2$ labels are of type F_4 while the remaining $v - 2$ labels are R, L, S, or E. An encoding that uses 1 bit for label F_4 and 3 bits each for the other labels guarantees a $4v - 8$ bit encoding.

3.3 Quadrilateral Grids

Instead of fixing together faces the Face Fixer scheme can also fix together patches of faces. Then we have to describe in addition the interior of these patches. If a patch is a rectangular quadrilateral grid this can be done very efficiently through the number of rows and columns in this grid. The beethoven bust and the shark model in Figure 4 for example, contain large patches of quadrilateral grids.

We introduce the label $QG_{r,l,h}$ to include such a *quad grid* into the active boundary. The associated integer values r, l, and h count the number of quadrangles that this grid extends to the right, to the left, and across as seen from the active gate (see Figure 4).

Optimal selection of a set of non-overlapping quad grids on the model is not only NP-hard, we also lack a well-defined optimality criterium. Including quad grids into the active boundary breaks up the regularity of the label stream, which in turn hampers subsequent arithmetic coding. However, first results using greedy methods are promising: The connectivity of the teapot, for example, compresses down to 1.069 bpv using 10 quad grids, for the shark 1.374 bpv, for the galleon 2.190 bpv, and for the beethoven bust 2.591 bpv.

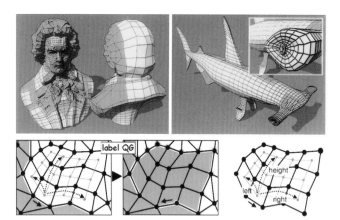

Figure 4: The beethoven bust and the shark model with quad grids marked in yellow (top). The label QG encodes a quad grid by specifying its left and right extend and its height (bottom).

4 PROPERTIES AND STRUCTURES

The Face Fixer scheme as presented so far allows to efficiently compress and uncompress the connectivity of a polygon mesh. However, polygonal models have geometry data associated with each vertex that specifies their physical location in 3D. Additional property data, such as normals, colours, and texture coordinates, is often attached to the vertices, the faces, or the corners of the mesh. To establish a connection between the geometry and property data and the vertex, face, or corner they are associated with, we define an implicit ordering on the occurrence of these mesh elements. Such an ordering can be derived using any deterministic mesh traversal that starts at a known point. Then the encoder stores the geometry or property values in the order in which the mesh features they are attached to are encountered during the traversal. Decoding performs the same traversal and re-assigns the data to the appropriate places.

Compression schemes that use the traversal order induced by the connectivity encoder to attach geometry and property data to the mesh are called *one-pass* coders. Carefully designed [7], they can combine connectivity, geometry and property information into a single bit-stream, which makes it possible to *stream* a mesh across a network. Then decompression can reconstruct the mesh incrementally as the bits are received. Time-critical applications benefit from such a scheme as transmission and reconstruction of the mesh can run in parallel. Other one-pass encoders [25] keep connectivity data separate from the rest in order to compress each more efficiently.

Reconstructing the polygon mesh in a single pass forces the predictive encoding for geometry and property data to make its estimations with incomplete neighbourhood information. A *multi-pass* coder stores the connectivity data separately from property and geometry data and traverses the mesh two or more times during encoding and decoding. The decoder first reconstructs the complete connectivity information before re-attaching geometry and property data to their appropriate location. In this case the mesh traversal used to establish the implicit ordering of geometry and property data can be different from the one used by the connectivity encoder.

4.1 Predictive Compression

The Face Fixer scheme can be combined with previously proposed techniques for predictive compression of geometry and property data [3, 24, 25]. Since the prediction rules of these schemes assume meshes with triangle connectivity, we could simply triangulate the polygons using a deterministic strategy that is solely based on the connectivity. However, even though this paper does not address pre-

dictive compression, we believe that the recovered polygon information can be utilized for more accurate geometry prediction.

For high-quality polygonal models like those in the Viewpoint Premier collection [28], faces are nearly planar and convex. Although a face may be not be not perfectly planar, major discontinuities are improbable to occur across it—otherwise it would likely have been triangulated when the model was designed. This can lead to an improvement in predictive geometry encoding: After the positions of three vertices of a planar face are known, the 3D problem of predicting the coordinates for the remaining vertices around the face reduces to 2D. The embedding planes of multiple neighbouring faces around a vertex give additional hints for predicting its location.

The convexity constraint can lead to further improvements in the accuracy of the prediction. The *parallelogram* rule introduced by Touma and Gotsman [25] uses the assumption that adjacent triangles form a parallelogram for predictive coding. While two adjacent triangles can violate this assumption quite drastically, a convex quadrangle can not. Their approach could be extended to define a *pentagon* or a *hexagon* rule for higher degree faces.

4.2 Vertex and Face Properties

A vertex-based property assignment is commonly used to achieve visually smooth transitions across face boundaries. In the same way the geometry data is shared by all faces around each vertex to avoid cracks in the surface, a common normal, colour, or texture coordinate eliminates discontinuities when interpolated shading (e.g. Gouraud shading) is applied. Geometry data and property data associated with a vertex are stored in the order the vertices are encountered during the traversal of the mesh.

A typical example for a face-based property assignment is a precomputed radiosity solution. Each face has assigned a colour that corresponds to the amount of light it emits or transmits. The property data associated with a face is stored in the order the faces are encountered during the traversal of the mesh. Obviously this is independent from the degree of the face. Here lies another advantage of the Face Fixer method over encoding schemes that first triangulate the input mesh. Splitting a face of degree n into $n - 2$ triangles creates $n - 2$ copies of its properties. Instead of encoding these properties once, they need to be encoded $n - 2$ times.

4.3 Corner Properties

A corner-based property assignment becomes necessary to reflect physical discontinuities in the underlying 3D model. Vertices that lie along such a discontinuity have usually more than one associated normal, colour or texture coordinate, each of which they share with a disjoint set of adjacent corners. Five of our example models have vertices with multiple normals (see Table 3).

We need to establish a mapping between a property value and the set of corners it is associated with. Our approach is a simple but effective improvement on work by Taubin et al. [23]. They store a *discontinuity bit* with every corner that is "0" when this corner uses the same property as the previous corner in counterclockwise order and a "1" otherwise. Then the property data associated with a set of corners is stored in the order in which the corresponding corners marked with "1" are encountered during the traversal of the mesh. This approach requires as many bits as the mesh has corners.

Based on the observation that not all vertices have multiple properties, we propose a similar marking scheme that uses *vertex bits* and *corner bits*. We use one bit per vertex to distinguish vertices with a single property ("1") from those with multiple properties ("0"). The corners around every vertex with multiple properties are marked as described above (see Figure 5). We store the property data in the same order as the corresponding "1" bits appear in the bit sequence. The results in Table 3 show that this encoding gives savings of 20 % to 70 % over the method proposed by Taubin et al. [23].

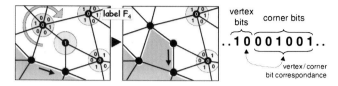

Figure 5: Encoding the mapping from properties to sets of corners.

name	vertices with n normals						vertex bits	corner bits
	$n = 1$	$n = 2$	$n = 3$	$n = 4$	$n = 5$	$n = 6$		
triceratops	2585	232	14	1	–	–	2832	980
galleon	1146	894	308	9	16	–	2372	4756
beethoven	1838	681	118	14	2	2	2655	3235
sandal	1120	1227	274	15	–	–	2636	6150
shark	1985	575	34	1	–	–	2560	2300

Table 3: Example results for encoding multiple vertex normals. The number of vertex bits and corner bits are reported that need to be recorded during the mesh traversal to establish a mapping between each normal and the set of corners sharing it.

4.4 Group Structures

Structural information that classifies groups of faces of a polygonal model into logical units is present in many file formats. Such face groupings allow to assign qualitative information to otherwise nameless polygons. Typically they establish a mapping between a meaningful part of the real world object and the set of faces of the polygonal model representing this part. We created and colour-coded such structural information for the popular teapot mesh and the cow mesh (see Figure 2). Many other well-known polygonal models, such as the triceratops, the cessna, the beethoven bust, and the galleon mesh contain similar group structures.

The triceratops mesh for example has six groups that classify each face as either skin, horn, toe, mouth, eye, or nose. The 58 faces that belong to the mouth-group form a single connected patch on the triceratops mesh. The 149 faces of the horn-group form three such patches and the 205 faces of the toe-group form fifteen.

The galleon model has a total of 17 groups. But this model consists of 12 unconnected components, which capture some of the group structure. The six sails, the three masts, the rig, and the lamp are separate components and form a group each. The body of the galleon however is one component with six groups: the hull, the keel, the deck, the aft, the windows, and the rig.

Encoding such structural information present in a polygon mesh has not been addressed by previously reported compression schemes. In a naive approach, we have a list of groups and assign a group index to every face. These group indices can then be treated like any other face property. For models with k groups and f faces such an encoding requires at least $f \log k$ bits.

When a model consists of several mesh parts we can improve on the above by specifying for each component the number of groupings it contains. For mesh parts whose faces belong all to the same group no additional information needs to be recorded. For mesh parts with group structures we need only as many bits per face as necessary to distinguish among the groups of this component. This is the approach we will compare our results against.

The concept of a *super face* is an natural extension of the Face Fixer scheme that leads to more compact and elegant encodings of face groupings. A super face is a collection of faces that is contained inside a single closed boundary loop. The representation power of super faces is illustrated in Figure 6: A simple super face composed of 9 faces (case A), a super face with a non-manifold vertex (case B), a super face with a non-manifold edge (case C), and a super face that contains another while being adjacent to a third (case D).

We introduce a new label SF to encode super face structure on the mesh. When the active gate is adjacent to a super face the active boundary is extended around the entire super face and the new gate is pushed on the stack. The super face is cut out of the polygon mesh and its boundary becomes the active boundary with the gate being the same as before (see Figure 7). The super face, which itself may contain other super faces, is first processed in its entirety before the encoding continues on the boundary that was pushed on the stack. The inverse operation used for decoding simply 'fixes' the super face back into the mesh. The length of the super face boundary is not encoded explicitly, but is directly related to the cost of encoding a super face. In addition to the label SF there is one additional label of types R, L, S, or E per super face boundary edge.

We use super faces to encode the group structure of a polygon mesh by declaring each group boundary a super face boundary. This results in super faces corresponding to cases A, B, and D. Ideally we would like a one to one mapping from groups to super faces. But when the faces of a group are not all adjacent, like the three horns of the triceratops, a group is represented by more than one super face. We could connect the three horns using non-manifold super face edges (case C) along a shortest path across the mesh. However, this requires additional computation and is expensive for distant patches because of the increasing length of the super face boundary.

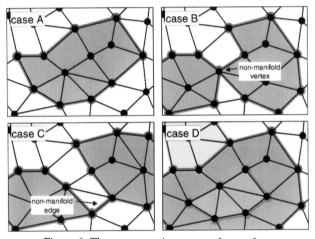

Figure 6: The representation power of super faces.

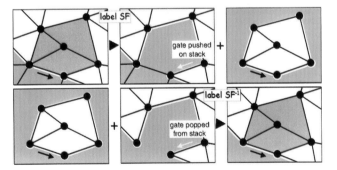

Figure 7: The label SF for encoding and decoding super faces.

Instead of storing one group index per face, we store one group index per super face and one group index per mesh component. Table 4 lists results for our pool of example meshes. Although more bits are needed to include the super face structure into the connectivity encoding, the savings in the number of necessary group references lead to superior compression rates overall.

Hierarchical Super Faces. The group structures that we have discussed so far are flat structures without a hierarchy. Suppose the

name	bpv without super faces			bpv with super faces		
	conn.	grouping	total	conn.	grouping	total
triceratops	2.115	8502	5.117	2.484	(23 + 1) * 3	2.509
galleon	2.595	2640	3.708	2.701	(10 + 12) * 5	2.747
cessna	2.841	15538	6.990	3.457	(137 + 11) * 6	3.694
beethoven	2.890	5470	4.950	3.081	(12 + 8) * 4	3.111
sandal	2.602	27	2.612	2.602	(0 + 9) * 3	2.612
shark	1.670	7686	4.672	1.962	(11 + 1) * 3	1.976
al	2.926	6039	4.595	3.051	(23 + 21) * 6	3.124
cupie	2.307	5060	4.003	2.387	(17 + 6) * 4	2.418
tommygun	2.611	5036	3.818	2.823	(12 + 39) * 4	2.872
cow	2.213	17412	8.209	2.346	(7 + 1) * 3	2.354
teapot	1.669	3870	4.924	1.853	(7 + 1) * 3	1.874

Table 4: Example results for encoding the grouping structure on a mesh together with the connectivity. The middle columns reflect the number of bits required for all indices into the group list. Both bit counts exploit the fact that the group structure is partly captured through the component structure of the models.

hierarchical structure of a world map with the oceans being the lowest level containing continents and islands. The continents themselves are subdivided into countries, some of which are composed of states, then counties, etc. Super faces can be used to efficiently encode such hierarchical structures on a polygon mesh.

Corner Properties Revisited. Group boundaries in a polygonal model often reflect discontinuities in the represented real-world object, which in turn is reason to associate multiple properties to sets of corners around a vertex. A substantial number of polygon meshes from the Viewpoint Premier collection [28] have vertices with multiple properties only along group boundaries. These meshes share a single normal, colour, or texture coordinate among all corners around a vertex that belong to the same group. In this case the super face structure is sufficient to establish the mapping between the property data and the appropriate set of corners. No additional information like corner or vertex bits is required.

5 SUMMARY

We have presented a new compression algorithm that encodes the connectivity of surface meshes directly in their polygonal representation. This has several benefits compared to methods that compress pre-triangulated polygon meshes: The original connectivity is preserved. Properties associated with faces and corners need not to be replicated. Subsequent stripification algorithms can generate better triangle strips. Predictive coding for geometry and property data can exploit additional convexity and planarity constraints.

Our method also improves on approaches that triangulate meshes prior to compression, but recover the polygons by marking edges. Although the freedom to triangulate polygons on demand can lead to compact encodings for the triangulated mesh, for example using Touma and Gotsman's scheme [25], the number of bits required to mark the edges would be as high as 3 bpv. This holds true especially for meshes with low triangle counts, as there is less connectivity information to compress. For the case of quadrangular meshes the Edgebreaker extensions [13, 15] give better encodings.

We have also introduced a method to encode structures on a polygon mesh. Such structures can specify classifications of faces, hierarchies, smoothing groups, or mesh partitions. The concept of super faces naturally extends our algorithm and leads to elegant and efficient encodings of such structural information—this has not been addressed by previous compression schemes. The edge-based nature of Face-Fixer combined with reverse decoding make the implementation of super faces extremely simple.

The techniques presented here lead to more compact and complete representations of polygonal models. The model collection

from Viewpoint [28], for example, consists of data sets that contain few triangles, but are rich in structural information and associated properties. Especially with such 3D content moving towards networked environments, our methods will find many applications.

We owe a debt of gratitude to many people for their thoughts and time. We especially thank Davis King and Jarek Rossignac for discussions, Mike Maniscalco and Stefan Gumhold for tips on arithmetic coding, and Viewpoint Datalabs for the polygon models.

References

[1] C. Bajaj, V. Pascucci, and G. Zhuang. Progressive compression and transmission of arbitrary triangular meshes. In *Visualization 99*, pages 307–316, 1999.

[2] D. Cohen-Or, D. Levin, and O. Remez. Progressive compression of arbitrary triangular meshes. In *Visualization 99 Conference Proceedings*, pages 67–72, 1999.

[3] M. Deering. Geometry compression. In *SIGGRAPH 95*, pages 13–20, 1995.

[4] M. Denny and C. Sohler. Encoding a triangulation as a permutation of its point set. In *Proc. of 9th Canadian Conf. on Comp. Geom.*, pages 39–43, 1997.

[5] F. Evans, S. S. Skiena, and A. Varshney. Optimizing triangle strips for fast rendering. In *Visualization 96 Conference Proceedings*, pages 319–326, 1996.

[6] L. Guibas and J. Stolfi. Primitives for the manipulation of general subdivisions and the computation of Voronoi Diagrams. *ACM ToG*, 4(2):74–123, 1985.

[7] S. Gumhold and W. Strasser. Real time compression of triangle mesh connectivity. In *SIGGRAPH 98 Conference Proceedings*, pages 133–140, 1998.

[8] H. Hoppe. Progressive meshes. In *SIGGRAPH 96*, pages 99–108, 1996.

[9] M. Isenburg and J. Snoeyink. Mesh collapse compression. In *Proceedings of SIBGRAPI 99*, Campinas, Brazil, pages 27–28, 1999.

[10] M. Isenburg and J. Snoeyink. Spirale reversi: Reverse decoding of the Edgebreaker encoding. Technical Report TR–99–08, Computer Science, UBC, 1999.

[11] K. Keeler and J. Westbrook. Short encodings of planar graphs and maps. In *Discrete Applied Mathematics*, pages 239–252, 1995.

[12] D. King and J. Rossignac. Guaranteed 3.67v bit encoding of planar triangle graphs. In *Proc. of 11th Canadian Conf. on Comp. Geom.*, pages 146–149, 1999.

[13] D. King, J. Rossignac, and A. Szymczak. Connectivity compression for irregular quadrilateral meshes. Technical Report TR–99–36, GVU, Georgia Tech, 1999.

[14] D. G. Kirkpatrick. Optimal search in planar subdivisions. *SIAM Journal of Computing*, 12(1):28–35, 1983.

[15] B. Kronrod and C. Gotsman. Efficient coding of non-triangular meshes. In *Proc. of 16th Europ. Workshop on Computational Geometry*, pages 24–26, 2000.

[16] J. Li, C. C. Kuo, and H. Chen. Mesh connectivity coding by dual graph approach. Contribution Document MPEG98/m3530 Tokyo, mar 1998.

[17] R. Parajola and Rossignac. Compressed progressive meshes. Technical Report TR–99–05, GVU, Georgia Tech, 1999.

[18] J. Rossignac. Edgebreaker: Connectivity compression for triangle meshes. *IEEE Transactions on Visualization and Computer Graphics*, 5(1), 1999.

[19] J. Rossignac and A. Szymczak. Wrap&zip: Linear decoding of planar triangle graphs. *The Journal of Computational Geometry, Theory and Applications*, 1999.

[20] J. Snoeyink and M. van Kreveld. Linear-time reconstruction of Delaunay triangulations with applications. In *Proc. of Europ. Symp. Alg.*, pages 459–471, 1997.

[21] D. M. Y. Sommerville. *An Introduction to the Geometry of N Dimensions*. Dutton Publications, New York, 1929.

[22] G. Taubin, A. Guéziec, W.P. Horn, and F. Lazarus. Progressive forest split compression. In *SIGGRAPH 98 Conference Proceedings*, pages 123–132, 1998.

[23] G. Taubin, W.P. Horn, F. Lazarus, and J. Rossignac. Geometry coding and VRML. *Proceedings of the IEEE*, 86(6):1228–1243, 1998.

[24] G. Taubin and J. Rossignac. Geometric compression through topological surgery. *ACM Transactions on Graphics*, 17(2):84–115, 1998.

[25] C. Touma and C. Gotsman. Triangle mesh compression. In *Graphics Interface 98 Conference Proceedings*, pages 26–34, 1998.

[26] G. Turan. Succinct representations of graphs. *Dis. Apl. Math.*, 8:289–294, 1984.

[27] W.T. Tutte. A census of planar triangulations. *Cnd. Jrn. Math.*, 14:21–38, 1962.

[28] Viewpoint. *Premier Catalog (2000 Edition) www.viewpoint.com*.

[29] I. H. Witten, R. M. Neal, and J. G. Cleary. Arithmetic coding for data compression. *Communications of the ACM*, 30(6):520–540, 1987.

[30] M. Woo, J. Neider, and T. Davis. *Open GL Programming Guide*. A.W., 1996.

Progressive Geometry Compression

Andrei Khodakovsky   Peter Schröder   Wim Sweldens
Caltech   Caltech   Bell Laboratories

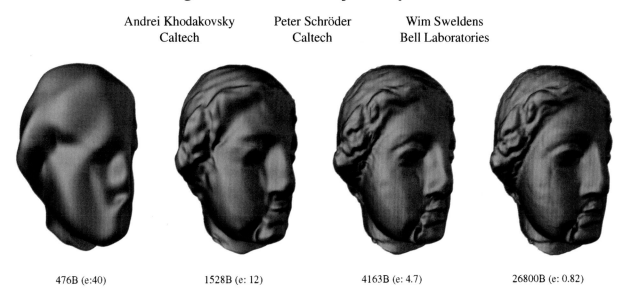

| 476B (e:40) | 1528B (e: 12) | 4163B (e: 4.7) | 26800B (e: 0.82) |

Figure 1: *Partial bit-stream reconstructions from a progressive encoding of the Venus head model. File sizes are given in bytes and relative L^2 reconstruction error in multiples of 10^{-4} The rightmost reconstruction is indistinguishable from the original.*

Abstract

We propose a new progressive compression scheme for arbitrary topology, highly detailed and densely sampled meshes arising from geometry scanning. We observe that meshes consist of three distinct components: geometry, parameter, and connectivity information. The latter two do not contribute to the reduction of error in a compression setting. Using semi-regular meshes, parameter and connectivity information can be virtually eliminated. Coupled with semi-regular wavelet transforms, zerotree coding, and subdivision based reconstruction we see improvements in error by a factor four (12dB) compared to other progressive coding schemes.

CR Categories and Subject Descriptors: I.3.5 [**Computer Graphics**]: Computational Geometry and Object Modeling - *hierarchy and geometric transformations*; G.1.2 [**Numerical Analysis**]: Approximation - *approximation of surfaces and contours, wavelets and fractals*; I.4.2 [**Image Processing and Computer Vision**]: Compression (Coding) - *Approximate methods*

Additional Keywords: Compression algorithms, signal processing, wavelets, subdivision surfaces, semi-regular meshes, zerotree coding, hierarchical representations

1 Introduction

Today we can accurately acquire finely detailed, arbitrary topology surfaces with millions and most recently billions [22] of vertices. Such models place large strains on computation, storage, transmission, and display resources. Compression is essential in these

settings and in particular *progressive* compression, where an early, coarse approximation can subsequently be improved through additional bits. While compression of *images* has a long history and has achieved a high level of sophistication, compression of *surfaces* is relatively new and still evolving rapidly.

Compression is always a tradeoff between accuracy and bit rate, i.e., bits per vertex. This tradeoff is the subject of classical rate-distortion theory. While rate-distortion curves are common in the image coding literature they have only recently appeared in geometry coding. This is partially due to the fact that the error for images is easily measured using the L^2 norm of the difference between original and approximation, while measuring error for surfaces is more involved. Since there is no immediate correspondence between the original and compressed surface, one cannot simply subtract one surface from another. This difficulty is typically addressed by computing a geometry error using, for example, Hausdorff distance. Such error metrics do not depend on the particular sample locations or connectivity, but instead measure the distance between the geometric shapes. This is important since the original and compressed mesh may have very different sample locations and connectivity, especially in a progressive setting. By sample location we mean the precise location of the vertex *within* the surface.

How low can such errors be? Consider a continuous physical surface, such as the Venus sculpture whose scan generated the mesh in Figure 1. Given that the source geometry is continuous, any digital representation, such as a triangle mesh, has some error E associated with it. This error has three components due to sampling, discretization, and quantization. Sampling error E_s arises from acquisition noise. Discretization error E_d is due to the fact that a triangulation with edge length h can approximate a smooth geometry no better than $O(h^2)$. Finally, a finite bit representation for the vertex positions leads to quantization error E_q. The sampling and triangulation of the model fix E_s and E_d. A standard float representation typically leads to a quantization error much smaller than $E_s + E_d$. All existing single rate coders proceed by first quantizing the vertex positions more coarsely leading to a quantization error $E'_q \approx E_s + E_d$ followed by lossless encoding of the connectivity and quantized vertex positions. Existing progressive coders aim to eventually recover the quantized sample locations and original connectivity. For small meshes with carefully layed out connectivity and sample locations this is very appropriate. The situation is different for highly detailed, densely sampled meshes coming from 3D scanning: Since distortion is measured as geometric distance the sample locations and connectivity can be treated as additional degrees of freedom to improve the rate-distortion performance. As long as the final result has geometric error on the order of the original E, the actual sample locations and connectivity do not matter. We will call the information contained in the sample locations, the *parameter* information. For example, by letting the vertices slide *within* the surface we only change the parameter information and not the geometric fidelity.

In particular, we propose a new progressive geometry compression method which is based on smooth semi-regular meshes, i.e., meshes built by successive triangle quadrisection starting from a coarse irregular mesh. Almost all vertices in a semi-regular mesh have valence six and their sample locations can easily be estimated. Hence, semi-regular meshes allow us to eliminate almost all *parameter* and connectivity information. As we illustrate below, parameter and connectivity information make up a considerable fraction of the bit budget in existing coders, but do not contribute at all to reducing geometric error. Consequently our rate-distortion curves are significantly better than those of existing coders. For most models, our error is about four times smaller at comparable bit rates, a remarkable 12 dB improvement!

Semi-regular meshes additionally allow for wavelet transforms and zerotree coders. Zerotrees are amongst the best image coding algorithms today. Wavelets have superior decorrelation properties and allow for subdivision based reconstruction. This means that in regions where the encoder sets wavelet coefficients to zero the decoder uses subdivision to reconstruct the geometry. Hence even highly compressed surfaces are still smooth and visually pleasing. Figure 1 shows a sequence of progressive reconstructions of the compressed Venus model at different bitrates.

Goals and Contributions The main contribution of this paper is the observation that parameter information makes up a significant fraction of the bit budget while not contributing to error reduction at all. This motivates our compression algorithm based on semi-regular meshes.

As input our algorithm takes an irregular mesh describing a 2-manifold (possibly with boundary) and produces successive approximations employing semi-regular meshes with little parameter and connectivity information. The coder first produces a hierarchical approximation of the surface which is subsequently encoded with a zerotree progressive coder. Novel aspects of the algorithm include

- reducing parameter information through the use of semi-regular meshes;

- a Loop based wavelet transform for high order decorrelation and subdivision based reconstruction;

- a novel zerotree hierarchy for primal semi-regular triangle meshes of arbitrary topology.

We emphasize that our target application is the compression of densely sampled, highly detailed surfaces. Our algorithm is not effective when the input geometry is well described by a small, carefully layed out mesh. In this case progressive coding is generally questionable and non-progressive coders are more appropriate and perform exceedingly well.

1.1 Review of Related Work

Mesh Compression: Algorithms for efficient encoding of arbitrary connectivity meshes have been described both for the progressive and non-progressive setting (for an excellent overview of 3D geometry compression see [36]). Most of the early efforts concentrated on finding efficient encodings for mesh connectivity with the current state of the art at around 2-6b/v (bits per vertex) [37, 13, 35, 29, 28]. Vertex positions are dealt with by performing an initial quantization followed by predictive coding induced by the traversal order of the connectivity encoding.

In contrast to single target rate coders, progressive coders aim to code for a range of rates by allowing reconstruction of intermediate shapes using a prefix of the encoded bit stream. Such coding schemes are typically based on mesh simplification techniques. Examples include progressive meshes [26, 23, 16], independent set vertex removal strategies [4], topological surgery [34], and topological layering [1]. Connectivity bits increase to around 4-10b/v in these schemes. Prediction of vertex positions is now more naturally performed in a hierarchical fashion as induced by the associated mesh simplification. Examples include centroid predictors [34, 4] as well as higher order predictors [26]. To date, progressivity in these coders has typically been focused on connectivity encoding. Rate-distortion theory however says that coordinate values should be progressively quantized [23, 17] as well: to minimize error at a given rate one must trade off additional quantization bits for already present vertices against bits for new vertices and their connectivity.

Wavelets It is well known from image coding that wavelet representations are very effective in decorrelating the original data [8, 6], greatly facilitating subsequent entropy coding. In essence, coarser level data provides excellent predictors for finer level data, leaving only generally small prediction residuals for the coding step. For tensor product surfaces many of these ideas can be applied in a straightforward fashion [8, 33, 12]. However, the arbitrary topology surface case is much more challenging. To begin with, wavelet decompositions of general surfaces were not known until the pioneering work in [25]. These constructions were subsequently applied to progressive approximation of surfaces [2] as well as data *on* surfaces [31, 19].

Multiresolution surface representations based on subdivision [39] and local frame details are closely related to our wavelet constructions and have proven to be very powerful in a variety of circumstances. However, they require the initial surface to be represented by a semi-regular mesh. This has led to the development of a number of algorithms for remeshing [10, 20, 21, 18].

Zerotree Coders Some of the best wavelet based progressive coders are based on zerotrees [5, 32, 30]. They effectively exploit the fact that wavelet coefficients at finer scales tend to be smaller in magnitude than coefficients at coarser scales in the same region. A zerotree coder encodes the location of coefficients below threshold in subtrees. Standard zerotree coders for images are based on a dual formulation, i.e., coefficients are associated with faces. For primal hierarchical mesh decompositions using face splits (e.g., quadrisection of triangles) the data however lives at vertices, not faces. We show in Section 3.4 how to build zerotree coders for primal hierarchies.

Irregular Subdivision Our separation of parameter versus geometry information is partially inspired by the work done on irregular subdivision [14] and intrinsic curvature normal flow [7]. They point out that without the parameter side information, it is impossible to build high order schemes converging to smooth meshes. Irregular parameter information is inherently hard to encode and hinders the performance of irregular mesh coders.

2 Geometry, Parameter, and Connectivity Information

Elimination of parameter and connectivity information is a key ingredient of our algorithm. In this section we go into more detail regarding parameter and connectivity information and how to eliminate it.

Previous compression approaches have typically treated triangle meshes as consisting of *two* distinct components: connectivity and vertex positions. State of the art coders are able to encode connectivity of irregular meshes with 2b/v or even less. Hence, it is argued, vertex positions are much more expensive and their coding needs further advancement, for example through better predictors.

The main insight of this paper is that there are actually *three* components: connectivity, geometry, and *parameter* information. The parameter information captures where the sample locations are *within* the surface while the geometry information captures the geometry *independent* of the sample locations used. So far parameter and geometry information were treated together.

Consider a vertex of a particular Venus head triangulation. Moving this vertex slightly *within* the surface, does not change the discretization error or geometry information. It only affects the parameter information. Alternatively, moving the vertex normal to the surface clearly changes the error and geometry information, but leaves parameter information unchanged. This illustrates that while geometry and parameter information are globally intertwined they disconnect locally: infinitesimally, we may think of parameter information as being described by displacements in the tangent plane to the surface. Geometry information on the other hand is normal to the surface. This implies that from a rate distortion point of view bits should be allocated preferentially to the local normal direction. For smooth parameterizations this occurs naturally since prediction residuals in the tangent plane will be small.

Sphere Example To illustrate the power of the distinction between geometry, parameter, and connectivity information we consider three triangulations of a sphere (Figure 2). All three meshes contain the same geometry information and carry the same discretization error E_d with no sampling noise. The first two meshes have semi-regular connectivity but different parameter information. The middle one was generated by jiggling the sample locations within the sphere, thereby adding significant parameter information. The rightmost has irregular connectivity and parameter information.

Figure 3 shows the respective rate-distortion curves when using the state of the art non-progressive coder of Touma and Gotsman (TG) [37]. We always show non-progressive curves dashed since these points are not achievable in a progressive manner. In case of the smooth semi-regular mesh, the TG coder correctly noticed that it contains almost no connectivity information (0.1 b/v) and almost no parameter information. Its performance is essentially limited by the quality of the predictor used. The TG coder for the non-smooth semi-regular sphere is worse illustrating the bit penalty for parameter information. The TG coder for the irregular mesh (right) illustrates the additional overhead from irregular connectivity. This example demonstrates the tremendous pay off of reducing both connectivity and parameter information in a mesh.

Finally the small curve near the y-axis shows the result of applying our coder to the smooth semi-regular mesh. It can approximate the sphere with a relative error of $5 \cdot 10^{-5}$ using 166 bytes or .5 b/v. This it not surprising since a sphere has very little geometric information and a smooth semi-regular mesh is essentially optimal for our coder. This is where the high order decorrelation and subdivision based reconstruction really pays off. The same effect we see here so pronounced for the sphere, can also be observed in smooth, regularly sampled regions of more general surfaces, see Section 4.

3 Algorithm Components

The algorithm accepts as input an arbitrary connectivity 2-manifold (with boundary) triangulation. In a first step we compute a smooth

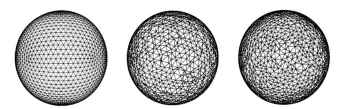

Figure 2: *Three spherical meshes each with 2562 vertices: smooth semi-regular (left), non-smooth semi-regular (middle), irregular (right). They have the same geometry information. The middle one also has parameter information while the right one has parameter and connectivity information.*

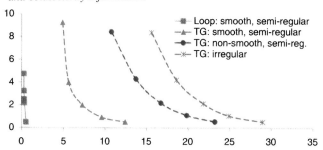

Figure 3: *Rate distortion curves for the triangle meshes from Figure 2 measured in relative L^2 error on a scale of 10^{-4} as a function of rate in b/v for TG coordinate quantization levels of $8 - 12b$.*

global parameterization using the MAPS algorithm [21]. This allows us to compute successive adaptive approximations with semi-regular connectivity. These semi-regular approximations are subsequently wavelet transformed and progressively compressed using zerotrees. The coarsest level connectivity is encoded using a standard non-progressive mesh encoder [37]. The decoder may produce intermediate approximations from any prefix of the bitstream.

We need to define the distance $d(X, Y)$ between two surfaces X and Y. Let $d(x, Y)$ be the Euclidean distance from a point x on X to the closest point on Y. Then the L^2 distance $d(X, Y)$ is given by

$$d(X, Y) = \left(\frac{1}{\text{area}(X)} \int_{x \in X} d(x, Y)^2 dx \right)^{1/2}.$$

This distance is not symmetric and we symmetrized it by taking the max of $d(X, Y)$ and $d(Y, X)$. For triangulations this distance can be computed using the METRO tool [3]. All the L^2 errors reported here are relative with respect to the bounding box diagonal on a scale of 10^{-4}, while rate is reported in b/v with respect to the number of vertices in the original input mesh.

3.1 Parameterization

As a first step, we compute a smooth parameterization of our input triangulation using MAPS [21]. An important feature of MAPS is its ability to automatically align iso-parameter lines of the semi-regular mesh with sharp features of the original input surface helping to avoid large wavelet coefficients near creases.

MAPS builds a bijective map between the input mesh T and a coarse base domain B. One can then apply quadrisection in the base domain B and use the mapping to build semi-regular approximations of T. These approximations have some remeshing error E_r with respect to T. While this error can be made arbitrarily small, it does not make sense to make the remeshing error E_r smaller than the discretization error E_d. This roughly occurs when the triangles from the semi-regular mesh are about the same size as the triangles of the input mesh. Using smaller triangles only serves to produce a better approximation of the input mesh, not necessarily of the original unknown geometry.

Of course one does not know E_d. An order estimate of E_d can be computed by measuring the distance between the input mesh T and a much finer mesh S obtained by Butterfly subdividing T. The latter serves as a proxy for the unknown original geometry. Once our semi-regular mesh error E_r is below the estimated discretization error E_d there is no need to further refine the semi-regular mesh. Hence our rate distortion curves will asymptotically not go to zero, but converge to the E_d estimate. Table 1 gives the E_d estimate, the minimum remeshing error, and the connectivity coding cost in bytes of the base domain B for various models. The connectivity was encoded using the TG coder.

	Feline	Bunny	Horse	Venus	Fandisk
# Vert.	49864	34835	48485	50002	6475
E_d (10^{-5})	7.3	9.4	6.0	5.5	28
E_r (10^{-5})	6.3	7.4	5.1	4.2	4.8
# Base Vert.	250	127	112	196	73
Base conn. (B)	122	76	62	72	46

Table 1: *Statistics for example meshes.*

3.2 Wavelet Transform

The wavelet transform replaces the original mesh with a coarsest mesh and a sequence of wavelet coefficients expressing the difference between successive levels. Since we deal with piecewise smooth models, neighboring vertices are highly correlated. The wavelet transform removes a large amount of this correlation. The distribution of wavelet coefficients is centered around zero and their magnitude decays at finer levels with the rate of decay related to the smoothness of the original surface. This behavior of the magnitude of wavelet coefficients is the key to progressive coding and justifies the choice of the zerotree coder for the bit encoding of coefficients.

Several methods for building wavelet transforms on semi-regular meshes exist [25, 31]. These are typically based on interpolating subdivision schemes such as Butterfly [9, 38]. A detailed description of the construction of lifted Butterfly wavelets can be found in [31]. The advantage of lifted wavelets is that both forward and inverse transforms can be computed with finite filters.

We use a novel Loop [24] wavelet transform, which has the advantage that the inverse transform uses Loop subdivision. Experimentally, we found it has rate distortion curves essentially identical to Butterfly, but typically better visual appearance.

The choice of Loop subdivision fixes the low pass reconstruction filter $\mathbf{P}$ in a wavelet construction. We require a high pass reconstruction filter $\mathbf{Q}$. Together they define the inverse wavelet transform

$$\mathbf{p}^{j+1} = \begin{bmatrix} \mathbf{P} & \mathbf{Q} \end{bmatrix} \begin{bmatrix} \mathbf{p}^j \\ \mathbf{d}^j \end{bmatrix}, \tag{1}$$

where $\mathbf{p}^j$ are the usual control points and $\mathbf{d}^j$ the wavelet coefficients at level j. For performance reasons we would like $\mathbf{Q}$ to have small support. One way to achieve this is to apply a quadrature mirror construction [27], deriving a high pass from a low pass filter. The result is shown in the regular case in Figure 4. Note that a globally consistent choice of the sign-flipping direction is possible only for orientable surfaces. Though we can use the same stencils in the general case, the wavelet subbands corresponding to edges of a certain orientation are well-defined only for orientable surfaces.

Around irregular vertices $\mathbf{P}$ is modified as usual. For edges immediately adjacent to an irregular vertex, $\mathbf{Q}$ must be modified as well. The only taps of the $\mathbf{Q}$ filter that can fall onto irregular vertices are the two -6 coefficients left and right of the center. If one of them is irregular we essentially "open up" that part of the filter and parameterize the coefficients by edge number, counting from the "10" (Figure 4, right). If an irregular vertex has valence less

than six this leads to the stencil folding over on itself, while for valences larger than six a gap is left. There is currently no theory available for wavelet constructions around irregular vertices. The only justification of the "trick" we used is that it does not impact the numerically computed condition numbers of our transform. Finally, boundaries are dealt with in the usual way through reflection.

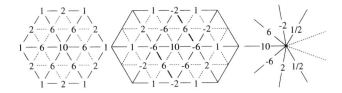

Figure 4: *Low (left) and high (middle) pass Loop reconstruction filters in the regular case. For irregular vertices the high pass filter is opened as indicated on the right.*

The forward wavelet transform, which goes from finer to coarser levels, is defined as the solution $[\mathbf{p}^j, \mathbf{d}^j]$ of the linear system in Eq. 1 for a given $\mathbf{p}^{j+1}$. Consequently computing the forward wavelet transform requires the solution of sparse linear systems. To solve these systems we use a bi-conjugate gradient solver [11] with diagonal preconditioning. We found the condition number for up to a 7 level transform to be no worse than 30 depending on the model.

Of course solving a linear system makes the forward transform slower than the inverse transform. This is acceptable as encoding is typically done once off-line while decoding happens frequently and in real time. For the Venus model the Loop forward transform, for example, takes 30s on a 550Mhz Pentium II Xeon while the inverse transform takes 2.5s. In case symmetry is important one can use a lifted Butterfly wavelet for which both forward and inverse transforms take about 2.5s.

The decorrelating power of the wavelet transform is illustrated in Figure 5. On the left is the histogram of the magnitude of Venus vertex positions. On the right is a histogram of the magnitude of the wavelet coefficients. Clearly a large amount of correlation was removed and the first order entropy has decreased considerably.

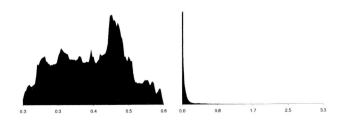

Figure 5: *Left: histogram of vertex position magnitudes for Venus. Right: histogram of the wavelet coefficient magnitudes, showing the decorrelation power of the wavelet transform.*

3.3 Vector Valued Wavelet Coefficients

Since our wavelet coefficients are vector valued, it is not immediately clear how they should be quantized. There is a fair amount of correlation between the x, y, and z wavelet components. We found that representing the wavelet coefficients in a local frame [39] induced by the surface tangent plane makes the components much more independent. In particular, we find that the variance of normal wavelet components is on average twice as large as the variance of the tangential components. Recalling the earlier geometry versus parameter distinction this is exactly what we want. In a smooth semi-regular mesh, the geometry information (normal component) is much larger than the parameter information (tangential component). Figure 6 illustrates this by showing the histograms of the polar angles θ (the angle from the z of normal axis) of the wavelet coefficients in global and local coordinate frames. The distribution becomes very non-uniform in the local frame with peaks around 0 and π indicating that most of the wavelet vectors lie in the normal direction. The angle along the equator is fairly uniformly distributed both in the global and local frame, hence the choice of basis vectors in the tangent plane is not important. Recall that parameter,

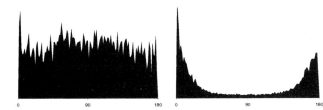

Figure 6: *Histograms of wavelet coefficient polar θ angles for the Venus head model in global (left) and local (right) frames. Coefficients lie mostly in the normal direction.*

i.e., tangential, information does not contribute to the error metric. Unfortunately, we cannot just ignore tangential wavelet components since this argument only holds in the infinitesimal limit. Especially at coarser levels, tangential wavelet coefficients can still contain some geometric information. However, we did find that the error metric is much less sensitive to quantization error of tangential versus normal wavelet components. Thus, we can further improve the error curves by more coarsely quantizing the tangential component.

A basic operation in a scalar zerotree coder is the *coefficient significance test*, i.e., checking its magnitude against a threshold. If it is below, the coefficient is added to a zerotree, else the location and sign of the coefficient need to be transmitted. For the vector case this becomes more difficult and we examined three quantization options. (1) Spherical cells are natural as we can use the magnitude for the significance test. We deal with the quantized angular components as "generalized" signs. (2) For cubical cells we divide the cube into 64 subcubes. Coefficients in the 8 internal cubes are insignificant and all the others are significant; their cell number again is an analog of the angular component. (3) We can deal with each vector component independently and encode it separately, reducing the vector case to three independent scalar passes.

We have compared all three cases and found that three scalar passes results in the best rate distortion curves for all models we considered. Experimentally, we found that quantization cells for the tangential component were best taken to be 4 times larger than those for the normal component.

3.4 Zerotree Coding

Given that we settled on scalar quantization, our coder consists of three independent zerotree coders. The bits from the three coders are interleaved to maintain progressivity.

A general principle of wavelet coefficient encoding is to send the highest order bits of the largest magnitude coefficients first. They will make the most significant contributions towards reducing error. Let $T_0 = \max\{|c_i|\}$ be the maximum magnitude of all coefficients, then in a first pass the coder should send the locations (index i) of *newly significant* coefficients, $|c_i| > T_0/2$. Doing so naïvely is expensive. However, if source and receiver agree on a canonical traversal order the source only has to send the result of the significance test $S(i) = (|c_i| > T)$ and, if true, the sign bit of c_i. If coefficients can be organized into canonical sets such that with high probability all coefficients in a given set are simultaneously below

threshold, a few set-based significance tests can enumerate the locations of the relevant coefficients. The decay properties of wavelet coefficients make their hierarchical tree organization the natural set structure [32, 30, 5]. Coding consists of a number of passes with exponentially decreasing thresholds $T_{j+1} = T_j/2$. In each pass significance bits are sent for newly significant coefficients. Additionally, refinement bits are sent for those coefficients which became significant in an earlier pass. Since source and receiver already agreed on locations of the latter, no location bits have to be sent for them. The number of such bit plane passes depends on the final quantization level. The decoder can reconstruct the geometry associated with any prefix of the bitstream by running an inverse wavelet transform on the coefficient bits seen so far.

The main distinction of our setting from the image case is the construction of the zerotrees. For images, one associates the coefficients with a quadrilateral face and the trees follow immediately from the face quadtree. While this works also for dual, i.e., face based subdivision schemes, our triangular transform is primal, i.e, vertex based.

The main insight is that while scale coefficients are associated with vertices, wavelet coefficients have a one-to-one association with edges of the coarser mesh. Vertices do not have a tree structure, but the edges do. Each edge is the parent of four edges of the same orientation in the finer mesh as indicated in Figure 7. Hence, each edge of the base domain forms the root of a zerotree; it groups all the wavelet coefficients of a fixed wavelet subband from its two incident base domain triangles. The grouping is consistent for arbitrary semi-regular meshes, i.e., no coefficient is accounted for multiple times or left out.

Figure 7: *A coarse edge (left) is parent to four finer edges of the same orientation (right).*

For brevity we do not give the complete coder/decoder algorithm here, but refer the interested reader to the pseudo code in [30], which is identical to our implementation with the above quadtree definition.

A final question concerns the transmission of the scale coefficients from the coarsest level. These are quantized uniformly. Experimentally, we found that it is best to send 4 bit planes initially with the base domain connectivity. Each remaining bitplane is sent as the zerotrees descend another bit plane.

The zerotree encoding (10 passes) of the Venus model takes 1s while decoding takes about 0.6s bringing the total decompression time to about 3.1s. Of course the low rate models can be decompressed faster.

3.5 Entropy Coding

The zerotree algorithm is very effective at exploiting parent-child coefficient correlations, minimizing the amount of encoded significance bits. However, the output of the zerotree coder can still be compressed further through arithmetic coding, which allows for a fractional number of bits per symbol.

The zerotree coder output contains three different types of information, significance bits, refinement bits and sign bits. Refinement and sign bits tend to be uniformly distributed; hence they are not entropy coded. Significance bits on the other hand can be further entropy coded. For early bitplanes most coefficients are insignificant resulting in mostly zero bits. For later bitplanes many coefficients become significant, resulting in mostly one bits. An arithmetic coder naturally takes advantage of this.

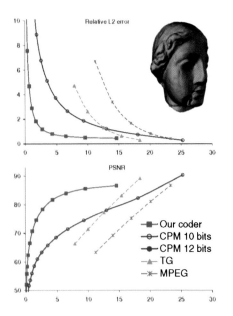
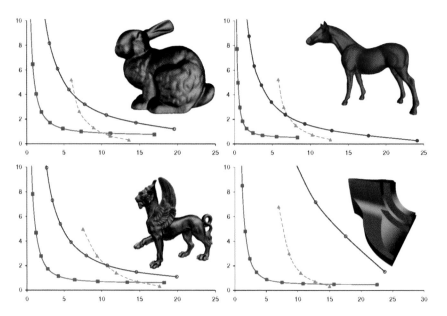

Figure 8: *Rate-distortion curves.*

We found that encoding of the significance bits in groups further improves performance of entropy coding [30]. Because children of any node always appear together during a zerotree pass we group their significance bits to form symbols of a 2^j alphabet ($j = 4, 3, 2, 1$). The actual number of bits of the alphabet is the number of children which were left insignificant at the previous pass. This grouping exploits correlations between magnitudes of spatially close wavelet coefficients.

4 Results

We compare our Loop based coder against known state of the art coders for different models. The coders we used are:

- **TG:** The Touma-Gotsman coder, which is a non progressive coder. It can be operated at different rates by changing the coordinate quantization between 8 and 12 bits.

- **CPM:** The compressed progressive mesh coder of Pajarola and Rossignac [26]. It can start with various quantization sizes. We found 10 or 12 to work best (and always show the best one).

- **MPEG:** The non-progressive coder from the MPEG4 standard which is based on topological surgery [35].

Figure 8 (left) shows the different curves for the Venus model for bitrates up to 25b/v. The top left shows relative L^2 error in units of 10^{-4}. The bottom left shows the same numbers but in a PSNR scale where $\text{PSNR} = 20 \log_{10} \text{peak}/d$, peak is the bounding box diagonal and d is the L^2 error. One can see that our progressive coder is about 12dB or a factor 4 better than the progressive CPM coder. As expected the non-progressive coders are much worse at lower rates and slightly better at higher rates. Our curve converges to the remeshing error which is where it crosses the TG curve. Given that the remeshing error is comparable to the discretization error, any compression with smaller error is only resolving a particular triangulation more accurately, but not increasing the geometric fidelity.

Figure 8 (right) shows the rate distortion curves for several additional models. Our curves are again significantly better. Typically the TG coder crosses our curve below the discretization error. For the fandisk, which is a model with creases, we used a tagged Loop transform which preserves the creases. The fandisk does not have

that many triangles which is why the TG coder shows better rate-distortion performance than the CPM coder.

Figure 9 shows renderings of the different compressed versions of the model. This demonstrates the visual benefits of using subdivision based reconstruction. Note that the feline dataset has non-trivial genus (tail section), while the bunny has a number of holes on the bottom. For purposes of comparison (in the case of the Venus head) we have also rendered a number of partial bitstream reconstructions produced with the CPM coder (Figure 10) at file sizes comparable to our reconstructions (Figure 1). One could argue that the results of a more traditional progressive mesh coder could be improved by a smoothing post-process. However, even at very low bit rates, bit-plane progressivity in our coder implies that we see high order bits of significant coefficients at fine levels of the hierarchy early on. The resulting reconstructions always carry more detail than a straightforward Loop smoothing of some triangle mesh would capture. Finally Table 2 gives numerical error values for our coder at a variety of bit rates for the different models.

b/v	1/4	1/2	1	2	4	8
venus	15	6.1	3.1	1.60	0.85	0.55
feline	32	13	5.8	2.5	1.25	0.75
horse	9.7	4.5	2.0	1.05	0.70	0.55
bunny	22	10.8	5.1	2.5	1.40	0.95
fandisk		52	11.9	3.5	1.00	0.60

Table 2: *Relative L^2 error in units of 10^{-4} of our coder at various bitrates.*

5 Conclusion and Future Work

In this paper we described a progressive compression algorithm based on semi-regular meshes, wavelet transforms, and zerotree coders. Our rate distortion curves are significantly better than the best known progressive and non-progressive coders. This was achieved by explicitly treating sample locations and mesh connectivity as degrees of freedom of the coder. The progressive reconstructions especially at very low bit rates can be of astonishingly high visual quality.

There are several directions for future work:

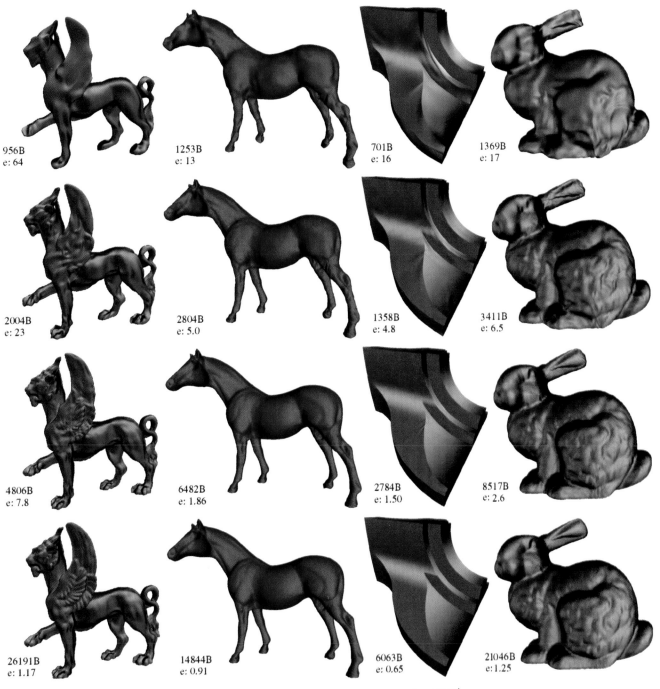

956B
e: 64

1253B
e: 13

701B
e: 16

1369B
e: 17

2004B
e: 23

2804B
e: 5.0

1358B
e: 4.8

3411B
e: 6.5

4806B
e: 7.8

6482B
e: 1.86

2784B
e: 1.50

8517B
e: 2.6

26191B
e: 1.17

14844B
e: 0.91

6063B
e: 0.65

21046B
e: 1.25

Figure 9: *File size in bytes and errors in units of* 10^{-4}.

- A mathematically sound theory for the construction of Loop wavelets around extraordinary vertices, including stability analysis.

- Construction of Loop wavelet transforms for adaptive semi-regular meshes. While all our reconstructions are performed adaptively, currently only lifted wavelets allow for adaptive analysis.

- Design of wavelet filters more suitable for geometry. Careful examination of reconstructed geometry reveals some ringing artifacts with our current wavelets.

- Even for our semi-regular meshes, there is still a fair amount of tangential information especially on the coarse levels. Recent

work by Guskov et al. [15] shows that it is possible to construct *normal meshes*, i.e., meshes in which all wavelet coefficients lie exactly in the normal direction.

- The issues we discuss in this paper regarding geometry versus parameterization led to ideas such as coarsely quantizing the tangential components. These ideas can also be used to further improve irregular mesh coders.

Acknowledgments Andrei Khodakovsky was partially supported through an internship at Lucent Technologies. Other support came from NSF (ACI-9624957, ACI-9721349, DMS-9872890, DMS-9874082), Alias|Wavefront, a Packard Fellowship, and the SGI-Utah Visual Supercomputing Center. Special thanks to Cici Koenig,

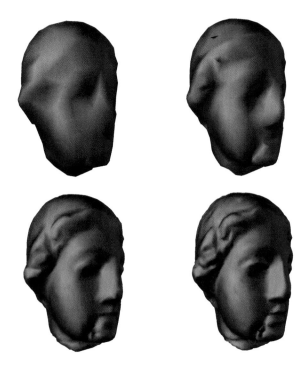

Figure 10: *Partial CPM reconstructions, error in units of* 10^{-4} *(compare to Fig. 1).*

Igor Guskov, Mathieu Desbrun, Aaron Lee, and Martin Vetterli. Datasets are courtesy Cyberware, the Stanford program in Computer Graphics and Hugues Hoppe. Our implementation uses an arithmetic coder of Geoff Davis and John Danskin. We are particularly grateful to Renato Pajarola, Craig Gotsman, and Gabriel Taubin for providing us with executables of their mesh compression algorithms.

References

[1] BAJAJ, C. L., PASCUCCI, V., AND ZHUANG, G. Progressive Compression and Transmission of Arbitrary Triangular Meshes. *IEEE Visualization '99* (1999), 307–316.

[2] CERTAIN, A., POPOVIC, J., DEROSE, T., DUCHAMP, T., SALESIN, D., AND STUETZLE, W. Interactive Multiresolution Surface Viewing. *Proceedings of SIGGRAPH 96* (1996), 91–98.

[3] CIGNONI, P., ROCCHINI, C., AND SCOPIGNO, R. Metro: Measuring Error on Simplified Surfaces. *Computer Graphics Forum 17*, 2 (1998), 167–174.

[4] COHEN-OR, D., LEVIN, D., AND REMEZ, O. Progressive Compression of Arbitrary Triangular Meshes. *IEEE Visualization '99* (1999), 67–72.

[5] DAVIS, G., AND CHAWLA, S. Image Coding Using Optimized Significance Tree Quantization. In *Prodeedings Data Compression Conference*, 387–396, 1997.

[6] DAVIS, G., AND NOSRATINIA, A. Wavelet-based Image Coding: An Overview. *Applied Computational Control, Signals, and Circuits 1*, 1 (1998).

[7] DESBRUN, M., MEYER, M., SCHRÖDER, P., AND BARR, A. H. Implicit Fairing of Irregular Meshes Using Diffusion and Curvature Flow. *Proceedings of SIGGRAPH 99* (1999), 317–324.

[8] DEVORE, R. A., JAWERTH, B., AND LUCIER, B. J. Surface Compression. *Computer Aided Geometric Design 9* (1992), 219–239.

[9] DYN, N., LEVIN, D., AND GREGORY, J. A. A Butterfly Subdivision Scheme for Surface Interpolation with Tension Control. *ACM Transactions on Graphics 9*, 2 (1990), 160–169.

[10] ECK, M., DEROSE, T., DUCHAMP, T., HOPPE, H., LOUNSBERY, M., AND STUETZLE, W. Multiresolution Analysis of Arbitrary Meshes. *Proceedings of SIGGRAPH 95* (1995), 173–182.

[11] GOLUB, G. H., AND LOAN, C. F. V. *Matrix Computations*, 2nd ed. The John Hopkins University Press, Baltimore, 1983.

[12] GROSS, M. H., STAADT, O. G., AND GATTI, R. Efficient Triangular Surface Approximations Using Wavelets and Quadtree Data Structures. *IEEE Transactions on Visualization and Computer Graphics 2*, 2 (1996).

[13] GUMHOLD, S., AND STRASSER, W. Real Time Compression of Triangle Mesh Connectivity. *Proceedings of SIGGRAPH 98* (1998), 133–140.

[14] GUSKOV, I., SWELDENS, W., AND SCHRÖDER, P. Multiresolution Signal Processing for Meshes. *Proceedings of SIGGRAPH 99* (1999), 325–334.

[15] GUSKOV, I., VIDIMCE, K., SWELDENS, W., AND SCHRÖDER, P. Normal Meshes. *Proceedings of SIGGRAPH 00* (2000).

[16] HOPPE, H. Efficient Implementation of Progressive Meshes. *Computers & Graphics 22*, 1 (1998), 27–36.

[17] KING, D., AND ROSSIGNAC, J. Optimal Bit Allocation in 3D Compression. Tech. Rep. GIT-GVU-99-07, Georgia Institute of Technology, 1999.

[18] KOBBELT, L., VORSATZ, J., LABSIK, U., AND SEIDEL, H.-P. A Shrink Wrapping Approach to Remeshing Polygonal Surfaces. *Computer Graphics Forum 18* (1999), 119 – 130.

[19] KOLAROV, K., AND LYNCH, W. Compression of Functions Defined on Surfaces of 3D Objects. In *Proc. of Data Compression Conference*, J. Storer and M. Cohn, Eds., 281–291, 1997.

[20] KRISHNAMURTHY, V., AND LEVOY, M. Fitting Smooth Surfaces to Dense Polygon Meshes. *Proceedings of SIGGRAPH 96* (1996), 313–324.

[21] LEE, A. W. F., SWELDENS, W., SCHRÖDER, P., COWSAR, L., AND DOBKIN, D. MAPS: Multiresolution Adaptive Parameterization of Surfaces. *Proceedings of SIGGRAPH 98* (1998), 95–104.

[22] LEVOY, M. The Digital Michelangelo Project. In *Proceedings of the 2nd International Conference on 3D Digital Imaging and Modeling*, October 1999.

[23] LI, J., AND KUO, C. Progressive Coding of 3-D Graphic Models. *Proceedings of the IEEE 86*, 6 (1998), 1052–1063.

[24] LOOP, C. Smooth Subdivision Surfaces Based on Triangles. Master's thesis, University of Utah, Department of Mathematics, 1987.

[25] LOUNSBERY, M., DEROSE, T. D., AND WARREN, J. Multiresolution Analysis for Surfaces of Arbitrary Topological Type. *ACM Transactions on Graphics 16*, 1 (1997), 34–73. Originally available as TR-93-10-05, October, 1993, Department of Computer Science and Engineering, University of Washington.

[26] PAJAROLA, R., AND ROSSIGNAC, J. Compressed Progressive Meshes. Tech. Rep. GIT-GVU-99-05, Georgia Institute of Technology, 1999.

[27] RIEMENSCHNEIDER, S. D., AND SHEN, Z. Wavelets and Pre-Wavelets in Low Dimensions. *J. Approx. Th. 71*, 1 (1992), 18–38.

[28] ROSSIGNAC, J. Edgebreaker: Connectivity Compression for Triangle Meshes. *IEEE Transactions on Visualization and Computer Graphics 5*, 1 (1999), 47–61.

[29] ROSSIGNAC, J., AND SZYMCZAK, A. Wrap&Zip: Linear Decoding of Planar Triangle Graphs. Tech. Rep. GIT-GVU-99-08, Georgia Institute of Technology, 1999.

[30] SAID, A., AND PEARLMAN, W. A New, Fast, and Efficient Image Codec Based on Set Partitioning in Hierarchical Trees. *IEEE Transaction on Circuits and Systems for Video Technology 6*, 3 (1996), 243–250.

[31] SCHRÖDER, P., AND SWELDENS, W. Spherical Wavelets: Efficiently Representing Functions on the Sphere. *Proceedings of SIGGRAPH 95* (1995), 161–172.

[32] SHAPIRO, J. Embedded Image-Coding using Zerotrees of Wavelet Coefficients. *IEEE Transactions on Signal Processing 41*, 12 (1993), 3445–3462.

[33] STAADT, O. G., GROSS, M. H., AND WEBER, R. Multiresolution Compression And Reconstruction. *IEEE Visualization '97* (1997), 337–346.

[34] TAUBIN, G., GUEZIEC, A., HORN, W., AND LAZARUS, F. Progressive Forest Split Compression. *Proceedings of SIGGRAPH 98* (1998), 123–132.

[35] TAUBIN, G., AND ROSSIGNAC, J. Geometric Compression Through Topological Surgery. *ACM Transactions on Graphics 17*, 2 (1998), 84–115.

[36] TAUBIN, G., AND ROSSIGNAC, J., Eds. *3D Geometry Compression*. No. 21 in Course Notes. ACM Siggraph, 1999.

[37] TOUMA, C., AND GOTSMAN, C. Triangle Mesh Compression. *Graphics Interface '98* (1998), 26–34.

[38] ZORIN, D., SCHRÖDER, P., AND SWELDENS, W. Interpolating Subdivision for Meshes with Arbitrary Topology. *Proceedings of SIGGRAPH 96* (1996), 189–192.

[39] ZORIN, D., SCHRÖDER, P., AND SWELDENS, W. Interactive Multiresolution Mesh Editing. *Proceedings of SIGGRAPH 97* (1997), 259–268.

Spectral Compression of Mesh Geometry

Zachi Karni[1]   Craig Gotsman[2]

Computer Science Department
Technion – Israel Institute of Technology
Haifa 32000, Israel

Abstract

We show how spectral methods may be applied to 3D mesh data to obtain compact representations. This is achieved by projecting the mesh geometry onto an orthonormal basis derived from the mesh topology. To reduce complexity, the mesh is partitioned into a number of balanced submeshes with minimal interaction, each of which are compressed independently. Our methods may be used for compression and progressive transmission of 3D content, and are shown to be vastly superior to existing methods using spatial techniques, if slight loss can be tolerated.

CR Categories and Subject Descriptors: I.3.3 [Computer Graphics]: Picture/Image Generation.

Additional Keywords: Compression Algorithms, Signal Processing.

1. INTRODUCTION

With the advent of the Web and the increase in demand for 3D content, it is becoming very important to compress 3D mesh data for efficient transmission. The basic content of a 3D mesh dataset is the topology, i.e. the connectivity information of the mesh structure, and the geometry, i.e. the 3D coordinates of the mesh vertices. All of the works to date on mesh compression [1,3,4,5,8,10,11,13,17,18,21,22] have concentrated mostly on efficient coding of the mesh topology, and the secondary coding of the geometry is driven by this. For example, the early mesh compression schemes of Deering [5] and Chow [3] and the later scheme of Taubin and Rossignac [21] order the vertices according to the topological information, and then code them using a simple linear predictor. Similarly, the mesh compression scheme of Touma and Gotsman [22] codes the topology as a traversal of the vertices, and the vertex coordinates are coded by predicting them along this traversal using the so-called "parallelogram rule",

[1]zachi_k@cs.technion.ac.il
[2]gotsman@cs.technion.ac.il

which better captures the geometry of the mesh surface. In all cases, the prediction errors are then entropy-coded. Due to the topology coding driving the geometry coding, and not the opposite, the geometry code is not optimal. Ironically, the geometric data contains far more information than the topological data (15 bits/vertex vs. 3 bits/vertex on the average), so more effort should be invested in reducing the geometry code than the topology code, but this seems to have been neglected for the most part by contemporary mesh compression algorithms.

While the existing mesh compression algorithms are advertised as being lossless, from a pure theoretical point of view, they are actually lossy. This is because the vertex coordinates are quantized to finite precision before the actual coding. Typical 3D mesh geometry is quantized to 10-14 bits per coordinate, predictive coding subsequently reducing this to approximately half. At these quantization levels, the decoded mesh is usually visually indistinguishable from the original, justifying the use of the term "lossless". More significant loss may be introduced, and the code size reduced, by performing coarser quantization, but this results in a model with a blocky structure, which is very different from the original. Hence these algorithms are not suitable for lossy compression, due to their non-graceful degradation. This paper proposes a mesh geometry compression technique which degrades gracefully, based on spectral methods.

Many compression techniques for traditional media, such as images, employ spectral methods to achieve impressive lossy compression ratios, e.g. the popular JPEG method which relies on the discrete cosine transform. These involve expressing the data as a linear combination of a set of orthogonal basis functions, each basis function characterized by a "frequency". The underlying assumption is that a relatively good approximation may be obtained using only a small number of low-frequency basis functions. JPEG typically reduces image storage requirements by a factor of 20 relative to the raw RGB data. The next section shows how to extend classical Fourier theory to the case of 3D meshes. Subsequent sections show how to apply this to 3D mesh coding. Similarly to JPEG, we are able to obtain very significant compression ratios at the expense of a very small loss in mesh quality. For example, in many cases the code size may be reduced by a factor of 2 or 3 relative to the lossless version, with an almost unnoticeable damage to mesh appearance.

Due to the assumption that the "low frequency" coefficients contribute more to the mesh data than the "high frequency" ones, the codes generated by our algorithm may be employed in a progressive manner. For instance, a rough approximation of the model may be reconstructed using a small number of spectral coefficients, and this progressively refined by increasing the number of coefficients used in the reconstruction.

Spectral codes are useful also in other applications where precise accuracy is not important, e.g. rapid previewing and product visualization for e-commerce.

2. MESH SPECTRA

We start by showing how to extend the classical Fourier analysis to 3D mesh data. Imagine a simple graph consisting of n vertices connected in a cycle. The adjacency matrix A of this graph is the circulant $n \times n$ matrix induced by the vector [1 0 1] (where the zero coincides with the diagonal). The so-called Laplacian operator associated with A is $L = I - \frac{1}{2}A$, and is the analog of the second spatial derivative. As is well-known in matrix theory [16], the traditional cosine basis functions of the one-dimensional Fourier transform are none other than the eigenvectors of this L. The associated eigenvalues are the squared frequencies. Since the rows of L sum to zero, L is singular and has a vanishing eigenvalue, which corresponds to an eigenvector of constant values. The projection of any real n-dimensional vector on this basis vector is just the DC component (mean) of the vector.

Analogously, the Fourier basis functions for 2D signals are obtained as the eigenvectors of the Laplacian matrix of the graph with the topology of a 2D grid: $A_{ij} = 1$ for entries (i,j) such that vertex i and vertex j are neighbors on the grid and $L = I - \frac{1}{4}A$. Because of the regular structure of the 2D grid, these are just the 2D cosine functions used in JPEG.

This classical spectral theory may be extended naturally to more general graph topologies [2], and, in particular, to arbitrary 3D mesh structures [20]. If A is the adjacency matrix as defined by the n-vertex mesh topology, i.e.

$$A_{ij} = \begin{cases} 1 & i \text{ and } j \text{ are neighbors} \\ 0 & \text{otherwise} \end{cases}$$

and D is the diagonal matrix such that $D_{ii} = 1/d_i$, where d_i is the degree (valence) of vertex i, then $L = I - DA$ is the mesh Laplacian:

$$L_{ij} = \begin{cases} 1 & i = j \\ -1/d_i & i \text{ and } j \text{ are neighbors} \\ 0 & \text{otherwise} \end{cases}$$

See Fig. 1 for an example. If vertex i has no neighbors, L_{ii} is set to zero. The eigenvectors of L form an orthogonal basis of R^n. The associated eigenvalues may be considered *frequencies*, and the three projections of each of the coordinate vectors of a 3D mesh geometry vector on the basis functions are the *spectrum* of the geometry. The essential observation is that geometries that are smooth relative to the mesh topology should yield spectra dominated by the low-frequency components. By "smooth relative to the mesh topology" we mean that the local geometry, as defined by topological neighborhoods in the mesh, is such that the coordinates of a vertex are very close to the average coordinates of the vertex's neighbors, hence the Laplacian operator, when applied to the mesh geometry, will yield very small absolute values. Note

that there is a separate spectrum for each of the x, y and z components of the geometry, and they could behave differently, depending on the directional geometric properties (e.g. curvature) of the mesh.

Recent years have seen an increase of interest in signal processing approaches [20,6] to 3D mesh manipulation, and their extension to multiresolution analyses [15,9]. However, to the best of our knowledge, this work is the first in which they are exploited for compression purposes.[1]

Fig. 2 shows a decimated *horse* mesh containing 2,978 vertices, a visualization of the some of the basis functions, and reconstruction of the horse using a small number of the low-frequency basis functions. Note how smooth these reconstructions are, due to the smooth nature of the low-frequency basis functions.

3. MESH PARTITIONING

Computing the spectral basis functions involves computing the eigenvectors of a $n \times n$ matrix. Ordinarily, this would require $O(n^3)$ time, which is prohibitive. However, since the Laplacian matrix is sparse (each row has only six non-zero entries on the average), this can be done in $O(n)$ time using multi-resolution methods [9,15]. Nonetheless, when n is large, the numerical stability of these methods breaks down, due to adjacent eigenvalues becoming too close. Hence it is practically impossible to compute Laplacian eigenvectors for meshes containing more than 1,000 vertices, and the mesh must be partitioned into submeshes, each of which is treated separately. This, of course, may result in a degradation in coding quality due to "edge-effects" along submesh boundaries, but has the advantage that local properties of the mesh may be captured better. In order to minimize damage, the partition should be well balanced, i.e. that each submesh contain approximately the same number of vertices, and also the number of edges straddling the different submeshes, the *edgecut*, be minimized. A optimal solution to this problem is NP-Complete [7], and algorithms approximating the optimum are an active branch of graph algorithmic research. An algorithm that performs reasonably well on meshes of up to 100,000 vertices is MeTiS [14], for which an optimized linear-time implementation is available. It seems that METIS gives some preference to minimizing the edge-cut over balancing the partition, which is the preference in our application as well. In particular, if the mesh consists of a number of connected components, MeTiS will prefer to partition into these components, unless the balance is significantly violated. Fig. 3 shows partitions generated by MeTiS for the (non-decimated) *horse* and *bunny* models. On these models MeTiS requires less than a second to run on a 350 MHz machine.

---

[1] As this paper went to press, we discovered that [12] addresses this issue.

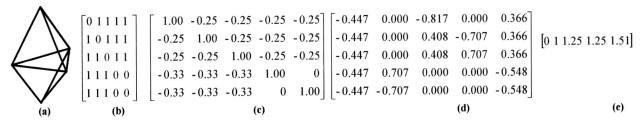

Figure 1: Spectral analysis of a simple 3D mesh containing 5 vertices. **(a)** Mesh. **(b)** Adjacency matrix A. **(c)** Laplacian L. **(d)** Laplacian (column) eigenvectors and **(e)** eigenvalues. Note that the first eigenvector has constant (DC) values and a vanishing eigenvalue.

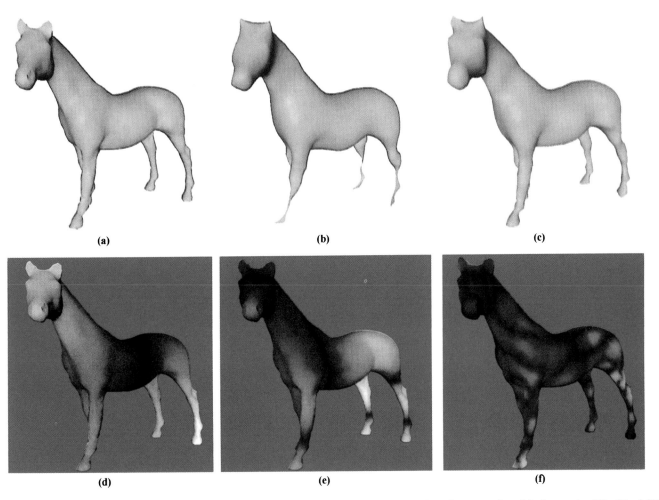

Figure 2: Approximation of the decimated *horse* model containing 2,978 vertices. **(a)** The original. **(b)** Reconstruction of the horse using 100 of the 2,978 basis functions. **(c)** Reconstruction of the horse using 200 basis functions. Note that both are smooth, and how the fine details gradually appear as more basis functions are used. **(d)** Second basis function. Eigenvalue = 4.9×10^{-4}. The grayscale intensity of a vertex is proportional to the scalar value of the basis function at that coordinate. **(e)** Tenth basis function. Eigenvalue = 6.5×10^{-2}. **(f)** Hundredth basis function. Eigenvalue = 1.2×10^{-1}. Note how higher frequencies (color bands) appear in the higher-order basis functions.

4. SPECTRAL CODING

4.1 A Visual Metric

In order to measure the loss resulting from a non-perfect reconstruction, a metric is required which captures well the visual difference between the original M^1 and its approximation M^2. The simplest measure is just the RMS geometric distance between corresponding vertices in both models. While this does give some indication of geometric closeness, it does not capture the more subtle visual properties the human eye appreciates, such as smoothness. This may be captured by a Laplacian operator, which takes into account both the topology and geometry. The value of this geometric Laplacian at vertex v_i is

$$GL(v_i) = v_i - \frac{\sum_{j \in n(i)} l_{ij}^{-1} v_j}{\sum_{j \in n(i)} l_{ij}^{-1}},$$

where $n(i)$ is the set of indices of the neighbors of vertex i, and l_{ij} is the geometric distance between vertices i and j.

Hence we have chosen to use a metric which is the simple average of the norm of the geometric distance between models and the norm of the Laplacian difference (v is the vertex set of M):

$$(1) \qquad \left\| M^1 - M^2 \right\| = \frac{1}{2n} \left(\left\| v^1 - v^2 \right\| + \left\| GL(v^1) - GL(v^2) \right\| \right).$$

Fig. 4 shows the original *horse* model, and two reconstructions of it. It is clear that the second reconstruction is closer to the original than the first. A simple geometric difference does not capture this, but our visual metric does.

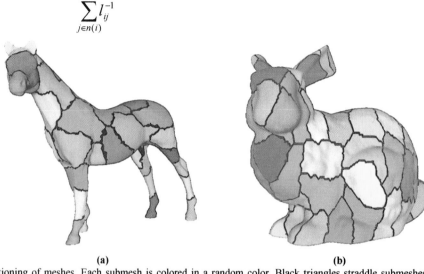

(a)   **(b)**

Figure 3: MeTiS partitioning of meshes. Each submesh is colored in a random color. Black triangles straddle submeshes. *Edgecut* is the percentage of edges straddling submeshes. The smaller, the better. *Balance* is the ratio of the largest submesh to the average submesh size (in vertices). The closer to unity, the better. **(a)** *Horse* model: 19,851 vertices, 59,547 edges, 40 submeshes, edgecut = 4.2%, balance = 1.03. Runtime = 0.28 sec on a 350 MHz machine. **(b)** *Bunny* model: 34,834 vertices, 104,288 edges, 70 submeshes, edgecut =5.5%, balance = 1.03. Runtime = 0.47 sec on a 350 MHz machine.

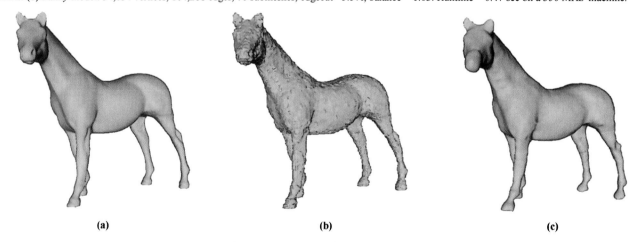

(a)   **(b)**   **(c)**

Figure 4: A simple visual metric: **(a)** Original model M^1. **(b)** Approximation M^2 to M^1. **(c)** Approximation M^3 to M^1. It is obvious that M^3 is visually closer to M^1 than M^2, yet $\|v^1 - v^2\| = \|v^1 - v^3\| = 0.10$. However introducing the geometric Laplacian component of Eq. (1) yields $\|M^1 - M^2\| = 0.16$ and $\|M^1 - M^3\| = 0.07$, which better reflects the visual distance.

4.2 Coefficient Coding

The first step in coding the spectral coefficients is to uniformly quantize them to finite precision. This, of course, introduces some loss into the code. Typical quantization levels are between 10 and 16 bits. The second step is to truncate the coefficient vector. The resulting set of integers is then entropy coded using a Huffman or arithmetic coder [19]. It is possible to optimize the tradeoff between coefficient quantization level and the truncation by taking either a small number of high-precision coefficients, or a large number of low-precision coefficients. In practice, the input parameter to the compression procedure is the desired visual distance d from the original. The mesh is partitioned into k submeshes, such that each submesh contains approximately 500 vertices. The visual distance d is divided by $\sqrt{k}$, and the number of retained coefficients per coordinate per submesh chosen so that the RMS of the truncated coefficients does not exceed this value.

5. EXPERIMENTAL RESULTS

We present numerical results for the *horse* and *bunny* models shown in Fig. 5. These models are relatively smooth, but also have some fine details. Our compression results are compared with results obtained using commercial compression software of Virtue Ltd. (www.virtue3d.com), which incorporates the Touma-Gotsman (TG) compression algorithm [22], and is widely considered to do a very good job. This software is meant primarily for lossless compression, but can introduce loss by aggressively quantizing the geometry before coding.

Fig. 6 shows a "rate-distortion" graph for each of the models. There we plot the visual distance between the original and the decoded version of the model, as described in Eq. (1), vs. the code size. The main result is that in the lossy domain, we are able to achieve codes of approximately half to a third the size of those of the TG method for comparable visual distance. In the lossless domain, the code lengths converge to comparable values. Fig. 7 shows lossy versions of the *horse* and *bunny* models reconstructed by our algorithm, and models reconstructed by the TG algorithm, when compressed with significant quantization in order to achieve the same code size. The superiority of our reconstructions is obvious. Additionally, when our lossy reconstructions are losslessly compressed using the TG algorithm, the code size is still 1.6 and 2.5 times larger than ours.

We should emphasize that although we compare our results to those of the TG algorithm, it is not a fair comparison, since the TG algorithm is not progressive, and there is no immediate way to continuously increase model quality by increasing the number of code bits.

Animated GIFs showing progressive reconstruction of the horse and bunny models as the number of spectral coefficients is increased may be found at http://www.cs.technion.ac.il/~gotsman/siggraph2000/demos

(a)   (b)

Figure 5: Models used in our experiments. **(a)** *Horse*: 19,851 vertices, 59,547 edges. **(b)** *Bunny*: 34,834 vertices, 104,288 edges.

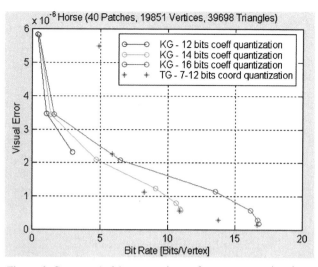
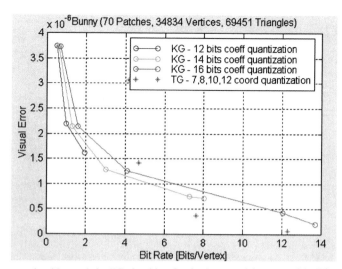

Figure 6: Geometry (only) compression performance comparison between our algorithm and the TG algorithm for the *horse* and *bunny* models. Visual losslessness is achieved at visual error of approximately 0.03 for *horse* and 0.02 for *bunny*. The best performance from our algorithm is achieved when the spectral coefficients are quantized to 14 bits.

6. DISCUSSION AND CONCLUSION

We have presented an algorithm for spectral coding of the geometric information in 3D meshes. This algorithm is similar in spirit to lossy JPEG coding of images, in the sense that it partitions the model into manageable and local submeshes, and represents each as a compact linear combination of orthogonal basis functions. The basis functions are eigenvectors of the topological Laplacian of the submesh.

In contrast to lossless coding, which is relatively well defined, lossy coding introduces a major (open) question of how to measure the loss (sometimes called *distortion*) present in the reconstructed signal. If not carefully addressed, it can be extremely hard to quantify lossy coding algorithm results. We presented a simple metric which we believe captures well the visual distance between models. Although it is far from perfect, and can still be fine-tuned, we do not believe that it will be possible to design a single metric that will be agreeable to the subjective visual systems of multiple observers.

Progressive transmission of 3D meshes is easy using the spectral methods presented here. First the compact mesh topology would be transmitted, and then the spectral coefficients of the geometry streamed, the low order coefficient first. As more and more coefficients are received, they are used to obtain a better approximation to the original.

Our results are seen to be excellent for relatively smooth models. We performed a limited number of experiments also on CAD-type models, containing sharp edges and folds. Here our results were not significantly better than the TG algorithm. This is due to the very high frequencies present in the models, forcing the coding of a very large number of coefficients. More work is required to overcome these difficulties.

We believe that ultimately it will be neccesary to employ mesh partition algorithms which are geometry-dependent, cutting the mesh along sharp folds. Since this partition will no longer be based purely on the mesh topology, and as only the topology is available at the decoder before geometry decoding, it will be neccesary to include this partition information as part of the code. This will theoretically increase the code size, but, fortunately, it seems that this overhead may be minimized by polygonal group coding, such as that of Isenberg and Snoeyink [11], which requires approximately 0.2 bits/vertex.

An alternative way to perform lossy compression of 3D mesh data is through mesh simplification, where the number of mesh vertices is reduced and topology modified, explicitly reducing the information present in the data set. It is also possible to modify even the remaining vertices, further reducing information, as is done in Khodakovsky et al [12]. The relationship between compression thru simplification and our spectral methods, which preserve the number of mesh vertices and mesh topology, has yet to be investigated. On the other hand, it would be interesting to check whether new mesh simplification methods may be obtained using spectral methods.

In practice, the mesh topology is coded and decoded separately from the geometry (e.g. using any of the algorithms of [1,8,11,13,17,18,21,22]). Since some of the topology coding algorithms permute the mesh vertices at the decoder, the geometric coordinate list must be permuted accordingly before coding. The decoder also runs the deterministic mesh partitioning algorithm and eigenvector computation algorithms based only on the topology information, in order to decode the geometry.

There are tradeoffs in many places in the encoding and decoding procedures between the time and space complexities, the code size and visual loss. There is still work to be done in order to fine-tune the parameters and optimize the results. As client CPU power seems to be increasing faster than network bandwidth, we believe that even complex decoding procedures will ultimately be tolerable, as long as the corresponding encoders produce very short codes. Nonetheless, as we have demonstrated, our results are extremely good even without significant optimizations.

Modern signal processing has embraced multiresolution methods (e.g. wavelets) as an alternative to classical Fourier theory. The main motivation is that basis functions with local support better capture the local features of the signal, hence the need for artificial signal partitioning is eliminated. Much effort has been invested in designing orthogonal multiresolution 2D basis functions, and these will be used for wavelet image coding in JPEG 2000. Designing orthogonal multiresolution basis functions for arbitrary 3D mesh topologies has so far proved to be elusive, but, when discovered, might yield results better than those presented here.

Optimization algorithms for mesh partitioning proved very useful in our compression application, and we believe that partitioning methods which achieve compact edgecuts should be useful for other 3D mesh applications, particularly efficient rendering.

Future work will include the extension of spectral coding theory to 3D mesh animation sequences.

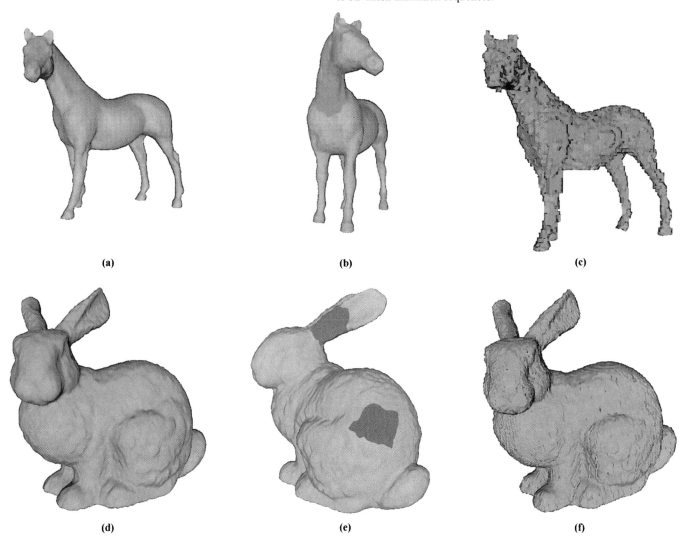

(a) (b) (c)

(d) (e) (f)

Figure 7: Some representative results of our spectral coding procedure: **(a)** Reconstructed *horse* (original in Fig. 5(a)) from code of 7,400 bytes (3.0 bits/vertex). Number of submeshes = 40, number of coefficients per coordinate per patch ranges from 66 to 221, average is 145. This horse compresses losslessly by the TG algorithm to 18,635 bytes (7.5 bits/vertex). **(b)** Same reconstruction as (a). The minimal (66 coefficients) complexity patch is in the hoof area, and the maximal (221 coefficients) complexity patch is the neck, due to the curvature. **(c)** Reconstructed horse from code of 10,100 bytes (4.0 bits/vertex) generated directly by the TG algorithm with significant geometry quantization. **(d)** Reconstructed *bunny* (original in Fig. 4(b)) from code of 17,900 bytes (4.1 bits/vertex). Number of submeshes = 70, number of coefficients per coordinate per patch ranges from 69 to 144, average is 97. This bunny compresses losslessly by the TG algorithm to 28,361 bytes (6.5 bits/vertex). **(e)** Same reconstruction as (d). The minimal (69) complexity patch is in the lower back area, and the maximal (144) complexity patch is the ear, due to the curvature and sharp edges. **(f)** Reconstructed bunny from code of 18,032 bytes (4.1 bits/vertex) generated directly by TG algorithm with significant geometry quantization.

7. ACKNOWLEDGEMENTS

Thanks to Leif Kobbelt and Gabriel Taubin for helpful discussions on the topic of this paper.

8. REFERENCES

[1]   V. Bajaj, V. Pascucci and G. Zhuang. Single resolution compression of arbitrary triangular meshes with properties. Proceedings of the Data Compression Conference, Snowbird, 1999.

[2]   N. Biggs. Alegbraic Graph Theory (2nd Ed.). Cambridge University Press, 1993.

[3]   M. Chow. Geometry compression for real-time graphics. Proceedings of Visualization '97, IEEE, 1997.

[4]   D. Cohen-Or , O. Remez, and D. Levin, Progressive compression of arbitrary triangular meshes. Proceedings of Visualization '99, IEEE, 1999.

[5]   M. Deering, Geometry compression, Proceedings of SIGGRAPH '95, pp. 13-20, ACM, 1995.

[6]   M. Desbrun, M. Meyer, P. Schroeder and A. Barr. Implicit fairing of irregular meshes using diffusion and curvature flow. Proceedings of SIGGRAPH '99, pp. 317-324, ACM, 1999.

[7]   M. Garey and D. Johnson, Computers and intractability: A guide to the theory of NP-completeness, Addison-Wesley, 1978.

[8]   S. Gumhold and W. Strasser. Real time compression of triangle mesh connectivity. Proceedings of SIGGRAPH '98, pp. 133-140, ACM, 1998.

[9]   I. Guskov, W. Sweldens and P. Schroeder. Multiresolution signal processing for meshes. Proceedings of SIGGRAPH '99, pp. 325-334, ACM, 1999.

[10] M. Isenburg and J. Snoeyink. Mesh collapse compression. Proceedings of SIBGRAPHI'99 – 12th Brazilian Symposium on Computer Graphics and Image Processing, pp.27-28, 1999.

[11] M. Isenberg and J. Snoeyink. FaceFixer: Compressing polygon meshes with properties. Proceedings of SIGGRAPH 2000.

[12] A. Khodakovsky, P. Schroeder and W. Sweldens. Progressive geometry compression. Proceedings of SIGGRAPH 2000.

[13] D. King and J. Rossignac. Guaranteed 3.67v bit encoding of planar triangle graphs. In Proceedings of 11th Canadian Conference on Computation Geometry, pp.146-149, 1999.

[14] G. Karypis and V. Kumar. MeTiS: A software package for partitioning unstructured graphs, partitioning meshes, and computing fill-reducing orderings of sparse matrices. Version 4.0, Univ. of Minnesota, Dept. of Computer Science, 1998. Available at http://www-users.cs.umn.edu/~karypis/metis/metis.html

[15] L. Kobbelt, S. Campanga, J. Vorsatz and H.-P. Seidel. Interactive multi-resolution modeling on arbitrary meshes. Proceedings of SIGGRAPH '98, pp. 105-114, ACM, 1998.

[16] P. Lancaster and M. Tismenetsky. The theory of matrices. (2nd Ed.), Academic Press, 1985.

[17] J. Li and C.-C. Kuo, A dual graph approach to 3D triangular mesh compression, In Proceedings of the IEEE International Conference on Image Processing, Chicago, 1998.

[18] J. Rossignac. Edgebreaker: Connectivity compression for triangle meshes. IEEE Transactions on Visualization and Computer Graphics, 5(1), 1999.

[19] D. Salomon. Data compression: The complete reference. Springer Verlag, 1998.

[20] G. Taubin. A signal processing approach to fair surface design. Proceedings of SIGGRAPH '95, pp. 351-358, ACM, 1995.

[21] G. Taubin and J. Rossignac. Geometric compression through topological surgery. ACM Transactions on Graphics, 17(2):84-115, 1998.

[22] C. Touma and C. Gotsman. Triangle mesh compression. In Proceedings of Graphics Interface '98, pp. 26-34, 1998.

Surface Light Fields for 3D Photography

Daniel N. Wood[1]   Daniel I. Azuma[1]   Ken Aldinger[1]

Brian Curless[1]   Tom Duchamp[1]   David H. Salesin[1,2]   Werner Stuetzle[1]

[1]University of Washington   [2]Microsoft Research

Abstract

A *surface light field* is a function that assigns a color to each ray originating on a surface. Surface light fields are well suited to constructing virtual images of shiny objects under complex lighting conditions. This paper presents a framework for construction, compression, interactive rendering, and rudimentary editing of surface light fields of real objects. Generalizations of vector quantization and principal component analysis are used to construct a compressed representation of an object's surface light field from photographs and range scans. A new rendering algorithm achieves interactive rendering of images from the compressed representation, incorporating view-dependent geometric level-of-detail control. The surface light field representation can also be directly edited to yield plausible surface light fields for small changes in surface geometry and reflectance properties.

CR Categories: I.3.2. [Computer Graphics]: Picture/Image Generation–
Digitizing and scanning, Viewing algorithms

Keywords: surface light fields, 3D photography, lumigraph, light field, function quantization, principal function analysis, view-dependent level-of-detail, image-based rendering, wavelets.

1 Introduction

Recent advances in digital cameras, 3D laser scanners and other imaging technology are enabling us to capture enormous quantities of geometric and radiance data with unprecedented ease and accuracy. These advances hold great promise for *3D photography*, the process by which both the shape and appearance of physical objects are modeled and realistically rendered. But to make 3D photography truly practical, quite a few open problems still need to be solved.

First, we need a good representation for those 3D datasets. The framework described in this paper is based on the *surface light field*, a term coined by Miller *et al.* [22]. The surface light field is a function that assigns an RGB value to every ray leaving every point on a surface. When constructed from observations made of an object, a surface light field encodes sufficient information to construct realistic images of the object from arbitrary viewpoints. Surface texture, rapid variation in specularity, and global effects like interreflection and shadowing are all correctly represented. Some of these properties can be seen in Figure 1.

However, a good representation by itself is only half the story. Because the datasets acquired by 3D photography techniques are so large, good *compression* algorithms are needed. Furthermore, we need algorithms to *render* those datasets efficiently, ideally at interactive speeds. To this end, we need to develop *level-of-detail*

Figure 1 Images of a surface light field demonstrating detailed surface texture, rapid changes in specular properties, and interreflections. The specular variations occur, for example, in the gold paint on the tail of this porcelain fish. The tail also reflects light onto the body, as indicated by the reddish hue on the side of the fish in the left panel.

controls for the rendering process, with shape and appearance under independent control. Finally, just as in traditional 2D photography, accurately capturing the real world is not sufficient for many applications; a useful representation for the results of 3D photography should also be *editable*.

In this paper, we address each of these problems. In particular, our contributions include:

Estimation/compression. Our raw data consists of a set of 2D digital color photographs of an object together with a collection of laser range scans. To make a surface light field tractable for rendering, the data must fit into main memory. To this end we present two new algorithms that simultaneously estimate and compress the surface light field. The first is a generalization of vector quantization; the second is a generalization of principal component analysis.

Rendering. We demonstrate an algorithm that can render our surface light fields at interactive frame rates. Evaluation of the surface color takes time proportional to the occupied screen space. The amount of time required to render the underlying geometry is controlled using a new view-dependent level-of-detail algorithm for meshes with subdivision connectivity. The level of geometric approximation does not affect the sharpness of the surface texture.

Editing. Our representation of surface light fields allows editing, using 3D analogs of image processing algorithms to filter reflected light, and modifications of surface geometry. We can simulate changes in the reflectance properties of the surface, and we can generate plausible images of the object after it has been deformed or moved relative to its environment.

1.1 Related work

Surface light fields fit into the broad framework of *image-based* rendering schemes. Image-based methods take a collection of photographs as input, construct a representation of the surface color or radiance, and use it to synthesize new images from arbitrary viewpoints. The methods tend to differ in the number of input images they use, the representation of the data, the degree to which they incorporate geometric information about the object into the image representation, and the compression techniques they employ. Our own approach leverages high-resolution geometry to improve image quality while affording a compact representation.

Levoy and Hanrahan [17] acquire many hundreds of images, which are resampled to lie on a regular grid in a two-plane parameterization. New images are computed by interpolation between ray samples, using essentially no geometric data. They apply vector quantization to obtain compressed representations of light fields. Gortler *et al.* [12] present a similar two-plane parameterization that they call a *lumigraph*, in which they interpolate image samples via a hierarchical *push-pull* algorithm. They use approximate surface geometry derived from photograph silhouettes (or higher-resolution geometry in the case of synthetic data) to perform a depth correction that substantially reduces ghosting and blurring artifacts. In both these methods, the representation restricts the viewpoint to lie outside of the convex hull of the object. Magnor and Girod [20, 21] develop an MPEG-like scheme for compressing two-plane light fields that produces better compression ratios than those obtained by Levoy and Hanrahan. Our approach depends on both high-resolution geometry and dense sets of images. It removes the convex hull restriction of the two-plane light field and admits a new form of compressed representation that can be rendered in real time. For comparable data sizes, our representation yields sharper images and greater compression ratios than two-plane representations.

View-dependent texture mapping [7, 8, 26] is a kind of light field that does not require resampling the input images. This approach uses geometric information to re-project each input image into the desired camera viewpoint. The re-projected input images are then blended together using weights based on the view direction primarily, and possibly other factors such as sampling rate. Because the blending in view-dependent texture mapping incorporates visibility information, this approach supports rendering within the convex hull of the object. In practice, view-dependent texture mapping has been used with fewer images and surfaces that are less specular than those demonstrated with two-plane light fields, though this is not a fundamental limitation. As noted in Debevec *et al.* [8], a surface light field can be viewed as a distillation of view-dependent texture mapping into a more efficient representation.

Miller *et al.* [22] use surface light fields to render solutions to synthetic (non-diffuse) global illumination problems. They apply JPEG-like image compression techniques to sets of texture maps. Their technique achieves compression rates for surface light fields that are comparable to those of Levoy and Hanrahan's vector quantization method. Walter *et al.* [31] also use surface light fields to approximate solutions to global illumination problems. Their representation involves basis functions derived from hardware lighting models, which provides very fast rendering, but does not support textured surfaces, nor can it adequately model complex phenomena such as rapidly varying specularity. In addition, problems exist in the 3D photography realm that do not arise with synthetic data: most importantly, neither a surface parameterization nor the radiance along arbitrary rays are known *a priori* and must instead be constructed.

Nishino *et al.* [23, 24] generate surface light fields of real objects, though their images are relatively dense in only one rotational direction. Geometric information is represented by a coarse triangular mesh. They construct a set of texture maps for each triangle by projecting each image onto the mesh. Compression is achieved by performing a principal component analysis on each set of textures. (Interestingly, the vectors in their analysis are formed by holding a direction fixed and letting surface location vary. This is the opposite of our analysis in Section 4.6, where, to form a vector, we fix a surface location and let direction vary.) Their approach successfully models objects with simple geometric structure and smoothly varying specularity. However, it has not been demonstrated on objects that exhibit both high geometric complexity and rapid BRDF variation, nor does it provide real-time rendering.

Inverse rendering is an alternative to generating a surface light field. The goal of these techniques is to estimate the surface BRDF from images and geometric data. Previous work on inverse rendering [28, 33] has assumed that the BRDF is piecewise linear with respect to a coarse triangulation of the surface. Our techniques require no such assumptions, and, of course, inverse rendering does not solve the re-rendering problem—a non-interactive global illumination algorithm is required to produce photorealistic results. Recent work has extended interactive rendering techniques to a wider range of lighting models and environments. Cabral *et al.* [3] describe a technique for using radiance environment maps to render objects under arbitrary lighting conditions and with any isotropic BRDF. Heidrich *et al.* [13] use texture mapping hardware for the same purpose but allow a different class of BRDFs. However, these two methods do not handle global effects like shadows or interreflection.

1.2 Overview

We have developed algorithms for acquiring light field data of real objects, and for estimating, compressing, rendering, and editing their surface light fields. We have tested these algorithms on two objects, a small ceramic fish with a shiny surface and detailed texture, and a marble elephant with more complex geometry and less pronounced specular highlights.

The following sections describe these new algorithms in detail. We begin by describing our representation of surface light fields (Section 2). Next, we discuss our data acquisition process (Section 3). We then describe our algorithms for estimating and compressing surface light fields and compare the quality of these methods to two-plane light fields of similar size (Section 4). Finally, we discuss our algorithms for rendering and editing surface light fields (Sections 5 and 6), and present ideas for future research (Section 7).

2 Representation

Roughly speaking, a surface light field is a function that associates a color to every ray originating from a surface. Our algorithm for constructing images from a surface light field relies on a good parameterization of an object's surface mesh M. The methods of either Eck *et al.* [9] or Lee *et al.* [16] yield a parameterization

$$\varphi : K_0 \rightarrow M \subset \mathbb{R}^3, \qquad (1)$$

whose domain K_0 is a triangular mesh with a small number of faces, called a *base mesh*. We use a variant of the algorithm of Lee *et al.* to parameterize our scanned geometry.

The parameterization allows us to represent the surface light field as a function

$$L : K_0 \times S^2 \rightarrow RGB, \qquad (2)$$

where S^2 denotes the sphere of unit vectors in $\mathbb{R}^3$. Radiance is represented by points in $\mathbb{R}^3$ corresponding to RGB triples. If u is a point on the base mesh and ω is an outward pointing direction at the surface point $\varphi(u)$, then $L(u, \omega)$ is the RGB value of the

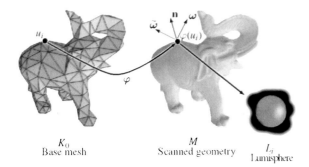

$$K_0$$
Base mesh
$$M$$
Scanned geometry
$$L_i$$
Lumisphere

Figure 2 Representation of the surface light field. Points u on the base mesh, K_0, are mapped to the geometric surface, M, by φ. The lumisphere, L_i at the grid point u_i, represents the radiance leaving surface point $\varphi(u_i)$. Directions are denoted by ω, or $\tilde{\omega}$ after reflection through the surface normal $\mathbf{n}$ as described in Section 4.4.

light ray starting at $\varphi(u)$ and traveling in direction ω. Although $L(u, \omega)$ has no physical interpretation when ω is inward pointing, our compression, rendering, and editing techniques rely on L being defined over the entire direction sphere.

We make the simplifying assumption that $L(u, \omega)$ is piecewise linear in ω. To make this more precise we have to define what we mean by a piecewise-linear function on S^2. It is not difficult to verify that the map

$$h(\omega) \equiv \frac{(\sin^{-1}\omega_x, \ \sin^{-1}\omega_y, \ \sin^{-1}\omega_z)}{|\sin^{-1}\omega_x| + |\sin^{-1}\omega_y| + |\sin^{-1}\omega_z|} \quad (3)$$

is a homeomorphism between S^2 and the regular octahedron with vertices $(\pm 1, \pm 1, \pm 1)$. We use h because it introduces less distortion than radial projection and yet can be evaluated quickly using a lookup table for $\sin^{-1}$.

Composition with h induces a bijection between functions on the octahedron and functions on the sphere. We say that a function $F(\omega)$ is *piecewise linear* if it is piecewise linear with respect to an s-times-subdivided octahedron, *i.e.*, the mesh resulting from s four-to-one subdivisions of the octahedron. We call a piecewise-linear RGB-valued function a *lumisphere*, and we let C_{PL}^s denote the vector space of all lumispheres.

With these definitions, the surface light field L can be represented by a function, whose domain is K_0 and whose range is C_{PL}^s, that sends a point u on K_0 to the lumisphere $L(u, \cdot)$. This definition can be described compactly in mathematical notation as follows:

$$K_0 \rightarrow C_{PL}^s : u \mapsto L(u, \cdot) \quad (4)$$

We have chosen subdivision level $s = 3$ in all our examples. In this case the space of lumispheres has dimension $3 \times 258 = 774$. We arrived at this value experimentally. Setting $s = 2$ results in noticeable degradation in the image quality, while $s = 4$ gives little improvement at the expense of higher dimension.

It is useful to think of a surface light field as a lumisphere-valued texture map, which assigns a lumisphere instead of a single color to each texel. There is one rectangular texture map for each triangle in K_0. The K_0 triangle is mapped to the lower-left corner of its rectangle, and the upper right corner is unused. (For compactness we store pairs of texture maps interleaved in memory.) As in conventional texture mapping, each texture map is divided into square texels, and these texels define a partition of each face of K_0 into cells. The surface light field L is thus piecewise-constant with respect to this partition of K_0. Let u_i denote the center of the i-th cell. Cell dimensions (correspondng to the texture map resolution)

are chosen so that the images $\varphi(u_i)$ and $\varphi(u_j)$ of any two adjacent grid points u_i and u_j are separated by at most one pixel in the image plane of each camera. We denote the lumisphere at the grid point u_i by L_i—that is, $L_i(\omega) \equiv L(u_i, \omega)$.

Figure 2 illustrates key aspects of our notation.

3 Data acquisition

Acquiring the raw data to build a surface light field for a real object requires four steps: (1) range scanning the object, (2) building a mesh to represent its geometry, (3) capturing a collection of images of the object, and (4) registering the images to the mesh. Because the techniques presented in this paper do not depend on the specifics of our acquisition process, we present only a brief summary here of the procedure that we have used successfully.

Range scanning. We took a number of range scans of each object using a Cyberware Model 15 scanner. Glossy objects like the fish and elephant are not ideal candidates for laser scanning. To improve laser returns, we coated them with a removable powder. The fish was built from 36 scans, and the elephant from 49.

Reconstructing the geometry. The scans were registered using a small number of hand-selected point correspondences to initialize a global iterated closest-points algorithm [2, 10]. The registered scans were merged into a single triangle mesh using the volumetric method described by Curless and Levoy [6]. The final meshes representing the surfaces of the fish and elephant contain 129,664 triangles and 311,376 triangles, respectively.

Acquiring the photographs. We used a camera attached to a spherical gantry arm to capture photographs from poses spaced roughly evenly over the sphere. The camera positions were known relative to one another, but not relative to the objects being photographed. We took 638 photographs of the fish and 388 photographs of the elephant, together with photographs of a calibration pattern, which we used to determine the intrinsic camera parameters using Tsai's method [30]. During acquisition, the camera and gantry arm occasionally cast shadows onto the object. Because we wanted to capture the object under fixed lighting conditions, we manually removed photographs taken under those circumstances.

Registering the photographs to the geometry. We registered the set of photographs to the reconstructed mesh with user assistance. By hand-selecting correspondences between points on the mesh and points on a small subset of the photographs, we generated a list of 3D point-to-ray correspondences. We then registered the photographs to the geometry using an iterated closest-points algorithm.

4 Estimation and compression

Once we have acquired the raw image and geometric data, we must estimate a surface light field that approximates that input. This section describes three estimation techniques; the latter two directly create compressed representations.

4.1 Assembling data lumispheres

The first step in the estimation process is the construction of a useful intermediate representation, consisting of a *data lumisphere* for each grid point in the surface light field. A data lumisphere is a set of samples from a full lumisphere, each consisting of a color and a direction corresponding to an observation of a grid point. We use $\mathcal{L}_i$ to denote the data lumisphere associated with point u_i on the base mesh. Assembling data lumispheres is a resampling problem that we solve separately for each grid point on the base mesh K_0.

Consider a fixed grid point u_i, and let c_{ij} denote the RGB value of the point in the j-th photograph defined by the ray from $\varphi(u_i)$ to the

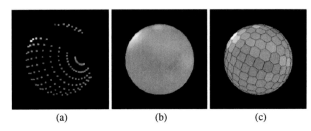

(a)   (b)   (c)

Figure 3 Lumispheres from a point under the elephant's trunk. (The surface normal points directly out of the page.) The swath of missing points were occluded by the trunk. (a) Data lumisphere. (b) Faired piecewise-linear lumisphere. (c) Faired lumisphere with vertices shown as constant-colored Voronoi regions (used for illustration only).

location of the j-th camera. The value c_{ij} is computed by bilinear interpolation in the j-th photograph. Some or all of the c_{ij} might be invalid because the point $\varphi(u_i)$ may not be visible from the j-th camera position. If $\varphi(u_i)$ is visible, we find the direction vector ω_{ij} from $\varphi(u_i)$ to the location of camera j and add the pair (c_{ij}, ω_{ij}) to the data lumisphere $\mathcal{L}_i$ for grid point u_i. Figure 3(a) shows the data lumisphere for a point on our elephant.

To determine if $\varphi(u_i)$ is occluded with respect to the j-th camera, we render, from the perspective of that camera, both the original mesh M and additional geometry that conservatively bounds the platform on which the object rests. (Because the platform obscures parts of the objects in some photographs, we add geometry representing the platform to ensure that we do not project the platform onto the object.) The depth buffer gives us a *depth image*, which we compare to the depth of each point $\varphi(u_i)$ to determine if it is visible.

4.2 Pointwise fairing

Our first estimation algorithm, *pointwise fairing*, constructs a piecewise-linear lumisphere from each data lumisphere independently at each surface point. If the data covered the entire direction sphere, we could estimate L_i using the standard least-squares procedure of setting L_i to be the lumisphere in C_{PL}^s that best approximates the data lumisphere:

$$L_i = \underset{F \in C_{PL}^s}{\operatorname{argmin}} E_{\text{dist}}(F, \mathcal{L}_i) \qquad (5)$$

The argmin notation evaluates to the value of its subscript that minimizes the expression to which it is applied. Here, F is a lumisphere, and $E_{\text{dist}}(F, \mathcal{L}_i)$ measures how well F approximates $\mathcal{L}_i$:

$$E_{\text{dist}}(F, \mathcal{L}_i) \equiv \frac{1}{|\mathcal{L}_i|} \sum_{j \in \text{visible cameras}} |F(\omega_{ij}) - c_{ij}|^2 \qquad (6)$$

where $|\mathcal{L}_i|$ is the number of observed color values in the data lumisphere $\mathcal{L}_i$.

But the physical light field at any point on the surface is only defined on the hemisphere of outward pointing directions. Moreover, due to self-occlusion and constraints on the camera poses, the data samples often do not cover the entire direction hemisphere (see Figure 3). The fitting problem (Equation (6)) is under-determined, and it is therefore necessary to regularize it by adding a fairing term. We use a discrete approximation to the thin-plate energy:

$$E_{\text{thin}}(F) \equiv \frac{N_s}{4\pi} \sum_k |\Delta_{PL} F(\omega_k)|^2 . \qquad (7)$$

The sum ranges over the vertices of the s-times-subdivided octahedron (with N_s vertices, each corresponding to a direction ω_k),

and Δ_{PL} denotes the umbrella Laplacian [29]. The regularized error function is then

$$E_\lambda(F, \mathcal{L}_i) \equiv E_{\text{dist}}(F, \mathcal{L}_i) + \lambda E_{\text{thin}}(F) . \qquad (8)$$

We use conjugate gradients to find the lumisphere F that minimizes Equation (8). Figures 3(b) and 3(c) show the faired lumisphere generated from the data lumisphere in Figure 3(a). The fairing term dampens the directional variation in the fitted lumisphere. It has little physical significance, and our data is relatively free of noise; we therefore choose λ small so that E_{dist} dominates. Note that our fairing procedure assigns values to $L(u, \omega)$ at all directions $\omega \in S^2$, including directions far away from any observations, and even directions pointing into the object.

Figure 4 illustrates the effects and the limitations of pointwise fairing. Figure 4(a) shows one of the actual photographs of the fish, and Figure 4(b) shows the same view of the uncompressed light field generated from all the photographs. The light field rendered in Figure 4(c) was generated after all photographs from viewpoints inside a cone of radius 10° about the viewing direction were removed. There is little degradation. In Figure 4(d) the radius of the cone was increased to 20°. Clearly the gap in directions has become too large for pointwise fairing to accurately approximate the actual surface light field.

4.3 Compression overview

Because C_{PL}^s is a high-dimensional space, a complete pointwise-faired surface light field may be very large. To generate a more compact surface light field, we will represent each lumisphere as a weighted sum of a small number of prototype lumispheres using two distinct methods, one analogous to vector quantization, and the other analogous to principal component analysis. Each lumisphere L_i can then be replaced by an index (as in vector quantization) or a set of coefficients (as in principal component analysis) indicating contributions from the prototypes.

A naive application of vector quantization or principal component analysis might treat as input the pointwise-faired lumispheres viewed as vectors in the space C_{PL}^s. Observe, however, that the RGB values for at least half of each lumisphere—corresponding to directions pointing into the object—are mostly fiction generated by the fairing process. If we were to apply vector quantization or principal component analysis to the pointwise-faired lumispheres, these fabricated values would have the same influence as values in directions where we actually have data. This is clearly undesirable.

A more principled compression approach would use only observed data. The data, however, is an irregular and incomplete sampling of each lumisphere. We have therefore developed two new estimation/compression methods, *function quantization* and *principal function analysis*, which are similar in spirit to vector quantization and principal component analysis, but are driven by irregularly spaced data and avoid the intermediate pointwise-fairing step.

Before discussing our compression algorithms, we present two transformations of the surface light field that increase spatial coherence among lumispheres, thereby making them more compressible.

4.4 Median removal and reflection

The first transformation is *median removal*. Let m_i denote the RGB value obtained by computing the median color of data lumisphere $\mathcal{L}_i$ (separately for each color channel). We use the median rather than the mean because it is robust against outliers and more accurately represents the bulk of the data. The collection of median values can be viewed as a texture map over the surface, roughly encoding the diffuse component of the surface light field. We store this "diffuse" texture map separately and then encode the residual

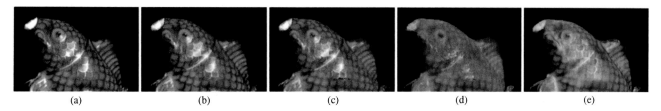

| (a) | (b) | (c) | (d) | (e) |

Figure 4 Analysis of estimation with missing data. (a) Photograph taken by a selected camera. (b) Faired surface light field using all photographs. (c) Faired surface light field after first removing from the input data all photographs in a cone of radius $10°$ about the direction shown. (d) Faired surface light field with a cone of radius $20°$ removed. (e) Compressed surface light field with principal function analysis of order 3 after first removing the same cone of radius $20°$. Note that the compressed surface light field reproduces the specularity of the input better than the pointwise-faired version when a significant portion of the input data is removed.

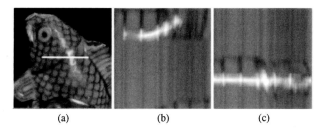

| (a) | (b) | (c) |

Figure 5 Increasing lumisphere coherence via reflection reparameterization. (a) Surface light field. (b) Transect of $L(u, \omega)$. (c) Transect of $\widetilde{L}(u, \widetilde{\omega})$. Horizontal axis shows position of u along white line across fish (a). Vertical axis shows position of ω (b) or $\widetilde{\omega}$ (c) on a user-selected great circle. Note that in the right panel the specular highlights are much better aligned.

surface light field after subtracting the diffuse component. This serves two purposes. First, if we compress only the residual surface light field, any diffuse texture will be exactly preserved. Second, the residual will be more compressible if the specular behavior of the surface is simpler than the diffuse (*e.g.*, an object with diffuse texture and a glossy coat.) Median removal before compression is analogous to mean-removed vector quantization [11].

The second transformation, *reflection*, is a reparametrization of the lumispheres. Let **n** be the unit surface normal at a surface. Then for a direction $\omega \in S^2$, let $\widetilde{\omega}$ be the reflection of ω about the normal **n** (transformed quantities will always be denoted with a tilde '$\sim$'):

$$\widetilde{\omega} \equiv 2(\mathbf{n} \cdot \omega)\mathbf{n} - \omega. \qquad (9)$$

Similarly, the reflected (and median-removed) surface light field $\widetilde{L}$ is defined at each grid point by:

$$\widetilde{L}_i(\widetilde{\omega}) \equiv L_i(\omega) - m_i. \qquad (10)$$

Where, by Equation (9), ω is $\widetilde{\omega}$ reflected around the surface normal, $\mathbf{n}_i$, at the i-th grid point. Obviously, $\widetilde{L}$ (plus the diffuse texture map) contains the same information as L. To see why we expect the reflected reparameterization to increase spatial coherence, consider the three elements that determine the lumisphere L_i at a point: the incoming radiance, the BRDF and the normal. First, assume that the incoming radiance at two points u_i and u_j is the same; this is approximately true for points that are nearby relative to the sources of light illuminating them. Second, assume that the BRDF is reflective. A *reflective BRDF* [3] is one that reflects the incoming radiance through the surface normal and then convolves with a "direction-invariant" filter (*i.e.,* a space-invariant filter, where space is restricted to the surface of the sphere of directions S^2). As observed by Rusinkiewicz [27], many BRDFs are approximately reflective. If these two assumptions hold, the reflected lumispheres

$\widetilde{L}_i$ and $\widetilde{L}_j$ will be the same even if the normals $\mathbf{n}_i$ and $\mathbf{n}_j$ are different. For an example, consider the case of a perfect mirror surface and an environment that is infinitely far away. Ignoring non-local effects such as occlusions and interreflections, all of the reparametrized lumispheres will agree on their overlap because they contain parts of the same environment map. If the surface had some roughness, then the lumispheres would be blurred, reflected images of the environment, but they would still roughly agree on the overlap. Figure 5 illustrates the effect of reparameterization for the fish, whose environment consists of several small light sources.

We always estimate and store median-removed and reflected lumispheres; however, the transformations have no effect on the pointwise-fairing algorithm.

4.5 Function quantization

Function quantization is a generalization of vector quantization to the case of irregularly sampled data. The goal is to construct a *codebook* comprised of a collection of prototype lumispheres (*codewords*) $\{P_0, \ldots, P_n\}$ and a map assigning to each grid point $u_i \in K_0$ a codeword index k_i, and thereby a codeword P_{k_i}. For a given n, the codebook and map should minimize the combined energy over all data lumispheres, *i.e.*, $\sum_i E_\lambda(P_{k_i}, \widetilde{\mathcal{L}}_i)$. This formulation is different from vector quantization in that the inputs (data lumispheres) are not vectors.

Function quantization starts with an initial codebook consisting of a single lumisphere and a small *training set* of randomly selected grid points. It proceeds by alternating between *codebook fitting* and *codeword splitting*, until the codebook reaches a user-specified size.

Codebook fitting is accomplished via Lloyd iteration [11], *i.e.,* by repeatedly applying the following two steps:

1. **Projection:** For each grid point u_i in the training set, find the index k_i of the closest codeword:

$$k_i = \underset{k}{\operatorname{argmin}} E_\lambda(P_k, \widetilde{\mathcal{L}}_i). \qquad (11)$$

   This partitions the training set into clusters of grid points that project to the same codeword.

2. **Optimization:** For each cluster, find the best piecewise-linear lumisphere:

$$P_k = \underset{F \in C_{PL}^s}{\operatorname{argmin}} \sum_{i \in \text{cluster } k} E_\lambda(F, \widetilde{\mathcal{L}}_i), \qquad (12)$$

   where the summation is over all of the data lumispheres $\widetilde{\mathcal{L}}_i$ in the k-th cluster.

We perform the optimization steps using conjugate gradients. The iteration terminates when the decrease in error between successive codebooks falls below a user-defined threshold. Then, if the

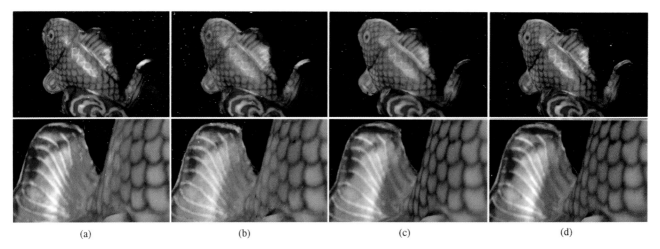

Figure 6 Comparison of different estimation techniques applied to the fish. (a) Pointwise faired surface light field. (b) Function quantization with 1024 codewords. (c) Principal function analysis with subspace dimension 2. (d) Principal function analysis with subspace dimension 5.

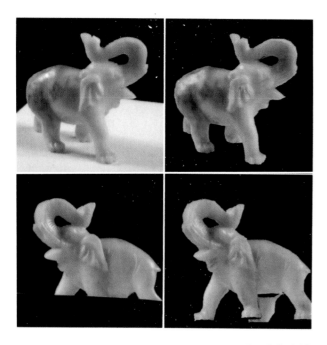

Figure 7 Comparison of compressed elephant surface light field with input photographs. Left: Elephant photographs. Right: Elephant surface light field (5.3 megabytes encoded with principal function analysis, subspace dimension $q = 2$). Note that the image on the bottom right shows a part of the elephant that was occluded in the corresponding photograph. Also note that some points on the very bottom of the elephant were not seen by any camera (using our conservative approximation of the platform) and are black.

codebook is smaller than desired, codeword splitting doubles the codebook size by cloning each codeword and adding a small perturbation to the clone. After a codebook of the desired size has been found, codewords are assigned to all grid points by projecting all the corresponding data lumispheres (not just those in the training sample) onto the codebook.

4.6 Principal function analysis

Principal function analysis, based on principal component analysis, is an alternative to function quantization. For a given set of data vectors and a given approximation dimension q, principal component analysis finds the q-dimensional affine subspace that best approximates the data vectors in the least squares sense. As in the case of function quantization, we must generalize this approach to the case of irregularly sampled data.

Our goal, then, is to find the q-dimensional subspace $V \subset C_{PL}^s$ that best approximates all of the data lumispheres in the training set. Each lumisphere $\widetilde{L}_i$ is represented by the point $F \in V$ that minimizes $E_\lambda(F, \widetilde{L}_i)$. We call F the *projection of $\widetilde{L}_i$ onto V*, or $\pi_V(\widetilde{L}_i)$. Overloading E_λ, we view it as a function of q-dimensional subspaces of C_{PL}^s; it measures how well a subspace approximates the data lumispheres in the training set, *i.e.,*

$$E_\lambda(V) \equiv \frac{1}{T} \sum_i E_\lambda(\pi_V(\widetilde{L}_i), \widetilde{L}_i). \qquad (13)$$

The summation is over all grid point indices in the training set, and T is the size of the training set.

While principal component analysis reduces to an eigenvalue problem, we have not succeeded in finding a corresponding formulation for minimizing the functional defined in equation (13). We have therefore taken a different approach.

Each q-dimensional affine subspace of C_{PL}^s can be expressed as the affine span of $q + 1$ prototype functions, and E_λ can be regarded as a functional on the space of $(q + 1)$-tuples of prototypes. Since E_λ depends only on the affine span of the prototypes, minimizing E_λ will not uniquely determine the prototypes.

To address the uniqueness problem, we consider a new functional:

$$E_{\lambda,\mu}(P_0, \ldots, P_q) \equiv E_\lambda(V) + \mu \sum_{k \in 0, \ldots, q} \|P_k - P_{mean}\|^2 \qquad (14)$$

where $P_0, \ldots, P_q$ are the prototypes defining V, and P_{mean} is their mean, and where the projection $\pi_V(\widetilde{L}_i)$ of a data lumisphere $\widetilde{L}_i$ is restricted to lie inside the convex hull of the prototypes. (The squared norm of a lumisphere, $\|F\|^2$, is the sum of the squared norms of the vertex values divided by the number of vertices.) This additional spring energy term penalizes widely-spaced prototypes. Minimizing it is a non-linear optimization problem, which we solve via conjugate gradients. After the subspace has been determined by selection of the prototypes, we assign barycentric coordinates to all grid points by projecting all corresponding data lumispheres (again, not just those in the training sample) onto the subspace.

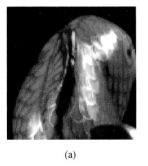

(a)

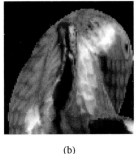

(b)

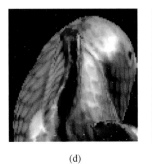

(d)

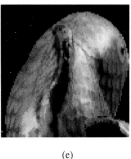

(e)

Figure 8 Comparison of a surface light field with a geometry-corrected two-plane light field. (a) Photograph. (b) Surface light field pointwise faired (180 MB). (c) Two-plane light field uncompressed (180 MB).

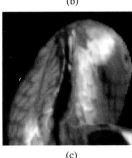

(d) Surface light field compressed using principal function analysis of dimension 5 (2.5 MB). (e) Surface light field compressed using function quantization with 1024 codewords (2.7 MB). (f) Two-plane light field compressed using vector quantization with 16384 codewords (8.1 MB).

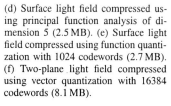

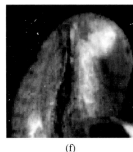

(c)

(f)

4.7 Compression results

We tested the various estimation and compression algorithms on the surface light fields of both the fish and elephant. Figure 6 compares results of the different methods. Figure 6(a) shows two views of the uncompressed (pointwise-faired) fish, the entire model (top) and a closeup of the tail fin (bottom). This data set contains 176 MB of color data, plus 0.7 MB for geometry and normals. Figure 6(b) demonstrates function quantization with 1024 codewords, resulting in a color data size of 2.7 MB. Figures 6(c) and (d) illustrate principal function analysis with subspace dimensions 2 and 5, resulting in color data sizes of 1.7 MB and 2.3 MB, respectively. Note that the 2-dimensional principal function analysis example, with its total file size of 2.4 MB (1.7 MB color + 0.7 MB geometry), results in more than 70:1 compression.

Overall, principal function analysis leads to smoother images than function quantization; function quantization introduces artifacts such as jagged edges on the fish's tail. However, function quantization is more accurate, better preserving the color of highlights and effects such as interreflections that are lost during principal function analysis.

Not surprisingly, increasing the dimension of the subspace in principal function analysis improves the quality of the results; *e.g.*, dimension 5 produces highlights substantially sharper and brighter than dimension 2. Rendering time, however, is asymptotically linear in the dimension q. Currently, other costs dominate when the dimension is low, and in our examples, dimensions 2 and 5 can be rendered at roughly the same speed. By contrast, the rendering time for a function-quantized surface light field is independent of codebook size (ignoring the effect of the memory hierarchy). The complementary strengths of function quantization and principal function analysis suggest a hybrid approach (see Section 7).

We achieved similar compression results with the elephant. A pointwise-faired elephant requires 409 MB of color data and 1.6 MB of geometric data. Applying principal function analysis with a 2-dimensional subspace compresses the elephant's color data to 3.7 MB.

Figure 7 compares synthesized images of the elephant with the photographs. The compressed surface light field captures most of the features of the input data, but the highlights are less bright. In addition to the lower dimension of the subspace, the lower fidelity may be a result of the fact that the scanned geometry of the elephant appeared to be of lower quality than that of the fish. Errors in the geometry, particularly the normals, adversely affect the quality of the compression. Note also that, even though the bottom reconstruction includes the feet of the elephant, which were not visible in the corresponding photograph, our compression algorithm succeeds in inferring plausible shading and highlights for that part of the model. The compressed representation is essentially a learned model of lumispheres; the unseen portions of data lumispheres are filled in by finding the closest lumisphere in the model. Figures 4(d) and (e) also show that principal function analysis can produce more realistic highlights than pointwise fairing given incomplete data lumispheres.

We have done an informal comparison of image quality between a surface light field and a two-plane light field. We constructed a two-plane light field of the fish with six slabs arranged along the faces of a cube. The resolution of the light field, 400^2 for the far plane and 8^2 for the near plane, was chosen to approximately match the corresponding resolutions of the surface light field: the far-plane resolution matches the input photograph resolution, and the near-plane resolution approximately matches the surface light field's directional resolution. The resulting raw data size is about 180 MB, the same size as our pointwise-faired (*i.e.*, uncompressed) surface light field. The input images were resampled into the two-plane parameterization offline using the scanned fish geometry and view-dependent texture mapping. We then compressed the data using the vector quantization technique (and software) of Levoy and Hanrahan [17], using their default settings: a codebook of 16384 $2\times2\times2\times2\times3$ codewords (*i.e.*, 2×2 camera positions, 2×2 image pixels and 3 color channels). All of the renderings of two-plane light fields use the geometry correction technique of Gortler *et al.* [12].

Figure 8 compares images generated from uncompressed and compressed surface light fields with corresponding images generated from the two-plane light field. The uncompressed data sets give reproductions of similar quality, although the two-plane light field's quadralinear interpolation has different filtering characteristics. When compressed, the surface light field produces more compelling reproductions even though the compressed two-plane light field data (8.1 MB + geometry) is more than 3 times the size of the compressed surface light field (2.5 MB + geometry).

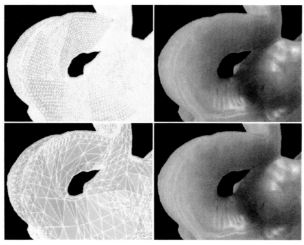

	Model	Faces	False color (secs/frame)	Light field (secs/frame)
top	uniform	102,400	0.36	0.59
bottom	LOD	5823	0.07	0.31

Figure 9 View-dependent level-of-detail. Left: Geometry visualization. Right: Surface light field. Top: Uniform subdivision, $r = 4$. Bottom: View-dependent level-of-detail with error terms chosen to match the uniform subdivision. Shown in the table, very bottom, are rendering times, first for false color only (the step that uses geometry), and second for the entire surface light field rendering algorithm.

The near-plane resolution of the two-plane light field we constructed, though comparable in angular resolution to our surface light field, is lower than those demonstrated by Gortler *et al.* and Levoy and Hanrahan. We have observed that lowering this resolution results in artifacts such as erroneous interpolation among rays that strike quite different surface points due to occlusion. Azuma [1] discusses this effect and other difficulties inherent in reduction of the near-plane resolution.

5 Rendering

In this section we present an interactive surface light rendering algorithm. Our implementation runs entirely in software and achieves interactive rates on PC-class hardware without 3D acceleration.

5.1 Basic algorithm

Rendering a surface light field from an arbitrary viewpoint is conceptually straightforward. Each pixel in the image plane of the camera defines an incoming ray in some direction ω. Suppose the ray intersects the mesh at a point $\varphi(u_i)$, corresponding to a point $u_i \in K_0$. Then the RGB value of the pixel is $L(u_i, \omega)$. Since we actually encode the reparameterized surface light field $\widetilde{L}(u_i, \widetilde{\omega})$ at each point, we must reflect the viewing ray about the normal before looking up the RGB value. To facilitate this process, we compute and store a *normal map* $\mathbf{n}(u)$ over the surface, so that we can quickly determine the normal $\mathbf{n}(u_i)$ at a grid point.

We render the surface light field in two passes. In the first pass we determine, for each pixel of the virtual camera, the point u_i corresponding to the surface point $\varphi(u_i)$ seen at that pixel, encoded as a face ID and barycentric coordinates. We do this efficiently by rendering the mesh in false color with Gouraud shading, using two of the framebuffer's four color channels to encode the index of the base mesh face, and the remaining two to encode the barycentric coordinates within the face.

In the second pass, we scan the frame buffer. For each pixel in the virtual camera we incrementally compute the direction ω of the incoming (viewing) ray using a single 3-vector addition at each pixel. We compute $\widetilde{\omega}$ by reflecting through the surface normal $\mathbf{n}(u_i)$ at $\varphi(u_i)$. Finally, we evaluate $\widetilde{L}(u_i, \widetilde{\omega})$ by looking up the lumisphere associated with u_i and evaluating the piecewise-linear function in direction space. These operations can be done quickly with just a few floating-point operations.

5.2 View-dependent refinement of geometry

One feature of the surface light field representation is the decoupling of the surface geometry from the light field. For best results, we can render the surface geometry at the highest resolution during the first pass of the rendering algorithm, but this can be costly. Alternatively, we can render a simplified mesh (*e.g.*, the embedding of the base mesh triangles in $\mathbb{R}^3$) and still achieve a compelling result because surface light fields, like bump-mapped lighting, suggest more geometric detail than is actually present. However, this simplified mesh introduces some distortion; moreover, the coarse silhouettes are often objectionable. Instead, we have explored a middle ground between those two extremes: *view-dependent refinement* of the subdivision-connectivity surface mesh.

Most current methods for real-time, view-dependent simplification of geometry, such as those presented by Hoppe [15] and Xia and Varshney [32], employ progressive mesh representations and adapt the level of detail using edge collapses and vertex splits. For a texture-mapped surface, however, these operations can cause considerable parametric distortion, especially near the boundaries of parameter domains, placing significant constraints on the simplification [5]. Therefore, we restrict the mesh used for rendering to have four-to-one subdivision connectivity [18], and refine the mesh by adding and removing lazy wavelets [4]. This allows us to modify the geometric detail almost independently of the parameterization.

We approximate the map $\varphi : K_0 \rightarrow M \subset \mathbb{R}^3$ by a piecewise-linear map $\varphi_r : K_r \rightarrow \mathbb{R}^3$ on the simplicial complex K_r obtained by applying r four-to-one subdivisions to the base complex K_0 and setting $\varphi_r(v) = \varphi(v)$ for each vertex v of K_r. The subdivision level r is a user-defined parameter ($r = 4$ in Figure 9). We then compute the lazy-wavelet expansion of φ_r, expressing it as a sum of hat functions. Adapting the mesh can now be formulated as finding a partial sum of those hat functions, satisfying a set of view-dependent properties.

Figure 10 (a) Lazy wavelet addition and subtraction. The support of the added hat function is shown in blue. (b) T-vertices (circled in red) are eliminated by adding edges.

The retriangulation procedure is an incremental algorithm that exploits frame-to-frame coherence, similar to algorithms described by Hoppe [15] and Xia and Varshney [32]. To compute the approximation for a frame, we begin with the approximation computed for the previous frame and modify it by applying the *lazy-wavelet addition* and *lazy-wavelet subtraction* operations, illustrated in Figure 10(a), according to view-dependent criteria. To reduce the appearance of "popping," we spread the visual effect of each operation over time by geomorphing [14]. In a second quick pass over the mesh, we add temporary edges to eliminate cracks caused by "T-vertices," as shown in Figure 10(b).

Our criteria for wavelet addition and subtraction are the same three view-dependent refinement criteria described by Hoppe [15]: (1) removing wavelets that are completely backfacing, (2) removing wavelets lying completely outside the view frustum, and (3) maintaining a screen-space error bound. To accelerate computation of screen-space error, we construct, in preprocessing, a bounding volume around the set of geometric error vectors associated with a wavelet addition. We have found that an ellipsoid aligned to the surface normal generally provides a tighter bound than the shape used by Hoppe, while not adding significantly to the cost of projecting the error volume. Because coarse silhouettes tend to be more noticeable than interior distortion, we use a smaller error tolerance near the silhouette [19]. Finally, to reduce the number of wavelet addition and subtraction operations that must be considered, we enforce one additional property: A hat function at level $\ell \leq r$, centered at an edge of $K_{\ell-1}$, may appear in the sum only if the hat functions centered at the endpoints of the edge appear in the sum.

The results of view-dependent level-of-detail are illustrated in Figure 9, showing a close-up of the elephant's trunk. While achieving high accuracy, the top renderings using uniform subdivision render fairly slowly due to the large number of triangles. The bottom renderings, using the view-dependent level-of-detail algorithm with error threshholds set to match the fine geometry renderings, are obtained with far fewer triangles yielding moderately improved frame rates with little visual difference.

The close-up views shown in Figure 9 benefit greatly from the view frustum test, which causes a considerable fraction of the model to be coarsened. In the other common case, where the entire model is visible, using view-dependent level-of-detail does not give as significant of a performance benefit, but it does no worse than a static model. Of course, if the model is very distant, the level-of-detail algorithm will generate a very coarse approximation.

6 Editing

Just as the decoupling of surface geometry and the light field allows us to refine the geometry independently, we are now able to perform editing operations that are not commonly possible in an image-based rendering context. In this section we describe three such operations: lumisphere editing, rotating the object relative to its environment, and deforming the geometry.

By performing simple image processing directly on the lumispheres, we can simulate changes in surface properties, such as sharpening of specular highlights. We demonstrate this particular operation in Figures 11(a) and (b), where the highlights in the original rendering (a) have been brightened and sharpened (b). We achieve this effect by applying Perlin's bias function [25] to the values of every lumisphere. For compressed surface light fields, we can quickly approximate this by adjusting the prototype lumispheres. (For principal function analysis, this is only an approximation because the bias function is non-linear.)

The other two editing operations we illustrate, rotation of geometry relative to its environment and general deformation, fit into one conceptual framework: a transformation is applied to define a new surface. The new surface can be represented by a modified embedding of the base mesh $\varphi' : K_0 \to \mathbb{R}^3$. (Rotation is just a special case of general deformation.)

Our goal then is to compute the corresponding surface light field $L'(u, \omega)$, and our solution is operationally very simple. We compute the new surface normal field $\mathbf{n}'(u)$ and then set $L'(u, \omega) = \widetilde{L}(u, \widetilde{\omega}')$, where $\widetilde{\omega}'$ is the reflection of ω through the new normal.

Figures 11 and 12 demonstrate the geometric edits. Figure 11(a) shows the original elephant; (c) and (d) show the elephant rotated

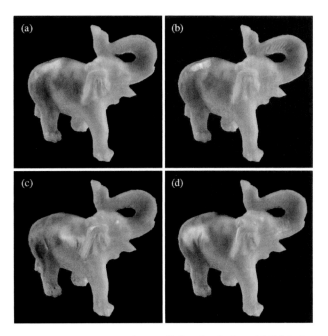

Figure 11 Editing operations applied to the elephant. (a) Original elephant. (b) Sharper and brighter highlights. (c) Environment rotated. (d) Environment rotated to another position.

Figure 12 A volumetric deformation applied to the fish. (Original on left.)

relative to its environment. Figure 12(a) shows the fish as it was originally; Figure 12(b) shows it after deformation, with its head bent to the side.

Our method for computing the new surface light field L' from the original L is justified if the environment is infinitely far away, if there is no occlusion, shadowing or interreflection, and if the BRDFs for all surface points are reflective. These are the same assumptions that motivate our reflection transformation described in Section 4.4. Even if all of these requirements are met, there is an additional problem. For any grid point $u_i \in K_0$, the camera directions represented in the data lumisphere fall inside a hemisphere. After editing, however, there will in general be viewing directions that require values of $L'(u_i, \omega)$ for directions outside this hemisphere. In fact, if we rotate the object by 180 degrees, we will need values exactly on the opposite hemisphere. Operationally, however, inferring these values is not a problem. The estimation techniques guarantee that lumispheres are well-defined everywhere, albeit not necessarily realistic.

7 Future work

We envision a number of areas for future work:

Combining function quantization and principal function analysis. Our two compression methods can be considered extrema of a spectrum: Function quantization fits the data by a collection of 0-dimensional spaces, whereas principal function analysis uses a single higher-dimensional space. We could do both: fit a collection of higher dimensional spaces. That approach might work well if the data lumispheres lie on a low-dimensional curved manifold in lumisphere space.

Wavelet representation of a surface light field. Constructing a wavelet expansion of the surface light field $L(u, \omega)$ might result in better compression than function quantization or principal function analysis, and would support progressive transmission and performance-tuned rendering [4].

Hole filling using texture synthesis. We have no method for assigning lumispheres to surface points not visible in any of the cameras, like those on the bottom of the elephant in Figure 7. A texture synthesis algorithm, suitably extended to operate on lumispheres instead of colors and with textures defined on general surfaces instead of the plane, could be used to fill these holes.

Acknowledgements

We would like to thank Marc Levoy for the use of the Stanford spherical gantry and other equipment. This work was supported by an NSF grant (DMS-9803226) and an Osberg Family Fellowship, as well as industrial gifts from Intel, Microsoft, and Pixar.

References

[1] D. I. Azuma. Interactive Rendering of Surface Light Fields. Technical Report UW-CSE-2000-04-01, Department of Computer Science and Engineering, University of Washington, April 2000.

[2] P. J. Besl and N. D. McKay. A Method for Registration of 3-D Shapes. *IEEE Transactions on Pattern Analysis and Machine Intelligence*, 14(2):239–256, February 1992.

[3] B. Cabral, M. Olano, and P. Nemec. Reflection Space Image Based Rendering. In *SIGGRAPH 98 Conference Proceedings*, Annual Conference Series, pages 165–170, August 1999.

[4] A. Certain, J. Popović, T. DeRose, T. Duchamp, D. Salesin, and W. Stuetzle. Interactive Multiresolution Surface Viewing. In *SIGGRAPH 96 Conference Proceedings*, Computer Graphics Annual Conference Series, pages 91–98, August 1996.

[5] J. Cohen, M. Olano, and D. Manocha. Appearance-Preserving Simplification. In *SIGGRAPH 98 Conference Proceedings*, Annual Conference Series, pages 115–122. ACM SIGGRAPH, July 1998.

[6] B. Curless and M. Levoy. A Volumetric Method for Building Complex Models from Range Images. In *SIGGRAPH 96 Conference Proceedings*, Annual Conference Series, pages 303–312, August 1996.

[7] P. E. Debevec, C. J. Taylor, and J. Malik. Modeling and Rendering Architecture from Photographs: A Hybrid Geometry- and Image-Based Approach. In *SIGGRAPH 96 Conference Proceedings*, Annual Conference Series, pages 11–20, August 1996.

[8] P. E. Debevec, Y. Yu, and G. D. Borshukov. Efficient View-Dependent Image-Based Rendering with Projective Texture-Mapping. *Eurographics Rendering Workshop 1998*, pages 105–116, June 1998.

[9] M. Eck, T. DeRose, T. Duchamp, H. Hoppe, M. Lounsbery, and W. Stuetzle. Multiresolution Analysis of Arbitrary Meshes. In *SIGGRAPH 95 Conference Proceedings*, Annual Conference Series, pages 173–182, August 1995.

[10] H. Gagnon, M. Soucy, R. Bergevin, and D. Laurendeau. Registration of Multiple Range Views for Automatic 3-D Model Building. In *IEEE Conf. Computer Vision and Pattern Recognition*, pages 581–586, June 1994.

[11] A. Gersho and R. M. Gray. *Vector Quantization and Signal Compression*. Kluwer Academic Publishers, 1991.

[12] S. J. Gortler, R. Grzeszczuk, R. Szeliski, and M. F. Cohen. The Lumigraph. In *SIGGRAPH 96 Conference Proceedings*, Annual Conference Series, pages 43–54, August 1996.

[13] W. Heidrich and H.-P. Seidel. Realistic, Hardware-Accelerated Shading and Lighting. *Proceedings of SIGGRAPH 99*, pages 171–178, August 1999.

[14] H. Hoppe. Progressive Meshes. In *SIGGRAPH 96 Conference Proceedings*, Annual Conference Series, pages 99–108, August 1996.

[15] H. Hoppe. View-Dependent Refinement of Progressive Meshes. In *SIGGRAPH 97 Conference Proceedings*, Annual Conference Series, pages 189–198, August 1997.

[16] A. W. F. Lee, W. Sweldens, P. Schroeder, L. Cowsar, and D. Dobkin. MAPS: Multiresolution Adaptive Parameterization of Surfaces. In *SIGGRAPH 98 Conference Proceedings*, Annual Conference Series, pages 95–104, July 1998.

[17] M. Levoy and P. Hanrahan. Light Field Rendering. In *SIGGRAPH 96 Conference Proceedings*, Annual Conference Series, pages 31–42, August 1996.

[18] M. Lounsbery, T. D. DeRose, and J. Warren. Multiresolution Analysis for Surfaces of Arbitrary Topological Type. *ACM Transactions on Graphics*, 16(1):34–73, January 1997.

[19] D. Luebke and C. Erikson. View-Dependent Simplification of Arbitrary Polygonal Environments. In *SIGGRAPH 97 Conference Proceedings*, Annual Conference Series, pages 199–208, August 1997.

[20] M. Magnor and B. Girod. Adaptive Block-Based Light Field Coding. *Proc. 3rd International Workshop on Synthetic and Natural Hybrid Coding and Three-Dimensional Imaging*, pages 140–143, September 1999.

[21] M. Magnor and B. Girod. Hierarchical Coding of Light Fields with Disparity Maps. *Proc. IEEE International Conference on Image Processing*, pages 334–338, October 1999.

[22] G. S. P. Miller, S. Rubin, and D. Ponceleon. Lazy Decompression of Surface Light Fields for Precomputed Global Illumination. *Eurographics Rendering Workshop 1998*, pages 281–292, June 1998.

[23] K. Nishino, Y. Sato, and K. Ikeuchi. Appearance compression and synthesis based on 3D model for mixed reality. In *Proceedings of IEEE ICCV'99*, pages 38 – 45, September 1999.

[24] K. Nishino, Y. Sato, and K. Ikeuchi. Eigen-Texture Method: Appearance Compression based on 3D Model. *Proc. of Computer Vision and Pattern Recognition*, 1:618–624, June 1999.

[25] K. Perlin and E. M. Hoffert. Hypertexture. *Computer Graphics (Proceedings of SIGGRAPH 89)*, 23(3):253–262, July 1989.

[26] K. Pulli, M. Cohen, T. Duchamp, H. Hoppe, L. Shapiro, and W. Stuetzle. View-based Rendering: Visualizing Real Objects from Scanned Range and Color Data. *Eurographics Rendering Workshop 1997*, pages 23–34, June 1997.

[27] S. M. Rusinkiewicz. A New Change of Variables for Efficient BRDF Representation. In *Eurographics Rendering Workshop 1998*, pages 11–22. Eurographics, June 1998.

[28] Y. Sato, M. D. Wheeler, and K. Ikeuchi. Object Shape and Reflectance Modeling from Observation. In *SIGGRAPH 97 Conference Proceedings*, Annual Conference Series, pages 379–388, August 1997.

[29] G. Taubin. A Signal Processing Approach to Fair Surface Design. In *SIGGRAPH 95 Conference Proceedings*, Annual Conference Series, pages 351–358. ACM SIGGRAPH, August 1995.

[30] R. Y. Tsai. An Efficient and Accurate Camera Calibration Technique for 3D Machine Vision. In *Proceedings of IEEE Conference on Computer Vision and Pattern Recognition*, pages 364–374, 1986.

[31] B. Walter, G. Alppay, E. P. F. Lafortune, S. Fernandez, and D. P. Greenberg. Fitting Virtual Lights For Non-Diffuse Walkthroughs. In *SIGGRAPH 97 Conference Proceedings*, Annual Conference Series, pages 45–48, August 1997.

[32] J. C. Xia and A. Varshney. Dynamic View-Dependent Simplification for Polygonal Models. In *IEEE Visualization '96*. IEEE, October 1996.

[33] Y. Yu, P. Debevec, J. Malik, and T. Hawkins. Inverse Global Illumination: Recovering Reflectance Models of Real Scenes From Photographs. In *SIGGRAPH 98 Conference Proceedings*, Annual Conference Series, pages 215–224, August 1999.

Dynamically Reparameterized Light Fields

Aaron Isaksen[†*]   Leonard McMillan[†]   Steven J. Gortler[‡]

[†]Laboratory for Computer Science
Massachusetts Institute of Technology

[‡]Division of Engineering and Applied Sciences
Harvard University

Abstract

This research further develops the light field and lumigraph image-based rendering methods and extends their utility. We present alternate parameterizations that permit 1) interactive rendering of moderately sampled light fields of scenes with significant, unknown depth variation and 2) low-cost, passive autostereoscopic viewing. Using a dynamic reparameterization, these techniques can be used to interactively render photographic effects such as variable focus and depth-of-field within a light field. The dynamic parameterization is independent of scene geometry and does not require actual or approximate geometry of the scene. We explore the frequency domain and ray-space aspects of dynamic reparameterization, and present an interactive rendering technique that takes advantage of today's commodity rendering hardware.

CR Categories: I.3.3 [Computer Graphics]: Picture/Image Generation—Viewing Algorithms I.3.6 [Computer Graphics]: Methodology and Techniques—Graphics data structures and data types

Additional Keywords: Image-based rendering, light field, lumigraph, ray space analysis, frequency domain analysis, autostereoscopic displays, synthetic aperture, depth of field, multitexturing

1   Introduction

The light field [13] and lumigraph [7] rendering methods synthesize novel images from a database of reference images. In these systems, rays of light are stored, indexed, and queried using a two-parallel plane parameterization [8]. Novel images exhibiting view-dependent shading effects are synthesized from this ray database by querying it for each ray needed to construct a desired view.

Several several shortcomings of the light field and lumigraph methods are addressed in this paper. At low to moderate sampling rates, a light field is only suitable for storing scenes with an approximately constant depth. A lumigraph uses depth-correction to reconstruct scenes with greater depth variation. However, it requires an approximate geometry of the scene which may be hard to obtain. Both systems exhibit static focus because they only produce a single reconstruction for a given queried ray. Thus, the pose and

---

focal length of the desired view uniquely determine the image that is synthesized.

This paper presents solutions to the shortcomings stated above. Our goal is to represent moderately sampled light fields with wide variations in depth, without requiring geometry. This requires a more flexible parameterization of the ray database, based on a general mathematical formulation for a planar data camera array. To render novel views, our parameterization uses a generalized depth-correction based on focal surfaces. Because of the additional degrees of freedom expressed in the focal surfaces, we can interactively render images with dynamic photographic effects, such as depth-of-field and apparent focus. The presented dynamic reparameterization is as efficient as the static lumigraph and light field parameterizations, but permits more flexibility at almost no cost. To enable this additional flexibility, we do not perform aperture filtering as presented in [13]. We present a frequency domain analysis to explain the trade-offs of this omission.

Furthermore, our reparameterization techniques allow us to create directly-viewable light fields which are passively autostereoscopic. By using a fly's-eye lens array attached to a flat display surface, the computation for synthesizing a novel view can be solved directly by the optics of the display device. This three-dimensional display, based on integral photography [24, 16], requires no eye-tracking or special hardware attached to a viewer, and it can be viewed by multiple viewers simultaneously under variable lighting conditions.

2   Background

A continuous representation of a ray database would be sufficient for generating any desired ray. However, continuous databases are impractical or unattainable for all but the most trivial cases. In practice, we must work with finite representations in the form of discretely-sampled ray databases.

As with any sampling of a continuous signal, the issues of 1) choosing an appropriate initial sampling density and 2) defining a method for reconstructing the continuous signal are crucial factors in effectively representing the original signal. In the context of light fields and lumigraphs, researchers have explored various parameterizations and methods to facilitate better or more practical sampling [3, 22, 20, 4]. Other parameterizations have been presented to decrease the dimensionality of the light field, giving up vertical parallax and the ability to translate into the scene [21].

The choice of a ray database parameterization also affects the reconstruction methods that can be used in synthesizing desired views. Even with properly sampled data, a poor reconstruction filter can introduce post-aliasing artifacts into the result [15].

The two-parallel-plane parameterization of a ray database has a substantial impact on the choice of reconstruction filters. In the original light field system, a ray is parameterized by a predetermined entrance plane and exit plane (also referred to as the st and uv planes using lumigraph terminology). Figure 1 shows a typical moderate sampling on the st plane and three possible highly sampled exit planes, uv_1, uv_2, and uv_3. To reconstruct a desired ray

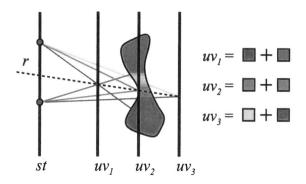

Figure 1: The parameterization of the exit plane, or uv plane, affects the reconstruction of a desired ray r. Here, the light field would be best parameterized using the uv_2 exit plane.

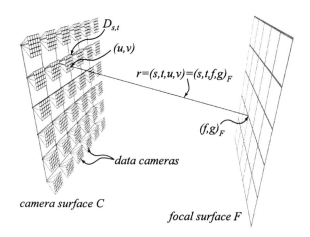

Figure 2: Our parameterization uses a camera surface C, a collection of data cameras $D_{s,t}$, and a dynamic focal surface F. Each ray r with coordinates (s, t, u, v) intersects the focal surface F at $(f, g)_F$ and is therefore also named $(s, t, f, g)_F$.

r which intersects the entrance plane at (s, t) and the exit plane at (u, v), a renderer combines samples with nearby (s, t) and (u, v) values. However, only the standard light field parameterized using exit plane uv_2 will give a satisfactory reconstruction. This is because the plane uv_2 well approximates the geometry of the scene,

The original light field system addresses this reconstruction problem by aperture filtering the ray database. Aperture filtering bandlimits the ray database with a low-pass prefilter. This removes high-frequency data that can not be reconstructed from a given sampling without aliasing. In Figure 1, aperture filtering on a ray database parameterized by either the exit plane uv_1 or uv_3 would store only a blurred version of the scene. Thus, any synthesized view of the scene will appear defocused. No post-processing can recover information that has been lost by aperture filtering. Because a particular fixed exit plane must be determined before performing aperture filtering, one can only represent scenes which can be sufficiently approximated by a single, fixed exit plane. In order to produce light fields that capture the full depth range of a deep scene without noticeable defocusing, the original light field system would require impractically large sampling rates.

The lumigraph system is able to reconstruct deep scenes stored at practical sampling rates by using depth-correction. In this process, the exit plane intersection coordinates (u, v) of each desired ray r are mapped to new coordinates (u', v') to produce an improved ray reconstruction. This mapping requires an approximate depth per ray, which can be efficiently stored as a polygonal model of the scene. If the geometry correctly approximates the scene, the reconstructed images will always appear in focus. The approximate geometry requirement imposes some constraints on the types of light fields that can be captured. Geometry is readily available for synthetic light fields, but acquiring geometry is difficult for photographically-acquired ray databases.

Both the light field and lumigraph systems are fixed-focus systems. That is, they will always produce the same result for a given geometric ray r. This is unlike a physical lens system which exhibits different behaviors depending on the focus setting and aperture size. In addition to proper reconstruction of a novel view, we would like to produce photographic effects such as variable focus and depth-of-field at interactive rendering rates. Systems have been built to render these types of lens effects using light fields, but this work was designed only for synthetic scenes where an entire light field is rendered for each desired image [11].

3 Focal Surface Parameterization

Our parameterization of ray databases is analogous to a two-dimensional array of pinhole cameras treated as a single optical

system with a discrete synthetic aperture. Each constituent pinhole camera captures a focused image, and the camera array acts as a discrete aperture in the image formation process. By using an arbitrary focal surface, we can establish correspondences between the rays from different pinhole cameras.

In the two-parallel-plane ray database parameterization there is an entrance plane, with parameters (s, t) and an exit plane with parameters (u, v). Each ray r is uniquely determined by the 4-tuple (s, t, u, v).

Our parameterization is best described in terms of a camera surface, a 2-D array of data cameras and images, and a focal surface (see Figure 2). The camera surface C, parameterized by coordinates (s, t), is identical in function to the entrance plane of the standard parameterization. Each data camera $D_{s,t}$ represents a captured image taken from a given grid point (s, t) on the camera surface. Each $D_{s,t}$ can have a unique orientation and internal calibration, although we typically capture the light field using a common orientation and intrinsic parameters for the data cameras. We index each pixel in the data camera images using image coordinates (u, v), and we can think of each pixel (u, v) in a camera $D_{s,t}$ as a ray $r = (s, t, u, v)$. Samples in the ray database exist for values of (s, t) if there is a data camera $D_{s,t}$. The focal surface F is a dynamic two-dimensional manifold parameterized by coordinates $(f, g)_F$. Because the focal surface changes dynamically, we subscript the coordinates to tell us which focal surface we are using. Each ray (s, t, u, v) also intersects the focal surface F, and thus has an alternate naming $(s, t, f, g)_F$.

For each $D_{s,t}$ we define a mapping $\mathbf{M}_{s,t}^{F \to D} : (f, g)_F \to (u, v)$. This mapping tells us which data camera ray intersects the focal surface F at $(f, g)_F$. In other words, if $(f, g)_F$ was an imageable point on F, then the image of this point in camera $D_{s',t'}$ would lie at (u', v'), as in Figure 3. Given that we know the projection mapping $\mathbf{P}_{s,t} : (X, Y, Z) \to (u, v)$ which describes how three-dimensional points are mapped to pixels in the data camera $D_{s,t}$, and we know $\mathbf{T}_F : (f, g)_F \to (X, Y, Z)$ which maps points $(f, g)_F$ on the focal surface F to three-dimensional points in space, the mapping $\mathbf{M}_{s,t}^{F \to D}$ is easily determined, $\mathbf{M}_{s,t}^{F \to D} = \mathbf{P}_{s,t} \circ \mathbf{T}_F$.[1] Since the data cameras do not move or change their calibration, $\mathbf{P}_{s,t}$ is con-

---

[1] Since we create the focal surface at run time, we know $\mathbf{T}_F$. Likewise, $\mathbf{P}_{s,t}$ is known for synthetic light fields. For captured light fields, $\mathbf{P}_{s,t}$ can either be assumed or calibrated using readily available camera calibration techniques [26, 28].

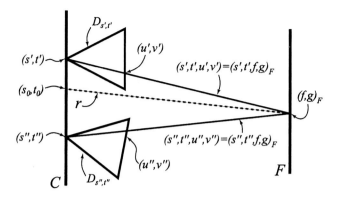

Figure 3: Given a ray $r = (s_0, t_0, f, g)_F$, we find the rays (s', t', u', v') and (s'', t'', u'', v'') in the data cameras $D_{s',t'}$ and $D_{s'',t''}$ which intersect F at the same point $(f, g)_F$.

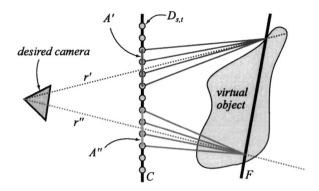

Figure 4: For each desired ray, our synthetic aperture system centers the aperture at the intersection of the ray with the camera surface. Thus the ray r' uses the aperture A' while r'' uses A''. The ray r' will appear in focus, while r'' will not.

stant for each data camera $D_{s,t}$. For a dynamic focal surface, we will modify the mapping $\mathbf{T}_F$, which changes the placement of the focal surface. A static $\mathbf{T}_F$ with a focal surface that conforms to the scene geometry gives us a depth-correction identical to the lumigraph [7].

To reconstruct a ray r from the ray database, we use a generalized depth-correction. We first find the intersections of r with C and F. This gives us the 4-D ray coordinates $(s_0, t_0, f, g)_F$ as in Figure 3. Using cameras near (s_0, t_0), say $D_{s',t'}$ and $D_{s'',t''}$, we apply $\mathbf{M}_{s',t'}^{F \rightarrow D}$ and $\mathbf{M}_{s'',t''}^{F \rightarrow D}$ to $(f, g)_F$, giving us (u', v') and (u'', v''), respectively. This gives us two rays (s', t', u', v') and (s'', t'', u'', v'') which are stored as the pixel (u', v') in the data camera $D_{s',t'}$ and (u'', v'') in the data camera $D_{s'',t''}$. We can then apply a filter to combine the values for these two rays. In the diagram, we have used two rays, although in practice, we can use more rays with appropriate filter weights.

4 Variable Aperture and Focus

We can use our dynamic parameterization to efficiently create images that simulate variable focus and variable depth-of-field. This allows us to create focused images of moderately sampled scenes with large depth variation without requiring geometric information. In addition, this new parameterization provides the user significant artistic expression when composing novel images.

4.1 Variable Aperture

In a traditional camera, the aperture controls the amount of light that can enter the optical system. It also influences the extent of depth-of-field present in the images. With smaller apertures, more of the scene appears in focus; larger apertures produce images with a narrow range of focus. We simulate synthetic apertures not to affect exposure, but to control the amount of depth-of-field present in an image.

We can interactively emulate a depth-of-field effect by combining rays from several cameras. In Figure 4, we are trying to reconstruct two rays, r' and r''. In this example, the extent of our synthetic apertures A' and A'' is four data cameras. We center the synthetic apertures at the intersection of r' and r'' with the camera surface C. We then recall ray database samples by applying $\mathbf{M}_{s,t}^{F \rightarrow D}$ for all (s, t) such that $D_{s,t}$ lies within the aperture. These samples are combined to create a single reconstructed ray.

Note that r' intersects F near the surface of the virtual object, whereas r'' does not. Our synthetic aperture reconstruction will

cause r' to appear in focus, while r'' will not. The size of the synthetic aperture affects the amount of depth-of-field.

It is important to note that our model is not necessarily equivalent to an aperture attached to the desired camera. For example, if one rotates the desired camera, our effective aperture remains parallel to the camera surface. Modeling the aperture on the camera surface and not on the desired camera makes the ray reconstruction more efficient and still produces the desired depth-of-field effect (See Figure 5). A more realistic and complete lens model is given in [11], although this is less efficient to render and impractical for captured light fields.

We do not weight the queried samples that fall within the synthetic aperture equally. Using a dynamic filter that controls the weighting, we can improve the frequency response of our reconstruction. In Figure 6, we attempt to reconstruct the pink dotted ray $r = (s_0, t_0, f, g)_F$. We use a two-dimensional function $w(x, y)$ to describe the point-spread function of the synthetic aperture. Typically w has a maximum at $w(0, 0)$ and is bounded by a square of width δ. The filter is defined such that $w(x, y) = 0$ whenever $x \leq -\delta/2$, $x \geq \delta/2$, $y \leq -\delta/2$, or $y \geq \delta/2$. The filters should also be designed so that the sum of sample weights will add up to 1. That is, $\sum_{i=-\infty}^{\infty} \sum_{j=-\infty}^{\infty} w(x+i, y+j) = 1$ for all $(x, y) \in \Re^2$.

We use the aperture filter on the ray $r = (s_0, t_0, f, g)_F$ as follows. The center of the aperture filter is translated to the point (s_0, t_0). Then, for each camera $D_{s,t}$ that is inside the aperture, we will construct a ray $(s, t, f, g)_F$ and then calculate (s, t, u, v) using the appropriate mapping $\mathbf{M}_{s,t}^{F \rightarrow D}$. Then each ray (s, t, u, v) is weighted by $w(s - s_0, t - t_0)$ and all weighted rays within the aperture are summed together. [2]

Our system can create arbitrarily large synthetic apertures. The size of the aperture is only limited to the extent to which there are cameras on the camera surface. With sufficiently large apertures, we can see through objects, as in Figure 7. One problem with making large apertures occurs when the aperture function falls outside the populated region of the camera surface. When this occurs, the weighted samples will not add up to one. This creates a vignetting effect where the image darkens when using samples near the edges of the camera surface. This can be solved by either adding more data cameras to the camera surface or by reweighting the samples on a pixel by pixel basis so the weights always add up to one.

---

[2] One could also use the aperture function $w(x, y)$ as a basis function at each sample to reconstruct the continuous light field, although this is not computationally efficient.

Figure 5: By changing the shape and width of the dynamic aperture filter, we can interactively change the amount of depth of field.

4.2 Variable Focus

Photographers using cameras can not only change the depth-of-field, but they vary what is in focus. Using our dynamic parameterization, one can create the same effect at run-time by modifying the focal surface. As before, a ray r is defined by its intersections with the camera surface C and focal surface F and can be written $(s_0, t_0, f, g)_F$. The mapping $\mathbf{M}_{s,t}^{F \to D}$ tells us which ray (s, t, u, v) in the data camera $D_{s,t}$ approximates $(s_0, t_0, f, g)_F$.

When the focal surface is changed to F', the same ray r now intersects a different focal surface at a different point $(f', g')_{F'}$. This gives us a new coordinate $(s_0, t_0, f', g')_{F'}$ for the ray r. The new mapping $\mathbf{M}_{s,t}^{F' \to D}$ gives us a pixel (u', v') for each data camera $D_{s,t}$ within the aperture.

In Figure 9, we have three focal surfaces, F_1, F_2, and F_3. Note that for a single ray r, we reconstruct the sample using different pixels, depending on which focal surface we use. For example, if we are using focal surface F_n, then we will use the rays (s', t', u'_n, v'_n) and (s'', t'', u''_n, v''_n).

Note that this selection is a dynamic operation. In the light field and lumigraph systems, the ray r would always return the same reconstructed sample. As we see in Figure 8, we can effectively control which part of the scene is in focus by simply moving the focal surface. If the camera surface is too sparsely sampled, then the

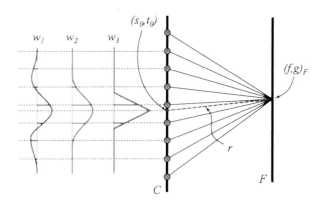

Figure 6: By changing the shape of our aperture filter, we can control the quality of reconstruction and the amount of depth-of-field. In this figure, filter w_1 will reconstruct r by combining six rays, w_2 will combine four rays, and w_3 will combine two.

Figure 7: With a very large aperture, we can see through objects. No one image in the light field sees the entire hillside.

out-of-focus objects can appear aliased. This aliasing is analyzed in Section 6.

Many scenes can not be brought entirely into focus with a single focal plane. As in Figure 9, the focal surfaces do not have to be planar. One could create a focal surface out of a parameterized surface patch that passes through key points in a scene, a polygonal model, or a depth map. Analogous to depth-corrected lumigraphs, this would insure that all visible surfaces are in focus. But, in reality, these depth maps would be hard and/or expensive to obtain with captured data sets. However, using a system similar to ours, a user can dynamically modify a non-planar focal surface until a satisfactory image is produced.

4.3 Multiple Apertures and Focal Surfaces

In general, we may like to have more than just the points near a single surface in clear focus. One solution is to use a different focal surface and aperture for each ray, something not available to real cameras. In a real lens system, only one continuous plane is in focus at one time. However, since we are not confined by physical optics, we can have two or more distinct regions that are in focus. Using a real camera, this can be done by first taking a set of pictures with different planes of focus, and then taking the best parts of each image and compositing them together as a post-process [17]. Using our parameterization, one can choose an aperture and focal surface on a per region or per pixel basis. We have previously described methods for rendering with multiple focal surfaces [12]. Multiple apertures would be useful to help reduce vignetting near the edges of the camera surfaces. If the aperture passes near the edge of the camera surface, then one could reduce its size so that it remains inside the boundary.

Figure 8: By varying the placement of the focal surface, one can interactively control what appears in focus.

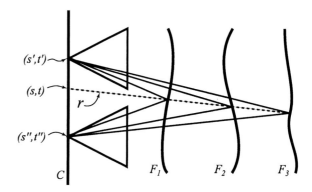

Figure 9: By changing the shape or placement focal surfaces, we can dynamically control which samples in each data camera will contribute to the reconstructed ray.

5 Ray-Space Analysis

It is instructive to consider the effects of dynamic reparameterization on light fields when viewed from ray space [13, 7] and, in particular, within epipolar plane images (EPIs) [2]. It is well-known that 3-D structures of the observed scene are directly related to features within these particular light field slices. The two-parallel plane parameterization is particularly suitable for analysis under this regime as shown by [8]. Our system can also be analyzed in ray space, especially when the focal surface is planar. In our analysis, we consider a 2-D subspace of rays corresponding to fixed values of t and g on a dynamic focal plane F. When the focal surface is parallel to the camera surface, the sf slice is identical to an EPI.

A dynamically reparameterized light field with four point features is shown in Figure 10a. The dotted point is a point at infinity. A light field parameterized with the focal plane F_1 will have a sf_1 ray-space slice similar to Figure 10b. Each point feature corresponds to a linear feature in ray space, where the slope of the line indicates the relative depth of the point. Vertical features in the slice represent points on the focal plane; features with positive slopes represent points that are further away and negative slopes represent points that are closer. Points infinitely far away will have a slope of 1 (for example, the dashed line) Although not shown in

the figure, variation in color along the line in ray space represents the view-dependent radiance of the point. If the same set of rays is reparameterized using a new focal plane F_2 that is parallel to the original F_1 plane, the sf_2 slice shown in Figure 10c results. These two slices are related by a shear transformation along the dashed line. If the focal plane is oriented such that it is not parallel with the camera surface, as with F_3, then the sf slice is transformed non-linearly, as shown in Figure 10d. However, each horizontal line of constant s in Figure 10d is a linearly transformed (i.e. scaled and shifted) version of the corresponding horizontal line of constant s in Figure 10b. In summary, dynamic reparameterization of light fields amounts to a simple transformation of ray space. When the focal surface remains perpendicular to the camera surface but its position is changing, this results in a shear transformation of ray space.

Changing the focal plane position thus affects which ray-space features will be axis-aligned. Thus, we can use a separable, axis-aligned reconstruction filter along with the focal plane to select which features will be axis-aligned, allowing us to dynamically select which features will be properly reconstructed. Equivalently, one can interpret focal plane changes as aligning the reconstruction filter to a particular feature slope, while keeping the ray space parameterization constant.

Under the interpretation that a focal plane shears ray space and keeps uses axis-aligned reconstruction filters, our aperture filtering methods amount to varying the extent of the reconstruction filters along the s dimension. In Figure 10e, the dashed horizontal lines depict the s extent of three different aperture filters (we assume they are infinitely thin in the f_1 dimension). When creating a line image from the ray-space using the three filters, we construct line images as shown in Figure 10f. Varying the extent of the aperture filter has the effect of "blurring" features located far from the focal plane while features located near on the focal plane will be relatively sharp. However, the filter will reduce the amount of view-dependent radiance for features aligned with the filter. If we shear ray space to produce the parameterization of Figure 10c and use the same three filters, we produce the line images of Figure 10g.

6 Frequency Domain Analysis

Ray space transformations have other effects on the reconstruction process. Since shears can arbitrarily modify the relative sampling frequencies between dimensions in ray space, they present considerable difficulties when attempting to bandlimit the source signal. Furthermore, any attempt to bandlimit the sampled function based on any particular parameterization will severely limit the fidelity of the reconstructed signals from the light field.

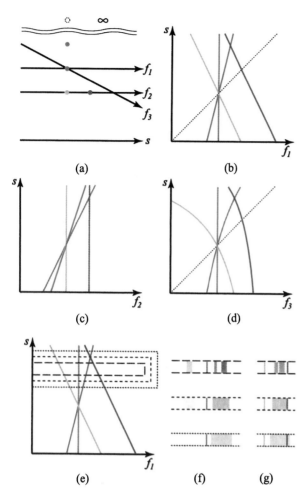

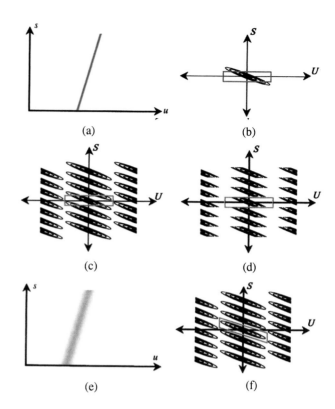

Figure 10: **(a)** A light field of four points, with 3 different focal planes. **(b,c,d)** sf slices using the three focal planes. **(e)** Three aperture filters drawn on the ray space of (b). **(f)** Line images constructed using the aperture filters of (e); red feature is in focus. **(g)** Line images constructed using the aperture filters of (e) but the ray space diagram of (c); orange and green features are in focus.

Figure 11: **(a)** su slice of a single feature. **(b)** Frequency domain power spectrum of (a). Aperture prefilter drawn in blue. **(c)** Power spectrum after typical sampling. Traditional reconstruction filter shown in red. **(d)** Power spectrum of sampled data after prefilter of (b). Traditional reconstruction filter shown in red. **(e)** In space domain, the result of (d) is a blurred version of (a). **(f)** By using alternative reconstruction function filter, we can accurately reconstruct (a).

In this section, we will analyze the frequency-domain dual of a dynamically reparameterized light field. Whereas in section 5 we interpreted dynamic reparameterization as ray space shearing, in this section we will interpret the ray space as fixed (using dimensions s and u) and instead shear the reconstruction filters.

Consider an 'ideal' continuous light field of a single feature located slightly off the u plane as shown in the EPI of Figure 11a. In the frequency domain, this su slice will have the power spectrum shown in Figure 11b. The blue box represents a bandlimiting prefilter. Sampling generates copies of this spectrum as shown in Figure 11c. Typical light fields have a higher sampling density on the data camera images than on the camera surface, and our example reflects this convention. If the data camera images are adequately sampled, there will be no overlap between the copies in the horizontal direction of the frequency domain. If we attempt to reconstruct this signal with the separable reconstruction filter under the original parameterization shown by the red box in Figure 11c, the resulting image will exhibit considerable post-aliasing, because of the high-frequency leakage from the other copies. This quality degradation will show up as ghosting in the reconstructed image, where multiple copies of a feature can be faintly seen. Note that this ghosting is a form of post-aliasing; the original sampling process has not lost any information.

One method for remedying this problem is to apply an aggressive bandlimiting pre-filter to the continuous signal before sampling. This approach is approximated by the aperture-filtering step described in [13]. When the resulting bandlimited light field is sampled using the prefilter of Figure 11b, the power spectrum shown in Figure 11d results. This signal can be reconstructed exactly with an ideal separable reconstruction filter as indicated by the red box. However, the resulting EPI, shown in Figure 11e, contains only the low-frequency portion of the original signal energy, giving a blurry image.

Dynamic reparameterization allows many equally valid reconstructions of the light field. The shear transformation of the ray-space filter effectively allows for the application of reconstruction filters that would be non-separable in the original parameterization. Thus, using dynamic reparameterization, the spectrum of the single point can be recovered exactly without post-aliasing using the filter indicated by the red box in Figure 11f.

Issues are more complicated in the case when multiple point features are represented in the light field, as shown in the su slice in Figure 12a. The power spectrum of this signal is shown in Figure 12b. After sampling, multiple copies of the original signal's spectrum interact, causing a form of pre-aliasing that cannot be undone by processing. Dynamic reparameterization allows for a single feature from the spectrum to be extracted, as shown by the red box overlaid on Figure 12c. However, some residual energy from the other points will also be captured, and will appear in the recon-

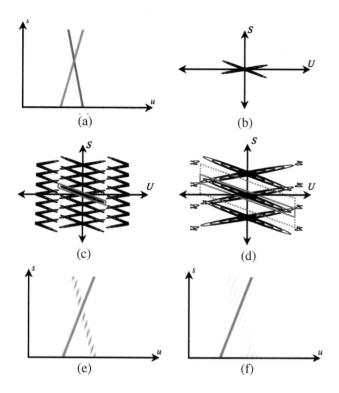

Figure 12: **(a)** su slice of two features. **(b)** Frequency domain power spectrum of the features. **(c)** Frequency domain power spectrum, the red box represents a possible reconstruction filter. **(d)** Wide aperture reconstruction corresponds to the thinner filters in frequency domain. **(e)** Result of small aperture reconstruction. **(f)** Result of large aperture reconstruction.

structed image as ghosting (see Figure 12e).

One method for reducing this artifact is to increase the size of the synthetic aperture. In the frequency domain, this reduces the width of the reconstruction filters as shown in Figure 12d. Using this approach, we can, in the limit, reduce the contribution of spurious features to a small fraction of the total extracted signal energy. The part we cannot extract is the result of the pre-aliasing. By choosing sufficiently wide reconstruction apertures (or narrow in the frequency domain), the effect of the pre-aliasing can be made imperceptible (below our quantization threshold). Figure 12f is reconstructed by using a wider aperture than that in Figure 12e. Note that the aliasing in Figure 12f has less energy and is more spread out than in Figure 12e.

This leads to a general trade-off that must be considered when working with moderately sampled light fields. We can either 1) apply prefiltering at the cost of limiting the range of images that can be synthesized from the light field and endure the blurring and attenuation artifacts that are unavoidable in deep scenes or 2) endure some aliasing artifacts in exchange for greater flexibility in image generation. The visibility of aliasing artifacts can be effectively limited by selecting appropriate apertures for a given desired image.

7 Rendering

As in the lumigraph and light field systems, we can construct a desired image by querying rays from the ray database. Given arbitrary cameras, camera surfaces, and focal surfaces, one can ray-trace the desired image. If the desired camera, data cameras, camera surface, and focal surface are all planar, then a texture mapping approach can be used similar to that proposed by the lumigraph system. We

extend the texture mapping method using multi-texturing for rendering with arbitrary non-negative aperture filters, including bilinear and higher order filters.

7.1 Memory Coherent Ray Tracing

We first describe a memory coherent ray tracing method with the following pseudo-code. Instead of rendering pixel by pixel in the desired image, we can render the contribution of each data camera sequentially. This causes us to write to each pixel in the desired image many times.

The intersection techniques are those used in standard ray tracing. In the following description, a ray $r = (s, t, u, v)$ has a color $c(r) = c(s, t, u, v)$. Likewise, a pixel (x, y) in the desired image has a color $c(x, y)$. Let K be the desired camera with a center of projection o and pixels (x, y) on its image plane. Let $w(x, y)$ be the aperture weighting function, where δ is the width of the aperture.

Initialize the frame buffer to black
For each data camera $D_{s,t}$
    $R_C :=$ a polygon on C defined by $\{(s \pm \delta/2, t \pm \delta/2)\}$
    $R_K :=$ projection of R_C onto the desired image plane
    For each pixel (x, y) within R_K
        $r :=$ the ray through o and (x, y)
        Intersect r with C and F to get (s', t') and $(f, g)_F$
        $(u, v) := \mathbf{M}_{s,t}^{F \to D}(f, g)_F$
        $weight := w(s' - s, t' - t)$
        $c(x, y) := c(x, y) + weight * c(s, t, u, v)$

7.2 Texture Mapping

Although the ray tracing method is simple to understand and easy to implement, there are more efficient methods for rendering when the camera surface, image surface, and focal surface are planar. We extend the lumigraph texture mapping approach [7] to support dynamic reparameterization. We render the contribution of each data camera $D_{s,t}$ using multi-texturing and an accumulation buffer [9]. Our method works with arbitrary non-negative aperture functions.

Multi-texturing, supported by Microsoft Direct3D 7's texture stages [14], allows a single polygon to have multiple textures and multiple projective texture coordinates. At each pixel, two sets of texture coordinates are calculated, and then two texels are accessed. The two texels are multiplied, and the result is stored in the frame buffer. We write to the frame buffer using the Direct3D alpha mode "source + destination," which makes the frame buffer act as a 8-bit, full-color accumulation buffer.

Our rendering technique is illustrated in Figure 13. For each camera $D_{s,t}$, we create a rectangular polygon $R_{s,t}^C$ on the camera surface with coordinates $\{(s \pm \delta/2, t \pm \delta/2)\}$. We then project this polygon on to the desired camera K's image plane using a projection matrix $\mathbf{P}_{C \to K}$, giving us a polygon $R_{s,t}^K$. This polygon $R_{s,t}^K$ represents the region of the image plane which uses samples from the data camera $D_{s,t}$. That is, only pixels inside polygon $R_{s,t}^K$ will use texture from data camera $D_{s,t}$.

We then project $R_{s,t}^K$ onto the focal plane F using a planar homography $\mathbf{H}_{K \to F}$, a 3x3 matrix which changes one projective 2-D basis to another. This projection is done from the desired camera K's point of view. The resulting polygon $R_{s,t}^F$ lies on the focal plane F. Finally, we use the mapping $\mathbf{M}_{s,t}^{F \to D}$ to calculate the (u, v) pixel values for the polygon. This gives us a polygon $R_{s,t}^D$, which represents the (u, v) texture coordinates for polygon $R_{s,t}^F$.

We can compose many of these operations into a single matrix, which takes us directly from polygon $R_{s,t}^C$ to texture coordinates $R_{s,t}^D$. This matrix $\mathbf{M}_{s,t}^{C \to D}$ can be written as $\mathbf{M}_{s,t}^{C \to D} = \mathbf{M}_{s,t}^{F \to D} \mathbf{H}_{K \to F} \mathbf{P}_{C \to K}$.

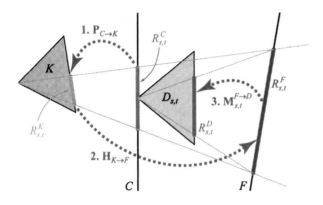

Figure 13: Projection matrices and planar homographies allow us to render the image using texture mapping on standard commodity PC rasterizing hardware.

This process gives us the correct rays (s, t, u, v), but we still require the appropriate weights from the aperture filter. Because we are drawing a polygon with the shape of the aperture filter, we can simply modulate the texture $D_{s,t}$ with the aperture filter texture A. For $D_{s,t}$ we use the projective texture coordinates $R_{s,t}^D$; for the aperture filter A, we use the texture coordinates $\{(\pm\delta/2, \pm\delta/2)\}$.

Initialize the frame buffer to black
For each data camera $D_{s,t}$
    $R_{s,t}^C :=$ polygon on C defined by $\{(s \pm \delta/2, t \pm \delta/2)\}$
    $R_{s,t}^D := \mathbf{M}_{s,t}^{F \to D} \mathbf{H}_{K \to F} \mathbf{P}_{C \to K} R_{s,t}^C$
    Render $R_{s,t}^C$ using...
        texture $D_{s,t}$
        projective texture coordinates $R_{s,t}^D$
        modulated by aperture texture A
    Accumulate rendered polygon into frame buffer

Using this method, dynamically reparameterized light fields can be rendered in real-time on readily available PC graphics cards that support multi-texturing. Frame rate decreases linearly with the number of data cameras that fit inside the aperture functions, so narrow apertures render faster. Vignetting occurs near the edges of the camera surface when using wide filters.

7.3 Using the Focal Surface as a User Interface

In typical light field representations, there is no explicit depth information making it difficult to navigate about an object using a keyboard or mouse. For example, it can be hard to rotate the camera about an object when we don't know where it is located in space. Head tracking can make navigation simpler, although specialized tracking hardware is considerably less accessible [19]. We have found the focal surface can be used to help navigate about an object in the light field. When we move the focal surface so that a particular pixel p belonging to that object is in focus, we can find the 3-D position P of p using the equation $P = \mathbf{H}_{K \to F} p$. Once we know the effective 3-D position of the object, we can rotate (or some other transformation) relative to that point.

8 Autostereoscopic Light Fields

Our flexible reparameterization framework allows for other useful reorganizations of light fields. One interesting reparameterization permits direct viewing of a light field. The directly-viewed light field is similar to an integral or lenticular photograph. In integral photography, a large array of small lenslets, usually packed in a

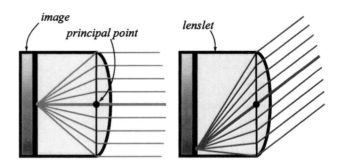

Figure 14: Each lenslet in the lens array acts as a view-dependent pixel. One can determine which color will be seen by drawing a ray through the principal point of the lenslet.

hexagonal grid, is used to capture and display an autostereoscopic image [16, 24]. Traditionally, two identical lens arrays are used to capture and display the image: this requires difficult calibration and complicated optical transfer techniques [27]. Furthermore, the viewing range of the resulting integral photograph mimics the configuration of the capture system. Holographic stereograms [10] also can present directly-viewed light fields, although the equipment and precision required to create holographic stereograms can be prohibitive. Using our reparameterizations, we can capture a scene using light field capture hardware, reparameterize it using our techniques, and thus create novel 3-D views which can be redisplayed using standard lens arrays with few restrictions. This makes it much easier to create integral photographs since a light field is much easier to collect and a variety of different integral photographs can be created from the same light field.

In an integral photograph, a single lenslet acts as a view-dependent pixel, as seen in Figure 14. For each lenslet, the focal length of the lens is equal to the thickness of the lens array. A reparameterized light field image is placed behind the lens array, such that a subset of the ray database lies behind each lenslet. When the lenslet is viewed from a particular direction, the entire lenslet takes on the color of a single point in the image. To predict which color will be seen from a particular direction, we use a paraxial lens approximation [23]. We can draw a line parallel to the viewing direction which passes through the principal point of the lenslet. This line will intersect the image behind the lenslet at some point; this point determines the view-dependent color. If the viewing direction is too steep, then the intersection point might fall under a neighboring lenslet. This causes a repeating "zoning" pattern which can be eliminated by limiting the viewing range or by embedding blockers in the lens array.

Since each lenslet acts as a view-dependent pixel, the entire lens array acts as a view-dependent, autostereoscopic image. The complete lens array system can be seen in Figure 16. Underneath each lenslet is a view of the object from a virtual camera located at each lenslet's principal point.

To create the autostereoscopic image from a dynamically reparameterized light field, we position a model of the lens array into our light field scene. This is analogous to positioning a desired camera to take a standard image. We then create an array of tiny sub-images, each the size of a lenslet. Each sub-image is created using our dynamically reparameterized light field system, with the focal surface passing through the object of interest. Each sub-image is taken from the principal point of a lenslet, with the image plane parallel to the flat face of the lens array. The sub-images are then composited together to create a large image, as in the background of Figure 15, which can be placed under the lens array.

The placement and orientation of the lens array determines if the viewed light field will appear in front or behind the display. If the

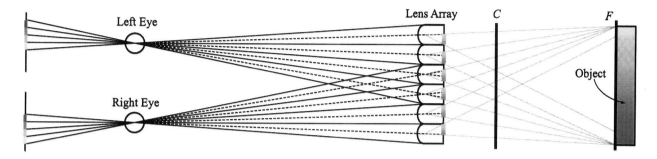

Figure 16: A light field can be reparameterized into a directly viewed light field, which operates on the principals of integral photography.

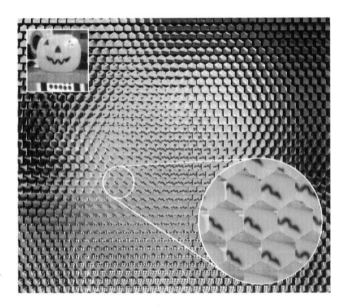

Figure 15: An autostereoscopic light field is drawn in the background. The scene is a three-dimensional version of the small inset picture in the upper left corner. The zoom is 400% magnification.

lens array is placed in front of the object, then the object will appear behind the display. Because the lens array image is rendered from a light field and not directly from an integral camera, we can place the lens array image behind the captured object, and the object will appear to float in front of the display.

9 Results

The light field data sets shown in this paper were created as follows. The tree data set was rendered in Povray 3.1. It is composed of 256 (16 x 16) images with resolutions of 320 x 240. The captured data sets were acquired with an Electrim EDC1000E CCD camera (654 x 496) with a fixed-focal length 16mm lens mounted on an X-Y motion platform from Arrick Robotics (30" x 30" displacement). For each set we captured either 256 (16 x 16) or 1024 (32 x 32) pictures. To calibrate the camera, we originally used a Faro Arm (a sub-millimeter accurate contact digitizer) to measure the spatial coordinates of targets on a three-dimensional calibration pattern. Using an image of the targets, we used the Tsai-Lenz camera calibration algorithm [26] which reported focal length, CCD sensor element aspect ratio, principle point, and extrinsic rotational orientation. The radial lens distortion reported for our lens was less than

1 pixel per 1000 pixels, and we decided not to correct for it. Finally, we resampled the raw 654 x 496 images down to 327 x 248 before using them as input to the renderer.

Recently, we have experimented with an alternative calibration method that requires no 3D measurements and uses the actual light field images rather than images of a special calibration object. This approach has some similarities with a family of techniques known as "self-calibration" [5]. However, our light field capture system, where a non-rotating camera is translated in a plane, is a degenerate case for true self-calibration [25]. Instead, we align the epipolar geometries of the source images rather than compute an actual calibration. Our method amounts to a two-axis rectification [1]. If the camera's optical axis is roughly perpendicular to the plane of motion and the X-Y platform's motion is reasonably accurate, then such a rectification is easily found. We find the epipolar planes induced by the horizontal and vertical camera motion by tracking a few corresponding image points. This can be done either automatically or by hand. The images are then rectified by a rotating their epipoles onto the line at infinity. The final rectified images will have valid horizontal and vertical EPI structures and can be immediately used in our light field viewer. However, when a user navigates within the scene they might notice a projective distortion of the space. This distortion can be ameliorated by allowing the user to interactively adjust the focal length of the data cameras. Otherwise, the focal length can be estimated by measuring a few points in the scene. In our experiments, it has been easy to create light fields using this method, and the final results are comparable to our strictly calibrated data sets.

Our autostereoscopic images were printed at 300dpi on a Tektronics Phaser 440 dye-sublimation printer and use a Fresnel Technologies #300 Hex Lens Array, with approximately 134 lenses per square inch [6].

10 Future Work

Light fields contain a large amount of redundancy which we would like to exploit. We would like to develop an algorithm for optimally selecting a focal plane, perhaps using auto-focus techniques similar to those used in consumer camcorders. Currently, the focal plane must be placed manually. In addition, we believe there is some promise in using our reparameterization techniques for passive depth-from-focus or depth-from-defocus vision algorithms [18]. In the left column of Figure 17, we have created two images with different focal surfaces and a large aperture. We then apply a gradient magnitude filter to these images, which give us the output to the right. These edge images tell us where in-focus, high-frequency energy exists. We would also like to experiment with depth-from-defocus by comparing two images with slightly different focal planes or apertures.

Figure 17: We believe our techniques can be used in a depth-from-focus or depth-from-defocus vision system. By applying a gradient magnitude filter on an image created with a wide aperture, we can detect in-focus regions.

Figure 18: Moving the focal plane within a deep scene.

11 Conclusion

Previous implementations have tried to solve focusing problems in undersampled light fields by 1) using scenes that were roughly planar, 2) using aperture filtering to bandlimit the input data, or 3) using approximate geometry for depth-correction. Unfortunately, most scenes can not be confined to a single plane, aperture filtering can not be undone or controlled at run time, and proxy surfaces can be difficult to obtain. We have presented a new parameterization that enables dynamic, run-time control of the sample reconstruction. This allows the user to modify focus and depth-of-field dynamically. This new parameterization allows light fields to capture deep scenes at moderate sampling rates. In addition, we have presented a strategy for creating directly-viewable light fields. These passive, autostereoscopic light fields can be viewed without head-mounted hardware by multiple viewers simultaneously under variable lighting conditions.

12 Acknowledgments

This work was supported by NTT, Fresnel Technologies, Hughes Research, and an NSF fellowship. Thanks to Ramy Sadek and Annie Sun Choi for illustrations, assistance, support, and proofreading. Thanks to Robert W. Sumner for his LaTeX experience and to Chris Buehler for many helpful light field discussions and DirectX help. Thanks to Neil Alexander for the "Alexander Bay" tree scene and to Christopher Carlson for permission to use Bumpé in our scenes. Finally, thanks to the entire MIT LCS Computer Graphics Group, especially Bryt Bradley for her administrative support.

References

[1] Nicholas Ayache and Charles Hansen. Rectification of images for binocular and trinocular stereovision. In *ICPR88*, pages 11–16, 1988.

[2] R.C. Bolles, H.H. Baker, and D.H. Marimont. Epipolar-plane image analysis: An approach to determining structure from motion. *IJCV*, 1(1):7–56, 1987.

[3] Emilio Camahort, Apostolos Lerios, and Donald Fussell. Uniformly sampled light fields. *Eurographics Rendering Workshop 1998*, pages 117–130, 1998.

[4] J.-X. Chai, X. Tong, S.-C. Chan, and H.-Y. Shum. Plenoptic sampling. In *SIGGRAPH 2000*, 2000.

[5] Olivier D. Faugeras. What can be seen in three dimensions with an uncalibrated stereo rig? In *ECCV92*, pages 563–578, 1992.

[6] Fresnel Technologies. *#300 Hex Lens Array*, 1999. http://www.fresneltech.com.

[7] Steven J. Gortler, Radek Grzeszczuk, Richard Szeliski, and Michael F. Cohen. The lumigraph. *SIGGRAPH 96*, pages 43–54, 1996.

[8] Xianfeng Gu, Steven J. Gortler, and Michael F. Cohen. Polyhedral geometry and the two-plane parameterization. *Eurographics Rendering Workshop 1997*, pages 1–12, June 1997.

[9] Paul E. Haeberli and Kurt Akeley. The accumulation buffer: Hardware support for high-quality rendering. *SIGGRAPH 90*, 24(4):309–318, 1990.

[10] Michael Halle. The generalized holographic stereogram. Master's thesis, Program in Media Arts and Sciences, Massachusetts Institute of Technology, 1991.

[11] Wolfgang Heidrich, Philipp Slusalek, and Hans-Peter Seidel. An image-based model for realistic lens systems in interactive computer graphics. *Graphics Interface '97*, pages 68–75, 1997.

[12] Aaron Isaksen, Leonard McMilland, and Steven J. Gortler. Dynamically reparameterized light fields. Technical Report LCS-TR-778, Massachusetts Institute of Technology, May 1999.

[13] Marc Levoy and Pat Hanrahan. Light field rendering. *SIGGRAPH 96*, pages 31–42, 1996.

[14] Microsoft Corporation. *Microsoft DirectX 7.0*, 1999. http://www.microsoft.com/directx.

[15] Don P. Mitchell and Arun N. Netravali. Reconstruction filters in computer graphics. *SIGGRAPH 88*, 22(4):221–228, 1988.

[16] Takanori Okoshi. *Three-Dimensional Imaging Techniques*. Academic Press, Inc., New York, 1976.

[17] Paul Haeberli. A multifocus method for controlling depth of field. Technical report, SGI, October 1994. http://www.sgi.com/grafica/depth/index.html.

[18] A.P. Pentland. A new sense for depth of field. *PAMI*, 9(4):523–531, July 1987.

[19] Matthew J.P. Regan, Gavin S.P. Miller, Steven M. Rubin, and Chris Kogelnik. A real time low-latency hardware light-field renderer. *SIGGRAPH 99*, pages 287–290, 1999.

[20] Hartmut Schirmacher, Wolfgang Heidrich, and Hans-Peter Seidel. Adaptive acquisition of lumigraphs from synthetic scenes. *Computer Graphics Forum*, 18(3):151–160, September 1999. ISSN 1067-7055.

[21] Heung-Yeung Shum and Li-Wei He. Rendering with concentric mosaics. *SIGGRAPH 99*, pages 299–306, 1999.

[22] Peter-Pike Sloan, Michael F. Cohen, and Steven J. Gortler. Time critical lumigraph rendering. *1997 Symposium on Interactive 3D Graphics*, pages 17–24, April 1997. ISBN 0-89791-884-3.

[23] Warren J. Smith. *Practical Optical System Layout*. McGraw-Hill, 1997.

[24] R. F. Stevens and N. Davies. Lens arrays and photography. *Journal of Photographic Science*, 39(5):199–208, 1991.

[25] Peter Sturm. Critical motion sequences for monocular self-calibration and uncalibrated euclidean reconstruction. In *CVPR97*, pages 1100–1105, 1997.

[26] R.Y. Tsai. An efficient and accurate camera calibration technique for 3-d machine vision. In *CVPR*, pages 364–374, 1986.

[27] L. Yang, M. McCormick, and N. Davies. Discussion of the optics of a new 3d imaging system. *Applied Optics*, 27(21):4529–4534, 1988.

[28] Z.Y. Zhang. Flexible camera calibration by viewing a plane from unknown orientations. In *ICCV*, pages 666–673, 1999.

Plenoptic Sampling

Jin-Xiang Chai*   Xin Tong   Shing-Chow Chan†   Heung-Yeung Shum‡

Microsoft Research, China

Abstract

This paper studies the problem of **plenoptic sampling** in image-based rendering (IBR). From a spectral analysis of light field signals and using the sampling theorem, we mathematically derive the analytical functions to determine the **minimum sampling rate** for light field rendering. The spectral support of a light field signal is bounded by the minimum and maximum depths only, no matter how complicated the spectral support might be because of depth variations in the scene. The minimum sampling rate for light field rendering is obtained by compacting the replicas of the spectral support of the sampled light field within the smallest interval. Given the minimum and maximum depths, a reconstruction filter with an optimal and constant depth can be designed to achieve anti-aliased light field rendering.

Plenoptic sampling goes beyond the minimum number of images needed for anti-aliased light field rendering. More significantly, it utilizes the scene depth information to determine the **minimum sampling curve** in the joint image and geometry space. The minimum sampling curve quantitatively describes the relationship among three key elements in IBR systems: scene complexity (geometrical and textural information), the number of image samples, and the output resolution. Therefore, plenoptic sampling bridges the gap between image-based rendering and traditional geometry-based rendering. Experimental results demonstrate the effectiveness of our approach.

Keywords: sampling, plenoptic sampling, spectral analysis, plenoptic functions, image-based rendering.

1 Introduction

Image-based modeling and rendering techniques have recently received much attention as a powerful alternative to traditional geometry-based techniques for image synthesis. Instead of geometrical primitives, a collection of sample images are used to render novel views. Previous work on image-based rendering (IBR) reveals a continuum of image-based representations [15, 14] based on the tradeoff between how many input images are needed and how much is known about the scene geometry.

At one end, traditional texture mapping relies on very accurate geometrical models but only a few images. In an image-based rendering system with depth maps, such as 3D warping [18], view

---

*Currently at Carnegie Mellon University. jchai@cs.cmu.edu

†Visiting from University of Hong Kong. scchan@eee.hku.hk

‡{xtong,hshum}@microsoft.com

interpolation [7], view morphing [21] and layered-depth images (LDI) [22], LDI tree [6], etc., the model consists of a set of images of a scene and their associated depth maps. When depth is available for every point in an image, the image can be rendered from any nearby point of view by projecting the pixels of the image to their proper 3D locations and re-projecting them onto a new picture.

At the other end, light field rendering uses many images but does not require any geometrical information. Light field rendering [16] generates a new image of a scene by appropriately filtering and interpolating a pre-acquired set of samples. Lumigraph [10] is similar to light field rendering but it applies approximated geometry to compensate for non-uniform sampling in order to improve rendering performance. Unlike light field and Lumigraph where cameras are placed on a two-dimensional manifold, Concentric Mosaics system [23] reduces the amount of data by only capturing a sequence of images along a circular path. Light field rendering, however, typically relies on oversampling to counter undesirable aliasing effects in output display. Oversampling means more intensive data acquisition, more storage, and more redundancy. To date, little research has been done on determining the lower bound or the minimum number of samples needed for light field rendering.

Sampling analysis in IBR is a difficult problem because it involves the complex relationship among three elements: the depth and texture information of the scene, the number of sample images, and the rendering resolution. The topic of prefiltering a light field has been explored in [16]. Similar filtering process has been previously discussed by Halle [11] in the context of Holographic stereograms. A parameterization for more uniform sampling [4] has also been proposed. From an initially undersampled Lumigraph, new views can be adaptively acquired if the rendering quality can be improved [20]. An opposite approach is to start with an oversampled light field, and to cull an input view if it can be predicted by its neighboring frames [12, 24]. Using a geometrical approach and without considering textural information of the scene, Lin and Shum [17] recently studied the number of samples needed in light field rendering with constant depth assumption and bilinear interpolation. However, a mathematical framework has not been fully developed for studying the sampling problems in IBR.

In this paper, we study *plenoptic sampling*, or how many samples are needed for plenoptic modeling [19, 1]. Plenoptic sampling can be stated as:

How many samples of the plenoptic function (e.g., from a 4D light field) and how much geometrical and textural information are needed to generate a continuous representation of the plenoptic function?

Specifically, our objective in this paper is to tackle the following two problems under plenoptic sampling, with and without geometrical information:

- Minimum sampling rate for light field rendering;

- Minimum sampling curve in joint image and geometry space.

We formulate the sampling analysis as a high dimensional signal processing problem. In our analysis, we assume Lambertian surfaces and uniform sampling geometry or lattice for the light field.

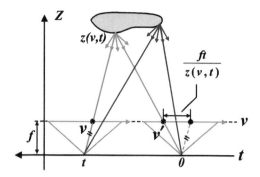 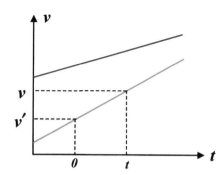

Figure 1: An illustration of 2D light field or EPI: (a) a point is observed by two cameras 0 and t; (b) two lines are formed by stacking pixels captured along the camera path. Each line has a uniform color because of Lambertian assumption on object surfaces.

Rather than attempting to obtain a closed-form general solution to the $4D$ light field spectral analysis, we only analyze the bounds of the spectral support of the light field signals. A key analysis to be presented in this paper is that the spectral support of a light field signal is bounded by only the minimum and maximum depths, irrespective of how complicated the spectral support might be because of depth variations in the scene. Given the minimum and maximum depths, a reconstruction filter with an optimal and constant depth can be designed to achieve anti-aliased light field rendering.

The minimum sampling rate of light field rendering is obtained by compacting the replicas of the spectral support of the sampled light field within the smallest interval without any overlap. Using more depth information, plenoptic sampling in the joint image and geometry space allows us to greatly reduce the number of images needed. In fact, the relationship between the number of images and the geometrical information under a given rendering resolution can be quantitatively described by a minimum sampling curve. This minimal sampling curve serves as the design principles for IBR systems. Furthermore, it bridges the gap between image-based rendering and traditional geometry-based rendering.

Our approach is inspired by the work on motion compensation filter in the area of digital video processing, in which depth information has been incorporated into the design of the optimal motion compensation filter [25, 9]. In digital video processing, global constant depth and arbitrary motion are considered for both static and dynamic scenes, whereas in our work, we analyze static scenes with an arbitrary geometry and with uniformly sampled camera setups.

The remainder of this paper is organized as follows. In Section 2, a spectral analysis of $4D$ light field is introduced and the bounds of its spectral support are determined. From these bounds, the minimum sampling rate for light field rendering can be derived analytically. Plenoptic sampling in the joint image and geometry space is studied in Section 3. The minimum sampling curves are deduced with accurate and approximated depths. Experimental results are presented in Section 4. Finally we conclude our paper in Section 5.

2 Spectral analysis of light field

2.1 Light field representation

We begin by briefly reviewing the properties of light field representation. We will follow the notations in the Lumigraph paper [10]. In the standard two-plane ray database parameterization, there is a camera plane, with parameter (s, t), and a focal plane, with parameter (u, v). Each ray in the parameterization is uniquely determined by the quadruple (u, v, s, t). We refer the reader to Figure 2(a) of [10] for more details.

A two dimensional subspace given by fixed values of s and t resembles an image, whereas fixed values of u and v give a hypo-

thetical radiance function. Fixing t and v gives rise to an epipolar image, or EPI [3]. An example of a 2D light field or EPI is shown in Figure 1. Note that in our analysis we define (u, v) in the local coordinates of (s, t), unlike in conventional light field where (u, v, s, t) are defined in a global coordinate system.

Assume the sample intervals along s and t directions be Δs and Δt, respectively, the horizontal and vertical disparities between two grid cameras in the (s, t) plane are determined by $k_1 \Delta s f / z$ and $k_2 \Delta t f / z$, respectively, where f denotes the focal length of the camera, z is the depth value and $(k_1 \Delta s, k_2 \Delta t)$ is the sample interval between two grid points (s, t).

Similarly, we assume that the sample intervals along u and v directions be Δu and Δv, respectively. A pinhole camera model is adopted to capture the light field. What a camera sees is a blurred version of the plenoptic function because of finite camera resolution. A pixel value is a weighted integral of the illumination of the light arriving at the camera plane, or the convolution of the plenoptic function with a low-pass filter.

2.2 A framework for light field reconstruction

Let $l(u, v, s, t)$ represent the continuous light field, $p(u, v, s, t)$ the sampling pattern in light field, $r(u, v, s, t)$ the combined filtering and interpolating low-pass filter, and $i(u, v, s, t)$ the output image after reconstruction. Let L, P, R and I represent their corresponding spectra, respectively. In the spatial domain, the light field reconstruction can be computed as

$$i(u, v, s, t) = r(u, v, s, t) * [l(u, v, s, t)p(u, v, s, t)] \quad (1)$$

where $*$ represents the convolution operation.

In the frequency domain, we have

$$I(\Omega_u, \Omega_v, \Omega_s, \Omega_t) = R(\Omega_u, \Omega_v, \Omega_s, \Omega_t)(L(\Omega_u, \Omega_v, \Omega_s, \Omega_t) \\ *P(\Omega_u, \Omega_v, \Omega_s, \Omega_t)) \quad (2)$$

The problem of light field reconstruction is to find a reconstruction filter $r(u, v, s, t)$ for anti-aliased light field rendering, given the sampled light field signals.

2.3 Spectral support of light fields

In this section, we will introduce the spectral supports of continuous light field $L(\Omega_u, \Omega_v, \Omega_s, \Omega_t)$ and sampled light field $L(\Omega_u, \Omega_v, \Omega_s, \Omega_t) * P(\Omega_u, \Omega_v, \Omega_s, \Omega_t)$.

2.3.1 Spectral support of continuous light field

We assume that the depth function of the scene is equal to $z(u, v, s, t)$. As shown in Figure 1(a), the same 3D point is observed at v' and v in the local coordinate systems of cameras 0 and

t, respectively. The disparity between the two image coordinates can be computed easily as $v - v' = ft/z$. Figure 1(b) shows an EPI image where each line represents the radiance observed from different cameras. For simplicity of analysis, the BRDF model of a real scene is assumed to be Lambertian. Therefore, each line in Figure 1(b) has a uniform color.

Therefore, the radiance received at the camera position (s, t) is given by

$$l(u, v, s, t) = l(u - \frac{fs}{z(u, v, s, t)}, v - \frac{ft}{z(u, v, s, t)}, 0, 0)$$

and its Fourier transform is

$$L(\Omega_u, \Omega_v, \Omega_s, \Omega_t) = \int_{-\infty}^{\infty} \int_{-\infty}^{\infty} \int_{-\infty}^{\infty} l(u, v, s, t)e^{-j\Omega^T \mathbf{x}} d\mathbf{x}$$
$$e^{-j(\Omega_s s + \Omega_t t)} ds dt \quad (3)$$

where $x^T = [u, v]$ and $\Omega^T = [\Omega_u, \Omega_v]$.

However, computing the Fourier transform (3) is very complicated, and we will not go into the details of its derivation in this paper. Instead, we will analyze the bounds of the spectral support of light fields. Also for simplicity, it is assumed that samples of the light field are taken over the commonly used rectangular sampling lattice.

2.3.2 Spectral support of sampled light field

Using the rectangular sampling lattice, the sampled light field $l_s(u, v, s, t)$ is represented by

$$l_s(u, v, s, t) = l(u, v, s, t) \sum_{n_1, n_2, k_1, k_2 \in Z}$$
$$\delta(u - n_1\Delta u)\delta(v - n_2\Delta v)\delta(s - k_1\Delta s)\delta(t - k_2\Delta t) \quad (4)$$

and its Fourier transform is

$$L_s(\Omega_u, \Omega_v, \Omega_s, \Omega_t) = \sum_{m_1, m_2, l_1, l_2 \in Z}$$
$$L(\Omega_u - \frac{2\pi m_1}{\Delta u}, \Omega_v - \frac{2\pi m_2}{\Delta v}, \Omega_s - \frac{2\pi l_1}{\Delta s}, \Omega_t - \frac{2\pi l_2}{\Delta t}) \quad (5)$$

The above equation indicates that $L_s(\Omega_u, \Omega_v, \Omega_s, \Omega_t)$ consists of replicas of $L(\Omega_u, \Omega_v, \Omega_s, \Omega_t)$, shifted to the $4D$ grid points

$$(2\pi m_1/\Delta u, 2\pi m_2/\Delta v, 2\pi l_1/\Delta s, 2\pi l_2/\Delta t),$$

where $m_1, m_2, l_1, l_2 \in Z$, and Z is the set of integers.

These shifted spectra, or replicas, except the original one at $m_1 = m_2 = l_1 = l_2 = 0$, are called the alias components. When L is not bandlimited outside the Nyquist frequencies, some replicas will overlap with the others, creating aliasing artifacts.

In general, there are two ways to combat aliasing effects in output display when we render a novel image. First, we can increase the sampling rate. The higher the sampling rate, the less the aliasing effects. Indeed, uniform oversampling has been consistently employed in many IBR systems to avoid undesirable aliasing effects. However, oversampling means more effort in data acquisition and requires more storage. Though redundancy in the oversampled image database can be partially eliminated by compression, excessive samples are always wasteful.

Second, light field signals can also be made bandlimited by filtering with an appropriate filter kernel. Similar filtering has to be performed to remove the overlapping of alias components during reconstruction or rendering. The design of such a kernel is, however, related to the depth of the scene. Previous work on Lumigraph shows that approximate depth correction can significantly improve

the interpolation results. The questions are: is there an optimal filter? Given the number of samples captured, how accurately should the depth be recovered? Similarly, given the depth information one can recover, how many samples can be removed from the original input?

2.4 Analysis of bounds in spectral support

2.4.1 A model of global constant depth

Let us first consider the simplest scene model in which every point is at a constant depth (z_0). The first frame is chosen as the reference frame, and $l(u, v, 0, 0)$ denotes the 2D intensity distribution within the reference frame. The 4D Fourier transform of the light field signal $l(u, v, s, t)$ with constant depth is

$$L(\Omega_u, \Omega_v, \Omega_s, \Omega_t) = \int_{-\infty}^{\infty} \int_{-\infty}^{\infty} l(u, v, 0, 0)e^{-j(\Omega_u u + \Omega_v v)} du dv$$
$$\int_{-\infty}^{\infty} e^{-j(\frac{f}{z_0}\Omega_u + \Omega_s)s} ds \int_{-\infty}^{\infty} e^{-j(\frac{f}{z_0}\Omega_v + \Omega_t)t} dt$$
$$= 4\pi^2 L'(\Omega_u, \Omega_v)\delta(\frac{f}{z_0}\Omega_u + \Omega_s)\delta(\frac{f}{z_0}\Omega_v + \Omega_t)$$

where $L'(\Omega_u, \Omega_v)$ is the 2D Fourier transform of continuous signal $l(u, v, 0, 0)$ and $\delta(\cdot)$ is the 1D Dirac delta function. To keep notation, representations and illustration simple, the following discussion will focus on the projection of the support of $L(\Omega_u, \Omega_v, \Omega_s, \Omega_t)$ onto the (Ω_v, Ω_t) plane, which is denoted by $L(\Omega_v, \Omega_t)$.

Under the constant depth model, the spectral support of the continuous light field signal $L(\Omega_v, \Omega_t)$ is defined by a line $\Omega_v f/z_0 + \Omega_t = 0$, as shown in Figure 2(b). The spectral support of the corresponding sampled light field signals is shown in Figure 2(c). Note that, due to sampling, replicas of $L(\Omega_v, \Omega_t)$ appear at intervals $2\pi m_2/\Delta v$ and $2\pi l_2/\Delta t$ in the Ω_v and Ω_t directions, respectively.

Figure 6(a) shows a constant depth scene (a1), its EPI image (a2), and the Fourier transform of the EPI (a3). As expected, the spectral support is a straight line.[1]

2.4.2 Spatially varying depth model

Now it is straightforward to observe that any scene with a depth between the minimum z_{min} and the maximum z_{max} will have its continuous spectral support bounded in the frequency domain, by two lines $\Omega_v f/z_{min} + \Omega_t = 0$ and $\Omega_v f/z_{max} + \Omega_t = 0$. Figure 6(b3) shows the spectral support when two planes with constant depths are in the scene. Adding another tilted plane in between (Figure 6(c1)) results in no variations in the bounds of the spectral support, even though the resulting spectral support (Figure 6(c3)) differs significantly from that in Figure 6(c2). This is further illustrated when a curved surface is inserted in between two original planes, as shown in Figure 6(d1). Even though the spectral supports differ significantly, Figures 6(b3), (c3) and (d3) all have the same bounds.

Another important observation is that geometrical information can help to reduce the bounds of the spectral support in the frequency domain. As will be illustrated in the following section, the optimal reconstruction filter is determined precisely by the bounds of the spectral support. And these bounds are functions of the minimum and maximum depths of the scene. If some information on the scene geometry is known, we can decompose the scene geometry into a collection of constant depth models on a block-by-block basis. Each model will have a much tighter bound than the original model. How tight the bound is will depend on the accuracy

---

[1] The ringing effect in the vicinity of the horizontal and vertical axes is caused by convolving with $\sin(\Omega_v)/\Omega_v$ because of the rectangular image boundary.

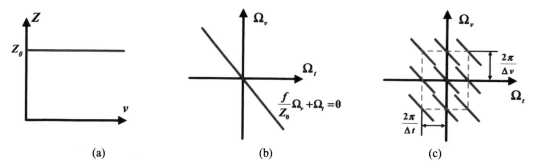

Figure 2: Spectral support of light field signals with constant depth: (a) a model of constant depth; (b) the spectral support of continuous light field signals; (c) the spectral support of sampled light field signals.

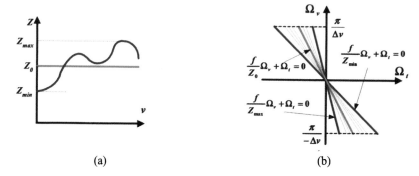

Figure 3: Spectral support for light field signal with spatially varying depths: (a) a local constant depth model bounded by z_{min} and z_{max} is augmented with another depth value z_0; (b)spectral support is now bounded by two smaller regions, with the introduction of the new line of z_0.

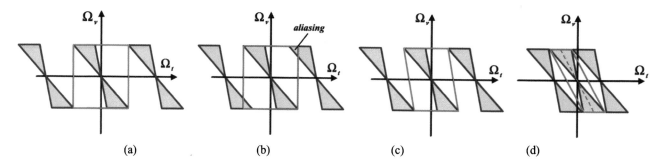

Figure 4: Three reconstruction filters with different constant depths: (a) infinite depth; (b) infinite depth (aliasing occurs); (c) maximum depth; (d) optimal depth at z_c.

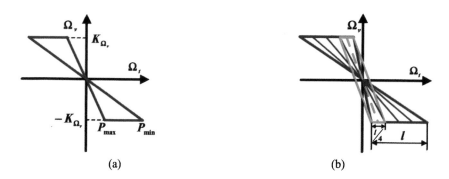

Figure 5: (a) The smallest interval that replicas can be packed without any overlap is $P_{max}P_{min}$, determined by the highest frequency K_{Ω_v}. (b) A spectral support decomposed into multiple layers.

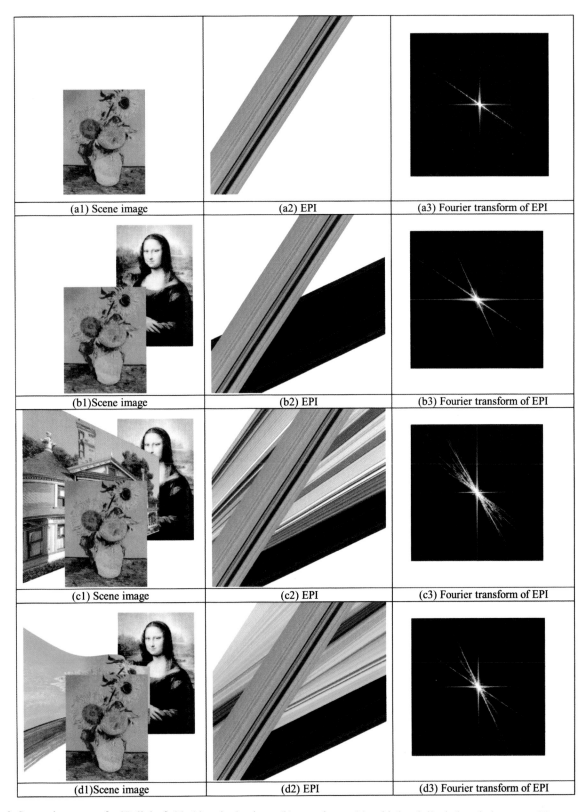

Figure 6: Spectral support of a 2D light field: (a) a single plane; (b) two planes; (c) a third and tilted plane in between; (d) a curved surface in between.

of the geometry. Figure 3 illustrates the reduction in bounds, from $[z_{min}, z_{max}]$ to $\max([z_{min}, z_0], [z_0, z_{max}])$, with the introduction of another layer.

2.4.3 A model with truncating windows

Because of the linearity of the Fourier transform, the spectral support of the EPI image for a scene with two constant planes will be two straight lines. However, this statement is true only if these two planes do not occlude each other. For synthetic environments, we can construct such EPI images on different layers by simply ignoring the occlusion.

In practice, we can represent a complicated environment using a model with truncating windows. For example, we can approximate an environment using truncated and piece-wise constant depth segments. Specifically, suppose the depth can be partitioned as

$$z(v) = z_i, \text{ for } v_i \leq v < v_{i+1}, \, i = 1, \cdots, N_d$$

where v_1 and v_{N_d+1} are the smallest and largest v of interest respectively. Then

$$l(v,t) = l_i(v - ft/z_i, 0), \text{ if } v_i \leq v < v_{i+1}$$

and

$$
\begin{aligned}
L(\Omega_v, \Omega_t) &= \sum_{i=1}^{N_d} \exp(-j\frac{v_i + v_{i+1}}{2}(\Omega_v + \Omega_t z_i/f)) \\
&\quad \frac{2\sin(\frac{v_{i+1}-v_i}{2}(\Omega_v + \Omega_t z_i/f))}{f\Omega_v/z_i + \Omega_t} L_i(-\Omega_t z_i/f) \\
&\equiv \sum_{i=1}^{N_d} Q_i(\Omega_v, \Omega_t)
\end{aligned}
\tag{6}
$$

where L_i is the $1D$ Fourier transform of l_i.

In (6), because the function $\frac{\sin x}{x}$ decays fast, and $L_i(-\Omega_t z_i/f)$ also decreases fast when $|\Omega_t|$ grows, the spectral support of $Q_i(\Omega_v, \Omega_t)$ will look like a narrow ellipse. Nevertheless, because of high frequency leak, cut-off frequency should be used in the sampling analysis.

An example of two constant planes in an environment is shown in Figures 6(b1) (original image), 6(b2) (EPI) and 6(b3) (spectral support). Note that the shape of each of the two spectral supports, i.e., two approximated lines, is not significantly affected by occlusion because the width of each spectral support is not too large.

2.5 A reconstruction filter using a constant depth

Given a constant depth, a reconstruction filter can be designed. Figure 4 illustrates four different designs of reconstruction filters oriented to different constant depths. Aliasing occurs when replicas overlap with the reconstruction filters in the frequency domain (Ω_t and Ω_v), as shown in Figure 4(a)(b)(d). Anti-aliased light field rendering can be achieved by applying the optimal filter as shown in Figure 4(c), where the optimal constant depth is defined as the inverse of average disparity d_c, i.e.,

$$d_c = \frac{1}{z_c} = (\frac{1}{z_{min}} + \frac{1}{z_{max}})/2.$$

Figure 7 shows the effect of applying reconstruction filters with different constant depths. As we sweep through the object with a constant depth plane, the aliasing effect is the worst at the minimum and maximum depths. The best rendering quality is obtained at the optimal depth (Figure 7(b)), not at the focal plane as has been commonly assumed in light field [16] or Lumigraph [10] rendering. In fact, the optimal depth can be used as a guidance for selecting

the focal plane. For comparison, we also show the rendering result using average depth in Figure 7(c).

Similar sweeping effects have also been discussed in the dynamically reparameterized light field [13]. However, an analytical solution using the minimum and maximum depths has never been presented before.

2.6 Minimum sampling rate for light field rendering

With the above theoretical analysis, we are now ready to solve the problem of the minimum sampling rate for light field rendering. Since we are dealing with rectangular sampling lattice, the Nyquist sampling theorem for 1D signal applies to both directions v and t. According to the Nyquist sampling theorem, in order for a signal to be reconstructed without aliasing, the sampling frequency needs to be greater than the Nyquist rate, or two times that of the Nyquist frequency. Without loss of generality, we only study the Nyquist frequency along the Ω_t direction in the frequency domain. However, the Nyquist frequency along the Ω_v direction can be analyzed in a similar way.

The minimum interval, by which the replicas of spectral support can be packed without any overlapping, can be computed as shown in Figure 5(a)

$$|P_{max}P_{min}| = K_{\Omega_v} fh_d = 2\pi K_{f_v} fh_d \tag{7}$$

where

$$h_d = \frac{1}{z_{min}} - \frac{1}{z_{max}},$$

and

$$K_{f_v} fh_d = \min(B_v^s, 1/(2\Delta v), 1/(2\delta v))$$

is the highest frequency for the light field signal, which is determined by the scene texture distribution (represented by the highest frequency B_v^s), the resolution of the sampling camera (Δv), and the resolution of the rendering camera (δv). The frequency B_v^s can be computed from the spectral support of the light field. Our formulation takes the rendering resolution into account because rendering at a resolution higher than the output resolution is wasteful. For simplicity, we assume $\delta v = \Delta v$ from now on.

The minimum sampling rate is equivalent to the maximum camera spacing Δt_{max}, which can be computed as

$$\Delta t_{max} = \frac{1}{K_{f_v} fh_d}. \tag{8}$$

The minimum sampling rate can also be interpreted in terms of the maximum disparity defined as the projection error using the optimal reconstruction filter for rendering. From Equation 8, we have the maximum disparity

$$\Delta t_{max} fh_d/2 = \frac{1}{2K_{f_v}} = \max(\Delta v, 1/(2B_v^s)). \tag{9}$$

Therefore, the disparity is less than 1 pixel (i.e., the camera resolution) or half cycle of the highest frequency ($1/B_v^s$ is defined as a cycle) presented in the EPI image because of the textural complexity of the observed scene.

If the textural complexity of the scene is not considered, the minimum sampling rate for light field rendering can also be derived in the spatial domain. For example, by considering the light field rendering as a synthetic aperture optical system, we present an optical analysis of light field rendering in Appendix A.

The maximum camera spacing will be larger if the scene texture variation gets more uniform, or if the rendering camera resolution becomes lower. By setting the higher frequency part of the spectrum to zero so that $B_v^s < 1/(2\Delta v)$, we can reduce the minimum sampling rate. One way to reduce B_v^s is to apply a low-pass filter to

  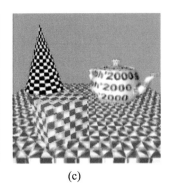 

(a)   (b)   (c)   (d)

Figure 7: Sweeping a constant depth plane through an object: (a) at the minimum depth; (b) at the optimal plane; (c) at the average distance between minimum and maximum depths; (d) at the maximum depth. The best rendering quality is achieved in (b).

the input v-t image. This approach is similar to prefiltering a light field (see Figure 7 in [16]).

In particular, the minimum sampling rate is also determined by the relative depth variation $f(z_{min}^{-1} - z_{max}^{-1})$. The closer the object gets to the camera, the smaller the z_{min} is, and the higher the minimum sampling rate will be. As f gets larger, the sampling camera will cover a more detailed scene, but the minimum sampling rate needs to be increased. Therefore, the plenoptic sampling problem should not be considered in the image space alone, but in the joint image and geometry space.

3 Minimum sampling in the joint image and geometry space

In this section, we will study the minimum sampling problem in the joint geometry and image space. Since the CPU speed, memory, storage space, graphics capability and network bandwidth used vary from users to users, it is very important for users to be able to seek the most economical balance between image samples and depth layers for a given rendering quality.

It is interesting to note that the minimum sampling rate for light field rendering represents essentially one point in the joint image and geometry space, in which little amount of depth information has been utilized. As more geometrical information becomes available, fewer images are necessary at any given rendering resolution. Figure 8 illustrates the minimum sampling rate in the image space, the minimum sampling curve in the joint image and geometry space, and minimum sampling curves at different rendering resolutions. Any sampling point above the minimum sampling curve (e.g., Figure 8b) is redundant.

3.1 Minimum sampling with accurate depth

From an initial set of accurate geometrical data, we can decompose a scene into multiple layers of sub-regions. Accordingly, the whole spectral support can be decomposed into multiple layers (see Figure 5b) due to the correspondence between a constant depth and its spectral support. For each decomposed spectral support, an optimal constant depth filter can be designed. Specifically, for each depth layer $i = 1, \ldots, N_d$, the depth of optimal filter is described as follows

$$\frac{1}{z_i} = \lambda_i \frac{1}{z_{min}} + (1 - \lambda_i) \frac{1}{z_{max}} \tag{10}$$

where

$$\lambda_i = \frac{i - 0.5}{N_d}$$

Therefore a depth value can be assigned to one of the depth layers $z = z_i$ if

$$\frac{-h_d}{2N_d} \leq \frac{1}{z} - \frac{1}{z_i} \leq \frac{h_d}{2N_d}. \tag{11}$$

The layers are quantized uniformly in the disparity space. This is because perspective images have been used in the light fields. If we use parallel projection images instead, the quantization should be uniform in the depth space [5].

Similar to Equation 8, the minimum sampling in the joint image and accurate depth space is obtained when

$$\frac{\Delta t}{N_d} = \frac{1}{K_{f_v} f h_d}, \ N_d \geq 1 \tag{12}$$

where N_d and Δt are the number of depth layers and the sampling interval along the t direction, respectively. The interval between replicas is uniformly divided into N_d segments.

The number of depth layers needed for scene representation is a function of the sampling and rendering camera resolution, the scene's texture complexity, the spacing of the sampling cameras and the depth variation relative to the focal length.

3.1.1 Applications

Based on the above quantitative analysis in the joint image and depth space for sufficient rendering, a number of important applications can be explored.

- **Image-based geometry simplification.** Given the appropriate number of image samples an average user can afford, the minimum sampling curve in the joint space determines how much depth information is needed. Thus, it simplifies the original complex geometrical model to the minimum while still guaranteeing the same rendering quality.

- **Geometry-based image database reduction.** In contrast, given the number of depth layers available, the number of image samples needed can also be reduced to the minimum for a given rendering resolution. The reduction of image samples is particularly useful for light field rendering.

- **Level of details (LOD) in joint image and depth space.** The idea of LOD in geometry space can be adopted in our joint image and geometry space. When an object becomes farther away, its relative size on screen space diminishes so that the number of required image samples or the number of required depth layers can be reduced accordingly. Zooming-in onto and zooming-out of objects also demand a dynamic change in the number of image samples or depth layers.

- **Light field with layered depth.** A general data structure for the minimum sampling curve in the joint image and geometry space can be light field with layered depth. With different numbers of images and depth layers used, the trade-off between rendering speed and data storage has to be studied.

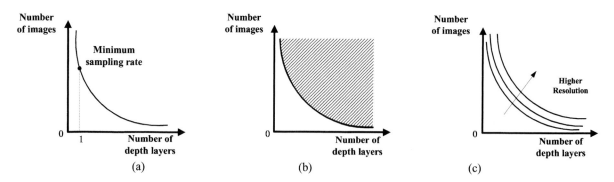

Figure 8: Plenoptic sampling: (a) the minimum sampling rate in image space; (b) the minimum sampling curve in the joint image and geometry space (any sampling point above the curve is redundant); (c) minimum sampling curves at different rendering resolutions.

3.2 Minimum sampling with depth uncertainty

Another aspect of minimum sampling in the joint image and geometry space is related to depth uncertainty. Specifically, minimum sampling with depth uncertainty describes the quantitative relationship between the number of image samples, noisy depth and depth uncertainty. It is important to study this relationship because in general the recovered geometry is noisy as modeling a real environment is difficult. Given an estimated depth z_e and its depth uncertainty $\Delta\eta$, the depth value should be located within the range $(z_e - \Delta\eta, z_e + \Delta\eta)$. The maximum camera spacing can be computed as

$$\Delta t_{max} = \min_{z_e} \frac{(z_e + \Delta\eta)(z_e - \Delta\eta)}{2fK_{f_v}\Delta\eta} = \frac{\min_{z_e} z_e^2 - \Delta\eta^2}{2fK_{f_v}\Delta\eta}. \quad (13)$$

In addition, geometrical uncertainty also exists when an accurate model is simplified. Given the correct depth z_0 and an estimated depth z_e, the maximum camera spacing can be computed as

$$\Delta t_{max} = \min_{z_e} \frac{z_e z_0}{2fK_{f_v}|z_e - z_0|}. \quad (14)$$

3.2.1 Applications

Knowledge about the minimum number of images under noisy depth has many practical applications.

- **Minimum sampling rate.** For a specific light field rendering with no depth maps or with noisy depth maps, we can determine the minimum number of images for antialiased light field rendering. Redundant image samples can then be left out from the sampled database for light field rendering.

- **Rendering-driven vision reconstruction.** This is a very interesting application, considering that general vision algorithms would not recover accurate scene depth. Given the number of image samples, how accurately should the depth be recovered to guarantee the rendering quality? Rendering-driven vision reconstruction is different from classical geometry-driven vision reconstruction in that the former is guided by the depth accuracy that the rendering process can have.

4   Experiments

Table 1 summarizes the parameters of each light field data set used in our experiments. We assume that the output display has the same resolution as the input image. Furthermore, without taking into consideration the actual texture distribution, we assume that the highest frequency in images is bounded by the resolution of the capturing camera.

We have used different settings of focal length for the Head, the Statue and the Table. We put the focal plane slightly in front of the Head. A smaller focal length will reduce the minimum sampling rate. For the Statue, the focal plane is set approximately at its forehead. In fact, we have set the focal length (3000) very close to the optimal (3323). Because the Table scene has significant depth variations, a small camera focal length was used so that each image can cover a large part of the scene.

First, we compare the rendering quality along the minimal sampling curve in the joint image and geometry space, with the best rendering quality we can obtain with all images and accurate depth. According to our theory (Eq (12)), the number of images is inversely proportional to the number of depth layers in use. The rendering results corresponding to five different image and depth combinations along the minimum sampling curve are shown in Figures 11(A)-(E). For example, C(7,8) represents the rendering result using 7 layers of depth and 8×8 images. In contrast, Figure 11(F) shows the best rendering output one can achieve from this set of data: accurate depth and all 32×32 images[2]. The quality of the rendered images along the minimal sampling curve is almost indistinguishable[3] from that of using all images and accurate depth.

Figure 12(a) compares the rendering quality using different layers of depth and a given number of image samples. With 2×2 image samples of the Head, images (A)-(E) in Figure 12(a) show the rendered images with different layers of depth at 4, 8, 10, 12, and 24. According to Eq (12), the minimum sampling point with 2×2 images of the Head is at approximately 12 layers of depth. Noticeable visual artifacts can be observed when the number of depth is below the minimal sampling point, as shown in images (A)-(C) of Figure 12(a). On the other hand, oversampling layers of depth does not improve the rendering quality, as shown in the images (D) and (E).

With the minimal sampling curve, we can now deduce the minimum number of image samples at any given number of depth layers available. For the Table scene, we find that 3 bits (or 8 layers) of depth information is sufficient for light field rendering when combined with 16×16 image samples (shown in image (D) of Figure 12(b)). When the number of depth layers is below the minimal sampling point, light field rendering produces noticeable artifacts, as shown in images (A)-(C) of Figure 12(b).

Given a single depth layer, our analysis (Eq 12) shows that the number of images for antialiased rendering of the table scene requires 124×124 images. Note that conventional light field may require even a larger number of images without using the optimal depth. This very large set of light field data is due to the signifi-

---

[2]We were not able to use all 64×64 images with accurate depth because of memory limitations.

[3]There exists little discrepancy because of the fact that we can not apply the optimal reconstruction filter in rendering.

(a)   (b)

Figure 9: Comparison between conventional light field with 48×48 images and rendering with 16×16 images and 3 bits of depth: (a) artifacts are visible on the left with conventional rendering, (b) but not present with additional geometrical information because minimum sampling requirement is satisfied.

cant depth variations in the Table scene. This perhaps explains why inside-looking-out light field rendering has not been used often in practice. Also according to our analysis, using 3 bits (8 layers) of depth helps to reduce the number of images needed by a factor of 60, to 16×16 images. For comparison, Figure 9(a) shows conventional light field rendering with 48×48 images and Figure 9(b) shows the rendering result with 16×16 images plus 3 bits of depth. Visual artifacts such as double images at the edge of the wall are clearly visible in Figure 9(a). They are not present in Figure 9(b).

Experiments using depth with uncertainty also demonstrate the effectiveness of our analysis. Due to space limitation, we will not present any results of minimum sampling curve using depth with uncertainty.

5 Conclusion and future work

In this paper we have studied the problem of plenoptic sampling. Specifically, by analyzing the bounds of spectral support of light field signals, we can analytically compute the minimum sampling rate of light field rendering. Our analysis is based on the fact that the spectral support of a light field signal is bounded by only the minimum and maximum depths, irrespective of how complicated the spectral support might be because of depth variations in the scene. Given the minimum and maximum depths, a reconstruction filter with an optimal constant depth can be designed for anti-aliased light field rendering. The minimum sampling rate for light field rendering is obtained by compacting the replicas of the spectral support of the sampled light field within the smallest interval. Our work provides a solution to overcoming the oversampling problem in light field capturing and rendering.

By studying plenoptic sampling in the joint image and geometry space, we have also derived the minimum sampling curve which quantitatively describes the relationship between the number of images and the information on scene geometry, given a specific rendering resolution. Indeed, minimum sampling curves with accurate depth and with noisy depth serve as the design principles for a number of applications. Such interesting applications include image-based geometry simplification, geometry-assisted image dataset reduction, rendering-driven vision reconstruction, in addition to depth-assisted light field compression, or the minimum sampling rate for light field rendering.

While we have studied minimum sampling using light fields in this paper, the very idea of plenoptic sampling is also applicable

to other IBR systems, e.g. concentric mosaics, layered-depth image, view interpolation, and image warping, to name a few. With plenoptic sampling, there are a number of exciting areas for future work.

For example, we have used depth value in this paper to encode the geometry information. Depth is also used in image-assisted geometry simplification. However, no surface normal has been considered. In the future, we would like to experiment with different techniques to generate image-assisted geometry simplification using geometrical representations other than depth. We plan to incorporate the surface normal into image-based polygon simplification. The efficiency of geometry simplification can be further enhanced by considering the standard techniques in geometrical simplification, e.g. visibility culling.

Another interesting line of future work is on how to design a new rendering algorithm for the joint image and geometry representation. The complexity of the rendering algorithm should be proportional to the number of depth in use. In addition, error-bounded depth reconstruction should be considered as an alternative to traditional vision reconstruction, if the reconstruction result is to be used for rendering. Given the error bounds that are tolerable by the rendering algorithms, the difficulty of vision reconstruction can be much alleviated.

Lastly, we plan to study view-dependent plenoptic sampling. Current analysis of plenoptic sampling is based on the assumption that the surface is diffuse and little view-dependent variance can occur. It is conceivable that view dependent surface property will increase the minimum sampling rate for light field.

6 Acknowledgements

The authors benefited from discussions with Zhouchen Lin on truncated models and Tao Feng on optical analysis of light field rendering. Mr. Yin Li's incredible help on preparing Siggraph video is greatly appreciated. The last author also wishes to thank Pat Hanrahan for his helpful discussion on the minimum sampling of concentric mosaics while visiting Stanford in April 1999. Finally, the authors thank Siggraph reviewers' comments which have tremendously helped to improve the final manuscript.

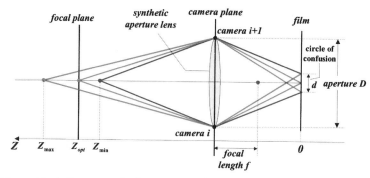

Figure 10: A discrete synthetic aperture optical system for light field rendering.

References

[1] E. H. Adelson and J. Bergen. The plenoptic function and the elements of early vision. In *Computational Models of Visual Processing*, pages 3–20. MIT Press, Cambridge, MA, 1991.

[2] M. Bass, editor. *Handbook of Optics*. McGraw-Hill, New York, 1995.

[3] R. C. Bolles, H. H. Baker, and D. H. Marimont. Epipolar-plane image analysis: An approach to determining structure from motion. *International Journal of Computer Vision*, 1:7–55, 1987.

[4] E. Camahort, A. Lerios, and D. Fussell. Uniformly sampled light fields. In *Proc. 9th Eurographics Workshop on Rendering*, pages 117–130, 1998.

[5] J.-X. Chai and H.-Y. Shum. Parallel projections for stereo reconstruction. In *Proc. CVPR 2000*, 2000.

[6] C. Chang, G. Bishop, and A. Lastra. Ldi tree: A hierarchical representation for image-based rendering. *SIGGRAPH'99*, pages 291–298, August 1999.

[7] S. Chen and L. Williams. View interpolation for image synthesis. *Computer Graphics (SIGGRAPH'93)*, pages 279–288, August 1993.

[8] T. Feng and H.-Y. Shum. An optical analysis of light field rendering. Technical report, Microsoft Research, MSR-TR-2000-38, May 2000.

[9] B. Girod. Motion compensation: visual aspects, accuracy, and fundamental limits. In *Motion Analysis and Image Sequence Processing*. Kluwer, 1995.

[10] S. J. Gortler, R. Grzeszczuk, R. Szeliski, and M. F. Cohen. The lumigraph. In *Computer Graphics Proceedings, Annual Conference Series*, pages 43–54, Proc. SIGGRAPH'96 (New Orleans), August 1996. ACM SIGGRAPH.

[11] M. Halle. Holographic stereograms as discrete imaging systems. In *Proc. SPIE Vol.2176, Practical Holography VIII*, pages 73–84, May 1994.

[12] V. Hlavac, A. Leonardis, and T. Werner. Automatic selection of reference views for image-based scene representations. In *Proc. ECCV*, pages 526–535, 1996.

[13] A. Isaksen, L. McMillan, and S. Gortler. Dynamically reparameterized light fields. Technical report, Technical Report MIT-LCS-TR-778, May 1999.

[14] S. Kang. A survey of image-based rendering techniques. In *VideoMetrics, SPIE Vol. 3641*, pages 2–16, 1999.

[15] J. Lengyel. The convergence of graphics and vision. Technical report, IEEE Computer, July 1998.

[16] M. Levoy and P. Hanrahan. Light field rendering. In *Computer Graphics Proceedings, Annual Conference Series*, pages 31–42, Proc. SIGGRAPH'96 (New Orleans), August 1996. ACM SIGGRAPH.

[17] Z.-C. Lin and H.-Y. Shum. On the numbers of samples needed in light field rendering with constant-depth assumption. In *Proc. CVPR 2000*, 2000.

[18] W. Mark, L. McMillan, and G. Bishop. Post-rendering 3d warping. In *Proc. Symposium on I3D Graphics*, pages 7–16, 1997.

[19] L. McMillan and G. Bishop. Plenoptic modeling: An image-based rendering system. *Computer Graphics (SIGGRAPH'95)*, pages 39–46, August 1995.

[20] H. Schirmacher, W. Heidrich, and H. Seidel. Adaptive acquisition of lumigraphs from synthetic scenes. In *Eurographics'99*, pages 151–159, Sept 1999.

[21] S. M. Seitz and C. M. Dyer. View morphing. In *Computer Graphics Proceedings, Annual Conference Series*, pages 21–30, Proc. SIGGRAPH'96 (New Orleans), August 1996. ACM SIGGRAPH.

[22] J. Shade, S. Gortler, L.-W. He, and R. Szeliski. Layered depth images. In *Computer Graphics (SIGGRAPH'98) Proceedings*, pages 231–242, Orlando, July 1998. ACM SIGGRAPH.

[23] H.-Y. Shum and L.-W. He. Rendering with concentric mosaics. In *Proc. SIGGRAPH 99*, pages 299–306, 1999.

[24] P. P. Sloan, M. F. Cohen, and S. J. Gortler. Time critical lumigraph rendering. In *Symposium on Interactive 3D Graphics*, pages 17–23, Providence, RI, USA, 1997.

[25] A. Tekal. *Digital Video Processing*. Prentice Hall, 1996.

A An optical analysis of light field rendering

Similar to [16, 13], we consider the light field rendering system as a discrete synthetic aperture optical system, as shown in Figure 10. Analogous to the Gaussian optical system, we can define the following optical parameters:

- Focal length f;
- Smallest resolvable feature (on the image plane) d;
- Aperture D. Distance between two adjacent cameras;
- Circle of confusion $c = d/f$;
- Hyperfocal distance $D_H = D/c$.

Let the plane of perfect focus be at the distance z_{opt}, the minimum and maximum distances at which the rendering is acceptable be z_{min} and z_{max}, respectively. The following relations exist ([2], vol. 1, p.1.92)

$$z_{min} = \frac{D_H z_{opt}}{D_H + z_{opt}}, \quad \text{and} \quad z_{max} = \frac{D_H z_{opt}}{D_H - z_{opt}},$$

which lead to,

$$\frac{1}{z_{opt}} = (\frac{1}{z_{min}} + \frac{1}{z_{max}})/2$$
$$\frac{1}{D_H} = (\frac{1}{z_{min}} - \frac{1}{z_{max}})/2$$

Therefore, to have the best rendering quality, no matter which optical system is used, the focus should be always at z_{opt}. Moreover, to guarantee the rendering quality, D_H has to be satisfied, i.e.,

$$\frac{D}{d/f} = (\frac{1}{z_{min}} - \frac{1}{z_{max}})/2 \quad (15)$$

In other words, given the minimum and maximum distances, the maximum camera spacing can be determined in order to meet the specified rendering quality. The hyperfocal distance describes the relationship among the rendering resolution (circle of confusion), the scene geometry (depth of field) and the number of images needed (synthetic aperture). Intuitively, the minimum sampling rate is equivalent to having the maximum disparity less than the smallest resolvable feature on the image plane, e.g, camera resolution or one pixel, i.e., $d = \delta_v = 1$. The same result was also obtained by Lin and Shum [17] using a geometrical approach.

Equation 15, not surprisingly, is almost exactly the same as Equation 8 because $D_H = 2/h_d$. However, our approach using spectral analysis of light field signals incorporates the textural information in the sampling analysis. More detailed optical analysis of light field rendering can be found in [8].

	Focal length	Maximum depth	Minimum depth	(u, v) interval	(s, t) interval	Pixels per image	Image per slab	Spacing Δt_{max}
Head	160.0	308.79	183.40	0.78125	1.5625	256×256	64×64	4.41
Statue	3000.0	5817.86	2326.39	15.625	31.25	256×256	64×64	40.38
Table	350.0	3235.47	362.67	2.4306	7.29	288×288	96×96	5.67

Table 1: A summary of parameters used in three data sets in our experiments.

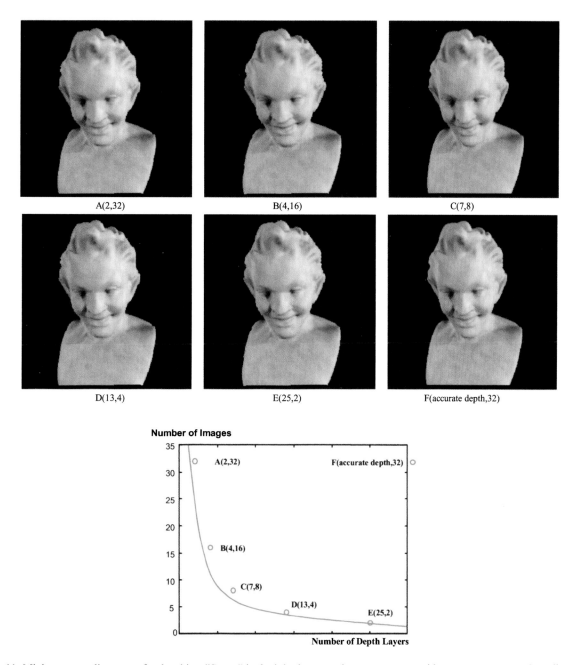

Figure 11: Minimum sampling curve for the object "Statue" in the joint image and geometry space with accurate geometry. Sampling points in the figure have been chosen to be slightly above the minimum sampling curve due to quantization.

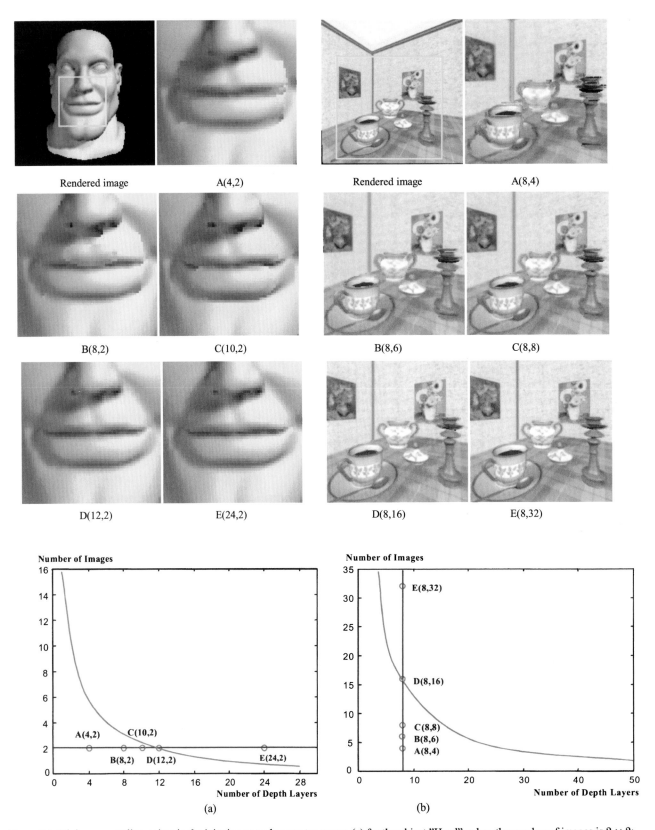

Figure 12: Minimum sampling points in the joint image and geometry space: (a) for the object "Head", when the number of images is 2×2; (b) for the "Table" scene, when the number of depth layers is 8.

An Autostereoscopic Display

Ken Perlin, Salvatore Paxia, Joel S. Kollin

Media Research Laboratory*, Dept. of Computer Science, New York University

ABSTRACT

We present a display device which solves a long-standing problem: to give a true stereoscopic view of simulated objects, without artifacts, to a single unencumbered observer, while allowing the observer to freely change position and head rotation.

Based on a novel combination of temporal and spatial multiplexing, this technique will enable artifact-free stereo to become a standard feature of display screens, without requiring the use of special eyewear. The availability of this technology may significantly impact CAD and CHI applications, as well as entertainment graphics. The underlying algorithms and system architecture are described, as well as hardware and software aspects of the implementation.

Keywords

graphics hardware, hardware systems, object tracking, optics, user interface hardware, virtual reality.

1 INTRODUCTION

1.1 Prior and Related Work

Computer graphics, even when rendered in high quality, still appears flat when displayed on a flat monitor. Various approaches toward creating true stereoscopy have been proposed so that the objects we simulate will look as though they are really in front of us [Okoshi, Lipton]. These fall into various categories.

The most common form of stereo display uses shuttered or passively polarized eyewear, in which the observer wears eyewear that blocks one of two displayed images from each eye. Examples include passively polarized glasses, and rapidly alternating shuttered glasses [Lipton85]. These techniques have become workhorses for professional uses, such as molecular modeling and some subfields of CAD. But they have not found wide acceptance for three dimensional viewing among most students, educators, graphic designers, CAD users (such as engineers and architects), or consumers (such as computer games players). Studies have shown that observers tend to dislike wearing any invasive equipment over their eyes, or wearing anything that impairs their general ambient visual acuity [Drascic]. This consideration has motivated a number of *non-invasive* approaches to stereoscopic display that do not require the observer to don special eyewear.

*Mailing Address: 719 Broadway, 12ᵗʰ Floor, New York, NY 10003

URL: http://www.mrl.nyu.edu/perlin/

A graphical display is termed *autostereoscopic* when all of the work of stereo separation is done by the display [Eichenlaub98], so that the observer need not wear special eyewear. A number of researchers have developed displays which present a different image to each eye, so long as the observer remains fixed at a particular location in space. Most of these are variations on the *parallax barrier* method, in which a fine vertical grating or lenticular lens array is placed in front of a display screen. If the observer's eyes remain fixed at a particular location in space, then one eye can see only the even display pixels through the grating or lens array, and the other eye can see only the odd display pixels. This set of techniques has two notable drawbacks: *(i)* the observer must remain in a fixed position, and *(ii)* each eye sees only half the horizontal screen resolution.

Holographic and pseudo-holographic displays output a partial light-field, computing many different views simultaneously. This has the potential to allow many observers to see the same object simultaneously, but of course it requires far greater computation than is required by two-view stereo for a single observer. Generally only a 3D lightfield is generated, reproducing only horizontal, not vertical parallax.

A display which creates a light field by holographic light-wave interference was constructed at MIT by [Benton]. The result was of very low resolution, but it showed the eventual feasibility of such an approach. Discrete light-field displays created by [Moore], and the recent work by Eichenlaub [Eichenlaub99], produce up to 24 discrete viewing zones, each with a different computed or pre-stored image. As each of the observer's eyes transitions from zone to zone, the image appears to jump to the next zone. A sense of depth due to stereo disparity is perceived by any observer whose two eyes are in two different zones.

Direct volumetric displays have been created by a number of researchers, such as [Downing], [Williams] and [Woodgate]. One commercial example of such a display is [Actuality]. A volumetric display does not create a true lightfield, since volume elements do not block each other. The effect is of a volumetric collection of glowing points of light, visible from any point of view as a glowing ghostlike image.

Autostereoscopic displays that adjust in a coarse way as the observer moves have been demonstrated by [Woodgate]. The Dresden display [Schwerdtner] mechanically moves a parallax barrier side-to-side and slightly forward/back, in response to the observer's position. Because of the mechanical nature of this adjustment, there is significant "settling time" (and therefore latency) between the time the observer moves and the time the screen has adjusted to follow. In both of these displays, accuracy is limited by the need to adjust some component at sub-pixel sizes.

1.2 Goals

The goals of our research have been to present a single observer with an artifact-free autostereoscopic view of simulated or remotely transmitted three dimensional scenes. The observer should be able to move or rotate their head freely in three dimensions, while always perceiving proper stereo separation. The subjective experience should simply be that the monitor is displaying a three dimensional object. In order to be of practical benefit, we sought a solution that could be widely adopted without great expense. We also wanted a solution that would not suffer from the factor-of-two loss of horizontal resolution which is endemic to parallax barrier systems.

These goals imposed certain design constraints. The user responsive adjustment could not contain mechanically moving parts, since that would introduce unacceptable latency. The mechanism could not rely on very high cost components. We also wanted the device to be able to migrate to a flat screen technology. Because we made certain simplifying design decisions for our first prototype, our initial test system displays only monochromatic images. However, this is not an inherent limitation of the technique.

1.3 Significance

The significance of this work is in that it enables a graphic display to assume many of the properties of a true three dimensional object. An unencumbered observer can walk up to an object and look at it from an arbitrary distance and angle, and the object will remain in a consistent spatial position. For many practical purposes, the graphic display subjectively *becomes* a three dimensional object. When combined with haptic response, this object could be manipulated in many of the ways that a real object can. Ubiquitous non-invasive stereo displays hold the promise of fundamentally changing the graphical user interface, allowing CAD program designers, creators of educational materials, and authors of Web interfaces (to cite only some application domains) to create interfaces which allow users to interact within a true three dimensional space.

2 PRINCIPLE

COMBINE SPATIAL MULTIPLEXING WITH TEMPORAL MULTIPLEXING

2.1 High level approach

We addressed our design goals by creating a modified parallax barrier that combines spatial multiplexing and temporal multiplexing. Since no fixed parallax barrier geometry could accommodate arbitrary observer position and orientation, we create a dynamically varying parallax barrier, one that continually changes the width and positions of its stripes as the observer moves. The use of a virtual dynamic parallax barrier is reminiscent of work by [Moore] and [Eichenlaub99], but to very different ends - instead of using a fixed dynamic pattern to create a fixed set of viewpoints, our goal is to create a result which is continually exact for one moving user.

As we shall show, each dynamic stripe needs to be highly variable in its width, in order to accommodate many different positions and orientations of the observer. For this reason, we make the dynamic stripes rather large, and use a correspondingly large gap between the display screen and the light-blocking parallax barrier.

Because the stripes are large enough to be easily visible, we need to make them somehow unnoticeable. To do this, we rapidly animated them in a lateral direction. The observer then cannot perceive the individual stripes, just as a passenger in a car speeding alongside a picket fence cannot see the individual fence posts.

This large-stripe approach requires each stripe to be composed from some number of very slender *microstripes*, each of which is an individually switchable liquid crystal display element. To sum up: we use a dynamic parallax barrier consisting of very large stripes, which are made out of many slender ones, and we move these large stripes so rapidly across the image that the observer cannot perceive them.

2.2 Three phases

In a perfect world, a temporally multiplexed system could be made from just two alternating phases. Parallax barrier systems depend on the distance E between an observer's two eyes (generally about 2.5 inches). Suppose that a display screen D inches away from the observer showed alternating stripes of a left and a right image. Suppose also that a light-blocking shutter were placed G inches in front of this display screen in a "picket fence" stripe pattern. If the width of each shutter stripe were chosen as E*G/D, and the width of each image stripe as E*G/(D-G), then during phase 1 the observer's left eye would be able to see half of one image through the clear stripes, and the observer's right eye would be able to see half of the other image through the clear stripes [Figure 1a]. If the light-blocking shutter were then flipped, and the display screen pattern simultaneously changed, then the observer would see the remainder of each respective image [Figure 1b]. If this flipping were done fast enough, then the observer would perceive two complete independent images, each visible only to one eye. The problem with this scenario is that the observer would need to be in precisely the correct position; the slightest deviation to the left or right would result in the wrong eye seeing a sliver of the wrong image.

For this reason, we animate the stripes in three phases. During each phase, the light-blocking shutter lets through only one third of each stripe. After each phase the stripe pattern is shifted laterally. Over the course of three phases, the observer's left eye sees one entire image, and the observer's eye sees a different entire image. The use of three phases guarantees that there is room for error in the observer's lateral position [Figures 2a,2b,2c].

2.3 Varying distance

The observer can be at a wide range of distances, since we can always vary the stripe width so as to equal E*G/D, as described above. [Figure 3a] shows the observer relatively far; [Figure 3b] shows the observer much closer. Microstripe resolution puts a practical upper limit on the observer distance, since the stripes become narrower as the observer's distance to the screen increases.

This upper limit increases linearly both with the gap between the display and shutter, and with the shutter resolution. In practice, we have set these so as to be able to handle an observer up to about five feet away.

2.4 Head rotation

In previous autostereoscopic techniques based on parallax barriers, all stripes were required to be of equal width. This presents a problem if the observer's head is facing off to the side. This will often be true when the observer has other displays or paperwork in his field of view, or is engaged in conversation with a colleague. In this case, one of the observer's eyes will be perhaps an inch or so closer to the screen than the other. When this happens, it no longer suffices for the barrier stripes to be all of equal width. Rather, in this case the stripes should vary in width in a perspective-linear pattern [Figure 4].

Our dynamically varying stripe generation handles this case accurately. Given any two eye positions, we compute and display the proper perspective linear stripe pattern. The mathematics to support this are developed in the next section.

2.5 Positioning the stripes

In this section we develop the mathematics needed to properly place the stripes. To make the light blocking work properly, we need to interleave the left and right images on the display and also to create a corresponding set of opaque/clear stripes on the optical shutter. To compute where the stripes should go, we use a system of crossed lines:

Starting from the *right* eye and the left-most point on the display, draw a straight line, and see where it crosses the shutter. Then draw a line from the *left* eye through this point on the shutter, and see where this new line hits the display. This process is continued, always starting with this next point over on the display, to produce an effective pattern of left/right image display stripes and light-blocking shutter stripes for that pair of eye positions.

Starting at one side of the display, we cross the lines on the shutter as follows:

1. Draw a line from x_n on the display, through the shutter, to the right eye;

2. Draw a line from the left eye, through the shutter, to x_{n+1} on the display;

3. Iterate

[Figures 5a, 5b] show how we construct a sequence of stripe positions from two eye positions (shown as a green and red dot, respectively), a display surface (shown as the bottom of the two horizontal lines) and a shutter surface (shown as the top of the two horizontal lines). Starting from the left side of the display screen, we calculate the line of sight through the shutter to the right eye. Then we compute the line of sight from the left eye, through this point, down onto the display screen. [Figure 5a] shows this process after one iteration; [Figure 5b] shows the same process after three iterations. In these figures, the positions at which the shutter needs to be transparent are circled in gray.

We now describe the mathematical details for this process. To place the stripes properly on the display screen, assume the two eye positions are: $\mathbf{p}=(p_x,p_y)$ and $\mathbf{q}=(q_x,q_y)$, that the display screen is on the line $y=0$, and that the shutter is on the line $y=1$. Given a location $(x,0)$ on the display screen, we find the line-of-sight location $f_p(x)$ on the shutter that lies between display screen location $(x,0)$ and eye position $\mathbf{p}$ by linear interpolation:

$$f_p(x) = p_x\, p_y^{-1} + x\, (1 - p_y^{-1})$$

Given a location $(x,1)$ on the shutter, we can find the corresponding line-of-sight location on the display screen by inverting the above equation:

$$f_p^{-1}(x) = (x - p_x\, p_y^{-1}) / (1 - p_y^{-1})$$

Therefore, given a location x_n on the display screen that is visible through a clear stripe on the shutter from both $\mathbf{p}$ and $\mathbf{q}$, the next such location is given first by finding the location on the shutter

$f_p(x_n)$ in the line-of-sight from $\mathbf{p}$, and then finding the corresponding location on the display screen which is in the line-of-sight from $\mathbf{q}$:

$$x_{n+1} = f_q^{-1}(f_p(x_n))$$

which expands out to:

$$(p_x\, p_y^{-1} + x\, (1 - p_y^{-1}) - q_x\, q_y^{-1}) / (1 - q_y^{-1})$$

This can be expressed as a linear equation $x_{n+1} = A\, x_n + B$, where:

$$A = x\, (1 - p_y^{-1}) / (1 - q_y^{-1})$$
$$B = (p_x\, p_y^{-1} - q_x\, q_y^{-1}) / (1 - q_y^{-1})$$

The nth location in the sequence of stripe locations on the display screen can be calculated by iterating $x_{n+1} = A\, x_n + B$:

$$x_0 = 0 \quad x_1 = B \quad x_2 = AB + B$$
$$x_3 = A^2 B + AB + B$$
$$x_n = B\, (A^{n-1} + ... + A + 1)$$

In the above sequence, the even terms locate the centers of those portions of the image visible from the right eye, and the odd terms locate the centers of those portions of the image visible from the left eye. The openings in the shutter are centered at

$$f^{-1}_q(x_0),\ f^{-1}_q(x_2),\ \text{etc.}$$

3 IMPLEMENTATION

Various physical arrangements could be used to implement this technique. For our first implementation, we used an approach that would allow us the greatest flexibility and ability to conduct tests. For the display screen, we used a Digital Light Processor (DLP) micro-mirror projector from Texas Instruments [TexasInstr], because DLP projectors handle R,G,B sequentially. This allowed us to use color to encode the three time-sequential phases. We used a Ferroelectric Liquid Crystal (FLC) element from [Displaytech] to shutter the start/stop time of each temporal phase.

For the light-blocking shutter, we had a custom pi-cell liquid crystal screen built to our specifications by [LXD], which we drove from power ICs mounted on a custom-made Printed Circuit Board (PCB). To control the sub-frame timings, we used a Field Programmable Gate Array (FPGA) from [Xilinx]. These were all driven from a Pentium II PC, running OpenGL in Windows NT.

3.1 Architecture

As flowcharted in [Figure 8] the steps to display a frame are:

(1) An eye tracker locates the observer's eyes, and sends this information to the CPU.

(2) The main CPU uses the eye tracker info to render two 3D scenes: one as seen from each eye.

(3) The main CPU also uses the eye tracker info to compute, for each of three phases, the proper left/right alternation pattern. These are interleaved into three successive time phases as red, green, and blue, respectively.

(4) The main CPU also uses the eye info to compute the three phases of stripe on the light shutter. These are encoded into three one-dimensional bit-maps, each indicating an on-off pattern for the shutter micro-stripes at one of the three phases. These bit-maps are shipped to the FPGA.

(5) The FPGA sends the three bit-patterns to the pi-cell light shutter in rotating sequence, every 1/180 second. The timing for this is controlled by the DLP projector, which produces a signal every time its color wheel advances.

(6) The DLP projector displays the three image phases in succession. The color wheel on the projector is removed, so that each of the red, green, and blue components displays as a gray scale image.

(7) The FLC element is modulated by the FPGA to block the light from the DLP projector lens in a 180 Hz square wave pattern. This allows finer control over timing.

(8) A rear projection screen (RPS) diffuses the image from the DLP projector.

(9) The pi-cell light shutter positioned in front of the RPS displays a different horizontally varying on-off pattern every 1/180 second.

Steps (5) through (9) above are part of the ``real-time subsystem'' which is monitored by the FPGA. These parts of the process are monitored continuously by the FPGA to synchronize all the events which must occur simultaneously 180 times per second.

Creating the three phased images

We use OpenGL to encode the red/green/blue sub-images which the DLP projector will turn into time sequential phases. To do this, we first render the compute separate left and right images in OpenGL, into off-screen buffers, as show in [Figures 6a,6b].

Then we slice each of these into their component image stripes, and reconstruct into three interleaved images that will be displayed in rapid sequence, as red, green, and blue components, as shown in [Figures 7a,7b,7c], respectively.

If this image were simply displayed on an unenhanced monitor, it would appear as in [Figure 9]. When filtered through the light-blocking shutter, each of the observer's eyes will reconstruct a complete image from a single viewpoint. If the DLP projector's color wheel were engaged, then the left and right eyes would see [Figure 10a] and [Figure 10b], respectively. With the color wheel removed, each of the observer's eyes simply sees the correct stereo component image of [Figure 6a] and [Figure 6b], respectively.

Timing requirements

There are two types of timing we need to address for this display: frame time, and shutter switching time.

In order to prevent eyestrain due to movement latency, we ideally want to maintain a frame refresh rate of at least 60 Hz, with a latency within 1/60 second between the moment the observer's head moves and the moment the correct image is seen. This consideration drove the timing design goals for the display: to be able to respond within the 1/60 interval from one screen refresh to the next. Within this time window, we make standard assumptions: that there is a known and fixed small latency to compute a frame, and that a Kalman filter [Grewal] can extrapolate from recent eye-tracking samples to predict reasonable eye positions at the moment of the next display refresh. If the user's head is moving, then the host computer should ideally compute the left and right images and merge them within this 1/60 second window.

The real-time subsystem maintains a more stringent schedule: a synchronous 180 Hz cycle. The pattern on the light-shutter needs to switch at the same moment that the DLP projector begins its red, green, or blue component. This timing task is handled by the FPGA, which reads a signal produced by the projector every time it the color wheel cycles (about once every 1/180 second) and responds by cycling the light shutter pattern. To help tune the on/off timing, the FPGA modulates a ferro-electric optical switch which is mounted in front of the projector lens.

The main CPU is not involved at all in this fine-grained timing. The only tasks required of the CPU are to produce left/right images, to interleave them to create a red/green/blue composite, and to put the result into an on-screen frame buffer, ideally (but not critically) at 60 frames per second.

3.2 The Parts

The essential components we used to implement this process are shown in the photograph [Figure 11] below. In this section, each is described in some detail.

FPGA

Every 1/180 of a second (three times per frame, from the observer's point of view), we need to update the light shutter with a different phase pattern of on/off stripes. To do this quickly enough, we built an ISA interface board with a non volatile Xilinx 95C108 PLD and a reconfigurable Xilinx XC4005E FPGA. The PLD is used to generate the ISA Bus Chip Select signals and to reprogram the FPGA. The XC4005E is large enough to contain six 256 bit Dual Ported RAMs (to double buffer the shutter masks needed for our three phases), the ISA Bus logic, and all the hardware needed to process the DLP signals and drive the pi-cell. When loaded with the three desired patterns from the main CPU, this chip continually monitors the color wheel signals from the DLP projector. Each time it detects a change from red to green, green to blue, or blue to red, it sends the proper signals to the Supertex HV57708 high voltage Serial to parallel converters mounted on the Pi-cell, switching each of the light shutter's 256 microstripes on or off.

Pi-cell

A standard twisted nematic liquid crystal display (such as is widely used in notebook computers) does not have the switching speed we need; requiring about 20 msec to relax from its on state to its off state after charge has been removed. Instead, we use a pi-cell, which is a form of liquid crystal material in which the crystals twist by $180°$ (hence the name) rather than that $90°$ twist used for twisted nematic LC displays.

Pi-cells have not been widely used partly because they tend to be bistable - they tend to snap to either one polarization or another This makes it difficult to use them for gray scale modulation. On the other hand, they will relax after a charge has been removed far more rapidly than will twisted nematic - a pi-cell display can be driven to create a reasonable square wave at 200 Hz. This is precisely the characteristic we need - an on-off light blocking device that can be rapidly switched. Cost would be comparable to that of twisted nematic LC displays, if produced at comparable quantities.

[Figure 12a] and [Figure 12b] show the pi-cell device that was manufactured for us by [LXD]. The image to the left shows the size of the screen, the close-up image to the right shows the individual microstripes and edge connectors. The active area is 14"x12", and the microstripes run vertically, 20 per inch. The microstripe density could easily have exceeded 100 per inch, but the density chosen required us to drive only 256 microstripes, and was sufficient for a first prototype. Edge connectors for the even microstripes run along the bottom; edge connectors for the odd microstripes run along the top. We used four power chips to maintain the required 40 volts, each with 64 pin-outs. Two chips drive the 128 even microstripes from a PCB on the top of the shutter, the other two drive the 128 odd microstripes from a PCB along the bottom. To turn a microstripe transparent, we drive it with a 5 volt square wave at 180 Hz. To turn a microstripe opaque, we drive it with a 40 volt square wave at 180 Hz.

Ferro-electric optical switch

A ferro-electric liquid crystal (FLC) will switch even faster than will a pi-cell, since it has a natural bias that allows it to be actively driven from the on-state to the off-state and back again. A ferro-electric element can be switched in 70 microseconds. Unfortunately ferro-electric elements are very delicate and expensive to manufacture at large scales, and would therefore be impractical to use as our light shutter. However, at small sizes they are quite practical and robust to work with. We use a small ferro-electric switch over the projector lens, manufactured by Displaytech [Displaytech], to provide a sharper cut-off between the three phases of the shutter sequence. We periodically close this element between the respective red, green, and blue phases of the DLP projector's cycle. While the FLC is closed, we effect the pi-cell microstripes transitions (which require about 1.2 ms).

User tracking

After surveying a number of different non-invasive eye tracking technologies available, we settled on the use of retroreflective camera based tracking. Because the back of the human eyeball is spherical, the eye will return light directly back to its source.

A system based on this principle sends a small infrared light from the direction of a camera during only the even video fields. The difference image between the even and odd video fields will show only two glowing spots, locating the observer's left and right eyes, respectively. By placing two such light/camera mechanisms side-by-side, and switching them on during opposite fields (left light on during the even fields, and right light on during the odd fields), the system is able to simultaneously capture two parallax displaced images of the glowing eye spots. The lateral shift between the respective eye spots in these two images is measured, to calculate the distance of each eye.

The result is two (x,y,z) triplets, one for each eye, at every video frame. A Kalman filter [Grewal] is used to smooth out these results and to interpolate eye position during the intermediate

fields. A number of groups are planning commercial deployment of retroreflective-based tracking in some form, including IBM [Flickner]. For calibration tests we used the DynaSite from Origin Systems [Origin], which requires the user to wear a retroreflective dot, but does not block the user's line of sight.

The user tracking provides as a pair of 3D points, one for each eye. As noted above, this information is used in three ways. *(i)* Each of these points is used by OpenGL as the eye point from which to render the virtual scene into an offscreen buffer; *(ii)* The proper succession lateral locations for left/right image interleaving is calculated, which is used to convert the left/right offscreen images into the three temporally phased images; *(iii)* The proper positions for the light shutter transitions are calculated. This information is converted to three one dimensional bit-maps, each indicating an on-off pattern for the shutter micro-stripes at one of the three phases. This information is sent to the FPGA, which then sends the proper pattern to the light shutter every 1/180 second, synchronously with the three phases of the DLP projector.

3.3 Experience

The goals of this current research version of the system were *(i)* low latency and *(ii)* absence of artifacts. In this section we discuss how well our experience matched those goals.

The most important question to answer is: ``does it work?'' The answer is yes. As we expected, the experience is most compelling when objects appear to lie near the distance of the display screen, so that stereo disparity is reasonably close to focus (which is always in the plane of the projection screen). When the system is properly tuned, the experience is compelling; as an observer looks around an object, it appears to float within the viewing volume. The observer can look around the object, and can position himself or herself at various distances from the screen as well. Special eyewear is not required.

The system always kept up with the renderer. Our software-implemented renderer did not achieve a consistent 60 frames per second, but rather something closer to 30 frames per second. In practice this meant that if the observer darted his/her head about too quickly, the tracker could not properly feed the display subsystem when the user moved his/her head rapidly.

The more critical issue is that of position-error based artifacts. Not surprisingly, we have found that it is crucial for the system to be calibrated accurately, so that it has a correct internal model of the observer's position. If the tracker believes the observer is too near or far away, then it will produce the wrong size of stripes, which will appear to the observer as vertical stripe artifacts (due to the wrong eye seeing the wrong image) near the sides of the screen. If the tracker believes the observer is displaced to the left or right, then this striping pattern will cover the entire display. We found in practice that a careful one-time calibration removed all such artifacts. This emphasizes the need for good eye position tracking.

One artifact we observed, which is exhibited by all polarization-based stereoscopic displays, is a small amount of ghosting - a faint trace of the wrong image is seen by each eye. This ghosting becomes noticeable when a bright object is placed against a black background. This is at least partly due to imperfections in the polarization; some light is scattered in the optical shutter and therefore becomes wrongly polarized. Some of this ghosting may also be due to imperfections in the timing, so that some light from the wrong phase gets through while the pi-cell shutter is still settling. In ongoing work, we plan to test this hypothesis by systematically varying the timing of the ferroelectric switch.

4 ONGOING WORK

We are designing an alternate version of this display that will work in full color with current stereo-ready CRT monitors. This will require a more sophisticated light-blocking shutter, since CRT monitors use a progressive scan, rather than displaying an entire image at once. For this reason, this version of the shutter will have separately addressable multiple bands from top to bottom, triggered at different times within the CRT monitor's scan cycle. This version would be in full color, since it will create phase differences by exploiting the time variation between different portions of the full-color CRT's vertical scan, instead of relying on sequential R,G,B to produce time phases.

In parallel, we are working with manufacturers of rapidly switchable flat-panel displays, to create a flat panel version. This version would be in full color, since it would not rely on sequential R,G,B. One of our goals for this flat-panel based version is a hand-held "gameboy" or "pokémon" size platform, for personal autostereoscopic displays. The costs of the pi-cell light shutter and its associated control electronics is roughly proportional to display area, which leads us to believe that portable hand-held autostereoscopic displays can be a practical low cost platform. This configuration will also depend on the success of ongoing work in the development of low cost eye position tracking for handheld platforms.

One of our current projects will use this display platform for teleconferencing. With a truly non-invasive stereoscopic display, two people having a video conversation can perceive the other as though looking across a table. Each person's image is transmitted to the other via a video camera that also captures depth [Kanade95]. At the recipient end, movements of the observer's head are tracked, and the transmitted depth-enhanced image is interpolated to create a proper view from the observer's left and right eyes, as in [Chen]. Head movements by each participant reinforce the sense of presence and solidity of the other, and proper eye contact is always maintained.

We plan to implement an API for game developers, so that users of accelerator boards for two-person games can make use of the on-board two-view hardware support provided in those boards to simultaneously accelerate left and right views in our display. We are also investigating variants of this system for two observers.

ACKNOWLEDGEMENTS

This work was supported by the NYU Center for Advanced Technology, NY3D Inc., and the Interval Research. The authors would also like to thank Clilly Castiglia, Chris Poultney, Jay Konopka, Michael Wahrman Dennis Zorin, and everyone else on the 12th floor who provided their time, effort and moral support.

References

Actuality Systems: http://actuality-systems.com/

S. Benton, T.E. Slowe, A.B. Kropp, and S.L. Smith, Micropolarizer-based Multiple-Viewer Autostereoscopic display. SPIE Proceedings Volume 3639: Stereoscopic Displays and Virtual Reality Systems VI, (SPIE January 1999) paper 3639-10.

S. Benton. The Second Generation of the MIT Holographic Video System. In: J. Tsujiuchi, J. Hamasaki, and M. Wada, eds. +Proc. of the TAO First International Symposium on Three Dimensional Image Communication Technologies. Tokyo, 6-7 December 1993. Telecommunications Advancement Organization of Japan, Tokyo, 1993, pp. S-3-1-1 to -6.

R. Börner. Three Autostereoscopic 1.25m Diagonal Rear Projection Systems with Tracking Features. IDW'97, Proc. of 4th Int'l Display Workshop, Nagoya, Japan, Nov. 1997, p.835-838

S. Chen and L. Williams. View Interpolation for Image Synthesis. Computer Graphics (SIGGRAPH 93 Conference Proc.) p.279-288.

Displaytech: http://www.displaytech.com/shutters.html

Elizabeth Downing et.al. A Three-Color, Solid-State, Three-Dimensional Display. Science 273,5279 (Aug. 30, 1996), pp. 1185-118.

D. Drascic, J. Grodski. Defence Teleoperation and Stereoscopic Video. Proc SPIE Vol. 1915, Stereoscopic Displays and Applications IV, pages 58-69, San Jose, California, Feb 1993.

J. Eichenlaub. Multiperspective Look-around Autostereoscopic Projection Display using an ICFLCD. Proc. SPIE Vol. 3639, p. 110-121, Stereoscopic Displays and Virtual Reality Systems VI, John O. Merritt; Mark T. Bolas; Scott S. Fisher; Eds.

J. Eichenlaub, Lightweight Compact 2D/3D Autostereoscopic LCD Backlight for Games, Monitor, and Notebook Applications. Proc. SPIE Vol. 3295, p. 180-185, in Stereoscopic Displays and Virtual Reality Systems V, Mark T. Bolas; Scott S. Fisher; John O. Merritt; Eds. April 1998.

M. Flickner: http://www.almaden.ibm.com/cs/blueeyes/find.html

M. Grewal, A. Andrews, Kalman Filtering: Theory and Practice, Prentice Hall, 1993.

T. Kanade, et al. Development of a Video Rate Stereo Machine. Proc. of International Robotics and Systems Conference (IROS-95), Pittsburgh, PA, August 7-9, 1995.

L. Lipton, et. al., U.S. Patent #4,523,226, Stereoscopic Television System, June 11,1985

L. Lipton, and J. Halnon. Universal Electronic Stereoscopic Display. Stereoscopic Displays and Virtual Reality Systems III, Vol. 2653, pp. 219-223, SPIE, 1996

LXD: http://www.lxdinc.com/

J.R. Moore, N.A. Dodgson, A.R.L. Travis and S.R. Lang. Time-Multiplexed Color Autostereoscopic Display. Proc. SPIE 2653, SPIE Symposium on Stereoscopic Displays and Applications VII, San Jose, California, Jan 28-Feb 2, 1996, pp. 10-19.

Okoshi, T. Three-Dimensional Imaging Techniques. Academic Press, New York 1976. ISBN 0-12-525250-1.

Origin Systems: http://www.orin.com/3dtrack/dyst.htm

A. Schwerdtner and H. Heidrich. Dresden 3D display (D4D). SPIE Vol. 3295, p. 203-210, Stereoscopic Displays and Virtual Reality Systems V, Mark T. Bolas; Scott S. Fisher; John O. Merritt; Eds.

P. St.-Hillaire, M. Lucente, J.D. Sutter, R. Pappu, C.J.Sparrell, and S. Benton. Scaling up the MIT Holographic Video System. Proc. of the Fifth International Symposium on Display Holography (Lake Forest College, July 18-22, 1994), SPIE, Bellingham, WA, 1995.

Texas Instruments: http://www.ti.com/dlp

R. Williams. Volumetric Three Dimensional Display Technology in D. McAllister (Ed.) Stereo Computer Graphics and other True 3D Technologies, 1993

G. J. Woodgate, D. Ezra, et.al. Observer-tracking Autostereoscopic 3D display systems. Proc. SPIE Vol. 3012, p.187-198, Stereoscopic Displays and Virtual Reality Systems IV, Scott S. Fisher; John O. Merritt; Mark T. Bolas; Eds.

Xilinx: http://www.xilinx.com/

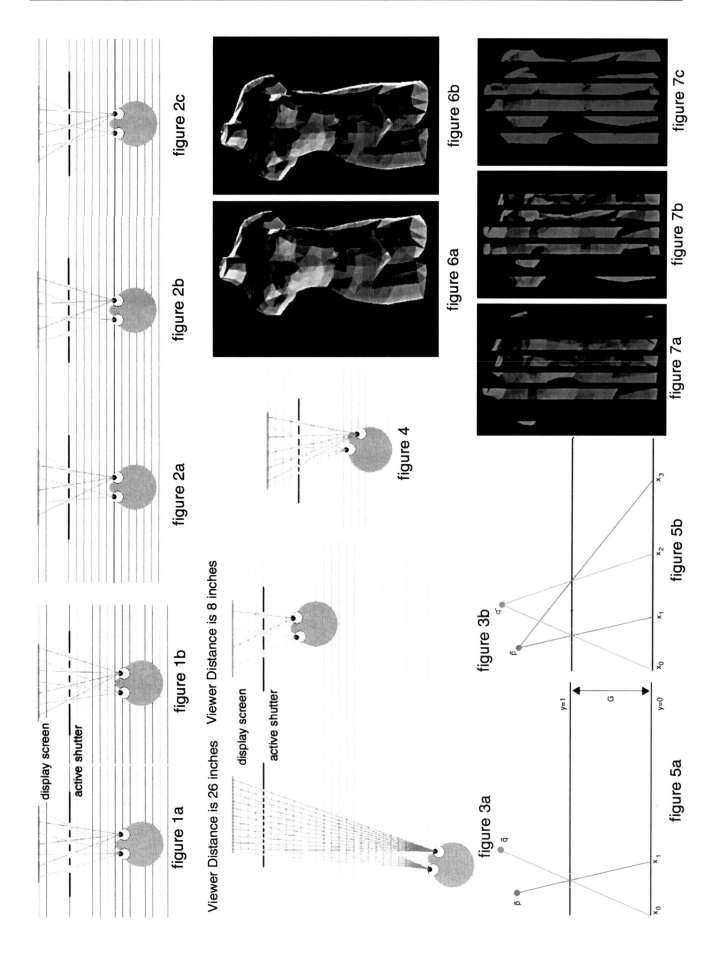

figure 2c

figure 2b

figure 2a

figure 1b

figure 1a

display screen

active shutter

Viewer Distance is 26 inches   Viewer Distance is 8 inches

display screen

active shutter

figure 4

figure 3a

figure 3b

figure 5a

figure 5b

figure 6a

figure 6b

figure 7a

figure 7b

figure 7c

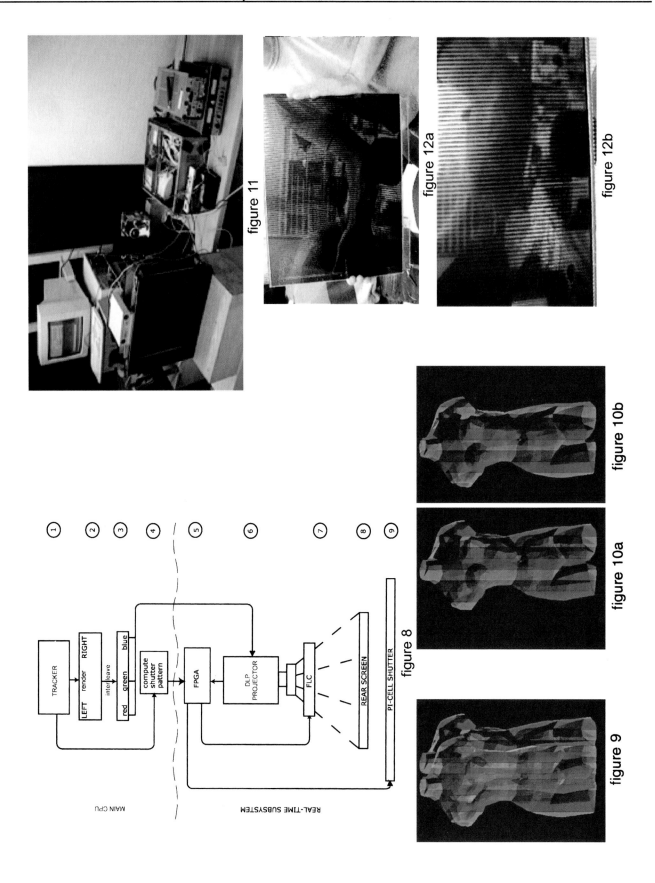

figure 11

figure 12a

figure 12b

figure 10b

figure 10a

figure 8

figure 9

Silhouette Clipping

Pedro V. Sander   Xianfeng Gu   Steven J. Gortler   Hugues Hoppe   John Snyder

Harvard University   Microsoft Research

Abstract

Approximating detailed models with coarse, texture-mapped meshes results in polygonal silhouettes. To eliminate this artifact, we introduce silhouette clipping, a framework for efficiently clipping the rendering of coarse geometry to the exact silhouette of the original model. The coarse mesh is obtained using progressive hulls, a novel representation with the nesting property required for proper clipping. We describe an improved technique for constructing texture and normal maps over this coarse mesh. Given a perspective view, silhouettes are efficiently extracted from the original mesh using a precomputed search tree. Within the tree, hierarchical culling is achieved using pairs of anchored cones. The extracted silhouette edges are used to set the hardware stencil buffer and alpha buffer, which in turn clip and antialias the rendered coarse geometry. Results demonstrate that silhouette clipping can produce renderings of similar quality to high-resolution meshes in less rendering time.

Keywords: Level of Detail Algorithms, Rendering Algorithms, Texture Mapping, Triangle Decimation.

1   Introduction

Rendering detailed surface models requires many triangles, resulting in a geometry processing bottleneck. Previous work shows that such models can be replaced with much coarser meshes by capturing the color and normal fields of the surface as texture maps and normal maps respectively [2, 3, 20, 26]. Although these techniques offer a good approximation, the coarse geometry betrays itself in the polygonal silhouette of the rendering. This is unfortunate since the silhouette is one of the strongest visual cues of the shape of an object [14], and moreover the complexity of the silhouette is often only $O(\sqrt{n})$ on the number n of faces in the original mesh.

In this paper, we introduce *silhouette clipping*, a framework for efficiently clipping the rendering of coarse geometry to the exact silhouette of the original model. As shown in Figure 1, our system performs the following steps.

Preprocess   Given a dense original mesh:

- Build a *progressive hull* representation of the original mesh and extract from it a coarse mesh, which has the property that it encloses the original, allowing proper clipping (Section 3).
- Construct a texture map and/or normal map over each face of the coarse mesh by sampling the color and/or normal field of the original mesh (Section 4).
- Enter the edges of the original mesh into a search tree for efficient runtime extraction of silhouette edges (Section 5).

http://cs.harvard.edu/~{pvs,xgu,sjg}
http://research.microsoft.com/~{hoppe,johnsny}

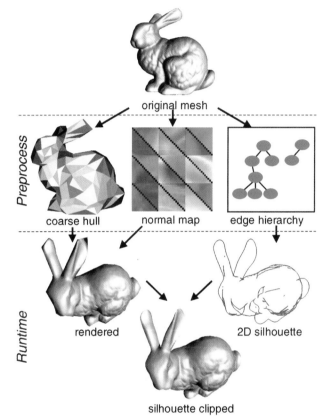

Figure 1: Overview of steps in silhouette clipping.

Runtime   Then, for a given viewpoint:

- Extract the silhouette edges from the search tree (Section 5).
- Create a mask in the stencil buffer by drawing the silhouette edges as triangle fans. Optionally, draw the edges again as antialiased lines to set the alpha buffer (Section 6).
- Render the coarse mesh with its associated texture/normal maps, but clipped and antialiased using the stencil and alpha buffers.

Contributions   This paper describes:

- The framework of silhouette clipping, whereby low-resolution geometry is rendered with a high-resolution silhouette.
- A progressive hull data structure for representing a nested sequence of approximating geometries. Within the sequence, any coarser mesh completely encloses any finer mesh.
- A new method for associating texel coordinates on the coarse model with positions on the original model. The association is based on the simple idea of shooting along an interpolated surface normal.
- A scheme for efficiently extracting the silhouette edges of a model under an arbitrary perspective view. It is inspired by previous work on backface culling [13, 15], but uses a convenient "anchored cone" primitive and a flexible n-ary tree to reduce extraction time.

- An efficient technique for setting the stencil buffer given the silhouette edges. Special care is taken to overcome rasterization bottlenecks by reducing triangle eccentricities.

- An improvement for efficiently antialiasing the silhouette with little additional cost.

- Demonstrations that silhouette clipping produces renderings of similar quality to high-resolution meshes in less time.

Limitations

- Only the exterior silhouette is used for clipping and antialiasing. Internal silhouettes retain their polygonalized appearance from the coarse model.

- As in other texture mapping schemes, some minor texture slipping can occur, depending on the accuracy of the coarse model.

- Efficiency depends on a relative sparsity of silhouettes, and therefore breaks down for extremely rough geometry like trees or fractal mountains.

- The approach only works for static models represented by closed, oriented, 2-dimensional manifolds.

- The stencil setting method assumes that the viewpoint is outside the convex hull of the original model.

2 Previous Work

Level of Detail/Simplification Level-of-detail (LOD) techniques adapt mesh complexity to a changing view. The simplest approach precomputes a set of view-independent meshes at different resolutions from which an appropriate approximation is selected based on viewer distance (see survey in [10]). A more elaborate approach, termed view-dependent LOD [12, 18, 27], locally adapts the approximating mesh. Areas of the surface can be kept coarser if they are outside the view frustum, facing away from the viewer, or sufficiently far away. In particular, the view-dependent error metric of Hoppe [12] automatically refines near mesh silhouettes. However, a cascade of dependencies between refinement operations causes refinement in areas adjacent to the silhouette, increasing rendering load. Also, the efficiency of these systems relies on time-coherence of the viewing parameters.

With silhouette clipping, fewer polygons need to be processed since silhouettes are obtained as a 2D post-process. Antialiasing is achieved by processing only the silhouette edges rather than supersampling the entire frame buffer.

Texturing Maruya [20] and Soucy et al. [26] define textures over a coarse domain by following invertible mappings through a simplification process. The shape of the final parametrization is influenced by the fairly arbitrary sequence of simplification steps.

Cignoni et al. [2] describe a simple method for defining a parametrization using only the geometry of the coarse and fine models. Each position on the coarse model is associated with its closest point on the fine model. This method often creates mapping discontinuities in concave regions (Figure 4). In Section 4 we present a method that instead shoots rays along the interpolated surface normal. Although not guaranteed to produce a one-to-one mapping, our parametrization has far fewer discontinuities.

Silhouette Extraction Silhouette information has been used to enhance artistic renderings of 3D objects [6, 7, 19]. Blythe et al. [1] describe a multipass rendering algorithm to draw silhouettes in the screen. Other work highlights the visible silhouette by rendering thickened edges [24] or backfaces [23] translated slightly towards the viewpoint. These works require the traversal of the entire geometric object.

A number of algorithms exist for extracting silhouette edges from polyhedral models. Markosian et al. [19] describe a probabilistic algorithm that tests random subsets of edges and exploits

view coherence to track contours. Their method is not guaranteed to find all of the silhouette components, and is too slow for models of high geometric complexity. Gooch et al. [7] extract silhouette edges efficiently using a hierarchical Gauss map. Their scheme is applicable only to orthographic views, whereas ours works for arbitrary perspective views.

Backface Culling Our method for fast silhouette extraction is inspired by previous schemes for fast backface culling. Kumar et al. [15] describe an exact test to verify that all faces are backfacing. They reduce its large cost by creating a memory-intensive auxiliary data structure that exploits frame-to-frame coherence. Johannsen and Carter [13] improve on this by introducing a conservative, constant-time backfacing test. The test is based on bounding the "backfacing viewpoint region" with a constant number of half spaces. In our system we use an even simpler anchored cone test primitive.

Johannsen and Carter do not address hierarchy construction, while Kumar et al. build their hierarchy using a dual space gridding that does not explicitly take into account the extraction cost. We describe a general bottom-up clustering strategy, similar to Huffman tree construction, that is greedy with respect to predicted extraction cost. In the results section we report the advantage of using our method over that of Johannsen and Carter.

Silhouette Mapping Our earlier system [8] performs silhouette clipping using an approximate silhouette, obtained using interpolation from a fixed number of precomputed silhouettes.

3 Progressive Hull

In order to be properly clipped by the high-resolution silhouette, the coarse mesh should completely enclose the original mesh M^n. In this section we show how such a coarse mesh can be obtained by representing M^n as a *progressive hull* — a sequence of nested approximating meshes $M^0 \ldots M^n$, such that

$$\mathcal{V}(M^0) \supseteq \mathcal{V}(M^1) \ldots \supseteq \mathcal{V}(M^n)$$

where $\mathcal{V}(M)$ denotes the set of points interior to M. A related construction for the special case of convex sets was explored in [4].

Interior volume To define interior volume, we assume that M^n is oriented and closed (i.e. it has no boundaries). In most cases, it is relatively clear which points lie in $\mathcal{V}(M)$. The definition of interior is less obvious in the presence of self-intersections, or when surfaces are nested (e.g. concentric spheres). To determine if a point $\mathbf{p} \in \mathbf{R}^3$ lies in $\mathcal{V}(M)$, select a ray from $\mathbf{p}$ off to infinity, and find all intersections of the ray with M. Assume without loss of generality that the ray intersects the mesh only within interiors of faces (i.e. not on any edges). Each intersection point is assigned a number, $+1$ or -1, equal to the sign of the dot product between the ray direction and the normal of the intersected face. Let the *winding number* $w_M(\mathbf{p})$ be the sum of these numbers [22]. Because the mesh is closed, it can be shown that $w_M(\mathbf{p})$ is independent of the chosen ray. To properly interact with the stencil algorithm described later in Section 6, we define interior volume using the *positive winding rule* as $\mathcal{V}(M) = \{\mathbf{p} \in \mathbf{R}^3 : w_M(\mathbf{p}) > 0\}$. Note that this description only defines interior volume; it is not used in actual processing.

Review of progressive mesh The progressive hull sequence is an adaptation of the earlier *progressive mesh* (PM) representation [11] developed for level-of-detail control and progressive transmission of geometry. The PM representation of a mesh M^n is obtained by simplifying the mesh through a sequence of n *edge collapse* transformations (Figure 3), thus defining a dense family of approximating meshes $M^0 \ldots M^n$.

For the purpose of level-of-detail control, edge collapses are selected so as to best preserve the appearance of the mesh during simplification (e.g. [3, 10, 11, 17]). We show that proper constraints on

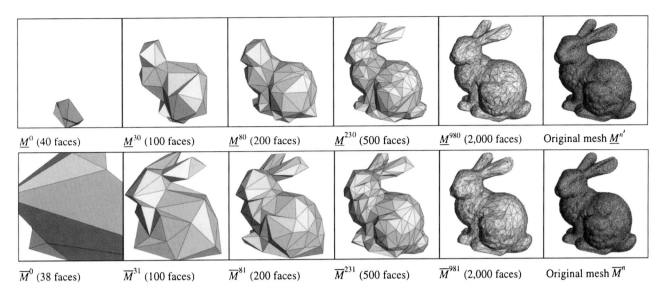

$\underline{M}^0$ (40 faces) $\underline{M}^{30}$ (100 faces) $\underline{M}^{80}$ (200 faces) $\underline{M}^{230}$ (500 faces) $\underline{M}^{980}$ (2,000 faces) Original mesh $\underline{M}^{n'}$

$\overline{M}^0$ (38 faces) $\overline{M}^{31}$ (100 faces) $\overline{M}^{81}$ (200 faces) $\overline{M}^{231}$ (500 faces) $\overline{M}^{981}$ (2,000 faces) Original mesh $\overline{M}^n$

Figure 2: Example of progressive inner and outer hulls. The original mesh has 69,674 faces; n'=34,817; n=34,818.

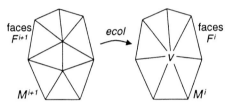

Figure 3: The edge collapse transformation.

the selection of edge collapse transformations allow the creation of PM sequences that are progressive hulls.

Progressive hull construction For the PM sequence to be a progressive hull, each edge collapse transformation $M^{i+1} \rightarrow M^i$ must satisfy the property $\mathcal{V}(M^i) \supseteq \mathcal{V}(M^{i+1})$. A sufficient condition is to guarantee that, at all points in space, the winding number either remains constant or increases:

$$\forall \mathbf{p} \in \mathbf{R}^3 , \; w_{M^{i+1}}(\mathbf{p}) \geq w_{M^i}(\mathbf{p}) .$$

Intuitively, the surface must either remain unchanged or locally move outwards everywhere.

Let F^{i+1} and F^i denote the sets of faces in the neighborhood of the edge collapse as shown in Figure 3, and let $\mathbf{v}$ be the position of the unified vertex in M^i. For each face $f \in F^{i+1}$, we constrain $\mathbf{v}$ to lie outside the plane containing face f. Note that the outside direction from a face is meaningful since the mesh is oriented. The resulting set of linear inequality constraints defines a feasible volume for the location of $\mathbf{v}$. The feasible volume may be empty, in which case the edge collapse transformation is disallowed. The transformation is also disallowed if either F^i or F^{i+1} contain self-intersections[1]. If $\mathbf{v}$ lies within the feasible volume, it can be shown that the faces F^i cannot intersect any of the faces F^{i+1}. Therefore, $F^i \cup flip(F^{i+1})$ forms a simply connected, non-intersecting, closed mesh enclosing the difference volume between M^i and M^{i+1}. The winding number $w(\mathbf{p})$ is increased by 1 within this difference volume and remains constant everywhere else. Therefore, $\mathcal{V}(M^i) \supseteq \mathcal{V}(M^{i+1})$.

The position $\mathbf{v}$ is found with a linear programming algorithm, using the above linear inequality constraints and the goal function of minimizing volume. Mesh volume, defined here as $\int_{\mathbf{p} \in \mathbf{R}^3} w_M(\mathbf{p})d\mathbf{p}$,

is a linear function on $\mathbf{v}$ that involves the ring of vertices adjacent to $\mathbf{v}$ (refer to [9, 17]).

As in earlier simplification schemes, candidate edge collapses are entered into a priority queue according to a cost metric. At each iteration, the edge with the lowest cost is collapsed, and the costs of affected edges are recomputed. Various cost metrics are possible. We obtain good results simply by minimizing the increase in volume, which matches the goal function used in positioning the vertex.

Inner and outer hulls The algorithm described so far constructs a *progressive outer hull* sequence $\overline{M}^0 \supseteq \ldots \supseteq \overline{M}^n$. By simply reversing the orientation of the initial mesh, the same construction gives rise to an *progressive inner hull* sequence $\underline{M}^0 \subseteq \ldots \subseteq \underline{M}^{n'}$. Combining these produces a single sequence of hulls

$$\underline{M}^0 \subseteq \ldots \subseteq \underline{M}^{n'} = \overline{M}^n \subseteq \ldots \subseteq \overline{M}^0$$

that bounds the original mesh from both sides, as shown in Figure 2. (Although the surface sometimes self-intersects, interior volume defined using the winding number rule is still correct.)

We expect that this representation will also find useful applications in the areas of occlusion detection and collision detection, particularly using a selective refinement framework [12, 27].

4 Texture Creation

As in [2, 20, 26], we create a texture tile over each face of the simplified mesh, and pack these tiles into a rectangular texture image. As illustrated in Figure 1, all tiles are right triangles of uniform size. The problem of texture creation is to fill these tiles using texel values (colors or normals) sampled from the original mesh. Inspired by Cignoni et al. [2], our approach constructs a parametrization from the simplified mesh to the original mesh based solely on their geometries (i.e. independent of the simplification algorithm). Whereas Cignoni et al. use a closest-point parametrization, we base our parametrization on a normal-shooting approach, which significantly reduces the number of discontinuities in the parametrization (see Figures 4 and 5).

Given the original mesh and a triangle T of the simplified mesh, we must determine how to calculate the values assigned to each texel. Our normal-shooting algorithm performs the following steps to compute the color or normal at each texel t of T:

---

[1] We currently hypothesize that preventing self-intersections in F^i and F^{i+1} may be unnecessary.

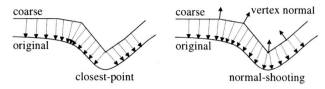

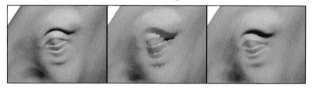

Figure 4: Closest-point parametrization often produces discontinuities not present with normal-shooting.

(a) original mesh   (b) closest-point   (c) normal-shooting

Figure 5: Comparison of texturing the coarse mesh using the closest-point parametrization and our normal-shooting parametrization. Note the parametric discontinuities in the concave regions for closest-point.

- Calculate the barycentric coordinates of t within the triangle T.

- Calculate the position $\mathbf{p}$ and normal $\vec{\mathbf{n}}$ by interpolating the positions and normals of the vertices of T.

- Shoot a ray from $\mathbf{p}$ in the $-\vec{\mathbf{n}}$ direction. This ray will intersect the original mesh at a particular point $\mathbf{q}$. In the extremely rare event of a ray failing to hit the original model, we instead use the closest point to $\mathbf{p}$.

- Given the triangle and barycentric coordinates of $\mathbf{q}$ in the original model, interpolate the prelit color or normal of its three vertices, and store the result in t.

We adjust the sampling resolution on the texture tiles depending on the complexities of the original and simplified meshes. For the models in Section 7, we sampled 512 texels per coarse face on the bunny and holes, but only 128 texels on the dragon, parasaur, and knot since these have many more coarse faces. These resolutions are enough to capture the desired level of detail. To allow bilinear interpolation on the resulting texture, we appropriately pad the triangle texture tiles.

5 Fast Silhouette Extraction

We consider each geometric edge in the mesh to consist of a pair of opposite-pointing *directed edges*. For a given mesh and viewpoint $\mathbf{p}$, the 3D silhouette is the subset of directed edges whose left adjacent face is frontfacing and whose right adjacent face is backfacing. More formally, a directed edge e is on the silhouette if and only if

$$\mathbf{p} \in \text{frontfacing}(e.f_1) \quad \text{and} \quad \mathbf{p} \notin \text{frontfacing}(e.f_2),$$

where the region

$$\text{frontfacing}(f) = \{\mathbf{p} \in \mathbf{R}^3 \mid (\mathbf{p} - f.\mathbf{v}) \cdot f.\vec{\mathbf{n}} \geq 0\}$$

in which $f.\mathbf{v}$ is any vertex of f, and $f.\vec{\mathbf{n}}$ is its outward facing normal.

Runtime Algorithm Applying this test to all edges in a brute-force manner proves to be too slow. Instead, our approach is to enter the edges into a hierarchical search tree, or more properly, a forest. Each node in the forest contains a (possibly empty) list of edges to test. Let the *face cluster* $F(n)$ for a node n be the set of faces attached to edges contained in that node and in all of its descendants. If for a given viewpoint we can determine that the faces in $F(n)$ are entirely frontfacing or entirely backfacing, then

none of the edges contained in the node's subtree can be silhouettes, and thus the depth-first traversal skips the subtree below n. The basic structure of the algorithm is as follows:

```
procedure findSilhouetteEdges(node n, viewpoint p)
    if ( p ∈ frontfacing(F(n)) or p ∈ backfacing(F(n)) )
        return;    // skip this subtree
    for  edges e in  n.E
        if ( p ∈ frontfacing(e.f₁) and p ∉ frontfacing(e.f₂) )
            output(e);
    for  children c in  n.C
        findSilhouetteEdges(c,p);
```

The frontfacing and backfacing regions of a face cluster F are defined as

$$\text{frontfacing}(F) = \bigcap_{f \in F} \text{frontfacing}(f) \quad \text{and}$$

$$\text{backfacing}(F) = \bigcap_{f \in F} \overline{\text{frontfacing}(f)}.$$

To make hierarchical culling efficient, we need a fast, constant-time algorithm to conservatively test $\mathbf{p} \in \text{frontfacing}(F)$ and $\mathbf{p} \in \text{backfacing}(F)$. We do this by approximating these regions using two open-ended *anchored cones*, a_f and a_b, satisfying

$$a_f \subset \text{frontfacing}(F) \quad \text{and} \quad a_b \subset \text{backfacing}(F)$$

as shown in Figure 6. Each anchored cone a is specified by an anchor origin $a.\mathbf{o}$, normal $a.\vec{\mathbf{n}}$, and cone angle $a.\theta$. The construction of these cones will be presented shortly.

Each region test then reduces to

$$\mathbf{p} \in a \quad \Leftrightarrow \quad \cos^{-1}\left(\frac{\mathbf{p} - a.\mathbf{o}}{\|\mathbf{p} - a.\mathbf{o}\|} \cdot a.\vec{\mathbf{n}}\right) \leq a.\theta.$$

For efficiency and to reduce storage, we store in our data structure the scaled normal $a.\vec{\mathbf{n}}_s = a.\vec{\mathbf{n}}/\cos(a.\theta)$. With careful precomputation, the above test can be then implemented with two dot products and no square roots or trigonometric operations, via

$$\mathbf{p} \in a \quad \Leftrightarrow \quad (\mathbf{p} - a.\mathbf{o}) \cdot a.\vec{\mathbf{n}}_s \geq 0 \quad \text{and}$$

$$\left((\mathbf{p} - a.\mathbf{o}) \cdot a.\vec{\mathbf{n}}_s\right)^2 \geq \|\mathbf{p} - a.\mathbf{o}\|^2.$$

Because we construct a_f and a_b to have the same cone angle and opposite cone normals, we can test for inclusion in *both* anchored cones with just two dot products. This is made possible by precomputing and storing the "anchor separation" $d = (a_f.\mathbf{o} - a_b.\mathbf{o}) \cdot a_f.\vec{\mathbf{n}}$. For reference, the final node data structure is:

```
struct node
    vector scaledNormal;        //n⃗ₛ
    point ffAnchor;             // a_f.o
    point bfAnchor;             // a_b.o
    float AnchorSeparation;     // d
    edgeList E;
    childPointerList C;
```

Anchored Cone Construction We first find the cone having the largest angle θ inside the frontfacing region. It can be shown that the central axis $\vec{\mathbf{n}}$ of such a cone has the following property: if one associates a point on the unit sphere with each face normal in the cluster, and computes the 3D convex hull of this pointset, $\vec{\mathbf{n}}$ must pass through the closest point from the origin to that convex hull. We therefore use Gilbert's algorithm [5] which directly finds this closest point in linear time. (Note that an open-ended cone exists

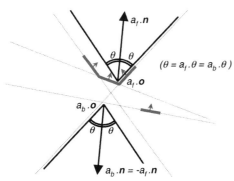

Figure 6: Anchored cones provide conservative bounds on the frontfacing and backfacing regions of a set of faces, illustrated here in 2D for the 4 oriented line segments in blue.

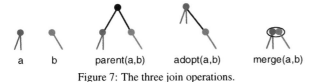

Figure 7: The three join operations.

if and only if the convex hull does not contain the origin.) The largest cone angle θ is then easily computed as the complement of the maximum angle from $\vec{n}$ to the set of face normals. In fact, θ is also the complement of the angular distance of $\vec{n}$ to any vertex in the closest simplex found by Gilbert's algorithm.

For a given node, we assign

$$a_f.\vec{n} = -a_b.\vec{n} = \vec{n}$$
$$a_f.\theta = a_b.\theta = \theta \ .$$

We then find the best cone origins, $a_f.\mathbf{o}$ and $a_b.\mathbf{o}$, by solving the linear programs

$$a_f.\mathbf{o} = \operatorname*{argmin}_{\mathbf{o}\in\text{frontfacing}(F)} \vec{n}\cdot\mathbf{o} \quad \text{and} \quad a_b.\mathbf{o} = \operatorname*{argmin}_{\mathbf{o}\in\text{backfacing}(F)} -\vec{n}\cdot\mathbf{o} \ .$$

Tree Construction We construct our trees in a bottom-up greedy fashion much like the construction of Huffman trees. We begin with a forest where each edge is in its own node. Given any two nodes (a,b), we allow the following three join operations (see Figure 7).

- parent(a,b): creates a new node with two children a and b.

- adopt(a,b): gives node b to node a as an additional child node.

- merge(a,b): creates a new node whose edge and child lists are the union of those from a and b.

Given these possible join operations, the algorithm is as follows:

```
Forest buildOptimalForest(Forest forest)
    candidates = buildJoinCandidates(forest);
    candidates.heapify();
    while (joinOp = candidates.removeTop())
        if ( joinOp.cost > 0 ) break;
        forest.applyJoin(joinOp);
        candidates.updateCosts(joinOp);
    return forest;
```

Candidate join operations are ordered in the heap by their predicted decrease in silhouette extraction cost. The silhouette extraction cost is computed as follows.

The cost of a forest is simply the sum of the costs of its roots:

$$\text{forestCost} = \sum_r \text{rootCost}(r) \ .$$

The cost of a root node is some constant k_a for the anchored cone tests, plus the possible cost of testing its edges and its children:

$$\text{rootCost}(r) = k_a + P(r)\left(k_e\,|r.E| + \sum_{c\in r.C} \text{nodeCost}(c,\{r\}) \right) \ ,$$

where k_e is the cost for testing an edge, and $P(r)$ is the probability of the node r not being culled[2]. To compute $P(r)$, one must assume some probability distribution over the viewpoints. We assume a uniform distribution over a large sphere U, in which case

$$P(r) = \frac{vol(U - r.a_f - r.a_b)}{vol(U)} \ .$$

The cost of a non-root node n with ancestor set A is computed recursively as:

$$\text{nodeCost}(n,A) = k_a + P(n\,|\,A)\left(k_e\,|n.E| + \sum_{c\in n.C} \text{nodeCost}(c,\{n\}\cup A) \right)$$

where $P(n\,|\,A)$ is the probability of the node n not being culled given that its ancestors A were also not culled. If one assumes that both anchored cones of a child are contained in its parent's, then

$$P(n\,|\,A) = \frac{vol(U - n.a_f - n.a_b)}{vol(U - p.a_f - p.a_b)}$$

where p is n's immediate parent. While this containment must be true of a node's respective frontfacing and backfacing regions, it is not necessarily true for their approximating anchored cones. In practice, numerical experiments have shown this approximation to be reasonable.

In principle one might consider all n^2 pairs of forest roots for candidate join operations. For computational efficiency during the preprocess, we limit the candidate set in the following way. A candidate graph is initialized with a graph vertex for each root in the initial forest, each representing a single mesh edge. Two vertices in the graph are linked if their corresponding mesh edges share the same mesh vertex, or if adjacent mesh faces have normals within an angular threshold[3]. Then during tree construction, when two roots are joined, their vertices and links are merged in the candidate graph.

6 Stencil Setting

The 3D silhouette extracted in the previous section is a set of directed edges. Since the mesh is closed and the silhouette edges separate frontfacing triangles from backfacing ones, the number of silhouette edges adjacent to any vertex must be even. Therefore the edges can be organized (non-uniquely) into a set of closed contours. Each such contour projects into the image plane as an oriented 2D polygon, possibly with many loops, and possibly self-intersecting. The winding number of this polygon at a 2D image location corresponds to the number of frontfacing surface layers that are seen along the ray from the viewpoint through that image location [19]. Our approach is to accumulate these winding numbers in the hardware *stencil buffer* for all contours in the 3D silhouette. Then, we clip the coarse geometry to the external silhouette of the original geometry by only rendering the coarse model where the stencil buffer values are positive.

---

[2] We have found that setting $k_a/k_e = 4/3$ gives us the best results.

[3] In practice we have found that ignoring similarity of normals (i.e., only considering mesh proximity) still provides search trees that are almost as good, with far less preprocessing time.

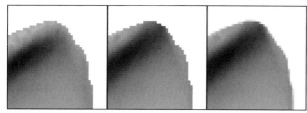

(a) original mesh   (b) binary stencil   (c) alpha matte

Figure 8: Comparison of rendering the bunny ear using the original mesh (69,674 face model), and using a coarse hull (500 face model) whose silhouette is (b) clipped to the stencil buffer and (c) antialiased using the alpha buffer.

Basic Algorithm The directed silhouette edges are organized into closed contours using a hash table. (For each directed edge, the hash key is the vertex index of the source vertex.) In order to render the winding number of each contour into the stencil buffer, we use a variation of the standard stencil algorithm for filling concave polygons [21]. Each edge contour is drawn as a fan of triangles about an arbitrary center point, which we choose to be the 3D centroid of the contour vertices. The orientation of each triangle determines whether its rendered pixels increment or decrement the stencil buffer values. To avoid testing triangle orientations in the CPU, we instead render the triangles twice, first with backface culling and stencil mode set to increment, and then with frontface culling and stencil mode set to decrement, as shown in the pseudocode below. The triangles are drawn as triangle fans for efficiency.

```
procedure setStencil(contours C, viewpoint p)
    setStencilToZero(boundingBox(C));
    cullFace(BACKFACE);
    for contours c in C
        point q = centroid(c.E);
        for edges e in c.E
            triangle t = makeTriangle(q, e.v₁, e.v₂);
            rasterizeToStencil(t, INCREMENT);
    cullFace(FRONTFACE);
    for contours c in C
        point q = centroid(c.E);
        for edges e in c.E
            triangle t = makeTriangle(q, e.v₁, e.v₂);
            rasterizeToStencil(t, DECREMENT);
    setDrawingToPositiveStencil();
```

Although the graphics hardware clips triangle fans to the view frustum, the setStencil algorithm remains correct even if parts of the model lie behind the viewer, as long as the viewer remains outside the convex hull of the object. This can be tracked efficiently by the test used in [25].

Loop Decomposition The basic algorithm described so far tends to draw many long, thin triangles. On many rasterizing chips (e.g. NVIDIA's TNT2), there is a large penalty for rendering such eccentric triangles. It is easy to show that the setStencil algorithm behaves best when the screen-space projection of q has a y coordinate at the median of the contour vertices. Choosing q as the 3D centroid of the contour vertices serves as a fast approximation.

To further reduce the eccentricity of the fan triangles, we break up each large contour into a set of smaller loops. More precisely, we pick two vertices on the contour, add to the data structure two opposing directed edges between these vertices, and proceed as before on the smaller loops thus formed.

When tested with the NVIDIA's TNT2, loop decomposition gave speedups of up to a factor of 2.3 on models that are raster bound on the stencil setting stage.

Model	Bunny	Dragon	Parasaur	Knot	Holes3
	Model complexities (number of faces)				
Original mesh	69,674	400,000	43,886	185,856	188,416
Coarse hull	500	4,000	1,020	928	500
	System timings (milliseconds)				
Original rendering	34.7	204.7	20.63	81.12	90.3
Silhouette extraction	4.5	24.2	4.0	6.5	4.0
Stencil setting	2.7	21.5	2.0	2.8	1.0
Coarse rendering	4.8	5.2	4.9	4.9	4.4
Total*	7.8	50.3	6.9	10.3	5.5
Speedup factor	4.4	4.1	3.0	7.9	16.4
(Antialiasing)	+3.0	+22.5	+2.9	+3.4	+1.5

Table 1: Timings of steps in our silhouette clipping scheme, and comparison with rendering the original mesh. *Total frame times are less than the sum due to parallelism between CPU and graphics.

Model	Bunny	Dragon	Parasaur	Knot	Holes3
Total faces	69,674	400,000	43,866	185,856	188,416
Total edges	104,511	600,000	65,799	278,784	282,624
	Silhouette extraction statistics				
Silhouette edges	3,461	23,493	3,227	3,291	1,737
Tested edges	10,256	67,934	10,938	13,134	5,976
Tested nodes	4,282	26,291	3,538	7,926	4,594
	Silhouette extraction times (milliseconds)				
Our search tree	4.1	28.2	4.3	6.4	3.3
Brute-force	20.4	117.3	12.5	50.6	51.4
Speedup factor	5.0	4.2	2.9	7.9	15.6

Table 2: Statistics of our silhouette extraction algorithm.

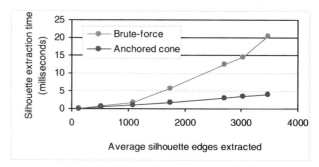

Figure 9: Comparison of the average silhouette extraction time with our algorithm and the brute-force algorithm, using bunny approximations with 500, 4,000, 20,000, 50,000, and 69,674 faces.

Antialiasing Although many graphics systems can antialias line segments, triangle antialiasing requires framebuffer supersampling which slows rendering except on high-end workstations. As a result, the silhouette typically suffers from aliasing artifacts (Figure 8a). The stencil buffer algorithm described in the previous section creates a *binary* pixel mask, therefore the coarse mesh clipped to this mask exhibits the same staircase artifacts (Figure 8b).

We can antialias the silhouette by applying line antialiasing on the silhouette contour. First, the silhouette edges are rendered as antialiased line segments into the alpha buffer (using glBlend(GL_ONE,GL_ZERO)). Second, the stencil buffer is computed as in the previous section. This binary stencil is then transferred to the alpha buffer, i.e. pixels interior to the silhouette are assigned alpha values of 1. Finally, the low-resolution geometry is rendered with these alpha buffer values using the *over* operation (glBlend(GL_DST_ALPHA,GL_ONE_MINUS_DST_ALPHA)). The result is shown in Figure 8c. As the timings in Table 1 reveal, silhouette antialiasing adds little to the overall time. Note that antialiased silhouette clipping on multiple models involves the non-commutative *over* operation, and thus requires visibility sorting [25].

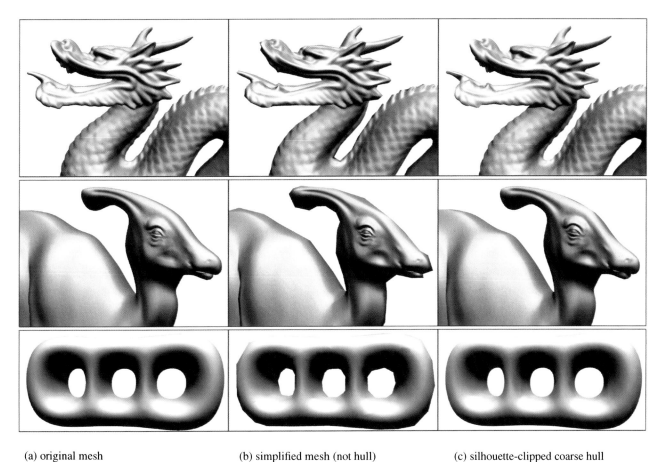

| (a) original mesh | (b) simplified mesh (not hull) | (c) silhouette-clipped coarse hull |

Figure 10: Comparison of rendering the original mesh, a normal-mapped simplified mesh without the progressive hull constraints, and a coarse hull with the same number of faces but with silhouette clipping.

7 Results

We tested our framework on the five models of Table 1. The bunny and dragon are from 3D scans at Stanford University. (The dragon was simplified to 400,000 faces; the four boundaries in the base of the bunny were closed.) The parasaur is from the Viewpoint library. The 3-holed torus and knot are subdivision surfaces tessellated finely to obtain an accurate silhouette. We used normal maps for all of our examples.

Preprocessing a model consists of building a coarse hull, the normal and/or texture map, and the edge search structures. This takes between 30 minutes and 5 hours depending on model complexity.

We have focused our effort on optimizing the runtime algorithm. Times for the substeps of our scheme are shown in Table 1. These are obtained on a PC with a 550MHz Pentium III and a Creative Labs Annihilator 256 graphics card based on the NVIDIA GeForce 256 GPU. The execution times represent averages over many random views of the models. Note that the expense of extracting silhouette edges is significantly reduced due to parallelism between the CPU and GPU. For instance, silhouette extraction is nearly free for the bunny. We compare our approach of silhouette-clipping a coarse hull with rendering the original mesh, and find speedups of approximately 3 to 16. For rendering both the coarse hulls and the original meshes, we use precomputed triangle strips.

Figure 10 compares the image quality of the silhouette-clipped coarse hull with a simplified mesh of the same complexity and the original mesh. Figure 11 indicates that given a fixed amount of resources, our system can render a model with a silhouette of much higher resolution than the brute-force method.

As shown in Table 2, our hierarchical culling scheme results in explicit silhouette testing of only a small fraction of the edges, particularly on the smooth models. In all cases, our extraction time is much lower than the brute-force approach of explicitly testing all edges. It works much like a quadtree search algorithm, which can find all cells that touch a line in $O(\sqrt{n})$ time. Figure 9 shows this comparison as a function of silhouette complexity for several simplified bunny meshes. The graph indicates that the time for our algorithm increases linearly on the number m of silhouette edges in the model, whereas the brute-force time increases linearly on the total number n of edges, which in this case is quadratic on m.

We implemented Johannsen and Carter's backface culling algorithm and modified it to extract silhouettes, in order to compare it with our silhouette extraction scheme. For this comparison we measured computation based on the number of edges explicitly tested and nodes traversed. We did not use wall-clock time because our implementation of Johannsen and Carter was not overly optimized. For bunnies with 500, 4000, 20,000, 50,000, and 69,674 faces, our speedup factors were 1.1, 1.3, 1.5, 2.0, and 2.1, respectively.

8 Summary and Future Work

We have shown that silhouette clipping is a practical framework for rendering simplified geometry while preserving the original model silhouette. The operations of extracting silhouette edges and setting the stencil buffer can be implemented efficiently at runtime. With little added cost, silhouette clipping also permits antialiasing of the silhouette, a feature previously available only through expensive supersampling. Several areas for future work remain.

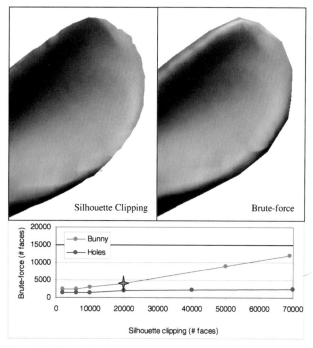

Figure 11: Comparison between silhouette clipping and brute-force rendering. The x-axis represents the resolution of the model used for silhouette extraction. The resolution of the coarse hull was fixed at 500 faces. The curves represent configurations that take the same amount of time to render. The star represents the configuration used in the bunny ear example shown above.

The complexity of the extracted silhouette should be adapted to the view, since it is obviously unnecessary to extract thousands of edges from an object covering a few pixels. Given a set of LOD meshes, our framework can use these for silhouette extraction by creating for each one a corresponding coarser hull. Alternatively, all of the silhouette meshes and their associated coarse hulls could be extracted from a single progressive hull. A related idea is to perform higher-order interpolation on the silhouette using projected derivatives or curvatures in addition to 2D points. This would result in smoother silhouettes without extracting more silhouette edges.

Currently, silhouette clipping only improves the appearance of exterior silhouettes. We have considered several approaches for dealing with interior silhouettes. One possibility is to exploit the winding number computed in the stencil buffer. Another approach partitions the mesh and applies silhouette clipping to each piece independently. We have performed initial experiments along these lines, but have not yet obtained a satisfactory solution.

Since the exterior silhouette of a shape is determined by its visual hull [16], silhouette extraction is unaffected by any simplification of the original mesh that preserves its visual hull. As an example, the interior concavity of a bowl can be simplified until it spans the bowl's rim. Such simplification offers an opportunity for further reducing silhouette extraction cost.

Acknowledgments

For the models we would like to thank Stanford University and Viewpoint DataLabs. We would also like to thank the MIT Laboratory for Computer Science for use of their equipment. The first three authors have been supported in part by the NSF, Sloan Foundation, and Microsoft Research.

References

[1] BLYTHE, D., GRANTHAM, B., NELSON, S., AND MCREYNOLDS, T. Advanced graphics programming techniques using OpenGL. avail from www.opengl.org.

[2] CIGNONI, P., MONTANI, C., ROCCHINI, C., AND SCOPIGNO, R. A general method for preserving attribute values on simplified meshes. In *Visualization '98 Proceedings*, IEEE, pp. 59–66.

[3] COHEN, J., OLANO, M., AND MANOCHA, D. Appearance-preserving simplification. *SIGGRAPH '98*, 115–122.

[4] DOBKIN, D. P., AND KIRKPATRICK, D. Determining the separation of preprocessed polyhedra – a unified approach. *ICALP-90, LNCS 443* (1990), 400–413.

[5] GILBERT, E. G., JOHNSON, D., AND KEERTHI, S. A Fast Procedure for Computing the Distance Between Complex Objects in Three-Dimensional Space. *IEEE Journal Of Robotics and Automation*, 2 (April 1988), 193–203.

[6] GOOCH, A., GOOCH, B., SHIRLEY, P., AND COHEN, E. A Non-Photorealistic Lighting Model for Automatic Technical Illustration. *SIGGRAPH 98*, 447–452.

[7] GOOCH, B., SLOAN, P., GOOCH, A., SHIRLEY, P., AND RIESEN-FELD, R. Interactive Technical Illustration. *ACM Symposium on Interactive 3D graphics 1999*, 31–38.

[8] GU, X., GORTLER, S., HOPPE, H., MCMILLAN, L., BROWN, B., AND STONE, A. Silhouette Mapping. Technical Report TR-1-99, Department of Computer Science, Harvard University, March 1999.

[9] GUÉZIEC, A. Surface simplification with variable tolerance. In *Proceedings of the Second International Symposium on Medical Robotics and Computer Assisted Surgery* (November 1995), pp. 132–139.

[10] HECKBERT, P., AND GARLAND, M. Survey of polygonal surface simplification algorithms. In *Multiresolution surface modeling (SIGGRAPH '97 Course notes #25)*. ACM SIGGRAPH, 1997.

[11] HOPPE, H. Progressive meshes. *SIGGRAPH '96*, 99–108.

[12] HOPPE, H. View-dependent refinement of progressive meshes. *SIGGRAPH '97*, 189–198.

[13] JOHANNSEN, A., AND CARTER, M. B. Clustered Backface Culling. *Journal of Graphics Tools 3*, 1 (1998), 1–14.

[14] KOENDERINK, J. J. What does the occluding contour tell us about solid shape. *Perception 13* (1984), 321–330.

[15] KUMAR, S., MANOCHA, D., GARRETT, W., AND LIN, M. Hierarchical Back-Face Computation. *Eurographics Rendering Workshop 1996*, 235–244.

[16] LAURENTINI, A. The visual hull concept for silhouette based image understanding. *IEEE PAMI 16*, 2 (1994), 150–162.

[17] LINDSTROM, P., AND TURK, G. Fast and memory efficient polygonal simplification. In *Visualization '98 Proceedings*, IEEE, pp. 279–286.

[18] LUEBKE, D., AND ERIKSON, C. View-dependent simplification of arbitrary polygonal environments. *SIGGRAPH '97*, 199–208.

[19] MARKOSIAN, L., KOWALSKI, M., TRYCHIN, S., AND HUGUES, J. Real time non photorealistic rendering. *SIGGRAPH '97*, 415–420.

[20] MARUYA, M. Generating texture map from object-surface texture data. *Computer Graphics Forum (Proceedings of Eurographics '95) 14*, 3 (1995), 397–405.

[21] NEIDER, J., DAVIS, T., AND WOO, M. *OpenGL Programming Guide, Second Edition*. Addison-Wesley, 1997.

[22] NEWELL, M. E., AND SEQUIN, C. The Inside Story on Self-Intersecting Polygons. *Lambda 1*, 2 (1980), 20–24.

[23] RASKAR, R., AND COHEN, M. Image Precision Silhouette Edges. *ACM Symposium on Interactive 3D Graphics 1999*, 135–140.

[24] ROSSIGNAC, J., AND VAN EMMERIK, M. Hidden contours on a frame-buffer. *Proceedings of the 7th Workshop on Computer Graphics Hardware* (1992).

[25] SNYDER, J., AND LENGYEL, J. Visibility Sorting and Compositing without Splitting for Image Layer Decompositions. *SIGGRAPH '98*, 219–230.

[26] SOUCY, M., GODIN, G., AND RIOUX, M. A texture-mapping approach for the compression of colored 3D triangulations. *The Visual Computer 12* (1986), 503–514.

[27] XIA, J., AND VARSHNEY, A. Dynamic view-dependent simplification for polygonal models. In *Visualization '96 Proceedings*, IEEE, pp. 327–334.

Surfels: Surface Elements as Rendering Primitives

Hanspeter Pfister *   Matthias Zwicker †   Jeroen van Baar*   Markus Gross†

Abstract

Surface elements (surfels) are a powerful paradigm to efficiently render complex geometric objects at interactive frame rates. Unlike classical surface discretizations, i.e., triangles or quadrilateral meshes, surfels are point primitives without explicit connectivity. Surfel attributes comprise depth, texture color, normal, and others. As a pre-process, an octree-based surfel representation of a geometric object is computed. During sampling, surfel positions and normals are optionally perturbed, and different levels of texture colors are prefiltered and stored per surfel. During rendering, a hierarchical forward warping algorithm projects surfels to a z-buffer. A novel method called visibility splatting determines visible surfels and holes in the z-buffer. Visible surfels are shaded using texture filtering, Phong illumination, and environment mapping using per-surfel normals. Several methods of image reconstruction, including supersampling, offer flexible speed-quality tradeoffs. Due to the simplicity of the operations, the surfel rendering pipeline is amenable for hardware implementation. Surfel objects offer complex shape, low rendering cost and high image quality, which makes them specifically suited for low-cost, real-time graphics, such as games.

CR Categories: I.3.3 [Computer Graphics]: Picture/Image Generation – Viewing Algorithms; I.3.6 [Computer Graphics]: Methodology and Techniques – Graphics Data Structures and Data Types.

Keywords: Rendering Systems, Texture Mapping.

---

*MERL, Cambridge, MA. Email: [pfister,jeroen]@merl.com
†ETH Zürich, Switzerland. Email: [zwicker,gross]@inf.ethz.ch

1 Introduction

3D computer graphics has finally become ubiquitous at the consumer level. There is a proliferation of affordable 3D graphics hardware accelerators, from high-end PC workstations to low-priced gamestations. Undoubtedly, key to this success is interactive computer games that have emerged as the "killer application" for 3D graphics. However, interactive computer graphics has still not reached the level of realism that allows a true immersion into a virtual world. For example, typical foreground characters in real-time games are extremely minimalistic polygon models that often exhibit faceting artifacts, such as angular silhouettes.

Various sophisticated modeling techniques, such as implicit surfaces, NURBS, or subdivision surfaces, allow the creation of 3D graphics models with increasingly complex shapes. Higher order modeling primitives, however, are eventually decomposed into triangles before being rendered by the graphics subsystem. The triangle as a rendering primitive seems to meet the right balance between descriptive power and computational burden [7]. To render realistic, organic-looking models requires highly complex shapes with ever more triangles, or, as Alvy Ray Smith puts it: "Reality is 80 million polygons" [26]. Processing many small triangles leads to bandwidth bottlenecks and excessive floating point and rasterization requirements [7].

To increase the apparent visual complexity of objects, texture mapping was introduced by Catmull [3] and successfully applied by others [13]. Textures convey more detail inside a polygon, thereby allowing larger and fewer triangles to be used. Today's graphics engines are highly tailored for high texture mapping performance. However, texture maps have to follow the underlying geometry of the polygon model and work best on flat or slightly curved surfaces. Realistic surfaces frequently require a large number of textures that have to be applied in multiple passes during rasterization. And phenomena such as smoke, fire, or water are difficult to render using textured triangles.

In this paper we propose a new method of rendering objects with rich shapes and textures at interactive frame rates. Our rendering architecture is based on simple surface elements (*surfels*) as rendering primitives. Surfels are point samples of a graphics model. In a preprocessing step, we sample the surfaces of complex geometric models along three orthographic views. At the same time, we perform computation-intensive calculations such as texture, bump, or displacement mapping. By moving rasterization and texturing from

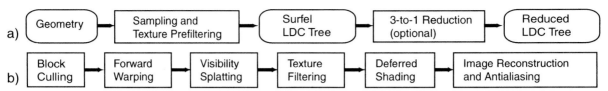

Figure 2: *Algorithm overview: a) Preprocessing. b) Rendering of the hierarchical LDC tree.*

the core rendering pipeline to the preprocessing step, we dramatically reduce the rendering cost.

From a modeling point of view, the surfel representation provides a mere discretization of the geometry and hence reduces the object representation to the essentials needed for rendering. By contrast, triangle primitives implicitly store connectivity information, such as vertex valence or adjacency – data not necessarily available or needed for rendering. In a sense, a surfel relates to what Levoy and Whitted call the *lingua franca* of rendering in their pioneering report from 1985 [18].

Storing normals, prefiltered textures, and other per surfel data enables us to build high quality rendering algorithms. Shading and transformations applied per surfel result in Phong illumination, bump, and displacement mapping, as well as other advanced rendering features. Our data structure provides a multiresolution object representation, and a hierarchical forward warping algorithm allows us to estimate the surfel density in the output image for speed-quality tradeoffs.

The surfel rendering pipeline complements the existing graphics pipeline and does not intend to replace it. It is positioned between conventional geometry-based approaches and image-based rendering and trades memory overhead for rendering performance and quality. The focus of this work has been interactive 3D applications, not high-end applications such as feature films or CAD/CAM. Surfels are not well suited to represent flat surfaces, such as walls or scene backgrounds, where large, textured polygons provide better image quality at lower rendering cost. However, surfels work well for models with rich, organic shapes or high surface details and for applications where preprocessing is not an issue. These qualities make them ideal for interactive games.

2 Related Work

The use of points as rendering primitives has a long history in computer graphics. As far back as 1974, Catmull [3] observed that geometric subdivision may ultimately lead to points. Particles were subsequently used for objects that could not be rendered with geometry, such as clouds, explosions, and fire [23]. More recently, image-based rendering has become popular because its rendering time is proportional to the number of pixels in the source and output images and not the scene complexity.

Visually complex objects have been represented by dynamically generated image sprites [25], which are quick to draw and largely retain the visual characteristics of the object. A similar approach was used in the Talisman rendering system [27] to maintain high and approximately constant frame rates. However, mapping objects onto planar polygons leads to visibility errors and does not allow for parallax and disocclusion effects. To address these problems, several methods add per-pixel depth information to images, variously called layered impostors [24], sprites with depth, or layered depth images [25], just to name a few. Still, none of these techniques provide a complete object model that can be illuminated and rendered from arbitrary points of view.

Some image-based approaches represent objects without explicitly storing any geometry or depth. Methods such as view interpolation and Quicktime VR [5] or plenoptic modeling [21] create new views from a collection of 2D images. Lightfield [17] or lumigraph [9] techniques describe the radiance of a scene or object as a function of position and direction in a four- or higher-

dimensional space, but at the price of considerable storage overhead. All these methods use view-dependent samples to represent an object or scene. However, view-dependent samples are ineffective for dynamic scenes with motion of objects, changes in material properties, and changes in position and intensities of light sources.

The main idea of representing objects with surfels is to describe them in a view-independent, object-centered rather than image-centered fashion. As such, surfel rendering is positioned between geometry rendering and image-based rendering. In volume graphics [16], synthetic objects are implicitly represented with surface voxels, typically stored on a regular grid. However, the extra third dimension of volumes comes at the price of higher storage requirements and longer rendering times. In [8], Perlin studies "surflets," a flavor of wavelets that can be used to describe free-form implicit surfaces. Surflets have less storage overhead than volumes, but rendering them requires lengthy ray casting.

Our research was inspired by the following work: Animatek's Caviar player [1] provides interactive frame rates for surface voxel models on a Pentium class PC, but uses simplistic projection and illumination methods. Levoy and Whitted [18] use points to model objects for the special case of continuous, differentiable surfaces. They address the problem of texture filtering in detail. Max uses point samples obtained from orthographic views to model and render trees [20]. Dally et al. [6] introduced the delta tree as an object-centered approach to image-based rendering. The movement of the viewpoint in their method, however, is still confined to particular locations. More recently, Grossman and Dally [12] describe a point sample representation for fast rendering of complex objects. Chang et al. [4] presented the LDI tree, a hierarchical space-partitioning data structure for image-based rendering.

We extend and integrate these ideas and present a complete point sample rendering system comprising an efficient hierarchical representation, high quality texture filtering, accurate visibility calculations, and image reconstruction with flexible speed-quality tradeoffs. Our surfel rendering pipeline provides high quality rendering of exceedingly complex models and is amenable for hardware implementation.

3 Conceptual Overview

Similar to the method proposed by Levoy and Whitted [18], our surfel approach consists of two main steps: sampling and surfel rendering. Sampling of geometry and texture is done during preprocessing, which may include other view-independent methods such as bump and displacement mapping. Figure 2 gives a conceptual overview of the algorithm.

The sampling process (Section 5) converts geometric objects and their textures to surfels. We use ray casting to create three orthogonal layered depth images (LDIs) [25]. The LDIs store multiple surfels along each ray, one for each ray-surface intersection point. Lischinski and Rappaport [19] call this arrangement of three orthogonal LDIs a *layered depth cube (LDC)*. An important and novel aspect of our sampling method is the distinction between sampling of *shape*, or geometry, and *shade*, or texture color. A surfel stores both shape, such as surface position and orientation, and shade, such as multiple levels of prefiltered texture colors. Because of the similarities to traditional texture mipmaps we call this hierarchical color information a *surfel mipmap*.

From the LDC we create an efficient hierarchical data structure for rendering. Chang et al.[4] introduce the LDI tree, an octree with an LDI attached to each octree node. We use the same hierarchical space-partitioning structure, but store an LDC at each node of the octree (Section 6). Each LDC node in the octree is called a *block*. We call the resulting data structure the *LDC tree*. In a step called *3-to-1 reduction* we optionally reduce the LDCs to single LDIs on a block-by-block basis for faster rendering.

The rendering pipeline (Section 7) hierarchically projects blocks to screen space using perspective projection. The rendering is accelerated by block culling [12] and fast incremental forward warping. We estimate the projected surfel density in the output image to control rendering speed and quality of the image reconstruction. A conventional z-buffer together with a novel method called *visibility splatting* solves the visibility problem. Texture colors of visible surfels are filtered using linear interpolation between appropriate levels of the surfel mipmap. Each visible surfel is shaded using, for example, Phong illumination and reflection mapping. The final stage performs image reconstruction from visible surfels, including hole filling and antialiasing. In general, the resolution of the output image and the resolution of the z-buffer do not have to be the same.

4 Definition of a Surfel

We found the term surfel as an abbreviation for *surface element* or *surface voxel* in the volume rendering and discrete topology literature. Herman [15] defines a surfel as an oriented $(n-1)$-dimensional object in R^n. For $n = 3$, this corresponds to an oriented unit square (voxel face) and is consistent with thinking of voxels as little cubes. However, for our discussion we find it more useful to define surfels as follows:

A surfel is a zero-dimensional n-tuple with shape and shade attributes that locally approximate an object surface.

We consider the alternative term, point sample, to be too general, since voxels and pixels are point samples as well.

5 Sampling

The goal during sampling is to find an optimal surfel representation of the geometry with minimum redundancy. Most sampling methods perform object discretization as a function of geometric parameters of the surface, such as curvature or silhouettes. This *object space* discretization typically leads to too many or too few primitives for rendering. In a surfel representation, object sampling is aligned to *image space* and matches the expected output resolution of the image.

5.1 LDC Sampling

We sample geometric models from three sides of a cube into three orthogonal LDIs, called a *layered depth cube (LDC)* [19] or *block*. Figure 3 shows an LDC and two LDIs using a 2D drawing. Ray

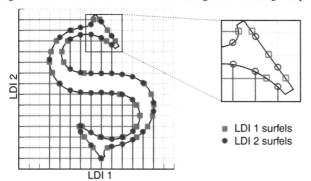

Figure 3: *Layered depth cube sampling (shown in 2D).*

casting records all intersections, including intersections with backfacing surfaces. At each intersection point, a surfel is created with floating point depth and other shape and shade properties. Perturbation of the surface normal or of the geometry for bump and displacement mapping can be performed on the geometry before sampling or during ray casting using procedural shaders.

Alternatively, we could sample an object from predetermined directions on a surrounding convex hull using orthographic depth images [6, 12]. However, combining multiple reference images and eliminating the redundant information is a difficult problem [21], and sampling geometry with reference images works best for smooth and convex objects. In addition, LDC sampling allows us to easily build a hierarchical data structure, which would be difficult to do from dozens of depth images.

5.2 Adequate Sampling Resolution

Given a pixel spacing of h_0 for the full resolution LDC used for sampling, we can determine the resulting sampling density on the surface. Suppose we construct a Delaunay triangulation on the object surface using the generated surfels as triangle vertices. As was observed in [19], the imaginary triangle mesh generated by this sampling process has a maximum sidelength s_{max} of $\sqrt{3}h_0$. The minimum sidelength s_{min} is 0 when two or three sampling rays intersect at the same surface position.

Similarly to [12], we call the object *adequately sampled* if we can guarantee that at least one surfel is projected into the support of each output pixel filter for orthographic projection and unit magnification. That condition is met if s_{max}, the maximum distance between adjacent surfels in object space, is less than the radius r'_{rec} of the desired pixel reconstruction filter. Typically, we choose the LDI resolution to be slightly higher than this because of the effects of magnification and perspective projection. We will revisit these observations when estimating the number of projected surfels per pixel in Section 7.2.

5.3 Texture Prefiltering

A feature of surfel rendering is that textures are prefiltered and mapped to object space during preprocessing. We use *view-independent* texture filtering as in [12]. To prevent view-dependent texture aliasing we also apply per-surfel texture filtering during rendering (see Sections 7.4 and 7.6).

To determine the extent of the filter footprint in texture space, we center a circle at each surfel on its tangent plane, as shown in Figure 4a. We call these circles *tangent disks*. The tangent disks are

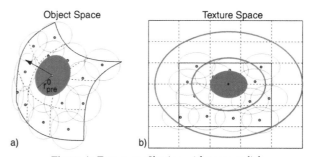

Figure 4: *Texture prefiltering with tangent disks.*

mapped to ellipses in texture space (see Figure 4b) using the predefined texture parameterization of the surface. An EWA filter [14] is applied to filter the texture and the resulting color is assigned to the surfel. To enable adequate texture reconstruction, the elliptical filter footprints in texture space must overlap each other. Consequently, we choose $r^0_{pre} = s_{max}$, the maximum distance between adjacent surfels in object space, as the radius for the tangent disks. This usually guarantees that the tangent disks intersect each other in object space and that their projections in texture space overlap.

Grossman and Dally [12] also use view-independent texture filtering and store one texture sample per surfel. Since we use a modified z-buffer algorithm to resolve visibility (Section 7.3), not all surfels may be available for image reconstruction, which leads to texture aliasing artifacts. Consequently, we store several (typically three or four) prefiltered texture samples per surfel. Tangent disks with dyadically larger radii $r_{pre}^k = s_{max} 2^k$ are mapped to texture space and used to compute the prefiltered colors. Because of its similarity to mipmapping [13], we call this a *surfel mipmap*. Figure 4b shows the elliptical footprints in texture space of consecutively larger tangent disks.

6 Data Structure

We use the LDC tree, an efficient hierarchical data structure, to store the LDCs acquired during sampling. It allows us to quickly estimate the number of projected surfels per pixel and to trade rendering speed for higher image quality.

6.1 The LDC Tree

Chang et al. [4] use several reference depth images of a scene to construct the LDI tree. The depth image pixels are resampled onto multiple LDI tree nodes using splatting [29]. We avoid these interpolation steps by storing LDCs at each node in the octree that are subsampled versions of the highest resolution LDC.

The octree is recursively constructed bottom up, and its height is selected by the user. The highest resolution LDC — acquired during geometry sampling — is stored at the lowest level $n = 0$. If the highest resolution LDC has a pixel spacing of h_0, then the LDC at level n has a pixel spacing of $h_n = h_0 2^n$. The LDC is subdivided into blocks with user-specified dimension b, i.e., the LDIs in a block have b^2 layered depth pixels. b is the same for all levels of the tree. Figure 5a shows two levels of an LDC tree with $b = 4$ using a 2D drawing. In the figure, neighboring blocks are differently shaded,

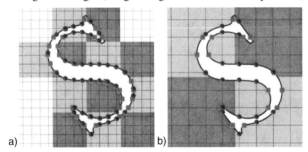

Figure 5: *Two levels of the LDC tree (shown in 2D).*

and empty blocks are white. Blocks on higher levels of the octree are constructed by subsampling their children by a factor of two. Figure 5b shows level $n = 1$ of the LDC tree. Note that surfels at higher levels of the octree reference surfels in the LDC of level 0, i.e., surfels that appear in several blocks of the hierarchy are stored only once and shared between blocks.

Empty blocks (shown as white squares in the figure) are not stored. Consequently, the block dimension b is not related to the dimension of the highest resolution LDC and can be selected arbitrarily. Choosing $b = 1$ makes the LDC tree a fully volumetric octree representation. For a comparison between LDCs and volumes see [19].

6.2 3-to-1 Reduction

To reduce storage and rendering time it is often useful to optionally reduce the LDCs to one LDI on a block-by-block basis. Because this typically corresponds to a three-fold increase in warping speed, we call this step *3-to-1 reduction*. First, surfels are resampled to integer grid locations of ray intersections as shown in Figure 6. Currently we use nearest neighbor interpolation, although a more

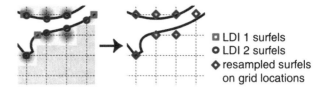

Figure 6: *3-to-1 reduction example.*

sophisticated filter, e.g., splatting as in [4], could easily be implemented. The resampled surfels of the block are then stored in a single LDI.

The reduction and resampling process degrades the quality of the surfel representation, both for shape and for shade. Resampled surfels from the same surface may have very different texture colors and normals. This may cause color and shading artifacts that are worsened during object motion. In practice, however, we did not encounter severe artifacts due to 3-to-1 reduction. Because our rendering pipeline handles LDCs and LDIs the same way, we could store blocks with thin structures as LDCs, while all other blocks could be reduced to single LDIs.

As in Section 5.2, we can determine bounds on the surfel density on the surface after 3-to-1 reduction. Given a sampling LDI with pixel spacing h_0, the maximum distance between adjacent surfels on the object surface is $s_{max} = \sqrt{3} h_0$, as in the original LDC tree. The minimum distance between surfels increases to $s_{min} = h_0$ due to the elimination of redundant surfels, making the imaginary Delaunay triangulation on the surface more uniform.

7 The Rendering Pipeline

The rendering pipeline takes the surfel LDC tree and renders it using hierarchical visibility culling and forward warping of blocks. Hierarchical rendering also allows us to estimate the number of projected surfels per output pixel. For maximum rendering efficiency, we project approximately one surfel per pixel and use the same resolution for the z-buffer as in the output image. For maximum image quality, we project multiple surfels per pixel, use a finer resolution of the z-buffer, and high quality image reconstruction.

7.1 Block Culling

We traverse the LDC tree from top (the lowest resolution blocks) to bottom (the highest resolution blocks). For each block, we first perform view-frustum culling using the block bounding box. Next, we use *visibility cones*, as described in [11], to perform the equivalent of backface culling of blocks. Using the surfel normals, we precompute a visibility cone per block, which gives a fast, conservative visibility test: no surfel in the block is visible from any viewpoint within the cone. In contrast to [11], we perform all visibility tests hierarchically in the LDC tree, which makes them more efficient.

7.2 Block Warping

During rendering, the LDC tree is traversed top to bottom [4]. To choose the octree level to be projected, we conservatively estimate for each block the number of surfels per pixel. We can choose one surfel per pixel for fast rendering or multiple surfels per pixel for supersampling. For each block at tree level n, the number of surfels per pixel is determined by i_{max}^n, the maximum distance between adjacent surfels in image space. We estimate i_{max}^n by dividing the maximum length of the projected four major diagonals of the block bounding box by the block dimension b. This is correct for orthographic projection. However, the error introduced by using perspective projection is small because a block typically projects to a small number of pixels.

For each block, i_{max}^n is compared to the radius r_{rec}' of the desired pixel reconstruction filter. r_{rec}' is typically $\frac{\sqrt{2}}{2} s_o$, where s_o

is the sidelength of an output pixel. If i_{max}^n of the current block is larger than r'_{rec} then its children are traversed. We project the block whose i_{max}^n is smaller than r'_{rec}, rendering approximately one surfel per pixel. Note that the number of surfels per pixel can be increased by requiring that i_{max}^n is a fraction of r'_{rec}. The resulting i_{max}^n is stored as i_{max} with each projected surfel for subsequent use in the visibility testing and the image reconstruction stages. The radius of the actual reconstruction filter is $r_{rec} = \max(r'_{rec}, i_{max})$ (see Section 7.6).

To warp a block to screen space we use the optimized incremental block warping by Grossman and Dally, presented in detail in [11]. Its high efficiency is achieved due to the regularity of LDCs. It uses only 6 additions, 3 multiplications, and 1 reciprocal per sample. The LDIs in each LDC block are warped independently, which allows us to render an LDC tree where some or all blocks have been reduced to single LDIs after 3-to-1 reduction.

7.3 Visibility Testing

Perspective projection, high z-buffer resolution, and magnification may lead to undersampling or holes in the z-buffer. A z-buffer pixel is a *hole* if it does not contain a visible surfel or background pixel after projection. Holes have to be marked for image reconstruction. Each pixel of the z-buffer stores a pointer to the closest surfel and the current minimum depth. Surfel depths are projected to the z-buffer using nearest neighbor interpolation.

To correctly resolve visibility in light of holes, we scan-convert the orthographic projection of the surfel tangent disks into the z-buffer. The tangent disks have a radius of $r_t^n = s_{max}2^n$, where s_{max} is the maximum distance between adjacent surfels in object space and n is the level of the block. We call this approach *visibility splatting*, shown in Figure 7. Visibility splatting effectively sepa-

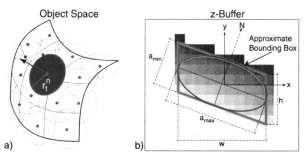

a)   b)

Figure 7: *Visibility splatting.*

rates visibility calculations and reconstruction of the image, which produces high quality images and is amenable to hardware implementation [22].

After orthographic projection, the tangent disks form an ellipse around the surfel, as shown in Figure 7b. We approximate the ellipse with a partially axis-aligned bounding box, shown in red. The bounding box parallelogram can be easily scan-converted, and each z-buffer pixel is filled with the appropriate depth (indicated by the shaded squares in the figure), depending on the surfel normal N. This scan conversion requires only simple setup calculations, no interpolation of colors, and no perspective divide.

The direction of the minor axis a_{min} of the projected ellipse is parallel to the projection of the surfel normal N. The major axis a_{max} is orthogonal to a_{min}. The length of a_{max} is the projection of the tangent disk radius r_t^n, which is approximated by i_{max}. This approximation takes the orientation and magnification of the LDC tree during projection into account. Next, we calculate the coordinate axis that is most parallel to a_{min} (the y-axis in Figure 7). The short side of the bounding box is axis aligned with this coordinate axis to simplify scan conversion. Its height h is computed by intersecting the ellipse with the coordinate axis. The width w of the

bounding box is determined by projecting the vertex at the intersection of the major axis and the ellipse onto the second axis (the x-axis in Figure 7).

$\frac{\partial z}{\partial x}$ and $\frac{\partial z}{\partial y}$ are the partial derivatives of the surfel depth z with respect to the screen x and y direction. They are constant because of the orthographic projection and can be calculated from the unit normal N. During scan conversion, the depth at each pixel inside the bounding box is calculated using $\frac{\partial z}{\partial x}$ and $\frac{\partial z}{\partial y}$. In addition, we add a small threshold to each projected z value. The threshold prevents surfels that lie on the foreground surface to be accidentally discarded. Pixels that have a larger z than the z values of the splatted tangent disk are marked as holes.

If the surface is extremely bent, the tangential planes do not cover it completely, potentially leaving tears and holes. In addition, extreme perspective projection makes orthographic projection a bad approximation to the actual projected tangent disk. In practice, however, we did not see this as a major problem. If the projected tangent disk is a circle, i.e., if N is almost parallel to the viewing direction, the bounding box parallelogram is a bad approximation. In this case, we use a square bounding box instead.

Using a somewhat related approach, Grossman and Dally [12] use a hierarchical z-buffer for visibility testing. Each surfel is projected and the hole size around the surfel is estimated. The radius of the hole determines the level of the hierarchical z-buffer where the z-depth of the surfel will be set. This can be regarded as visibility splatting using a hierarchical z-buffer. The advantage is that the visibility splat is performed with a single depth test in the hierarchical z-buffer. However, the visibility splat is always square, essentially representing a tangential disk that is parallel to the image plane. In addition, it is not necessarily centered around the projected surfel. To recover from those drawbacks, [12] introduces weights indicating coverage of surfels. But this makes the reconstruction process more expensive and does not guarantee complete coverage of hidden surfaces.

7.4 Texture Filtering

As explained in Section 5.3, each surfel in the LDC tree stores several prefiltered texture colors of the surfel mipmap. During rendering, the surfel color is linearly interpolated from the surfel mipmap colors depending on the object minification and surface orientation. Figure 8a shows all visible surfels of a sampled surface projected to the z-buffer. The ellipses around the centers of the surfels mark the projection of the footprints of the highest resolution texture prefilter (Section 5.3). Note that during prefiltering, we try to guarantee that the footprints cover the surface completely. In figure 8b

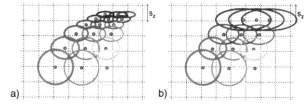

a)   b)

Figure 8: *Projected surfel mipmaps.*

the number of samples per z-buffer pixel is limited to one by applying z-buffer depth tests. In order to fill the gaps appearing in the coverage of the surface with texture footprints, the footprints of the remaining surfels have to be enlarged. If surfels are discarded in a given z-buffer pixel, we can assume that the z-buffer pixels in the 3x3 neighborhood around it are not holes. Thus the gaps can be filled if the texture footprint of each surfel covers at least the area of a z-buffer pixel. Consequently, the ellipse of the projected footprint has to have a minor radius of $\sqrt{2}s_z$ in the worst case, where s_z is the z-buffer pixel spacing. But we ignore that worst case and use $\frac{\sqrt{2}}{2}s_z$, implying that surfels are projected to z-buffer pixel centers.

Figure 8b shows the scaled texture footprints as ellipses around projected surfels.

To select the appropriate surfel mipmap level, we use traditional *view-dependent* texture filtering, as shown in Figure 9. A circle with

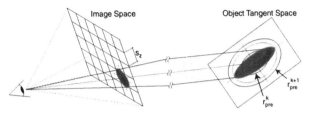

Figure 9: *Projected pixel coverage.*

radius $\frac{\sqrt{2}}{2}s_z$ is projected through a pixel onto the tangent plane of the surface from the direction of the view, producing an ellipse in the tangent plane. In this calculation, the projection of the circle is approximated with an orthographic projection. Similar to isotropic texture mapping, the major axis of the projected tangent space ellipse is used to determine the surfel mipmap level. The surfel color is computed by linear interpolation between the closest two mipmap levels with prefilter radii r_{pre}^k and r_{pre}^{k+1}, respectively.

7.5 Shading

The illumination model is usually applied before visibility testing. However, deferred shading after visibility testing avoids unnecessary work. Grossman and Dally [12] perform shading calculations in object space to avoid transformation of normals to camera space. However, we already transform the normals to camera space during visibility splatting (Section 7.3). With the transformed normals at hand, we use cube reflectance and environment maps [28] to calculate a per-surfel Phong illumination model. Shading with per-surfel normals results in high quality specular highlights.

7.6 Image Reconstruction and Antialiasing

Reconstructing a continuous surface from projected surfels is fundamentally a scattered data interpolation problem. In contrast to other approaches, such as splatting [29], we separate visibility calculations from image reconstruction [22]. Z-buffer pixels with holes are marked during visibility splatting. These hole pixels are not used during image reconstruction because they do not contain any visible samples. Figure 10 shows the z-buffer after rendering of an object and the image reconstruction process.

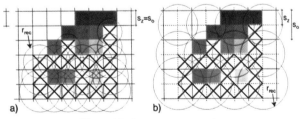

Figure 10: *Image reconstruction.*

The simplest and fastest approach, shown in Figure 10a, is to choose the size of an output pixel s_o to be the same as the z-buffer pixel size s_z. Surfels are mapped to pixel centers using nearest neighbor interpolation, shown with color squares in the figure. Holes are marked with a black X. Recall that during forward warping each surfel stores i_{max}, an estimate of the maximum distance between adjacent projected surfels of a block. i_{max} is a good estimate for the minimum radius of a pixel filter that contains at least one surfel. To interpolate the holes, we use a radially symmetric Gauss filter with a radius r_{rec} slightly larger than i_{max} positioned at hole pixel centers. Alternatively, to fill the holes we implemented

the pull-push algorithm used by Grossman and Dally [12] and described by Gortler et al.[9].

A high quality alternative is to use supersampling, shown in Figure 10b. The output image pixel size s_o is any multiple of the z-buffer pixel size s_z. Dotted lines in the figure indicate image-buffer subpixels. Rendering for supersampling proceeds exactly the same as before. During image reconstruction we put a Gaussian filter at the centers of all output pixels to filter the subpixel colors. The radius of the filter is $r_{rec} = \max(r'_{rec}, i_{max})$. Thus r_{rec} is at least as large as $r'_{rec} = \frac{\sqrt{2}}{2}s_o$, but it can be increased if i_{max} indicates a low density of surfels in the output image.

It is instructive to see how the color of an output pixel is determined for regular rendering and for supersampling in the absence of holes. For regular rendering, the pixel color is found by nearest neighbor interpolation from the closest visible surfel in the z-buffer. The color of that surfel is computed by linear interpolation between two surfel mipmap levels. Thus the output pixel color is calculated from two prefiltered texture samples. In the case of supersampling, one output pixel contains the filtered colors of one surfel per z-buffer subpixel. Thus, up to eight prefiltered texture samples may contribute to an output pixel for 2×2 supersampling. This produces image quality similar to trilinear mipmapping.

Levoy and Whitted [18] and Chang et al. [4] use an algorithm very similar to Carpenter's A-Buffer [2] with per-pixel bins and compositing of surfel colors. However, to compute the correct per pixel coverage in the A-buffer requires projecting all visible surfels. Max [20] uses an output LDI and an A-buffer for high quality anti-aliasing, but he reports rendering times of 5 minutes per frame. Our method with hierarchical density estimation, visibility splatting, and surfel mipmap texture filtering offers more flexible speed-quality tradeoffs.

8 Implementation and Results

We implemented sampling using the Blue Moon Rendering Tools (BMRT) ray tracer [10]. We use a sampling resolution of 512^2 for the LDC for 480^2 expected output resolution. At each intersection point, a Renderman shader performs view-independent calculations, such as texture filtering, displacement mapping, and bump mapping, and prints the resulting surfels to a file. Pre-processing for a typical object with 6 LOD surfel mipmaps takes about one hour.

A fundamental limitation of LDC sampling is that thin structures that are smaller than the sampling grid cannot be correctly represented and rendered. For example, spokes, thin wires, or hair are hard to capture. The rendering artifacts are more pronounced after 3-to-1 reduction because additional surfels are deleted. However, we had no problems sampling geometry as thin as the legs and wings of the wasp shown in Figure 1 and Figure 12.

The surfel attributes acquired during sampling include a surface normal, specular color, shininess, and three texture mipmap levels. Material properties are stored as an index into a table. Our system does currently not support transparency. Instead of storing a normal we store an index to a quantized normal table for reflection and environment map shading [28]. Table 1 shows the minimum storage requirements per surfel. We currently store RGB colors as 32-bit integers for a total of 20 Bytes per surfel.

Data	Storage
3 texture mipmap levels	3×32 bits
Index into normal table	16 bit
LDI depth value	32 bit
Index into material table	16 bit
Total per sample:	20 Bytes

Table 1: *Typical storage requirements per surfel.*

Table 2 lists the surfel objects that we used for performance analysis with their geometric model size, number of surfels, and file size

Figure 11: *Tilted checker plane. Reconstruction filter: a) Nearest neighbor. b) Gaussian filter. c) Supersampling.*

before and after 3-to-1 reduction. All models use three LODs and three surfel mipmap levels. The size of the LDC tree is about a factor of 1.3 larger than the LDC acquired during sampling. This

Data	# Polys	3 LDIs	3-to-1 Reduced
Salamander	81 k	112 k / 5 MB	70 k / 3 MB
Wasp	128 k	369 k / 15 MB	204 k / 8 MB
Cab	155 k	744 k / 28 MB	539 k / 20 MB

Table 2: *Geometric model sizes and storage requirements (# surfels / file size) for full and 3-to-1 reduced LDC trees.*

overhead is due to the octree data structure, mainly because of the pointers from the lower resolution blocks to surfels of the sampled LDC. We currently do not optimize or compress the LDC tree.

Figure 1 shows different renderings of surfel objects, including environment mapping and displacement mapping. Figure 12 shows an example of hole detection and image reconstruction. Visibility splatting performs remarkably well in detecting holes. However, holes start to appear in the output image for extreme closeups when there are less than approximately one surfel per 30 square pixels.

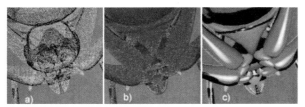

Figure 12: *Hole detection and image reconstruction. a) Surfel object with holes. b) Hole detection (hole pixels in green). c) Image reconstruction with a Gaussian filter.*

To compare image quality of different reconstruction filters, we rendered the surfel checker plane shown in Figure 11. There is an increasing number of surfels per pixel towards the top of the image, while holes appear towards the bottom for nearest neighbor reconstruction. However, a checker plane also demonstrates limitations of the surfel representation. Because textures are applied during sampling, periodic texture patterns are stored explicitly with the object instead of by reference. In addition, flat surfaces are much more efficiently rendered using image space rasterization, where attributes can be interpolated across triangle spans.

Table 3 shows rendering performance broken down into percentages per major rendering tasks. The frame rates were measured on a 700 MHz Pentium III system with 256 MB of SDRAM using an unoptimized C version of our program. All performance numbers are averaged over one minute of an animation that arbitrarily rotates

Data	WRP	VIS	SHD	REC	CLR	fps
Output image: 256 × 256						
Salamander	39%	3%	28%	17%	13%	11.2
Wasp	61%	4%	21%	8%	8%	6.0
Cab	91%	2%	5%	1%	1%	2.5
Output image: 480 × 480						
Salamander	14%	18%	31%	22%	16%	4.6
Wasp 3to1	29%	17%	29%	15%	9%	2.7
Wasp 3LDI	48%	13%	22%	11%	6%	2.0
Wasp SS	15%	22%	28%	18%	16%	1.3
Cab	74%	7%	11%	5%	3%	1.4
Output image: 1024 × 1024						
Salamander	5%	14%	26%	32%	23%	1.3
Wasp	13%	19%	25%	26%	17%	1.0
Cab	16%	36%	24%	16%	8%	0.6

Table 3: *Rendering times with breakdown for warping (WRP), visibility splatting (VIS), Phong shading (SHD), image reconstruction (REC), and framebuffer clear (CLR). Reconstruction with pull-push filter. All models, except Wasp 3LDI, are 3-to-1 reduced. Wasp SS indicates 2x2 supersampling.*

the object centered at the origin. The animation was run at three different image resolutions to measure the effects of magnification and holes.

Similar to image-based rendering, the performance drops almost linearly with increasing output resolution. For 256^2 or object minification, the rendering is dominated by warping, especially for objects with many surfels. For 1024^2, or large object magnification, visibility splatting and reconstruction dominate due to the increasing number of surface holes. The performance difference between a full LDC tree (Wasp 3LDI) and a reduced LDC tree (Wasp 3to1) is mainly in the warping stage because fewer surfels have to be projected. Performance decreases linearly with supersampling, as shown for 2x2 supersampling at 480^2 resolution (Wasp SS). The same object at 1024^2 output resolution with no supersampling performs almost identically, except for slower image reconstruction due to the increased number of hole pixels.

To compare our performance to standard polygon rendering, we rendered the wasp with 128k polygons and 2.3 MB for nine textures using a software-only Windows NT OpenGL viewing program. We used GL_LINEAR_MIPMAP_NEAREST for texture filtering to achieve similar quality as with our renderer. The average performance was 3 fps using the Microsoft OpenGL implementation (opengl32.lib) and 1.7 fps using Mesa OpenGL. Our unoptimized surfel renderer achieves 2.7 fps for the same model, which compares favorably with Mesa OpenGL. We believe that further optimization will greatly improve our performance.

Choosing the block size b for the LDC tree nodes has an influence on block culling and warping performance. We found that a block size of $b = 16$ is optimal for a wide range of objects. However, the frame rates remain practically the same for different choices of b due to the fact that warping accounts for only a fraction of the overall rendering time.

Because we use a z-buffer we can render overlapping surfel objects and integrate them with traditional polygon graphics, such as OpenGL. However, the current system supports only rigid body animations. Deformable objects are difficult to represent with surfels and the current LDC tree data structure. In addition, if the surfels do not approximate the object surface well, for example after 3-to-1 reduction or in areas of high curvature, some surface holes may appear during rendering.

9 Future Extensions

A major strength of surfel rendering is that in principal we can convert any kind of synthetic or scanned object to surfels. We would like to extend our sampling approach to include volume data, point clouds, and LDIs of non-synthetic objects. We believe that substantial compression of the LDC tree can be achieved using run length encoding or wavelet-based compression techniques. The performance of our software renderer can be substantially improved by using Pentium III SSE instructions. Using an occlusion compatible traversal of the LDC tree [21], one could implement order-independent transparency and true volume rendering.

Our major goal is the design of a hardware architecture for surfel rendering. Block warping is very simple, involving only two conditionals for z-buffer tests [11]. There are no clipping calculations. All framebuffer operations, such as visibility splatting and image reconstruction, can be implemented using standard rasterization and framebuffer techniques. The rendering pipeline uses no inverse calculations, such as looking up textures from texture maps, and runtime texture filtering is very simple. There is a high degree of data locality because the system loads shape and shade simultaneously and we expect high cache performance. It is also possible to enhance an existing OpenGL rendering pipeline to efficiently support surfel rendering.

10 Conclusions

Surfel rendering is ideal for models with very high shape and shade complexity. As we move rasterization and texturing from the core rendering pipeline to the preprocessing step, the rendering cost per pixel is dramatically reduced. Rendering performance is essentially determined by warping, shading, and image reconstruction — operations that can easily exploit vectorization, parallelism, and pipelining.

Our surfel rendering pipeline offers several speed-quality trade-offs. By decoupling image reconstruction and texture filtering we achieve much higher image quality than comparable point sample approaches. We introduce visibility splatting, which is very effective at detecting holes and increases image reconstruction performance. Antialiasing with supersampling is naturally integrated in our system. Our results demonstrate that surfel rendering is capable of high image quality at interactive frame rates. Increasing processor performance and possible hardware support will bring it into the realm of real-time performance.

11 Acknowledgments

We would like to thank Ron Perry and Ray Jones for many helpful discussions, Collin Oosterbaan and Frits Post for their contributions to an earlier version of the system, and Adam Moravanszky and Simon Schirm for developing a surfel demo application. Thanks also to Matt Brown, Mark Callahan, and Klaus Müller for contributing code, and to Larry Gritz for his help with BMRT [10]. Finally, thanks to Alyn Rockwood, Sarah Frisken, and the reviewers for their constructive comments, and to Jennifer Roderick for proofreading the paper.

References

[1] Animatek. Caviar Technology. Web page. http://www.animatek.com/.

[2] L. Carpenter. The A-buffer, an Antialiased Hidden Surface Method. In *Computer Graphics*, volume 18 of *SIGGRAPH '84 Proceedings*, pages 103–108. July 1984.

[3] E. E. Catmull. *A Subdivision Algorithm for Computer Display of Curved Surfaces*. Ph.D. thesis, University of Utah, Salt Lake City, December 1974.

[4] C.F. Chang, G. Bishop, and A. Lastra. LDI Tree: A Hierarchical Representation for Image-Based Rendering. In *Computer Graphics*, SIGGRAPH '99 Proceedings, pages 291–298. Los Angeles, CA, August 1999.

[5] S. E. Chen. Quicktime VR – An Image-Based Approach to Virtual Environment Navigation. In *Computer Graphics*, SIGGRAPH '95 Proceedings, pages 29–38. Los Angeles, CA, August 1995.

[6] W. Dally, L. McMillan, G. Bishop, and H. Fuchs. The Delta Tree: An Object-Centered Approach to Image-Based Rendering. Technical Report AIM-1604, AI Lab, MIT, May 1996.

[7] M. Deering. Data Complexity for Virtual Reality: Where do all the Triangles Go? In *IEEE Virtual Reality Annual International Symposium (VRAIS)*, pages 357–363. Seattle, WA, September 1993.

[8] D. Ebert, F. Musgrave, D. Peachey, K. Perlin, and S. Worley. *Texturing & Modeling - A Procedural Approach*. AP Professional, second edition, 1994.

[9] S. Gortler, R. Grzeszczuk, R. Szeliski, and M. Cohen. The Lumigraph. In *Computer Graphics*, SIGGRAPH '96 Proceedings, pages 43–54. New Orleans, LS, August 1996.

[10] L. Gritz. Blue Moon Rendering Tools. Web page. http://www.bmrt.org/.

[11] J. P. Grossman. *Point Sample Rendering*. Master's thesis, Department of Electrical Engineering and Computer Science, MIT, August 1998.

[12] J. P. Grossman and W. Dally. Point Sample Rendering. In *Rendering Techniques '98*, pages 181–192. Springer, Wien, Vienna, Austria, July 1998.

[13] P. Heckbert. Survey of Texture Mapping. *IEEE Computer Graphics & Applications*, 6(11):56–67, November 1986.

[14] P. Heckbert. *Fundamentals of Texture Mapping and Image Warping*. Master's thesis, University of California at Berkeley, Department of Electrical Engineering and Computer Science, June 17 1989.

[15] G. T. Herman. Discrete Multidimensional Jordan Surfaces. *CVGIP: Graphical Modeling and Image Processing*, 54(6):507–515, November 1992.

[16] A. Kaufman, D. Cohen, and R. Yagel. Volume Graphics. *Computer*, 26(7):51–64, July 1993.

[17] M. Levoy and P. Hanrahan. Light Field Rendering. In *Computer Graphics*, SIGGRAPH '96 Proceedings, pages 31–42. New Orleans, LS, August 1996.

[18] M. Levoy and T. Whitted. The Use of Points as Display Primitives. Technical Report TR 85-022, The University of North Carolina at Chapel Hill, Department of Computer Science, 1985.

[19] D. Lischinski and A. Rappoport. Image-Based Rendering for Non-Diffuse Synthetic Scenes. In *Rendering Techniques '98*, pages 301–314. Springer, Wien, Vienna, Austria, June 1998.

[20] N. Max. Hierarchical Rendering of Trees from Precomputed Multi-Layer Z-Buffers. In *Rendering Techniques '96*, pages 165–174. Springer, Wien, Porto, Portugal, June 1996.

[21] L. McMillan and G. Bishop. Plenoptic Modeling: An Image-Based Rendering System. In *Computer Graphics*, SIGGRAPH '95 Proceedings, pages 39–46. Los Angeles, CA, August 1995.

[22] V. Popescu and A. Lastra. High Quality 3D Image Warping by Separating Visibility from Reconstruction. Technical Report TR99-002, University of North Carolina, January 15 1999.

[23] W. T. Reeves. Particle Systems – A Technique for Modeling a Class of Fuzzy Objects. In *Computer Graphics*, volume 17 of *SIGGRAPH '83 Proceedings*, pages 359–376. July 1983.

[24] G. Schaufler. Per-Object Image Warping with Layered Impostors. In *Rendering Techniques '98*, pages 145–156. Springer, Wien, Vienna, Austria, June 1998.

[25] J. Shade, S. J. Gortler, L. He, and R. Szeliski. Layered Depth Images. In *Computer Graphics*, SIGGRAPH '98 Proceedings, pages 231–242. Orlando, FL, July 1998.

[26] A. R. Smith. Smooth Operator. *The Economist*, pages 73–74, March 6 1999. Science and Technology Section.

[27] J. Torborg and J. Kajiya. Talisman: Commodity Real-Time 3D Graphics for the PC. In *Computer Graphics*, SIGGRAPH '96 Proceedings, pages 353–364. New Orleans, LS, August 1996.

[28] D. Voorhies and J. Foran. Reflection Vector Shading Hardware. In *Computer Graphics*, Proceedings of SIGGRAPH 94, pages 163–166. July 1994.

[29] L. Westover. Footprint Evaluation for Volume Rendering. In *Computer Graphics*, Proceedings of SIGGRAPH 90, pages 367–376. August 1990.

QSplat: A Multiresolution Point Rendering System for Large Meshes

Szymon Rusinkiewicz
Marc Levoy
Stanford University[†]

Abstract

Advances in 3D scanning technologies have enabled the practical creation of meshes with hundreds of millions of polygons. Traditional algorithms for display, simplification, and progressive transmission of meshes are impractical for data sets of this size. We describe a system for representing and progressively displaying these meshes that combines a multiresolution hierarchy based on bounding spheres with a rendering system based on points. A single data structure is used for view frustum culling, backface culling, level-of-detail selection, and rendering. The representation is compact and can be computed quickly, making it suitable for large data sets. Our implementation, written for use in a large-scale 3D digitization project, launches quickly, maintains a user-settable interactive frame rate regardless of object complexity or camera position, yields reasonable image quality during motion, and refines progressively when idle to a high final image quality. We have demonstrated the system on scanned models containing hundreds of millions of samples.

Categories and Subject Descriptors: I.3.3 [Computer Graphics]: Picture/Image Generation – Display Algorithms; I.3.5 [Computer Graphics]: Computational Geometry and Object Modeling – Curve, surface, solid, and object representations; I.3.6 [Computer Graphics]: Methodology and Techniques – Graphics data structures and data types.

Keywords: Rendering systems, Spatial data structures, Level of detail algorithms, Compression algorithms

1 Introduction

A significant recent trend in computer graphics has been the shift towards using sampled representations of real objects during rendering. An example of this trend has been the increased use of 3D scanning systems, which produce three-dimensional sampled models of physical objects. One problem with 3D scanners, however, is handling

---

[†] Stanford Computer Graphics Lab
Gates Building 3B
Stanford University
Stanford, CA 94305
{smr,levoy}@graphics.stanford.edu

the large amounts of data they produce. Over the past several years, improvements in the hardware and software components of 3D scanning systems have increased the practically attainable sizes of scanned meshes to hundreds of millions of samples.

Current workstations can not display meshes of this size in real time, and the running time and space requirements of traditional mesh simplification and progressive display algorithms make these approaches impractical for scanned meshes containing more than a few million samples. Moreover, many such techniques focus on optimizing the placement of individual edges and vertices, expending a relatively large amount of effort per vertex. Scanned data, however, has a large number of vertices and their locations are often imprecise due to noise. This suggests an alternative approach in which individual points are treated as relatively unimportant, and consequently less effort is spent per primitive. Recent research employing this paradigm includes the spline-fitting system by Krishnamurthy and Levoy [Krishnamurthy 96], the range image merging system by Curless and Levoy [Curless 96], and Yemez and Schmitt's rendering system based on octree particles [Yemez 99]. These algorithms do not treat range data as exact, and in fact do not preserve the 3D locations of any samples of the original mesh.

Following this trend of algorithms with low per-primitive cost, we have developed a new algorithm for interactive display of large meshes. The implementation, dubbed QSplat, was designed during the course of a large 3D digitization project [Levoy 00]. Because it uses a simple rendering algorithm based on traversing a bounding sphere hierarchy, it is suitable for browsing the models generated during this project, which contain 100 million to 1 billion samples. Additionally, QSplat does not maintain the connectivity of the input mesh (which in the case of scanned data inherently is only useful to resolve depth discontinuities and has little other meaning), instead relying on a point-based representation and splat rendering. As a result, our system has lower preprocessing and rendering costs than comparable polygon-based systems. QSplat launches quickly, adjusts level of detail to maintain an interactive frame rate, and has a compact in-memory and on-disk representation.

In this paper, we present the QSplat data structure and rendering algorithm and discuss some of the tradeoffs and design decisions involved in making it practical for large meshes. We describe the rendering performance of the system, and discuss its preprocessing costs. Finally, we consider its relation to previous algorithms for displaying large meshes, and describe some future extensions for rendering other kinds of large geometric data sets.

2 QSplat Data Structure and Algorithms

QSplat uses a hierarchy of bounding spheres [Rubin 80, Arvo 89] for visibility culling, level-of-detail control, and rendering. Each node of the tree contains the sphere center and radius, a normal, the width of a normal cone [Shirman 93], and optionally a color. One could generate such a bounding sphere hierarchy from polygons, voxels, or point clouds, though for our application we only needed an algorithm for generating the hierarchy from triangular meshes. The hierarchy is constructed as a preprocess, and is written to disk.

2.1 Rendering Algorithm

Once the hierarchy has been constructed, the following algorithm is used for display:

```
TraverseHierarchy(node)
{
    if (node not visible)
        skip this branch of the tree
    else if (node is a leaf node)
        draw a splat
    else if (benefit of recursing further is too low)
        draw a splat
    else
        for each child in children(node)
            TraverseHierarchy(child)
}
```

We now examine several stages of this basic algorithm in detail.

Visibility Culling: As we recurse the bounding sphere hierarchy, we cull nodes that are not visible. Frustum culling is performed by testing each sphere against the planes of the view frustum. If the sphere lies outside, it and its subtree are discarded and not processed further. If the sphere lies entirely inside the frustum, this fact is noted and no further frustum culling is attempted on the children of the node.

We also perform backface culling during rendering, using the normal and cone of normals stored at each node. If the cone faces entirely away from the viewer, the node and its subtree are discarded. We also detect the case of a cone pointing entirely towards the viewer, and mark its children as not candidates for backface culling.

Determining When to Recurse: The heuristic used by QSplat to decide how far to recurse is based on projected size on the screen. That is, a node is subdivided if the area of the sphere, projected onto the viewing plane, exceeds a threshold. The cutoff is adjusted from frame to frame to maintain a user-selected frame rate. We currently use a simple feedback scheme that adjusts the threshold area by the ratio of actual to desired rendering time on the previous frame. Funkhouser and Séquin have demonstrated a predictive algorithm for LOD control that results in smaller frame-to-frame variation of rendering times [Funkhouser 93]; however, we have not implemented this. We also have not incorporated any algorithm for smooth transitions as sections of the model change from one level of detail to another, such as the geomorphs in Hoppe's progressive mesh system [Hoppe 98]. Given the modest changes in appearance as we refine and the quick changes in viewpoint typical in our application, we have not found the absence of smoothing visually significant; other applications, however, might benefit from smoother transitions.

Although screen-space area is the most popular metric for LOD control, other heuristics have been proposed for determining how far to recurse [Duchaineau 97, Hoppe 97]. Within the framework of our system, one could incorporate rules for recursing further around silhouette edges (using per-node normals), in areas of high curvature (using normal cone widths), or in the central "foveal" region of the screen (which uses only projected position).

The above implementation of frame rate control is used during interactive manipulation of the model. Once the user stops moving the mouse, we redraw the scene with successively smaller thresholds until

a size of one pixel is reached. Figure 1 shows a sample scene rendered by QSplat at several levels of refinement.

Drawing Splats: Once we have either reached a leaf node or decided to stop recursing, we draw a splat representing the current sphere [Westover 89]. The size of the splat is based on the projected diameter of the current sphere, and its color is obtained from a lighting calculation based on the current per-sphere normal and color. Splats are drawn with Z-buffering enabled to resolve occlusion. We discuss the shape of each splat in Section 3.3.

2.2 Preprocessing Algorithm

Our preprocessing algorithm begins with a triangular mesh representing the model to be encoded. Although one could build up a QSplat hierarchy directly from a point cloud, starting with a mesh makes it easy to compute the normals at each node. If we did not have a mesh, we would have to compute normals by fitting a plane to the vertices in a small neighborhood around each point. Beginning with a mesh also makes it possible to assign sphere sizes to the input vertices (which become the leaf nodes in our bounding sphere hierarchy) such that no holes are left during rendering. In order to guarantee this, the sizes must be chosen such that if two vertices are connected by an edge of the original mesh, the spheres placed at those vertices are large enough to touch. Our current algorithm makes the size of the sphere at a vertex equal to the maximum size of the bounding spheres of all triangles that touch that vertex. This is a conservative method – it may result in spheres that are too large, but is guaranteed not to leave any holes.

Once we have assigned leaf sphere sizes, we use the following algorithm to build up the rest of the tree:

```
BuildTree(vertices[begin..end])
{
    if (begin == end)
        return Sphere(vertices[begin])
    else
        midpoint = PartitionAlongLongestAxis(vertices[begin..end])
        leftsubtree = BuildTree(vertices[begin..midpoint])
        rightsubtree = BuildTree(vertices[midpoint+1..end])
        return BoundingSphere(leftsubtree, rightsubtree)
}
```

The algorithm builds up the tree by splitting the set of vertices along the longest axis of its bounding box, recursively computing the two subtrees, and finding the bounding sphere of the two children spheres. As the tree is built up, per-vertex properties (such as normal and color) at interior nodes are set to the average of these properties in the subtrees. When the recursion reaches a single vertex, we simply create a sphere whose center is the position of the vertex. Because the total size of a tree depends on the branching factor at each node, we combine nodes in the tree to increase the average branching factor to approximately 4. This reduces the number of interior nodes, thereby reducing the storage requirements for the tree. The final step of preprocessing is quantizing all of the properties at each node, as described in Section 3.1.

3 Design Decisions and Tradeoffs

Let us now consider some of the decisions made in the implementation of QSplat that make it suitable for our application of visualizing large scanned data sets. We describe how tradeoffs in quantization, file layout, splat shape, and the choice of splatting were affected by our goals of fast rendering and compact representation.

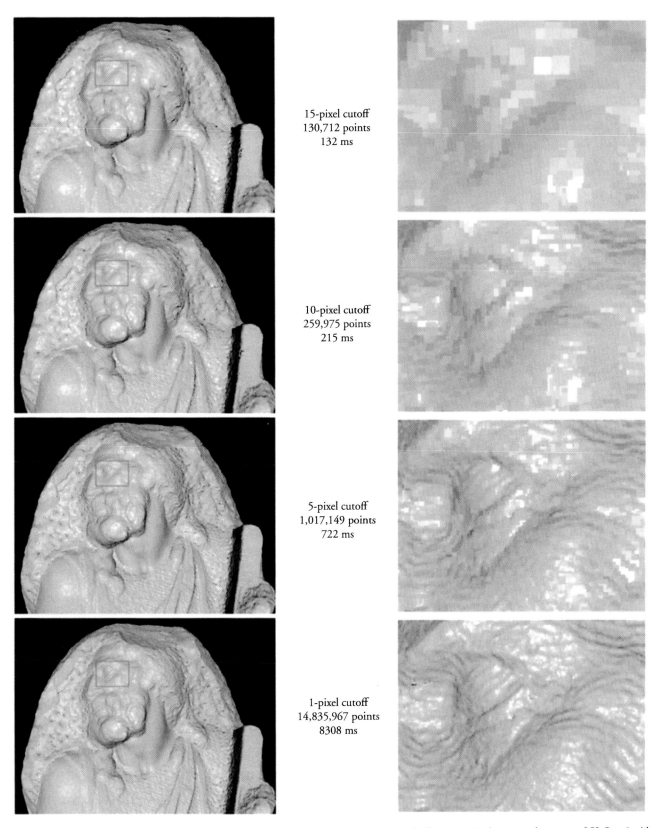

Figure 1: A model of Michelangelo's statue of St. Matthew rendered by QSplat at several levels of refinement. Rendering was done on an SGI Onyx2 with InfiniteReality graphics, at a screen resolution of 1280x1024. The model was generated from a mesh with 127 million samples, representing a statue 2.7 meters tall at 0.25 mm resolution. The images at right are closeups of the outlined areas at left.

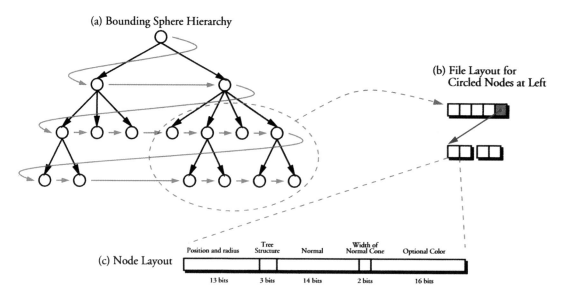

Figure 2: QSplat file and node layout. (a) The tree is stored in breadth-first order (i.e., the order given by the red arrows). (b) The link from parent to child nodes is established by a single pointer from a group of parents to the first child. The pointer is not present if all of the "parent" siblings are leaf nodes. All pointers are 32 bits. (c) A single quantized node occupies 48 bits (32 without color).

3.1 Node Layout and Quantization

The layout of each node in the bounding sphere hierarchy is shown in Figure 2c. A node contains the location and size of a sphere relative to its parent, a normal, the width of a cone of normals, an optional color, and a few bits used in representing the structure of the tree. We discuss the structure of the tree and the layout of nodes within the file in Section 3.2.

Position and radius: The position and radius of each sphere is encoded relative to its parent in the bounding sphere hierarchy. In order to save space, these quantities are quantized to 13 values. That is, the radius of a sphere can range from $^1/_{13}$ to $^{13}/_{13}$ of the radius of its parent, and the offset of the center of a sphere relative to the center of its parent (in each of X, Y, and Z) is some multiple of $^1/_{13}$ of the diameter of the parent sphere. The quantization proceeds top-down, so the position and size of a child sphere is encoded relative to the quantized position of its parent; thus, quantization error does not propagate down the mesh. In order to guarantee that the quantization process does not introduce any holes, the quantized radius is always rounded up to the nearest representable value that ensures that the quantized sphere completely encloses the true sphere.

Note that not all of the 13^4 possible combinations of (x, y, z) center offset and radius ratio are valid, since many result in child spheres that are not enclosed by their parents. In fact, only 7621 of the possible combinations are valid, which means that we can encode the quantized position and radius using only 13 bits (using a lookup table). For a parent sphere of radius 1, this encoding scheme gives a mean quantization error of 0.04 in the x, y, and z components of a child sphere, and a mean error of 0.15 in the child sphere's radius. The error in the radius is larger than the error in position because the radius is first increased by the quantization error in the position of the sphere (to ensure that the quantized sphere encloses the true sphere), and is then always rounded up to the next representable value. We could obtain lower quantization error in the radius by not insisting that the quantized sphere completely enclose the original. Doing so, however, would introduce the possibility that spheres that should touch no longer do so after the quantization. This could produce holes in our renderings.

The idea of representing geometric quantities such as sphere positions by encoding them incrementally, thereby essentially spreading out the bits of the quantities among the levels in the hierarchy, represents a departure from traditional approaches to mesh compression, which rely on encoding the differences between vertex positions along some path along the edges of the mesh [Taubin 98]. This "hierarchical delta coding" is, in fact, closer to the wavelet representation of geometry used in the multiresolution analysis of Eck et. al. [Eck 95]. Our space requirement of 13 bits per node appears competitive with state-of-the-art geometric compression methods, which average 9-15 bits per vertex depending on initial quantization of vertex positions. This is not an entirely valid comparison, however, since traditional geometric compression methods also represent mesh connectivity (which we discard), and since our 13 bits per node also includes sphere radius.

The position and radius of each node are decoded on-the-fly during rendering. Because of this, our data structure is not only compact on disk, but also requires less memory during rendering than methods that must decompress their data before rendering.

Normals: The normal at each node is stored quantized to 14 bits. The representable normals correspond to points on a 52×52 grid on each of the 6 faces of a cube, warped to sample normal space more uniformly. A lookup table is used during rendering do decode the representable normals. In practice the use of only $52 \cdot 52 \cdot 6 = 16224$ different normals (leading to a mean quantization error of approximately 0.01 radian) produces no visible artifacts in the diffuse shading component, but some banding artifacts are visible around specular highlights in broad areas of low curvature. It would be possible to eliminate these artifacts, as well as achieve better compression, by moving to an incremental encoding of each normal relative to the normal of the parent sphere. This would, however, increase the computational complexity of the inner loop of the algorithm, resulting in a time-space tradeoff. Unlike the range of node positions, the space of normals is bounded, so a fixed quantization table suffices for encoding the normals of arbitrary scenes. Therefore, at this time we have chosen to use a fixed quantization for the normals, which requires only a single table lookup at run time. As processor speed increases, we anticipate that the incremental quantization scheme will become more attractive.

Colors: Colors are currently stored quantized 5-6-5 to 16 bits. As in the case of normals, an incremental encoding of colors would save space but be more expensive at run time.

Normal cones: After some experimentation, we have decided to quantize the width of the cone of normals at each node to just 2 bits. The four representable values correspond to cones whose half-angles have sines of $^1/_{16}$, $^4/_{16}$, $^9/_{16}$, and $^{16}/_{16}$. On typical data sets, backface culling with these quantized normal cones discards over 90 percent of nodes that would be culled using exact normal cone widths. Note that we are always conservative in representing normal cone widths, so we never discard geometry that should be displayed. As with normals and colors, the normal cone widths could be represented relative to the widths at the parent nodes, but this would slow down rendering.

3.2 File Layout and Pointers

The nodes of the bounding sphere hierarchy are laid out (both in memory and on disk) in breadth-first order. A primary consequence of this is that the first part of the file contains the entire mesh at low resolution. Thus, we only need to read in the first part of a file in order to visualize the model at low resolution; we see greater detail as more of the file is read in from disk. We currently use OS-provided memory mapping as the basis for working-set management, so high-resolution data for a given section of the model is read in from disk when the user looks at it. This progressive loading is important for usability with large models, for which the time to load the entire data set from disk may be several minutes. Because data is loaded as it is needed, rendering performance will be lower the first time the user zooms in on some area of the model – due to our feedback-based approach to frame rate control, there is a glitch in the frame rate. Subsequent frames that touch the same area of the model, however, are rendered at full speed. Speculative prefetching has been explored as a method for reducing this performance variation [Funkhouser 92, Funkhouser 96, Aliaga 99], but we currently do not implement this.

Several pointerless schemes have been proposed for tree encoding, including linear octrees and methods based on complete trees [Samet 90]. These data structures, however, are inappropriate for our application. Linear octrees and related ideas require the entire tree to be traversed to recover its structure, which is impractical in our system. Data structures based on complete trees can be used for partial traversals, but because the algorithm we use to generate our trees is based on axis-aligned bisections, we can not guarantee that the resulting trees will be complete and balanced. Furthermore, modifying the preprocessing algorithm to generate complete trees would not be desirable, since putting an equal number of vertices in each subtree can potentially put the splitting planes significantly off-center. Given the amount of quantization we perform on child sphere centers, this could lead to significant inaccuracies in the compressed tree.

Although we can not use pointerless encodings for our trees, we should at least attempt to minimize the number of pointers required. Given that we store the tree in breadth-first order, it is sufficient to have one pointer for each group of siblings in the tree (i.e. children of a single parent sphere), that points to the children of these nodes. Furthermore, that pointer is not necessary if none of these spheres have children (i.e. they are all leaf nodes). Using this scheme, approximately 8 to 10 percent of the total storage cost is devoted to pointers, which we judged to be sufficiently small that we did not pursue more complicated schemes for reducing pointer costs further. In order to be able to traverse the tree, we store at each node two bits encoding the number of children of the node (0, 2, 3, or 4 children – nodes with a single child are not permitted), and one bit indicating whether all children of this node are leaf nodes.

The total storage requirements for a tree may now be computed as the number of nodes in the tree multiplied by the cost per node, plus the overhead due to pointers. For a tree with average branching factor 3.5, the total number of nodes will be 1.4 times the number of leaf nodes, making the net storage requirements for the entire tree approximately 9 bytes times the number of leaf nodes, or 6 bytes if colors are not stored.

3.3 Splat Shape

The choice of kernel used to represent a rendered point sample can have a significant effect on the quality of the final image. The simplest, fastest option is a non-antialiased OpenGL point, which is rendered as a square. A second choice is an opaque circle, which may be rendered as a group of small triangles or, less expensively in most OpenGL implementations, as a single texture-mapped polygon. Another possibility is a fuzzy spot, with an alpha that falls off radially with a Gaussian or some approximation. The particular approximation we use is a spline in opacity that falls to $^1/_2$ at the nominal radius of the splat. These last two options will be slower to draw, since they require sending more data to the graphics pipeline. In addition, drawing a Gaussian splat requires special care regarding the order in which the splats are drawn, because of the interaction between blending and Z-buffering. Levoy and Whitted discuss this problem in the context of a software-only renderer [Levoy 85]; they propose an approach based on buckets to ensure that both occlusion and blending happen correctly. In OpenGL we can use multipass rendering to implement the correct behavior. For the first pass, depth is offset away from the viewer by some amount z_0, and we render only into the depth buffer. For the second pass we turn off depth offset and render additively into the color buffer, with depth comparison but not depth update enabled. This has the effect of blending together all splats within a depth range z_0 of the surface, while maintaining correct occlusion. Figure 3 compares these three choices of splat kernel. Because per-splat drawing time on current hardware is different for each kernel, we present comparisons at both constant splat size and constant running time.

Another option we have in choosing splat shape is the choice of whether the splats are always round (or square in the case of OpenGL points) or elliptical. In the latter case, the normal at each node is used to determine the eccentricity and orientation of the ellipse. When the normals point towards the viewer, the splats will be circular. Otherwise, the minor axis of each ellipse will point along the projection of the normal onto the viewing plane, and the ratio of minor to major axes will equal $\hat{\mathbf{n}} \cdot \hat{\mathbf{v}}$, where $\mathbf{n}$ is the normal of the splat and $\mathbf{v}$ is a vector pointing towards the viewer. This improves the quality of silhouette edges compared to circular splats, reducing noise and thickening. We compare the use of circular and elliptical splats in Figure 4.

Because we construct our bounding sphere hierarchy such that spheres placed along a continuous surface will never leave holes, we can guarantee that the square and circular kernels will always result in hole-free reconstructions. Our approximation to a Gaussian kernel is also guaranteed to produce full opacity in areas that started out as continuous surfaces. When we move to elliptical kernels, we can no longer guarantee hole-free reconstructions because normals need not be continuous along the surface. In practice, we do occasionally see holes when using elliptical kernels, especially around silhouette edges. We have found that restricting the maximum foreshortening of ellipses (e.g. clamping the maximum ratio of major to minor axis to 10) fills in practically all of these holes.

3.4 Consequences of a Point-Based System

The fact that QSplat uses points as its rendering primitives makes it most suitable for certain kinds of scenes. In particular, point render-

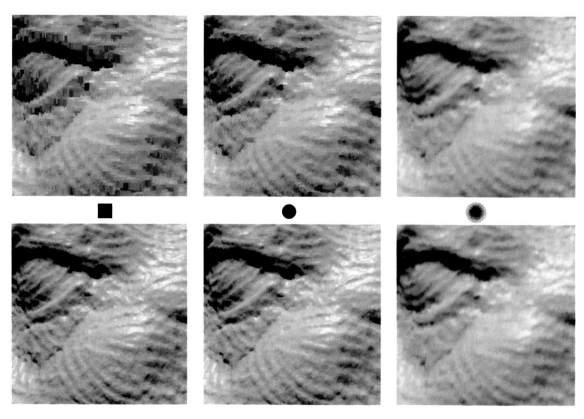

Figure 3: Choices for splat shape. We show a scene rendered using squares, circles, and Gaussians as splat kernels. In the top row, each image uses the same recursion threshold of 20 pixels. Relative to squares, circles take roughly twice as long to render, and Gaussians take approximately four times as long. The Gaussians, however, exhibit significantly less aliasing. In the bottom row, the threshold for each image is adjusted to produce the same rendering time in each case. According to this criterion, the square kernels appear to offer the highest quality.

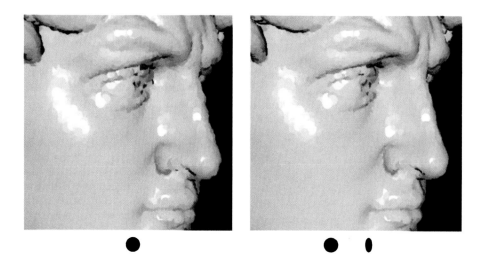

Figure 4: Circular vs. elliptical splats. In the left image, all splats are circular with diameter 20 pixels. In the right image, we draw elliptical splats rotated and foreshortened depending on per-node normals. This reduces thickening and noise around silhouette edges. Recursion depth has deliberately been limited to make the splats large enough to see in this visualization.

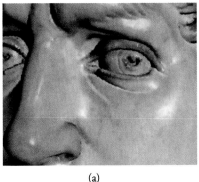

(a)

Points

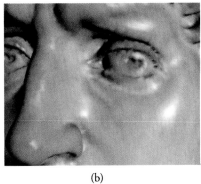

(b)

Polygons – same number of primitives as (a)
Same rendering time as (a)

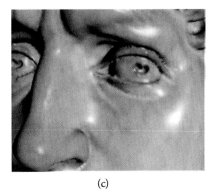

(c)

Polygons – same number of vertices as (a)
Twice the rendering time of (a)

Figure 5: Comparison of renderings using point and polygon primitives.

ing systems are most effective for objects with uniformly-sized geometric detail, and in applications where it is not necessary to look at the model at significantly higher resolution than the spacing between samples. If the model has large, flat or subtly curved surfaces, polygonal models can be more compact and faster to draw. Similarly, if it is necessary to zoom in such that the spacing of samples is large compared to pixel size, polygons offer higher visual quality, especially near sharp edges and corners. Figure 5 shows a comparison between point- and polygon-based renderings.

QSplat was developed with the intent of visualizing scanned models that contained significant amounts of fine detail at scales near the scanning resolution. We used the Volumetric Range Image Processing (VRIP) system [Curless 96] to merge raw scans into our final models, and the marching cubes algorithm [Cline 88] to extract a polygonal mesh. Since the latter produces samples with a uniform spacing, point rendering was well-suited for our application domain. For scenes with large, smooth regions, we expect that QSplat would be less effective relative to polygon-based systems. The visual quality of the resulting models would still be good, however, if the large polygons were diced, as in the REYES architecture [Cook 87]. For applications containing both high-frequency detail and large flat regions, hybrid point/polygon schemes might be appropriate.

4 Performance

As described in Section 3, the goal of interactivity dictated many design decisions for our system. In addition to these, we have optimized our implementation in several ways in order to increase the size of the models we can visualize.

4.1 Rendering Performance

The majority of rendering time in our system is spent in an inner loop that traverses the hierarchy, computes the position and radius of each node, performs visibility culling, and decides whether to draw a point or recurse further. This inner loop was tuned to eliminate expensive operations, especially at lower levels of the tree. For example, we do not perform an exact perspective divide at the low levels of the tree, switching to an approximation when the screen-space size of a node reaches a few pixels. As a result, on average our algorithm can render between 1.5 and 2.5 million points per second on an SGI Onyx2 once data has been read in from disk. The exact rate varies depending on caching effects (for example, we observe a speedup when the working

set fits in L2 cache) and how much data is culled at which levels in the tree.

Our display rate may be compared to the 480 thousand polygons per second (on identical hardware) reported by Hoppe for his implementation of progressive meshes [Hoppe 98] or the 180 thousand polygons per second for the ROAM system [Duchaineau 97]. For our application, we typically use frame rates of 5-10 Hz, meaning that we draw 200 to 300 thousand points per frame during interactive rendering. Note that unlike the above two systems, QSplat makes no explicit use of frame-to-frame coherence, such as cached lists of primitives likely to be visible. QSplat's rendering performance is summarized in Figure 6.

The simplicity of our algorithm makes it well suited for implementation on low-end machines. As an extreme example, we have implemented QSplat on a laptop computer with no 3D graphics hardware (366 MHz Intel Pentium II processor, 128 MB memory). Because rendering is performed in software, the system is fill limited. For a typical window size of 500x500 and frame rate of 5 Hz, the implementation can traverse 250 to 400 thousand points per second, has a 40 million pixel per second fill rate, and typically draws 50 to 70 thousand splats per frame. At this resolution the implementation is still comfortably usable. Although most present desktop systems do have 3D graphics hardware, the same is not true for portable and handheld systems, and in applications such as digital television set-top boxes. We believe that QSplat might be well-suited for such environments.

4.2 Preprocessing Performance

Although preprocessing time is not as important as rendering time, it is still significant for practical visualization of very large meshes. Hoppe reports 10 hours as the preprocessing time for a progressive mesh of 200 thousand vertices [Hoppe 97]. Luebke and Erikson report 121 seconds as the preprocessing time for 281 thousand vertices for their implementation of hierarchical dynamic simplification [Luebke 97]. In contrast, our preprocessing time for 200 thousand vertices is under 5 seconds (on the same hardware). Figure 6 presents some statistics about the preprocessing time and space requirements of the models used in this paper's figures.

Another class of algorithms with which we can compare our preprocessing time is algorithms for mesh simplification and decimation. Although these algorithms have different goals than QSplat, they are also commonly used for generating multiresolution representations or simplifying meshes for display. Lindstrom and Turk have published a comparison of several recent mesh simplification meth-

| | David's head, 1mm, color | | David, 2mm | | St. Matthew, 0.25mm | |

Typical performance

	Interactive	Static	Interactive	Static	Interactive	Static
Traverse tree	22 ms	448 ms	30 ms	392 ms	27 ms	951 ms
Compute position and size	19 ms	126 ms	30 ms	307 ms	31 ms	879 ms
Frustum culling	1 ms	4 ms	1 ms	3 ms	1 ms	3 ms
Backface culling	1 ms	22 ms	2 ms	25 ms	1 ms	35 ms
Draw splats	77 ms	364 ms	46 ms	324 ms	50 ms	1281 ms
Total rendering time	**120 ms**	**838 ms**	**109 ms**	**1051 ms**	**110 ms**	**3149 ms**
Points rendered	**125,183**	**931,093**	**267,542**	**2,026,496**	**263,915**	**8,110,665**

Preprocessing statistics

Input points (= leaf nodes)	2,000,651	4,251,890	127,072,827
Interior nodes	974,114	2,068,752	50,285,122
Bytes per node	6	4	4
Space taken by pointers	1.3 MB	2.7 MB	84 MB
Total file size	**18 MB**	**27 MB**	**761 MB**
Preprocessing time	**0.7 min**	**1.4 min**	**59 min**

Figure 6: Typical QSplat rendering and preprocessing statistics for three models. The columns marked "interactive" indicate typical performance when the user is manipulating the model. The columns labeled "static" are typical of performance when the user has stopped moving the mouse and the scene has refined to its highest-quality version. Variation of up to 30% has been observed in these timings, depending on details such as cache performance. All times were measured on an SGI Onyx2 with InfiniteReality graphics; rendering was done at 1280x1024 resolution.

ods [Lindstrom 98]. They report times of between 30 seconds and 45 minutes for simplification of a bunny mesh with 35000 vertices. One method that paper did not consider was the voxel-based simplification of Rossignac and Borrel [Rossignac 93], which takes under one second on identical hardware to that used by Lindstrom and Turk. Our preprocessing time for this mesh is 0.6 seconds. Thus, our algorithm is significantly faster than most of the contemporary mesh decimation algorithms, and competitive with Rossignac and Borrel's method.

5   Previous Work

Previous approaches for representing and displaying large models can be grouped into point rendering, visibility culling, level-of-detail control, and geometric compression.

5.1   Point Rendering

Computer graphics systems traditionally have used triangles as rendering primitives. In an attempt to decrease the setup and rasterization costs of triangles for scenes containing a large amount of geometry, a number of simpler primitives have been proposed. The use of points as a display primitive for continuous surfaces was introduced by Levoy and Whitted [Levoy 85], and more recently has been revisited by Grossman and Dally [Grossman 98]. Point rendering has been incorporated into commercial products – the Animatek Caviar system, for example, uses point rendering for animated characters in video games [Animatek]. Particles have also been used in more specialized contexts, such as rendering fire, smoke, and trees [Csuri 79, Reeves 83, Max 95].

A concept related to point rendering is *splatting* in volume rendering [Westover 89]. For large volumes, it is natural to use a hierarchical

data structure to achieve compression of regions of empty space, and Laur and Hanrahan have investigated hierarchical splatting for volumes represented using octrees [Laur 91]. Although splatting is best suited to the case in which the projected voxel size is on the order of the pixel size, other regimes have also been examined. The *dividing cubes* algorithm proposed by Cline et. al. is intended for use when voxels are larger than pixels [Cline 88]. For voxels smaller than pixels, Swan et. al. have proposed algorithms for producing correctly antialiased results [Swan 97].

5.2   Visibility Culling

Frustum and backface culling algorithms, such as those used by QSplat, have appeared in a large number of computer graphics systems. Hierarchical frustum culling based on data structures such as octrees has been a standard feature of most systems for rendering large scenes [Samet 90]. Backface culling of primitives is commonly implemented in hardware, and Kumar and Manocha have presented an algorithm for hierarchical backface culling based on cones of normals [Kumar 96].

Another class of visibility culling algorithms includes methods for occlusion culling. Greene et. al. describe a general algorithm to discard primitives that are blocked by closer geometry using a hierarchical Z-buffer [Greene 93]. Other, more specialized occlusion algorithms can also be used if the scene is highly structured. Systems for architectural flythroughs, for example, often use the notion of *cells* and *portals* to cull away entire rooms that are not visible [Teller 91]. QSplat currently does not perform any sort of occlusion culling – it would provide minimal benefit for viewing the scanned models we are considering. Occlusion culling would, however, be a useful addition for scenes of greater depth complexity.

5.3 Level of Detail Control

Rendering a large data set at low magnification will often cause primitives to be smaller than output device pixels. In order to minimize rendering time in these cases, it is desirable to switch to a lower-resolution data set with primitives that more closely match the output display resolution. Among LOD algorithms, one may differentiate those that store entire objects at discrete levels of detail from methods that perform finer-grained LOD control. The algorithms in the latter class can control the number of primitives continuously, minimizing "popping" artifacts, and often vary the level of detail throughout the scene to compensate for the varying magnification of perspective projection.

Multiresolution analysis represents an object as a "base mesh," with a series of corrections stored as wavelet coefficients [Eck 95]. Certain et al. have implemented a real-time viewer based on multiresolution meshes that can select an arbitrary number of wavelet coefficients to be used, and so draw a mesh with any desired number of polygons [Certain 96]. Their viewer also includes features such as progressive transmission and separate sets of wavelet coefficients for geometry and color.

Progressive meshes use a base mesh together with a series of vertex split operations [Hoppe 96]. Progressive meshes have been incorporated into a real-time viewer that performs view-dependent refinement for real-time flythroughs of scenes of several million polygons [Hoppe 97, Hoppe 98]. The viewer can not only select an arbitrary number of polygons to draw, but also refine different parts of an object to different resolutions. Other recent systems that allow level of detail to vary throughout the scene include the *ROAM* terrain rendering system [Duchaineau 97], and *LDI trees* [Chang 99]. The implementation of LOD control in QSplat has the same goal as these systems, permitting the level of detail to vary smoothly throughout a scene according to projected screen size.

5.4 Geometric Compression

The goal of geometric compression is to reduce the storage and memory requirements of large meshes, as well as their transmission costs. Deering has presented a system for compression of mesh connectivity, vertex locations, colors, and normals, which was later implemented in hardware [Deering 95]. More recent research, such as the *Topological Surgery* scheme by Taubin and Rossignac, has focused on reducing the cost of representing mesh connectivity and improving the compression of vertex positions [Taubin 98]. Pajarola and Rossignac have applied compression to progressive meshes, yielding a scheme that combines level-of-detail control and progressive refinement with a compact representation [Pajarola 99]. Their algorithm, however, has higher preprocessing and decoding costs than QSplat.

6 Conclusions and Future Work

The QSplat system has demonstrated real-time progressive rendering of large models. QSplat's architecture matches the rendering speed of state-of-the-art progressive display algorithms, has preprocessing times comparable to the fastest presently-available mesh decimators, and achieves compression ratios close to those of current geometric compression techniques.

Because the QSplat viewer is lightweight and can be implemented on low-cost hardware, we believe it has the potential for permitting 3D rendering in applications where it was previously impractical, for example built-in kiosks in museums. On May 6, 1999, we set up QSplat on a computer in the Medici Chapel in Florence, displaying our partially-completed computer model of the statue of Dawn, and we let the tourists play (see Figure 7).

Figure 7: Tourists in the Medici Chapel using QSplat to fly around our 3D model of Michelangelo's statue of Dawn. We simplified the interface to only allow rotating, translating, and relighting the model. Nevertheless, some tourists managed to get the viewer into various confusing states, typically by zooming in too far. This underscores the need for a simple, robust, and constrained user interface. We found that most tourists appreciated having a computer model of the statue at which they were looking; having the capability to see the statue from other views, and to change its virtual lighting, made looking at the statue a more active, hands-on experience.

Several previously-introduced techniques could be incorporated into the present QSplat framework to make it more time and space efficient:

- Huffman coding [Huffman 52] or another lossless compression scheme could be used to make the current representation more compact. This would be useful for offline storage or transmission across low-bandwidth communications links, but would require the model to be decompressed before rendering.

- For cases when rendering speed is more important than compact representation, the algorithm could be sped up by eliminating the compression and incremental encoding of sphere positions and sizes (as described in Section 3.1), and simply storing these quantities as floats. In addition, *normal masks* and *visibility masks*, such as those used by Grossman and Dally, could speed up rendering if there is a significant amount of large-scale occlusion [Zhang 97, Grossman 98]. A further gain in speed could be achieved by parallelizing the rendering algorithm, distributing portions of the tree to different processors. We can already parallelize our preprocessing algorithm by breaking up the mesh into tiles, though we have reported single-processor results in this paper.

- Further analysis is necessary to understand the temporal coherence and caching behavior of QSplat. A large amount of systems research has been done on frame rate control and working set management techniques in terrain rendering and architectural walkthrough systems [Funkhouser 96], and those algorithms would improve the smoothness of user interaction with QSplat.

The following are potential areas of future research for combining the QSplat approach with different kinds of algorithms within computer graphics:

- The bounding sphere hierarchy used by QSplat is well-suited as an acceleration data structure for ray tracing. Potentially, this could be used for high-quality renderings with advanced rendering effects of models stored in the QSplat format.

- Instancing would be easy to incorporate into our tree-based data structure and rendering algorithm, greatly reducing the memory requirements for many classes of procedurally-defined scenes. This could be thought of as a new form of view-dependent sprite, permitting efficient inclusion of geometry at multiple locations within a scene.

- Items other than normals and colors could be stored at each node. Transparency (alpha), BRDFs, and BTDFs would be obvious candidates that would increase the visual complexity representable by QSplat, giving it capabilities similar to those of modern volumetric renderers [Kajiya 89]. More complicated objects such as light fields, view-dependent textures, spatially-varying BRDFs, and layered depth images could potentially also be stored at each node, creating hybrids of point rendering systems and contemporary image-based renderers.

Acknowledgments

Thanks to Dave Koller, Jonathan Shade, Matt Ginzton, Kari Pulli, Lucas Pereira, James Davis, and the whole DMich gang. The Digital Michelangelo Project was sponsored by Stanford University, Interval Research Corporation, and the Paul Allen Foundation for the Arts.

References

[Aliaga 99] Aliaga, D., Cohen, J., Wilson, A., Baker, E., Zhang, H., Erikson, C., Hoff, K., Hudson, T., Stuerzlinger, W., Bastos, R., Whitton, M., Brooks, F., and Manocha, D. "MMR: An Interactive Massive Model Rendering System Using Geometric and Image-Based Acceleration," *Proc. Symposium on Interactive 3D Graphics*, 1999.

[Animatek] AnimaTek International, Inc., "Caviar Technology," Web page: http://www.animatek.com/products_caviar.htm

[Arvo 89] Arvo, J. and Kirk, D. "A Survey of Ray Tracing Acceleration Techniques," *An Introduction to Ray Tracing*, Glassner, A. S. ed., Academic Press, 1989.

[Certain 96] Certain, A., Popović, J, DeRose, T., Duchamp, T., Salesin, D., and Stuetzle, W. "Interactive Multiresolution Surface Viewing," *Proc. SIGGRAPH*, 1996.

[Chang 99] Chang, C., Bishop, G., and Lastra, A. "LDI Tree: A Hierarchical Representation for Image-Based Rendering," *Proc. SIGGRAPH*, 1999.

[Cline 88] Cline, H. E., Lorensen, W. E., Ludke, S., Crawford, C. R., and Teeter, B. C. "Two Algorithms for the Three-Dimensional Reconstruction of Tomograms," *Medical Physics*, Vol. 15, No. 3, 1988.

[Cook 87] Cook, R., Carpenter, L., and Catmull, E. "The Reyes Image Rendering Architecture," *Proc. SIGGRAPH*, 1987.

[Csuri 79] Csuri, C., Hackathorn, R., Parent, R., Carlson, W., and Howard, M. "Towards an Interactive High Visual Complexity Animation System," *Proc. SIGGRAPH*, 1979.

[Curless 96] Curless, B. and Levoy, M. "A Volumetric Method for Building Complex Models from Range Images," *Proc. SIGGRAPH*, 1996.

[Deering 95] Deering, M. "Geometry Compression," *Proc. SIGGRAPH*, 1995.

[Duchaineau 97] Duchaineau, M., Wolinsky, M., Sigeti, D,. Miller, M., Aldrich, C., and Mineev-Weinstein, M. "ROAMing Terrain: Real-time Optimally Adapting Meshes," *Proc. Visualization*, 1997.

[Eck 95] Eck, M., DeRose, T., Duchamp, T., Hoppe, H., Lounsbery, M., and Stuetzle, W. "Multiresolution Analysis of Arbitrary Meshes," *Proc. SIGGRAPH*, 1995.

[Funkhouser 92] Funkhouser, T., Séquin, C., and Teller, S. "Management of Large Amounts of Data in Interactive Building Walkthroughs," *Proc. Symposium on Interactive 3D Graphics*, 1992.

[Funkhouser 93] Funkhouser, T. and Séquin, C. "Adaptive Display Algorithm for Interactive Frame Rates During Visualization of Complex Virtual Environments," *Proc. SIGGRAPH*, 1993.

[Funkhouser 96] Funkhouser, T. "Database Management for Interactive Display of Large Architectural Models," *Graphics Interface*, 1996.

[Greene 93] Greene, N., Kass, M., and Miller, G. "Hierarchical Z-buffer Visibility," *Proc. SIGGRAPH*, 1993.

[Grossman 98] Grossman, J. and Dally, W. "Point Sample Rendering," *Proc. Eurographics Rendering Workshop*, 1998.

[Hoppe 96] Hoppe, H. "Progressive Meshes," *Proc. SIGGRAPH*, 1996.

[Hoppe 97] Hoppe, H. "View-Dependent Refinement of Progressive Meshes," *Proc. SIGGRAPH*, 1997.

[Hoppe 98] Hoppe, H. "Smooth View-Dependent Level-of-Detail Control and its Application to Terrain Rendering," *Proc. Visualization*, 1998.

[Huffman 52] Huffman, D. "A Method for the Construction of Minimum Redundancy Codes," *Proc. IRE*, Vol. 40, No. 9, 1952.

[Kajiya 89] Kajiya, J. and Kay, T. "Rendering Fur with Three Dimensional Textures," *Proc. SIGGRAPH*, 1989.

[Krishnamurthy 96] Krishnamurthy, V. and Levoy, M. "Fitting Smooth Surfaces to Dense Polygon Meshes," *Proc. SIGGRAPH*, 1986.

[Kumar 96] Kumar, S., Manocha, D., Garrett, W., and Lin, M. "Hierarchical Back-Face Computation," *Proc. Eurographics Rendering Workshop*, 1996.

[Laur 91] Laur, D. and Hanrahan, P. "Hierarchical Splatting: A Progressive Refinement Algorithm for Volume Rendering," *Proc. SIGGRAPH*, 1991.

[Levoy 85] Levoy, M. and Whitted, T. "The Use of Points as a Display Primitive," *Technical Report TR 85-022*, University of North Carolina at Chapel Hill, 1985.

[Levoy 00] Levoy, M., Pulli, K., Curless, B., Rusinkiewicz, S., Koller, D., Pereira, L., Ginzton, M., Anderson, S., Davis, J., Ginsberg, J., Shade, J., and Fulk, D. "The Digital Michelangelo Project: 3D Scanning of Large Statues," *Proc. SIGGRAPH*, 2000.

[Lindstrom 98] Lindstrom, P. and Turk, G. "Fast and Memory Efficient Polygonal Simplification," *Proc. Visualization*, 1998.

[Luebke 97] Luebke, D., and Erikson, C. "View-Dependent Simplification of Arbitrary Polygonal Environments," *Proc. SIGGRAPH*, 1997.

[Max 95] Max, N. and Ohsaki, K. "Rendering Trees from Precomputed Z-buffer Views," *Proc. Eurographics Rendering Workshop*, 1995.

[Pajarola 99] Pajarola, R. and Rossignac, J. "Compressed Progressive Meshes," *Technical Report GIT-GVU-99-05*, Georgia Institute of Technology, 1999.

[Reeves 83] Reeves, W. "Particle Systems – A Technique for Modeling a Class of Fuzzy Objects," *Proc. SIGGRAPH*, 1983.

[Rossignac 93] Rossignac, J. and Borrel, P. "Multi-Resolution 3D Approximations for Rendering Complex Scenes," *Geometric Modeling in Computer Graphics*, 1993.

[Rubin 80] Rubin, S. M. and Whitted, T. "A 3-Dimensional Representation for Fast Rendering of Complex Scenes," *Proc. SIGGRAPH*, 1980.

[Samet 90] Samet, H. *Applications of Spatial Data Structures*, Addison-Wesley, 1990.

[Shirman 93] Shirman, L. and Abi-Ezzi, S. "The Cone of Normals Technique for Fast Processing of Curved Patches," *Proc. Eurographics*, 1993.

[Swan 97] Swan, J., Mueller, K., Möller, T., Shareef, N., Crawfis, R., and Yagel, R. "An Anti-Aliasing Technique for Splatting," *Proc. Visualization*, 1997.

[Taubin 98] Taubin, G. and Rossignac, J. "Geometric Compression Through Topological Surgery," *ACM Trans. on Graphics*, Vol. 17, No. 2, 1998.

[Teller 91] Teller, S. and Séquin, C. "Visibility Preprocessing for Interactive Walkthroughs," *Proc. SIGGRAPH*, 1991.

[Westover 89] Westover, L. "Interactive Volume Rendering," *Proc. Volume Visualization Workshop*, University of North Carolina at Chapel Hill, 1989.

[Yemez 99] Yemez, Y. and Schmitt, F. "Progressive Multilevel Meshes from Octree Particles," *Proc. 3D Digital Imaging and Modeling*, 1999.

[Zhang 97] Zhang, H. and Hoff, K. "Fast Backface Culling Using Normal Masks," *Proc. Symposium on Interactive 3D Graphics*, 1997.

A Fast Relighting Engine for Interactive Cinematic Lighting Design

Reid Gershbein   Pat Hanrahan
Stanford University

Abstract

We present new techniques for interactive cinematic lighting design of complex scenes that use procedural shaders. Deep-framebuffers are used to store the geometric and optical information of the visible surfaces of an image. The geometric information is represented as collections of oriented points, and the optical information is represented as bi-directional reflection distribution functions, or BRDFs. The BRDFs are generated by procedurally defined surface texturing functions that spatially vary the surfaces' appearances.

The deep-framebuffer information is rendered using a multi-pass algorithm built on the OpenGL graphics pipeline. In order to handle both physically-correct as well as non-realistic reflection models used in the film industry, we factor the BRDF into independent components that map onto both the lighting and texturing units of the graphics hardware. A similar factorization is used to control the lighting distribution. Using these techniques, lighting calculations can be evaluated 2500 times faster than previous methods. This allows lighting changes to be rendered at rates of 20Hz in static environments that contain millions of objects with dozens of unique procedurally defined surface properties and scores of lights.

CR Categories: I.3.3 [Computer Graphics]: Picture/Image Generation;

Keywords: Animation, Illumination, Image-based Rendering, Optics, Rendering Hardware, Rendering, Texture Mapping

1 Introduction

Cinematography and lighting are extremely important aspects of movie making, as shown by the visual richness of the computer animated movie *Toy Story 2* and the special effects in *Star Wars: The Phantom Menace*. The cinematic goals of an animated computer-generated film are the same as a live-action picture: add depth and clarity to the images, create mood and atmosphere, and focus the viewer's attention on the action [5]. The similarities between the real and virtual media do not end there. Both use elaborate sets and perhaps thousands of props and characters; both use visually complex materials and detailed surfaces; and both require scores of light sources.

However, there is one aspect of designing and evaluating lighting in computer-generated films that is different than a live-action film. In a live-action film the lights are moved and positioned by the grips

©2000 ACM 0-58113-208-5/00/0007 $5.00

and the visual result can be seen immediately by the cinematographer. Currently, the opposite is true for computer-generated cinematography. After the cinematographer directs the lighting artist to move a light, the scene must be rendered again. This is a major bottleneck because production rendering systems require minutes to hours to render scenes of movie complexity. The slow rendering rate limits the turnaround time and, ultimately, the productivity of the lighting artist. Moreover, since lighting artists are responsible for creating the final visual appearance of the film, lighting is one of the final stages in production and is done under extreme time pressure. Thus, building an interactive cinematic lighting system would greatly benefit the computer animation industry.

The goals of interactive lighting design are easy to state. What a lighting artist wants is the ability to add, remove, and change the position of a light in real-time. It should also be possible to modify any of the light's attributes such as beam width, fall-off or flap position. Hard and soft shadows are also important. Finally, it is important that the quality of the final image be maintained; approximations that reduce quality are undesirable.

It should be noted that it is rare to change the surface properties of the objects and characters in the scene during the lighting phase. Controlling the look by changing the lights is part of the artistic legacy of traditional film making and is emulated by computer animation production houses. Controlling surface properties on a shot by shot basis is largely impractical in the real-world; and even in the world of computers the properties of most characters are set once and not changed as the characters are reused in different shots. Most previous computer lighting design systems allow modification of *both* surface and light source properties and, unlike our system, have not been optimized for only lighting design.

In this paper, we present a simple rendering engine for interactive lighting design. Like previous systems it uses a deep-framebuffer to store the geometric and optical information of the visible surfaces from a fixed viewpoint. One main innovation is to treat this deep-framebuffer as a set of oriented surface samples so that they may be rendered using the OpenGL graphics pipeline. The state of the graphics pipeline is set to evaluate the reflection from the oriented surface sample due to a single light source. The second innovation is that the optical properties of a surface sample are reduced to only the bi-directional reflection distribution function (BRDF). All spatially varying procedural and texture-mapped surface attributes are evaluated during the process of producing the deep-framebuffer. Our experience is that this leads to a significant speedup, since the majority of the time spent in most surface shaders goes into calculating textures and not reflection models. The final innovation is to enhance the builtin OpenGL BRDF and light source models to be more like those used in production quality rendering systems. Inspired by techniques recently developed by Heidrich and Seidel[14], we factor the BRDF and light source into independent components that may be evaluated using multiple rendering passes that use both the lighting and texturing units. This collection of simple techniques increase the rate at which lighting calculations are computed by at least three orders of magnitude and allow the system to render 512 by 256 images of arbitrarily complex environments with procedural surface and lighting functions at approximately 20 Hz.

2 Related Work

Good examples of current lighting simulation systems are those available for buildings and theatrical sets. Lightscape [1] and Radiance [27] are among the best of the systems designed to accurately predict the lighting in architectural spaces. They allow the designer to select a light fixture from a catalog, and they use the outgoing spectral distribution of the light source during the simulation. They also model the effects of skylighting and have the capability to simulate indirect lighting. These systems focus on physical simulation, and do not support programmable shading languages. Dorsey *et al.* have built a system for designing opera lighting [9] [8]. A major feature of this system is its ability to choreograph the complex time-dependent changes in lighting throughout the production.

Barzel discusses the controls and features of the light source model used at Pixar Animation Studios [2]. This model emphasizes the computer cinematographer's need for precise control over the shape and pattern of the light and its interaction with an object. Our system is designed to control light sources such as these.

There have been a number of methods proposed for quickly rendering changes in lighting based on using *linearity* and *basis images*. Linearity implies that the image formed from two lights is the sum of the images formed from each light separately. Linearity also implies that the effect of a change in color or intensity of a light can be efficiently recomputed by scaling the basis image [8].

Interactive methods have been developed for controlling light positions and parameters using inverse methods. Poulin and Fournier present a technique for determining light positions based on the position and orientation of a highlight or shadow boundary [20]. Schoeneman *et al.* describe a system in which the user paints over the image to brighten or darken different regions, and the system solves for the colors and intensities of a set of fixed lights using a constrained least squares approach[22]. In a system presented by Kawai *et al.*, the user specifies desired features of the lighting, such as visual clarity or contrast, and an optimization procedure is used to search for surface properties, such as reflectivities, and light properties, such as colors, intensities, and directions, that maximize the quality of the lighting [15]. All these techniques are important and useful, but in isolation none of them solve the cinematic lighting problem, especially in scenes with more complex shading models and descriptions.

A major method used to accelerate rendering for design purposes is to fix the camera position and create a "deep-framebuffer" image. A deep-framebuffer image contains all the information needed to rerender the scene, assuming only surface properties and light sources are changed. They do this by precomputing all the geometric information and storing it at each pixel. This precomputation makes it unnecessary to repeat geometric calculations such as tessellating the surface, transforming positions, and removing hidden surfaces during rerendering. The oldest technique of this type is orientation coding [3] [25] [13], where a normal vector is stored in the framebuffer and the lighting calculation is tabulated in the colormap. To change the surface or lighting attributes involves only recomputing the colormap entries. The natural extension of this technique is the G-buffer [21]. In the G-buffer, a collection of framebuffers is allocated, one per attribute. The information available in these framebuffers is available for shading calculations. This technique was considerably extended by Sequin and Smyrl [24]; in their system they store a ray tree at each pixel and reevaluate the ray tree to recompute the effects due to changes in surface properties or lights. Perhaps the most sophisticated deep-framebuffer system is the one built by Briere and Poulin [4]. In their system, visibility structures are stored that accelerate the recomputation of shadows and others effects due to reflection and transparency. As a result their system is able to handle a simple moving environment. Unfortunately, the data structures they use require a great deal of memory,

and so their system is impractical for very complex scenes.

The lighting system discussed in this paper is designed to be used with procedural shaders [19] [6] [12] [26]. Using procedural shaders significantly complicates the system design for several reasons. First, the lighting system must be general enough to handle arbitrary shading programs. Second, profiles of rendering systems show that 70-90% of the time is spent evaluating procedural shaders. Thus, a simple minded deep-framebuffer approach is only likely to speed up rendering time by 10-30% (the cost of all other calculations).

Guenter *et al.* have described an approach to incrementally evaluate procedural shaders by using partial evaluation and generalized shader specialization[11]. Although this method is very general, it is quite complex. Specialized versions of the shaders must be created for all combinations of surface and light parameters. In additional, partial evaluation requires a complex caching scheme that uses a lot of memory and is relatively difficult to manage. The combination of the methods used in this paper are much simpler, and as a result much easier to adapt to hardware.

Finally, this paper builds on techniques for hardware accelerated point rendering, or splatting [16][10][28]. The advantage of point rendering is that it is a forward mapping technique that runs very efficiently on graphics pipelines. Current widely available commodity graphics cards can render approximately 5 million points per second [7] and in the near future systems may be able to render 50 million or more points per second. The disadvantage of point rendering is that artifacts such as gaps may occur during the rendering process. However, in lighting design the view point is fixed, so no resampling is required. Thus point rendering is a very simple way of building a high performance rendering engine.

3 Lighting Design Process

Sharon Calahan has written an excellent overview chapter on cinematic lighting design in the context of computer graphics [5]. Her chapter describes the goals of lighting and how it contributes to storytelling. She also outlines the process used by professional lighting artists.

There are two scenarios in which a lighting artist works. In the first stage, called *master lighting*, the artist places lights that provide the background lighting for the set and props of the sequence. When working on the master lighting, the artist judges the lighting by rendering the static scene from a few camera positions that are characteristic of those used during the sequence. The second stage, called *shot lighting*, occurs when the artist is working on an animated sequence with a continuous camera position. Shots tend to last between one to ten seconds. In this stage the lighting artists concentrates on lighting the characters and telling the story.

A lighting artist typically uses a key-frame system in which they choose a few key locations in the animation, creates the lighting they desire for these frames, and then renders the entire animated sequence to judge the lighting for the entire shot. This means that the lighting artist spends most of their time designing the lighting for a single image from a fixed viewpoint. Thus, our design decision to optimize our system for a fixed viewpoint matches well existing production practices.

4 Relighting Engine

In this section we describe the basic operation of our lighting design system and our relighting engine. The system has three major stages:

- The first stage converts a shot from a given viewpoint to a deep-framebuffer. During this process the rendering system is used to partially evaluate the shading.

- The second stage is the lighting design stage. This stage takes as input the deep-framebuffer and outputs a set of lights. This system is built upon a hardware-assisted real-time rendering system so that light sources may be interactively moved and their properties changed.

- In the third stage the set of lights are added to the scene graph and the final rendering is performed.

4.1 Deep-Framebuffer

The first step in our system is the generation of the deep-framebuffer. Each pixel in the deep-framebuffer represents a visible surface element and contains all the geometric and optical information needed to perform subsequent lighting calculations.

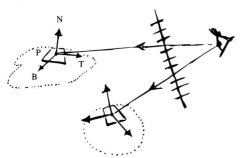

Figure 1: Each sample in the deep-framebuffer stores the world space position, surface normal, tangent, and bitangent vectors of the visible surface.

The geometric information associated with a sample defines the local coordinate system used for shading a point on the surface. This information includes the position, normal, tangent, and bitangent vectors, see Figure 1, all represented in world space coordinates.

For relighting purposes, the only optical information needed is the bi-directional reflection distribution function (BRDF). The BRDF is defined to be the ratio of reflected radiance to the differential incoming irradiance and represents the percentage of light energy reflected in a given outgoing direction for each incoming direction. Figure 2 shows the important direction vectors used in the computation of BRDFs.

In our approach, each BRDF F is represented as a linear combination of primitive BRDFs F_i multiplied by color reflectances C_i

$$ F(x, y, w_i, w_o) = \sum_i C_i(x, y) F_i(w_i, w_r, s(x, y)) $$

In our system, the primitive BRDFs include the common diffuse and specular (Phong) models, and less common models such as the Cook-Torrance, Oren-Nayar, and a model appropriate for materials such as velvet [17], Specular BRDF models are typically parameterized by a single number, the specularity or roughness, that characterizes the size of the highlight on the surface. Specifically, each deep-framebuffer sample stores an array of n BRDF terms; each term includes a color reflectance, the type of the primitive BRDF, and any associated parameters associated with that primitive BRDF.

Typically, final renderings are done with a production high quality rendering system. Thus, it is necessary to adapt the rendering system to output a deep-framebuffer; this is usually very straightforward. Because we have targeted our system for cinematic lighting, we use rendering systems that have programmable shading languages. To generate the deep-framebuffers, surface shaders that normally output only a final color are modified to output the geometric and optical information described above. In the case of

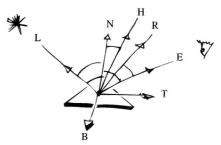

Figure 2: The major vectors required for the evaluation of the BRDF. N, L, and E represent the surface normal, the incoming direction from the light source, and the outgoing direction to the eye, respectively. H is the halfway vector between L and E, and R is the reflection of L about the surface normal N.

PIXAR's RenderMan shading language [26], this simply requires inserting "print" commands in the right places. However, for the examples used in this paper, we have used a locally written ray tracer as the final rendering system. This ray tracer is similar to RenderMan in that it uses a shading language for creating different surface and lighting models, but the shading language subsystem has been modified to output the required geometric and optical information directly to a file. This system also uses dynamically loaded libraries of C code to evaluate built-in and programmed BRDF models, and this same code may be used by a software-only implementation of the relighting system.

The surface sample points and BRDFs are sent down the graphics pipeline to compute lighting. The vertex transformation unit is used to transform the world space location of the point into the shading coordinate system and the lighting unit is used to evaluate the product of the point's BRDF and the radiance from a single light source. Finally, the texturing and compositing features of the fragment processing pipeline are used to modulate the reflected light and blend the result into the framebuffer.

4.2 Reflection Functions

In order to accelerate rendering we factor the color reflectance and BRDF into a form suitable for hardware acceleration.

Deep-framebuffer systems store parameters as images. In our system this image data is converted to texture maps. We store each color reflectance C_i in a texture map in which the location of the color component is the location of its image sample (x, y). When the points are fed into the graphics pipeline, the texture coordinates of each point are set to (x, y) and the color looked up and then used to modulate the color of the lit point.

Heidrich and Seidel recently have shown how a physically-based reflection model may be mapped onto the OpenGL graphics pipeline. The key idea is to factor the reflection model into a product of simpler lower-dimensional terms. Although the general BRDF is a function of 4 dimensions, each term in the factorization is typically a function of only one or two dimensions. For example, the Cook-Torrance reflection model is the product of three terms: a micro-facet distribution function $D(N \cdot H)$, a Fresnel term $F(H \cdot L)$, and a self-shadowing term $S(E \cdot N)S(L \cdot N)$. The micro-facet distribution function and Fresnel term are one-dimensional functions and the self-shading term is a two-dimensional function (actually this may be simplified into a product of one-dimensional functions). The advantage of this factorization is that these lower-dimensional terms may be stored in texture maps.

Building upon their work, we map each reflection function term F_i stored in the deep-framebuffer is mapped to a product of simpler factors. The terms themselves are associated with different stages of the graphics pipeline; BH is a term computed by the host processor, BL by the lighting unit, and BT by texture lookup unit.

$$F_i = (\prod_i BH_i(\theta_i)) \cdot (\prod_j BL_j(\theta_j)) \cdot (\prod_k BT_k(\theta_k))$$

Using this representation, a product of the form $BH \cdot BL \cdot BT$ may be computed using a single rendering pass. If multiple BH, BL or BT factors are required, then multiple passes are used. Note that in general, BH terms are to be avoided if possible, since they do not use the graphics hardware. BL factors are computed using the lighting engine and all that is required is that the normal be passed with each point and the light position be set properly. BT factors are the most complex. To evaluate these terms requires that the texture coordinates of the point be set to the appropriate dot product between two lighting vectors. As a preprocess we must also tabulate the BT factor and store it as a texture map. Note that on newer graphics hardware with multitexturing units, multiple textures may be applied in a single pass and this may reduce the total number of passes.

Our current system uses the following factorization which is automatically created from the relighting engine based on the deep-framebuffer. It is very easy to add additional factorizations or other terms as new reflection models are developed. As future work, it may be possible to compute such a factorization automatically.

$$\begin{aligned} F =& C_D \cdot BL_D(L \cdot N) + C_S \cdot BL_S(N \cdot H, s) + \\ & C_{CT} \cdot BT_{FD}(L \cdot H, N \cdot H) \cdot BT_G(N \cdot L, N \cdot E) + \quad (1) \\ & C_{LN} \cdot BH_{LN}(L \cdot N, k) + C_{EN} \end{aligned}$$

BL_D and BL_S are the standard OpenGL diffuse and specular functions. Following the factorization of the Cook-Torrance reflection model used by Heidrich and Siedel [14], BT_{FD} stores the product of the Fresnel term $F(L \cdot H)$ and the microfacet distribution function $D(N \cdot H)$, and BT_G stores the geometry term $G(N \cdot L, N \cdot E)$. Finally, BH_{LN} and C_{EN} compute reflection components used in the Minneart reflection model [18] (the Minneart model is useful for modeling materials such as velvet [17]). The Minneart model is a sum of two terms $L \cdot N^k$ and $E \cdot N^l$. Since $L \cdot N^k$ cannot be evaluated using the lighting unit, we elected to compute this on the host (although we could have also used a texture map). C_{EN} represents the function $E \cdot N^l$; Because the viewpoint is fixed, $E \cdot N$ is constant for each sample and may be precomputed and stored in a single texture map. Figure 4 shows the the factorization and the resulting passes used for a typical scene. Figure 3 shows the pseudo-code for the multi-pass algorithm.

4.3 Light Sources

Our system is designed to use light sources such as those described by Barzel [2]. The key feature of these light source models is the extreme flexibility in creating lighting distributions. The basic source model specifies the directional beam distribution and the intensity fall-off with distance from the source. Then this spatial lighting distributing is modulated using a set of attenuators. These include procedurally defined superelliptical blockers, "cookie" textures, slide textures, noise textures, and projected shadow mattes.

To implement such lights in real-time we use projective texturing algorithms [23]. To use projective textures in lighting, texture coordinate matrix is set to projectively transform the world space position of the sample into the light coordinate system. The resulting texture map look up is used to specify the color and intensity of the light or the color and alpha of an attenuator. We model a Barzel light as an initial distribution and a product of textures

$$L(x, \omega) = L_s(x, \omega)(\prod_i A_i(\omega))$$

```
/*   Fb = Framebuffer */

Fb = CCT;
BindBTTextures(FD);
Fb = Fb * RenderTextureBRDFPoints(BTFD);
BindBTTextures(G);
Fb = Fb * RenderTextureBRDFPoints(BTG);

BindTexture(CD);
Fb = Fb + RenderHardwareBRDFPoints(BLD);
BindTexture(CS);
Fb = Fb + RenderHardwareBRDFPoints(BLS);

BindTexture(CLN);
Fb = Fb + RenderHostBRDFPoints(BHLN);
BindTexture(CEN);
Fb = Fb + RenderNoBRDFPoints();

BindProjectiveTexture();
Fb = Fb * RenderProjectiveImage();

RenderShadowMap();
Fb = Fb * RenderShadowImage();

If have texture image of previous lights
        Fb = Fb + ImageOfPreviousLights;
```

Figure 3: Psuedo-code for the multi-pass algorithm that corresponds to the pipeline shown in figure 4.

Here L_s is the beam distribution from a point source and A_i are color attenuation maps as a function of direction.

This factorization allows very complex lights to be rendered using multiple passes. However, an important optimization is to pre-multiply fixed terms together into a single projected texture map so that it may be rendered with a single pass. Another useful mode in the design process is to allow only a single term to be modified. For example, the user changes the shape or size of a single blocker or moves a single attenuator with respect to the light. This mode requires only two passes, one for the static terms and one for the dynamic term.

The computation of shadows requires two additional passes. The algorithm we use takes advantage of hardware z-buffering, depth comparisons, and the SGI OpenGL shadow extension. The first pass of the shadow algorithm creates a shadow depth map from the viewpoint of the light source. In second pass the points are rendered from the eye point, but also transformed into the light source coordinate system. If the depth of the point is less than the corresponding shadow map depth, then the point is in shadow and its alpha value is set to zero, otherwise the alpha value is set to one. Other approaches for computing shadows are available if this functionality is not supported by the graphics hardware, but it is assumed that these features will appear in commodity graphics hardware within the next year.

Finally, we exploit the linearity of the contribution of the individual lights. This property allows us to generate an image of the combined result of the new light source with the previously placed lights by adding the image of the new light to the image of previously computed lighting effects. In our system, this is done by storing the previously computed image as a texture and adding it to the result of the newly computed image in a final pass.

4.4 Performance Optimizations

In order to minimize the total number of primitives processed by the graphics hardware, we cull points that do not contribute to a particular reflection function. This culling is easily performed by checking the color reflectance map: if the color is black (0), then

Rendering	Lights	Time (s)	Speedup
Geometry + Texturing + Lighting	10	121	1:1
Texturing + Lighting	10	51	2.4:1
Lighting (sw)	10	13	9.3:1
Lighting (sw)	1	1.3	93:1
Lighting (hw)	10	0.5	242:1
Lighting (hw)	1	0.05	2420:1
Lighting + Shadows (hw)	1	0.25	484:1

Table 1: Time to render the scene in Figure 4.

that point is culled. Additionally, if the properties of the point are static (this is always the case unless texture coordinates need to be recomputed), we store points in a display list to maximize rendering rate, Finally, we can partition the points by object and only rendering a subset of the points that come from a particular object. This is very useful since it speeds up the system and since lights are often defined object by object.

Another major method used to increase performance is to reorder the calculation to maximize coherence. For example, SGI's Performer and many other scene graph libraries reorder primitives by texture maps; that is, all the primitives that use the same texture map are drawn together. We have found that we can significantly speedup rendering by reordering the points by the material properties. In one sense this is done by reordering the shading calculation so that all diffuse calculations are done in one pass and all specular calculations are done in another pass. As a further optimization, we quantize material parameters such as the specular exponent to reduce the number of different materials and to reorder rendering so that all points with the same properties are rendered together. Since there is substantial cost to switching material properties, this is a significant speedup. In the case of the specular exponent, we found applying a logarithmic transformation before quantization is also useful.

5 Results

We have implemented a simple lighting design system using our rendering engine. A detailed discussion of all the features of this system is beyond the scope of this paper. In this section we describe various experiments we did to estimate the performance of the system and to validate our design decisions.

We created a simple test scene typical of a set (see Figure 4). All the shaders are programmed in a shading language very similar to the RenderMan shading language; this scene contains 104 objects, 2.2 million micro-triangles, and 13 distinct surface shaders. Figure 5 presents timings of various stages. We timed how long it took to render the scene using the ray tracer and how long it took to render the scene using our deep-framebuffer. We also compared the time it took to render the deep-framebuffer using software vs. hardware. All timings were done using a Onyx2 with a 195 MHZ MIPS R10000 and an InfiniteReality2 Graphics Subsystem. The final image size was 512 by 256 which represents 131,072 samples; a detailed breakdown of the number of points required per pass is shown in figure 4. The shadow timing includes the generation of a shadowmap from 100,000 polygons of geometry.

There are seven separate passes in figure 4, not including shadow computations (the two passes of BT_{FD} and BT_G are merged together in the diagram). The average number of points rendered per pass is 48,210.

Some results stand out. First, in this scene approximately 42% of the time is spent in geometry processing and 58% in shading. Second, of the shading, 25% of the time is spent evaluating the reflection model and 75% of the time is spent evaluating spatially varying textures that control the reflection model. Third, as expected, there is linear speedup in the number of lights; that is, in a

scene consisting of ten lights, moving one light is exactly ten times faster than rendering all the lights. Finally, the hardware version is 27.5 times faster than the software system. Overall the hardware relighting system runs 2000 times faster than the software batch renderer. Moreover, the lighting design system runs at roughly 20 Hz, fast enough for interactive use.

6 Summary and Discussion

We have described and implemented a simple rendering engine for interactive lighting design. The system meets our original goals which were to accept scene descriptions with programmable shaders from a production rendering system; and to allow a lighting artist to position the light source and modify all the major light properties in real-time without compromising image quality. Figure 5 shows examples of lighting created using our system. Although our example set is relatively simple, we believe our system will scale to movie-complexity scenes since the rendering time only depends on the output complexity of the deep-framebuffer.

The shadow computation is dependent on the input complexity of the scene, while all other computations are based on the output complexity of the deep-framebuffer. Therefore, the shadow algorithm does not scale as well as the other computations with increases in scene complexity. We are currently exploring new image and point-based methods for shadow approximations.

The key to our system is adapting deep-framebuffer technology to modern graphics hardware. Over the past several years we have built a series of more and more complex software-only rendering engines for lighting design with limited success. There is no silver bullet: interactive relighting requires lots of floating point operations and today's graphics hardware delivers more flops per dollar than conventional CPUs. For example, a 1999 single chip graphics accelerator from NVIDIA is rated by the manufacturer at 50 gigaflops and costs tens of dollars. (We are currently in the process of porting our system from the SGI IR used in this paper to a PC.) In the future the gap between graphics hardware and the main processor is predicted to be even larger, and so our approach will be even more attractive. For example, a hardware system capable of rendering 50 million points per second would allow us to do more than 20 passes at 20 Hz on a 512 by 256 image. Finally, graphics hardware vendors are introducing new features such as multitexturing and texture combiners that support advanced shading and even programmablity. With hardware assistance, we believe interactive lighting design will soon be as common as interactive 3d painting.

Acknowledgements

We would like to thank Matt Pharr and Craig Kolb for co-developing the technique of separating surface texturing from the lighting calculations. Julie Dorsey for discussions on lighting design systems. Pixar's RenderMan Graphics R&D group for years of discussions on production lighting and rendering systems. Kekoa Proudfoot and Bill Mark for their discussions on real-time programmable shading systems and graphics hardware. Sudeep Rangaswamy for creating the chair, table and bookshelf models in our test images. Reid would like to thank Sharon Calahan for her guidance and teaching of cinematography and lighting design during the productions *A Bug's Life* and *Toy Story 2*. This research was supported by NSF contract number CCR-9508579-001, and DARPA contracts DABT63-96-C-0084-P00002 and DABT63-95-C-0085-P00006.

References

[1] Lightscape visualization system.

[2] Ronen Barzel. Lighting controls for computer cinematography. *Journal of Graphics Tools*, 2(1):1–20, 1997.

[3] J. F. Blinn. Raster graphics. In K. Booth, editor, *Tutorial: Computer Graphics*. IEEE Computer Society, 1979.

[4] Normand Briere and Pierre Poulin. Hierarchical view-dependent structures for interactive scene manipulation. In *Computer Graphics Annual Conference Series 1996*, pages 83–90. Siggraph, August 1996.

[5] Sharon Calahan. Storytelling through lighting, a computer perspective. In Tony Apodaca and Larry Gritz, editors, *Advanced Renderman: Creating CGI for Motion Pictures*, pages 337–382. Morgan Kaufman Publishers, San Francisco, 1999.

[6] Robert L. Cook. Shade trees. In Hank Christiansen, editor, *Computer Graphics (SIGGRAPH '84 Proceedings)*, volume 18, pages 223–231, July 1984.

[7] NVIDIA Corporation. *GeForce 256 Graphics Accelerator Specifications*, December 1999.

[8] J. Dorsey, J. Arvo, and D. Greenberg. Interactive design of complex time-dependent lighting. *IEEE Computer Graphics and Applications*, 15(2):26–36, March 1995.

[9] Julie O'B. Dorsey, Francois X. Sillion, and Donald P. Greenberg. Design and simulation of opera lighting and projection effects. *Computer Graphics*, 25(4):41–50, July 1991.

[10] J.P. Grossman and Willian J. Dally. Point sample rendering. In George Drettakis and Nelson Max, editors, *Eurographics Rendering Workshop*, Eurographics, pages 181–192, 1998.

[11] Brian Guenter, Todd B. Knoblock, and Erik Ruf. Specializing shaders. In *Computer Graphics Annual Conference Series 1995*, pages 343–350. Siggraph, August 1995.

[12] Pat Hanrahan and Jim Lawson. A language for shading and lighting calculations. In Forest Baskett, editor, *Computer Graphics (SIGGRAPH '90 Proceedings)*, volume 24, pages 289–298, August 1990.

[13] Paul S. Heckbert. Techniques for real-time frame buffer animation. In *Computer FX 84 Conference*, October 1984.

[14] Wolfgang Heidrich and Hans-Peter Seidel. Realistic, hardware-accelerated shading and lighting. In Alyn Rockwood, editor, *Computer Graphics (SIGGRAPH '99 Proceedings)*, pages 171–178, August 1999.

[15] John K. Kawai, James S. Painter, and Michael F. Cohen. Radioptimization - goal based rendering. In *Computer Graphics Annual Conference Series 1993*, pages 147–154. Siggraph, August 1993.

[16] Marc Levoy and Turner Whitted. The use of points as a display primitive. Technical Report 85-022, UNC-Chapel Hill Computer Science, 1985.

[17] Rong Lu, Jan J. Koenderink, and Astrid M. Kappers. Optical properties (bidirectional reflection distribution functions) of velvet. In *Applied Optics*, volume 37, pages 5974–5984, 1998.

[18] M. Minnaert. The reciprocity principle in lunar photometry. In *Astrophys. J.*, volume 93, pages 403–410, 1941.

[19] Ken Perlin. An image synthesizer. *Computer Graphics*, 19(3):287–296, July 1985.

[20] Pierre Poulin and A. Fournier. Lights from highlights and shadows. In *1992 Symposium on Interactive 3D Graphics*, pages 31–38, March 1992.

[21] Takafumi Saito and Tokiichiro Takahashi. Comprehensible rendering of 3-d shapes. In *Computer Graphics Annual Conference Series 1990*, pages 197–206, August 1990.

[22] Chris Schoeneman, Julie Dorsey, Brian Smits, James Arvo, and Donald Greenberg. Painting with light. In *Computer Graphics Annual Conference Series 1993*, pages 143–146. Siggraph, August 1993.

[23] Mark Segal, Carl Korobkin, Rolf van Widenfelt, Jim Foran, and Paul Haeberli. Fast shadows and lighting effects using texture mapping. In *Computer Graphics Annual Conference Series 1992*, pages 249–252, July 1992.

[24] Carlo H. Sequin and Eliot K. Smyrl. Parameterized ray tracing. In *Computer Graphics Annual Conference Series 1989*, pages 307–314. Siggraph, July 1989.

[25] Kenneth R. Sloan and Christopher M. Brown. Color map techniques. *Computer Graphics and Image Processing*, 10:297–317, 1979.

[26] Steve Upstill. *The RenderMan Companion*. Addison Wesley, 1992.

[27] Gregory J. Ward. The radiance lighting simulation and rendering system.

[28] Lee Westover. Footprint evaluation for volume rendering. *Computer Graphics*, 24(4):367–376, August 1990.

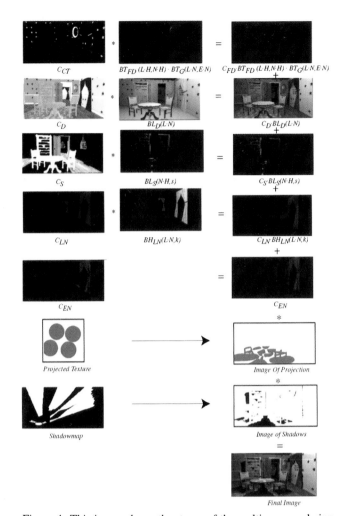

Figure 4: This image shows the stages of the multi-pass rendering algorithm. The number of points rendered per row are: row 1 = 17,302 points, row 2 = 129,604 points, row 3 = 39,006 points, row 4 = 10,246 points, row 5 = 10,246 points, row 6 (projective texture) = 131,072 points, row 7 (shadow map) = 131,072.

Figure 5: This is an example of lighting designed using our system. It took 2 hours to create, contains 60 lights (mostly to simulate inter-reflection effects), and defines an early morning mood.

Relief Texture Mapping

Manuel M. Oliveira[†]   Gary Bishop[‡]   David McAllister[‡]

University of North Carolina at Chapel Hill

Figure 1. Town rendered using conventional texture mapping. The façades and brick walls represented with one texture each.

Figure 2. Same view as in Figure 1 rendered using relief texture mapping. Both scenes contain the same number of polygons. Notice the bricks standing out and the protruding dormers.

ABSTRACT

We present an extension to texture mapping that supports the representation of 3-D surface details and view motion parallax. The results are correct for viewpoints that are static or moving, far away or nearby. Our approach is very simple: a *relief texture* (texture extended with an orthogonal displacement per texel) is mapped onto a polygon using a two-step process: First, it is converted into an ordinary texture using a surprisingly simple 1-D forward transform. The resulting texture is then mapped onto the polygon using standard texture mapping. The 1-D warping functions work in texture coordinates to handle the parallax and visibility changes that result from the 3-D shape of the displacement surface. The subsequent texture-mapping operation handles the transformation from texture to screen coordinates.

CR Categories and Subject Descriptors: I.3.3 [Computer Graphics]: Picture/Image Generation I.3.6 [Computer Graphics]: Methodologies and Techniques; I.3.7 [Computer Graphics]: Three-Dimensional Graphics and Realism.

[†] Now at the Computer Science Department
SUNY at Stony Brook, Stony Brook, NY, 11794-4400
oliveira@cs.sunysb.edu   http://www.cs.sunysb.edu/~oliveira

[‡] UNC Department of Computer Science
CB #3175, Sitterson Hall, Chapel Hill, NC, 27599-3175
{bishop | davemc}@cs.unc.edu   http://www.cs.unc.edu/~ibr

Additional Keywords: Image-Based Rendering, Texture Mapping, Range Images, Rendering.

1. INTRODUCTION

Texture mapping has long been used to enhance the realism of computer-generated images by adding 2-D details to object surfaces [1]. For instance, it can be used to correctly simulate a picture on a wall, or the label on a can. Unfortunately, texture mapping is not as effective for adding 3-D details to a surface. When seen by a moving observer, the absence of parallax reveals the flatness of the surface. Such flatness is also evidenced when the surface is observed from an oblique angle (Figure 1).

A much more convincing illusion of 3-D surface detail can be achieved by using a height field in conjunction with a texture map. A height field is a scalar field of distances between surface points and their orthogonal projections onto a plane that forms its algebraic basis. Unfortunately, rendering height fields is much more difficult than texture mapping. The planar-projective transform of texture mapping has a very convenient inverse formulation. This allows direct computation of texture coordinates from screen coordinates, thus allowing efficient implementation as well as accurate resampling and filtering. Height-field rendering allows no such inverse formulation directly. Multiple samples from the height field may be mapped to the same pixel in the final image. Assuring correct visibility requires either a search for the closest surfaces (essentially a ray-tracing strategy) or a direct forward mapping [11].

We present an extension to texture mapping for representing three-dimensional surface details and view motion parallax. This new approach, called *relief texture mapping*, results from a factorization of the 3-D image-warping equation of McMillan and

Bishop into a pre-warp followed by standard texture mapping. The pre-warp is applied to images with per-texel displacements and handles only the parallax effects resulting from the direction of view and the displacements of texture elements; the subsequent texture-mapping operation handles scaling, rotation, and the remaining perspective transformation.

The pre-warping equations have a very simple 1-D structure that enables the pre-warp to be implemented using only 1-D image operations along rows and columns and requires interpolation between only two adjacent texels at a time. This allows efficient implementation in software and should allow a simple and efficient hardware implementation. The texture-mapping hardware already very common in graphics systems efficiently implements the final texture mapping stage of the warp.

In recent years, image-based modeling and rendering (IBMR) techniques have gained considerable attention in the graphics community because of their potential to create very realistic images. We hope to help to bridge the gap between IBMR and conventional polygonal rendering techniques by casting a subset of IBMR as an extension of texture mapping. Such a hybrid system can offer much of the photo-realistic promise of IBMR while retaining the advantages of polygonal rendering. In section 4.4, we present an example of a real environment modeled and rendered using relief texture mapping.

We demonstrate a software implementation of our method and show that it significantly increases the expressive power of conventional texture mapping. Our approach also dramatically reduces the polygonal count required to model a scene, while preserving its realistic look. Figure 2 shows the use of our approach for the same viewpoint used to create Figure 1. The two scenes used to render these images were modeled using the same number of polygons. In the example of Figure 2, each façade and brick wall is represented with a single relief texture. Notice the bricks standing out of the wall and the protruding dormers. In the original model of the town, each house consists of a few thousand polygons, whereas the corresponding relief texture representation uses only seven polygons per house.

The new results presented in this paper are:

- An extension to texture mapping that supports view motion parallax (Section 3);
- An exact factorization of the 3-D image warping equation [11] into a 1-D pre-warp followed by a planar projective mapping (Section 3.1);
- After rotations are factored out, 3-D warps reduce to a 2-D problem, regardless of the coordinate systems associated with the source and target images (section 3.1); and
- A 1-D image reconstruction algorithm that handles an arbitrary number of self-occlusions without requiring extra storage or depth comparison (section 3.3.2).

2. RELATED WORK

3-D Image Warping. Three-dimensional image warping [11] is a geometric transformation that maps a source image with depth i_s into a target image i_t. The geometric content of the scene is represented implicitly by combining depth information with a camera model associated with the source image. Thus, let $\dot{x}$ be a point in Euclidean space whose projection on the image plane of

i_s has coordinates (u_s, v_s). The projection of $\dot{x}$ into an arbitrary target image plane, $\vec{x}_t$, is given by:

$$\vec{x}_t \doteq P_t^{-1} P_s \vec{x}_s + P_t^{-1}(\dot{C}_s - \dot{C}_t)\delta_s(u_s, v_s) \tag{1}$$

where $\doteq$ is projective equivalence, *i.e.*, the same except for a scalar multiple, P_k is a 3x3 camera matrix associated with image i_k, $\vec{x}_s = \begin{bmatrix} u_s & v_s & 1 \end{bmatrix}^T$, $\dot{C}_k$ is the center of projection (COP) of the pinhole camera associated with image i_k and $\delta_s(u_s, v_s)$ is the *generalized disparity* of source pixel (u_s, v_s) [11]. Equation (1) shows that the target image can be obtained by applying a planar perspective transformation to the source image followed by a per-pixel shift proportional to $\delta_s(u_s, v_s)$ in the direction of the *epipole*[1] of the target image. Such a factorization is often referred to as *plane-plus-parallax* in the computer vision literature [15].

Texture mapping is a special case of 3-D image warping for which all pixels of the source image share a single disparity value [11]. This fact will be exploited in section 3.1 for the derivation of the pre-warping equations.

Sprites with Depth. *Sprites with depth* [17] enhance the descriptive power of traditional sprites with out-of-plane displacements per pixel. Such a technique is based on the *plane-plus-parallax* factorization [15] mentioned before. In a first step, the displacement information associated with the source image is forward mapped using a 2-D transformation to compute an intermediate displacement map. In the second pass, each pixel of the desired image is transformed by a homography (planar perspective projection) and the resulting coordinates are used to index the displacement map computed in the first pass. The retrieved displacement value is then multiplied by the epipole of the target image and added to the result of the homography. These new coordinates are used to index the color of the desired pixel.

Although such an approach may sound similar to ours at first, it differs in some fundamental aspects. Sprites with Depth are an approximation to the 3-D image warping process. Our method, on the other hand, is based on an exact factorization of the 3-D image warping equation [11], takes advantage of texture mapping hardware, uses an efficient image reconstruction strategy and naturally integrates itself with popular graphics APIs such as OpenGL [21].

View-dependent Texture Mapping. New views of a scene can be rendered by compositing multiple textures based on the observer's viewpoint, which are then mapped onto a polygonal model. In [4], a model-based stereo algorithm is used to compute depth maps from pairs of images. Once a depth map associated with a particular image has been computed, new views of the scene can be rendered using several image-based rendering techniques.

1-D Perspective Projection. Robertson [14] showed how hidden-point removal and perspective projection of height images could be performed on scanlines or columns. This approach explores the separability of perspective projection into orthogonal components. First, the image is rotated to align its lower edge with the lower edge of the viewing window. Then, a horizontal compression is applied to each scanline so that all points that may potentially occlude each other

---

[1]   The projection of one camera's center of projection into the image plane of another camera.

fall along the same column. 1-D vertical perspective projection is applied to the columns of the intermediate image in back-to-front order, thus performing hidden-point removal. Finally, 1-D horizontal perspective projection is applied to the resulting image, incorporating compensation for the compression applied in the second step [14].

Serial Warps. Image operations such as texture mapping and image warping involve transformations among pairs of coordinates. Catmull and Smith [2] showed how affine and perspective transformations applied to planar surfaces and to bilinear and biquadratic patches can be decomposed into a series of 1-D operations over rows and columns. Later, Smith [18] showed that texture mapping onto planar quadric and superquadric surfaces, and planar bicubic and biquadratic image warps are two-pass transformable.

Serial warps suffer from a problem commonly referred to as *bottleneck*, the collapse of the intermediate image into an area much smaller than the final image [2]. Non-injective 2-D mapping may also map multiple samples to the same pixel on the screen, a situation known as *foldover* [2]. The major sources of bottlenecks are *image rotations* and *perspective distortions* [20]. In combination with rotations, perspective distortions can cause the intermediate image to twist, leading to loss of information and introducing severe artifacts in the final image [13].

3. RELIEF TEXTURE MAPPING

A *relief texture* is a texture extended with orthogonal displacements per texel, and has some interesting properties. For instance, when the viewer is far away from the represented surface, it can be rendered as a regular texture. As the viewer approaches the surface, the relief texture can be warped before being mapped onto a polygon and, when the viewer is extremely close, the relief texture can be rendered as a mesh of micro-polygons.

Image-based rendering techniques can generate very realistic views by warping images and Equation (1) concisely describes the warping process. Ideally, from a conventional rendering point-of-view, the mapping expressed by Equation (1) should be factored so to allow conventional texture mapping to be applied after the shift in the direction of the epipole. Such an approach is the opposite of the conventional plane-plus-parallax decomposition, in the sense that shifts take place prior to the homography (Figure 3), and presents several advantages. First, it can benefit from the texture mapping hardware in graphics systems to perform the final transformation and filtering. Secondly, the warp can be implemented using 1-D image operations along rows and columns, requiring interpolation between only two adjacent texels at a time. This property greatly simplifies the tasks of reconstruction and filtering of the intermediate image [5] and should allow a simple and efficient hardware implementation. Thirdly, the approach naturally integrates itself with popular graphics APIs such as OpenGL [21].

During the warp, texels move only horizontally and vertically in texture space by amounts that depend on their orthogonal displacements and on the viewing configuration. The warp

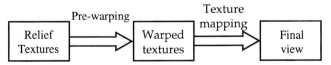

Figure 3. Relief texture mapping: pre-warping followed by standard texture mapping.

implements no rotations (which are subsequently performed as part of the conventional texture mapping operation) and the resulting serial warps do not suffer from bottlenecks or from image twists. Figure 3 shows a flowchart for the relief texture-mapping algorithm resulting from such an ideal factorization. Section 3.1 explains how such a factorization is obtained.

3.1 Pre-Warping Equations

In order to obtain the ideal factorization, one needs to find a pre-warp p so that the composition $m \circ p$, where m is a standard texture-mapping transformation, is equivalent to the 3-D image warp w. Thus, let $(u_i, v_i) = (u_s + \Delta u, v_s + \Delta v)$ be the intermediate coordinates obtained after shifting source pixel (u_s, v_s) by $(\Delta u, \Delta v)$. The equivalence between the composed mapping $m \circ p$ and w can be expressed as:

What coordinates (u_i, v_i) should the source pixels (u_s, v_s) have so that a view of such a flat distorted image on the source image plane from the target COP would be identical to a 3-D image warp of the source image onto the target image plane?

While perspective projection images with depth can be used as source images for such a purpose, the use of parallel projection images with depth presents some advantages. For instance, they have constant sampling density across the entire image. Also, the perpendicular relationship between sampling rays and image plane can be exploited to produce a simple and efficient rendering algorithm (Section 4.1).

Given a parallel projection camera model (Figure 4), the coordinates of a point $\dot{x}$ in Euclidean space are given by:

$$\dot{x} = \dot{C}_s + \begin{bmatrix} a_{si} & b_{si} & f_{si} \\ a_{sj} & b_{sj} & f_{sj} \\ a_{sk} & b_{sk} & f_{sk} \end{bmatrix} \begin{bmatrix} u_s \\ v_s \\ displ(u_s,v_s) \end{bmatrix} = \dot{C}_s + P'_s \vec{x}'_s$$

where vectors $\vec{a}_s$ and $\vec{b}_s$ form a basis for the plane of the source image. The lengths of these vectors are the horizontal and vertical sample spacing in the Euclidean space, respectively. $\vec{f}_s$ is a unit vector perpendicular to the plane defined by $\vec{a}_s$ and $\vec{b}_s$, $\dot{C}_s$ is the origin of the source image plane, and $displ(u_s, v_s)$ is the orthogonal displacement, or height, associated with source pixel (u_s, v_s). The reprojected coordinates of $\dot{x}$ into a target perspective projection camera (Figure 5) are given by[2]

$$u_t = \frac{Au_s + Bv_s + D + C'displ(u_s,v_s)}{Iu_s + Jv_s + L + K'displ(u_s,v_s)} \quad (2a)$$

$$v_t = \frac{Eu_s + Fv_s + H + G'displ(u_s,v_s)}{Iu_s + Jv_s + L + K'displ(u_s,v_s)} \quad (2b)$$

where $A = \vec{a}_s \cdot (\vec{b}_t \times \vec{c}_t)$, $B = \vec{b}_s \cdot (\vec{b}_t \times \vec{c}_t)$, $C' = \vec{f}_s \cdot (\vec{b}_t \times \vec{c}_t)$, $D = (\dot{C}_s - \dot{C}_t) \cdot (\vec{b}_t \times \vec{c}_t)$, $E = \vec{a}_s \cdot (\vec{c}_t \times \vec{a}_t)$, $F = \vec{b}_s \cdot (\vec{c}_t \times \vec{a}_t)$, $G' = \vec{f}_s \cdot (\vec{c}_t \times \vec{a}_t)$, $H = (\dot{C}_s - \dot{C}_t) \cdot (\vec{c}_t \times \vec{a}_t)$, $I = \vec{a}_s \cdot (\vec{a}_t \times \vec{b}_t)$, $J = \vec{b}_s \cdot (\vec{a}_t \times \vec{b}_t)$, $K' = \vec{f}_s \cdot (\vec{a}_t \times \vec{b}_t)$, $L = (\dot{C}_s - \dot{C}_t) \cdot (\vec{a}_t \times \vec{b}_t)$

---

[2] We preserved the original notation used in [13] for easy reference by interested readers.

Figure 4. Parallel projection camera model.

and $\vec{c}_t$ is a vector from the target COP to the origin of the target image plane (Figure 5).

The corresponding texture mapping expressions are obtained from Equations (2a) and (2b) by letting $displ(u_s, v_s) = 0$ for all source pixels. Thus, the problem of finding the desired warp can be modeled as

$$\frac{Au_i + Bv_i + D}{Iu_i + Jv_i + L} = \frac{Au_s + Bv_s + D + C'displ(u_s, v_s)}{Iu_s + Jv_s + L + K'displ(u_s, v_s)} \quad (3a)$$

$$\frac{Eu_i + Fv_i + H}{Iu_i + Jv_i + L} = \frac{Eu_s + Fv_s + H + G'displ(u_s, v_s)}{Iu_s + Jv_s + L + K'displ(u_s, v_s)}. \quad (3b)$$

The pre-warp associated with the ideal factorization is then obtained by solving the system above for u_i and v_i:

$$u_i = \frac{u_s + k_1 displ(u_s, v_s)}{1 + k_3 displ(u_s, v_s)} \quad (4a)$$

$$v_i = \frac{v_s + k_2 displ(u_s, v_s)}{1 + k_3 displ(u_s, v_s)} \quad (4b)$$

where k_1, k_2 and k_3 are constants for the given configuration of source and target cameras and, together with $displ(u_s, v_s)$, determine the amount of change $(\Delta u, \Delta v)$ in the coordinates of the source texels. A formal proof of the 1-D nature of the pre-warping equations can be found in [13].

Such a factorization proves to have many desirable properties. In particular, the coordinates of a pixel in the intermediate image can be computed independently from each other, *i.e.*, u_i does not depend on v_s and v_i does not depend on u_s. Also, when $displ_s(u_s, v_s) = 0$ no computation is required.

The evaluation of Equations (4a) and (4b) can be reduced to two additions, two multiplications and three lookup operations by quantizing the displacement values (in a pre-processing step) and storing the reciprocal of the denominator of Equation (4a) and the expressions $k_1 displ(u_s, v_s)$ and $k_2 displ(u_s, v_s)$ in lookup tables. We have used a uniform quantization scheme in which a quantized displacement is recovered as $displ' = min + qi * qs$, where min is the minimum displacement value, $qs = (max - min) / 254$ is the quantization step and

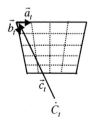

Figure 5. Pinhole camera model [11].

$qi = int((displ(u_s, v_s) - min) / qs)$ is the quantization index. The indices were stored in the alpha channel of the relief texture with one value reserved for transparency. In practice, this uniform quantization scheme works very well and the results are virtually indistinguishable from those obtained with the actual displacement values. Moreover, such a strategy reduces the storage requirements of relief textures to essentially the same as conventional textures (the values of *min* and *qs* need to be saved) and it also helps to improve cache coherence, since the displacement and color data associated with a texel are always used together. This scheme uses the alpha channel of source textures only and the alpha channel of the pre-warped textures can still be used for antialiasing and transparency.

The Coefficients of the Pre-Warping Equations. The amount of shift $(\Delta u, \Delta v)$ to be applied to a source texel does not depend on the parameters of the target camera except for its COP [13]. Therefore, one can freely specify the parameters $\vec{a}_t$, b_t and $\vec{c}_t$ which define a temporary target camera used only for the purpose of the pre-warp and which usually differs from the virtual camera used for the visualization of the final scene. By appropriately choosing such parameters, it is possible to eliminate several of the coefficients in Equations (3a) and (3b) by forcing the corresponding scalar triple products to have the form $\vec{v} \cdot (\vec{v} \times \vec{w})$ or $\vec{w} \cdot (\vec{v} \times \vec{w})$. Such a procedure leads to a drastic simplification of the expressions used to compute coefficients k_1, k_2 and k_3. For instance, the condition $\vec{a}_t = \alpha \vec{a}_s$, $b_t = \beta b_s$ and $\vec{c}_t = \gamma(C_s - C_t)$, for nonzero $\alpha, \beta, \gamma \in \Re$, eliminates coefficients B, D, E, H, I and J and is trivially satisfied by letting source and target image planes coincide, including their origins and basis vectors (Figure 6). The subscripts of all vectors can then be dropped without risk of confusion and the coefficients of Equations (4a) and (4b) become

$$k_1 = \frac{\vec{f} \cdot (\vec{b} \times \vec{c})}{\vec{a} \cdot (\vec{b} \times \vec{c})}, \quad k_2 = \frac{\vec{f} \cdot (\vec{c} \times a)}{\vec{a} \cdot (\vec{b} \times \vec{c})} \text{ and } k_3 = \frac{1}{\vec{c} \cdot \vec{f}}.$$

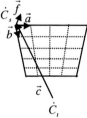

Figure 6. Parallel and perspective projection cameras sharing the same image plane (origin, $\vec{a}$ and $\vec{b}$ vectors).

Occlusion-Compatible Ordering. The COP of a parallel projection image is at infinity. Its epipole is the projection of the other camera's COP onto the plane of the parallel projection image. By similarity of triangles, whenever two samples fall along the same viewing ray, the one whose projection is closer to the epipole is also closer to the viewer (Figure 7). Thus, an occlusion-compatible order [11] (essentially a painter's algorithm) for parallel projection images with depth is obtained by warping pixels from the borders towards the epipole.

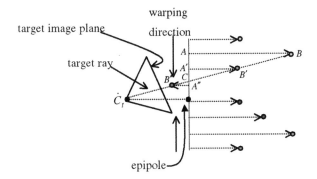

Figure 7. Triangles ABC, $A'B'C$ and $A''B''C$ are similar. Similarity of triangles guarantees that occlusion compatible order is achieved by warping from the borders towards the epipole.

3.2 Reconstructing Pre-warped Textures

Section 3.1 has shown how to determine the coordinates of infinitesimal points in the intermediate image from points in the source image. Determining these is only the beginning of the image-warping process. The more expensive step is reconstruction and resampling onto the pixel grid of the intermediate image. The simplest and most common approaches to reconstruction and resampling are splatting and meshing. Splatting requires spreading each input pixel over several output pixels to assure full coverage and proper interpolation. Meshing requires rasterizing a quadrilateral for each pixel in the NxN input texture.

The special structure of our pre-warp equations allows us to implement reconstruction and resampling as a two-pass process using 1-D transforms along rows and columns [2]. The reader should make a clear distinction between the two steps of our method: pre-warping followed by texture mapping, and the two phases used to implement the pre-warping step itself. Such phases consist of a horizontal pass and a vertical pass.

3.2.1 Two-pass Reconstruction

Assuming that the horizontal pass takes place first, the steps of a two-pass reconstruction algorithm are illustrated in Figure 8. Figure 8(a) shows two source texels A and B and their positions after the pre-warp (outlined circles). The first texel of each row is moved to its final column (Figure 8(b)) and, as the subsequent texels are warped, color and final row coordinates are interpolated during rasterization (Figure 8(c)). Fractional coordinate values (for both rows and columns) are used for filtering purposes in a similar way as described in [5]. Notice that adjacent texels are usually warped to adjacent positions and the situation shown in Figure 4-3(c) is used to stress the interpolation scheme. The warp may, however, map adjacent texels to relatively distant positions if such texels are at different sides of a depth discontinuity. Let texel C be right above texel B after all rows have been warped (Figure 8(d)). During the vertical pass, texels are moved to their final row coordinates (Figure 8(e)) and colors are interpolated (Figure 8(f)). Figure 9 illustrates the stages of the two-pass warp and reconstruction for the case of a building façade. Figure 9(a) shows a source relief texture. Figures 9(b) and 9(c) present the results of the horizontal and vertical passes, respectively. The final view of the texture-mapped polygon, whose borders are shown in red, is presented in Figure 9(d). A pseudocode for a two-pass reconstruction algorithm that disregards filtering issues for simplicity is presented in Figure 10.

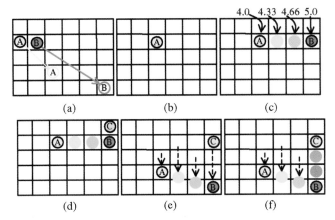

Figure 8. Warping of one texel. (a) Source texels A and B and their final positions after the warp. (b) The first texel of the current row is moved to its final column. (c) Next texel is moved to its final column and color and final row coordinates are interpolated during rasterization. (d) After all rows have been warped, texel C is adjacent to texel B. (e) Along each column, texels are moved to their final rows. (f) Color is interpolated during rasterization.

There are advantages in computing both coordinates of pre-warped texels in the first step of the algorithm. For instance, it avoids nonlinear distortions in the final image that would otherwise be introduced if row coordinates were computed during the second pass using interpolated displacement values [13].

We have compared the results produced by this algorithm with the results of rendering relief textures as meshes of micropolygons. The results are essentially the same in most cases. Improper color interpolation may happen across depth discontinuities, where no information about the surface is available, and are the major source of artifacts in images produced by two-pass 1-D

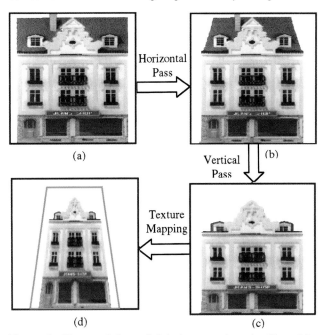

Figure 9. Stages of the relief texture-mapping algorithm. (a) Source relief texture. (b) Image produced by the horizontal pass. (c) Pre-warped texture obtained after the vertical pass. (d) Final view, showing the borders of the texture-mapped polygon.

reconstruction strategies. In practice, however, depth discontinuities are frequently associated with either smooth color changes or sharp color transitions matching the discontinuities. In both cases, the results produced by the 1-D approach are similar to the ones obtained with a 2-D warp followed by the rasterization of 2-D micropolygons. The examples shown in this paper and the accompanying animations were rendered with the two-pass reconstruction algorithm described.

```
get U_in, V_in, C_in, D_in
U_next = Equation_5a(U_in,D_in)
V_next = Equation_5b(V_in,D_in)
for (U_out = integer(U_prev+1); U_out ≤ U_next; U_out++)
        linearly interpolate C_out between C_prev and C_in
        linearly interpolate V_out between V_prev and V_in
        put C_out, V_out at U_out
U_prev=U_next; V_prev=V_next; C_prev=C_in
```

Figure 10. Pseudocode for a first-pass left-to-right horizontal warp and resampling of one texel with coordinates (U, V), color C and displacement D. No antialiasing computed for simplicity.

3.2.2 Pipelined Reconstruction

The overwriting of texels during the first pass may cause self-occlusions. Although bottlenecks [2] are not an issue during the pre-warp step and, in practice, self-occlusions seem not to introduce noticeable artifacts in the pre-warped textures, we present a solution that is capable of handling an arbitrary number of foldovers and that does not require depth comparison. It consists of interspersing the horizontal and vertical warps and is related to the work described in [10]. As before, assume the horizontal pass is completed first and the rows are processed in occlusion-compatible order. As the horizontal warp produces each intermediate texel, this is immediately rasterized into the appropriate column. Since each vertical warp receives and processes its texels in occlusion-compatible order, correct visibility is preserved in the output. Also, because each texel is processed immediately after its generation, no information is overwritten and self-occlusions are avoided. The steps of the algorithm are illustrated in Figure 11, where gray circles represent the texels previously warped to the corresponding columns.

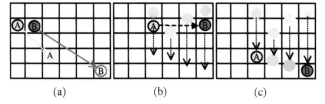

(a)   (b)   (c)

Figure 11. Pipelined reconstruction: (a) Two adjacent texels and their final positions. (b) and (c) Horizontal and vertical interpolation interspersed.

4. MODELING

Relief textures can be used as modeling primitives by simply instantiating them in a scene in such a way that the reprojected surfaces match the surfaces of the objects to be modeled. During the pre-warp, however, samples may have their coordinates mapped beyond the limits of the original texture. This corresponds, in the final image, to have samples projecting outside the limits of the polygon to be texture-mapped (Figure 12 (left)). The occurrence of such situations depends

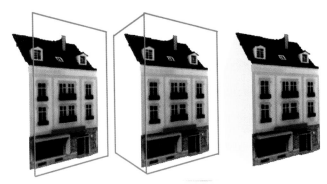

Figure 12. An extra quadrilateral is used to texture map outliers (center). Final view rendered with additional sidewall (right).

on the viewpoint and on the size of the displacements. This is similar to what happens when a light field [9] consisting of a single light slab is viewed from oblique angles.

The problem of incomplete views can be overcome if extra perpendicular polygons are texture-mapped with the outliers. This situation is illustrated in Figure 12 (center). The final result, rendered with an additional sidewall (pentagon), is shown in Figure 12 (right). The details of the technique will be explained next, in the context of the more general problem of rendering three-dimensional objects from arbitrary viewpoints.

4.1 Object Representation

Several researchers have used image-based techniques to represent objects [9] [7] [8] [16] [12]. Relief texture mapping can also be used to render complex three-dimensional shapes. Figure 13 shows a relief texture representation of an object originally modeled with 35,280 polygons. It consists of six relief textures acquired from the faces of the object's bounding box. New views of the object can be obtained by pre-warping these textures and mapping the resulting images onto the faces of the box. But just warping each relief texture to its original face of the box is not enough to produce the desired result. Some samples may project onto other faces, depending on the viewpoint (Figure 14).

One solution to this problem is to pre-warp adjacent faces to the desired ones. The perpendicular orientation between faces allows such mappings to be performed using the same pre-warping equations (Equations (4a) and (4b)). The concept will be explained in 2-D. Its generalization to 3-D is straightforward. Figure 14 shows a division of the object space into numbered regions. If the viewer is in an odd region, the three closest faces are classified as *front*, *left*, and *right* with respect to the viewpoint.

Figure 13. Object represented by six relief textures associated with the faces of a bounding box.

Thus, for instance, if the viewer is in region (1), face *a* is *front*, face *d* is *left*, and face *b* is *right*. In this case, faces *left* and *right* are pre-warped to the image plane of *front*. Then *front* is pre-warped to its own image plane, overwriting all samples except the ones intended to fill holes. If, however, the viewer is in an even region, the two closest faces are classified as *left* and *right*. For instance, if the viewer is in region (6), face *c* is *left* and face *d* is *right*. *left* is pre-warped to the image plane of *right*, then *right* is pre-warped to its own image plane. Likewise, *right* is pre-warped to the image plane of *left*, and then *left* is pre-warped to its own image plane. Notice that at most three polygons (in the full 3-D version of the algorithm) need to be displayed.

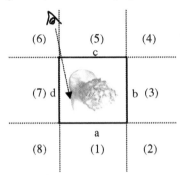

Figure 14. Samples from one face can project onto another. Letters identify the faces, and numbers identify regions used to define the faces that should be pre-warped from each region.

The perpendicular orientation between adjacent faces can be exploited to pre-warp a face to its adjacent image plane as if it were the adjacent face itself. When the viewer is in an odd region, the displacement values associated with *left* and *right* are converted to column indices for *front*, while their column indices can be used as displacement for *front* (Figure 15). Thus, *left* and *right* can be pre-warped to *front* as if they were *front* themselves. The even region is similar.

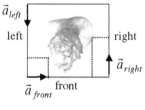

Figure 15. Height values from *left* and *right* become columns for *front*. Columns from *left* and *right* become height for *front*.

Figure 16 shows the statue rendered as two texture-mapped quadrilaterals (*left* and *right*), whose boundaries are shown to the right. The corresponding pre-warped textures are shown in Figure 17 and provide a clear illustration of the factorization of the planar perspective, which is compensated by the texture map stage of the warp.

4.1.1 Handling Surface Discontinuities

Treating relief textures as continuous surfaces may not be desirable in some situations. Improper reconstruction of originally non-connected surfaces may lead to the occurrence of "skins". The assumption about surface continuity can be relaxed if surfaces that would otherwise be rendered as "skins" had been appropriately sampled by adjacent relief textures. In this case,

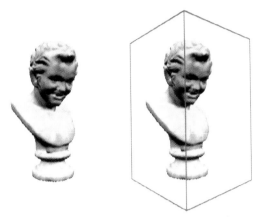

Figure 16. View of the statue (left) obtained by texture mapping two quads, whose boundaries are shown to the right.

Figure 17. Pre-warped textures used to produce Figure 16.

texels belonging to non-connected surfaces should not be interpolated during the pre-warp. A simple way to achieve this is to use depth thresholds to identify and mark such discontinuities during a pre-processing step. Figure 18 shows the rendering of a rat before and after skin removal. In the accompanying videotape, the skins between the façade and the roof of the *jeans shop store* were removed and the resulting hole was seamlessly filled by adding an extra conventionally texture-mapped polygon.

4.2 Correct Occlusion

The relief texture-mapping algorithm, as described so far, does not handle interpenetrating polygons appropriately. Thus, for example, consider intersecting a planar polygon with the bounding box used to represent the statue shown in Figure 13. Since the intersection between two polygons defines a straight line, the resulting occlusion pattern will not match the perceived depth of the associated relief textures. In order to solve this problem, corrected depth values accounting for the perceived off-the-plane displacements must be computed (Figure 19). Thus, let $\dot{x}$ be a point in 3-space associated with texel t, whose coordinates in the source texture are (u_s, v_s). The Z coordinate of $\dot{x}$ in camera space when observed from a virtual COP $\dot{C}$ is given by

$$Z_{\dot{x}} = c_1 + u_s c_2 + v_s c_3 + displ(u_s, v_s)c_4$$

where $c_1 = \vec{c} \cdot \vec{n}$, $c_2 = \vec{a}_s \cdot \vec{n}$, $c_3 = \vec{b}_s \cdot \vec{n}$ and $c_4 = \vec{f}_s \cdot \vec{n}$ are

Figure 18. Renderings of a rat before (a) and after (b) surface discontinuity identification.

constants for a given viewing configuration, $\vec{n}$ is the unit vector normal to the image plane of the virtual camera, $\vec{c} = \dot{C}_s - \dot{C}$, and $\dot{C}_s$, $\vec{a}_s$, $\vec{b}_s$ and $\vec{f}_s$ are the camera parameters associated with the relief texture. Let (u_j, v_j) be the coordinates of texel t' obtained after pre-warping t. Notice that the perceived depth at t' is $Z_{\dot{x}}$ and such value can be interpolated along rows and columns in the same way as described for color in section 3.2. Alternatively, one can compute and interpolate only the difference Δz between the actual polygon depth at t' and its perceived depth, which can be encoded using a smaller number of bits. Since t' is on the polygon to be texture mapped, its Z coordinate in the virtual camera space can be expressed as $Z_{t'} = c_1 + u_j c_2 + v_j c_3$. During the pre-warp, Δz values can be linearly interpolated along rows and columns. The interpolated values can be used to compute the amount by which the depth buffer must be changed to produce correct visibility. Figure 19 shows the statue rendered with an interpenetrating polygon seen from different distances. In this example, Δz was interpolated and the resulting values were quantized using the same strategy described in section 3.1 before being used to modulate the depth buffer.

Figure 19. Depth-correction using 8-bit quantized Δz values.

4.3 Multiresolution

Image pyramids have been long used in computer graphics for antialiasing [19]. Representing relief textures using fixed resolution causes a constant amount of work to be carried out during the pre-warp, independently of the number of pixels covered on the screen. The use of *relief texture pyramids* can be used not only to reduce aliasing but also to keep the warping cost proportional to the texture contribution to the final image.

Level i of a relief texture pyramid is constructed by averaging color and depth data associated to groups of $2^i x 2^i$ adjacent texels from the highest resolution relief texture (level zero). The lengths of vectors $\vec{a}$ and $\vec{b}$ are doubled from level i to level $i+1$ in order to compensate for the halving of the number of texels in each dimension, so that the spatial coverage of the relief texture remains unchanged. Figure 20 shows a statue rendered using the first four levels of a texture pyramid.

Although mip-mapping is frequently used in computer graphics to reduce aliasing artifacts introduced by texture minification, bilinear interpolation is the preferred image resampling strategy during the texture mapping stage of the relief texture-mapping algorithm. It produces sharper images, is less prone to undesirable blurring due to polygon orientation and is computationally less expensive than trilinear interpolation. An in-depth discussion of this subject can be found in [13].

Figure 20. Textured LODs obtained by relief texture mapping the first four levels of a relief texture map pyramid. Relief texture resolution: 256x256 texels (left) down to 32x32 texels (right).

4.4 Modeling Immersive Environments

Relief texture mapping can be used not just to represent objects, but complete environments. This is useful for the many applications of computer graphics that require immersive virtual environments. Moreover, the relief textures used to represent a whole environment can be generated nearly automatically, making this an elegant method of representing acquired real scenes.

In our experiments, a laser rangefinder and a digital camera were used to scan the environment. The resulting data were then projected onto relief textures instantiated at user-defined locations (Figure 22 (left)). Registration is naturally enforced by the depth information associated with the samples (Figure 22 (right)).

Figure 23 shows two renderings of a partial model of Sitterson Hall's reading room obtained using the three relief textures depicted in Figure 22 and an extra polygon representing the ceiling. Notice the parallax effect that allows the plaque on the wall to become visible in the image to the right.

5. RESULTS

For a typical 256x256-texel relief texture mapped onto a single quadrilateral (*e.g.*, Figure 9) using the two-pass approach described in Section 3.2.1, the current software prototype, written in C++, achieves an average frame rate of 9.42 frames per second. Such measurements were performed on a Pentium II PC running at 400MHz with an Intergraph graphics accelerator (Intense 3D RealiZm II VX113A-T) with 16 MB of texture memory and 16MB of frame buffer memory. The final view of the surface was displayed on a 512x512-pixel window. The percentage of the rendering time spent with pre-warping and resampling, loading pre-warped textures into texture memory, and the actual texture mapping operation are shown in Table 1. Notice that, since the pre-warping and resampling operations dominated the rendering time, one can expect a considerable speedup from a hardware implementation of the algorithm. Also notice that pre-warping cost is independent of the dimensions of the output window.

When a large number of texels have zero displacement, such as the case of the brick texture shown in Figure 21, speed-ups of over 100% were verified in the current software prototype by just skipping the unnecessary transformations.

Table 1: Percentage of the average rendering time associated with the steps of the relief texture-mapping algorithm (one relief texture mapped onto one quadrilateral).

Pre-warping and resampling	Loading warped textures into texture memory	Actual texture mapping operation	Others
94.10%	2.65%	0.066%	3.18%

6. LIMITATIONS

A relief texture is a single-layer image representation. If multiple layers of surfaces are required (*e.g.*, in the case of objects containing holes), alternative representations such as LDI's [17] or image-based objects [12] should probably be preferred. Although parallel projection LDIs can be rendered in occlusion compatible order, the existence of multiple samples along each ray introduces ambiguity about which samples should be connected, making 1-D interpolation and mesh-based reconstruction impractical. In many cases, the rendering of several layers each consisting of individual relief textures can be used to achieve similar results. Objects, on the other hand, consist of six perpendicular relief textures and such a representation is equivalent to a multi-layer representation [13].

In some applications, it may not be possible to constrain the viewpoint from crossing the plane of a relief texture. In such a case, the relief texture-mapped polygon will not be rendered even if the represented surface may still be visible. In these cases, relief textures should to be rendered as meshes of micro-polygons.

Ideally, only texels that effectively contribute to some screen fragments should be pre-warped. While such a strategy would make optimal use of the pre-warping, in practice this is not feasible, since it would require an inverse mapping. Alternatively, one can consider selecting the most appropriate level of a relief texture pyramid by using the projected area (in screen space) of the quadrilateral to be texture mapped.

7. SUMMARY AND FUTURE WORK

We have presented an extension to texture mapping that supports the representation of 3-D surface details and view motion parallax. It results from an exact factorization of the 3-D image warping equation [11] into a pre-warp followed by conventional texture mapping. We have shown that, from a conventional rendering perspective, such a new factorization presents several advantages over the conventional plane-plus-parallax factorization. The simple pre-warping functions allow surface reconstruction (color and depth) to be performed in 1-D. This property should allow a simple and efficient hardware implementation.

One important area for investigation is the design of efficient hardware implementations for relief texture mapping using our pre-warping functions. Adding this pre-warping capability to the texture memory of a graphics accelerator may allow this approach to become as commonly used as conventional texture mapping.

Automatic acquisition of relief textures from 3-D environments is another important area for exploration. Other avenues for exploration involve the use of normal maps [6] [3] for view-dependent lighting and the use of relief textures for geometry simplification.

Acknowledgements

We would like to thank Chris Dwyer, Anselmo Lastra, Steve Molnar, Lars Nyland, Jason Smith and Mary Whitton for their assistance and suggestions, and the anonymous reviewers for their insightful comments. Special thanks go to Frederick P. Brooks, Jr. for his detailed critique of an earlier draft of this paper. Cássio Ribeiro designed *Relief Town*. The UNC IBR group provided the reading room data set. De Espona Infográfica provided the other models.

This work was sponsored by CNPq/Brazil under Process # 200054/95, DARPA under order # E278 and NFS under grant # MIP-9612643.

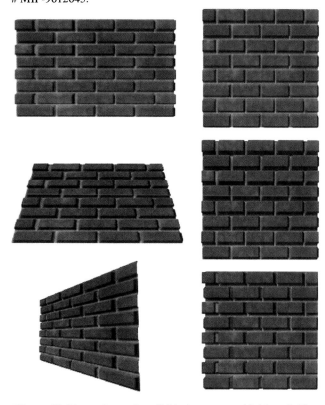

Figure 21. Three views of a relief texture-mapped brick wall. The images on the left show one quadrilateral texture-mapped with the corresponding pre-warped images shown to the right. Brick texels have zero displacement and, therefore, do not move.

References

[1] Catmull, E. A Subdivision Algorithm for Computer Display of Curved Surfaces. Ph.D. Dissertation, Department of Computer Science, University of Utah, December 1974.

[2] Catmull, E., Smith, A. 3D Transformations of Images in Scanline Order. *Proc. SIGGRAPH 80* (Seattle, Washington, July 14-18, 1980), pp. 279-285.

[3] Cohen, J., Olano, M., Manocha, D. Appearance-Preserving Simplification. *Proc. SIGGRAPH 98* (Orlando, FL, July 19-24, 1998), pp. 115-122.

[4] Debevec, P., Taylor, C., Malik, J. Modeling and Rendering Architecture from Photographs: A hybrid geometry- and image-based approach. *Proc. SIGGRAPH 96* (New Orleans, LA, August 4-9, 1996), pp. 11-20.

[5] Fant, Karl. A Nonaliasing, Real-Time Spatial Transform Technique. IEEE CG&A, Vol. 6, No 1, January 1986, pp. 71-80.

[6] Fournier, A. Normal Distribution Functions and Multiple Surfaces. *Graphics Interface '92 Workshop on Local Illumination*. pp. 45-52.

[7] Gortler, S., et al.. The Lumigraph. *Proc. SIGGRAPH 96* (New Orleans, LA, August 4-9, 1996), pp. 43-54.

[8] Grossman, J., Dally, W. Point Sample Rendering. *Proceedings of the 9th Eurographics Workshop on Rendering*. Vienna, Austria, June 1998. *Rendering Techniques '98*, Springer-Verlag, pp. 181-192.

[9] Levoy, M., Hanrahan, P. Light Field Rendering *Proc. SIGGRAPH 96* (New Orleans, LA, August 4-9, 1996), pp. 31-42.

[10] Max, N. A One-Pass Version of Two-Pass Image Resampling. Journal of Graphics Tools, Vol. 3, No. 1, pp. 33-41.

[11] McMillan, L. An Image-Based Approach to Three-Dimensional Computer Graphics. Ph.D. Dissertation. UNC Computer Science Technical Report TR97-013, April 1997.

[12] Oliveira, M., Bishop, G. Image-Based Objects. Proceedings of 1999 ACM Symposium on Interactive 3D Graphics. pp. 191-198.

[13] Oliveira, M. Relief Texture Mapping. Ph.D. Dissertation. UNC Computer Science Technical Report TR00-009. March 2000. http://www.cs.unc.edu/~ibr/pubs/oliveira-diss/TR00-009.pdf.

[14] Robertson, P. Fast Perspective Views of Images Using One-Dimensional Operations. IEEE CG&A, vol. 7, pp. 47-56, Feb. 1987.

[15] Sawhney, H. 3D Geometry from Planar Parallax. In IEEE CVPR'94, pages 929-934. IEEE Computer Society, Seattle, Washington, June 1994.

[16] Schaufler, G. Per-Object Image Warping with Layered Impostors. *Proceedings of the 9th Eurographics Workshop on Rendering*. Vienna, Austria, June 1998. *Rendering Techniques '98*, Springer-Verlag, pp. 145-156.

[17] Shade, J., et al. Layered Depth Images. *Proc. SIGGRAPH 98* (Orlando, FL, July 19-24, 1998), pp. 231-242.

[18] Smith, Alvy Ray. Planar 2-Pass Texture Mapping and Warping. *Proc. SIGGRAPH 87* (Anaheim, CA, July 27-31, 1987), pp. 263-272.

[19] Williams, L. Pyramidal Parametrics. *Proc. SIGGRAPH 83* (Detroit, MI, July 25-29, 1983), pp. 1-11.

[20] Wolberg, George. Separable Image Warping with Spatial Lookup Tables. *Proc. SIGGRAPH 89* (Boston, MA, July 31-4 August, 1989), pp. 369-378.

[21] Woo, M., et al. OpenGL Programming Guide. 2nd edition. Addison Wesley, 1997.

Figure 22. Modeling of an immersive environment using three relief textures (left). The dashed lines represent two extra polygons used to capture outliers. Registration is enforced by the depth information (right).

Figure 23. Sitterson Hall's reading room rendered using relief texture mapping. Notice the parallax effect that allows the plaque on the wall to become visible in the image to the right. The partial model of the reading room used to render these images consists of three 256x256 relief textures and six quadrilaterals.

SIGGRAPH

Image-Based Visual Hulls

Wojciech Matusik*
Laboratory for Computer Science
Massachusetts Institute of Technology

Chris Buehler*
Laboratory for Computer Science
Massachusetts Institute of Technology

Ramesh Raskar‡
Department of Computer Science
University of North Carolina - Chapel Hill

Steven J. Gortler†
Division of Engineering and Applied Sciences
Harvard University

Leonard McMillan*
Laboratory for Computer Science
Massachusetts Institute of Technology

Abstract

In this paper, we describe an efficient image-based approach to computing and shading visual hulls from silhouette image data. Our algorithm takes advantage of epipolar geometry and incremental computation to achieve a constant rendering cost per rendered pixel. It does not suffer from the computation complexity, limited resolution, or quantization artifacts of previous volumetric approaches. We demonstrate the use of this algorithm in a real-time virtualized reality application running off a small number of video streams.

Keywords: Computer Vision, Image-Based Rendering, Constructive Solid Geometry, Misc. Rendering Algorithms.

1 Introduction

Visualizing and navigating within virtual environments composed of both real and synthetic objects has been a long-standing goal of computer graphics. The term "Virtualized Reality™", as popularized by Kanade [23], describes a setting where a real-world scene is "captured" by a collection of cameras and then viewed through a virtual camera, as if the scene was a synthetic computer graphics environment. In practice, this goal has been difficult to achieve. Previous attempts have employed a wide range of computer vision algorithms to extract an explicit geometric model of the desired scene.

Unfortunately, many computer vision algorithms (e.g. stereo vision, optical flow, and shape from shading) are too slow for real-time use. Consequently, most virtualized reality systems employ off-line post-processing of acquired video sequences. Furthermore, many computer vision algorithms make unrealistic simplifying assumptions (e.g. all surfaces are diffuse) or impose impractical restrictions (e.g. objects must have sufficient non-periodic textures) for robust operation. We present a new algorithm for synthesizing virtual renderings of real-world scenes in real time. Not only is our technique fast, it also makes few simplifying assumptions and has few restrictions.

*(wojciech | cbuehler | mcmillan)@graphics.lcs.mit.edu
†sjg@cs.harvard.edu
‡raskar@cs.unc.edu

©2000 ACM 0-58113-208-5/00/0007 $5.00

Figure 1 - The intersection of silhouette cones defines an approximate geometric representation of an object called the visual hull. A visual hull has several desirable properties: it contains the actual object, and it has consistent silhouettes.

Our algorithm is based on an approximate geometric representation of the depicted scene known as the visual hull (see Figure 1). A visual hull is constructed by using the visible silhouette information from a series of reference images to determine a conservative shell that progressively encloses the actual object. Based on the principle of *calculatus eliminatus* [28], the visual hull in some sense carves away regions of space where the object "is not".

The visual hull representation can be constructed by a series of 3D constructive solid geometry (CSG) intersections. Previous robust implementations of this algorithm have used fully enumerated volumetric representations or octrees. These methods typically have large memory requirements and thus, tend to be restricted to low-resolution representations.

In this paper, we show that one can efficiently render the exact visual hull without constructing an auxiliary geometric or volumetric representation. The algorithm we describe is "image based" in that all steps of the rendering process are computed in "image space" coordinates of the reference images.

We also use the reference images as textures when shading the visual hull. To determine reference images that can be used, we compute which reference cameras have an unoccluded view of each point on the visual hull. We present an image-based visibility algorithm based on epipolar geometry and McMillan's occlusion compatible ordering [18] that allows us to shade the visual hull in roughly constant time per output pixel.

Using our *image-based visual hull* (IBVH) algorithm, we have created a system that processes live video streams and renders the observed scene from a virtual camera's viewpoint in real time. The resulting representation can also be combined with traditional computer graphics objects.

2 Background and Previous Work

Kanade's virtualized reality system [20] [23] [13] is perhaps closest in spirit to the rendering system that we envision. Their initial implementations have used a collection of cameras in conjunction with multi-baseline stereo techniques to extract models of dynamic scenes. These methods require significant off-line processing, but they are exploring special-purpose hardware for this task. Recently, they have begun exploring volume-carving methods, which are closer to the approach that we use [26] [30].

Pollard's and Hayes' [21] immersive video objects allow rendering of real-time scenes by morphing live video streams to simulate three-dimensional camera motion. Their representation also uses silhouettes, but in a different manner. They match silhouette edges across pairs of views, and use these correspondences to compute morphs to novel views. This approach has some limitations, since silhouette edges are generally not consistent between views.

Visual Hull. Many researchers have used silhouette information to distinguish regions of 3D space where an object is and is not present [22] [8] [19]. The ultimate result of this carving is a shape called the object's *visual hull* [14]. A visual hull always contains the object. Moreover, it is an equal or tighter fit than the object's convex hull. Our algorithm computes a view-dependent, sampled version of an object's visual hull each rendered frame.

Suppose that some original 3D object is viewed from a set of reference views R. Each reference view r has the silhouette s_r with interior pixels covered by the object. For view r one creates the cone-like volume vh_r defined by all the rays starting at the image's point of view p_r and passing through these interior points on its image plane. It is guaranteed that the actual object must be contained in vh_r. This statement is true for all r; thus, the object must be contained in the volume $vh_R = \bigcap_{r \in R} vh_r$. As the size of R goes to infinity, and includes all possible views, vh_R converges to a shape known as the visual hull vh_∞ of the original geometry. The visual hull is not guaranteed to be the same as the original object since concave surface regions can never be distinguished using silhouette information alone.

In practice, one must construct approximate visual hulls using only a finite number of views. Given the set of views R, the approximation vh_R is the best conservative geometric description that one can achieve based on silhouette information alone (see Figure 1). If a conservative estimate is not required, then alternative representations are achievable by fitting higher order surface approximations to the observed data [2].

Volume Carving. Computing high-resolution visual hulls can be tricky matter. The intersection of the volumes vh_r requires some form of CSG. If the silhouettes are described with a polygonal mesh, then the CSG can be done using polyhedral CSG, but this is very hard to do in a robust manner.

A more common method used to convert silhouette contours into visual hulls is volume carving [22] [8] [29] [19] [5] [27]. This method removes unoccupied regions from an explicit volumetric representation. All voxels falling outside of the projected silhouette cone of a given view are eliminated from the volume. This process is repeated for each reference image. The resulting volume is a quantized representation of the visual hull according to the given volumetric grid. A major advantage of our view-dependent method is that it minimizes artifacts resulting from this quantization.

CSG Rendering. A number of algorithms have been developed for the fast rendering of CSG models, but most are ill suited for our task. The algorithm described by Rappoport [24],

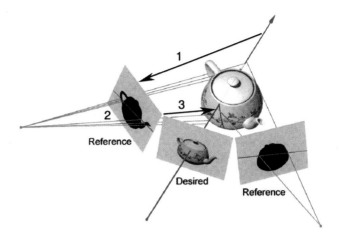

Figure 2 – Computing the IBVH involves three steps. First, the desired ray is projected onto a reference image. Next, the intervals where the projected ray crosses the silhouette are determined. Finally, these intervals are lifted back onto the desired ray where they can be intersected with intervals from other reference images.

requires that each solid be first decomposed to a union of convex primitives. This decomposition can prove expensive for complicated silhouettes. Similarly, the algorithm described in [11] requires a rendering pass for each layer of depth complexity. Our method does not require preprocessing the silhouette cones. In fact, there is no explicit data structure used to represent the silhouette volumes other than the reference images.

Using ray tracing, one can render an object defined by a tree of CSG operations without explicitly computing the resulting solid [25]. This is done by considering each ray independently and computing the interval along the ray occupied by each object. The CSG operations can then be applied in 1D over the sets of intervals. This approach requires computing a 3D ray-solid intersection. In our system, the solids in question are a special class of cone-like shapes with a constant cross section in projection. This special form allows us to compute the equivalent of 3D ray intersections in 2D using the reference images.

Image-Based Rendering. Many different image-based rendering techniques have been proposed in recent years [3] [4] [15] [6] [12]. One advantage of image-based rendering techniques is their stunning realism, which is largely derived from the acquired images they use. However, a common limitation of these methods is an inability to model dynamic scenes. This is mainly due to data acquisition difficulties and preprocessing requirements. Our system generates image-based models in real-time, using the same images to construct the IBHV and to shade the final rendering.

3 Visual-Hull Computation

Our approach to computing the visual hull has two distinct characteristics: it is computed in the image space of the reference images and the resulting representation is viewpoint dependent. The advantage of performing geometric computations in image space is that it eliminates the resampling and quantization artifacts that plague volumetric approaches. We limit our sampling to the pixels of the desired image, resulting in a view-dependent visual-hull representation. In fact, our IBVH representation is equivalent to computing exact 3D silhouette cone intersections and rendering the result with traditional rendering methods.

Our technique for computing the visual hull is analogous to finding CSG intersections using a ray-casting approach [25].

Given a desired view, we compute each viewing ray's intersection with the visual hull. Since computing a visual hull involves only intersection operations, we can perform the CSG calculations in any order. Furthermore, in the visual hull context, every CSG primitive is a generalized cone (a projective extrusion of a 2D image silhouette). Because the cone has a fixed (scaled) cross section, the 3D ray intersections can be reduced to cheaper 2D ray intersections. As shown in Figure 2 we perform the following steps: 1) We project a 3D viewing ray into a reference image. 2) We perform the intersection of the projected ray with the 2D silhouette. These intersections result in a list of intervals along the ray that are interior to the cone's cross-section. 3) Each interval is then lifted back into 3D using a simple projective mapping, and then intersected with the results of the ray-cone intersections from other reference images. A naïve algorithm for computing these IBVH ray intersections follows:

```
IBVHisect (intervalImage &d, refImList R)
  for each referenceImage r in R
    computeSilhouetteEdges (r)
  for each pixel p in desiredImage d do
    p.intervals = {0..inf}
  for each referenceImage r in R
    for each scanline s in d
      for each pixel p in s
        ray3D  ry3 = compute3Dray(p,d.camInfo)
        lineSegment2D l2 = project3Dray(ry3,r.camInfo)
        intervals int2D = calcIntervals(l2,r.silEdges)
        intervals int3D = liftIntervals(int2D,r.camInfo,ry3)
        p.intervals = p.intervals ISECT int3D
```

To analyze the efficiency of this algorithm, let n be the number of pixels in a scanline. The number of pixels in the image d is $O(n^2)$. Let k be the number of reference images. Then, the above algorithm has an asymptotic running time $O(ikn^2)$, where i is the time complexity of the `calcIntervals` routine. If we test for the intersection of each projected ray with each of the e edges of the silhouette, the running time of `calcIntervals` is $O(e)$. Given that l is the average number of times that a projected ray intersects the silhouette[1], the number of silhouette edges will be $O(ln)$. Thus, the running time of `IBVHisect` to compute all of the 2D intersections for a desired view is $O(lkn^3)$.

The performance of this naïve algorithm can be improved by taking advantage of incremental computations that are enabled by the epipolar geometry relating the reference and desired images. These improvements will allow us to reduce the amortized cost of 1D ray intersections to $O(l)$ per desired pixel, resulting in an implementation of `IBVHisect` that takes $O(lkn^2)$.

Given two camera views, a reference view r and a desired view d, we consider the set of planes that share the line connecting the cameras' centers. These planes are called *epipolar planes*. Each epipolar plane projects to a line in each of the two images, called an *epipolar line*. In each image, all such lines intersect at a common point, called the *epipole*, which is the projection of one of the camera's center onto the other camera's view plane [9].

As a scanline of the desired view is traversed, each pixel projects to an epipolar line segment in r. These line segments emanate from the epipole e_{dr}, the image of d's center of projection onto r's image plane (see Figure 3), and trace out a "pencil" of epipolar lines in r. The slopes of these epipolar line segments will either increase or decrease monotonically depending on the direction of traversal (Green arc in Figure 3). We take advantage of this monotonicity to compute silhouette intersections for the whole scanline incrementally.

---

[1] We assume reference images also have $O(n^2)$ pixels.

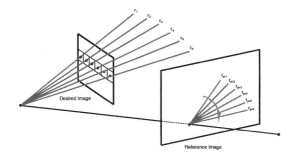

Figure 3 – The pixels of a scanline in the desired image trace out a pencil of line segments in the reference image. An ordered traversal of the scanline will sweep out these segments such that their slope about the epipole varies monotonically.

The silhouette contour of each reference view is represented as a list of edges enclosing the silhouette's boundary pixels. These edges are generated using a 2D variant of the marching cubes approach [16]. Next, we sort the $O(nl)$ contour vertices in increasing order by the slope of the line connecting each vertex to the epipole. These sorted vertex slopes divide the reference image domain into $O(nl)$ bins. Bin B_i has an extent spanning between the slopes of the ith and $i+1$st vertex in the sorted list. In each bin B_i we place all edges that are intersected by epipolar lines with a slope falling within the bin's extent[2]. During `IBVHisect` as we traverse the pixels along a scanline in the desired view, the projected corresponding view rays fan across the epipolar pencil in the reference view with either increasing or decreasing slope. Concurrently, we step through the list of bins. The appropriate bin for each epipolar line is found and it is intersected with the edges in that bin. This procedure is analogous to merging two sorted lists, which can be done in a time proportional to the length of the lists ($O(nl)$ in our case).

For each scanline in the desired image we evaluate n viewing rays. For each viewing ray we compute its intersection with edges in a single bin. Each bin contains on average $O(l)$ silhouette edges. Thus, this step takes $O(l)$ time per ray. Simultaneously we traverse the sorted set of $O(nl)$ bins as we traverse the scanline. Therefore, one scanline is computed in $O(nl)$ time. Over n scanlines of the desired image, and over k reference images, this gives a running time of $O(lkn^2)$. Pseudocode for the improved algorithm follows.

```
IBVHisect (intervalImage &d, refImList R){
  for each referenceImage r in R
    computeSilhouetteEdges (r)
  for each pixel p in desiredImage d do
    p.intervals = {0..inf}
  for each referenceImage r in R
    bins b = constructBins(r.caminfo, r.silEdges, d.caminfo)
    for each scanline s in d
      incDec order = traversalOrder(r.caminfo,d.caminfo,s)
      resetBinPositon(b)
      for each pixel p in s according to order
        ray3D  ry3 = compute3Dray(p,d.camInfo)
        lineSegment2D l2 = project3Dray(ry3,r.camInfo)
        slope m = ComputeSlope(l2,r.caminfo,d.caminfo)
        updateBinPosition(b,m)
        intervals int2D = calcIntervals(l2,b.currentbin)
        intervals int3D = liftIntervals(int2D,r.camInfo,ry3)
        p.intervals = p.intervals ISECT int3D
```

---

[2] Sorting the contour vertices takes $O(nl \log(nl))$ and binning takes $O(nl^2)$. Sorting and binning over k reference views takes $O(knl \log(nl))$ and $O(knl^2)$ correspondingly. In our setting, $l << n$ so we view this preprocessing stage as negligible.

It is tempting to apply further optimizations to take greater advantage of epipolar constraints. In particular, one might consider rectifying each reference image with the desired image prior to the ray-silhouette intersections. This would eliminate the need to sort, bin, and traverse the silhouette edge lists. However, a call to liftInterval would still be required for each pixel, giving the same asymptotic performance as the algorithm presented. The disadvantage of rectification is the artifacts introduced by the two resampling stages that it requires. The first resampling is applied to the reference silhouette to map it to the rectified frame. The second is needed to unrectify the computed intervals of the desired view. In the typical stereo case, the artifacts of rectification are minimal because of the closeness of the cameras and the similarity of their pose. But, when computing visual hulls the reference cameras are positioned more freely. In fact, it is not unreasonable for the epipole of a reference camera to fall within the field of view of the desired camera. In such a configuration, rectification is degenerate.

4 Visual-Hull Shading

The IBVH is shaded using the reference images as textures. In order to capture as many view-dependent effects as possible a view-dependent texturing strategy is used. At each pixel, the reference-image textures are ranked from "best" to "worst" according to the angle between the desired viewing ray and rays to each of the reference images from the closest visual hull point along the desired ray. We prefer those reference views with the smallest angle [7]. However, we must avoid texturing surface points with an image whose line-of-sight is blocked by some other point on the visual hull, regardless of how well aligned that view might be to the desired line-of-sight. Therefore, visibility must be considered during the shading process.

When the visibility of an object is determined using its visual hull instead of its actual geometry, the resulting test is conservative– erring on the side of declaring potentially visible points as non-visible. We compute visibility using the visual hull, VH_R, as determined by IBVHisect. This visual hull is represented as intervals along rays of the desired image d. Pseudocode for our shading algorithm is given below.

```
IBVHshade(intervalImage &d, refImList R){
  for each pixel p in d do
    p.best = BIGNUM
  for each referenceImage r in R do
    for each pixel p in d do
      ray3D ry3 = compute3Dray(p,d.camInfo)
      point3 pt3 = front(p.intervals,ry3)
      double s = angleSimilarity(pt3,ry3,r.camInfo)
      if isVisible(pt3,r,d)
        if (s < p.best)
          point2 pt2 = project(pt3,r.camInfo)
          p.color = sample_color(pt2,r)
          p.best = s
}
```

The front procedure finds the front most geometric point of the IBVH seen along the ray. The IBVHshade algorithm has time complexity $O(vkn^2)$, where v is the cost for computing visibility of a pixel.

Once more we can take advantage of the epipolar geometry in order to incrementally determine the visibility of points on the visual hull. This reduces the amortized cost of computing visibility to $O(l)$ per desired pixel, thus giving an implementation of IBVHshade that takes $O(lkn^2)$.

Consider the visibility problem in flatland as shown in Figure 4. For a pixel p, we wish to determine if the front-most point on the visual hull is occluded with respect to a particular reference image by any other pixel interval in d.

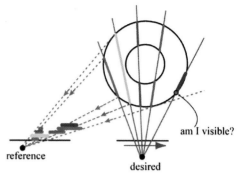

Figure 4 – In order to compute the visibility of an IBVH sample with respect to a given reference image, a series of IBVH intervals are projected back onto the reference image in an occlusion-compatible order. The front-most point of the interval is visible if it lies outside of the unions of all preceding intervals.

Efficient calculation can proceed as follows. For each reference view r, we traverse the desired-view pixels in front-to-back order with respect to r (left-to-right in Figure 4). During traversal, we accumulate coverage intervals by projecting the IBVH pixel intervals into the reference view, and forming their union. For each front most point, pt3, we check to see if its projection in the reference view is already covered by the coverage intervals computed thus far. If it is covered, then pt3 is occluded from r by the IBVH. Otherwise, pt3 is not occluded from r by either the IBVH or the actual (unknown) geometry.

```
visibility2D(intervalFlatlandImage &d, referenceImage r){
  intervals coverage = <empty>
  for each pixel p in d do \\front to back in r
    ray2D ry2 = compute2Dray(p,d.camInfo)
    point2 pt2 = front(p.intervals,ry2);
    point1D p1 = project(pt2,r.camInfo)
    if contained(p1,coverage)
      p.visible[r] = false
    else
      p.visible[r] = true
    intervals tmp =
            prjctIntrvls(p.intervals,ry2,r.camInfo)
    coverage = coverage UNION tmp
}
```

This algorithm runs in $O(nl)$, since each pixel is visited once, and containment test and unions can be computed in $O(l)$ time.

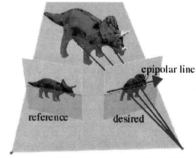

Figure 5 – Ideally, the visibility of points in 3D could be computed by applying the 2D algorithm along epipolar planes.

In the continuous case, 3D visibility calculations can be reduced to a set of 2D calculations within epipolar planes (Figure 5), since all visibility interactions occur within such planes. However, the extension of the discrete 2D algorithm to a complete discrete 3D solution is not trivial, as most of the discrete pixels in our images do not exactly share epipolar planes. Consequently, one must be careful in implementing conservative 3D visibility.

First, we consider each of the intervals stored in d as a solid frustum with square cross section. To determine visibility of a (square) pixel p correctly we consider S_p, the set of all possible epipolar planes which touch p. There are at least two possible definitions for whether p is visible: (1) p is visible along **all** planes in S_p, (2) p is visible along **any** plane in S_p. Clearly the first definition results in more pixels that are labeled not visible, therefore, it is better suited when using a large number of reference images. With a small number of reference images, the second definition is preferred. Implementing efficient exact algorithms for these visibility definitions is difficult, therefore, we use conservative algorithms; if the pixel is truly invisible we never label it as visible. However, the algorithms could label some pixel as invisible though it is in fact visible.

An algorithm that conservatively computes visibility according to the first definition is performed as follows. We define an epipolar wedge starting from the epipole e_{rd} in the desired view extending out to a one pixel-width interval on the image boundary. Depending on the relative camera views, we traverse the wedge either toward or away from the epipole [17]. For each pixel in this wedge, we compute visibility with respect to the pixels traversed earlier in the wedge using the 2D visibility algorithm. If a pixel is computed as *visible* then no geometry within the wedge could have occluded it in the reference view. We use a set of wedges whose union covers the whole image. A pixel may be touched by more than one wedge, in these cases its final visibility is computed as the *AND* of the results obtained from each wedge.

The algorithm for the second visibility definition works as follows. We do not consider all possible epipolar lines that touch pixel p but only some subset of them such that at least one line touches each pixel. One such subset is all the epipolar lines that pass through the centers of the image boundary pixels. This particular subset completely covers all the pixels in the desired image; denser subsets can also be chosen. The algorithm computes `visibility2D` for all epipolar lines in the subset. Visibility for a pixel might be computed more than once (e.g., the pixels near the epipole are traversed more often). We *OR* all obtained visibility results. Since we compute `visibility2D` for up to *4n* epipolar lines in k reference images the total time complexity of this algorithm is $O(lkn^2)$. In our real-time system we use small number of reference images (typically four). Thus, we use the algorithm for the second definition of visibility.

The total time complexity of our IBVH algorithms is $O(lkn^2)$, which allows for efficient rendering of IBVH objects. These algorithms are well suited to distributed and parallel implementations. We have demonstrated this efficiency with a system that computes IBVHs in real time from live video sequences.

Figure 6 – Four segmented reference images from our system.

5 System Implementation

Our system uses four calibrated Sony DFW500 FireWire video cameras. We distribute the computation across five computers, four that process video and one that assembles the IBVH (see Figure 6). Each camera is attached to a 600 MHz desktop PC that captures the video frames and performs the following processing

steps. First, it corrects for radial lens distortion using a lookup table. Then it segments out the foreground object using background-subtraction [1] [10]. Finally, the silhouette and texture information are compressed and sent over a 100Mb/s network to a central server for IBVH processing.

Our server is a quad-processor 550 MHz PC. We interleave the incoming frame information between the 4 processors to increase throughput. The server runs the IBVH intersection and shading algorithms. The resulting IBVH objects can be depth-buffer composited with an OpenGL background to produce a full scene. In the examples shown, a model of our graphics lab made with the Canoma modeling system was used as a background.

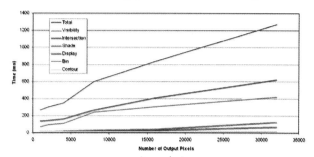

Figure 7 – A plot of the execution times for each step of the IBVH rendering algorithm on a single CPU. A typical IBVH might cover approximately 8000 pixels in a 640 × 480 image and it would execute at greater than 8 frames per second on our 4 CPU machine.

In Figure 7, the performances of the different stages in the IBVH algorithm are given. For these tests, 4 input images with resolutions of 256 × 256 were used. The average number of times that a projected ray crosses a silhouette is *6.5*. Foreground segmentation (done on client) takes about 85 ms. We adjusted the field of view of the desired camera, to vary the number of pixels occupied by the object. This graph demonstrates the linear growth of our algorithm with respect to the number of output pixels.

6 Conclusions and Future Work

We have described a new image-based visual-hull rendering algorithm and a real-time system that uses it. The algorithm is efficient from both theoretical and practical standpoints, and the resulting system delivers promising results.

The choice of the visual hull for representing scene elements has some limitations. In general, the visual hull of an object does not match the object's exact geometry. In particular, it cannot represent concave surface regions. This shortcoming is often considered fatal when an accurate geometric model is the ultimate goal. In our applications, the visual hull is used largely as an imposter surface onto which textures are mapped. As such, the visual hull provides a useful model whose combination of accurate silhouettes and textures provides surprisingly effective renderings that are difficult to distinguish from a more exact model. Our system also requires accurate segmentations of each image into foreground and background elements. Methods for accomplishing such segmentations include chromakeying and image differencing. These techniques are subject to variations in cameras, lighting, and background materials.

We plan to investigate techniques for blending between textures to produce smoother transitions. Although we get impressive results using just 4 cameras, we plan to scale our system up to larger numbers of cameras. Much of the algorithm parallelizes in a straightforward manner. With k computers, we expect to achieve $O(n^2 l \log k)$ time using a binary-tree based structure.

Figure 8 - Example IBVH images. The upper images show depth maps of the computed visual hulls. The lower images show shaded renderings from the same viewpoint. The hull segment connecting the two legs results from a segmentation error caused by a shadow.

7 Acknowledgements

We would like to thank Kari Anne Kjølaas, Annie Choi, Tom Buehler, and Ramy Sadek for their help with this project. We also thank DARPA and Intel for supporting this research effort. NSF Infrastructure and NSF CAREER grants provided further aid.

8 References

[1] Bichsel, M. "Segmenting Simply Connected Moving Objects in a Static Scene." *IEEE PAMI* 16, 11 (November 1994), 1138-1142.

[2] Boyer, E., and M. Berger. "3D Surface Reconstruction Using Occluding Contours." *IJCV* 22, 3 (1997), 219-233.

[3] Chen, S. E. and L. Williams. "View Interpolation for Image Synthesis." *SIGGRAPH 93*, 279-288.

[4] Chen, S. E. "Quicktime VR – An Image-Based Approach to Virtual Environment Navigation." *SIGGRAPH 95*, 29-38.

[5] Curless, B., and M. Levoy. "A Volumetric Method for Building Complex Models from Range Images." *SIGGRAPH 96*, 303-312.

[6] Debevec, P., C. Taylor, and J. Malik, "Modeling and Rendering Architecture from Photographs." *SIGGRAPH 96*, 11-20.

[7] Debevec, P.E., Y. Yu, and G. D. Borshukov, "Efficient View-Dependent Image-based Rendering with Projective Texture Mapping." *Proc. of EGRW* 1998 (June 1998).

[8] Debevec, P. *Modeling and Rendering Architecture from Photographs*. Ph.D. Thesis, University of California at Berkeley, Computer Science Division, Berkeley, CA, 1996.

[9] Faugeras, O. *Three-dimensional Computer Vision: A Geometric Viewpoint*. MIT Press, 1993.

[10] Friedman, N. and S. Russel. "Image Segmentation in Video Sequences." *Proc 13th Conference on Uncertainty in Artifical Intelligence* (1997).

[11] Goldfeather, J., J. Hultquist, and H. Fuchs. "Fast Constructive Solid Geometry Display in the Pixel-Powers Graphics System." *SIGGRAPH 86*, 107-116.

[12] Gortler, S. J., R. Grzeszczuk, R. Szeliski, and M. F. Cohen. "The Lumigraph." *SIGGRAPH 96*, 43-54.

[13] Kanade, T., P. W. Rander, and P. J. Narayanan. "Virtualized Reality: Constructing Virtual Worlds from Real Scenes." *IEEE Multimedia* 4, 1 (March 1997), 34-47.

[14] Laurentini, A. "The Visual Hull Concept for Silhouette Based Image Understanding." *IEEE PAMI* 16,2 (1994), 150-162.

[15] Levoy, M. and P. Hanrahan. "Light Field Rendering." *SIGGRAPH 96*, 31-42.

[16] Lorensen, W.E., and H. E. Cline. "Marching Cubes: A High Resolution 3D Surface Construction Algorithm." *SIGGRAPH 87*, 163-169.

[17] McMillan, L., and G. Bishop. "Plenoptic Modeling: An Image-Based Rendering System." *SIGGRAPH 95*, 39-46.

[18] McMillan, L. *An Image-Based Approach to Three-Dimensional Computer Graphics*, Ph.D. Thesis, University of North Carolina at Chapel Hill, Dept. of Computer Science, 1997.

[19] Moezzi, S., D.Y. Kuramura, and R. Jain. "Reality Modeling and Visualization from Multiple Video Sequences." *IEEE CG&A* 16, 6 (November 1996), 58-63.

[20] Narayanan, P., P. Rander, and T. Kanade. "Constructing Virtual Worlds using Dense Stereo." *Proc. ICCV* 1998, 3-10.

[21] Pollard, S. and S. Hayes. "View Synthesis by Edge Transfer with Applications to the Generation of Immersive Video Objects." *Proc. of VRST*, November 1998, 91-98.

[22] Potmesil, M. "Generating Octree Models of 3D Objects from their Silhouettes in a Sequence of Images." *CVGIP* 40 (1987), 1-29.

[23] Rander, P. W., P. J. Narayanan and T. Kanade, "Virtualized Reality: Constructing Time Varying Virtual Worlds from Real World Events." *Proc. IEEE Visualization* 1997, 277-552.

[24] Rappoport, A., and S. Spitz. "Interactive Boolean Operations for Conceptual Design of 3D solids." *SIGGRAPH 97*, 269-278.

[25] Roth, S. D. "Ray Casting for Modeling Solids." *Computer Graphics and Image Processing*, 18 (February 1982), 109-144.

[26] Saito, H. and T. Kanade. "Shape Reconstruction in Projective Grid Space from a Large Number of Images." *Proc. of CVPR*, (1999).

[27] Seitz, S. and C. R. Dyer. "Photorealistic Scene Reconstruction by Voxel Coloring." *Proc. of CVPR* (1997), 1067-1073.

[28] Seuss, D. "The Cat in the Hat," *CBS Television Special* (1971).

[29] Szeliski, R. "Rapid Octree Construction from Image Sequences." *CVGIP: Image Understanding* 58, 1 (July 1993), 23-32.

[30] Vedula, S., P. Rander, H. Saito, and T. Kanade. "Modeling, Combining, and Rendering Dynamic Real-World Events from Image Sequences." *Proc. 4th Intl. Conf. on Virtual Systems and Multimedia* (Nov 1998).

Efficient Image-Based Methods for Rendering Soft Shadows

Maneesh Agrawala
Pixar Animation Studios

Ravi Ramamoorthi
Stanford University*

Alan Heirich   Laurent Moll
Compaq Computer Corporation

Figure 1: *A plant rendered using our interactive layered attenuation-map approach (left), rayshade (middle), and our efficient high-quality coherence-based raytracing approach (right). Note the soft shadows on the leaves. To emphasize the soft shadows, this image is rendered without cosine falloff of light intensity. Model courtesy of O. Deussen, P. Hanrahan, B. Lintermann, R. Mech, M. Pharr, and P. Prusinkiewicz.*

Abstract

We present two efficient image-based approaches for computation and display of high-quality soft shadows from area light sources. Our methods are related to shadow maps and provide the associated benefits. The computation time and memory requirements for adding soft shadows to an image depend on image size and the number of lights, not geometric scene complexity. We also show that because area light sources are localized in space, soft shadow computations are particularly well suited to image-based rendering techniques. Our first approach—*layered attenuation maps*—achieves interactive rendering rates, but limits sampling flexibility, while our second method—*coherence-based raytracing* of depth images—is not interactive, but removes the limitations on sampling and yields high quality images at a fraction of the cost of conventional raytracers. Combining the two algorithms allows for rapid previewing followed by efficient high-quality rendering.

CR Categories: I.3.7 [*Computer Graphics*]: Three-Dimensional Graphics and Realism—Shadowing, Raytracing

Keywords: Shadows, Raytracing, Image-Based Rendering

1   Introduction

Soft shadows from area light sources can greatly enhance the visual realism of computer-generated images. However, accurately computing penumbrae can be very expensive because it requires

*(maneesh,ravir)@graphics.stanford.edu   (Alan.Herich,Laurent.Moll)@compaq.com
Address: Gates Wing 3B-386, Stanford University, Stanford, CA 94305.

determining visibility between every surface point and every light. The cost of many soft shadow algorithms grows with the geometric complexity of the scene. Algorithms such as ray tracing [5], and shadow volumes [6], perform visibility calculations in object-space, against a complete representation of scene geometry. Moreover, some interactive techniques [12, 27] precompute and display soft shadow textures for each object in the scene. Such approaches do not scale very well as scene complexity increases.

Williams [30] has shown that for computing hard shadows from point light sources, a complete scene representation is not necessary. He performs the visibility calculations in image space, against *shadow maps*—image-based representations of scene geometry. Although the shadows may suffer undersampling, bias, and aliasing artifacts, the cost of the algorithm is relatively independent of scene complexity. Further, it is possible to implement this method as a post-shading pass that modulates a shadowless rendering from the base renderer to include shadows. This makes it simple to add the method to any existing renderer, without modifying the base renderer, and does not limit the approach to particular geometric primitives. In this paper, we describe two efficient image-based techniques for rendering soft shadows that can be seen as logical extensions of Williams' approach.

In both methods, shadows are computed in image space. Therefore the time and memory requirements for adding soft shadows to an image are dependent only on image complexity and the number of lights, not geometric scene complexity. Neither algorithm computes per object textures, so texture mapping is not a bottleneck for us. This independence from geometric scene complexity allows us to efficiently compute soft shadows for large scenes, including those which have complex patterns of self-shadowing.

We will also show that soft shadows are a particularly good application for image-based rendering approaches. Since area light sources are localized in space, visibility changes relatively little across them. The depth complexity of the visible or partially visible scene as seen from a light (and stored in our shadow maps) is generally very low. Further, shadow maps rendered from the light source sparsely sample surfaces that are oblique to the light source. However, these surfaces are less important to sample well, because they are precisely the surfaces that are dimly lit.

The contributions of this paper are the two algorithms summarized below, which represent two ends of a spectrum.

Layered Attenuation Maps: Our first approach achieves interactive rendering rates but limits sampling flexibility, and can therefore generate undersampling and banding artifacts. We precompute a modified layered depth image (LDI) [25] by warping and combining depth maps rendered from a set of locations on the light source. The LDI stores both depth information and layer-based *attenuation maps* which can be thought of as projective soft shadow textures. During display, the proper attenuation is selected from the LDI in real time in software, and is used to modulate normal rendering without shadows. The precomputation is performed in a few seconds, and soft shadows are then displayed at several frames a second. Since the light source sample positions are chosen a priori, they are correlated for each surface location and this correlation can appear as banding in the final image.

Coherence-Based Raytracing: Our second approach removes limitations on sampling and yields high quality images, suitable for high resolution prerendered animations, but is not interactive. We precompute shadow maps from a few points on the light, often the boundary vertices. To shade a surface point, we trace shadow rays through the shadow maps rather than the scene geometry. The shadows rays are decorrelated since they are chosen independently for each surface point, and therefore banding is replaced by noise. While the general approach to ray tracing depth images is well-known[1] [15, 16, 18, 20], we develop several novel acceleration techniques for accelerating shadow ray computations.

The visible portion of a light source tends to change very little for surface points close to one another. We describe a new image-based technique for exploiting this coherence when sampling visibility along shadow rays. Our image-based raytracing approach with coherence-based sampling produces soft shadows at a fraction of the cost of conventional raytracers. While we combine both the image-based ray-tracing and sampling algorithms in a single renderer, they can be used independently (i.e. a standard geometric ray tracer might incorporate our coherence-based sampling method).

Our algorithms can be combined in an interactive lighting system; our fast layered attenuation map method can be used to interactively set the viewing transformation, and position the light source and geometry. Our coherence-based raytracing method can then be used to quickly generate final high-quality images. This is the approach we took to produce the results in this paper, and we believe this approach has many applications to lighting design.

The rest of this paper is organized as follows. Section 2 reviews previous work on soft shadows. Section 3 presents preliminaries, while Section 4 describes our interactive layered attenuation map algorithm. In section 5, we describe coherence-based raytracing of depth images. The results are presented in Section 6, and Section 7 discusses future work and conclusions.

2 Previous Work

There is a vast literature on shadow algorithms, which we touch on only briefly. Although a decade old, the survey by Woo et al. [32] is still an excellent reference.

2.1 Object-Based Methods

Soft shadows can be computed using object-space methods such as distributed ray tracing [5] and radiosity with discontinuity meshing [11, 17] or backprojection [7, 29]. Stark et al.[28] describe analytic methods for computing soft shadows. These approaches are computationally intensive and are not suitable for fast soft shadow generation for complex scenes.

Herf and Heckbert [12] combine a number of shadow images for each receiver using an accumulation buffer [9]. The method is

object-based, and the precomputation time can grow quadratically with the number of objects being shadowed, making it impractical for large scenes. Furthermore, a separate (generally large) texture is created for each shadowed object. Our layered attenuation map approach is analogous in that we combine a similar number of depth images rendered from different points on the light. However, we improve on Herf and Heckbert's method by precomputing image-based textures simultaneously for the entire scene.

Soler and Sillion [27] use convolution on blocker images to compute fast approximate soft shadows. A primary advantage of their technique is that sampling artifacts that sometimes occur when averaging hard shadows are avoided. A disadvantage of their method is that they cluster geometry in object-space and the clusters cannot shadow themselves; to correct this for complex objects like plants or trees would require a very large number of clusters for the leaves. This increased number of clusters can greatly increase the computation time, obviating the benefits of the method. Separate textures are needed for each cluster being shadowed, which can strain the texture mapping hardware for complex objects. Furthermore, robust error control and automated clustering algorithms can be complicated to implement [26].

Hart et al. [10] develop a view dependent method to accelerate soft shadow computations for a standard ray tracer. They precompute a blocker list of geometry, stored in object space, for each image pixel by tracing a small number (often only one) of shadow rays to the light. When a blocker is found, they check if adjacent image pixels also "see" the same blocker using a recursive 4-connect flood-fill algorithm. The main stage of their algorithm first projects and clips each blocker to the light source and then computes the irradiance from the remaining portion of the light. While this method can greatly accelerate shadow computation, it is not well-suited for handling large amounts of tiny blocker geometry. As the size of geometric elements decreases, the probability that a blocker is missed in the blocker list precomputation phase increases, which can result in light leaks. Moreover, the storage of the blocker list and the projection and clipping of each blocker against the light source can become very expensive. While our coherence-based sampling bears some similarities to this approach, we remove two limitations. First, our approach is view independent. From a given set of precomputed shadows maps we can generate shadows for any view of the scene. Second, since our algorithm is image-based, its cost is independent of scene complexity. Small triangles are not a bottleneck for our coherence-based raytracing approach.

2.2 Image-Based Methods

Williams' shadow map algorithm [30] is an image-based alternative to object-space methods. Visibility along a shadow ray is determined by precomputing a shadow map from the light and then comparing the depth of each pixel in the final image to the corresponding depth in the shadow map. Percentage-closer filtering can be used for antialiasing [23] and projective textures [24] can be used for hardware implementation. Forward shadow mapping [33] is an alternative implementation when texture-mapping represents a bottleneck for normal rendering of the scene. All of these methods render hard shadows from point light sources.

Chen and Williams [2] describe a simple extension to shadow mapping for rendering soft shadows. They render a few key shadow maps at the vertices of the light source and then use view interpolation to compute shadow maps for each sample location on the interior. To render soft shadows, they simply perform the standard shadow map test on each interpolated map to compute average visibility. The view interpolation method suffers from two drawbacks. First, the final image must be projected into each interpolated shadow map independently. These projections can become expensive since they are required for each view in an interactive session. Second, like our layered attenuation map algorithm, banding artifacts can appear in the shadows, since the light source sam-

---

[1]McMillan [20] calls this inverse warping.

ple positions are chosen a priori.

Lischinski and Rappoport [16] use hierarchical raytracing of depth images as one of several image-based techniques for computing secondary rays in synthetic scenes. Keating and Max [14] point out that light leaks are a problem with this approach because each depth sample is treated independently as a 2D surface unconnected with adjacent samples. They extend Lischinski and Rappoport's method by aggregating adjacent depth samples into discrete depth buckets, forming relatively large flat surfaces. While this approach reduces light leaks, as the authors point out, it can also completely change the scene geometry. It is unclear how such changes affect the final image. While our raytracing algorithm is also based on that of Lischinski and Rappoport, we reduce the light leak problem by reconstructing more accurate surfaces from the depth samples. We also introduce several new acceleration techniques that improve the efficiency of the hierarchical algorithm, especially when using multiple reference shadow maps.

Guo [8] accelerates raytracing by using image-space coherence to reduce the number of primary rays traced without affecting the number of shadow rays traced per primary ray. Our coherence-based raytracing method exploits visibility coherence among shadow rays to reduce the number of shadow rays traced per primary ray. It may be possible to combine our approach with Guo's to exploit coherence for both shadow rays and primary rays.

3 Preliminaries

Irradiance from an area light source on a surface is given by

$$E = \int_{A_{light}} \left[\frac{L \cos \theta_i \cos \theta_l}{\pi r^2} \right] V \, dA \tag{1}$$

where L is the radiance output from the light source, θ_i is the incident angle, and θ_l is the angle made with the light normal [3]. We are primarily concerned with the change in binary visibility V. In a post-shading approach, the lighting term is computed separately from visibility and is often approximated by treating the area light as a point light source. We can then independently compute an average visibility that attenuates the shadowless rendering.

$$ATT = \frac{1}{A} \int_A V \, dA \tag{2}$$

It is also possible to implement both of our methods within the normal shading pass of the base renderer and compute equation 1 directly. For simplicity and efficiency, our layered attenuation map algorithm takes the former approach, separating visibility from lighting. For high quality results, our coherence-based raytracing algorithm takes the latter approach, directly computing equation 1. As in most soft shadow approaches, multiple lights are handled independently.

The integral in equation 2 is evaluated using quadrature by sampling a number of points on the light source. We assume there is a mapping from the unit square to the light source such that a uniform sampling of the square will uniformly sample the light. To choose N^2 sample locations on the light source, we stratify the unit square into NxN cells and choose some jittered sample location within each cell. In our layered attenuation map approach, the same sample points on the light are used for shadowing each surface point. In contrast, our ray tracing algorithm chooses which points to sample on the light separately for each surface point, and thereby removes the banding artifacts that can appear in the former approach.

4 Layered Attenuation Maps

In this section, we describe our algorithm for precomputing and displaying layered attenuation maps. The reader will want to refer to the illustrations in figures 2 thru 6.

Figure 2: **Left:** *A schematic of the scene used to illustrate the layered attenuation map algorithm.* **Right:** *The scene without shadows,*

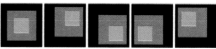

Figure 3: *Images taken from the light source center (leftmost) and the four corners (line 3 of the precomputation pseudocode).*

Figure 4: *Images in figure 3 are warped to the light center (line 5 precomputation pseudocode). On top, we show the first layer after warping, and below, the second layer. Yellow indicates absence of a second layer i.e. only one layer present. Regions not visible from a given light position show up as holes (black) when warped.*

Figure 5: *Images in figure 4 are combined to form layered attenuation maps (lines 6 and 7 of the pseudocode). From left to right, layer 1, the texture on layer 1 (white indicates fully visible), layer 2 (yellow indicates absence of a second layer), and the texture on layer 2. Note that the completely occluded green square is not present at all.*

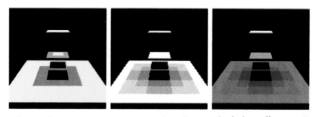

Figure 6: **Left:** *A visualization; white denotes the light, yellow: regions with only one layer, red: the first of two layers, blue: the second of two layers, black: umbral regions behind the last layer in the LDI, and magenta: when a point is between two layers (which happens for a very small region of the green square—at its edges—since it is culled from the LDI).* **Middle:** *Attenuation map. This modulates the basic image.* **Right:** *The final image.*

Precomputation: During the precomputation phase, we build the layered attenuation maps. This data structure consists of a separate list of layers for each pixel. Each layer stores depth, and the attenuation or fraction of the light that is visible from that point.

```
procedure Precompute
1    foreach light sample l_i
2        Viewpoint ← l_i
3        Render(SCENE)
4        foreach pixel (x, y)
5            (x', y') ← WarpCenter(x, y, z(x, y))
6            Insert((x', y'),z,ε)
7    Process Attenuation Maps
```

For each of a number of samples (typically 64) on the light, we render an image looking into the scene along the normal to the light at the sample location. In line 5 of the pseudocode, we transform the pixel into a central reference frame—the view from the light's center. For planar light sources, this warp is especially simple, being given by

$$\mathbf{dp} = -\frac{\mathbf{dv}}{z} \qquad (3)$$

where $\mathbf{dp}$ is the vector disparity (change) in pixels, $\mathbf{dv}$ is the (known) vector difference in viewing positions. z is measured from the viewpoint into the scene, and is the same for both views. In general, a projective transformation is required.

In line 6, we insert the transformed pixel into the *layered-depth image* (LDI). In our algorithm, each layer contains a depth value and an integer count. If the transformed depth value is already in the LDI (to tolerance ϵ), we simply increment the count of the appropriate layer by one. The count corresponds to the number of light samples visible to a point in a given layer at a given pixel. If the depth does not exist in the layer list, we add a new layer to the list, setting its count to one.

Holes, or gaps, can occur when warping image-based representations of large objects in line 5. Splatting is often used to combat this problem. Since our viewpoints on the light are all close to each other (assuming the light is a relatively small finite object), we adopt a simple strategy. For each transformed (fractional) point, the four neighboring (integer) pixels are considered in line 6 of the pseudocode. To avoid double-counting, we increment the count for a given layer at a given pixel at most once for each viewpoint. Note that this splatting can slightly overestimate object size, making the shadows appear somewhat lighter.

Finally, line 7 computes an attenuation map by dividing the count in a layer by the total number of samples used in the outer loop. This corresponds to the fraction of the light that is visible.

Display: As shown in the pseudocode below, in the display phase of the algorithm, the scene is first rendered normally with lighting. Note that we do not interfere with the texture path, so the normal rendering can include textures.

procedure Display
```
1   RenderWithLightingAndTextures(SCENE)
2   foreach pixel (x, y)
3       (x', y', z') ← WarpLDI((x, y, z(x, y)))
4       layer ← Layer((x', y'),z',ε)
5       color ← color * AttMap((x', y'),layer)
```

In line 3, each pixel is then projected back to the viewpoint at the center of the light source, and is associated with the nearest pixel in the precomputed LDI. The appropriate projection matrix is continuously updated during an interactive session.

In line 4, the list of layers at the corresponding pixel in the LDI is traversed and depths are compared with the transformed depth from the input pixel using a tolerance (shadow bias) ϵ. If no depth matches, the rendered point is not visible from anywhere on the light, and the attenuation applied in the next step is 0. In line 5, the base color of the image pixel is modulated by the attenuation map corresponding to the layered attenuation map for *layer* computed in the previous step.

Discussion: The time for precomputation is proportional to the number of light source samples used, while the time for display is proportional to the average depth complexity of the LDI. The precomputation can be performed quickly because we use only fast image warping operations instead of slower raytracing or backprojection. The display phase can be carried out at interactive rates because the depth complexity of the LDI is very low. Since the light samples are close together, and the LDI only stores points visible from somewhere on the light, the average number of layers in our representation is significantly less than for an LDI that represents the entire scene. As we will see in section 6.1, LDI depth complexity increases slowly after the first few light samples i.e. very few new layers are created in line 6 of the precomputation pseudocode.

We need to render the scene from many light sample locations to precompute accurate attenuation maps. If rendering the scene separately for each sample is expensive, we may instead warp depth images from key locations such as the corners of the light. In our implementation, this is not an issue because we use standard graphics hardware as the base renderer—for line 3 precomputation, and line 1 display. However, all other parts of our precomputation and display routines are implemented entirely in software.

To implement the precomputation and display routines in hardware would require hardware support for LDI creation and lookup. This is somewhat complicated because the depth complexity of LDIs is not fixed a priori. For soft shadows, however, the final depth complexity of the LDIs tends to be very low. Therefore, it may be possible to limit the number of layers and implement the display phase in hardware by combining shadows separately computed for each layer—either using the accumulation buffer and the SGI shadow map extensions, or using a programmable image-compositing framework [13].

5 Coherence-Based Raytracing

The layered attenuation map method is suitable for rapid previewing because of its fast precomputation phase and its interactive display phase—whose time complexity is independent of the number of light source samples. However, final images for applications such as prerendered animation, require high quality antialiased artifact-free shadows. To render such images efficiently, we have developed a coherence-based raytracing algorithm.

The algorithm combines two independent image-based methods: a hierarchical raytracing technique and a coherence-based sampling technique. We begin by precomputing shadow maps from several locations in the scene. Our raytracing algorithm places no restrictions on the position and orientation of the reference views; we typically use views from the exterior vertices of the light. To shade a surface point, we compute visibility along each shadow ray by tracing it through each shadow map, until either an intersection is found or we pass through all the shadow maps. Our coherence-based sampling algorithm reduces the number of shadow rays cast to a light source by sampling light source visibility only where changes in visibility are most likely.

For the layered attenuation map approach, the light source sampling is done during precomputation. On the other hand, it is done during display in the coherence-based ray tracing method, making the precomputation phase independent of the number of light source samples, and the display time proportional to the number of shadow rays traced.

5.1 Raytracing Depth Images

Raytracing depth images is a well known technique [15, 20] . After a quick summary of the algorithm, we describe several new modifications to it, which improve both its accuracy and efficiency.

To trace a shadow ray against a single reference image (shadow map), we can first project it onto the reference image plane, and then step along this *epipolar ray* from pixel to pixel, checking for intersections with the scene geometry—represented as depths in the shadow map. The intersection calculation is performed in two phases. The first phase is a quick *overlap test* to determine if intersection is possible. As we step along the ray, we maintain the epipolar depth interval $[Z_{enter}, Z_{exit}]$ of the shadow ray that spans the current reference pixel. If the corresponding reference image depth Z_{ref} is inside the epipolar depth interval, the second phase of the intersection test is performed to determine the exact point of intersection.

Recently, several papers [1, 16, 18] have described a hierarchical version of this raytracing algorithm that is similar to earlier work on raytracing height fields [22]. As a pre-process, two quadtrees are constructed from the reference image, one storing maximum depth values and one storing minimum depth values. The hierarchical algorithm performs the overlap test in a coarse-to-fine manner using these quadtrees. Thus, the raytracer can efficiently skip over large sections of the ray that cannot contain intersections. At the leaf-node level the exact intersection test is applied as before. Our pseudocode is adapted from [16]:

procedure Trace(QTreesNode,Ray,Z_{enter},Z_{exit})
1   **if**(Leaf(QTreesNode))
2   check for exact intersection
3   **else**
4   RefIntrvl ← [QTreesNode(MIN),QTreesNode(MAX)]
5   EpiIntrvl ← [Z_{enter},Z_{exit}]
6   **if**(OverLap(EpiIntrvl,RefIntrvl))
7   **foreach** non-empty Child of QTreesNode
8   Update(Z_{enter},Z_{exit})
9   Trace(Child,Ray,Z_{enter},Z_{exit})

The exact intersection test requires reconstructing a surface from the depth values stored in the reference image. Two common reconstruction techniques are triangulation[19] and bilinear interpolation[18, 21]. However, both methods impose costly exact intersection checks. A much simpler approach is to assume each reference image depth pixel represents a plane, which we call a *floor*, that runs parallel to the reference image plane. The floors are connected at their edges with vertical planes we call *walls*[2]. Although the floors-and-walls approach may yield a blocky surface reconstruction compared to triangulation or bilinear interpolation, in practice we have found that such artifacts are easy to control by generating higher resolution reference images.

Assuming every pair of adjacent reference pixels is connected with a wall yields incorrect intersections at silhouette edges of unconnected objects. We mitigate the problem by assuming adjacent reference image pixels are connected only if they differ in depth by less than a user specified *gap bias*. We check for intersections with walls only when adjacent reference pixels are connected.

In the next two subsections, we describe new methods for accelerating the hierarchical traversal and for efficiently combining information from multiple reference images.

5.1.1 Accelerating the Hierarchical Traversal

Hierarchical Connectedness: By traversing the epipolar ray in a coarse-to-fine manner, the hierarchical algorithm can quickly eliminate sections of the epipolar ray that cannot possibly intersect scene geometry. However, the only way to find an intersection is to recurse through the min/max quadtrees all the way to the finest level and then perform the exact intersection test. If it is not necessary to determine the exact point of intersection, we can modify the algorithm to determine whether or not the ray is blocked before descending to the finest level.

When building the min/max quadtrees, we also build a connectedness quadtree. At the leaf level, each pixel is connected to itself. At the next level, we determine whether each group of four adjacent pixels form a single surface by checking if their depths fall within the gap bias. We continue computing connectedness in this manner all the way to the root of the tree. At any stage in the hierarchical traversal, if the epipolar depth interval contains the corresponding reference image min/max interval and the connectedness quadtree reports that all four children of the current node are connected, then the ray must intersect some geometry within the node. Thus, it is possible to report that the ray is blocked without recursing to the finest level of the quadtree.

---

[2]To compute the exact intersection, we first check if reference image depth Z_{ref}, lies within the epipolar depth interval for the leaf node pixel. If so, the ray intersects the floor. At the exiting edge of the pixel we look up the reference depth for the adjacent pixel Z_{ref2} and if Z_{exit} lies within [Z_{ref}, Z_{ref2}], the ray intersects a wall. Linear interpolation can be used to find the exact point of intersection along the ray if necessary.

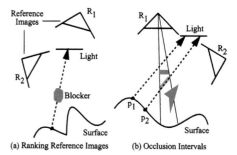

(a) Ranking Reference Images   (b) Occlusion Intervals

Figure 7: *Handling multiple reference images. In (a) reference image R_1's image plane is more perpendicular to the ray than R_2's image plane and therefore yields a shorter epipolar ray. We rank R_1 higher than R_2 since it is faster to traverse and more likely to yield an intersection. In (b) the shadow ray starting at p_1 is a clear miss in R_1 since it never passes behind geometry. Since the ray is entirely visible in R_1 we do not need to trace it in any other reference image and can immediately declare the ray unblocked. For the shadow ray starting at p_2 only the green occlusion interval found in R_1 is traced in R_2.*

Min/Max Clipping: The epipolar ray is initially clipped to the viewing frustum of the reference image. We can aggressively reduce the length of the epipolar ray by clipping it against the min/max bounds of the current node in the min/max quadtrees. By clipping the epipolar ray upon entering the Trace procedure, at every level of the recursion we ensure that the overlap test is always performed against the smallest possible piece of the epipolar ray[3].

5.1.2 Efficiently Combining Multiple Reference Images

Using a single reference image, it is possible to miss intersections. If the desired ray intersects geometry that is not visible in the reference view due to occlusion, the intersection can not be found. Using multiple reference images that capture different portions of the scene geometry can mitigate this problem. However, multiple views generally contain redundant information about the scene as well[4]. Our layered attenuation map algorithm handles this redundancy by creating an LDI that only retains a single sample at each depth. A drawback of the LDI approach is that it requires resampling the reference images which can reduce numerical accuracy. We take a two pronged solution that avoids this resampling. First we rank the reference images so the that images most likely to generate an intersection are traversed first. We adapt Chang's[1] approach of ranking the reference images by the length of the clipped epipolar ray in each image (see figure 7(a)). As soon as an intersection is found we move on to the next shadow ray. Second, for each reference image after the first, we only trace portions of the ray that were not visible in the previous images.

Clear Miss: Shadow ray computation requires traversing the epipolar ray in every reference image, until some intersection is found. For blocked shadow rays, the loop over reference images can be exited early, as soon as the intersection is found. This type of early exit is sometimes possible for unblocked rays as well. If we traverse an epipolar ray in one reference image and find no intervals in which it passes behind occluding geometry, the entire ray was visible in the reference view. We can safely report that the shadow ray is not blocked. This type of *clear miss* allows us to exit the function early, without traversing the epipolar ray in any other reference image.

Occlusion Intervals: As we traverse the epipolar ray in some reference image, the overlap test forces the recursion all the way

---

[3]Marcato[18] performs this clipping only once at the coarsest level of the recursion.

[4]Choosing the optimal set of reference views to cover the space of a given scene while minimizing redundant information is a difficult problem which we do not address in this paper.

down to the leaf level each time the ray enters and exits a region behind occluding geometry, We determine that an intersection did not occur at such silhouette boundaries only after we perform the exact intersection test which includes a check for connectedness. As we traverse the ray, we store a list of these *occlusion intervals* in which the ray passes behind occluding geometry. These are the only intervals that need to be checked in the other reference images[5] as shown in figure 7(b).

5.2 Sampling the Light Source

Stochastic raytracers typically distribute shadow rays independently over the entire light source for each surface point in the scene. Yet, visibility as a function of the position of the surface point tends to change slowly. Moreover, object-space rendering algorithms such as z-buffered scan conversion or REYES [4] shade a single surface at a time, moving from surface point to surface point in some continuous order. Thus, the surface points are generally processed in groups that lie close to one another. In this section we develop a technique for exploiting this coherence to reduce the region of the light source for which we cast shadow rays.

As described in section 3, sampling the light source requires a mapping from the unit square to the surface of the light source. We consider the set of cells stratifying the unit square as a 2D image array covering the light source. The *visibility image* is a binary image storing whether or not each light source cell is blocked. The key idea of our algorithm is to predict the visibility image for surface point p_i based on the light source visibility for the previous surface points. The algorithm is described in the following pseudocode:

procedure SoftShad

```
1   BlockerPtsList ← ∅
2   foreach surface point p_i
3       Predict(p_i,BlockerPtsList,VisImg,cellsTodo,cellsUsePrev)
4       cellsDone ← ∅
5       while not empty(cellsTodo)
6           l_j ← cellsTodo.dequeue
7           blockPt = Trace(ray(p_i,l_j))
8           Update(BlockerPtsList,blockPt,l_j)
9           if(isBlocked(blockPt) != VisImg[l_j])
10              VisImg[l_j] ← isBlocked(blockPt)
11              foreach cell l_k adjacent to l_j
12                  if(l_k in cellsUsePrev)
13                      cellsTodo.enqueue(l_k)
14          cellsDone.enqueue(l_j)
15      color_i ← Shade(VisImg)
```

The BlockerPtsList stores the intersection point for each occluded shadow ray we have traced. Initially it is the empty set (line 1) and we insert new blocker points every time we trace a shadow ray (line 7). Blocker points that are no longer relevant are removed in the Predict procedure (line 3) as described in section 5.2.2.

Figure 8: *Predicted Visibility Image. Gray boxes represent occluded cells, and white boxes represent unoccluded cells. Each cell marked with an X is initially placed in the cellsTodo list by the Predict procedure. Blues X's represent cells at edges between occluded and unoccluded regions, while red X's represent cells at the exterior edges of the light source. Cells that do not contain an X are initially placed in the cellsUsePrev list.*

We generate a predicted visibility image by projecting each point in the current BlockerPtsList onto the light source. Assuming a planar light source, the appropriate projection matrix is formed using p_i as the center of projection and the light source as the image. In the predict procedure, we also build two lists of light source

---

[5]Chang[1] also computes occlusion intervals, but uses them to invalidate intersections along the epipolar ray, rather than as an acceleration technique.

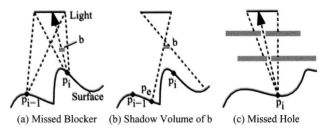

(a) Missed Blocker (b) Shadow Volume of b (c) Missed Hole

Figure 9: *Prediction errors. In (a) the blocker point b is not seen from surface point p_{i-1}. We predict the light is completely unblocked at p_i and never trace the ray through b. By increasing the surface sampling density so that p_i falls on p_e, the edge of the shadow volume due to b (shown in(b)), the blocker is found. In (c), a ray starting at p_i passes through the aligned holes in the blockers. To ensure that this ray is traced, we must increase the light source sampling density.*

cells based on our confidence of the predicted visibility. We assume that changes in visibility are most likely to occur in two places—at the boundaries between blocked and unblocked regions on the interior of the light source and at the exterior edges of the light source. If the predicted visibility for each interior cell is the same as the predicted visibility value of all of its neighboring cells, we are confident of the prediction and we add the cell to the cellsUsePrev list. Otherwise, the cell is at an edge between blocked and unblocked regions, confidence is low, so we add the cell to the cellsTodo list. Since we cannot examine a complete neighborhood for the cells on the exterior edges of the light source, we add all of these cells to the cellsTodo list. This is illustrated in figure 8. If the BlockerPtsList is empty, we put all of the light source cells in the cellsTodo list.

The main loop of the algorithm (lines 5 – 14) traces shadow rays for each light source cell in the cellsTodo list. When the value of a traced ray differs from the prediction held in the corresponding visibility image cell (line 9) we move any adjacent cell (considering all 8 neighbors) in the cellsUsePrev list to the cellsTodo list. As we find prediction errors, we spread out the lower confidence values to the neighboring cells using an 8-connect flood-fill algorithm. The main loop ends when we have processed all cells in the cellsTodo list, and we then shade the surface point using the current version of the visibility image.

5.2.1 Prediction Errors

As shown in figure 9(a),(c) there are two types of errors that may occur with our prediction technique; 1) *missed blocker:* a ray inside a region of the frustum predicted as unblocked is actually blocked and 2) *missed hole:* a ray inside a region of the frustum predicted as blocked is unblocked. Both types of prediction errors can lead to visible artifacts if the ray containing the blocker or the hole is predicted with high confidence and is not traced.

There is a fundamental difference between these two errors. The missed blocker error can be diminished by increasing surface sampling density. Reducing the missed hole error requires increased light sampling. To better understand this difference, we simplify the situation. Assume the light source is entirely visible from p_{i-1} and there is some small object b blocking a ray between p_i and some point on the interior of the light. The missed blocker error occurs because b is completely inside the frustum of p_i but outside the frustum of p_{i-1}, as shown in figure 9(a). Thus, our prediction for p_i requires that we only trace rays to the edges of the light source and since each of these traced rays agrees with our predicted visibility (unblocked), we never trace the ray through b.

Consider however, the shadow volume due to b and its intersection with the surface P. There must be some point p_e on the edge of the intersection that lies between p_i and p_{i-1}. Since p_e is on the surface of the shadow volume, the ray with origin at p_e and passing though b must intersect the edge of the light source (figure 9(b)). Since we always trace rays for points on the edge of the light source we correctly find the blocker b. As long as the surface points are sufficiently close to one another, this property holds regardless of the direction (on the surface) in which we approach p_i. Therefore, if we increase the surface sampling density, we reduce the missed blocker errors. A similar argument applies when regions of the light source are empty rather than the entire light source. Note that, if the distance between the current surface point and the previous surface point is larger than a given tolerance, we disregard the predicted visibility and trace all the shadow rays.

While it may seem a similar argument would apply to missed holes, there is a special case when multiple holes align to allow shadow rays to reach the interior of the light unoccluded. Suppose as in figure 9(c), at surface point p_i the holes in the two blockers align so that a single shadow ray to the interior of the light source is unblocked. For every surface point in any neighborhood of p_i, every shadow ray to the light is blocked. There is no surface point for which a shadow ray to an exterior edge of the light "sees" the hole. To ensure this ray is traced, we must increase light source sampling density. This in turn increases the precision of our predicted visibility since our blocker points list samples the surfaces more finely and we project them onto the light more accurately.

5.2.2 Updating the Blocker Points List

A drawback of our coherence-based sampling approach is that we must store and projectively warp each point in the blocker points list. Storing the list requires that the raytracer explicitly compute intersection points. Therefore, we cannot use the hierarchical connectedness optimization described in section 5.1.1. While warping a single point is relatively fast, if the blocker points list is large, the time to warp every point in the list can be significant.

We have designed several optimizations that limit the size of the blocker points list. We remove any blocker point that projects to a point outside the light source. This maintains some locality within the list and ensures that it stays relatively small. Often, multiple blocker points will warp to the same cell of the light. This is especially true for cells at edges between blocked and unblocked regions, since these are exactly the cells that we trace for every surface point. Such blocker points essentially provide redundant information and generally lie very close to each other in object space. One option is to keep only one of the blocker points that warp to the same light source cell. We generalize this approach. In each cell, we maintain a higher resolution grid (typically 3x3) and within each high resolution cell we keep only a single blocker point. With these optimizations, the size of the blocker points list is at most the light sampling resolution times the high resolution grid resolution. In contrast, Hart et al. [10] precompute and store blocker lists of geometry for each pixel in the final image. Their lists can contain redundancies and the size of each list is limited only by image resolution and the total number of shadow rays traced in their precomputation phase.

As a side benefit, we can use our high resolution grid to directly insert cells into the cellsDone list. Before prediction, we compute a jittered sample location for each cell of the light source. During the prediction phase, if a blocker point warps to a high-resolution cell containing a sample location, we place the corresponding light source cell in the cellsDone list. In this case, the blocker point lies close enough to the ray we would trace that we can assume the ray is blocked.

6   Results

Our results are presented in figures 1, 12, 13, and 14. Each image was originally rendered at 512x512 pixels and uses the equivalent of 256 light source samples. Some images have been cropped to preserve space, but the timings in figure 10 are for the entire un-cropped image. The light is rectangular for each of these scenes. It lies directly above the center of the geometry for the plant and the

flower, and is displaced toward the head of the dragon. We have deliberately shown extremely complex examples. The light position is chosen so that almost all the geometry either casts shadows or is itself shadowed. Also, our viewpoints have been picked so that almost the entire geometry and shadow region is visible. Soft shadows for these scenes would be expensive to generate by object-space methods, including the interactive approaches of Herf and Heckbert [12] or Soler and Sillion [27], since the scenes contain a large number of triangles, and complex self-shadowing interactions. Further, the triangles are typically very small, especially for the dragon and the flower, making these scenes difficult to handle by an approach that stores geometric information per pixel such as that of Hart et al. [10]. For quality comparisons, we have included images generated by rayshade.

Performance: Layered Attenuation Maps   Our layered attenuation map approach is implemented using standard graphics hardware under OpenGL as the base renderer. No special features, such as antialiasing, or shadow mapping extensions, are used. The hardware is used only for rendering shadowless images; the other parts of our precomputation and display phases work entirely in software. The running times for the precomputation phase on an SGI Onyx 2 Infinite Reality, and with an LDI size of 512x512, are shown in the left of figure 10. The main operations are software warping of rendered images and insertion into the LDI (lines 5 and 6 of the precomputation pseudocode), so the running time is largely independent of scene complexity. We see that coarse shadows (64 light samples), that may be suitable for most previewing work, can be precomputed in between 5 and 10 seconds, while higher-quality versions (256 samples) can be precomputed in about half a minute. Regardless of light sampling density, images with soft shadows can be displayed interactively at 5-10 frames per second, with the appropriate attenuation being chosen in real time in software.

Performance: Coherence-Based Raytracing   Our coherence based sampling technique is designed to work with object-space rendering algorithms that shade and render the scene surface by surface. We have implemented our algorithm within the shading pass of Pixar's PhotoRealistic Renderman which is based on the REYES [4] object-space rendering algorithm. In the REYES algorithm, geometric primitives are split into micropolygons that are shaded and then scan converted to create the final image. Micropolygons are shaded in a coherent manner, in groups that lie close to one another both in screen space and on the geometric primitive. Thus, lighting tends to change slowly from micropolygon to micropolygon. Since the micropolygons are shaded before computing their visibility, we compute soft shadows for every surface in the viewing frustum regardless of whether it is visible or not[6]. In contrast, standard raytracing renderers and the post-shading approach used with layered attenuation maps only perform the soft shadow computation on visible points. Therefore, direct comparisons between the running times of our coherence-based approach and other methods is difficult.

Running times and speedups for our coherence-based raytracing algorithm are presented in figure 10. The precomputation consists of rendering shadow maps at a resolution of 1024x1024 from the four corners of the light and constitutes a small fraction of the total running time. Note that the no-acceleration column refers to standard hierarchical image-based raytracing without any of our new acceleration techniques. Adding our raytracing acceleration techniques alone, without coherence-based sampling, provides a fairly consistent speedup of around 2.20x across the three scenes, regardless of light source sampling density. Much of this performance increase is due to the clear miss optimization which allows

---

[6]Rendering the plant, flower and dragon in Renderman at 512x512 image resolution requires shading 765134, 1344886 and 772930 surface samples respectively.

Layered Attenuation Maps			
Scene	Triangles	# Light Samp.	Precom. Time (s)
Plant	5247	64	6.0
		256	22.4
Flower	35109	64	7.4
		256	28.1
Dragon	77890	64	7.7
		256	29.4

Coherence-Based Raytracing						
Scene	Precom.. Time (s)	# Light Samp.	No Accel t(1000 s)	RT accel speedup	Accel + Coherence	
					speedup	rays
Plant	236	64	8.36	2.14x	**7.74x**	28.80
		256	33.30	2.16x	**8.52x**	88.74
		1024	131.96	2.16x	**10.12x**	287.59
Flower	332	64	4.59	2.15x	**3.64x**	34.86
		256	18.20	2.18x	**3.82x**	120.29
		1024	71.42	2.14x	**3.95x**	424.24
Dragon	140	64	3.92	2.28x	**10.59x**	27.57
		256	15.42	2.27x	**12.96x**	79.86
		1024	61.93	2.27x	**15.18x**	249.45

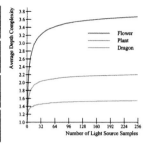

Figure 10: Left: *Precomputation times (in seconds) for our layered attenuation map approach on an SGI Onyx2 Infinite Reality. The major operations are image-based—warping rendered images and inserting into the LDI—so running time grows slowly with increased geometric scene complexity. The scenes can be displayed at 5-10 frames per second after precomputation is completed.* **Middle:** *Performance of Coherence-Based Raytracing on a 300 Mhz processor. The no acceleration column refers to hierarchical raytracing without any of our acceleration techniques and provides a baseline set of running times. The next two columns show the speedups achieved by including our raytracing accelerations and then both the accelerations and the coherence-based sampling. The final column shows the average number of rays actually traced with coherence-based sampling.* **Right:** *Increase in average depth complexity over non-empty LDI pixels in our layered attenuation map as a function of number of light samples. After the first few samples, the complexity increases very slowly. The flower has a lot more very small geometry, and so the final average visible depth complexity is higher, though even in this case, it is fairly low. This graph is a more meaningful measure of scene complexity than simple polygon count; the size of the LDI is proportional to this complexity.*

the algorithm to efficiently process many of the unoccluded shadow rays without visiting all four shadow maps.

As we increase the number of light samples, sizes of the fully blocked and unblocked areas on the light source grow faster than the lengths of the edges between them. We exploit this perimeter versus area growth ratio with our coherence-based sampling algorithm since we initially trace shadow rays only at the edges between blocked and unblocked regions. For all three scenes, we see that the speedups increase as we increase the light source sampling rate. Similarly, the ratio of average rays traced to the total number of light source samples decreases. If we increase the light source sampling rate by 4x, the running time of the original hierarchical raytracer and even that of the version with accelerations, but without coherence-based sampling, increase by roughly 4x. When we add coherence-based sampling however, the increase in running time is significantly smaller (i.e. the speedup increases as we increase the light source sampling density, especially for the plant and dragon). We have observed that adding coherence-based sampling causes no noticeable difference in image quality compared to hierarchical raytracing without coherence-based sampling (figure 13).

The speedup due to coherence-based sampling is relatively low for the flower scene. We believe this is largely due to the thin (typically much smaller than a pixel) geometry of the branches in the head of the flower. For points in the penumbra region on the ground plane, there are few large regions of the light source that are either fully occluded or unoccluded. Since most of the light source is at an edge between occluded and unoccluded regions, the coherence-based sampling approach provides little benefit. In contrast, the coherence-based approach achieves the largest speedups for the dragon scene. Although the triangles are still very small, this scene tends to contain larger blocked and unblocked regions on the light source.

Asymptotically, coherence-based sampling will make the number of rays traced proportional to the square-root of the number of light samples, rather than the number of samples (because, in the limit, the number of rays traced depends on the length of the perimeter between blocked and unblocked regions, not area). In the limit, we therefore expect a 4x increase in light source sampling to cause the number of rays actually traced to increase by only 2x, not 4x. At the light source sampling densities we've tested, we see an increase of a little more than 3x.

6.1 Discussion

In some respects, soft shadow representation is a model application for the use of image-based representations.

Depth Complexity: Since the light is localized in space, samples on it are close together, and visibility does not change significantly between the samples. This means the depth complexity of the completely and partially visible portions of the scene, as seen from the light, is very low, as seen in the graph in figure 10. Note that geometry that is occluded from everywhere on the light is completely excluded from our image-based representations. Therefore, as compared to an LDI that represents the entire scene, the LDIs in our layered attenuation map approach require significantly fewer layers. Furthermore, the complexity of the representation increases very slightly after the first few samples on the light. In the context of coherence-based raytracing, this low complexity means a sparse set of shadow maps suffices to produce high-quality results.

Sampling: Since our shadow maps are rendered from points on the light, surfaces whose normals make large angles to that of the light are sampled poorly. Since only a single LDI is used, this is more of an issue for layered attenuation maps than for coherence-based raytracing. However, these surfaces will also usually be very dimly lit—because of cosine falloff in light intensity—diminishing the visibility of sampling artifacts, as seen in the left of figure 11.

Artifacts: The images produced by both of our algorithms look very plausible when seen by themselves, and are also very close to those produced by rayshade. However, our layered attenuation map method produces some artifacts:

- **Insufficient Depth Sampling:** If the LDI samples depths of some surfaces insufficiently, we will not be able to tell whether a point in the final image occurs on, above, or below the surface, as seen in the left of figure 11. This is less of a problem with coherence-based raytracing since we do not resample into a single LDI. Therefore, those shadow maps that better sample the surfaces in question are used to generate the shadows. Note that since both of our algorithms require the use of error tolerances, we cannot use mid-point shadows [31]. Therefore, both methods require the user to specify a value for shadow bias.

- **Insufficient Attenuation Map Sampling:** Even if a surface has constant depth, insufficient sampling can cause blockiness when the attenuation map is magnified and reprojected. As shown in the right of figure 11, simple bilinear filtering of four neighboring attenuation map values—analogous to percentage-closer filtering [23]—for each image pixel can diminish the visibility of the artifacts. However, the results may still be inaccurate because a limited number of samples

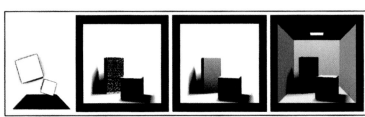

Figure 11: *Artifacts.* **Left:** *Insufficient depth sampling. Leftmost is the precomputed texture for layer 1 using layered attenuation maps. The sides of the large box are very poorly sampled. Next is the attenuation map, which has artifacts on the poorly sampled side. Similar artifacts are produced by the SGI (hard) shadow map hardware. However, coherence-based raytracing (third image) is able to do a much better job. Including cosine-falloff of light intensity, the final image produced by our layered attenuation map algorithm is shown rightmost, and the artifacts are considerably diminished.* **Right:** *Insufficient attenuation map sampling. Left is a thumbnail of the scene. The middle shows an extreme closeup of the ground which indicates blocky textures from magnification and reprojection. In the rightmost image, simple bilinear filtering reduces the perceptibility of the artifacts. Models courtesy of Peter Shirley.*

are available for reconstruction. Since coherence-based raytracing does not precompute textures, and thereby predetermine their resolution and sampling pattern, this is not an issue for that method.

- **Banding:** Since the same light samples are used for all surfaces, banding may occur as seen in figure 15. Note that banding is present in the attenuation map, and can therefore not be removed simply by post-filtering on the attenuation map, similar to that discussed above. In the coherence-based raytracing method, banding is replaced by noise since light samples are decorrelated for all surface points.

These artifacts are somewhat more apparent in high resolution images than at the size of the images in the printed version of this paper. To clearly show the artifacts here, we have zoomed very close. Similarly, to show banding, we have reduced the number of light source samples in figure 15 only.

As can be seen from the results, sampling artifacts are generally not a problem with coherence-based raytracing, so this technique is suitable for producing final high-quality images.

7 Conclusions and Future Work

We have described two efficient image-based methods for computing soft shadows. These methods can be seen as extensions of an extremely popular technique for hard shadows—shadow maps—and produce results significantly faster than traditional approaches. The algorithms can be combined for rapid previewing followed by efficient high-quality rendering. We have also demonstrated how soft shadows are an ideal application for image-based approaches. As future work, we would like to investigate better sampling strategies, the use of adaptive biases, and hardware implementation of the display phase for layered attenuation maps.

Acknowledgements: We are indebted to Tom Lokovic for developing the hierarchical connectedness acceleration for the raytracing approach and for implementing an initial version of coherence-based raytracing in Pixar's Photorealistic Renderman. Special thanks to Reid Gershbein, Tony Apodaca, Mark VandeWettering and Craig Kolb for initial discussions, and to Bill Mark, James Davis, and Pat Hanrahan for reviewing early drafts. The Siggraph reviewers provided many helpful comments.

References

[1] L. W. Chang. Combining multiple reference images in an inverse warper. M.eng. thesis, MIT, 1998.

[2] S. E. Chen and L. Williams. View interpolation for image synthesis. In *SIGGRAPH 93 proceedings*, pages 279–288, 1993.

[3] M. F. Cohen and J. R. Wallace. *Radiosity and Realistic Image Synthesis*. Academic Press, 1993.

[4] R. L. Cook, L. Carpenter, and E. Catmull. The Reyes image rendering architecture. In *SIGGRAPH 87 proceedings*, pages 95–102, 1987.

[5] R. L. Cook, T. Porter, and L. Carpenter. Distributed ray tracing. In *SIGGRAPH 84 proceedings*, pages 137–145, 1984.

[6] F. C. Crow. Shadow algorithms for computer graphics. In *SIGGRAPH 77 proceedings*, pages 242–248, 1977.

[7] G. Drettakis and E. Fiume. A fast shadow algorithm for area light sources using backprojection. In *SIGGRAPH 94 proceedings*, pages 223–230, 1994.

[8] B. Guo. Progressive radiance evaluation using directional coherence maps. In *SIGGRAPH 98 Proceedings*, pages 255–266, 1998.

[9] P. E. Haeberli and K. Akeley. The accumulation buffer: Hardware support for high-quality rendering. In *SIGGRAPH 90 proceedings*, pages 309–318, 1990.

[10] D. Hart, P. Dutre, and D. P. Greenberg. Direct illumination with lazy visibility evaluation. In *SIGGRAPH 99 proceedings*, pages 147–154, 1999.

[11] P. Heckbert. Discontinuity meshing for radiosity. In *Eurographics Rendering Workshop 92 proceedings*, pages 203–226, May 1992.

[12] P. Heckbert and M. Herf. Simulating soft shadows with graphics hardware. Technical Report CMU-CS-97-104, Carnegie Mellon University, 1997.

[13] A. Heirich and L. Moll. Scalable distributed visualization using off-the-shelf components. In *Symposium on Parallel Visualization and Graphics*, pages 55–60, 1999.

[14] B. Keating and N. Max. Shadow penumbras for complex objects by depth-dependent filtering of multi-layer depth images. In *Eurographics Rendering Workshop 99 proceedings*, 1999.

[15] S. Laveau and O. Faugeras. 3D scene representation as a collection of images and fundamental matrices. Technical Report 2205, INRIA, February 1994.

[16] D. Lischinski and A. Rappoport. Image-based rendering for non-diffuse synthetic scenes. In *Eurographics Rendering Workshop 98 proceedings*, pages 301–314, 1998.

[17] D. Lischinski, F. Tampieri, and D. P. Greenberg. Discontinuity meshing for accurate radiosity. *IEEE Computer Graphics and Applications*, 12(6):25–39, November 1992.

[18] R.W. Marcato, Jr. Optimizing an inverse warper. M.eng. thesis, MIT, 1998.

[19] W. R. Mark, L. McMillan, and G. Bishop. Post-rendering 3D warping. In Michael Cohen and David Zeltzer, editors, *1997 Symposium on Interactive 3D Graphics*, pages 7–16, April 1997.

[20] L. McMillan. *An Image–Based Approach to Three–Dimensional Computer Graphics*. Phd thesis, Department of Computer Science, University of North Carolina, 1997.

[21] L. McMillan and G. Bishop. Plenoptic modeling: An image-based rendering system. In *SIGGRAPH 95 Proceedings*, pages 39–46, 1995.

[22] F. K. Musgrave, C. E. Kolb, and R. S. Mace. The synthesis and rendering of eroded fractal terrains. In *SIGGRAPH 89 proceedings*, pages 41–50, 1989.

[23] W. T. Reeves, D. H. Salesin, and R. L. Cook. Rendering antialiased shadows with depth maps. In *SIGGRAPH 87 proceedings*, pages 283–291, 1987.

[24] M. Segal, C. Korobkin, R. van Widenfelt, J. Foran, and P. E. Haeberli. Fast shadows and lighting effects using texture mapping. In *SIGGRAPH 92 proceedings*, pages 249–252, 1992.

[25] J. W. Shade, S. J. Gortler, L. He, and R. Szeliski. Layered depth images. In *SIGGRAPH 98 proceedings*, pages 231–242, 1998.

[26] C. Soler and F. X. Sillion. Automatic calculation of soft shadow textures for fast, high-quality radiosity. In *Eurographics Rendering Workshop 98 proceedings*, pages 199–210, 1998.

[27] C. Soler and F. X. Sillion. Fast calculation of soft shadow textures using convolution. In *SIGGRAPH 98 proceedings*, Computer Graphics Proceedings, Annual Conference Series, pages 321–332, 1998.

[28] M. Stark, E. Cohen, T. Lyche, and R. F. Riesenfeld. Computing exact shadow irradiance using splines. In *SIGGRAPH 99 proceedings*, 1999.

[29] A. J. Stewart and S. Ghali. Fast computation of shadow boundaries using spatial coherence and backprojection. In *SIGGRAPH 94 proceedings*, pages 231–238, 1994.

[30] L. Williams. Casting curved shadows on curved surfaces. In *SIGGRAPH 78 proceedings*, pages 270–274, 1978.

[31] A. Woo. *Graphics Gems III*, chapter The Shadow Depth Map Revisited, pages 338–342. Academic Press, 1992.

[32] A. Woo, P. Poulin, and A. Fournier. A survey of shadow algorithms. *IEEE Computer Graphics and Applications*, 10(6):13–32, November 1990.

[33] H. Zhang. Forward shadow mapping. In *Eurographics Rendering Workshop 98 proceedings*, pages 131–138, 1998.

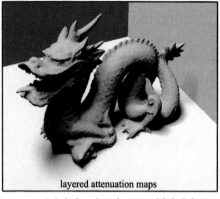  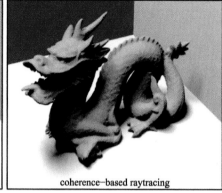

layered attenuation maps   rayshade   coherence–based raytracing

Figure 12: *Soft shadows for a dragon model shaded using a Lambertian model. The rayshade and layered attenuation map images were rendered with 256 light source samples. The coherence–based raytracing image used an average of only 79.86 light source samples. Splatting in the layered attenuation map method slightly increases the brightness of the shadow at the front of the dragon and the artifacts around the rear foot of the dragon are due to undersampling and shadow bias errors. Also, the color of the white floor and wall in the layered attenuation map method is slightly darker since the base hardware renderer does not do per–pixel lighting. Model courtesy of Stanford Scanning Repository.*

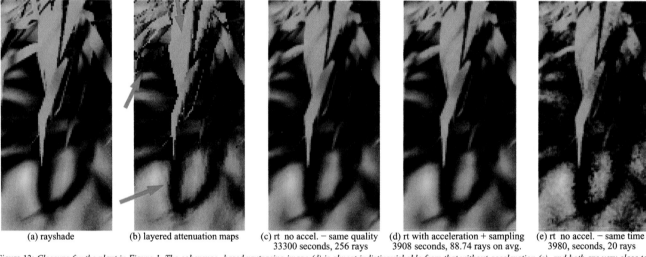

(a) rayshade   (b) layered attenuation maps   (c) rt no accel. – same quality 33300 seconds, 256 rays   (d) rt with acceleration + sampling 3908 seconds, 88.74 rays on avg.   (e) rt no accel. – same time 3980, seconds, 20 rays

Figure 13: *Closeups for the plant in Figure 1. The coherence–based raytracing image (d) is almost indistinguishable from that without acceleration (c), and both are very close to the image produced by rayshade (a). Our coherence–based method is 8.52 times faster than the unaccelerated hierarchical raytracer (c). An equal time comparison is provided in (e). Note that the times listed are for the entire image, not just the closeups. At the scale of the closeup, there are some artifacts for our layered attenuation map approach (b), as indicated by the red arrows. However, at normal scales as in Figure 1 these artifacts are less prominent, and are usually tolerable for interactive applications.*

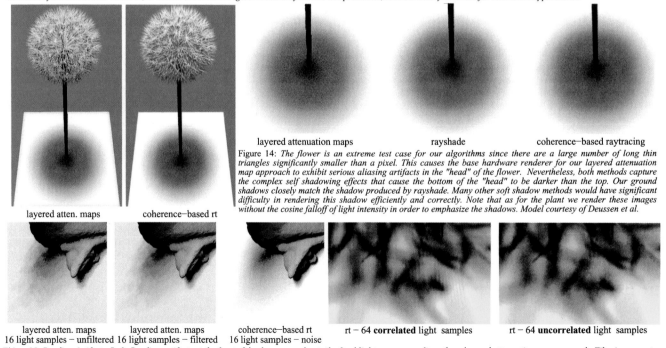

layered atten. maps   coherence–based rt

layered attenuation maps   rayshade   coherence–based raytracing

Figure 14: *The flower is an extreme test case for our algorithms since there are a large number of long thin triangles significantly smaller than a pixel. This causes the base hardware renderer for our layered attenuation map approach to exhibit serious aliasing artifacts in the "head" of the flower. Nevertheless, both methods capture the complex self shadowing effects that cause the bottom of the "head" to be darker than the top. Our ground shadows closely match the shadow produced by rayshade. Many other soft shadow methods would have significant difficulty in rendering this shadow efficiently and correctly. Note that as for the plant we render these images without the cosine falloff of light intensity in order to emphasize the shadows. Model courtesy of Deussen et al.*

layered atten. maps 16 light samples – unfiltered   layered atten. maps 16 light samples – filtered   coherence–based rt 16 light samples – noise   rt – 64 **correlated** light samples   rt – 64 **uncorrelated** light samples

Figure 15: *Banding Artifacts. **Left:** Banding artifacts at the front of the dragon are due to the fixed light source sampling of our layered attenuation map approach. Filtering cannot eliminate the banding artifacts. The banding is replaced by noise when the light source samples are chosen independently for each surface point as with our coherence–based raytracing approach.*

Deep Shadow Maps

Tom Lokovic   Eric Veach

Pixar Animation Studios*

Abstract

We introduce *deep shadow maps*, a technique that produces fast, high-quality shadows for primitives such as hair, fur, and smoke. Unlike traditional shadow maps, which store a single depth at each pixel, deep shadow maps store a representation of the fractional visibility through a pixel at all possible depths. Deep shadow maps have several advantages. First, they are prefiltered, which allows faster shadow lookups and much smaller memory footprints than regular shadow maps of similar quality. Second, they support shadows from partially transparent surfaces and volumetric objects such as fog. Third, they handle important cases of motion blur at no extra cost. The algorithm is simple to implement and can be added easily to existing renderers as an alternative to ordinary shadow maps.

1 Introduction

Rendering hair, fur, and smoke is difficult because accurate self-shadowing is so important to their appearance [2]. To demonstrate this, Figure 1 shows a small patch of curly hair rendered both with and without shadows. Notice that the shadows cast by portions of the hair onto itself have a great influence on the overall illumination and apparent realism of the rendering.

Traditional shadow maps [11] need very high resolutions to capture this type of self-shadowing accurately. Many more depth samples must also be accessed during shadow lookups to compensate for the higher frequencies in the shadow map. This is especially obvious in animations, where inadequate sampling results in *sparkling* (a distracting artifact caused by rapidly changing noise patterns).

Furthermore, shadow maps cannot handle volumetric effects such as clouds or smoke. Traditional approaches such as integrating the atmospheric density along each shadow ray are very inefficient, simply because there can be a large number of shadow tests along each primary ray.

We propose a new type of shadow map to solve these problems, the *deep shadow map*. Rather than storing a single depth at each pixel, a deep shadow map stores a *fractional visibility function* (or simply *visibility function*) that records the approximate amount of light that passes through the pixel and penetrates to each depth. The visibility function takes into account not only the opacities of the surfaces and volume elements encountered, but also their coverage of the pixel's filter region. This allows deep shadow maps to accurately represent the partial attenuation that occurs as light passes

*email: tdl@pixar.com, ericv@pixar.com

Figure 1: *Hair rendered with and without self-shadowing.*

through dense hair and fog.

Compared to ordinary shadow maps, deep shadows have the following advantages:

- They support semitransparent surfaces and volumetric primitives such as smoke.

- For high-quality shadows, they are smaller than equivalent shadow maps by an order of magnitude and are significantly faster to access.

- Unlike ordinary shadow maps, they support mip-mapping. This can dramatically reduce lookup costs when objects are viewed over a wide range of scales.

In addition, deep shadow maps can efficiently support high-quality motion blurred shadows. While this effect is also possible with ordinary shadow maps, the large filter widths required have made this technique quite expensive in the past.

In the following section, we discuss previous work and explain why traditional shadow maps are not appropriate for fine geometry such as hair and fur. Section 3 defines deep shadow maps and presents algorithms for creating and using them, while Section 4 describes their advantages and limitations. We then discuss some of the more practical implementation issues, and present the results from several experiments.

2 Background and Related Work

Traditional shadow maps [11] are generated by placing a camera (the *shadow camera*) at the light source origin such that the objects casting shadows are within the field of view. The result is a rectangular array of pixels where each pixel stores the depth of the closest visible surface. To determine whether a given point P is in shadow, it is transformed into the coordinate system of the shadow camera and its depth is compared to the corresponding value from the shadow map. Higher-quality antialiased shadows are possible with *percentage closer filtering* [9], which examines depth samples within a given filter region and computes the fraction that are closer than a given depth z. This process relies heavily on stratified sampling [7], both in generating the original shadow map and in selecting a random subset of the depth samples for filtering.

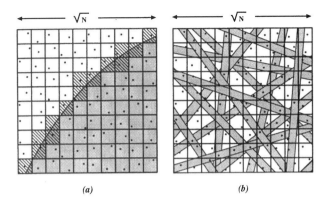

Figure 2: *Variance contributions to stratified sampling. (a) When a single silhouette edge passes through the filter region, $O(N^{1/2})$ samples contribute to the variance. (b) When the filter region is covered with fine geometry, all N samples contribute to the variance, resulting in a much larger expected error.*

While shadow maps are very good for rendering shadows of large objects, they do not work as well for finely detailed geometry such as hair. This is because stratified sampling does not work very well when there are many discontinuities crossing the filter region [7]. As a result, many more samples are required in order to reduce noise artifacts such as sparkling to an acceptable level.

To understand why this is so, consider Figure 2a. Here we show an isolated silhouette edge crossing the filter region for a shadow lookup, evaluated using N samples jittered over a $\sqrt{N} \times \sqrt{N}$ grid. The depth of each sample is obtained from the shadow map (whose resolution may be much finer than the sample grid). Using percentage closer filtering, each sample contributes either 0 or 1 to the average shadow value depending on the relative z values of the shadow map and the test point P.

In this situation, observe that the only samples that contribute to the variance are the ones whose cells are crossed by the silhouette edge. There are only $O(N^{1/2})$ of these, and further analysis [7] shows that the expected error in this case is $O(N^{-3/4})$. Thus stratification yields much better results near large silhouette edges than unstratified Monte Carlo sampling, which has an expected error of $O(N^{-1/2})$.

In the case of hair or fur, however, the filter region is crossed by many silhouette edges (see Figure 2b). In this case, every one of the N cells is crossed by an edge, and the corresponding expected error is $O(N^{-1/2})$. Thus in the case of very fine geometry, stratified sampling is no better than unstratified sampling.

These error bounds have a dramatic effect on the number of samples required to reduce noise below a given threshold. For example, to achieve an expected error of 1%, approximately $N = 140$ samples are needed near an isolated silhouette, while $N = 2500$ samples are required near a point that is 50% obscured by dense fur.[1] Furthermore, if the same amount of shadow detail is desired in both cases (*i.e.* the same filter size in world space), then the underlying shadow map resolution must be increased by the same factor. To gain any benefit from stratification, the shadow map would need to be fine enough to resolve the silhouettes of individual hairs, and the filter region small enough that only a few edges cross it. Since these conditions are rarely satisfied in practice, shadow maps for high-quality hair rendering are typically large and slow.

We briefly mention some other possible shadow techniques (the

---

[1] These estimates assume that the silhouette edge is horizontal and has a random vertical position, in which case the constant factors for the expected error are $1/\sqrt{6}$ and $1/2$ respectively.

classic survey is [13]). Ray casting can generate accurate shadows, but on furry objects with millions of hairs it is too expensive in terms of time and memory. This is particularly true when hair receives shadows from fog or smoke, since ray marching is performed once for every hair sample. It is also difficult, other than by using an expensive area light source, to "soften" shadows for artistic purposes. In the case of standard shadow maps this can be achieved by simply increasing the filter width. Kajiya and Kay used ray-cast shadows on a volumetric hair representation [2], but their rendering times were relatively long.

Another possible approach to hair self-shadowing is to precompute the shadow density as a 3D texture. This technique has been used with some success for clouds (*e.g.* [3]) and for hybrid volume and surface rendering of medical datasets [5]. The main drawback of this approach is that 3D textures have a relatively coarse resolution, and in particular they have limited range and low accuracy in z (which creates bias problems). A 3D texture with sufficient detail to capture accurate surface shadows of complex geometry would be prohibitively large.

Multi-layer Z-buffers [6] and *layered depth images* [10] store information at multiple depths per pixel, but are geared toward rendering opaque surfaces from new viewpoints rather than shadow evaluation. Keating and Max [4] apply multi-layer depth images to the problem of shadow penumbras, but their technique otherwise has the same limitations as ordinary shadow maps.

3 Deep Shadow Maps

3.1 Definition

A deep shadow map is a rectangular array of pixels in which every pixel stores a *visibility function*. Intuitively, a visibility function is defined by considering a beam of light that starts at the shadow camera origin and passes through the given pixel. The function value at a given depth is simply the fraction of the beam's initial power that penetrates to that depth. Note that the beam is not necessarily square; it can be shaped and weighted according to any desired pixel filter. Figure 3 gives several examples, showing how visibility functions can account for semitransparent surfaces, pixel coverage, and smoke. Each visibility function starts off with a value of 1, and decreases with depth as various types of blockers are encountered. If all light is blocked, the function drops off to a value of 0.

To make this definition more precise, consider a ray that starts at the shadow camera origin and passes through the point (x, y) on the image plane. Some fraction of the light emitted along this ray will be attenuated by surfaces or by volumetric scattering and absorption. The fraction of light that penetrates to a given depth z is known as the *transmittance* $\tau(x, y, z)$. We refer to τ as a *transmittance function* when we wish to consider the transmittance at a fixed image point (x, y) as a function of z.

The visibility function for each pixel is now obtained by filtering the nearby transmittance functions and resampling at the pixel center. This is easier to understand if we restrict our attention to a particular depth z. The transmittance at every point in this z-plane is given by $\tau(x, y, z)$, and the visibility function $V_{i,j}$ for each pixel is obtained by filtering these values:

$$V_{i,j}(z) = \int_{-r}^{r} \int_{-r}^{r} f(s,t)\, \tau(i + \tfrac{1}{2} - s, j + \tfrac{1}{2} - t, z)\, ds\, dt \,,$$

where $(i + \tfrac{1}{2}, j + \tfrac{1}{2})$ is the pixel center, f is the desired bandlimiting pixel filter (centered around the origin), and r is the filter radius. This definition is similar to ordinary image filtering, except that it applies to every z value separately.

Notice that visibility functions are closely related to the *alpha channels* used for image compositing. The alpha channel of an im-

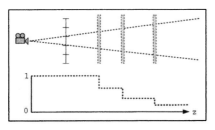

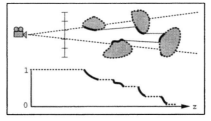

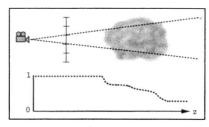

(a) A stack of semitransparent objects   (b) Partial coverage by opaque blockers   (c) Volume attenuation due to smoke

Figure 3: *Visibility functions in flatland. Each diagram shows a beam of light that starts at the shadow camera origin (i.e. the light source) and passes through a single pixel of the deep shadow map, accompanied by that pixel's visibility function. (**a**) The beam's power is reduced as it passes through consecutive semitransparent surfaces. (**b**) The blockers are opaque, but each covers only part of the pixel's area; the emphasized segments of the function correspond to visible portions of the blockers. (**c**) Passage through smoke reduces the beam's power in a more continuous manner.*

age accounts for attenuation due to both semitransparent surfaces and partial coverage of pixels, but is equal to the fraction of light blocked rather than the fraction of light transmitted. The alpha channel also stores just a single value per pixel, corresponding to the light blocked at the plane $z = \infty$. Thus the relationship between visibility functions and alpha channels can be expressed as:

$$\alpha_{i,j} = 1 - V_{i,j}(\infty) .$$

A deep shadow map is equivalent to computing the approximate value of $1 - \alpha$ at all depths, and storing the result as a function of z. In this way each pixel contains the combined attenuation and coverage information for every depth.

3.2 Sampling

In this section we describe how deep shadow maps can be generated using the facilities of any standard renderer. Our strategy is similar to ordinary image sampling. To generate a deep shadow map, we select a set of sample points across the shadow camera's image plane (for example, 16 samples per pixel on a jittered grid). For each sample point we determine the corresponding transmittance function, which describes the light falloff along a particular primary ray. Finally, the visibility function for each pixel is computed by taking a weighted combination of the transmittance functions at nearby sample points.

We first describe how to compute a single transmittance function. Given an image point (x, y), we compute the surfaces and volume elements intersected by the corresponding primary ray. The surface intersections can be found using either a ray tracer or an ordinary scan conversion renderer, and we assume that the properties of volumetric objects can be evaluated at any points desired. The transmittance function at the point (x, y) can then be expressed as the product of a *surface transmittance function* τ^s and a *volume transmittance function* τ^v, as described below.

Surface transmittance is estimated using all of the surface intersections along the primary ray at (x, y). Each *surface hit* has a depth value z_i^s and an opacity O_i. These are composited in the usual way, starting with a transparency of 1 and multiplying by $1 - O_i$ at each surface hit, to yield a piecewise constant function τ^s (see Figure 4a). Notice that each surface hit generates two vertices with the same z value, in order to represent the discontinuous steps as a piecewise linear curve.[2] The "vertices" at $z = 0$ and $z = \infty$ are represented implicitly and are not part of the output.

---

[2]The wasted space in this representation is removed during the compression phase, which approximates the average of many discrete steps with a single linear segment. A true "step" in the compressed output function would occur only for a surface exactly parallel to the xy-plane.

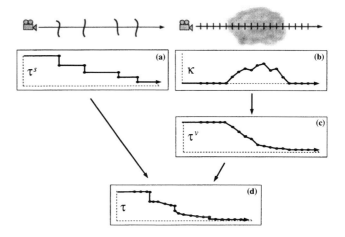

Figure 4: *Constructing a transmittance function. (**a**) The object intersections along a given ray yield the surface transmittance function τ^s, which has a discontinuity at the depth of each surface. (**b**) The extinction function κ is obtained by sampling the atmospheric density at regular intervals along the ray. (**c**) The extinction function is integrated and exponentiated to yield the volume transmittance τ^v. (**d**) The surface transmittance and volume transmittance are multiplied to obtain the final transmittance function τ for each ray.*

To estimate the volume transmittance, we sample the atmospheric density at regular intervals along the ray. Each *volume sample* has a depth value z_i^v and an *extinction coefficient* κ_i that measures the light falloff per unit distance along the ray. We linearly interpolate between these samples to yield the *extinction function* κ (see Figure 4b). The fraction of light that penetrates to a given depth z is then given by the formula[3]

$$\tau^v(z) = \exp(-\int_0^z \kappa(z') \, dz') .$$

Since this function is not piecewise linear, we approximate it by evaluating the transmittance at each vertex of the extinction function and linearly interpolating. We do this by computing the transmittance of each linear segment as

$$T_i = \exp(-(z_{i+1}^v - z_i^v)(\kappa_{i+1} + \kappa_i)/2)$$

and compositing as we did for the surface transparencies, except that we interpolate between vertices rather than forcing discrete

---

[3]If the shadow camera is not orthographic, a correction factor is needed for each ray to account for the relationship between depth and distance.

steps. This yields the volume transmittance function τ^v (see Figure 4c). We then merge the surface and volume components by multiplying them:

$$\tau(z) = \tau^s(z)\,\tau^v(z)$$

(see Figure 4d). Since this function is again not piecewise linear, we evaluate it at the combined vertices of τ^s and τ^v and interpolate linearly between them.

Finally, we describe how the transmittance functions are combined to yield the visibility function $V_{i,j}$ for an entire pixel. At each depth z the nearby transmittance functions are filtered just like ordinary image samples:

$$V_{i,j}(z) = \sum_{k=1}^{n} w_k\,\tau_k(z) , \qquad (1)$$

where n is the number of transmittance functions within the filter radius around $(i + \frac{1}{2}, j + \frac{1}{2})$, and w_k is the normalized filter weight for each corresponding sample point (x_k, y_k). The result is a piecewise linear function that has approximately n times as many vertices as the transmittance functions do. This function takes into account not only the light attenuation due to semitransparent surfaces and fog, but also the fractional coverage of these features.

3.3 Compression

Visibility functions sampled in this way may have a large number of vertices, depending on the filter radius and the number of samples per shadow pixel. Fortunately these functions are generally quite smooth, making them easily compressed. The compressed functions are stored as an array of floating-point pairs, each containing a z value and a fractional visibility V.

It is very important that the compression method preserve the z values of important features, since even small errors in z can lead to undesirable self-shadowing artifacts. The method must also be appropriate for the unbounded domain $z \in [0, \infty)$. These facts preclude the use of compression methods based on a fixed or hierarchical set of basis functions (e.g. a wavelet basis). It also implies that the L_1 and L_2 error metrics are unsuitable, since visibility errors are important even if they occur over a very small range of z values. Instead we use the L_∞ error metric (maximum error), and compress functions using the simple greedy algorithm described below.

Given a visibility function V and an error tolerance ϵ (see Figure 5a), our algorithm outputs a new visibility function V' such that

$$\left| V'(z) - V(z) \right| \le \epsilon \qquad \text{for all } z$$

and where V' typically has a much smaller number of control points (Figure 5d). The main feature of the algorithm is that it is incremental: It reads and writes control points one at a time in increasing z order, and requires only a constant amount of state information.

The basic idea is that at each step, the algorithm draws the longest possible line segment that stays within the error bounds (similar to hitting a ball through as many wickets as possible in a game of croquet). The origin of the current segment is fixed, and we only need to choose the direction and length of the segment. To simplify the implementation, we restrict the output z values to be a subset of the input z values.

Let the origin of the current output segment be (z_i', V_i'). At every step we maintain the range of permissible slopes $[m_{lo}, m_{hi}]$ for the segment. Each new control point (z_j, V_j) of the input function V imposes a constraint on the current slope range by forcing the segment to pass through the *target window* defined by the wedge from the segment origin to the two points $(z_j, V_j \pm \epsilon)$ (see Figure 5b). The current slope range is initialized to $[-\infty, \infty]$, and is intersected

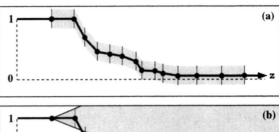

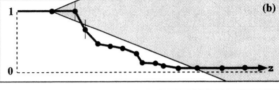

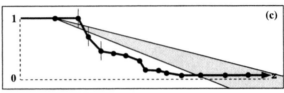

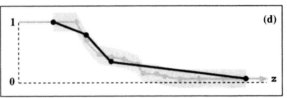

Figure 5: *Our compression algorithm. (a) A piecewise linear curve and an illustration of its error bound. (b) Each input vertex defines a target window that constrains the slope of the next output segment. (c) The current slope range is intersected with each target window until it would become empty. (d) The output segment is extended to the current z value with a slope equal to the midpoint of the current slope range, and this process is repeated.*

with each target window in succession until further progress would make it empty (see Figure 5c). We then output the line segment with slope $(m_{lo} + m_{hi})/2$ terminating at the z value of the last control point visited. The endpoint of this segment becomes the origin of the next segment, and the entire process is repeated. Note that the midpoint slope rule attempts to center each segment within the allowable error bounds.

This algorithm is fast, simple to implement, and requires constant storage. Slightly better approximations could be obtained by doing a least-squares fit once the z values of the control points have been chosen. However, the basic algorithm satisfies the given error criteria and generates very good approximations in practice.

3.4 Lookups

Like textures, deep shadows are accessed by applying a reconstruction and resampling filter to a rectangular array of pixel values. In our case the pixel values are obtained by evaluating the visibility functions at a constant depth z. Given a point (x, y, z) at which to perform the lookup and a two-dimensional filter kernel f, the filtered shadow value is given by

$$V(x, y, z) = \frac{\sum_{i,j} w_{i,j} V_{i,j}(z)}{\sum_{i,j} w_{i,j}}$$

where $w_{i,j} = f(i + \frac{1}{2} - x, j + \frac{1}{2} - y)$ is the filter weight for pixel (i, j), and the sum is over all pixels within the filter radius.

Evaluating each visibility function requires a search through its data points to determine which segment contains the given z value. This can be done using a linear or binary search, depending on the number of data points. In our implementation, we take advantage of the fact that many shadow lookups are often done at nearby z values by storing a pointer with each pixel to the most recently accessed segment. On each lookup we search linearly either forward or backward from this position in order to reduce the average cost of visibility function evaluations.

4   Discussion

One of the main advantages of deep shadows over regular shadow maps is that they support prefiltering. Each deep shadow map pixel summarizes many individual depth samples in such a way that evaluating the visibility function at a given z value is equivalent to percentage closer filtering all of the depth samples within the pixel's filter radius (to within the tolerance used for compression). Prefiltering is important because accurate shadows require large numbers of depth samples, as we saw in Section 2. This is equally true for both ordinary shadow maps and deep shadow maps.

Although deep shadows do not reduce the number of depth samples that must be taken from the scene, they greatly reduce the amount of data that must be accessed during filtering. For example, recall that in order to compute a shadow of dense hair with an expected error of 1%, approximately $N = 2500$ samples are needed. Using a deep shadow map with 250 samples per pixel, we would need to filter only $N = 10$ pixels to achieve the required accuracy. Furthermore deep shadows can be mip-mapped (see Section 5.3), and thus accurate shadows require only a constant number of pixel accesses even when filter widths are very large.

Prefiltering not only makes shadow lookups faster, but also allows deep shadows to be much smaller than the equivalent high-resolution depth map. This is an advantage when deep shadow maps are written, stored, and cached in memory. Note that the advantages of prefiltering are completely dependent on compression. If we did not compress the visibility functions at all, then each pixel would contain the data from all the underlying samples and would not be any smaller.

Fortunately, at any sampling rate there is an error tolerance that allows significant compression without compromising shadow quality. Specifically, recall from Section 2 that shadows of detailed geometry have an expected error of $O(N^{-1/2})$, where N is the number of samples per deep shadow pixel. This error is a measure of the noise inherent in the sampled visibility function. Since there is no point in preserving noise, this suggests that $O(N^{-1/2})$ is a suitable tolerance for compression. The tolerance we actually use is $0.25/\sqrt{N}$, which is about half of the maximum expected noise magnitude of $0.5/\sqrt{N}$.[4]

Using this tolerance, we can show that deep shadows are asymptotically much smaller than regular shadow maps. Since each visibility function decreases monotonically from 1 to 0 (assuming that the filter function has no negative lobes), and the function decreases by at least the compression tolerance at each vertex, the compressed function can have at most $O(N^{1/2})$ vertices. The corresponding regular shadow map uses $O(N)$ storage for the depth values in each pixel, and so the deep shadow map must be smaller by at least a factor of $\Omega(N^{1/2})$.

---

[4]Recall that the expected error is only $O(N^{-3/4})$ when the shadow geometry is simple, which suggests that a compression tolerance of $O(N^{-1/2})$ is too large in this case. But since N must be chosen large enough to control the noise artifacts in the worst-case pixels, there is little benefit to compressing more accurately than this.

The compression ratios are even better when the visibility functions are asymptotically piecewise smooth (which is the usual case). A simple Taylor series argument shows that in this case the compression error decreases quadratically in the number of output vertices, so that functions can be compressed with a tolerance of $O(N^{-1/2})$ using only $O(N^{1/4})$ vertices. Thus deep shadow maps are typically smaller than their regular counterparts by at least a factor of $\Omega(N^{3/4})$. This is a substantial advantage when many samples per pixel are used (say $N = 250$).

The main disadvantage of deep shadow maps is that they are significantly more expensive to compute than a regular shadow map of the same pixel resolution (because many more samples per pixel are taken). This contradicts the conventional assumption that shadow map generation is cheap [9]. On the other hand, they are typically no more expensive to compute than a shadow map with the same number of depth samples, and they are considerably cheaper to store and access. Note that generating more depth samples is relatively inexpensive in a scanline renderer, since it does not increase the shading cost.

Another potential issue with deep shadows is bias. Because filtering is performed at a constant z depth, large objects may suffer from incorrect self-shadowing. Although this artifact also occurs with normal shadow maps, deep shadows exacerbate the problem because they encourage the use of large filter widths.

However, it is important to realize that the bias problems are no worse than they would be for an ordinary shadow map at the same filter width. The main limitation of deep shadow maps compared to high-resolution ordinary shadow maps is that the minimum filter width is larger (because each deep shadow pixel summarizes many depth samples). However, this can be considered an advantage: It provides deep shadows with an extra degree of freedom to control the tradeoff between shadow detail and noise. The deep shadow resolution should be chosen according to the minimum filter width desired (i.e. shadow detail), while the number of samples per pixel should be determined by the maximum acceptable noise. This strategy allows the depth samples that are required only for accuracy purposes to be represented very compactly, with bias problems that are no worse than they would be for a regular shadow map of the same pixel resolution.

5   Implementation Issues

5.1   Incremental Updates

Recall that each visibility function is defined as the weighted average of n piecewise linear transmittance functions, according to equation (1). The naïve way to generate this function is to sort all of the input vertices and process them in z order, evaluating the n contributing functions at each vertex. Unfortunately this approach has $O(n^2)$ complexity: there are $O(n)$ input vertices, and $O(n)$ work is needed to compute the weighted average at each one. This is quite inefficient when large numbers of samples per pixel are used.

Instead, we describe an $O(n \log n)$ sweep algorithm that has a constant update cost per vertex. The algorithm is easier to understand if we first suppose that the transmittance functions are piecewise constant. In this case, we can efficiently compute the output function as follows. At $z = 0$, the weighted average is easily computed as $V(0) = 1$. We then process all of the input vertices in increasing z order, which can be done in $O(\log n)$ time per vertex by storing the next vertex of each transmittance function in a heap. For every vertex, we update the current sum V by simply subtracting out this transmittance function's old contribution and adding in its new contribution. That is,

$$V' = V + w_j(\tau_j' - \tau_j)$$

where w_j is the filter weight for the chosen transmittance function, τ_j is the old value of this function and τ_j' is its new value.

This method can be extended to piecewise linear functions by using a similar technique to keep track of the output function's current value and slope. The update for each vertex consists of two steps: First, we extend the output function (using its current position and slope) to the z value of the next input vertex, and then we update the current output slope using the method described above. (Vertical steps are handled as a special case, by updating the current position rather than the current slope.)

This technique is much more efficient than computing the weighted averages directly, and makes the algorithm practical even when very large numbers of samples per pixel are used. Note that all of the transmittance functions do not need to be stored simultaneously as the deep shadow map is rendered; it is sufficient to store only the previous several scanlines, as determined by the filter radius.

5.2 Colored Shadows

Colored shadows are supported by simply encoding a different visibility function for each color channel (one each for red, green, and blue). The compression algorithm processes all the channels simultaneously, and starts a new segment whenever any of the three functions would exceed its error threshold. The output is a sequence of tuples (z, V_R, V_G, V_B). Notice that with this representation, three-channel maps are only twice as large as one-channel maps.

To reduce storage even further, our format allows each pixel to encode either one or three visibility functions depending on its needs. If all three channels happen to be the same, we store only one channel and set a flag indicating that this pixel is monochrome.

5.3 Mip-mapping

Since deep shadow maps are filtered like textures, it is straightforward to apply mip-mapping [12]. Starting with the highest-resolution deep shadow map, each new mip-map level is obtained by averaging and downsampling the previous level by a factor of two. Each pixel is defined by taking the average of four visibility functions, and recompressing the result.

To avoid the accumulation of too much error, the compression tolerance can be reduced on each successive level. For example, if the error threshold is cut if half each time, the total error will be at most twice that permitted for the highest-resolution map. This method corresponds to the analysis of Section 4, which suggests that the compression tolerance should be $O(N^{-1/2})$ in the number of contributing depth samples N. The storage per sample increases somewhat at coarser levels, but since the functions being compressed are asymptotically piecewise smooth, their compressed size is $O(N^{1/4})$ (see Section 2). This implies that the number of vertices per visibility function doubles once for every two mip-map levels, and that the full mip-map is approximately $1/(1 - \sqrt{2}/4) \approx 1.55$ times as large as the base level (rather than the $4/3$ ratio for an ordinary mip-map).

Mip-mapped deep shadows are filtered just like mip-mapped textures, including anisotropic filters, lerping between levels, etc. [1].

5.4 Tiling and Caching

We store deep shadow maps in a tiled format, similar to those for textures [8]. This lets us load and cache only the deep shadow map tiles that are actually accessed.

One important difference is that unlike textures, deep shadow map tiles and pixels require varying amounts of storage in memory. To deal with this, our file format includes a *tile directory* that specifies the starting offset and size of every tile. Similarly, each tile has a table indicating the starting position and size of every pixel. Tile caching is handled by providing a fixed number of tile slots; when a tile fault occurs, the slot chosen for replacement is resized if necessary to hold the incoming tile. In this way, each tile slot grows to accommodate the largest tile it has seen. (Optionally the tile slots could also be resized when the incoming tile is significantly smaller.)

5.5 Motion Blur

It is easy to support motion blur in deep shadow maps by simply associating a random time with every shadow image sample (and its corresponding transmittance function). When these samples are averaged together into visibility functions, they account for the average coverage over time as well as over the image plane.

While motion blur is also possible with ordinary shadow maps, it is very expensive because of the large filter widths needed for adequate anti-aliasing. Deep shadow maps do much of this filtering in advance, and thus reduce the number of pixels that need to be accessed for each lookup.

Motion-blurred shadows produced in this way are strictly correct only when the receiving object is stationary with respect to the shadow camera. In particular, moving objects cast incorrect shadows onto other moving objects (and onto themselves). This happens because the deep shadow map effectively blurs an object's shadow over the entire shutter interval, allowing one object to cast shadows onto other objects at a different times. However, even the ability to cast shadows onto stationary objects is useful, and the results are often acceptable even when the receiving object is moving.

6 Results

We have implemented deep shadow maps in a highly optimized scanline renderer that also supports traditional shadow maps. We present experiments comparing these two techniques in terms of time and storage space. We also illustrate two additional capabilities of deep shadows: volumetric shadows and inexpensive motion blur.

Figure 6a shows a ball covered with 50,000 hairs. The individual hairs are significantly narrower than a pixel, and combine to form tufts and curls of various densities. The scene is illuminated by three spotlights, each of which casts shadows.

We have rendered this scene under various conditions to compare the performance of deep shadow maps with traditional shadow maps. Figure 6b shows a magnified view of the shadow cast by the hairball, rendered using a 512×512 normal shadow map. Shadow filtering was done using 16 samples per lookup on a jittered grid; using more samples does not increase the shadow quality due to the coarse resolution of the underlying shadow map. This image has obvious noise artifacts that would be unacceptable if animated. In order to eliminate these artifacts, Figure 6c was rendered using a $4k \times 4k$ shadow map with 400 samples per lookup for percentage closer filtering. The noise artifacts are much improved, but shadow filtering times were much longer (559 seconds *vs.* 19 seconds). Figure 6d was rendered using a 512×512 deep shadow map with 256 samples per pixel (the same number of depth samples as the previous case). Even though the deep shadows were much faster (37 seconds) and required only one-sixth the storage space, the shadow quality is actually slightly better than the $4k \times 4k$ shadow map image (because deep shadows consider every depth sample rather than randomly selecting a subset of them for filtering).

Figure 7 summarizes the results of similar tests at various maximum noise levels. Each row compares a deep shadow map to a normal shadow map with the same number of depth samples; in the deep shadow this was achieved by holding the resolution constant at 256×256 and adjusting the number of samples per pixel (as shown

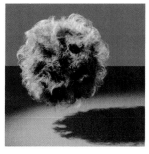
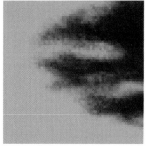

(a) Ball with 50,000 hairs   *(b)* 512×512 *Normal shadow map*   *(c)* $4k \times 4k$ *Normal shadow map*   *(d)* 512×512 *Deep shadow map*

Figure 6: *Hair ball and magnified shadows demonstrating noise from various methods.*

		Time (sec)		Space (MB)	
Samples	*Error*	*Normal*	*Deep*	*Normal*	*Deep*
2×2	25.00 %	34	45	0.34	0.49
4×4	12.50 %	39	46	1.34	0.79
8×8	6.25 %	60	45	5.34	1.18
16×16	3.12 %	145	46	21.34	1.53
32×32	1.56 %	554	46	85.34	1.84
64×64	0.78 %	2414	45	341.34	2.20

Figure 7: *Comparison of deep shadows and normal shadows for the scene in Figure 6. The error column shows the expected error $0.5/\sqrt{N}$ associated with the given sampling density.*

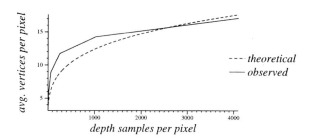

Figure 8: *Theoretical and observed growth rates of deep shadow maps. (The theoretical growth rate of $O(N^{1/4})$ is taken from Section 4.)*

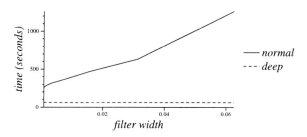

Figure 9: *Filtering time as a function of filter width (expressed as a fraction of the shadow map size). While both methods access a constant number of pixels per lookup, larger filter widths result in worse cache coherence for normal shadow maps and slightly better cache coherence for deep shadow maps.*

in the first column). This column also represents the number of samples used for normal shadow map filtering, chosen to achieve the same accuracy as the deep shadow map at its minimum filter size. The second column shows the corresponding worst-case expected error level of $0.5/\sqrt{N}$; the deep shadows were compressed using an error tolerance of half this amount. All tests used the same absolute filter width, equal to the pixel size of a 256×256 shadow map. The shadow evaluation times were measured by rendering an image using each technique and subtracting the time for an image without shadows.

Observe that normal shadow maps become much more expensive as the error threshold decreases, while the deep shadow map filtering times are virtually constant. Normal shadow maps are only faster at 4×4 and fewer samples, sampling rates that are much too low for use in animations. In our implementation deep shadows have not been as extensively optimized as normal shadow maps, and it is likely that further speed improvements will be found. Shadow generation time was similar for both methods and is not shown; the compression overhead for deep shadows was negligible.

Notice that deep shadow maps grow very slowly in size as the error threshold decreases. The deep shadow sizes do not include mip-map overhead, which would make them approximately 1.5 times larger (see Section 5.3). Figure 8 plots the growth of the deep shadow map size with respect to the number of depth samples per pixel. About 40% of the pixels in this deep shadow map contain hair, while the rest contain simple geometry. Notice that the average number of vertices per compressed visibility function closely matches the $O(N^{1/4})$ behavior predicted in Section 4.

Figure 9 shows how both methods perform when a fixed accuracy is desired, but progressively larger filter widths are applied. In this case the number of filter samples for normal shadow maps can be held fixed. A single shadow map of each type was rendered to support the smallest desired filter size, and the same shadow maps were used to render progressively larger blurs. The filtering time

for the normal shadow map grows rapidly with the amount of blur, even though the number of filter samples was held constant at 8×8. This can be attributed to worse cache performance as the filter region spans larger and larger portions of the shadow map. With the deep shadow map, on the other hand, mip-mapping allows the filtering times to be virtually constant. (In theory the cache performance of deep shadows is actually better at very large filter widths, since the lower-resolution mip-map levels contain fewer pixels.)

Figure 10 illustrates the importance of self-shadowing to the appearance of volumetric objects, while Figure 11 demonstrates that a single deep shadow map can be used for both volumetric and surface shadows. Finally, Figure 12 demonstrates the artifacts that occur when shadows are not motion blurred; this effect appears as strobing when animated. Unlike normal shadow maps, deep shadows allow motion blur to be added without incurring an extra filtering cost.

391

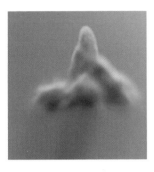

Figure 10: Cloud with and without self-shadowing.

Figure 11: A cloud with pipes. Notice the shadows cast from surfaces onto volumetric objects and vice versa. A single deep shadow map contains the shadow information for the cloud as well as the pipes.

7   Conclusion and Future Work

A nice feature of deep shadow maps is their generality: they support ordinary surfaces, volumetric objects, dense fur, and even motion blur, effects that would normally be handled using different techniques. With deep shadows they can all be combined in a single compact data structure, and rendered efficiently under a wide range of viewing and filtering conditions.

Carrying this idea further, deep shadow maps are an attractive representation for arbitrary volumetric data: fog densities, approximate illumination information, and so on. In this context, a deep shadow map can be viewed as a two-dimensional *function image* of piecewise linear one-dimensional functions. This representation is sparse in z, which allows it to take advantage of any smoothness in the raw data, while it is discrete in x and y (and allows binary search in z) in order to facilitate fast lookups. The domain can easily be mapped to a frustum or an orthographic space, and has the advantage of having an arbitrary extent and resolution in one of its dimensions. Three-dimensional filtering would be an easy extension, since the adjacent data values in z can be found without searching and the representation is sparse in this direction.

Although the function image representation may not achieve quite as much compression as a three-dimensional octree or wavelet expansion, and it is not quite as fast to index as a three-dimensional grid, it is an excellent compromise that retains most of the benefits of both of these extremes. We expect that deep shadow maps and their underlying representation will find other interesting applications in the future.

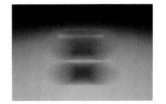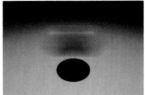

Figure 12: Rapidly moving sphere with and without motion blur.

Acknowledgements

Thanks to Adam Woodbury for modeling the cloud in Figure 10, Christian Hill and Brad Winemiller for production help, and Rob Cook and Matt Pharr for valuable comments on early drafts of the paper.

References

[1] Paul S. Heckbert. Survey of texture mapping. *IEEE Computer Graphics and Applications*, 6(11):56–67, November 1986.

[2] James T. Kajiya and Timothy L. Kay. Rendering fur with three dimensional textures. In *Computer Graphics (SIGGRAPH '89 Proceedings)*, volume 23, pages 271–280, July 1989.

[3] James T. Kajiya and Brian P. Von Herzen. Ray tracing volume densities. In *Computer Graphics (SIGGRAPH '84 Proceedings)*, volume 18, pages 165–174, July 1984.

[4] Brett Keating and Nelson Max. Shadow penumbras for complex objects by depth-dependent filtering of multi-layer depth images. In *Eurographics Rendering Workshop 1999*, pages 205–220, New York, June 1999. Springer-Verlag.

[5] Marc Levoy. *Display of Surfaces from Volume Data*. Ph.D. thesis, University of North Carolina at Chapel Hill, 1989.

[6] Nelson Max. Hierarchical rendering of trees from precomputed multi-layer Z-buffers. In *Eurographics Rendering Workshop 1996*, pages 165–174, New York, June 1996.

[7] Don P. Mitchell. Consequences of stratified sampling in graphics. In *SIGGRAPH 96 Proceedings*, pages 277–280. Addison Wesley, August 1996.

[8] Darwyn R. Peachey. Texture on demand. Unpublished manuscript, 1990.

[9] William T. Reeves, David H. Salesin, and Robert L. Cook. Rendering antialiased shadows with depth maps. In *Computer Graphics (SIGGRAPH '87 Proceedings)*, volume 21, pages 283–291, July 1987.

[10] Jonathan W. Shade, Steven J. Gortler, Li-wei He, and Richard Szeliski. Layered depth images. In *SIGGRAPH 98 Proceedings*, pages 231–242. Addison Wesley, July 1998.

[11] Lance Williams. Casting curved shadows on curved surfaces. *Computer Graphics (SIGGRAPH '78 Proceedings)*, 12(3):270–274, August 1978.

[12] Lance Williams. Pyramidal parametrics. *Computer Graphics (SIGGRAPH '83 Proceedings)*, 17(3):1–11, July 1983.

[13] Andrew Woo, Pierre Poulin, and Alain Fournier. A survey of shadow algorithms. *IEEE Computer Graphics and Applications*, 10(6):13–32, November 1990.

Tangible Interaction + Graphical Interpretation:
A New Approach to 3D Modeling

David Anderson[1], James L. Frankel[1,4], Joe Marks[1],
Aseem Agarwala[1], Paul Beardsley[1], Jessica Hodgins[2], Darren Leigh[1],
Kathy Ryall[3], Eddie Sullivan[1], Jonathan S. Yedidia[1]

[1]MERL—Mitsubishi Electric Research Laboratory   [2]Georgia Institute of Technology
[3]University of Virginia   [4]Frankel and Associates, Inc.

Contact: marks@merl.com

Abstract

Construction toys are a superb medium for creating geometric models. We argue that such toys, suitably instrumented or sensed, could be the inspiration for a new generation of easy-to-use, tangible modeling systems—especially if the tangible modeling is combined with graphical-interpretation techniques for enhancing nascent models automatically. The three key technologies needed to realize this idea are embedded computation, vision-based acquisition, and graphical interpretation. We sample these technologies in the context of two novel modeling systems: physical building blocks that self-describe, interpret, and decorate the structures into which they are assembled; and a system for scanning, interpreting, and animating clay figures.

CR Categories: I.3.6 [Computer Graphics]: Methodology and Techniques—interaction techniques.

Keywords: Applications, Geometric Modeling, Graphics Systems, HCI (Human-Computer Interface), Shape Recognition, User Interface Hardware.

Additional Keywords: Embedded Computation, Tangible User Interfaces, Perceptual User Interfaces, Transmedia.

1 Introduction

Artists using standard 3D modeling packages must specify precisely the geometric and material properties of the models they create, and therein lies much of the complexity and tedium of using those tools. By contrast, children playing with construction toys like Lego™ and K'nex™ make simple models easily, and use their imaginations to fill in the details. We would like to transform computer-based geometric modeling into that same kind of playful, tactile experience but without sacrificing the ability to create the interesting geometric detail and movement that make 3D graphics and animation compelling. To retain the tactile experience of model manipulation, we look to tangible-interface technology; and to create detailed, fully realized models, we use new methods for graphically interpreting a nascent model by recognizing and augmenting its salient features.

This combination of *tangible interaction* and *graphical interpretation* is investigated in a pair of case studies. Tangible modeling can be approached in two ways: either by directly instrumenting the modeling medium with embedded computation or by using external sensors to capture the geometry. Our first system consists of computational building blocks assembled into physical structures that in their aggregate determine and communicate their own geometric arrangement. A rule-based system interprets these structures as buildings, parses their architectural features, then adds geometric detail and decorative enhancements (Figures 1 and 4). Our second system uses simple and robust computer vision to capture volumetric scans of clay models of such common toy-like objects as people, animals, trees, houses, cars, and boats. A volumetric matching algorithm allows us to recognize, interpret, and animate the clay models (Figure 2).

2 Computational Building Blocks

The vision of a tangible 3D geometric modeling system that uses building blocks with embedded computation has been pursued by several groups over the past 20 years. Research on this topic began with the pioneering projects of Aish [1, 2] and of Frazer [15, 16, 12, 14, 13], and was renewed more recently by Dewey and Patera [7, 3].[1]

All of these systems take advantage of the idea that completely and robustly determining the geometry of a tangible model follows naturally if the model is built from rigidly connected building blocks of known size and shape. Recovering 3D geometry is then reduced to the problem of determining the identity and connectivity of the blocks and communicating that information to a host computer. However, these systems differ significantly in the details of their design and implementation. A broad range of solutions have been tried for these fundamental engineering problems:

- *How do blocks connect?* Blocks that can stack only vertically have a low "constructive versatility" relative to, say, Lego™ blocks (a pair of standard 2 × 4 Lego™ blocks can connect in 184 different configurations). Simple, symmetrical connectors are the key to achieving high constructive versatility.

- *How are blocks powered?* Self-powered blocks allow use of simpler connectors but increase the cost, maintenance,

---

[1]The AlgoBlock [31] and Triangles [18, 19] systems are similar in architecture to the tangible modelers cited above. However, their target application is visual/tangible programming, not geometric modeling; and both systems enable the general description of 2D structure only, not 3D.

Two other tangible modeling systems deserve mention. The "Active Lego™ Baseplate Project" at MIT [23] addressed the issue of 3D geometric modeling, but it was only a paper design and was never implemented. The Monkey™ is a posable articulated linkage that is used for keyframing and performance capture [10]; it is a successful product.

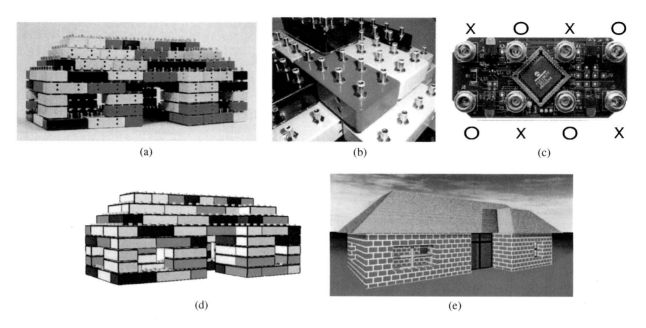

Figure 1: (a) a physical block structure comprising 98 blocks; (b) a close-up of the blocks; (c) a bottom view of the circuit board inside each block; and renderings of the virtual model recovered from the structure, one literal (d) and one interpreted (e). The literal rendering uses associated shapes and colors to render the blocks. The virtual model is augmented automatically for the interpreted rendering.

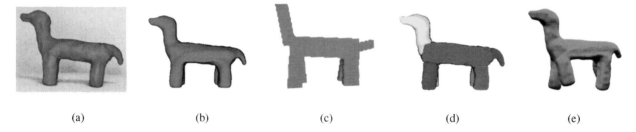

Figure 2: (a) a clay model; (b) its volumetric scan, computed from silhouette information; (c) the best match for it from a small library of object templates; (d) the constituent parts of the interpreted virtual model; and (e) a frame from an automatically generated animation of the virtual model running.

and complexity of the individual blocks. Externally powered blocks require connectors that handle the distribution of power.

- *How do blocks communicate?* The earliest systems used simple electronics to create a circuit-switched network in a block structure. Recent systems have used a microcontroller in each block, and a variety of message-passing architectures for communication.

- *How is geometry computed?* There are two general strategies for computing connectivity, and thereby geometry. At one extreme the connectivity computation can be controlled centrally by the host computer; at the other extreme, it can be organized as a distributed computation among the computing elements in the blocks.

The system we have developed is just one point in a large space spanned by the dimensions of connection, communication, and computation, but it illustrates well the various design and engineering issues involved. Its distinctive characteristics include the following:

- *Very simple physical/electrical connection:* We have based the physical design of our blocks on the popular Lego™ block. Although this choice achieves much greater constructive versatility than any previous system, it comes at the price of extremely simple connectors. Our standard block has eight plugs on the top, and eight jacks on the bottom. The plugs and jacks have only two conductors each, one for power distribution and one for bidirectional signals.

- *Asynchronous, distributed communication:* These simple connectors make it impossible to have a common bus linking all our blocks (in addition to point-to-point connections). The software of many previous systems was simplified by using such a bus for global synchronization and communication. All communication in our block structures is based on asynchronous message passing between physically connected blocks.

- *Parallel, distributed computation of structure:* Our design goal was to build self-describing structures of up to 500 blocks. To complete the distributed computation of structure for a 500-block model in a reasonable time we had to exploit parallelism, which further complicated an already complicated distributed computation.

- *Automatic detailing:* A modeling system that makes it easy to create coarse models will be of limited use if the refinement of the models requires learning a complex user interface such as that found in today's animation and CAD systems. Automatic detailing based on graphical interpretation can make block structures look less blocky and more interesting. As an illustration of what is possible, our system interprets a block structure as a building; it identifies walls, roofs, windows, doors, and other features, and augments them with additional geometric and surface detail in various styles to produce more interesting models.

2.1 System description

For economy and ease of development, we used mostly off-the-shelf components in the construction of our building-block prototypes (Figure 1(b)). A block consists of a 100mm (L) × 50mm (W) × 25mm (H) plastic box that is drilled to accommodate slightly modified DC power connectors. Eight plugs are on top of the block, and eight jacks are on the bottom. The dimensions of the box and the locations of the plugs and jacks are such that our building blocks fit together like Lego™ blocks.

Each connector has just two conductors. However, instead of using one for power and one for ground, we use the inner pin as a signal line for bidirectional communication, and the outer sleeve for power distribution. Each block is wired internally so that connectors with power and ground on their outer sleeves, respectively, are arranged in an alternating pattern, as shown in Figure 1(c). The polarity of the connector sleeves marked 'X' is different from that of the sleeves marked 'O.' Thus each block has at least one connection to power and one to ground in any typical Lego™-block structure, i.e., one in which no block is connected at only one corner or at only diagonally opposite corners. There is no way to tell a priori which connector sleeves have power or ground, but this problem is solved by the use of a full-wave bridge rectifier.

We chose the PIC16F877 microcontroller as the best single-chip solution to the various design problems posed by our application. Its features include: a relatively large number of I/O pins (16 are required for communication, and it has 33); compact size; low-power, high-speed (20 Mhz) CMOS technology; an 8-bit RISC CPU; 8K × 14-bit words of FLASH program memory; 368 × 8-bit bytes of data memory (RAM); 256 × 8-bit bytes of EEPROM data memory; a hardware Universal Synchronous Asynchronous Receiver Transmitter (USART) that we use for debugging; and interrupt handling. The program and data in each block's microcontroller are identical except for a unique ID number.

We left several pads in the periphery of our custom circuit board to accommodate such additional transducers and sensors inside a block as speakers, and proximity and touch detectors. Alternatively, the board can be trimmed to fit inside a 2 × 2 building block without affecting its basic functionality.

2.2 Geometry determination

A fully assembled block structure computes its own geometry in three phases. When a block is powered on, it immediately enters Phase 1 of the geometry-determination algorithm. Lacking a global communication bus, the switching on of electrical power is the only source of synchronization, which is necessarily approximate because of small delays in power propagation throughout a block structure.

All 16 signal lines in a block are normally held high by pull-up resistors. Phase 1 begins with each block pulling its top signal lines (those in the plugs) low. Each block then tests its bottom signal lines (those in the jacks) to determine and record which of them have been pulled low by some other block. After a short delay to ensure that the approximately synchronized blocks do not try

to drive shared signal lines simultaneously in both directions, this test is then repeated with the roles of top and bottom lines reversed. Thus when Phase 1 is complete, each block has identified in parallel which of its lines are *connected*, i.e., are attached to other blocks, but it does not know the identity of these neighboring blocks.

After another short delay, each block enters Phase 2 of the algorithm during which blocks communicate with their neighbors over the connected lines found in Phase 1. At the start of Phase 2, each block listens on its connected bottom lines for transmitted packets that contain the ID of the transmitting block and the number of the connector over which it is transmitting.[2] The receiving block records this information with its own ID number and the number of the connector over which it received the transmission. The combined data form a complete record of a single connection between two blocks. When a block has successfully received a transmission on all of its connected bottom lines, it begins transmitting on its connected top lines, iterating through them in order. Connectivity information, therefore, flows initially through the block structure from bottom to top, with the potential for significant parallel communication.

After a block has completed the first half of Phase 2, it knows to which connector of which block each of its own bottom connectors is attached. During the second half of Phase 2, the procedure is repeated with blocks listening on their top connected lines and transmitting on their bottom connected lines. Thus, at the end of Phase 2, each block has acquired and recorded in its database complete knowledge about all of its connected lines: the IDs of the connected pair of blocks and the connector numbers by which they are attached. Each connected line that is processed successfully in Phase 2 is termed *valid*.

In Phase 3, the connectivity information determined in Phase 2 is communicated to the host computer through the *drain*, a special block that runs slightly different software and has a serial connection to the host computer. In addition to mediating communication between a block structure and the host, the drain also supplies power to the blocks and may be attached to any part of the structure. During Phase 3 all blocks listen for messages on all of their valid lines. When a *request-to-drain* message is received, a block transmits packets containing all of its connectivity information on its *drain connector*, the one from which it received the request-to-drain message. When the block has successfully completed these transmissions, it forwards the request-to-drain message on the first of its valid lines, and enters a message-forwarding mode. If it receives a packet containing connectivity information, it stores and forwards it on its drain connector; if it receives subsequent request-to-drain messages, it responds with an *already-drained* message; when it receives an already-drained or *done* message, it forwards the request-to-drain message on its next valid line or sends a done message on its drain connector when all its valid lines have been processed.

The first request-to-drain message is injected into the structure by the drain, and permission to drain then percolates through the block structure in a preorder traversal of the blocks. Although this traversal is performed sequentially—only one block has permission to drain at any point in time—the forwarding of messages towards the drain is pipelined, thereby achieving some parallelism in this phase as well.

At the end of Phase 3 the host computer should have complete connectivity information for the block structure. (In fact, it should have redundant information because each connectivity datum is reported twice, once by each of the two blocks involved. This re-

---

[2]Transmitted packets may be missed if the receiving microcontroller is busy when transmission commences. Noise may also corrupt a message. Therefore all packets transmitted in Phases 2 and 3 have checksums and are acknowledged, and faulty transmissions are retried after an appropriate timeout.

dundancy contributes to the robustness of the system, but it can be eliminated for greater efficiency.) The host also has shape data for each block, indexed by ID. These data are recorded when a block is programmed. A straightforward recursive procedure ought now to give the 3D structure of the block structure, which can then be used to produce a geometric scene description suitable as input to a variety of common 3D graphics applications. However, occasionally the host does not obtain complete information: due to mechanical stresses in the structure, some connections fail (about 0.5% of them on average) such that their connectivity data are not acquired. Our geometry-recovery procedure therefore determines the most likely block structure given potentially incomplete connectivity data.

The block structure in Figure 1(a) contains 98 blocks. The time required for this structure to compute its own geometry is 35 seconds. The structure in Figure 4(c) contains 560 blocks and requires 53 minutes for geometry determination. Almost all of the time is spent in Phase 3 of the algorithm.

2.3 Graphical interpretation

For a *literal rendering* of the block structure, the host uses associated values for the rendering attributes of each block, such as shape, color, and texture. Figure 1(d) shows a literal rendering of the block structure in Figure 1(a); color and shape values have been chosen to mimic the physical blocks.

Examples of *graphical interpretations* are shown in Figures 1(e) and 4(b) and (d). To produce these enhanced renderings, our system generates a description of a block structure as a set of logical axioms, one to assert the existence and location of each block. These axioms serve as input to a logic program written in Prolog that can identify architectural features of a block structure. For example, the rules in Figure 3 compute which blocks constitute the walls and roof of a structure, interpreted as a building.[3] Recognized structural elements can be decorated with additional geometry and surface detail to enhance the visual appearance of the rendered model.

To validate the ability of the computer to generate interpreted renderings, we handcrafted a few distinct styles that can be applied to block structures automatically. For a fully realized application, we would develop more interactive user interfaces for customizing and applying these interpretive styles. We return to this point in the concluding section of the paper.

3 Clay

Using external sensors to capture geometry is the alternative technology for supporting tangible modeling. For our second case study, we were inspired by the ancient myth of Pygmalion, whose sculpture of a woman was brought to life by Venus [24]. We set ourselves the goal of bringing clay models to life automatically. Although any practical application would divide this task more evenly between user and computer, we tried to fully automate the system in order to explore the limits of the technology, just as we did in our previous case study. In the following subsections we present the details of the hardware and software used to scan, recognize, interpret, and animate 3D clay models.

---

[3]In the early 70's Winston developed a landmark program that could learn about simple architectural structures from positive and negative examples of those structures [33]. However, the robust recognition of the important structural elements in our block models requires hand-crafted rules of much greater complexity than those that could be learned by Winston's approach.

```
% wall/1 finds sets of blocks that form walls. A wall is defined to be
% a contiguous set of blocks that lie flush against some vertical plane,
% and that constitute a given fraction of the structure.
wall(WALL_BLOCKS) :-
    structure_bbox(X_MIN, X_MAX, _, _, Z_MIN, Z_MAX),
    candidate_planes(X_MIN, X_MAX, Z_MIN, Z_MAX, U, V, W, R),
    lies_flush_against(U, V, W, R, PLANE_BLOCKS),
    contiguous_subsets(PLANE_BLOCKS, PLANE_BLOCKS_SUBSETS),
    member(WALL_BLOCKS, PLANE_BLOCKS_SUBSETS),
    big_enough(WALL_BLOCKS).

% wall_tops/1 finds the blocks that are the tops of walls.
wall_tops(WALL_TOPS) :-
    setof(BLOCK,
        WALL_BLOCKS ^
            (wall(WALL_BLOCKS),
             member(BLOCK, WALL_BLOCKS),
             not_overhung(BLOCK, WALL_BLOCKS)),
        WALL_TOPS).

% roof_blocks/1 computes the set of blocks make up the roof, which is
% defined to be those blocks that rest directly or indirectly on the tops of
% walls. The indirectly resting blocks are computed by grow_roof/2.
roof_blocks(ROOF_BLOCKS) :-
    findall(BLOCK1,
        (wall_tops(WT_BLOCKS),
         member(WT_BLOCK, WT_BLOCKS),
         on_top_of(BLOCK1, WT_BLOCK)),
        BASE_BLOCKS_BAG),
    setof(BLOCK2,
        member(BLOCK2, BASE_BLOCKS_BAG),
        BASE_BLOCKS),
    grow_roof(BASE_BLOCKS, ROOF_BLOCKS).

grow_roof(NASCENT_ROOF_BLOCKS, FINAL_ROOF_BLOCKS) :-
    member(BLOCK1, NASCENT_ROOF_BLOCKS),
    on_top_of(BLOCK2, BLOCK1),
    not member(BLOCK2, NASCENT_ROOF_BLOCKS),
    grow_roof([BLOCK2 | NASCENT_ROOF_BLOCKS], FINAL_ROOF_BLOCKS),
    !.

grow_roof(ROOF_BLOCKS, ROOF_BLOCKS).
```

Figure 3: Recognizing the structural elements of a block structure by logic programming.

3.1 System description and geometry determination

Our scanning system consists of a motorized rotary table, a consumer-quality digital camera, a laser striper (optional), and a host computer (Figure 5). The camera is calibrated from an image of an object of known dimensions. The clay model to be scanned is placed upright and face forward on the rotary table. (It is convenient for the matching process to have models placed in a known orientation. Inferring orientation automatically is certainly feasible but seems unnecessary for modeling applications that involve cooperative users.) The camera captures an image sequence of the model as it rotates, and a volumetric scan is generated from silhouettes [4]. This approach worked well on the majority of models we scanned, but when significant concavities were present (e.g., the door and windows of the house in Figure 8), the laser striper could be used to refine the shape of the model.[4] The use of silhouettes and laser striping is well suited to our smooth-surfaced, single-color clay models; however, systems that rely on surface-color variation [29] or uncalibrated systems that require a significant number

---

[4]Affordable 3D scanning systems that operate on the same principles as our laboratory system are now available commercially from Geometrix, Sanyo, and others.

(a)   (b)

(c)   (d)

Figure 4: (a) a model of a castle comprising 118 blocks, and (b) an interpreted rendering of it. The automatic enhancements in this graphical interpretation include the addition of turrets, roofs, windows, archways, a portcullis, and a flagpole in appropriate locations, as well as the selection of suitable surface properties and features for all the geometry. The 560-block model in (c)—a 12-inch ruler is included to show scale—was built as a challenging virtual environment for Quake II, the data format for which is another output option in our system. Applying the same interpretive style to this larger model to get the rendering in (d) requires changing only one numerical parameter indicative of building scale: it specifies the smallest number of blocks in the structure that can constitute a distinct architectural feature.

of point matches between surface features to be visible in the image sequence [11, 22] would likely encounter difficulty.

3.2 Graphical interpretation

The technical novelty in our system lies in our approach to model recognition and interpretation, both of which are accomplished by comparing a set of parameterized object templates to a scanned clay model. The templates are deformed to match the model, and the matching score determines how the model is classified.[5]

---

[5]Brooks' ACRONYM system [5] is an early example of the use of parameterized models (generalized cylinders) for object recognition. Solina et al. [30] describe how to recover parametric models (superquadrics with global deformations) from range data by minimizing surface distances, which is similar to our maximization of volumetric overlap. Surveys of

The templates are articulated linkages in which the links are truncated rectangular pyramids, or *beams*. A beam is completely defined by 10 numbers that specify the positions and dimensions of two parallel *base* rectangles. By requiring that the bases always be orthogonal to some major axis, a beam can be efficiently rasterized in three dimensions, which is important for the efficiency of the matching algorithm described below. A linkage is formed by connecting beams at the corners or centers of any of their six faces. Figure 6 shows representative templates for the 13 object categories currently recognized by our system. For each category there are 10 actual templates, created by hand, that differ only in the relative

---

other related work on shape recovery and object recognition from image and range data can be found in more recent papers, e.g., [8, 9]. Finally, an application closely related to ours, shape-based indexing and retrieval of mechanical objects, is discussed in [6].

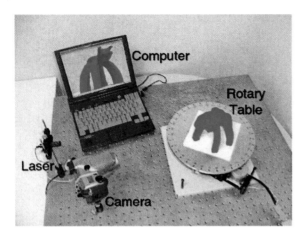

Figure 5: A low-cost scanning system.

proportions and orientations of their constituent beams: they provide multiple starting points for the matching algorithm, thereby reducing its chance of being confounded by matches that are locally optimal but globally inferior. A complete set of templates for a single category is shown in Figure 7.

Each biped template comprises six beams. Hence there would seem to be $6 \times 10 = 60$ parameters available for deforming a template. However, many of the parameters are constrained relative to each other. Some of these constraints derive implicitly from the enforced connectedness of beams in an articulated linkage. Others are the result of explicit programmer-specified constraints that apply to beam-size parameters, e.g., a constraint that the dimensions of the base rectangles for both arm beams be the same. When these constraints are applied, the number of free parameters for a biped template reduces to a more manageable 25. By modifying these parameters the computer can attempt to deform a template to best match a given clay model.

Quantifying the notion of a best match in an objective function is the essential problem in this optimization-based approach. Our objective function has terms for the following characteristics of a voxel-based match:

- *Superposition:* Each voxel occupied by both the rasterized object template and the scanned clay model contributes +1 to the objective-function score.

- *Excess:* This term penalizes voxels occupied by the rasterized template but not by the clay model. A simple approach would be to add a score of -1 for each such voxel. A much better idea is to add a score of $-r$, where r is the distance to the nearest occupied voxel in the clay model. This value can be computed for each voxel by an efficient two-pass algorithm [28]. The advantage of this distance-based penalty is that its gradient still gives useful information even when there is minimal overlap between the template and clay model.

- *Deformation:* Without some penalty for excessive deformation, templates can sometimes achieve excellent superposition and excess scores through absurd contortions. Deformation beyond a certain threshold is therefore penalized by an exponential function of the distance between the original and current parameter vectors.

Dividing the superposition and excess terms by the number of occupied voxels in the scanned volume normalizes for the volume of the clay model; dividing the deformation term by the number of beam vertices normalizes for the complexity of the object template.

Given this objective function, the matching algorithm is straightforward. First, the object template is adjusted for fit: the template is scaled in all three dimensions so that the beam endpoints lie just within the bounding box of the scanned model. (There is no need to normalize for orientation because we assume that scanned models have been placed upright and facing forward.) Matching is then just a matter of gradient descent using the negative of the objective function above. We use the conjugate-gradient method of gradient descent [26], approximating partial derivatives of the objective function by central differences. For best results we run the gradient-descent algorithm to quiescence three times in succession: first, we vary only the location parameters of the object template, then only the size parameters, and finally the location parameters again. We also schedule the relative weights of the objective-function terms over the three runs; the superposition and excess terms decrease in significance, and the deformation term increases. Good values for the weights were determined empirically for a small subset of the clay models, and then applied uniformly to all the models in our experiments. Matching is performed against a total of 130 object templates, 10 from each of the 13 categories shown in Figure 6.

Figure 8 shows the 16 clay models on which we tested our system. Each model is from one of the 13 object categories listed in Figure 6, with some duplication. These categories were based on the objects that figured most often in an informal survey of children's drawings. The artists who created the models worked independently of the programmer who fashioned the object templates, so that sometimes there are significant differences in the artists' and programmer's conceptions of a modeled object, e.g., compare the clay model of the Insect in Figure 8 with the corresponding object template in Figure 6. Each volumetric scan of a clay model was computed from 180 images, taken a uniform 2° apart. An additional 180 images were taken with the laser stripe on, though this additional data improved the scan significantly for only one of the reported models (the indented windows and door of the house were found). The scanned volumes were subsampled to a resolution of $128 \times 128 \times 128$ voxels for the purposes of matching.

Table 1 lists the top two matches for each clay model; Figure 9 illustrates the best matches graphically. Matching a single clay model against all 130 object templates took an average of 85 minutes on a 200 MHz Pentium Pro PC, and required rasterizing about 100,000 object templates; the bulk of the time was spent in the rasterization step. The top match was correct for 14 of the 16 clay models.

An examination of the two matching errors was instructive. Although the Insect template deformed to cover the Insect model almost perfectly, the degree of deformation was sufficient to result in the Quadruped and Chair templates receiving better matching scores. Reducing the deformation penalty would cause the Insect template to match best, but would also cause many incorrect best matches for the other clay models. The failure of the Car template to be the best match for the Car #1 model is due to a limitation of our modeling language for articulated linkages: one beam can attach to another only at the four corners or center of one of its faces. The offset of Car #1's wheels are such that the Car template cannot deform to cover them very well with its wheel beams constrained to attach as they do.

When the best-matching template has been found for a given clay model, an interpretation step parses the model into its constituent parts. For example, if a model is recognized as a biped, the match between the clay model and the deformed biped template is used to identify the model voxels that constitute the head, arms, legs, and torso. This voxel classification is based on the shortest distance from each voxel to each beam through clay-occupied space. Voxels are then assigned to their closest beams, with ties broken by distance to the beams' center axes. Once the best match is known, parsing takes about a minute. The 14 correctly matched models were all parsed acceptably well. Sample parses are shown

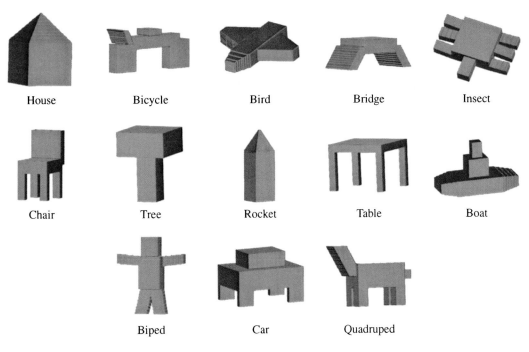

Figure 6: Representative templates from 13 categories of toy-like objects.

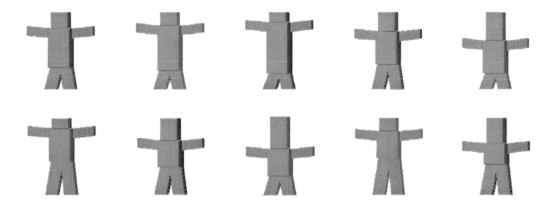

Figure 7: The 10 templates for the Biped category.

in Figure 2(d) and Figure 10.

With this information we can bring a clay model to (virtual) life. We did this automatically for the quadruped shown in Figure 2. The body measurements, masses, and moments of inertia were computed from the parse of the clay model. These values were passed as input to a control and simulation system for a four-legged robot, which adapted an existing control system to the dynamics of this particular clay model [20, 27]. The motion data computed by the simulation were then used to animate the object template, which in turn was used to animate the scanned volume by moving its voxels in rough concert with the beams of the template to which they were assigned in the parsing phase. However, care must be taken to avoid the introduction of tears and cracks in the model as it deforms. Such unwanted artifacts will appear if each voxel maintains position relative to just its associated beam. It is better to have all beams influence the movement of a voxel in inverse proportion to the square of their distance from the voxel; this reduces tears at the junctions of different model regions. (See Figure 2 and the companion videotape.) Related work on animating volumetric objects is described in [17].

An alternative and more general way to bring these models to life is with keyframes specified by the user. Commercial animation packages are notoriously complex because of the large number of features that must be provided. However, these clay models have been parsed by the computer and, therefore, the internal skeletal structure and kinematics are already known. The skeleton should allow the construction of an intuitive animation interface for this specific character. The user need only specify the motion of the skeleton because the internal details of the motion of the clay can be computed automatically using heuristic algorithms as was done for the quadruped or a more general physical simulation of clay [32]. Examples of this approach are shown on the companion video.

4 Conclusions and future work

In our case studies we have investigated the combination of tangible modeling and graphical interpretation. Tangible modeling

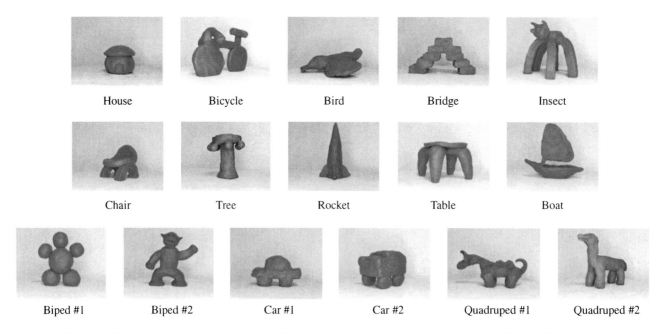

Figure 8: Examples from the image sequences for the 16 clay models captured by the camera illustrated in Figure 5.

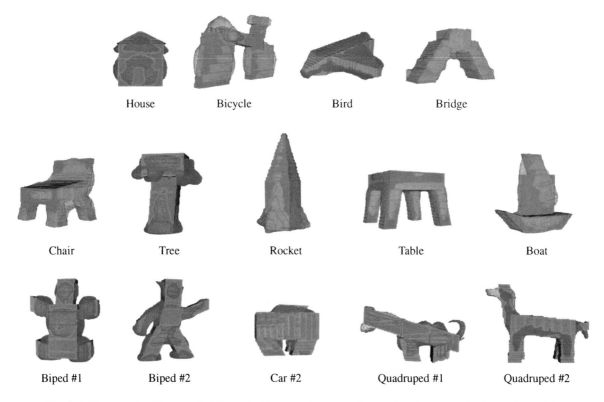

Figure 9: Best matches illustrated: deformed object templates superimposed on the scanned volumetric models.

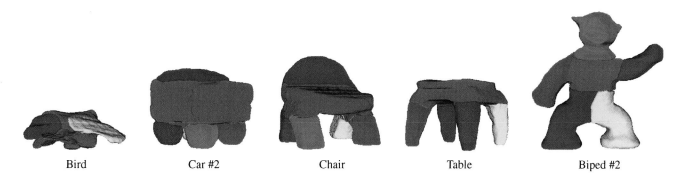

Bird   Car #2   Chair   Table   Biped #2

Figure 10: Sample parses of five clay models. The colored regions correspond to specific beams in the corresponding best-matching object template.

Clay Models	Object Templates Ranked by Score	
	First	Second
House	House(105)	Car(77)
Bicycle	Bicycle(87)	Boat(47)
Bird	Bird(79)	Insect(76)
Bridge	Bridge(115)	Insect(104)
Insect	*Q'ped(54)*	*Chair(50)*
Chair	Chair(78)	Bird(56)
Tree	Tree(82)	Biped(71)
Rocket	Rocket(89)	Q'ped(87)
Table	Table(107)	Car(102)
Boat	Boat(92)	Bicycle(31)
Biped #1	Biped(82)	Q'ped(67)
Biped #2	Biped(98)	Q'ped(76)
Car #1	*Boat(105)*	*Car(80)*
Car #2	Car(115)	Chair(92)
Q'ped #1	Q'ped(86)	Insect(55)
Q'ped #2	Q'ped(113)	Bicycle(71)

Table 1: The best-matching object templates for all the clay models, along with the matching scores. Of the 16 models, 14 were matched correctly; the entries for the two erroneous matches are shown in italics.

makes it easy for the user to create simple geometry quickly; the computer performs the tedious detailing tasks via graphical interpretation. Combined, these two ideas make for a new, more accessible approach to 3D modeling. As with recent sketch-based systems [34, 21], some generality is sacrificed in return for dramatically simpler interfaces that are accessible to unskilled and untrained users.

However, the modeling systems we have developed are only research prototypes. To make a truly useful and affordable system, more investigation is required. Our current work and future plans include:

- *Alternative architectures for embedded computation:* The most significant practical problem with our computational building blocks is that of power supply: the 560-block model in Figure 4(c) required a peak current of 8 amps at 13.8 volts to determine its geometry and to illustrate algorithmic progress via the blocks' LEDs. To reduce the power requirements (and thereby the cost) of the blocks, we are looking at ways of capturing a block structure using only a bare minimum of active components in each block. We are also considering the design of embedded computation architectures that make use of a broadcast medium. And to realize

a more interactive experience, we are exploring hardware and software modifications that allow for interactive, incremental adjustment of the physical models.

- *Applications ancillary to geometric modeling:* We have built blocks with LEDs, speakers, switches, and motion sensors that support "world-in-miniature" interaction metaphors for virtual environments in which our miniature worlds are physical rather than virtual [25]. We are also exploring game applications that make use of these same sensors and actuators.

- *Interactive embodiments of graphical interpretation:* In our case studies, we focused on fully automatic graphical interpretation with the goal of understanding the limits of such an approach. We plan to study semi-automatic systems in which the computer plays a more assistive role. For example, it would be straightforward for our interpretation systems to prompt the user for help with ambiguous interpretations (e.g., "Is this part of the wall or roof?" or "Is this a quadruped or a chair?") or with a choice of enhancement (e.g., "Do you want a portcullis or a drawbridge here?" or "Do you want the quadruped to run or gallop?"). This kind of user input would do much to address problems of brittleness and speed in our prototypes.

More interestingly, we could develop mixed-initiative systems that make more use of the fully automatic algorithms we have developed. For example, a mixed-initiative system might begin by prompting the user for all stylistic and aesthetic choices, but then begin making suggestions that are consistent with the user's previous selections. Our case studies show that these kinds of systems can be built, and hold promise to enable a new paradigm of computer-assisted graphical-interpretation applications.

5 Acknowledgments

Special thanks to Christopher Marks, whose playful blending of the real and virtual inspired this work. We also want to thank Emily Anderson, Lynn Anderson, Bob Bell, Dirk Brinkman, Audrey Hodgins, Clifton Leigh, Neil McKenzie, Egon Pasztor, Hanspeter Pfister, Rusty Ventura, Dick Waters, Jonathan Wolff, and Bill Yerazunis for their last-minute help, encouragement, and advice, and Altec Plastics, Flextronics, and Switchcraft for satisfying our unusual requirements. And thanks to the anonymous SIGGRAPH reviewers for helpful suggestions and comments.

References

[1] R. Aish. 3D input for CAAD systems. *Computer-Aided Design*, 11(2):66–70, Mar. 1979.

[2] R. Aish and P. Noakes. Architecture without numbers – CAAD based on a 3D modelling system. *Computer-Aided Design*, 16(6):321–328, Nov. 1984.

[3] G. Anagnostou, D. Dewey, and A. Patera. Geometry-defining processors for engineering design and analysis. *The Visual Computer*, 5:304–315, 1989.

[4] B. G. Baumgart. Geometric modeling for computer vision. Technical Report AIM-249, AI Laboratory, Stanford Univ., Oct. 1974.

[5] R. Brooks. Model-based 3D interpretations of 2D images. *IEEE Trans. on Pattern Analysis and Machine Intelligence*, 5(2):140–150, 1983.

[6] G. Cybenko, A. Bhasin, and K. D. Cohen. Pattern recognition of 3D CAD objects: Towards an electronic Yellow Pages of mechanical parts. *Smart Engineering Systems Design*, 1:1–13, 1997.

[7] D. Dewey and A. Patera. Geometry-defining processors for partial differential equations. In B. Alder, editor, *Special Purpose Computers*, pages 67–96. Academic Press, 1988.

[8] S. Dickinson, A. Pentland, and A. Rosenfeld. From volumes to views: An approach to 3D object recognition. *Computer Vision, Graphics, and Image Processing: Image Understanding*, 55(2):130–154, 1992.

[9] S. J. Dickinson and D. Metaxas. Integrating qualitative and quantitative shape recovery. *Intl. Journal of Computer Vision*, 13(3):311–330, 1994.

[10] C. Esposito, W. B. Paley, and J. Ong. Of mice and monkeys: A specialized input device for virtual body animation. In *Proc. of Symposium on Interactive 3D Graphics*, pages 109–114, 213, Monterey, California, Apr. 1995.

[11] A. W. Fitzgibbon, G. Cross, and A. Zisserman. Automatic 3D model construction for turn-table sequences. In *Proc. of SMILE Workshop*, Freiburg, Germany, June 1998.

[12] J. Frazer. Use of simplified three-dimensional computer input devices to encourage public participation in design. In *Proc. of Computer Aided Design 82*, pages 143–151. Butterworth Scientific, 1982.

[13] J. Frazer. *An Evolutionary Architecture*. Architectural Association, London, 1994. Describes several tangible modelers developed by Frazer's group from 1979 onwards.

[14] J. Frazer, P. Coates, and J. Frazer. Software and hardware approaches to improving the man-machine interface. In *Proc. of the First International IFIP Conf. on Computer Applications in Production and Engineering*, pages 1083–94, Amsterdam, Holland, 1983. North Holland.

[15] J. Frazer, J. Frazer, and P. Frazer. Intelligent physical three-dimensional modelling system. In *Proc. of Computer Graphics 80*, pages 359–370. Online Publications, 1980.

[16] J. Frazer, J. Frazer, and P. Frazer. New developments in intelligent modelling. In *Proc. of Computer Graphics 81*, pages 139–154. Online Publications, 1981.

[17] N. Gagvani, D. Kenchammana-HoseKote, and D. Silver. Volume animation using the skeleton tree. In *Proc. of the IEEE Symposium on Volume Visualization*, pages 47–53, Research Triangle Park, NC, Oct. 1998.

[18] M. G. Gorbet and M. Orth. Triangles: Design of a physical/digital construction kit. In *Proc. of DIS 97*, pages 125–128, Amsterdam, Holland, Mar. 1997. ACM.

[19] M. G. Gorbet, M. Orth, and H. Ishii. Triangles: Tangible interface for manipulation and exploration of digital information topography. In *Proc. of CHI 98*, pages 49–56, Los Angeles, California, Apr. 1998. ACM.

[20] J. K. Hodgins and N. S. Pollard. Adapting simulated behaviors for new characters. In *Proc. of SIGGRAPH 97*, pages 153–162, Los Angeles, California, Aug. 1997.

[21] T. Igarashi, S. Matsuoka, and H. Tanaka. Teddy: A sketching interface for 3D freeform design. In *Proc. of SIGGRAPH 99*, pages 409–416, Los Angeles, California, Aug. 1999.

[22] S. B. Kang. Quasi-euclidean recovery from unknown but complete orbital motion. Technical Report TR 97-10, Compaq CRL, 1997.

[23] F. Martin and R. Borovoy. The active LEGO baseplate project. http://fredm.www.media.mit.edu/people/fredm/projects/ab/, 1994.

[24] Ovid. Metamorphoses:X. Rome, 1 AD.

[25] R. Pausch, T. Burnette, D. Brockway, and M. E. Weiblen. Navigation and locomotion in virtual worlds via flight into hand-held miniatures. In *Proc. of SIGGRAPH 95*, pages 399–400, Los Angeles, California, Aug. 1995.

[26] W. H. Press, B. P. Flannery, S. A. Teukolsky, and W. T. Vetterling. *Numerical Recipes in C*. Cambridge University Press, 1988.

[27] M. H. Raibert. *Legged Robots That Balance*. MIT Press, Cambridge, 1986.

[28] J. C. Russ. *The Image Processing Handbook*. CRC Press, 1998.

[29] S. M. Seitz and C. R. Dyer. Photorealistic scene reconstruction by voxel coloring. *International Journal of Computer Vision*, 35(2):151–173, 1999.

[30] F. Solina and R. Bajcsy. Recovery of parametric models from range images: The case for superquadrics with global deformations. *IEEE Trans. on Pattern Analysis and Machine Intelligence*, 12(2):131–146, 1990.

[31] H. Suzuki and H. Kato. AlgoBlock: A tangible programming language — a tool for collaborative learning. In *Proc. of the 4th European Logo Conference*, pages 297–303, 1993.

[32] D. Terzopoulos and K. Fleischer. Deformable models. *The Visual Computer*, 4(6):306–331, December 1988.

[33] P. H. Winston. Learning structural descriptions from examples. In P. H. Winston, editor, *The Psychology of Computer Vision*. McGraw-Hill, New York, 1975.

[34] R. C. Zeleznik, K. Herndon, and J. F. Hughes. SKETCH: An interface for sketching 3D scenes. In *Proc. of SIGGRAPH 96*, pages 163–170, New Orleans, Louisiana, Aug. 1996.

Accessible Animation and Customizable Graphics via Simplicial Configuration Modeling

Tom Ngo,* Doug Cutrell,† Jenny Dana, Bruce Donald,‡ Lorie Loeb,§ and Shunhui Zhu#

Interval Research Corporation, 1801 Page Mill Rd., Palo Alto, CA 94304-1216

{ngo,jdana}@interval.com

Abstract

Our goal is to embed free-form constraints into a graphical model. With such constraints a graphic can maintain its visual integrity—and break rules tastefully—while being manipulated by a casual user. A typical parameterized graphic does not meet these needs because its configuration space contains nonsense images in much higher proportion than desirable images, and the casual user is apt to ruin the graphic on any attempt to modify or animate it.

We therefore model the small subset of a given graphic's configuration space that maps to desirable images. In our solution, the basic building block is a simplicial complex—the most practical data structure able to accommodate the variety of topologies that can arise. The configuration-space model can be built from a cross product of such complexes. We describe how to define the mapping from this space to the image space. We show how to invert that mapping, allowing the user to manipulate the image without understanding the structure of the configuration-space model. We also show how to extend the mapping when the original parameterization contains hierarchy, coordinate transformations, and other nonlinearities.

Our software implementation applies simplicial configuration modeling to 2D vector graphics.

CR Categories and Subject Descriptors: I.3.6 [Computer Graphics]: Methodology and Techniques – Graphics Data Structures and Data Types, Interaction Techniques; I.3.8 [Computer Graphics]: Applications.

Keywords: Animation with constraints, geometric modeling, weird math, WWW applications

---

* Corresponding author.
† Present address: NetLens, 10975 N. Wolfe Rd., Cupertino, CA 95014, doug@netlens.com.
‡ Present address: Dartmouth Computer Science Dept., 6211 Sudikoff Lab., Rm. 113, Hanover, NH 03755, brd@cs.dartmouth.edu.
§ Present address: Stanford Computer Science Dept., Stanford, CA 94304, lorie@graphics.stanford.edu.
# Present address: Integral Development Corp., 156 University Ave., Palo Alto, CA 94301, shunhui.zhu@integral.com.

1 Introduction

1.1 Goal

Constraints often provide coherence and creative freedom. That principle has been exploited pervasively in computer graphics since the days of Ivan Sutherland's Sketchpad system [18], in forms ranging from user-specified constraints such as those found in CAD systems [3] and dataflow systems [9] to constraint-inference engines [10] Even bitmap-based tools such as Painter [14] empower the user's creativity by constraining the modifications she can make to an image.

We are interested in how to re-parameterize graphical models so that they are constrained enough to hold their visual form when modified or animated by a casual user. Target applications include creativity software, dynamic clip art, cartoons, performance-based avatars, and charts. Most existing parameterized representations (e.g., 2D vector graphics, NURBS surfaces, and CSG) are not constraining enough to meet our requirements. Consider the spline-based example in Figure 1. In that diagram, the blue cube represents the configuration space of the spline. Each configuration is a set of numerical values for the parameters of the spline (the coordinates of its control points). Most configurations correspond to meaningless scribbles. A rare few generate humanoid shapes.

Our task, then, is *configuration modeling*: representing a subset of the configuration space of an existing parameterized graphic. Because this subset can have arbitrarily topology, our modeling scheme must not impose any a priori restrictions on topology. Moreover, the resulting re-parameterization might not map in any convenient way to a user's "mental parameterization." We therefore seek to shield the user from knowing the structure of the parameterization by allowing for direct manipulation of the graphical object. We refer to such direct manipulation as *tugging*.

Configuration modeling is a fundamental open problem in computer graphics; the need to represent a subset of a graphical object's configuration space is pervasive.[1] Although our test implementation is designed for 2D spline-based graphics, we expect simplicial configuration modeling to be applicable to other forms of parameterized graphics, including morphs, physically based models, and so forth.

1.2 Structure of paper

Section 2 describes a configuration-modeling pipeline in a qualitative way. Quantitative and other algorithmic details are deferred for the appendices. Section 3 discusses how the re-parameterization used in configuration modeling can be used in concert with domain-specific techniques, primarily to incorporate hierarchy. Section 4 describes selected pieces of

---

[1] The technique might also be applied to objects that are not graphical, such as parameterized sounds.

content made using our authoring system. Section 5 compares our technique with related work, employing the modeling abstractions introduced in earlier sections. Section 6 recapitulates our main contributions and lists avenues of future work.

2 Qualitative description

2.1 Configuration-modeling pipeline

Any configuration-modeling technique can be described in terms of the modeling pipeline depicted in Figure 2. The rightmost component in that pipeline, the *image space*, represents the space of all possible images that can be rendered on the display device. The middle component, the *configuration space*, represents the freedom in the given parameterized image: a configuration is a set of parameter values, one for each parameter. Its dimensions are therefore called *configuration parameters*, or simply *parameters*.

The mapping from the configuration space to the image space is the *rendering map*. It determines how the parameter values in a configuration are interpreted to generate an image on the display device; thus, it subsumes all processes normally associated with modeling, rendering, and display. Together, these two spaces and the intervening map define a parameterized graphic—an object whose re-parameterization is the goal of our work.

The leftmost component of the pipeline is the *state space*. The mapping from it to the configuration space is the *re-parameterization map*. The goal in configuration modeling is to define a state space and re-parameterization map so that the range of the map is a set of desirable configurations.

Thus, a state determines[2] a configuration under the re-parameterization map, and a configuration determines an image under the rendering map. Most computer graphics research, including work on modeling, rendering, and display, is concerned with the rendering map. This paper describes an approach to defining the re-parameterization map.

2.2 Nature of the configuration parameters

As we have described it, configuration-modeling tasks usually involve continuous configuration parameters: geometry (e.g., 2D or 3D coordinates of control points or lengths of line segments), colors, and even physical parameters such as forces and masses in a relaxed mesh. In most such cases, it is appropriate to define a re-parameterization map that is a function.

A significant twist on configuration modeling can arise when continuous configuration parameters represent coordinate transformations. Consider a gedanken experiment in which the original parameterized image is a closed 2D spline. The goal in this experiment is to build a configuration model that represents a complete human walk cycle in profile, a complete crawl cycle, and any gait between walking and crawling. The state space is isomorphic to a square: one dimension represents progress in the gait cycle; the other, interpolation between walking and crawling. Assuming that a walk cycle covers more horizontal distance than a crawl cycle, the path through the state space depicted in Figure 3 produces a net horizontal translation. Thus, the addition of a

global horizontal translation is required to avoid representing configurations that differ from each other only by translation. Moreover, the horizontal-translation variable is not a function of state: it experiences hysteresis.

When a discrete parameter is present, one can arrange for the re-parameterization map to map patches of the state space to values of the discrete parameter.

2.3 Structure of the state space

In our solution, the state space is represented by a data structure that is topologically general and computationally practical: the simplicial complex [15]. For convenience in expressing certain common relationships, we allow for a cross product of simplicial complexes.

Combinatorially, a *simplicial complex* S can be specified[3] by a set V of symbols, and subsets of V chosen so that none is a subset of any other. Each of those subsets is called a *simplex*: a point, a line segment, a triangle, a tetrahedron, or a higher-order simplex, depending on the number of symbols in the subset. The standard embedding of that combinatorial object is then the subset Λ of R^V such that every λ in Λ lies in a simplex.[4] A vector λ lies in a simplex s if each of its coordinates lies in the unit interval [0,1], the coordinates sum to unity, and all coordinates corresponding to symbols outside the simplex are zero. The coordinates corresponding to symbols inside the simplex are called *barycentric coordinates*. We use the combinatorial representation of a simplex as shorthand for its standard embedding.

Suppose, for example, that the simplicial complex S_1 comprises the set of symbols $\{o,p,q,r\}$ and simplices $\{\{o,p,q\},\{q,r\}\}$. It consists of a triangle $\{o,p,q\}$ and a line segment $\{q,r\}$. Using the symbol ordering (o,p,q,r), the points $(^3/_4,^1/_8,^1/_8,0)$ and $(0,0,^1/_3,^2/_3)$ both lie in the standard embedding of this simplicial complex because $(^3/_4,^1/_8,^1/_8)$ lies in $\{o,p,q\}$, and so forth. Thus, a simplicial complex can be used as a data structure for generating interpolation weights; the simplices restrict certain groups of weights from being simultaneously non-zero.

We define the state space Ψ to be a cross product of k simplicial complexes: $\Psi=S_1 \times S_2 \times \ldots \times S_k$. We use the term *state* to denote an element of the state space. Thus, a state ψ lies in the state space Ψ if it can be expressed as a tuple $(\lambda_1;\lambda_2;\ldots;\lambda_k)$ such that each λ_i lies in the corresponding simplicial complex S_i. We use the term *vertex* to refer to a "corner" of the state space, i.e., a state $\psi=(\lambda_1;\lambda_2;\ldots;\lambda_k)$ in which each λ_i has exactly one coordinate equal to 1.

Suppose, for example, that a state space is equal to $S_1 \times S_2$, where S_1 is as defined above, and S_2 comprises the set of symbols $\{u,v,w\}$ and the simplices $\{\{u,v\},\{v,w\}\}$. Using the symbol ordering $(o,p,q,r; u,v,w)$, the points $(^1/_4,^1/_2,^1/_4,0; ^3/_7,^4/_7,0)$ and $(0,0,1,0; 0,1,0)$ both lie in the state space. The latter is a vertex.

We use the term *zone* to refer to a linear region of the state space,

---

[2] We will later introduce hysteresis into the re-parameterization map, so the word "determine" is used loosely.

[3] Only top-level simplices—simplices that are not sub-faces of other simplices—are specified by the user and explicitly represented in the implementation.

[4] The notation R^V denotes a Euclidean space whose $|V|$ dimensions are named according to the symbols in V.

i.e., a tuple of simplices, with one simplex taken from each factor in the cross product of simplicial complexes. Thus, the state space $S_1 \times S_2$ contains four zones.

2.4   Re-parameterization map

We use re-parameterization maps of various levels of complexity, depending on the nature of the configuration parameters. In its simplest form, a re-parameterization map on a k-factor state space is specified by an arbitrary configuration for each vertex in the state space, and is k-linear within each zone (linear within each factor simplex). Thus, a re-parameterization map for the state space $S_1 \times S_2$ would be specified by twelve independent configurations: one for each symbol pair in the cross product $\{o,p,q,r\} \times \{u,v,w\}$. Configurations admitted by the map would be of the form

$$x' = \Sigma_{a \in \{o,p,q,r\}} \Sigma_{b \in \{u,v,w\}} \lambda_1[a] \, \lambda_2[b] \, x[a][b]$$

where square brackets denote indexing by the symbols in the set $\{o,p,q,r\} \cup \{u,v,w\}$, $x[a][b]$ denotes the configuration associated with symbols a and b, and the state $\psi = (\lambda_1; \lambda_2)$ lies in the state space $S_1 \times S_2$. In our current software implementation, those twelve configurations are supplied by an artist with a drawing tool. In other systems they might be automatically generated.

A re-parameterization map can also take more complicated forms if the configuration space contains some discrete parameters, or some parameters control coordinate transformations.

In the case of a discrete parameter, one can tessellate the state space into regions, each of which maps to a different value of the parameter. We have implemented a form of such a discrete map in which the regions are zones and the discrete parameter controlled the front-to-back permutation ordering of the primitives in a 2D vector graphic.

Appendix A.2 describes the case of a continuous parameter that represents a coordinate transformation and therefore can undergo hysteresis.

2.5   Forward process: "driving"

We use the term *driving* to describe any process in which a sequence of states, generated either automatically or interactively, is used to compute a sequence of configurations, and hence an animation. Driving can be used in many ways.

Clip motions. A sequence of states can be used to animate any simplicial configuration model whose state space is compatible[5] with it, and therefore can be used as a clip motion. The term "clip motion" has been used previously in a different way. In Litwinowicz' Inkwell system [13], for example, a clip motion is a collection of animated Coons patches that can be textured differently to generate different characters. By contrast, two simplicial configuration models can use the same clip motion if they have isomorphic state spaces, even if they bear no

geometric resemblance.

Factor synchronization. If two configuration models are authored with state spaces whose cross products have one or more factors in common (e.g., $S_1 \times S_2$ and $S_2 \times S_3$), then the barycentric coordinates associated with the two instances of the shared factors (e.g., S_2) can be synchronized. This is useful when two models contain some logical dependency; for example, the position of a drawn shadow can be synchronized with the position of a light source.

Factor sharing is also critical in abating the exponential explosion that can occur when a model contains many degrees of freedom. In a model with hierarchy, it is typical for different graphical elements to depend on different—but overlapping—sets of hierarchical levels. Consider a human figure: trousers could depend on the knee and hip degrees of freedom; a T-shirt, on the hip and shoulders; and a scarf, on the shoulders and neck. Without factor sharing, each element would need to be re-parameterized with a state space that includes factors associated with every joint. With it, each element's state space needs to include only the factors on which it depends.

Algorithmic behavior. Some or all of the factors in a model can be driven algorithmically. We have implemented, for instance, a behavior that executes cartoon-like squash and stretch, taking into account the magnitude and direction of flight, and impacts with the ground. This behavior can be applied to any model that contains a squash-and-stretch factor in its state space that is isomorphic to the one expected by the behavior. Because it interfaces with the model at the level of state—not geometry—it is sufficiently general to be applied to both a soft, round beach ball and a rigid block of wood. Moreover, the same behavior code can be used either interactively (for performance or play) or offline (for authoring).

2.6   Inverse process: "tugging"

Tugging means inverting the re-parameterization map so that a user or some exogenous process can manipulate the model through some of its configuration parameters, rather than its state. The system answers each requested change in configuration with a change in state that matches the request as closely as possible. The configuration parameters being manipulated are often an (x,y) pair;[6] we refer to them collectively as the *tug point*.

The algorithms for tugging, described in Appendix A.1, address two principal challenges.

1.   The re-parameterization map on a zone is often ill-conditioned. We invert it safely using the Moore-Penrose inverse [7].

2.   At boundaries between zones, the re-parameterization map contains discontinuities in the first derivative. Our algorithms handle these discontinuities seamlessly, so that inter-zone boundaries—and therefore the structure of the state space—can be transparent to the user.

---

[5] For example, if two simplicial configuration models can use the same clip motion if they have state spaces that are isomorphic to each other, even if their appearance is radically different. The condition for compatibility is weaker than isomorphism: the clip motion can also be used for a model whose state space is a superset of the aforementioned isomorphic state spaces.

[6] The number of configuration parameters in the tug point could be more or less than two. For example, a mixing station or armature could control many parameters simultaneously. In a 3D environment, the tug point might often be a (x,y,z) point. Non-geometric parameters such as colors can also be tugged.

Because configuration parameters are generally more intuitive to use than states, tugging is the primary mechanism by which both users and software interact with the graphic. Like driving, tugging can be used in many ways.

Direct manipulation. The user specifies desired configuration changes by dragging the tug point with a pointing device. This style of interaction obviates the need for (but still permits the creation of) separate graphical user-interface elements. It is also well suited for performance-driven animation.

Combination with factor sharing. When factor sharing makes objects in a scene mutually dependent, tugging can be used to control any of the objects.

Simple software control. The graphic is regarded as a software object whose tug point is its interface. This technique permits an algorithmic behavior to be designed for reusability. We have implemented, for instance, a dynamic behavior that simulates a mass in a viscous medium, attached to a user-translatable anchor point through a damped spring. It can be used for any graphic with an (x,y) tug point and a 2D translation, regardless of state-space topology.

Factor locking. Barycentric coordinates associated with one or more of the factors in a state space can be constrained not to change during a tug. In our system, the author can arrange for certain factors to be locked whenever a given point is tugged.

Hybrid driving and tugging. One or more factors can be driven algorithmically while others are tugged. This is useful in arranging for a combination of interactivity and autonomous behavior.

3 Hybridizing with domain-specific techniques

Configuration modeling is best suited for describing relatively free-form interdependencies that are difficult to express algebraically. When constraints are more easily described by domain-specific techniques such as articulated-figure kinematics, the domain-specific techniques are preferable. In addition, a mechanism to make one model depend on another improves model reusability: for example, a model of an eye might be made once and used with many faces.

One approach to addressing these needs would be to use configuration modeling and an existing domain-specific technique independently. For example, to develop a human character in a 2D vector-based system, one might use standard forward and inverse kinematics for articulated figures to define a complete skeleton, and express fragments of clothing using independent re-parameterized models, each in the local coordinate system of a different rod in the skeleton. In this approach, clothing would not automatically deform in response to skeletal movements.

Another approach would be to incorporate curvilinear interpolation into the re-parameterization map, which is linear on each simplex as we have presented it. For instance, to mitigate the foreshortening effects characteristic of linear interpolation in Cartesian coordinates, one might make the re-parameterization map polynomial or transcendental on each simplex. We have considered employing simplicial splines with differential constraints at boundaries. Librande and Poggio have successfully developed a curvilinear re-parameterization

technique that employs radial basis functions on a hypercube [12].

Instead of either approach, we place parameterized, domain-specific coordinate transformations in the original model. Thus, the coordinate transformations are executed in the rendering map, but because they are parameterized, their behavior can be influenced during re-parameterization. Structural hierarchy is permitted in several ways: control points, entire models, and coordinate transformations can depend on other coordinate transformations. This technique simultaneously addresses the needs for reusability and for domain-specific constraints. In addition, we find that it permits the use of re-parameterization to break rules imposed by the domain-specific constraints.

To amplify the last point, consider a 2D vector-based arm drawn as one spline around two rotational joints. Parts of the spline are represented in a forearm coordinate system; others are in an upper-arm coordinate system; yet others are in absolute coordinates. Rotating the two joints without re-parameterizing any spline coordinates causes the curve to move roughly as the outline of an arm, but with artifacts: the spline folds incorrectly at the elbow.

Re-parameterization allows the artifact to be removed. In addition, it permits the artist to arrange for the shoulder to dislocate artfully by adjusting translational joint parameters[7] in the extreme poses. Specifically, one might create a state space with topology {{elbow1,elbow2}, {elbow2,elbow3}} × {{shoulder1,shoulder2}, {shoulder2,shoulder3}}: simple bilinear interpolation in each of four zones generated from a 3×3 grid of example configurations. By arranging for the nine configurations to differ only in their shoulder- and elbow-joint parameters, one would obtain the coarse movement described above. The artifact repair and joint dislocation would be brought about by adjusting the spline coordinates in each of the nine configurations.

4 Results

We implemented an authoring system for the re-parameterization of 2D vector graphics via simplicial configuration modeling. We also implemented a number of smaller applications in which novice users could manipulate models created in the authoring system. The authoring system and applications were written for the Win32 operating system and the Microsoft Foundation Classes. For smooth real-time animation, a Pentium-class processor with a clock speed of at least 266 MHz is required. Rendering—not tugging—is the slow step.

Figure 4 shows selected content authored in our system.

The fern, Figure 4d, exemplifies free-form constraints. It was authored using twenty-one drawings of the fern in different

---

[7] Our domain-specific coordinate transformation has four parameters. It represents a translatable rubber sheet that stretches along a preferred axis whose orientation is variable. When these transformations are chained, the origin of each rubber sheet is expressed in the coordinate system of the preceding transformation but the orientation and stretch are in absolute coordinates.

positions. Tugging its tip elicits flowing undulations. A flattened diagram of its single-factor kite-shaped state space is in Figure 5. Moving along the "kite tail" from its tip to the "kite body" corresponds to unfurling of the fern from seed to seedling. Vertical movements within the "kite" region correspond roughly to further unfurling; and horizontal movements, to graceful swaying from left to right.

The beach scene, Figure 4a, demonstrates factor synchronization. It has five factors: two for the sun position, one for the shoreline shape, one for the castle shape, and one for the motion of the waves. The first four factors are linear chains of three, two, three, and four symbols each; the fifth is a single triangle. Each object in the scene depends on a different subset of the factors. They are interrelated in several ways; for example, the position of the sun, its reflection, and the castle's shadow are mutually dependent and all can be tugged.

The Trapeze Guy, Figure 4b, illustrates how a simple behavior (the mass-spring dynamical system described in Section 2.6) can be reused [19]. The Trapeze Guy's state space is a ring of eight symbols (which represents rotation about the trapeze), crossed with a linear chain of five symbols (which represents, roughly, the distance of the character's feet from the trapeze). The user-translatable anchor point of the mass-spring system is attached to the trapeze; the dynamically controlled mass, to a tug point near the character's feet. His body swings about as the user moves the trapeze. In the spirit of free-form constraints, an open red mouth and beads of sweat added to some of the forty authored configurations add to the comedy.

Our most complex piece is the cartoon character model, Figure 4c. It contains extensive factor synchronization and hybridization using the modified form of articulated-figure kinematics described in Section 3. Its fourteen separate simplicial configuration models represent body parts such as arms, legs, eyes, and eyelids. They share subsets of the twelve factors, with the greatest amount of sharing used for axial rotation as well as left-right and part-to-part coordination of the eyes. One of the more interesting factors is the one that governs the shape of the mouth: it contains four triangles and two tetrahedra, assembled into a kite-like structure.

Articulation in each limb and the attachment of facial parts to the head are both accomplished using the hybrid scheme described in Section 3. In both cases, the visual integrity of the cartoon depended critically on the re-parameterization component of the hybrid scheme, without which the coordination of body parts is only approximate.

5   Related work

In computer graphics, simplicial complexes have been used principally for modeling 3D geometry. Hoppe et al. [8] exploited the well-understood topological properties of simplicial complexes to regulate changes to mesh representations of surfaces. Edelsbrunner [5] used a multi-resolution approach (α-shapes) to track scale-dependent topological changes in the Delaunay triangulation of a multi-scale point-data set.

We use simplicial complexes to meet a goal much closer to that of Librande and Poggio [12], whose work may be described in the language of configuration modeling. Viewed from that perspective, their technique prescribes a state space that is a

hypercube, and therefore cannot represent topological holes. Representational power resides in the re-parameterization map, whose form is a superposition of radial basis functions, whereas ours is only piecewise linear. Thus, their system is geometrically flexible but—in comparison to ours—topologically restricted. Holes are important, for example, when rotational degrees of freedom are involved. Indeed, recent work by Rademacher on view-dependent deformations [17] essentially employed simplicial configuration modeling. Rademacher's work exemplifies how an artist's expressiveness can be layered onto geometric relationships through the use of example-based modeling.

Gleicher and Witkin [6] influenced us to ensure that any simplicial configuration model is, without any special effort on the part of the artist, responsive to direct manipulation. Pai [16], among others, has applied similar concepts to robot control; his methods are based much more on half-space penalty functions.

Also related are constraint-based systems that require the user to specify constraints explicitly, either algorithmically or through a more graphical interface. Such systems are ideal when the desired constraints are relatively easy to state, as in industrial CAD [3], diagramming tools [1], and 3D animation tools that permit entry of algebraic constraints [2]. By reducing cognitive burden on the user, the work of Kurlander and Feiner on constraint inference [10] challenges our distinction between explicit and free-form constraints.

Techniques for multi-target interpolation [4,11] are complementary to simplicial configuration modeling in the sense that each represents a new class of parameterized models to which the structured interpolation implied by simplicial configuration modeling may be applied. In fact, the present work is part of a growing interest in structured interpolation between examples, either digitally captured or created by an artist.

6   Epilogue

We have identified the challenge of configuration modeling, which we believe to be an important open problem in computer graphics. To address this challenge, we have proposed to use a modeling primitive based on the simplicial complex. This choice leads to topological generality.

We have shown how to run the maps from state space to image space both forward (by driving) and in reverse (by tugging). We have identified a number of ways in which driving and tugging lead to economies related to reusability of code and content. We have shown why the need for hysteresis arises in configuration modeling and have proposed techniques for obtaining it. We have demonstrated how domain-specific coordinate transformations can be used in harmony with configuration modeling in a manner that exploits the strengths of both.

Today's simplicial configuration models are characterized by low simplex counts and labor-intensive authoring—much like the first polygonal models in 3D graphics. If configuration modeling addresses a genuine need, one might expect to see further developments along lines analogous to the ones that have permitted polygonal models to grow in complexity by orders of magnitude. These might include semi-automated authoring using high-level primitives and capture of configuration models from video sources.

Acknowledgments

We thank Subutai Ahmad, Neal Bhadkamkar, Frank Brooks, Michele Covell, Frank Crow, Kevin Hunter, Yan-Bin Jia, Scott Klemmer, Andrew Kunz, Bud Lassiter, Golan Levin, Joy Mountford, Chris Seguine, Malcolm Slaney, and Meg Withgott for their thoughtful contributions to this work. We also thank the reviewers for their many useful and constructive suggestions.

A Appendices

A.1 Tugging algorithms

This appendix describes how to invert the re-parameterization map. Given a requested change in one or more configuration parameters, the goal is to compute a state change that satisfies the request as closely as possible. We describe cases in order of increasing complexity. Following Gleicher and Witkin [6], we use local solutions instead of global ones to provide temporal continuity in animation.

One factor, one zone. In a single-factor model that contains one simplex, the re-parameterization map is linear. Let x be a vector whose coordinates are the configuration parameters to be changed, and let Δx be the desired change. A state is said to *improve upon* the current state if it maps to a configuration x' for which $(x'-x) \cdot \Delta x > 0$.

Let λ be the state in barycentric coordinates. To constrain the barycentric coordinates to sum to unity, we use the redundant coordinate system ρ, defined by $\lambda_i = \rho_i + (1-R)/k$, where k is the number of symbols in the simplex and $R = \Sigma_i \rho_i$, summed over all symbols in the simplex.

The state change is then $\Delta \rho = J^{\ddagger} \Delta x$, where the components of the Jacobian J are the partial derivatives of x with respect to ρ, and the symbol $\ddagger$ denotes Moore-Penrose inversion, which handles rank-deficient matrices by giving special treatment to singularities [7].

If the requested state change $\Delta \rho$ would cause the state to exit the simplex, travel is halted at the simplex boundary. At the simplex boundary, one or more barycentric coordinates are zero. The Jacobian computation is repeated with the corresponding symbols in the simplex omitted from the computation, i.e., constraining the state to lie in the subface. If a boundary of that subface is encountered, the procedure continues in subfaces of decreasing dimensionality until a subface of dimensionality zero is encountered.

Multiple factors, one zone. When k factors are involved, the re-parameterization map is k-linear. Let x and Δx be defined as above, but let each ρ_i in the tuple $(\rho_1; \rho_2; \dots; \rho_k)$ be the state coordinates from factor i. The state change is then $[\Delta \rho_1^T | \Delta \rho_2^T | \dots | \Delta \rho_k^T]^T = [J_1 | J_2 | \dots | J_k]^{\ddagger} \Delta x$, where each Jacobian J_i is defined as above with respect to the corresponding ρ_i while keeping ρ_j fixed for all $j \neq i$. In a multilinear map, rectilinear movements produce linear effects, but diagonal movements can produce polynomial effects because each Jacobian J_i depends on every ρ_j for all $j \neq i$. Therefore, local optima exist.

Factor locking. To lock factor i, i.e., prevent ρ_i from changing during tugging, we merely omit ρ_i and J_i from the equation given above. Multiple omissions lock multiple factors. When one factor is driven while another is tugged, we interleave steps of driving and tugging.

One factor, multiple zones. This is the piecewise linear case. In contrast with the linear case, a simplex boundary can be the portal to one or more neighboring simplices. When the state arrives at a simplex boundary, we first identify neighboring simplices, i.e., ones that share the subface in which the state resides. We remove from consideration each neighboring simplex[8] that contains no states that improve upon the current state. (Because the re-parameterization map is linear on the neighboring simplex, it is sufficient to test each vertex in the neighboring simplex that lies outside the current subface.) If zero neighboring simplices remain, tugging proceeds in the subface, as in the linear case. If one neighboring simplex remains, tugging proceeds in that simplex.[9]

The subcase in which multiple neighboring simplices remain is one for which we have discussed and implemented various heuristics, but that we have not yet encountered in practice. We leave as an open problem the development of a universally acceptable way either to choose an appropriate neighboring simplex, or to control the topology of the state space so that this subcase cannot arise.

Multiple factors, multiple zones. This is the piecewise multilinear case. It raises additional issues that are also open problems. As in the piecewise linear case, the only challenges that are not present in the purely multilinear case arise at boundaries between zones. If the state encounters a zone boundary that is a simplex boundary in only one of the factors, the decision reduces to the one-factor, multiple-zone case. At a zone boundary that is a simplex boundary in more than one factor—this case does arise in practice—the decision is more complicated. The remainder of this section discusses that decision.

Recall that in a state space formed from the cross product of k simplicial complexes, a zone is a k-tuple of simplices, with one simplex taken from each factor. In the situation under consideration, the state lies on a subface in more than one of those simplices. Another zone is considered to be a neighbor if at least one of the simplices is replaced by a neighboring simplex that shares one of those subfaces.

One difficulty arises because the re-parameterization map associated with a zone can be polynomial for moves that are not rectilinear. The simple test used in the piecewise linear case to determine whether a neighboring simplex should be eliminated does not necessarily work. A neighboring zone can contain states that improve upon the current state even if none of its vertices do. We have therefore replaced the global test over vertices by a local test: we compute the anticipated state change from Δx in each neighboring zone and eliminate any neighboring zone from which the state would immediately exit.

The second difficulty is that the test given above may admit multiple neighboring zones. This particular difficulty has not occurred for us in practice, but a universally acceptable solution (or way to guarantee that the situation is never encountered) would be desirable for the sake of completeness.

A.2 Re-parameterization map with hysteresis

This appendix shows how to define a re-parameterization map with hysteresis. We have developed re-parameterization maps with three differing levels of hysteresis.

A *conservative* map is one for which traversing a closed loop in the state space always produces a closed loop in the configuration space. Outside of this appendix, all re-parameterization maps described in

---

[8] Moving into such a simplex cannot produce any movement in the direction of the requested configuration change.

[9] Infinite looping is prevented by eliminating a simplex from consideration for the duration of a single tugging step once it has been exited.

this paper are conservative.

A *semi-conservative* map is one for which traversing a closed loop in the state space can be guaranteed to produce a closed loop in the configuration space only if the loop in state space crosses no zone boundaries.

A *non-conservative* map is one for which traversing a closed loop in the state space can never be guaranteed to produce a closed loop in the configuration space.

We describe semi-conservative and non-conservative maps. Each of these developments requires to departures from the mechanisms put forth outside this appendix.

First, we modify the definition of a simplicial complex. A simplicial complex is normally defined as a union of simplices in which each simplex is an open set. Instead, we define each top-level simplex as a closed set, deliberately creating redundancy at shared subfaces. Under this definition, every state on a shared subface has one or more siblings that have the same barycentric coordinates but are associated with different top-level simplices.

Second, we distinguish between the *relative* values of a configuration parameter (which are present in the range of the map) and the *actual* values (which are supplied to the rendering map and may differ from the relative values).

Semi-conservative map. Suppose x is a continuous configuration parameter for which we wish to define a semi-conservative map. In each zone, we permit the author to specify an arbitrary, relative value of x at every vertex. Thus, a vertex can have a different relative value of x in every zone of which it is a member. We define the re-parameterization map to be multi-linear within each zone, just as in the conservative case, but possibly discontinuous at zone boundaries. As the state moves continuously within a zone, the infinitesimal changes in the relative value of x are accumulated into the actual value of x; but when it moves from one zone to another, the non-infinitesimal changes in the relative value of x are ignored.

A semi-conservative map could be used, for example, to control the rotation of a 2D wheel on or near a high-friction 1D surface. The parameters of the wheel are (x,y,θ), where x and y are the position of the wheel's center and θ is its rotation angle. For x and y, the re-parameterization map is conservative and defined so that a zone boundary maps to a horizontal line just above the surface. For θ, the map is semi-conservative. It is defined so that the relative value of θ is constant in the zone above the surface, and linearly related to x in the zone on the surface. The wheel exhibits the physically correct hysteresis that results from rotating only when moved horizontally while in contact with the surface.

Non-conservative map. Suppose, now, that x is a continuous configuration parameter for which we wish to define a non-conservative map. In each zone, we permit the author to specify an arbitrary relative-value difference Δx at every edge (ordered vertex pair). When the state moves within a zone from barycentric-coordinate vector λ to barycentric-coordinate vector λ', we accumulate into the actual value of x the following quantity:

$$\Delta X(\lambda,\lambda') = \Sigma_v \Sigma_{v'} \lambda(v) \, \Delta x(v,v') \, \lambda'(v'),$$

where each sum is over all vertices in the zone, each $\Delta x(v,v')$ is an relative-value difference supplied by the author, and $\lambda(v)$ is a scalar quantity extracted from the vector λ by multiplying together all components of λ associated with symbols in the symbol tuple v. As with the semi-conservative case, we do not change the actual value of x when crossing a zone boundary.

This procedure has a number of attractive properties. First, it produces hysteresis. Second, $\Delta X(\lambda,\lambda')$ is a smooth function of λ and λ'. Third, when moving from one vector (v) to another (v') it produces a change in x equal to the one specified by the author, i.e., $\Delta x(v,v')$. Fourth, under some circumstances[10] we have been able to show that a linear path through the state space can be executed in any number of smaller steps without affecting the total change in x. Fifth, when the values of $\Delta x(v,v')$ are conservative (i.e., $\Delta x(v,v')$ + $\Delta x(v',v'') = \Delta x(v,v'')$ for any v, v', and v''), the procedure reduces to the semi-conservative case.

A non-conservative map could be used to provide the hysteresis called for in Figure 3.

References

[1] Aldus Corp. IntelliDraw. Computer Program (1992).

[2] Alias|Wavefront Corp. PowerAnimator 9. Computer Program (1998).

[3] Autodesk Inc. AutoCAD 2000. Computer Program (2000).

[4] Shenchang Eric Chen, Lance Williams. View interpolation for image synthesis. In James T. Kajiya, ed., SIGGRAPH 93 Conference Proceedings, Annual Conference Series, pages 279-288. ACM SIGGRAPH, Addison Wesley, August 1993. ISBN 0-201-58889-7.

[5] Herbert Edelsbrunner, Ernst P. Mücke. Three-dimensional alpha shapes. ACM Transactions on Graphics, *13 (1)*, pp. 43-72 (January 1994). ISSN 0730-0301.

[6] Michael Gleicher, Andrew Witkin. Through-the-lens camera control. In Edwin E. Catmull, editor, *Computer Graphics* (SIGGRAPH 92 Conference Proceedings), volume 26, 2 (July 1992), ACM SIGGRAPH, New York, 1992, pages 331-340. ISBN 0-201-51585-7.

[7] Gene H. Golub, Charles F. Van Loan. Matrix Computations, p. 243. Johns Hopkins University Press, Baltimore, MD (1989).

[8] Hugues Hoppe, Tony DeRose, Tom Duchamp, John McDonald, Werner Stuetzle. Mesh optimization. In James T. Kajiya, ed., SIGGRAPH 93 Conf. Proceedings, Annual Conference Series, pages 19-26. ACM SIGGRAPH, Addison Wesley, Aug 1993. ISBN 0-201-58889-7.

[9] Michael Kass. CONDOR: Constraint-based dataflow. In Edwin C. Catmull, editor, Computer Graphics (SIGGRAPH 92 Conference Proceedings), volume 26, pages 321-330. Addison Wesley, July 1992. ISBN 0-89791-479-1.

[10] David Kurlander, Steve Feiner. Inferring constraints from multiple snapshots. ACM Transactions on Graphics, *12 (4)*, pp. 277-304 (October 1993). ISSN 0730-0301.

[11] Seungyong Lee, George Wolberg, Sung Yong Shin. Polymorph: morphing among multiple images. IEEE *Computer Graphics and Applications*, 18(1), pp.58-71 (January-February 1998).

[12] Steve E. Librande. Example-based character drawing. Master's thesis, Media Arts and Science, MIT (1992).

[13] Peter C. Litwinowicz. Inkwell: a 2 ½-D animation system. In Thomas W. Sederberg, editor, Computer Graphics (SIGGRAPH 91 Conference Proceedings), volume 25, pages 113-122. Addison Wesley, July 1991. ISBN 0-201-56291-X.

[14] MetaCreations Corp. Painter 6. Computer Program (1999).

[15] James R. Munkres. Elements of Algebraic Topology. Addison-Wesley, Reading, MA (1984).

[16] Dinesh K. Pai. Least constraint: a framework for the control of complex mechanical systems. In Proc. American Control Conf., Boston, MA, 1615--1621 (June 1991).

[17] Paul Rademacher. View-dependent geometry. In Alyn Rockwood, editor, SIGGRAPH 99 Conference Proceedings, Annual Conference Series, pages 439-446. ACM SIGGRAPH, Addison Wesley, August 1999. ISBN 0-201-48560-5.

[18] Ivan E. Sutherland. Sketchpad: A man-machine graphical communication system. Ph.D. thesis, Dept. of E.E., MIT (1963).

[19] Andrew Witkin, Kurt Fleischer, Alan Barr. Energy constraints on parameterized models. In Maureen C. Stone, editor, Computer Graphics (SIGGRAPH 87 Conference Proceedings), volume 21, pages 225-232. ACM, July 1987. ISBN 0-89791-227-6.

---

[10]We have shown this property for the case of linear movement in one factor.

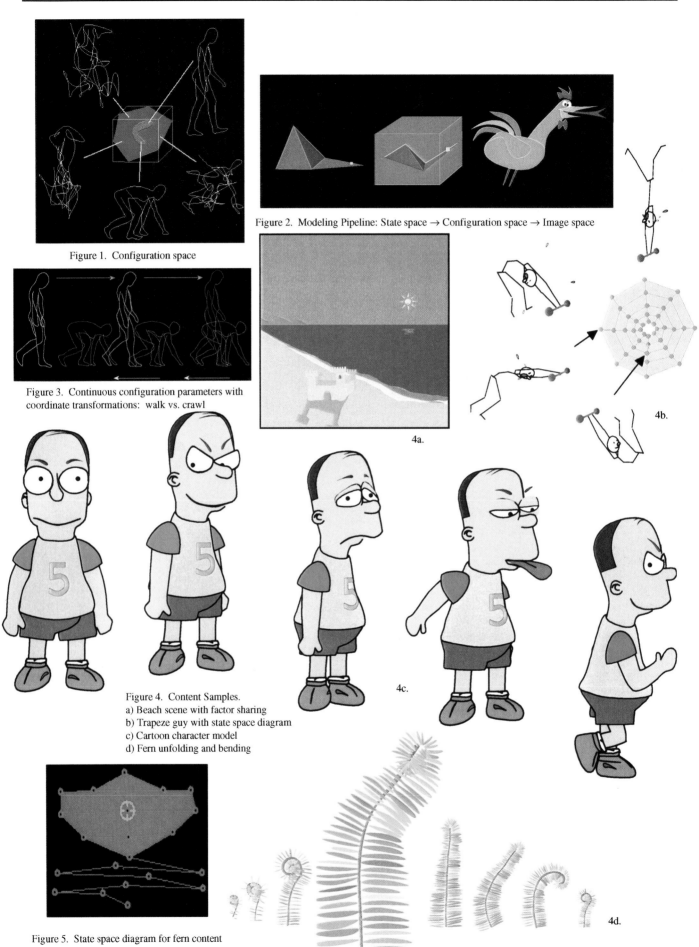

Figure 1. Configuration space

Figure 2. Modeling Pipeline: State space → Configuration space → Image space

Figure 3. Continuous configuration parameters with coordinate transformations: walk vs. crawl

4a.

4b.

4c.

Figure 4. Content Samples.
a) Beach scene with factor sharing
b) Trapeze guy with state space diagram
c) Cartoon character model
d) Fern unfolding and bending

4d.

Figure 5. State space diagram for fern content

Example-Based Hinting of TrueType Fonts

Douglas E. Zongker[1,2]   *Geraldine Wade*[1]   *David H. Salesin*[1,2]

[1]Microsoft Corporation   [2]University of Washington

Abstract

Hinting in TrueType is a time-consuming manual process in which a typographer creates a sequence of instructions for better fitting the characters of a font to a grid of pixels. In this paper, we propose a new method for automatically hinting TrueType fonts by transferring hints of one font to another. Given a hinted source font and a target font without hints, our method matches the outlines of corresponding glyphs in each font, and then translates all of the individual hints for each glyph from the source to the target font. It also translates the control value table (CVT) entries, which are used to unify feature sizes across a font. The resulting hinted font already provides a great improvement over the unhinted version. More importantly, the translated hints, which preserve the sound, hand-designed hinting structure of the original font, provide a very good starting point for a professional typographer to complete and fine-tune, saving time and increasing productivity. We demonstrate our approach with examples of automatically hinted fonts at typical display sizes and screen resolutions. We also provide estimates of the time saved by a professional typographer in hinting new fonts using this semi-automatic approach.

CR Categories: I.7.4 [Document and Text Processing]: Electronic Publishing

Keywords: automatic hinting, digital typography, gridfitting, shape matching

1 Introduction

The demand for high-quality hinted fonts is outstripping the ability of digital typography houses to produce them. Hinting is a painstaking manual process that can only be done well by a handful of highly skilled professionals. It requires a blend of typographical artistry with technological ability. In order to provide a full appreciation of the hinting problem, we begin here with a review of how digital fonts are scan-converted onto a raster display.

In digital typography, each character in a font is described by a set of *outlines*, usually represented by splines. When the character is rendered onto a grid of pixels, the outlines are scaled to the desired size, and then each pixel whose center lies inside of an outline is set to black. When fonts are displayed at sufficiently high resolutions this approach works beautifully. But for sizes below about 150 ppem,[1] severe aliasing problems can result when this naive outline filling process is applied, especially for delicate features such as serifs. Figure 1 shows an example. The left image is generated by the naive algorithm. This pixel pattern does not look much like a lowercase 'a'. A simple *dropout control* mechanism added to the fill algorithm turns on additional pixels to preserve the character's topology, resulting in the center image. The right image, though, shows the work of an experienced hinter. The pixel pattern has been subtly altered to both improve readability and better preserve the character of the original outline.

Figure 1 Outline for the Palatino Italic 'a', along with the pixel pattern generated by rasterizing the outlines for display of 18-point text on a 72 dpi device. The left image shows the results of the naive fill algorithm. The middle image shows the result of enabling the rasterizer's dropout control mechanism. The right image shows the results of hinting the character by hand.

The hinting process is not just about optimizing individual characters. The hinter must balance the needs of a single glyph with the desire for *consistency* across all the characters of a font. It is important, for example, to ensure that all the vertical stems of a font are the same number of pixels wide at a given size. If the scaling and rounding process produced one-pixel-wide stems on some characters and two-pixel-wide stems on others, then a passage of text would look blotchy and be difficult to read. The goal of the hinter is to produce a smooth transition from very high sizes, where merely filling the outlines suffices and hinting is unnecessary, down to lower sizes, where legibility must be preserved even when that means a departure from the outlines drawn by the original font designer.

Although the ever-improving resolution of hardcopy devices is beginning to approach the point at which hinting is not necessary, the technology is not there yet: 10- or 12-point text on a 300 or even 600 dpi printer still needs hinting for best results. More importantly, the increasing emphasis on reading text on-screen—from visions of the "paperless office" to the emergence and proliferation of hand-held computers and eBooks—means that more and more text is being viewed on devices in the 72–100 dpi range. Though resolutions of these displays are improving as well, for the foreseeable future hinting will be an absolute necessity in order to provide clear, legible text.

Although attempts have been made to design automated hinting systems in the past [2, 5], even the best of these produce hints that are good, but still not up to the standards of professional typographers. This previous work assumed that in order to be useful, an autohinter had to be a monolithic, self-contained package: outlines in, quality hints out. That is an admirable goal, and it may be achieved someday. However, given the detailed, aesthetically-based nature of the work, we think that it is currently more useful to view the autohinter as one piece of a system that includes a human hinter.

The subject of this paper, then, is not a tool for automatically *generating* hints so much as a tool for automatically *translating* hints from one font to another. An important advantage of this approach is that it preserves the basic strategy and structure of the original hints, which were hand crafted by a professional typographer for each individual glyph of the font. Generally, these translated hints provide an excellent starting point for a human to fine-tune and adjust. We demonstrate our approach with examples of automatically hinted fonts at typical display sizes and screen resolutions. We also provide estimates of the time saved by a professional typographer in hinting new fonts using this semi-automatic approach.

2 Background

There are two major font standards in widespread use today: Type 1 and TrueType. Type 1 fonts [1], often called "PostScript fonts," were developed by Adobe and are popular in the world of publishing. Printing applications were the target when this system was developed, though utilities are now available to enable on-screen display of Type 1 fonts. The TrueType format [3], originally developed by Apple, was intended to unify type on the screen and on paper, and is used in both the Macintosh and Windows operating systems. TrueType has something of a reputation for being of low quality, but this is mostly due to the fact that TrueType was always an open standard while Type 1 was not, and so the public domain is flooded with a large number of poorly designed, unhinted TrueType fonts. The TrueType standard does contain extensive facilities for high-quality hinting, though, and more and more quality fonts are now available in TrueType.

Though both formats represent characters as spline-based outlines, the hinting styles are radically different. Hinting for Type 1 fonts works by marking sections of the outline as corresponding to particular typographic features of the character—stems, bowls, counters, and so on. It is the job of the rasterizer to take advantage of these *hints* about the character shape to produce the best possible pattern of pixels. This scheme has the advantage that enhancements to the rasterizer can produce improvements to all fonts on the system, but means that a designer of digital type cannot specify exactly what an outline will look like when rendered at a given size.

The TrueType font technology takes a different approach. Instead of leaving control over the glyph's final appearance to the rasterizer, a TrueType font contains explicit instructions about how particular control points should be shifted to fit the pixel grid. These instructions take the form of a *program* in a special, TrueType-specific bytecode language. Since both the behavior of each instruction and the rasterizing algorithm are defined in the TrueType standard, the designer of a TrueType font can predict exactly which pixels will be turned on for a character at a given size, no matter what the output device is.

In TrueType, each contour of an outline is specified with a sequence of point positions. (See the outline curves of Figure 3 for some examples.) Each point is flagged as either *on-curve* or *off-curve*. TrueType defines the outline as follows:

- Two successive on-curve points are connected with a straight line segment.

- When an off-curve point falls between two on-curve points, the three are treated as the control points for a quadratic Bézier segment.

- When two adjacent off-curve points appear, the midpoint of the segment connecting them is treated as an implicit on-curve point between them, allowing reduction to the case above.

The glyph renderer starts by scaling the outlines to a particular size, then executing the attached program to shift control points around

in a size-specific way before filling the altered outline. By itself, this approach cannot produce the necessary consistency among different characters of a font, or even between different parts of the same character, since each action is necessarily local. Global synchronization of outline alterations is achieved through use of the *control value table*, or CVT. This is a shared table of distances, which can be referenced by instructions in each glyph's program. When the rendering is initialized for a given size, the values in the CVT are scaled and rounded to the current grid size. Point movements can then be constrained by CVT entries. For instance, a person writing hints for TrueType may decide to use CVT 81 to represent, say, the width of vertical black stems in lowercase letters. He or she will then write instruction sequences for all appropriate lowercase letters, all referring to CVT entry 81, so that all the vertical black stems at a given size will have the same width.

The TrueType language is an assembly-style stack-based language. The intent of the designers of TrueType was not to make typographers learn and write in the TrueType language itself, but rather to facilitate the development of high-level languages and tools that generate TrueType code. The Visual TrueType (VTT) package from Microsoft [7] is such a tool. VTT provides a high-level language, called *VTT Talk*, for expressing relationships between points. VTT Talk provides statements for expressing the following classes of hints:

- *Link* constraints: the vertical or horizontal distance between a pair of knots is constrained by an entry in the CVT.

- *Dist* constraints: the "natural" vertical or horizontal distance between a pair of knots is maintained, so that if one point is moved the other moves in parallel.

- *Interpolate* constraints: a knot's fractional distance between two parent knots is maintained.

- *Anchors*: specific knots can be rounded to the nearest gridline, or to a gridline specified by a CVT entry.

These types of hints are demonstrated visually for two characters from the Georgia Roman font in Figure 6. The VTT Talk hints are compiled into a TrueType program stored in the font file. One advantage of working with VTT Talk is that each statement simply asserts a relationship between two points, and there is little dependence on the order of the statements. If one statement is omitted, the meaning of the others is unchanged. In contrast, TrueType assembler is a sequential language that maintains a fairly complex state. Most instructions in TrueType have side effects that modify this state. If we tried to translate the assembler code directly, and were for some reason unable to translate a particular instruction—for instance, due to a sufficiently large difference in the matched glyphs' outlines—the effects of subsequent instructions could change entirely.

Our approach is primarily motivated by the work of Hersch and Betrisey [4, 6]. In their method, hints are generated for each glyph by matching its outline to a human-constructed generic model of that character's shape (for example, a generic uppercase roman 'B'). The model consists of two representations of the generic character shape. The *skeleton* model builds the character out of solid parts, labeled as stems, bowls, serifs, and so on. The *contour* model is an outline representation of the character, constructed to have as few control points as possible while still spanning the space of possible character shapes. The correspondences between the two models are known, being specified by hand when the model is built. In their method, the outlines of the glyph to be hinted are matched to the corresponding contour model by a fairly complex process that takes into account both global and local features. Points are classified by their position relative to the baseline, cap-height and x-height lines, and left and right sidebearings. Local features distinguishing points are based on the curvature, direction, and orientation of the adjacent curve segments. Once the correspondence between the unknown

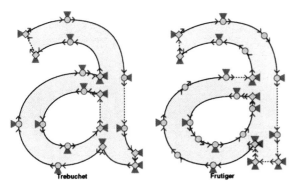

Figure 2 Features used for matching on-curve points. Diamonds indicate corner points; circles indicate smooth points. Incoming and outgoing directions are quantized to the eight compass directions, indicated with blue arrows. Local extrema are shown with red triangles. Each point is also marked to indicate whether the segments on each side are curved (solid lines) or straight (dashed lines).

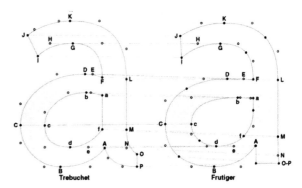

Figure 3 The final match for the two 'a' glyphs. On-curve knots are solid dots; off-curve knots are open circles.

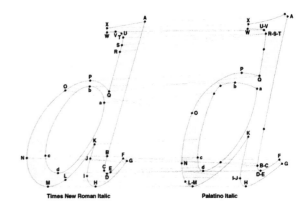

Figure 4 Results of matching for a more complex pair of glyphs. No matches involve off-curve knots in this example, so these knots are not shown.

outline and the model outline is established, the known correspondence between the model outline and the model skeleton can be used to label parts of the unknown outline as belonging to significant features such as stems and serifs. From this labeling a set of Type 1-style hints for the new outline can be derived.

3 Method

Hersch and Betrisey's work requires a manually constructed model in order to link points on the outline with the "semantic" features needed for hinting. Hinting in TrueType does not require an explicit labeling of these features; this information is implicitly used by the human typographer when deciding on a hinting strategy for the character, but the end result expressed in the font is just a set of relationships, or constraints, between control points. These constraints obviate the need for the skeleton model—once we find the correspondence between a contour model and the outlines of the target glyph, we can immediately produce hints for the target outline without transitively applying a second correspondence.

We've therefore reduced our needs to having a contour model with control-point-level hints attached to it. A shortcut now becomes obvious: use an already hinted TrueType font as the model! This has a number of advantages over using a specialized model built expressly for the auto-hinter. First, we already have a wide variety of fonts from which to choose as templates. Moreover, choosing a template close to the target font will increase the likelihood of a good match and consequently the quality of the resulting hints. This raises the possibility of having the template font be selected from the library automatically, or even choosing different template fonts for different characters of the target. Another advantage of using real hinted fonts as templates is that typographers, rather than computer scientists, can build templates using tools they already know; furthermore, each typographer can build templates to suit his or her own hinting style.

3.1 Matching the outlines

Suppose now that we have two glyphs representing a single character. One, the *source outline*, will be the hinted character that we are taking hints from. The goal is to translate those hints to refer to control points on the *target outline*. In the illustration here we'll show the process of translating hints from the lowercase 'a' of Trebuchet to the 'a' of Frutiger.

Our algorithm attempts to match up explicit on-curve knots using features such as contour direction and the presence of extrema. The on-curve knots typically have far more significance to the shape and extents of the contour. Once a match is computed between the

on-curve knots, we attempt to pair up the remaining knots by simply counting the number of off-curve knots between each pair of matched on-curve knots. If the numbers are equal, we pair the off-curve knots based solely on their order. Only a very small fraction of hints involve these off-curve knots, but we want to preserve as many of the source hints as possible.

Many glyphs are defined by multiple contours, but there are no restrictions on what order the contours are listed in. Therefore, our first task is to determine which contour goes with which in the two glyphs. We do this be enumerating all the possibilities for a one-to-one pairing of the contours. (The hinter rejects input outline pairs with differing numbers of contours.) For each pairing we calculate a score as follows. Suppose that the target character is scaled and translated so that its bounding box is equal to that of the source character. For each individual contour within the characters, we sum together the absolute values of the differences between corresponding sides of the *contour* bounding boxes. This value, summed over all the contours gives the score for the match, with the lowest value being the best match. While this is a factorial-time algorithm, we have not found the running time to be a problem—for the Latin character sets we have been using it is rare to find a character with more than five contours.

The next step, the heart of the algorithm, is to match up the knots on each pair of contours. We begin by identifying a number of features at each knot, and assigning a point score for matching that feature:

1. Each knot has an incoming and an outgoing *direction,* based on the tangents of the curves touching that knot. The direction is quantized to one of eight possibilities, corresponding to the eight compass directions. A pair of knots is assigned from 200 to -200 points based on the similarity of each direction. For example, a knot with an incoming direction of "north," gets 200

points when matched with another "north" knot, 100 points for a "northeast" or "northwest" match, 0 points for "east" or "west", −100 points for "southeast" or "southwest", and −200 points for matching "south" knot. This score is calculated for both incoming and outgoing direction.

2. Each knot can be flagged as a local minimum or maximum in each of the x or y directions. A knot with one of these flags will contribute 150 points when matched with a knot with the same flag, or −150 points when matched to the opposite flag. A knot may not be an extremum at all in a given direction, in which case any match will not produce a score for this category.

3. Finally, each knot has a flag to indicate whether the incoming and outgoing lines are straight (within some tolerance) or curved. Matching these flags produces a score of 100 points, but not matching them produces no penalty.

Figure 2 shows our two 'a' characters, marked with the features used for matching.

To generate these matches, we pick an arbitrary starting knot on each contour to be matched, and pair these knots. We then go around the source contour, pairing each knot with the knot on the target curve whose fractional arc length relative to the starting knot is closest to that of the source knot. This generates a match with one pair for each source knot. We can sum the local-feature score of each pair to rate the quality of the overall match. We generate a match using each knot on the target outline as the starting point. The five matches with the highest local-feature scores go on to the next stage.

In this final stage, we attempt to improve the scores of these five best matches by small perturbations of the pairings. We remove knot pairs with a negative local-feature score, look for matches for unpaired source knots, and shift existing pairs to adjacent target knots, all subject to the constraint that the match respect the ordering of knots around the contour: if knot B follows knot A in the source contour, then the partner of knot B should not come before the partner of knot A on the target contour. Once we've performed this local improvement on each of the five top matches, we select the match with the highest final score as our final match.

The results of this matching algorithm are shown in Figure 3. These heuristics work well for a wide variety of character styles, including roman, bold, and italic characters. A matching for a more complex pair of glyphs is shown in Figure 4.

3.2 Hint translation

Having produced a match between the knots of the source character outline and those of the target outline, we're now ready to translate the hints themselves. We parse the source font's VTT Talk hints and copy them to the target font, replacing knot numbers as appropriate according to our match. If we do not have a match for a knot referenced in a particular statement, we simply copy the source statement unchanged, but comment it out, to mark it as a place that may need special attention by a person reviewing the font.

3.3 CVT translation

The CVT is a central feature of the TrueType hinting mechanism, and no TrueType autohinting scheme would be complete without addressing it. In VTT Talk, entries of the CVT are used via statements such as `YLink(14,0,87)`, which says, in effect, "move knot 0 up or down so that its vertical distance from knot 14 is equal to CVT entry 87." Our matcher allows us to translate the references to specific knots to their analogues in the new font, and we can certainly keep using the same CVT entry numbers as in the original font. The question is, what *values* do we put in those entries? The old entries tell us little, since they represent distances measured in the source font, which may bear little or no relation to distances in the target font.

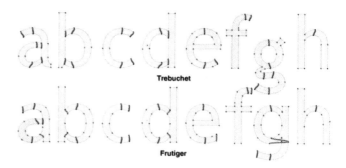

Figure 5 The top row shows characters from the font Trebuchet. The typographer has used CVT entry 87 to control the height of round, black features in lowercase letters, indicated by the green links between control points. The bottom row shows Frutiger, along with the uses of CVT entry 87 as transferred from Trebuchet by our autohinter. Red lines indicate where hints were automatically discarded because the natural distance between the points was too different from the value in the CVT table.

glyph	references to CVT entry 87					
'a'	75*	143	143	156	156	164
'b'	111*	113*	156	156		
'c'	156	156	160	172		
'd'	111*	113*	156	156		
'e'	156	156	193*			
'f'	155	156				
'g'	45*	45*	111*	156	156	178
'h'	156					

Table 1 Some of the references to CVT entry 87 when translating Trebuchet hints to Frutiger. For each pair of points whose vertical distance is constrained by this CVT entry, the natural distance between the points in the Frutiger glyphs is listed. The value given to entry 87 is the median of these natural distances, 156 units in this case. The starred values are outliers.

The solution comes from recognizing that the major reason the CVT is used is to take a set of distances that are *approximately* the same in the outline, and force them to be *exactly* the same number of pixels in the rendered bitmap. Since the goal is to provide this consistency while changing the outlines as little as possible, the CVT entry will generally contain some average value, which is close to all the distances it is going to be used to constrain. We can look at all the uses of a particular CVT entry to estimate what its value should be.

Let's look at how this works on our 'a' character. The person hinting Trebuchet chose to use CVT entry 87 to represent the height of round, black features in lowercase characters. Accordingly, most of the lowercase letters that have round parts reference CVT 87, as we see in the top row of Figure 5. The 'a' glyph alone uses entry 87 six times—that is, there are six pairs of knots in the 'a' whose distance is constrained by CVT entry 87.

Table 1 shows the "natural" distances between each of these pairs in Trebuchet for characters 'a' through 'h'. One pair of points in the 'a' is 75 units apart vertically in the unhinted outline, another is 143 units, and so on. To determine the overall value to place in the CVT entry, we take the median of all these individual guesses, which in this case is 156 units. The starred numbers in the listing indicate those uses of the CVT entry where the natural outline distance differs by more than 20% from the median value. We label these *outliers,* and we remove (comment out) the hints corresponding to these uses during the translation process, as they usually represent cases where the shape of the target character differs enough from that of the source character that the CVT constraint is inappropriate. These commented-out constraints correspond to the red lines in the lower row of Figure 5. Note that Trebuchet has a so-called *spectacle g,* while Frutiger has a *multi-story g.* In this case, it is likely that two the forms of the 'g' require entirely different hinting strategies, since many of the hints of the source 'g' are simply not appropriate for the target character shape. These inappropriate

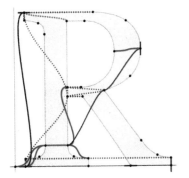
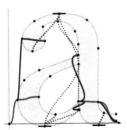

Figure 6 A visualization of the VTT Talk hints created by a professional hinter for two characters of Georgia Roman. *Link* constraints are shown in green, *dist* constraints in blue, and *interpolate* constraints in purple. Solid lines indicate x-direction constraints, while dashed lines indicate y constraints. *Anchors* are indicated with small "wings" on the anchored knot.

source font	target font	success rate (%)	review & cleanup (min.)	manual hinting (min.)	savings (%)
Sylfaen Sans	Sylfaen Sans Bold	84%	5.9	9.4	37%
Georgia Italic	Georgia Bold Italic	86%	6.7	7.9	15%
Georgia Roman	Georgia Bold	93%	4.6	7.1	35%
Georgia Roman	Bodoni	78%	3.3	3.3	0%
Georgia Roman	Calisto	74%	3.0	4.3	30%
Georgia Roman	Perpetua	76%	1.2	2.7	56%
Georgia Roman	Revival	82%	1.3	2.3	43%

Table 2 Times for hinting a sample of representative characters, both starting with the autohinted font and starting with no hints at all.

hints are automatically discarded by the outlier mechanism. Only *link* constraints, which reference the CVT, are eliminated. Other types of hints do not refer to the CVT, and so are never discarded as long as there are matches for the points they constrain.

4 Results

Our program takes two TrueType fonts as input: a source font, from which the hints are transferred; and a target font, which is hinted by the program. The program takes under a minute to match the outlines, translate the hints, and create the new CVT for a 256-character font. Once the target font is hinted, it still needs to be reviewed by hand and corrected by an experienced typographer. Even minor errors in the translated hints or CVT can take a considerable amount of time to identify and correct, so the translation has to be highly accurate in order to be useful.

Figure 7 shows how the set of manually-defined hints for two glyphs from Georgia Roman, 'R' and 'a', have been automatically transferred to five different fonts. Figures 8 and 9 compare the unhinted versions of Sylfaen Sans Bold and Georgia Bold, respectively, to the versions hinted automatically, at 16, 17, and 19 ppem, the most commonly used on-screen sizes. In these examples it is clear that most of the objectionable artifacts in the unhinted versions have already been corrected by the automatic hinting. Note, for instance, the improved 'O' shapes and the much more uniform stem weights in both fonts. Still, the autohinted versions are not perfect; note for instance where the bowl of the Georgia Bold 'b' has narrowed unacceptably, especially at lower sizes. Imperfections like these will need to be corrected by hand.

We evaluated our method by using the program to transfer hints between three pairs of fonts within the same family (Sylfaen Sans Bold from Sylfaen Sans, Georgia Bold from Georgia, and Georgia Bold Italic from Georgia Italic) as well as four target fonts from a source font of a different font family (Bodoni, Calisto, Perpetua, and Revival—all from Georgia). Table 2 summarizes the results of

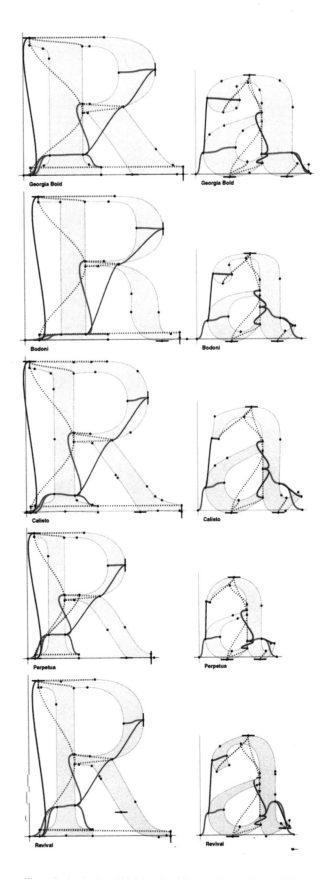

Figure 7 Visualization of hints transferred from the Georgia Roman of Figure 6 to five other fonts.

415

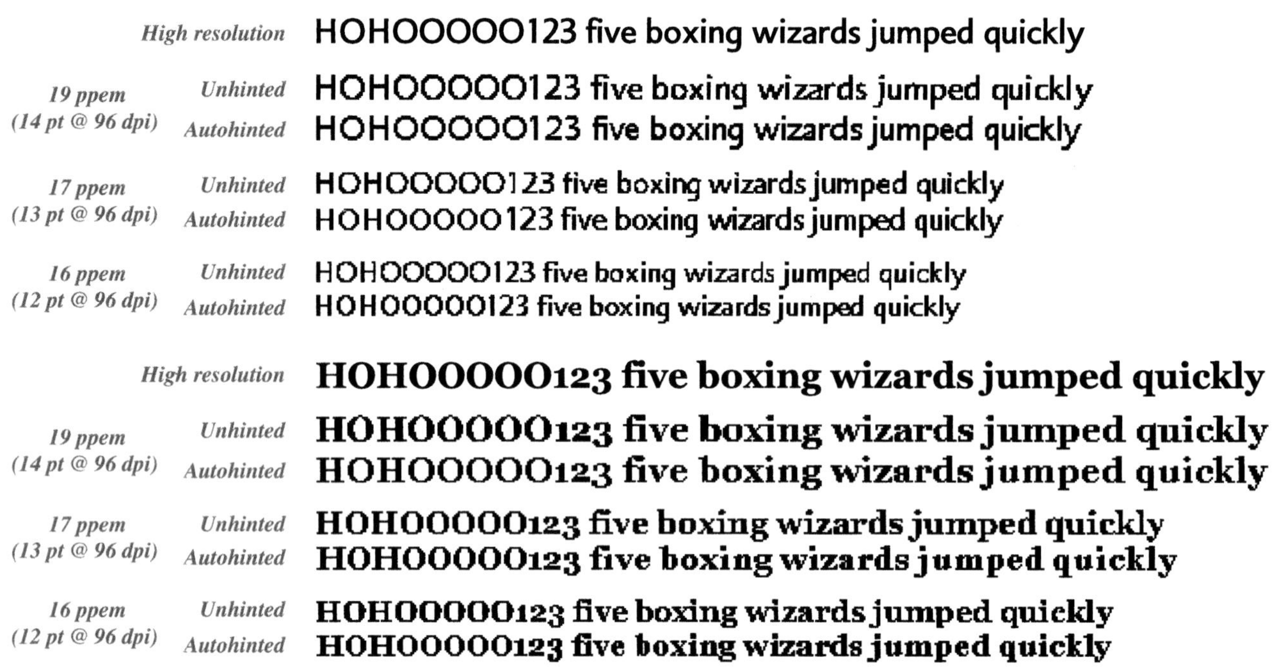

	High resolution	HOHOOOOO123 five boxing wizards jumped quickly
19 ppem *(14 pt @ 96 dpi)*	*Unhinted*	HOHOOOOO123 five boxing wizards jumped quickly
	Autohinted	HOHOOOOO123 five boxing wizards jumped quickly
17 ppem *(13 pt @ 96 dpi)*	*Unhinted*	HOHOOOOO123 five boxing wizards jumped quickly
	Autohinted	HOHOOOOO123 five boxing wizards jumped quickly
16 ppem *(12 pt @ 96 dpi)*	*Unhinted*	HOHOOOOO123 five boxing wizards jumped quickly
	Autohinted	HOHOOOOO123 five boxing wizards jumped quickly
	High resolution	**HOHOOOOO123 five boxing wizards jumped quickly**
19 ppem *(14 pt @ 96 dpi)*	*Unhinted*	**HOHOOOOO123 five boxing wizards jumped quickly**
	Autohinted	**HOHOOOOO123 five boxing wizards jumped quickly**
17 ppem *(13 pt @ 96 dpi)*	*Unhinted*	**HOHOOOOO123 five boxing wizards jumped quickly**
	Autohinted	**HOHOOOOO123 five boxing wizards jumped quickly**
16 ppem *(12 pt @ 96 dpi)*	*Unhinted*	**HOHOOOOO123 five boxing wizards jumped quickly**
	Autohinted	**HOHOOOOO123 five boxing wizards jumped quickly**

Figure 8 Sylfaen Sans Bold (top), and Georgia Bold (bottom), each autohinted by transferring hints from the corresponding roman typeface.

these tests. In each case, just the alphanumeric glyphs were hinted. The "success rate" column gives the percentage of these 62 glyphs in which the transferred hints basically worked. More specifically, for a "successful" glyph, the overall appearance of the glyph conformed to the original outline at high sizes (38 ppem and above) without any stretching or distortion, whereas below 38 ppem there might be some cleaning up to do, but no major reshaping or rethinking of the hints. If a glyph did not conform to its original outline at high sizes or required major reshaping at low sizes, then it was considered "unsuccessful." As can be seen from the table, the hinter had a fairly high success rate by this measure, especially when hinting characters within the same font family.

The next column gives an estimate of the number of minutes required for an experienced typographer to review the results of the autohinter and clean up any problems in the transferred hints. The figures in this column were estimated by performing this process on some 3 to 11 representative glyphs in the target font. These same glyphs were also manually hinted by the same typographer and the times required reported in the following column. Finally, the rightmost column provides an estimate of the overall time savings provided by the example-based hinter.

Note that the very high success rate of the hinter translates into a more moderate overall time savings, since even a perfectly-hinted font requires time to review, and since a few small problems in the hints can be time-consuming to correct. Still, these savings are significant, considering that a full font of 256 characters can take on the order of 20–40 hours for a skilled professional to produce.

5 Conclusion

We have adapted the earlier work of Hersch and Betrisey on automatic hinting through shape matching to create a useful production tool for hinting TrueType fonts. Instead of using hand-created templates for each character to be hinted, we use an existing, hinted font as the template, allowing the hints of one font to be transferred to another. This translation process includes estimation of the control value table entries used to unify feature sizes across a font. The matching algorithm, while simple, works well for a wide variety of character shapes, including serifed and italic fonts.

The hint transfer itself is somewhat less successful, owing primarily to the different strategies used in hinting different styles of characters (e.g., modern serif vs. oldstyle serif). The technique is already quite useful for transferring hints between members of the same family (a roman to a bold, for instance). We expect that transferring hints between fonts of different families will become more and more practical as more fonts are hinted with the VTT tool, so that the hinter has a larger selection of source fonts to choose from and can pick one that is more similar to the target font.

An important advantage of our approach over previous autohinters is that it preserves the hand-crafted hinting strategy, built by a professional typographer, in the newly hinted font. Thus, the translated hints provide a good starting point and generally require only minor cleanup and adjustment. With time, we expect this work to evolve into a highly practical tool for speeding the creation of production-quality digital fonts.

Acknowledgements

We are indebted to Michael Duggan, Greg Hitchcock, and Beat Stamm of the Microsoft eBooks group for the many long discussions about hinting, VTT, TrueType, and typography in general.

References

[1] Adobe Systems, Inc. *Adobe Type 1 Font Format*, March 1990.

[2] Sten F. Andler. Automatic generation of gridfitting hints for rasterization of outline fonts or graphics. In *Proceedings of the International Conference on Electronic Publishing, Document Manipulation, and Typography*, pages 221–234, September 1990.

[3] Apple Computer, Inc. *The TrueType Font Format Specification*, 1990. Version 1.0.

[4] Claude Bétrisey. *Génération Automatique de Contraintes pour Caractères Typographiques à l'Aide d'un Modèle Topologique*. PhD thesis, École Polytechnique Fédérale de Lausanne, 1993.

[5] Roger D. Hersch. Character generation under grid constraints. In *Proceedings of SIGGRAPH 87*, pages 243–252, July 1987.

[6] Roger D. Hersch and Claude Bétrisey. Model-based matching and hinting of fonts. In *Proceedings of SIGGRAPH 91*, pages 71–80, July 1991.

[7] Beat Stamm. Visual TrueType: A graphical method for authoring font intelligence. In R. D. Hersch, J. André, and H. Brown, editors, *Electronic Publishing, Artistic Imaging, and Digital Typography*, pages 77–92, March/April 1998.

Image Inpainting

Marcelo Bertalmio and Guillermo Sapiro*
Electrical and Computer Engineering, University of Minnesota

Vicent Caselles and Coloma Ballester
Escola Superior Politecnica, Universitat Pompeu Fabra

Abstract

Inpainting, the technique of modifying an image in an undetectable form, is as ancient as art itself. The goals and applications of inpainting are numerous, from the restoration of damaged paintings and photographs to the removal/replacement of selected objects. In this paper, we introduce a novel algorithm for digital inpainting of still images that attempts to replicate the basic techniques used by professional restorators. After the user selects the regions to be restored, the algorithm automatically fills-in these regions with information surrounding them. The fill-in is done in such a way that isophote lines arriving at the regions' boundaries are completed inside. In contrast with previous approaches, the technique here introduced does not require the user to specify where the novel information comes from. This is automatically done (and in a fast way), thereby allowing to simultaneously fill-in numerous regions containing completely different structures and surrounding backgrounds. In addition, no limitations are imposed on the topology of the region to be inpainted. Applications of this technique include the restoration of old photographs and damaged film; removal of superimposed text like dates, subtitles, or publicity; and the removal of entire objects from the image like microphones or wires in special effects.

CR Categories: I.3.3 [Computer Graphics]: Picture/Image Generation—; I.3.4 [Computer Graphics]: Graphics Utilities—; I.4.4 [Image Processing and Computer Vision]: Restoration—; I.4.9 [Image Processing and Computer Vision]: Applications—;

Keywords: Image restoration, inpainting, isophotes, anisotropic diffusion.

1 Introduction

The modification of images in a way that is non-detectable for an observer who does not know the original image is a practice as old as artistic creation itself. Medieval artwork started to be restored as early as the Renaissance, the motives being often as much to bring medieval pictures "up to date" as to fill in any gaps [1, 2]. This practice is called *retouching* or *inpainting*. The object of inpainting is to reconstitute the missing or damaged portions of the work, in order to make it more legible and to restore its unity [2].

The need to retouch the image in an unobtrusive way extended naturally from paintings to photography and film. The purposes remain the same: to revert deterioration (e.g., cracks in photographs or scratches and dust spots in film), or to add or remove elements (e.g., removal of stamped date and red-eye from photographs, the infamous "airbrushing" of political enemies [3]).

Digital techniques are starting to be a widespread way of performing inpainting, ranging from attempts to fully automatic detection and removal of scratches in film [4, 5], all the way to software tools that allow a sophisticated but mostly manual process [6].

In this article we introduce a novel algorithm for automatic digital inpainting, being its main motivation to replicate the basic techniques used by professional restorators. At this point, the only user interaction required by the algorithm here introduced is to mark the regions to be inpainted. Although a number of techniques exist for the semi-automatic detection of image defects (mainly in films), addressing this is out of the scope of this paper. Moreover, since the inpainting algorithm here presented can be used not just to restore damaged photographs but also to remove undesired objects and writings on the image, the regions to be inpainted must be marked by the user, since they depend on his/her subjective selection. Here we are concerned on how to "fill-in" the regions to be inpainted, once they have been selected.[1] Marked regions are automatically filled with the structure of their surrounding, in a form that will be explained later in this paper.

2 Related work and our contribution

We should first note that classical image denoising algorithms do not apply to image inpainting. In common image enhancement applications, the pixels contain both information about the real data and the noise (e.g., image plus noise for additive noise), while in image inpainting, there is no significant information in the region to be inpainted. The information is mainly in the regions surrounding the areas to be inpainted. There is then a need to develop specific techniques to address these problems.

Mainly three groups of works can be found in the literature related to digital inpainting. The first one deals with the restoration of films, the second one is related to texture synthesis, and the third one, a significantly less studied class though very influential to the work here presented, is related to disocclusion.

Kokaram et al. [5] use motion estimation and autoregressive models to interpolate losses in films from adjacent frames. The basic idea is to copy into the gap the right pixels from neighboring frames. The technique can not be applied to still images or to films where the regions to be inpainted span many frames.

---

*Electrical and Computer Engineering, University of Minnesota, Minneapolis, MN 55455, USA, {marcelo,guille}@ece.umn.edu

[1] In order to study the robustness of the algorithm here proposed, and not to be too dependent on the marking of the regions to be inpainted, we mark them in a very rough form with any available paintbrush software. Marking these regions in the examples reported in this paper just takes a few seconds to a non-expert user.

Hirani and Totsuka [7] combine frequency and spatial domain information in order to fill a given region with a selected texture. This is a very simple technique that produces incredible good results. On the other hand, the algorithm mainly deals with texture synthesis (and not with structured background), and requires the user to select the texture to be copied into the region to be inpainted. For images where the region to be replaced covers several different structures, the user would need to go through the tremendous work of segmenting them and searching corresponding replacements throughout the picture. Although part of this search can be done automatically, this is extremely time consuming and requires the non-trivial selection of many critical parameters, e.g., [8]. Other texture synthesis algorithms, e.g., [8, 9, 10], can be used as well to re-create a pre-selected texture to fill-in a (square) region to be inpainted.

In the group of disocclusion algorithms, a pioneering work is described in [11]. The authors presented a technique for removing occlusions with the goal of image segmentation.[2] The basic idea is to connect T-junctions at the same gray-level with elastica minimizing curves. The technique was mainly developed for simple images, with only a few objects with constant gray-levels, and will not be applicable for the examples with natural images presented later in this paper. Masnou and Morel [12] recently extended these ideas, presenting a very inspiring general variational formulation for disocclusion and a particular practical algorithm (not entirely based on PDE's) implementing some of the ideas in this formulation. The algorithm performs inpainting by joining with geodesic curves the points of the isophotes (lines of equal gray values) arriving at the boundary of the region to be inpainted. As reported by the authors, the regions to be inpainted are limited to having simple topology, e.g., holes are not allowed.[3] In addition, the angle with which the level lines arrive at the boundary of the inpainted region is not (well) preserved: the algorithm uses straight lines to join equal gray value pixels. These drawbacks, which will be exemplified later in this paper, are solved by our algorithm. On the other hand, we should note that this is the closest technique to ours and has motivated in part and inspired our work.

2.1 Our contribution

Algorithms devised for film restoration are not appropriate for our application since they normally work on relatively small regions and rely on the existence of information from several frames.

On the other hand, algorithms based on texture synthesis can fill large regions, but require the user to specify what texture to put where. This is a significant limitation of these approaches, as may be seen in examples presented later in this paper, where the region to be inpainted is surrounded by hundreds of different backgrounds, some of them being structure and not texture.

The technique we propose does not require any user intervention, once the region to be inpainted has been selected. The algorithm is able to simultaneously fill regions surrounded by different backgrounds, without the user specifying "what to put where." No assumptions on the topology of the region to be inpainted, or on the simplicity of the image, are made. The algorithm is devised for inpainting in structured regions (e.g., regions crossing through boundaries), though it is not devised to reproduce large textured areas. As we will discuss later, the combination of our proposed approach with texture synthesis techniques is the subject of current research.

---

[2]Since the region to be inpainted can be considered as occluding objects, removing occlusions is analogous to image inpainting.

[3]This is not intrinsic to the general variational formulation they propose, only to the specific discrete implementation they perform.

3 The digital inpainting algorithm

3.1 Fundamentals

Let Ω stand for the region to be inpainted, and $\partial\Omega$ for its boundary (note once again that no assumption on the topology of Ω is made). Intuitively, the technique we propose will prolong the isophote lines arriving at $\partial\Omega$, while maintaining the angle of "arrival." We proceed drawing from $\partial\Omega$ inward in this way, while curving the prolongation lines progressively to prevent them from crossing each other.

Before presenting the detailed description of this technique, let us analyze how experts inpaint. Conservators at the Minneapolis Institute of Arts were consulted for this work and made it clear to us that inpainting is a very subjective procedure, different for each work of art and for each professional. There is no such thing as "the" way to solve the problem, but the underlying methodology is as follows: (1.) The global picture determines how to fill in the gap, the purpose of inpainting being to restore the unity of the work; (2.) The structure of the area surrounding Ω is continued into the gap, contour lines are drawn via the prolongation of those arriving at $\partial\Omega$; (3.) The different regions inside Ω, as defined by the contour lines, are filled with color, matching those of $\partial\Omega$; and (4.) The small details are painted (e.g. little white spots on an otherwise uniformly blue sky): in other words, "texture" is added.

A number of lessons can immediately be learned from these basic inpainting rules used by professionals. Our algorithm simultaneously, and iteratively, performs the steps (2.) and (3.) above.[4] We progressively "shrink" the gap Ω by prolonging inward, in a smooth way, the lines arriving at the gap boundary $\partial\Omega$.

3.2 The inpainting algorithm

We need to translate the manual inpainting concepts expressed above into a mathematical and algorithmic language. We proceed to do this now, presenting the basic underlying concepts first. The implementation details are given in the next section.

Let $I_0(i,j) : [0,M] \times [0,N] \to \mathbb{R}$, with $[0,M] \times [0,N] \subset \mathbb{N} \times \mathbb{N}$, be a discrete 2D gray level image. From the description of manual inpainting techniques, an iterative algorithm seems a natural choice. The digital inpainting procedure will construct a family of images $I(i,j,n) : [0,M] \times [0,N] \times \mathbb{N} \to \mathbb{R}$ such that $I(i,j,0) = I_0(i,j)$ and $lim_{n\to\infty} I(i,j,n) = I_R(i,j)$, where $I_R(i,j)$ is the output of the algorithm (inpainted image). Any general algorithm of that form can be written as

$$ I^{n+1}(i,j) = I^n(i,j) + \Delta t I^n_t(i,j), \forall(i,j) \in \Omega \qquad (1) $$

where the superindex n denotes the inpainting "time" n, (i,j) are the pixel coordinates, Δt is the rate of improvement and $I^n_t(i,j)$ stands for the update of the image $I^n(i,j)$. Note that the evolution equation runs only inside Ω, the region to be inpainted.

With this equation, the image $I^{n+1}(i,j)$ is an improved version of $I^n(i,j)$, with the "improvement" given by $I^n_t(i,j)$. As n increases, we achieve a better image. We need now to design the update $I^n_t(i,j)$.

As suggested by manual inpainting techniques, we need to continue the lines arriving at the boundary $\partial\Omega$ of the region Ω to be inpainted (see point (2) in Section 3.1). In other words, we need to smoothly propagate information from outside Ω into Ω (points (2) and (3) in Section 3.1). Being $L^n(i,j)$ the information that we want to propagate, and $\overrightarrow{N}^n(i,j)$ the propagation direction, this means that we must have

---

[4]In the discussion section we will argue how both steps can be performed separately, and we will also discuss step (4.).

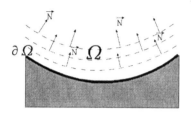

Figure 1: Propagation direction as the normal to the signed distance to the boundary of the region to be inpainted.

Figure 2: Unsuccessful choice of the information propagation direction. Left: detail of the original image, region to be inpainted is in white. Right: restoration.

$$I_t^n(i,j) = \overrightarrow{\delta L^n}(i,j) \cdot \overrightarrow{N}^n(i,j), \qquad (2)$$

where $\overrightarrow{\delta L^n}(i,j)$ is a measure of the change in the information $L^n(i,j)$.[5] With this equation, we estimate the information $L^n(i,j)$ of our image and compute its change along the $\overrightarrow{N}$ direction. Note that at steady state, that is, when the algorithm converges, $I^{n+1}(i,j) = I^n(i,j)$ and from (1) and (2) we have that $\overrightarrow{\delta L^n}(i,j) \cdot \overrightarrow{N}^n(i,j) = 0$, meaning exactly that the information L has been propagated in the direction $\overrightarrow{N}$.

What is left now is to express the information L being propagated and the direction of propagation $\overrightarrow{N}$.

Since we want the propagation to be smooth, $L^n(i,j)$ should be an image smoothness estimator. For this purpose we may use a simple discrete implementation of the Laplacian: $L^n(i,j) := I_{xx}^n(i,j) + I_{yy}^n(i,j)$ (subscripts represent derivatives in this case). Other smoothness estimators might be used, though satisfactory results were already obtained with this very simple selection.

Then, we must compute the change $\overrightarrow{\delta L^n}(i,j)$ of this value along $\overrightarrow{N}$. In order to do this we must first define what the direction $\overrightarrow{N}$ for the 2D information propagation will be. One possibility is to define $\overrightarrow{N}$ as the normal to the signed distance to $\partial\Omega$, i.e., at each point (i,j) in Ω the vector $\overrightarrow{N}(i,j)$ will be normal to the "shrinked version" of $\partial\Omega$ to which (i,j) belongs, see Figure 1. This choice is motivated by the belief that a propagation normal to the boundary would lead to the continuity of the isophotes at the boundary. Instead, what happens is that the lines arriving at $\partial\Omega$ curve in order to align with $\overrightarrow{N}$, see Figure 2. This is of course not what we expect. Note that the orientation of $\partial\Omega$ is not intrinsic to the image geometry, since the region to be inpainted is arbitrary.

If isophotes tend to align with $\overrightarrow{N}$, the best choice for $\overrightarrow{N}$ is then the isophotes directions. This is a bootstrapping problem: having the isophotes directions inside Ω is equivalent to having the inpainted image itself, since we can easily recover the gray level image from its isophote direction field (see the discussion section and [13]).

---

[5]Borrowing notation from continuous mathematics, we could also write $\overrightarrow{\delta L^n}(i,j)$ as ∇L.

We use then a time varying estimation of the isophotes direction field: for any given point (i,j), the discretized gradient vector $\nabla I^n(i,j)$ gives the direction of largest spatial change, while its 90 degrees rotation $\nabla^\perp I^n(i,j)$ is the direction of smallest spatial change, so the vector $\nabla^\perp I^n(i,j)$ gives the isophotes direction. Our field $\overrightarrow{N}$ is then given by the time-varying $\overrightarrow{N}(i,j,n) = \nabla^\perp I^n(i,j)$. We are using a time-varying estimation that is coarse at the beginning but progressively achieves the desired continuity at $\partial\Omega$, instead of a fixed field $\overrightarrow{N}(i,j)$ that would imply to know the directions of the isophotes from the start.

Note that the direction field is not normalized, its norm is the norm of the gradient of $I^n(i,j)$. This choice helps in the numerical stability of the algorithm, and will be discussed in the following subsection.

Since we are performing inpainting along the isophotes, it is irrelevant if $\nabla^\perp I^n(i,j)$ is obtained as a clockwise or counterclockwise rotation of $\nabla I^n(i,j)$. In both cases, the change of $I^n(i,j)$ along those directions should be minimum.

Recapping, we estimate a variation of the smoothness, given by a discretization of the 2D Laplacian in our case, and project this variation into the isophotes direction. This projection is used to update the value of the image inside the region to be inpainted.

To ensure a correct evolution of the direction field, a diffusion process is interleaved with the image inpainting process described above.[6] That is, every few steps (see below), we apply a few iterations of image diffusion. This diffusion corresponds to the periodical curving of lines to avoid them from crossing each other, as was mentioned in Section 3.1. We use anisotropic diffusion, [14, 15], in order to achieve this goal without losing sharpness in the reconstruction. In particular, we apply a straightforward discretization of the following continuous-time/continuous-space anisotropic diffusion equation:

$$\frac{\partial I}{\partial t}(x,y,t) = g_\epsilon(x,y)\kappa(x,y,t)\,|\nabla I(x,y,t)|\,, \forall(x,y) \in \Omega^\epsilon \quad (3)$$

where Ω^ϵ is a dilation of Ω with a ball of radius ϵ, κ is the Euclidean curvature of the isophotes of I and $g_\epsilon(x,y)$ is a smooth function in Ω^ϵ such that $g_\epsilon(x,y) = 0$ in $\partial\Omega^\epsilon$, and $g_\epsilon(x,y) = 1$ in Ω (this is a way to impose Dirichlet boundary conditions for the equation (3)).[7]

3.3 Discrete scheme and implementation details

The only input to our algorithm are the image to be restored and the mask that delimits the portion to be inpainted. As a preprocessing step, the *whole* original image undergoes anisotropic diffusion smoothing. The purpose of this is to minimize the influence of noise on the estimation of the direction of the isophotes arriving at $\partial\Omega$. After this, the image enters the inpainting loop, where only the values inside Ω are modified. These values change according to the discrete implementation of the inpainting procedure, which we proceed to describe. Every few iterations, a step of anisotropic diffusion is applied (a straightforward, central differences implementation of (3) is used; for details see [14, 15]). This process is repeated until a steady state is achieved.

Let $I^n(i,j)$ stand for each one of the image pixels inside the region Ω at the inpainting "time" n. Then, the discrete inpainting equation borrows from the numerical analysis literature and is given by

$$I^{n+1}(i,j) = I^n(i,j) + \Delta t I_t^n(i,j), \forall(i,j) \in \Omega \quad (4)$$

---

[6]We can also add the diffusion as an additional term in $I_t^n(i,j)$, the results being very similar.

[7]Other filters, e.g., form mathematical morphology, can be applied as well, though we found the results obtained with this equation satisfactory.

where

$$I_t^n(i,j) = \left(\overrightarrow{\delta L^n}(i,j) \cdot \frac{\overrightarrow{N}(i,j,n)}{\left| \overrightarrow{N}(i,j,n) \right|} \right) \left| \nabla I^n(i,j) \right|, \quad (5)$$

$$\overrightarrow{\delta L^n}(i,j) := (L^n(i+1,j) - L^n(i-1,j), L^n(i,j+1) - L^n(i,j-1)), \quad (6)$$

$$L^n(i,j) = I_{xx}^n(i,j) + I_{yy}^n(i,j), \quad (7)$$

$$\frac{\overrightarrow{N}(i,j,n)}{\left| \overrightarrow{N}(i,j,n) \right|} := \frac{(-I_y^n(i,j), I_x^n(i,j))}{\sqrt{(I_x^n(i,j))^2 + (I_y^n(i,j))^2}}, \quad (8)$$

$$\beta^n(i,j) = \overrightarrow{\delta L^n}(i,j) \cdot \frac{\overrightarrow{N}(i,j,n)}{\left| \overrightarrow{N}(i,j,n) \right|}, \quad (9)$$

and

$$\left| \nabla I^n(i,j) \right| = \begin{cases} \sqrt{(I_{xbm}^n)^2 + (I_{xfM}^n)^2 + (I_{ybm}^n)^2 + (I_{yfM}^n)^2}, \\ \quad \text{when } \beta^n > 0 \\ \sqrt{(I_{xbM}^n)^2 + (I_{xfm}^n)^2 + (I_{ybM}^n)^2 + (I_{yfm}^n)^2}, \\ \quad \text{when } \beta^n < 0 \end{cases} \quad (10)$$

We first compute the 2D smoothness estimation L in (7) and the isophote direction $\overrightarrow{N}/\left| \overrightarrow{N} \right|$ in (8). Then in (9) we compute β^n, the projection of $\overrightarrow{\delta L}$ onto the (normalized) vector $\overrightarrow{N}$, that is, we compute the change of L along the direction of $\overrightarrow{N}$. Finally, we multiply β^n by a *slope-limited* version of the norm of the gradient of the image, $\left| \nabla I \right|$, in (10). [8] A central differences realization would turn the scheme unstable, and that is the reason for using slope-limiters. The subindexes b and f denote backward and forward differences respectively, while the subindexes m and M denote the minimum or maximum, respectively, between the derivative and zero (we have omitted the space coordinates (i,j) for simplicity); see [16] for details. Finally, let us note that the choice of a non-normalized field $\overrightarrow{N}$ instead of a normalized version of it allows for a simpler and more stable numerical scheme; see [17, 18].

Note once again that when the inpainting algorithm arrives to steady state, that is, $I_t = 0$, we have geometrically solved $\nabla(\text{Smoothness}) \cdot \nabla^{\perp} I = 0$, meaning that the "smoothness" is constant along the isophotes. [9]

When applying equations (4)-(10) to the pixels in the border $\partial \Omega$ of the region Ω to be inpainted, known pixels from outside this region are used. That is, conceptually, we compute equations (4)-(10) in the region Ω^{ϵ} (an ϵ dilation of Ω), although we update the values only inside Ω (that is, (4) is applied only inside Ω). The information in the narrow band $\Omega^{\epsilon} - \Omega$ is propagated inside Ω. Propagation of this information, both gray-values and isophotes directions, is fundamental for the success of the algorithm.

In the restoration loop we perform A steps of inpainting with (4), then B steps of diffusion with (3), again A steps of (4), and so on. The total number of steps is T. This number may be pre-established, or the algorithm may stop when changes in the image are below a given threshold. The values we use are: $A = 15, B = 2$, at speed $\Delta t = 0.1$. The value of T depends on the size of Ω.

---

[8]Note that $\left| \nabla I \right| = \left| \nabla^{\perp} I \right|$.

[9]This type of information propagation is related and might be applicable to velocity fields extension in level-set techniques [19, 20].

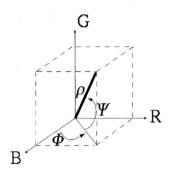

Figure 3: Relation between the (R, G, B) color model and the one used in this article,$(\rho, sin\phi, sin\psi)$.

If Ω is of considerable size, a *multiresolution* approach is used to speed-up the process.[10]

Color images are considered as a set of three images, and the above described technique is applied independently to each one. To avoid the appearance of spurious colors, we use a color model which is very similar to the LUV model, with one luminance and two chroma components. See Figure 3.

4 Results

The CPU time required for inpainting depends on the size of Ω. In all the color examples here presented, the inpainting process was completed in less than 5 minutes (for the three color planes), using non-optimized C++ code running on a PentiumII PC (128Mb RAM, 300MHz) under Linux. All the examples use images available from public databases over the Internet. The main examples here presented, and additional ones, can be seen at http://www.ece.umn.edu/users/marcelo/restoration.html, where in addition to the original and inpainted images reproduced below, the evolution process can be observed.

Figure 4 shows, on the left, a synthetic image with the region to inpaint in white. Here Ω is large (30 pixels in diameter) and contains a hole. The inpainted reconstruction is shown on the right. Notice that contours are recovered, joining points from the inner and outer boundaries. Also, these reconstructed contours follow smoothly the direction of the isophotes arriving at $\partial \Omega$ (the algorithm reported in [12] will fail with this type of data).

Figure 5 shows a deteriorated B&W image (first row) and its reconstruction (second row). As in all the examples in this article, the user only supplied the "mask" image (last row). This mask was drawn manually, using a paintbrush-like program. The variables were set to the values specified in the previous section, and the number of iterations T was set to 3000. When multiresolution is not used, the CPU time required by the inpainting procedure was approximately 7 minutes. With a 2-level multiresolution scheme, only 2 minutes were needed. Observe that details in the nose and right eye of the middle girl could not be completely restored. This is in part due to the fact that the mask covers most of the relevant information, and there is not much to be done without the use of high level prior information (e.g., the fact that it is an eye). These minor errors can be corrected by the manual procedures mentioned in the introduction, and still the overall inpainting time would be reduced by orders of magnitude. This example was tested and showed to be robust to initial conditions inside the region to be inpainted.

Figure 6 shows a vandalized image and its restoration, followed by an example where overimposed text is removed from the image.

---

[10]We basically use the converged result of a lower resolution stage to initialize the higher one, as classically done in image processing.

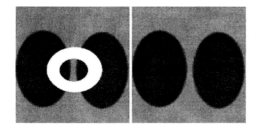

Figure 4: Synthetic example: Ω is shown in white. Topology is not an issue, and the recovered contours smoothly continue the isophotes.

These are typical examples where texture synthesis algorithms as those described in the introduction can not be used, since the number of different regions to be filled-in is very large.

The next figure shows the progressive nature of the algorithm, several intermediate steps of the inpainting procedure are shown, removing painted text over a natural scene.

Finally, Figure 8 shows an entertainment application. The bungee cord and the knot tying the man's legs have been removed. Given the size of Ω a 2-level multiresolution scheme was used. Here it becomes apparent that it is the user who has to supply the algorithm with the masking image, since the choice of the region to inpaint is completely subjective.

5   Conclusions and future work

In this paper we have introduced a novel algorithm for image inpainting that attempts to replicate the basic techniques used by professional restorators. The basic idea is to smoothly propagate information from the surrounding areas in the isophotes direction. The user needs only to provide the region to be inpainted, the rest is automatically performed by the algorithm in a few minutes. The inpainted images are sharp and without color artifacts. The examples shown suggest a wide range of applications like restoration of old photographs and damaged film, removal of superimposed text, and removal of objects. The results can either be adopted as a final restoration or be used to provide an initial point for manual restoration, thereby reducing the total restoration time by orders of magnitude.

One of the main problems with our technique is the reproduction of large textured regions, as can be seen in Figure 9. The algorithm here proposed is currently being tested in conjunction with texture synthesis ideas to address this issue. We are mainly investigation the combination of this approach with the reaction-diffusion ideas of Kass and Witkin and of Turk. An ideal algorithm should be able to automatically switch between textured and geometric areas, and select the best suited technique for each region.

We would also like to investigate how to inpaint from partial degradation. In the example of the old photo for example, ideally the mask should not be binary, since some underlying information exists in the degraded areas.

The inpainting algorithm here presented has been clearly motivated by and has borrowed from the intensive work on the use of Partial Differential Equations (PDE's) in image processing and computer vision. When "blindly" letting the grid go to zero, the inpainting technique in equations (4)-(10) naively resembles a third order equation, for which too many boundary conditions are imposed (being all of them essential). Although theoretical results for high order equations are available, e.g., [21], and some properties like preservation of the image moments can be immediately proved for our corresponding equation (this was done by A. Bertozzi), fur-

ther formal study of our "high order equation" is needed (see also [22, 23]). Nevertheless, this suggests the investigation of the use of lower, second order, PDE's to address the inpainting problem. We can split the inpainting problem into two coupled variational formulations, one for the isophotes direction (point (2) in Section 3.1) and one for the gray-values, consistent with the estimated directions (point (3) in Section 3.1). The corresponding gradient descent flows will give two coupled second order PDE's for which formal results regarding existence and uniqueness of the solutions can be shown. This is reported in [24].

Acknowledgments

This work started when the authors were visiting the Institute Henri Poincare in Paris, France. We thank the organizers of the quarter on "Mathematical Questions in Signal and Image Processing" and the Institute for their hospitality and partial financial support. We would like to thank Tom Robbins and Elizabeth Buschor from the Upper Midwest Conservation Association for their help in linking our work with actual art restoration and conservation. Amy Miller, of Photo-Medic, kindly provided the damaged photograph shown in the examples. We also thank Dr. Santiago Betelu, Prof. Stan Osher, Prof. Eero Simoncelli, and Prof. Andrea Bertozzi for very interesting discussions and feedback. The reviewers provided many useful ideas. This work was partially supported by a grant from the Office of Naval Research ONR-N00014-97-1-0509, the Office of Naval Research Young Investigator Award, the Presidential Early Career Awards for Scientists and Engineers (PECASE), a National Science Foundation CAREER Award, by the National Science Foundation Learning and Intelligent Systems Program (LIS), and Universidad de la Republica (Uruguay).

References

[1] S. Walden. *The Ravished Image*. St. Martin's Press, New York, 1985.

[2] G. Emile-Male. *The Restorer's Handbook of Easel Painting*. Van Nostrand Reinhold, New York, 1976.

[3] D. King. *The Commissar Vanishes*. Henry Holt and Company, 1997.

[4] A.C. Kokaram, R.D. Morris, W.J. Fitzgerald, P.J.W. Rayner. *Detection of missing data in image sequences*. IEEE Transactions on Image Processing 11(4), 1496-1508, 1995.

[5] A.C. Kokaram, R.D. Morris, W.J. Fitzgerald, P.J.W. Rayner. *Interpolation of missing data in image sequences*. IEEE Transactions on Image Processing 11(4), 1509-1519, 1995.

[6] C. Braverman. *Photoshop retouching handbook*. IDG Books Worldwide, 1998.

[7] A. Hirani and T. Totsuka. *Combining Frequency and spatial domain information for fast interactive image noise removal*. Computer Graphics, pp. 269-276, SIGGRAPH 96, 1996.

[8] A. Efros and T. Leung, "Texture synthesis by non-parametric sampling," *Proc. IEEE International Conference Computer Vision*, pp. 1033-1038, Corfu, Greece, September 1999.

[9] D. Heeger and J. Bergen. *Pyramid based texture analysis/synthesis*. Computer Graphics, pp. 229-238, SIGGRAPH 95, 1995.

[10] E. Simoncelli and J. Portilla. *Texture characterization via joint statistics of wavelet coefficient magnitudes*. 5th IEEE Int'l Conf. on Image Processing, Chicago, IL. Oct 4-7, 1998.

[11] M. Nitzberg, D. Mumford, and T. Shiota, *Filtering, Segmentation, and Depth*, Springer-Verlag, Berlin, 1993.

[12] S. Masnou and J.M. Morel. *Level-lines based disocclusion*. 5th IEEE Int'l Conf. on Image Processing, Chicago, IL. Oct 4-7, 1998.

[13] C. Kenney and J. Langan. *A new image processing primitive: reconstructing images from modified flow fields*. University of California Santa Barbara Preprint, 1999.

[14] P. Perona and J. Malik *Scale-space and edge detection using anisotropic diffusion*. IEEE-PAMI 12, pp. 629-639, 1990.

[15] L. Alvarez, P.L. Lions, J.M. Morel. *Image selective smoothing and edge detection by nonlinear diffusion*. SIAM J. Numer. Anal. 29, pp. 845-866, 1992.

[16] S. Osher and J. Sethian. *Fronts propagating with curvature dependent speed: algorithms based on Hamilton-Jacobi formulations*. Journal of Computational Physics, 79:12-49, 1988.

[17] A. Marquina and S. Osher. *Explicit algorithms for a new time dependent model based on level set motion for nonlinear deblurring and noise removal*. UCLA CAM Report 99-5, January 1999.

[18] L. Rudin, S. Osher and E. Fatemi. *Nonlinear total variation based noise removal algorithms*. Physica D, 60, pp. 259-268, 1992.

[19] S. Osher, personal communication, October 1999.

[20] H. K. Zhao, T. Chan, B. Merriman, and S. Osher, "A variational level-set approach to multiphase motion," *J. of Computational Physics* **127**, pp. 179-195, 1996.

[21] A. Bertozzi *The mathematics of moving contact lines in thin liquid films*. Notices Amer. Math. Soc., Volume 45, Number 6, pp. 689-697, June/July 1998.

[22] J. Tumblin and G. Turk, "LCIS: A boundary hierarchy for detail-preserving contrast reduction," Computer Graphics, pp. 83-90, SIGGRAPH 99, 1999.

[23] T. Chan and J. Shen, "Mathematical models for local deterministic inpaintings," *UCLA CAM TR* **00-11**, March 2000.

[24] C. Ballester, M. Bertalmio, V. Caselles, G. Sapiro, and J. Verdera, "Filling-in by joint interpolation of vector fields and grey levels," *University of Minnesota IMA TR*, April 2000.

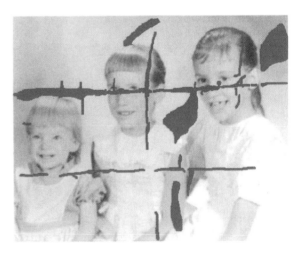

Figure 5: Restoration of an old photograph.

Figure 6: Restoration of a color image and removal of superimposed text.

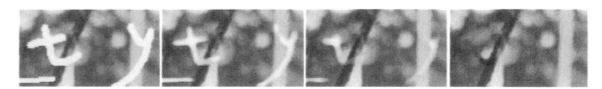

Figure 7: Progressive nature of the algorithm. Several intermediate steps of the reconstruction are shown.

Figure 8: The bungee cord and the knot tying the man's feet have been removed.

Figure 9: Limitations of the algorithm: texture is not reproduced.

Interactive Multi-Pass Programmable Shading

Mark S. Peercy, Marc Olano, John Airey,* P. Jeffrey Ungar

SGI

Abstract

Programmable shading is a common technique for production animation, but interactive programmable shading is not yet widely available. We support interactive programmable shading on virtually any 3D graphics hardware using a scene graph library on top of OpenGL. We treat the OpenGL architecture as a general SIMD computer, and translate the high-level shading description into OpenGL rendering passes. While our system uses OpenGL, the techniques described are applicable to any retained mode interface with appropriate extension mechanisms and hardware API with provisions for recirculating data through the graphics pipeline.

We present two demonstrations of the method. The first is a constrained shading language that runs on graphics hardware supporting OpenGL 1.2 with a subset of the ARB imaging extensions. We remove the shading language constraints by minimally extending OpenGL. The key extensions are *color range* (supporting extended range and precision data types) and *pixel texture* (using framebuffer values as indices into texture maps). Our second demonstration is a renderer supporting the RenderMan Interface and RenderMan Shading Language on a software implementation of this extended OpenGL. For both languages, our compiler technology can take advantage of extensions and performance characteristics unique to any particular graphics hardware.

CR categories and subject descriptors: I.3.3 [Computer Graphics]: Picture/Image generation; I.3.7 [Image Processing]: Enhancement.

Keywords: Graphics Hardware, Graphics Systems, Illumination, Languages, Rendering, Interactive Rendering, Non-Realistic Rendering, Multi-Pass Rendering, Programmable Shading, Procedural Shading, Texture Synthesis, Texture Mapping, OpenGL.

1 INTRODUCTION

Programmable shading is a means for specifying the appearance of objects in a synthetic scene. Programs in a special purpose language, known as *shaders*, describe light source position and emission characteristics, color and reflective properties of surfaces, or transmittance properties of atmospheric media. Conceptually, these programs are executed for each point on an object as it is being rendered to produce a final color (and perhaps opacity) as seen from a given viewpoint. Shading languages can be quite general, having

---

*Now at Intrinsic Graphics

constructs familiar from general purpose programming languages such as C, including loops, conditionals, and functions. The most common is the RenderMan Shading Language [32].

The power of shading languages for describing intricate lighting and shading computations been widely recognized since Cook's seminal shade tree research [7]. Programmable shading has played a fundamental role in digital content creation for motion pictures and television for over a decade. The high level of abstraction in programmable shading enables artists, storytellers, and their technical collaborators to translate their creative visions into images more easily. Shading languages are also used for visualization of scientific data. Special *data shaders* have been developed to support the depiction of volume data [3, 8], and a texture synthesis language has been used for visualizing data fields on surfaces [9]. Image processing scripting languages [22, 31] also share much in common with programmable shading.

Despite its proven usefulness in software rendering, hardware acceleration of programmable shading has remained elusive. Most hardware supports a parametric appearance model, such as Phong lighting evaluated per vertex, with one or more texture maps applied after Gouraud interpolation of the lighting results [29]. The general computational nature of programmable shading, and the unbounded complexity of shaders, has kept it from being supported widely in hardware. This paper describes a methodology to support programmable shading in interactive visual computing by compiling a shader into multiple passes through graphics hardware. We demonstrate its use on current systems with a constrained shading language, and we show how to support general shading languages with only two hardware extensions.

1.1 Related Work

Interactive programmable shading, with dynamically changing shader and scene, was demonstrated on the PixelFlow system [26]. PixelFlow has an array of general purpose processors that can execute arbitrary code at every pixel. Shaders written in a language based on RenderMan's are translated into C++ programs with embedded machine code directives for the pixel processors. An application accesses shaders through a programmable interface extension to OpenGL. The primary disadvantages of this approach are the additional burden it places on the graphics hardware and driver software. Every system that supports a built-in programmable interface must include powerful enough general computing units to execute the programmable shaders. Limitations to these computing units, such as a fixed local memory, will either limit the shaders that may be run, have a severe impact on performance, or cause the system to revert to multiple passes within the driver. Further, every such system will have a unique shading language compiler as part of the driver software. This is a sophisticated piece of software which greatly increases the complexity of the driver.

Our approach to programmable shading stands in contrast to the programmable hardware method. Its inspiration is a long line of interactive algorithms that follow a general theme: treat the graphics hardware as a collection of primitive operations that can be used to build up a final solution in multiple passes. Early examples of this model include multi-pass shadows, planar reflections, highlights on top of texture, depth of field, and light maps [2, 10]. There has been a dramatic surge of research in this area over the past few years. Sophisticated appearance computations, which had previously been available only in software renderers, have been mapped to generic graphics hardware. For example, lighting per pixel, general bidirectional reflectance distribution functions, and bump mapping now run in real-time on hardware that supports none of those effects natively [6, 17, 20, 24].

Consumer games like ID Software's Quake 3 make extensive use of multi-pass effects [19]. Quake 3 recognizes that multi-pass provides a flexible method for surface design and takes the important step of providing a scripting mechanism for rendering passes, including control of OpenGL blending mode, alpha test functions, and vertex texture coordinate assignment. In its current form, this scripting language does not provide access to all of the OpenGL state necessary to treat OpenGL as a general SIMD machine.

A team at Stanford has been investigating real-time programmable shading. Their focus is a framework and language that explicitly divides operations into those that are executed at the vertex processing stage in the graphics pipeline and those that are executed at the fragment processing stage [25].

The hardware in all of these cases is being used as a computing machine rather than a special purpose accelerator. Indeed, graphics hardware has been used to accelerate techniques such as back-projection for tomographic reconstruction [5] and radiosity approximations [21]. It is now recognized that some new hardware features, such as multi-texture [24, 29], pixel texture [17], and color matrix [23], are particularly valuable for supporting these advanced computations interactively.

1.2 Our Contribution

In this paper, we embrace and extend previous multi-pass techniques. We treat the OpenGL architecture as a SIMD computer. OpenGL acts as an assembly language for shader execution. The challenge, then, is to convert a shader into an efficient set of OpenGL rendering passes on a given system. We introduce a compiler between the application and the graphics library that can target shaders to different hardware implementations.

This philosophy of placing the shading compiler above the graphics API is at the core of our work, and has a number of advantages. We believe the number of languages for interactive programmable shading will grow and evolve over the next several years, responding to the unique performance and feature demands of different application areas. Likewise, hardware will increase in performance and many new features will be introduced. Our methodology allows the languages, compiler, and hardware to evolve independently because they are cleanly decoupled.

This paper has three main contributions. First, we formalize the idea of using OpenGL as an assembly language into which programmable shaders are translated, and we show how to apply dynamic tree-rewriting compiler technology to optimize the mapping between shading languages and OpenGL (Section 2). Second, we demonstrate the immediate application of this approach by introducing a constrained shading language that runs interactively on most current hardware systems (Section 3). Third, we describe the color range and pixel texture OpenGL extensions that are necessary and sufficient to accelerate fully general shading languages (Section 4). As a demonstration of the viability of this solution, we present a complete RenderMan renderer including full support of the RenderMan Shading Language running on a software im-

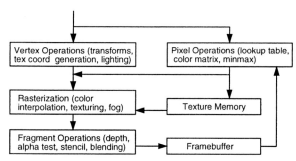

Figure 1: A simplified block diagram of the OpenGL architecture. Geometric data passes through the vertex operations, rasterization, and fragment operations to the framebuffer. Pixel data (either from the host or the framebuffer) passes through the pixel operations and on to either texture memory or through the fragment pipeline to the framebuffer.

plementation of this extended OpenGL. We close the paper with a discussion (Section 5) and conclusion (Section 6).

2 THE SHADING FRAMEWORK

There is great diversity in modern 3D graphics hardware. Each graphics system includes unique features and performance characteristics. Countering this diversity, all modern graphics hardware also supports the basic features of the OpenGL API standard.

While it is possible to add shading extensions to graphics hardware, OpenGL is powerful enough to support shading with no extensions at all. Building programmable shading on top of standard OpenGL decouples the hardware and drivers from the language, and enables shading on every existing and future OpenGL-based graphics system.

A compiler turns shading computations into multiple passes through the OpenGL rendering pipeline (Figure 1). This compiler can produce a general set of rendering passes, or it can use knowledge of the target hardware to pick an optimized set of passes.

2.1 OpenGL as an Assembly Language

One key observation allows shaders to be translated into multi-pass OpenGL: a single rendering pass is also a general SIMD instruction — the same operations are performed simultaneously for all pixels in an object. At the simplest level, the framebuffer is an accumulator, texture or pixel buffers serve as per-pixel memory storage, blending provides basic arithmetic operations, lookup tables support function evaluation, the alpha test provides a variety of conditionals, and the stencil buffer allows pixel-level conditional execution. A shader computation is broken into pieces, each of which can be evaluated by an OpenGL rendering pass. In this way, we build up a final result for all pixels in an object (Figure 2). There are typically several ways to map shading operations into OpenGL. We have implemented the following:

Data Types: Data with the same value for every pixel in an object are called *uniform*, while data with values that may vary from pixel to pixel are called *varying*. Uniform data types are handled outside the graphics pipeline. The framebuffer retains intermediate varying results. Its four channels may hold one quadruple (such as a homogeneous point), one triple (such as a vector, normal, point, or color) and one scalar, or four independent scalars. We have made no attempt to handle varying data types with more than four channels. The framebuffer channels (and hence independent scalars or

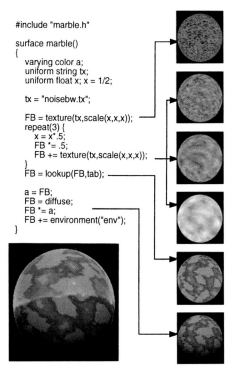

```
#include "marble.h"

surface marble()
{
    varying color a;
    uniform string tx;
    uniform float x; x = 1/2;

    tx = "noisebw.tx";

    FB = texture(tx,scale(x,x,x));
    repeat(3) {
        x = x*.5;
        FB *= .5;
        FB += texture(tx,scale(x,x,x));
    }
    FB = lookup(FB,tab);

    a = FB;
    FB = diffuse;
    FB *= a;
    FB += environment("env");
}
```

Figure 2: SIMD Computation of a Shader. Some of the different passes for the shader written in ISL listed on the left are shown as thumbnails down the right column. The result of the complete shader is shown on the lower left.

the components of triples and quadruples) can be updated selectively on each pass by setting the write-mask with `glColorMask`.

Variables: Varying global, local, and temporary variables are transferred from the framebuffer to a named texture using `glCopyTexSubImage2D`, which copies a portion of the framebuffer into a portion of a texture. In our system, these textures can be one channel (intensity) or four channels (RGBA), depending on the data type they hold. Variables are used either by drawing a textured copy of the object bounding box or by drawing the object geometry using a projective texture. The relative speed of these two methods will vary from graphics system to graphics system. Intensity textures holding scalar variables are expanded into all four channels during rasterization and can therefore be restored into any framebuffer channel.

Arithmetic Operations: Most arithmetic operations are performed with framebuffer blending. They have two operands: the framebuffer contents and an incoming fragment. The incoming fragment may be produced either by drawing geometry (object color, a texture, a stored variable, etc.) or by copying pixels from the framebuffer and through the pixel operations with `glCopyPixels`. Data can be permuted (*swizzled*) from one framebuffer channel to another or linearly combined more generally using the color matrix during a copy. The framebuffer blending mode, set by `glBlendEquation`, `glBlendFunc`, and `glLogicOp`, supports overwriting, addition, subtraction, multiplication, bit-wise logical operations, and alpha blending. Unextended OpenGL does not have a divide blend mode. We handle divide using multiplication by the reciprocal. The reciprocal is computed like other mathematical functions (see below). More complicated binary operations are reduced to a combination of these primitive operations. For example, a dot product of two vectors is

a component-wise multiplication followed by a pixel copy with a color matrix that sums the resulting three components together.

Mathematical and Shader Functions: Mathematical functions with a single scalar operand (e.g. sin or reciprocal) use color or texture lookup tables during a framebuffer-to-framebuffer pixel copy. Functions with more than one operand (e.g. atan2) or a single vector operand (e.g. normalize or color space conversion) are broken down into simpler monadic functions and arithmetic operations, each of which can be supported in a pass through the OpenGL pipeline. Some shader functions, such as texturing and diffuse or specular lighting, have direct correspondents in OpenGL. Often, complex mathematical and shader functions are simply translated to a series of simpler shading language functions.

Flow Control: Stenciling, set by `glStencilFunc` and `glStencilOp`, limits the effect of all operations to only a subset of the pixels, with other pixels retaining their original framebuffer values. We use one bit of the stencil to identify pixels in the object, and additional stencil bits to identify subsets of those pixels that pass varying conditionals (*if-then-else* constructs and loops). One stencil bit is devoted to each level of nesting. Loops with uniform control and conditionals with uniform relations do not need a stencil bit to control their influence because they affect all pixels.

A two step process is used to set the stencil bit for a varying conditional. First, the relation is computed with normal arithmetic operations, such that the result ends up in the alpha channel of the framebuffer. The value is zero where the condition is true and one where it is false. Next, a pixel copy is performed with the alpha $> .5$ test enabled (set by `glAlphaFunc`). Only fragments that pass the alpha test are passed on to the stenciling stage of the OpenGL pipeline. A stencil bit is set for all of these fragments. The stencil remains unchanged for fragments that failed the alpha test. In some cases, the first operation in the body of the conditional can occur in the same pass that sets the stencil.

The passes corresponding to the different blocks of shader code at different nesting levels affect only those pixels that have the proper stencil mask. Because we are executing a SIMD computation, it is necessary to evaluate both branches of *if-then-else* constructs whose relation varies across an object. The stencil compare for the *else* clause simply uses the complement of the stencil bit for the *then* clause. Similarly, it is necessary to repeat a loop with a varying termination condition until all pixels within the object exit the loop. This requires a test that examines all of the pixels within the object. We use the *minmax* function from the ARB imaging extension as we copy the alpha channel to determine if any alpha values are non-zero (signifying they still pass the looping condition). If so, the loop continues.

2.2 OpenGL Encapsulation

We encapsulate OpenGL instructions in three kinds of rendering passes: *GeomPasses*, *CopyPasses*, and *CopyTexPasses*. GeomPasses draw geometry to use vertex, rasterization, and fragment operations. CopyPasses copy a subregion of the framebuffer (via `glCopyPixels`) back into the same place in the framebuffer to use pixel, rasterization, and fragment operations. A stencil allows the CopyPass to avoid operating on pixels outside the object. CopyTexPasses copy a subregion of the framebuffer into a texture object (via `glCopyTexSubImage2D`) and also utilize pixel operations. There are two subtypes of GeomPass. The first draws the object geometry, including normal vectors and texture coordinates. The second draws a screen-aligned bounding rectangle that covers the object using stenciling to limit the operations to pixels on the object. Each pass maintains the relevant OpenGL state for its path through the pipeline. State changes on drawing are minimized by only setting the state in each pass that is not default and immediately restoring that state after the pass.

2.3 Compiling to OpenGL

The key to supporting interactive programmable shading is a compiler that translates the shading language into OpenGL assembly. This is a CISC-like compiler problem because OpenGL passes are complex instructions. The problem is somewhat simplified due to constraints in the language and in OpenGL as an instruction set. For example, we do not have to worry about instruction scheduling since there is no overlap between rendering passes.

Our compiler implementation is guided by a desire to retarget the compiler to easily take advantage of unique features and performance and to pick the best set of passes for each target architecture. We also want to be able to support multiple shading languages and adapt as languages evolve. To help meet these goals, we built our compiler using an in-house tool inspired by the iburg code generation tool [11], though we use it for all phases of compilation. This tool finds the least-cost covering of a tree representation of the shader based on a text file of patterns.

A simple example can show how the tree-matching tool operates and how it allows us to take advantage of extensions to OpenGL. Part of a shader might be matched by a pair of texture lookups, each with a cost of one, or by a single multi-texture lookup, also with a cost of one. In this case, multi-texture is cheaper because it has a total cost of one instead of two. Using similar matching rules and semantic actions, the compiler can make use of fragment lighting, light texture, noise generation, divide or conditional blends, or any other OpenGL extension [16, 27].

The entire shader is matched at once, giving the set of matching rules that cover the shader with the least total cost. For example, the computations surrounding the above pair of texture lookups expand the set of possible matching rules. Given operation A, texture lookup B, texture lookup C, and operation D, it may be possible to do all of the operations in four separate passes (A,B,C,D), to do the surrounding operations separately while combining the texture lookups into one multi-texture pass for a total cost of three (A,BC,D), or to combine one computation with each texture lookup for a cost of two (AB,CD). By considering the entire shader we can choose the set of matching rules with the least overall cost.

When we use the tool for final OpenGL pass generation, we currently use the number of passes as the cost for each matching rule. For performance optimization, the costs should correspond to predicted rendering speed, so the cost for a GeomPass would be different from the cost for a CopyPass or a CopyTexPass.

The pattern matching happens in two phases, *labeling* and *reducing*. Labeling is done bottom-up through the abstract syntax tree, using dynamic programming to find the least-cost set of pattern match rules. Reducing is done top-down, with one semantic action run before the node's children are reduced and one after. The iburg-like label/reduce tool proved useful for more than just final pass selection. We use it for shader syntax checking, constant folding, and even memory allocation (although most of the memory allocation algorithm is in the code associated with a small number of rules). The ease of changing costs and creating new matching rules allows us to achieve our goal of flexible retargeting of the compiler for different hardware and shading languages.

2.4 Scene Graph Support

Since objects may be rendered multiple times, it is necessary to retain geometry data and to deliver it repeatedly to the graphics hardware. In addition, shaders need to be associated with objects to describe their appearances, and the shaders and objects need to be translated into OpenGL passes to render an image. Our framework supports these operations in a scene graph used by an application through the addition of new scene graph containers and new traversals.

In our implementation, we have extended the Cosmo3D scene graph library [30]. Cosmo3D uses a familiar hierarchical scene graph. Internal nodes describe coordinate transformations, while the leaves are *Shape* nodes, each of which contains a list of *Geometry* and an *Appearance*. Traversals of the scene graph are known as *actions*. A *DrawAction*, for example, is applied to the scene graph to render the objects into a window.

We have implemented a new appearance class that contains shaders. When included in a shape node, this appearance completely describes how to shade the geometry in the shape. The shaders may include a list of active light shaders, a displacement shader, a surface shader, and an atmosphere shader. In addition, we have implemented a new traversal, known as a *ShadeAction*. A ShadeAction converts a scene graph containing shapes with the new appearance into another Cosmo3D scene graph describing the multiple passes for all of the objects in the original scene graph. (The transformation of scene graphs is a powerful, general technique that has been proposed to address a variety of problems [1].) The key element of the ShadeAction is the shading language compiler that converts the shaders into multiple passes. A ShadeAction may treat multiple objects that share the same shader as a single, combined object to minimize overhead. A DrawAction applied to this second scene graph renders the final image.

The scene graph passes information to the compiler including the matrix to transform from the object's coordinate system into camera space and the screen space footprint for the geometry. The footprint is computed during the ShadeAction by projecting a 3D bounding box of the geometry into screen space and computing an axis-aligned 2D bounding box of the eight projected points. Only pixels within the 2D bounding box are copied on a CopyPass or drawn on the quad-GeomPass to minimize unnecessary data movement when shading each object.

We provide support for debugging at the single-step, pass-by-pass level through special hooks inserted into the DrawAction. Each pass is held in an extended Cosmo3D *Group* node, which invokes the debugging hook functions when drawn. Each pass is also tagged with the line of source code that generated it, so everything from shader source-level debugging to pass-by-pass image dumps is possible. Hooks at the per-pass level also let us monitor or estimate performance. At the coarsest level, we can find the number of passes executed, but we can also examine each pass to record details like pixels written or time to draw.

3 EXAMPLE: INTERACTIVE SL

We have developed a constrained shading language, called ISL (for Interactive Shading Language) [25] and an ISL compiler to demonstrate our method on current hardware. ISL is similar in spirit to the RenderMan Shading Language in that it provides a C-like syntax to specify per-pixel shading calculations, and it supports separate light, surface, and atmosphere shaders. Data types include varying colors, and uniform floats, colors, matrices, and strings. Local variables can hold both uniform and varying values. Nestable flow control structures include loops with uniform control, and uniform and varying conditionals. There are built-in functions for diffuse and specular lighting, texture mapping, projective textures, environment mapping, RGBA one-dimensional lookup tables, and per-pixel ma-

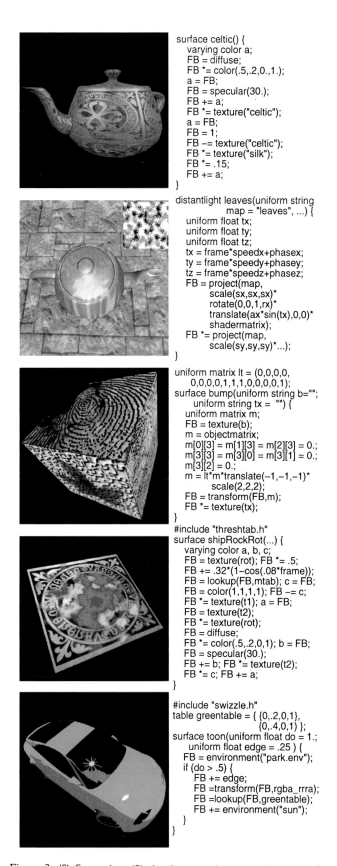

```
surface celtic() {
    varying color a;
    FB = diffuse;
    FB *= color(.5,.2,0.,1.);
    a = FB;
    FB = specular(30.);
    FB += a;
    FB *= texture("celtic");
    a = FB;
    FB = 1;
    FB -= texture("celtic");
    FB *= texture("silk");
    FB *= .15;
    FB += a;
}

distantlight leaves(uniform string
        map = "leaves", ...) {
    uniform float tx;
    uniform float ty;
    uniform float tz;
    tx = frame*speedx+phasex;
    ty = frame*speedy+phasey;
    tz = frame*speedz+phasez;
    FB = project(map,
        scale(sx,sx,sx)*
        rotate(0,0,1,rx)*
        translate(ax*sin(tx),0,0)*
        shadermatrix);
    FB *= project(map,
        scale(sy,sy,sy)*...);
}

uniform matrix lt = (0,0,0,0,
        0,0,0,0,1,1,1,0,0,0,0,1);
surface bump(uniform string b="";
        uniform string tx = "") {
    uniform matrix m;
    FB = texture(b);
    m = objectmatrix;
    m[0][3] = m[1][3] = m[2][3] = 0.;
    m[3][3] = m[3][0] = m[3][1] = 0.;
    m[3][2] = 0.;
    m = lt*m*translate(-1,-1,-1)*
        scale(2,2,2);
    FB = transform(FB,m);
    FB *= texture(tx);
}

#include "threshtab.h"
surface shipRockRot(...) {
    varying color a, b, c;
    FB = texture(rot); FB *= .5;
    FB += .32*(1-cos(.08*frame));
    FB = lookup(FB,mtab); c = FB;
    FB = color(1,1,1); FB -= c;
    FB *= texture(t1); a = FB;
    FB = texture(t2);
    FB *= texture(rot);
    FB = diffuse;
    FB *= color(.5,.2,0,1); b = FB;
    FB = specular(30.);
    FB += b; FB *= texture(t2);
    FB *= c; FB += a;
}

#include "swizzle.h"
table greentable = { {0,.2,0,1},
                     {0,.4,0,1} };
surface toon(uniform float do = 1.;
        uniform float edge = .25 ) {
    FB = environment("park.env");
    if (do > .5) {
        FB += edge;
        FB =transform(FB,rgba_rrra);
        FB =lookup(FB,greentable);
        FB += environment("sun");
    }
}
```

Figure 3: ISL Examples. ISL shaders are shown to the right of each image. Ellipses denote where parameters and statements have been omitted. Some tables are in header files.

trix transformations. In addition, ISL supports uniform shader parameters and a set of uniform global variables (shader space, object space, time, and frame count).

We have intentionally constrained ISL in a number of ways. First, we only chose primitive operations and built-in functions that can be executed on any hardware supporting base OpenGL 1.2 plus the color matrix extension. Consequently, many current hardware systems can support ISL. (If the color matrix transformation is eliminated, ISL should run anywhere.) This constraint provides the shader writer with insight into how limited precision of current commercial hardware may affect the shader. Second, the syntax does not allow varying expressions of expressions, which ensures that the compiler does not need to create any temporary storage not already made explicit in the shader. As a result, the writer of a shader knows by inspection the worst-case temporary storage required by the shading code (although the compiler is free to use less storage, if possible). Third, arbitrary texture coordinate computation is not supported. Texture coordinates must come either from the geometry or from the standard OpenGL texture coordinate generation methods and texture matrix.

One consequence of these design constraints is that ISL shading code is largely decoupled from geometry. For example, since shader parameters are uniform there is no need to attach them directly to each surface description in the scene graph. As a result, ISL and the compiler can migrate from application to application and scene graph to scene graph with relative ease.

3.1 Compiler

We perform some simple optimizations in the parser. For instance, we do limited constant compression by evaluating at parse time all expressions that are declared uniform. When parameters or the shader code change, we must reparse the shader. In our current system, we do this every time we perform a ShadeAction. A more sophisticated compiler, such as the one implemented for the RenderMan Shading Language (Section 4) performs these optimizations outside the parser.

We expand the parse trees for all of the shaders in an appearance (light shaders, surface shader, and atmosphere shader) into a single tree. This tree is then labeled and reduced using the tree matching compiler tool described in Section 2.3. The costs fed into the labeler instruct the compiler to minimize the total number of passes, regardless of the relative performance of the different kinds of passes.

The compiler recognizes and optimizes subexpressions such as a texture, diffuse, or specular lighting multiplied by a constant. The compiler also recognizes when a local variable is assigned a value that can be executed in a single pass. Rather than executing the pass, storing the result, and retrieving it when referenced, the compiler simply replaces the local variable usage with the single pass that describes it.

3.2 Demonstration

We have implemented a simple viewer on top of the extended scene graph to demonstrate ISL running interactively. The viewer supports mouse interaction for rotation and translation. Users can also modify shaders interactively in two ways. They can edit shader text files, and their changes are picked up immediately in the viewer. Additionally, they can modify parameters by dragging sliders, rotating thumb-wheels, or entering text in a control panel. The viewer creates the control panel on the fly for any selected shader. Changes to the parameters are seen immediately in the window. Examples of the viewer running ISL are given in Figures 2 and 3.

4 EXAMPLE: RENDERMAN SL

RenderMan is a rendering and scene description interface standard developed in the late 1980s [14, 28, 32]. The RenderMan standard includes procedural and bytestream scene description interfaces. It also defines the RenderMan Shading Language, which is the *de facto* standard for programmable shading capability and represents a well-defined goal for anyone attempting to accelerate programmable shading.

The RenderMan Shading Language is extremely general, with control structures common to many programming languages, rich data types, and an extensive set of built-in operators and geometric, mathematical, lighting, and communication functions. The language originally was designed with hardware acceleration in mind, so complicated or user-defined data types that would make acceleration more difficult are not included. It is a large but straightforward task to translate the RenderMan Shading Language into multi-pass OpenGL, assuming the following two extensions:

Extended Range and Precision Data Types: Even the simplest RenderMan shaders have intermediate computations that require data values to extend beyond the range [0-1], to which OpenGL fragment color values are clamped. In addition, they need higher precision than is found in current commercial hardware. With the *color range* extension, color data can have an implementation-specific range to which it is clamped during rasterization and framebuffer operations (including color interpolation, texture mapping, and blending). The framebuffer holds colors of the new type, and the conversion to a displayable value happens only upon video scan-out. We have used the color range extension with an IEEE single precision floating point data type or a subset thereof to support the RenderMan Shading Language.

Pixel Texture: RenderMan allows texture coordinates to be computed procedurally. In this case, texture coordinates cannot be expected to change linearly across a geometric primitive, as required in unextended OpenGL. This general two-dimensional indirection mechanism can be supported with the OpenGL pixel texture extension [17, 18, 27]. This extension allows the (possibly floating point) contents of the framebuffer to be used as texture indices when pixels are copied from the framebuffer. The red, green, blue, and alpha channels are used as texture coordinates s, t, r, and q, respectively. We use pixel texture not only to index two dimensional textures but also to index extremely wide one-dimensional textures. These wide textures are used as lookup tables for mathematical functions such as sin, reciprocal, and sqrt. These can be simple piecewise linear approximations, starting points for Newton iteration, components used to construct the more complex mathematical functions, or even direct one-to-one mappings for a reduced floating point format.

4.1 Scene Graph Support

The RenderMan Shading Language demands greater support from the scene graph library than ISL because geometry and shaders are more tightly coupled. *Varying parameters* can be supplied as four values that correspond to the corners of a surface patch, and the parameter over the surface is obtained through bilinear interpolation. Alternatively, one parameter value may be supplied per control point for a bicubic patch mesh or a NURBS patch, and the parameter is interpolated using the same basis functions that define the surface. We associate a (possibly empty) list of named parameters with each surface to hold any parameters provided when the surface is defined. When the surface geometry is tessellated to form *GeoSets* (triangle strip sets and fan sets, etc.), its parameters are transferred to the GeoSets so that they may be referenced

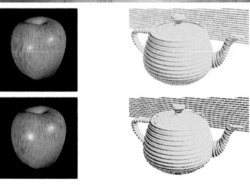

Figure 4: RenderMan SL Examples. The top and bottom images of each pair were rendered with PhotoRealistic RenderMan from Pixar and our multi-pass OpenGL renderer, respectively. No shaders use image maps, except for the reflection and depth shadow maps generated on the fly. The wood floor, blue marble, red apple, and wood block print textures all are generated procedurally. The velvet and brushed metal shaders use sophisticated `illuminance` blocks for their reflective properties. The specular highlight differences are due to Pixar's proprietary specular function; we use the definition from the RenderMan specification. The blue marble, wood floor, and apple do not match because of differences in in the `noise` function. Other discrepancies typically are due to limited precision lookup tables used to help evaluate mathematical functions. (Credit: LGParquetPlank by Larry Gritz, SHWvelvet and SHWbrushedmetal by Stephen Westin, DPBlueMarble by Darwin Peachey, eroded from the RenderMan companion, JMredapple by Jonathan Merritt, and woodblockprint by Scott Johnston. Courtesy of the RenderMan Repository http://www.renderman.org.)

and drawn as vertex colors by the passes produced by the compiler. Similarly, a shader may require derivatives of surface properties, such as the partial derivatives of the position (dP/du and dP/dv) either as global variables or through a differential function such as `calculatenormal`. A shader may also use derivatives of user-supplied parameters. The compiler can request from the scene graph any of these quantities evaluated over a surface at the same points used in its tessellation. As with any other parameter, they are computed on the host and stored in the vertex colors for the surface. Where possible, lazy evaluation ensures that the user does not pay in time or space for this support unless requested.

4.2 Compiler

Our RenderMan compiler is based on multiple phases of the tree-matching tool described in Section 2.3. The phases include:

Parsing: convert source into an internal tree representation.
Phase0: detect errors
Phase1: perform context-sensitive typing (e.g. noise, texture)
Phase2: detect and compress uniform expressions
Phase3: compute "difference trees" for Derivatives
Phase4: determine variable usage and live range information
Phase5: identify possible OpenGL instruction optimizations
Phase6: allocate memory for variables
Phase7: generate optimized, machine specific OpenGL

The mapping of RenderMan to OpenGL follows the methodology described in Section 2.1. Texturing and some lighting carry over directly; most math functions are implemented with lookup tables; coordinate transformations are implemented with the color matrix; loops with varying termination condition are supported with minmax; and many built-in functions (including illuminance, solar, and illuminate) are rewritten in terms of simpler operations. Features whose mapping to OpenGL is more sophisticated include:

Noise: The RenderMan SL provides band-limited `noise` primitives that include 1D, 2D, 3D, and 4D operands and single or multiple component output. We use floating point arithmetic and texture tables to support all of these functions.

Derivatives: The RenderMan SL provides access to surface-derivative information through functions that include `Du`, `Dv`, `Deriv`, `area`, and `calculatenormal`. We dedicate a compiler phase to fully implement these functions using a technique similar that described by Larry Gritz [12].

A number of optimizations are supported by the compiler. Uniform expressions are identified and computed once for all pixels. If texture coordinates are linear functions of s and t or vertex coordinates, they are recognized as a single pass with some combination of texture coordinate generation and texture matrix. Texture memory utilization is minimized by allocating storage based on single-static assignment and live-range analysis [4].

4.3 Demonstration

We have implemented a RenderMan renderer, complete with shading language, bytestream, and procedural interfaces on a software implementation of OpenGL including color range and pixel texture. We experimented with subsets of IEEE single precision floating point. An interesting example was a 16 bit floating point format with a sign bit, 10 bits of mantissa and 5 bits of exponent. This format was sufficient for most shaders, but fell short when computing derivatives and related difference-oriented functions such as `calculatenormal`. Our software implementation supported other OpenGL extensions (cube environment mapping, fragment lighting, light texture, and shadow), but they are not strictly necessary as they can all be computed using existing features.

ISL Image	celtic	leaves	bump	rot	toon
MPix Filled	2.8	4.3	1.2	2.2	1.9
Frames/Second	6.8	7.3	9.6	12.5	4.6
RSL Image	teapots	apple	print		
MPix Filled	500	280	144		

Table 1: Performance for 512x512 images on Silicon Graphics Octane/MXI

The RenderMan bytestream interface was implemented on top of the RenderMan procedural interface. When data is passed to the procedural interface, it is incorporated into a scene graph. Higher order geometric primitives not native to Cosmo3D, such as trimmed quadrics and NURBS patches are accommodated by extending the scene graph library with parametric surface types, which are tessellated just before drawing. At the WorldEnd procedural call, this scene graph is rendered using a ShadeAction that invokes the RenderMan shading language compiler followed by a DrawAction.

To establish that the implementation was correct, over 2000 shading language tests, including point-feature tests, publicly available shaders, and more sophisticated shaders were written or obtained. The results of our renderer were compared to Pixar's commercially available PhotoRealistic RenderMan renderer. While never bit-for-bit accurate, the shading is typically comparable to the eye (with expected differences due, for instance, to the `noise` function). A collection of examples is given in Figure 4. We focused primarily on the challenge of mapping the entire language to OpenGL, so there is considerable room for further optimization.

There are a few notable limitations in our implementation. Displacement shaders are implemented, but treated as bump mapping shaders; surface positions are altered only for the calculation of normals, not for rasterization. True displacement would have to happen during object tessellation and would have performance similar to displacement mapping in traditional software implementations. Transparency is not implemented. It is possible, but requires the scene graph to depth-sort potentially transparent surfaces. Pixel texture, as it is implemented, does not support texture filtering, which can lead to aliasing. Our renderer also does not currently support high quality pixel antialiasing, motion blur, and depth of field. One could implement all of these through the accumulation buffer as has been demonstrated elsewhere [13].

5 DISCUSSION

We measured the performance of several of our ISL and RenderMan shaders (Table 1). The performance numbers for millions of pixels filled are conservative estimates since we counted all pixels in the object's 2D bounding box even when drawing object geometry that touched fewer pixels.

5.1 Drawbacks

Our current system has a number of inefficiencies that impact our performance. First, since we do not use deferred shading, we may spend several passes rendering an object that is hidden in the final image. There are a variety of algorithms that would help (for example, visibility culling at the scene graph level), but we have not implemented any of them.

Second, the bounding box of objects in screen space is used to define the active pixels for many passes. Consequently pixels within the bounding box but not within the object are moved unnecessarily. This taxes one of the most important resources in hardware: bandwidth to and from memory.

Third, we have only included a minimal set of optimization rules in our compiler. Many current hardware systems share frame-buffer and texture memory bandwidth. On these systems, storage and retrieval of intermediate results bears a particularly high price. This is a primary motivation for doing as many operations per pass as possible. Our iburg-like rule matching works well for the pipeline of simple units found in standard OpenGL, but more complex units (as found in some new multitexture extensions, for example) require more powerful compiler technology. Two possibilities are surveyed by Harris [15].

5.2 Advantages

Our methodology allows research and development to proceed in parallel as shading languages, compilers, and hardware independently evolve. We can take advantage of the unique feature and performance needs of different application areas through specialized shading languages.

The application does not have to handle the complexities of multipass shading since the application interface is a scene graph. This model is a natural extension of most interactive applications, which already have a retained mode interface of some sort to enable users to manipulate their data. Applications still retain the other advantages of having a scene graph, like occlusion culling and level of detail management.

As mentioned, we have only implemented a few of the many possible compiler optimizations. As the compiler improves, our performance will improve, independent of language or hardware.

Finally, the rapid pace of graphics hardware development has resulted in systems with a diverse set of features and relative feature performance. Our design allows an application to use a shading language on all of the systems, and still take advantage of many of their unique characteristics. Hardware vendors do not need to create the shading compiler and retained data structures since they operate above the level of the drivers. Further, since complex effects can be supported on unextended hardware, designers are free to create fast, simple hardware without compromising on capabilities.

6 CONCLUSION

We have created a software layer between the application and the hardware abstraction layer to translate high-level shading descriptions into multi-pass OpenGL. We have demonstrated this approach with two examples, a constrained shading language that runs interactively on current hardware, and a fully general shading language. We have also shown that general shading languages, like the RenderMan Shading Language, can be implemented with only two additional OpenGL extensions.

There is a continuum of possible languages between ISL and the RenderMan Shading Language with different levels of functionality. We have applied our method to two different shading languages in part to demonstrate its generality.

There are many avenues of future research. New compiler technology can be developed or adapted for programmable shading. There are significant optimizations that we are investigating in our compilers. Research is also needed to understand what hardware features are best for supporting interactive programmable shading. Finally, given examples like the scientific visualization constructs described by Crawfis that are not found in the RenderMan shading language [9], we believe the wide availability of interactive programmable shading will spur exciting developments in new shading languages and new applications for them.

References
[1] BIRCH, P., BLYTHE, D., GRANTHAM, B., JONES, M., SCHAFER, M., SEGAL, M., AND TANNER, C. An OpenGL++ Specification. SGI, March 1997.

[2] BLYTHE, D., GRANTHAM, B., KILGARD, M. J., MCREYNOLDS, T., NELSON, S. R., FOWLER, C., HUI, S., AND WOMACK, P. Advanced graphics programming techniques using OpenGL: Course notes. In Proceedings of SIGGRAPH '99 (July 1999).

[3] BOCK, D. Tech watch: Volume rendering. Computer Graphics World 22, 5 (May 1999).

[4] BRIGGS, P. Register Allocation via Graph Coloring. PhD thesis, Rice University, April 1992.

[5] CABRAL, B., CAM, N., AND FORAN, J. Accelerated volume rendering and tomographic reconstruction using texture mapping hardware. 1994 Symposium on Volume Visualization (October 1994), 91–98. ISBN 0-89791-741-3.

[6] CABRAL, B., OLANO, M., AND NEMEC, P. Reflection space image based rendering. Proceedings of SIGGRAPH 99 (August 1999), 165–170.

[7] COOK, R. L. Shade trees. Computer Graphics (Proceedings of SIGGRAPH 84) 18, 3 (July 1984), 223–231. Held in Minneapolis, Minnesota.

[8] CORRIE, B., AND MACKERRAS, P. Data shaders. Visualization '93 1993 (1993).

[9] CRAWFIS, R. A., AND ALLISON, M. J. A scientific visualization synthesizer. Visualization '91 (1991), 262–267.

[10] DIEFENBACH, P. J., AND BADLER, N. I. Multi-pass pipeline rendering: Realism for dynamic environments. 1997 Symposium on Interactive 3D Graphics (April 1997), 59–70.

[11] FRASER, C. W., HANSON, D. R., AND PROEBSTING, T. A. Engineering a simple, efficient code generator generator. ACM Letters on Programming Languages and Systems 1, 3 (September 1992), 213–226.

[12] GRITZ, L., AND HAHN, J. K. BMRT: A global illumination implementation of the RenderMan standard. Journal of Graphics Tools 1, 3 (1996), 29–47.

[13] HAEBERLI, P. E., AND AKELEY, K. The accumulation buffer: Hardware support for high-quality rendering. Computer Graphics (Proceedings of SIGGRAPH 90) 24, 4 (August 1990), 309–318.

[14] HANRAHAN, P., AND LAWSON, J. A language for shading and lighting calculations. Computer Graphics (Proceedings of SIGGRAPH 90) 24, 4 (August 1990), 289–298.

[15] HARRIS, M. Extending microcode compaction for real architectures. In Proceedings of the 20th annual workshop on Microprogramming (1987), pp. 40–53.

[16] HART, J. C., CARR, N., KAMEYA, M., TIBBITTS, S. A., AND COLEMAN, T. J. Antialiased parameterized solid texturing simplified for consumer-level hardware implementation. 1999 SIGGRAPH / Eurographics Workshop on Graphics Hardware (August 1999), 45–53.

[17] HEIDRICH, W., AND SEIDEL, H.-P. Realistic, hardware-accelerated shading and lighting. Proceedings of SIGGRAPH 99 (August 1999), 171–178.

[18] HEIDRICH, W., WESTERMANN, R., SEIDEL, H.-P., AND ERTL, T. Applications of pixel textures in visualization and realistic image synthesis. 1999 ACM Symposium on Interactive 3D Graphics (April 1999), 127–134. ISBN 1-58113-082-1.

[19] JAQUAYS, P., AND HOOK, B. Quake 3: Arena shader manual, revision 10. In Game Developer's Conference Hardcore Technical Seminar Notes (December 1999), C. Hecker and J. Lander, Eds., Miller Freeman Game Group.

[20] KAUTZ, J., AND MCCOOL, M. D. Interactive rendering with arbitrary brdfs using separable approximations. Eurographics Rendering Workshop 1999 (June 1999). Held in Granada, Spain.

[21] KELLER, A. Instant radiosity. Proceedings of SIGGRAPH 97 (August 1997), 49–56.

[22] KYLANDER, K., AND KYLANDER, O. S. Gimp: The Official Handbook. The Coriolis Group, 1999.

[23] MAX, N., DEUSSEN, O., AND KEATING, B. Hierarchical image-based rendering using texture mapping hardware. Rendering Techniques '99 (Proceedings of the 10th Eurographics Workshop on Rendering) (June 1999), 57–62.

[24] MCCOOL, M. D., AND HEIDRICH, W. Texture shaders. 1999 SIGGRAPH / Eurographics Workshop on Graphics Hardware (August 1999), 117–126.

[25] OLANO, M., HART, J. C., HEIDRICH, W., MCCOOL, M., MARK, B., AND PROUDFOOT, K. Approaches for procedural shading on graphics hardware: Course notes. In Proceedings of SIGGRAPH 2000 (July 2000).

[26] OLANO, M., AND LASTRA, A. A shading language on graphics hardware: The PixelFlow shading system. Proceedings of SIGGRAPH 98 (July 1998), 159–168.

[27] OPENGL ARB. Extension specification documents. http://www.opengl.org/Documentation/Extensions.html, March 1999.

[28] PIXAR. The RenderMan Interface Specification: Version 3.1. Pixar Animation Studios, September 1999.

[29] SEGAL, M., AKELEY, K., FRAZIER, C., AND LEECH, J. The OpenGL Graphics System: A Specification (Version 1.2.1). Silicon Graphics, Inc., 1999.

[30] SGI TECHNICAL PUBLICATIONS. Cosmo 3D Programmer's Guide. SGI Technical Publications, 1998.

[31] SIMS, K. Particle animation and rendering using data parallel computation. Computer Graphics (Proceedings of SIGGRAPH 90) 24, 4 (August 1990), 405–413.

[32] UPSTILL, S. The RenderMan Companion. Addison-Wesley, 1989.

The WarpEngine: An Architecture for the Post-Polygonal Age

Voicu Popescu, John Eyles, Anselmo Lastra, Joshua Steinhurst, Nick England, Lars Nyland
University of North Carolina at Chapel Hill

ABSTRACT

We present the WarpEngine, an architecture designed for real-time image-based rendering of natural scenes from arbitrary viewpoints. The modeling primitives are real-world images with per-pixel depth. Currently they are acquired and stored off-line; in the near future real-time depth-image acquisition will be possible, and WarpEngine is designed to render in immediate mode from such data sources.

The depth-image resolution is locally adapted by interpolation to match the resolution of the output image. 3D warping can occur either before or after the interpolation; the resulting warped/interpolated samples are forward-mapped into a warp buffer, with the precise locations recorded using an offset. Warping processors are integrated on-chip with the warp buffer, allowing efficient, scalable implementation of very high performance systems. Each chip will be able to process 100 million samples per second and provide 4.8GigaBytes per second of bandwidth to the warp buffer.

The WarpEngine is significantly less complex than our previous efforts, incorporating only a single ASIC design. Small configurations can be packaged as a PC add-in card, while larger deskside configurations will provide HDTV resolutions at 50 Hz, enabling radical new applications such as 3D television.

WarpEngine will be highly programmable, facilitating use as a test-bed for experimental IBR algorithms.

KEYWORDS: Graphics hardware, image-based rendering.

1 INTRODUCTION

Research efforts in interactive 3D computer-graphics have been targeted at providing high-quality, high-resolution images. This goal has proven elusive: renderings that can be mistaken for photographs can usually be obtained only by sacrificing interactivity.

This problem, and the extreme difficulty of modeling natural environments, motivated research on image-based rendering. Although the image-based primitives are novel, conventional polygon-based graphics hardware has been used for the rendering. Few attempts have been made to take advantage of the new image-based primitives with novel hardware.

{popescu, jge, lastra, jsteinhu, nick, nyland}@cs.unc.edu
Sitterson Hall, CB#3175, CS UNC, Chapel Hill, 27599, NC

In this paper, we present the WarpEngine architecture for rendering directly from an image-based representation, specifically from images with per-pixel depth [McMillan95]. The prototype that we plan to build promises high performance at HDTV resolution, as well as extensive programmability to support research in algorithms for image-based rendering.

We first review related work in image-based rendering (and graphics hardware that uses image-based primitives). Then we present the algorithm on which the WarpEngine is based, followed by a detailed architectural description of the machine. We close with proposed future work and conclusions.

1.1 Related Work

The spectrum of image-based approaches ranges from those that exclusively use images to those that re-project acquired imagery onto geometric models.

[Chen95] employed 360° panoramas, stitched together from overlapping photographs. A panorama offers a realistic view of the scene, but the user has a correct 3D perspective only from a single location. However, using inexpensive hardware, the user can view, at interactive rates, outdoor or indoor scenes that are hard to model as a collection of polygons.

Image morphing approaches [Wolberg90, Beier92, Chen93, Seitz96] allow some range of motion but the transformation of the reference views to the desired views is *approximated* by interpolation. To maintain a high update rate, the Talisman architecture [Torborg96] reused portions of rendered images by re-projecting to a new, nearby, view using a 2D warp.

The Lumigraph [Gortler96] and Light Field [Levoy96] densely sample light rays to create a ray database. Unfortunately, the database of rays grows quite large for bigger viewing volumes. [Regan99] describes low-latency rendering hardware for a one-axis light field.

At the other end of the spectrum are methods based largely on geometry. Texture mapping is the most common way to incorporate images in the scene description. The *Façade* system [Debevec96] represents the scene with an approximate geometric model (semi-automatically created) texture-mapped, in a view-dependent fashion, from photographs.

McMillan and Bishop's [McMillan95] method is in the middle of the spectrum, representing the scene as a collection of images that in addition to color also store depth at each pixel. The desired view is generated by a 3D-warp of the depth images.

We have chosen image-based rendering by 3D warping (IBRW) as the basis for the WarpEngine. There are two reasons for this: (1) the storage and bandwidth requirements are manageable, and (2) laser rangefinders [K2T, Beraldin92, Cyra] and other range-acquisition equipment [Kanade99, Minolta] are rapidly improving and appearing on the commercial market. Some instruments can even acquire range in real time. Such a "depth camera" coupled with the WarpEngine will enable extraordinary applications: a spectator of a live event will not be confined to the view of the TV camera; he or she can choose any seat in the arena, and even venture onto the stage or court.

1.2   3D Image Warping

McMillan and Bishop show in [McMillan95] how to compute the desired image coordinates of a depth image sample using the 3D warping equations

$$u_2 = \frac{w_{11} + w_{12} \cdot u_1 + w_{13} \cdot v_1 + w_{14} \cdot \delta(u_1, v_1)}{w_{31} + w_{32} \cdot u_1 + w_{33} \cdot v_1 + w_{34} \cdot \delta(u_1, v_1)}$$
$$v_2 = \frac{w_{21} + w_{22} \cdot u_1 + w_{23} \cdot v_1 + w_{24} \cdot \delta(u_1, v_1)}{w_{31} + w_{32} \cdot u_1 + w_{33} \cdot v_1 + w_{34} \cdot \delta(u_1, v_1)} \tag{1}$$

where u_2, v_2 are the desired image coordinates, u_1, v_1 the original (reference) image coordinates, the w's are transformation constants obtained from the reference and desired image camera parameters, and $\delta(u_1, v_1)$ is the generalized disparity at sample (u_1, v_1), which is defined as the ratio between the distance to the reference image plane and $z_{eye}(u_1, v_1)$.

The warping equation is equivalent to the vertex transformation commonly used in computer graphics, but allows one to take advantage of the regular structure of images to perform incremental transformation. The warped coordinates of a sample can be computed with six adds, five multiplies[1], and one divide.

Reconstructing by simply setting a desired image pixel to the color of the sample that warps within its boundary results in holes thus not acceptable. Also, more than one visible sample can warp to the same pixel, and simply discarding all but one sample produces aliasing. Reconstruction is a challenging task when warping images with depth; we analyze it in more detail next.

1.3   Reconstruction

The 3D warping equation is a forward mapping that takes samples from the reference domain and maps them to the destination domain. An inverse mapping (as in conventional texturing) would be ideal. Unfortunately there is no analytically computable inverse for 3D warping (there is a rather costly search procedure described in [McMillan97]).

Reconstruction for IBRW is mainly done in one of two ways [Mark97, McMillan97]: with splats or with a polygonal mesh.

A splat [Westover90] is a representation of the projected shape of the reference sample. The original use for splats was to render transparency for volume rendering; thus the splats were blended in front-to-back order. For IBRW, we do not want to blend samples that are at different depths. Rather we want to overwrite samples that should be hidden and only blend samples that represent the same surface. This is very difficult to do because in IBRW we have no information about surfaces. To prevent samples of hidden surfaces from showing through, the sizes of the splats are overestimated [Shade98], thus overlapping splats may incorrectly erase visible samples, resulting in aliasing.

Good reconstruction can be obtained by connecting the samples of the reference image into a polygonal mesh. Not all samples should be connected, of course; in Section 2.1 we present a simple method for detecting depth discontinuities. With meshing, continuity of the surfaces is maintained where desired, and hardware acceleration increases performance. On WarpEngine, we connect samples, but avoid the overhead of general polygonal rendering.

1.4   Why WarpEngine?

One might ask, why build the WarpEngine if existing graphics hardware can be used for IBRW? One reason is performance; another is efficiency.

Assume that 1280 by 1024 is the targeted resolution and that on average we warp twice the reference samples as the desired resolution. Two triangles need to be rendered for every warped sample. The average number of triangles per second to sustain a frame rate of 30 Hz is

$$N \approx 1280 \times 1024 \times 2 \times 2 \times 30 \approx 157\, Mtris/s$$

Neither high-end systems like PixelFlow [Molnar92] or InfiniteReality [Montrym97], nor the rapidly improving PC 3D graphics accelerators, can produce the necessary performance. Moreover, we speculate that it will take years for them to reach this sustained level of performance. Even then, it will take more hardware than on a machine optimized for IBRW. We believe that WarpEngine is more efficient because it takes advantage of the regularity of image-based primitives and of the small screen-size of the warped samples.

More needs to be said to explain the number of reference-image samples required at each frame. This number depends on the scene and on how it is modeled. One must process (on average) more than one reference image sample per desired image location because:

- there are surfaces that are redundantly captured in more than one reference image;

- there are surfaces captured in the reference images that are not visible in the desired image (depth complexity is greater than one);

- there are surfaces that were better sampled in the reference image than in the desired image, which leads to more than one visible sample per desired image pixel.

Two input samples per output pixel is a reasonable lower bound; in practice we have found it difficult to use fewer. With real-time depth-image updates (immediate mode), the number of samples will be determined by the number, resolution and update rates of the cameras.

The most viable alternative to IBRW is to simplify triangle meshes in order to reduce the polygon count, and thus meet our performance goals with conventional graphics hardware (in fact, other members of our team are investigating this approach). However, simplified meshes are less well suited to real-time depth updates because of the pre-processing required.

2   RENDERING ALGORITHM

We wish to treat the depth image as connected (as in the mesh approach) in order to prevent samples of hidden surfaces from showing through. The triangles resulting from the mesh method are very small in screen space; thus scan conversion time is dominated by setup. Instead of conventional scan conversion, we propose simply bilinearly interpolating between connected samples in reference image domain, reducing *per-sample* setup.

---

[1] If w_{34} is non-zero (non-zero translation from reference position) one could save a multiply by dividing all w's by w_{34}.

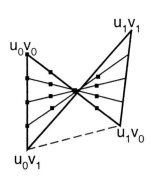

Figure 1. Once warped, the four neighboring reference-image samples u_0v_0, u_1v_0, u_1v_1, and u_0v_1 may form a concave quad. Interpolating in desired-image space produces the sub-samples shown with little squares, which is different from the projection of the surface on the image plane.

When interpolating in reference-image space and then warping, the surface projection is approximated better, but at higher computational cost.

The algorithm is:

> *For all adjacent, connected samples*
> > *Bilinearly interpolate color and depth to obtain subsamples*
> > *Warp resulting subsamples to desired image space*
> > *Z-composite warped subsamples into the warp buffer*

In order to reduce aliasing, we warp into a sub-pixel resolution *warp buffer* (usually 2x2), then filter to produce the final image in the frame buffer. The sub-samples are z-buffered.

The interpolation factor (number of subsamples created in each of x and y directions) is critical in order to ensure that (1) back surfaces do not show through, and (2) we do not generate too many subsamples. We describe the computation of the interpolation factor in more detail in Section 3.3.

Recall that the reference-image depth information is stored as generalized disparity that is proportional to $1/z_{eye}$, which is linear in image space. Consequently, if the four neighboring samples are planar, the sub-samples resulting from the interpolation are correctly located on the same plane. If the samples are not coplanar, the sub-samples define a general bilinear patch. Adjacent patches exhibit C^0 continuity.

An alternative rendering algorithm, to save the cost of warping the sub-samples (dominated by the inverse computation, see Equation 1) is to *first* warp the reference-image samples and *then* interpolate. This still avoids the triangle setup costs. Just as when interpolation is done in reference-image space, if the original samples lie on a plane, the sub-samples are also on the plane.

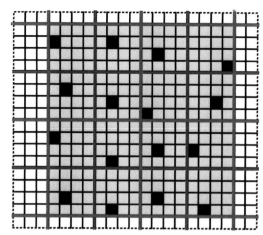

Figure 3. In the warp buffer fragment shown, the green lines define the warp buffer locations. The blue lines delimit the output pixels, which span four warp buffer locations each. The fine black lines show the virtual subdivision of the warp buffer locations corresponding to the two 2-bit offset values. The locations at which these samples warped are shown by black squares and are recorded to a precision of $1/8^{th}$ of a pixel. There is exactly one sample per warp buffer location.

The output pixel is reconstructed using a two-pixel wide kernel, with a half pixel (one warp buffer location) overlap. The kernel is shown in gray. The 16 color samples are weighted according to their position inside the warp buffer location, as modified by the offsets. The reconstruction is equivalent to reconstructing from an 8x8 supersampled buffer that is sparsely populated, without having to explicitly allocate the dense buffer or to search for the locations that are populated.

However the similarity between the two methods ends when the four original samples are not coplanar and the resulting screen-space quad might be concave (resulting in a "bow tie", see Figure 1). Our simulations show that this is a very infrequent case, which usually occurs between silhouette samples that were marked as disconnected anyway.

2.1 Determining Connectivity

We devised a robust and inexpensive way of detecting which samples should not be connected by interpolation, based on the surface curvature (see also [McAllister99]). At every reference image sample we compute the second derivative[2] of the generalized disparity along four directions: E-W, SE-NW, N-S, and SW-NE. If the surface sampled is planar the second derivative is exactly zero. If it exceeds a threshold (which is unique per scene) the samples are marked as disconnected (see Figure 2).

2.2 Reconstruction Using Offsets

We want to render high-quality, antialiased images. Conventional jittered supersampling is not an option because of the *forward-mapping* nature of the warping process; warping produces sub-samples that do not correspond exactly with the centers of warp-buffer locations. Even with a 2x2 warp buffer, aliasing is greater than we wish.

Our proposed alternative is to compute the *(x, y)* location of the warp to a precision higher than that of the warp buffer, and store that more precise location as an offset from the corner of the warp

Figure 2. The vertical and horizontal depth discontinuities are marked in green and red, respectively. The detection algorithm works well in spite of the great range of distances in the image.

---

[2] difference of neighboring differences

Offset	Viewpoint Rotated	Viewpoint Translated	Zoom
4x4			1x
			8x
1x1 (none)			1x
			8x

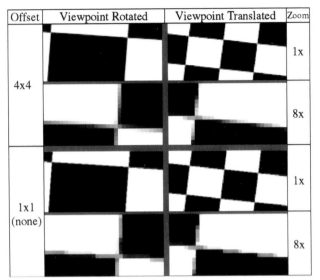

Figure 4. Antialiasing using offsets. These images were rendered from a depth image of a checkerboard. The left column is just rotated, the right also translated. We show both original and 8X zoomed versions. All images used a *2x2* warp buffer. The upper set was rendered with two bits for each of x and y offset. The lower set used no offsets and exhibits more aliasing.

buffer location. The *offsets* are used during reconstruction to obtain better filtering and a higher-quality final image. We have found that a 2-bit offset in each of *x* and *y* (total of 4 bits per warp buffer location) provides good results. This, combined with a 2x2 warp buffer, locates the warped subsamples to within one-eight of a pixel (see Figure 3). The results are illustrated in Figure 4.

Offsets are, of course, not equivalent to higher warp buffer resolution. Although its location is recorded more precisely, only one sample is stored at each warp buffer location. In the expected case, when the sampling resolution of the desired image is within a factor of two of that of the reference images, the 2x2 warp buffer with 4x4 offsets provides a good reconstruction. Outside that interval, other reference images should be used. One could increase the resolution of the warp buffer to accommodate even bigger sampling mismatches, but this comes at a substantial additional cost, not only in memory, but also in warping since more reference image samples must be used.

The offset reconstruction also has good temporal antialiasing properties. Antialiasing by jittered supersampling or coverage-mask-based methods suffer from the problem of collinear

sampling locations within a pixel. No matter how the sampling locations are chosen, at least two of them are collinear in jittered supersampling and *k* are collinear when *kxk* subpixel masks are computed. If from one frame to the next all collinear sampling locations move from one side to the other of a slowly moving edge, the change in color of the output pixel is too abrupt. Using 2x2 pixel kernels with 2x2 warpbuffer and 4x4 offsets guarantees 16 intermediate levels (when an edge moves slowly enough). We refer the reader to the conference-proceedings videotape and DVD-ROM, which illustrate the dynamic antialiasing properties of our algorithm. Also the conference-proceedings CD-ROM includes the antialiasing examples. Please look at the images on the CD to see the full effects of the antialiasing. Figures 5, 6, and 10 (at the end of the paper) show images of various test scenes rendered with the WarpEngine simulator.

3 WarpEngine ARCHITECTURE

3.1 Overview

The hardware architecture must provide sufficient warping power for all required reference-image samples and sufficient bandwidth to the warp buffer.

We decided to partition the reference images into 16x16-sample *tiles* (with a 15x15 payload) and to use these as the basic rendering primitive. Tiles provide several important advantages:

- we can selectively use portions of reference images as needed for adequate sampling and coverage of visible surfaces (Section 3.3);

- one can easily estimate the screen area a tile transforms to, enabling efficient high-level parallelism (Section 3.1.3);

- tiles are small enough that the same interpolation factor can be used for all samples, enabling SIMD low-level parallelism (Section 3.1.1).

Figure 6. The upper image was rendered on the WarpEngine simulator. For comparison, the lower image was rendered directly from the geometric model.

Figure 5. Eurotown images were made from reference depth images placed on a regular grid. Only the reference images of the current grid-cell were used to render each frame.

3.1.1 Warping and Interpolation

All the samples of a tile can be warped and interpolated with the same set of instructions so a SIMD implementation is, we believe, the most efficient. We opted for an array of simple byte-wide processors, similar to the one used in PixelFlow [Molnar92]. For a computation that can be efficiently mapped, a SIMD array provides efficient use of silicon, since control is factored out over all the processors. A large array of simple processors is more easily programmable than a complex pipelined processor. The programmability is necessary for use of the WarpEngine as a research tool.

A SIMD array equal in size to the reference-image-tile maps very efficiently, since the warping calculation is the same for every pixel, with minimal branching required. Nearest neighbor Processing Element (PE) connectivity provides each PE with access to the three other samples needed for interpolation.

3.1.2 Warp Buffer

The biggest design concern was providing sufficient warp buffer bandwidth. We assume the maximum resolution to be HDTV (approximately 2K x 1K pixels) and 60 Hz update rate; we assume again that one needs to use at least two reference-image samples per output pixel. This implies that at least 240 million reference samples per second must be warped. In our simulations, a 2x2 warp buffer resolution required in some cases an average interpolation factor of 4x4. Thus, for each warped reference-image pixel, 16 warped samples are generated, and the warp buffer must process approximately 4 billion warped samples per second. Each sample is about 12 bytes in size (4 bytes RGB; 4 bytes Z-buffer; 4 bytes X and Y values, including offsets). Assuming a depth complexity of two, and that 50% of the hidden samples initially pass the Z-comparison test, an average of 10 byte accesses is required per warped sample. Thus total warp buffer bandwidth is about 40 GigaBytes/sec.

To achieve this enormous warp-buffer bandwidth, a very large number of commodity DRAMs is required (well over 100); similarly, the warping/interpolation processors would require hundreds of pins dedicated to interfacing with the warp-buffer. By placing the warp buffer on-chip, that is, on the same ASIC as the processors that generate the warped samples, very wide and fast memory interfaces can be used.

3.1.3 Region-Based Rendering

With current technology, a single ASIC can provide neither sufficient processing power nor sufficient warp buffer memory[3]. Thus multiple ASICs are required, and some form of high-level parallelism must be employed. Partitioning the warp buffer into contiguous screen regions with each region assigned to an ASIC (screen-space subdivision) is appealing, because the typical 16x16-sample tile intersects only one screen region and therefore needs to be processed by a single ASIC (tiles that overlap region boundaries are assigned to multiple regions). By contrast, with interleaving, each tile would need to be processed by many or all of the ASICs.

For partitioning by screen-space subdivision, primitives must be sorted by screen region[4]. Using tiles as the rendering primitive means that sorting is performed on 256 samples at a time; the number of tiles per frame ranges from a few thousand to a maximum of a few tens of thousands (depending on screen resolution) so the computational and memory burden of sorting is considerably less than for the general polygon-rendering case. By assigning multiple screen regions to each ASIC, a smaller number of ASICs is sufficient; however this requires sorting into buckets corresponding to screen regions [Ellsworth97], because an ASIC must process all primitives in a given region before moving to its next assigned region.

The sort first, sort middle, sort last taxonomy developed to describe object-parallel polygon-rendering architectures [Molnar94], can also be applied to IBR architectures. Sorting by reference-image tiles is sort first from the point of view of reference-image samples, since after a tile has been assigned to a screen region, it is known a priori that its sub-samples will warp to the desired screen region (those that do not can be discarded, since the tile will be assigned to all pertinent regions). In polygon rendering, sort first [Mueller95] is prone to load-balancing difficulties; this is not be a problem for IBR, since reference-image tiles and interpolation factors are chosen to sample the destination image uniformly. We believe that sort first is an attractive approach for the WarpEngine, because it makes scaling of the system relatively painless. Performance is increased by adding additional ASICs, and assigning fewer screen regions to each ASIC. Screen-space subdivision requires a central processor, perhaps the host, which can perform the tile sorting, or a way of distributing these tasks across the multiple ASICs.

3.1.4 Processing Warped Sub-Samples

It is straightforward to build a region-sized on-chip warp buffer with very high performance. Since each warped sample maps to only one location in the warp buffer, the warp buffer can be partitioned, with a *sample processor* assigned to each partition. Very high numbers of samples can be processed by instantiating more sample processors, processing simultaneous streams of warped samples. Load-balancing can be achieved by sub-pixel interleaving the partitions and providing input FIFOs for the sample processors. The region size is determined by the silicon budget for the warp buffer, independently of the number of partitions.

The sample processors are very simple: they combine a new warped sample with the previous contents of the warp buffer location, using a z-compare operation. Since the sample processors' memory interface does not cross chip boundaries, it can be very wide and very fast; thus the sample processors are not bandwidth limited.

3.2 WarpEngine Implementation

Our architecture, the *WarpEngine*, consists of one or more identical *Nodes* (typically 4 to 32); each Node consists of an ASIC and a Tile Cache. The ASIC contains:

• a <u>16x16 SIMD Warp Array</u>, for warping and interpolating reference-image samples;

---

[3] As silicon technology improves, a full-sized warp buffer becomes feasible (on an embedded-DRAM process).

[4] For tiles, this is efficiently done by warping the 4 corners, using both the tile's minimum and maximum disparity values; the resulting 8 points define the tile's screen-space bounding box.

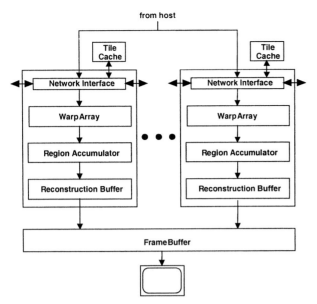

Figure 7. Block diagram of the WarpEngine

- a <u>Region Accumulator</u>, which includes a double-buffered warp buffer for a 128x128 screen region and 4 sample processors for resolving visibility;

- a <u>Reconstruction Buffer</u>, for computing final pixel values;

- a <u>Network Interface</u>, which connects the Nodes together into a high-bandwidth ring, and provides a connection to the host, a connection to each of the Warp Arrays, and a connection to the <u>Tile Cache</u>.

The Tile Cache is a commodity DRAM device; it is used for caching both reference-image tiles and instructions. A double-buffered Frame Buffer receives the final pixel values from the Nodes for display.

The basic operation of the system is as follows (see Figure 7):

- The host determines which reference-image tiles are to be used to compute the destination image, and computes the screen-space bounding box for each of these tiles. For each screen region, the host maintains a *bin*; each bin contains pointers to the tiles whose bounding boxes intersect that screen region.

- For each screen region, the host assigns a Node to be responsible for that screen region. The host sends each tile in the region's bin to the Node. (Tiles are cached in each node's Tile Cache. If a tile is resident in one of the caches, the host instructs the Network Interface to forward it to the appropriate Node. If not, the host must send the tile data to the Node).

- Each tile received by each Node is loaded into the Warp Array, which performs the warping and interpolation calculations for the tile, and forwards the warped samples to the Region Accumulator.

- The Region Accumulator collects the warped samples into its sub-pixel resolution warp buffer.

- After all tiles in the region's bin have been processed, the Region Accumulator swaps its buffers and initializes the visibility buffer, in preparation for processing the next screen region.

- Concurrently with processing the next screen region, the Region Accumulator steals memory cycles to send the previous region's data to the Reconstruction Buffer. The Reconstruction Buffer computes the final pixel values for the region and forwards them to the Frame Buffer.

- After all regions have been processed and the final pixel values calculated and forwarded to the Frame Buffer, the Frame Buffer swaps buffers.

The system can function in *retained* mode, in which there is a fixed set of reference images describing an environment, or *immediate* mode, in which new reference images are being received "on the fly".

3.2.1 Warp Array

The Warp Array (see Figure 8) consists of 256 processing elements (PEs), arranged as a 16x16-pixel array. Each PE consists of a simple byte-wide ALU and 160 bytes of local memory partitioned as: 128 bytes main memory, 16 bytes IO Buffer, 16 bytes Sample Buffer.

A distributed linear expression evaluator provides values of the linear expression Ax+By+C to each PE simultaneously, in byte-serial form (*x* and *y* represent the position of the PE in the 16x16 array). It is used for very fast computation of the linear part of the numerator and denominator of the warp-equation expressions (see Equation 1). Each PE includes a byte-wide connection to its neighbor in each dimension. Clock rate for the PE and local memory will be at 300 MHz or more.

The IO Buffer is used for inputting reference-image tiles (from the Tile Cache or host, via the Network Interface) via a 300 MByte/sec interface. The Sample Buffer is used for exporting warped samples to the Region Accumulator, over the sample port, via an on-chip 4.8 GigaByte/sec interface. Access to these buffers may occur simultaneously with accessing of the main memory by the ALU, so that the next tile may be loaded during processing of the current one, and one set of interpolated samples can be computed while the previous set is being output to the Region Accumulator.

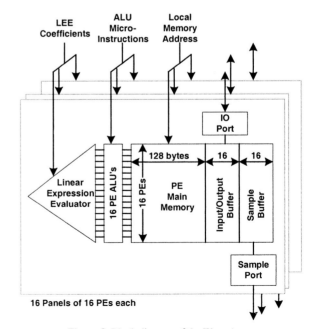

Figure 8. Block diagram of the Warp Array

3.2.2 Region Accumulator

The Region Accumulator (Figure 9) consists of a large SRAM warp buffer (the Region Buffer) and a set of 4 Sample Processors, which combine warped samples into Region Buffer memory.

The Region Buffer contains data for a 128x128-screen region, at 2x2 sub-pixel resolution; a half-pixel wide boundary is added, to allow reconstruction kernels up to two pixels wide. The Region Buffer is partitioned into 4 sections, interleaved 2x2 across the sub-pixel grid.

Each word of Region Buffer memory is divided into three fields. Two double-buffered fields (the RGB/Offset/Present fields) include RGB values, the offsets used for reconstruction, and a *present* bit (used to avoid z-buffer initialization). One buffer is used for accumulating samples for the current region, while the other buffer contains the previous region's values for output.

The third field contains values that are not required for reconstruction and need not be double-buffered. Besides z value, we are reserving space for measures such as the quality of each sample [Mark99]. If the z of two samples are similar, the sample processor gives preference to the better sample. The quality of the sample is derived differently according to the scene. In the context of imperfect registration characteristic to our (and probably all) current depth-image acquisition devices, we obtained better results when we consistently chose the samples of *one* sampling location and used the additional samples from other images just to fill in holes. Synthetic data simulates perfect registration and the quality of the samples was derived from the interpolation factor of the tile it belonged to: the closer the interpolation factor was to 2x2, the higher the quality[5].

A 128-bit wide memory interface provides read/write access to all three buffers in parallel.

Each Sample Processor processes a sample every two clock cycles; this is the maximum possible rate, since 2 Region Buffer accesses (1 read and 1 write) are required for each sample. The Sample Processor is pipelined, so that each computation has several cycles to execute, while sustaining the rate of a sample every two clock cycles. Thus 4 Sample Processors handle an aggregate rate of 2 samples per clock cycle, or 600 million samples/sec at 300 MHz.

The back buffer outputs samples from the previous region to the Reconstruction Buffer, via a shift path that spans all 4 partitions of the Region Accumulator. A small fraction of memory cycles are stolen from the Sample Processors, to feed this scan-out path.

3.2.3 Reconstruction buffer

The Reconstruction Buffer accepts the stream of final warped subsample values from the Region Accumulator, and filters them to produce final pixel values for the 128x128 pixel region. The Reconstruction Buffer includes two scan-line-sized accumulators, and four simple processors. For each RGB/Offset/Present value, each color component is multiplied by a weight from the filtering kernel and added to a sum. Normalization by the sum of weights produces the final pixel value, which is output from the ASIC to the Frame Buffer. The filter kernel is 2x2 pixels in size, with 4x4 sub-pixel resolution. The two 2-bit offset values select the proper kernel element within each sub-pixel.

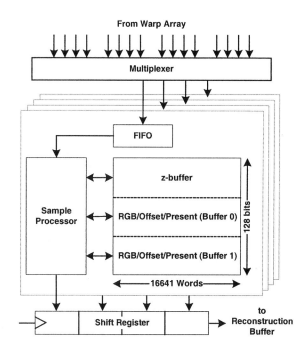

Figure 9. Block diagram of the Region Accumulator

3.2.4 Frame Buffer

The Frame Buffer is a straightforward assembly of commodity DRAMs and programmable parts. It must absorb the full bandwidth of the Reconstruction Buffers on all Nodes, so the peak output rate of the Nodes must be tuned to avoid over-running the Frame Buffer.

3.3 Host and Software

The host is responsible for determining which reference-image tiles will be used to compute the current destination image, for sorting the tiles according to screen region, and for sending the tiles to the WarpEngine Nodes. The host must also determine the interpolation factor for each chosen tile and send instructions to control the warping and interpolation, but these instructions are cached in the Tile Caches and should not represent a significant computational or bandwidth burden for the host.

3.3.1 Retained Mode

Since all reference images are available beforehand, and since the depth discontinuities in the reference images do not depend on the desired view, surface connectivity is estimated as a pre-process. This frees the Warp Array of an additional task at the price of a few additional connectivity bits per reference-image sample.

Determining which tiles are needed for the current image begins with choosing the tiles that are visible. This is done efficiently by subdividing each reference image down to 16x16 tiles in quad-tree fashion and recursively testing whether rectangular sub-images of the image are visible. The visibility test itself is identical to the bucket sorting of tiles: the 4 corners of the sub-image are warped with the minimum and then the maximum disparity of the sub-image. The bounding box of the 8 resulting points is a conservative estimate of the screen area covered by the sub-image. If the sub-image is a tile (a leaf in the quad-tree) it is also assigned to the appropriate screen region bin(s).

---

[5] A 2x2 interpolation factor implies destination image sampling close to reference image sampling, which is desirable.

Depending on the scene, a large number of tiles can be visible and warping all of them is inefficient. Not all visible tiles are needed for the current frame since some tiles sample the same surfaces. Choosing among the visible tiles is not a trivial task. First one needs to determine which tiles sample the same surfaces and then choose among the several candidate tiles according to a quality metric.

The algorithm we use approximates each visible tile by two triangles. The triangles are transformed, projected and scan-converted according to the desired view. The z-buffer test is fuzzy and when two samples are close, the one that belongs to a better tile wins. A better tile is a tile whose approximating triangles have a desired-image size closer to 16x16, which implies a reference-image sampling close to the destination-image sampling. After all visible tiles are processed the chosen tiles are the tiles that have at least one sample left in the tile-choosing buffer.

Scene		Tiles	Overlap factor	Interpolation Factor
Reading room	w/o t.c.	6246	1.28	2.3x2.5
	w/ t.c.	4863	1.32	2.4x2.6
Eurotown	w/o t.c.	15050	1.23	2.2x2.4
	w/ t.c.	6736	1.44	2.6x2.9
Helicopter	w/o t.c.	9101	1.47	2.5x3.7
	w/ t.c.	4976	1.61	3.3x4.8

Table 1. Simulation results on three test scenes at VGA resolution (see Color Plates 3-5) with and without tile choosing.

Table 1 shows the average number of visible tiles in our simulations and the number of tiles chosen by the algorithm. It also shows the *overlap factor*, the average number of regions a tile mapped to in our simulations. The number of chosen tiles is high due to the tiles that have depth discontinuities and for which the triangle approximation breaks. Such tiles are conservatively chosen since the algorithm cannot establish their potential redundancy. We are currently investigating splitting the tiles that have depth discontinuities into depth-discontinuity-free tiles, whenever possible. We believe that this will reduce the total number of chosen tiles since the algorithm presented above will now eliminate more redundant tiles. The overlap factor also will be lower since tiles with depth discontinuities have an unnecessarily large screen-space bounding box.

The host needs to determine the interpolation factor for each chosen tile. The ideal interpolation factor is the minimum value for which surface continuity is preserved. We first find the maximum changes in disparity along each direction, then we use them to estimate the maximum screen-space distance between two neighboring samples. The maximum one-pixel disparity variation is computed as a pre-process, taking into consideration depth discontinuities. Table 1 shows the average of the interpolation factors used in the simulations shown on the video.

Frame-to-frame coherence can be exploited to minimize bandwidth requirements by storing each rendered tile in the Tile Cache of the WarpEngine Node that rendered it[6]. A large

percentage of these tiles can then be used in rendering the same region for the next frame, and many of the remainder can be re-distributed using the Network Interface and used by other WarpEngine Nodes for other regions. Only a relatively small percentage of the tiles will need to be sent from the host; in fact, with a modest number of reference images, it should be possible to cache all the reference-image tiles. A PC's AGP interface should provide plenty of bandwidth for sending missing tiles and pointers to cached tiles[7].

3.3.2 Immediate Mode

For immediate-mode, frame-to-frame coherence cannot be utilized as effectively, since users may wander into areas of the environment that have not been previously sampled in reference images, and the environment itself may indeed be in flux (persons moving, for example). This means that bandwidth requirements from the host will be much higher. In the worst case, it may be necessary on each frame to send every tile from the host to the WarpEngine, and to render every tile.

Within the next few years, we do not expect real-time depth-image acquisition at better than VGA resolution. We can build an immediate-mode system with 20 WarpEngine Nodes that contains a full-screen-sized warp buffer; this means that bucket sorting is not required. Similarly, the low-resolution yields a manageable amount of data. If one data stream provides 640*480 pixels at 30Hz, this is 36,000 tiles/sec or 72 megabytes/sec. For an immediate mode system with four such data streams, a single high-end PC host with an AGP 4X Interface could handle routing tiles to the WarpEngine Nodes. Silicon technology (for the WarpEngine ASIC) and interface technology (for data bandwidth) should scale as depth-image acquisition scales. We are also investigating the possibility of decompressing tiles within the Warp Array.

Another difference is that the PEs will have to compute connectivity information. This is not a serious performance loss since the computation required is simple enough: two adds and a compare for each of the four directions along which connectivity is estimated; a PE can easily get the disparities of the neighboring samples through the closest-neighbor communication paths. Also the host cannot approximate the interpolation factor as described in 3.3.1 since the tile information needed cannot be pre-computed. Our solution is to let the Warp Array estimate the interpolation factor: after all PEs warp their sample, using the inter-PE paths, the Warp Array establishes the maximum distance between consecutive warped samples, in both directions. This produces interpolation-factors that are close to ideal, as described in 3.3.1.

3.4 Performance Considerations

The performance estimates are based on our WarpEngine functional-block-level software simulator. The Warp Array performance was measured with a cycle-accurate simulator. The Warp Engine system has two basic performance limits: the number of tiles per second that can be warped and interpolated, and the number of regions per second for which final pixel values can be reconstructed and forwarded to the Frame Buffer. The first defines the maximum achievable rendering rate, while the second defines the maximum achievable update rate for a given screen-size.

---

[6] Using a 64-MegaBit SDRAM chip as the Tile Cache, each WarpEngine node can cache up to 4,096 reference-image tiles (each tile contains, 256 pixels, each with 4 bytes of color and connectivity, and 4 bytes of disparity).

[7] AGP 2X presently supports peak data transfer rates of 533 MBytes/sec, with a future 4X extension to 1066 MBytes/sec planned. Actual usable throughputs are 50-80% of the peak rate.

3.4.1 Tile Warping/Interpolation Performance

We have found that the Warp Array will require 1878 cycles to perform a 3D image warp for all samples in a tile, using fixed-point arithmetic as described in [Mark99].

If interpolation is done after warping, the interpolated samples will be computed and output to the Region Accumulator one sample at a time (over the entire tile). Outputting one sample for the entire tile requires 256 clock cycles (one cycle per PE). The time to actually compute each interpolated sample from the warped samples will be significantly less. Table 1 indicates that, on average, interpolation generates about 8 sub-samples, so about 8 * 256 = 2K cycles are required to interpolate and output the warped samples. The Region Accumulator can process up to two samples per clock cycle, assuming decent load-balancing, so it is very likely that the one sample per cycle peak output rate of the Warp Array can be sustained. The total time per tile is therefore about 4K cycles, or about 75K tiles per second, per Node. Table 1 shows a typical overlap factor of less than 1.5, so the net performance will be 50K tiles per second per Node. Table 1 shows that at VGA resolutions 5K tiles are typically required to render a scene; we believe that these numbers extrapolate to higher resolutions. Using these assumptions, we computed the following performance numbers for some typical system configurations:

Screen size	Tiles/ frame	Nodes	Sub-samples/sec	Update rate
640x480	5K	3	307 M	30
1280x1024	20K	16	1.6 G	40
2048x1024	32K	32	3.2 G	50

Table 2. Projected performance of typical system configurations.

These numbers show that 4 Nodes can easily handle VGA output resolution loads and that 32 Nodes make a quite powerful system capable of high update rates at HDTV resolution.

If interpolation is done before warping (which we do not think is necessary), it takes on average 8200 cycles to interpolate and warp the same average number of 8 sub-samples. However, there is enough time for the warped sub-samples to be forwarded to the Region Accumulator so no additional cycles are needed. This indicates that interpolation and then warping is feasible but it requires on average twice as many Nodes for the same performance.

3.4.2 Reconstruction Performance

The Reconstruction Buffer operates on the back buffer. It requires 64K clock cycles to compute final pixel values for a region, which is pipelined with the time to render another region. Only if the next region is assigned fewer than 16 tiles (less than it takes to *cover* the region) will the reconstruction time affect performance.

4 FUTURE WORK

The programmability and high-performance of the WarpEngine will allow us to conduct many experiments. Thus far we have not attempted to generate view dependent effects. If provided with the necessary BRDF information, perhaps as a shader program, the Warp Array could compute the view dependent color [Olano98]. Similarly, one could experiment with changing the original lighting conditions of the reference images.

Tile-choosing is a very important and difficult problem, similar to the visibility and level-of-detail problems in conventional rendering. Our tile-choosing is presently complicated by having to detect and resolve inconsistencies between the samples of the same surface seen in several reference images. Dealing separately with view-dependencies will simplify tile-choosing.

Another challenging problem is encountered at the silhouettes. Since photographs or antialiased renderings are used, the color of a silhouette sample is a blend between the color of the front and back surfaces. When warping the depth image, this blended color persists on both the front and the back surfaces, which are no longer adjacent. To prevent this, we discard the silhouette samples, and rely on other reference images to provide replacement samples. For very thin features however, correct samples cannot be found in any of the reference images, causing the thin features to disappear. This comes at no surprise since, in order to respect the Nyquist sampling-rate criterion, the reference images should sample the scene at least twice as densely as the output image. We could, of course, use higher-resolution reference images, but practical considerations will usually prevent this.

An alternative approach, at least in retained mode, is to detect the thin features and model them with tiles from higher resolution images closer to the objects. For example, a light pole that projects one-pixel wide in the desired image can be extracted from a reference image that sees it as several pixels wide. Detecting the thin features can be done relatively easily using the depth-discontinuity detection method described. For efficient tile utilization, the reference-image coordinates of the samples can be stored explicitly, which allows packing the pole samples on one tile, at the price of more data per tile and slightly longer warping time.

An attractive alternative use for the WarpEngine architectural ideas is in a hybrid geometry/image-based rendering machine, which uses images as impostors to bound the total number of polygons [Aliaga99].

5 CONCLUSIONS

The WarpEngine is a 3D graphics hardware architecture designed specifically for rendering by warping images with depth. It might be argued that warping and then interpolating is equivalent to creating a quadrilateral mesh and rendering it on conventional polygon-rendering hardware. There is some truth to this, but the WarpEngine ASIC is a quad renderer particularly optimized for this application. This is because the quads formed by warping the samples of a reference-image tile are of small and uniform size, and conveniently grouped into square arrays, so a SIMD array provides particularly efficient processing. Furthermore, bilinearly interpolating between warped samples (a forward-mapping) requires minimal setup costs, unlike conventional scan conversion (which is a reverse-mapping), further optimizing the processing of tiny quads. Finally, the SIMD array allows flexible programmability, facilitating experimentation with new algorithms. And integration of the SIMD array with the on-chip warp buffer obviates bandwidth concerns and the use of off-chip memory (except for the frame buffer), and the partitioning facilitates scalability to very high performance levels.

The WarpEngine will be implemented using a single custom ASIC, replicated as necessary to meet the desired resolution and warping performance. We expect the ASIC to measure about 12 mm by 16 mm when fabricated on a 0.18-micron process, and to run at 300 MHz or higher. A small 4-node system could fit on a board inside a PC, while a 32-node system will be in a workstation-sized enclosure. We expect to begin layout of the WarpEngine ASIC later this year.

Building the WarpEngine will provide us with insights applicable not only to IBRW architectures but also to architectures for conventional polygon-based rendering, particularly when rendering small polygons.

We expect that the WarpEngine, coupled with image-based modeling or real-time depth imaging, will render images that look truly photorealistic, leading to a dramatically heightened sense of presence for applications like visual simulation and tele-presence, and enabling entirely new applications such as 3D TV.

ACKNOWLEDGEMENTS

We would like to thank Gary Bishop and John Poulton for their encouragement at early stages of this work, David McAllister for his important contributions to depth-image acquisition, and Henry Fuchs for his useful critique of earlier versions of this paper. Special thanks to Mary Whitton for organizing the SIGGRAPH-submission event here at UNC. Support was provided by DARPA, order number E278, and NSF grant number MIP-9612643.

REFERENCES

[Aliaga99] Aliaga D. and Lastra A., "Automatic Image Placement to Provide a Guaranteed Frame Rate", *Proc. SIGGRAPH '99*, 307-316 (1999).

[Beier92] Beier T. and Neely S., "Feature-Based Image Metamorphosis", *Proc. SIGGRAPH '92*, 35-42 (1992).

[Beraldin92] Beraldin J.-A., Rioux M., Blais F., Domey J., and Cournoyer L., "Registered Range and Intensity Imaging at 10-Mega Samples per Second", *Opt. Eng.*, **31**(1): p. 88-94 (1992).

[Chen93] Chen S. and Williams L., "View Interpolation for Image Synthesis", *Proc. SIGGRAPH '93*, 279-288 (1993).

[Chen95] Chen S., "Quicktime VR - An Image-Based Approach to Virtual Environment Navigation", *Proc. SIGGRAPH '95*, 29-38 (1995).

[Cyra] The Cyrax System, in http://www.cyra.com/.

[Debevec96] Debevec P., Taylor C., and Malik J., "Modeling and Rendering Architecture from Photographs: A Hybrid Geometry and Image-Based Approach", *Proc. SIGGRAPH '96*, 11-20 (1996).

[Ellsworth97] Ellsworth D., *Polygon Rendering for Interactive Visualization on Multicomputers*, PhD thesis, University of North Carolina at Chapel Hill, 1997.

[Gortler96] Gortler S., Grzeszczuk R., Szeliski R., and Cohen M., "The Lumigraph", *Proc. SIGGRAPH '96*, 43-54 (1996).

[Kanade99] Kanade T., Rander P., Vedula S., and Saito H., "Virtualized Reality: Digitizing a 3D Time-Varying Event As Is and in Real Time", *Mixed Reality, Merging Real and Virtual Worlds*, Y. Ohta and H. Tamura, Editors. Springer-Verlag. p. 41-57 (1999).

[K2T] *Scene Modeler*, http://www.k2t.com/.

[Levoy96] Levoy M. and Hanrahan P., "Light Field Rendering", *Proc. SIGGRAPH '96*, 31-42 (1996).

[Mark97] Mark W., McMillan L., and Bishop G., "Post-Rendering 3D Warping", *1997 Symposium on Interactive 3D Graphics*, 7-16 (1997).

[Mark99] Mark W., *Post-Rendering 3D Image Warping: Visibility, Reconstruction, and Performance for Depth-Image Warping*, PhD thesis, University of North Carolina at Chapel Hill, 1999.

[McAllister99] McAllister, D., Nyland L., Popescu V., Lastra A., McCue C., "Real-Time Rendering of Real-World Environments", *Rendering Techniques '99, Proc. Eurographics Workshop on Rendering*, 145-160, (1999).

[McMillan95] McMillan L. and Bishop G., "Plenoptic Modeling: An Image-Based Rendering System", *Proc. SIGGRAPH '95*, 39-46 (1995).

[McMillan97] McMillan L., *An Image-Based Approach to Three-Dimensional Computer Graphics*, PhD thesis, University of North Carolina at Chapel Hill, 1997.

[Minolta] *Minolta 3D 1500*, in http://www.minolta3d.com/.

[Molnar92] Molnar S., Eyles J., and Poulton J., "PixelFlow: High-speed Rendering using Image Composition", *Proc. SIGGRAPH '92*, 231-240 (1992).

[Molnar94] Molnar S., Cox M., Ellsworth D., and Fuchs H., "A Sorting Classification of Parallel Rendering", *IEEE Computer Graphics and Aplications*, 14(4), 23-32 (1994)

[Montrym97] Montrym J., Baum D., Dignam D., and Migdal C., "InfiniteReality: A Real-Time Graphics System", *Proc. SIGGRAPH '97*, 293-302 (1997).

[Mueller95] Mueller C., "The Sort-First Rendering Architecture for High-Performance Graphics", *1995 Symposium on Interactive 3D Graphics*, 75-84 (1995).

[Olano98] Olano M. and Lastra A., "A Shading Language on Graphics Hardware: The PixelFlow Shading System", *Proc. SIGGRAPH 98*, (1998).

[Regan99] Regan M., Miller G., Rubin S., and Kogelnik C., "A Real Time Low-Latency Hardware Light-Field Renderer", *Proc. SIGGRAPH '99*, 287-290 (1999).

[Seitz96] Seitz S. and Dyer C., "View Morphing: Synthesizing 3D Metamorphoses Using Image Transforms", *Proc. SIGGRAPH '96*, 21-30 (1996).

[Shade98] Shade J., Gortler S., He L., and Szeliski R., "Layered Depth Images", *Proc. SIGGRAPH '98*, 231-242 (1998).

[Torborg96] Torborg J. and Kajiya J., "Talisman: Commodity Real-time 3D Graphics for the PC", *Proc. SIGGRAPH '96*, 353-364 (1996).

[Westover90] Westover L., "Footprint Evaluation for Volume Rendering", *Proc. SIGGRAPH '90*, 367-376 (1990).

[Wolberg90] Wolberg G., *Digital Image Warping*, IEEE Computer Society Press, Los Alamitos California, 1990.

Figure 10. These images were rendered with the WarpEngine simulator. The reference depth images were created by registering color images with the range information acquired by our laser range finder. The range finder captured data from two positions in the center of the room. We are missing some data, on the ceiling for example.

Pomegranate: A Fully Scalable Graphics Architecture

Matthew Eldridge   Homan Igehy   Pat Hanrahan

Stanford University*

Abstract

Pomegranate is a parallel hardware architecture for polygon rendering that provides scalable input bandwidth, triangle rate, pixel rate, texture memory and display bandwidth while maintaining an immediate-mode interface. The basic unit of scalability is a single graphics pipeline, and up to 64 such units may be combined. Pomegranate's scalability is achieved with a novel "sort-everywhere" architecture that distributes work in a balanced fashion at every stage of the pipeline, keeping the amount of work performed by each pipeline uniform as the system scales. Because of the balanced distribution, a scalable network based on high-speed point-to-point links can be used for communicating between the pipelines.

Pomegranate uses the network to load balance triangle and fragment work independently, to provide a shared texture memory and to provide a scalable display system. The architecture provides one interface per pipeline for issuing ordered, immediate-mode rendering commands and supports a parallel API that allows multiprocessor applications to exactly order drawing commands from each interface. A detailed hardware simulation demonstrates performance on next-generation workloads. Pomegranate operates at 87–99% parallel efficiency with 64 pipelines, for a simulated performance of up to 1.10 billion triangles per second and 21.8 billion pixels per second.

CR Categories: I.3.1 [Computer Graphics]: Hardware Architecture—Parallel Processing

Keywords: Graphics Hardware, Parallel Computing

1 Introduction

The performance of interactive graphics architectures has been improving at phenomenal rates over the past few decades. Not only have the speed improvements kept up with or exceeded Moore's Law, but each successive generation of graphics architecture has expanded the feature set. Despite these great improvements, many applications cannot run at interactive rates on modern hardware. Examples include scientific visualization of large data sets, photo-realistic rendering, low-latency virtual reality, and large-scale display systems. A primary goal in graphics research is finding ways to push this performance envelope, from the details of the chip architecture to the overall system architecture.

The past few years have also marked a turning point in the history of computer graphics. Two decades ago, interactive 3D graph-

---

*{eldridge,homan,hanrahan}@graphics.stanford.edu

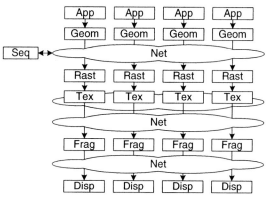

Figure 1: Each Pomegranate pipeline is composed of five stages: geometry (Geom), rasterization (Rast), texture (Tex), fragment (Frag) and display (Disp). A network (Net) connects the pipelines and a sequencer (Seq) orders their execution of multiple graphics streams submitted by the application threads (App).

ics systems were found only at large institutions. As semiconductor technologies improved, graphics architects found innovative ways to place more functionality on fewer chips, and interactive graphics workstations made their way to the desktops of engineers. Today, the entire graphics pipeline can be placed on a single chip and sold at a mass-market price point. Because of the enormous economies of scale afforded by commoditization, this trend has a significant impact on how high-end systems must be built: it is much more cost effective to design a single low-end, high-volume system and replicate it in an efficient manner in order to create high-end, low-volume systems. For example, supercomputers used to be designed with unique, proprietary architectures and esoteric technologies. With the commoditization of microprocessors, these designs were replaced by highly parallel multiprocessor systems that made use of microprocessor technology. The Pomegranate architecture provides a way of scaling the base unit of a single graphics pipeline to create higher performance systems.

Pomegranate is composed of n graphics pipelines interconnected by a scalable point-to-point network, as depicted in figure 1. Each pipeline accepts standard, immediate-mode OpenGL commands from a single context as well as parallel API commands for ordering the drawing commands of the context with the drawing commands of other contexts. As with any parallel system, Pomegranate will only operate efficiently if the load is balanced across its functional units. However, graphics primitives can vary substantially in the amount of processing time they require. Furthermore, the amount of work a primitive will require is not known a priori. Distributing and balancing this workload in a dynamic fashion while minimizing work replication is a key innovation of the Pomegranate architecture and directly contributes to its scalability. A novel serial ordering mechanism is used to maintain the order specified by the OpenGL command stream, and a novel parallel ordering mechanism is used to interleave the work of multiple graphics contexts. Because the use of broadcast communication is minimized in both

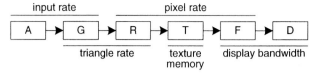

Figure 2: The serial graphics pipeline consists of an application (A), a geometry processor (G), a rasterizer (R), a texture processor (T), a fragment processor (F) and a display processor (D). The units with a direct impact on each scalability measure are underlined.

the data distribution and the ordering, Pomegranate is able to scale to a high degree of parallelism.

In addition to scalability, an equally important characteristic of the Pomegranate architecture is its compatibility with a modern graphics API. OpenGL has strict ordering semantics, meaning that all graphics commands must appear to execute in the order they are specified. For example, two overlapping polygons must appear on the screen in the order they were submitted by the user, and a state change command applies to all subsequent primitives. This constraint forces any parallel OpenGL hardware architecture to be capable of maintaining the serial order specified by the application. This restriction is one of the major obstacles to building a scalable OpenGL hardware renderer. As an analogy, C has become the de facto standard for programming, and as a result microprocessor architects focus the bulk of their efforts addressing the difficulties it introduces — pointer aliasing, limited instruction-level parallelism, strict order of operations, etc. Similarly, we felt it was important to design within the ordering constraints of OpenGL. In addition to specifying ordered semantics, OpenGL is an immediate-mode interface. Commands that are submitted by the application are drawn more or less immediately thereafter. APIs that are built around display lists, scene graphs, or frame semantics all provide the opportunity for the hardware to gather up a large number of commands and partition them among its parallel units. An immediate-mode interface does not enable this approach to extracting parallelism, and thus provides a further challenge.

A fully scalable graphics architecture should provide scalability on the five key metrics depicted in figure 2: input rate, triangle rate, rasterization rate, texture memory and display bandwidth.

- *Input rate* is the rate at which the application can transmit commands (and thus primitives) to the hardware.

- *Triangle* rate is the rate at which geometric primitives are assembled, transformed, lit, clipped and set up for rasterization.

- *Pixel rate* is the rate at which the rasterizer samples primitives into fragments, the texture processor textures the fragments and the fragment processor merges the resultant fragments into the framebuffer.

- *Texture memory* is the amount of memory available to unique textures.

- *Display bandwidth* is the bandwidth available to transmit the framebuffer contents to one or more displays.

Pomegranate provides near-linear scalability in all five metrics while maintaining an ordered, immediate-mode API.

We motivate our discussion of Pomegranate by suggesting two possible implementations: a scalable graphics pipeline and a multi-pipeline chip. A scalable graphics pipeline could be flexibly deployed at many levels of parallelism, from a single pipeline solution with performance comparable to a modern graphics accelerator up to a 64 pipeline accelerator with "supercomputer" performance.

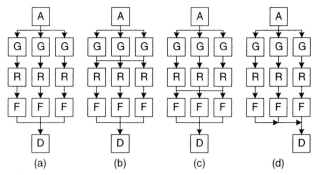

Figure 3: Sort-first (a) sorts triangles before the geometry stage. Sort-middle (b) sorts triangles between geometry and rasterization. Sort-last fragment (c) sorts fragments between rasterization and fragment processing. Sort-last image (d) sorts pixels between fragment processing and the display. The texture stage has been eliminated in this diagram, but in practice will either be located at the end of the rasterization stage or the beginning of the fragment stage.

The incremental cost of the Pomegranate pipeline over a traditional graphics pipeline is the area required for approximately 1MB of buffering, 256KB for supporting 64 contexts, and the area and pins of a high-speed network interface. We estimate that the incremental cost of the Pomegranate pipeline is an additional 200 pins and $50mm^2$ for memory in a modern $0.18\mu m$ process. A network chip, replicated as necessary to interconnect all of the pipelines, would weigh in at approximately 1000 pins, which is feasible. Our second possible implementation is a single chip with multiple Pomegranate pipelines. In such a chip the Pomegranate architecture would be leveraged as a practical method for using the hundreds of millions of transistors which will soon be practical in even a consumer-level graphics accelerator. Current graphics accelerators already stretch the capabilities of VLSI tools and engineers with their size and complexity. Pomegranate would enable the design of a comparatively smaller pipeline which could then be replicated to consume the available transistor count, rather than requiring the design of a huge monolithic pipeline.

In this paper, we will first briefly review previous work in parallel graphics architectures. Then, we will give an overview of the Pomegranate architecture and the details of its key components, describing how work is distributed in a balanced way at each stage of the pipeline to give scalable performance in each of the five metrics. Next, we describe the serial ordering algorithm that maintains the serial order mandated by a single OpenGL context as well as a parallel ordering algorithm that interleaves work according to the order specified by a parallel API. Finally, we present results from a detailed hardware simulation that demonstrates Pomegranate's scalability and compares it to traditional parallel graphics architectures.

2 Background

2.1 Parallel Graphics Architectures

There are a number of published systems that use parallelism to achieve high performance levels. How this parallelism is organized has a direct effect on the scalability of these architectures. Molnar et al. describe a taxonomy for classifying parallel rendering architectures as sort-first, sort-middle or sort-last based on where they transition from object-space parallelism to screen-space parallelism [9]. A variation of this taxonomy is illustrated in figure 3. All of these architectures typically exploit parallelism at each of the geometry, rasterization and fragment stages, either in object-space (assigning work by primitive) or in screen-space (assigning work by screen location). Historically, while addressing scalable triangle rate and pixel rate, most architectures have used a single host interface, replicated texture memory across the rasterizers, and shared a single bus for display, all of which eventually limit the system's capabilities.

In a *sort-first* architecture, the screen is subdivided so that each graphics pipeline is responsible for a fraction of the pixels. The application processor distributes primitives only to the overlapping pipelines. Because the overlap computation can be time-consuming, it is usually amortized over groups of primitives. The primary advantage of this technique is its ability to use relatively standard graphics pipelines as its building block, with only glue logic for the display, and a straightforward mechanism of providing ordering. A major challenge of sort-first architectures has been the load balancing of both triangle work and pixel work. One scheme is to dynamically subdivide the screen into a small number of large tiles [12]. These schemes typically require a retained-mode interface with frame semantics so that each tile comprises an equal amount of work, and finding an efficient, accurate estimator of work is challenging. Another scheme is to subdivide the screen into a large number of small regions and either statically or dynamically assign the regions. While such schemes work with immediate-mode interfaces, minimizing overlap while balancing the load across a wide variety of workloads is difficult.

As with sort-first architectures, *sort-middle* architectures exploit image parallelism by dividing responsibility for primitive rasterization and fragment processing in image-space. However, any geometry unit is allowed to process any primitive. Thus, a sort must occur between the geometry units and the rasterizers, which are responsible for specific areas of the screen. Generally, the partitioning of the screen has been done on a very fine granularity. For example, 2-pixel wide stripes are used on the SGI Infinite Reality [11] to ensure a good load balance of pixel work across all rasterizers. While providing excellent load balancing of pixel work, these small tiles impose a high cost in redundant triangle work because every triangle is assumed to overlap every tile. This broadcast of triangle work sets an upper limit on the triangle rate the system can sustain. However, this broadcast mechanism does provide a natural point to return the primitives processed by the parallel geometry stage to their specified serial order. Larger tiles have been used to remove this broadcast limitation at the cost of large reorder buffers [7]. Minimizing redundant work due to primitives overlapping multiple tiles while efficiently addressing the temporal load imbalances of an immediate-mode API is a major challenge for these systems.

Unlike the sort-first and sort-middle architectures, *sort-last* architectures exploit object parallelism in both the geometry and rasterization stages. In *fragment sorting* architectures, any primitive may be given to any geometry unit, and each geometry unit distributes its work to a single rasterization unit. The rasterization units then distribute the resultant fragments to the specific fragment processor responsible for the corresponding region of the screen. Because each fragment is communicated only once from a single rasterizer to a single fragment processor, no broadcast is involved. The Evans & Sutherland Freedom 3000 [1] and the Kubota Denali [2] are both examples of fragment sorting architectures. The advantage of these architectures is that they potentially have greater triangle scalability than sort-middle since each triangle is processed by only one geometry and rasterization unit. However, even though a fine image-space interleaving ensures load balancing at the fragment processors, there is little or no flexibility to load balance rasterization work. If a few large primitives are submitted, they may push the system significantly out of balance as one or a few rasterizers are given much more work to do than the other rasterizers. This is problematic since primitive sizes are not known a priori.

A second variation of sort-last architectures are *image composition* architectures such as PixelFlow [10]. Multiple independent graphics pipelines render a fraction of the scene into independent

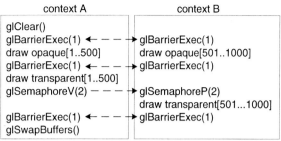

Figure 4: The scene to be rendered consists of 1000 opaque primitives and 1000 transparent primitives. The opaque primitives are rendered with depth buffering enabled, and the transparent primitives are rendered in back to front order. The pseudocode uses two contexts to submit this scene in parallel. The first barrier ensures that the clear performed by context A is complete before context B starts drawing. The second barrier ensures that all the opaque primitives are drawn before any transparent primitives. The semaphore pair ensures that context A's half of the transparent primitives are drawn first. The final barrier ensures that all drawing is done before the swapbuffers occurs.

framebuffers. Then, these framebuffers are composited based on color and depth to form a final image for display. Image composition architectures are a significant departure from the architectures discussed so far because they forfeit ordering altogether in order to scale to higher levels of performance. As with fragment sorting architectures, large primitives can cause significant load imbalance in image composition architectures. Furthermore, while the displays on the previous architectures could be made scalable using approaches similar to Pomegranate, image composition displays are difficult to scale robustly.

2.2 Parallel Interface

While building internally parallel graphics hardware is challenging in its own right, recent graphics accelerators outstrip the ability of the host interface to supply them with data (e.g. NVIDIA's GeForce256). Igehy et al. introduced a parallel API for graphics to address this bandwidth limitation [7]. The parallel API extends OpenGL with synchronization primitives that express ordering relationships between two or more graphics contexts that simultaneously submit commands to the hardware. The significance of these primitives is that they do not execute at the application level, which allows the application threads to execute past the synchronization primitives and continue submitting work. These synchronization commands are then later executed by the graphics system. This allows the programmer to order the execution of the various contexts without being reduced to using a serial interface. The primitives we focus our attention on are barriers and semaphores.

A barrier synchronizes the execution of multiple graphics contexts, ensuring that all of the commands executed by any of the contexts previous to the barrier have completed before any of the commands subsequent to the barrier have any effect. A barrier is defined with `glBarrierCreate` (*name, count*), which associates a graphics barrier that has *count* contexts participating in it with *name*. A graphics context enters a barrier by calling `glBarrierExec` (*name*). A semaphore provides a point-to-point ordering constraint, and acts as a shared counter. A semaphore "V" (or up) operation atomically increments the counter. A semaphore "P" (or down) operation blocks until the counter is greater than zero, and then atomically decrements the counter. A semaphore is defined with `glSemaphoreCreate` (*name, initialCount*), V'd by `glSemaphoreV` (*name*) and P'd by `glSemaphoreP` (*name*). Figure 4 provides an example of the use of these primitives.

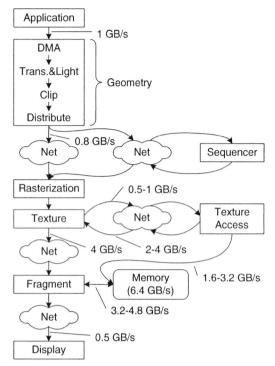

Figure 5: The Pomegranate pipeline. The bandwidth requirements of the communication channels are labeled.

3 Pomegranate Architecture

The Pomegranate architecture is composed of graphics pipelines and a high-speed network which connects them. The pipeline, shown in figure 5, is composed of five stages: geometry, rasterization, texture, fragment and display. The geometry stage receives commands from an application; transforms, lights and clips the primitives; and sends screen-space primitives to the rasterizer. The rasterizer performs rasterization setup on these primitives, and scan converts them into untextured fragments. The texturer applies texture to the resultant fragments. The fragment processor receives textured fragments from the texturer and merges them with the framebuffer. The display processor reads pixels from the fragment processor and sends them to a display. The network allows each pipeline of the architecture to communicate with all the other pipelines at every stage. For example, each geometry processor can distribute its transformed primitives over *all* the rasterizers.

Pomegranate achieves its scalability through a combination of a parallel host interface and multiple types of communication between the functional units.

- Each geometry unit has a host interface that may receive graphics commands simultaneously and independently. Ordering constraints between different graphics contexts may be specified by parallel API commands. This provides scalability of *input rate*. Because the geometry unit is limited by the interface speed, there is no purpose in distributing commands from a single interface across multiple geometry units. The application must therefore provide a balanced number of triangles to each interface. This provides scalability of *triangle rate*.

- A virtual network port allows each geometry unit to transmit screen-space primitives to any rasterizer. There is no constraint on this mapping, thus allowing the geometry units to load balance triangle work among rasterizers. This provides scalability of *triangle rate*.

- The sequencer, shared among all pipelines, determines the interleaving of the execution of the primitives emitted by each geometry unit. It allows multiple contexts to simultaneously submit commands to the hardware and to have their order of execution described by the parallel API. This provides scalability of *input rate*.

- Each rasterizer scan converts screen-space triangles into untextured fragments, and then passes them to the texturer where they are textured. The geometry units may load balance the amount of pixel work sent to each rasterizer in addition to the number of triangles. The geometry units may also subdivide large triangles so that their work is distributed over all the rasterizers. This provides scalability of *pixel rate*.

- Textures are distributed in a shared fashion among the pipeline memories, and each texture processor has a network port for reading and writing of remote textures. This provides scalability of *texture memory*.

- Each texture processor has a network port that enables it to route its resultant fragments to the appropriate fragment processor according to screen-space location. This sorting stage performs the object-space to image-space sort, and allows the unconstrained distribution of triangles between the geometry and rasterization stages that balances object-space parallelism. Fine interleaving of the fragment processors load balances screen-space parallelism and provides scalability in *pixel rate*.

- Each display unit has a network port that allows it to read pixels from all of the fragment processors and output them to its display. This provides scalability of *display bandwidth*.

The Pomegranate architecture faces the same implementation challenges as other parallel graphics hardware: load balancing and ordering. Load balancing issues arise every time that work is distributed. The four main distributions of work are: primitives to rasterizers by the geometry processors; remote texture memory accesses by the texturers; fragments to fragment processors by the texturers; and pixel requests to the fragment processors by the display engine. Additionally a balanced number of primitives must be provided to each geometry processor, but that is the responsibility of the application programmer.

Two distinct ordering issues arise in Pomegranate. First, the primitives of a single graphics context will be distributed twice, first over the rasterizers, and then over the fragment processors. This double distribution results in the work for a single context arriving out of order at the fragment processors, where it must be reordered. Second, each serial graphics context will execute its own commands in order, but it must in turn be interleaved with the other graphics contexts to provide parallel execution in accordance with any parallel API commands. In this section, we discuss in detail the different stages of the pipeline and their mechanisms for load balancing, and defer the discussion of maintaining a correct serial and parallel order and the associated sequencer unit until later.

3.1 Network

Central to the Pomegranate architecture is a scalable network that supports the balanced distribution of work necessary for load balancing and the synchronization communication necessary for ordering. We chose to implement the network as a multi-stage butterfly, depicted in figure 6. A discussion of other candidate networks is beyond this paper, and readers are encouraged to see the text by Duato, Yalmanchili and Ni [4] for a deeper discussion of high-performance scalable interconnects.

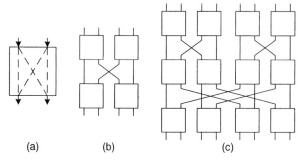

Figure 6: The butterfly network is composed of a single building block (a) which may be cascaded into a multi-stage network to support an arbitrary number of inputs (b & c), with a number of stages that grows logarithmically with the number of inputs.

Networks, and butterflies in particular, are notorious for suffering severe performance penalties under imbalanced loads and increasing latency with increasing utilization. Pomegranate's network usage is engineered to be both uniform and latency tolerant to avoid these problems. For example, in an n-pipeline system, a geometry unit will send $1/n$th of its triangles to each rasterizer. This distribution pattern occurs similarly during texture, fragment and display communication, and is balanced over very fine time scales. Furthermore, the algorithms used in Pomegranate are designed to be able to tolerate latency through the use of buffering.

At the heart of a butterfly network is a $k \times k$ switch ($k = 2$ for figure 6). Every cycle, this switch is able to read a single quantum of data (a *flit*) from each of its input channels and write a flit to each of its output channels. Internally, the switch must arbitrate its outputs according to the requests of incoming packets, which are composed of multiple flits. Channels are virtualized to provide multiple virtual channels per physical channel to increase the likelihood that an output channel will have a packet that needs it on every cycle [3]. Virtual channels are critical to large butterfly networks as they increase bandwidth efficiency from the range of 25% to over 75%.

In order to scale a butterfly network beyond the k inputs and outputs of a single switch, an additional stage of switches is introduced. The first stage routes based on the most significant digits of the destination address, and the second stage routes based on the least significant digits. An n-interface network may be constructed using $\log_k n$ stages of n/k switches. As the number of interfaces increases the aggregate bandwidth available increases linearly, while the cost increases as $n \log_k n$.

The multiple networks of figure 5 are actually virtualized ports within a single unified network. Two messages from the same source to the same destination, e.g. geometry processor 0 to rasterizer 3, are guaranteed to arrive in order, but no other ordering guarantees are made by the network. A unified network allows the network to be used efficiently for all types of traffic, rather than having some networks left idle while other networks are overloaded with traffic. In order to support the expected workload and network inefficiencies, each channel runs at 10 GB/sec. Each channel is 32 bits wide and operates at 2.5 GHz. Each 160-bit flit in our system is transferred over 5 32-bit clocks, and thus the switching logic runs at 500 MHz. We use 4×4 switches and 16 virtual channels per physical channel, each capable of buffering 16 flits. Ignoring contention, each hop through a switch imposes 8 flits of latency. Packets are constrained to be an integral number of flits, with a 24 bit header in the first flit, which imposes a small overhead.

3.2 Geometry

The geometry unit consists of a DMA engine, a transform and lighting engine, a clip processor and a distribution processor. Each geometry unit supports a single hardware context, although the context may be virtualized.

- The DMA engine is responsible for transferring blocks of commands across the host interface and transferring them to the transform and lighting engine. In our model the host interface bandwidth is 1 GB/sec. This is representative of AGP 4x, a current graphics interface.

- The transform and lighting (T&L) engine is a vertex parallel vector processor. It transforms, culls and lights the primitives. Clipping is not performed in the T&L engine because it introduces a potentially large number of new vertices and corresponding primitives which must be correctly ordered in the primitive stream. Deferring this generally infrequent operation to a dedicated clip processor greatly simplifies the T&L engine. The T&L engine has a maximum performance of 20 million transformed and lit vertices per second.

- The clip processor performs geometric clipping for any primitives that intersect a clipping plane. Computation of the clip state for each vertex is performed by the T&L engine, so the clip processor's fast path has no computation. After geometric clipping, the clip processor subdivides large primitives into multiple smaller primitives by specifying the primitives multiple times with different rasterization bounding boxes. This subdivision ensures that the work of rasterizing a large triangle can be distributed over all rasterizers. Large primitives are detected by the signed area computation of back-face culling and subdivided according to a primitive-aligned 64×64 stamp.

- The distribution processor distributes the clipped and subdivided primitives to the rasterizers. This is Pomegranate's first "sort". Because the rasterizers are primitive parallel (object-space parallel) rather than fragment parallel (image-space parallel), the distribution processor has the freedom to distribute primitives as it sees fit.

The distribution processors transmit individual vertexes with meshing information over the network to the rasterizers. A vertex with 3D texture coordinates is 228 bits plus 60 bits for a description of the primitive it is associated with and its rasterization bounding box, resulting in 320 bit (2 flit) vertex packets. At 20 Mvert/sec, each distribution processor generates 0.8 GB/sec of network traffic. The distribution processor generates additional network traffic in two cases. First, large primitives are subdivided to ensure that they present a balanced load to all the rasterizers. In such a case the additional network traffic is unimportant, as the system will be rasterization limited. Second, commands that modify rasterizer state (e.g. the texture environment) must be broadcast to all the rasterizers.

The distribution processor governs its distribution of work under conflicting goals. It would like to give the maximum number of sequential triangles to a single rasterizer to minimize the transmission of mesh vertexes multiple times and to maximize the texture cache efficiency of the rasterizer's associated texture processor. At the same time it must minimize the number of triangles and fragments given to each rasterizer to load balance the network and allow the reordering algorithm, which relies on buffering proportional to the granularity of distribution decisions, to be practical. The distribution processor balances these goals by maintaining a count of the number of primitives and an estimate of the number of fragments sent to the current rasterizer. When either of these counts exceeds a limit, the distribution processor starts sending primitives to a new rasterizer. While the choice of the next rasterizer to use could be based on feedback from the rasterizers, a simple round-robin mechanism with a triangle limit of 16 and a fragment limit of 4096 has proven effective in practice. When triangles are small, and thus each rasterizer gets very few fragments, performance is geometry limited and the resulting inefficiencies at the texture cache are unimportant. Similarly, when triangles are large, and each rasterizer gets few triangles, or perhaps even only a piece of a very large triangle, the performance is rasterization limited and the inefficiency of transmitting each vertex multiple times is inconsequential.

3.3 Rasterizer

The rasterizer scan converts triangles, as well as points and lines, into a stream of fragments with color, depth and texture coordinates. The rasterizer emits 2×2 fragment "quads" at 100 MHz and requires 3 cycles for triangle setup, for a peak fill rate of 400 Mpixel/sec. Partially covered quads can reduce the rasterizer's efficiency to 100 Mpixel/sec in the worst case. We achieve 1.34 to 3.95 fragments per quad for the scenes in this paper. Each rasterizer receives primitives from all the geometry processors and receives execution order instructions from the sequencer (see section 4). Each of the geometry units maintains its own context, and thus each rasterizer maintains n contexts, one per geometry processor. The fragment quads emitted by the rasterizer are in turn textured by the texture processor.

3.4 Texture

The texture stage consists of two units, the texture processor which textures the stream of quads generated by the rasterizer, and the texture access unit which handles texture reads and writes. The input to the rasterization stage has already been load balanced by the distribution processors in the geometry stage, so each texture processor will receive a balanced number of fragments to texture.

In order to provide a scalable texture memory, textures are distributed over all the pipeline memories in the system. Igehy et al. have demonstrated a prefetching texture cache architecture that can tolerate the high and variable amount of latency that a system with remote texture accesses, such as Pomegranate, is likely to incur [6]. Igehy et al. subsequently showed that this cache architecture could be used very effectively under many parallel rasterization schemes, including an object-space parallel rasterizer similar to Pomegranate [5]. Based on these results, we distribute our textures according to 4×4 texel blocks. Texture cache misses to a non-local memory are routed over the network to the texture access unit of the appropriate pipeline. The texture access unit reads the requested data and returns it to the texture processor, again over the network. A texture cache miss requires that a 160-bit texture request be sent over the network, which will be followed by a 640-bit reply, for a total of 800 bits of network traffic per 16 texels, or 6.25 bytes per texel. If we assume 1–2 texels of memory bandwidth per fragment, our rasterizer requires 4–8 bytes of texture memory bandwidth and 6.25–12.5 bytes of network bandwidth per fragment. At 400 Mpixel/sec, this becomes 1.6–3.2 GB/sec of memory bandwidth and 2.5–5 GB/sec of network bandwidth.

After texturing the fragments, the texture processor routes the fragment quads to the appropriate fragment processors. The fragment processors finely interleave responsibility for pixel quads on the screen. Thus, while the texture engine has no choice in where it routes fragment quads, the load it presents to the network and all of the fragment processors will be very well balanced. A quad packet contains 4 fragment colors, 4 corresponding sample masks, the depth of the lower-left fragment, the depth slopes in x and y and the location of the quad on the screen. This representation encodes a quad in 241 bits, or 320 bits (2 flits) on the network. Due to network packet size constraints, this is only twice the size of an individually encoded fragment, which is transmitted as 1 flit. At 100

Mquad/sec, the texture processor sends 4 GB/sec of traffic to the fragment processors. Just as the distribution processor broadcasts rasterization state changes to the rasterizers, the texture processor must also broadcast fragment processor state changes.

3.5 Fragment

The fragment stage of the pipeline consists of the fragment processor itself and its attached memory system. The fragment processor receives fragment quads from the texture processor and performs all the per-fragment operations of the OpenGL pipeline, such as depth-buffering and blending. The memory system attached to each fragment processor is used to store the subset of the framebuffer and the texture data owned by this pipeline.

The use of fragment quads, in addition to reducing network bandwidth, allows efficient access to the memory system by grouping reads and writes into 16-byte transactions. Each pixel quad is organized by pixel component rather than by pixel, so, for example, all of the depth components are contiguous and may be accessed in a single transaction. This improves Pomegranate's efficiency in the peak performance case of fully covered fragment quads, and when fragment quads are only partially covered Pomegranate is already running beneath peak pixel rates, so the loss of memory efficiency is not as important.

The memory system provides 6.4 GB/sec of memory bandwidth. At 400 Mpixel/sec and 8 to 12 bytes per pixel (a depth read, depth write, and color write), fragment processing utilizes 3.2 to 4.8 GB/sec. When combined with texture accesses of 1.6 to 3.2 GB/sec and display accesses of 0.5 GB/sec, the memory system bandwidth is overcommitted. Memory access is given preferentially to the display processor, since it must always be serviced, then to the fragment processor, because it must make forward progress for the texture processor to continue making forward progress, and finally the texture access unit. The majority of our results are not memory access limited.

Pomegranate statically interleaves the framebuffer at a fragment quad granularity across all of the fragment processors. This image-space parallel approach has the advantage of providing a near perfect load balance for most inputs. As with the rasterizers, the fragment processors maintain the state of n hardware contexts. While the rasterizers will see work for a single context from any particular geometry unit, the fragment processor will see work for a single context from all the texture processors because the geometry stage's distribution processor distributes work for a single context over all the rasterizers.

3.6 Display

The display processor is responsible for retrieving pixels from the distributed framebuffer memory and outputting them to a display. Each pipeline's display processor is capable of driving a single display. The display processor sends pipelined requests for pixel data to all of the fragment processors, which in turn send back strips of non-adjacent pixels. The display processor reassembles these into horizontal strips for display. Unlike the use of the network everywhere else in Pomegranate, the display system is very sensitive to latency — if pixels arrive late, gaps will appear in the displayed image. We address this issue with a combination of buffering, which enables the display processor to read ahead several scanlines, and a priority channel in the network. Dally has shown that a bounded percentage of the traffic on a network can be made high priority and delivered with guaranteed latency [3]. At a display resolution of 1920×1280 and a 72 Hz refresh rate, the display bandwidth is 0.5 GB/sec, 5% of Pomegranate's per-pipeline bandwidth.

4 Ordering

Ordered execution of the application command stream must be maintained everywhere its effects are visible to the user. The work distribution algorithms described in the previous section explain

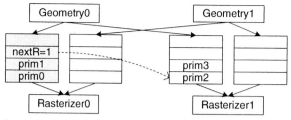

Figure 7: Geometry processor 0 distributes its first 2 primitives to rasterizer 0, and its second two primitives to rasterizer 1. It expresses the ordering constraint between them with a `NextR` command.

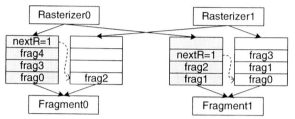

Figure 8: Rasterizer 0 and rasterizer 1 simultaneously process the primitives distributed to them by geometry processor 0. After rasterizing primitive 1, rasterizer 0 broadcast a `NextR` to all the fragment processors, announcing that they should now process fragments from rasterizer 1. The texture processors have been omitted for clarity.

how the Pomegranate architecture scales performance, but the constraint of ordering was ignored. By far the most prevalent place this constraint is exposed is the OpenGL API itself, which is stateful. For example, a `glBlendFunc` command modifies the blending state for all subsequent primitives and no previous primitives. Second, many commands (i.e. points, lines, triangles) modify the contents of the framebuffer, and these modifications must occur in order at each pixel. Finally, changes to the texture memory must be ordered.

Pomegranate faces two distinct ordering issues. First, the commands for a single context are distributed over all the rasterizers, which in turn distribute their fragments over all the fragment processors. This double sort means that the original order of the command stream must be communicated to the fragment processors to allow them to merge the fragments in the correct order. Second, the operations of different contexts must be interleaved in a manner that observes constraints specified by the parallel API.

4.1 Serial Ordering

The key observation to implementing ordering within a single context is that every place work is distributed, the ordering of that work must be distributed as well. The first distribution of work is performed by the distribution processor, which distributes blocks of primitives over the rasterizers. Every time it stops sending primitives to the current rasterizer and starts sending primitives to a new rasterizer it emits a `NextR` command to the current rasterizer, announcing where it will send subsequent primitives. Figure 7 shows the operation of this mechanism. These `NextR` commands provide a linked list of the primitive order across the rasterizers. The rasterizers in turn broadcast the `NextR` commands to all the fragment processors. Each rasterizer has dedicated command buffering for each geometry unit, so that the commands from different geometry units may be distinguished.

The fragment processors each have dedicated buffering for receiving commands from each of the rasterizers, as illustrated in figure 8. Each fragment processor processes commands from a single

rasterizer at a time. When a fragment processor receives a `NextR` command, it ceases listening to the current rasterizer and starts listening to the specified next rasterizer. This is analogous to following the linked list of `NextR` commands emitted by the distribution processor. While a fragment processor will only ever process commands from a single rasterizer at any point in time, all of the rasterizers can continue to make forward progress and transmit fragments to the fragment processors where they will be buffered.

The Pomegranate architecture is designed with the expectation that the same parts which construct the base units are repeated to create larger, more powerful systems. As part of this assumption, the amount of buffering at the input of each fragment processor is fixed. However, this buffering is always divided evenly among all the rasterizers, so as the number of pipelines increases the buffering available per rasterizer at each fragment processor shrinks. However, the increase in the number of pipelines matches this decrease, and the total amount of buffering per rasterizer across all fragment processors remains constant.

The amount of traffic generated by `NextR` commands from a geometry unit to a rasterizer is limited. When the scene is triangle limited, one single-flit `NextR` packet is sent to a rasterizer for every 16 two-flit vertex packets sent to a rasterizer. This represents an overhead of approximately 3%, which remains constant as the system scales. The `NextR` messages from the rasterizers to the fragment processors, on the other hand, represent a potential broadcast in the system because each rasterizer must broadcast each `NextR` it receives to all the fragment processors. Fortunately, this broadcast may be avoided by employing a lazy algorithm. Because `NextR` commands take only a few bits to encode, we can include space for a potential `NextR` command in every fragment quad without increasing its size in network flits. Because the fragment processors have very finely interleaved responsibility for quads on the screen, chances are that a fragment quad will be sent to the fragment processor shortly after the `NextR` command is observed by the rasterizer. A timeout ensures that a `NextR` command that is waiting to piggyback on a fragment quad is not excessively delayed, prompting the rasterizer to send as many outstanding `NextR` commands as possible in a single network packet.

In general, the fragment processors operate independently, each processing fragments at its own rate. The exception is when a command observes or modifies shared state beyond that on a single fragment processor, the fragment processors must be synchronized. Pomegranate uses an internal fragment barrier command, `BarrierF`, to support this synchronization. For example, `glFinish` has an implementation similar to this pseudocode:

```
glFinish( ) {
    BarrierF
    hardware writeback to device driver
}
```

The `BarrierF` ensures that all previous operations by this context are complete before the writeback signaling completion of the `glFinish` occurs.

A similar issue arises at the rasterizers. If a command modifies the current texture state, which is shared among the multiple rasterizers, it must be executed in the correct serial order with respect to the other commands from that context. Pomegranate enforces this constraint with an internal `BarrierR` command which forces all of the rasterizers to synchronize. A texture modification command can be bracketed between `BarrierR` commands and thus be made atomic within the hardware. For example, `glTexImage2D` has an implementation similar to this pseudocode:

```
glTexImage2D( ) {
    BarrierR
    texture download
```

```
        BarrierR
    }
```

The initial `BarrierR` ensures that all previous commands for this context are complete on all rasterizers before the texture download starts so that the new texture does not appear on any previous primitives. The final `BarrierR` ensures no subsequent commands for this context are executed on any rasterizer before the texture download completes so that the old texture does not appear on any subsequent primitives.

4.2 Parallel Ordering

The internal hardware commands `NextR`, `BarrierR` and `BarrierF` suffice to support serial ordering semantics. The extension of the hardware interface to a parallel API requires additional support. The parallel API requires that some or all of the graphics resources must be virtualized, and more importantly, subject to preemption and context switching. Imagine an application of $n + 1$ graphics contexts running on a system that supports only n simultaneous contexts. If a graphics barrier is executed by these $n + 1$ contexts, at least one of the n running contexts must be swapped out to allow the $n + 1$th context to run. Furthermore, the parallel API introduces the possibility of deadlock. Imagine an incorrectly written graphics application that executes a `glSemaphoreP` that never receives a corresponding `glSemaphoreV`. At the very least, the system should be able to preempt the deadlocked graphics context and reclaim those resources. Resolving the preemption problem was one of the most difficult challenges of the Pomegranate architecture.

One solution to the preemption problem is the ability to read back all of the state of a hardware context and then restart the context at a later time. Although this may seem straightforward, it is a daunting task. Because a context may block at any time, the preempted state of the hardware is complicated by partially processed commands and large partially-filled FIFOs. As a point of comparison, microprocessor preemption, which has a much more coherent architecture compared to a graphics system, is generally viewed by computer architects as a great complication in high-performance microprocessors.

A second approach to the preemption problem is to resolve the API commands in software, using the preemption resources of the microprocessor. With this approach, even though ordering constraints may be specified to the hardware, every piece of work specified has been guaranteed by the software to eventually execute. Figure 9 illustrates this approach. Each graphics context has an associated submit thread that is responsible for resolving the parallel API primitives. The application thread communicates with the submit thread via a FIFO, passing pointers to blocks of OpenGL commands and directly passing synchronization primitives. If the submit thread sees a pointer to a block of OpenGL commands, it passes this directly to the hardware. If the submit thread sees a parallel API command, it actually executes the command, possibly blocking until the synchronization is resolved. This allows the application thread to continue submitting OpenGL commands to the FIFO beyond a blocked parallel API command. In addition to executing the parallel API command, the submit thread passes the hardware a sequencing command that maintains the order resolved by the execution of the parallel API command. The important part of this hardware sequencing command is that even though an ordering is specified, the commands are guaranteed to be able to drain: the hardware sequencing command for a `glSemaphoreP` will not be submitted until the hardware sequencing command for the corresponding `glSemaphoreV` is submitted. Thus, a blocked context is blocked entirely in software, and software context switching and resource reclamation may occur.

In order to keep hardware from constraining the total number of barriers and semaphores available to a programmer, the inter-

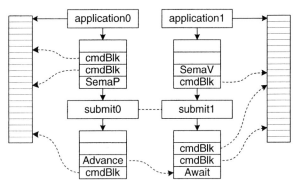

Figure 9: Each graphics context has an associated submit thread which is responsible for resolving the parallel API primitives. In this figure submit thread 0 is blocked waiting to resolve a semaphore P that will be released by context 1. Both application threads are continuing to submit work, and the hardware is continuing to consume work.

nal hardware sequencing mechanism is based on a single sequence number per hardware context. Upon executing a `glSemaphoreV` operation, the submit thread increments the hardware context's sequence number by one to indicate a new ordering boundary, annotates the semaphore with a (*ctx*, *seq*) pair and issues an `AdvanceContext` (*ctx*, *seq*) command to the hardware. Upon completing the `glSemaphoreP` operation, the signaled submit thread removes the corresponding (*ctx*, *seq*) annotation from the semaphore and issues a `AwaitContext` (*ctx*, *seq*) command to the hardware. A similar mechanism is used to implement barriers.[1] The sequence numbers are associated with a particular hardware context, not with a virtual graphics context, and when a context switch occurs, it is not reset. This allows us to express dependencies for contexts that have been switched out of the hardware, and thus execute an $n + 1$ context barrier on n context hardware.

Given the `AdvanceContext`/ `AwaitContext` commands for expressing ordering constraints among contexts, Pomegranate now needs a way of acting on these constraints. The sequencer unit provides a central point for resolving these ordering constraints and scheduling the hardware. The distribution processors at the end of the geometry stage, each of which is dedicated to a single hardware context, inform the sequencer when they have work available to be run and what ordering constraints apply to that work. The sequencer then chooses a particular order in which to process work from the various contexts and broadcasts this sequence to all of the rasterizers, which, along with all the subsequent stages of the pipeline, are shared among all the contexts.

Whenever a distribution processor starts emitting primitives, it sends a `Start` command to the sequencer to indicate that it has work available to be scheduled. In addition, the distribution processor transmits all `AdvanceContext` and `AwaitContext` commands for its context to the sequencer, which in turn enforces the ordering relationships expressed by these commands when making its scheduling decisions. The counterpart of the `Start` command is the `Yield` command which the distribution processors broadcast to all the rasterizers at the end of a block of work. When a rasterizer encounters a `Yield` it reads the next execute command from the sequencer and starts executing that context. The `Yield` com-

---

[1]The first $n - 1$ submit threads to arrive at the barrier execute an `AdvanceContext` to create a sequence point and block. The last context to arrive at the barrier executes an `AwaitContext` on the previous $n - 1$ contexts, an `AdvanceContext` to create its own sequence point and then unblocks the waiting contexts. The $n - 1$ waiting contexts then each execute an `AwaitContext` on the nth context's just created sequence point, for a total of n `AdvanceContexts` and n `AwaitContexts`.

scene	March	Nurbs	Tex3D
input	400^3 volume	1632 patches, 8 passes	256^3 volume
output	$2.5K \times 2K$	$2.5K \times 2K$	$1K \times 1K$
triangles	1.53M	6.68M	512
fragments	10.4M	5.81M	92.5M

Table 1: Benchmark scenes.

	entries	bytes/entry	bytes
Primitive	4096	120	480K
Texture	256	72	18K
Fragment	16384	32	512K

Table 2: Total FIFO sizes for each of functional unit. The FIFO size is listed as the total number of commands it can contain.

mand provides context switching points to support ordering and to allow the pipelines to be shared. First, if a context waits on another context, it must then yield to allow the rasterizers to work on other contexts, which will eventually allow this context to run again. Second, a context must occasionally yield voluntarily, to allow the hardware to be shared among all the contexts so that a single context does not unfairly monopolize the machine. The frequency of these yields is determined by the relationship of the triangle rate of the geometry units to the command buffering provided at each rasterizer. In our implementation, a context yields once it has sent one `NextR` command to each rasterizer. Because the sequencer is decoupled from the rasterizers, it will make scheduling decisions as far in advance as it can, limited only by the available information from the distribution processors and the available buffering for execution commands at the rasterizers.

5 Results

We have implemented an OpenGL software device driver and hardware simulator to verify our architecture. Our system supports all of the major functionality of OpenGL.

The Pomegranate hardware is modeled under an event-driven simulator. The simulator is composed of multiple independent threads of execution which communicate with each other via events. Threads advance events and await on events to coordinate their execution. The simulator provides a shared global knowledge of time, so threads may both wait for other threads to complete a task, as well as simply wait for time to pass, to model clock cycles, etc. The simulator is non-preemptive and a particular thread of execution only ceases execution when it explicitly waits for time to pass or waits on a semaphore.

Our simulator masquerades as the system OpenGL dynamic library on Microsoft Windows NT and SGI IRIX operating systems. Application parallelism is supported through additional functions exported by our OpenGL library that allow the creation of user threads within our simulator. This simulation methodology allows us to deterministically simulate Pomegranate, which aids both debugging and analysis of performance. In particular, performance problems can be iteratively analyzed by enabling more and more instrumentation in different areas of the hardware, with the confidence that subsequent runs will behave identically.

We analyzed Pomegranate's performance with three applications, shown in table 1. The first, March, is a parallel implementation of marching cubes [8]. The second, Nurbs, is a parallel patch evaluator and renderer. The final, Tex3D, is a 3D texture volume renderer.

- March extracts and draws an isosurface from a volume data set. The volume is subdivided into 12^3 voxel subcubes that are processed in parallel by multiple application threads. Each subcube is drawn in back to front order, allowing the use of transparency to reveal the internal structure of the volume. The parallel API is used to order the subcubes generated by

each thread in back to front order. Note that while March requires a back to front ordering, there are no constraints between cubes which do not occlude each other, so substantial inter-context parallelism remains for the hardware.

- Nurbs uses multiple application threads to subdivide a set of patches and submit them to the hardware. We have artificially chosen to make Nurbs a totally ordered application in order to stress the parallel API. Such a total order could be used to support transparency. Each patch is preceded by a semaphore P and followed by a semaphore V to totally order it within the work submitted by all the threads. Multiple passes over the data simulate a multipass rendering algorithm.

- Tex3D is a 3D texture volume renderer. Tex3D draws a set of back to front slices through the volume along the viewing axis. Tex3D represents a serial application with very high fill rate demands and low geometry demands, and it is an example of a serial application that can successfully drive the hardware at a high degree of parallelism.

We measure Pomegranate's performance on these scenes in four ways. First we examine Pomegranate's raw scalability, the speedup we achieved as a function of the number of pipelines. Next we examine the load imbalance across the functional units, which will determine the best achievable speedup for our parallel system. Then we quantify the network bandwidth demanded by the different stages of the pipeline and analyze the lost performance due to network imbalance. Finally we compare Pomegranate's performance to simulations of sort-first, sort-middle and sort-last architectures.

All of these simulations are based on the parameters outlined in our description of the architecture, and the FIFO sizes listed in table 2. The primitive FIFO is the FIFO at the input to the rasterizer, and determines how many primitives a geometry unit can buffer before stalling. The texture FIFO is the FIFO that receives texture memory requests and replies and determines how many outstanding texture memory requests the texture system can have. The final major FIFO is the fragment FIFO, which is where the fragment processors receive their commands from the texture processors. The n pipeline architecture uses the same FIFOs as the 1 pipeline architecture, but divides them into n pieces. The FIFO sizes have been empirically determined.

5.1 Scalability

Our first measure of parallel performance is speedup, presented for our scenes in figure 10. Nurbs exhibits excellent scalability, despite presenting a totally ordered set of commands to the hardware. At 64 processors the hardware is operating at 99% efficiency, with a triangle rate of 1.10 Gtri/sec and a fill rate of 0.96 Gpixel/sec. The only application tuning necessary to achieve this level of performance is picking an appropriate granularity of synchronization. Because Nurbs submits all of its primitives in a total order, the sequencer has no available parallel work to schedule, and is always completely constrained by the API. This results in only 1 geometry unit being schedulable at any point in time, and the other geometry units will only make forward progress as long as there is adequate buffering at the rasterizers and fragment processors to receive their commands. This requirement is somewhat counterintuitive, as the

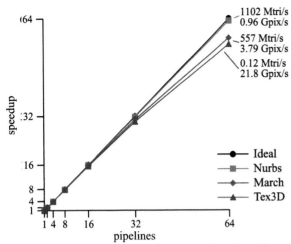

Figure 10: Pomegranate speedup vs. number of pipelines.

pipelines	4	16	64
Geometry	1.00/1.00	1.00/1.00	1.00/1.00
Rasterizer	1.00/1.00	1.00/1.00	0.98/1.02
Fragment	1.00/1.00	0.99/1.01	0.99/1.01
Network	0.98/1.04	0.97/1.27	0.95/2.63

Table 3: Load balance for Nurbs. Each entry in the table presents the minimum/maximum work done by any functional unit as a fraction of the average work per functional unit. Geometry work is measured in triangles; rasterization and composition work is measured in fragment quads. The network imbalance is measured in bytes of traffic per pipeline.

pipelines	4	16	64
Geometry	0.00/4.00	0.00/16.0	0.00/64.0
Rasterization	1.03/1.00	1.00/1.00	1.00/1.00
Texture	1.00/1.00	1.00/1.00	0.99/1.00
Fragment	1.00/1.00	1.00/1.00	1.00/1.01
Network	1.00/1.01	1.00/1.04	0.99/1.15

Table 4: Load balance for Tex3D. Each entry in the table presents the minimum/maximum work done by any functional unit , as a fraction of the average work per functional unit. Geometry work is measured in triangles; rasterization and composition work is measured in fragment quads.

usual parallel programming rule is to use the largest possible granularity of work.

March runs at a peak of 557 Mtri/sec and 3.79 Gpixel/sec in a 64-pipeline architecture, a $58\times$ speedup over a single pipeline architecture. While this scalability is excellent, it is substantially less than that of Nurbs. If we examine the granularity of synchronization, the problem becomes apparent. Nurbs executes a semaphore pair for every patch of the model, which corresponds to every 512 triangles. March, on the other hand, executes 3 semaphore pairs for every 12^3 voxel subcube of the volume, and the average subcube only contains 38.8 triangles. Thus, the number of synchronization primitives executed per triangle is more than an order of magnitude greater than that of Nurbs. Furthermore, there is high variance in the number of triangles submitted between semaphores. These effects cause March to encounter scalability limitations much sooner than Nurbs despite its much weaker ordering constraints.

Tex3D runs at 21.8 Gpixel/sec on a 64-pipeline Pomegranate, with a tiny 0.12 Mtri/sec triangle rate, a $56\times$ speedup over a single pipeline architecture. Tex3D scales very well, considering that it is a serial application. If Tex3D's input primitives were skewed towards smaller triangles it would rapidly become limited by the geometry rate of a single interface and execution time would cease improving as we add pipelines.

5.2 Load Balance

In order to achieve a high parallel efficiency, the work performed by the hardware must be balanced across the functional units and communication must be balanced across the network. Table 3 presents the load imbalance for Nurbs on our architecture with 4, 16, and 64 pipelines. The load balance is within a few percent for all the functional units. This indicates that Pomegranate's methodology for distributing work is providing us with an excellent load balance. By the time Nurbs reaches 64 pipelines the network is significantly out of balance. This is an artifact of Nurbs's relatively low network usage, as it is geometry limited, and the asymmetry of the network traffic generated by the sequence processor, as discussed in section 5.3. The results for March are not shown, but they are qualitatively similar.

Table 4 shows the load imbalance for Tex3D. Despite all of the application commands arriving through a single interface, the subsequent rasterization and fragment stages still receive an extremely balanced load. The texture load imbalance is the ratio of the most texture requests handled by a pipeline to the average. Numbers close to 1 indicate that the shared texture memory is working effectively, because all of the texture requests are well distributed over the pipelines. Tex3D's network imbalance is becoming significant

by the time we reach 64 pipelines. This large asymmetry is the result of all of the primitives entering through a single interface and being distributed from a single geometry unit. As Pomegranate is scaled, the total rasterization speed increases, but the entire geometry traffic is borne by a single pipeline.

5.3 Network Utilization

There are five main types of network traffic in Pomegranate: geometry, sequencer, texture, fragment and display. Geometry traffic is comprised of vertexes transmitted from the geometry processor to the rasterizers and the NextR ordering commands, as well as any state commands, textures, etc. for the subsequent stages. Sequencer traffic is the communication between the distribution processors and the sequencer as well as the sequencer and the rasterizers, and encapsulates all the traffic which allows the hardware to be shared among multiple contexts and the parallel API commands. Texture traffic is made up of the texture request and texture reply traffic generated by each texture processor. Fragment traffic is composed of the quads emitted by the texture processors and sent to the fragment processors. Display traffic is the pixel read requests and replies between the display processors and the fragment processors. The network bandwidth for each traffic type across our scenes on a 64-pipeline Pomegranate is presented in table 5. The sequencer numbers are extremely skewed because there is a single sequencer in the system, so all sequencing information from the distribution processors flows into a single point, and all sequencing decisions for the rasterizers flow back out of that point, which introduces a broadcast into the system. A future version of Pomegranate will use a low bandwidth broadcast ring connecting all the pipelines specifically for the distribution of the sequencing information.

5.4 Comparison

We compare Pomegranate's performance to 4 other parallel graphics architectures:

Sort-First introduces a communication stage between the DMA units and transform & lighting in the geometry processor. The screen is statically partitioned in 32×32 tiles among the pipelines. The screen-space bounding boxes of blocks of 16 vertexes are used to route primitives to pipelines.

	March	Nurbs	Tex3D
Geometry	0.84/0.85	0.54/0.58	0.01/0.93
Sequence	0.02/1.06	0.05/2.95	0.00/0.14
Texture	0/0	0/0	3.00/3.01
Fragment	1.82/1.84	1.19/1.20	3.31/3.32
Total	2.68/3.71	1.78/4.67	6.33/7.26

Table 5: The network traffic by type for each of our scenes on a 64-pipeline Pomegranate. Each row corresponds to a particular type of traffic and each pair of numbers is the average/maximum amount of traffic per pipeline of that type in gigabytes per second. These simulations do not include a display processor.

Sort-Middle Tiled is a sort-middle architecture with the screen statically partitioned in 32×32 tiles among the rasterizers. Individual primitives are only transmitted to the rasterizers whose tiles they overlap.

Sort-Middle Interleaved partitions the screen in 2×2 tiles to ensure rasterization and fragment load balancing. Each geometry processor broadcasts its primitives to all rasterizers.

Sort-Last Fragment partitions the screen in 2×2 tiles among the fragment processors. Each rasterizer is responsible for all the primitives transformed by its corresponding geometry processor.

All of these architectures are built on top of the Pomegranate simulator, and only differ in how the network is deployed to interconnect the various components. We provide each of these architectures, although not Pomegranate, with an ideal network — zero latency and infinite bandwidth — to illustrate fundamental differences in the work distribution. All of these architectures have been built to support the parallel API and a shared texture memory. The ordering mechanisms necessary to support the parallel API are borrowed from Pomegranate, although they are deployed in different places in the pipeline.

Our simulator requires substantial time to run — over 24 hours for some the 64 pipeline simulations. In order to provide these results across all these architectures we were forced to reduce the size of the benchmarks for the remaining simulations. Point simulations of the full data sets give us confidence that the results presented here are quantitatively very similar to the results for the full scenes used in the previous sections.

Figure 11a shows the performance of all of these architectures for the March data set. As March runs, all of the primitives are clustered along the isosurface, which results in high screen-space temporal locality. Sort-first, which uses coarse-grained screen-space parallelism for both geometry and rasterization, is most severely impacted because *temporal locality causes spatial load imbalances over short periods of time*, the length of which are determined by the amount of FIFOing available. Sort-middle tiled employs object-space parallelism for the geometry stage, and because this scene is not rasterization limited, exhibits substantially more scalability than sort-first, although its limitations are exposed at higher levels of parallelism. Sort-middle interleaved behaves much more poorly than sort-middle tiled because it broadcasts triangle work to every rasterizer, and each rasterizer can process a limited number of triangles per second. Sort-last and Pomegranate both scale very well because they rasterize each triangle only once (eliminating redundant work) and use object-space parallelism for rasterization (eliminating any issues with temporal locality). The main difference between Pomegranate and sort-last, the balancing of fragment work across rasterizers by the geometry processors, does not matter here because the triangles are relatively uniformly sized.

Nurbs, shown in figure 11b, exhibits much worse scalability for sort-first and sort-middle than March, and in fact even slows down at high degrees of parallelism. The granularity of work for Nurbs is a patch, which exhibits a great degree of temporal locality in screen-space, even greater than March, which explains the performance at low degrees of parallelism. However, unlike March, Nurbs is a totally ordered application, and when combined with architectures that use screen-space parallelism for geometry or rasterization, the result is hardware that performs almost no better than the serial case. As the number of pipelines increases, the system is capable of processing more work. However, the amount of FIFOing available from each pipeline to each tile decreases, reducing the window over which temporal load imbalance may be absorbed. The hump in performance at moderate numbers of pipelines is a result of these effects. As with March, sort-last and Pomegranate exhibit excellent scalability.

Unlike March and Nurbs, Tex3D, shown in figure 11c, is a completely rasterization limited application. The speedup for sort-first and sort-middle tiled here is limited purely by the rasterization load balance of the entire frame, illustrating that even scenes which appear very well balanced in screen-space may suffer large load imbalances due to tiling patterns at high degrees of parallelism. Sort-middle interleaved, which was previously limited by its reliance on broadcast communication, is now limited by texture cache performance, which is severely compromised by the use of extremely fine-grained rasterization. Each triangle is so large in this application that it serializes sort-last at the fragment processor stage: the fragment FIFOs provide elasticity for the rasterizers to continue ordered rasterization on subsequent triangles while the current triangle is merged with the framebuffer, but when a single large triangle fills up the entire FIFO this elasticity is lost and the rasterizers are serialized. If we greatly increase the buffering at the fragment processors, shown by the "sort-last big" curve, so that sort-last is no longer serialized by the large primitives, the fundamental problem with sort-last is exposed: imbalances in triangle size cause load imbalances across the rasterizers. In Tex3D at 64 pipelines, the worst rasterizer has almost twice the work of an average rasterizer. Many applications (e.g. architectural walkthroughs) have a few very large polygons and exhibit much more severe imbalance in rasterization work than the relatively innocuous Tex3D. Pomegranate addresses this fundamental problem by load balancing both the number of triangles and the number of fragments across the rasterizers, and exhibits excellent scalability on Tex3D.

6 Discussion

Pomegranate was designed to support an immediate-mode parallel graphics interface and uses high-speed point-to-point communication to load balance work across its pipelines. Our results have demonstrated the quantitative impact of these choices, and we will now revisit their qualitative benefits and costs.

6.1 OpenGL and the Parallel API

The decision to support OpenGL, a strict serial API, has proven somewhat complicated to implement, but has not resulted in a performance impact. In fact, Nurbs, which totally orders the submission of its work across all contexts, achieves almost perfectly linear speedup, despite its very strong ordering constraints. The expense of supporting ordering is FIFOs which allow the various pipeline stages to execute commands in application order.

While it may be necessary for the application programmer to choose an appropriate granularity of parallelism, particularly in a strongly ordered scene, it is not required that the application balance fragment work, only primitive work. This is a desirable feature, as in general application programmers have little knowledge of the amount of fragment work that will be generated by a primitive, but they are well aware of the number of primitives being submitted.

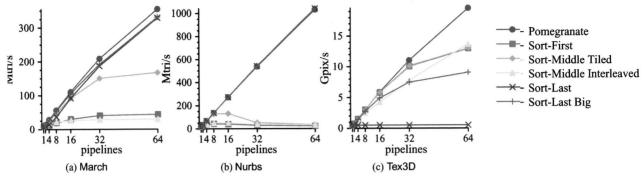

Figure 11: Performance of each architecture on each scene.

6.2 Communication

Pomegranate uses a network to interconnect all the pipeline stages. This approach to interconnecting a graphics system has become much more practical recently due to the advent of high-speed point-to-point signaling, which reduces the cost of providing the multiple high bandwidth links necessary in such a network. Nonetheless, we expect the cost of the network to dominate the cost of implementing an architecture like Pomegranate.

Pomegranate only achieves high scalability when it is able to use the network as a point-to-point communication mechanism. Every time broadcast communication is performed, scalability will be lost. However, some commands must be broadcast. Commands that modify the state of a particular context (e.g. `glBlendFunc`) must be broadcast to all of the units using that state. The command distribution could potentially be implemented lazily, but is still fundamentally a broadcast communication, which will impose a scalability limit. Most high performance applications already try to minimize the frequency of state changes to maximize performance. It remains to be seen how the potentially greater cost of state changes in Pomegranate would impact its scalability.

7 Conclusions

We have introduced Pomegranate, a new fully scalable graphics architecture. Simulated results demonstrate performance of up to 1.10 billion triangles per second and 21.8 billion pixels per second in a 64-way parallel system.

Pomegranate uses a high-speed point-to-point network to interconnect its pipeline stages, allowing each pipeline stage to provide a temporally balanced work load to each subsequent stage, without requiring broadcast communication. A novel ordering mechanism preserves the serial ordered semantics of the API while allowing full parallel execution of the command stream. Hardware support for a parallel host interface allows Pomegranate to scale to previously unreached levels of performance for immediate-mode applications.

8 Acknowledgments

We would like to acknowledge the numerous helpful comments the reviewers made that have improved this work. We would like to thank Greg Humphreys, John Owens and the rest of the Stanford Graphics Lab for their reviews of this paper and their insights. This work was supported by the Fannie and John Hertz Foundation, Intel and DARPA contract DABT63-95-C-0085-P00006.

References

[1] Freedom 3000 Technical Overview. Technical report, Evans & Sutherland Computer Corporation, October 1992.

[2] Denali Technical Overview. Technical report, Kubota Pacific Computer Inc., March 1993.

[3] William J. Dally. Virtual–Channel Flow Control. *IEEE Transactions on Parallel and Distributed Systems*, pages 194–205, March 1992.

[4] José Duato, Sudhakar Yalmanchili, and Lionel Ni. *Interconnection Networks: an Engineering Approach*. IEEE Computer Society Press, 1997.

[5] Homan Igehy, Matthew Eldridge, and Pat Hanrahan. Parallel Texture Caching. *1999 SIGGRAPH / Eurographics Workshop on Graphics Hardware*, pages 95–106, August 1999.

[6] Homan Igehy, Matthew Eldridge, and Kekoa Proudfoot. Prefetching in a Texture Cache Architecture. *1998 SIGGRAPH / Eurographics Workshop on Graphics Hardware*, pages 133–142, August 1998.

[7] Homan Igehy, Gordon Stoll, and Pat Hanrahan. The Design of a Parallel Graphics Interface. *SIGGRAPH 98 Conference Proceedings*, pages 141–150, July 1998.

[8] William E. Lorensen and Harvey E. Cline. Marching Cubes: A High Resolution 3D Surface Construction Algorithm. *Computer Graphics (SIGGRAPH 87 Conference Proceedings)*, pages 163–169, July 1987.

[9] Steven Molnar, Michael Cox, David Ellsworth, and Henry Fuchs. A Sorting Classification of Parallel Rendering. *IEEE Computer Graphics and Applications*, pages 23–32, July 1994.

[10] Steven Molnar, John Eyles, and John Poulton. PixelFlow: High-Speed Rendering Using Image Composition. *Computer Graphics (SIGGRAPH 92 Conference Proceedings)*, pages 231–240, July 1992.

[11] John S. Montrym, Daniel R. Baum, David L. Dignam, and Christopher J. Migdal. InfiniteReality: A Real-Time Graphics System. *SIGGRAPH 97 Conference Proceedings*, pages 293–302, August 1997.

[12] Rudrajit Samanta, Jiannan Zheng, Thomas Funkhouser, Kai Li, and Jaswinder Pal Singh. Load Balancing for Multi-Projector Rendering Systems. *1999 SIGGRAPH / Eurographics Workshop on Graphics Hardware*, pages 107–116, August 1999.

Illuminating Micro Geometry Based on Precomputed Visibility

Wolfgang Heidrich*   Katja Daubert   Jan Kautz   Hans-Peter Seidel

Max-Planck-Institute for Computer Science

Abstract

Many researchers have been arguing that geometry, bump maps, and BRDFs present a hierarchy of detail that should be exploited for efficient rendering purposes. In practice however, this is often not possible due to inconsistencies in the illumination for these different levels of detail. For example, while bump map rendering often only considers direct illumination and no shadows, geometry-based rendering and BRDFs will mostly also respect shadowing effects, and in many cases even indirect illumination caused by scattered light.

In this paper, we present an approach for overcoming these inconsistencies. We introduce an inexpensive method for consistently illuminating height fields and bump maps, as well as simulating BRDFs based on precomputed visibility information. With this information we can achieve a consistent illumination across the levels of detail.

The method we propose offers significant performance benefits over existing algorithms for computing the light scattering in height fields and for computing a sampled BRDF representation using a virtual gonioreflectometer. The performance can be further improved by utilizing graphics hardware, which then also allows for interactive display.

Finally, our method also approximates the changes in illumination when the height field, bump map, or BRDF is applied to a surface with a different curvature.

CR Categories: I.3.1 [Computer Graphics]: Hardware Architecture—Graphics processors; I.3.3 [Computer Graphics]: Picture/Image Generation—Bitmap and frame buffer operations; I.3.7 [Computer Graphics]: Three-Dimensional Graphics and Realism—Color, Shading, Shadowing and Texture

Keywords: Illumination Effects, Monte Carlo Techniques, Graphics Hardware, Frame Buffer Tricks, Reflectance & Shading Models, Texture Mapping

1 Introduction

Geometry, bump maps and bidirectional reflectance distribution functions (BRDFs) are often considered different levels of detail for the same surface structure. Although there has been a considerable amount of work on generating smooth transitions between

*MPI for Computer Science, Im Stadtwald, 66123 Saarbrücken, Germany, {heidrich,daubert,jnkautz,hpseidel}@mpi-sb.mpg.de

©2000 ACM 0-58113-208-5/00/0007 $5.00

these levels [19, 1], the fundamental problem of inconsistent illumination algorithms for the representations still remains.

For example, both simulated and measured BRDFs typically respect not only direct illumination, but also shadowing and masking effects of the micro geometry, as well as indirect illumination resulting from light that scatters between the micro surfaces. Geometry based representations usually consider direct illumination and shadowing/masking, but the indirect illumination is often neglected for performance reasons. Similarly, techniques for shadowing [19] and masking [1] in bump maps have been developed, but most applications do not use them; techniques for light scattering in bump maps have not been available so far. The importance of this indirect, scattered light to the overall appearance is illustrated in Figure 1.

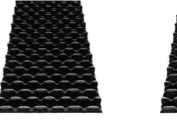

| (a) without scattering | (b) with scattering |

Figure 1: *Indirect light in height fields can have a strong impact on the overall appearance.*

With the advent of new, inexpensive computer graphics hardware that supports both bump mapping (see [23], [22], and [10] for some possible implementations) and rendering with arbitrary BRDFs [15, 10], some newly gained interest in making the transitions consistent has evolved. In this paper we introduce a single, efficient, but high-quality method for illuminating height field geometry and bump maps, as well as for precomputing BRDFs and even higher dimensional data structures. The method is suitable for both ray-tracing and hardware-accelerated rendering.

Our algorithm is based on precomputation and reuse of visibility information in height fields, simulates both shadowing and indirect illumination, and is able to approximate the illumination as the underlying base geometry changes. Thus it is capable of consistently illuminating height field geometry, bump maps, and BRDFs. The main contributions of this paper are:

- An algorithm for efficient computation of indirect light in height fields, based on precomputed visibility information.

- An efficient representation for shadowing and masking in bump maps.

- Hardware-accelerated versions of the above algorithms, using a generalization of Monte Carlo algorithms known as the "Method of Dependent Tests".

- Techniques to approximate the changes in illumination when the height field is applied to a curved surface.

- Application of all methods to simulate BRDFs and render other high dimensional data structures such as light fields and bidirectional texture functions (BTFs).

Throughout this paper we will only deal with height field geometry, which also means that the simulated BRDFs can only originate from height fields. Furthermore, we assume that the bump heights are relatively small compared to their distance from light sources and other objects, so that the only occlusions occurring within a hight field are caused by parts of the same height field, but not by any other geometry in the scene.

The remainder of this paper is organized as follows: In Section 2 we briefly discuss related work. Then, we introduce our data structures for precomputed visibility and their applications to computing indirect illumination in Section 3. We also describe how to make use of graphics hardware for further performance improvements and interactive viewing (Section 3.3), and introduce new data structures for shadowing and masking in Section 4. We then discuss how to adapt both the scattering and the shadow data structures to varying base geometry (Section 5), and finally conclude with some results and a discussion (Section 6).

2   Related Work

Articles that discuss enhancing the original bump map algorithm [2] represent some of the work most closely related to ours. For example, Max [19] shows how to compute the self-shadowing of bump maps with a so-called "horizon map". This horizon map describes the horizon for a small number of directions (8 in the original paper) at each point in the height field. During rendering, the shadow test then simply determines whether the light direction is above or below the (interpolated) horizon. Stewart [26, 27] introduced a hierarchical approach to determine the visibility in terrains both for occlusion culling and shading. More recently, Stewart used a similar idea to simulate the shadowing in cloth [28].

For the shadowing part of our paper, we use a concept similar to the original horizon map, but in a different representation of the horizon that allows for a highly efficient shadow test, which can also be performed with graphics hardware. In addition, we discuss how the data structure can be adapted to different curvatures of the underlying base geometry.

Masking is in a sense a dual problem to shadowing: where shadowing means that a light ray does not hit a specific surface point because it is occluded by some portion of the height field, masking means that the viewing ray does not hit the point for the same reason. In order to incorporate masking in bump maps, Becker and Max [1] introduced *redistribution bump mapping*, which adjusts the distribution of normals in the bump map with the viewing angle. Another possibility is to blend in coarse approximations of the height field as a displacement map. In our implementation, we take this latter approach, although using the results from Becker and Max should also be possible. Furthermore, we can reuse the horizon data structures, which we also apply for shadowing, to compute BRDFs.

So far, there has been little work on computing the indirect illumination in height fields and bump maps. Although Mostefaoui et al. [20] do integrate the indirect illumination at micro geometry scale into a global illumination simulation, their method relies on both precomputed data (BTFs) and a full geometric description of the features. It does not address the problem of precomputing these BTFs, or of computing the illumination in bump maps.

Several approaches for simulating BRDFs have been proposed in the past. The method by Cabral et al. [3] is based on horizon maps, while Becker and Max [1] use the normal distribution in a bump map. Our method is most closely related to the one from Westin et al. [31], which is based on ray-tracing. At the same time,

we borrow the idea of using precomputed visibility information in bump maps from Cabral et al. [3], although our data structures are more comprehensive than simple horizon maps in order to account for indirect illumination.

For the hardware-accelerated variants of our algorithms we require some way of rendering bump mapped surfaces. Any of the recently published algorithms (e.g. [10, 22, 23]) will be sufficient. Mathematically, the hardware implementation of indirect illumination uses a generalization of Monte Carlo integration known as the *Method of Dependent Tests* [7]. This method, which is described in more detail in Section 3.1, uses the same random sampling pattern for estimating an integral at all different points (the indirect illumination in all different points of a height field, in our case). Several other hardware-based algorithms have implicitly used the Method of Dependent Tests in the past, for example most algorithms using the accumulation buffer [9] or the Instant Radiosity algorithm by Keller [16]. Another example is the transillumination method [29], an algorithm for global illumination computations, which is based on propagating light from all surfaces in one direction. Our method improves on this by using precomputed visibility that can be reused for many light paths, and allows for the use of graphics hardware.

While our algorithms yield a significant performance improvement for the generation of single images, they are even more attractive for the computation of higher dimensional data structures such as BRDFs, light fields [18, 8], volume representations [21], and spatially variant BRDFs or bidirectional texture functions (BTFs, [5]), because this allows for a reuse of the precomputed visibility information. Thus, the costly precomputation of visibility can be amortized over a larger amount of reuses. For the same reason our methods are even more attractive if applied to periodic height fields.

3   Light Scattering in Height Fields

To compute the indirect illumination in a height field, we have to solve an integral equation called the Rendering Equation [13]. This requires integrating over the incident illumination in each point of the height field, which can, for example, be achieved with Monte Carlo ray-tracing. The most expensive part of this integration is typically the visibility computation, which determines the surface visible from a given surface point in a certain direction. This is the part that depends on the complexity of the scene, while the computation of the local interaction of the light with the surface has a constant time complexity.

In the case of small-scale height fields that describe the irregularities of a surface, we can make two simplifying assumptions. Most importantly, we only deal with cases where the visibility inside the height field is completely determined by the height field itself, and not by any external geometry. This is equivalent to requesting that no external geometry penetrates the convex hull of the height field, which is a reasonable assumption for the kind of small surface structures that we are targeting. It allows us to precompute the visibility information, and afterwards combine it to a variety of different paths, so that the cost of its computation can be amortized over a larger number of light paths.

Secondly, in the case where we want to use our method to compute a BRDF, we request that the height field geometry is small compared to the remainder of the scene, and therefore any incoming direct light can be assumed parallel. This is necessary simply because the BRDF by definition is a function of *exactly one* incoming direction and *exactly one* outgoing direction. This assumption is not necessary for the other levels of detail, i.e. bump maps and displacement maps.

The visibility restriction requests that no other geometry in the scene will act as an occluder between two points in the height field. If we now assume the height field is attached to a specific, fixed base geometry, we can, for a given point **p** on the height field, and a given direction $\vec{d}$, precompute whether the ray originating at $\mathbf{p}$ in direction $\vec{d}$ hits some other portion of the height field, or not. Furthermore, if it does intersect with the height field, we can precompute the intersection point and store it in a data base. Since this intersection point is some point in the same height field, it is unambiguously characterized by a 2D texture coordinate.

Figure 2: *One of the scattering textures S_i for the triangular height field on the right.*

Now imagine having a set D of N uniformly distributed directions, and having precomputed the visible surface point for every direction $\vec{d} \in D$ and for every grid point in the height field texture. If the height field is periodic, this has to be taken into account for determining this visibility information. Also, for the moment we assume that the height field is applied to a specific base geometry, typically a flat surface. Section 5 deals with an adaptation to varying base geometries.

We store this precomputed data as a set of N texture maps S_i; for each direction $\vec{d_i} \in D$ there is one 2D texture with two components representing the 2D coordinates of the visible point. Each of these textures is parameterized the same way the height field is, i.e. the 2D texture coordinates directly correspond to height field positions $\mathbf{p}$. The texture value also corresponds to a point in the height field and represents the surface point $\mathbf{q}$ that is visible from $\mathbf{p}$ in direction $\vec{d_i}$. Note again, that these visibility textures are only valid for a given, predefined base geometry to which the height field is attached. Section 5 will describe how this information can be used to illuminate the height field when it is attached to other geometries.

By chaining together this visibility information, we can now generate a multitude of different light paths for computing the indirect illumination in the height field. This way, it is possible to implement variants of many existing Monte Carlo algorithms, using the precomputed data structures instead of on-the-fly visibility computations. Below, for example, we outline a simple path tracing algorithm that computes the illumination at a given surface point, but ignores indirect light from geometry other than the height field:

```
radiance( p, v⃗ ) {
    L:= direct illumination( p );
    i:= random number in [1...N];
    if(q := S_i[p] is valid height field coord.){
        L:= L + f_r(p,v⃗,d⃗_i) · cos(∠(d⃗_i,n⃗_p))·
                radiance( q, -d⃗_i );
    }
    return L;
}
```

In this algorithm, $\vec{n}_p$ is the bump map normal in point $\mathbf{p}$, and $f_r(\mathbf{p}, \vec{v}, \vec{d_i})$ is the BRDF of the height field in that point. The direct illumination in each point is computed using a bump mapping technique.

Of course the visibility information for direction S_i is only known at discrete height field grid positions. At other points, we

can only exactly reconstruct the direct illumination, while the indirect light has to be interpolated. For example, we can simply use the visibility information of the closest grid point as $S_i[\mathbf{p}]$. This nearest-neighbor reconstruction of the visibility information corresponds to a quantization of texture coordinates, so that these always point to grid points of the height field. For higher quality, we can also choose a bilinear interpolation of the indirect illumination from surrounding grid points. In our implementation, we use the nearest-neighbor approach for all secondary intersections by simply quantizing the texture coordinates encoded in the visibility textures S_i. On the other hand, we use the interpolation method for all primary intersections to avoid blocking artifacts. Figure 1b shows a result of this method. For more complex examples, see Section 6.

The simple algorithm above ignores shadowing, but with the technique described in Section 4, which is similar to the one introduced by Max [19], shadows can also be included.

Using similar methods, other Monte Carlo algorithms like distribution ray-tracing [4] can also be built on top of this visibility information. The advantage of using precomputed visibility for the light scattering in height fields, as described in this section, is that the visibility information is reused for different paths. Therefore, the cost of computing it can be amortized over several uses.

3.1 The Method of Dependent Tests

As mentioned above, we have to solve the Rendering Equation [13] in order to determine the indirect illumination in a height field. Based on the precomputed visibility information, we solve the Rendering Equation by Monte Carlo integration of the incident illumination at any given surface point, and obtain the reflected radiance for that point and a given viewing direction.

In general, however, we do not only want to compute the reflected light for a single point on the height field, but typically for a large number of points. With standard Monte Carlo integration, we would use different, statistically independent sample patterns for each of the surface points we are interested in.

The Method of Dependent Tests [7] is a generalization of Monte Carlo techniques that uses the same sampling pattern for all surface points. More specifically, we choose the same set of directions for sampling the incident light at all surface points. For example, as depicted in Figure 3, for all points $\mathbf{p}$ in the height field, we collect illumination from the same direction $\vec{d_i}$.

As pointed out by Keller [17], there are several instances in the computer graphics literature, where the Method of Dependent Tests has been applied implicitly [9, 16]. For example, one of the standard algorithms for the accumulation buffer [9] is a depth-of-field effect, which uses identical sampling patterns of the lens aperture for all pixels. It has been shown by Sobol [25] that the Method of Dependent Tests is an unbiased variant of Monte Carlo integration. Recently, hierarchical versions of the Method of Dependent Tests have been proposed [11, 17], but we do not currently make use of these results.

3.2 Dependent Test Implementation of Light Scattering in Height Fields

Based on the Method of Dependent Tests, we can rewrite Monte Carlo algorithms as a sequence of SIMD operations that operate on the grid cells of the height field. Consider the light path in Figure 3. Light hits the height field from direction $\vec{l}$, scatters at each point in direction $-\vec{d_i} \in D$, and leaves the surface in the direction of the viewer $\vec{v}$.

Since all these vectors are constant across the height field, the only varying parameters are the surface normals. More specifically, for the radiance leaving a grid point $\mathbf{p}$ in direction $\vec{v}$, the important

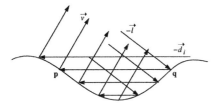

Figure 3: *With the Method of Dependent Tests, the different paths for the illumination in all surface points are composed of pieces with identical directions.*

varying parameters are the normal $\vec{n}_p$, the point $\mathbf{q} := S_i[\mathbf{p}]$ visible from $\mathbf{p}$ in direction $\vec{d}_i$, and the normal $\vec{n}_q$ in that point.

In particular, the radiance in direction $\vec{v}$ caused by light arriving from direction $\vec{l}$ and scattered once in direction $-\vec{d}_i$ is given by the following formula.

$$L_o(\mathbf{p}, \vec{v}) = f_r(\vec{n}_p, \vec{d}_i, \vec{v}) < \vec{n}_p, \vec{d}_i > \cdot$$
$$\left(f_r(\vec{n}_q, \vec{l}, -\vec{d}_i) < \vec{n}_q, \vec{l} > \cdot L_i(\mathbf{q}, \vec{l}) \right). \quad (1)$$

Usually, the BRDF is written as a 4D function of the incoming and the outgoing direction, both given relative to a local coordinate frame where the local surface normal coincides with the z-axis. In a height field setting, however, the viewing and light directions are given in some global coordinate system that is not aligned with the local coordinate frame, so that it is first necessary to perform a transformation between the two frames. To emphasize this fact, we have denoted the BRDF as a function of the incoming and outgoing direction as well as the surface normal. If we plan to use an anisotropic BRDF on the micro geometry level, we would also have to include a reference tangent vector.

Note that the term in parenthesis is simply the direct illumination of a height field with viewing direction $-\vec{d}_i$, with light arriving from $\vec{l}$. If we precompute this term for all grid points in the height field, we obtain a texture L_d containing the direct illumination for each surface point. This texture can be generated using a bump mapping step where an orthographic camera points down onto the height field, but $-\vec{d}_i$ is used as the viewing direction for shading purposes.

Once we have L_d, the second reflection is just another bump mapping step with $\vec{v}$ as the viewing direction and $\vec{d}_i$ as the light direction. This time, the incoming radiance is not determined by the intensity of the light source, but rather by the content of the L_d texture. For each surface point $\mathbf{p}$ we look up the corresponding visible point $\mathbf{q} = S_i[\mathbf{p}]$. The outgoing radiance at $\mathbf{q}$, which is stored in the texture as $L_d[\mathbf{q}]$, is at the same time the incoming radiance at $\mathbf{p}$.

Thus, we have reduced computing the once-scattered light in each point of the height field to two successive bump mapping operations, where the second one requires an additional indirection to look up the illumination. We can easily extend this technique to longer paths, and also add in the direct term at each scattering point. This is illustrated in the Figure 4.

For the total illumination in a height field, we sum up the contributions for several such paths (some 40-100 in most of our scenes). This way, we compute the illumination in the complete height field at once, using two SIMD-style operations on the whole height field texture: bump mapping for direct illumination, using two given directions for incoming and outgoing light, as well as a lookup of the indirect illumination in a texture map using the precomputed visibility data in form of the textures S_i.

This is in itself a performance improvement over the regular Monte Carlo algorithms presented before, because the illumination

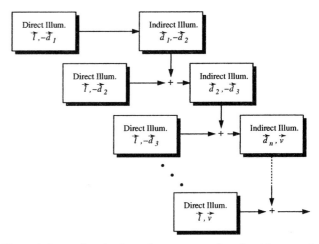

Figure 4: *Extending the dependent test scattering algorithm to multiple scattering. Each box indicates a texture that is generated with regular bump mapping.*

in one grid cell will contribute to many other points on the surface in the final image via light scattering. In contrast to standard Monte Carlo, our dependent test approach avoids recomputing this contribution for each individual pixel.

What remains to be done is an efficient test of whether a given point lies in shadow with respect to the light direction $\vec{l}$. While it is possible to interpolate this information directly from the visibility database S_i, we can also find a more efficient, although approximate representation, that will be described in Section 4.

3.3 Use of Graphics Hardware

In addition to the above-mentioned performance improvements we get from the implementation of the Method of Dependent Tests in software, we can also utilize graphics hardware for an additional performance gain. In recent graphics hardware, both on the workstation and on the consumer level, several new features have been introduced that we can make use of. In particular, we assume a standard OpenGL-like graphics pipeline [24] with some extensions as described in the following.

Firstly, we assume the hardware has some way of rendering bump maps. This can either be supported through specific extensions (e.g. [22]), or through the OpenGL imaging subset [24], as described by Heidrich and Seidel [10]. Any kind of bump mapping scheme will be sufficient for our purposes, but the kind of reflection model available in this bump mapping step will determine what reflection model we can use to illuminate our hight field.

Secondly, we will need a way of interpreting the components stored in one texture or image as texture coordinates pointing into another texture. One way of supporting this is the so-called *pixel texture* extension [12, 10], which performs this operation during transfer of images into the frame buffer, and is currently only available on some high-end SGI machines. Alternatively, we can use *dependent texture lookups*, a variant of multi-texturing, that has recently been announced by several vendors for the next generation of consumer level hardware (the Matrox G400 offers a restricted version of this today). With dependent texturing, we can map two or more textures simultaneously onto an object, where the texture coordinates of the second texture are obtained from the components of the first texture. This is exactly the feature we are looking for. In case we have hardware that supports neither of the two, it is quite simple, although not very fast, to implement the pixel texture extension in software: the framebuffer is read out to main memory, and each pixel is replaced by a value looked up from a texture, using the previous contents of the pixel as texture coordinates.

Using these two features, dependent texturing and bump mapping, the implementation of the dependent test method as described above is simple. As mentioned in Section 3.2 and depicted in Figure 3, the scattering of light via two points **p** and **q** in the height field first requires us to compute the direct illumination in **q**. If we do this for all grid points we obtain a texture L_d containing the reflected light caused by the direct illumination in each point. This texture L_d is generated using the bump mapping mechanism the hardware provides. Typically, the hardware will support only diffuse and Phong reflections, but if it supports more general models, then these can also be used for our scattering implementation.

The second reflection in **p** is also a bump mapping step (although with different viewing- and light directions), but this time the direct illumination from the light source has to be replaced by a per-pixel radiance value corresponding to the reflected radiance of the point **q** visible from **p** in the scattering direction. We achieve this by bump mapping the surface with a light intensity of 1, and by afterwards applying a pixel-wise multiplication of the value looked up from L_d with the help of dependent texturing. Figure 5 shows how to conceptually set up a multi-texturing system with dependent textures to achieve this result.

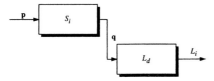

Figure 5: *For computing the indirect light with the help of graphics hardware, we conceptually require a multi-texturing system with dependent texture lookups. This figure illustrates how this system has to be set up. Boxes indicate one of the two textures, while incoming arrows signal texture coordinates and outgoing ones mean the resulting color values.*

The first texture is the S_i that corresponds to the scattering direction d_i. For each point **p** it yields **q**, the point visible from **p** in direction d_i. The second texture L_d contains the reflected direct light in each point, which acts as an incoming radiance at **p**.

By using this hardware approach, we treat the graphics board as a SIMD-like machine which performs the desired operations, and computes one light path for each of the grid points at once. As shown in Section 6, this use of hardware dramatically increases the performance over the software version to an almost interactive rate.

4   Approximate Bump Map Shadows

As mentioned in Section 3.1, we can simply use scattering information stored in S_i for determining the shadows cast in a height field. For example, to determine if a given grid point **p** lies in shadow for some light direction, we could simply find the closest direction $\vec{d_i} \in D$, and use texture S_i to determine whether **p** sees another point of the height field in direction $\vec{d_i}$.

For a higher quality test, we can precompute a triangulation of all points points on the unit sphere corresponding to the unit vectors $\vec{d_i}$ (since the set of directions is the same for all surface points, this is just one triangle mesh for all points on the height field). The same triangulation will later be used in Section 5 for other purposes. Based on this mesh, we can easily determine the three directions $\vec{d_i}$ that are closest to any given light direction, and then interpolate those directions' visibility values. This yields a visibility factor between 0 and 1 defining a smooth transition between light and shadow.

Although this approach works, we have also implemented a more approximate method that is better suited for hardware implementation and much faster.

We start by projecting all the unit vectors for the sampling directions $\vec{d_i} \in D$ of the upper hemisphere over the shading normal into the tangent plane, i.e. we drop the z coordinate of $\vec{d_i}$ in the local coordinate frame. Then we fit an ellipse containing as many of those 2D points that correspond to unshadowed directions as possible, without containing too many shadowed directions. This ellipse is uniquely determined by its (2D) center point **c**, a direction $(a_x, a_y)^T$ describing the direction of the major axis (the minor axis is then simply $(-a_y, a_x)^T$), and two radii r_1 and r_2, one for the extent along each axis.

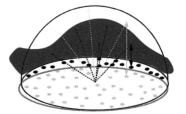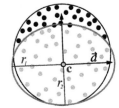

Figure 6: *For the shadow test we precompute 2D ellipses at each point of the height field, by fitting them to the projections of the scattering directions into the tangent plane.*

For the fitting process, we begin with the ellipse represented by the eigenvectors of the covariance matrix of all points corresponding to unshadowed directions. We then optimize the radii with a local optimization method. As an optimization criterion we try to maximize the number of light directions inside the ellipse while at the same time minimizing the number of shadowed directions inside it.

Once we have computed this ellipse for each grid point in the height field, the shadow test is simple. The light direction $\vec{l}$ is also projected into the tangent plane, and it is checked whether the resulting 2D point is inside the ellipse (corresponding to a lit point) or not (corresponding to a shadowed point). This approach is similar to the one described by Max [19] using horizon maps. Only here the horizon map is replaced by a map of ellipses, each uniquely determined by 6 parameters.

Both the projection and the in-ellipse test can mathematically be expressed very easily. First, the 2D coordinates l_x and l_y have to be transformed into the coordinate system defined by the axes of the ellipse:

$$l_x' := < \left(\begin{array}{c} a_x \\ a_y \end{array} \right), \left(\begin{array}{c} l_x - c_x \\ l_y - c_y \end{array} \right) >, \qquad (2)$$

$$l_y' := < \left(\begin{array}{c} -a_y \\ a_x \end{array} \right), \left(\begin{array}{c} l_x - c_x \\ l_y - c_y \end{array} \right) > \qquad (3)$$

Afterwards, the test

$$1 - \frac{(l_x')^2}{r_1^2} - \frac{(l_y')^2}{r_2^2} \geq 0 \qquad (4)$$

has to be performed.

To map these computations to graphics hardware, we represent the six degrees of freedom for the ellipses as 2 RGB textures. Then the required operations to implement Equations 2 through 4 are simple dot products as well as additions and multiplications. Both Westermann et al. [30] and Heidrich and Seidel [10] have shown how such operations can be implemented on graphics hardware. This is possible using the OpenGL imaging subset [24], available on most contemporary workstations, but also using some vendor specific extensions, such as the *register combiner* extension from NVIDIA [22]. Depending on the exact graphics hardware available, the implementation details will have to vary slightly. Thus, they are omitted from this paper, and we refer the interested reader to our technical report [14].

5 Varying the Base Geometry

So far we have only considered the case where the height field is attached to a base geometry of a fixed, previously known curvature, typically a planar object. However, if we plan to use the same height field for different geometric objects, the valleys in a height field widen up or narrow down depending on the local curvature of the object, and the height field can be locally stretched in a non-uniform fashion. This affects both the casting of shadows and the scattering of indirect light. For the shadows, it is obvious that narrower valleys will cause more regions to be shadowed, while in wider valleys more regions are lit.

For the scattering part, the opposite is true. For a point on the bottom of a narrow valley, a large proportion of the solid angle is covered by other portions of the height field, and therefore the impact of indirect light is strong. On the other hand, in a wide valley, most of the light will be reflected back into the environment rather than remaining inside the height field.

In this section we discuss adaptations of the previously described algorithms and data structures to the case where the base geometry changes. To this end, we will assume that the curvature of this base geometry is small compared to the features in the height field. It is then a reasonable assumption that the visibility does not change as the surface is bent. This means that two points in the height field that are mutually visible for a planar base geometry, are also mutually visible in the curved case. Obviously, this assumption breaks down for extreme curvatures, but it generally holds for small ones.

First let us consider the data structures and algorithms for computing scattered, indirect light. Since we have assumed that no extreme changes in visibility occur, the precomputed visibility data i.e. the textures S_i are still valid as the underlying geometry changes. However, as depicted in Figure 7, some parameters of the illumination change. Firstly, there is no longer a fixed global direction $\vec{d}_i$ corresponding to each texture S_i. Rather, the direction changes as a parameter of the curvature and of the distance between two mutually visible points, and becomes different for every point on the surface. Secondly, the normal (and therefore the angles between the normal and other vectors) changes as a function of the same parameters.

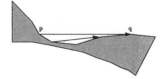

Figure 7: *The directions $\vec{d}_i$ change on a per-pixel basis if the height field is applied to a curved base geometry. The rate of change depends on the distance of two points from each other.*

These changes remove the coherence that we used to map the algorithm to graphics hardware, since now all directions need to be computed for each individual height field point.This requires operations that are currently not possible with graphics hardware. On the other hand, the abovementioned changes are quite easy to account for in a software renderer.

However, there is a third change due to the curvature, which affects all our Monte Carlo algorithms. The set of directions D used to be a uniform sampling of the directional sphere for the case of a given, fixed base geometry. Now, when the height field is applied to a geometry with slightly changed curvature or a non-uniformly scaled one, the directions change as mentioned above. The rate of change depends on the distance of the two mutually visible points. Therefore, the directions do not change uniformly, and, as a consequence, the sampling of directions is no longer uniform. In Monte Carlo terms, this means that the importance of the individual directions has changed, and that this importance has to be taken into account for the Monte Carlo integration. Different light paths can no longer be summed up with equal weight, but have to be weighted by the importance of the respective path. This importance has to be computed for every individual point in the height field.

This requires us to develop an estimate for the importance of a given sample direction, which is explained in the following. We start by interpreting the unit directions $d_i \in D$ for the original geometry as points on the unit sphere, and generate a triangulation of these. Since the sampling of directions is uniform in this planar case, the areas of the triangle fans surrounding any direction d_i will be approximately the same for all d_i, see Figure 8.

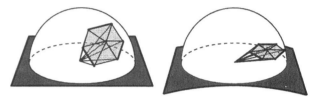

Figure 8: *When a height field is applied to a different base geometry, the importance of the individual directions changes, which is indicated by a change of area of the triangulated unit directions on the sphere.*

Now, if we gradually bend the underlying surface, the points corresponding to the directions will slowly move either towards the horizon or towards the zenith, depending on the sign of the curvature we apply. Note that a change in visibility means that during this movement the triangle mesh folds over at a given point. As mentioned above, we are going to ignore this situation, and restrict ourselves to small curvatures which do not cause such visibility changes.

In this case, the sole effect of the moving points on the unit sphere is that the areas of the triangle fans surrounding each direction change (see Figure 8). This change of area is an estimate for the change in sampling rate, and therefore an estimate for the importance of a particular direction in the curved case. Thus, if we apply a height field to a curved surface, we weight all light paths by the relative area of the triangle fan surrounding the chosen direction.

Now that we have dealt with the adaptation of the scattering data structures, we also have to take care of the shadowing. If we compute the shadows directly from the S_i, as described at the beginning of Section 4, then no changes are required. However, if we are using the 2D ellipses introduced at the end of Section 4, then these ellipses have to be adapted to the local surface curvature.

Starting from the updated scattering directions d_i, we can fit a different ellipse for each point and each surface curvature. However, precomputing and storing this information for a lot of different curvatures is both memory and time consuming. We therefore only precompute a total of five different ellipses: the original one for zero curvature, one each for a slight positive and a slight negative curvature in each of the parametric directions. From this data we can then generate a linear approximation of the changes of ellipse parameters under any given curvature. Again, this only works reasonably as long as the radii of curvature are large compared to the height field features (i.e. as long as the curvatures are small), but for large curvatures we will run into visibility changes anyway.

6 Results

We have implemented the approaches described in this paper both in software, and for two different kinds of graphics hardware. Firstly, we use the SGI Octane, which provides support for pixel textures, but does not have advanced features like multi-texturing, which would help us to reduce the number of rendering passes. On this platform we have implemented the Phong reflection model using the normal map approach described by Heidrich and Seidel [10]. Heidrich and Seidel also describe ways of incorporating other reflection models as well as environment maps through the use of pixel textures. We have not made use of these results.

Secondly, we have used an NVIDIA GeForce 256 with DDR RAM. This graphics board supports multi-texturing with very flexible ways of combining the resulting colors for each fragment (via NVIDIA's register combiner extension [22]). This allows us to perform bump mapping with local illumination and the Phong model in one pass, and helps us to efficiently implement the shadow test. However, the GeForce does not support dependent texture lookups, so that the scattering had to be implemented essentially using a software version of the pixel texture extension.

The first tests we have performed are designed to show whether we can use precomputed visibility to consistently illuminate geometry and bump maps, and also to simulate BRDFs. Figure 9 shows some curved geometry to which the triangular height field from Figure 2 has been applied. In this height field, the faces pointing in one direction are red, and the faces pointing in the other are white. The top row of Figure 9 shows the results of applying the geometry as a displacement map. On the left side, which does not include scattering but shadowing and masking, the separation of the colors becomes apparent, since the top of the geometry is more reddish, while the bottom is white. Due to color bleeding, the image including the scattering term on the right is more homogeneous. The bottom row of the figure shows the geometry with a BRDF that has been computed from the same height field using graphics hardware. Both the version with and the one without scattering show the same kind of behavior as the geometry-based rendering, which illustrates that our technique can be used for smooth transitions between levels of detail.

Both for the rendering of the geometry-based image and for the generation of the BRDF, we first had to generate the visibility data, namely the textures S_i and the ellipse data structures for the shadows. The two leftmost columns of Table 1 show the timings for this precomputation phase and a number of different height fields. The memory requirements for the data structures are quite low: for the scattering in a 32×32 height field with 100 sample directions we generate 100 two-component textures with a size of $32 \times 32 \times 2$ Bytes, which amounts to less than 2 MB of data for the whole scattering information. The shadowing data structure simply consists of two three-component textures, yielding $32 \times 32 \times 6 = 6144$ Bytes.

After the data structures are precomputed, we can efficiently compute images with scattering (100 samples) and shadowing/masking from them using either a software or a hardware renderer. The times for computing the scattering terms in the height field are listed in the third and fourth column of Table 1.

Note that the timings for hardware rendering of small (32×32) height fields including a one-time scattering are well below one second. Thus, we can generate images of scattered height fields at interactive frame rates, although not quite fast enough for applications like games.

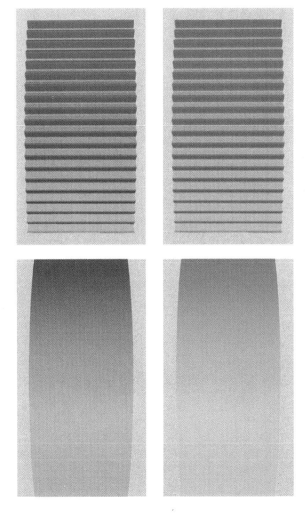

Figure 9: *A comparison of geometry (top) and BRDF (bottom). Left side: without indirect light, right side: with indirect light.*

Height Field	S_i	Shadows	SW	HW
Triangles (32×32)	27	32	10	0.48
Bricks (128×128)	1029	194	12	2.10
Bumps (32×32)	109	65	8	0.48

Table 1: *Timings for precomputation and rendering of different height fields in seconds.*

However, we can use the hardware algorithm to compute higher-dimensional data structures, such as light fields [8, 18] and both space variant and space invariant BRDFs. For example, we can generate a light field consisting of 32×32 images of a height field including scattering terms in just about 6-8 minutes.

As we move to BRDFs, a single BRDF sample is the average radiance from a whole image of the height field. Thus, if we would like to compute a dense, regular mesh of samples for a BRDF, we have to compute a 4-dimensional array of images, and then average the radiance of each image. The BTF [5], on the other hand, is a 6-dimensional data structure obtained by omitting the averaging step, and storing the images directly. These operations can become prohibitively expensive: even for relatively small BRDF resolutions such as 16^4, this would take about 7-8 hours. However, as other researchers have pointed out before [3, 31], it is not necessary to compute this large number of independent samples. Since BRDFs are typically smooth functions, it is sufficient to compute several hundred random samples, and project those into a hierarchical basis such as spherical harmonics.

Using our approach, this small number of samples can be generated within several minutes. To further improve the performance slightly, we can completely get rid of geometry for the computation of BRDF samples, and work in texture space. As described in Sections 3.2 and 3.3, the Method of Dependent Tests already operates in texture space. Only in the last step, when we want to display the result, we normally have to apply this texture to geometry. For the BRDF computation, however, we are only interested in the average of the radiances for the visible surface points. Therefore, if we manage to solve the masking problem by some other means, we do not have to use geometry at all. The masking problem can be solved by using the same data structures as used for the shadow test, only with the viewing direction instead of the light direction. This technique was first proposed by Cabral et al. [3] for their method of shadowing bump maps.

Figure 10: *Three bump-mapped spheres. Bottom left: with shadows only. Top: with shadows and indirect light bouncing off other parts of the bump map. Bottom right: with additional indirect light looked up from an environment map.*

Figure 10 shows some more examples for our technique. The bottom left sphere is rendered with a bump map using only direct light and our shadow test. The top sphere uses the same bump map, but also includes indirect light reflected from other portions of the bump map up to a path length of 4. Finally, in the bottom right sphere, we also include indirect illumination from other parts of the scene, which, in this case, is represented as an environment map, similarly to the method described by Debevec [6]. This is implemented by querying the environment map every time the visibility textures S_i indicate that no intersection occurs with the height field for the given direction.

Figure 11 demonstrates the effect of different curvatures of the underlying geometry, that other researchers have neglected so far. Note that the red faces receive only indirect illumination through scattering from the white faces. We can clearly see the reduced scattering in the case where the curved base geometry causes the valleys to widen up, and at the same time we can see that more regions are shadowed for this case.

Finally, Figures 12 and 13 show some more complicated examples. Figure 12 depicts a backyard scene in which every object except for the floor and the bin has been bump-mapped. This image took 16.2 minutes to render in a resolution of 640×400 pixels.

Figure 11: *Changes of indirect light and shadows as the curvature of the base geometry changes. Note that the red faces are exclusively illuminated indirectly via the light scattered from the white faces.*

The scene has been rendered in software with our methods for shadowing and scattering. Figure 13 shows an image of a terrain model rendered with hardware acceleration and bump shadows in real time ($\approx$ 20 fps. on a GeForce 256).

7 Conclusion

In this paper, we have described an efficient method for illuminating height fields and bump maps based on precomputed visibility information. The algorithm simulates both self shadowing of the height field, as well as indirect illumination bouncing off height field facets. This allows us to use geometry, bump maps, and BRDFs as different levels of detail for a surface structure, and to consistently illuminate these three representations.

Using the Method of Dependent Tests, which is a generalization of Monte Carlo techniques, it is possible to map these methods onto graphics hardware. These techniques exploit the new bump mapping features of recent graphics boards, as well as dependent texture mapping, which is currently available only on some high-end systems, but will be a standard feature of the commodity hardware shipping at the end of the year.

Both the software and the hardware implementation of our algorithms can be used to efficiently precompute BRDFs and higher dimensional data structures such as BTFs or shift-variant BRDFs. Finally, we are also able to approximate the effects of different curvatures of the underlying base geometry, which to some extent change shadowing and light scattering in a height field, and therefore also affects representations like the BRDF. This is the first time in the literature that these effects are simulated.

There is a potential for extending the techniques described in this paper in several ways. First of all, we would like to be able to deal with other geometry than height fields, since materials such as cloth and porous materials cannot be represented in this form. In principle it should be easy to extend our algorithms to arbitrary geometry, however. In order to utilize graphics hardware, we have to find an appropriate 2D parameterization for the object so that all surface points can be represented in a texture. The next step could then be to extend the method to participating media, for example to simulate sub-surface scattering. It would also be interesting to explore whether it is useful to apply the developed methods to compute global illumination in macroscopic scenes along the lines of the transillumination method [29].

Finally, a hierarchical version of the Method of Dependent Tests has recently been introduced by Heinrich [11] and Keller [17]. Heinrich proved that this method is optimal for a certain class of functions fulfilling some smoothness criteria, and Keller extended this work to other classes of functions. It would be interesting to see if these results can be utilized to further improve the performance of our algorithm.

8 Acknowledgments

We would like to thank Alexander Keller for pointing out the relationship between our algorithms and the Method of Dependent Tests. Furthermore, we would like to thank him, Michael McCool, and the anonymous reviewers for their valuable comments.

References

[1] B. Becker and N. Max. Smooth transitions between bump rendering algorithms. In *Computer Graphics (SIGGRAPH '93 Proceedings)*, pages 183–190, August 1993.

[2] J. Blinn. Simulation of wrinkled surfaces. In *Computer Graphics (SIGGRAPH '78 Proceedings)*, pages 286–292, August 1978.

[3] B. Cabral, N. Max, and R. Springmeyer. Bidirectional reflection functions from surface bump maps. In *Computer Graphics (SIGGRAPH '87 Proceedings)*, pages 273–281, July 1987.

[4] R. Cook, T. Porter, and L. Carpenter. Distributed ray tracing. In *Computer Graphics (SIGGRAPH '84 Proceedings)*, pages 137–45, July 1984.

[5] K. Dana, B. van Ginneken, S. Nayar, and J. Koenderink. Reflectance and texture of real world surfaces. *ACM Transactions on Graphics*, 18(1):1–34, January 1999.

[6] P. Debevec. Rendering synthetic objects into real scenes: Bridging traditional and image-based graphics with global illumination and high dynamic range photography. In *Computer Graphics (SIGGRAPH '98 Proceedings)*, pages 189–198, July 1998.

[7] A. Frolov and N. Chentsov. On the calculation of certain integrals dependent on a parameter by the Monte Carlo method. *Zh. Vychisl. Mat. Fiz.*, 2(4):714 – 717, 1962. (in Russian).

[8] S. Gortler, R. Grzeszczuk, R. Szelinski, and M. Cohen. The Lumigraph. In *Computer Graphics (SIGGRAPH '96 Proceedings)*, pages 43–54, August 1996.

[9] P. Haeberli and K. Akeley. The accumulation buffer: Hardware support for high-quality rendering. In *Computer Graphics (SIGGRAPH '90 Proceedings)*, pages 309–318, August 1990.

[10] W. Heidrich and H.-P. Seidel. Realistic, hardware-accelerated shading and lighting. In *Computer Graphics (SIGGRAPH '99 Proceedings)*, August 1999.

[11] S. Heinrich. Monte Carlo Complexity of Global Solution of Integral Equations. *Journal of Complexity*, 14:151–175, 1998.

[12] Silicon Graphics Inc. *Pixel Texture Extension*, December 1996. Specification document, available from http://www.opengl.org.

[13] J. Kajiya. The rendering equation. In *Computer Graphics (SIGGRAPH '86 Proceedings)*, pages 143–150, August 1986.

[14] J. Kautz, W. Heidrich, and K. Daubert. Bump map shadows for OpenGL rendering. Technical Report MPI-I-2000-4-001, Max-Planck-Institut für Informatik, Saarbrücken, Germany, 2000.

[15] J. Kautz and M. McCool. Interactive rendering with arbitrary BRDFs using separable approximations. In *Rendering Techniques '99 (Proc. of Eurographics Workshop on Rendering)*, pages 247 – 260, June 1999.

[16] A. Keller. Instant radiosity. In *Computer Graphics (SIGGRAPH '97 Proceedings)*, pages 49–56, August 1997.

[17] A. Keller. Hierarchical monte carlo image synthesis. *Mathematics and Computers in Simulation*, 2000. preprint available from http://www.uni-kl.de/AG-Heinrich/Alex.html.

[18] M. Levoy and P. Hanrahan. Light field rendering. In *Computer Graphics (SIGGRAPH '96 Proceedings)*, pages 31–42, August 1996.

[19] N. Max. Horizon mapping: shadows for bump-mapped surfaces. *The Visual Computer*, 4(2):109–117, July 1988.

[20] L. Mostefaoui, J.-M. Dischler, and D. Ghazanfarpou. Rendering inhomogeneous surfaces with radiosity. In *Rendering Techniques '99 (Proc. of Eurographics Workshop on Rendering)*, pages 283–292, June 1999.

[21] F. Neyret. Modeling, animating, and rendering complex scenes using volumetric textures. *IEEE Transactions on Visualization and Computer Graphics*, 4(1), January – March 1998.

[22] NVIDIA Corporation. *NVIDIA OpenGL Extension Specifications*, October 1999. Available from http://www.nvidia.com.

[23] M. Peercy, J. Airey, and B. Cabral. Efficient bump mapping hardware. In *Computer Graphics (SIGGRAPH '97 Proceedings)*, pages 303–306, August 1997.

[24] M. Segal and K. Akeley. *The OpenGL Graphics System: A Specification (Version 1.2)*, 1998.

[25] I. Sobol. The use of ω^2-distribution for error estimation in the calculation of integrals by the monte carlo method. In *U.S.S.R. Computational Mathematics and Mathematical Physics*, pages 717–723, 1962.

[26] J. Stewart. Hierarchical visibility in terrains. In *Rendering Techniques '97 (Proc. of Eurographics Workshop on Rendering)*, pages 217–228, June 1997.

[27] J. Stewart. Fast horizon computation at all points of a terrain with visibility and shading applications. *IEEE Transactions on Visualization and Computer Graphics*, 4(1):82–93, March 1998.

[28] J. Stewart. Computing visibility from folded surfaces. *Computers and Graphics*, 1999. preprint obtained from http://www.dgp.toronto.edu/people/JamesStewart/.

[29] L. Szirmay-Kalos, T. Fóris, L. Neumann, and B. Csébfalvi. An Analysis of Quasi-Monte Carlo Integration Applied to the Transillumination Radiosity Method. *Computer Graphics Forum (Proc. of Eurographics '97)*, 16(3):271–282, August 1997.

[30] R. Westermann and T. Ertl. Efficiently using graphics hardware in volume rendering applications. In *"Computer Graphics (SIGGRAPH '98 Proceedings)"*, pages 169–178, July 1998.

[31] S. Westin, J. Arvo, and K. Torrance. Predicting reflectance functions from complex surfaces. In *Computer Graphics (SIGGRAPH '92 Proceedings)*, pages 255–264, July 1992.

Figure 12: *A more complex scene where all surfaces are bump mapped, including shadowing and indirect light.*

Figure 13: *A terrain model with bump map shadowing rendered in realtime with graphics hardware.*

Lapped Textures

Emil Praun   Adam Finkelstein   Hugues Hoppe
Princeton University   Microsoft Research
http://www.cs.princeton.edu/~{emilp,af}   http://research.microsoft.com/~hoppe

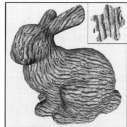

Figure 1: Four different textures pasted on the bunny model. The last picture illustrates changing local orientation and scale on the body.

Abstract

We present a method for creating texture over an arbitrary surface mesh using an example 2D texture. The approach is to identify interesting regions (*texture patches*) in the 2D example, and to repeatedly paste them onto the surface until it is completely covered. We call such a collection of overlapping patches a *lapped texture*. It is rendered using compositing operations, either into a traditional global texture map during a preprocess, or directly with the surface at runtime. The runtime compositing approach avoids resampling artifacts and drastically reduces texture memory requirements.

Through a simple interface, the user specifies a tangential vector field over the surface, providing local control over the texture scale, and for anisotropic textures, the orientation. To paste a texture patch onto the surface, a *surface patch* is grown and parametrized over texture space. Specifically, we optimize the parametrization of each surface patch such that the tangential vector field aligns everywhere with the standard frame of the texture patch. We show that this optimization is solved efficiently as a sparse linear system.

Keywords: Texture synthesis, texture mapping, parametrizations.
URL: http://www.cs.princeton.edu/gfx/proj/lapped_tex

1 Introduction

This paper describes a method for creating a texture over an arbitrary surface mesh, using a given example 2D texture (Figure 1). Computer graphics applications often use surface textures to give the illusion of fine detail without explicit geometric modeling. There exist several schemes for synthesizing texture on the 2D plane based on example texture. However, these methods cannot be readily extended to cover surfaces of arbitrary topology because such surfaces lack continuous parametrizations over the plane.

©2000 ACM 0-58113-208-5/00/0007 $5.00

Our approach to this problem relies on the observation that even though a global parametrization may not exist, any manifold surface may be *locally* mapped onto the 2D plane. We repeatedly paste small regions of the example texture (*texture patches*) onto parts of the mesh that can be easily mapped (*surface patches*), until the entire mesh is covered with a series of overlapping texture patches, called collectively a *lapped texture*. The perceptibility of seams is reduced by applying alpha-blending at the edges of the pasted texture patches. The user provides local control over the orientation and scale of the synthesized texture by specifying a tangential vector field over the mesh surface.

For each paste operation, we form a surface patch on the mesh by growing a region homeomorphic to a disc. The surface patch is parametrized into texture space so as to locally align the axes of the texture patch with the surface tangential vector field. We cast this as an optimization of a least squares functional. Unlike other approaches that rely on an explicit fairness functional for minimizing texture distortion, the fairness comes from the underlying vector field. Our optimization is therefore extremely fast, as it only involves solving a sparse linear system.

We have tested our method by applying more than sixty textures over seven models, and found that it works surprisingly well. Figure 1 shows a bunny model covered using four different example textures. The fifth bunny has the same texture as the fourth, but the tangential vector field has been modified on the body. As shown in Figure 7, our scheme applies a variety of isotropic and anisotropic textures over complex, organic surfaces in a natural fashion.

Lapped textures embody the simple idea of texturing a surface with overlapping patches. Efficient implementation of this idea is straightforward. Precomputation of patch placements takes only minutes, and the resulting texture displays in real time. Little human effort is necessary to delineate a texture patch and specify texture direction and scale. Because a single texture patch is instantiated many times over the mesh, a large surface may be covered using a compact texture footprint. Finally, the method extends trivially to bump maps, displacement maps, and other surface appearance fields.

The contributions of this paper are: (1) the idea of covering an arbitrary surface using overlapping copies of a texture patch, (2) a fast parametric optimization that allows control over the local texture orientation and scale, (3) a simple scheme for specifying the vector field necessary for this control, and (4) a method of rendering the texture in real time through the composition of precomputed, overlapping surface patches.

2 Previous work

Previous methods for generating texture by example work mainly on images, and are difficult to extend to surfaces. Conversely, the methods proposed for texturing surfaces are mainly procedural in nature, and therefore difficult to control. None of these methods provide convenient control over local orientation and scale. We address the problem of generating texture by example on complex surfaces, while providing control over local orientation and scale.

Texture synthesis The problem of synthesizing textures in 2D has been studied extensively. Heeger and Bergen [8] perturb a noisy image in order to match the histograms of the original image and its steerable pyramid representation with the corresponding histograms of the generated image. They report good results with stochastic textures, but cannot produce realistic replicas of more structured textures such as bricks. DeBonet [2] synthesizes texture from a wide variety of input images by shuffling elements in the Laplacian pyramid representation. Recently, Efros and Leung [5] proposed a scheme based on non-parametric sampling. They grow the texture one pixel at a time, creating for each target pixel a probability distribution based on windows of the original image. The scheme is relatively slow, but produces impressive results for a large class of input images. Xu et al. [20] developed a 2D texture synthesis scheme based on the random motion of image blocks; their prototype inspired us to consider texturing surface meshes using overlapping patches.

Many 2D texture synthesis schemes can be extended to 3D using *solid textures:* the color function is defined over a volume, and then sampled on the surface. Heeger and Bergen [8] and Dischler et al. [4, 7] propose schemes that apply spectral and histogram analysis to produce a volume-filling function.

A different class of methods synthesizes texture based on a few parameters, instead of by example. Pioneering work in this area by Perlin [15] and subsequent extensions by Worley [19] generate a color defined over the volume using a noise function. In a different approach, reaction-diffusion and biologic evolution can procedurally texture surfaces in 3D directly [6, 17, 18]. The main drawback of these methods is the difficulty of controlling the input parameters in order to get the desired visual result. This parameter-to-visual-appearance feedback loop is further hindered by the long simulation times necessary to produce an image. Also, these methods explore a limited space of possible textures. Of these techniques, perhaps the most suitable for the problem we address is that of Fleischer et al. [6]; while their method is designed to produce geometric detail, it might be adapted so that each of their cell models carries a texture patch, and gets aligned locally to a direction field.

Neyret and Cani [12] introduce a scheme for texturing a mesh with a given set of triangular texture tiles. They partition the mesh into a coarse tiling, where each triangular tile is as close to equilateral as possible. Each surface tile is assigned one of the given texture tiles, subject to continuity constraints across tile boundaries. The user chooses a priori the number of distinct tile boundaries, and creates a set of tiles that match all possible boundary conditions.

Surface parametrization for texture mapping In seeking a surface parametrization for texture mapping, the primary objective is to minimize distortion. The usual strategy is to define an energy functional for the mapping, and to try to minimize it. In early work in this area, Bennis et al. [1] "flatten" a series of user-defined patches via optimization. Maillot et al. [10] propose as a deformation functional the Green-Lagrange tensor from elasticity theory. They discretize the problem by meshing the surface, placing on each mesh edge a spring of nonzero rest length. To prevent surface buckling, they also measure squared differences of signed face areas. They minimize the energy functional using a nonlinear optimization procedure, which makes the method relatively slow.

Lévy and Mallet [9] propose a functional that combines orthogonality and homogeneous spacing of isoparametric curves. Although the resulting functional is nonlinear, it can be minimized iteratively as a sequence of linear problems by solving alternately for the s and the t parametric coordinates.

Pedersen [13, 14] extends texture mapping and cut-and-paste operations to a broader class of surfaces (including implicit surfaces). He positions a meshed version of a square domain onto the surface and allows the vertices of this regular parametrization to slide over the surface, while minimizing the energy of an associated mesh of springs. Arbitrarily-shaped regions of the sliding patch are cut and pasted, using curve-drawing on the surface to define alpha masks. The sliding patch is translated, rotated, scaled and even warped through the manipulation of the control points defining the parametrization. This is probably the closest work to our own. The main difference is that Pedersen's system is designed to be an interactive paint system while ours is aimed at the automatic texturing of objects. Another difference is our use of a tangential vector field to guide the texture orientation and scale during the parametrization process.

3 Our Approach

Our approach consists of identifying a set of broad features from the example texture ("texture patches"), and then repeatedly pasting them onto "surface patches" grown on the mesh, until the mesh is completely covered. Here is an overview of our procedure:

Cut texture patches from input texture	(Figure 2a, § 3.1)
Specify direction and scale fields over mesh	(Figure 2a, § 3.2)
Repeat	
Select random texture patch $\mathcal{T}$	
Select random uncovered location $\mathcal{L}$ for paste	
Grow surface patch $\mathcal{S}$ around $\mathcal{L}$ to size of $\mathcal{T}$	(§ 3.3)
Flatten $\mathcal{S}$ over $\mathcal{T}$	(§ 3.4)
Record paste operation	(§ 3.5)
Update face coverages	(§ 3.6)
Until the mesh is covered	(Figure 2b, § 3.6)

For recording the paste operations and rendering the final model, we propose two completely different approaches which are presented and compared in Section 4.

3.1 Creating the texture patches

For highly structured textures, the texture patch boundaries should avoid cutting across important features, so as to minimize obtrusive seams in the resulting lapped texture. For example, in a brick texture, the patch boundary should not intersect the bricks but instead follow the grout. The user manually outlines image regions using a commercial drawing package. This outlining process is facilitated by gradient-seeking tools such as the "edge finder" in Microsoft PhotoDraw. The first six examples in Figure 7 were created this way.

For homogeneous or stochastic textures, the outline of the texture patch is less important, so we use a set of predefined shapes, such as a circle or an irregular "splotch".

In either case, the texture patch is assigned an alpha mask that falls off near the patch boundary (e.g. over a distance of 3 pixels).

3.2 Establishing local orientation and scale

The desired orientation and scale for the texture are specified over the mesh as a tangential vector field. Specifically, each mesh face is assigned a vector **T** within its plane (Figure 2). The direction of **T** is the desired the texture "up" direction, and the magnitude of **T** is the desired local uniform scaling.

A simple choice for the tangential vector field is to project the global up direction onto the surface, and then normalize the resulting tangent vector. More often, the user needs more control

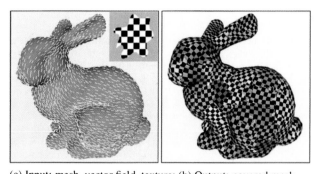

(a) Input: mesh, vector field, texture; (b) Output: covered mesh

Figure 2: Process overview. The inputs are a triangle mesh, a tangential vector field defined on this mesh, and a texture cut into patches. The patches are pasted onto the mesh until it is covered.

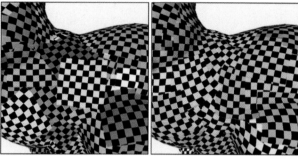

(a) Align only patch center   (b) Align locally to field

Figure 3: Continuity of the texture direction is improved when the optimization aligns the entire surface patch with the vector field rather than just its center.

over the vector field. With our interface, the user specifies vectors at a few faces. We interpolate vectors at the remaining faces using Gaussian radial basis functions, where radius is defined as distance over the mesh, as computed using Dijkstra's algorithm. The user has control over the spatial extent and weight of each basis function.

We convert the tangential vector $\mathbf{T}$ at each face into a tangential basis $(\mathbf{S}, \mathbf{T})$ by using the "right" direction $\mathbf{S} = \mathbf{T} \times \hat{\mathbf{N}}$, where $\hat{\mathbf{N}}$ is the unit face normal (see Figure 5). The user could alternatively specify this tangential basis directly for local control of a full linear transform for the texture, including shearing and non-uniform stretching. However, we have found this additional flexibility to be unnecessary in our experiments.

For isotropic textures, the orientations of the paste operations are unimportant. For such cases, we only specify a scaling field over the mesh (and in most cases it is a global constant). During the growth of surface patches (described in the next section), a local orientation field is instead defined through propagation. That is, the center face of the patch is assigned an arbitrary tangent direction, and the direction of each subsequently added face is computed by projecting onto its face plane the average direction of neighboring faces already in the patch.

3.3 Growing the surface patch

For each paste operation, we grow a surface patch on the mesh by successively adding faces, and form an initial parametrization ϕ of the surface patch into texture space. The parametrization $\phi : R^3 \rightarrow R^2$ is a piecewise linear map specified by texture coordinates assigned to the surface patch vertices. The growth of the surface patch is guided so that its image through ϕ fully covers the texture patch. We next present the details.

First, a random point is chosen on a triangle face that is not yet fully textured, using the coverage test presented in Section 3.6. (Early in the process we give higher priority both to areas of high curvature and to discontinuities in the direction field – where the parametrization is difficult – with the hope that any distorted regions will be covered over later.) The triangle is mapped to texture space such that the chosen point maps to the texture patch center, and the face tangential basis $(\mathbf{S}, \mathbf{T})$ maps to the texture space standard axes $(\hat{\mathbf{s}}, \hat{\mathbf{t}})$.

Next, the surface patch is grown around this seed face, one triangle at a time. Faces are added in order of increasing distance from the center face, but subject to three constraints. First, the surface patch is required to be homeomorphic to a disc. The adjacent figure illustrates a problem that may arise when this constraint is not enforced: the optimization of Section 3.4 maps a tubular patch to a thin vertical band due to the

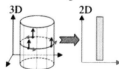

circular dependency in the specified texture $\mathbf{S}$ direction (in red). Second, the patch is only grown over an edge if the edge is still partially inside the texture patch, since there is no point in growing the surface patch beyond the image region that will be pasted. This test is made efficient using the polygonal hull representation discussed later in this section. Third, patch growth is stopped when distortion becomes excessive, which can occur in surface areas with high curvature. In these cases where we are unable to extend the surface patch to fully cover the texture patch, the pasted texture lacks an alpha falloff across one or more edges. We find that the few noticeable artifacts from these "hard edges" are less objectionable than distorted texture.

When a face is added to the patch, the newly added vertex is assigned an initial parametrization using the heuristic in [10]. Specifically, for each face that contains the new vertex and an already mapped edge, we predict the parametrization of the new vertex by extending the edge with a triangle similar to the face in 3D. The new vertex is assigned the centroid of these predictions. Note that for texture pasting, we do not prevent the patch from folding or wrapping over itself in texture space.

To determine if we need to grow the patch over a given edge, we test to see if the edge intersects the interior of a **polygonal hull** of the texture patch. We first construct a polygon with vertices at all the boundary pixels (in blue), and then we conservatively simplify it, allowing it only to grow (red outline). Sander *et al.* [16] construct conservative approximations of polyhedral surface meshes using *progressive hull* simplification. We adapt their construction to the 2D setting. Simplification is done using a sequence of edges collapses, but with the constraint that the resulting vertex lie within the correct half-spaces of the previous model. In 3D this involves linear programming, but in 2D it reduces to just the 3 cases illustrated in Figure 4. The simplification operations are prioritized according to the area they add to the polygon interior. Operations that would give rise to self-intersections are disallowed.

Once the surface patch stops growing, we optimize the map ϕ as discussed in the next section. The optimization may sometimes uncover parts of the texture patch. When this occurs, we further grow the patch and optimize again.

(i) Both angles convex (ii) Convex - concave (iii) Both concave No self intersections

Figure 4: Simplification of the outer hull polygon. The thick edge is replaced with the thin lines, thereby removing one vertex.

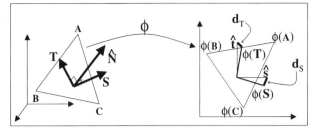

Figure 5: The optimization process minimizes the differences $(\mathbf{d}_S, \mathbf{d}_T)$ between the texture coordinate axes $(\hat{\mathbf{s}}, \hat{\mathbf{t}})$ and the images $(\phi(\mathbf{S}), \phi(\mathbf{T}))$ in texture space of the user-specified vectors $(\mathbf{S}, \mathbf{T})$.

3.4 Optimizing the surface patch parametrization

Having formed a surface patch together with its initial parametrization ϕ, we optimize ϕ so as to locally match both the orientation and scale of the texture with the vector field defined on the surface. More precisely, we attempt to match the images of the surface tangent vectors $(\mathbf{S}, \mathbf{T})$ with the texture coordinate axes $(\hat{\mathbf{s}}, \hat{\mathbf{t}})$. Figure 3 shows the importance of aligning the vector field over the whole patch, as opposed to just at its center.

For each mesh face $f = \{\mathbf{A}, \mathbf{B}, \mathbf{C}\}$, the "up" vector $\mathbf{T}$ lies within the face plane. We can therefore express it using its barycentric coordinates with respect to the vertex positions[1]:

$$\mathbf{T} = \alpha \mathbf{A} + \beta \mathbf{B} + \gamma \mathbf{C}, \quad \text{where} \quad \alpha + \beta + \gamma = 0 .$$

Since the map ϕ is linear over the face, the image $\phi(\mathbf{T})$ is therefore a linear function of the vertex parametrizations $\phi(\mathbf{A})$, $\phi(\mathbf{B})$, and $\phi(\mathbf{C})$. As shown in Figure 5, we define the difference vector

$$\mathbf{d}_T = \alpha \, \phi(\mathbf{A}) + \beta \, \phi(\mathbf{B}) + \gamma \, \phi(\mathbf{C}) - \hat{\mathbf{t}} ,$$

and we do likewise for the difference vector $\mathbf{d}_S$. Our optimization problem is to find the vertex parametrizations that minimize the least squares functional

$$\sum_f \|\mathbf{d}_S\|^2 + \|\mathbf{d}_T\|^2 .$$

The minimum of this function is unique up to a translation. We therefore add a positional constraint to fix the location of the patch center. The exact solution to the minimization problem only requires solving a sparse linear system. Since we begin with a reasonable approximation of the solution, we use a conjugate-gradient iterative solver, which is faster than an explicit solver like Gaussian elimination.

Note that the functional does not include any explicit "fairness" term to penalize distortion in the parametrization. Instead, continuity of the parametrization across mesh edges relies on the continuity of the user-provided tangential vector field. Unlike many local edge-spring functionals, our functional does not have local minima when the face orientations flip, and thus avoids "buckling" artifacts. Finally, the parametrization is well-behaved even though the patch boundary is left unconstrained.

3.5 Recording the paste operations

The paste operation sends image samples from the texture patch onto the surface patch using ϕ^{-1}. Section 4 presents two schemes for recording these paste operations.

---

[1]Given a set of points P in general position, any vector in the affine subspace spanning P is uniquely expressed as a linear combination of P, and these barycentric coordinates sum to zero.

3.6 Computing face coverages

To decide where to apply paste operations (Section 3.3), we need to know if a face is already fully covered by texture. We answer this query using a rasterization algorithm. After each paste operation, we render all the patch faces in an offscreen buffer, with the parametrization from Section 3.4. (In the rare case that the patch overlaps itself in texture space, we compute the coverage in several passes, for subsets of non-overlapping faces.) Each face in the patch is rendered using all paste operations that overlap it. We use the R and G color channels to store the face ID, and the B channel to accumulate the opaque regions of the paste operations. To determine the coverage of a face, we divide the number of covered pixels (in the B channel) by the number of pixels in the triangle. For each faces that is not fully covered, we remember an uncovered point inside the face, in order to start a future paste operation centered there. When all faces are fully covered, we are done pasting.

4 Texture storage and rendering

We propose two approaches for representing the textured object. The first approach constructs a traditional surface parametrization using a texture atlas, and pre-renders the lapped texture into this atlas. The second and more interesting approach uses the hardware graphics pipeline to composite the texture patches at runtime.

Rendering with a texture atlas Previous approaches for storing texture on meshes use a texture atlas (e.g. [3, 10, 16]). An atlas is a collection of charts that map regions of the surface to subsets of a texture unit square, such that no two distinct surface points map to the same texture point (see Figure 6b). Ideally, the charts should have low parametric distortion, and should have uniform resolution across the mesh.

To build an atlas, we use a method similar to Maillot *et al.* [10]. We segment the mesh into regions by bounding each region's space of face normals, flatten each region using relaxation, and let the user arrange the flattened pieces. To grow and flatten the surface regions, we use the algorithm described in Section 3.3 (for the case of isotropic textures), but with two additional constraints. We require the normals of the added faces to be within a certain angle from the one of the center face. And, we prevent overlaps by checking for intersections using a spatial hash table. The next step is to arrange the chart images inside the unit square. Packing a set of non-convex polygons into a given 2D domain is a well-studied problem in computational geometry known as "pants packing" [11] due to its application in the clothing industry. Since the problem is NP-hard, an exact solution cannot generally be computed. Heuristic algorithms for arranging on the order of a hundred polygons with no initial layout produce significantly worse results than a trained human. Therefore, we let the user manually arrange the charts.

The atlas is represented using sets of texture coordinates at the mesh vertices. During a preprocess, the texture paste operations are composited into the atlas charts. At runtime, the mesh is rendered using ordinary texture mapping.

(a) Runtime pasting   (b) Rendering with a texture atlas

Figure 6: Comparison of our two texture representations. The atlas representation is more portable but may have sampling problems.

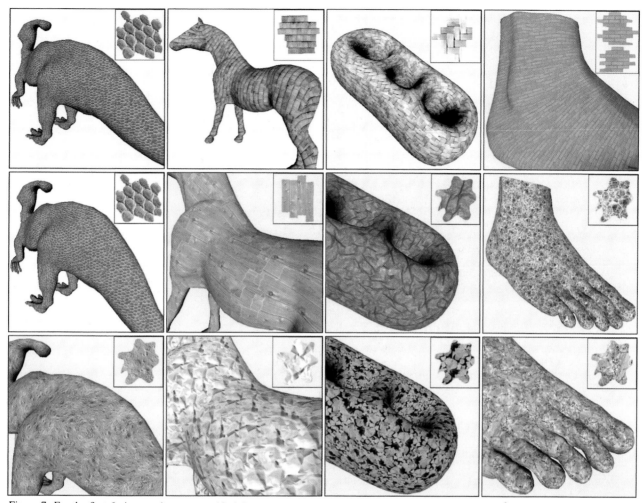

Figure 7: For the first 6 pictures the user specified the texture patch boundary and a vector field over the mesh. The remaining pictures are examples of isotropic textures, and are generated automatically. The two upper dinosaurs are frames from an animation of the tail (see video).

Runtime pasting of lapped textures   Our preferred approach for rendering the lapped texture is to record the parameters for each paste operation (texture patch index, list of surface patch faces, and texture coordinates for vertices), and to render these surface patches at runtime with alpha blending enabled.

With runtime pasting, each face of the model is rendered several times, once for each surface patch to which the face belongs. This increases the load on the graphics system, in terms of both geometry processing and rasterization. To reduce this overhead, during a preprocess we remove for a given paste operation any faces that are completely occluded by subsequent paste operations; such faces are detected through a rasterization algorithm as in Section 3.6. With this optimization, the average number of times that each face gets rendered ranges between 1.5 and 3.2, depending on the texture scale and the model. Graphics systems have begun to support *multitexturing*, whereby the rasterizer can directly evaluate a complicated shading expression involving several texture lookups (recently, as many as four). Although not used in our current prototype, this multitexturing capability could reduce the number of times each face is rendered.

Since our flattening process may produce texture coordinates outside the unit square, we use texture coordinate clamping. For proper interaction of blending and mipmapping, the texture patch must have a border of transparent pixels at all mipmap levels finer than 2x2. We therefore build the mipmap levels explicitly.

Tradeoffs of rendering approaches   Compared to the atlas, runtime pasting requires little texture memory, since it only involves storing the initial texture patches (and often there is only one such patch). As in ordinary 2D texture tiling, large amounts of apparent texture can be created with little actual texture memory usage. The randomness of our surface patch construction makes repetitiveness of the texture less obvious than with ordinary 2D tiling.

Runtime pasting offers better visual quality because it does not suffer from several problems inherent to a texture atlas (Figure 6):

• *Sampling.* The use of an atlas adds one more resampling step, thus inherently degrading the texture image quality. The quality is improved by increasing the texture resolution, but this further reduces the ratio of apparent texture to texture memory usage.

• *Discontinuities.* The tri-linear interpolation filter used to sample the texture does not match exactly at chart boundaries.

• *Mipmapping problems.* At coarser mipmap levels, distinct charts of the atlas are wrongly averaged together.

The disadvantages of the runtime pasting approach are the following. As discussed above, rendering is likely slower since faces are drawn multiple times (though multitexturing may alleviate this). Also, the storage format for the model is somewhat less portable since it involves textures with alpha. Finally, each face must be rendered with different textures in a specific order, and some rendering systems may not guarantee the order in which overlapping polygons are drawn.

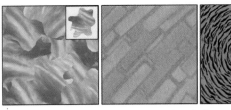

Figure 8: Limitations of our method: (a) Strong low-frequency components, (b) Boundary mismatch, (c) Singularity point.

5 Results

Several textured meshes are shown in Figure 7. In all the examples, the synthesized texture is generated from a single texture patch extracted from the example texture (except the brick foot which uses two). It takes the user about 15 minutes to create a non-trivial direction field for the meshes shown. The growth and parametrization of the patches takes between 20 seconds and 6 minutes to compute on a 733 MHz Pentium III with a GeForce graphics card. Except where noted, all of the examples shown in the paper and the accompanying video tape use runtime pasting rather than the atlas approach. The meshes used in this paper average 5000 faces. Since each face is rendered on average two or three times, all of the lapped textures shown here display in real time. For homogeneous textures we can use a generic texture patch boundary (e.g., the splotch), and switch between different texture examples instantaneously at runtime.

Figure 8 shows some of the limitations of lapped textures. Patch seams become noticeable when the texture patch has strong low frequency components. Seams are also apparent when viewing highly structured textures up close. For anisotropic textures, the user-specified vector field generally has singularity points, since of course one cannot smoothly comb a hairy ball. Sometimes, visual artifacts are caused by poor vector field sampling near these points due to the presence of large faces; we reduce such artifacts by locally subdividing the mesh.

6 Summary and future work

We have introduced lapped textures, a new approach for covering arbitrary triangle meshes with an example 2D texture. The approach is to apply copy/paste operations to cover the surface with overlapping texture patches, using alpha blending to hide seams. The paste operation relies on a new, fast, robust flattening scheme that simultaneously minimizes distortion of the texture and matches local orientation and scale specified by the user.

Our scheme proves to be highly practical, allowing the creation of complex textures on meshes at a fraction of the user effort required by 3D painting. Lapped textures can be used as a starting point for further manual painting (e.g. for unique details such as the mouth and eyes of a bunny).

This work suggests a number of areas for future investigation:

Fine-tuning patch placement. It may be beneficial to fine-tune the placement of the surface patches so that sharp texture features align across patch boundaries (Figure 8b). Initially, we anticipated that this process would be absolutely necessary to make patch boundaries unobtrusive; we were pleasantly surprised to find that the method works quite well without this embellishment. Nonetheless, we still believe it could enhance the results.

Greater automation. We believe that methods to reduce user interaction would make this system even more practical. For example, we have considered automatic texture patch creation, automatic equalization of low-frequency information in these patches (Figure 8a), and automatic direction field construction using surface curvatures.

Other texture types. Within the lapped texture framework, we are now exploring several other types of textures, including animated, volumetric and view-dependent textures.

Acknowledgements

We thank Harry Shum for demonstrating a prototype 2D texture synthesis scheme [20] that largely inspired this work. Thanks to Viewpoint DataLabs and Stanford University for the surface meshes, and Michael Cohen and Rico Malvar for proposing the name "lapped textures".

Emil Praun was supported in part by a Microsoft Research internship. The research of Adam Finkelstein is supported by an NSF CAREER Award and an Alfred P. Sloan Fellowship.

References

[1] BENNIS, C., VÉZIEN, J.-M., IGLÉSIAS, G., AND GAGALOWICZ, A. Piecewise surface flattening for non-distorted texture mapping. *Computer Graphics (Proceedings of SIGGRAPH 91)* 25, 4, 237–246.

[2] BONET, J. S. D. Multiresolution sampling procedure for analysis and synthesis of texture images. *Computer Graphics (Proceedings of SIGGRAPH 97)*, 361–368.

[3] CIGNONI, P., MONTANI, C., ROCCHINI, C., AND SCOPIGNO, R. A general method for preserving attribute values on simplified meshes. In *IEEE Visualization* (1998), pp. 59–66.

[4] DISCHLER, J. M., GHAZANFARPOUR, D., AND FREYDIER, R. Anisotropic solid texture synthesis using orthogonal 2D views. *Computer Graphics Forum* 17, 3 (1998), 87–96.

[5] EFROS, A. A., AND LEUNG, T. K. Texture synthesis by non-parametric sampling. In *IEEE International Conference on Computer Vision* (Sept. 1999).

[6] FLEISCHER, K., LAIDLAW, D., CURRIN, B., AND BARR, A. Cellular texture generation. *Computer Graphics (Proceedings of SIGGRAPH 95)*, 239–248.

[7] GHAZANFARPOUR, D., AND DISCHLER, J.-M. Generation of 3D texture using multiple 2D models analysis. *Computer Graphics Forum 15*, 3 (1996), 311–324.

[8] HEEGER, D. J., AND BERGEN, J. R. Pyramid-based texture analysis/synthesis. *Computer Graphics (Proceedings of SIGGRAPH 95)*, 229–238.

[9] LÉVY, B., AND MALLET, J.-L. Non-distorted texture mapping for sheared triangulated meshes. *Computer Graphics (Proceedings of SIGGRAPH 98)*, 343–352.

[10] MAILLOT, J., YAHIA, H., AND VERROUST, A. Interactive texture mapping. *Computer Graphics (Proceedings of SIGGRAPH 93)*, 27–34.

[11] MILENKOVIC, V. J. Rotational polygon containment and minimum enclosure. *Proc. of the 14th Annual Symp. on Computational Geometry, ACM* (June 1998).

[12] NEYRET, F., AND CANI, M.-P. Pattern-based texturing revisited. *Computer Graphics (Proceedings of SIGGRAPH 99)*, 235–242.

[13] PEDERSEN, H. K. Decorating implicit surfaces. *Computer Graphics (Proceedings of SIGGRAPH 95)*, 291–300.

[14] PEDERSEN, H. K. A framework for interactive texturing operations on curved surfaces. *Computer Graphics (Proceedings of SIGGRAPH 96)*, 295–302.

[15] PERLIN, K. An image synthesizer. *Computer Graphics (Proceedings of SIGGRAPH 85) 19*, 3, 287–296.

[16] SANDER, P., GU, X., GORTLER, S., HOPPE, H., AND SNYDER, J. Silhouette clipping. *Computer Graphics (Proceedings of SIGGRAPH 2000)*.

[17] TURK, G. Generating textures for arbitrary surfaces using reaction-diffusion. *Computer Graphics (Proceedings of SIGGRAPH 91) 25*, 4, 289–298.

[18] WITKIN, A., AND KASS, M. Reaction-diffusion textures. *Computer Graphics (Proceedings of SIGGRAPH 91) 25*, 4, 299–308.

[19] WORLEY, S. P. A cellular texture basis function. *Computer Graphics (Proceedings of SIGGRAPH 96)*, 291–294.

[20] XU, Y., GUO, B., AND SHUM, H.-Y. Chaos mosaic: Fast and memory efficient texture synthesis. Tech. Rep. MSR-TR-2000-32, Microsoft Research, 2000.

Seamless Texture Mapping of Subdivision Surfaces by Model Pelting and Texture Blending

Dan Piponi and George Borshukov

MVFX, a division of Manex Entertainment

Abstract

Subdivision surfaces solve numerous problems related to the geometry of character and animation models. However, unlike on parametrised surfaces there is no natural choice of texture coordinates on subdivision surfaces. Existing algorithms for generating texture coordinates on non-parametrised surfaces often find solutions that are locally acceptable but globally are unsuitable for use by artists wishing to paint textures. In addition, for topological reasons there is not necessarily any choice of assignment of texture coordinates to control points that can satisfactorily be interpolated over the entire surface. We introduce a technique, *pelting*, for finding both optimal and intuitive texture mapping over almost all of an entire subdivision surface and then show how to combine multiple texture mappings together to produce a seamless result.

Keywords: Curves & Surfaces, Texture Mapping, Physically Based Animation

1 Introduction

Subdivision surfaces [5], [6] possess unique advantages over traditionally used NURBS surfaces that make them ideal for animated models. Complex models can be modeled with the efficiency of polygons and the smoothness of NURBS and other spline surfaces. Multi-limbed characters can be created using a single, contiguous mesh when using subdivision surfaces, something that is, in most cases, not possible using a single NURBS or other type of parametrised surface.

The most obvious advantage of using a single mesh to define, for example, a humanoid model, can be seen during the deformation or rigging process. Keeping closed seams and tangency between multiple NURBS patches, trimmed or untrimmed, becomes very difficult in areas where multiple joints exert influence over vertices of these multiple surfaces. With subdivision surfaces, the use of a single polygon mesh to define the head, torso, arms, and legs makes skeletal binding and weighting a much simpler and more effective process.

However, in order to apply surface detail with 2 dimensional texture maps [4],[12] the surface must be parametrised. Spline patches come with a natural parametrisation, but there is no such natural

---

0

parametrisation on subdivision surfaces. In fact, as subdivision surfaces may have arbitrary topologies, there may in fact be no global parametrisation over the entire surface. In this paper we look at an approach to providing parametrisations for regions of subdivision surfaces and combining these into one continuous colour map on the surface. Much of our discussion also applies to polygonal models however subdivision surfaces have some extra complications making them more instructive to consider.

2 Background

Traditionally the way to represent the geometry of CG creatures is through the use of NURBS [9]. Unfortunately, there are many difficulties with arranging separate NURBS together so that they define a single smooth surface. The problems of arranging NURBS to abut against each other with a shared tangent are well known to those who have worked with commercial modelling packages. However, even when these problems have been solved there are difficulties with arranging textures to vary continuously over the seams between patches. Renderers need to sample texture values over a region in order to interpolate cleanly, anti-alias, and to calculate quantities like normals for correct lighting of displacement maps. As a result even when the geometry of NURBS join cleanly with a common tangent the surface detail can appear to have 'tears' along seams. Subdivision surfaces can provide a way to solve all of these problems resulting in texture and displacements that are continuous over the entire surface.

Subdivision surfaces are constructed by starting with a polygonal mesh that forms a manifold, M^0. A subdivision process is applied to this mesh to produce a new higher resolution mesh M^1 and then this process is iterated to form meshes $M^0, M^1, \ldots$ that better approximate the limiting mesh M^∞ [6], [7]. The subdivision scheme is chosen in such a way that under reasonable conditions the limiting surface is smooth.

In this paper we consider only Catmull-Clark surfaces but the techniques extend naturally to other subdivision schemes. (For clarity of exposition we consider mainly Catmull-Clark surfaces derived from quadrilateral meshes. After the first Catmull-Clark refinement any polygonal mesh becomes a quadrilateral mesh anyway [22].)

Unfortunately, assigning texture coordinates to a subdivision surface can be a difficult problem. Firstly, there is a purely topological problem. There is no way to assign texture coordinates to a sphere, for example, in such a way that the assignment is continuous and every point is assigned a unique pair of texture coordinates. Even worse - by the Borsuk-Ulam theorem [19] it is guaranteed that there are antipodal points on the sphere that are mapped to the same texture coordinates. So attempting to map a sphere using one global coordinate system is doomed to catastrophic failure. This problem is well known from cartography. Similar results hold for models with topologies other than that of the sphere. There are a number of ways to sidestep this problem:

- Use texture mappings with discontinuities

- Change the topology of the surface maps

- Use 3d solid textures rather than 2d textures

- Don't seek a global texture map but instead use multiple local textures

We consider these options in turn. It is difficult to ensure that texture mappings with discontinuities look seamless because renderers require continuous functions in order to calculate normals for bump mapping or sample areas for anti-aliasing (this is similar to the aforementioned problem with joining NURBS surfaces).

There are a number of approaches to changing the topology of the underlying objects. One approach to changing the model is to break it into individual pieces that can each be globally texture mapped - unfortunately this gives the problem of arranging that there are no seams between pieces. One can arrange for pieces to overlap but now we run into many of the same problems found with NURBS and additionally we lose the advantages of being able to work with a single model. Another approach can be best illustrated with a cylinder. A cylinder may be formed by rolling a sheet of paper, so that the opposite ends of the paper overlap. However, this *overwrapping* still requires breaking and rebuilding the original geometry and does not generalise easily to all topologies.

Using a solid texture for the entire model is inefficient and cumbersome. It is far easier for artists to paint 2d texture maps with familiar painting tools.

We chose the fourth approach because we found we could work uniformly with surfaces of any topology and always guarantee a final colour map that was completely smooth. In addition we found the task of managing multiple overlapping textures to be much easier than that of managing overlapping geometries because the former has no impact on the work of modellers or animators. (Note that from a mathematical viewpoint these approaches may be similar.)

We broke the problem down into two stages:

- Finding a way to texture regions on the model in a fashion that is intuitive for artists to work with and

- Joining together different regions in a completely seamless way

Assigning texture coordinates to a subdivision surface consists of two parts - assigning values to control vertices on the zeroth refinement of the mesh and a technique for interpolating these values over the surface. Therefore, we need to consider interpolation schemes. Stam [22] describes a set of basis functions that parametrise patches on the subdivision surface corresponding to each quadrilateral in the zeroth refinement. This parametrisation defines a pair of coordinates on the surface to $[0, 1] \times [0, 1]$. Using these values we may bilinearly interpolate scalar values assigned at the vertices of the quadrilateral to define scalar fields over each patch and hence over the entire surface. Denote the set of functions on the subdivision surface obtained in this way by $L(M^\infty)$. Unfortunately, these fields are only guaranteed to be C^1 differentiable [1] on the interior of each patch. They have discontinuities in the first derivative along the edges and so texture coordinates chosen from $L(M^\infty)$ can result in texture maps that look unattractive. (Actually, these discontinuities are not necessarily a problem for single images, but they have a tendency to look bad when animated.)

According to [7] another technique for assigning texture coordinates to points on a subdivision surface is to consider scalar values assigned at vertices to be coordinates in an extra dimension. For

---

[1] C^0 means continuous. C^n means the nth derivative exists and is continuous.

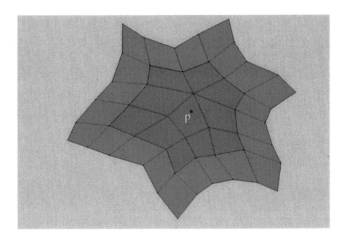

Figure 1: The domain of control of p

example a vertex at (x, y, z) with texture coordinates (s, t) is considered to be a point (x, y, z, s, t). We then apply the subdivision process in the dimensionally extended space - 5 dimensional in this example. Each point in the subdivision surface (x', y', z', s', t') defines a point in 3D (x', y', z') with texture coordinates (s', t'). Under reasonable conditions these fields are C^1 over the entire subdivision surface. Denote the set of functions produced this way by $S(M^\infty)$. Our goal is to produce texture coordinate functions that lie in $S(M^\infty)$. It is useful to introduce the idea of the *domain of control* of a point p on M^∞. This is the set of control points that determine the value at p of a scalar field in $S(M^\infty)$. In Figure 1 we illustrate the domain of control of an example point - the vertices inside and on the boundary of the red region form the domain of control.

3   Texture Mapping Creatures

We now turn to the problem of assigning surface detail to a subdivision surface. Much of what we discuss applies equally well to polygonal models, however, the interpolation scheme that we use for subdivision surface texturing causes some extra complications that are not present in polygonal models. Typical methods included projection, solid textures [20] or two-part texturing [3]. These methods can be difficult to use with complex surfaces, so we chose to use 2 dimensional texture mapping using texture coordinate fields defined over the surface. We now look at the problem of choosing how to assign texture coordinates to control vertices. Even on a region that has no topological obstruction to being continuously texture mapped there is no *natural* choice of such texture coordinates. This makes the problem of choosing texture coordinates for subdivision surfaces similar to that for implicit surfaces or for surfaces derived from point coulds [13], [14],[15],[8]. One useful characteristic of any technique for assigning texture coordinates to a surface is to ensure that distances between points on the surface are represented accurately in the distances between the corresponding points in the texture space. (For surfaces with non-zero implicit curvature there will always be some distortion of distances [21].) This makes it much easier for artists to work with a 2 dimensional texture because the image they paint closely reflects how it will look in 3D. It also ensures uniformity in the look of the surface and efficiency in the storage of texture information. One approach to achieving this is to define a function that represents the extent to which distances are distorted by the texture mapping function. One can then find the mapping that minimises this parametric distortion. Ma [17] describes an algorithm that minimises a discrete

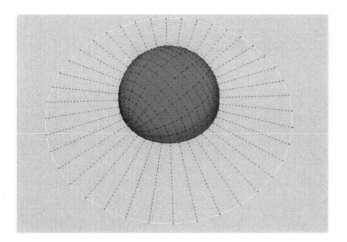

Figure 2: A pelting frame. The surrounding circle is the frame and the dashed lines represent the springs instantiated around the edge of the model and along the edges of the model.

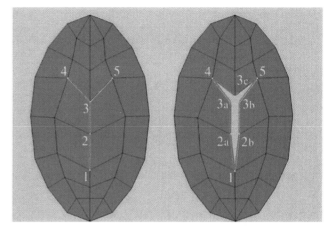

Figure 3: An example cut

approximation to a distortion measure on a grid. There are a number of different candidates for a measure of distortion such as the *Green-Lagrange deformation tensor* [18], [2]. An elementary approach is to consider the lengths of the edges of the polygon mesh in texture space and make the functional the sum of the squares of the deviations of the lengths of the edges.

$$E = \sum_{\text{edges } e} \frac{(L_e - l_e)^2}{L_e} \qquad (1)$$

where L_e is the length of edge e and l_e is the distance between the two points in texture space. (Dividing by L_e provides a certain amount of invariance with respect to the details of the tesselation. Splitting an edge into two pieces by adding a new vertex in the middle will make no difference to the minimum value of E.) We can then use standard "black box" minimisation techniques to minimise this function.

Unfortunately, this is not necessarily adequate. This is a complex search problem with many local minima - especially for complex surfaces. Sometimes 'buckling' [18] can occur during minimisation. In addition, minima do not necessarily preserve approximate symmetries in the original model that artists involved in a production desire. Sometimes there are other factors that artists feel are more important than minimising distortion including aesthetic aspects of the resulting texture mappings. In short, many of the existing techniques provide mappings that are locally good but globally over the whole model the result is not suitable for production work - especially with complex models. We now consider a way to deal with all of these issues.

There are a number of different types of terms that can be added to Equation 1 in order to eliminate problems, for example, terms to prevent faces 'flipping' [18] or angular variation. We use a different approach. Equation 1 is formally identical to the total energy of a collection of springs that obey Hooke's law except that the dynamics is described only in 2D. Temporarily we will work with texture coordinates that lie in a 3D space. The resulting energy can now be minimised by deriving equations of motion from Equation 1, adding damping terms, and running a dynamics solver until a steady state is achieved [1]. Suppose we have a model that is topologically equivalent to a disk. We can add springs to the boundary of this disk with the opposing ends of these springs attached to a surrounding fixed frame. (See Figure 2 for an example using a hemisphere model.)

What this does is ensure that the edges of region to be textured

are 'spread out' and it pulls the entire system out of local minima. The fact that we have extended the system to 3 dimensions is significant. If the orientation of a face in the 2D texture space is opposite to what it should be at the global minimum then it will often be caught in a local minimum because in order to 'flip' it over one or two vertices will have to actually pass through other edges in the polygon in order to reach the global minimum and hence pass through a higher energy state. In 3D no such flipping is necessary because each face can smoothly rotate to its correct orientation. With suitable choice of spring length and stiffness the system quickly achieves a state where it is almost flat and now texture coordinates may be applied by planar projection.

There is, of course, another way of looking at this: we are carrying out a simulation of a procedure traditionally used to stretch out animal hides for tanning. As a result the user can intuitively interact with the minimisation procedure and if starting with a creature model can arrange to end up with a texture that is in the form a pelt. We call this technique *pelting*.

The dynamics model we have just described is very elementary. In principle it could be made much more sophisticated - in particular we could add extra springs arranged so as to minimise shearing of the texture. However we have found that in practice the strength of the pelting process is that it quickly finds a global texture mapping that is an excellent starting point for a subsequent local refinement. For this reason the precise details of the dynamics used are relatively unimportant.

4 The Pelting Procedure in Detail

For a model topologically equivalent to a sphere we need only make one cut in order to have a model that is topologically equivalent to a disk. Before the cutting procedure is described there is an important point to make: these cuts are for the sake of generating texture coordinates only. After our procedure is described we will show how texture coordinates can be transferred back to the original *uncut* model in a way that provides smooth colour mapping.

A cut is a collection of edges that form a connected tree. In our pelting tool the user indicates this set of edges and the software operates on the model by duplicating the edges and vertices as in figure Figure 3. Although we have illustrated point 2, say, as duplicated into distinct points 2a and 2b, these two points actually have the same location in 3D space. The cutting process changes the connectivity of the faces, edges and vertices only. The edges around the cut form a topological circle and we walk around this circle connecting each vertex (via a connecting spring) to a corresponding point in the frame. We ensure that the stiffness of each spring and the spacing between the connecting points on the frame is proportional to the spacing between the other ends of the springs in the original model. A spring is then instantiated along each edge in the original model with stiffness proportional to the edge length. A mass is placed at each vertex and the outer frame is held fixed. (We chose to use an equal mass at each vertex. One could choose the mass of each vertex in such a way that the mass density per unit area of the model is approximately constant but in practice we found this unnecessary.) The user can then adjust various parameters such as spring stiffness and frame configuration and run the simulation in order to find a pelt that is optimal. For alternative topologies we can use more than one frame but the principles are the same. The user can make alterations to the geometry of the frame before or even during the minimisation. Our first test was with a model for a rat-like creature. (See Figure 4 (a,c).)

Once the model is stretched out flat the user can make manual adjustments if required and then texture coordinates can be applied using planar projection. In addition, further modifications may be carried out using algorithms more suited to local refinement. (See Figure 4 (b).) These assigned texture coordinates may now be transferred back to the original model. Note that as the vertices in the original cut were duplicated there is no unique way to transfer texture coordinates back to the original model at these points. We assign texture coordinates at these points completely arbitrarily (we see later why this is acceptable). At this stage what we have is the original model with texture coordinates assigned to all vertices. Unfortunately, in the region of the cut we will have an unsightly seam because (1) we have assigned arbitrary texture coordinates to some vertices and (2) we will be interpolating between texture coordinates that correspond to opposite sides of the flattened model.

5 Blending Textures

Fortunately, there is a way to deal with this problem. We can split up the surface into a number of pieces, each of which is a topological disk, and then generate texture coordinates for each piece. (Again we stress that although we are talking about splitting up the model our ultimate goal is to leave the original model intact.) If we split up the model into non-overlapping pieces we face the problem that the domain of control of points near the boundary may in fact lie in a neighbouring region. So we choose to work with a set of overlapping pieces.

There is a standard technique used in topology for dealing with functions on arbitrary topological surfaces that are defined on overlapping pieces. Suppose we have a manifold M and that we can express it as a union of open subsets [2]

$$M = \bigcup_{i \in I} U_i$$

(I is some indexing set.) We choose the sets U_i so that they are all topological disks. Suppose we can find texture coordinates s_i and t_i on each U_i so that any function f_i on U_i can be written as $f_i(s_i, t_i)$ (Each U_i is called a *chart* and the whole collection is called an *atlas* [18], [19].)

Suppose we have a set of continuous functions $b_i : M \to R$ such that each b_i is zero outside of U_i and

$$\sum_{i \in I} b_i(p) = 1$$

[2] An open set is one where for every point there is a real ϵ such that it has a ball of radius ϵ around it that is completely contained in the set. As we are dealing with *compact* manifolds we are guaranteed that we can write M as a union of a finite number of sets. [19]

(Traditionally such a set of b_i is called a *partition of unity* [19] but we will call the b_i *blend functions*.) Given any continuous function f on M the functions $b_i f$ have the property

$$\sum_{i \in I} b_i f = f$$

and each $b_i f$ is zero outside of U_i. This gives a way to write any function on M as a sum of functions of s_i and t_i. Conversely, given a collection of continuous functions $f_i : U_i \to R$ we can construct the function

$$f = \sum_{i \in I} b_i f_i$$

and it is guaranteed to be continuous over the entire manifold. This gives a way to build a continuous function on the whole manifold out of the individual pieces. More generally by choosing blend functions that are themselves C^n we can build functions that are C^n out of individual pieces.

Our problem now is to build blend functions out of the functions contained in the sets $L(M^\infty)$ and $S(M^\infty)$ because these are the functions we are able to specify using control points.

Although it makes sense to use smooth functions for texture coordinates - when blending two different but similar functions it is acceptable to use functions in $L(M^\infty)$. This is because, as we will see later, we will be blending textures that are approximately equal on the overlap making the discontinuity in the derivative of the texture small.

We will now consider in detail how to construct blend functions for the pelting procedure above.

In our scheme we will use two regions: U_0 and U_1. U_0 will correspond to the pelt that we have described above and U_1 is a region that we will call the *patch*. We will have two sets of texture coordinates: (s_0, t_0) and (s_1, t_1). (s_0, t_0) are the coordinates derived by the pelting process above and (s_1, t_1) are discussed below. In this case we have only two blend functions $b_0(p)$ and $b_1(p) = 1 - b_0(p)$.

We discuss first how we construct control points for the blend function b_0 because this scheme determines how we choose the patch U_1.

In any overlap between the pelt and the patch regions we require a polygon over which both of the texture maps interpolate correctly because this gives a region over which we may smoothly switch from one texture map to another. Consider Figure 5. This represents a region spanning both sides of a cut (which is represented by ej). As discussed above we assign arbitrary values for the pelt texture coordinates to e and j and texture coordinates derived from the planar projection of the pelt at a, b, c, d, f, g, h and i (and similarly on the opposite site of the cut). The domain of control of the points on the interior of polygon *chid* includes e and j so we know that the pelt texture coordinates interpolated here will have an arbitrary component and so will not represent the planar projection. The polygon closest to the cut that is a good representation is *bghc*. So in order to make the patch as small as possible we make the patch extend out as far as a and f so that on *bghc* the patch texture coordinates are also good. We now define the blend function to be the function in $L(M^\infty)$ that has control value 1 at a, b, f, and g and zero on c, d, e, h, i, j. Over *bghc* the blend function can be used to smoothly interpolate between the two textures and outside this region either one or the other texture mapping will be used. In this way we define a smooth transition between two texture maps by defining one extra scalar field and more importantly: not changing the geometry of the model in any way. In practice we design our textures so that the two different texture maps map into textures so that on *bghc* they approximate each other.

When the topology of the faces is more complex than in this diagram a more complex definition is required. Call the set of vertices and edges in the cut C_0. Define C_n for $n > 0$ to be the loop of

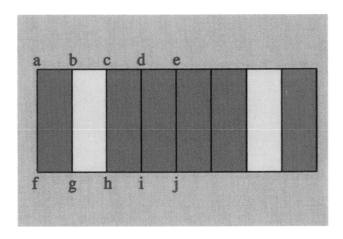

Figure 5: Regions of the blend function

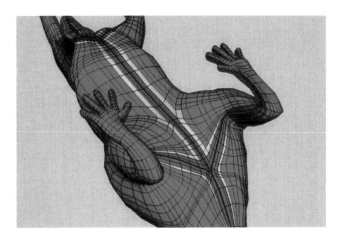

Figure 6: The regions of the blend function over the example rat model

edges and vertices that goes completely around C_{n-1}, containing the smallest area, that does not share any vertices with it. We are now in a position to define the patch - it is the region enclosed by C_4. Vertices within and including C_2 are given blend functon value 0 and those outside and including C_3 are given value 1. It can be seen that the region between C_2 and C_3 contains no points whose domain of control intersects with the cut. If we choose models with all vertices at least trivalent (at least three edges meeting at each vertex) and with every polygon a quadrilateral (after one Catmull-Clark subdivision all faces are quadrilateral) then there are guaranteed to be no isolated vertices between C_2 and C_3. This means that every vertex between and including C_2 and C_3 can be unambiguously assigned blend value 0 or 1 by the above method. On the other hand if other polygons are present we can interpolate blend values to vertices between C_2 and C_3 by any reasonable scheme - e.g. by taking the average of the values at nearest neighbours.

We can assign texture coordinates to the patch by detaching it from the full model and applying the pelting procedure to it. We then transfer the texture coordinates assigned to the patch back onto the full model. This mapping is extended to the entire model to produce (s_1, t_1) - assigning texture coordinates arbitrarily to points not in the patch. At this stage we now have two global sets of texture coordinates, and a global blending function that seamlessly blends between texture maps rendered using these coordinates in such a way that the regions with arbitrary texture coordinates are invisible.

The procedure for painting the models typically went as follows: once texture coordinates have been assigned to the model through the pelt int is roughly painted directly in a 3d paint package. The resulting low resolution texture map was then transferred to a 2d paint package where additional detail was applied. Using the texture coordinates derived from the pelting process we are able to render the patch region of the model after it has been flattened by pelting. As a result of the scheme described above the edges of the patch will be textured correctly. The final task of the artist is then to paint the small region of the patch in the immediate vicinity of the cut.

Implementing the texture blending is easily achieved with modern shaders [10] or with multipass texturing.

Although we have concentrated on the implementation details for subdivision surfaces a simplified scheme can be implemented for use with polygon models using linear interpolation of texture coordinates.

In Figure 5 we mark the region textured solely by the patch texture in red, that using solely the pelt texture in green and the region in which blending occurs in yellow. In Figure 6 we show how these regions extend over a large portion of our example model.

6 Results

We implemented the system to set up the dynamics using MEL scripting and C++ plug-ins within Alias-Wavefront's *Maya* and the dynamics solver used was the standard one in *Maya*. On an R10000 SGI O2 it took under a minute to find a good texture mapping for the 11000 polygon rat model and we were able to find good texture mappings for models such as the alien creature example with no difficulty. We used *Flesh* from Digits 'n' Art software to carry out local refinement on the final texture mappings and the initial 3d model painting. (See Figure 7.) We were able to implement the rendering using Pixar's *Renderman* which supports Catmull-Clark surfaces, multiple scalar attributes at control vertices, and both the $L(M^\infty)$ and $S(M^\infty)$ interpolation schemes. The resulting mappings were found to be very suitable for work with 2D paint packages such as Adobe *Photoshop* or with scans of real paint and brush. For the alien creature example we added geometric detail to the 6500 polygon model by using a displacement map painted using the same set of texture coordinates.

7 Conclusions and Future Research

We have found a way to texture map the entire surface of subdivision surfaces without modifying the model. We have used a dynamics solver to find optimal texture mappings and have used two techniques to find a good global solution: solving in 3D instead of 2D and using springs and a frame to impose boundary conditions. We have also introduced a scheme for blending smoothly between different texture mappings on a subdivision surface.

We would like to reimplement the dynamics more directly and efficiently (possibly replacing it with a more specialised statics solver that could work in real time) so that we can allow users to manipulate texture maps directly and easily as if they were rubber sheets [16]. We would also like to implement the entire blending process in an automatic way so that the user simply paints in 3D on a single model and the software automatically updates the (possibly multiple) texture map contributing to each point [11]. Although the technique has only been applied in the case of two regions it generalises to multiple regions by using multiple blend functions. We would like to find good ways to enable the user to define such regions with various types of cuts allowing extremely complex topologies to be dealt with efficiently.

One difficulty is with finding ways to make the cutting and blending scheme compatible with level of detail (LOD) techniques. LOD methods substitute low resolution proxies for models whenever

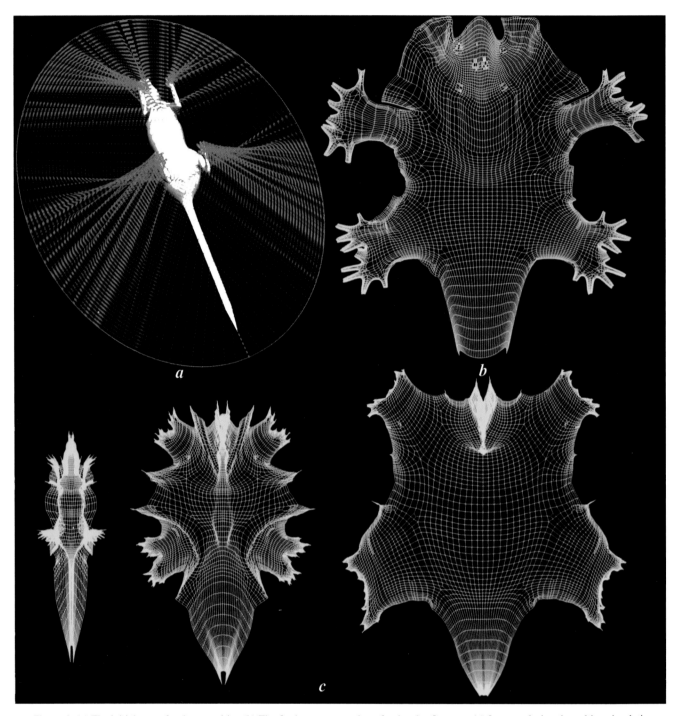

Figure 4: (a) The initial setup for the rat pelting (b) The final texture mapping after local refinement (c) 3 stages during the pelting simulation

high resolution details are not required. Unfortunately, the patch is itself a high resolution detail and so model simplification tends to remove it entirely. For very low resolution substitutes where the seam is too small to be noticeable we have used pelting combined with the earlier mentioned overwrapping approach in production.

We have had great success using pelting within a production environment. Animators and modelers have found it easy to generate texture mappings and 2D and 3D painters have found the mappings extremely well adapted to their needs. We believe the future of character animation lies with subdivision surfaces and pelting has played a major role in allowing us to move along this path.

8 Acknowledgements

Thanks to John Tissavary, Brett Hartshorne, Dan Klem, Mauricio Baiocchi among the artists who worked with and constructively criticised our work. A special thanks goes to Devorah Petty for both modelling and painting the alien model. Thanks also to Peter Plevritis for testing our approach in production.

References

[1] David Baraff and Andrew Witkin. Dynamic simulation of non-penetrating flexible bodies. In *SIGGRAPH '92 Conference Proceedings*, Annual Conference Series, pages 303–308. ACM SIGGRAPH, July 1992.

[2] Chakib Bennis, Jean-Marc Vézien, and Gérard Iglésias. Piecewise surface flattening for non-distorted texture mapping. In *SIGGRAPH '91 Conference Proceedings*, Annual Conference Series, pages 237–246. ACM SIGGRAPH, July 1991.

[3] E. Bier and K. Sloan. Two-part texture mapping. *IEEE Computer Graphics and Applications*, pages 40–53, September 1986.

[4] J.F. Blinn and M.E. Newell. Texture and reflection in computer generated images. *Communications of the ACM,19,10*, pages 542–547, October 1976.

[5] E. Catmull. *A subdivision algorithm for the computer display of curved surfaces*. PhD thesis, University of Utah, December 1974.

[6] E. Catmull and J. Clark. Recursively generated b-spline surfaces on arbitrary topological meshes. *Computer Aided Design, 10(6):350-355*, 1978.

[7] Tony DeRose, Michael Kass, and Tien Truong. Subdivision surfaces in character animation. In *SIGGRAPH '98 Conference Proceedings*, Annual Conference Series, pages 85–94. ACM SIGGRAPH, July 1998.

[8] Helaman Ferguson, Alyn Rockwood, and Jordan Cox. Topological design of sculptured surfaces. In *SIGGRAPH '92 Conference Proceedings*, Annual Conference Series, pages 149–156. ACM SIGGRAPH, July 1992.

[9] J. Foley and A. van Dam. *Computer Graphics: Principles and Practice*. Addison-Wesley, 1990.

[10] Pat Hanrahan. A language for shading and lighting calculations. In *SIGGRAPH '90 Conference Proceedings*, Annual Conference Series, pages 289–298. ACM SIGGRAPH, August 1990.

[11] Pat Hanrahan and Paul E. Haeberli. Direct WYSIWYG painting and texturing on 3D shapes. In *SIGGRAPH '90 Conference Proceedings*, Annual Conference Series, pages 215–223. ACM SIGGRAPH, August 1990.

[12] P. S. Heckbert. Survey of texture mapping. *IEEE Computer Graphics and Applications*, pages 215–223, August 1990.

[13] Hans Køhling Pedersen. Decorating implicit surfaces. In *SIGGRAPH '95 Conference Proceedings*, Annual Conference Series, pages 291–300. ACM SIGGRAPH, August 1995.

[14] V. Krishnamurthy and M. Levoy. Fitting smooth surfaces to dense polygon meshes. In *SIGGRAPH '96 Conference Proceedings*, Annual Conference Series, pages 313–324. ACM SIGGRAPH, aug 1996.

[15] A. W. F. Lee, W. Sweldens, P. Schröder, L. Cowsar, and D. Dobkin. Maps: Multiresolution adaptive parameterization of surfaces. In *SIGGRAPH '98 Conference Proceedings*, Annual Conference Series, pages 95–104. ACM SIGGRAPH, 1998.

[16] Peter Litwinowicz and Gavin Miller. Efficient techniques for interactive texture placement. In *SIGGRAPH '94 Conference Proceedings*, Annual Conference Series, pages 119–122. ACM SIGGRAPH, 1994.

[17] S.D. Ma and H. Lin. Optimal texture mapping. In *EUROGRAPHICS '88*, September 1988.

[18] Jérôme Maillot, Hussein Yahia, and Anne Verroust. Interactive texture mapping. In *SIGGRAPH '93 Conference Proceedings*, Annual Conference Series, pages 27–34. ACM SIGGRAPH, August 1993.

[19] C. R. F. Maunder. *Algebraic Topology*. Dover, 1996.

[20] D. Peachey. Solid texturing of complex surfaces. *Computer Graphics 19(3)*, pages 253–260, July 1984.

[21] M. Spivak. *A Comprehensive Introduction to Differential Geometry*. Publish or Perish, Inc., 1979.

[22] Jos Stam. Exact evaluation of catmull-clark subdivision surfaces at arbitrary parameter values. In *SIGGRAPH '98 Conference Proceedings*, Annual Conference Series. ACM SIGGRAPH, 1998.

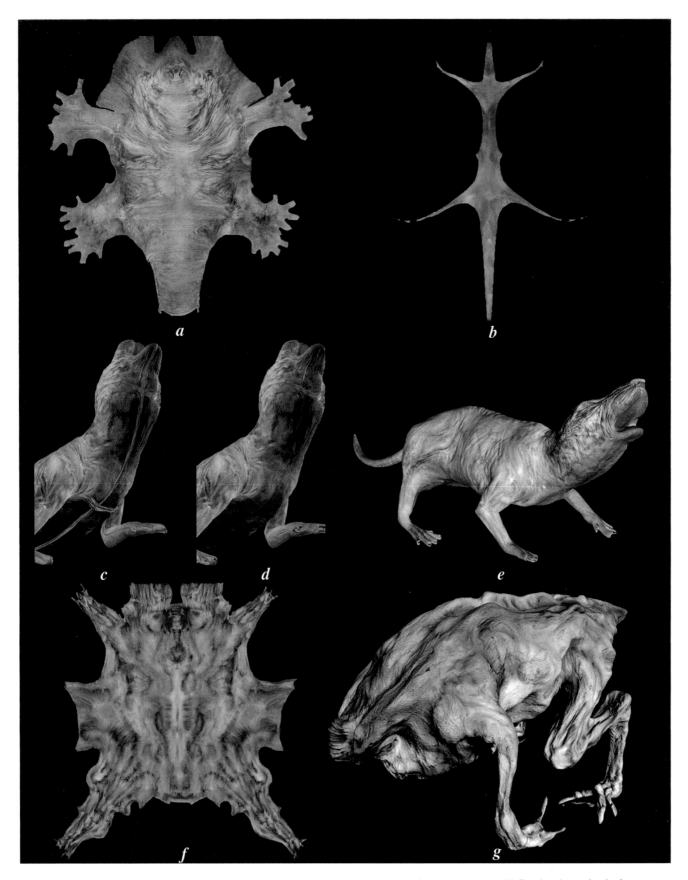

Figure 7: (a) Pelt texture for rat (b) Seam texture (c) Rendered rat using only pelt texture (note the seam) (d) Rendered rat using both textures (e) The final rat (f) Pelt texture for alien (g) Rendered alien (6500 polygons)

Fast Texture Synthesis using Tree-structured Vector Quantization

Li-Yi Wei   Marc Levoy

Stanford University *

 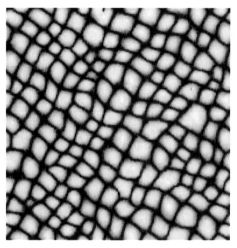

Figure 1: *Our texture generation process takes an example texture patch (left) and a random noise (middle) as input, and modifies this random noise to make it look like the given example texture. The synthesized texture (right) can be of arbitrary size, and is perceived as very similar to the given example. Using our algorithm, textures can be generated within seconds, and the synthesized results are always tileable.*

Abstract

Texture synthesis is important for many applications in computer graphics, vision, and image processing. However, it remains difficult to design an algorithm that is both efficient and capable of generating high quality results. In this paper, we present an efficient algorithm for realistic texture synthesis. The algorithm is easy to use and requires only a sample texture as input. It generates textures with perceived quality equal to or better than those produced by previous techniques, but runs two orders of magnitude faster. This permits us to apply texture synthesis to problems where it has traditionally been considered impractical. In particular, we have applied it to constrained synthesis for image editing and temporal texture generation. Our algorithm is derived from Markov Random Field texture models and generates textures through a deterministic searching process. We accelerate this synthesis process using tree-structured vector quantization.

---
*Gates Computer Science Building, Stanford, CA 94305
Email: {liyiwei | levoy}@graphics.stanford.edu
WWW: http://graphics.stanford.edu/projects/texture/

Keywords: Texture Synthesis, Compression Algorithms, Image Processing

1   Introduction

Texture is a ubiquitous visual experience. It can describe a wide variety of surface characteristics such as terrain, plants, minerals, fur and skin. Since reproducing the visual realism of the physical world is a major goal for computer graphics, textures are commonly employed when rendering synthetic images. These textures can be obtained from a variety of sources such as hand-drawn pictures or scanned photographs. Hand-drawn pictures can be aesthetically pleasing, but it is hard to make them photo-realistic. Most scanned images, however, are of inadequate size and can lead to visible seams or repetition if they are directly used for texture mapping.

Texture synthesis is an alternative way to create textures. Because synthetic textures can be made any size, visual repetition is avoided. Texture synthesis can also produce tileable images by properly handling the boundary conditions. Potential applications of texture synthesis are also broad; some examples are image denoising, occlusion fill-in, and compression.

The goal of texture synthesis can be stated as follows: Given a texture sample, synthesize a new texture that, when perceived by a human observer, appears to be generated by the same underlying stochastic process. The major challenges are 1) modeling- how to estimate the stochastic process from a given finite texture sample and 2) sampling- how to develop an efficient sampling procedure to produce new textures from a given model. Both the modeling and sampling parts are essential for the success of texture synthesis: the visual fidelity of generated textures will depend primarily on the accuracy of the modeling, while the efficiency of the sampling procedure will directly determine the computational cost of texture generation.

In this paper, we present a very simple algorithm that can efficiently synthesize a wide variety of textures. The inputs consist of an example texture patch and a random noise image with size specified by the user (Figure 1). The algorithm modifies this random noise to make it look like the given example. This technique is flexible and easy to use, since only an example texture patch (usually a photograph) is required. New textures can be generated with little computation time, and their tileability is guaranteed. The algorithm is also easy to implement; the two major components are a multiresolution pyramid and a simple searching algorithm.

The key advantages of this algorithm are quality and speed: the quality of the synthesized textures are equal to or better than those generated by previous techniques, while the computation speed is two orders of magnitude faster than those approaches that generate comparable results to our algorithm. This permits us to apply our algorithm in areas where texture synthesis has traditionally been considered too expensive. In particular, we have extended the algorithm to constrained synthesis for image editing and motion texture synthesis.

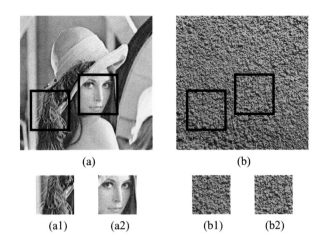

(a)   (b)

(a1)   (a2)   (b1)   (b2)

Figure 2: *How textures differ from images. (a) is a general image while (b) is a texture. A movable window with two different positions are drawn as black squares in (a) and (b), with the corresponding contents shown below. Different regions of a texture are always perceived to be similar (b1,b2), which is not the case for a general image (a1,a2). In addition, each pixel in (b) is only related to a small set of neighboring pixels. These two characteristics are called stationarity and locality, respectively.*

1.1 Previous Work

Numerous approaches have been proposed for texture analysis and synthesis, and an exhaustive survey is beyond the scope of this paper. We briefly review some recent and representative works and refer the reader to [8] and [12] for more complete surveys.

Physical Simulation: It is possible to synthesize certain surface textures by directly simulating their physical generation processes. Biological patterns such as fur, scales, and skin can be modeled using reaction diffusion [26] and cellular texturing [27]. Some weathering and mineral phenomena can be faithfully reproduced by detailed simulations [5]. These techniques can produce textures directly on 3D meshes so the texture mapping distortion problem is avoided. However, different textures are usually generated by very different physical processes so these approaches are applicable to only limited classes of textures.

Markov Random Field and Gibbs Sampling: Many algorithms model textures by Markov Random Fields (or in a different mathematical form, Gibbs Sampling), and generate textures by probability sampling [6, 28, 20, 18]. Since Markov Random Fields have been proven to be a good approximation for a broad range of textures, these algorithms are general and some of them produce good results. A drawback of Markov Random Field sampling, though, is that it is computationally expensive: even small texture patches can take hours or days to generate.

Feature Matching: Some algorithms model textures as a set of features, and generate new images by matching the features in an example texture [9, 4, 22]. These algorithms are usually more efficient than Markov Random Field algorithms. Heeger and Bergen [9] model textures by matching marginal histograms of image pyramids. Their technique succeeds on highly stochastic textures but fails on more structured ones. De Bonet [4] synthesizes new images by randomizing an input texture sample while preserving the cross-scale dependencies. This method works better than [9] on structured textures, but it can produce boundary artifacts if the input texture is not tileable. Simoncelli and Portilla [22] generate textures by matching the joint statistics of the image pyramids. Their method can successfully capture global textural structures but fails to preserve local patterns.

1.2 Overview

Our goal was to develop an algorithm that combines the advantages of previous approaches. We want it to be efficient, general, and able to produce high quality, tileable textures. It should also be user friendly; i.e., the number of tunable input parameters should be minimal. This can be achieved by a careful selection of the texture modeling and synthesis procedure. For the texture model, we use Markov Random Fields (MRF) since they have been proven to cover the widest variety of useful texture types. To avoid the usual computational expense of MRFs, we have developed a synthesis procedure which avoids explicit probability construction and sampling.

Markov Random Field methods model a texture as a realization of a *local* and *stationary* random process. That is, each pixel of a texture image is characterized by a small set of spatially neighboring pixels, and this characterization is the same for all pixels. The intuition behind this model can be demonstrated by the following experiment (Figure 2). Imagine that a viewer is given an image, but only allowed to observe it through a small movable window. As the window is moved the viewer can observe different parts of the image. The image is stationary if, under a proper window size, the observable portion always appears similar. The image is local if each pixel is predictable from a small set of neighboring pixels and is independent of the rest of the image.

Based on these locality and stationarity assumptions, our algorithm synthesizes a new texture so that it is locally similar to an example texture patch. The new texture is generated pixel by pixel, and each pixel is determined so that local similarity is preserved between the example texture and the result image. This synthesis procedure, unlike most MRF based algorithms, is completely deterministic and no explicit probability distribution is constructed. As a result, it is efficient and amenable to further acceleration.

The remainder of the paper is organized as follows. In Section 2, we present the algorithm. In Section 3, we demonstrate synthesis results and compare them with those generated by previous approaches. In Section 4, we propose acceleration techniques. In Sections 5 and 6, we discuss applications, limitations, and extensions.

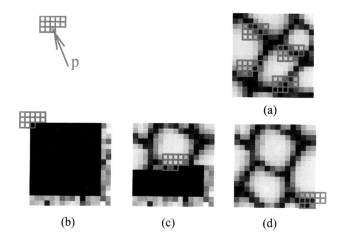

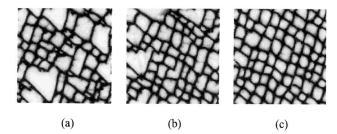

Figure 4: *Synthesis results with different neighborhood sizes. The neighborhood sizes are (a) 5x5, (b) 7x7, (c) 9x9, respectively. All images shown are of size 128x128. Note that as the neighborhood size increases the resulting texture quality gets better. However, the computation cost also increases.*

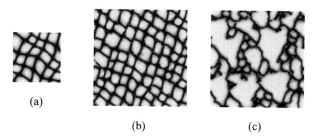

Figure 5: *Causality of the neighborhood. (a) sample texture (b) synthesis result using a causal neighborhood (c) synthesis result using a noncausal neighborhood. Both (b) and (c) are generated from the same random noise using a 9x9 neighborhood. As shown, a noncausal neighborhood is unable to generate valid results.*

Figure 3: *Single resolution texture synthesis. (a) is the input texture and (b)-(d) show different synthesis stages of the output image. Pixels in the output image are assigned in a raster scan ordering. The value of each output pixel p is determined by comparing its spatial neighborhood $N(p)$ with all neighborhoods in the input texture. The input pixel with the most similar neighborhood will be assigned to the corresponding output pixel. Neighborhoods crossing the output image boundaries (shown in (b) and (d)) are handled toroidally, as discussed in Section 2.4. Although the output image starts as a random noise, only the last few rows and columns of the noise are actually used. For clarity, we present the unused noise pixels as black. (b) synthesizing the first pixel, (c) synthesizing the middle pixel, (d) synthesizing the last pixel.*

2 Algorithm

Using Markov Random Fields as the texture model, the goal of the synthesis algorithm is to generate a new texture so that each local region of it is similar to another region from the input texture. We first describe how the algorithm works in a single resolution, and then we extend it using a multiresolution pyramid to obtain improvements in efficiency. For easy reference, we list the symbols used in Table 1 and summarize the algorithm in Table 2.

Symbol	Meaning
I_a	Input texture sample
I_s	Output texture image
G_a	Gaussian pyramid built from I_a
G_s	Gaussian pyramid built from I_s
p_i	An input pixel in I_a or G_a
p	An output pixel in I_s or G_s
$N(p)$	Neighborhood around the pixel p
$G(L)$	Lth level of pyramid G
$G(L, x, y)$	Pixel at level L and position (x, y) of G
{RxC,k}	(2D) neighborhood containing k levels, with size RxC at the top level
{RxCxD,k}	3D neighborhood containing k levels, with size RxCxD at the top level

Table 1: *Table of symbols*

2.1 Single Resolution Synthesis

The algorithm starts with an input texture sample I_a and a white random noise I_s. We force the random noise I_s to look like I_a by transforming I_s pixel by pixel in a raster scan ordering, i.e. from top

to bottom and left to right. Figure 3 shows a graphical illustration of the synthesis process.

To determine the pixel value p at I_s, its spatial neighborhood $N(p)$ (the L-shaped regions in Figure 3) is compared against all possible neighborhoods $N(p_i)$ from I_a. The input pixel p_i with the most similar $N(p_i)$ is assigned to p. We use a simple L_2 norm (sum of squared difference) to measure the similarity between the neighborhoods. The goal of this synthesis process is to ensure that the newly assigned pixel p will maintain as much local similarity between I_a and I_s as possible. The same process is repeated for each output pixel until all the pixels are determined. This is akin to putting together a jigsaw puzzle: the pieces are the individual pixels and the fitness between these pieces is determined by the colors of the surrounding neighborhood pixels.

2.2 Neighborhood

Because the set of local neighborhoods $N(p_i)$ is used as the primary model for textures, the quality of the synthesized results will depend on its size and shape. Intuitively, the size of the neighborhoods should be on the scale of the largest regular texture structure; otherwise this structure may be lost and the result image will look too random. Figure 4 demonstrates the effect of the neighborhood size on the synthesis results.

The shape of the neighborhood will directly determine the quality of I_s. It must be causal, i.e. the neighborhood can only contain those pixels preceding the current output pixel in the raster scan ordering. The reason is to ensure that each output neighborhood $N(p)$ will include only already assigned pixels. For the first few rows and columns of I_s, $N(p)$ may contain unassigned (noise) pixels but as the algorithm progresses all the other $N(p)$ will be completely "valid" (containing only already assigned pixels). A non-

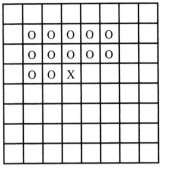

Figure 6: *A causal multiresolution neighborhood with size {5x5,2}. The current level of the pyramid is shown at left and the next lower resolution level is shown at right. The current output pixel p, marked as X, is located at (L, x, y), where L is the current level number and (x, y) is its coordinate. At this level L of the pyramid the image is only partially complete. Thus, we must use the preceding pixels in the raster scan ordering (marked as O). The position of the parent of the current pixel, located at $(L + 1, \frac{x}{2}, \frac{y}{2})$, is marked as Y. Since the parent's level is complete, the neighborhood can contain pixels around Y, marked by Q. When searching for a match for pixel X, the neighborhood vector is constructed that includes the O's, Q's, and Y, in scanline order.*

causal $N(p)$, which always includes unassigned pixels, is unable to transform I_s to look like I_a (Figure 5). Thus, the noise image is only used when generating the first few rows and columns of the output image. After this, it is ignored.

2.3 Multiresolution Synthesis

The single resolution algorithm captures the texture structures by using adequately sized neighborhoods. However, for textures containing large scale structures we have to use large neighborhoods, and large neighborhoods demand more computation. This problem can be solved by using a multiresolution image pyramid [3]; computation is saved because we can represent large scale structures more compactly by a few pixels in a certain lower resolution pyramid level.

The multiresolution synthesis algorithm proceeds as follows. Two Gaussian pyramids, G_a and G_s, are first built from I_a and I_s, respectively. The algorithm then transforms G_s from lower to higher resolutions, such that each higher resolution level is constructed from the already synthesized lower resolution levels. This is similar to the sequence in which a picture is painted: long and thick strokes are placed first, and details are then added. Within each output pyramid level $G_s(L)$, the pixels are synthesized in a way similar to the single resolution case where the pixels are assigned in a raster scan ordering. The only modification is that for the multiresoltion case, each neighborhood $N(p)$ contains pixels in the current resolution as well as those in the lower resolutions. The similarity between two multiresolution neighborhoods is measured by computing the sum of the squared distance of all pixels within them. These lower resolution pixels constrain the synthesis process so that the added high frequency details will be consistent with the already synthesized low frequency structures.

An example of a multiresolution neighborhood is shown in Figure 6. It consists of two levels, with sizes 5x5 and 3x3, respectively. Within a neighborhood, we choose the sizes of the lower levels so that they are about half the sizes of the previous higher resolution levels. For clarity, we use the symbol {RxC,k} to indicate multires-

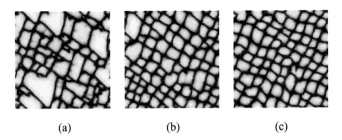

Figure 7: *Synthesis results with the same neighborhood, but different numbers of pyramid levels (a) 1 level, (b) 2 levels, (c) 3 levels. Except for the lowest resolution, which is synthesized with a 5x5 single resolution neighborhood, each pyramid level is synthesized using the multiresolution neighborhood shown in Figure 6. Note that as the number of pyramid levels increases, the image quality improves.*

olution neighborhoods which contain k levels with size RxC at the top level.

Figure 7 shows results of multiresolution synthesis with different numbers of pyramid levels. Note that Figure 7 (c), although synthesized with a small {5x5,2} multiresolution neighborhood, looks comparable with Figure 4 (c), which was generated with a larger 9x9 single resolution neighborhood. This demonstrates a major advantage of multiresolution synthesis: moderately small neighborhoods can be used without sacrificing synthesis qualities.

2.4 Edge Handling

Proper edge handling for $N(p)$ near the image boundaries is very important. For the synthesis pyramid the edge is treated toroidally. In other words, if $G_s(L, x, y)$ denotes the pixel at level L and position (x, y) of pyramid G_s, then $G_s(L, x, y) \equiv G_s(L, x \bmod M, y \bmod N)$, where M and N are the number of rows and columns, respectively, of $G_s(L)$. Handling edges toroidally is essential to guarantee that the resulting synthetic texture will tile seamlessly.[1]

For the input pyramid G_a, toroidal neighborhoods typically contain discontinuities unless I_a is tileable. A reasonable edge handler for G_a is to pad it with a reflected copy of itself. Another solution is to use only those $N(p_i)$ completely inside G_a, and discard those crossing the boundaries. Because a reflective edge handler may introduce discontinuities in the derivative, we adopt the second solution which uses only interior blocks.

2.5 Initialization

Natural textures often contain recognizable structures as well as a certain amount of randomness. Since our goal is to reproduce realistic textures, it is essential that the algorithm capture the random aspect of the textures. This notion of randomness can sometimes be achieved by entropy maximization [28], but the computational cost is prohibitive. Instead, we initialize the output image I_s as a white random noise, and gradually modify this noise to look like the input texture I_a. This initialization step seeds the algorithm with sufficient entropy, and lets the rest of the synthesis process focus on the transformation of I_s towards I_a. To make this random noise a better initial guess, we also equalize the pyramid histogram of G_s with respect to G_a [9].

---

[1]The multiresolution algorithm is also essential for tileability if a causal neighborhood is used. Since a single resolution causal neighborhood $N(p)$ contains only pixels above p in scanline order, the vertical tileability may not be enforced. A multiresolution neighborhood, which contains symmetric regions at lower resolution levels, avoids this problem.

The initial noise affects the synthesis process in the following way. For the single resolution case, neighborhoods in the first few rows and columns of I_s contain noise pixels. These noise pixels introduce uncertainty in the neighborhood matching process, causing the boundary pixels to be assigned semi-stochastically (However, the searching process is still deterministic. The randomness is caused by the initial noise). The rest of the noise pixels are overwritten directly during synthesis. For the multiresolution case, however, more of the noise pixels contribute to the synthesis process, at least indirectly, since they determine the initial value of the lowest resolution level of G_s.

2.6 Summary of Algorithm

We summarize the algorithm in the following pseudocode.

function $I_s \leftarrow$ TextureSynthesis(I_a, $outputSize$)
1    $I_s \leftarrow$ Initialize($outputSize$);
2    $G_a \leftarrow$ BuildPyramid(I_a);
3    $G_s \leftarrow$ BuildPyramid(I_s);
4   **foreach** level L from lower to higher resolutions of G_s
5   **loop** through all pixels (x_s, y_s) of $G_s(L)$
6          $C \leftarrow$ FindBestMatch(G_a, G_s, L, x_s, y_s);
7          $G_s(L, x_s, y_s) \leftarrow C$;
8    $I_s \leftarrow$ ReconPyramid(G_s);
9   **return** I_s;

function $C \leftarrow$ FindBestMatch(G_a, G_s, L, x_s, y_s)
1    $N_s \leftarrow$ BuildNeighborhood(G_s, L, x_s, y_s);
2    $N_a^{best} \leftarrow$ null; $C \leftarrow$ null;
3   **loop** through all pixels (x_a, y_a) of $G_a(L)$
4       $N_a \leftarrow$ BuildNeighborhood(G_a, L, x_a, y_a);
5   **if** Match(N_a, N_s) > Match(N_a^{best}, N_s)
6          $N_a^{best} \leftarrow N_a$; $C \leftarrow G_a(L, x_a, y_a)$;
7   **return** C;

Table 2: *Pseudocode of the Algorithm*

The architecture of this algorithm is flexible; it is composed from several orthogonal components. We list these components as follows and discuss the corresponding design choices.

Pyramid: The pyramids are built from and reconstructed to images using the standard routines **BuildPyramid** and **ReconPyramid**. Various pyramids can be used for texture synthesis; examples are Gaussian pyramids [20], Laplacian pyramids [9], steerable pyramids [9, 22], and feature-based pyramids [4]. A Gaussian pyramid, for example, is built by successive filtering and downsampling operations, and each pyramid level, except for the highest resolution, is a blurred and decimated version of the original image. Reconstruction of Gaussian pyramids is trivial, since the image is available at the highest resolution pyramid level. These different pyramids give different trade-offs between spatial and frequency resolutions. In this paper, we choose to use the Gaussian pyramid for its simplicity and greater spatial localization (a detailed discussion of this issue can be found in [19]). However, other kinds of pyramids can be used instead.

Neighborhood: The neighborhood can have arbitrary size and shape; the only requirement is that it contains only valid pixels. A noncausal/symmetric neighborhood, for example, can be used by extending the original algorithm with two passes (Section 5.1).

Synthesis Ordering: A raster scan ordering is used in line 5 of the function **TextureSynthesis**. This, however, can also be extended. For example, a spiral ordering can be used for constrained texture

synthesis (Section 5.1). The synthesis ordering should cooperate with the **BuildNeighborhood** so that the output neighborhoods contain only valid pixels.

Searching: An exhaustive searching procedure **FindBestMatch** is employed to determine the output pixel values. Because this is a standard process, various point searching algorithms can be used for acceleration. This will be discussed in detail in Section 4.

3 Synthesis Results

To test the effectiveness of our approach, we have run the algorithm on many different images from standard texture sets. Figure 8 shows examples using the MIT VisTex set [16], which contains real world textures photographed under natural lighting conditions. Additional texture synthesis results are available on our project website.

A visual comparison of our approach with several other algorithms is shown in Figure 9. Result (a) is generated by Heeger and Bergen's algorithm [9] using a steerable pyramid with 6 orientations. The algorithm captures certain random aspects of the texture but fails on the dominating grid-like structures. Result (b) is generated by De Bonet's approach [4] where we choose his randomness parameter to make the result look best. Though capable of capturing more structural patterns than (a), certain boundary artifacts are visible. This is because his approach characterizes textures by lower frequency pyramid levels only; therefore the lateral relationship between pixels at the same level is lost. Result (c) is generated by Efros and Leung's algorithm [6]. This technique is based on the Markov Random Field model and is capable of generating high quality textures. However, a direct application of their approach can produce non-tileable results.[2]

Result (d) is synthesized using our approach. It is tileable and the image quality is comparable with those synthesized directly from MRFs. It took about 8 minutes to generate using a 195 MHz R10000 processor. However, this is not the maximum possible speed achievable with this algorithm. In the next section, we describe modifications that accelerate the algorithm greatly.

4 Acceleration

Our deterministic synthesis procedure avoids the usual computational requirement for sampling from a MRF. However, the algorithm as described employs exhaustive searching, which makes it slow. Fortunately, acceleration is possible. This is achieved by considering neighborhoods $N(p)$ as points in a multiple dimensional space, and casting the neighborhood matching process as a nearest-point searching problem [17].

The nearest-point searching problem in multiple dimensions is stated as follows: given a set S of n points and a novel query point Q in a d-dimensional space, find a point in the set such that its distance from Q is lesser than, or equal to, the distance of Q from any other point in the set. Because a large number of such queries may need to be conducted over the same data set S, the computational cost can be reduced if we preprocess S to create a data structure that allows fast nearest-point queries. Many such data structures have been proposed, and we refer the reader to [17] for a more complete reference. However, most of these algorithms assume generic inputs and do not attempt to take advantage of any special structures they may have. Popat [20] observed that the set S of spatial neighborhoods from a texture can often be characterized well by

---
[2]Though not stated in the original paper [6], we have found that it is possible to extend their approach using multiresolution pyramids and a toroidal neighborhood to make tileable textures.

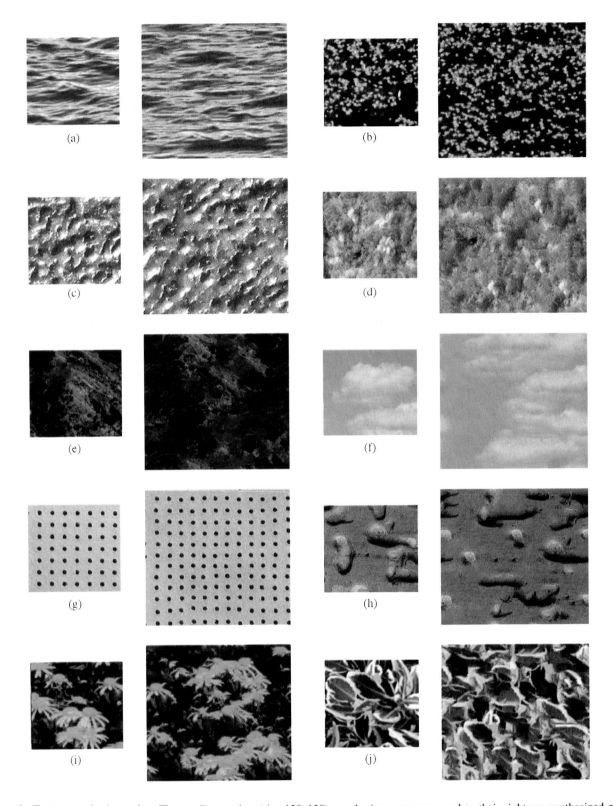

Figure 8: Texture synthesis results. The smaller patches (size 128x128) are the input textures, and to their right are synthesized results (size 200x200). Each texture is generated using a 4-level Gaussian pyramid, with neighborhood sizes {3x3,1}, {5x5,2}, {7x7,2}, {9x9,2}, respectively, from lower to higher resolutions. VisTex textures: (a) Water 0000 (b) Misc 0000 (c) Metal 0004 (d) Fabric 0015 (e) Terrain 0000 (f) Clouds 0000 (g) Tile 0007 (h) Stone 0002 (i) Flowers 0000 (j) Leaves 0009.

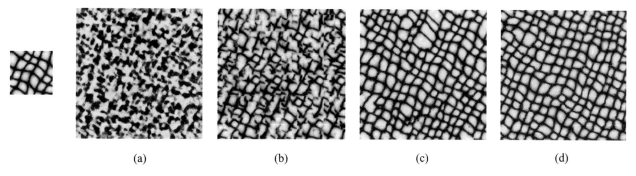

(a)   (b)   (c)   (d)

Figure 9: *A comparison of texture synthesis results using different algorithms: (a) Heeger and Bergen's method [9] (b) De Bonet's method [4] (c) Efros and Leung's method [6] (d) Our method. Only Efros and Leung's algorithm produces results comparable with ours. However, our algorithm is two orders of magnitude faster than theirs (Section 4). The sample texture patch has size 64x64, and all the result images are of size 192x192. A 9x9 neighborhood is used for (c), and (d) is synthesized using the same parameters as indicated in the caption of Figure 8.*

a clustering probability model. Taking advantage of this clustering property, we propose to use tree-structured vector quantization (TSVQ, [7]) as the searching algorithm [25].

4.1 TSVQ Acceleration

Tree-structured vector quantization (TSVQ) is a common technique for data compression. It takes a set of training vectors as input, and generates a binary-tree-structured codebook. The first step is to compute the centroid of the set of training vectors and use it as the root level codeword. To find the children of this root, the centroid and a perturbed centroid are chosen as initial child codewords. A generalized Lloyd algorithm [7], consisting of alternations between centroid computation and nearest centroid partition, is then used to find the locally optimal codewords for the two children. The training vectors are divided into two groups based on these codewords and the algorithm recurses on each of the subtrees. This process terminates when the number of codewords exceeds a pre-selected size or the average coding error is below a certain threshold. The final codebook is the collection of the leaf level codewords.

The tree generated by TSVQ can be used as a data structure for efficient nearest-point queries. To find the nearest point of a given query vector, the tree is traversed from the root in a best-first ordering by comparing the query vector with the two children codewords, and then follows the one that has a closer codeword. This process is repeated for each visited node until a leaf node is reached. The best codeword is then returned as the codeword of that leaf node. Unlike full searching, the result codeword may not be the optimal one since only part of the tree is traversed. However, the result codeword is usually close to the optimal solution, and the computation is more efficient than full searching. If the tree is reasonably balanced (this can be enforced in the algorithm), a single search with codebook size $|S|$ can be achieved in time $O(log|S|)$, which is much faster than exhaustive searching with linear time complexity $O(|S|)$.

To use TSVQ in our synthesis algorithm, we simply collect the set of neighborhood pixels $N(p_i)$ for each input pixel and treat them as a vector of size equal to the number of pixels in $N(p_i)$. We use these vectors $\{N(p_i)\}$ from each $G_a(L)$ as the training data, and generate the corresponding tree structure codebooks $T(L)$. During the synthesis process, the (approximate) closest point for each $N(p)$ at $G_s(L)$ is found by doing a best-first traversal of $T(L)$. Because this tree traversal has time complexity $O(log N_L)$ (where N_L is the number of pixels of $G_a(L)$), the synthesis procedure can be executed very efficiently. Typical textures take seconds to generate; the exact timing depends on the input and output image sizes.

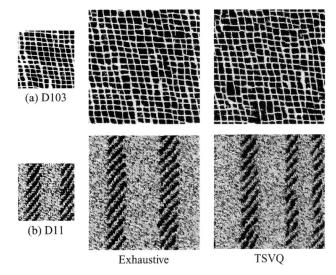

(a) D103

(b) D11

Exhaustive   TSVQ

Figure 10: *Accelerated synthesis using TSVQ. The original Brodatz textures, with size 128x128, are shown in the left column. The results generated by exhaustive searching and TSVQ are shown in the middle and right columns, respectively. All generated images are of size 200x200. The average running time for exhaustive searching is 360 seconds. The average training time for TSVQ is 22 seconds and the average synthesis time is 7.5 seconds.*

4.2 Acceleration Results

An example comparing the results of exhaustive searching and TSVQ is shown in Figure 10. The original image sizes are 128x128 and the resulting image sizes are 200x200. The average running time for exhaustive searching is 360 seconds. The average training time for TSVQ is 22 seconds and the average synthesis time is 7.5 seconds. The code is implemented in C++ and the timings are measured on a 195MHz R10000 processor. As shown in Figure 10, results generated with TSVQ acceleration are roughly comparable in quality to those generated from the unaccelerated approach. In some cases, TSVQ will generate more blurry images. We fix this by allowing limited backtracking in the tree traversal so that more than one leaf node can be visited. The amount of backtracking can be used as a parameter which trades off between image quality and computation time. When the number of visited leaf nodes is equal to the codebook size, the result will be the same as the exhaustive searching case.

One disadvantage of TSVQ acceleration is the memory require-

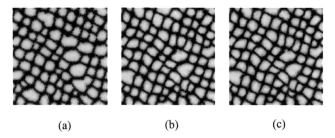

(a)   (b)   (c)

Figure 11: *TSVQ acceleration with different codebook sizes. The original image size is 64x64 and all these synthesized results are of size 128x128. The number of codewords in each case are (a) 64 (b) 512 (c) 4096 (all).*

Algorithm	Training Time	Synthesis Time
Efros and Leung	none	1941 seconds
Exhaustive Searching	none	503 seconds
TSVQ acceleration	12 seconds	12 seconds

Table 3: *A breakdown of running time for the textures shown in Figure 9. The first row shows the timing of Efros and Leung's algorithm. The second and third rows show the timing of our algorithm, using exhaustive searching and TSVQ acceleration, respectively. All the timings were measured using a 195 MHz R10000 processor.*

ment. Because an input pixel can appear in multiple neighborhoods, a full-sized TSVQ tree can consume $O(d * N)$ memory where d is the neighborhood size and N is the number of input image pixels. Fortunately, textures usually contain repeating structures; therefore we can use codebooks with fewer codewords than the input training set. Figure 11 shows textures generated by TSVQ with different codebook sizes. As expected the image quality improves when the codebook size increases. However, results generated with fewer codewords such as (b) look plausible compared with the full codebook result (c). In our experience we can use codebooks less than 10 percent the size of the original training data without noticeable degradation of quality of the synthesis results. To further reduce the expense of training, we can also train on a subset rather than the entire collection of input neighborhood vectors.

Table 3 shows a timing breakdown for generating the textures shown in Figure 9. Our unaccelerated algorithm took 503 seconds. The TSVQ accelerated algorithm took 12 seconds for training, and another 12 seconds for synthesis. In comparison, Efros and Leung's algorithm [6] took half an hour to generate the same texture (the time complexity of our approach over Efros and Leung's is $O(logN)/O(N)$ where N is the number of input image pixels). Because their algorithm uses a variable sized neighborhood it is difficult to accelerate. Our algorithm, on the other hand, uses a fixed neighborhood and can be directly accelerated by any point searching algorithm.

5   Applications

One of the chief advantages of our texture synthesis method is its low computational cost. This permits us to explore a variety of applications, in addition to the usual texture mapping for graphics, that were previously impractical. Presented here are constrained synthesis for image editing and temporal texture generation.

5.1   Constrained Texture Synthesis

Photographs, films and images often contain regions that are in some sense flawed. A flaw can be a scrambled region on a scanned photograph, scratches on an old film, wires or props in a movie

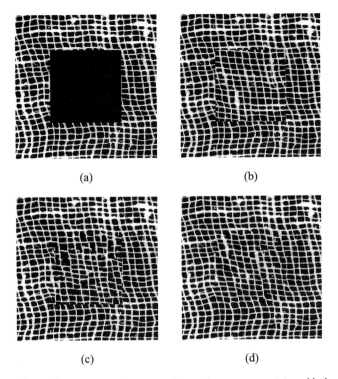

(a)   (b)

(c)   (d)

Figure 12: *Constrained texture synthesis. (a) a texture containing a black region that needs to be filled in. (b) multiresolution blending [3] with another texture region will produce boundary artifacts. (c) A direct application of the algorithm in Section 2 will produce visible discontinuities at the right and bottom boundaries. (d) A much better result can be generated by using a modification of the algorithm with 2 passes.*

film frame, or simply an undesirable object in an image. Since the processes causing these flaws are often irreversible, an algorithm that can fix these flaws is desirable. For example, Hirani and Totsuka [10] developed an interactive algorithm that finds translationally similar regions for noise removal. Often, the flawed portion is contained within a region of texture, and can be replaced by constrained texture synthesis [6, 11].

Texture replacement by constrained synthesis must satisfy two requirements: the synthesized region must look like the surrounding texture, and the boundary between the new and old regions must be invisible. Multiresolution blending [3] with another similar texture, shown in Figure 12 (b), will produce visible boundaries for structured textures. Better results can be obtained by applying our algorithm in Section 2 over the flawed regions, but discontinuities still appear at the right and bottom boundaries as shown in Figure 12 (c). These artifacts are caused by the causal neighborhood as well as the raster scan synthesis ordering.

To remove these boundary artifacts a noncausal (symmetric) neighborhood must be used. However, we have to modify the original algorithm so that only valid (already synthesized) pixels are contained within the symmetric neighborhoods; otherwise the algorithm will not generate valid results (Figure 5). This can be done with a two-pass extension of the original algorithm. Each pass is the same as the original multiresolution process, except that a different neighborhood is used. During the first pass, the neighborhood contains only pixels from the lower resolution pyramid levels. Because the synthesis progresses in a lower to higher resolution fashion, a symmetric neighborhood can be used without introducing invalid pixels. This pass uses the lower resolution information to "extrapolate" the higher resolution regions that need to be replaced. In the

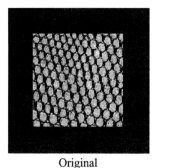 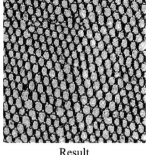

Original   Result

Figure 13: *Image extrapolation of Brodatz texture D36. The original image is on the left and the synthesized result is on the right. The black region is filled in so that it looks consistent with the rest of the image.*

second pass, a symmetric neighborhood that contains pixels from both the current and lower resolutions is used. These two passes alternate for each level of the output pyramid. In the accelerated algorithm, the analysis phase is also modified so that two TSVQ trees corresponding to these two kinds of neighborhoods are built for each level of the input pyramid. Finally, we also modify the synthesis ordering in the following way: instead of the usual raster-scan ordering, pixels in the filled regions are assigned in a spiral fashion. For example, the hole in Figure 12 (a) is replaced from outside to inside from the surrounding region until every pixel is assigned (Figure 12 (d)). This spiral synthesis ordering removes the directional bias which causes the boundary discontinuities (as in Figure 12 (c)).

With a slight change of the synthesis ordering, the algorithm can be applied to other applications, such as the image extrapolation shown in Figure 13. The algorithm could also be extended as an interactive tool for image editing or denoising [15].

5.2 Temporal Texture Synthesis

The low cost of our accelerated algorithm enables us to consider synthesizing textures of dimension greater than two. An example of 3D texture is a temporal texture. Temporal textures are motions with indeterminate extent both in space and time. They can describe a wide variety of natural phenomena such as fire, smoke, and fluid motions. Since realistic motion synthesis is one of the major goals of computer graphics, a technique that can synthesize temporal textures would be useful. Most existing algorithms model temporal textures by direct simulation; examples include fluid, gas, and fire [23]. Direct simulations, however, are often expensive and only suitable for specific kinds of textures; therefore an algorithm that can model general motion textures would be advantageous [24].

Temporal textures consist of 3D spatial-temporal volume of motion data. If the motion data is local and stationary both in space and time, the texture can be synthesized by a 3D extension of our algorithm. This extension can be simply done by replacing various 2D entities in the original algorithm, such as images, pyramids, and neighborhoods, with their 3D counterparts. For example, the two Gaussian pyramids are constructed by filtering and downsampling from 3D volumetric data; the neighborhoods contain local pixels in both the spatial and temporal dimension. The synthesis progresses from lower to higher resolutions, and within each resolution the output is synthesized slice by slice along the time domain.

Figure 14 shows synthesis results of several typical temporal textures: fire, smoke, and ocean waves (animations available on our webpage). The resulting sequences capture the flavor of the original motions, and tile both spatially and temporally. This technique is also efficient. Accelerated by TSVQ, each result frame took about

20 seconds to synthesize. Currently all the textures are generated automatically; we plan to extend the algorithm to allow more explicit user controls (such as the distribution and intensity of the fire and smoke).

6 Conclusions and Future Work

Textures are important for a wide variety of applications in computer graphics and image processing. On the other hand, they are hard to synthesize. The goal of this paper is to provide a practical tool for efficiently synthesizing a broad range of textures. Inspired by Markov Random Field methods, our algorithm is general: a wide variety of textures can be synthesized without any knowledge of their physical formation processes. The algorithm is also efficient: by a proper acceleration using TSVQ, typical textures can be generated within seconds on current PCs and workstations. The algorithm is also easy to use: only an example texture patch is required.

The basic version of our algorithm (Section 2) relates to an earlier work by Popat and Picard [20] in that a causal neighborhood and raster scan ordering are used for texture synthesis. However, instead of constructing explicit probability models, our algorithm uses deterministic searching. This approach shares the simplicity of Efros and Leung [6], but uses fix-sized neighborhoods which allow TSVQ acceleration. The fact that such a simple approach works well on many different textures implies that there may be computational redundancies in other texture synthesis techniques. This algorithm shares some of the same limitations as Markov Random Field approaches: in particular, only local and stationary phenomena can be represented. Other visual cues such as 3D shape, depth, lighting, or reflection can not be captured by this simple model.

Aside from constrained synthesis and temporal textures, numerous applications of our approach are possible. Other potential applications/extensions are:

Multidimensional texture: The notion of texture extends naturally to multi-dimensional data. One example was presented in this paper - motion sequences. The same technique can also be directly applied to solid textures or animated solid texture synthesis. We are also trying to extend our algorithm for generating structured solid textures from 2D views [9].

Texture compression/decompression: Textures usually contain repeating patterns and high frequency information; therefore they are not well compressed by transform-based techniques such as JPEG. However, codebook-based compression techniques work well on textures [1]. This suggests that textures might be compressable by our synthesis technique. Compression would consist of building a codebook, but unlike [1], no code indices would be generated; only the codebook would be transmitted and the compression ratio is controlled by the number of codewords. Decompression would consist of texture synthesis. This decompression step, if accelerated one more order of magnitude over our current software implementation, could be usable for real time texture mapping. The advantage of this approach over [1] is much greater compression, since only the codebook is transmitted.

Motion synthesis/editing: Some motions can be efficiently modeled as spatial-temporal textures. Others, such as animal or human motion, are too highly structured for such a direct approach. However, it might be possible to encode their motion as joint angles, and then apply texture analysis-synthesis to the resulting 1D temporal motion signals.

Modeling geometric details: Models scanned from real world objects often contain texture-like geometric details, making the

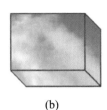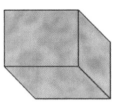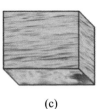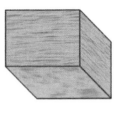

(a)   (b)   (c)

Figure 14: *Temporal texture synthesis results. (a) fire (b) smoke (c) ocean waves. In each pair of images, the spatial-temporal volume of the original motion sequence is shown on the left, and the corresponding synthesis result is shown on the right. A 3-level Gaussian pyramid, with neighborhood sizes {5x5x5,2}, {3x3x3,2}, {1x1x1,1}, are used for synthesis. The original motion sequences contain 32 frames, and the synthesis results contain 64 frames. The individual frame sizes are (a) 128x128 (b) 150x112 (c) 150x112. Accelerated by TSVQ, the training times are (a) 1875 (b) 2155 (c) 2131 seconds and the synthesis times per frame are (a) 19.78 (b) 18.78 (c) 20.08 seconds. To save memory, we use only a random 10 percent of the input neighborhood vectors to build the (full) codebooks.*

models expensive to store, transmit or manipulate. These geometric details can be represented as displacement maps over a smoother surface representation [13]. The resulting displacement maps should be compressable/decompressable as 2D textures using our technique. Taking this idea further, missing geometric details, a common problem in many scanning situations [14], could be filled in using our constrained texture synthesis technique.

Direct synthesis over meshes: Mapping textures onto irregular 3D meshes by projection often causes distortions [21]. These distortions can sometimes be fixed by establishing suitable parameterization of the mesh, but a more direct approach would be to synthesize the texture directly over the mesh. In principle, this can be done using our technique. However, this will require extending ordinary signal processing operations such as filtering and downsampling to irregular 3D meshes.

Acknowledgments

We would like to thank Kris Popat and Alyosha Efros for answering questions about their texture synthesis works, Phil Hubbard for his help on the writing of the paper, and the anonymous reviewers for their comments. The texture thumbnail shown in Figure 1 was acquired from Jeremy De Bonet's webpage. Special thanks to members of the Stanford Graphics Group. This research was supported by Intel, Interval, and Sony under the Stanford Immersive Television Project.

References

[1] A. C. Beers, M. Agrawala, and N. Chaddha. Rendering from compressed textures. *Proceedings of SIGGRAPH 96*, pages 373–378, August 1996.

[2] P. Brodatz. *Textures: A Photographic Album for Artists and Designers*. Dover, New York, 1966.

[3] P. J. Burt and E. H. Adelson. A multiresolution spline with application to image mosaics. *ACM Transactions on Graphics*, 2(4):217–236, Oct. 1983.

[4] J. S. De Bonet. Multiresolution sampling procedure for analysis and synthesis of texture images. In T. Whitted, editor, *SIGGRAPH 97 Conference Proceedings*, Annual Conference Series, pages 361–368. ACM SIGGRAPH, Addison Wesley, Aug. 1997.

[5] J. Dorsey, A. Edelman, J. Legakis, H. W. Jensen, and H. K. Pedersen. Modeling and rendering of weathered stone. *Proceedings of SIGGRAPH 99*, pages 225–234, August 1999.

[6] A. Efros and T. Leung. Texture synthesis by non-parametric sampling. In *International Conference on Computer Vision*, volume 2, pages 1033–8, Sep 1999.

[7] A. Gersho and R. M. Gray. *Vector Quantization and Signal Compression*. Kluwer Academic Publishers, 1992.

[8] R. Haralick. Statistical image texture analysis. In *Handbook of Pattern Recognition and Image Processing*, volume 86, pages 247–279. Academic Press, 1986.

[9] D. J. Heeger and J. R. Bergen. Pyramid-Based texture analysis/synthesis. In R. Cook, editor, *SIGGRAPH 95 Conference Proceedings*, Annual Conference Series, pages 229–238. ACM SIGGRAPH, Addison Wesley, Aug. 1995.

[10] A. N. Hirani and T. Totsuka. Combining frequency and spatial domain information for fast interactive image noise removal. *Computer Graphics*, 30(Annual Conference Series):269–276, 1996.

[11] H. Igehy and L. Pereira. Image replacement through texture synthesis. In *International Conference on Image Processing*, volume 3, pages 186–189, Oct 1997.

[12] H. Iversen and T. Lonnestad. An evaluation of stochastic models for analysis and synthesis of gray scale texture. *Pattern Recognition Letters*, 15:575–585, 1994.

[13] V. Krishnamurthy and M. Levoy. Fitting smooth surfaces to dense polygon meshes. *Proceedings of SIGGRAPH 96*, pages 313–324, August 1996. ISBN 0-201-94800-1. Held in New Orleans, Louisiana.

[14] M. Levoy, K. Pulli, B. Curless, S. Rusinkiewicz, D. Koller, L. Pereira, M. Ginzton, S. Anderson, J. Davis, J. Ginsberg, J. Shade, and D. Fulk. The Digital Michelangelo Project: 3D scanning of large statues. To appear in Proceedings of SIGGRAPH 2000.

[15] T. Malzbender and S. Spach. A context sensitive texture nib. In *Proceedings of Computer Graphics International*, pages 151–163, June 1993.

[16] MIT Media Lab. Vision texture. http://www-white.media.mit.edu/vismod/-imagery/VisionTexture/vistex.html.

[17] S. Nene and S. Nayar. A simple algorithm for nearest neighbor search in high dimensions. *IEEE Transactions on Pattern Analysis and Machine Intelligence*, 19:989–1003, 1997.

[18] R. Paget and I. Longstaff. Texture synthesis via a noncausal nonparametric multiscale Markov random field. *IEEE Transactions on Image Processing*, 7(6):925–931, June 1998.

[19] A. C. Popat. *Conjoint Probabilistic Subband Modeling*. PhD thesis, Massachusetts Institute of Technology, 1997.

[20] K. Popat and R. Picard. Novel cluster-based probability model for texture synthesis, classification, and compression. In *Visual Communications and Image Processing*, pages 756–68, 1993.

[21] M. Segal, C. Korobkin, R. van Widenfelt, J. Foran, and P. E. Haeberli. Fast shadows and lighting effects using texture mapping. *Computer Graphics (Proceedings of SIGGRAPH 92)*, 26(2):249–252, July 1992.

[22] E. Simoncelli and J. Portilla. Texture characterization via joint statistics of wavelet coefficient magnitudes. In *Fifth International Conference on Image Processing*, volume 1, pages 62–66, Oct. 1998.

[23] J. Stam and E. Fiume. Depicting fire and other gaseous phenomena using diffusion processes. *Proceedings of SIGGRAPH 95*, pages 129–136, August 1995.

[24] M. Szummer and R. W. Picard. Temporal texture modeling. In *International Conference on Image Processing*, volume 3, pages 823–6, Sep 1996.

[25] L. Wei. Deterministic texture analysis and synthesis using tree structure vector quantization. In *XII Brazilian Symposium on Computer Graphics and Image Processing*, pages 207–213, October 1999.

[26] A. Witkin and M. Kass. Reaction-diffusion textures. In T. W. Sederberg, editor, *Computer Graphics (SIGGRAPH '91 Proceedings)*, volume 25, pages 299–308, July 1991.

[27] S. P. Worley. A cellular texture basis function. In H. Rushmeier, editor, *SIGGRAPH 96 Conference Proceedings*, Annual Conference Series, pages 291–294. ACM SIGGRAPH, Addison Wesley, Aug. 1996.

[28] S. Zhu, Y. Wu, and D. Mumford. Filters, random fields and maximun entropy (FRAME) - towards a unified theory for texture modeling. *International Journal of Computer Vision*, 27(2):107–126, 1998.

Video Textures

Arno Schödl[1,2]   *Richard Szeliski*[2]   *David H. Salesin*[2,3]   *Irfan Essa*[1]

[1]Georgia Institute of Technology   [2]Microsoft Research   [3]University of Washington

Abstract

This paper introduces a new type of medium, called a *video texture*, which has qualities somewhere between those of a photograph and a video. A video texture provides a continuous infinitely varying stream of images. While the individual frames of a video texture may be repeated from time to time, the video sequence as a whole is never repeated exactly. Video textures can be used in place of digital photos to infuse a static image with dynamic qualities and explicit action. We present techniques for analyzing a video clip to extract its structure, and for synthesizing a new, similar looking video of arbitrary length. We combine video textures with view morphing techniques to obtain *3D video textures*. We also introduce *video-based animation*, in which the synthesis of video textures can be guided by a user through high-level interactive controls. Applications of video textures and their extensions include the display of dynamic scenes on web pages, the creation of dynamic backdrops for special effects and games, and the interactive control of video-based animation.

CR Categories and Subject Descriptors:
H.5.1 [Information Interfaces]: Multimedia Information Systems—video
I.3.3 [Computer Graphics]: Picture/Image Generation—display algorithms
I.4.9 [Image Processing and Computer Vision]: Applications

Keywords: Animation, image-based rendering, morphing, multimedia, natural phenomena, texture synthesis, video-based rendering, video-based animation, video sprites, view morphing.

1 Introduction

A picture is worth a thousand words. And yet, there are many phenomena, both natural and man-made, that are not adequately captured by a single static photo. A waterfall, a flickering flame, a flag flapping in the breeze—each of these phenomena has an inherently dynamic quality that a single image simply cannot portray.

The obvious alternative to static photography is video. But video has its own drawbacks. If we want to store video on a computer or some other storage device, we are forced to use a video clip of finite duration. Hence, the video has a beginning, a middle, and an end. The video becomes a very specific embodiment of a very specific period of time. Although it captures the time-varying behavior of the phenomenon at hand, the video lacks the "timeless" quality of the photograph.

In this work, we propose a new type of medium, which is in many ways intermediate between a photograph and a video. This new

medium, which we call a *video texture*, provides a continuous, infinitely varying stream of video images. (We use the term "video texture" because of the strong analogy to image textures, which usually repeat visual patterns in similar, quasi-periodic ways.) The video texture is synthesized from a finite set of images by randomly rearranging (and possibly blending) original frames from a source video.

Video textures occupy an interesting niche between the static and the dynamic realm. Whenever a photo is displayed on a computer screen, a video texture might be used instead to infuse the image with dynamic qualities. For example, a web page advertising a scenic destination could use a video texture of a beach with palm trees blowing in the wind rather than a static photograph. Or an actor could provide a dynamic "head shot" with continuous movement on his home page. Video textures could also find application as dynamic backdrops or foreground elements for scenes composited from live and synthetic elements, for example, in computer games.

The basic concept of a video texture can be extended in several different ways to further increase its applicability. For backward compatibility with existing video players and web browsers, finite duration *video loops* can be created to play continuously without any visible discontinuities. The original video can be split into independently moving *regions*, and each region can be analyzed and rendered independently. We can also use computer vision techniques to separate objects from the background and represent them as *video sprites*, which can be rendered at arbitrary image locations. Multiple video sprites or video texture regions can be combined into a complex scene.

Video textures can also be combined with stereo matching and view morphing techniques to produce *three-dimensional video textures* that can be rendered from continually varying viewpoints. Most interesting, perhaps, is the ability to put video textures under interactive control—to drive them at a high level in real time. For instance, by interactively specifying a preferred segment within a source video, a jogger can be made to speed up and slow down according to the position of an interactive slider. Alternatively, an existing video clip can be shortened or lengthened by removing or adding video texture in the middle. We call these forms of high-level control *video-based animation*.

Creating video textures and applying them in all of these ways requires solving a number of problems. The first difficulty is in locating potential transition points in the video sequences, i.e., places where the video can be looped back on itself in a minimally obtrusive way. A second challenge is in finding a sequence of transitions that respects the global structure of the video. Even though a given transition may, itself, have minimal artifacts, it could lead to a portion of the video from which there is no graceful exit, and therefore be a poor transition to take. A third challenge is in smoothing visual discontinuities at the transitions—we solve this problem using morphing techniques. A fourth problem is in automatically factoring video frames into different regions that can be analyzed and synthesized independently. Furthermore, the various extensions described above involve new, additional challenges: creating good, fixed-length cycles; separating video texture elements from their backgrounds so that they can be used as video sprites; applying view morphing to video imagery; and generalizing the transition metrics to incorporate real-time user input.

In some cases, our solutions to these problems are (in retrospect) quite simple. We thus feel that the primary contribution of this paper may lie not so much in the technical solutions to each of these individual problems *per se*, but rather in the overall paradigm of reusing video frames to create video textures, video sprites, and video-based animation.

1.1 Related work

Increasingly, computer graphics is turning toward image-based modeling and rendering techniques [7, 13], where images captured from a scene or object are used as an integral part of the rendering process, sometime obviating the need for geometry altogether [5]. As Debevec points out [13], this trend parallels the one that occurred in music synthesis a decade ago, when sample-based synthesis replaced more algorithmic approaches like frequency modulation. To date, image-based rendering techniques have mostly been applied to still scenes such as architecture [8, 18], although they have also been used to cache and accelerate the renderings produced by conventional graphics hardware [27, 32].

Our work generalizes image-based rendering to the temporal domain. It can thus be thought of as a kind of "video-based rendering." A similar idea has been used in video games, in which hand-generated video loops have been created to simulate natural phenomena like fire or water. However, there has been little previous work on automatically generating motion by reusing captured video. Probably the work most closely related to our own is "Video Rewrite" [3], in which video sequences of a person's mouth are extracted from a training sequence of the person speaking and then reordered in order to match the phoneme sequence of a new audio track. Related 3D view interpolation techniques have also been applied to multiple video streams in the *Virtualized Reality* [16] and *Immersive Video* [19] projects. Pollard *et al.* [23] introduced the term "video sprite" for applying such techniques to an alpha-matted region of the video rather than to the whole image. Finkelstein *et al.* [10] also used alpha-matted video elements in their earlier multiresolution video work, which they called "video clip-art."

Video textures can also be thought of as a temporal extension of 2D image texture synthesis. The multiscale-sampling techniques used for texture synthesis [6, 9, 12] have in fact been directly extended by Bar-Joseph into the space-time domain [1]. Bar-Joseph's work focuses on texture-type motions with limited semantic content such as fire or water close-ups, which are well modeled by the hierarchy of filter responses used for texture synthesis. Our approach can deal with these kinds of phenomena, but also deals with much more structured motions such as repetitive human actions. In this context, some of our analysis resembles earlier work in finding cycles in repetitive motions and "rectifying" these cycles into truly periodic sequences [20, 22, 25]. Our work also has some similarity to the "motion without movement" technique [11], in which patterns in an image appear to move continuously without changing their positions.

1.2 System overview

Given a small amount of "training video" (our input video clip), how do we generate an infinite amount of similar looking video? The general approach we follow in this paper is to find places in the original video where a transition can be made to some other place in the video clip without introducing noticeable discontinuities.

Our system is thus organized into three major components (Figure 1).

The first component of the system *analyzes* the input video to find the good transition points, and stores these in a small data table that

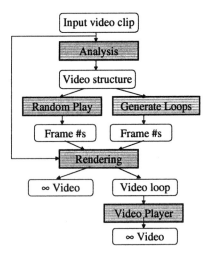

Figure 1 *System overview diagram.* An input video clip is fed into the *Analysis* component, which finds good transition points where the video can be looped back on itself. These transitions (the *Video structure*) are fed to one of two *Synthesis* components: either *Random Play*, which sequences the transitions stochastically; or *Generate Loops*, which finds a set of transitions that together create a single overall video loop of a given length. The *Rendering* component takes the generated sequence of frames, together with the original video clip, and produces either an infinite video texture sequence, or a video loop that can be played indefinitely by a standard *Video Player* in "loop" mode.

becomes part of the video texture representation. This analysis component may also optionally trim away parts of the input video that are not needed, or segment the original video into independently moving pieces, in order to more easily analyze (and find the repetition in) these individual regions.

The second component of our system *synthesizes* new video from the analyzed video clip, by deciding in what order to play (or shuffle) the original video frames (or pieces thereof). We have developed two different approaches to perform this sequencing. The first approach is *random play*, which uses a Monte-Carlo (stochastic) technique to decide which frame should be played after a given frame, using the table of frame-to-frame similarities computed by the analysis algorithm. The second approach selects a small number of transitions to take in such a way that the video is guaranteed to loop after a specified number of frames. The resulting *video loop* can then be played by a conventional video player in "loop" mode.

Once the set of frames to be played has been selected, the *rendering* component puts together the frames (or frame pieces) in a way that is visually pleasing. This process may be as simple as just displaying or outputting the original video frames, or it may involve cross-fading or morphing across transitions and/or blending together independently moving regions.

The remainder of this paper describes, in more detail, the representation used to capture the structure of video textures (Section 2), our process for extracting this representation from source video (Section 3), and for synthesizing the video texture (Section 4). The rendering algorithms used to composite video sprites together and to smooth over visual discontinuities are described next (Section 5). The discussion of our basic results (Section 6) is followed by a description of some further extensions (Section 7). These include the extraction and rendering of video sprites, changing viewpoints using image-based rendering techniques, and the creation of video-based animation. The video clips associated with these results can be viewed on the CD-ROM, DVD, and Video Conference Proceedings. We conclude with a discussion of the potential of video textures and some ideas for future research.

2 Representation

Our video textures are essentially Markov processes, with each state corresponding to a single video frame, and the probabilities corresponding to the likelihood of transitions from one frame to another.

In practice, we have found two alternate (and equivalent) representations to be useful for storing these video textures. One is as a matrix of probabilities (Figure 3), in which each element P_{ij} of the matrix describes the probability of transitioning from frame i to frame j. The other is as a set of explicit *links* (Figure 6) from one frame i to another j, along with an associated probability. The first representation is advantageous when the matrix is dense, as the indices do not need to be stored explicitly. However, in most cases the set of allowable transitions is relatively sparse, and so the second representation is preferred.

In many cases, better results can be achieved by splitting the original video into regions and computing a video texture for each region separately. As discussed in more detail in Section 7.3, we sometimes also segment the video into different video sprite elements, each with its own affiliated alpha channel and compute a video texture for each sprite separately. In this case, additional information is stored along with the links to describe how the relative position of the sprite is changed as the link is crossed.

3 Analysis: Extracting the video texture

The first step in creating a video texture from an input video sequence is to compute some measure of similarity between all pairs of frames in the input sequence. In our current implementation, we use L_2 distance, since it is simple and works well in practice.

Before computing these distances, we often equalize the brightness in the image sequence (based on some background portions that do not change) in order to remove visual discontinuities that would otherwise appear when jumping between different parts of the input video. If the camera also has a small amount of jitter (e.g., from being handheld or shot in high wind conditions), we run video stabilization software over the sequence.

Once the frame-to-frame distances have been computed, we store them in the matrix

$$D_{ij} = \|\mathcal{I}_i - \mathcal{I}_j\|_2, \tag{1}$$

which denotes the L_2 distance between each pair of images $\mathcal{I}_i$ and $\mathcal{I}_j$. During the new video synthesis, the basic idea will be to create transitions from frame i to frame j anytime the successor of i is similar to j—that is, whenever $D_{i+1,j}$ is small.

A simple way to do this is to map these distances to probabilities through an exponential function,

$$P_{ij} \propto \exp(-D_{i+1,j}/\sigma). \tag{2}$$

All the probabilities for a given row of P are normalized so that $\sum_j P_{ij} = 1$. At run time, the next frame to display after frame i is selected according to the distribution of P_{ij}. The σ parameter controls the mapping between L_2 distance and relative probability of taking a given transition. Smaller values of σ emphasize just the very best transitions, while larger values of σ allow for greater variety at the cost of poorer transitions. We typically (but not always) set σ to a small multiple of the average (non-zero) D_{ij} values, so that the likelihood of making a transition at a given frame is fairly low.

3.1 Preserving dynamics

Of course, video textures need to preserve more than just similarity across frames: the dynamics of motion need to be preserved as well. Consider, for example, a swinging pendulum (Figure 2). Each frame

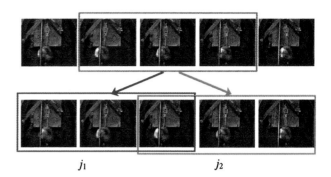

Figure 2 *Finding good transitions in a pendulum sequence.* Frame i in the top row matches both frames j_1 and j_2 of the bottom row very closely. However, of these two possibilities, only frame j_2 comes from a sequence with the correct dynamics. The two possibilities are disambiguated by considering the sequence of frames surrounding i, j_1, and j_2. Frames $i - 1$, i, and $i + 1$ match $j_2 - 1, j_2$, and $j_2 + 1$ but not $j_1 - 1, j_1$, and $j_1 + 1$.

of the left-to-right swing will have a corresponding frame in the right-to-left swing that looks very similar (indicated by the blue arrow in Figure 2). However, transitioning from frame i in the left-to-right swing to a frame that looks very similar to $i + 1$ in the right-to-left swing will create an abrupt and unacceptable change in the pendulum's motion.

One possible way to overcome this problem might be to match velocities (e.g., using optical flow computed at each frame), in addition to matching the visual similarity between frames. However, flow computations can be quite brittle (they can be almost arbitrary in the absence of texture), so we have opted for the following simpler alternative.

We solve the problem of preserving dynamics by requiring that for a frame to be classified as similar to some other frame, not only the frames themselves, but also temporally adjacent frames within some weighted window must be similar to each other. In other words, we match subsequences instead of individual frames. Such a subsequence match can be achieved by filtering the difference matrix with a diagonal kernel with weights $[w_{-m}, \ldots, w_{m-1}]$,

$$D'_{ij} = \sum_{k=-m}^{m-1} w_k D_{i+k,j+k}. \tag{3}$$

In practice, we use $m = 1$ or 2, corresponding to a 2- or 4-tap filter, with binomial weights. (Making the filter even-length allows the decision to transition from some frame i to some other frame j to be determined as much by the similarity of i and $j - 1$ as by the similarity of $i + 1$ and j, removing any asymmetry in this decision.) After filtering and computing the probabilities from the filtered difference matrix, the undesired transitions no longer have high probability.

Figure 3 shows this behavior using two-dimensional images of the D_{ij} and P_{ij} tables for the pendulum sequence of Figure 2. (These images bear some resemblance to those found in earlier papers on the analysis of periodic motion [20, 22, 25].) Here, the new probabilities P'_{ij} are computed from the dynamics-preserving distances D'_{ij} in the same way as P_{ij} were computed from D_{ij} (in equation (2)). In the original unfiltered tables, the periodic nature of the pendulum is readily visible, as is the tendency to match both forward and backward swings. After filtering, only swings in the same direction are matched. (The bright knots are where the pendulum pauses at the ends of its swing, and hence has more self-similarity.) The accompanying video clips show how false jumps are eliminated.

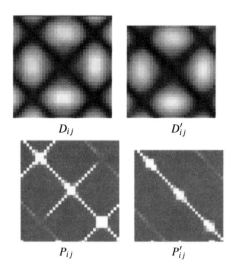

D_{ij} D'_{ij}

P_{ij} P'_{ij}

Figure 3 *Unfiltered and filtered distance matrix and transition probabilities for the clock pendulum sequence.* While the filtering has only a moderate effect on the distance table, the effect becomes pronounced when passed through the exponential function. The filtered images are slightly smaller because the filter kernel has to fit completely into the matrix and thus frames near the beginning and the end are thrown away.

Figure 4 *First and last frame of clock sequence with dead-end.* A hand moves into the field of view at the end. If only instantaneous transition costs are used, the video texture will get stuck in the last frame.

3.2 Avoiding dead ends and anticipating the future

The decision rule we have described so far looks only at the local cost of taking a given transition. It tries to match the appearance and dynamics in the two frames, but gives no consideration to whether the transition might, for example, lead to some portion of the video from which there is no graceful exit—a "dead end," in effect (Figure 4).

Much better results can be achieved by planning ahead—by trying to predict the anticipated (increased) "future cost" of choosing a given transition, given the future transitions that such a move might necessitate.

More precisely, let D''_{ij} be the *anticipated future cost* of a transition from frame $i-1$ to frame j, i.e., a cost that reflects the expected average cost of future transitions. We define D''_{ij} by summing over all future anticipated costs,

$$D''_{ij} = (D'_{ij})^p + \alpha \sum_k P''_{jk} D''_{jk}. \tag{4}$$

Here, p is a constant used to control the tradeoff between taking multiple good (low-cost) transitions versus a single, poorer one. (Higher p favors multiple good transitions; lower p favors a single poorer one.) The constant α is used to control the relative weight of future transitions in the metric. For convergence, we must choose $0 < \alpha < 1$ (in practice, we use $0.99 \leq \alpha \leq 0.999$). The probabil-

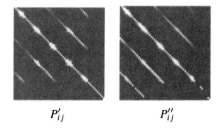

P'_{ij} P''_{ij}

Figure 5 *Probability matrices for clock sequence with dead end.* The original probability matrix causes the player to run to the end and get stuck. The new matrix based on future costs causes the system to "jump out" early, before getting stuck in the dead end.

ities P''_{jk} are defined as before, but using D'' instead of D',

$$P''_{ij} \propto \exp(-D''_{i+1,j}/\sigma). \tag{5}$$

The pair of equations (4) and (5) can be solved using a simple iterative algorithm, i.e., by alternating the evaluation of (4) and (5). Unfortunately, this algorithm is slow to converge.

A faster variant on equation (4) can be derived by making the following observation. As $\sigma \to 0$, the P''_{jk} in equation (5) will tend to 1 for the best transition, and 0 otherwise. We can therefore replace equation (4) with

$$D''_{ij} = (D'_{ij})^p + \alpha \min_k D''_{jk}. \tag{6}$$

This equation is known in the reinforcement learning community as Q-learning [15]. It corresponds to finding the best possible continuation (path) through a graph with associated costs on edges, and has been proven to always converge.

We can further increase the computational efficiency of the algorithm by being selective about which rows in D''_{ij} are updated at each step. Heuristically speaking, the lowest cost path often involves a transition from a frame near the end of the sequence, and the cost of this transition has to be propagated forward. We initialize with $D''_{ij} = (D'_{ij})^p$ and define

$$m_j = \min_k D''_{jk}. \tag{7}$$

Iterating from the last row to the first, we alternately compute

$$D''_{ij} = (D'_{ij})^p + \alpha m_j \tag{8}$$

and update the corresponding m_j entries using equation (7). We repeat these sweeps from back to front until the matrix entries stabilize.

Figure 5 shows the probability tables before and after applying the future cost computation. The original probability matrix causes the player to run to the end and get stuck. The new matrix based on future costs causes the system to "jump out" early, before getting stuck in the dead end.

3.3 Pruning the transitions

While the above techniques can be used to produce perfectly good video textures, it is often desirable to prune the set of allowable transitions, both to save on storage space, and to improve the quality of the resulting video (suppressing non-optimal transitions).

We have examined two pruning paradigms:

1. Select only local maxima in the transition matrix for a given source and/or destination frame.

2. Set all probabilities below some threshold to zero.

The first strategy finds just the "sweet spots" in the matrix of possible transitions between frames, since often a whole neighborhood of frames has good and very similar transitions to some other neighborhood of frames, and only the best such transition needs to be kept. This can be combined with the second strategy, which is applied after the first. Both strategies are generally applied after the future cost computation has been done.

In the case of video loops, which are described in Section 4.1, we use a slightly different pruning strategy. For video loops, we would like to find sequences of frames that can be played continuously with low *average cost*, defined as the sum of all the transition costs D'_{ij}, divided by the total length of the sequence. It is straightforward to show that the average cost of a sequence of transitions is just the weighted average of the average costs of the transitions. Thus, for video loops, after pruning all transitions that are not local minima in the distance matrix, we compute the average cost for each transition, and keep only the best few (typically around 20).

4 Synthesis: Sequencing the video texture

Once the analysis stage has identified good transitions for the video texture, we need to decide in what order to play the video frames. For this *synthesis stage*, we have developed two different algorithms: *random play* and *video loops*.

Random play is very simple to describe. The video texture is begun at any point before the last non-zero-probability transition. After displaying frame i, the next frame j is selected according to P_{ij}. Note that usually, $P_{i,i+1}$ is the largest probability, since $D'_{ii} = 0$ (however, this is not necessarily true when using the anticipated future cost D''_{ij}, which is how the system avoids dead ends). This simple Monte-Carlo approach creates video textures that never repeat exactly and is useful in situations in which the video texture can be created on the fly from the source material.

When a conventional digital video player is used to show video textures, it is necessary to create video loops that do in fact repeat with a fixed period. In this case the video texture can be played in standard "loop mode" by such a player. Generating such loops with the highest possible quality is actually a rather difficult problem, to which we devote the rest of this section.

4.1 Video loops

Consider a loop with a single transition $i \rightarrow j$, from *source frame* i to *destination frame* j, which we call a *primitive loop*. In order for the single transition to create a (non-trivial) cycle we must have $i \geq j$. Thus, the *range* of this loop is $[j, i]$. The *cost* of this loop is the filtered distance between the two frames D'_{ij}.

One or more primitive loops can be combined to create additional cyclic sequences, called *compound loops*. To add one (primitive or compound) loop to another, their ranges must overlap. Otherwise, there is no way to play the first loop after the second has played. The resulting compound loop has a range that is the union of the ranges of the two original loops, and a length and cost that is the sum of the original lengths and costs. Compound loops may contain several repeated instances of the same primitive loop, and can thus be represented by a multiset, where the ordering of the loops is not important.

Forward transitions $i \rightarrow j$, where $i + 1 < j$, can be added into a cycle as well. Although we have an algorithm that efficiently checks whether a multiset of forward and backward jumps is playable, the dynamic programming algorithm described below, which finds the

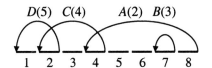

length	A(2)	B(3)	C(4)	D(5)
1		$B(3)$		
2		$B^2(6)$		$D(5)$
3		$B^3(9)$	$C(4)$	
4		$B^4(12)$		$D^2(10)$
5	$A(2)$	$B^5(15)$	$CD(9)$	$CD(9)$
6	$AB(5)$	$AB(5)$	$C^2(8)$	$D^3(15)$
		$\vdots$		

Figure 6 *Dynamic programming table for finding optimal loops.* Each entry lists the best compound loop of a given length that includes the primitive loop listed at the top of the column. Total costs are shown in parentheses.

lowest cost compound loop of a given length, does not work with forward jumps, and we currently have no suitable extension. Our algorithm for creating compound loops of minimal average cost therefore considers only *backward transitions* (transitions $i \rightarrow j$ with $i \geq j$).

In the remainder of this section we present the two algorithms we need to generate *optimal loops*—that is, video loops with minimal cost for a given sequence length. The first algorithm selects a set of transitions that will be used to construct the video loop. The second algorithm orders these transitions in a legal fashion—that is, in an order that can be played without any additional transitions.

4.2 Selecting the set of transitions

The most straightforward way to find the best compound loop of a given length L is to enumerate all multisets of transitions of total length L, to select the legal ones (the compound loops whose ranges form a continuous set), and to keep the best one. Unfortunately, this process is exponential in the number of transitions considered.

Instead, we use a dynamic programming algorithm. Our algorithm constructs a table of L rows, where L is the maximum loop length being considered, and N columns, where N is the number of transitions, or primitive loops, being considered (see Figure 6). The algorithm builds a list of the best compound loop of a given length that contains at least one instance of the primitive loop listed at the top of the column. Each cell in the table lists the transitions in the compound loop and the compound loop's total cost.

The algorithm works by walking through the table, updating cells one row at a time. For each cell, it examines all compound loops of shorter length in that same column, and tries to combine them with compound loops from columns whose primitive loops have ranges that overlap that of the column being considered. (This assures that the created compound loops are actually playable, since the ranges of the constituent compound loops must overlap.) For example, the entry in row 5 column C is obtained by combining the entry in row 3 column C with the entry in row 2 column D, which is possible since primitive loops C and D have ranges that overlap and have lengths that sum to 5. The combination with the lowest total cost becomes the new entry.

For each of the LN cells examined, the algorithm must combine at most $L - 1$ compound loops from its column with at most $N - 1$ entries from the other columns. The total computational complexity of the algorithm is therefore $O(L^2N^2)$, with a space complexity of

$O(LN)$. Note that the full descriptions of the compound loops need not be stored during the computation phase: only backpointers to the originating cells (constituent compound loops) are needed.

4.3 Scheduling the primitive loops

After finding the list of primitive loops in the lowest cost compound loop, the transitions have to be scheduled in some order so that they form a valid compound loop. This is done as follows (we use the scheduling of $\{ABCD\}$ in this example):

1. Schedule the transition that starts at the very end of the sequence as the very first transition to be taken. This would be A in our example.

2. The removal of this transition $i \to j$ may break the remaining primitive loops into one or more sets of continuous ranges. In our example, the removal of A breaks the remaining loops into two continuous-range sets $\{C, D\}$ and $\{B\}$. Frame j is always contained in the first such set and we schedule next any transition from this set whose source frame occurs after j. In our example, C is the only transition that meets these criteria.

3. Repeat the previous step, removing transitions $i \to j$ until there are no more primitive loops left in the first range. In our example, D would be removed next by this repeated step.

4. Schedule any primitive loop in each of the following disjoint ranges, using the algorithm beginning at step 2. In our example, B is the only primitive loop left.

5. Continue with step 2 until all primitive loops are removed.

In our example, the loops are scheduled in the order A, C, D, B.

The computational complexity of this algorithm is quadratic in the number of transitions in the compound loop. The scheduling algorithm can either be run in a deterministic fashion (e.g., taking the first legal transition encountered), or in a stochastic fashion (randomly selecting from the legally available transitions). The latter variant, which utilizes transitions with precisely the same frequency as in the compound loop, is an alternative to the Monte-Carlo sequencing algorithm presented earlier.

5 Rendering

Although we favor transitions that introduce only small discontinuities in the motion, there are cases where no unnoticeable transitions are available in the sequence. This section describes techniques for disguising discontinuities in the video texture, and for blending independently analyzed regions together.

Instead of simply jumping from one frame to another when a transition is made, the images of the sequence before and after the transition can be blended together with standard *cross-fading*: frames from the sequence near the source of the transition are linearly faded out as the frames from the sequence near the destination are faded in. The fade is positioned so that it is halfway complete where the transition was scheduled.

Although cross-fading of the transitions avoids abrupt image changes, it temporarily blurs the image if there is a misalignment between the frames. The transition from sharp to blurry and back again is sometimes noticeable. In some situations, this problem can be addressed by taking very frequent transitions so that several frames are always being cross-faded together, maintaining a more or less constant level of blur.

Our implementation of the cross-fading algorithm supports multiway cross-fades, i.e., more than two subsequences can be blended

together at a time. The algorithm computes a weighted average of all frames participating in a multi-way fade,

$$B(x, y) = \sum_i \alpha_i \, \mathcal{I}_i(x, y), \qquad (9)$$

where the blending weights α_i are derived from the shifted weighting kernels associated with each participating frame, normalized such that $\sum_i \alpha_i = 1$.

Another approach to reducing the blurriness of the transitions is to *morph* the two sequences together, so that common features in the two sets of frames are aligned. The method we use is based on the *de-ghosting* algorithm described by Shum and Szeliski [29] and is also related to automatic morphing techniques [2].

To perform the de-ghosting, we first compute the optical flow between each frame $\mathcal{I}_i$ participating in the multi-way morph and a reference frame $\mathcal{I}_R$ (the reference frame is the one that would have been displayed in the absence of morphing or cross-fading). For every pixel in $\mathcal{I}_R$, we find a *consensus* position for that pixel by taking a weighted average of its corresponding positions in all of the frames $\mathcal{I}_i$ (including $\mathcal{I}_R$). Finally, we use a regular inverse warping algorithm to resample the images such that all pixels end up at their consensus positions. We then blend these images together.

When the video texture consists of several independently analyzed regions, the rendering algorithm blends these regions together smoothly. We use the *feathering* approach commonly used for image mosaics [31], where the contribution of a given region (our analysis regions are typically overlapping) tapers gradually towards its edge.

6 Basic results

The accompanying video clips (available on the CD-ROM, DVD, and Video Conference Proceedings) demonstrate several different video textures produced by the methods described so far. Here, we summarize these basic results; in the next section, we develop some extensions to the basic algorithms and show some additional results.

Candle flame. A 33-second video of a candle flame was turned into four different video textures: one random play texture; and three different video loops, each containing three different primitive loops. One of the video loops repeats every 426 frames. The other two repeat every 241 frames; these each use the same set of three primitive loops, but are scheduled in a different order. In the figure at right, the position of the frame currently being displayed in the original video clip is denoted by the red bar. The red curves show the possible transitions from one frame in the original video clip to another, used by the random play texture.

Clock. This example shows the necessity for both the preservation of dynamics and the future cost computation. The input video sequence shows a clock with a swinging pendulum. Without considering dynamics, a forward-swinging pendulum is likely to match equally well with a backward-swinging frame, causing unnatural jumps in the motion. Adding in the temporal filtering solves this problem. At the end of the input video, a hand moves into the frame. Without the future cost computation, the video texture will reach a dead end, from which no transition to the earlier video will work without a visual jump. The future cost computation solves this problem by increasing the probability of a transition before the hand comes into frame.

Flag. A 38-second video of a flying flag was cyclified using the lowest average cost loop contained in the video. Video textures were created using no fading, cross-fading, and morphing. Cross-fading improves the quality of the transition, at the cost of a small amount of blurring. Morphing works even better at re-

moving the jump without introducing blur, even though the alignment is one stripe off the geometrically correct alignment. The wrong alignment that causes a fold to magically disappear during transition is almost invisible to the unsuspecting observer.

Campfire. A 10-second video of a campfire was cyclified using a single transition. The transition is hardly visible without crossfading, but crossfading over four frames hides it entirely. Although the configuration of the flames never replicates even approximately, the transition is well hidden by the high temporal flicker.

Portrait. A 25-second video of a woman posing for a portrait was turned into a random-play video texture with 20 transitions. Although the frames across the transitions are already quite similar, the morphing performs a subtle alignment of details, such as the eye positions, which hides the transitions

almost entirely. Such video textures could be useful in replacing the static portraits that often appear on web pages.

Waterfall. This example of a waterfall works less well. The original 5 minute video sequence never repeats itself, and yet, unlike the campfire, there is a great deal of continuity between the frames, making it difficult to find any unnoticeable transitions. Our best result was obtained by selecting a 6-

second source clip, and using cross-fading with frequent transitions so that averaging is always performed across multiple subsequences at once. Although the resulting video texture is blurrier than the original video clip, the resulting imagery is still fairly convincing as a waterfall.

Blowing grass. Here is another example that does not work well as a video texture. Like the waterfall sequence, the original 43-second video of blowing grass never repeats itself. Unlike the waterfall sequence, blurring several frames together does not produce acceptable

results. Our automatic morphing also fails to find accurate correspondences in the video frames. The best we could do was to crossfade the transitions (using a 4-second clip as the source), which creates occasional (and objectionable) blurring as the video texture is played.

7 Extensions

In this section, we present several extensions to the basic idea of video textures: *sound synthesis*, in which an audio track is re-rendered along with the video texture; *three-dimensional video textures*, in which view interpolation techniques are applied to simulate 3D motion; *motion factorization*, in which the video frames are factored into separate parts that are analyzed and synthesized independently; and *video-based animation*, in which video texture is modified under interactive control.

7.1 Sound synthesis

Adding sound to video textures is relatively straightforward. We simply take the sound samples associated with each frame and play them back with the video frames selected to be rendered. To mask any popping effects, we use the same multi-way cross-fading algorithm described in Section 5. The resulting sound tracks, at least in the videos for which we have tried this (*Waterfall* and *Bonfire*), sound very natural.

7.2 Three-dimensional video textures

Video textures can be combined with traditional image-based rendering algorithms such as view interpolation [5, 18, 24] to obtain *three-dimensional video textures*. These are similar to the 3D video-based characters demonstrated in several video-based view interpolation systems [16, 19, 23], except that they are based on synthetic video textures instead of captured video clips.

3D Portrait. We created a three-dimensional video texture from three videos of a smiling woman, taken simultaneously from three different viewing angles about 20 degrees apart. We used the center camera to extract and synthesize the video texture, and the first still from each camera to estimate a 3D depth map, shown here.

(As an alternative, we could have used some other 3D image-based modeling technique [21].) We then masked out the background using background subtraction (a clear shot of the background was taken before filming began). To generate each new frame in the 3D video animation, we mapped a portion of the video texture onto the 3D surface, rendered it from a novel viewpoint, and then combined it with the flat image of the background warped to the correct location, using the algorithm described in [26].

7.3 Motion factorization

For certain kinds of more complex scenes, we can divide the original video into independently moving parts, and analyze each one separately. This kind of *motion factorization* decreases the number of frame samples necessary to synthesize an interesting video texture. Interdependencies between different parts of the synthesized frames could later be added with supplemental constraints.

The simplest form of motion factorization is to divide the frame into independent regions of motion, either manually or automatically.

Swings. In this example, the video of two children on swings is manually divided into two halves: one for each swing. These parts are analyzed and synthesized independently, then recombined into the final video texture. The overall video texture is significantly superior to

the best video texture that could be generated using the entire video frame.

Balloons. For this example, we developed an automatic segmentation algorithm that separates the original video stream into regions that move independently. We first compute the variance of each pixel across time, threshold this image to obtain connected regions of motion, and use connected component  labeling followed by a morphological dilation to obtain the five region labels (shown as color regions in this still). The independent regions are then analyzed and synthesized separately, and then recombined using feathering.

Motion factorization can be further extended to extract independent *video sprites* from a video sequence. For instance, we can use background subtraction or blue-screen matting [30] to identify connected portions of the video image that change with time and to extract these portions as foreground elements with alpha. To create a video sprite, we first factor out the positional information by placing the element's centroid at the origin in each frame. We call this *registering* the element. We also store the *velocity* of the sprite at each frame, defined as the difference in the unregistered elements' centroid positions. In the analysis phase the distance between frames is computed as a linear combination of the registered elements' colors, alphas, and moving directions and speeds. The synthesis phase is performed by utilizing the optimal transitions computed by the analysis and adding back in the stored velocities across the transitions.

Fish. We used background subtraction to create a video sprite of a fish, starting from 5 minutes of video of a fish in a tank. Unfortunately, fish are uncooperative test subjects who frequently visit the walls of the fish tank, where they are hard to extract from the scene because of reflec-  tions in the glass. We therefore used as source material only those pieces of video where the fish is swimming freely. (This requires generalizing the future cost computation to handle the possibility of multiple dead ends, but is otherwise straightforward.)

Using this technique, the fish swims freely in two-dimensional space. Ideally, we would like to constrain its motion—for example, to the boundaries of a fish tank. The next section describes approaches to this problem.

7.4 Video-based animation

Instead of using visual smoothness as the only criterion for generating video, we can also add some user-controlled terms to the error function in order to influence the selection of frames.

The simplest form of such user control is to interactively select the set of frames S in the sequence that are used for synthesis. In this case, we perform the analysis phase as before, optionally pruning the list of transitions. In the synthesis stage, however, we recompute the probabilities of the transitions, using a modified form of equation (5), which takes into account the distance from the destination of the transition to the set of user-specified frames S:

$$P_{ij} \propto \exp\left(-(D''_{i+1,j}/\sigma + w\,\text{distance}(j,S))\right) \quad (10)$$

Here, w trades off the weight of the user-control against the smoothness of the transitions.

Runner. We took 3 minutes of video of a runner on a treadmill, starting at a slow jog and then gradually speeding up to a fast run. As the user moves a slider selecting a certain region of the video (the black region of the slider in the fig-  ure), the synthesis attempts to select frames that remain within that region, while at the same time using only fairly smooth transitions to jump forward or backward in time. The user can therefore control the speed of the runner by moving the slider back and forth, and the runner makes natural-looking transitions between the different gaits.

We expect it will be possible to extend this type of *parametric motion control* to other types of movements as well, thereby allowing much greater directorial control in the post-processing phase of video production.

Watering can. As another example, we took a 15-second clip of a watering can pouring water into a birdbath. The central portion of this video, which shows the water pouring as a continuous stream, makes a very good video texture. We can therefore shorten or extend the pouring sequence by using the same technique as we did for the  runner, only advancing the slider automatically at a faster or slower speed. Thus, the same mechanism can be used to achieve a natural-looking *time compression* or *dilation* in a video sequence.

Mouse-controlled fish. Instead of directly specifying a preferred range of frames, we can select frames based on other criteria. For example, in order to interactively guide the path of  the fish presented earlier with a mouse, we could give preference to frames in which the fish's video sprite has a certain desired velocity vector.

In particular, if x is the current position of the fish, y the desired position of the fish (say the mouse location), and v_i the velocity at frame i, then we can use the following distance function:

$$D'_{ij} = w_1\,\|\mathcal{I}_i - \mathcal{I}_j\|_2 + w_2\,E(v_i, v_j) + w_3\,E(y - x, v_j) \quad (11)$$

where w_1, w_2, w_3 are user-specified weights, $\|\mathcal{I}_i - \mathcal{I}_j\|_2$ is a modified image distance metric that takes into account the difference in the two image sprites' alpha channels, and $E(v, v')$ is a "velocity error function". In our current implementation, E is proportional to the angle between v and v'.

In the runner example (Equation 10), in order to achieve interactive performance we added the extra error term to D''_{ij} directly, instead of adding the term to D'_{ij} and re-running the precomputed future cost computation. It turns out that this technique does not work so well for directed movement: the system has trouble finding good sequences on the fly that will avoid later bad transitions. To do this right, a larger-scale anticipated future cost computation is required. We therefore compute the future cost D''_{ij} from D'_{ij} using the techniques described in Section 3.2. Unfortunately, we have to do this precomputation for all possible values of E. In practice, we perform the precomputation for a set of eight different directions and discretize the user input to one of these directions on the fly, choosing the precomputed probability table accordingly.

Fish tank. The final example we show is a complete fish tank, populated with artificial fish sprites. The tank includes two sets of bubbles, two independently swaying plants, and a small number of independently moving fish. The fish can also be scripted to follow a path (here, the SIGGRAPH "2000" logo), using the same techniques described for the mouse-controlled fish.

8 Discussion and future work

In his 1966 science-fiction short story, "Light of Other Days," Bob Shaw describes a material called *slow glass*, which traps photons coming into it, and emits them a year or two later [28]. Slow glass can be exposed in scenic locations (such as a woodland lake) and then placed on people's walls, where it gives a three-dimensional illusion of having a scenic view of your own.

Video textures (which were partially inspired by this story) share some of the characteristic of slow glass, but also differ in important ways. Like slow glass, they are an attempt to capture the inherent dynamic characteristics of a scene. (Using a video camera array to capture a time-varying light field [17] would be another approach, but capturing enough data to play back for a year would be prohibitively expensive.) Video textures attempt to capture the inherent *characteristics* of a dynamic scene or event, without necessarily capturing all of the stochastically-varying detail inherent in a particular segment of time.

Video textures also have the potential to give the artist creative control over the appearance of the dynamic events they are depicting. By capturing a wide variety of similar looking video that is periodic or quasi-periodic, the user can then select which portions to use, and blend smoothly between different parameter settings. The video texture analysis and synthesis software takes care of making these transitions smooth and creating segments of the desired duration.

How well do video textures work? For motions that are smooth and repetitive or quasi-repetitive, such as the kids on the swing, the candle flame, the swaying balloons, the runner, and the smiling woman, the illusion works quite well. For complex stochastic phenomena with little discernible structure, like the water pouring out of the can, it also works well. We run into trouble when the phenomena are complex but also highly structured, like the grass blowing in the wind (we have also thus far failed at creating a convincing video texture for waves on a beach). Other highly structured phenomena like full-body human motion will also likely fail, unless we start using some higher-level motion and structure analysis.

Our work suggests a number of important areas for future work:

Better distance metrics. To create video textures, we need a distance metric that reliably quantifies the perceived discontinuity of a frame transition. For most of our examples we used a simple L_2 distance between images. Finding better features and distance functions will be crucial for improving the quality of video textures and for increasing their applicability. We have some initial promising results applying a wavelet-based distance metric [14] to some of our sequences. We have also improved the metric for the fish example by modeling it as a linear combination of several features and learning the coefficients from hand-labeled training transitions.

Better blending. To suppress residual visual discontinuities, we are currently using blending and morphing. We would like to explore techniques that allow for blending and morphing separately in different frequency bands both in space and time, perhaps using multiresolution splining techniques [4].

Maintaining variety. A significant problem with generating long (infinite) sequences of video from the same set of frames is that, after a while, the algorithm will find some optimal paths and more or less play the same series of frames over and over again. This requires that in addition to σ, which controls randomness, we define a parameter that penalizes a lack of variety in the generated sequences. Such a parameter would enforce that most (if not all) of the frames of the given input sequence are sometimes played and probabilistically vary the generated order of frames.

Better tools for creative control. Another important area of future research will be the addition of more creative control over video textures. An alternative to interactively controlling the parameters in a video animation would be to specify control points or keyframes as in conventional keyframe animation. For this, we need to develop optimization techniques that generate smoothly playing video textures that obey user-supplied constraints. Better video animation control would enable us to generate complex scenes such as crowds; the animation controller could also be enhanced to include behavioral aspects such as flocking.

While many areas remain to be explored, we believe that video textures provide an interesting new medium with many potential applications, ranging from simple video portraits to realistic video synthesis. Video textures are just one example of the more general class of techniques we call video-based rendering. By re-using real-world video footage (in a manner analogous to image-based rendering), we can achieve a degree of photorealism and naturalness hard to match with traditional computer graphics techniques. We hope that this work will spur further research in this field, and that video textures, along with video-based rendering in general, will ultimately become an essential part of the repertoire of computer graphics techniques.

References

[1] Z. Bar-Joseph. Statistical learning of multi-dimensional textures. Master's thesis, The Hebrew University of Jerusalem, June 1999.

[2] D. Beymer. Feature correspondence by interleaving shape and texture computations. In *IEEE Computer Society Conference on Computer Vision and Pattern Recognition (CVPR'96)*, pages 921–928, San Francisco, California, June 1996.

[3] C. Bregler, M. Covell, and M. Slaney. Video rewrite: Driving visual speech with audio. *Computer Graphics (SIGGRAPH'97)*, pages 353–360, August 1997.

[4] P. J. Burt and E. H. Adelson. A multiresolution spline with applications to image mosaics. *ACM Transactions on Graphics*, 2(4):217–236, October 1983.

[5] S. E. Chen. QuickTime VR – an image-based approach to virtual environment navigation. *Computer Graphics (SIGGRAPH'95)*, pages 29–38, August 1995.

[6] J. De Bonet. Multiresolution sampling procedure for analysis and synthesis of texture images. *Computer Graphics (SIGGRAPH'97)*, pages 361–368, August 1997.

[7] P. Debevec *et al.*, editors. *Image-Based Modeling, Rendering, and Lighting*, SIGGRAPH'99 Course 39, August 1999.

[8] P. E. Debevec, C. J. Taylor, and J. Malik. Modeling and rendering architecture from photographs: A hybrid geometry- and image-based approach. *Computer Graphics (SIGGRAPH'96)*, pages 11–20, August 1996.

[9] A. A. Efros and T. K. Leung. Texture synthesis by non-parametric sampling. In *Seventh International Conference on Computer Vision (ICCV'99)*, pages 1033–1038, Kerkyra, Greece, September 1999.

[10] A. Finkelstein, C. E. Jacobs, and D. H. Salesin. Multiresolution video. *Proceedings of SIGGRAPH 96*, pages 281–290, August 1996. ISBN 0-201-94800-1. Held in New Orleans, Louisiana.

[11] W. T. Freeman, E. H. Adelson, and D. J. Heeger. Motion without movement. *Computer Graphics (Proceedings of SIGGRAPH 91)*, 25(4):27–30, July 1991.

[12] D. J. Heeger and J. R. Bergen. Pyramid-based texture analysis/synthesis. *Proceedings of SIGGRAPH 95*, pages 229–238, August 1995.

[13] *Workshop on Image-Based Modeling and Rendering*, Stanford University, March 1998. http://graphics.stanford.edu/workshops/ibr98/.

[14] C. E. Jacobs, A. Finkelstein, and D. H. Salesin. Fast multiresolution image querying. *Proceedings of SIGGRAPH 95*, pages 277–286, August 1995.

[15] L. P. Kaelbling, M. L. Littman, and A. W. Moore. Reinforcement learning: A survey. *Journal of Artificial Intelligence Research*, 4, 1996.

[16] T. Kanade, P. W. Rander, and P. J. Narayanan. Virtualized reality: constructing virtual worlds from real scenes. *IEEE MultiMedia Magazine*, 1(1):34–47, Jan-March 1997.

[17] M. Levoy and P. Hanrahan. Light field rendering. In *Computer Graphics Proceedings, Annual Conference Series*, pages 31–42, Proc. SIGGRAPH'96 (New Orleans), August 1996. ACM SIGGRAPH.

[18] L. McMillan and G. Bishop. Plenoptic modeling: An image-based rendering system. *Computer Graphics (SIGGRAPH'95)*, pages 39–46, August 1995.

[19] S. Moezzi *et al.* Reality modeling and visualization from multiple video sequences. *IEEE Computer Graphics and Applications*, 16(6):58–63, November 1996.

[20] S. A. Niyogi and E. H. Adelson. Analyzing and recognizing walking figures in xyt. In *IEEE Computer Society Conference on Computer Vision and Pattern Recognition (CVPR'94)*, pages 469–474, Seattle, Washington, June 1994.

[21] F. Pighin, J. Hecker, D. Lischinski, D. H. Salesin, and R. Szeliski. Synthesizing realistic facial expressions from photographs. In *Computer Graphics (SIGGRAPH'98) Proceedings*, pages 75–84, Orlando, July 1998. ACM SIGGRAPH.

[22] R. Polana and R. C. Nelson. Detection and recognition of periodic, nonrigid motion. *International Journal of Computer Vision*, 23(3):261–282, 1997.

[23] S. Pollard *et al.* View synthesis by trinocular edge matching and transfer. In *British Machine Vision Conference (BMVC98)*, Southampton, England, September 1998.

[24] S. M. Seitz and C. M. Dyer. View morphing. In *Computer Graphics Proceedings, Annual Conference Series*, pages 21–30, Proc. SIGGRAPH'96 (New Orleans), August 1996. ACM SIGGRAPH.

[25] S. M. Seitz and C. R. Dyer. View invariant analysis of cyclic motion. *International Journal of Computer Vision*, 25(3):231–251, December 1997.

[26] J. Shade, S. Gortler, L.-W. He, and R. Szeliski. Layered depth images. In *Computer Graphics (SIGGRAPH'98) Proceedings*, pages 231–242, Orlando, July 1998. ACM SIGGRAPH.

[27] J. Shade, D. Lischinski, D. Salesin, T. DeRose, and J. Snyder. Hierarchical images caching for accelerated walkthroughs of complex environments. In *Computer Graphics (SIGGRAPH'96) Proceedings*, pages 75–82, Proc. SIGGRAPH'96 (New Orleans), August 1996. ACM SIGGRAPH.

[28] B. Shaw. Light of other days. In *Other Days, Other Eyes*. Ace Books, New York, 1972. (also published in *Analog* and various sci-fi anthologies).

[29] H.-Y. Shum and R. Szeliski. Construction of panoramic mosaics with global and local alignment. *International Journal of Computer Vision*, 36(2):101–130, February 2000.

[30] A. R. Smith and J. F. Blinn. Blue screen matting. In *Computer Graphics Proceedings, Annual Conference Series*, pages 259–268, Proc. SIGGRAPH'96 (New Orleans), August 1996. ACM SIGGRAPH.

[31] R. Szeliski and H.-Y. Shum. Creating full view panoramic image mosaics and texture-mapped models. In *Computer Graphics (SIGGRAPH'97) Proceedings*, pages 251–258, Los Angeles, August 1997. ACM SIGGRAPH.

[32] J. Torborg and J. T. Kajiya. Talisman: Commodity realtime 3D graphics for the PC. In *Computer Graphics Proceedings, Annual Conference Series*, pages 353–363, Proc. SIGGRAPH'96 (New Orleans), August 1996. ACM SIGGRAPH.

Escherization

Craig S. Kaplan[1]   *David H. Salesin*[1,2]

[1]University of Washington   [2]Microsoft Corporation

Abstract

This paper introduces and presents a solution to the "Escherization" problem: given a closed figure in the plane, find a new closed figure that is similar to the original and tiles the plane. Our solution works by using a simulated annealer to optimize over a parameterization of the "isohedral" tilings, a class of tilings that is flexible enough to encompass nearly all of Escher's own tilings, and yet simple enough to be encoded and explored by a computer. We also describe a representation for isohedral tilings that allows for highly interactive viewing and rendering. We demonstrate the use of these tools—along with several additional techniques for adding decorations to tilings—with a variety of original ornamental designs.

CR Categories: I.3.5 [Computational Geometry and Object Modeling]: Geometric algorithms, languages and systems; I.3.8 [Computer Graphics]: Applications; J.5 [Arts and Humanities]: Fine arts; J.6 [Computer-Aided Engineering]: Computer-aided design (CAD).

Keywords: Tilings, tesselations, morphing, optimization, simulated annealing, Escher

1 Introduction

Tilings are as old as civilization. Our ancestors' earliest experience with tilings probably arose out of the quest for regularity in the construction of walls, floors, and ceilings. This regularity could at once simplify the task of construction and lend a sense of order and uniformity to the objects being constructed.

Historical uses of ornamental tilings abound; numerous examples from as early as the twelfth century survive today [15]. Perhaps the most renowned example is the Alhambra palace in Granada, Spain. The Moors who built the Alhambra became masters of geometric ornament, covering every surface of the palace with intricate tilings of astonishing beauty.

By the time the Dutch graphic artist M.C. Escher began studying the regular division of the plane in the first half of the twentieth century, tiling as an art form had passed mostly into history, to be replaced by the growing development of a systematic mathematical theory. Escher was deeply inspired by the interlocking geometric forms of the Moors but felt it a pity that they were forbidden by their religion from depicting real-world objects in their art [20]. He undertook as a personal quest the reinvention of geometric art, substituting easily-recognized motifs such as animal forms for the purity of the Moorish rosettes and poly-

gons. Escher arrived at each of his interlocking animal forms after a great deal of tinkering and manipulation. Over the years, he became more proficient at inventing new arrangements of motifs, developing his own "layman's theory" of tilings to track the ground he had covered and suggest new directions for exploration. He managed over his career to produce a notebook with more than a hundred of these ingenious, playful designs [18].

Figure 2 Escher's Escher Escherized.

Taking our inspiration from Escher and his elegant work, we attempt to solve the following problem in this paper:

> **Problem** ("ESCHERIZATION"): Given a closed plane figure S (the "goal shape"), find a new closed figure T such that:
> 1. T is as close as possible to S; and
> 2. copies of T fit together to form a tiling of the plane.

This problem is tricky in that for a sufficiently large perturbation of the goal shape, it is always possible to find a tiling in a trivial sense. (Let T, for example, be a square.) We need to formalize the measure of "closeness" in such a way that it both preserves the "essence" of the goal shape S and at the same time produces new shapes T that are known to tile.

This paper presents a solution to the Escherization problem that is able to find reasonable-looking tiles for many real-world shapes (see, for example, the "Escherized" version of Escher's own self-portrait, shown in Figure 2). Creating such tilings requires solving a number of subproblems, which we discuss in this paper. The first difficulty is in selecting a set of tiling types that are both simple enough to be encoded and manipulated by a computer, and flexible enough to express most of the ornamental designs we would like to create. A second problem is in finding consistent and complete parameterizations for these tilings—that is, parameterizations that are always guaranteed to produce correct tilings of a given type ("consistent") and that are furthermore capable of producing all tilings of that type ("complete"). Though fundamental to the analysis of patterns and tilings, to our knowledge this problem has never before been addressed for the types of tilings we consider. A third problem is in choosing a good measure of closeness. A fourth challenge is in designing an optimizer to search over all possible tiling types, their parameterizations, and tile shapes in order to find a good approximation to the goal tile. A fifth problem is in creating a representation for these tilings that allows for highly interactive viewing and editing. A final problem is in decorating and rendering the resulting tiles.

Unlike most research projects in computer graphics, this one is motivated more by intellectual curiosity than by practical import. Nevertheless, a solution to the Escherization problem does have certain applications in the real world. Tilings are of course useful as floor and wall coverings. In manufacturing, the outlines of tiles can be cut repeatedly out of stone using a process known as water-jet cutting. Automatically-designed tilings could just as easily be carved out of wood or even sewn into a quilt. This suggests a further application, proposed by Chow [5]: a tiling program could be used to lay out copies of a part to be cut out a sheet of some material. If the copies are arranged in a tiling, they can be cut from the sheet without creating any waste material (except around the outer edges of the sheet).

1.1 Related Work

Several authors have explored the possibility of creating ornament in various forms by computer. A paper at the second annual SIGGRAPH conference featured a system for drawing figures constrained to the seventeen planar symmetry groups [1]. More recently, Glassner examined the synthesis of frieze patterns [8] and aperiodic tilings [9, 10], which can be used for generating ornaments for bands and for the 2-D plane, respectively. Wong et al. investigated algorithms for computer-generated floral ornament [21] and surveyed other previous work in creating these kinds of ornamental designs.

In addition, software created specifically for allowing users to construct tilings of the plane has been around for at least twenty years. Chow had a very successful FORTRAN program [4] that let the user input the portion of the tile that is independent, i.e., not expressed in terms of some other portion of the tile. The program then filled in the remaining part of the tile and replicated it in the plane. Reptiles [14], by Huson and Friedrichs, is a complex system that understands a large class of mathematically-interesting tilings. Reptiles has since been expanded into Funtiles, an even more sophisticated tool that can create tilings in non-Euclidean geometries. Lee's TesselMania! is a marvelous program for giving children an understanding of symmetry and tilings.

A number of individuals are actively designing new Escher-like tilings, aided by illustration software. Crompton [6] has compiled an extensive list of recent contributions to tesselation-based art.

Still, none of these earlier efforts attempt in any way to find tilings automatically whose tiles approximate a particular goal shape, the work we describe here.

1.2 Overview

We begin with background on the mathematical theory of tilings, leading into a description of the "isohedral" tilings (Section 2), on which the rest of this work is based. We then address each of the remaining subproblems in turn: parameterizing the isohedral tilings (Section 3); developing a measure of "closeness" between two tiles (Section 4); designing an optimizer for finding the best tiles (Section 5); representing the resulting tilings for efficient editing and viewing (Section 6); and decorating and rendering the tiles (Section 7). We end with a discussion of our results (Section 8) and ideas for future work (Section 9).

2 Mathematical theory of tilings

In this section, we present background on only the parts of tiling theory necessary to understand the research work presented in the rest of this paper. Readers seeking a more in-depth analysis of tilings should consult the highly accessible treatise on tiling theory, Grünbaum and Shephard's *Tilings and Patterns* [11].

2.1 Tilings

A *tiling of the plane* is a collection of shapes, called *tiles*, that cover the plane without any gaps or overlaps. That is, every point in the plane is contained in at least one tile, and the intersection of any two tiles is a set with zero area (we regard tiles as closed sets, and allow them to intersect along their boundaries).

Given certain natural analytic restrictions on the shapes of tiles [11, sec 3.2], the intersection of any set of tiles will either be empty, a point, or a simple curve. When the intersection is a curve, we call that curve a *tiling edge*. When the intersection is a point, in which case that point will necessarily be a meeting place of at least three tiles, we call that point a *tiling vertex*.

Every tile can be decomposed, based on intersections with its neighbours, into a sequence of tiling vertices joined by tiling edges. These must be distinguished from the vertices and edges of the *tiles*

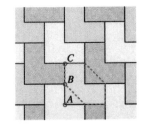

(if the tiles are in fact polygons), which we will call *shape vertices* and *shape edges*, respectively, to differentiate them from their tiling counterparts. Although the features of the tiling occupy the same positions as the features of the tiles, they may break down differently. For the blue tile in the tiling on the right, A is a shape vertex but not a tiling vertex, B is a tiling vertex but not a shape vertex, and C is both a tiling vertex and a shape vertex. We will also make use of the *tiling polygon*, the polygon formed by joining the tiling vertices that lie on a given tile, shown here as a red dashed line. This polygon is important in describing the structure of the tiling.

In many of the tilings we see every day on walls and streets, the tiles all have the same shape. If any given tile in a tiling is congruent to any other through a rigid motion of the plane, we say that the tiling is *monohedral*. Similarly, a *k-hedral* tiling is one in which every tile is congruent to one of k different prototiles. When $k = 2$, we also use the term *dihedral* to describe the tiling.

2.2 Isohedral tilings

A *symmetry* of a figure in the plane is a rigid motion of the plane that maps the figure onto itself. Every figure in the plane necessarily has an associated set of symmetries, even if it is just the trivial set containing the "identity" motion. It is easy to see that the symmetries of a figure have a natural group structure under composition of

Figure 3 Both of these tilings are monohedral, but the one on the left is isohedral and the one on the right is not. The reflection that maps tile A onto tile B is not a symmetry of the tiling on the right.

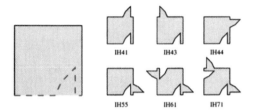

Figure 4 An isohedral tiling type imposes a set of adjacency constraints on the tiling edges of a tile. When the bottom edge of the square deforms into the dashed line, the other edges must respond in some way to preserve the tiling. The six resulting tiles here are from six different isohedral types.

rigid motions. The set of symmetries of a figure is therefore called the *symmetry group* of that figure. If the symmetry group of a figure contains linearly independent translations, we call that figure *periodic*.

For two congruent tiles A and B in a tiling, there will be some rigid motion of the plane that carries one onto the other (there may in fact be several). A somewhat special case occurs when the rigid motion is also a symmetry of the tiling. In this case, when A and B are brought into correspondence, the rest of the tiling will map onto itself as well. We then say that A and B are *transitively equivalent*.

Transitive equivalence is an equivalence relation that partitions the tiles into *transitivity classes*. When a tiling has only one transitivity class, we call the tiling *isohedral*. More generally, a k-isohedral tiling has k transitivity classes. An isohedral tiling is one in which a single prototile can cover the entire plane through repeated application of rigid motions from the tiling's symmetry group. Note that an isohedral tiling must be monohedral, though the converse is not true [11, p. 31], as Figure 3 illustrates.

We use the isohedral tilings as a mathematical basis for our exploration of computer generation of ornamental tilings. They achieve a satisfying balance between flexibility and convenience. On the one hand, they are capable of representing a wide subjective range of tilings. Of all the monohedral tilings in Escher's notebook, only one is not isohedral (the exception is based on a special mono- but not isohedral tiling first shown to Escher by Roger Penrose). Moreover, in Escher's dihedral tilings, tiles of each of the two motifs can be paired up to form a single "supertile" that tiles that plane isohedrally. On the other hand, the isohedral tilings can be classified into a small number of symbolically-encoded families (the following subsections give more details about this classification). It is therefore fairly easy to create a system to manipulate and render them.

2.3 Isohedral families

By definition, an isohedral tiling is bound by a set of geometric constraints: congruences between tiles must be symmetries of the tiling. Grünbaum and Shephard showed that those geometric constraints can be equated with a set of *combinatoric* constraints expressing the adjacency relationship between edges of a tile. They proved that these constraints yield a division of the isohedral tilings into precisely 93 distinct *types* or *families*,[1] referred to individually as IH1, ..., IH93 and collectively as IH [11, sec. 6.2]. Each family encodes information about how a tile's shape is constrained by the adjacencies it is forced to maintain with its neighbours. A deformation in a tiling edge is counterbalanced by deformations in other edges; which edges respond and in what way is dependent on the tiling type, as shown in Figure 4.

Isohedral tilings have the property that if you list the valence of each tiling vertex as you move around any given tile, the list will be consistent across all tiles in the tiling. This list is fundamental to the topological structure of the tiling and is called its *topological type*.

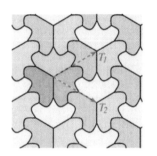

For example, the topological type of IH16, shown on the left, is 3^6, since there are 6 different tiling vertices around each tile, each of valence 3. Every isohedral tiling belongs to one of eleven different topological types [11, sec. 2.7].

In any periodic tiling, it is possible to identify a collection of tiles that together cover the plane using only the translations from the tiling's symmetry group. Any such collection that is connected and minimal in size is called a *translational unit* of the tiling. Within a translational unit, all tiles must have different orientations, which are referred to as the *aspects* of the tiling. IH16 has three aspects, shown in varying shades of blue above. These three tiles comprise one possible translational unit, with translation vectors T_1 and T_2.

2.4 Incidence symbols

The adjacency constraints between the tiling edges of a tile are summarized by an *incidence symbol*. Given a rendering of a tiling, the incidence symbol can be constructed in a straightforward way.

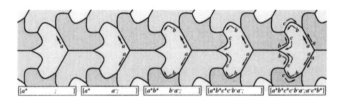

Figure 5 Five steps in the derivation of a tiling's incidence symbol.

Figure 5 shows five steps in the derivation of the incidence symbol for our sample tiling. To obtain the first part of the incidence symbol, pick an arbitrary tiling edge as a starting point, assign that edge a single-letter name, and draw an arrow pointing counterclockwise around the tile (step 1). We then copy the edge's label to all other edges of the tile related to it through a symmetry of the tiling (step 2). Should the edge get mapped to itself with a reversal of direction, it is given a double-headed arrow and becomes undirected. We then proceed counterclockwise around the tile to the next unlabeled edge (if there is one) and repeat the process (step 3). The first half of the symbol is obtained by reading off the assigned edge

---

[1] In tiling theory, seemingly arbitrary numbers like 93 are not uncommon; enumerations of families of tilings tend to have sets of constraints that collapse certain cases and fracture others.

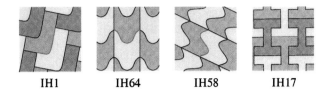

IH1   IH64   IH58   IH17

Figure 6 Examples (from left to right) of **J**, **U**, **S** and **I** edges. In each case, the tiling edge with the given shape is highlighted in red.

names (step 4). A directed edge is superscripted with a sign indicating the coherence of its arrow with the traversal direction. Here, a plus sign is used for a counterclockwise arrow and a minus sign for a clockwise arrow.

The second half of an incidence symbol records how, for each different name, a tiling edge of that name is related to the corresponding edge of the tile adjacent to it. To derive this part of the symbol, we copy the labeling of the tile to its neighbours (step 5). Then, for each unique edge letter assigned in the first step, we write down the edge letter adjacent to it in the tiling. If the original edge was directed, we also write down a plus or minus sign, depending on whether edge direction is respectively preserved or reversed across the edge. A minus sign is used if the arrows on the two sides of an edge are pointing in the same direction and a plus sign is used otherwise. For the running example, the incidence symbol turns out to be $[a^+b^+c^+c^-b^-a^-; a^-c^+b^+]$. Note that the incidence symbol is not unique; edges can be renamed and a different starting point can be chosen. But it can easily be checked whether two incidence symbols refer to the same isohedral type.

Every isohedral type is fully described in terms of a topological type and an incidence symbol. Enumerating all possible topological types and incidence symbols and then eliminating the ones that do not result in valid tilings or that are trivial renamings of other symbols leads to the classification given by Grünbaum and Shephard.

2.5 Tile shapes

Within a single isohedral type, tilings are distinguished from each other by their shapes, consisting of the positions of the tiling vertices and the shapes of the curves that join them. In the next section, we will address the question of finding, for each isohedral type, a parameterization of the tiling vertices that yields all and only those tiling polygons compatible with the type. To our knowledge, this problem has not been previously explored.

On the other hand, the constraints on the shapes of tiling edges are simple to describe. Although the underlying choice of how to represent a "curve" is left open, the tiling's symmetries imply a large reduction in the tiling edges' degrees of freedom. These constraints can be extracted directly from the tiling's incidence symbol. We enumerate four cases for the structure of a tiling edge. For each case, Figure 6 gives a tiling with such an edge.

If some directed edge is adjacent to itself without a flip, then a tile's neighbour across that edge is adjacent through a half-turn. This rotation forces the edge shape to itself be symmetric through a half-turn about its centre. We call such an edge an **S** edge as a visual mnemonic. Only half of an **S** edge is free; the other half must complete the rotational symmetry.

An undirected edge must look the same starting from either end, meaning it must have a line of mirror symmetry through its midpoint. If the edge is adjacent to an edge other than itself, it is free to take on any curve with this mirror symmetry. We call it a **U** edge. Again, only half of a **U** edge is free.

If an undirected edge is adjacent to itself, or if a directed edge is adjacent to itself with a change in sign, that edge must have both **S** symmetry and **U** symmetry. The only shape that has both is a straight line, leading us to call such an edge an **I** edge.

The remaining case is when a directed edge is adjacent to some other directed edge. Such an edge is free to take on any shape, and we call it a **J** edge.

Note also that if an edge x is adjacent to an edge y, then x and y have the same shape (even though they have different names). In this case, we need only specify one tiling edge, since the other is entirely constrained to it. Thus, the tiling edges of IH16 can be summarized by one curve: the shape of the edge labeled b. Edges labeled a are **I** edges and have no degrees of freedom, and edges labeled c are constrained to b.

3 Parameterizing the isohedral tilings

Like the shape vertices, tiling vertices cannot move independently of each other. Moving one tiling vertex forces the others to move to preserve the tiling. The exact nature of this movement depends on the tiling type in question. The incidence symbol for a tiling type implies a set of constraints on the tiling polygon's edge lengths and interior angles. Any tile of that type will have a tiling polygon that obeys those constraints.

If we hope to build a generative model of isohedral tilings, it is not sufficient to merely recognize the constraints on the shape vertices: we need a way to explicitly navigate the space of legal tiling polygons. For each isohedral type we need a parameterization of the tiling vertices for tilings of that type. The parameterization should be *complete*, in the sense that for every legal configuration of tiling vertices, there is a set of parameters that generates that configuration. We also require it to be *consistent*, in the sense that every set of parameters generates legal tiling vertices. To our knowledge, no tiling vertex parameterizations have ever been given for IH. They represent a nontrivial extension to the table of information about IH found in Grünbaum and Shephard.

We have developed a set of consistent and complete parameterizations for the isohedral types (of course, the history of tiling theory has experienced its share of imperfect analyses [11, Sec. 6.6]). They were derived by determining angle and length constraints from the incidence symbols and parameterizing the unconstrained degrees of freedom. In some cases, parameterizations are shared between tiling types: nine tiling types have squares as tiling polygons (implying a parameterization with zero parameters), and seven have parallelograms (implying two parameters). These easy parameterizations are balanced by tiling types with one-of-a-kind structure that can take some thought to derive. In all, the 93 isohedral types require 45 different parameterizations. Diagrams of the parameterizations appear in full in Figures 9 and 10.

To give the flavor of these parameterizations, here is a sketch of the derivation for our running example, IH16 (see Figure 7). We begin by placing at least enough tiles to completely surround one central tile, and marking up the tiles with the labels from the tiling's incidence symbol. Now consider the situation at tiling vertex A. This vertex is surrounded by three copies of the same angle from three different tiles, namely $\angle FAB$, the angle between the a edges. It follows that the tiling polygon must have a 120° angle at that vertex. The same observation applies to vertices C and E. Thus, $\triangle FAB$, $\triangle BCD$, and $\triangle DEF$ are all 120° isosceles triangles. Because these isosceles triangles can be constructed given only the edge opposite the 120° angle, the tiling polygon depends entirely on the "skeleton" triangle $\triangle BDF$. Furthermore, the incidence symbol reveals a line of bilateral symmetry in the tile across $\overline{AD}$, forcing $\triangle BDF$ to be isosceles. The only degrees of freedom left in the

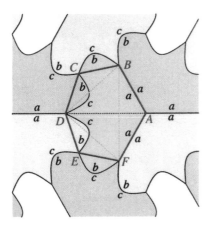

Figure 7 The diagram used to establish a tiling vertex parameterization for IH16. For simplicity, the arrows indicating edge direction have been left out of the diagram.

tiling polygon are the lengths of $\overline{AD}$ and $\overline{BF}$. However, as discussed in the next section, the shape comparison metric that we would like to use is independent of scale. We can factor out the dependence on scale by fixing $||\overline{BF}|| = 1$ and keeping just a single parameter: $v_0 \equiv ||\overline{AD}||$. Figure 8 shows tilings of type IH16 that can result from different values of this single parameter.

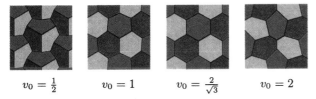

$$v_0 = \tfrac{1}{2} \qquad v_0 = 1 \qquad v_0 = \tfrac{2}{\sqrt{3}} \qquad v_0 = 2$$

Figure 8 Some examples of IH16 with different values for the single parameter in its tiling vertex parameterization.

4 The shape metric

The Escherization problem raises the difficult question of how to compare two shapes. An answer should be in the form of a metric that would take two outlines and return a nonnegative real number; zero would mean that the outlines are identical, and higher positive values would denote shapes that are increasingly dissimilar. To simplify the rest of the Escherization algorithm, we would also like the metric to be insensitive to rigid motion or scale of either of the shapes.

Fortunately, such metrics have been developed by computer vision researchers. We use the metric created by Arkin *et al.* for comparing polygons [2]. Their metric represents the input polygons as *turning functions*, functions that map fraction of arc length in a polygon to the angle of the polygon at that point. Turning functions are naturally translation and scale independent. Translation of a turning function corresponds to rotation of the polygon and movement of the point where the measurement of arc length begins. They compute the minimal L^2 distance between all translations of the two turning functions by proving that only a small number of such translations need to be checked.

Their algorithm is efficient and has a predictable run time: $O(n^2 \log n)$ in the total number of vertices n. The algorithm also corresponds fairly well to a subjective notion of the distance between two shapes. It is limited in its ability to cope with varying levels of detail across the shapes (which is a form of what they call "non-uniform noise"), but it is acceptable for our purposes.

We use the polygon comparison metric for both polygons and subdivision curves. In the case of subdivision curves, we first approximate the curve as a polygon with a large number of vertices and then make a call to the same routine.

5 Optimizing over the space of tilings

Armed with a set of tilings (the isohedral tiles), parameterizations over those tilings, and a good shape metric, we are now ready to address the problem of building an optimizer that can search over the space of those tilings to find an instance whose tiles are close to the goal shape.

Our optimizer is based on simulated annealing. It works roughly as follows:

```
function FINDOPTIMALTILING (GOALSHAPE, FAMILIES):
    INSTANCES ← CREATEINSTANCES (FAMILIES)
    while ||INSTANCES|| > 1 do
        for each i in INSTANCES do
            ANNEAL(i, GOALSHAPE)
        end for
        INSTANCES ← PRUNE(INSTANCES)
    end while
    return CONTENTS (INSTANCES)
end function
```

The optimizer takes as input a goal shape and a set of isohedral families in which to search for an optimal tiling. The optimizer begins by creating a set of multiple instances of tilings from each isohedral family. It then calls a re-entrant simulated annealing procedure to improve each one of these instances. (This ANNEAL() procedure is discussed in more detail below.) After each of the instances has been optimized to some degree, the instances are evaluated according to the shape metric, and the worst ones are removed. The annealing is continued on the remaining instances. This iterative process of alternately pruning the search space and then improving the remaining instances is repeated until just a single tiling instance is left. This tiling is returned as the optimal tiling.

The annealer is a re-entrant procedure, which works roughly like this:

```
procedure ANNEAL(TILING, GOALSHAPE):
    for j = 1 to N do
        while T > T_min do
            OPTIMIZETILING (TILING, GOALSHAPE, T)
            T ← REDUCE(T)
        end while
        SMOOTHEDGESHAPES (TILING)
        SPLITEDGESHAPES (TILING)
        (T, T_min) ← UPDATESCHEDULE (T, T_min)
    end for
    suspend
end procedure
```

The annealer takes a given tiling instance and a goal shape as input. It loops for a constant number of iterations to improve the tiling and then exits, maintaining its state, so that upon re-entry it can continue from where it left off, in the same cooling schedule. Within each iteration of the outer loop, the procedure takes a number of cooling steps, reducing the "temperature" at each step. Within this inner loop, it makes a call to a procedure that we have termed OPTIMIZETILING(). This procedure implements the "multidimensional minimization by simulated annealing combined with the downhill simplex method," as described by Press *et al.* [17]. The procedure attempts to improve all of the parameters of the tiling, including the parameterizations of the tiling vertices (discussed in Section 3) and the positions of the shape vertices of the tile. The procedure always accepts a downhill step (one that improves the tiling instance) and sometime accepts an uphill step, with probability depending on the temperature T. Once the temperature has

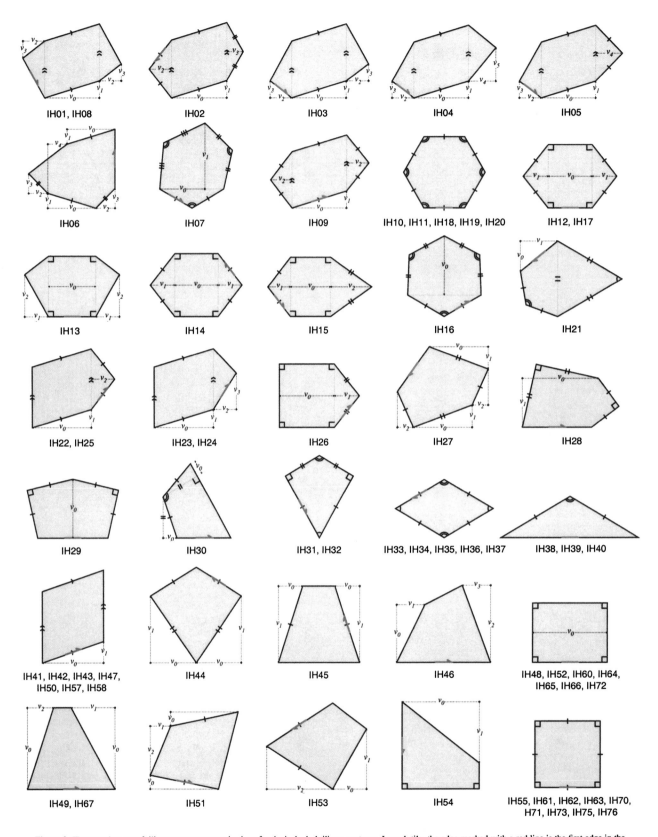

Figure 9 The complete set of tiling vertex parameterizations for the isohedral tilings, part one. In each tile, the edge marked with a red line is the first edge in the tiling type's incidence symbol. When that first edge is directed, the red line has an arrowhead. Labelled dotted lines represent parameter values, and are horizontal or vertical (with the exception of one guide line in the diagram for IH30). Since the diagrams are scale independent, distances that do not depend on parameters can be taken to have unit length. Tile edges cut with the same number of short lines have the same length, and edges cut with chevrons are additionally parallel. A single arc, a small square, and a double arc at vertices represent 60°, 90°, and 120° angles, respectively.

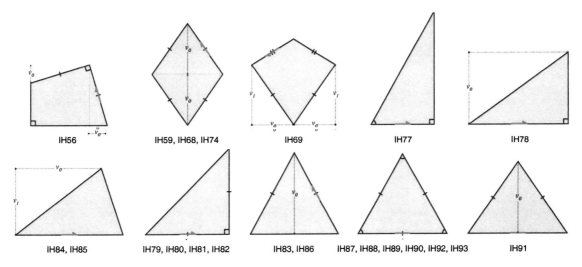

Figure 10 The complete set of tiling vertex parameterizations for the isohedral tilings, part two.

cooled to some minimum temperature T_{min}, we exit this inner loop. At this stage, we run through the vertices of the tile and remove any vertices that are nearly collinear with their neighbors, thereby eliminating any unnecessary degrees of freedom that may have been introduced into the tiling instance. Next, we subdivide each edge of the tiling, essentially doubling the number of variables over which we optimize in the next stage. Finally, we restart the cooling schedule, generally with some slightly lower temperatures T and T_{min}.

One additional part of the optimization, which is not shown in the pseudocode and which is optional, is to automatically convert the vertices of the tiles into control points for B-spline subdivision curves after a certain stage in the optimization. We can then additionally optimize over weights on each vertex that control the smoothness of the curve near that point.

Our use of simulated annealing is subject to the usual practicalities. First, the success of the optimization for a single instance of a single tiling type depends on the initial shape of the tiling polygon and the initial positions of the shape vertices. We therefore generally start with multiple instances for each tiling type. As with any simulating annealing algorithm, the choice of cooling schedule can also make a difference. We use a very simple approach where the temperature T is multiplied by a factor of ϕ after every N iterations, with $T = 0.1$, $N = 250$, and $\phi = 0.9$ to start. When the temperature reaches 5% of its initial value ($T_{min} = 0.05T$), the optimization resets, lowering the starting and minimum temperatures by a factor of 0.6, increasing the number of iterations N by a factor of 1.2, and reducing the temperature multiplier ϕ by a factor of 0.1. We did not spend a lot of time "optimizing" this cooling schedule, so other reasonable choices would probably work equally well or better.

6 Representation of isohedral tilings

We have developed a computer representation of isohedral tilings that allows us to express our Escherization algorithm efficiently and naturally. The key is to factor out the constraints on the tile imposed by adjacencies and internal symmetries, and to store only the minimal set of free parameters that encode the tile shape.

We break down the information associated with a tile into two components: the *tiling template* and the *tile instance*. The tiling template contains information about a tiling type in general. The tile instance refers to a template and contains a set of parameters for the tiling vertex parameterization, along with the minimal set of information required to reproduce the edge shapes. We first describe each of

```
template IH16 {
    topology 3^6                      [1]
    symbol [a+b+c+c-b-a-;a-c+b+]      [2]
    colouring 3 (1 2 3) (1 2 3) (1 2 3) [3]
    aspects 3                         [4]
    rules                             [5]
        aspect 2 1                    [6]
        aspect 3 6                    [7]
        translate T1 1,4              [8]
        translate T2 1,2              [9]
}
```

Figure 11 The tiling type information stored for IH16

these components in detail, and then show how they can be used to support efficient editing and viewing in an interactive system.

6.1 Tiling templates

Tiling templates are computed once ahead of time, and stored in a master file that is read in when the tile library is initialized. Figure 11 shows a sample entry from the template file. The complete set of templates is available on the proceedings CD-ROM.

Along with the topological type and incidence symbol (lines 1 and 2), we store additional static information that increases the efficiency and functionality of our system.

First, we add a `colouring` field (line 3) that provides a default rule for filling the interiors of tiles with colours. An *n-colouring* of a tiling is a set of symbols $\{c_1, \ldots, c_n\}$, together with a function f that assigns a colour c_i to each tile in the tiling. A *perfect colouring* is a colouring that respects the tiling's symmetry in the sense that symmetries act as permutations of the colours. Every perfect colouring of an isohedral tiling can be conveniently encoded as an assignment of different colours to the different aspects in a single translational unit, along with an assignment of different colour permutations to each of the two translation vectors. The colouring field in the template gives, in order, the number of colours, the assignment of colours to aspects, and the permutations of the assignment associated with the two translation vectors. This encoding can express a superset of the perfect colourings. In the case shown here, the permutations are both the identity. (In all of his drawings, Escher was careful to ensure that no two adjacent tiles ever shared the same colour. He also used the minimum number of colours necessary to satisfy this condition. The default colourings we provide in our tiling templates have both of these properties.)

Another line of the template (line 4) specifies the number of aspects in the tiling, in this case, 3.

The `rules` section (lines 5 through 9) gives a collection of rules that, when applied to a tiling polygon, yield transform matrices for all the aspects of a translational unit, as well as the two translation vectors. These transforms cannot be computed ahead of time, as they depend on the tiling polygon. Each rule is expressed as a sequence of hops across edges, starting from the first aspect in the translational unit at the origin.

Aspect 1 is always given the identity matrix as its transform, and the other aspect transforms are computed from it. In this example, the first rule (line 6) says that the transform for creating aspect 2 from the first aspect is just the transform that creates the symmetry across edge 1 of the first aspect in the tiling—that is, a reflection about the first edge, labelled a+, in the incidence symbol. Similarly, the second rule (line 7) says that the transform for creating aspect 3 from the first aspect is the transform that creates the symmetry across edge 6 of the first aspect in the tiling—here, a reflection about the edge labelled a-. Sometimes, more than a single hop is required. For instance, the rule "`aspect 2 1,2,3`" would specify a sequence of hops: first, across edge 1 of the first aspect in the tiling, then across edge 2 of the first aspect's neighboring tile, then across edge 3 of that neighbor's neighbor.

The two translation vectors are specified in the same way. Thus, following across edge 1 of the first aspect in the tiling, then across edge 4 of the first aspect's neighboring tile, gives the translation vector T_1.

One piece of per-tiling-type information missing from the template file is the set of tiling vertex parameterizations. The parameterizations are more easily described in code than in a table-driven format, and are embedded in the source code, each as a C++ class. A Python file that implements the parameterizations is available on the CD-ROM.

6.2 Tile instances

The tile is stored as a set of parameters for the tiling vertex parameterization, along with a hierarchical model whose leaves are *fundamental edge shapes*—the portions of the tiling edges that cannot be further decomposed by symmetries.

The fundamental edge shapes are simply stored as arrays of points. Each fundamental edge shape implicitly begins at $(0,0)$ and ends at $(1,0)$. By default, the points are interpreted as a sequence of line segments, but to increase the aesthetic appeal of our tilings we have implemented the ability to treat them as control points for a subdivision curve. As a further enhancement, each control point has an associated weight. The higher the weight, the more subdivision steps will go by before that point is averaged with its neighbours. In effect, the weight controls the sharpness of the curve near the control point, with maximum weight yielding a sharp corner that interpolates the control point.

To rebuild the tile shape, we apply the parameterization to obtain the positions of the tiling vertices, and transform the edge shapes into place between them.

There are at most three levels of transformation between a fundamental edge shape and a point on the outline of the tile. The first level takes into account the symmetries of **U** and **S** edges. Half of the **U** or **S** edge comes directly from the fundamental edge. The other half is derived from the first half as needed through rotation or reflection. **J** edges are passed unmodified through this level, and since **I** edges are immutable, all tiles share a single system-wide copy of an **I** edge.

At the next level up, we recognize that edges with different names in the incidence symbol may still have related shapes. In IH16, for

example, the edge named b+ is adjacent to c+, forcing the two edge shapes to be congruent. In this case, the two edges share the same shape passed up from the level below.

Finally, the topmost level maps the unit interval to an edge of the tiling polygon; this mapping will move an edge shape from its normalized coordinate system into a portion of the tile's outline. At this level, all edges with the same name in the incidence symbol share a lower-level shape object.

Specific tiles are stored in tile files, which are simply XML documents.

6.3 Interactive tools

To provide a convenient interface to the Escherization algorithm, and to explore the mathematical and aesthetic properties of isohedral tilings in general, we have constructed several graphical tools on top of the tile library and optimizer, using the free toolkits **GTK+** [19] and **GTK--** [12].

The simplest of these tools is a utility for tracing goal shapes from images. An image can be loaded into a viewer where the user can trace an outline of an image by hand. The outline can then be saved and passed to the optimizer.

The more sophisticated tool is a rich viewer and editor for tile files. The editor is highly responsive, running at interactive rates on an off-the-shelf Linux system with no graphics acceleration. Because of the deep sharing of information in the tile representation, when a part of the tile is edited, the system provides immediate feedback by showing all parts of the tile (and tiling) that are affected by the change.

When subdivision-based edges are enabled, we provide a novel gauge-based interface for editing weights on control points. The gauge pops up at the vertex location and is set with a radial motion. Setting weights integrates very comfortably with the general process of editing the vertices.

6.4 Filling a region with tiles

The most basic drawing operation for a tiling is to fill a region of the plane with copies of the tile. Beginning with a tile in its local coordinate system and a viewing region, we need to find the rigid motions to apply to the tile that replicate it across the region.

To find these motions, we project the viewing region's corners into the coordinate system formed by the tiling's translation vectors, derived from the template's rules. In that coordinate system, the translational units become lattice squares; the lattice squares that intersect the projection of the viewing region are the ones that need to be drawn. For each needed translation, we place a tile relative to the rigid motion formed by composing the translation with each of the aspect transforms in turn.

7 Decorations and rendering

The output of the core Escherization algorithm is a geometric description of a tile, not a finished ornamental design. To complete the Escherization process, we need to surround the core algorithm with tools to add decorations to tiles and create high-quality renderings of the results. We have explored the use of both vector-based and image-based decorations and rendering styles.

A tile maintains a set of *markings*, sequences of weighted subdivision control points with various drawing attributes. Markings can be open, closed or filled, polygonal or subdivided, and have variable line thickness, line colour and fill colour. The line and fill colours

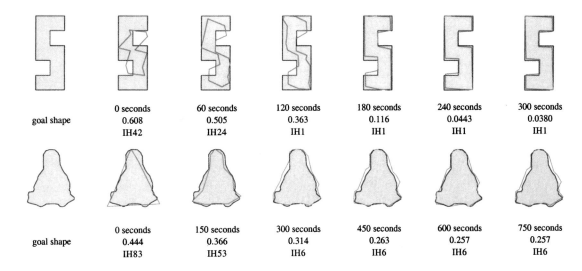

goal shape	0 seconds 0.608 IH42	60 seconds 0.505 IH24	120 seconds 0.363 IH1	180 seconds 0.116 IH1	240 seconds 0.0443 IH1	300 seconds 0.0380 IH1
goal shape	0 seconds 0.444 IH83	150 seconds 0.366 IH53	300 seconds 0.314 IH6	450 seconds 0.263 IH6	600 seconds 0.257 IH6	750 seconds 0.257 IH6

Figure 12 Timelines for two sample Escherization runs. Each step shows the current best tile in the system (in red) overlaid on the goal shape. The caption indicates the elapsed time, the score for that tile, and its isohedral type. The second goal shape is the penguin from Figure 15(c).

can also be mapped according to the tiling's colouring. The markings can be created and edited from within the interactive tool, and are stored in the tile file as fragments of XML. The editor can also render a tiling decorated with markings as PostScript.

It may also be desirable to fill the interior of a tile with image-based markings. We have implemented an image-based tiling renderer using **libart**, a freely-available image manipulation library [16]. The renderer takes a tile file and a set of images to serve as backdrops. For each tile in a region, it starts with the image backdrop for that tile's colour, applies a transparent wash of the tile colour, rasterizes the markings, draws an outline, and transforms the composited tile into its position in the final rendering.

The natural choice for an image-based marking is the interior of the goal shape in the image that was originally traced. Using the correspondence provided by the polygon comparison metric, we do a Beier-Neely style image warp [3] to deform the interior of the goal shape in the source image into the interior of the Escherized tile shape. When the deformation is not too great, we end up with an attractive tiling out of motifs that resemble the original image. When the automatically-determined correspondence produces too much distortion (which can happen when the goal shape and tile shape differ in level of detail), it can be edited by hand to create a better match.

To further increase the appeal of an image-based rendering, we apply various painterly effects to the warped tile image before replication. This post-processing step gives the artist creative control over the appearance of the final tiling, and can bring the result closer to the informal hand-drawn style of Escher's notebook drawings.

8 Results

We have used our Escherization implementation and decoration tools to produce a number of ornamental tilings from various sources of imagery.

Figure 12 shows snapshots from two sample runs of the Escherizer. The goal shape in the first run is a simple test polygon, part of a series used to verify and tune the optimizer. The second goal shape is a more typical outline traced from an image. The more complicated shape takes longer to run, and the convergence is not quite as complete (as should be expected from a real-world outline).

Figure 13 A comparison between the tile returned by the optimizer and the same tile with user modifications. Note also that the second tile has subdivision enabled.

Figure 13 shows the tile result produced by the optimizer for a teapot image, followed by the tile after a small amount of hand-tweaking in the interactive editor. Even when manual intervention improved the overall appeal of a tiling, Escherization did the hard work of determining how to make the goal shape fit together with itself in the first place. The edits shown here took a minute or two to perform and were fairly typical of our experience in creating tilings in this fashion.

The remaining results can be seen in Figures 14 and 15. Figures 15 (d) is rendered as line art, and the remaining examples use the image-based renderer. In all cases, the optimizer generated a tile shape that was then modified slightly in the editor. The source image was warped into the tile shape, and copies of the warped image were recoloured and edited to make the final rendering. The user intervention was primarily to exert creative control, and rarely to guide the optimization process. On some occasions, it was helpful to watch the optimizer discover a tiling type suitable for a given goal shape, then stop and restart it with many tilings of that type, resulting in a narrower and deeper search.

9 Discussion

Most outlines are not tiles. For just about any goal shape, an Escherizer will have to produce an approximation, and a better Escherizer will produce a closer approximation. A perfect Escherizer would determine the smallest distance over all possible tile shapes, and return the tiling that achieves that bound. Our imperfect optimizer, by contrast, coarsely samples the space of isohedral tilings in a directed fashion and returns the best sample it finds. Consequently, there are seemingly easy cases, such as the one in Figure 16 that our algorithm cannot successfully Escherize.

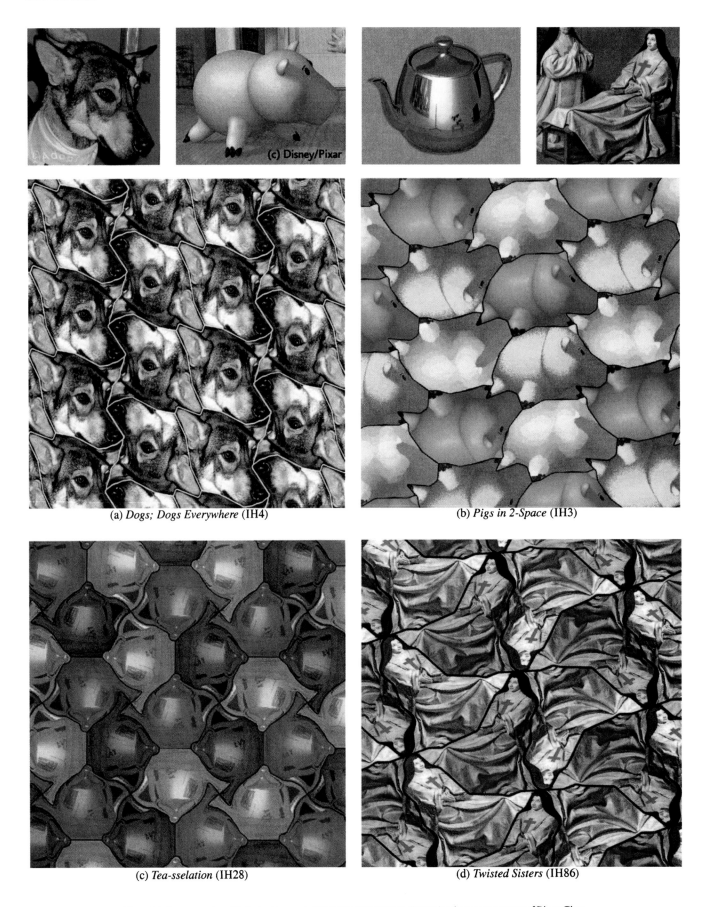

(a) *Dogs; Dogs Everywhere* (IH4)

(b) *Pigs in 2-Space* (IH3)

(c) *Tea-sselation* (IH28)

(d) *Twisted Sisters* (IH86)

Figure 14 Some examples of Escherized images and the tilings they generate. Hamm the pig appears courtesy of Disney/Pixar.

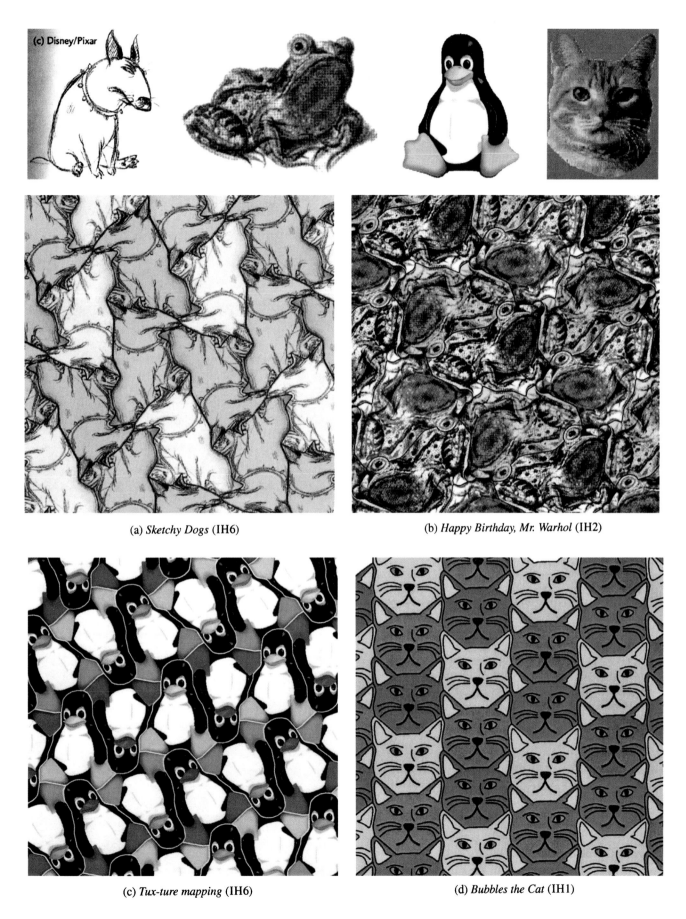

(a) *Sketchy Dogs* (IH6)

(b) *Happy Birthday, Mr. Warhol* (IH2)

(c) *Tux-ture mapping* (IH6)

(d) *Bubbles the Cat* (IH1)

Figure 15 More examples of Escherization. Tux the Penguin appears courtesy of Larry Ewing (lewing@isc.tamu.edu). Sketchy Dog appears courtesy of Disney/Pixar.

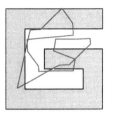

Figure 16 A tile for which Escherization performs badly, and a tiling that can be generated from it.

In practice, our Escherization system performs well on convex or nearly convex shapes. The shapes that tend to fail are the ones with long, complicated edges between the tiling vertices. It is difficult for the optimizer to come up with just right the sequence of vertex adjustments to push a tendril of detail out, especially when constrained by the "no non-uniform noise" condition of the metric. Furthermore, in our shape comparison metric, the importance of a section of outline is directly proportional to its fraction of the perimeter of the goal shape, even if from our own perspective outlines may obey different measures of significance. For example, the precise profile edge of a face in silhouette, descending along eyes, nose, and mouth, is much more important to us than the hairline. But to the current shape metric these might be relatively insignificant details. It would be valuable to investigate an extension to the polygon comparison metric wherein a section of outline could be assigned a measure of importance, a weight controlling which parts of the polygon should match more closely.

Moreover, although Escher's tiles are almost always immediately recognizable as particular kinds of animals, they generally bear little actual resemblance to a real image: they are more like conventionalizations, or cartoons. Our optimizer does not "understand" the shapes it is manipulating, so it has no way to deform them while preserving their essential recognizability. It must instead rely on a purely geometric notion of proximity.

All this being said, the Escherizer we have built performs remarkably well on many different shapes for which no tiling is obvious. Who would have guessed that a teapot could tile the plane? We certainly couldn't. Even when the optimizer fails to find an ideal tiling, it often finds a tiling that is close enough that it is easily converted into an acceptable result. Thus, it allows us to work in much the same way that Escher did, only with a very close starting point and more helpful interactive tools.

This research suggests many future directions, including generalizing our algorithms to handle multihedral and aperiodic tilings, parquet deformations [13, Chap. 10], or tilings over non-Euclidean domains, such as the hyperbolic plane [7]. Another intriguing idea is to allow some flexibility in the goal shape as well. For instance, instead of a 2D shape, we might use a 3D (and potentially parameterized) model and attempt to automatically discover a camera position from which the view of the model is most easily Escherized. Finally, along the lines of creating Escher tilings automatically is the problem of "automatic conventionalization": somehow creating not just the tile boundaries, but the line-art graphical decorations that go inside the tilings, more or less automatically from a reference image.

Acknowledgments

Many people contributed to the development of this research. Michael Noth and Jeremy Buhler collaborated on FuTile, the class project that ultimately led to our ongoing research in tilings. Branko Grünbaum motivated the use of isohedral tilings as a powerful and manageable system for ornamental design. Douglas Zongker sat in on many early discussions. Michael Cohen, Rick Szeliski and John Hughes participated in discussions and provided valuable feedback and insight that kept the project moving forward. Mike Ernst pointed us at the papers that led us to the polygon comparison metric. Dan Huttenlocher assisted us with the metric (and made his source code available). Tony DeRose filled in details on the implementation of subdivision curves. Zoran Popović helped with the taming of the continuous simulated annealing algorithm. Finally, Victor Ostromoukhov provided helpful feedback on a draft of this paper. This research was supported in part through industrial grants from Intel, Microsoft and Pixar.

References

[1] Howard Alexander. The computer/plotter and the 17 ornamental design types. *Proceedings of SIGGRAPH'75*, pages 160–167, 1975.

[2] E. M. Arkin, L. P. Chew, D. P. Huttenlocher, K. Kedem, and J. S. B. Mitchell. An efficiently computable metric for comparing polygonal shapes. *PAMI(13)*, pages 209–216, 1991.

[3] Thaddeus Beier and Shawn Neely. Feature-based image metamorphosis. *Proceedings of SIGGRAPH'92*, pages 35–42, 1992.

[4] William W. Chow. Automatic generation of interlocking shapes. *Computer Graphics and Image Processing*, 9:333–353, 1979.

[5] William W. Chow. Interlocking shapes in art and engineering. *Computer Aided Design*, 12:29–34, 1980.

[6] Andrew Crompton. Grotesque geometry. `http://dspace.dial.pipex.com/crompton/Home.shtml`.

[7] Douglas J. Dunham. Creating hyperbolic escher patterns. In H.S.M. Coxeter et al., editor, *M.C. Escher: Art and Science*, pages 241–247. Elsevier Science Publishers B.V., 1986.

[8] Andrew Glassner. Frieze groups. *IEEE Computer Graphics and Applications*, 16(3):78–83, May 1996.

[9] Andrew Glassner. Andrew glassner's notebook: Aperiodic tiling. *IEEE Computer Graphics & Applications*, 18(3):83–90, May – June 1998. ISSN 0272-1716.

[10] Andrew Glassner. Andrew glassner's notebook: Penrose tiling. *IEEE Computer Graphics & Applications*, 18(4), July – August 1998. ISSN 0272-1716.

[11] Branko Grünbaum and G. C. Shephard. *Tilings and Patterns*. W. H. Freeman, 1987.

[12] GTK--. `http://gtkmm.sourceforge.net`.

[13] Douglas Hofstadter. *Metamagical Themas: Questing for the Essence of Mind and Pattern*. Bantam Books, 1986.

[14] Daniel H. Huson and Olaf Delgado Friedrichs. Reptiles. `ftp://ftp.uni-bielefeld.de/pub/math/tiling/reptiles/`.

[15] Hans Van Lemmen. *Tiles: 1000 Years of Architectural Decoration*. Harry N. Abrams, Inc., 1993.

[16] Raph Levien. libart. `http://www.levien.com/libart/`.

[17] William H. Press, Saul A. Teukolsky, William T. Vetterling, and Brian P. Flannery. Numerical recipes in c: The art of scientific computing (2nd ed.). 1992. ISBN 0-521-43108-5. Held in Cambridge.

[18] Doris Schattschneider. *M.C. Escher: Visions of Symmetry*. W.H. Freeman, 1990.

[19] The GIMP toolkit. `http://www.gtk.org`.

[20] M.C. Escher (tran. Karin Ford). *Escher on Escher: Exploring the Infinite*. Henry N. Abrams, Inc., 1989.

[21] Michael T. Wong, Douglas E. Zongker, and David H. Salesin. Computer-generated floral ornament. *Proceedings of SIGGRAPH'98*, pages 423–434, 1998.

Shadows for Cel Animation

Lena Petrović *   Brian Fujito *   Lance Williams °   Adam Finkelstein *

* Princeton University
° Disney Feature Animation

Abstract

We present a semi-automatic method for creating shadow mattes in cel animation. In conventional cel animation, shadows are drawn by hand, in order to provide visual cues about the spatial relationships and forms of characters in the scene. Our system creates shadow mattes based on hand-drawn characters, given high-level guidance from the user about depths of various objects. The method employs a scheme for "inflating" a 3D figure based on hand-drawn art. It provides simple tools for adjusting object depths, coupled with an intuitive interface by which the user specifies object shapes and relative positions in a scene. Our system obviates the tedium of drawing shadow mattes by hand, and provides control over complex shadows falling over interesting shapes.

Keywords: Shadows, cel animation, inflation, sketching, NPR.
URL: http://www.cs.princeton.edu/gfx/proj/cel_shadows

1 Introduction

Shadows provide important visual cues for depth, shape, contact, movement, and lighting in our perception of the world [5, 17]. In cel animation, a moving figure and background scenery are illustrated in different layers with different styles, and therefore shadows play an especially crucial role by integrating the character into the background. According to Thomas and Johnston, two of Disney's most renowned animators, shadows were used in cel animation even from the very early days "because they anchored the figure to the ground. Without some kind of contact with the background, the characters seemed to float around, walking on air, no matter how much weight had been animated into their movements." [12] Traditionally, shadow mattes have been drawn by hand, and while modern digital image manipulation tools provide simple operations that assist in the creation of mattes, the process is still largely manual. In this paper, we present a semi-automatic method of creating shadow mattes from the hand-drawn outlines of moving figures. The process requires relatively little effort per frame, and generates plausible shadows cast by complex shapes over interesting background scenery such as walls, stairs and statues.

In rare cases where the shadow itself becomes a focal point for the viewer's attention, the shadow mattes *should* be drawn by hand, because they embody an artistic interpretation of the scene. In our work, we are addressing the rest of the shadow mattes – shadows that serve to anchor the character to the ground, enhance the form of the figure, or suggest lighting or mood. These represent the

©2000 ACM 0-58113-208-5/00/0007 $5.00

Figure 1: An example frame. (a) hand-drawn line art (b) shadow mattes created by our system (c) composited frame.

majority of the shadow mattes in cel animation, and the work of creating them is considerable. Unfortunately, it is not yet possible to *fully* automate the process of creating shadow mattes based on the line art; understanding the shapes suggested by the line art is tantamount to solving the computer vision problem, and is subject to ambiguities in interpretation. Thus, our system requires a small amount of user input – less effort than would be required to draw the mattes by hand. Once the user has set up the scene, it is easy to alter the lighting conditions to produce very different kinds of shadows. The benefits of such a system are a reduction in effort, an increase in control and flexibility, and the ability to create plausible shadow mattes even for complex character-scene interactions.

At a high level, our process works as follows. We begin with hand-drawn line art created by a traditional animator (Figure 1a), as well as hand-painted scenery created by a background artist. The user sketches over features in the painted background to establish the camera, ground plane, and background objects. Using character mattes integral to the compositing stage of the normal cel animation pipeline, we automatically "inflate" a 3D mesh for the character. The user specifies the depth for the character in the scene, as well as light positions. Next, based on the lights, the 3D character, and the background objects, the computer renders three types of shadow mattes for the character: *tone mattes* indicate both self-shadowing and shadows of other objects on the character (Figure 1b, blue); *contact shadow mattes* emphasize contact between the character and the ground (green); and *cast shadow mattes* specify shadows cast by the character onto the background scenery (red). Finally, we composite these mattes into the scene (Figure 1c) as part of the conventional cel animation pipeline.

The contributions of this work are: (1) application of "inflation" algorithms to create frame-by-frame 3D models from hand-drawn animation; (2) tools that allow the user to manipulate the inflated models of the artwork in three dimensions while preserving their image-space silhouettes; and (3) an intuitive user interface for describing shapes and relative 3D positions of both static and animated objects in the scene.

The remainder of this paper is organized as follows. In Section 2 we review related work. Section 3 describes the details of our process. In Section 4 we demonstrate the results of our working system. Section 5 concludes with observations and proposed areas of future work.

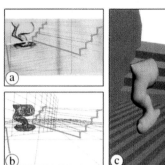

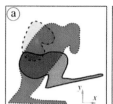
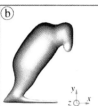
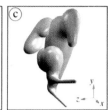

Figure 3: Building a three-layered character. (a) character mattes (b) middle-layer inflation (c) 3D character seen from side view.

Figure 2: Specifying background. (a) marking features in artwork (b) 3D scene in wireframe (c) flat-shaded side-view of 3D scene.

2 Related Work

A variety of previous efforts have applied computer graphics in cel animation. Researchers have automated the image processing and compositing aspects of cel animation [2, 7, 11, 15], in which the shadow mattes created by our system could replace hand-drawn mattes. For the cel animation industry, 3D techniques are becoming increasingly prominent in production. For example, in Disney's *Tarzan* [16], jungle backgrounds were built and painted in 3D with "Deep Canvas," to give extra depth to the scene and allow camera fly-throughs [9]. For *The Prince of Egypt* [13], DreamWorks used "Exposure," allowing them to fly cameras through a 3D scene with sequential background shots specified by manipulating a series of painted 2D background cards [8]. 3D methods have also been used for cel animation in research contexts, for example in the design of *multiperspective panoramas* (static background paintings that are appropriate for a moving camera [22]) or *view-dependent geometry* (3D models that change shape depending on view direction [6]). Previously, we showed how to apply texture to a hand-animated character by warping a 3D model to match the line art [1]. While this method could be adapted for creating plausible shadow mattes, the process requires too much human effort for this application; it would be easier generally to draw the shadow mattes by hand.

Since shading and tones enhance our understanding of 3D shape, a number of cel animation projects have applied 3D computer graphics for shading. In the extreme, a character (for example, the giant in *The Iron Giant* [18]) is modeled and animated entirely in 3D and then rendered with a "cartoon shader." Most characters in cel animation are not designed in 3D, and therefore to invoke 3D shading techniques, one must form some kind of 3D representation of the 2D artwork. This project grew out of previous work [19, 20] where we used pixel-based inflation schemes to automatically build 3D representations from 2D art, and then rendered tones and shadows with strictly 2D interactions. In this paper, we employ a 3D inflation technique, and develop technology that allows us to interactively stage a scene with 3D shadow interactions.

We adapt the inflation algorithm originally proposed by van Overveld and Wyvill [14], as implemented in a simpler form in the "Teddy" system of Igarashi *et al.* [4]. We use Teddy because it generates 3D forms that yield plausible tones and cast shadows. However, we modify their method to account for a perspective camera, requiring that the figure aligns with the artwork on its silhouette, as seen from the camera. The more significant departure from the Teddy system is that we build the character up in multiple layers, rather than extruding limbs from the main body. In our application, there are two advantages to the layer-based approach: it is more consistent with the cel animation pipeline, and it guarantees that the silhouette of each layer in the figure matches the line art.

Finally, our strategy for constructing the 3D scene is largely inspired by the "SKETCH" system of Zeleznik *et al.* [23].

3 The Process

Here we describe the process of creating shadow mattes based on hand-drawn art. Section 3.1 addresses construction of background scenery based on a few simple gestures by the user. Section 3.2 describes inflation of 3D characters from line art, and Section 3.3 presents tools for adjusting the relative depths of the 3D figures in the scene. Finally, Section 3.4 describes setting up lights, rendering shadow mattes, and compositing them into the artwork.

3.1 Constructing Background Scenery

The first stage of the process of creating the scene is to construct a background. In order to establish the relationship between the camera and the scene, we begin with several assumptions: a fixed field of view and aspect ratio for the camera (in our tests, $83°$ wide with an aspect of 4:3), and known camera roll and ground plane tilt (both are upright). These assumptions work for a broad class of scenes, and may be easily modified by the user to work for other scenes. Next, in order to establish the pitch of the camera relative to the ground plane, the user sketches over the background art a pair of parallel lines in the ground plane, for example the cyan lines in Figure 2a. In a perspective image, all parallel lines on the ground plane that intersect in the image plane will intersect on the horizon. Thus, even if the horizon is not visible in the scene we can find it by intersecting the parallel lines given by the user. The height h of the horizon relative to the center of the image determines[1] the pitch ϕ of the camera by the simple relationship:

$$\phi = \arctan{(h/d)}$$

where d is the distance from the camera to the image plane (which we set arbitrarily to 1). The only remaining camera parameters are its yaw and its height above the ground plane. Since at this stage there are no objects in the scene other than the ground plane, the yaw is arbitrary and we set it to zero. The camera height establishes a scale for the scene that is also arbitrary. For example, in Figure 1 we see a man in a room, but whether this room is the size of a bread box or a warehouse has no impact on the size or shape of his shadow projected onto the image plane. Thus, we arbitrarily choose the height of the camera, only taking care that the entire image plane is guaranteed to be above the ground plane. Now we establish a coordinate system for the scene: we take the origin to be the center of the image plane, the x and y axes to be, respectively, the horizontal and vertical axes of the image, and the -z axis to be the camera look direction.

Taking inspiration from the SKETCH system [23], we construct objects in the scene relative to the ground plane using simple gestures. Walls are built perpendicular to the ground by specifying the line of intersection with the ground plane. The user can create more complicated objects consisting of multiple polygonal faces

---

[1]This method fails for cameras that are looking straight up or straight down, and in these cases we would ask the user to set the pitch by hand.

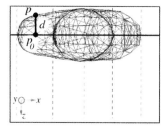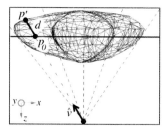

Figure 4: Inflating a 3D figure from 2D line art using perspective. Left: orthographic extrusion. Right: perspective extrusion.

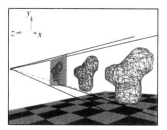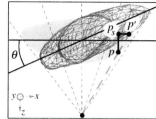

Figure 5: Adjusting depth. Left: ball grows as it moves back to contact point. Right: Depth-shear preserves perspective outline.

(such as stairs and boxes) by specifying two polylines on the object, starting with ground contact points. The object is constructed so that it conforms to the sketched lines and its neighboring polygonal faces are perpendicular. Figure 2 shows the user-identified features in the image: cyan for the ground lines, yellow for the wall line, and violet for the stairs. Smooth, organic 3D background objects, such as the statue in Figure 2, are built using the character inflation and placement methods described in Sections 3.2 and 3.3.

3.2 Inflating 3D Models

Having specified the background, the next step is to inflate the line art to form meshes representing the character in 3D. Our goal is to create 3D figures that cast plausible shadows under various lighting conditions. First, we convert the line art into *character mattes* – bitmaps that define regions of the image covered by the character. This process is performed as a normal aspect of the cel animation pipeline, because these mattes are used for filling and clipping when the character is composited into the scene. For further control in our system, we often divide the character mattes into multiple layers, so that each may be placed at a different depth. These separate layers help to cast plausible shadows under lighting conditions that reveal the geometry of the character. For the character in Figure 3, the arm (inflated from the yellow matte) could cast a shadow from an overhead light onto the leg (magenta). Layer mattes may need to be extended past visible boundaries to cast reasonable shadows. For example, a matte for the man's right arm in Figure 1 would extend into his body, with the body-arm boundary being preserved by placing the arm behind the body (as described in Section 3.3). Converting line art into character mattes must be a manual process, because it requires a visual interpretation of the scene. However, it is fairly easy to perform using digital image editing tools such as Adobe Photoshop. In some cases, these layer mattes may already be available to us, as animation houses may split characters into multiple layers for separate animation.[2]

Next we "inflate" each layer in the character matte to form rotund 3D shapes; for example the shape shown in Figure 3b is inflated from the cyan region in Figure 3a. Our inflation scheme is based on the Teddy system of Igarashi *et al.* [4], which finds the chordal axis of a closed curve, lifts it out of the plane, and lofts a surface between the curve and its axis. Many other inflation methods might be used at this stage. We chose Teddy because it is simple and fast, and produces smooth, bulky shapes that yield reasonable cast shadows and tone mattes. As input to Igarashi's algorithm, each layer in the character mattes should be described by a simple, closed, 2D polyline, i.e. there should be no holes. We use an automatic tracing tool to convert the matte to a closed curve, and then resample it as a polyline. Teddy then elevates a surface whose intersection with the image plane is the input polyline.

---

[2]This is more common in television animation where individual layers tend to be reused, but less common in feature animation.

If we were using an orthographic camera, we would be done. However, with a perspective camera, this scheme will not produce a 3D shape whose silhouette is exactly aligned with the original matte. Therefore, we adjust the resulting shape as follows. Every point p on the lofted surface is a signed distance d from its corresponding point p_0 in the image plane of the orthographic camera (Figure 4). For the perspective camera, we find the point p' on the ray from the camera to p_0:

$$p' = p_0 + d\hat{v}$$

where $\hat{v}$ is the normalized vector from the camera to p_0. By sending every point p in the Teddy-lofted surface through this transform, the silhouette of the resulting shape conforms exactly to the matte.

3.3 Specifying Depth

Now that we have inflated the layers of the character from the image plane, we need to give them depth in the 3D world while preserving their image plane projection. We provide two projection-preserving depth adjustments: *depth-translation* and *depth-shear*. While one could implement more sophisticated projection-preserving warps, we designed these methods to minimize user interaction.

Depth-translation moves the figure out of the image plane to varying depths in the scene; we maintain its image plane projection using a uniform scale about the camera center. The user specifies the translation in one of two ways. First, she can mark a contact point in the image plane, and the system pushes the object back into the scene until the marked point reaches the ground plane, as shown in Figure 5a. Second, the user can push the object towards or away from the camera via a manipulator, watching the object move in relation to other objects in the scene as well as an approximate shadow cast by an overhead light onto the ground plane.

We also allow the user to control the relative depth across a single object via a projection-preserving *depth-shear*, which provides fine control over how shadows will be cast by this figure. For example, in Figure 3c, the arm has been sheared so that the hand is closer to the image plane (to the left in this pose) than the rest of the arm. Nonetheless, the image-plane projection of this object must remain unchanged. The user specifies the shear via a manipulator that provides an axis and an angle θ. Our algorithm works as follows. For every point p on the unsheared object (light blue in Figure 5b), we calculate p_s, the point that would result from sending p through the conventional shear by θ. We take our final point p' to be the point on the ray extending from the camera through p that has the same z value (depth) as p_s.

Depth adjustment is generally specified separately for all layers. However, for any layer this information may be keyframed across time. For example, by specifying a contact point in two frames of the animation of the ball shown in Figure 7 we are able to implicitly set depths for the ball in all of the other frames. Likewise, the contact points for the stomping man are keyframed, even though his body remains at approximately constant depth.

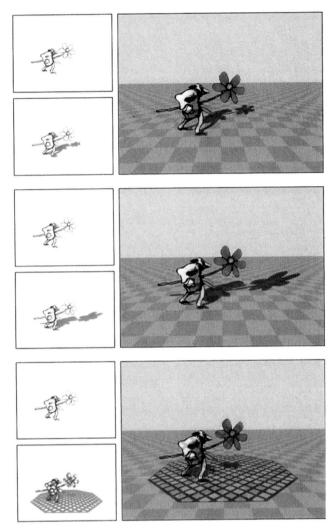

Figure 6: Specifying lights. From top to bottom: directional light, point light, gazebo gobo.

Figure 7: Bouncing ball casts shadow in desert scene.

3.4 "Lights ... Camera ... Action!"

Now that we have constructed a background set and positioned a 3D character in the scene, setting up lights and rendering shadow mattes is straightforward. As shown in Figure 6, we obtain different shadow effects by using directional lights, point lights, or by using a "gobo."[3] Within a range of lighting subjectively consistent with the painted background, lights may even be animated to provide fine control over where a shadow falls in the scene. When creating the sequence shown in Figure 8, we animated the light position to cause the shadow to fall on the legs of the statue early in the clip and extend up the stairs later.

To render the mattes for tones and cast shadows, we use a standard ray tracer with custom shaders. For example, for on-character tone mattes we have implemented a cartoon shader that thresholds all colors to either white or black based on a diffuse lighting calculation. Due to sampling and approximation errors in 3D mesh construction, it is possible that the 3D figure used to render tone mattes does not exactly align with the line art, causing a small gap between the tone matte and the line art. In these cases,

we apply morphological dilation to the tone matte, and then clip it to the original character matte. To accommodate this operation, we actually render a separate tone matte for each layer in the figure and perform dilation and clipping on each independently before combining them.

We render contact shadows in two passes. First, we place an orthographic camera in the ground plane, looking up at the character, and use a far clipping plane that is just above the ground. With this camera, we capture an image of parts of the character that nearly touch the ground. Second, we re-project the image onto the ground plane, and view it from the regular camera for the scene, giving us contact shadows. Final dilation of the resulting matte ensures that it emerges from beneath the character.

Now we are ready to composite the frame. Tone mattes modulate the character's color, while mattes for cast shadows and contact shadows darken the background painting. In some cases, we blur the mattes to suggest softer shadows. Finally, we composite the shadowed character over the shadowed background, and then add the line art.

4 Experimental Results

In this section, we describe the animations that we created using our system, as well as the time and effort for building these sequences.[4] The animations are shown on the video proceedings.

Figure 7 shows two frames from a 33-frame sequence of a bouncing ball. We built a ground plane (from the lines of the road) and inflated each ball mesh as a single, animated layer. Since parts of the ball go off-frame in the last five frames, we completed the character mattes (extending out of the frame) to get reasonable shadows. We specified the depth of the bouncing ball using ball-to-ground contact points in two frames, and interpolated and extrapolated depths for all other frames.

---

[3]A "gobo", referred to in live action film as a "cuckaloris" or "cookie", is a device for projecting a shadow pattern (such the foliage in Figure 9, or in this case a gazebo) onto a scene.

[4]Our system is implemented on a 400 MHz Pentium II PC as a series of plug-ins for Alias|Wavefront Maya. For matte editing and compositing we use Adobe Photoshop, Softimage Eddie and NothingReal Shake.

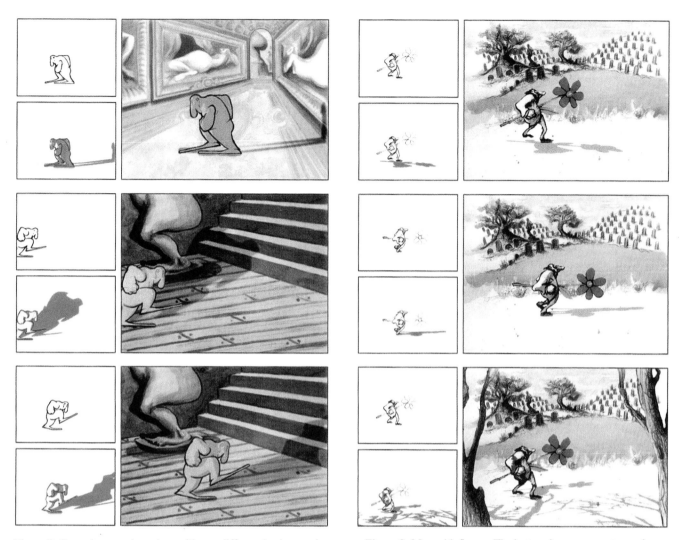

Figure 8: Stomping man in action, with two different backgrounds.

Figure 9: Man with flower. The bottom image uses a tree gobo.

Figure 8 shows three frames of a stomping man – one in a hallway and two near some stairs. For both scenes, we built the stomping man from a 16-frame, hand-drawn walk cycle. For each of the 16 frames, we split up the character into three or four layers (depending on the visibility of the far arm) and specified different relative depths and shears in each layer. Our system then built offset copies of these meshes to form 10 stomp cycles (160 frames). In the hallway scene, we placed a near-horizontal directional light that casts a long shadow breaking up the far wall. In the staircase scene, we subtly animated a point light, as described in Section 3.4.

In Figure 9 we show three test frames from a work in progress of an old man carring a flower. The upper two frames illustrate varying the light direction. Because of the style of the artwork, these frames do not use tone mattes. The bottom frame shows the body of the man and the ground receiving a shadow from a tree gobo.

The bulk of the human effort involved in our system consists of the following: (1) specifying the background – 1 or 2 minutes, even for complex scenes such as the stair scene; (2) creating character mattes – 2 minutes per layer per frame;[5] (3) specifying depth information for each layer – roughly 30 seconds per layer

per frame;[6] (4) specifying lights – under 1 minute. The human effort required to specify layer mattes and depth information may be substantial. However, several factors mitigate this cost. First, layer segmentation is only required insofar as the lighting and geometry demand it. Second, the task of layering and depth specification requires minimal artistic interpretation, and might be relegated to junior staff. Third, specifying depth using our interface is simple, so that even if the layers frequently change depth across frames, the work of adjusting layers is faster, simpler, and more easily adapted than drawing shadows by hand. Finally, once the scene has been established, changing the lighting is easy. Thus, in general, our system requires relatively little human effort, and allows users to cast interesting shadows that would otherwise be quite tedious to draw by hand.

The most computationally expensive aspect of our system is ray tracing shadow mattes, each of which takes roughly 45 seconds at 640×480.[7] This time is characteristic for ray-traced shadows; other rendering regimes (e.g. depth buffer shadows or shadows cast by area lights) could be expected to vary in computational expense.

---

[5]For the stomping man, it took 2 hours to build mattes for a 16-frame cycle with 4 layers. For the 9 other cycles, character mattes were simply offset with no human effort.

[6]For the entire ball sequence, the depths were specified in 1 minute using only two contact points. For the stomping man, setting depths took about 30 minutes for 16 frames; the remaining 144 frames were cycled.

[7]Computing shadows took less than 2 hours for the ball (33 frames, 3 mattes) and 12 hours for the stomping man (160 frames, 6 mattes).

5 Conclusion and Future Work

This paper presents a method for semi-automatic creation of shadow mattes for cel animation. The process reduces human effort normally required for painting shadow mattes. The system yields plausible shadows, even for complex characters and scenes. We show examples with dramatic lighting – directional lights and point lights casting very oblique shadows, and even gobos – in order to demonstrate the effectiveness of the method with such lights.

Setting up the scene and generating shadow mattes is relatively easy. Furthermore, once this task is accomplished it is trivial to subsequently change the lighting conditions and experiment with different effects. Thus, animators and directors can easily adjust the lighting (within a range consistent with the underlying painted artwork), in contrast to the traditional method wherein the shadow artist would redraw all of the mattes.

While the shadows in our examples are reasonable, there are some characters or background objects for which our inflation technique would be inappropriate. Either hand-drawn shadows or alternate modeling methods would address these problem cases.

This work suggests a number of areas for future investigation:

Applying computer vision techniques for understanding art. The most time-consuming aspect of our system is creation of layered character mattes. Applying computer vision techniques (e.g. [21, 24]) to automate layer specification would facilitate this process. Ultimately, tracking processes which adapt 3D models to drawn animation sequences [3] offer the potential of highly refined shadows and rendering effects.

Automatic light placement. Artists and directors accustomed to traditional hand-drawn techniques may be benefit from automatic light placement, based on either the background painting and its simple 3D model, or on crude hand-drawn samples (in the spirit of Schoeneman et al. [10]).

Shadow simplification. In traditional animation, hand-drawn shadows are often abstract rather than realistic. We would like to be able to simplify shadows, perhaps as a post-process in this system.

Acknowledgements

Many of the ideas in this paper were advanced at DreamWorks by Galen Gornowicz, Saty Raghavachary, and Gigi Yates. We are extremely grateful to Grady Klein and Rob Jensen for creating the hand-drawn characters and background scenery shown here. Thanks to Rick Szeliski and Mike Salisbury for helpful discussions about constructing the scene.

This work was supported by an NSF CAREER Award and an Alfred P. Sloan Fellowship.

References

[1] CORRÊA, W. T., JENSEN, R. J., THAYER, C. E., AND FINKELSTEIN, A. Texture mapping for cel animation. *Computer Graphics (Proceedings of SIGGRAPH 98)*, 435–446.

[2] FEKETE, J., BIZOUARN, E., COURNARIE, E., GALAS, T., AND TAILLEFER, F. TicTacToon: A paperless system for professional 2-D animation. *Computer Graphics (Proceedings of SIGGRAPH 95)*, 79–90.

[3] GORNOWICZ, G., AND WILLIAMS, L. Snap to it! Automatic 3D object and silhouette registration. Sketches and Applications, SIGGRAPH 2000.

[4] IGARASHI, T., MATSUOKA, S., AND TANAKA, H. Teddy: A sketching interface for 3D freeform design. *Computer Graphics (Proceedings of SIGGRAPH 99)*, 409–416.

[5] KERSTEN, D., MAMASSIAN, P., AND KNILL, D. C. Moving cast shadows induce apparent motion in depth. *Perception 26*, 2 (1997), 171–192. Also see: http://vision.psych.umn.edu/www/kersten-lab/demos/shadows.html.

[6] RADEMACHER, P. View-dependent geometry. *Computer Graphics (Proceedings of SIGGRAPH 99)*, 439–446.

[7] ROBERTSON, B. Disney lets CAPS out of the bag. *Computer Graphics World* (July 1994), 58–64.

[8] ROBERTSON, B. Mixed media. *Computer Graphics World* (Dec. 1998), 32–35.

[9] ROBERTSON, B. Deep background. *Computer Graphics World* (July 1999), 50–51.

[10] SCHOENEMAN, C., DORSEY, J., SMITS, B., ARVO, J., AND GREENBERG, D. Painting with light. *Computer Graphics (Proceedings of SIGGRAPH 93)*, 143–146.

[11] SHANTZIS, M. A. A model for efficient and flexible image computing. *Computer Graphics (Proceedings of SIGGRAPH 94)*, 147–154.

[12] THOMAS, F., AND JOHNSTON, O. *Disney Animation: The Illusion of Life*. Walt Disney Productions, New York, 1981.

[13] UNIVERSAL STUDIOS / DREAMWORKS. *The Prince of Egypt*. Movie, 1999.

[14] VAN OVERVELD, K., AND WYVILL, B. Polygon inflation for animated models: A method for the extrusion of arbitrary polygon meshes. *Journal of Vision and Computer Animation 18* (1997), 3–16.

[15] WALLACE, B. A. Merging and transformation of raster images for cartoon animation. *Computer Graphics (Proceedings of SIGGRAPH 81)*, 253–262.

[16] WALT DISNEY PRODUCTIONS. *Tarzan*. Movie, 1999.

[17] WANGER, L., FERWERDA, J., AND GREENBERG, D. Perceiving spatial relationships in computer-generated images. *IEEE Computer Graphics and Applications, 12*, 3 (1992), 44–58.

[18] WARNER BROTHERS. *The Iron Giant*. Movie, 1999.

[19] WILLIAMS, L. 3D rendering effects for 2D animation. Sketches and Applications, SIGGRAPH 1999.

[20] WILLIAMS, L. Shading in two dimensions. *Proceedings of Graphics Interface 91*, 143–151.

[21] WILLIAMS, L. R. Topological reconstruction of a smooth manifold-solid from its occluding contour. Tech. Rep. 94-04, University of Massachusetts, Amherst, MA, 1994.

[22] WOOD, D. N., FINKELSTEIN, A., HUGHES, J. F., THAYER, C. E., AND SALESIN, D. H. Multiperspective panoramas for cel animation. *Computer Graphics (Proceedings of SIGGRAPH 97)*, 243–250.

[23] ZELEZNIK, R. C., HERNDON, K. P., AND HUGHES, J. F. SKETCH: An interface for sketching 3D scenes. *Computer Graphics (Proceedings of SIGGRAPH 96)*, 163–170.

[24] ZHU, S., AND YUILLE, A. FORMS: A flexible object recognition and modelling system. *International Journal of Computer Vision 20*, 3 (1996), 187–212.

Illustrating smooth surfaces

Aaron Hertzmann   Denis Zorin

New York University

Abstract

We present a new set of algorithms for line-art rendering of smooth surfaces. We introduce an efficient, deterministic algorithm for finding silhouettes based on geometric duality, and an algorithm for segmenting the silhouette curves into smooth parts with constant visibility. These methods can be used to find all silhouettes in real time in software. We present an automatic method for generating hatch marks in order to convey surface shape. We demonstrate these algorithms with a drawing style inspired by *A Topological Picturebook* by G. Francis.

CR Categories and Subject Descriptors: I.3.3 [**Computer Graphics**]: Picture/Image Generation– *Display algorithms.*

Additional Keywords: Non-photorealistic rendering, silhouettes, pen-and-ink illustration, hatching, direction fields.

1 Introduction

Line art is one of the most common illustration styles. Line drawing styles can be found in many contexts, such as cartoons, technical illustration, architectural design and medical atlases. These drawings often communicate information more efficiently and precisely than photographs. Line art is easy to reproduce, compresses well and, if represented in vector form, is resolution-independent.

Many different styles of line art exist; the unifying feature of these styles is that the images are constructed from uniformly colored lines. The simplest is the style of silhouette drawing, which consists only of silhouettes and images of sharp creases and object boundaries. This style is often sufficient in engineering and architectural contexts, where most shapes are constructed out of simple geometric components, such as boxes, spheres and cylinders. This style of rendering captures only geometry and completely ignores texture, lighting and shadows. On the other end of the spectrum is the pen-and-ink illustration style. In pen-and-ink illustrations, variable-density hatching and complex hatch patterns convey information about shape, texture and lighting. While silhouette drawing is sufficient to convey information about simple objects, it is often insufficient for depicting objects that are complex or free-form. From many points of view, a smooth object may have no visible silhouette lines, aside from the outer silhouette (Figure 8), and all the information inside the silhouette is lost. In these cases, can be added to indicate the shape of the surface.

The primary goal of our work was to develop rendering techniques for automatic generation of line-art illustrations of piecewise-smooth free-form surfaces. When using conventional photorealistic rendering techniques (e.g. Z-buffer or ray tracing)

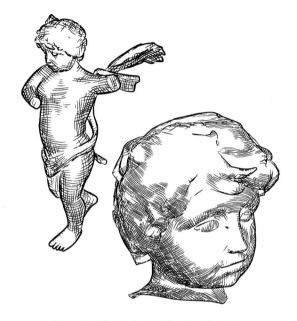

Figure 1: Illustrations of the Cupid mesh.

one can typically replace a smooth surface with a polygonal approximation, and thus reduce the problem to that of rendering polygonal meshes. This no longer true when our goal is to generate line drawings. Some differential quantities associated with the smooth surface must be recovered in order to generate visually pleasing hatch directions and topologically correct silhouette lines. Some of the problems that occur when a smooth surface is replaced by its polygonal approximation are discussed in greater detail in Section 4.

In this paper we address two general problems: computing silhouette curves of smooth surfaces, and generating smooth direction fields on surfaces that are suitable for hatching. The algorithms that we have developed can be used to implement a number of non-photorealistic rendering techniques. Our main focus is on a particular rendering style, which aims to communicate all essential information about the shape of the surface with a limited amount of hatching.

Contributions. *Algorithms.* To support rendering of smooth surfaces, we have developed a number of novel algorithms including:

- An efficient, deterministic algorithm for detecting silhouettes; (Section 4.3). In addition to non-photorealistic applications, this method can be used to accelerate computation of shadow volumes.
- An algorithm for cusp detection and segmentation of silhouette curves into smooth parts with constant visibility (Section 4.2).
- An algorithm for computing smooth direction fields on surfaces, suitable for use in hatching (Section 5). These fields have a wide range of uses, ranging from high-quality pen-and-ink rendering to interactive illustration and hatching.

An important feature of our approach is that any polygonal mesh can serve as input; the smooth surface that we render is inferred from the mesh. We do not assume an explicitly specified parameterization, which make our approach more general than previously developed techniques.

Rendering style. We have developed a new non-photorealistic rendering style based on the techniques of Francis [15], and influenced by the cartoons of Thomas Nast [34] and others.

The rules for drawing in this style are described in Section 6.

2 Previous Work

The methods used in nonphotorealistic rendering can be separated into two groups: image-space and object-space. The image-based approach is general and simple; however, it is not particularly suitable for generating concise line drawings of untextured smooth surfaces. Image-based techniques are presented in [5, 30, 7, 18, 6, 28]; these algorithms exploit graphics hardware to produce image precision silhouette images. Our technique is an object space method; it directly uses the 3D representation of objects, rather than their images. Winkenbach and Salesin [36] describe a method for producing appealing pen-and-ink renderings of smooth surfaces. Parametric lines on NURBS patches were used to determine the hatch directions and silhouette lines were computed using polyhedral approximation to the surface. Their main technical focus is on using the hatch density to render complex texture and lighting effects. Their system relied on a surface parameterization to produce hatch directions; however, such a parameterization does not exist for many types of surfaces, and can often be a poor indicator of shape when it does exist. Elber [12, 13] and Interrante [21] used principal curvature directions for hatching. Curvatures generally provide good hatch directions, but cannot be reliably or uniquely computed at many points on a surface. Our system makes use of the principle curvature directions, and uses an optimization technique to "fill in" the hatching field where it is poorly-defined. Deussen et al. [9] use intersections of the surfaces with planes; while being quite flexible, this approach requires segmentation of the surface into parts, where different groups of planes are used; the plane orientations computed using skeletons relate only indirectly to the local surface properties.

Our work also draws on techniques developed for vector field visualization [8, 22]. It should be noted that relatively little work has been done on generating fields on surfaces as opposed to visualization of existing fields. Elber [12, 13] discusses the relative merits of some commonly-used hatching fields (principle curvature directions, field of tangents to the isoparametric lines, the gradient field of the brightness).

Silhouette detection is an important component of many nonphotorealistic rendering systems. Markosian et al. [25] presented a randomized algorithm for locating silhouettes; this system is fast but does not guarantee that all silhouettes will be found. Gooch et al. [18] and Benichou and Elber [3] proposed the use of a Gauss map to efficiently locate all object silhouettes under orthographic projection. In this paper, we present a new method for silhouette detection that is fast, deterministic, and applicable to both orthographic and perspective projection.

Our method for computing the silhouette lines of free-form surfaces is closely related to the work of [14, 17] in computing silhouettes for NURBS surfaces.

3 Overview

In this section we present a general overview of our algorithms.

Surface representation. The input data for our system is a polygonal mesh that approximates a smooth surface. Polygonal meshes remain the most common and flexible form for approximating surfaces. However, information about differential quantities (normals, curvatures, etc.) associated with the original surface is lost. We need a way to estimate these quantities and compute, if necessary, finer approximations to the original smooth surface. This can be

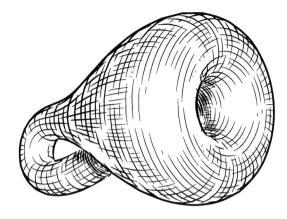

Figure 2: Klein bottle. Lighting and hatch directions are chosen to convey surface shape. Undercuts and Mach bands near the hole and the self-intersection enhance contrast.

done if we choose a method that allows us to construct a smooth surface from an approximating arbitrary polygonal mesh, and easily compute the associated differential quantities (normals, curvatures, etc.).

We use piecewise-smooth subdivision, similar to the algorithms presented in [20], with an important modification (Appendix A) to make the curvature well-defined and nonzero at extraordinary vertices. However, other ways of defining smooth surfaces based on polygonal meshes can be used, provided that all the necessary quantities can be computed.

Algorithms. Our rendering technique has three main stages: computation of a direction field on the surface, computation of the silhouette lines and generation of hatch lines.

Hatch direction field. This stage defines a view-independent field on the surface that can be used later to generate hatches. Rather than defining two separate directional fields, we define a single *cross field* (Section 5) for hatches and cross-hatches. The main steps of our algorithm are: smooth the surface if necessary; compute an initial approximation to the field in areas of the surface where it is well defined, initialize the directions arbitrarily elsewhere; optimize the directions in places where the cross field was not well defined.

Silhouette curve computation. We compute the curves in several steps (Section 4): compute boundary, self-intersection and crease curves, as well as boundaries of flat areas; compute silhouette curves as zero-crossings of the dot product of the normal with the view direction; find cusps, determine visibility, and segment the silhouette curves into smooth pieces.

Hatch generation. Our hatch generation algorithms follow some of the rules described by Francis [15] (Section 6). The surface is divided into four levels of brightness with corresponding levels of hatching: highlights and Mach bands (no hatching), midtones (single hatching), shadowed regions (cross-hatching), and undercuts (dense cross-hatching). Line thickness varies within each region according to the lighting. Undercuts and Mach bands are used to increase contrast where objects overlap. Lights are placed at the view position or to the side of the object. The hatching algorithm covers all hatch regions with cross-hatches, then removes hatches from the single hatch regions as necessary.

4 Computing Silhouette Drawings

In this section we describe algorithms for generating the simplest line drawings of smooth surfaces, which we call silhouette drawings. A silhouette drawing includes only the images of the most visually important curves on the surface: boundaries, creases, silhouette lines and self-intersection lines. Finding intersections of smooth surfaces is a complex problem, which we do not address in the paper. We find self-intersections of a mesh approximating the surface and assume that self-intersection lines of the mesh approximate the self-intersection curves of the surface sufficiently well. Boundary curves and creases are explicitly represented in the surface; thus, we focus our attention on the problem of computing the silhouette lines. We will refer to the creases, boundaries and self-intersection curves as *feature curves*.

Before proceeding, we recall several definitions[1]. First, we define more precisely what we mean by a piecewise-smooth surface. A piecewise-smooth surface can be thought of as a finite union of a number of smooth surfaces with boundaries. A smooth embedded surface is a subset M of $\mathbf{R}^3$ such that for any point $\mathbf{p}$ of this subset there is a neighborhood $U(\mathbf{p}) = \mathrm{Ball}_\epsilon(\mathbf{p}) \cap M$ and a C^1-continuous nondegenerate one-to-one map $\mathbf{F}(u, v)$ from a domain D in $\mathbf{R}^2$ onto $U(\mathbf{p})$. The domain D can be taken to be an open disk for interior points, and a half-disk (including the diameter, but excluding the circular boundary) for smooth boundary points. It follows from the definition that the normal $\mathbf{F}_u \times \mathbf{F}_v$ is defined and is nonzero everywhere on the surface. The direction of $\mathbf{F}_u \times \mathbf{F}_v$ at any point of the surface is independent, up to a sign, of the local parameterization $\mathbf{F}$ and is denoted $\mathbf{n}(\mathbf{p})$.

The *silhouette set* for the smooth surface is the set of points $\mathbf{p}$ of the surface such that $(\mathbf{n}(\mathbf{p}) \cdot (\mathbf{p} - \mathbf{c})) = 0$, where $\mathbf{c}$ is the viewpoint. The silhouette is in general a union of flat areas on the surface, curves and points. We isolate flat areas and consider them separately. Isolated silhouette points are unstable, and are not relevant for our purposes. For a surface that does not contain flat areas and is C^2, the silhouette for a general position of the viewpoint can be shown to consist of C^1 non-intersecting curves (silhouette curves).

An important role in our constructions is played by the *curvature* of the surface. More specifically, we are interested in principal curvatures and principal curvature directions. The two principal curvatures at a point $\mathbf{p}$ are maximal and minimal curvatures of the curves obtained by intersecting the surface with a plane passing through $\mathbf{p}$ and containing the normal to the surface. The principal curvature directions are the tangents to the curves for which the maximum and minimum are obtained; these directions are always orthogonal and lie in the tangent plane to the surface. The formulas expressing these quantities in terms of the derivatives of $\mathbf{F}$ are standard and can be found, for example, in [4]. The most important property of the principal curvatures that we use can be formulated as follows: *if a surface has principal curvatures κ_1 and κ_2, and the unit vectors along principal directions and the normal are used to define an orthonormal coordinate system (r, s, t), with r and s parameterizing the tangent plane then locally the surface is the graph of a function over the tangent plane*

$$t = \kappa_1 r^2 + \kappa_2 s^2 + o(r^2 + s^2) \tag{1}$$

It follows that principal curvatures and principal curvature directions locally define the best approximating quadratic surface.

4.1 Silhouettes of Meshes and Smooth Surfaces

The simplest approach to computing the silhouette curves would be to replace the smooth surface with its triangulation and find the silhouette edges of the triangular mesh. However, there are significant differences between the silhouettes of smooth surfaces and their approximating polygonal meshes (Figure 4). For polygonal meshes, complex cusps (Figure 3), where several silhouette chains meet, are stable, that is, do not disappear when the viewpoint is perturbed. Singularities of projections of polyhedra were studied

---

[1] We do not state rigorous mathematical definitions in complete detail; an interested reader can find them in most standard differential geometry texts.

in considerable detail (see a recent paper [2] for pointers); a simple classification in the two-dimensional case, which does not appear to be explicitly described elsewhere, can be found in [1]. For smooth surfaces, the only type of stable singularity is a simple cusp, as it was shown in the classic paper by Whitney [35]. As a consequence, silhouette curves on smooth surfaces are either closed loops, or start and end on feature lines, while on polygonal surfaces they may intersect, and their topology is more complex. Moreover, we observe

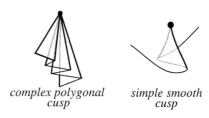

complex polygonal cusp   *simple smooth cusp*

Figure 3: *Left:* Complex cusps are stable on polygonal meshes. *Right:* Only simple cusps are stable on smooth surfaces.

that *no matter how fine the triangulation is, the topology of the silhouette of a polygonal approximation to the surface is likely to be significantly different from that of the smooth surface itself.* This does not present a problem for fixed-resolution images: if the distance between the projected silhouette of the mesh and the projected silhouette of the smooth surface is less than a pixel, the topological details cannot be distinguished. However, if we do want to generate resolution-independent images capturing the essential features of the silhouette of the smooth surface correctly, or apply line styles to the silhouette curves, the polygonal approximation cannot be used. (Figure 4). Similar observations were made in [5].

To preserve the essential topological properties of silhouettes, we compute the silhouette curves using an approach similar to the one used in [14, 17] for spline surfaces. Recall that the silhouette set of a surface is the zero set of the function $g(\mathbf{p}) = (\mathbf{n}(\mathbf{p}) \cdot (\mathbf{p} - \mathbf{c}))$ defined on the surface. The idea is to compute an approximation to this function and find its zero set. For each vertex $\mathbf{p}$ of the polygonal approximation, we compute the true surface normal and $g(\mathbf{p})$ at the vertex. Then the approximation to the function $g(\mathbf{p})$ is defined by linear interpolation of the values of the function. As the resulting function is piecewise-linear, the zero set will consist of line segments inside each triangle of the polygonal approximation. Moreover, we can easily enforce the general position assumption by picking arbitrarily the sign of the function $g(\mathbf{p})$ at vertices where it happens to be exactly zero. As a result, the line segments of the zero set connect points in the interior of the edges of the mesh, and form either closed loops or non-intersecting chains connecting points on the feature lines (Figure 4), similar in structure to the actual silhouette curves. We may miss narrow areas on the surface where the sign is different from surrounding areas. It is easy to see, however, that the silhouette curves we obtain by our method will have the same topology as the silhouette curves of some surface obtained by a small perturbation of the original. This means that we are guaranteed to have a plausible image of a surface, but it may not accurately reflect features of size on the order of the size of a triangle of the approximating mesh in some cases. The silhouette algorithm is described in greater detail in [19].

4.2 Cusp Detection

While the silhouette curves on the surface do not have singularities in a general position, the projected silhouette curves in the image plane do; there is a single stable singularity type, aside from terminating points at feature lines: a simple cusp (Figure 3). The most straightforward way to detect these singularities is to examine the

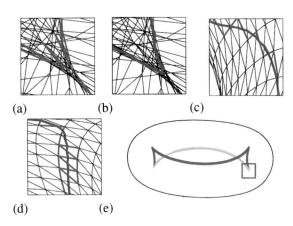

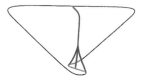

Figure 5: *Left:* Cusps are found as intersections of zero sets of two functions defined on the surface, the dot product of the normal with the viewing direction and the cusp function. The silhouette curve is shown in blue, the cusp zero set in red. *Right:* The same curves; view from a viewpoint different from the one that was used to compute the curves.

Figure 4: (a) Silhouette edges of a polygonal approximation produce jagged silhouette curves. (b) Our method produces smooth silhouette curves by inferring information about the smooth surface from the polygonal mesh. (c) The same curves shown from another viewpoint and overlayed. (d) A complex cusp occurs in the polygonal approximation when the surface is nearly parallel to the view direction. This does not occur in the smooth silhouette curve. (e) Smooth line drawing of the "smiling torus." The red box shows the location of the curves in (a)-(c).

tangents of the silhouette curves; cusps are the points where the tangent is parallel to the view direction. However, this approach is not numerically reliable, especially if the silhouette curves are approximated by polylines. We propose a new, numerically more robust way to find the cusps, using the following geometric observations.

Consider a silhouette point $\mathbf{p}$ with principal curvature directions $\mathbf{w}_1$ and $\mathbf{w}_2$ and principal curvatures κ_1 and κ_2. Let $\mathbf{c}$ be the viewpoint; since $\mathbf{p}$ is the silhouette point, the viewing direction $\mathbf{v} = \mathbf{c} - \mathbf{p}$ is in the tangent plane. Let $[c_1, c_2, 0]$ be the components of $\mathbf{c}$ with respect to the coordinates (r, s, t) associated with the principal curvature directions, computed by $c_1 = (\mathbf{v} \cdot \mathbf{w}_1)$ and $c_2 = (\mathbf{v} \cdot \mathbf{w}_2)$. As we have observed, $\mathbf{p}$ is a cusp when the tangent to the silhouette at $\mathbf{p}$ is parallel to the viewing direction $\mathbf{v}$. The tangent to the silhouette can easily be expressed in terms of curvature. Approximation (1) yields the following approximation to the normals in a small neighborhood near $\mathbf{p}$: $\mathbf{n}(r,s) = [-2\kappa_1 r, -2\kappa_2 s, 1]$. The equation of the 2nd order approximation to the silhouette curve is an implicit quadratic equation, $g(r,s) = (\mathbf{n}(r,s) \cdot \mathbf{v}(r,s)) = 0$, where $\mathbf{v}(r,s)$ is the viewing direction $\mathbf{c} - \mathbf{p}(r,s) = [c_1 - r, c_2 - s, -\kappa_1 r^2 - \kappa_2 s^2]$. We calculate the vector perpendicular to the silhouette at $\mathbf{p}$ as $\nabla g(0,0) = [-2\kappa_1 c_1, -2\kappa_2 c_2]$. The resulting condition for the viewing direction to be parallel to the silhouette tangent (or, equivalently, perpendicular to $\nabla g(0,0)$) to the viewing direction is $\kappa_1 c_1^2 + \kappa_2 c_2^2 = 0$. Therefore, we can define a parameterization-independent scalar function on the surface which we call the *cusp function*:

$$C(\mathbf{p}) = \kappa_1 \left(\mathbf{v} \cdot \mathbf{w}_1\right)^2 + \kappa_2 \left(\mathbf{v} \cdot \mathbf{w}_2\right)^2$$

where all quantities are evaluated at point $\mathbf{p}$. This function has the following important property: *cusps are contained in the intersection set of the two families of curves: one obtained as the zero set of the function* $g(\mathbf{p})$, *the other as the zero set of the cusp function* $C(\mathbf{p})$ (Figure 5). The zero set of $C(\mathbf{p})$ can be approximated in the same way as the zero set of $g(\mathbf{p})$; each triangle of the polygonal mesh may contain a single line segment approximating the zero set of $C(\mathbf{p})$ and another approximating the zero set of $g(\mathbf{p})$. This allows us to compute approximate cusp locations robustly, without introducing many spurious cusps, and at the same time using relatively coarse polygonal approximations to the smooth surface.

4.3 Fast Silhouette Detection

In the previous section, we have presented an algorithm for constructing approximations to the silhouette curves which, when implemented in the simplest way, requires complete traversal of the mesh. Such a traversal is unnecessary; typically, only a small percentage of mesh faces contain silhouettes [25, 23]. For polygonal meshes, a number of fast techniques were developed that allow one to avoid complete traversal. A stochastic algorithm was proposed in [25]. A deterministic algorithm based on the Gauss map was proposed in [3, 18], but is restricted to orthographic projection. We present a new deterministic algorithm for accelerated location of silhouettes, which works for both orthographic and perspective projection. This algorithm is equally suitable for finding silhouettes defined as zero sets, and for finding silhouette edges of polygonal meshes.

Our algorithm is based on the concept of *dual surfaces*. The points of the dual surface M' are the images of the tangent planes to a surface M under a duality map, which maps each plane $Ax + By + Cz + D = 0$ to the homogeneous point $[A, B, C, D]$. More explicitly, M' can be obtained by mapping each point of M to a homogeneous point $\mathbf{N} = [n_1, n_2, n_3, -(\mathbf{p} \cdot \mathbf{n})]$, where $\mathbf{n} = [n_1, n_2, n_3, 0]$ is the unit normal at $\mathbf{p}$. Note that the inverse is also true: each plane in the dual space corresponds to a point in the primal space. Let $\mathbf{C} = [c_1, c_2, c_3, c_4]$ be our viewpoint in the homogeneous form. Then the silhouette of the surface consists of all points $\mathbf{p}$ for which $\mathbf{C}$ is in the tangent plane at that point. For perspective projection, this means that $(\mathbf{C} \cdot \mathbf{N}) = (\mathbf{c} - \mathbf{p}) \cdot \mathbf{n} = 0$. For orthographic projection, the homogeneous formula is the same: $(\mathbf{C} \cdot \mathbf{N}) = (\mathbf{c} \cdot \mathbf{n}) = 0$, where $\mathbf{c}$ is interpreted as the view direction. Our algorithm is based on the following observation: *the image of the silhouette set of the surface with respect to the viewpoint* $\mathbf{C}$ *under the duality map is the intersection of the plane* $(\mathbf{C} \cdot \mathbf{x}) = 0$, *with the dual surface.* This fact allows us to reduce the problem of finding the silhouette to the problem of intersecting a plane with a surface (Figure 7), for which many space-partition-based acceleration techniques are available. However, an additional complication is introduced by the fact that some points of the dual surface may be at infinity. This does not allow us to consider only the finite part of the projective space, which can be identified with $\mathbf{R}^3$. However we can identify the whole 3D projective space with points of the unit hypersphere S^3, or, equivalently, of the boundary of a hypercube, in four-dimensional space. As four-dimensional space is somewhat difficult to visualize, we show the idea of the algorithm on a 2D example in Figure 6. In the 2D case, the problem is to compute all *silhouette points* on a curve, that is, the points for which the tangent line contains the viewpoint.

While the geometric background is somewhat abstract, the actual algorithm is quite simple. The input to the algorithm is a polygonal mesh, with normals specified at vertices, if we are computing silhouettes using zero-crossings. The normals are not necessary if we are locating the silhouette edges of the polygonal mesh. There are two parts to the algorithm: initialization of the spatial partition and

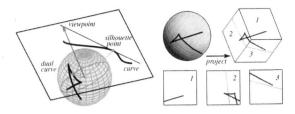

Figure 6: *Left*: Using a dual curve to find silhouette points. The figure shows a curve in the plane $z = 1$ and its dual on a sphere. The blue arrow is the vector c from the origin in 3D to the viewpoint in the plane, the blue circle is the intersection of the plane passing through the origin perpendicular to c with the unit sphere. The red points are a silhouette point and its dual. The silhouette point can be found by intersecting the blue circle with the dual curve and retrieving corresponding point on the original curve. *Right*: Reducing the intersection problem to planar subproblems. The upper hemisphere containing the dual curve is projected on the surface of cube and at most 5 (in this case 3) planar curve-line intersection problems are solved on the faces.

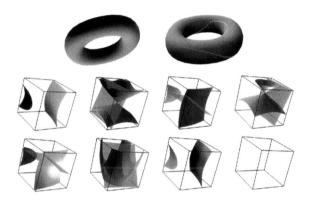

Figure 7: Silhouette lines under the duality map correspond to the intersection curve of a plane with the dual surface. *Top:* Torus shown from camera and side views. *Bottom:* The eight 3D faces of the hypercube, seven of which contain portions of the dual surface. The viewpoint dual is shown as a blue plane. Silhouettes occur at the intersection of the dual plane with the dual surface.

intersection of the dual surface with the plane corresponding to the viewpoint. The second part is fairly standard, so we focus on the first part.

Step 1: For each vertex $\mathbf{p}$ with normal $\mathbf{n}$, we compute the dual position $\mathbf{N} = [n_1, n_2, n_3, -(\mathbf{p} \cdot \mathbf{n})]$. The dual positions define the dual mesh which has different vertex positions but the same connectivity.

Step 2: Normalize each dual position $\mathbf{N}$ using l_∞-norm, that is, divide by $\max(|N_1|, |N_2|, |N_3|, |N_4|)$. After division, at least one of the components N_i, $i = 1..4$, becomes 1 or -1. The resulting four-dimensional point is on the surface of the unit hypercube. The three-dimensional face of the cube on which the vertex is located is determined by the index and sign of the maximal component.

Step 3: Each triangle of the dual mesh is assigned to a list for every three-dimensional face in which it has a vertex.

Step 4: An octtree is constructed for each three-dimensional face, and the triangles assigned to this face are placed into the octtree.

The second step of the algorithm, which is repeated for each frame, uses the octtree to find the silhouette edges for a given camera position by intersecting the dual plane with the dual surface.

We have implemented an interactive silhouette viewer based on the dual space method. In our tests, silhouette tests were performed

on twice as many triangles as there were actual triangles containing silhouettes, suggesting that performance is roughly linear in the number of silhouette triangles. This represents a substantial speedup over traversing the entire mesh. Silhouette edge detection and visibility calculations on the three-times subdivided Venus model ($\sim$90,000 triangles) can be performed at approximately 17 frames per second on a 225 MHz SGI Octane, without using graphics hardware, which is similar to the performance of the nondeterministic algorithm of [25].

4.4 Visibility

Before computing visibility, we separate the silhouette curves into segments. Visibility is determined for each segment. The following points are used to separate segments: cusps, silhouette-feature joints, and inverse images of silhouette-feature and silhouette-silhouette intersections in image space. Visibility can change only at these points, thus each segment is either completely visible or invisible.

Determining visibility is fundamentally difficult for smooth surfaces, because it cannot be inferred precisely from visibility of the approximating mesh. Our algorithm can only guarantee that the correct visibility will be produced if the mesh is sufficiently fine, using a theoretically-estimated required degree of refinement. However, the estimate is too conservative and difficult to compute to be practical; in our implementation, we refine the mesh to a fixed subdivision level.

Our visibility algorithm is based on the following observation: at any area on the surface, the rate of change of the normal is bounded by the maximal directional curvature. For a sufficiently fine triangulation, one can guarantee that for any triangle for which $(\mathbf{n} \cdot (\mathbf{p} - \mathbf{c}))$ changes sign, there is a silhouette edge of the polygonal approximation adjacent to a vertex of the triangle. We use the visibility of these edges to compute visibility of the silhouette curves. The visibility of the silhouette edges can be determined using known techniques (e.g. [25]).

For each curve we find visibility of all nearby silhouette edges (which is not necessarily consistent) and use the visibility of the majority of the edges to determine visibility of the chain. It is possible to show that this method will produce correct visibility for sufficiently fine meshes in the following sense: there is a smooth surface for which the precise projection has the same topology as the one computed by our method.

In practice, we have found that the algorithm performs well even without extra refinement near the silhouettes, provided that the original mesh is sufficiently close to the surface. An efficient algorithm with better-defined properties would be useful.

5 Direction Fields on Surfaces

Fields on surfaces. To generate hatches, we need to choose several direction fields on visible parts of the surface. The direction fields are different from the more commonly used vector fields: unlike a vector field, a direction field does not have a magnitude and does not distinguish between the two possible orientations.

The fields can either be defined directly in the image plane as in [31], or defined on the surface and then projected. The advantage of the former method is that the field needs to be defined and continuous only in each separate area of the image. However, it is somewhat more difficult to use the information about the shape of the objects when constructing the field, and the field must be recomputed for each image. We choose to generate the field on the surface first.

A number of different fields on surfaces have been used to define hatching directions. The most commonly-used field is probably the field of isoparametric lines; this method has obvious limitations,

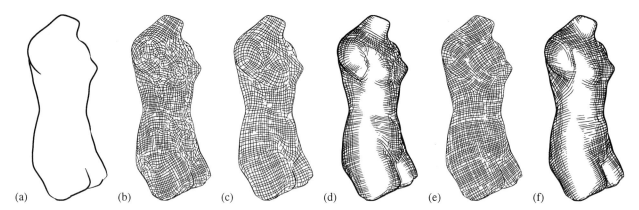

Figure 8: Direction fields on the Venus. (a) Silhouettes alone do not convey the interior shape of the surface. (b) Raw principle curvature directions produce an overly-complex hatching pattern. (c) Smooth cross field produced by optimization. Reliable principal curvature directions are left unchanged. Optimization is initialized by the principal curvatures. (d) Hatching with the smooth cross field. (e) Very smooth cross field produced by optimizing all directions. (f) Hatching from the very smooth field.

as the parameterization may be very far from isometric, and is not appropriate for surfaces lacking a good natural parameterization, such as subdivision surfaces and implicit surfaces. The successes and failures of this approach provide valuable clues for construction of fields for hatching.

The most natural geometric candidate is the pair of principal curvature direction fields [13, 21]. corresponding to the minimal and maximal curvatures[2]. We will refer to the integral lines of these fields as *curvature lines*. These fields do not depend on parameterization, capture important geometric features, and are consistent with the most common two-directional hatching pattern. However, they suffer from a number of disadvantages. All umbilical points (points with coinciding principal curvatures) are singularities, which means that the fields are not defined anywhere on a sphere and have arbitrarily complex structure on surfaces obtained by small perturbations of a sphere. On flat areas (when both curvatures are very small) the fields are likely to result in a far more complex pattern than the one that would be used by a human.

Other candidates include isophotes (lines of constant brightness) and the gradient field of the distance to silhouette or feature lines [25, 12]. Both are suitable for hatching in a narrow band near silhouettes or feature lines, but typically do not adequately capture shape further from silhouettes, nor are they suitable for cross-hatching.

Our approach is based on several observations about successes and failures of existing methods, as well as hatching techniques used by artists.

• *Cylindric surfaces.* Surface geometry is rendered best by principal curvature directions on cylindrical surfaces, that is, surfaces for which one of the principal curvatures is zero (all points of the surface are parabolic). This fact is quite remarkable: psychophysical studies confirm that even a few parallel curves can create a strong impression of a cylindrical surface with curves interpreted as principal curvature lines [32, 24]. Another important observation is that for cylinders the principal curvature lines are also geodesics, which is not necessarily true in general. Hatching following the principal curvature directions fails when the ratio of principal curvatures is close to one.
Deussen et al. [9] uses intersections of the surface with planes to obtain hatch directions; the resulting curves are likely to be locally close to geodesics on slowly varying surfaces.
• *Isometric parameterizations.* Isoparameteric lines work well as curvature directions when a parameterization exists and is close

to isometric, i.e. minimizes the metric distortion as described in, for example, [10, 27]. In this case, parametric lines are close to geodesics. Isoparametric lines were used by [36, 11].
• *Artistic examples.* We observe that artists tend to use relatively straight hatch lines, even when the surface has wrinkles. Smaller details are conveyed by varying the density and the number of hatch directions (Figure 9).

Figure 9: Almost all hatches in this cartoon by Thomas Nast curve only slightly, while capturing the overall shape of the surface. Note that the hatches often appear to follow a cylinder approximating the surface. Small details of the geometry are rendered using variations in hatch density.

These observations lead to the following simple requirements for hatching fields: *in areas where the surface is close to parabolic, the field should be close to principal curvature directions; on the whole surface, the integral curves of the field should be close to geodesic.* In addition, if the surface has small details, the field should be generated using a smoothed version of the surface.

Cross fields. While it is usually possible to generate two global direction fields for the two main hatch directions, we have observed that this is undesirable in general. There are two reasons for this: first, if we would like to illustrate nonorientable surfaces, such fields may not exist. Second, and more importantly, there are natural cross-hatching patterns that cannot be decomposed into two smooth fields even locally (Figure 10). Thus, we consider *cross fields*, that is, maps defined on the surface, assigning an unordered pair of perpendicular directions to each point.

Constructing Hatching Fields. Our algorithm is based on the considerations above and proceeds in steps.

---

[2]It is possible to show that for a surface in general position, these fields are always globally defined, excluding a set of isolated singularities.

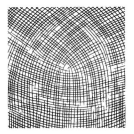

Figure 10: A cross-hatching pattern produced by our system on a smooth corner. This pattern cannot be decomposed into two orthogonal smooth fields near the corner singularity. The analytic expression for a similar field in the plane is $v_1(r, \theta) = [\cos(\theta/4), \sin(\theta/4)]$; $v_2(r, \theta) = [-\sin(\theta/4), \cos(\theta/4)]$. This field is continuous and smooth only if we do not distinguish between v_1 and v_2.

Step 1. Optionally, create a smoothed copy of the original mesh. The copy is used to compute the field. The amount of smoothing is chosen by the user, with regard to the smoothness of the original mesh, and the scale of geometric detail the user wishes to capture in the image. For example, no smoothing might be necessary for a close-up view of a small part of a surface, while substantial smoothing may be necessary to produce good images from a general view; in practice we seldom found this to be necessary.

Step 2. Identify areas of the surface which are sufficiently close to parabolic, that is, the ratio of minimal to maximal curvature is high, and at least one curvature is large enough to be computed reliably. Additionally, we mark as unreliable any vertex for which the average cross field energy of its incident edges exceeds a threshold, in order to allow optimization of vertices that begin singular.

Step 3. Initialize the field over the whole surface by computing principal curvature directions. If there are no quasi-parabolic areas, user input is required to initialize the field.

Step 4. Fix the field in quasi-parabolic areas and optimize the field on the rest of the vertices, which were marked as unreliable. This step is of primary importance and we describe it in greater detail.

Our optimization procedure is based on the observation that we would like the integral lines of our field to be close to geodesics. We use a similar, but not identical, requirement that the field is as close to constant as possible. Minimizing the angles between the world-space directions at adjacent vertices of the mesh is possible, but requires constrained optimization to keep the directions in the tangent planes. We use a different idea, based on establishing a correspondence between the tangent planes at different points of the surface, which, in some sense, corresponds to the minimal possible motion of the tangent plane as we move from one point to another. Then we only need to minimize the change of the field with respect to the corresponding directions in the tangent planes.

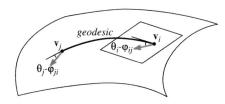

Figure 11: Moving vectors along geodesics.

Given two sufficiently close points $\mathbf{p}_1$ and $\mathbf{p}_2$ on a smooth surface, a natural way to map the tangent plane at $\mathbf{p}_1$ to the tangent plane at $\mathbf{p}_2$ is to transport vectors along the geodesics (Figure 11); for sufficiently close points there is a unique geodesic $\gamma(t)$, $t = 0..1$, connecting these points. This is done by mapping a unit

vector $\mathbf{u}_1$ in the tangent plane at $\mathbf{p}_1$ to a unit vector $\mathbf{u}_2$ in the tangent plane at $\mathbf{p}_2$, such that the angle between $\mathbf{u}_1$ and the tangent to the geodesic $\gamma'(0)$ is the same as the angle between $\mathbf{u}_2$ and $\gamma'(1)$. In discrete case, for adjacent vertices of the approximating mesh $\mathbf{v}_i$ and $\mathbf{v}_j$, we approximate the tangents to the geodesic by the projections of the edge $(\mathbf{v}_i, \mathbf{v}_j)$ into the tangent planes at the vertices. Let the directions of these projections be $\mathbf{t}_{ij}$ and $\mathbf{t}_{ji}$. Then a rigid transformation T_{ij} between the tangent planes is uniquely defined if we require that $\mathbf{t}_{ij}$ maps to $\mathbf{t}_{ji}$ and that the transformation preserves orientation. Then for any pair of tangent unit vectors $\mathbf{w}_i$ and $\mathbf{w}_j$ at $\mathbf{v}_i$ and $\mathbf{v}_j$ respectively, we can use $\|T_{ij}\mathbf{w}_i - \mathbf{w}_j\|$ to measure the difference between directions. One can show that the value of this expression is the same as $\|T_{ji}\mathbf{w}_j - \mathbf{w}_i\|$. To measure the difference between the values of the cross field at two points, we choose a unit tangent vector for each point. The vectors are chosen along the directions of the cross field. There are four possible choices at each point. We choose a pair of unit vectors for which the difference is minimal.

We now explicitly specify the energy functional. The cross field is described by a single angle θ_i for each vertex $\mathbf{v}_i$, which is the angle between a fixed tangent direction $\mathbf{t}_i$, and one of the directions of the cross field; we do not impose any limitations on the value of θ_i, and there are infinitely many choices for θ_i differing by $n\pi/2$ that result in the same cross field. Let φ_{ij} be the direction of the projection of the edge $(\mathbf{v}_i, \mathbf{v}_j)$ into the tangent plane at $\mathbf{v}_i$. Using this choice of coordinates, one can show that the quantity $\|T_{ij}\mathbf{w}_i - \mathbf{w}_j\|$ is equal to $\min_k \sqrt{2 - 2\cos((\theta_i - \varphi_{ij}) - (\theta_j - \varphi_{ji}) + k\pi/2)}$. Minimization of this quantity is equivalent to minimization of $E(i, j) = \min_k (-\cos((\theta_i - \varphi_{ij}) - (\theta_j - \varphi_{ji}) + k\pi/2))$, which is not differentiable. We observe, however, that $E_0(i, j) = -8E(i, j)^4 + 8E(i, j)^2 - 1$ is just $-\cos 4((\theta_i - \varphi_{ij}) - (\theta_j - \varphi_{ji}))$, and is a monotonic function of $E(i, j)$ on $[\sqrt{2}/2..1]$, the range of possible values of $E(i, j)$. Thus, instead of minimizing $E(i, j)$, we can minimize $E_0(i, j)$. We arrive at the following simple energy:

$$E_{\text{field}} = - \sum_{\text{all edges } (\mathbf{v}_i, \mathbf{v}_j)} \cos 4((\theta_i - \varphi_{ij}) - (\theta_j - \varphi_{ji}))$$

which does not require any constraints on the variables θ_i. Note that the values φ_{ij} are constant. Due to the simple form of the functional, it can be minimized quite quickly. We use a variant of the BFGS conjugate gradient algorithm described in [37] to perform minimization. For irregularly-sampled meshes, the energy may also be weighted in inverse proportion to edge length. We have not found this to be necessary for the meshes used in this paper. The result of the optimization depends on the threshold chosen to determine which vertices are considered unreliable; in the extreme cases, all vertices are marked as unreliable and the whole field is optimized, or all vertices are marked as reliable and the field remains unoptimized. Figure 8 shows the results for several thresholds.

6 Rendering Style

6.1 Style Rules

Our rendering style is based to some extent on the rules described by G. Francis in *A Topological picturebook* [15], which are in turn based on Nikolaïdes' rules for drawing drapes [26]. We have also used our own observations of various illustrations in similar styles. We begin our style description by defining undercuts and folds. A visible projected silhouette curve separates two areas of the image: one containing the image of the part of the surface on which the curve is located, the other empty or containing the image of a different part of the surface. We call the former area a *fold*. If the

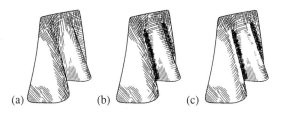

Figure 12: Hatching rules shown on drapes. (a) There are 3 main discrete hatch densities: highlights, midtones, and shadows, corresponding to 0, 1, and 2 directions of hatches. (b) Undercuts. (c) "Mach bands." Undercuts and Mach bands increase contrast where surfaces overlap.

latter area contains the image of a part of the surface, we call it an *undercut*.

We use the following rules, illustrated in Figure 12.

- The surface is separated into four levels of hatching: highlights and Mach bands (no hatching), midtones (single hatching), shadowed regions (cross-hatching), and undercuts (dense cross-hatching). Inside each area, the hatch density stays approximately uniform. The choice of the number of hatch directions used at a particular area of the surface is guided by the lighting and the following rules:
- If there is an undercut, on the other side of the silhouette from a fold, a thin area along the silhouette on the fold side is not hatched ("Mach band effect").
- Undercuts are densely hatched.
- Hatches are approximately straight; a hatch is terminated if its length exceeds a maximum, or if its direction deviates from the original by more than a fixed angle.
- Optionally, hatch thickness within each density level can be made inversely proportional to lighting; the resulting effect is rather subtle, and is visible only when the hatches are relatively thick.

6.2 Hatch Placement

The hatching procedure has several user-tunable parameters: basic hatch density specified in image space; the hatch density for undercuts; the threshold for highlights (the areas which receive no hatching); the threshold that separates single hatch regions from cross hatch regions; the maximum hatch length; the maximum deviation of hatches from the initial direction in world space. Varying these parameters has a considerable effect both on the appearance of the images and on the time required by the algorithm. Threshold values are usually chosen to divide the object more or less evenly between different hatching levels.

Once we have a hatching field, we can illustrate the surface by placing hatches along the field. We first define three intensity regions over the surface: no hatching (highlights and Mach bands), single hatching (midtones), and cross hatching (shadowed regions). Furthermore, some highlight and hatch regions may be marked as undercut regions. The hatching algorithm is as follows:

1. Identify Mach bands and undercuts.
2. Cover the single and cross hatch regions with cross hatches, and add extra hatches to undercut regions.
3. Remove cross-hatches in the single hatch regions, leaving only one direction of hatches.

6.3 Identifying Mach Bands and Undercuts

In order to identify Mach bands and undercuts, we step along each silhouette and boundary curve. A ray test near each curve point is used to determine if the fold overlaps another surface. Undercuts and Mach bands are indicated in a 2D grid, by marking every grid cell within a small distance of the fold on the near side of the surface as a Mach band, and by marking grid cells on the far side of the surface within a larger distance as undercuts. (This is the same 2D grid as used for hatching in the next section.)

6.4 Cross-hatching

We begin by creating evenly-spaced cross-hatches on a surface. We adapt Jobard and Lefers' method for creating evenly-spaced streamlines of a 2D vector field [22]. The hatching algorithm allows us to place evenly-spaced hatches on the surface in a single pass over the surface.

Our algorithm takes two parameters: a desired hatch separation distance d_{sep}, and a test factor d_{test}. The separation distance indicates the desired image-space hatch density; a smaller separation distance is used for undercuts. The algorithm creates a queue of surface curves, initially containing the critical curves (silhouettes, boundaries, creases, and self-intersections). While the queue is not empty, we remove the front curve from the queue and seed new hatches along it at points evenly-spaced in the image. Seeding creates a new hatch on the surface by tracing the directions of the cross-hatching field. Since the cross field is invariant to 90 degree rotations, at each step the hatch follows the one of four possible directions which has the smallest angle with the previous direction. Hatches are seeded perpendicular to all curves. Hatches are also seeded parallel to other hatches, at a distance d_{sep} from the curve. A hatch continues along the surface until it terminates in a critical curve, until the world-space hatch direction deviates from the initial hatch direction by more than a constant, or until it comes near a parallel hatch. This latter condition occurs when the endpoint of the hatch $\mathbf{p}_1$ is near a point $\mathbf{p}_2$ on another hatch, such that the following conditions are met:

- $||\mathbf{p}_1 - \mathbf{p}_2|| < d_{test}d_{sep}$, measured in image space.
- A straight line drawn between the two points in image space does not intersect the projection of any visible critical curves. In other words, hatches do not "interfere" when they are not nearby on the surface.
- The world space tangents of the two hatch curves are parallel, i.e. the angle between them is less than 45 degrees, after projection to the tangent plane at $\mathbf{p}_1$.

The search for nearby hatches is performed by placing all hatches in a 2D grid with grid spacing equal to d_{sep}. This ensures that at most nine grid cells must be searched to detect if there are hatches nearby the one being traced.

6.5 Hatch Reduction

Once we have cross-hatched all hatch regions, we remove hatches from the single hatch regions until they contain no cross-hatches. By removing hatches instead of directly placing single a hatch direction, we avoid the difficulty inherent in producing a consistent vector field on the surface. Our algorithm implicitly segments the visible single-hatch regions into locally-consistent single hatching fields. This allows us to take advantage of the known view direction and the limited extent of these regions.

The reduction algorithm examines every hatch on the surface and deletes any hatch that is perpendicular to another hatch. In particular, a hatch is deleted if it contains a point $\mathbf{p}_1$ nearby a point $\mathbf{p}_2$ on another hatch such that:

- $\mathbf{p}_1$ and $\mathbf{p}_2$ lie within the single hatch region.
- $||\mathbf{p}_1 - \mathbf{p}_2|| < 2d_{sep}$, measured in image space.
- A straight line drawn between the two points in image space does not intersect any visible critical curve.
- The world space tangents of the two hatch curves are perpendicular, i.e. the angle between them is greater than 45 degrees after projection to the tangent plane at $\mathbf{p}_1$.

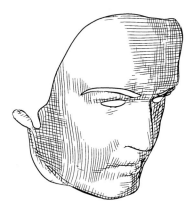

Deleting a hatch entails clipping it to the cross-hatch region; the part of the hatch that lies within the cross-hatch region is left untouched.

The order in which hatches are traversed is important; a naïve traversal order will usually leave the single hatch region uneven and inconsistent. We perform a breadth-first traversal to prevent this. A queue is initialized with a hatch curve. While the queue is not empty, the front curve is removed from the queue. If it is perpendicular to another curve in the single hatch region, then the curve is deleted, and all parallel neighbors of the hatch that have not been visited are added to the queue. When the queue is empty, a hatch that has not yet been visited is added to the queue, if any remain. The tests for perpendicular is as described above; the angle condition is reversed for the parallel test.

7   Results and Conclusions

Most of the illustrations in this paper were created using our system. Figures 1, 8 demonstrate the results for relatively fine meshes that define surfaces with complex geometry. Figures 2 and 13 show the results of using our system to illustrate several mathematical surfaces.

The time required to create an illustration varies greatly; while silhouette drawings can be computed interactively, and the field optimization takes very little time, hatching is still time-consuming, and can take from seconds to minutes, depending on hatch density and complexity of the model. Also, for each model the parameters of the algorithms (thresholds for hatching, position of the light sources, hatch density) have to be carefully chosen;

Future work. As we have already mentioned, improvements should be made to the silhouette visibility algorithm. Performance was not our goal for the hatching algorithm. It is clear that substantial speedups are possible. While the quality of fields generated by our algorithms is quite good, it would be desirable to reduce the number of parameters that may be tuned.

A more fundamental problem is the lack of control over the the number, type and placement of singularities of the generated field. As most surfaces of interest have low genus, the number of singularities can be very small for most surfaces.[3] However, the user currently has little control over their placement and additional support must be provided. Furthermore, the hatch reduction algorithm could be made more robust to irregular cross-hatching patterns, and the hatching could be improved reduce hatching artifacts, perhaps by employing the optimization technique of Turk and Banks [33].

---

[3]The relation between the numbers of singularities of different types is determined by the analogs of Euler formula; such formulas are known for vector and tensor fields; obtaining classification of singularities and a formula of this type for the cross fields described in the paper is an interesting mathematical problem.

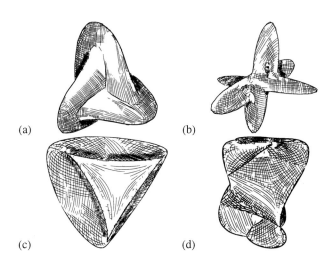

(a)   (b)   (c)   (d)

Figure 13: Several surfaces generated using G. Francis' generalization of Apéry's Romboy homotopy [16]. (a) Boy surface; (b) "Ida"; (c) Roman surface; (d) Etruscan Venus.

Acknowledgments

Our special thanks go to Jianbo Peng who implemented the dual surface silhouette detection algorithm. We are grateful to Pat Hanrahan, who suggested this research topic to us. We thank the anonymous reviewers for their comments. Chris Stolte participated in the project in its early stages.

This research was supported in part by the NSF grant DGE-9454173 and the NYU Center for Advanced Technology.

A C^2-surfaces based on subdivision

Commonly used subdivision surfaces, such as variants of Loop subdivision, produce either surfaces with curvatures that do not converge or have zero curvature at extraordinary vertices. There are fundamental reasons for this [29]. This property is rather undesirable, if we would like to compute silhouette curves, as it means either flat points or singular behavior near extraordinary points. We have developed a surface representation based on subdivision that produces surfaces that are everywhere C^2, do not have zero curvature at extraordinary vertices, and agree arbitrarily well with the limit surfaces produced by subdivision. This representation is described elsewhere [38]. However, for our purposes it is sufficient to have a way to compute curvatures for the surface associated with a mesh, and it is not necessary to have a complete surface evaluation algorithm.

The curvature computation that we propose is based on ideas from subdivision and is compatible with the curvature computations for subdivision surfaces in the regular case.

Consider a vertex $\mathbf{v}$ of the initial mesh of valence k. We will regard a part of the smooth surface corresponding to the 1-neighborhood of $\mathbf{v}$ as parameterized over a regular k-gon in the plane. Introduce the polar coordinates (r, φ) in the plane, with $u = r \cos \varphi$ and $v = r \sin \varphi$. then the second-order approximation to the surface can be written as

$$a_0 + (a_{11} \sin \varphi + a_{12} \cos \varphi)r + (a_{20} + a_{21} \sin 2\varphi + a_{22} \cos 2\varphi)r^2$$

A simple calculation shows that the least squares fit to $k + 1$ points of the 1-neighborhood $p_0 \ldots p_k$ assumed to be values at $(\sin(2\pi i/k), \cos(2\pi i/k))$, $i = 0..k$. with p_0 in the center, leads to

$$a_0 = p_0; \quad a_{20} = -p_0 + \frac{1}{k} \sum_i p_i$$

$$a_{11} = \frac{2}{k} \sum_i p_i \sin \frac{2\pi i}{k}; \quad a_{12} = \frac{2}{k} \sum_i p_i \cos \frac{2\pi i}{k}$$

$$a_{21} = \frac{2}{k} \sum_i p_i \sin \frac{4\pi i}{k}; \quad a_{22} = \frac{2}{k} \sum_i p_i \cos \frac{4\pi i}{k}$$

Note that the formulas for a_{11} and a_{21} coincide with the standard formulas for the tangents to the Loop subdivision surface, and a_{20}, a_{21}, a_{22}, with appropriate variable changes, produce second derivatives in the regular case. To make our calculations compatible with the Loop surface, we replace $a_0 = p_0$ with $a_0 = p_0^{limit}$, the limit position of the control point p_0. As a result, we obtain a set of simple rules for computing the coefficients of an approximating quadratic surface, which, after appropriate change of variables can be used to compute curvatures and is compatible with the Loop subdivision rules. In [38], we show that one can construct a C^2 surface which has precisely these curvatures at the vertices. A similar construction works for the boundary case. We should note that for valences $k = 3, 4$, the coefficients of the quadric are not independent, and thus not all possible local behaviors can be approximated well.

Given known partial derivatives $\mathbf{F}_u, \mathbf{F}_v, \mathbf{F}_{uu}, \mathbf{F}_{uv}, \mathbf{F}_{vv}$ of the local parameterization of the surface, the principal curvature directions and magnitudes can be computed as eigenvalues and eigenvectors of the following matrix:

$$\begin{pmatrix} E & F \\ F & G \end{pmatrix} \begin{pmatrix} L & M \\ M & N \end{pmatrix} \tag{2}$$

where $E = (\mathbf{F}_u \cdot \mathbf{F}_u)$, $F = (\mathbf{F}_v \cdot \mathbf{F}_u)$, $G = (\mathbf{F}_v \cdot \mathbf{F}_v)$, $L = (\mathbf{F}_{uu} \cdot \mathbf{n})$, $M = (\mathbf{F}_{uv} \cdot \mathbf{n})$, $N = (\mathbf{F}_{vv} \cdot \mathbf{n})$.

References

[1] I. A. Babenko. Singularities of the projection of piecewise-linear surfaces in $\mathbb{r}$span3. *Vestnik Moskov. Univ. Ser. I Mat. Mekh.*, 1991(2):72–75.

[2] Thomas F. Banchoff and Ockle Johnson. The normal Euler class and singularities of projections for polyhedral surfaces in 4-space. *Topology*, 37(2):419–439, 1998.

[3] Fabien Benichou and Gershon Elber. Output sensitive extraction of silhouettes from polygonal geometry. *Pacific Graphics '99*, October 1999. Held in Seoul, Korea.

[4] William M. Boothby. *An Introduction to Differentiable Manifolds and Riemannian Geometry*. Academic Press, 1986.

[5] Wagner Toledo Corrêa, Robert J. Jensen, Craig E. Thayer, and Adam Finkelstein. Texture Mapping for Cel Animation. In *SIGGRAPH 98 Conference Proceedings*, pages 435–446, July 1998.

[6] Cassidy Curtis. Loose and Sketchy Animation. In *SIGGRAPH 98: Conference Abstracts and Applications*, page 317, 1998.

[7] Philippe Decaudin. Cartoon-Looking Rendering of 3D-Scenes. Technical Report 2919, INRIA, June 1996.

[8] Thierry Delmarcelle and Lambertus Hesselink. The topology of symmetric, second-order tensor fields. In *Visualization '94*, pages 140–147, October 1994.

[9] Oliver Deussen, Jörg Harnel, Andreas Raab, Stefan Schlechtweg, and Thomas Strothotte. An Illustration Technique Using Hardware-Based Intersections. *Graphics Interface '99*, pages 175–182, June 1999.

[10] Matthias Eck, Tony DeRose, Tom Duchamp, Hugues Hoppe, Michael Lounsbery, and Werner Stuetzle. Multiresolution Analysis of Arbitrary Meshes. In *Computer Graphics Proceedings*, Annual Conference Series, pages 173–182. ACM Siggraph, 1995.

[11] Gershon Elber. Line art rendering via a coverage of isoparametric curves. *IEEE Transactions on Visualization and Computer Graphics*, 1(3):231–239, September 1995.

[12] Gershon Elber. Line Art Illustrations of Parametric and Implicit Forms. *IEEE Transactions on Visualization and Computer Graphics*, 4(1), January – March 1998.

[13] Gershon Elber. Interactive line art rendering of freeform surfaces. *Computer Graphics Forum*, 18(3):1–12, September 1999.

[14] Gershon Elber and Elaine Cohen. Hidden Curve Removal for Free Form Surfaces. In *Computer Graphics (SIGGRAPH '90 Proceedings)*, volume 24, pages 95–104, August 1990.

[15] George K. Francis. *A Topological Picturebook*. Springer-Verlag, New York, 1987.

[16] George K. Francis. The Etruscan Venus. In P. Concus, R. Finn, and D. A. Hoffman, editors, *Geometric Analysis and Computer Graphics*, pages 67–77. 1991.

[17] Amy Gooch. Interactive Non-Photorealistic Technical Illustration. Master's thesis, University of Utah, December 1998.

[18] Bruce Gooch, Peter-Pike J. Sloan, Amy Gooch, Peter Shirley, and Richard Riesenfeld. Interactive Technical Illustration. In *Proc. 1999 ACM Symposium on Interactive 3D Graphics*, April 1999.

[19] Aaron Hertzmann. Introduction to 3D Non-Photorealistic Rendering: Silhouettes and Outlines. In Stuart Green, editor, *Non-Photorealistic Rendering*, SIGGRAPH Course Notes. 1999.

[20] Hugues Hoppe, Tony DeRose, Tom Duchamp, Mark Halstead, Huber Jin, John McDonald, Jean Schweitzer, and Werner Stuetzle. Piecewise smooth surface reconstruction. In *Computer Graphics Proceedings*, Annual Conference Series, pages 295–302. ACM Siggraph, 1994.

[21] Victoria L. Interrante. Illustrating Surface Shape in Volume Data via Principal Direction-Driven 3D Line Integral Convolution. In *SIGGRAPH 97 Conference Proceedings*, pages 109–116, August 1997.

[22] Bruno Jobard and Wilfrid Lefer. Creating evenly-spaced streamlines of arbitrary density. In *Proc. of 8th Eurographics Workshop on Visualization in Scientific Computing*, pages 45–55, 1997.

[23] Lutz Kettner and Emo Welzl. Contour Edge Analysis for Polyhedron Projections. In W. Strasser, R. Klein, and R. Rau, editors, *Geometric Modeling: Theory and Practice*, pages 379–394. Springer Verlag, 1997.

[24] Pascal Mamassian and Michael S. Landy. Observer biases in the 3D interpretation of line drawings. *Vision Research*, (38):2817—2832, 1998.

[25] Lee Markosian, Michael A. Kowalski, Samuel J. Trychin, Lubomir D. Bourdev, Daniel Goldstein, and John F. Hughes. Real-Time Nonphotorealistic Rendering. In *SIGGRAPH 97 Conference Proceedings*, pages 415–420, August 1997.

[26] Kimon Nikolaïdes. *The Natural Way to Draw*. Houghton Mifflin, Boston, 1975.

[27] Hans Køhling Pedersen. A Framework for Interactive Texturing on Curved Surfaces. *Proceedings of SIGGRAPH 96*, pages 295–302, August 1996.

[28] Ramesh Raskar and Michael Cohen. Image Precision Silhouette Edges. In *Proc. 1999 ACM Symposium on Interactive 3D Graphics*, April 1999.

[29] Ulrich Reif. A degree estimate for polynomial subdivision surfaces of higher regularity. *Proc. Amer. Math. Soc.*, 124:2167–2174, 1996.

[30] Takafumi Saito and Tokiichiro Takahashi. Comprehensible Rendering of 3-D Shapes. In Forest Baskett, editor, *Computer Graphics (SIGGRAPH '90 Proceedings)*, volume 24, pages 197–206, August 1990.

[31] Michael P. Salisbury, Michael T. Wong, John F. Hughes, and David H. Salesin. Orientable Textures for Image-Based Pen-and-Ink Illustration. In *SIGGRAPH 97 Conference Proceedings*, pages 401–406, August 1997.

[32] Kent A. Stevens. Inferring shape from contours across surfaces. In Alex P. Pentland, editor, *From Pixels to Predicates*, pages 93–110. 1986.

[33] Greg Turk and David Banks. Image-Guided Streamline Placement. In *SIGGRAPH 96 Conference Proceedings*, pages 453–460, August 1996.

[34] J. Chal Vinson. *Thomas Nast: Political Cartoonist*. University of Georgia Press, Atlanta, 1967.

[35] Hassler Whitney. On singularities of mappings of euclidean spaces. I. Mappings of the plane into the plane. *Ann. of Math. (2)*, 62:374–410, 1955.

[36] Georges Winkenbach and David H. Salesin. Rendering Parametric Surfaces in Pen and Ink. In *SIGGRAPH 96 Conference Proceedings*, pages 469–476, August 1996.

[37] Ciyou Zhu, Richard H. Byrd, Peihuang Lu, and Jorge Nocedal. Algorithm 778: L-BFGS-B: Fortran subroutines for large-scale bound-constrained optimization. *ACM Trans. Math. Software*, 23(4):550–560, 1997.

[38] D. Zorin. Constructing curvature-continuous surfaces by blending. in preparation.

Non-Photorealistic Virtual Environments*

Allison W. Klein   Wilmot Li   Michael M. Kazhdan   Wagner T. Corrêa

Adam Finkelstein   Thomas A. Funkhouser

Princeton University

Abstract

We describe a system for non-photorealistic rendering (NPR) of virtual environments. In real time, it synthesizes imagery of architectural interiors using stroke-based textures. We address the four main challenges of such a system – interactivity, visual detail, controlled stroke size, and frame-to-frame coherence – through image based rendering (IBR) methods. In a preprocessing stage, we capture photos of a real or synthetic environment, map the photos to a coarse model of the environment, and run a series of NPR filters to generate textures. At runtime, the system re-renders the NPR textures over the geometry of the coarse model, and it adds dark lines that emphasize creases and silhouettes. We provide a method for constructing non-photorealistic textures from photographs that largely avoids seams in the resulting imagery. We also offer a new construction, *art-maps*, to control stroke size across the images. Finally, we show a working system that provides an immersive experience rendered in a variety of NPR styles.

Keywords: Non-photorealistic rendering, image-based rendering, texture mapping, interactive virtual environments.

Figure 1: A non-photorealistic virtual environment.

1 Introduction

Virtual environments allow us to explore an ancient historical site, visit a new home with a real estate agent, or fly through the twisting corridors of a space station in pursuit of alien prey. They simulate the visual experience of immersion in a 3D environment by rendering images of a computer model as seen from an observer viewpoint moving under interactive control by the user. If the rendered images are visually compelling, and they are refreshed quickly enough, the user feels a sense of presence in a virtual world, enabling applications in education, computer-aided design, electronic commerce, and entertainment.

While research in virtual environments has traditionally striven for photorealism, for many applications there are advantages to non-photorealistic rendering (NPR). Artistic expression can often convey a specific mood (e.g. cheerful or dreary) difficult to imbue in a synthetic, photorealistic scene. Furthermore, through abstraction and careful elision of detail, NPR imagery can focus the viewer's attention on important information while downplaying extraneous or unimportant features. An NPR scene can also suggest additional semantic information, such as a quality of "unfinishedness" that

*http://www.cs.princeton.edu/gfx/proj/NPRVE

may be desirable when, for example, an architect shows a client a partially-completed design. Finally, an NPR look is often more engaging than the prototypical stark, pristine computer graphics rendering.

The goal of our work is to develop a system for real-time NPR virtual environments (Figure 1). The challenges for such a system are four-fold: interactivity, visual detail, controlled stroke size, and frame-to-frame coherence. First, virtual environments demand interactive frame rates, whereas NPR methods typically require seconds or minutes to generate a single frame. Second, visual details and complex lighting effects (e.g. indirect illumination and shadows) provide helpful cues for comprehension of virtual environments, and yet construction of detailed geometric models and simulation of global illumination present challenges for a large virtual environment. Third, NPR strokes must be rendered within an appropriate range of sizes; strokes that are too small are invisible, while strokes that are too large appear unnatural. Finally, frame-to-frame coherence among strokes is crucial for an interactive NPR system to avoid a noisy, flickery effect in the imagery.

We address these challenges with image-based rendering (IBR). In general, IBR yields visually complex scenery and efficient rendering rates by employing photographs or pre-rendered images of the scene to provide visual detail. Not surprisingly, by using a hybrid NPR/IBR approach we are able to reap the benefits of both technologies: an aesthetic rendering of the scene, and visual complexity from a simple model. More subtly, each technology addresses the major drawbacks of the other. IBR allows us to render artistic imagery with complex lighting effects and geometric detail at interactive frame rates while maintaining frame-to-frame coherence. On the flipside, non-photorealistic rendering appeases many of the artifacts due to under-sampling in IBR, both by visually masking them and by reducing the viewer's expectation of realism.

At a high level, our system proceeds in three steps as shown in Figure 2. First, during off-line preprocessing, we construct an IBR model of a scene from a set of photographs or rendered images. Second, during another preprocessing step, we filter samples of the IBR model to give them a non-photorealistic look. The result is a non-photorealistic image-based representation (NPIBR) for use in interactive walkthroughs. Finally, during subsequent on-line sessions, the NPIBR model is resampled for novel viewpoints to reconstruct NPR images for display.

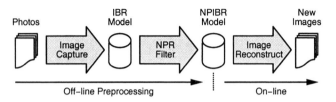

Figure 2: Overview of our approach.

This approach addresses many of the challenges in rendering NPR images of virtual environments in real-time. First, by executing the most expensive computations during off-line preprocessing, our system achieves interactive frame rates at run-time. Second, by capturing complex lighting effects and geometric detail in photographic images, our system produces images with visual richness not attainable by previous NPR rendering systems. Third, with appropriate representation, prefiltering, and resampling methods, IBR allows us to control NPR stroke size in the projected imagery. Fourth, by utilizing the same NPR imagery for many similar camera viewpoints rather than creating new sets of strokes for each view, our system acquires frame-to-frame coherence. Moreover, by abstracting NPR processing into a filtering operation on an image-based representation, our architecture supports a number of NPR styles within a common framework. This feature gives us aesthetic flexibility, as the same IBR model can be used to produce interactive walkthroughs in different NPR styles.

In this paper, we investigate issues in implementing this hybrid NPR/IBR approach for interactive NPR walkthroughs. The specific technical contributions of our work are: (1) a method for constructing non-photorealistic textures from photographs that largely avoids seams in images rendered from arbitrary viewpoints, and (2) a multiresolution representation for non-photorealistic textures (called *art-maps*) that works with conventional mip-mapping hardware to render images with controlled stroke size. These methods are incorporated into a working prototype system that supports interactive walkthroughs of visually complex virtual environments rendered in many stroke-based NPR styles.

The remainder of this paper is organized as follows. In Section 2 we review background information and related work. Sections 3-5 address the main issues in constructing, filtering, and resampling a hybrid NPR/IBR representation. Section 6 presents results of experiments with our working prototype system, while Section 7 contains a brief conclusion and discussion of areas for future work.

2 Related Work

The traditional strategy for immersive virtual environments is to render detailed sets of 3D polygons with appropriate lighting effects as the camera moves through the model [21]. With this approach, the primary challenge is constructing a digital representation for a complex, visually rich, real-world environment. Despite recent advances in interactive modeling tools, laser-based range-finders, computer vision techniques, and global illumination algorithms, it remains extremely difficult to construct compelling models with detailed 3D geometry, accurate material reflectance properties, and

realistic global illumination effects. Even with tools to create an attractive, credible geometric model, it must still be rendered at interactive frame rates, limiting the number of polygons and shading algorithms that can be used. With such constraints, the resulting imagery usually looks very plastic and polygonal, despite setting user expectations for photorealism.

In contrast, image-based modeling and rendering methods represent a virtual environment by its radiance distribution without relying upon a model of geometry, lighting, and reflectance properties [5]. An IBR system usually takes images (photographs) of a static scene as input and constructs a sample-based representation of the plenoptic function, which can be resampled to render photorealistic images for novel viewpoints. The important advantages of this approach are that photorealistic images can be generated without constructing a detailed 3D model or simulating global illumination, and the rendering time for novel images is independent of a scene's geometric complexity. The primary difficulty is storing and resampling a high-resolution representation of the plenoptic function for a complex virtual environment [23]. If the radiance distribution is under-sampled, images generated during a walkthrough contain noticeable aliasing or blurring artifacts, which are disturbing when the user expects photorealism.

In recent years, a few researchers have turned their attention away from photorealism and towards developing non-photorealistic rendering techniques in a variety of styles and simulated media, such as impressionist painting [13, 15, 20, 24], pen and ink [28, 33], technical illustration [11, 27], ornamentation [34], engraving [25, 26], watercolor [4], and the style of Dr. Seuss [18]. Much of this work has focused on creating still images either from photographs, from computer-rendered reference images, or directly from 3D models, with varying degrees of user-direction. One of our goals is to make our system work in conjunction with any of these technologies (particularly those that are more automated) to yield virtual environments in many different styles.

Several stroke-based NPR systems have explored time-changing imagery, confronting the challenge of frame-to-frame coherence with varying success. Winkenbach *et al.* [32] and later Curtis *et al.* [4] observed that applying NPR techniques designed for still images to time-changing sequences yields flickery, jittery, noisy animations because strokes appear and disappear too quickly. Meier [24] adapted Haeberli's "paint by numbers" scheme [13] in such a way that paint strokes track features in a 3D model to provide frame-to-frame coherence in painterly animation. Litwinowicz [20] achieved a similar effect on video sequences using optical flow methods to affix paint strokes to objects in the scene. Markosian [22] found that silhouettes on rotating 3D objects change slowly enough to give frame-to-frame coherence for strokes drawn on the silhouette edges. We exploit this property when drawing lines on creases and silhouettes at run-time. Kowalski *et al.* [18] extends these methods by attaching non-photorealistic "graftals" to the 3D geometry of a scene, while seeking to enforce coherence among the graftals between frames. The bulk of the coherence in our system comes from reprojection of non-photorealistic imagery, so the strokes drawn for neighboring frames are generally slowly-changing.

Several other researchers, for example Horry *et al.* [17], Wood *et al.* [35], and Buck *et al.* [1], have built hybrid NPR/IBR systems where hand-drawn art is re-rendered for different views. In this spirit our system could also incorporate hand-drawn art, although the drawing task might be arduous as a single scene involves many reference images.

In this paper, we present a system for real-time, NPR virtual environments. Rather than attempting to answer the question "how would van Gogh or Chagall paint a movie?" we propose solutions to some technical issues facing an artist wishing to use NPR styles in a virtual environment system. Two visual metaphors represent the extremes in a spectrum of aesthetics one could choose for an "artistic" immersive experience. On one extreme, we could imagine that an artist painted over the walls of the model. In this case, the visual effect is that as the user navigates the environment the detailed stroke work is more or less apparent depending on her distance from the various surfaces she can see. In the other extreme, we could imagine that as the user navigates the environment in real-time, a photograph of what is seen is captured, and an artist instantaneously paints a picture based on the photograph. In this case, the visual effect suffers from either flickering strokes (lack of frame-to-frame coherence) or the "shower door effect" (the illusion that the paintings are somehow embedded in a sheet of glass in front of the viewer). Our goal is to find a compromise between these two visual metaphors: we would like the stroke coherence to be on the surfaces of the scene rather than in the image plane, but we would like the stroke size to be roughly what would have been selected for the image plane rather than what would have been chosen for the walls. The difficult challenge is to achieve this goal while rendering images at interactive rates.

We investigate a hybrid NPR/IBR approach. Broadly speaking, the two main issues we address are: 1) constructing an IBR representation suitable for NPR imagery, and 2) developing a IBR prefiltering method to enable rendering of novel NPR images with controllable stroke-size and frame-to-frame coherence in a real-time walkthrough system. These issues are the topics of the following two sections.

3   Image-Based Representation

The first issue in implementing a system based on our hybrid NPR/IBR approach is to choose an image-based representation suitable for storing and resampling non-photorealistic imagery. Of course, numerous IBR representations have been described in the literature (see [5] for a survey); and, in principle, any of them could store NPR image samples of a virtual environment. However, not all IBR representations are equally well-suited for NPR walkthroughs. Specifically, an IBR method for interactive walkthroughs should have the following properties:

A1) **Arbitrary viewpoints:** The image reconstruction method should be able to generate images for arbitrary novel viewpoints within the interior of the virtual environment. This property implies a 5D representation of the plenoptic function capable of resolving inter-object occlusions. It also implies a prefiltered multiresolution representation from which novel views can be rendered efficiently from any distance without aliasing.

A2) **Practical storage:** The image-based representation should be small enough to fit within the capacity of common long-term storage devices (e.g., CD-ROMs), and the working set required for rendering any novel view should be small enough to fit within the memory of desktop computers. This property suggests methods for compressing image samples and managing multi-level storage hierarchies in real-time.

A3) **Efficient rendering:** The rendering algorithm should be very fast so that high-quality images can be generated at interactive frame rates. This property suggests a hardware implementation for resampling.

Additionally, the following properties are important for IBR representations used to store *non-photorealistic* imagery:

B1) **Homeomorphic reprojection:** The mapping of pixel samples onto any image plane should be homeomorphic so that strokes and textures in NPR imagery remain intact during image reconstruction for novel views. This property ensures that our method can work with a wide range of NPR filters.

B2) **Predictable reprojection:** The reprojected positions of pixel samples should be predictable so that the sizes and shapes of strokes in reconstructed NPR images can be controlled. This property allows the system to match the sizes and shapes of strokes in NPR images to the ones intended by the scene designer.

B3) **Filter Flexibility:** Pixel samples should be stored in a form that makes NPR filters simple and easy to implement so that support for multiple NPR styles is practical. This property provides scene designers with the aesthetic flexibility of experimenting with a variety of NPR styles for a single scene.

We have considered several IBR representations. QuickTime VR [2] is perhaps the most common commercial form of IBR, and its cylindrical panoramic images could easily be used to create NPR imagery with our approach. For instance, each panoramic image could be run through an off-the-shelf NPR image processing filter, and the results could be input to a QuickTime VR run-time viewer to produce an immersive NPR experience. While this method may be appropriate for some applications, it cannot be used for smooth, interactive walkthroughs, since QuickTime VR supports only a discrete set of viewpoints, and it would require a lot of storage to represent the interior of a complex environment, thereby violating properties 'A1' and 'A2' above.

Other IBR methods allow greater freedom of motion. However, in doing so, they usually rely upon more complicated resampling methods, which makes reconstruction of NPR strokes difficult for arbitrary viewpoints. As a simple example, consider adding cross-hatch strokes to an image with color and depth values for each pixel. As novel images are reconstructed from this representation, individual pixels with different depths get reprojected differently according to their flow fields; and, consequently, the cross-hatch stroke pattern present in the original depth image disintegrates for most views. This problem is due to a violation of property 'B1,' which is typical of most view-dependent IBR representations, including cylindrical panorama with depth [23], layered depth images [29], light fields [19], Lumigraphs [12], interpolated views [3], etc.

Our approach, based on textures, relies upon a hybrid geometry-and image-based representation. Radiance samples acquired from photographs are used to create textures describing the visual complexity of the scene, while a coarse 3D polygonal model is used to reason about the coverage, resolution, discontinuities, coherence, and projections of radiance samples for any given view. This approach satisfies all of the properties listed above. In particular, surface textures are a very compact form for the 5D plenoptic function, as inter-object occlusions are implicit in the hidden surface relationships between polygons of the coarse 3D model ('A1'). Also, storage and rendering can take advantage of the plethora of previous work in texture mapping [14], including multi-scale prefiltering methods ('A1'), texture compression and paging algorithms ('A2'), and texture rendering hardware implementations ('A3'), which are available in most commodity PC graphics accelerators today.

Textures are especially well-suited for NPR imagery, as the mapping from the texture sample space to the view plane is simply a 2D projective warp, which is both homeomorphic ('B1') and predictable ('B2'). As a consequence, our system can control the sizes and shapes of rendered strokes in reconstructed images by prefiltering NPR textures during a preprocessing step to compensate for the predictable distortions introduced by the projective mapping (the details of this method appear in the following section). Finally, we note that textures provide a simple and convenient representation for NPR filtering, as any combination of numerous commonly available image processing tools can be used to add NPR effects to texture imagery ('B3'). For instance, most of the NPR styles shown in this paper were created with filters in Adobe Photoshop.

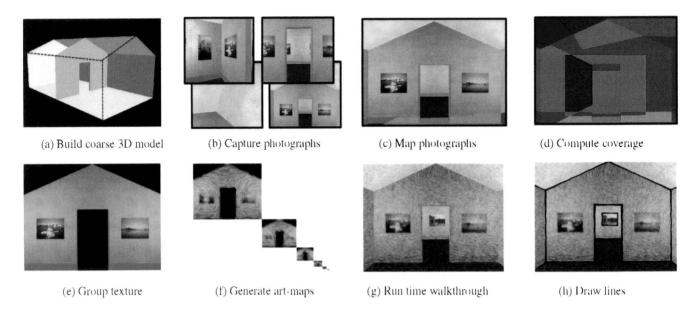

| (a) Build coarse 3D model | (b) Capture photographs | (c) Map photographs | (d) Compute coverage |
| (e) Group texture | (f) Generate art-maps | (g) Run time walkthrough | (h) Draw lines |

Figure 3: Our process. Steps (a) through (f) happen as pre-processing, enabling interactive frame rates at run-time in steps (g) and (h).

Our specific method for constructing textures from images proceeds as shown in Figure 3a-d. First, we construct a coarsely-detailed polygonal model using an interactive modeling tool (Figure 3a). To ensure proper visibility calculations in later stages, the model should have the property that occlusion relationships between polygons in the model match the occlusion relationships between the corresponding objects in the environment. Second, we capture images of the environment with a real or synthetic camera and calibrate them using Tsai's method [30] (Figure 3b). Third, we map the images onto the surfaces of the polygonal model using a beam tracing method [9] (Figure 3c). The net result is a coverage map in which each polygon is partitioned into a set of convex faces corresponding to regions covered by different combinations of captured images (Figure 3d). Fourth, we select a representative image for each face to form a view-independent texture map, primarily favoring normal views over oblique views, and secondarily favoring images taken from cameras closer to the surface. Finally, we fill faces not covered by any image with a texture hole-filling algorithm similar to the one described by Efros and Leung [8]. Note that view-dependent texture maps could be supported with our method by blending images from cameras at multiple discrete viewpoints (as in [6, 7]). However, we observe that NPR filtering removes most view-dependent visual cues, and blending reduces texture clarity, and thus we choose view-independence over blending in our current system.

4 Non-Photorealistic Filtering

The second step in our process is to apply NPR filters to texture imagery. Sections 4.1 and 4.2 address the two major concerns relating to NPR filtering: avoiding visible seams and controlling the stroke size in the rendered images.

4.1 Seams

Our goal is to enable processing of IBR textures with many different NPR filters. Some NPR filters might add artistic strokes (e.g., "pen and ink"), others might blur or warp the imagery (e.g., "ink blot"), and still others might change the average luminance (e.g.,

"impressionist") based on the pixels in the input texture. In all these cases, seams may appear in novel images anywhere two textures processed by an NPR filter independently are reprojected onto adjacent areas of the novel image plane. As a consequence, we must be careful about how to apply NPR filters so as to minimize noticeable resampling artifacts in rendered images.

The problem is best illustrated with an example. The simplest way to process textures would be to apply an NPR filter to each of the captured photographic images, and then map the resulting NPR images onto the surfaces of the 3D model as projective textures (as in [6, 7]). Unfortunately, this photo-based approach causes noticeable artifacts in reconstructed NPR images. For instance, Figure 4a shows a sample image reconstructed from photographic textures processed with a "ink blot" filter in Photoshop. Since each photographic texture is filtered independently and undergoes a different projective warp onto the image plane, there are noticeable seams along boundaries of faces where the average luminance varies ('A') and where the sizes and shapes of NPR strokes change abruptly ('B'). Also, since this particular NPR filter resamples the photographic images with a large convolution kernel, colors from occluding surfaces bleed across silhouette edges and map onto occluded surfaces, leaving streaks along occlusion boundaries in the reconstructed image ('C').

We can avoid many of these artifacts by executing the NPR filter on textures constructed for each surface, rather than for each photographic image. This approach ensures that most neighboring pixels in reprojected images are filtered at the same scale, and it avoids spreading colors from one surface to another across silhouette edges. Ideally, we would avoid all seams by creating a single texture image with a homeomorphic map to the image plane for every potential viewpoint. Unfortunately, this ideal approach is not generally possible, as it would require unfolding the surfaces of 3D model onto a 2D plane without overlaps. Instead, our approach is to construct a single texture image for each connected set of coplanar faces (Figure 3e), and then we execute the NPR filter on the whole texture as one image (Figure 4b). This method moves all potential seams due to NPR filtering to the polyhedral edges of the 3D model, a place where seams are less objectionable and can be masked by lines drawn over the textured imagery.

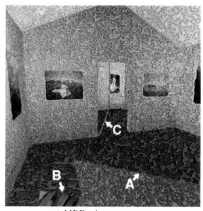

a) NPR photo textures

b) NPR surface textures

Figure 4: Applying NPR filters to surface textures avoids seams and warped strokes in reconstructed images.

Figure 5: Scene rendered with art-maps. The stroke size remains roughly constant across the image.

4.2 Art Maps

This section addresses the problem of placing strokes into the textures in such a way that we have control over stroke size in the final image. Our challenge is a fundamental tension between frame-to-frame coherence and stroke size appropriate for the image plane. As the user moves toward a surface, the strokes on that surface *must* change in order to maintain an appropriate size in the image plane. Unfortunately, this means that we must either slowly blend from one set of strokes to another set, or suffer from a "pop" when they all change at once. Preferring the former effect, our compromise is to choose slowly-changing strokes, with some amount of blurring as they change, and to allow stroke size to vary somewhat with a *range* of sizes nearly appropriate for the viewing plane.

Our solution relies on the observation that the stroke size problem is analogous to choice of filter for projected imagery in photorealistic environments using conventional texture mapping. As the user navigates a photorealistic environment, the goal of texture mapping hardware is to select for every pixel p a filter f for the texture such that the size of f varies with the size of the texture space pre-image of p. Likewise, our goal is to place each stroke s in the texture such that as the user navigates the environment, the relative sizes of s and f in texture space stay constant. Thus, our strategy for management of stroke size is to leverage the great deal of work on pre-filtering imagery for texture mapping, most notably mip-maps [31]).

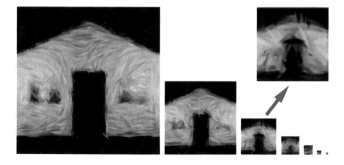

Figure 6: Art-maps work with conventional mip-mapping hardware to maintain constant stroke size at interactive frame rates.

We use a construction that we call "art-maps." The key idea is to apply strokes to each level of the mip-map, knowing that it is suitable for projection to the screen *at a particular size*. Figure 6 shows an example. To create this mip-map hierarchy, we simply filter the photorealistic images as in normal mip-mapping, but then apply an NPR filter to each level independently.

The strokes at each level of the mip-map hierarchy vary in size in powers of two relative to the whole image, just as pre-filtered mip-map levels vary the filter kernel size. Thus, when conventional texture mapping hardware selects a level of the mip-map hierarchy from which to sample a pixel, it will automatically choose a pixel from a set of strokes of the appropriate size. Furthermore, as it blends between levels of the mip-map hierarchy, it will likewise blend between strokes of appropriate size. So the effect is that strokes remain affixed to the surfaces in the scene, but as the user navigates through the environment, the strokes have roughly constant size in the image plane, as shown for example in Figure 5. Note that at locations marked 'D' and 'E' the stroke size is roughly the same. (In contrast, without art-maps, the strokes in these locations varies with the distance between the surface and the camera, as can be seen in Figure 4.) As the user moves toward a wall, the strokes shown for that wall will slowly blend from the strokes in one mip-map level to the next to maintain roughly constant image-space size. As the viewer moves, there is frame-to-frame coherence in the mip-map level chosen for the wall, and therefore there is visual coherence in the strokes. We suffer some amount of blending of strokes, because the mip-map level is generally non-integer; but we prefer this to either popping or lack of control over stroke size. The benefits of art-maps are that they are very simple to implement, and that they permit interactivity by relegating expensive NPR filtering to a preprocess and by exploiting texture mapping hardware for sampling at runtime.

A known problem for conventional mip-maps is that for very oblique polygons the mip-map is forced to choose between aliasing and blurring for one or both of the principle directions [14]. This problem is due to a round filter kernel in image space projected to a very oblong shape in texture space, which forces the use of a kernel that is either correctly sized in its long direction (giving aliasing in the short direction) or correctly sized in its short direction (giving blurring in the long direction). This filter problem manifests itself as stretched strokes when art-maps are applied (Figure 7a). A number of solutions to this problem have been proposed [14] – art-maps will work with any of them that stores multiple prefiltered

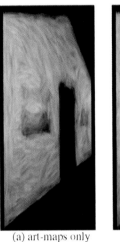  

(a) art-maps only   (b) with rip-maps   (c) varying strokes

Figure 7: Art maps using generalizations of mip-maps.

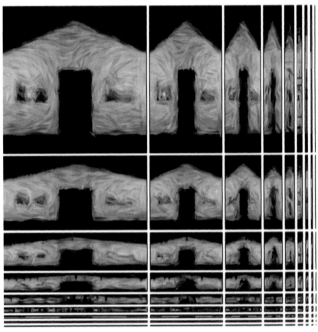

Figure 8: Art-maps can be applied to other, more generalized mip-mapping techniques such as RIP-maps.

versions of a texture (e.g., for different perspective warps). We have experimented with a generalization of mip-maps, called "rip-maps" [16]. As shown in Figure 8, rip-maps contain a cascading series of pre-filtered, off-angle images of the texture. An obliquely-projected texture may select one of the off-axis images from the rip-map; in the case of rip-maps with art-maps, the stroke shape will be corrected, as shown in Figure 7b. Our prototype renders this scene by recursively dividing textured polygons, selecting among rip-map textures in the subdivided regions. This method allows interactive control over stroke sizes in different areas of the image plane, as illustrated in Figure 7c; in this example, we use small strokes in the upper part of the image, and smoothly vary stroke size down to large strokes at the bottom of the image. Unfortunately, our current software implementation of rip-mapping is too slow for real-time rendering of complex scenes, and thus we use art-maps with conventional mip-mapping for our interactive walkthrough system. We note that it might still be possible to control the sizes of rendered strokes on a per-surface basis using various texture mapping parameters (e.g., LOD bias) that guide the selection of mip-map levels.

5 Interactive Walkthrough System

During the run-time phase, we simulate the experience of moving through a non-photorealistic environment by drawing surfaces of the coarse 3D model rendered with their art-map textures as the user moves a simulated viewpoint interactively.

Our run-time system loads all art-map levels for all surfaces into texture memory at startup. Then, for every novel viewpoint, it draws surfaces of the 3D model with standard texture mip-mapping hardware using the pre-loaded art-maps (as described in Section 4). The rendering process is fast, and it produces images with relatively high frame-to-frame coherence and nearly constant size NPR strokes, as blending between art-map levels is performed in texture mapping hardware on a per-pixel basis according to estimated projected areas.

To facilitate management of texture memory, we break up large textures into *tiles* before loading them into texture memory, and we execute view frustum culling and occlusion culling algorithms to compute a potentially visible set of surface tiles to render for every novel viewpoint [10]. These methods help keep the working set of texture data relatively small and coherent from frame-to-frame, and thus we can rely upon standard OpenGL methods to manage texture swapping when the total texture size exceeds texture memory.

Our hybrid geometry- and image-based approach allows us not only to render NPR textured surfaces, but also to augment the resulting images with additional visual information. For example, we sometimes apply photorealistic textures to an object in order to differentiate that object from others in the scene. We also use run-time geometric rendering to highlight interesting features of the environment. For instance, we draw wavy lines over silhouette edges and creases at the intersections of non-coplanar polygons, which helps mask objectionable artifacts due to seams and unnaturally hard edges at polygon boundaries. In our implementation, the lines are drawn as a 2D triangle strip following a sinusoidal backbone along the 2D projection of each visible edge in the 3D model. Since the frequency of the sine function is based on screen space distances, all of the lines drawn have a consistent "waviness," regardless of their orientation relative to the viewer. The lines help to clarify the geometry of the environment, especially when the NPR filter used is very noisy or produces low contrast textures. See Figure 3h for an example.

6 Experimental Results

We have implemented the methods described in the preceding sections in C++ on Silicon Graphics/Irix and PC Windows/NT computers and incorporated them into an interactive system for walkthroughs of non-photorealistic virtual environments.

To test the viability of our methods, we have performed experiments with several virtual environments rendered with different NPR styles. Tables 1 and 2 show statistics logged during our process for three of these environments, two of which are synthetic ("Museum" and "Gallery") and one of which is a real building captured with photographs ("Building"). All times were measured on a Silicon Graphics Onyx2 with a 195MHz R10000 CPU and Infinite-Reality graphics.

Examining the timing results in Table 2, we see that the preprocessing steps of our method can require several hours in all. Yet, we reap great benefit from this off-line computation. The re-

Model name	Number of polygons	Surface area (inches^2)	Number of photos	Number of faces	Number of textures	Total MBs of textures	Total MBs of art-maps
Gallery	192	2,574,400	46	414	73	82	109
Museum	76	421,520	93	282	42	104	138
Building	201	931,681	18	815	114	118	157

Table 1: Quantitative descriptions of test environments and preprocessing results.

Model name	Preprocessing								Run-time		
	Capture photos	Calibrate photos	Map photos	Create textures	Hole filling	Create art-maps	Run NPR filter	Total preprocessing	Draw images	Draw lines	Total per frame
Gallery	1m 40s	—	0.4s	3m 30s	2h 02m	10m	30m	2h 47m	0.017s	0.025s	0.042s
Museum	1m 52s	—	0.8s	2m 53s	3h 34m	8m	40m	4h 26m	0.017s	0.014s	0.031s
Building	2h	2h	5.8s	4m 22s	3h 40m	14m	50m	8h 48m	0.056s	0.037s	0.093s

Table 2: Timing results for each stage of our process.

sult is visually compelling imagery rendered at interactive frame rates with high frame-to-frame coherence during run-time. Average frame refresh times measured during interactive walkthroughs of each model are shown in the right-most column of Table 2. The corresponding frame rates range from 11 to 32 frames per second, which are adequate to provide a convincing illusion of presence as the user moves interactively through a non-photorealistic environment.

Another result is the demonstration of our system's flexibility in supporting interactive walkthroughs in many NPR styles. Figures 9a-c show screen shots of the walkthrough program with the "Museum" environment after processing with different NPR filters. Creating each new set of NPR textures took around 40 minutes of preprocessing time, as only the last step of the preprocess ("run NPR filter") had to be re-done for each one. Then, the run-time program could immediately provide interactive walkthroughs in the new style. Figures 9d-f show images of the "Building" environment rendered in a watercolor style from different viewpoints. Each image took less than 1/10th of a second to generate. Notice how the size of the strokes in all the images remains relatively constant, even for surfaces at different distances from the viewer.

The primary limitation on the complexity of virtual environments and the resolution of imagery rendered with our system is the capacity of graphics hardware texture memory. In order to maintain interactive frame rates, all texture data for every rendered image must fit into the texture cache on the graphics accelerator (64MB in our tests). As a result, the number of surfaces in the virtual environment and the resolution of captured textures must be chosen judiciously. So far, we have generally constructed group textures with each texel corresponding to a 2 by 2 inch region of a surface, and we decompose group textures into 512 by 512 pixel tiles that can be loaded and removed in the texture cache independently. With these resolutions, our test environments require between 109MB and 157MB of texture data with art-maps (see the right-most column of Table 1), of which far less than 64MB is required to render an image for any single novel viewpoint (due to view frustum culling and occlusion culling). In our experiments, we find that the standard OpenGL implementation of texture memory management is able to swap these textures fast enough for interactive walkthroughs, at least on a Silicon Graphics Onyx2 with InfiniteReality graphics. While the frame rate is not perfectly constant (there are occasionally "hiccups" due to texture cache faults), the frame rate is usually between 10 and 30 frames per second – yielding an interactive experience for the user. More sophisticated texture management and compression methods could be used to address this issue in future work.

7 Conclusion

This paper describes a system for real-time walkthroughs of non-photorealistic virtual environments. It tackles the four main challenges of such a system – interactivity, visual detail, controlled stroke size, and frame-to-frame coherence – through image-based rendering of non-photorealistic imagery. The key idea is that an image-based representation can be constructed off-line through a sequence of image capture and filtering steps that enable efficient reconstruction of visually detailed images from arbitrary viewpoints in any non-photorealistic style. The technical contributions of this work include a method for constructing NPR textures that avoids seams in novel images and a multiscale texture representation (*art-maps*) that provides control over the size of strokes during interactive rendering. This work suggests a number of areas for future investigation:

Augmenting the scene with geometry-based elements. Real-time NPR rendering of simple geometric objects in the scene – perhaps architectural accents such as a plant or a chair rendered in the NPR styles of Gooch *et al.* [11] or Kowalski *et al.* [18] – would enhance the sense of immersion while not greatly slowing our system.

View-dependent rendering. We have observed that many view-dependent geometric and lighting effects are visually masked by non-photorealistic rendering (see Section 3). Nonetheless, view-dependent texture mapping (e.g. [6, 7]) offers an opportunity to capture these effects for even better fidelity to the environment.

Better stroke coherence. As mentioned in Section 4.2, runtime blending between neighboring levels of the mip-map hierarchy causes visual blending between strokes in the art-maps. It may be possible to achieve better coherence between neighboring levels of the mip-maps, most likely by designing customized NPR filters that deliberately assign strokes in multiple levels of the art-maps at once. The desired visual effect might be that strokes grow and eventually split apart, rather than fading in, as the user approaches a surface.

Acknowledgements

The authors would like to thank several people for their assistance with this project: Lee Markosian taught us how to draw wavy lines quickly using triangle strips; Reg Wilson provided the implementation of Tsai's camera calibration algorithm; and John Hughes provided helpful discussion. This work was supported in part by Alfred P. Sloan Foundation Fellowships awarded to Adam Finkelstein and Thomas Funkhouser, an NSF CAREER grant for Adam Finkelstein, and generous gifts from Microsoft Corporation.

(a) Museum, drybrush

(b) Museum, pastel

(c) Museum, van Gogh

(d) Building, watercolor

(e) Building, watercolor

(f) Building, watercolor

Figure 9: Images of artistic virtual environments rendered during an interactive walkthrough.

References

[1] Buck, I., Finkelstein, A., Jacobs, C., Klein, A., Salesin, D. H., Seims, J., Szeliski, R., and Toyama, K. Performance-driven hand-drawn animation. *Proceedings of NPAR 2000* (June 2000).

[2] Chen, S. E. Quicktime VR - An image-based approach to virtual environment navigation. *Computer Graphics (SIGGRAPH 95)*, 29–38.

[3] Chen, S. E., and Williams, L. View interpolation for image synthesis. *Computer Graphics (SIGGRAPH 93)*, 279–288.

[4] Curtis, C. J., Anderson, S. E., Seims, J. E., Fleischer, K. W., and Salesin, D. H. Computer-generated watercolor. *Computer Graphics (SIGGRAPH 97)*, 421–430.

[5] Debevec, P. Image-based modeling, rendering, and lighting. *Course #35, SIGGRAPH 2000 Course Notes* (July 2000).

[6] Debevec, P. E., Taylor, C. J., and Malik, J. Modeling and rendering architecture from photographs: A hybrid geometry- and image-based approach. *Computer Graphics (SIGGRAPH 96)*, 11–20.

[7] Debevec, P. E., Yu, Y., and Borshukov, G. D. Efficient view-dependent image-based rendering with projective texture-mapping. *Eurographics Rendering Workshop* (June 1998), 105–116.

[8] Efros, A. A., and Leung, T. K. Texture synthesis by non-parametric sampling. *IEEE International Conference on Computer Vision* (1999).

[9] Funkhouser, T. A. A visibility algorithm for hybrid geometry- and image-based modeling and rendering. *Computers and Graphics, Special Issue on Visibility* (1999).

[10] Funkhouser, T. A., Teller, S. J., Sequin, C. H., and Khorramabadi, D. The UC Berkeley system for interactive visualization of large architectural models. *Presence 5*, 1 (January 1996).

[11] Gooch, A., Gooch, B., Shirley, P., and Cohen, E. A non-photorealistic lighting model for automatic technical illustration. *Computer Graphics (SIGGRAPH 98)*, 447–452.

[12] Gortler, S. J., Grzeszczuk, R., Szeliski, R., and Cohen, M. F. The lumigraph. *Computer Graphics (SIGGRAPH 96)*, 43–54.

[13] Haeberli, P. E. Paint by numbers: Abstract image representations. *Computer Graphics (SIGGRAPH 90)*, 207–214.

[14] Heckbert, P. Survey of texture mapping. *IEEE Computer Graphics and Applications* (Nov. 1986).

[15] Hertzmann, A. Painterly rendering with curved brush strokes of multiple sizes. *Computer Graphics (SIGGRAPH 98)*, 453–460.

[16] Hewlett Packard. HP PEX Texture Mapping, www.hp.com/mhm/WhitePapers/PEXtureMapping/PEXtureMapping.html.

[17] Horry, Y., ichi Anjyo, K., and Arai, K. Tour into the picture: Using a spidery mesh interface to make animation from a single image. *Computer Graphics (SIGGRAPH 97)*, 225–232.

[18] Kowalski, M. A., Markosian, L., Northrup, J. D., Bourdev, L., Barzel, R., Holden, L. S., and Hughes, J. Art-based rendering of fur, grass, and trees. *Computer Graphics (SIGGRAPH 99)*, 433–438.

[19] Levoy, M., and Hanrahan, P. Light field rendering. *Computer Graphics (SIGGRAPH 96)*, 31–42.

[20] Litwinowicz, P. Processing images and video for an impressionist effect. *Computer Graphics (SIGGRAPH 97)*, 407–414.

[21] Manocha, D. Interactive walkthroughs of large geometric databases. *Course #18, SIGGRAPH 2000 Course Notes* (July 2000).

[22] Markosian, L., Kowalski, M. A., Trychin, S. J., Bourdev, L. D., Goldstein, D., and Hughes, J. F. Real-time nonphotorealistic rendering. *Computer Graphics (SIGGRAPH 97)*, 415–420.

[23] McMillan, L., and Bishop, G. Plenoptic modeling: An image-based rendering system. *Computer Graphics (SIGGRAPH 95)*, 39–46.

[24] Meier, B. J. Painterly rendering for animation. *Computer Graphics (SIGGRAPH 96)*, 477–484.

[25] Mizuno, S., Okada, M., and ichiro Toriwaki, J. Virtual sculpting and virtual woodcut printing. *The Visual Computer 14*, 2 (1998), 39–51.

[26] Ostromoukhov, V. Digital facial engraving. *Computer Graphics (SIGGRAPH 99)*, 417–424.

[27] Saito, T., and Takahashi, T. NC machining with G-buffer method. *Computer Graphics (SIGGRAPH 91)*, 207–216.

[28] Salisbury, M. P., Wong, M. T., Hughes, J. F., and Salesin, D. H. Orientable textures for image-based pen-and-ink illustration. *Computer Graphics (SIGGRAPH 97)*, 401–406.

[29] Shade, J. W., Gortler, S. J., wei He, L., and Szeliski, R. Layered depth images. *Computer Graphics (SIGGRAPH 98)*, 231–242.

[30] Tsai, R. Y. A Versatile Camera Calibration Technique for High-Accuracy 3D Machine Vision Metrology Using Off-the-Shelf TV Cameras and Lenses. *IEEE Journal of Robotics and Automation 3*, 4 (Aug. 1987), 323–344.

[31] Williams, L. Pyramidal parametrics. *Computer Graphics (SIGGRAPH 83)*, 1–11.

[32] Winkenbach, G., and Salesin, D. H. Computer-generated pen-and-ink illustration. *Computer Graphics (SIGGRAPH 94)*, 91–100.

[33] Winkenbach, G., and Salesin, D. H. Rendering parametric surfaces in pen and ink. *Computer Graphics (SIGGRAPH 96)*, 469–476.

[34] Wong, M. T., Zongker, D. E., and Salesin, D. H. Computer-generated floral ornament. *Computer Graphics (SIGGRAPH 98)*, 423–434.

[35] Wood, D. N., Finkelstein, A., Hughes, J. F., Thayer, C. E., and Salesin, D. H. Multiperspective panoramas for cel animation. *Computer Graphics (SIGGRAPH 97)*, 243–250.

SIGGRAPH 2000 Committee

SIGGRAPH 2000 Conference Chair
Jackie White
California State University, Los Angeles

SIGGRAPH Conference
Chief Staff Executive
Dino Schweitzer
Capstone Management Group

Accounting / Conference Management /
Copy Coordination / Registration /
Marketing and Media
Smith, Bucklin, & Associates, Inc.

Art Gallery
Diane Gromala
Georgia Institute of Technology

Audio/Visual Support
AVW Audio Visual, Inc.

Community Outreach
Adele Newton
University of Toronto

Computer Animation Festival
Joe Takai
Industrial Light + Magic

Conference Administration
Capstone Management Group

Courses
Anselmo Lastra
University of North Carolina at Chapel Hill

Creative Applications Lab
Rob Lembree
Metro Link Incorporated

Educators Program
Valerie Miller
Georgia State University

Emerging Technologies:
Point of Departure
J. Jeffrey Close
Independent Consultant

Exhibition Management
Hall-Erickson, Inc.

Graphic Design / Editing / Web Site
Q LTD

GraphicsNet
Larry Kauffman
USA Group, Inc.

International
Marcelo Knorich-Zuffo
Universidade de São Paulo

Organizational Development
Gayle Magee
Independent Consultant

Panels
Aliza Corson
Walt Disney Feature Animation

Papers
Kurt Akeley
SGI

Pathfinders 2000
Kristen J. Stratton
Incentive Innovations

Publications
Stephen N. Spencer
University of Washington

Service Contractor
Freeman Decorating Company

SIGGRAPH TV/Online
Mary Nichols
Middle Tennessee State University

sigKIDS
Marc Barr
Middle Tennessee State University

Sketches & Applications
Tom Appolloni
Harris Corporation

Student Volunteers
Steve Talent
Motorola, Inc.

The Studio
Peter Braccio
Monterey Bay Aquarium Research
Institute

Travel Agent
Travel Technology Group, Ltd.

Web3D RoundUP
Timothy Childs
Eyematic Interfaces
Don Brutzman
Naval Postgraduate School

SIGGRAPH 99 Conference Chair
Warren N. Waggenspack, Jr.
Louisiana State University

SIGGRAPH 2001 Conference Chair
Lynn Pocock
New York Institute of Technology

SIGGRAPH Executive Committee

Chair
Judith R. Brown

Vice Chair
Alan Chalmers
University of Bristol

Director for Communications
Leo Hourvitz
Pulse Entertainment

Director for Education
Mike McGrath
Colorado School of Mines

Director for Professional Chapters
Colleen Cleary
Orange County (FL) Sheriff's Office

Director for Publications
Stephen N. Spencer
University of Washington

Director-at-Large
David Ebert
University of Maryland Baltimore County

Director-at-Large
Gudrun Enger
Metro Link Incorporated

Treasurer
Garry M. Paxinos
Metro Link Incorporated

Past Chair
Steve Cunningham
California State University, Stanislaus

SIGGRAPH 2000 Conference Chair
Jackie White
California State University Los Angeles

SIGGRAPH Conference
Chief Staff Executive (ex officio)
Dino Schweitzer
Capstone Management Group

Conference Advisory Group

Conference Advisory Group Chair
G. Scott Owen
Georgia State University

SIGGRAPH 99 Conference Chair
Warren Waggenspack
Louisiana State University

SIGGRAPH 2000 Conference Chair
Jackie White
California State University Los Angeles

SIGGRAPH 2001 Conference Chair
Lynn Pocock
New York Institute of Technology

SIGGRAPH 2002 Conference Chair
Tom Appolloni
Harris Corporation

SIGGRAPH Conference
Chief Staff Executive (Ex officio)
Dino Schweitzer
Capstone Management Group

Executive Committee Representative
Theresa-Marie Rhyne
Lockheed Martin Technical Services/
US EPA Scientific Visualization Center

Executive Committee Representative
Garry Paxinos
Metro Link Incorporated

Papers Committee

Chair

Kurt Akeley
SGI

Advisory Board

Eugene Fiume
University of Toronto

Patrick Hanrahan
Stanford University

Mark Segal
San Jose State University

Committee

Norman I. Badler
University of Pennsylvania

David C. Banks
Florida State University

David Baraff
Pixar Animation Studios

Edwin Catmull
Pixar Animation Studios

Frank Crow
Interval Research

Paul Debevec
USC Institute for Creative Technologies

Julie Dorsey
Massachusetts Institute of Technology

Gershon Elber
Technion - Israel Institute of Technology

Adam Finkelstein
Princeton University

Eugene Fiume
University of Toronto

Henry Fuchs
University of North Carolina at Chapel Hill

Andrew Glassner
Consultant

Steven J. Gortler
Harvard University

Larry Gritz
Pixar Animation Studios

Charles Hansen
University of Utah

Paul Heckbert
Carnegie-Mellon University

Jessica K. Hodgins
Georgia Institute of Technology

John Hughes
Brown University

Victoria Interrante
University of Minnesota

Hiroshi Ishii
Massachusetts Institute of Technology

David B. Kirk
NVIDIA Corporation

Leif P. Kobbelt
Max-Planck-Institut für Informatik

Marc Levoy
Stanford University

Dinesh Manocha
University of North Carolina
at Chapel Hill

Nelson Max
Lawrence-Livermore National
Laboratory

Michael D. McCool
University of Waterloo

Jarek Rossignac
Georgia Institute of Technology

Holly Rushmeier
IBM T.J. Watson Research Center

David H. Salesin
Microsoft Research and University of
Washington

Mark Segal
San Jose State University

Steven Seitz
Carnegie-Mellon University

John Snyder
Microsoft Research

Michiel van de Panne
University of Toronto

Luiz Velho
Instituto de Matematica Pura e Aplicada

Paper Reviewers

Agrawala, Maneesh
Airey, John
Alexa, Marc
Aliaga, Daniel
Amanatides, John
Amaya, Kenji
Amenta, Nina
Anderson, David
Anjyo, Ken
Apodaca, Tony
Arvo, Jim
Ashdown, Ian

Bajaj, Chandrajit
Bajura, Michael
Baker, Simon
Bala, Kavita
Balch, Tucker
Bao, Paul
Barrett, Bill
Barsky, Brian
Barzel, Ronen
Bastos, Rui
Beadouin-Lafon, Michael
Becker, Barry
Beier, Thad
Bekaert, Philippe
Bender, Walter
Benford, Steve
Benger, Werner
Berg, Alex
Bern, Marshall
Bernard, Marc
Bernardini, Fausto
Besl, Paul
Bindiganavale, Rama
Bishop, Gary
Blinn, Jim
Bloomenthal, Jules
Blythe, David
Bodenheimer, Bobby
Boissonnat, Jean-Daniel
Bookstein, Fred
de Boor, Carl
Borning, Alan
Bouatouch, Kadi
Boulic, Ronan
Bove, Michael
Bowskill, Jerry
Breen, David E.
Bregler, Christoph
Brinsmead, Duncan
Brogan, David
Bronskill, John
Browse, Roger
Bruderlin, Armin
Bruderlin, Beat
Brutzman, Don
Bryson, Steve
Buchanan, John

Buehler, Chris
Buxton, Bill
Cabral, Brian

Callet, Patrick
Calvert, Tom
Cani, Marie-Paule
Canny, John
Carmack, John
Carpenter, Loren
Carvalho, Paulo Cezar Pinto
Cassell, Justine
Chai, Jinxiang
Chang, Chu-Fei
Chen, Eric
Chen, Tsuhan
Chenney, Stephen
Chi, Ed
Chow, Mike
Christensen, Per H.
Chupa, Mike
Cignoni, Paolo
Cohen, Elaine
Cohen, Jonathan D.
Cohen, Michael F.
Cohen-Or, Daniel
Colucci, D'nardo
Cook, Rob
Coquillart, Sabine
Costa da Silva, Bruno
Costa, Monica
Cowan, William
Crawfis, Roger
Cremer, Jim
Curless, Brian
Curtis, Cassidy
Cutler, Larry

Dahmen, Wolfgang
Daly, Scott
Dana, Kristin
Daniilidis, Kostas
DeBonet, Jeremy
DeCarlo, Douglas
DeFanti, Thomas
DeRose, Tony
Deering, Michael
Delp, Scott
Desbrun, Mathieu
Dey, Tamal K.
Dischler, Jean-Michel
Donovan, Walt
Drebin, Bob
Drettakis, George
Drucker, Steven
Duchaineau, Mark
Duchamp, Tom
Duff, Tom
Durand, Frédo
Dyer, Charles R.

Ebert, David
Edelsbrunner, Herbert
Efros, Alyosha
Ehrlich, Charles
Erikson, Carl
Ertl, Thomas
Erturk, Hakan
Eschbach, Reiner
Eyles, John

Faloutsos, Petros
Farin, Gerald
Faust, Nickolas L.
Feiner, Steven
Feldman, Uri
Fieguth, Paul
de Figueiredo, Luiz Henrique
Fisher, Anath
Fishkin, Ken
Fitzmaurice, George
Fleischer, Kurt
Floater, Michael
de Floriani, Leila
Forrest, Robin
Forsberg, Andrew
Forsey, David
Foster, Nick
Fournier, Alain
Francis, George
Franklin, Randolph W.
Freeman, Bill
Frisken, Sarah
Fröhlich, Bernd
Funkhouser, Tom

Garland, Michael
Gleicher, Michael
Gomes, Jonas
Gordon, Dan
Goswami, Ambarish
Gotsman, Craig
Greene, Ned
Grimm, Cindy
Grimson, Eric
Grinstein, Georges
Gross, Markus
Grzeszczuk, Radek
Guenter, Brian
Gueziec, André
Guibas, Leonidas J.
Guimbretiere, Francois
Gumhold, Stefan
Guskov, Igor

Haeberli, Paul
Hahn, Tom
Haines, Eric
Hall, Roy
Halle, Michael
Hamann, Bernd

Paper Reviewers

Hanrahan, Pat
Hansen, Andrew J.
Harrison, Jason
Hart, John C.
Hauser, Helwig
Hawkins, Tim
Healey, Christopher
Hecker, Chris
Heeger, David
Hegron, Gerard
Heidrich, Wolfgang
Hersch, Roger
Hertzmann, Aaron
Hinckley, Ken
Hinton, Geoff
Hirota, Gentaro
Hobby, John
Hoff, Kenneth
Hong, Qin
Hoppe, Hugues
House, Donald H.
Hubbard, Philip
Hudson, Scott
Huh, Suejung

Igarashi, Takeo
Irani, Michal
Isaksen, Aaron
Isenburg, Martin

Jacobs, Chuck
Jensen, Henrik Wann
Jepsen, Mary Lou
Johnson, David E.
Jones, Lynette
Jouppi, Norman P.
Joy, Ken
Jüttler, Bert

Kajiya, Jim
Kalaiah, Aravind
Kang, Sing-Bing
Kass, Michael
Kautz, Jan
Keating, Brett
Keller, Alexander
Kim, Myung Soo
Kimia, Ben
Kindlman, Gordon
King, Davis
Klassen, R. Victor
Klein, Reinhard
Ko, Hyeong-Seok
Koch, Reinhard
Koditschek, Daniel E.
Kolb, Craig
Koller, David
Kowalski, Michael
Krishnamurthy, Venkat
Krishnan, Shankar

Kugler, Anders
Kumar, Subodh
Kurlander, David
Kurtenbach, Gord
Kutulakos, Kyros

Lafortune, Eric
Lai, Feipei
Laidlaw, David
Lalonde, Paul
Lappas, Tasso
Larsen, Eric
Laszlo, Joseph
Latombe, Jean-Claude
Lazarus, Francis
Leather, Mark
Lee, Seungyong
Leinhardt, Pascal
Lengyel, Jerome E.
Lensch, Hendrik
Lerios, Tolis
Levin, Adi
Levin, David
Levy, Bruno
Lew, Steven
Lin, Ming C.
Lindeberg, Tony
Lindholm, Erik
Lindstrom, Peter
Lischinski, Dani
Litwinowicz, Pete
Liu, Yanxi
Livingston, Mark
Loftin, Bowen
Lokovic, Tom
Loop, Charles
Lorensen, William
Lounsbery, Michael
Lubin, Jeffrey
Luebke, David

Ma, Kwan-Liu
MacIntyre, Blair
Magnenat-Thalmann, Nadia
Magnor, Marcus
Maillot, Jerome
Malik, Jitendra
Mallet, Jean-Laurent
Malvar, Henrique
Malzbender, Tom
Mammen, Abe
Mann, Stephen
Manocha, Dinesh K.
Mark, William R.
Markosian, Lee
Marks, Joe
Marschner, Steve
Marshall, Dana
Martin, Ralph
May, Steve

McAllister, David K.
McCann, John
McCann, Mary
McCormack, Joel
McGlone, Chris
McGrenere, Joanna
McMillan, Leonard
Meier, Barbara
Metaxas, Dimitris
Meyer, Gary
Migdal, Christopher
Milenkovic, Victor
Miller, Gavin
Mine, Mark
Minsky, Margaret
Mirtich, Brian
Mitchell, Don P.
Mitchell, Joe
Mitchell, Ross
Moher, Tom
Molnar, Steve
Monks, Michael
Morse, Bryan S.
Mortensen, Eric
Moshell, J. Michael
Mueller, Carl
Mumford, David
Munzner, Tamara
Myszkowski, Karol

Navazo, Isabel
Nawotki, Alexa
Neff, Michael
Neumann, Ulrich
Neyret, Fabrice
Ng-Thow-Hing, Victor
Ngo, Tom
Nishida, Shin'ya
Nishita, Tomoyuki

O'Brien, James
Olano, Marc
Olynyk, Kirk
Ostromoukhov, Victor
van Overveld, C.W.A.M.

Paget, Rupert
Pai, Dinesh K.
Painter, Jamie
Pajarola, Renato
Pandy, Marcus
Pandzic, Igor
Papakipos, Matt
Parent, Rick
Pasko, Alexander
Patrikalakis, Nicholas
Pattanaik, Sumanta N.
Pausch, Randy
Pedersen, Hans
Peercy, Mark

Paper Reviewers

Pelachaud, Catherine
Peng, Liang
Perlin, Ken
Petajan, Eric
Peters, Jörg
Pfister, Hanspeter
Pharr, Matt
Pierce, Jeff
Pighin, Frédéric
Pinhanez, Claudio
Playter, Robert
Pollard, Nancy S.
Popović, Zoran
Porter, Tom
Post, Frits
Poulin, Pierre
Prautzsch, Hartmut
Premože, Simon
Prentice, Stephen
Prevost, Scott
Prock, Andrew
Proffitt, Dennis
Prusinkiewicz, Przemyslaw
Pueyo, Xavier
Pulli, Kari
Puppo, Enrico
Purgathofer, Werner

Rademacher, Paul
Raghavachary, Saty
Rahimi, Ali
Raskar, Ramesh
Reddy, Martin
Regan, Matthew
Reif, Uli
Rheingans, Penny
Rhyne, Theresa-Marie
Rickel, Jeff
Rockwood, Alyn
Roddy, Brian
Rokne, Jon
Rose, Charles F.
Rosenthal, Charles
Rosenthal, Seth
Rumpf, Martin
Rusinkiewicz, Szymon
Rutman, Serge
Ryall, Kathy

Sabin, Malcolm
Salisbury, Kenneth
Salisbury, Mike
Samet, Hanan
Sato, Yoichi
Savage, Craig
Schaufler, Gernot
Scheepers, Ferdi
Schlick, Christophe
Schneider, Bengt-Olaf
Schödl, Arno
Schröder, Peter
Scopigno, Roberto
Searle, Anthony
Sedenberg, Tom

Seidel, Hans-Peter
Séquin, Carlo
Shade, Jonathan
Shakespeare, Robert
Shapiro, Art
Shapiro, Vadim
Shin, Sung Yong
Shinya, Mikio
Shirley, Peter
Shoup, Dick
Shum, Harry
Sibert, Linda
Siegel, Mel
Sillion, François
Silvers, Robert
Simoncelli, Eero
Singh, Karan
Slater, Mel
Sloan, Kenneth
Sloan, Peter-Pike
Slusallek, Philipp
Smith, Alvy Ray
Smith, Jeff
Smits, Brian
Snoeyink, Jack
Soler, Cyril
Spalter, Anne
Stalling, Detlev
Stam, Jos
State, Andrei
Stewart, James
Stolfi, Jorge
Stollnitz, Eric
Straßer, Wolfgang
Strauss, Paul
Stürzlinger, Wolfgang
Sugihara, Kokichi
Surati, Rajeev
Surazhsky, Tatiana
Suzuki, Hiromasa
Swan, Ed
Sweldens, Wim
Szeliski, Richard

Takala, Tapio
Tal, Ayellet
Taubin, Gabriel
Taylor, Camillo
Taylor, Russell
Tchou, Chris
Teller, Seth
Terzopoulos, Demetri
Thalmann, Daniel
Tolani, Deepak
Tombre, Karl
Torrance, Kenneth
Toyama, Kentaro
Trinkle, Jeff
Troscianko, Tom
Tu, Xiaoyuan
Tumblin, Jack
Turk, Greg
Turkowski, Ken

Underkoffler, John

Van Hook, Tim
VanGelder, Dirk
VandeWettering, Mark
Varshney, Amitabh
Veach, Eric
Venetsanopoulos, Anastasios N.
Verplank, Bill
Vicci, Leandra
Vidimče, Karl
Voorhies, Doug

Walter, Bruce
Wang, Wenping
Ward, Matt
Ware, Colin
Warren, Joe
Watson, Andrew
Weinstein, David
Welch, Greg
Westermann, Rüdiger
Westin, Stephen
Westover, Lee
Whitman, Scott
Whitted, Turner
Wilhelms, Jane
Williams, Lance
Willmott, Andrew
Winkenbach, Georges
Winner, Stephanie
Witkin, Andy
Wolberg, George
Wolters, Hans
Wood, Daniel Niklas
Wu, Xiaolin
Wu, Yin

Yu, Yizhou

Zabih, Ramin
Zatz, Harold
Zeilfelder, Frank
Zelesnick, Bob
Zhang, Hansong
Zhang, Zhengyou
Zheng, Jianmin
Zorin, Denis
Zyda, Michael

Courses Committee

Phil Amburn
Qualia Computing

Pere Brunet
Univ Politecnica de Catalunya

Lou Harrison
North Carolina State University

Barb Helfer
ACCAD, The Ohio State University

Alyce Kaprow
The New Studio

Anselmo Lastra
University of North Carolina at Chapel Hill

Steve May
Pixar Animation Studios

Harry Smith
University of North Carolina at Wilmington

Courses Reviewers

Ergun Akleman
Daniel Aliaga
Vinacua Alvar
Steve Anderson
Carlos Andujar
Dolors Ayala

William H. Bares
Daniel Bergeron
Gary Bishop
Dennis J. Bouvier
Ed Brabant
Jack Bresenham

Michael Capps
Wayne Carlson
Pete Carswell
Jim Chung
Alan Commike
Larry Cutler

Tim Davis
Tony DeRose
Dan Deter
Todd DeVriese
Martin Dulberg

David Ebert
David Ellsworth
Nick England
Jordi Esteve

Steven Feiner
Leila De Floriani
Ken Flurchick
Perales Francisco

Kevin Geiger
Robert Geitz
Meg Geroch
Jon Gladden
Andrew Glassner
Tim Glenn
Brian Green
Arthur Gregory
Ugur Gudukbay
Curry Guinn
Mary Beth Haggerty
Brad Hemminger
Dan Herman
Karl Hillesland
Larry Hodges
Kenneth Hoff
Jeff Hoffmeister
Leo Hourvitz
Donald House
Steve Hwan

Gil Irizarry

Tim Jacobs
Robert Joan-Arinyo
Robert Judd

Midori Kitagawa
Craig Kolb

Wm Leler
James Lester
Matt Lewis
James Lipscomb
Mark Livingston
Shaun Love

Michael Macedonia
William R. Mark
David K. McAllister
Ann McNamara
Tim Milliron

Isabel Navazo
Bob Nicoll
Lars Nyland

Marc Olano
Bill Oliver
Nick Orlans

Voicu Popescu
Dave Pratt
Xavier Pueyo
Enrico Puppo

Guido Quaroni

Saty Raghavachary
Tomas Recio
Dave Reed
Phil Ritzenthaler
Kevin Rodgers

Daniel Sanchez-Crespo
Rick Sayre
Roberto Scopigno
Scott Senften
Francisco Seron
Peter Shirley
Jeff Smith
Dana Smith
LLuís Solano
Gary Stelling
Antonio Susin
Ed Swan

Rasmus Tamstorf
Federico Thomas
Juan Carlos Torres
Dani Tost

Jim Vaigl
Marc Vigo
Manuel Vivo

Charles Wardin
Benjamin Watson
Greg Welch
Lee Westover
Mary Whitton
Doug Wiley
Adam Woodbury

R. Michael Young

Michael Zyda

Exhibitors

(as of 05 April 2000)

2d3
3Dlabs, Inc.
3DMetrics, Inc.
3D Pipeline Corporation
3D Nature
The 3D Shop
3D Systems
5D
Accom, Inc.
Addison-Wesley/New Riders
Adobe Systems, Inc.
Advanced Imaging Magazine
Advanced Media Production
Advanced Micro Devices
Advanced Rendering Technology
AJA Video
A K Peters, Ltd.
Alias|Wavefront
Alpha Processor, Inc.
Alternate Realities Corporation
American Cinematographer
ANDROME
Animation Magazine
Anthro Corporation
Appian Graphics
Arc Second, Inc.
ArchVision
Arete Entertainment
Artbeats Digital Film Library
ARTBYTE: The Magazine of Digital
Culture
The Art Institutes
Ascension Technology Corporation
AuSIM Engineering Solutions
auto·des·sys, Inc.
Autonomous Effects Inc.

B & H Photo-Video-Pro Audio
B & L Engineering
BARCO Projection Systems America
Baydel North America, Inc.
Big Idea Productions
blaxxun interactive
Blue Sky Studios, Inc.
Boris FX
BOXX Technologies, Inc.
BrassRing.com

Caligari Corporation
Cambridge University Press
CDAT
Cebas Computer
CELCO
Charles River Media
Chromatek Inc.
Chyron Corporation
CMP Media Inc.
Colorgraphic
Communication Arts

Compaq Computer Corporation
Computer Graphics Systems Development
Corporation
Computer Graphics World
The Coriolis Group
Crater Software
Creation Engine LLC
Creative Planet
Creature House Ltd.
Criterion Software Limited
CYBELIUS Software, Inc.
Cyberware
Cyberworld International
Cycore
Cyra Technologies, Inc.

Dell Computer Corporation
Desktop Engineering
Desktop Images
Digimation, Inc.
Digital Domain, Inc.
dhima & DIGITAL HOLLYWOOD
Digital Immersion Software Corporation
Digital Media Online
Dimension 3D-Systems GmbH
DISC, Incorporated
Discreet
Disti
DotVision, Inc.
DPS (Digital Processing Systems Inc.)
DreamSkills Productions

EDC of Mid-Florida
ednet
ELSA, Inc.
Elsevier Science
Essential Reality
Exabyte Corporation
Eyematic Interfaces Inc.

Fakespace, Inc.
Florida Center for Electronic
Communication
Fraunhofer CRCG, Inc.

Geometrix, Inc.
gettyone.com
Global Haptics, Inc.

Hash Inc.
Hewlett-Packard Company
The Hollywood Reporter
Hypercosm, Inc.

I.D. Magazine
IdN Magazine
IEEE Computer Society
IMAGICA Corporation
Imagina-INA

Immersion Corporation
Improv Technologies
Industrial Light & Magic
InSpeck, Inc. inc.
Intense3D
International Fine Arts College
InterSense, Incorporated
Intertec Publishing
i-O Display Systems, LLC

Journey Education Marketing
Junior Land Co. Ltd

Kaydara, Inc.
Kazoo 3D
Kingston Technology Company
Knowledge Industry Publications

Lake Technology Limited
LEGASYS International
Linker Systems, Inc.
LIPSinc.
LSI Logic Storage Systems

MacAcademy/Windows Academy
Mainframe Entertainment, Inc.
Manex Entertainment
MathEngine Inc.
Matrox
MaxVision Corporation
Measurand Inc.
Medea Corporation
MediaFORM
MENSI, Inc.
Meta Motion
Microboards Technology
Millimeter Magazine
Minicomputer Exchange, Inc.
Minolta Corporation
Miranda Technologies Inc.
Mississippi State University
MMS Multi Media Systems
Morgan Kaufmann Publishers, Inc
Motek
Motion Analysis Corporation
Multimedia Content Association of Japan
MUSE Technologies, Inc.

NEMO
Netmor
NewTek
Next Level Digital Academy
Next Limit SL
Nikkei Computer Graphics
NIST-Advanced Technology Program
Not a Number
Nothing Real
NVIDIA Corporation
n-vision, inc.

Exhibitors
(as of 05 April 2000)

NxView Technologies, Inc.

Okino Computer Graphics, Inc.
Ontario Film Development Corporation
Opticore
ORAD, Inc.
OTT-LITE Technology
PDI (Pacific Data Images)
Panoptic Vision
Panoram Technologies
Paraform
Parallax Inc.
Peachpit Press
Pepper's Ghost Productions
PhoeniX Technologies Incorporated
Phoenix Tools
Photron USA
Pixar Animation Studios
PixelFusion Limited
Pixologic, Inc
Play Incorporated
Polhemus, Inc.
Post Magazine
Professional Graphics World
Purdue University, Department of
Computer Graphics

Quantel Inc.

Raindrop Geomagic, Inc.
ReachIn Technologies
Real Vision, Inc.
Realviz
Reflex Inc.
RES Magazine
Research Systems
RHINO/Robert McNeel & Associates
Rhythm & Hues Studios
Right Hemisphere
Roland DGA Corporation

S3/Professional Graphics
San Francisco Imaging Inc.
Savannah College of Art and Design
SBS Technologies, Inc.
Scientific Placement, Inc.
SensAble Technologies
SENSE8 Product Line of EAI
SGI
Sharp Electronics Corporation
Sheridan College
Side Effects Software
Sierra Design Labs
Silicon Grail
SIMI Reality Motion Systems GmbH
SMPTE
SNELL & WILCOX Ltd.
Softimage Inc.
Solid Modeling Solutions

Sony Computer Entertainment, Inc.
Sony Electronics Inc.
Sony Electronics Inc.
Spatial Integrated Systems, Inc.
Springer-Verlag
Square
Steamboat Software, Inc.
Stratasys Inc.
Sun Microsystems, Inc.
Synthetik Software, Inc.
System Upgrade, Inc.
Systems in Motion

Texas Memory Systems, Inc.
Total Training
Toon Boom Technologies
Toyobo Co., Ltd.
Tricorder Technology
TRIMEDIA, INC.
Trimension Systems

University of Advancing Computer
Technology

Vancouver Film School
Vicon Motion Systems
Viewgraphics Inc.
Viewpoint Digital
Virtual Research Systems, Inc.
Virtual Technologies, Inc.
Vividata, Inc.

Wacom Technology
The Walt Disney Company
Wicks and Wilson Limited
Workstation Users Alliance, Inc.

Yannix Technology Corporation

Z Corporation
Zebra Imaging

SIGGRAPH Professional Chapters

California

Los Angeles ACM SIGGRAPH
Genny Yee, Chair
PO Box 9399
Marina del Rey, CA 90295
los_angeles_chapter@siggraph.org
www.siggraph.org/chapters/los_angeles

San Diego ACM SIGGRAPH
Alan Scrivener, Chair
10150 Waynecrest Lane
Santee, CA 92701
san_diego_chapter@siggraph.org
www.siggraph.org/chapters/san_diego

San Francisco ACM SIGGRAPH
Walter Beer, Chair
100 First St., Suite 100 - Box 347
San Francisco, CA 94105
san_francisco_chapter@siggraph.org
www.siggraph.org/chapters/sf

Silicon Valley ACM SIGGRAPH
Jenny Dana, Chair
PO Box 804
Mountain View, CA 94042-1205
silicon_valley_chapter@siggraph.org
www.siggraph.org/chapters/siliconv

Colorado

Denver/Boulder ACM SIGGRAPH
Inactive

District of Columbia

Washington, D.C. ACM SIGGRAPH
Mary Higgins, Chair
c/o SMS Interactive
85 South Bragg Street , Suite 500
Alexandria, VA 22312
washington_dc_chapter@siggraph.org
www.dcsiggraph.org

Florida

Ft. Lauderdale ACM SIGGRAPH
Francis X. McAfee, Chair
c/o Florida Center for Electronic
Communication
220 Southeast Second Avenue
Fort Lauderdale, FL 33301
fort_lauderdale_chapter@siggraph.org
www.siggraph.org/chapters/ftlsig/

Florida

Orlando ACM SIGGRAPH
Betsy Walton, Acting Chair
University of Central Florida
4000 Central Florida Blvd.
VAB 221A
Orlando, FL 32816
orlando_chapter@siggraph.org
www.siggraph.org/chapters/orlando/

Tampa Bay ACM SIGGRAPH
Blake Barr, Acting Chair
8401 15th Way North
St. Petersburg, Florida 33702
tampa_bay_chapter@siggraph.org
www.siggraph.org/chapters/tampa_bay

Georgia

Atlanta ACM SIGGRAPH
Inactive

Massachusetts

Boston ACM SIGGRAPH
Olin Lathrop, Chair
PO Box 194
Bedford, MA 01730
boston_chapter@siggraph.org
www.siggraph.org/chapters/boston

Michigan

Motown ACM SIGGRAPH
Ed McDonald, Chair
motown_chapter@siggraph.org

Minnesota

Minneapolis/St. Paul ACM SIGGRAPH
Stan Bissinger, Chair
5401 Elliot Ave. S.
Minneapolis, MN 55417
minneapolis-stpaul_chapter@siggraph.org
www.pixel8.com/siggraph/

Mississippi

Oktibbeha ACM SIGGRAPH
Paras Kaul, Chair
5631 SE Salmon Street
Mississippi State, MS 39762
+1-612-332-3361 Ext. 131 (Voice)
oktibbeha_chapter@siggraph.org
www.siggraph.org/chapters/oktibbeha

New Jersey

Princeton ACM SIGGRAPH
Douglas Dixon, Chair
P.O. Box 1324
Princeton, NJ 08542
princeton_chapter@siggraph.org
www.siggraph.org/chapters/princeton/

New Mexico

Rio Grande ACM SIGGRAPH
Inactive

New York

New York City ACM SIGGRAPH
Scott Lang, Chair
NYC ACM SIGGRAPH Chapter
ACM/Local Activities
1515 Broadway
New York, NY 10036
new_york_city_chapter@siggraph.org
www.siggraph.org/chapters/nyc

North Carolina

NC Research Triangle ACM SIGGRAPH
Carl Schmidt, Chair
Timeline Studios
114 MacKenan Drive, Suite 100
Cary, NC 27511
research_triangle_chapter@siggraph.org
www.siggraph.org/chapters/research_triangle

Pennsylvania

Pittsburgh ACM SIGGRAPH
Inactive

Texas

Dallas - Fort Worth ACM SIGGRAPH
G. Michael Youngblood, Acting Chair
dallas_fort-worth_chapter@siggraph.org
www.siggraph.org/chapters/dallas_fort-worth/

Houston ACM SIGGRAPH
Christine Rosso Paige, Acting Chair
The Art Institute of Houston
1900 Yorktown
Houston, TX 77056
houston_chapter@siggraph.org
www.siggraph.org/chapters/houston/

SIGGRAPH Professional Chapters

Utah

Wasatch Front ACM SIGGRAPH
Richard Coffey, Chair
50 South Central Campus Drive, Room 3190
Merrill Engineering Building
Salt Lake City, UT
wasatch_front_chapter@siggraph.org
www.perp.com/siggraph

Washington State

Seattle ACM SIGGRAPH
Steve Hollasch, Chair
Microsoft
One Microsoft Way
Redmond, WA 98052-6399
seattle_chapter@siggraph.org
www.siggraph.org/chapters/seattle/

Argentina

Buenos Aires ACM SIGGRAPH
Alejandro Beviglia, Chair
TucumBn 1625 PB "B"
1050 Buenos Aires, Argentina
buenos_aires_chapter@siggraph.org
www.siggraph.org.ar

Bulgaria

Sofia ACM SIGGRAPH
Gospodin Jelev, Chair
Dept of Prog & Computer Appl
Technical Univ. of Sofia
1756 Sofia,
Bulgaria
sofia_chapter@siggraph.org

Canada

Vancouver B.C. ACM SIGGRAPH
Graeme Gish, Chair
Vancouver Film School
420 Homer Street
Vancouver, B.C.
V6B 2V5
Canada
vancouver_bc_chapter@siggraph.org
fas.sfu.ca/cs/research/groups/GMRL/ACM-SIGGRAPH

Canada

Toronto ACM SIGGRAPH
Adele Newton, Chair
Newton Associates
6338 Snowflake Lane
Mississauga, Ontario
L5N 6G9
Canada
toronto_chapter@siggraph.org
www.siggraph.org/chapters/to

France

Paris ACM SIGGRAPH
Thierry Frey, Chair
c/o SUPINFOCOM - Terita 3000
2, rue Henri Matisse
59300 Aulnoye-lez-Valenciennes,
France
paris_chapter@siggraph.org
www.siggraph.org/chapters/paris/

Israel

Central Israel ACM SIGGRAPH
Ayellet Tal, Chair
Dept. of Electrical Engineering
Technion - Israel Institute of Technology
Haifa, Israel, 32000
Phone: +972-4-8294651
Fax: +972-4-8323041
central_israel_chapter@siggraph.org
www.ee.technion.ac.il/~ayellet/icgf/

Italy

Milano ACM SIGGRAPH - In Formation
Maria Grazia Mattei, Chair
MGM Digital Communication s.r.l.
via Vivaio 23
20122 Milano Italia
+39 2 798760 (Voice)
+39 2 798701 (Fax)
milano_chapter@siggraph.org

Japan

Tokyo ACM SIGGRAPH
Masa Inakage, Chair
c/o Yukiko Ozaki
Image Systems Engineering Division
IMAGICA Corporation
2-14-1,Higashi-Gotanda,Shinagawa-ku
Tokyo, 141
Japan
tokyo_chapter@siggraph.org
www.siggraph.org/chapters/tokyo

Mexico

Mexico City ACM SIGGRAPH
Gonzalo Leon, Chair
Calzada de las Aguilas #1124-E-202
Col. San Clemente
Mexico City 01740 D.F.
Mexico
mexico_city_chapter@siggraph.org
www.siggraph.org.mx

Singapore

Singapore ACM SIGGRAPH
Hock Soon Seah, Chair
Nanyang Technological University
Nanyang Avenue
Singapore 639798
Republic of Singapore
singapore_chapter@siggraph.org
www.siggraph.org.sg

Taiwan

Taipei ACM SIGGRAPH
Michael Huang, Chair
taipei_chapter@siggraph.org

In-Formation Chapters

Chennai ACM SIGGRAPH
K. Seshasai, Acting Chair
Digital Media Interactive
#1C 1st Floor JP Towers
Nungambakkam High Road
Chennai 600 034, India
chennai_chapter@siggraph.org

Long Island ACM SIGGRAPH Paul Lipsky, Acting Chair
long_island_chapter@siggraph.org

Rotterdam ACM SIGGRAPH
Richard E. Ouwerkerk, Acting Chair
Department of Arts and Architecture
Hogeschool Rotterdam & Omstreken
Scheepmakersstraat 7
PO Box 1272
3000 BG Rotterdam
The Netherlands
rotterdam_chapter@siggraph.org

Southern Germany ACM SIGGRAPH
Jan Weigner, Acting Chair
southern_germany_chapter@siggraph.org

Author Index

Cover Image Credits

Front Cover

"Stone Bunny"

This *lapped texture* model renders at 25 frames per second at a resolution of 1024x1024 pixels using ordinary texture mapping hardware on a PC. It is created by covering a 15,000-triangle mesh using 282 overlapping copies of the inset texture patch. The user spent 15 minutes specifying the desired texture direction over the surface. Then, automatic placement of the texture patches took 2 minutes of computation. Due to the overlapping texture patches, each face of the original mesh is rendered 1.6 times on average. Lapped textures allow large, arbitrary surfaces to be covered with a compact texture footprint. The bunny model is a simplified version of the original "Stanford Bunny" dataset created by Greg Turk.

Reference: "Lapped Textures," Emil Praun, Adam Finkelstein and Hugues Hoppe, pp. 465–470.

Frontispiece

A computer rendering made from a 3D model of Michelangelo's David. The model was built by scanning the statue using a laser triangulation rangefinder and assembling the resulting range images to form a seamless polygon mesh. The mesh contains 8 million polygons, each about 2.0 mm in size. The raw data from which the mesh was built contains 2 billion polygons, representing range samples spaced 0.25 mm apart on the statue surface. Although we also digitized the statue's color, the veining and reflectance shown here are artificial. The rendering includes simulated subsurface scattering, but with arbitrary parameters. Thanks to Henrik Wann Jensen for computing this image.

Reference: "The Digital Michelangelo Project: 3D Scanning of Large Statues," Marc Levoy, Kari Pulli, Brian Curless, Szymon Rusinkiewicz, David Koller, Lucas Pereira, Matt Ginzton, Sean Anderson, James Davis, Jeremy Ginsberg, Jonathan Shade, Duane Fulk, pp. 131–144.

Back Cover

First Row

A pirouette and promenade in five styles drawn from a space that contains ballet, modern dance, and a variety of body types. Style, choreography, and motion are all synthetic. Streamers show the trajectory of the left hand and foot. The motion-generating model and its "style knobs" are learned from unlabeled motion capture data.

Reference: "Style Machines," Matthew Brand, Aaron Hertzmann, pp. 183–192.

Second Row, Left

The complex soft shadows in this image were generated using an efficient image-based raytracing approach combined with a coherence-based light source sampling algorithm that uses visibility coherence to reduce the number of shadow rays cast into the scene. Note the large smooth penumbrae regions and how the leaves cast shadows on other parts of the plant. To emphasize the shadows the image has been generated without the usual cosine falloff of light intensity.

Reference: "Efficient Image-Based Methods for Rendering Soft Shadows," Maneesh Agrawala, Ravi Ramamoorthi, Alan Heirich, Laurent Moll, pp. 375–384.

Second Row, Center

The image shows sequences of meshes generated by the $\sqrt{3}$-subdivision scheme (top row) and by the Loop subdivision scheme (bottom row) applied to the same control mesh (upper left). Although the quality of the limit surfaces is the same (C^2, lower left), $\sqrt{3}$-subdivision uses an alternative refinement operator that increases the number of triangles slower than Loop's. The relative complexity of the corresponding meshes from both rows is (from left to right) $3/4 = 0.75$, $9/16 = 0.56$, and $27/64 = 0.42$. Hence, the new subdivision scheme yields a finer gradation of uniform hierarchy levels. (Original control mesh by Hughes Hoppe.)

Reference: "$\sqrt{3}$ Subdivision," Leif Kobbelt, pp. 103–112.

Second Row, Right

Stripes reflecting off a pie tin. The reflectance properties of this pie tin were first captured using the new environment matting techniques described in "Environment Matting Extensions: Towards Higher Accuracy and Real-Time Capture," by Chuang, Zongker, Hindorff, Curless, Salesin, and Szeliski. The pie tin image was then compositing in front of the striped background. These new techniques are able to accurately produce the stripes' oriented reflections in the tin.

Reference: "Environment Matting Extensions: Towards Higher Accuracy and Real-Time Capture," Yung-Yu Chuang, Douglas E. Zongker, Joel Hindorff, Brian Curless, David H. Salesin, Richard Szeliski, pp. 121–130.

Third Row, Left

"A Snowy North Pole"

This image shows the result of automatically adding a layer of slightly moist snow to an outdoor scene consisting of approximately 300,000 polygons. We use an importance-ordering technique that computes major details first, improving areas of lesser importance only if allowed time permits. We allocated this scene 4 hours to compute the depth and location of snow accumulation, and 10 hours to find and resolve areas of unstable (avalanching) snow.

Reference: "Computer Modeling of Fallen Snow," Paul Fearing, pp. 37–46.

Third Row, Center

"Virtual Environment with Van Gogh Brush Strokes"

This image shows a frame from an interactive walkthrough of a non-photorealistic virtual environment. Our system uses image-based rendering methods to achieve interactivity and frame-to-frame coherence. In addition, we introduce a method for maintaining appropriate stroke size as the user navigates through a scene. Our working system provides an immersive experience rendered in a variety of NPR styles.

Reference: "Non-Photorealistic Virtual Environments," Allison W. Klein, Wilmot Li, Michael M. Kazhdan, Wagner T. Corrêa, Adam Finkelstein and Thomas A. Funkhouser, pp. 527–534.

Third Row, Right

"Stomping Man"

This image is a composite of a hand-drawn artwork and computer-generated shadows. In conventional cel animation, shadows are drawn by hand, in order to provide visual cues about the spatial relationships and forms of characters in the scene. Our system creates shadows and tone mattes based on hand-drawn characters, given high-level guidance from the user about depths of various objects. The method employs a scheme for "inflating" a 3D figure based on 2D hand-drawn art, and provides simple tools for adjusting shapes and relative positions of objects in a scene. Our system obviates the tedium of drawing shadow mattes by hand, and provides control over complex shadows falling over interesting shapes.

Reference: "Shadows for Cel Animation," Lena Petrovic, Brian Fujito, Adam Finkelstein, Lance Williams, pp. 511–516.

Fourth Row

These images are stills from an animation of clouds created by using our simple and computationally inexpensive method. The cloud evolution is simulated using cellular automaton that simplifies the dynamics of cloud formation. The dynamics are expressed by several simple transition rules and their complex motion can be simulated with a small amount of computation. Realistic images are then created using one of the standard graphics APIs, OpenGL. This makes it possible to utilize graphics hardware, resulting in fast image generation. The proposed method can realize the realistic motion of clouds, shadows cast on the ground, and shafts of light through clouds.

Reference: "A Simple, Efficient Method for Realistic Animation of Clouds," Yoshinori Dobashi, Kazufumi Kaneda, Hideo Yamashita, Tsuyoshi Okita, Tomoyuki Nishita, pp. 19–28.

BRUCE SPRINGSTEEN

IN FOCUS 1980 – 2012
PHOTOGRAPHS BY DEBRA L. ROTHENBERG

To Elizabeth,
greetings from Asbury Park, NJ.

Debra L Rothenberg
1/18/14

by Debra L. Rothenberg

Turn the Page
PUBLISHING

Published by Turn the Page Publishing LLC
P. O. Box 3179
Upper Montclair, NJ 07043
www.turnthepagepublishing.com

ISBN-13: 978-1-938501-51-7

Bruce Springsteen In Focus 1980 – 2012
Photographs by Debra L. Rothenberg

Library of Congress Control Number 2013930889

Printed in Canada

Cover Illustration Design by Trace Hull
Design by Robin McGeever, McB Design
Artistic Advisor, Piero Ribelli
Photographs © Debra L. Rothenberg

August 9, 1987
The Stone Pony, Asbury Park, NJ

Bruce was on fire—again! Two feet in front of me, he struck his classic killer-guitar pose. This photo went on to become the official Stone Pony post card.

INTRODUCTION

I grew up in a household in Fair Lawn, New Jersey, where music played all the time. My parents and three older brothers were all into music, and from the moment I came home from school to the time I went to bed, music played on the stereo. My brothers thought they were the Beatles—they grew their hair long, covered their rooms with Beatles memorabilia, and they played musical instruments. Me? I tried to play the piccolo and flute, and failed miserably, then changed to the clarinet and played the only two songs I knew—"Twinkle, Twinkle Little Star" and "Mary Had a Little Lamb." In the marching band, I faked my way through, never really playing. It's safe to say my musical preferences back then were Barry Manilow, Barry Manilow, and Barry Manilow.

My father was a serious amateur photographer who could easily have gone pro. My mom was a lover of the arts, *all* arts, and taught high school English. When I was eight, I saw the movie, *Planet of the Apes*, and loved it so much (and still do), I decided to be a filmmaker. But doubt crept in when I was told the odds for success were 10,000 to one. I watched every movie possible (not easy back in the days before video and cable), and when I was in junior high, I bought a TV for my room, and would set my clock to watch movies in the middle of the night.

At 15, I decided still photography was the next best thing to movie making. I saved for my first SLR and a year later, my parents gave me a Minolta SLR. After coming down with mono and missing three months of school, it was a long time before I took my first photo. In order to graduate on time I had to attend summer school, and chose a printing class. The class met all day, every day, for six weeks, and though initially it was not how I wanted to spend my summer, this class changed my life.

It was 1978 and the instructor, John Heyn, was fresh out of college. When I walked into the classroom on the first day, I heard music playing on the stereo. I hated it. There was some guy named Bruce Springsteen mumbling from the speakers. All day we listened to this guy. The next day, the same

thing. I couldn't work with the distraction. Mr. Heyn said Bruce was from the Jersey Shore (as if that was going to make me like him). He kept playing the music, and I kept complaining, to which he said, "Rothenberg, by the end of the summer you're going to have all of his albums and a deposit down for his next tour." (In those days Ticketmaster accepted deposits for tickets.)

Mr. Heyn changed it up during week two, and we heard Southside Johnny and the Asbury Jukes, another Jersey Shore band. When I asked for more Bruce, Mr. Heyn looked at me and smiled.

John Heyn was also a photographer and brought in photos of Bruce in concert. He photographed The Stone Pony where Bruce played, the boardwalk and Madam Marie and other places mentioned in Bruce's songs. I wanted to know more. John told me how spectacular Bruce's concerts were, and I couldn't imagine it, as I had only been to one concert in my life—Barry Manilow.

A few weeks later, my brothers surprised me with a ticket to see Southside Johnny at the South Mountain Arena in South Orange, NJ. I brought my camera; this would be the first time I used it. I sent the photos to a magazine, but they were never published. So I continued listening to Bruce's music, and loved it. On weekends, my best friend, Lois Brunda, and I hung out and listened to Bruce and dreamed. I brought my camera everywhere. My life was breathing, photography, and Bruce Springsteen. Nothing else mattered.

A year later, Southside Johnny's manager called and asked to use one of the photos on his live album *Reach Up and Touch the Sky*. I made my first photo sale.

When summer school ended, I wanted to get to Asbury Park to see it for myself, but had to wait six long months before I could take my driving test. (I warned my mom if I passed, I was skipping school to drive down.) In February 1979, I passed the test on a slightly snowy day, picked up my friend Jeff Malc, and we drove to Asbury Park with windows open in my Dodge Dart listening to Bruce. We went a few more times in the summer, and I made Jeff pose in all the spots where Bruce was photographed.

In September, 1980, I arrived in college at the Rochester Institute of Technology in Rochester, NY. When I stepped out of the car, I looked up and saw a sign in a dorm window saying, "45 DAYS 'TIL THE RIVER." I knew I was going to like it there. Whoever lived in that room changed the number every day until Bruce's newest album was released.

The River Tour was announced shortly after my arrival, and Bruce was scheduled to play Rochester on December 2, 1980. I stood in line all night in the cold at the local record store to get tickets. As soon as I reached the counter, they sold out. I cried. Others began throwing records off the shelves in frustration. Back on campus, a student was selling tickets for $50 (original price $8.50). I didn't have the money and told him he would never get that amount. Because I was from New Jersey, he thought I knew what people would pay, so he gave me the pair for $30.

The following summer, Bruce opened the new Brendan Byrne Arena in East Rutherford, NJ. My friend, Marti, won the lottery for four tickets—three in row 13 and one in row 14. I was in row 14 on the aisle. Bruce was so close, looking right into my camera and grinning from ear to ear. At one point, Marti turned around and saw my eyes big and glassy and asked if I was doing drugs. "Bruce and photography are the only drugs I need," I answered.

Many times throughout college, I needed my Asbury Park/Stone Pony fix, so I'd jump in the car and drive seven or more hours to be where Bruce played. Too many of those times, I left at 1:45 a.m. to head back to Rochester, only to later learn Bruce showed up ten minutes after I left.

After graduation I landed a job in central New York, but every weekend, I was down the shore. My bad luck continued missing Bruce by minutes.

Later moving to Pennsylvania, I worked at a small newspaper and hated it, but was soon hired by a paper in Toms River. That's when my life began. Living in a small apartment on the bay in Seaside Heights, I shot any and every band that graced the stage at the Pony. Since I wasn't the best student in college, the Pony was my photo education. Studying the work of my favorite live concert photographer, Lynn Goldsmith, I hoped one day to shoot in big arenas half as well as she did. It was a dream I thought would never happen.

Hanging out with Billy Smith and Stephen Bumball, who ran the Asbury Park Rock and Roll Museum, I met all the local musicians and the amazing people who loved and supported the scene. For me, the clubs and the town were like Cheers—a place where everybody knew my name. Every night I saw friends and heard some of the best live music anywhere. And so it began.

Delia S. Rockenberg

3

THE RIVER TOUR 1980-1981

by Debra L. Rothenberg

The River Tour was announced shortly after my arrival at The Rochester Institute of Technology. Bruce was going to play Rochester on December 2, 1980.

During the first week of classes, I met a cute guy named John Ghosn, a transfer student from Long Island, who I wanted to get to know. When I said I was from New Jersey, he said, "Bruuuuuuce!" Then I liked him even more.

After scalping tickets to the concert, I called John and yelled, "We're going to see Bruce!" When the day arrived, John and I and his roommates went to the arena on a crisp, cold night. During the concert, Bruce kept talking about the snow, but we didn't understand (or care). All that mattered was seeing Bruce Springsteen and the E Street Band.

I was in my glory. John and I sang every song, danced, laughed, hugged, and cried. We also lost our voices. When we exited the arena, there was a lot of snow on the ground. Driving back to campus, we plowed into a snow bank and someone in the car asked, "Are we in heaven?" I remember thinking, it doesn't matter ... I just saw Bruce!

December 2, 1980—(Above) My first photo of Bruce. When I put the negative in the enlarger and raised the enlarger to the ceiling, he was the size of a penny, but I was beyond ecstatic because I just shot Bruce! I also thought this would be the best photo of Bruce I would ever take.

July 2, 1981—Brendan Byrne Arena
East Rutherford, NJ—Opening night

As I stood on my chair to get a better shot, Bruce looked directly into my camera. So many times he smiled and laughed and sang right to me. Thrilled isn't the word. It was my first time seeing him UP CLOSE. Bruce Springsteen and photography—I found my purpose.

A man jumped on stage to dance with Bruce. Security looked concerned, but Bruce didn't seem to mind—he ran all over the stage with the guy. He enjoyed sharing the spotlight with an eager fan.

My first published photo of Bruce, as it appeared in the September, 1981, issue of *New Jersey Monthly Magazine*.

Bruce slipped on his own sweat and slid off the stage. The band continued playing, and when he jumped back on stage, there was blood on his elbow. Clarence Clemons took him by the arm and Bruce told the audience he was going to take a break. When he came back, he was good as new. Who can fall off a high stage and keep playing? Bruce Springsteen can.

August 31, 1985
Giants Stadium
East Rutherford, NJ

I was standing alone on the side stage in an empty section. When Bruce came over, at first he looked a little surprised that no one else was there, and then he flashed THAT grin. To this day, this is one of my favorite photos.

BORN IN THE U.S.A. TOUR 1984-1985

by Caryn Rose

I f you were to ask people what comes to mind when they think of *Born in the U.S.A.*, most would recall the album cover, or the image of Springsteen live onstage with the now-iconic headband, cut-off shirt, and bulging muscles. It was a carefully cultivated, deliberate image, and to this day, concert-goers flock to Springsteen concerts all over the world dressed identically, paying homage to an image they may not have even been old enough to personally remember.

And, of course, the music: an album of almost solid hits, with seven Top Ten singles, performed in front of Springsteen's largest audience of his career.

Bruce Springsteen was no longer a cult favorite in a few East Coast cities; he was a bona fide rock and roll star. In those old-fashioned days before the Internet, ticket sales for his concerts literally took down phone circuits in cities across the country due to the unprecedented demand.

Despite the massive success of the album, the live shows still blazed with the same power that the E Street Band had been bringing to the faithful for years and years, even when bridging the gap from arenas to multi-night stadium runs. The tour successfully combined new hits with old favorites, and introduced material from *Nebraska* (the album immediately preceding *Born in the U.S.A.*) to a live audience for the first time. In the arenas, the sets were notable for a mid-show acoustic break, showcasing several songs from *Nebraska*, such as "Reason to Believe," "Atlantic City," and "Johnny 99," featuring only Bruce on acoustic guitar with new member Nils Lofgren—replacing the departed Steve Van Zandt—for backup.

Despite playing on the album, Steve Van Zandt made the decision to leave the E Street Band just as the success meter began to creep skyward. It was a surprise but also a relief when Nils Lofgren was announced as his replacement—a palpable relief among fans who knew that Lofgren was a real musician and not some LA session guy. It was also a surprise to see a woman break the E Street ranks

with the addition of Patti Scialfa on background vocals. Many fans hated that a woman had violated the NO GIRLS ALLOWED clubhouse of the E Street Band, but more fans loved what Patti brought to the live show. Bruce joked that they now had "someone there who can hit the high notes every night."

This was the tour of the mega-hit "Dancing In The Dark" (which was only kept from the number one spot by Prince's "When Doves Cry"), and the legendary "Pink Cadillac" stories: "In the beginning there was a Garden of Eden, there was a man, there was a woman, there was an apple, there was temptation, there was sin, and parked curbside there was a pink Cadillac," and how the actual location of the Garden of Eden was ten miles south of Jersey City, off the New Jersey Turnpike. ("That's why they call it the Garden State!") It was the tour that brought out two roadies dressed as a tree and a bear for the "Growin' Up" story. It was the tour of goofy dances—featuring the entire E Street Band, including Patti Scialfa, dancing to "Cadillac Ranch."

"Born in the U.S.A." would quickly become one of the most misunderstood songs in the history of rock and roll. Not all of the new fans took the time to understand the lyrics and misinterpreted the enormous American flag that served as a backdrop onstage. But no one could have anticipated that Springsteen would become a prop in the 1984 elections, with Reagan's attempt to co-op both Bruce and his song at an election stop in New Jersey (after repeated, and rebuffed, requests for an endorsement), and then Walter Mondale's attempt to grab the brass ring a few days later by falsely claiming that he had Springsteen's endorsement.

All of this was going on while Springsteen placed songs like "Seeds," and its dedication to the workers in the oil fields that inspired the song, in the setlist night after night. It was also the tour where "This Land Is Your Land" made a frequent appearance, dedicated to the steel workers and the family farmers, and the tour where "My Hometown" was introduced with a sincere and lengthy exhortation to support the local food banks who were now regular presences at shows, at Springsteen's specific invitation. (They were also the recipients of private donations from Springsteen, who realized he could do more good by giving the organizations exposure from his stage than just by handing them a check.) And of course, Springsteen's response to the Reagan speech playing "Johnny 99" and wondering what his favorite song was: "I don't think he's been listening to this one."

When the dust finally cleared, *Born in the U.S.A.* firmly established Bruce Springsteen as an international superstar with an audience of fans around the world. Springsteen was now a household name, and things would never be quite the same again. But many of the elements and themes which were introduced or came to the forefront in this period would accompany Springsteen for the rest of his career.

Caryn Rose *is a Brooklyn-based writer and novelist who documents rock and roll, baseball, and urban life. She has been writing about Bruce Springsteen for over 30 years, and has been a regular contributor to "Backstreets Magazine" since 2003.*

Working my second job as a staff photographer for a daily newspaper in Pennsylvania, I was miserable. I wanted to be back in New Jersey. I worked 12 hours a day in an awful town, going back and forth to my shoots, always listening to Bruce. Sometimes I cried, sometimes I smiled. Every day I dreamt of a better life; one where I was a better photographer shooting more music, and especially more Bruce.

One day I was in my apartment listening to the *Born in the USA* album. When "Dancing in the Dark" came on, I picked up a yard stick as my pretend guitar and jumped on the coffee table to dance to this happy song. But then I listened to the lyrics, and realized that Bruce was singing about my life. The beat was happy, but the lyrics were not. Bruce sings about getting up in the evening with nothing to say. I would get up in the afternoon and I had lots to say, but no one to say it to. Like the character in the song, I was also tired and not only bored with myself, but bored with living in this dumpy town and working for this newspaper. Every day, my editor had a different complaint. This town was carving me up, just the way Bruce described. When someone asked me how old I was, at first I couldn't remember, then said, "Twenty-four, but I feel like 40." It was this day that I knew I had to quit and leave the town, but was terrified I would never work as a photojournalist again. I gave two weeks notice, and as I handed the editor my keys, I quoted the last line of "Thunder Road." Saying the place was full of losers was harsh, but I did say it, adding that it was my time to pull out to win and head back to New Jersey.

I moved home to Fair Lawn, terrified. I met another out-of-work photographer who, like me, didn't have any money. We drove to the shore every day to look for work, then back to North Jersey for a $4 happy hour dinner at a local Mexican restaurant. Two weeks later, I landed a staff job at a newspaper at the Jersey Shore and found an apartment on the bay in Seaside Heights.

August 31, 1985
Giants Stadium, East Rutherford, NJ

Panic set in tonight. I forgot to turn my camera off and didn't check it before the concert. So, there I was in a side section all by myself with what I thought was a dead camera. But then I realized the Nikon FM didn't need a battery to work, and later I shot one of my favorite photos. As my female friends say when they see this photo, "Bruce looks mighty fine!"

THE MUSEUM VISIT 1987

In 1985, while I was still working for a newspaper in southwestern, Pennsylvania, I visited Asbury Park as often as possible. I met Billy Smith and Stephen Bumball, who later opened the Asbury Park Rock and Roll Museum, and who became my life-long friends. In 1986, when I landed my dream job working on staff at a Jersey Shore newspaper, I became a resident of Monmouth County and the museum became part of my life.

A labor of love for Billy and Steve, on July 4, 1986, the museum opened and people from all over the world came to see the amazing exhibits that paid homage to the local music scene. To this day, I still hear the excitement in my friends' voices when they talk about the day Bruce visited the museum. I arrived in Asbury Park a little late from a photo shoot, but in enough time to peek through the Palace's window to see Bruce walking to the museum with Billy and Steve. What a thrill for me to witness and document this special day.

The Museum Visit
by Billy Smith and Stephen Bumball

The highlight of all the years operating the Asbury Park Rock and Roll Museum was on 11/11/87, when Bruce Springsteen paid a call. Bruce was out and about in Asbury Park that week filming scenes for his "Tunnel of Love" video, and we were allowed on set to witness some of the filming.

Prior to Bruce's visit, several members of his band had toured the museum, as well as Jon Bon Jovi and Southside Johnny. But we were always asked what Bruce thought of the museum and we could never answer that. The media always referred to the museum as the "Springsteen Museum," and that may have bothered Bruce, but after hearing good things about it, we think Bruce eventually understood that our goal was to respect and honor all the local musicians. It wasn't all about him. We told Bruce many times that we were collecting the memorabilia, and he told us he read a 1979 *Asbury Park Press* article about the collection. At the time he wasn't nostalgic about the past and preferred not to look back, but when he visited our museum, he genuinely enjoyed seeing the collection and reminiscing with us.

Bruce spent about 45 minutes in the museum and before he left, he asked what we wanted for the museum. One of us jokingly suggested his Fender Esquire guitar and he laughed saying it would be hard to part with it.

But now we know how to answer when folks ask about Bruce—"Yes he was here, and he liked it."

November 11, 1987

Bruce visited the Asbury Park Rock and Roll Museum
with owners Stephen Bumball and Billy Smith,
which was located inside the Palace Amusements
in Asbury Park, NJ.

ONE STEP UP/TWO STEPS BACK 1988

The Wonder Bar

February 15, 1988, was a day I will never forget. I lived in Belmar, New Jersey, and it was three days before my 26th birthday. It was also President's Day and everyone had off. The weather was great, so I decided to drive to a boat show in Asbury Park. As I was driving along Main Street in Bradley Beach, I noticed everyone had their windows rolled down. There was a lot of holiday traffic, and it was unseasonably warm for February. On the other side of the street coming toward me was a gorgeous, old car. As the car moved closer, I glanced at the license plate to see what model it was—a 1957 Ford. I then looked at the driver and saw it was Bruce! As the car drove past me, Bruce turned and smiled. We were so close, Bruce and I could have reached out and touched hands. I watched in my rearview mirror as the car turned down a street heading toward the ocean. I rushed home to get my camera—the FIRST and LAST time I ever left home without it. I called Stephen Bumball and Billy Smith, and we met in Bradley Beach. After looking for the car with no luck, we went to Asbury Park's Boat Show. We parked outside the Wonder Bar and I saw THE car coming down the street. After parking, Bruce stepped out of the car, waved, laughed and said, "Hi there. Ya found me." I took my shot, and he went inside to film the video for "One Step Up/Two Steps Back."

Billy, Steve and I wanted to watch Bruce film the video, so we went into the bar. After a while, they asked us to leave, and we did, then came back in only to be thrown out again. After the third time, the director said, "Ok, I admire your tenacity. You can stay." For one scene they made up Bruce to look

like an old man, but that scene never made the final version of the video. After a while, they asked Billy to be in the video. Steve and I watched, happy for our friend, but a little jealous too. Later, the director asked us to walk by in the background. The Wonder Bar was freezing inside and we were anxious to be finished. We never saw Billy in the final version of the video but twenty years later, I saw myself and Steve in the background in a frame so quick that if you blink, you miss us.

TUNNEL OF LOVE EXPRESS TOUR 1988

by Bill Daverne

After the record-shattering Born in the U.S.A. Tour, one question was foremost in the minds of longtime Springsteen fans as well as those who had just jumped on board: What would come next and when?

We were all glued—especially those of us outside of New Jersey—to *Backstreets Magazine* and the photographs which always upped the anticipation. Bruce hopping on club stages down the Jersey Shore, often but not exclusively at The Stone Pony. And those pictures, by Debra Rothenberg, made it all real. She didn't know it, but she became a household name thousands of miles away. Bruce was clearly itching to produce the new blockbuster record and conquer the world yet again. Debra's club pictures were the proof.

Tunnel of Love, the album, added a new layer of sophistication to the Springsteen oeuvre. It was different; not at all what we expected. He had showed us again. Stepping out from stark romanticism, alluring despair, and rollicking rock, we got an artist coping with, and carping about, relationships. Tour? Usually they started quickly, or in the case of *The River* in 1980, even before the album was released. But ToL came in October, 1987, and no tour was on the horizon. Just Debra's club pix.

Finally, word came in early 1988. The ToL tour would start in the dead of winter in Worcester, Massachusetts, a place cold and uninviting that time of year. And February 25, 1988, was a bitterly cold Thursday night. But the night before was even colder and complicated by sleet and snow on the New York State Thruway, I-90, which took three of us east from Buffalo in a little Honda Prelude after crossing the border from Canada.

Once we arrived in Worcester, we decided to find a room, and two of us would sleep while the other joined the line. Despite being the driver, I drew the short straw, and my two pals headed for hotel warmth. There were people in line from at least fifteen states, some of them worried the partially-announced Tunnel of Love Express Tour might not make it to them (which was true for my fellow linemates from Canada and New Jersey, as it turned out), and others who had attended previous openers and wouldn't miss it for the world.

An ABC News satellite truck pulled up in the dark. They'd driven over from Boston after hearing there was a line-up and wanted a "hit" from us for *Good Morning, America.* The reporter told the camera the tour opener that day was the most anticipated music event in the world! We deafened people nationwide, cheering wildly. We were at the center of the musical universe. We had just been on national TV. Surely when the sun rose there'd be tickets for at least the early birds ....

There weren't, not even in the fabled "drop line." There were now hundreds more among us. We scattered seeking scalpers. My refreshed buddies appeared around 10 a.m. expecting to take over my spot in line. They got the bad news. They were stunned but rested, warm, and fed.

Many of us did find tickets, somehow. Scalpers had a field day. I was lucky and found a local stagehand who had an 18th row floor seat, dead-center, given as part of his pay. The $20 ticket cost me $188.

Sleep? Nope. We were in Springsteenland. We had tickets. We decided to find Bruce. I had previously run into *LA Times* music critic Robert Hilburn in the hotel lobby when ticket searching (he couldn't help me), so we knew we had the right hotel. We went up an elevator. The doors opened and we saw Springsteen's manager Jon Landau and some others, including Hilburn. I waved. He waved back with a smile. We stayed on the elevator. We rode back to the lobby. We decided we weren't stalkers after all.

I got to my seat as soon as the doors opened. There was a buzz outside and a bigger one inside. The stage was not right. There were two multi-keyboard stands, but no grand piano for Roy, no Hammond B-3 for Danny. There seemed to be too many microphones, and there was a little ticket booth on the right side of the stage.

As I drank it in, from behind came a polite tap on my shoulder. A woman, still in her 20s, younger than me, asked if I'd ever seen a Springsteen show. She was nervous. It was her first. She was a teacher. Her high school students had brought her. They had talked about Springsteen non-stop in class for two years, and had vowed to take her to the next show. They assured her it would change her life. This was it. She was afraid it wouldn't, and wanted advice on how to react, or whether I thought she could tell them the truth if she didn't like it. I told her there was no other place to be in the world at that moment. It was all more than worth it. She looked like she wanted to believe.

The show began like no other Springsteen show except for the standing ovations and cascading cacophony of "Bruuuuce" from all corners that drowned the stage as the E Street Band members appeared two at a time, bought 'tickets' from the booth and took up their unfamiliar positions, along with Patti Scialfa and the debuting Tunnel of Love Horns.

Previous shows got down to business. This one offered a passion play. Patti held helium-filled balloons. The extended intro to "Tunnel of Love" began to build as each musician took his station before Bruce suddenly appeared with a bouquet of roses, 'bought' his ticket, leaned into the mic and asked: "Are you ready for a date?" The balloons left Patti's grasp as he passed her. She was all smiles.

Bedlam. Bolo tie. No ripped jeans. And the roses were tossed into the crowd as the song bit.

The last E Street Tour for 11 long years had begun. It was an opening night like non previous, or since, with Patti the micro-mini-skirted femme fatale, the horn players perfectly punching the sound, with music well beyond the record we had come to hear. Beyond our imaginations. Beyond stunning.

At the intermission, the teacher behind me looked like she had barely survived a shipwreck, damp, flustered and hair beautifully askew. Her cheeks were tear-streaked. Her smile huge. She told me she hadn't believed me. She told me she'd never be the same. She had stopped being surprised, until now. It wasn't a dark ride.

Bill Daverne is a writer from a small town in Canada, who first heard the song "Born to Run" while hitchhiking during a bus strike in London, Ontario, in late September, 1975. He hasn't been the same since.

February 25, 1988
Opening night of the Tunnel of Love Tour
Worcester, Massachusetts

My friend, Stan Goldstein, loaded his car with four others—me, Billy Smith, Stephen Bumball, and Maureen Keuny, and we made the trek from the Jersey Shore to Worcester for an amazing opening night show. Bruce performed "Roulette" and "Be True," which have always been two of my favorites.

WORLD TOUR 1992

by Matty Karas

He walks onstage in dark jeans and an oversized button-up shirt, tucked in. The buckle of his worn-in leather belt is way off to the side, presumably to protect the back of his equally worn-in guitar. Motorcycle boots. Maybe a vest.

He is about to turn 43. He looks happy. Not rock and roll happy. Happy, happy.

The stage is boxy and bare—completely unadorned, unless you count amplifiers and microphones as decorations. There are more microphones than you're used to seeing. And there are unfamiliar faces: a baby-faced drummer whose last job, you may or may not know, was with the B-52's. A skinny-jeaned British guitarist, who looked like he might collapse under the weight of his own hair. Women galore.

House lights down, stage lights up. He counts: One! Two! One Two Three—

And then … no ka-boom. No thunderous snare drum exploding like Fourth of July firecrackers into "Born in the U.S.A." No drumroll hurtling like an out-of-control bobsled into "Born to Run." Tonight it's a single snare hit, purely functional—a pickup beat to let the rest of the band know when to come in. On the downbeat, a D chord rings out on three guitars (two electric, one acoustic). The tempo is neither fast nor slow, the volume neither loud nor soft. The feel is comfortable, *settled*, as if you've shown up in the middle of a long concert. Or a long career.

But you and he have got some catching up to do, and he isn't going to waste any time getting to it. After a short four-bar vamp on that D, he approaches the mic. Bruce Springsteen is ready to reintroduce himself.

It's summer, 1992. It's been nearly a decade since "Born in the U.S.A." turned him into a bona fide pop star. It's been four years since he and the E Street Band played their last concert, at a stadium in Buenos Aires. And it's been three years since—to the shock of fans from Argentina to Zimbabwe, from Alpha Centauri to Zeta Laporis—he gave the band its walking papers.

Since Bruce Springsteen last stood in front of you, the Berlin Wall has fallen and the Soviet Union has collapsed. McDonald's has started serving burgers in Moscow. The first Gulf War has begun and ended. Apartheid has been repealed. Pete Rose has been banned from baseball. The Chinese Army has rolled through Tiananmen Square. The World Wide Web has been created. *The Simpsons* and *Law & Order* have started historic runs that will carry television into the next century. Rodney King has been beaten senseless in Los Angeles, the officers who beat him have been acquitted (later convicted), and riots have torn apart America's second-largest city.

Guns N' Roses, Nirvana, grunge, Metallica, Garth Brooks, Mariah Carey, MC Hammer and Vanilla Ice have all staked their claim on the radio. Max Weinberg has entered, and dropped out of, law school. Clarence Clemons has co-starred with Rick Springfield in a TV pilot based on a comic book. Garry W. Tallent has moved to Nashville.

Bruce Springsteen has divorced, turned 40, remarried, become a father. He has abandoned his beloved New Jersey for a bourgeois house in the Hollywood hills that he bought with a truckload of hundred thousand dollar bills. He has all but disappeared from the pop charts. The two albums he made with studio musicians and released on the same day are proving no match, commercially speaking, for albums by Garth and Mariah and Billy Ray Cyrus and Def Leppard and Pearl Jam. He finds this latter fact funny. Truly, deeply funny. It might scare him, too; fear, after all, is where so much humor comes from. He is the last man standing in an alien world. He has been in hiding, and now he has come out into the light of the 1990s.

He is at the mic now, ready to testify.

The long night of music ahead will include some call-and-response gospel and soul, some R&B-infused pop, some dark folk-rock, awkward dancing, a chant of "no justice, no peace," the sampled voices of Los Angeles newscasters, and, of course, some rock, and rock and roll pomp and circumstance. And almost every minute of it, in one way or another, will be a testimony to the power of love. Because if one thing has changed in the years since the Cold War stopped raging and Ice Cube and AxlRose started raging and morning in America gave way to afternoon somewhere else, it is this: Bruce Springsteen is in love.

He is in love with his wife, who will make a cameo appearance onstage sometime tonight, maybe during "Human Touch," maybe during "Brilliant Disguise." For those few minutes, there will be 12 people onstage: six men, six women. You may or may not draw a conclusion from this.

He is in love with his children, whose births will be celebrated in song every night he is onstage for the next year.

And he is in love with rock and roll, in case there was any chance you'd forgotten. He's still just around the corner from the light of day, but he seems a little closer now.

He begins to sing a different kind of Bruce Springsteen anthem, something about all the hours he wasted waiting for his life to begin. There was a soul that needed to be saved, and it was his. He is singing about how sad it is to spend your life living in your own skin, without the company of a woman. But now he's got a new suit of clothes, a pretty red rose and—his voice has practically risen to a shout—a woman he can call his friend.

"These," he affirms, "are better days."

Matty Karas was the pop music critic for the "Asbury Park Press" during the Human Touch/Lucky Town era, and has worked as a writer, editor, and music programmer at MTV, VH1, Rhapsody, and Addicted to Noise.

June 29, 1992
Palais Omnisports De Paris-Bercy
Paris, France

This was my first time photographing Bruce outside of the U.S. I wasn't sure what to expect from the crowds or the new band. I thought the sound and arrangements might be new, but the songs were the same. Even though I missed the familiar faces of the E Street Band, I enjoyed the tour, and thought the crowds were amazing, especially in Spain and Paris.

On assignment for *Q Magazine*, I photographed several shows on the European leg: Paris, London, and Barcelona. It was during this time I came to realize why musicians used teleprompters. When I was in the photo pit in London, I thought we were in Paris. Bruce kept referencing London, and I said out loud, "London? We're in Paris." A fellow photographer corrected me and said, "We're in London."

The European audiences were on their feet the entire time, jumping, clapping, and singing every word, even though at times they got the words wrong. In Barcelona, "Hungry Heart" took on new meaning as the crowd sang words that didn't make sense, but it didn't matter. The people and their enthusiasm made the shows very special. Coming from New Jersey, I always thought the best crowds were in my home state, or even Philadelphia, but the European audiences had a different energy, and Bruce responded.

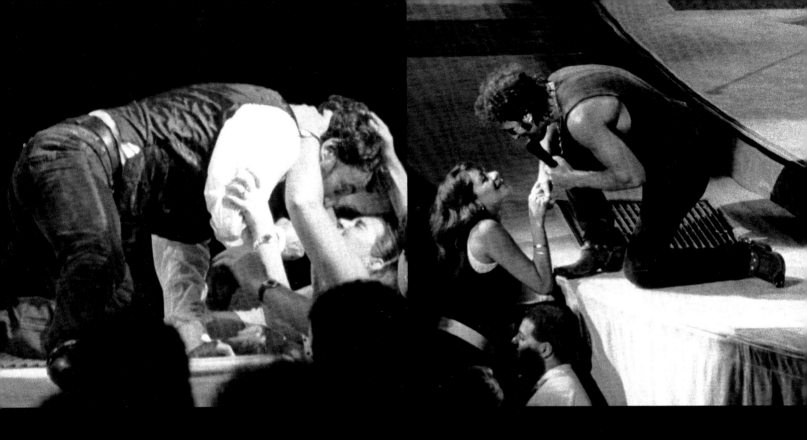

Bruce never hesitates to show his fans he loves them. Their joy is his joy. Through countless shows I have always loved those moments when a fan was brought on stage to bask in a little of Bruce's glory. Whether they sang a few bars with Bruce, strummed his guitar, or danced with him to "Dancing in the Dark," I always tried to capture these special moments.

June 29, 1992
Palais Omnisports de Paris-Bercy
Paris, France.

A great show with a rocking crowd, but I could tell the people in the front were frustrated because a barricade with a wide gap separated them from Bruce and the stage. I don't think Bruce liked the barricade either. Several times he ran through the crowd and high-fived those in front. Other times, he'd jump on a speaker to be as close to the crowd as possible. The audience danced and sang through the entire show.

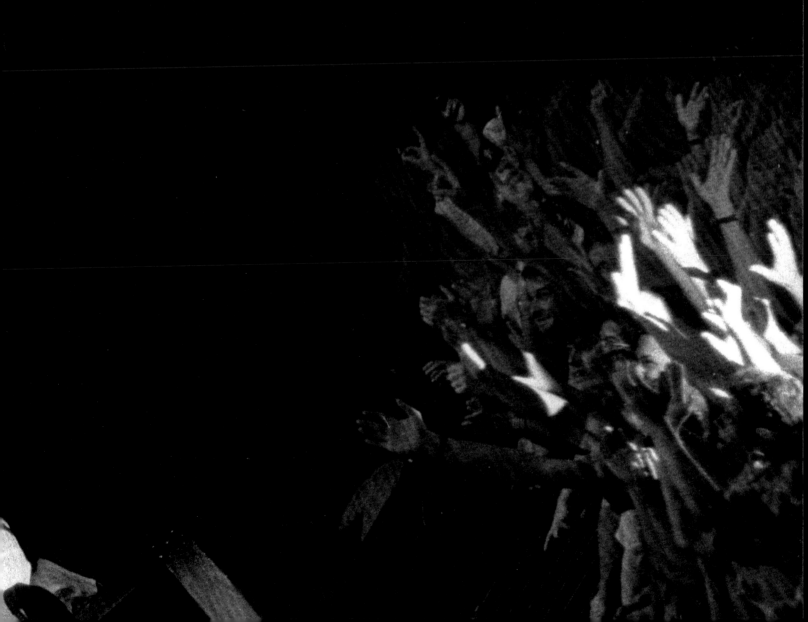

July 3, 1992
Plaza Monumental, Barcelona, Spain

Several journalists and I decided to drive from France to Spain, which turned out to be the drive from hell. Due to a transportation strike in France, the truck drivers abandoned their trucks all over the highways. It was the strangest thing I have ever seen—all these 18 wheelers with no drivers in sight. We maneuvered the car through the trucks, and at times had to get off the highway and drive through little towns trying to find the back roads to Barcelona. When we finally reached Spain, we kissed the ground. A typical ten hour drive from Paris to Barcelona took over 36 hours.

The show took place in a bull ring, and there were people on their balconies along the perimeter. The crowds and those watching from their apartments were electrifying. I can only imagine the feeling Bruce and the Band had on stage. I will never forget the energy and the connection of the crowd.

July 6, 1992 — London

August 28, 1992—Spectrum, Philadelphia, PA

I have to admit, I was preoccupied tonight. My mind was in other places. Looking through binoculars, I scanned the crowd watching everyone in the arena having the time of their lives, then I saw my good friend, Jeff Quinn, in the front row with his girlfriend and two other friends. They were jumping, screaming, and smiling. My focus and energy returned just seeing Jeff having the time of his life.

During intermission, I made my way over and asked how he got front row tickets. He said they were sitting in the worst seats in the arena when a man in black asked if they wanted to sit in the front row. Jeff kept asking, "Why? What's the catch?" The man said there was no catch, but they had to change tickets. Jeff didn't believe they were real so he made the man walk them to the front row. When they got to their seats, they realized THIS WAS REAL! Dead center for the entire show, Bruce sang directly to them and even took Jeff's girlfriend's hand. What made it even more special ... Jeff is from Bruce's home town—Freehold!

August 10, 1992—Brendan Byrne Arena, East Rutherford, NJ—Little Steven makes a guest appearance.

Somehow my camera malfunctioned and the result was a double exposure—a happy mistake.

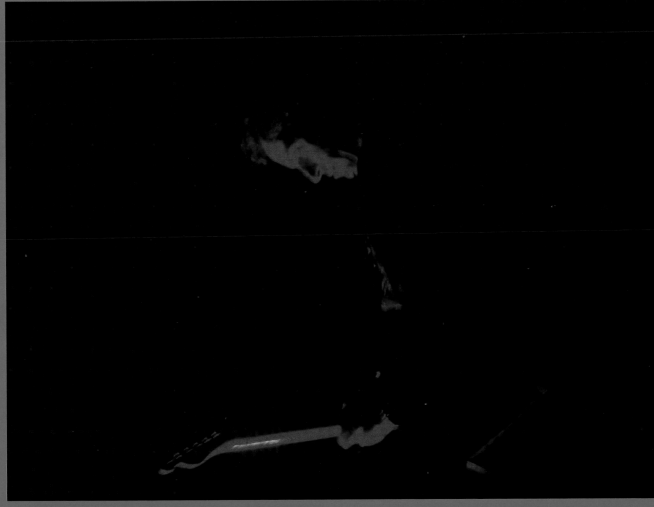

CLUBS

by Stan Goldstein

One of the treasures of being around the Jersey Shore bar scene in the 70s and 80s was catching a surprise appearance and jam by Bruce Springsteen.

Those magical moments would most likely be in the wee hours of the morning (bars were open until 3 a.m.), which would require a lot of waiting and patience, but the reward was oh, sooooo great! Bruce, who sometimes had been hanging around the bar for most of the night, would jump on stage with Cats on a Smooth Surface at The Stone Pony and play a few songs. After seeing Bruce in front of thousands of people at stadiums and arenas, this was a special treat played out in front of, sometimes, just dozens of people.

Debra Rothenberg was fortunate to capture many of those special moments, not just at The Stone Pony, but at other Jersey Shore night spots including McLoone's Rumrunner in Sea Bright, and Cheers in Long Branch.

These were the days before cell phones and the Internet, so there was no instant news of a Bruce spotting, except when you could find a pay phone and shout over the music. Mostly it was a lot of rumors, oh yeah, lots of rumors. You would get a phone call in the early evening saying, "I hear it's a definite that Bruce will be at The Stone Pony tonight, so you might want to check it out." Sometimes it would be true, but more times than not, it wasn't. You would be standing in a dark bar around 2 a.m. hoping he would show, but then say to yourself, "Guess it was a false alarm." Many Jersey Shore bar veterans would like to have a nickel for every time those "definites" didn't happen.

But when they did, those were nights to cherish forever. The excitement when Bruce took the stage was heart-pounding—you knew you were among an elite group, and your friends would be so jealous when they heard. Bruce would jam away, usually on some cover song but sometimes one of his own, and he'd be having nothing but fun.

I once heard Bruce say in an interview that he enjoyed playing to a small crowd at The Stone Pony as much as he did to 70,000 people in a stadium. It showed.

One rule was that if there was a Bruce rumor, you had to stay until the bar closed, whether it was 3 a.m. or 2 a.m. (they moved up the closing time sometime in the 1980s). The worst was when you left at 1:30 a.m. and Bruce walked in 15 minutes later. Talk about heartbreak.

On Sunday night, August 21, 1988, Debbie, a few friends and I were at The Stone Pony to see Cats on a Smooth Surface. It was getting late, around 1 a.m., and we looked at each other and asked, "Want to go?" almost breaking that cardinal rule. Thankfully, we hesitated and a few minutes later in through the front door walked Bruce, Patti Scialfa (their first time out together as a couple at the Jersey Shore), Ed Manion and Mark Pender, among others. (Bruce had finished the Tunnel of Love Tour three weeks earlier and was set to go out on the Amnesty Tour in less than two weeks.)

About a half hour later, right before closing time, Bruce jumped onstage to play "Stand by Me," and "Around and Around." Debbie shot one of her more famous photos of Bruce that evening, a close up of his face that still adorns The Stone Pony wall to this day.

Those surprise appearances are a rare occurrence today but they still do happen. You never quite know when Mr. Springsteen may get the urge to play.

Another one of the magical days was April 2, 2011, in Asbury Park. Bruce showed up as a surprise guest that afternoon at the Atonement Lutheran Church for a panel discussion on Asbury's West Side music scene and the racial and economic issues that had shaped the city's cultural and political history. He joined Nicky Addeo, Bobby Thomas (The Vibranaires), and Southside Johnny for a talk hosted by author Daniel Wolff.

Debbie was fortunate to be in town (although she had a little trouble finding the right church, there are quite a few in Asbury Park) and captured several great photos of this wonderful discussion in front of about 80 people.

Later that night, Debbie was right up front to capture the moment when Bruce played for the first time ever at the Wonder Bar. He joined Southside Johnny, Vini Lopez, Bobby Thomas, Billy Ryan, Ed Manion and others, as part of a special concert titled, "Nicky Addeo and Friends celebrate the Music of Asbury Park's Westside."

The pictures in this section are just the tip of the iceberg of some of those magical nights. We are so fortunate that Debbie was there to create this photographic record. Enjoy.

Stan Goldstein—A lifelong New Jersey Shore resident, Goldstein has been following the Asbury Park music scene and Bruce Springsteen for 30-plus years. He has attended more than 250 Springsteen shows dating back to a Monmouth Arts Center show in Red Bank in 1976. In 2002, he and friend Jean Mikle published the first edition of "Rock and Roll Tour of the Jersey Shore." Since 1999, Stan and Jean have provided tours for thousands of fans to the historical music sites at the Jersey Shore.

July 31, 1987
The Stone Pony, Asbury Park, NJ

The summer of 1987 was a magical time both in my career and in the friendships I made and the musicians I photographed. And it was the summer a dream came true.

I must have missed a Bruce appearance at The Stone Pony at least 18 times before tonight. I thought I'd never see him in a club. That all changed on this night, but not without some agita.

I met a few friends and we lined up early to see Marshall Crenshaw. I always loved Marshall's shows and his songs, so we wanted to get as close to the stage as possible. Marshall took to the stage and played a killer set. Unknown to me, Bruce was watching the show from the DJ booth. For the first encore, Marshall said something like, "I understand the most famous musician in the world is here—Bruce Springsteen." And then…nothing. No Bruce. I turned to my friend Debbie Mayer and said, "I can't believe it. He's here, I'm here, and he isn't going to play."

After the first song of Marshall's encore, he announced Bruce again, only this time, Bruce took the stage.

I was in my glory—right up front, Bruce just a few feet away on the stage with another one of my favorite performers. Even though he sang only three songs, "You Can't Sit Down," LaBamba," and "Twist and Shout," it was still magical.

After the show, my friend, Marty Venturo drove with me to my office and stayed up all night in the darkroom as I processed and printed the images. The following Monday, I called *Rolling Stone* to see if they were interested in the photos and they said no. I sent them anyway and later that week, Marty called to tell me my photo was in the latest issue. And that was the first of many more to come.

"I felt really high on life that night, even before Bruce came up. Back then we always used to pack [The Stone Pony] to the walls, but this was the first time Bruce came to see us, which blew my mind. I was debating about inviting him up … I was worried about possibly imposing on him, worried about him possibly blanking me! Anyway, I'm glad I did ask because the energy became explosive when he got up there. To just hang on and go with it was an amazing feeling. That was the summer "La Bamba" was out too. Fantastic, memorable stuff and, of course, I have a lot of fondness and admiration for Bruce."

~ Marshall Crenshaw, singer/songwriter

August 2, 1987
The Stone Pony, Asbury Park, NJ

I arrived late to the club because my friends and I heard that Bruce was playing at another club. I didn't get my usual front row spot. My friend, Marty Venturo, lifted me onto his shoulders so I could take this photo.

August 9, 1987
The Stone Pony, Asbury Park, NJ

Summer, 1987, was a magical time to be a Bruce Springsteen fan at the Jersey Shore. It was hard to tell when he would show up, or who he would show up to play with. Several times that summer it wasn't an uncommon sight to have almost the entire E Street Band rocking the stage at The Stone Pony. When I think about it, it was amazing—here was the biggest band in the world on a tiny stage in front of several hundred VERY lucky fans. I was not only listening to great music, but I had my camera every time, shooting my favorite performer while working on my craft and having my images seen worldwide. It was the beginning of my dream.

August 9, 1987—Dancing with Patti Scialfa at The Stone Pony, Asbury Park, NJ

"I will always look back on those early days of performing on the same stage as Bruce, from The Stone Pony to the Tradewinds, with a reverent smile. I went right from high school to performing in clubs, so those nights were literally my true school of rock … with the greatest teacher a musician could hope for, along with Bob Bandiera.

You can see how in awe I was of him, and right after this pic was taken, he invited me to sing the great Barrett Strong tune, 'Money (That's What I Want).'

I still get the chance to share a stage with Bruce on occasion, and I turn into that same awestruck young apprentice."

~ Ray Andersen, singer/songwriter
Cats on A Smooth Surface, Mr. Ray

The Stone Pony, with Ray Andersen (far left) and Vinny Daniele of Cats on a Smooth Surface (above) Summer, 1987

One of the most rocking, fun bands at the shore was Cats on a Smooth Surface. They were the house band for The Stone Pony every Sunday night, and thrilled their audiences every week with amazing covers of hit songs, with many of their originals also thrown in. Many a night, Bruce would jump on stage, knowing that whatever song he wanted to play, these seasoned pros would be able to back him.

August, 1987—Backstage at The Stone Pony, Asbury Park, NJ

August 21, 1987—The Stone Pony, Asbury Park, NJ

One of the ten best shows I have ever seen … and that was BEFORE Bruce came out. Little Steven's performance was unbelievable. This man is a showman; not only does he have songs that are excellent, his stage presence as a front man is incredible. When he is onstage as part of the E Street Band he is the side man, but when he is fronting his own band, you just can't take your eyes off him. The night only got that much better when Bruce came out and sang "Native American" and "Sun City," complete with the words written on a small piece of paper that he held in his hand.

August 22, 1987
The Stone Pony, Asbury Park, NJ

The anticipation was building in the club all night. Rumors were spreading. Then Bruce joined Levon Helm and his All Stars for two songs: "Up on Cripple Creek" and "Lucille." It was a great show, a hot night, made only hotter when Bruce got onstage.

November 20, 1987
The Stone Pony, Asbury Park, NJ

"Bruce is the real deal. When he jumps on stage, you feel like you're part of creating what music is supposed to be about. He raises the level of everyone on the stage. Whether he's playing at The Stone Pony, or at a small Christmas party for family and friends, he is just as intense as when he's playing in Giants Stadium. Even if there are just a couple of people in a small club, you'll see the veins in his neck pop out as he gets into the music we're performing. He's all about the music. It's very inspiring."

~ Hal B. Selzer
musician/Broadway performer

December 5, 1987

Someone once told me that Bruce doesn't like photos of himself smiling, but it's hard to shoot him on stage when he isn't smiling, because he smiles all the time. And so does his audience.

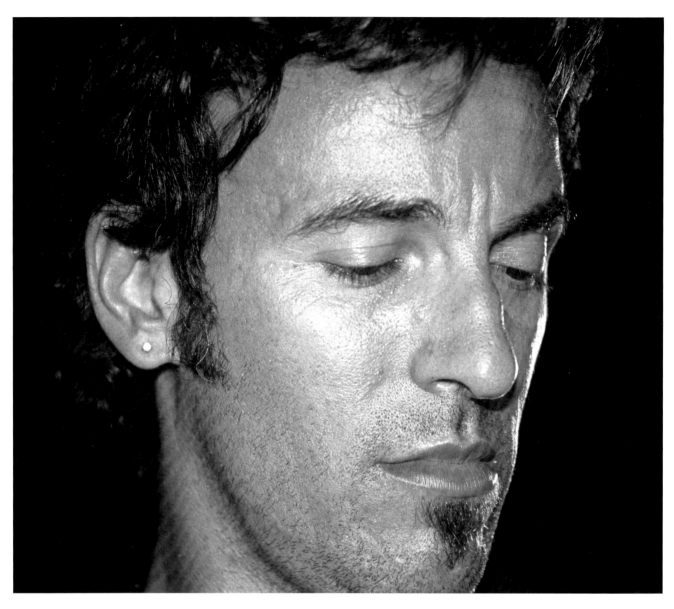

August 21, 1988
The Stone Pony, Asbury Park, NJ

This is one of my favorite photographs. I was at The Stone Pony with friends Stan, Billy, Steve, and Kathy Powers. We went almost every Sunday night, because we loved the regular house bands, Joey and the Works, and Cats on A Smooth Surface. It was a night we could all just hang out, be together, and hear good music. There would be many nights when we knew it was almost impossible for Bruce to show, and this was one of those nights because The Tunnel of Love Tour had just ended. It was getting late and we decided it was time to go when IN WALKED BRUCE.

I was dead center in front of the stage with a new macro lens in my bag, and decided to try to get as close as possible without being obnoxious. Bruce was so enthralled in his guitar playing he didn't even notice, or care.

June 2,1989, with "Killer Joe" Delia.

"Max and I were playing in my band, Killer Joe, right there in Bruce territory–The Stone Pony. It was a hot night, and the joint was jumping with good people groovin' to our music. This was one of those nights when there was a surprise visit. Bruce came in like a fireball, heating the place even more. Everyone was feeling it. We were all swimming in sound, good will, and our own sweat.

It was not the only night I've played with Bruce, before or since, and each time has been amazing. Debra captured how drenched in rock 'n' roll these nights were and still are."
     ~ Joe Delia, singer/songwriter

June 9,1989, with Nils Lofgren

June 24, 1989, with Bobby Bandiera.

Bobby Bandiera is possibly the best guitarist to come from the Jersey Shore. Seeing Bruce and Bobby share the stage is a musician's and music fan's dream. Bobby and Bruce probably know every song ever written, so you just never know what gem they are going to play.

"Bruce was very inspirational to my career, and still is."
~ Bobby Bandiera, singer/songwriter

July 1, 1989, with LaBamba at The Stone Pony, Asbury Park, NJ

I met a bunch of Europeans early in the day, and we were all having a great time listening to "La Bamba" (Richie Rosenberg), who always puts on a great show. Bruce jumped on stage to sing "Long Tall Sally," and I was able to capture my new friends in the front row, watching their favorite performer just inches away.

"A "Glory Days" moment for me when a very welcome friend joined LaBamba's Big Band on stage at The Pony. Just when you thought the energy on stage was at its peak, up jumps Bruce and the bar is raised to levels that were simply off the charts. My best memories of hangin' with Bruce in the early days were all the baseball games, movies, dinners, and parties that were as much fun as the partying on the stage."

~ Richie "LaBamba" Rosenberg

Trombonist Richie "LaBamba" Rosenberg has recorded and toured with Southside Johnny, Little Steven and Bruce. He is currently a member of the Basic Cable Band on CONAN.

July 9, 1989—The Stone Pony, Asbury Park, NJ
with Vinny Daniele

July 9, 1989—The Stone Pony, Asbury Park, NJ

Even in a small club playing to only a few hundred people, Bruce gives 100%.

July 23, 1989
The Stone Pony, Asbury Park, NJ

Bruce joined the local band, Cats on a Smooth Surface, and sang: "Old Time Rock and Roll," "Hound Dog," "From Small Things (Big Things One Day Come)," "Sweet Little 16," "Under the Boardwalk," "Glory Days," and "Carol." After shooting the first song, I started to sing along and dance, and actually not shoot—something I rarely do. Bruce walked over to me, looked at my camera, looked back at me, smiled and shouted, "DEBBIE!" (which really surprised me), and when he smiled again waiting for me to take his photo, I did!

Later, someone asked me if I had ever met him or knew him and how did he know my name. It was only then that I realized he probably saw the paper every day, and started to notice my photos. Being the only female shooting night after night, he must have figured out who I was.

Without Margaret Potter and her husband Tom, there may have never been a Bruce Springsteen as we know him. The Potters owned and opened the club called "The Upstage" in Asbury Park in 1968. At that time, clubs remained open until 5 a.m., and all the local musicians would hang out. Springsteen was a fixture at this club in the early 1970s. I became friendly with Margaret in 1986 after meeting her and then shooting portraits of her band and her album cover. She was also a hairdresser and many times I would go to her house and she would cut my hair. We talked about music and photography. Everyone on the local scene knew her and what a lovely person she was.

This night was one of my first at McLoone's Rum Runner in Sea Bright. The crowds who frequented The Stone Pony in Asbury Park rarely went a few miles north to McLoone's. I had received a call earlier in the day from someone telling me to be at the Rum Runner by eight, but not to tell anyone. I knew what that call meant. For a few hours, I did as instructed and didn't call anyone. Then I decided I didn't want to be at a club alone, so I called my friends and told them not to ask questions and just be there.

Bruce performed with Max Weinberg on drums and Tim McLoone's band for five songs: "Reddy Teddy," "Tobacco Road," "Under the Boardwalk," "Jersey Girl," and "Glory Days." The place was so crowded, and with everyone bouncing up and down, it felt like the floor was going to cave in.

January 21, 1991
With the legendary Margaret Potter

April 2, 2011
Atonement Lutheran Church, Asbury Park, NJ

Bruce Springsteen participated in a discussion on the history of race and music of Asbury Park's West Side with Southside Johnny and other local musicians.

I made my way back to Asbury Park for the first time in over 10 years to shoot all the local musicians from my past—the ones I shot night after night at The Stone Pony, and to see some old friends. I couldn't believe how different the town was. Stores and restaurants packed the boardwalk. People were on the beach. It seemed like a mini Greenwich Village. Everyone who had moved away came back for a benefit concert in honor of Butch Pielka, former co-owner of The Stone Pony, who was having medical issues. It was like going home for a family reunion. I had planned to go to the church to hear the discussion, but after visiting with an old friend, local musician Amy Broza, I lost track of time until Stan Goldstein texted me and said, "Where are you? Bruce is here."

I cut short my afternoon with Amy and headed to the church. The only problem was, I forgot which church because there's a church on every corner in this part of Asbury Park. When I finally found the right one, I made my way inside.

(Top) Bruce chats with former co-owner of the Asbury Park Rock and Roll Museum owner, Stephen Bumball at the Lutheran Church after "A Talk with Nicky Addeo and Friends," celebrating the music of Asbury Park's Westside.

(Right) Bruce talking with my friend Linda Thebold.

April 2, 2011 — The Wonder Bar, Asbury Park, NJ

Bruce performed at the Wonder Bar with Nicky Addeo and the Night Owls on the day I returned for the benefit/reunion for Butch Pielka, the former co-owner of The Stone Pony. It was my first time back in about a decade. It was so amazing to see old friends and listen to all the great bands from my youth.

Southside Johnny, Bruce, Billy Ryan

REUNION TOUR 1999-2000

by Bob Makin

In the middle of 1991, I was working extensively with Debra covering the rich and fertile New Jersey music scene like bees on honey, when my son, Matty, was born. Through the eyes of a Bruce Springsteen fan, I wrote an editorial for *East Coast Rocker/The Aquarian Weekly* about becoming a new father. I swore I would turn that "Little Gun" onto the Boss, and that's just what I did.

The torch was energetically passed eight years later, when Matty pumped his fist to the echoing encore of "Born to Run" with a broad smile on his young face. As his first Springsteen concert came to an end, I couldn't help but wonder if Debbie had been in the photographers' pit capturing the E Street Band's Reunion Tour as prolifically as we had all those late nights at The Stone Pony and the Brighton Bar. I'm glad to see that she did.

The reunion tour not only was a breath of fresh air because I brought Matty to his first Springsteen show, but also because it rejuvenated every Springsteen fan who longed for the greatest backing band of all time. Clarence, Steven, Danny, Max, Roy and now Patti, Nils and Soozie were more than just a backing band. They seemed to bring soulful roots, not only to Springsteen's music, but to the man himself. In the Reunion Tour, this was evidenced in the enthusiasm of the fans, as well as the working and personal relationships that have endured among the personnel.

When Bruce parted with the E Street Band at the turn of the '90s, he expressed a desire to be like Neil Young working with Crazy Horse when the mood and material matched their musical marriage. Because the Reunion Tour seemed to be a resounding professional and personal success for the participants, they have continued working together straight through the bitter passing of Danny in 2008 and Clarence in 2011. Only during a solo acoustic tour in support of the similarly arranged *Devils and Dust* disc, has Bruce opted not to work with the E Street Band, which morphed into the larger Seeger Sessions Band for that 2006 tour.

The sounds and images of Bruce Springsteen and the E Street Band have been embedded in me since the first time I heard and saw them in 1978 at the age of 14. And they will keep me forever young, no matter how old we all get. I don't know any Bruce fan who was not ecstatic that he remained loyal to the E Street Band, including original drummer, Vini "Mad Dog" Lopez (a longtime friend of mine), who has joined the band onstage on several occasions, most recently in the summer of 2012, at Jersey's MetLife Stadium.

Long live Bruce Springsteen and the E Street Band! May our memories help us endure the tough times ahead, as we turn to them for solace. And as they continue to march down their musical road, blasting such classics as "Badlands" and "Backstreets," may they also inspire us with performances of Bruce's new material, as it reflects the human condition and the compassion we must share.

If there was one thing I hope Matty gained from that night long ago in East Rutherford, it would be the compassion of Bruce Springsteen and the E Street Band. And for that, may their reunion last forever.

Bob Makin *was a reporter with "Home News Tribune," "Courier News," and "Asbury Park Press," and has been a music writer for 32 years, covering the New Jersey music scene and Bruce Springsteen for "The Aquarian Weekly," "East Coast Rocker," "Backstreets Magazine" and "Details."*

November 21, 1999—Pepsi Arena, Albany, NY

Shot during "10th Avenue Freeze Out." Any mention of the "Big Man," Clarence Clemons, always gets everyone on their feet. This was a great sight to see; Bruce and Clarence back on the stage, together again. A lot of my friends cried every night during this tour; they were afraid that they would never see the E Street Band again.

November 21, 1999—Pepsi Arena, Albany, NY

This was a special time. Bruce got the band back together for The Reunion Tour, making long-time fans very happy. The Internet was just starting to catch on, and there were several Springsteen groups for die hard fans. One of those fans, Amy Cavanaugh, a transplanted New Jerseyean, opened her house in Albany to the people from a group calling themselves RMAS for a preshow get together. She expected about 20 people to show up at her house … over 150 showed. It was a magical night and several long term relationships, including one marriage (Greg and Marilyn Weber), resulted from this get together.

August 21, 1999—Fleet Center, Boston, MA

116

"Sitting in on Bruce Springsteen's gig, to me, was akin to being shot from a cannon seventy feet into the air, knowing you will land on a football-sized cushion made of the thickest, softest material. The adrenaline rush was so intense, but there was no fear. You knew that no one was going to try to throw any curves at you. A truly joyous experience."

~ Bruce Hornsby, singer/songwriter

Bruce Hornsby and Jackson Browne join in.

July 1, 2000—Madison Square Garden, New York, NY

Bruce playing the piano. I believe this was a first for me, and it was special. This was the end of The Reunion Tour, and I was wandering all over the arena, running into friends, many I had not seen in years. For the last song, "Blood Brothers," I ended up in a section with my good friend, Pam Ross who, like many others, was crying … the tour was over. Sitting in our section was actor/writer/director Ed Burns, a big fan who spoke with us about the tour for so long after the show ended that security came over to us and told us we had to leave.

August 31, 1999—MCI Center, Washington, DC
I don't think there is another performer anywhere who plays to the people sitting behind the stage as much as Bruce does.

Singing to Obie, who is probably Bruce's oldest and biggest fan (and friend). Every long-time Bruce fan knows Obie. Bruce speaks of her often in concert, and it's always so lovingly. I think it says a lot about a person when they hit it big and never forget the people who were there for them from the beginning. Every show, he leaves front row tickets for her, and those lucky enough to observe them together see how much they still love and respect one another.

I had the pleasure of meeting Obie on this tour so it made photographing her even more special.

THE RISING TOUR 2002-2003

by Gary Wien

There were many aspects of The Rising Tour which I can still clearly remember, but the one that still stands out in my mind is the way Asbury Park played a major role. Maybe it was because of the subject matter of the album, which was so personal to those of us in the New York/New Jersey area; or the actual progress being made to bring the town back to its former glory; or the rehearsal shows in Asbury Park's Convention Hall, or the launch of the album at The Stone Pony and the madness of having *The Today Show* in town. Whatever the reason, Asbury Park played a rather significant role throughout The Rising Tour from the outdoor shows at Giants Stadium featuring a mini-boardwalk, to the way "My City of Ruins" was used across the country to help soothe the nation's fears after 9/11, becoming one of the highlights of each concert in the process.

The way the story goes, a few days after 9/11, a man drove by Springsteen and rolled down his car window and said, "We need you!" and ultimately inspired the collection of songs to be written. From my perspective, these songs put lyrics and music to the same feelings my friends and I were all experiencing. There was the beautiful "Empty Sky" above us which ushered in a strange, new world of quiet in the heavens in an area generally bustling with airplanes. I'll never forget the first airplane I saw in the sky when the ban on flights was finally lifted. It actually startled me the way seeing an airplane must have startled people in the first part of the 20th century. The haunting "You're Missing," which will always remind me of the days after the attacks, when survivors and family members of those who never returned posted photographs of their loved ones on community boards and building walls throughout New York City, hoping for a miracle. And "My City of Ruins," a song originally written about Asbury Park that was played at the legendary "Concert for New York," forever became part of 9/11.

For a Springsteen fan, the big news about *The Rising* album and tour was simply the fact that the E Street Band was back. This was the first album since *Tunnel of Love* to feature the band and, for whatever reason, the timing just seemed perfect for their return. America not only needed Springsteen's words and wisdom, but needed the whole crew behind him. We needed to believe that as much as our world had changed, some things would never change.

For a nation, the big news was that we had an artist eloquently describe the myriad of feelings we all experienced during the attacks and the immediate aftermath. His songs captured the heroism of the firefighters, police, and first responders; the conflicted world views we had as we sought revenge, unsure of how that could be possible; and, more importantly, hope for the future. As bad as this tragedy had been, Springsteen offered assurance that our nation would, rise again.

Every Springsteen concert is like a sing-along, but *The Rising* shows were something different. Fans didn't simply sing along, the weight of the tragedy was lifted somewhat by hearing thousands echoing the words. People have always said Springsteen shows were like a religious experience; during The Rising Tour, that experience was multiplied and the relief was amplified. It was as emotionally draining as a funeral and as wonderful as a wedding day.

The show I distinctly remember the most was July 24, 2003. This was one of the outdoor shows at Giants Stadium. It had rained a day or two before, but the weather was perfect on this day. As you pulled up near the stadium, the first thing to catch your eye was probably the largest banner you ever saw—50 x 200 feet saluting Bruce Springsteen and the E Street Band. The next was the mini-boardwalk (at 175,000 square feet, it really wasn't that mini) that took up a huge chunk of the stadium parking lot. The boardwalk opened in the afternoon and stayed open until the final minutes before the concert began. I remember there was a Ferris wheel, boardwalk games, a volleyball court on sand, and tons of boardwalk-style food available. Each night featured a different local artist playing on a large stage. On this night JoBonanno & the Godsons of Soul played. It was probably the first time I could recall anybody ever opening for Bruce.

Springsteen played 10 sold-out nights at Giants Stadium in 2003, and he probably could have had another 10 if he wanted. Fans from throughout the world always wanted to see him in New Jersey. There is the belief that the shows in Jersey are just more special. On this tour, that probably was the case. The shows were far more personal. Each night in New Jersey, Springsteen took a few minutes to talk about the changes happening in Asbury Park. You sensed his pride that the town was finally on its way back. He mentioned some of the restaurants and places to visit, and urged people to check them out. I'll never forget how humbled I was to hear him say those words just before playing "My City of Ruins."

That July 24th show was also the first time I ever heard "Sandy (4th of July, Asbury Park)" performed live. Several times in my life I just missed it—being at the show just before or just after he brought out the tune. For this tour, I think I was at the only show in New Jersey when it was played. It has always been one of my favorite songs because I've lived

the words in that song. The lyrics tell the story of just about every guy who grows up along the Jersey Shore. Springsteen was able to reach inside all of us like that with the songs on *The Rising*. While the album achieved an amazingly significant goal, the live performances on that tour went even higher. We needed Bruce then and he delivered. In my opinion, that album and that tour were probably his finest hour.

Gary Wien is a music journalist from Belmar, NJ—the town that put the E Street in E Street Band. He followed the Asbury Park music scene since his teenage days when he would often sneak into The Stone Pony, thanks to a magical key that somehow opened the back door. Wien won three Asbury Music Awards for Top Music Journalist for his work with "Upstage Magazine" and "AsburyMusic.com." He has also authored two books, is working on a third, and currently covers Jersey Shore music on his daily online radio show "ThePenguinRocks.com."

July 26, 2002—The Rising Tour at Convention Hall, Asbury Park, NJ

I brought a friend down to Asbury who had never seen or photographed Bruce. I knew Bruce would be coming out on the terrace after rehearsals, so we took our positions on the beach below. All of a sudden, the entire band came out. All around me were fellow photographers from *AP*, *The Asbury Park Press*, and *The Newark Star Ledger*. I think we were all a little surprised (I know I was). Just another way Bruce and the band get up close and personal with their fans.

Thousands of fans lined the beach during the warm up shows for The Rising Tour at Convention Hall.

July 29, 2002 — Asbury Park, NJ

In early 1999, I left Jersey Shore for NYC, and this was my first time back to Asbury Park. Bruce and the band were not only appearing live on The Today Show from the beach, but there would be a series of warm up shows at Convention Hall. People lined up for days hoping to get into the shows. More fans got shut out, but it didn't matter because Bruce opened the doors of the venue and large speakers were put outside so everyone on the beach could hear. The sound was perfect so no one was disappointed. After his performance, Bruce and the entire E Street Band came out to acknowledge and thank everyone for supporting them.

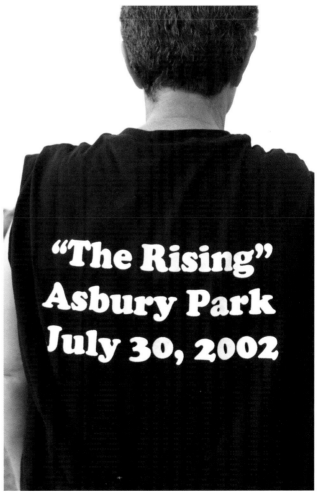

"The Rising"
Asbury Park
July 30, 2002

July 26, 2002—Greeting Fans in Asbury Park during the rehearsal shows.

*July 26, 2002—Convention Hall, Asbury Park, NJ—*Clarence Clemons told Bruce the chant he taught fans at their rehearsal concert, "You can only expect greatness from the E Street Band." Thousands of fans who lined the boardwalk and the beach began to chant along with Clarence. A priceless moment.

*July 26, 2002—*Bruce arriving at Convention Hall.

August 29, 2002—Bruce at the Video Music Awards at the Hayden Planetarium of the American Museum of Natural History in NYC.

Bruce and the band played for over an hour in the rain and never stopped, even when it poured. As miserable as it can be standing and shooting in the rain, all those bad feelings left the minute he took the stage.

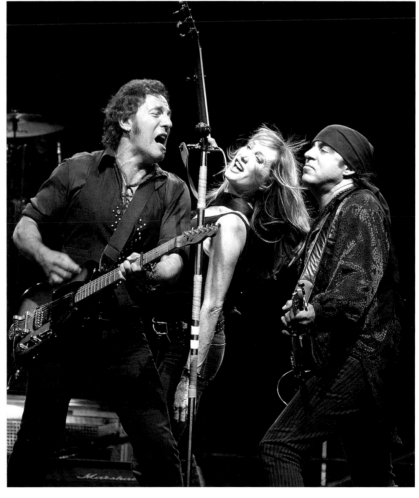

There was always at least one thing that Bruce did during each tour that I had to shoot. During The Rising Tour, it was when he flipped upside down holding the microphone stand. This was a crowd pleaser and the cheers went through the roof.

October 4, 2003—Last show of The Rising Tour, Shea Stadium, NYC

I almost didn't make this show. My cat died, I was sick. I went to the doctor and was told I had pneumonia. I didn't think I had the strength to make it. My mother, the coolest, rockin' mom in the U.S.A. said, "You have to go. This may be the last time you shoot the E Street band as you know them. Go and shoot the concert

then come home and get right into bed." I did just that ... I dragged myself to Queens, coughing the entire time. On the way home I was hoping to find a cab, but had no luck. My photographer friend, Gary Gershoff, who was also shooting the show, helped me to the subway, even carrying my camera bag for me. My mother knew best—I would have been very upset if I didn't get the last shot on this tour.

THE HOPE CONCERT 2003

The Hope Concert raised money for the Rock and Roll Music Fund

Asbury Jukes' guitarist, Bobby Bandiera, lent a hand on countless occasions to his fellow Jersey Shore musicians; now, some of those favors were returned. On April 29, 2003, at The Count Basie Theater in Red Bank, NJ, The Hope Concert raised money for the Rock and Roll Music Fund to benefit the ongoing care of Bandiera's son, Robert Bandiera, Jr.

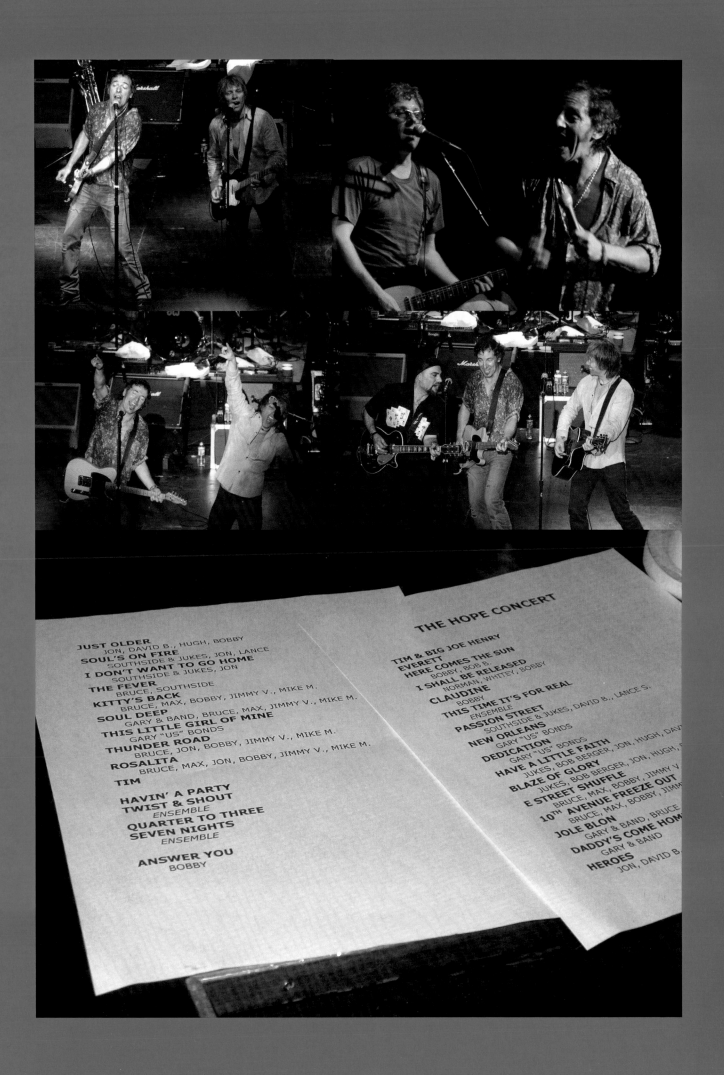

April 29, 2003—The Count Basie Theater, Red Bank, NJ, with Jon Bon Jovi.

What a thrill it was to see two hometown heroes perform together at The Hope Concert, a benefit for Robert Bandiera, Jr., the son of local band leader and guitarist, Bobby Bandiera, a longtime colleague of Springsteen and Bon Jovi.

"It doesn't get better than this—the Boss … and Bruce."
~ Gary "U.S." Bonds
singer/songwriter

Southside Johnny and Bruce

Jon Bon Jovi and Bruce

VOTE FOR CHANGE TOUR 2004

by Lisa Iannucci

In fall 2004, Bruce and a stellar cast of musical cohorts, including R.E.M., John Fogerty, Dixie Chicks, Pearl Jam, Jackson Browne, and Bonnie Raitt, joined forces for the Vote for Change Tour, and the result was a mind-blowing series of shows that were engaging, energizing, moving and inspiring.

The brainchild of MoveOn executive director, Eli Pariser, and sponsored by MoveOn, PAC, and ACT (America Coming Together), Vote for Change was a career highlight for Bruce and the E Street Band, showcasing the original lineup at their absolute best. The tour's official mission—to get voters out in the swing states—seemed to give way to the higher mission of rocking the house, and the band did just that. Night after night, they took advantage of the free-form setup to jam with other artists from the tour as well as "special guests" like Neil Young.

The shows were presented in revue fashion, and featured two core lineups that would cover key battleground states in the Midwest, East Coast, and the South. The E Street contingent also included Bright Eyes, R.E.M., and John Fogerty, who joined the band each night for a handful of classics like "Fortunate Son" and "Centerfield," and then stuck around to trade vocals with Bruce on "The Promised Land."

The tour was ostensibly about raising awareness and firing up the base, but with so much talent involved, it was inevitable it would become much more than that. Each night seemed to bring yet another unexpected collaboration and the mutual admiration of the participants for one another's work just upped the ante.

Night after night, there seemed to be a "pinch me" moment: Bruce joining R.E.M. for a transcendent "Man on the Moon," and Michael Stipe returning the favor on "Because the Night," or the look of pure joy on Mike Mills' face as he and Peter Buck joined the E Street Band for the set-closing "Born to Run." And the audience's response was equally impressive, though it was clear who the main attraction was

each evening. Hardcore Springsteen fans in attendance responded warmly to all of the artists onstage, and as each show drew to a conclusion with the entire ensemble onstage for the powerful one-two punch of "(What's so Funny 'Bout) Peace Love and Understanding" and Patti Smith's "People Have the Power," it was hard not to get caught up in the significance of the moment.

The supposed tour finale brought many of the artists from both lineups together for the first time for a televised five-hour marathon performance in the Nation's Capital. But the true tour finale for Bruce & Co. was held—where else?—in the swamps of Jersey. The finale featured a rare performance by Patti Scialfa and her band (which included her husband on guitar) as well as a guest appearance by Eddie Vedder, who joined the E Street Band for "No Surrender," "Darkness on the Edge of Town," and his own "Betterman," drawing a loud ovation from the audience. And that wasn't all: there was Little Steven joining Jackson Browne on Van Zandt's "I am a Patriot," and Bruce joining Browne on "Running on Empty." But when Browne walked out to join Bruce and the E Street Band on "Racing in the Street," there were gasps of delight from the crowd. In a tour filled with highlights, this was truly a once in a lifetime moment for many in attendance; the dream performance they never thought would actually happen.

In the end, the Vote for Change Tour more than lived up to its potential—it was a series of shows that brought the artists before audiences who weren't always familiar with their material, and pushed them to deliver consistently inspired performances. There was a dramatic urgency surrounding the shows, a momentous sense of occasion. And for Bruce and the E Street Band, Vote for Change was a challenge that elicited career performances from some already legendary musicians.

Lisa Iannucci is a writer/editor, librarian, archivist and activist currently working at the Asbury Park Public Library. Lisa followed the Jersey Shore music scene for 25 years and has contributed to "Backstreets Magazine" since 2001.

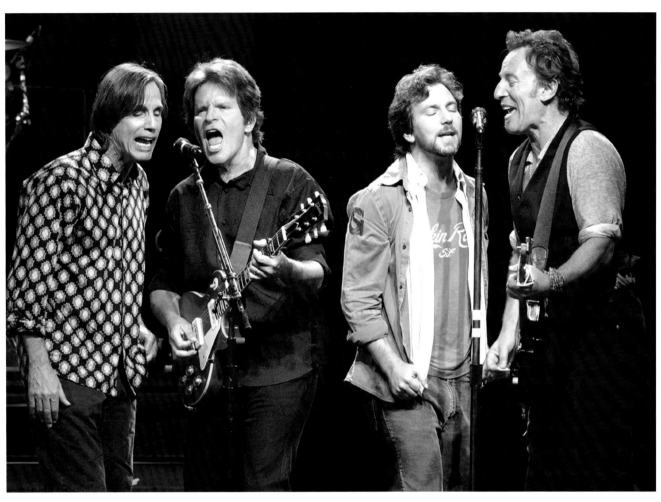

Jackson Browne, John Fogerty, Eddie Vedder

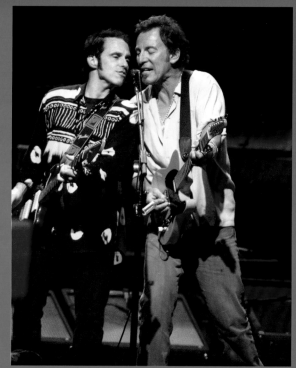

Nils Lofgren

Michael Stipe, Conor Oberst

Eddie Vedder

Jackson Browne

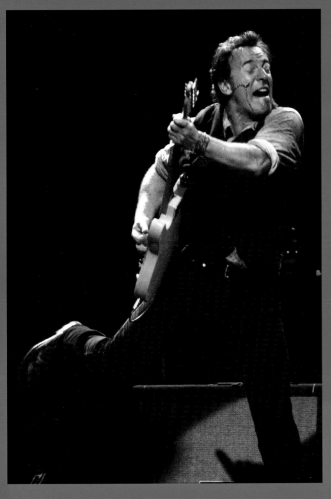

DEVILS AND DUST TOUR 2005

by Glenn Radecki

The Devils and Dust Tour was Springsteen's second solo outing, supporting an album of songs recorded with mostly acoustic instruments. Although it was far more diverse than the prior Ghost of Tom Joad Tour, an acoustic guitar would remain Bruce's primary instrument; but this time, he also brought along a bevy of other instruments as the tour explored not only the album, but also the dark corners of Bruce's extensive song catalog.

Although the song "Devils and Dust" had been written in 2003 as a commentary on the war in Iraq, the majority of the "new" songs dated back to *The Ghost of Tom Joad* period—songs that had been written during that tour or shortly thereafter. Themes regarding parents and children were woven through the album's key songs, including "Long Time Coming," "Black Cowboys," and "Jesus Was an Only Son."

When the tour was announced, the most exciting news was that Bruce would be taking a piano on the road in addition to his guitars. Although Springsteen had talked about composing songs on the piano, actual in-concert performances on the instrument were rare in the 1970s, and essentially non-existent in the 1980s and 1990s (with the November 1990 Christic Institute benefit shows a notable exception). Yet in recent years, Bruce had been playing the piano more, including a regular setlist feature for a significant part of The Rising Tour in which fan favorites from the back catalog were dusted off.

From the very start of the tour, which was in small theaters before moving to arenas in a scaled-down format, Bruce showed an interest in the entirety of his career when crafting each night's setlist. Naturally, a healthy portion of songs from *Devils and Dust* were in the set each night, and much of the recent *The Rising* album was heard in acoustic format for the first time. Given that it was a solo tour, it was no surprise that every song from *Nebraska* and all but one from *The Ghost of Tom Joad* were played. Also performed, however, was every song from *Tunnel of Love* and the first significant revisiting of material

from Bruce's two 1992 albums, *Human Touch* and *Lucky Town*. Fans had pined for another solo-piano reading of "Real World" since its breathtaking debut at the Christic Institute benefit shows in 1990, and sure enough, it came out at the second rehearsal show in Asbury Park and remained a frequent visitor to the set throughout the tour. A version of "My Beautiful Reward," played on the pump organ, served as a thematic link back to the 1992 tour, when the same song was played at the end of the show.

A large portion of the set each night was performed on acoustic guitar, but Bruce brought a passel of extra tools with him on the road. A custom-made stomp board was used for a new, almost undecipherable arrangement of "Reason to Believe," with Bruce singing into a distorted "bullet-microphone," the type usually used for harmonicas. A Gretsch electric guitar was used on "Part Man, Part Monkey" as well as "State Trooper." The grand piano was used often, with highlights ranging from "Backstreets" to "Mary's Place."

As the tour progressed, several additional instruments made their way on stage. An electric piano debuted on the first leg of the tour, which was used on songs that required a slightly different mood than the grand piano provided. As the tour progressed, a banjo would appear for "I'm on Fire," a dobro for "Johnny 99," an autoharp for "The New Timer," and on the final leg of the tour, a ukulele—reportedly, the instrument was a gift from Eddie Vedder. A pump organ that was first used to open the show was also played by Bruce for the ethereal "Dream Baby Dream," a song originally by the 70s synth-punk band Suicide. "Dream Baby Dream," which literally stunned the crowd upon its debut in Chicago in May to close the show, would remain the closing number for the balance of the tour.

Frequently, Bruce would comment to the crowd that at each show he would, "try to pull something different out of the box," and his enthusiasm for trying new things led to 140 different songs being played on the tour. His piano skills notably improved as the tour went on, but even on the occasions

when the right chords eluded him, he maintained a self-deprecating humor about the situation, noting that "any mistakes are intentional." His marked accessibility to fans, particularly before the concerts, allowed fans to cross many things off their wish-lists as requests were frequently acknowledged and granted.

Glenn Radecki is a Springsteen writer, researcher and statistician. He is a contributing writer for "Backstreets Magazine" and "Brucespringsteen.net." He will gladly take credit for giving Bruce the suggestion that he use a horn section on the 2012-13 world tour.

BRUCE SPRINGSTEEN TRIBUTE 2007

Bruce surprises the crowd at Carnegie Hall by performing at the Music for Youth Benefit

When I got the call to shoot this concert, I was excited—I was going to have the opportunity to hear other musicians and fans sing Bruce's songs. Steve Earle, Jesse Malin, The Hold Steady, Patti Smith, Pete Yorn, Odetta, and others did not disappoint. The biggest thrill for everyone was that Bruce showed up at the end and sang "The Promised Land" and "Rosalita."

"The Hold Steady played a Bruce tribute at Carnegie Hall in 2007. We did "Atlantic City," but at the end of the night, Bruce brought all the artists on stage and asked if anyone knew the words to "Rosalita." Saying "yes" was an understatement. I knew the words to the song by heart since the eighth grade. I got to sing the first verse and some of the ending, including the whole "Papa says he knows that you don't have any money,"—it gives me chills just thinking about it. It was a huge highlight in my time in music, and a memory I'll always treasure."
~ Craig Finn, singer/songwriter
The Hold Steady

"Talk about a dream; try to make it real." One of my favorite things about Bruce Springsteen is how he embodies the idea of being able to will (through perseverance, hard work, good luck) a vision into reality. Not only does he rejoice in that triumph, but he's also able to plumb the depressing depths and empathize with those who have failed (through weakness, adverse circumstances, bad luck) to do so. Playing with Bruce is eye-opening. In a split second you can catch a veiled glimpse of all the effort that goes into appearing so effortless, and all the authority that it commands."

~ Adam Garbinski, singer/songwriter
Adam & Dave's Bloodline

"Sometimes meeting your heroes can turn you off to their music. Meeting Bruce makes you respect him even more. The art and the artist."

~ Jesse Malin
singer/songwriter

TODAY SHOW

September 28, 2007—Rockefeller Plaza, NYC before the "Magic" Tour

This was Bruce and the Band's first time playing in Rockefeller Plaza and he was on fire! He sound checked five songs: "The Promised Land," "Radio Nowhere," "Livin' in the Future," "My Hometown," and "Long Walk Home." At 8 a.m., he came back and sang "The Promised Land." Then at 8:30 a.m., it was SHOWTIME—live on TV and he performed "The Promised Land," "Radio Nowhere," "Livin' in the Future," "My Hometown," and a killer version of "Night." When the TV show was over, we knew not to leave … he wasn't done. I was in the photo pen talking to another photographer and we were both hoping he'd sing "Last to Die," and at 9:30 a.m., Bruce came back and we heard the first chords. YES! When we began to sing along, Bruce looked confused and we later realized it was probably because we weren't supposed to know the words since the album hadn't released yet.

Bruce with Matt Lauer

LIGHT OF DAY

by Chris Rotolo

January 2012—Light of Day

Hunched over at the foot of Asbury Park's storied Paramount Theatre Stage, while jockeying for position with my fellow photojournalists, it was difficult not to focus on the muscle aches induced by a long weekend of live coverage. But it was well worth it when you attained that perfect angle, where the amber fluorescence of the house lighting catches a collection of dust particles wafting through the ether, casting an angelic glow about the featured artist's celebrated profile.

Behind me, the gentle residents of the front row hissed and shuffled in their seats, cursing my name with every breath—their worst fears realized—as some obnoxious, camera-toting cretin obstructed their view of this concert hall's grandiose stage. Hovering about this wonderful gathering of musicians, artists, and fans who came together to combat the devastating ailment of Parkinson's disease, was an air of tension and displeasure that didn't belong at an altruistic venture of this magnitude. The 12th Annual Light of Day Festival warranted better, the event's founder Bob Benjamin deserved more, and in the moments that followed, all of the negativity would melt into that aforementioned ether, fading away into oblivion with those clouds of dust, revealing to this penman the true healing powers of music.

As Joe Grushecky and the House Rockers gave way to the lavish crimson curtain dressed in gold and draped upon the venue's lauded planks, an unsuspecting congregate spoke casually of the sights and sounds that surrounded this wondrous weekend featuring such Garden State favorites of the old school and new guard as Southside Johnny, John Eddie, J.T. Bowen, Nicky Addeo, Robert Gordon, No Wine For Kittens, Tara Elliott, Quincy Mumford, Emily Grove, Outside The Box, Lost In Society, The Obvious, and many more. However, the best was yet to come.

With no introduction or adieu, the lights gave way to shade and the curtain ascended revealing the silhouette of a cowboy coated in plaid and denim with an acoustic six string slung over his shoulder. Asbury Park's favorite son, Bruce Springsteen, had arrived under the cover of darkness, but would invite us all to bask in the light of day.

The Boss would serenade the 1600-person assemblage for more than three hours, opening with "Incident On 57th Street," and concluding with an acoustic rendition of "Thunder Road." However, what's staggering to look back upon was not the music he chose to play, but what that music represented, how this showman was able to leap into the essence of those in attendance and replace any illness or ill will they may have had for 180 minutes and change.

Springsteen's offering altered moods, states of mind, and acted as a much needed escape for patrons with various afflictions, embodying the idea at the core of "Light of Day." The beloved Asbury bluesman has fought ailments and animosity with the influence of his artistic endeavors, displaying his grasp on the hearts and minds of generations of music enthusiasts. It was the closest thing to immortality any living being could ever hope to own, and I felt fortunate to have lived a chapter of his everlasting saga.

__Chris Rotolo__ is the Founder and Editor In Chief of "Speak Into My Good Eye," an online music news outlet centered in and focused on the storied Asbury Park, NJ music scene. Rotolo is currently an Assistant Editor in the "Asbury Park Press" Sports Department.

Bob Benjamin, Founder of Light of Day

I first saw Bruce Springsteen in February 1977, in Buffalo, where I was attending college. I met him briefly in Toronto later in the same month. In May of 1978, Bruce started his legendary Darkness on the Edge of Town Tour in Buffalo, and since it was summer break, I made sure I stayed to catch the show. At that time, the only hotel in Buffalo that bands would stay in was the Statler Hilton, so I decided to hang around the hotel until I met Bruce. Thirty-four years later I found myself on stage next to Bruce at the Paramount Theatre in Asbury Park at the 12th annual Light of Day concert. Light of Day is a series of shows I founded to fight Parkinson's disease. Bruce started reminiscing about our meeting in Buffalo. The dialogue took a comedic turn as you can see below:

Bruce: I met Bobby many, many years ago, I don't ...
Bob: Buffalo, New York ... 1978.
Bruce: Buffalo, New York in 1978?
Bob: It was opening day of the Darkness tour.
Bruce: It was opening day of the Darkness tour? What were you doing up there?
Bob: I was in college up there.
Bruce: You were in college ... right! And how did we end up meeting?
Bob: I was at the hotel. I was being a stalker.
Crowd breaks in loud applause and laughter.
Bruce: Stalkers, unite!
Bruce: When he was at the hotel being a stalker ... somehow we ended up sitting down at a table ...
Bob: You were starting to do merchandising for the first time.
Bruce: Right.
Bob: You were asking me what the fans wanted.
Bruce: Right! I had no clue! What do you put on a t-shirt? Only thing I remember thinking is ... Who's this kid? Anyway, he has stalked me, well let me see . . . 30 some years. He's given stalking a good name, that's all I can say. This is for you Bobby.

And Bruce launched into a heart-wrenching solo acoustic, sing-a-long version of "Thunder Road." There were not many dry eyes in the audience or onstage.

Bruce has now performed at nine of thirteen Light of Day shows. He has been incredibly gracious in welcoming me to the stage. Even though he knows I can't sing, he shares a mic with me. Thank you, Bruce, for being so gracious, for the music and for the inspiration.

Fans of the New Jersey Shore music scene know Bob Benjamin for his annual Light of Day concerts that raise money for research to cure Parkinson's disease and provide funds for the patient support programs of the ALS Association.

Joe D'Urso, Light of Day Board of Directors

Having a chance to share the stage with Bruce, well if someone would have told me when I was 15 that was going to ever happen, I would have thought them crazy. If someone would have told me that at 23-years-old, I would have said the same. But right around 24, I picked up a guitar, and with a few chords that I taught myself, plus years' worth of words scribbled in notebooks, I started making noise. Gradually it turned into music and with my band, Stone Caravan, I began putting out records in 1991 and I started going on tour in Europe in 1993. As of 2013, we have released 13 records and I have had the great fortune of performing in 24 countries. But to this day, one of my greatest joys is seeing Bruce "serenade" my music manager and dear friend, Bob Benjamin. It has brought tears to my eyes, as well as to the eyes of many folks who have been in theater, when we all sing "Thunder Road" as one voice.

Bruce with singer/songwriter Joe D'Urso

Bob and I, along with Tony Pallagrosi, Jean Mikle and a handful of other great Light of Day volunteers, have worked tirelessly to raise funds and awareness to find a cure for Parkinson's disease and to help our friend, Bob, and others, hopefully lead happier and healthier lives. Over the past 13 years, Bruce has been a tremendous friend to both Bob and Light of Day. I believe he has joined Joe Grushecky & The Houserockers on stage nine out of the 13 years, which tells you a lot about the strength of his ties to old friends and the Jersey Shore community. He is a special person, to say the least.

I've been a Bruce fan since I was 15-years-old when I heard his music coming from my sister's bedroom. Then I saw the film No Nukes, and I said, "Who the hell is this guy?" I started going to see Bruce and the E Streeters, along with Bob Seger, John Mellencamp and The Grateful Dead, and my love affair with music knew no equal in my life. After college I worked for almost ten years for Bruce's booking agents, Barry Bell and Frank Barsalona, which gave me the chance to work on four Bruce tours from 1988 to 1996. My time at Premier Talent working on Bruce's tours (and with many other great artists) was my graduate school and my doctorate all wrapped up in one. What a great place to observe, learn and see how the great ones, both in business and in music, did it right.

One night, at one of Bruce's Light of Day appearances, we were backstage before the show. It was right after the Vote for Change Tour and John Kerry had just lost the presidential election. Many of us were still licking our wounds and I thanked Bruce for being at Light of Day once again, and for being part of the direct lineage musician/activists like Woody Guthrie, Pete Seeger, and others who truly cared and put it on the line; even though they were fully aware that a backlash could occur. Bruce put down his drink and gave me a hug. Class act, great songwriter. Best rocker ever.

"It's like playing ball with Mickey Mantle."
~ Joe Grushecky
    singer/songwriter

"Playing with Bruce, for me, is always a great learning experience. I always come away a better musician every single time I play with him and learn his songs. It's loads of fun like an amusement ride—you don't want to get off. He always makes me laugh. As a drummer, never take your eyes off of him, cause he has a lot of cues to follow and they're different every night. Expect the unexpected. He doesn't even know what he's going to do. That's what makes it so much fun to play with him and the Patrón Tequila, which we both love."
~ Jeff "Joffo" Simmons
    drummer with Joe Grushecky
    and the Houserockers

"Bruce and I met in the 70's and our first meeting was immediately friendly. I've joined him on stage numerous times and it has always been fun, whether at The Stone Pony, or singing with him in front of 125,000 people in Holland. His venue sizes are just a little bit larger than mine! He is always very inviting and generous; you are his equal. Of course, you have to be able to hold your own, but he invites you in to enjoy what he is enjoying. I remember very vividly the Asbury Park Christmas shows just after 9/11. It was a painful time to say the very least. He called and asked me to be part of it and I sang my "New York Skyline" along with a few other songs for those nights. I was honored that he asked. He is a consistently big-hearted person."

      ~ Garland Jeffreys
         singer/songwriter

"Playing on stage with Bruce is like standing next to a volcano exploding into space. His power comes from a real place of fire and compassion. It's a wild ride and worth every minute of it."

      ~ Willie Nile
         singer/songwriter

"I loved going to the Light of Day shows in Asbury Park. There is always a real buzz about the place. Everyone is there to have a fun time, hear some great music and raise money for an important cause. Being in the front row for Bruce's two-hour guest slot with Joe Grushecky in January 2012, has to be one of the, admittedly, many highlights of the over 100 Bruce Springsteen concerts I've seen since 1981. We got "blessed" with tequila, and Bruce stood in my seat during "Waiting on a Sunny Day."

~ Philip Jump
    Badlands UK

APOLLO
APOLLO
SiriusXM Presents
BRUCE SPRINGSTEEN
AND THE E STREET BAND
Celebrating 10 Yrs of SiriusXM

THE APOLLO THEATER SHOW 2012

by Kiley Armstrong

On the blustery night of March 9, 2012, the man who succeeded James Brown as the undisputed Hardest Working Man in Show Business brought his unique brand of harmony, heart, and soul to Harlem's storied Apollo Theater. Following a profoundly punctuated two-year pause, Bruce Springsteen took the stage with the E Street Band in a prelude to their Wrecking Ball Tour.

"If you played in a bar on the central Jersey shore in the '60s and '70s, you played soul music," said Springsteen. "And we knew that way off, in some never-never land of rhythm and blues, there was a place called the Apollo. It was the home of the gods and the true temple of soul."

For his own debut at the hallowed hall, Springsteen brought not only the core members of the E Street Band, but a beefy brass pack, and other talented musicians to the jam-packed stage of the jewel-box beautiful, neo-classical theater. And they, in turn, were accompanied by another larger-than-life aura. The June 2011 passing of Big Man Clarence Clemons left a crater in the band and the E Street Nation. Looking reflective as they quietly entered the stage one by one, the musicians touched the Tree of Hope, a talisman to generations of Apollo performers.

Embracing the Apollo's history as a showplace for comedians as well as musicians, Springsteen got the ball rolling with tongue-in-cheek wit, poking fun at his larger-than-life reputation. Bathed in the spotlight on an otherwise darkened stage, he maintained a poker face as he roundly intoned a third-person introduction of a young man who was "Born in the U.S.A." and who, "arrived here tonight in his pink Cadillac. Winner of the Academy Award, he brought you such great hits as "Dancing in the Dark," "Born to Run," and "Hungry Heart." I'm talking about Mister Badlands ... the Jersey Devil Himself. The Hardest Working White Man in Show Business."

The audience was instantly at his mercy, locked into his radar as he powered into the setlist with his vein-popping intensity, igniting a fervent call to action with, "We Take Care of Our Own," followed by the defiantly delivered "Wrecking Ball" title track.

Springsteen looked ecstatic to be hitting the road with E Street once again. He raged as they sent the robber barons straight to Hell, spat in the face of these "Badlands" and, "... put a whoop-ass on the recession." He hosted a house party and a revival meeting with "Preacher Cindy" and washed away sorrow with a flood of communal joy.

And, as the crowd roared for more, he wove touching interludes into the musical mosaic. "We're glad to be here again. We've missed you," he told the audience. The moment fulfilled a promise made in November 2009, in Buffalo, N.Y., when he said, "Goodbye for a very little while. We love you! We'll be seeing you!"

Saying the fans were glad to see them again, too, would be a massive understatement. Clarence's nephew, Jake Clemons, gazed heavenward and kept the beat with his palm tapping over his heart. It was the perfect symbolism as he was warmly welcomed into the fold, both as an emotional ambassador for the Big Man beyond and as a versatile musician in his own right, bolstered from every direction by superbly seasoned Springsteen sidekicks.

An emotional hurdle for the fans and, undoubtedly, for E Street as well, was achieved during "My City of Ruins." It was the roll call, introducing each band member. "Are we missing anybody?" Springsteen asked three times, followed by 30 seconds of cheering as the audience paid tribute to Clemons, Danny Federici and other dearly departed. "That's right. We're missing a few. But the only thing I can guarantee tonight is that if you're here and we're here, they're here!"

Springsteen, who's imagined his characters in countless occupations over the decades, turned teacher for a time—backed by soft, rhythmic humming and finger-snapping as he schooled the fans on the Apollo's great past: Geography: "We learned the exact location of funky Broadway from Wilson Pickett." History: "Change is gonna come; Sam Cooke." Math: "Ninety-nine-and-a-half won't do; Wilson again." Religion: "Aretha Franklin." Sex education: "Marvin Gaye."

"We were imparted with the wisdom of Solomon (pause for emphasis) Burke. And of course there was the poetry of Smokey Robinson." Cue the opening lyrics of what came to be known as "The Apollo Medley"—a splash of Motown dappled with a breezy, Bronx/Jersey street-corner feel. "You got a smile so bright …"

Then it was time for the finale. The ending formalized the band's new beginning. The song choice answered stricken fans who had contemplated the question: Will they, can they, ever sing "Tenth Avenue Freeze Out" again? The story of Scooter and the Big Man was now doused with hard reality. But it also was instilled with catharsis: The crowd raised its collective voice in a tearful yet joyful noise, likely heard all the way to the heavens.

They sang about changes made uptown and when the Big Man joined the band. The music halted. Sixty seconds of cheering erupted. Scooter and the Big Man—forever—busting this city in half.
> "Oh, yeah!"
> "Oh, yeah!"
> "Oh, yeah!"
> "It's alright."

Kiley Armstrong, *a native of Plattsmouth, Nebraska, got hooked on the music culture as a kid when her dad took her and her best friend, Susan, to stake out the Dave Clark Five's middle-of-the-night airport arrival. She later became a writer and editor in New York. She'd like to thank the Bronx's best apostle, Mike Safferstein, for introducing her to the E Street Nation. She would have married him anyway, but it pushed his "plus" column way over the top.*

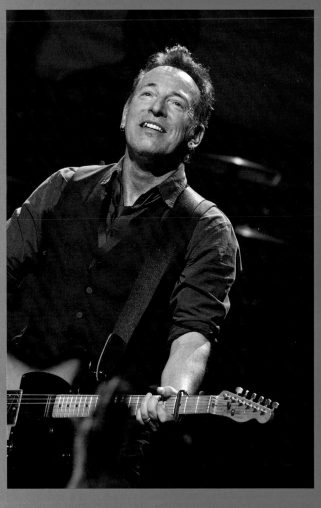

March 9, 2012, the "unofficial" start to the Wrecking Ball Tour at the legendary Apollo Theater in Harlem.

The show was broadcast on Sirius Satellite Radio (which also broadcasts E Street Radio) as part of their 10th Anniversary celebration. The concert was also my first show without Clarence Clemons. What would it be like? Clarence's nephew, Jake, was the new saxophone player, along with Eddie Manion—a musician I have known and admired since the first time I saw him in 1977. How would Jake handle it? He had tough shoes to fill. When the night was done, he filled them perfectly.

It was no secret to my long time Bruce friends that I wasn't a fan of his new CD, Wrecking Ball, but after tonight's show, my feelings changed. The band was tight, Bruce's voice sounded the way I loved it most—reminiscent of the late 70s and early 80s when I first heard him. Tonight he was ON FIRE— all over the stage, and even went up into the balcony. My eyes welled with tears hearing Jake play so beautifully and hearing the E Street Band the way I remember them, as the BEST band in the history of Rock and Roll.

LITTLE KIDS ROCK

October 16, 2012—Little Kids Rock Charity Event at the Hammerstein Ballroom in NYC

The Right to Rock Celebration, where Steven Van Zandt was honored as "Big Man of the Year" by the charity, Little Kids Rock, was a celebration of the man and his music by many of his friends. Bruce presented Little Steven with the award, and the night was just amazing. Dion, Gary "U.S." Bonds, Kris Allen, Tom Morello, Southside Johnny, Darlene Love, Jesse Malin, Bernie Williams, Ruben Blades, and the amazing talented kids from Little Kids Rock, were all there. Everyone sang a different Little Steven song and the Celebration raised over $800,000 to keep music in schools. It's been a long time since I have been so excited to shoot a show. This night was flawless.

Bruce presented Little Steven with the "Big Man of the Year Award" saying, "There's been no better bandmate, or wingman, or friend to me than Steve Van Zandt."

Seeing him present Little Steven with a beautiful, framed photo of their friend and bandmate, Clarence Clemons, was very emotional.

Bruce shared the stage with Little Steven and Southside Johnny, singing "It's Been a Long Time." And it had been a long time since I saw these three wonderful musicians sharing the stage. As I sat in the balcony next to Debbie Mayer, my good friend of 26 years, it made the moment even more special.

"Raise a Glass to the Comrades We Lost" hit home, as some of the musicians we grew up with from our Jersey Shore days were no longer here. Looking around, there were so many old friends in attendance, making the song even more poignant. John Cavanaugh, a Jersey Shore photographer, was also in the balcony. Usually when we are shooting concerts, we are crammed in with very little space or time to shoot. However, this night, for the first time in over twenty years, John and I had time not only to shoot, but to catch up. Every word in the song rang true.

With Kris Allen, winner of the eighth season of American Idol.

Tom Morello

"It's always a joy and honor to share the stage with Bruce Springsteen. He's as American as apple pie and just as sweet as pie too! He championed my induction into the Rock & Roll Hall of Fame. He's truly a fine, fine boy!"
    ~ Darlene Love, singer/actress

WRECKING BALL TOUR 2012

by Holly Cara Price

The Wrecking Ball Tour was groundbreaking in many ways for Bruce Springsteen. The album, released in March, 2012, was his first since 2009's *Working on a Dream*. This was also the first album without the mighty presence of Clarence Clemons by Bruce's side (Clemons, who died in the summer of 2011, appeared on only two songs on the record). *Wrecking Ball* is all about life and death, and how we should be taking care of each other in between, as noted with the album's opening jubilant cry, "We Take Care of Our Own." *Wrecking Ball* closed with the eerily beautiful "We Are Alive," in which Bruce celebrated ghosts from the past, including those who now inhabit his career—not just Clarence in 2011, but also Danny Federici, the longest running member of the E Street Band, who died in 2008.

It was anyone's guess how this would translate onstage; how Bruce would acknowledge the gaping loss of his onstage foil for the past 39 years. And he did not disappoint. He augmented the E Street Band with a full horn section (Jake Clemons, Ed Manion, Clark Gayton, Curt Ramm, and Barry Danielian), and a gospel choir (Cindy Mizelle, Curtis King, Michelle Moore), a percussionist (Everett Bradley), and the two musicians who had been a part of the albums and live show for the past several years, Soozie Tyrell on violin and guitar, and Charlie Giordano on organ, keyboards, and accordion. All of which translated to seventeen people onstage, making a joyful noise.

Far from playing just his new music and conducting this tour like business as usual, Bruce Springsteen confronted the changing landscape of the E Street Band head on, making it strikingly different from all other tours that have gone before. It resembles, in fact, a New Orleans jazz funeral which begins with slow hymns and the family walking to the cemetery. After the burial takes place and the final goodbyes are said, there is a marked change of tone amongst the mourners. The music takes a 180-degree turn from deep sadness to celebrating the life of the one who has left us, to dancing, to joy, to purifying catharsis. That's the closest I can come to describing the arc of this show.

As Springsteen tours are wont to do, this one has morphed and changed and grown with new song patterns and arrangements. As of this writing, the tour has traveled from arenas and stadiums in the U.S. to Europe and back again.

There will be more twists and turns and changes ahead. But the core of the show has always centered on the album's message of life and death, and how we care for each other in between. Bruce has never been more charged with the power and glory of his vision. He leaps and jumps and runs all over not just the stage, but the venue itself. He gazes deep into the eyes of fans, he grasps their hands. In arenas, he throws himself literally on top of the crowd and trusts them to hold him up, and carry him back to the stage. Yes, it's a concert, but it's also a medicine show in the traditional sense, bringing us the miracle cure of rock and soul music.

Holly Cara Price is a social media consultant and archival researcher. She writes about television, music, and books for The Huffington Post and delights in examining the slings and arrows of outrageous pop culture.

May 2, 2012 — Prudential Center, Newark, NJ
The final show of the first leg of the U.S. tour

I went with my friend Michael and our seats were waaaaaayyyy up high, higher than I have been in over 30 years. The sound was excellent and the song choices were fantastic. "Bishop Danced" hasn't been played since sometime in the 70's and then it was "It's Hard to Be a Saint in the City." There were a few signs being held up by fans for songs by Levon Helm, who had recently passed away, and Bruce and the band sang "The Weight." A few of my favorites of the night were "No Surrender," "Candy's Room" (a song I can listen to over and over), and "Talk to Me." I am still amazed every time I see Bruce jump into the audience to be carried back to the stage. I shoot MANY concerts each year and there are only a handful of musicians who get that close to their audience. It's one of the many things that make a Bruce Springsteen concert so amazing and special.

Bruce high-fiving his mother, Adele Springsteen, as he runs through the audience. Seeing his mother at shows has ALWAYS brought super loud cheers from the audience. She is loved by so many people. When I see her in the audience, I think how very fortunate Bruce is to have her there to see him doing the one thing he was put on this earth to do— perform. A feeling of happiness and sadness came over me, and my one regret has been that I never brought my mom to one of his concerts. She always wanted to go, but I thought it would have been too loud or too long. The look on both of their faces is something that is just so special. Seeing how proud and happy she is–you can't help but smile. There is nothing like making your mom proud and happy.

October 31, 2012—Rochester, NY

I would call this the show that almost wasn't. I had booked a plane ticket to arrive a few days before the concert, scheduled for October 30th, but then the unthinkable happened—Hurricane Sandy hit New Jersey, New York City, and so many other places, devastating the region. It was probably the worst storm we had ever seen in this area. My flight was canceled, so I booked the train and bus for Tuesday, just in case. Either would get me to Rochester with enough time to check into my hotel and get to the arena.

All day Monday, I was glued to my computer. When were they going to announce if the show was canceled or postponed? Friends were emailing back and forth all day. Finally, I received an e-mail and then a call—no show tomorrow night … it's now on Wednesday, Halloween. I called and changed my hotel room to the next night and began worrying if Greyhound or Amtrak would cancel too. My friend Mitch sent a storm photo of a boat on the train tracks, so I was almost sure Amtrak wouldn't be running. After being on hold with both the train and bus companies, I found out both were canceled. Well

… it looked like Rochester wouldn't be happening. Major stress set in. Rochester was an important show for me—I was going back to where it all began, almost 32 years ago. I posted a message on one of the Bruce groups on Facebook, and my e-mail flooded. Dozens of people in the group, many of whom I've never met, were determined to get me to Rochester. All of them had to go very far out of their way, and I didn't want to inconvenience anyone. Three, in particular, would not take no for an answer, even when I said it wasn't meant to be. My three angels Natalie Markova, Kathryn Hanson, and Janice Arlow Danckwerth came to my rescue, with Kathryn driving two hours out of her way to pick me up, and then another hour to get Janice. (Natalie left the Jersey Shore at 3:00 a.m. and met us in Rochester.) We pulled in about 4:30 p.m., and just as we turned the corner to go to the hotel, Janice yelled, "There's Bruce! Get out of the car!" I did, and walked to where he was standing, smiling and signing autographs. The man in front of me had Bruce's signature tattooed on his arm.

At 8:14 pm, Bruce and the band took the stage and opened with "Jersey Devil." After a dozen or so songs, it seemed as if his heart wasn't quite in it as usual. Who could blame him? He's a Jersey Shore guy, and Hurricane Sandy had ripped through his beloved state and county, destroying so much. I am sure his mind wasn't totally on performing, as much as mine wasn't totally on being in Rochester. But, as they say, "The show must go on."

As I stood a few sections away from the stage, I looked around the audience and realized even though I was in the same arena, and almost in the same seat I was in back in 1980, the audience had changed. We had all grown up, looked older, and almost everyone was wearing a wedding ring. There were kids with their parents, which I always loved to see. I met a nine-year-old, and this was her twelfth show.

When the first chords of "Cover Me" started, I went back decades in my mind. When Bruce sang about the rain, the snow, and the crazy wind blowing, I actually got a little nervous, and thought about what happened 32 years ago when I left this arena to go back to the college campus and our car slid into a snow bank. Did Bruce know something about the weather outside that I didn't know? Thankfully, NO! A total of 26 songs filled the night and the audience was on their feet for the whole concert.

The band was so tight; the horns were just amazing. Jake Clemons continued to impress everyone and is as loved as his Uncle Clarence. Bruce's voice was spectacular—just as great as when I heard him for the very first time.

Was it wrong for a 50-year-old woman to say a 63-year-old man was "cute?" Well, Bruce Springsteen looked so cute tonight. It was hard to believe that he is 63 when I watched him live on stage. He was all over the place—jumping on the piano, running through the audience and crowd surfing back to the stage, dancing with girls during "Dancing in the Dark," and having a young boy share his microphone during "Waiting on a Sunny Day." During "Land of Hope and Dreams," he talks a lot about trains. This train has been so much fun. My faith was rewarded and my dreams were never thwarted.

Just like he did 32 years ago and every tour in between, he didn't disappoint. I had so many dreams back then—dreams I never thought would ever become a reality, and Bruce Springsteen played a huge part in those dreams becoming my life. Bruce Springsteen and the E Street Band continue to be the best Rock and Roll band on the planet.

Wrecking Ball Tour, Rochester 2012
By Kathleen Smith, who danced on stage with Bruce 34 years ago

In 1978, I watched from the front row at St. Bonaventure University's Reilly Center as Bruce Springsteen tore through a nearly four-hour show. He jumped on speakers, played piano with his feet, ran the length of the stage repeatedly, and fed off the energy of 5,000 enthusiastic fans. He was the most charismatic performer I had ever seen, and a brief moment onstage with him near the end of the show undoubtedly was the highlight of my college experience. Thirty-four years later, my 17-year-old daughter, Kelly, and I attended his show in Rochester, New York. This was Kelly's second Bruce show, and she steadfastly insisted on trying to get into the "pit" by the front of the stage. Because I was bringing her younger sister for the first time, I bought regular arena seats and wished her good luck.

Many, many things contributed to what happened next to Kelly—she got a good number in the lottery; a group of veteran "pit" fans took her under their wing and supported her, literally and figuratively, in her dream to get onstage; and of course, Bruce saw and reacted to her sign.

When I saw her join him onstage for the dance, I realized with a surreal sense of déjà vu that she was about to experience the exact same magic that I had so many years before. Bruce's first question to Kelly was, "Is your mom here?" She pointed me out in the audience and waved.

Watching her, I was transported back in time to 1978, when I was a carefree 19-year-old to whom the redemptive power of Rock 'n' Roll was all that really mattered. It was both amazing and reassuring to me that, 34 years later, Bruce Springsteen still felt and shared that magic each and every time he performed. Thank you, Bruce.

Kelly Smith, age 17, on Dancing with Bruce

I was raised a Springsteen fan. One of my earliest memories was dancing in our living room to "Born in the U.S.A.," playing air guitar, and wearing the signature red bandanna around my head. I grew to learn and love so much of Bruce's music, influenced by my amazing mom. She took me to my first show when I was a freshman in high school—it was the first

concert I'd ever been to. Bruce's stage presence, energy, and stamina set the bar for all my future concert experiences. It's safe to say that none I've been to since have measured up to it.

Except, of course, my most recent Springsteen concert. I was lucky enough to get into the pit, and even though I was nervous to be by myself, I quickly learned that Bruce fans are the most amazing people on earth—they made me feel safe and welcome.

Six hours after I left school to get my wristband, the show started. Bruce worked his way through a somber, yet searing, set; Hurricane Sandy weighing heavily on everyone's mind. A couple of times he seemed to point or smile at me—and I was ready to die happy. He came back for his encore and the nice lady in front of me let me move closer, and I was right against the stage.

My sign read, "34 years ago my mom danced with you onstage—Can I?" He caught sight of it during "Thunder Road," and I saw him smile. During "Born to Run" he knelt in front of me and, as I strummed his guitar, he mouthed something that I couldn't understand. Finally, he launched into "Dancing in the Dark." I had this surreal sense the whole time, I couldn't even sing the lyrics. Steven gestured at me at one point, almost like he was saying, "Keep singing!" The band started into the instrumental and Bruce made his way over to me.

He smiled at me and I handed him my sign. He held it up as I clambered over the barrier, waited for a nod from the security guard, then climbed onstage. It all happened so fast—I didn't feel nervous at all. We started dancing, and he asked me if my mom was here. I pointed to her—I immediately spotted her and my sisters screaming and waving from their seats and said, "She's your biggest fan!" He smiled and told me I was sweet. He spun me a couple times, knelt down, and even kissed my hand. I went back to my seat shaking, with a huge grin on my face.

I had allowed myself to imagine getting pulled up onstage many times growing up, but I had never really believed it would happen. There was so much I wanted to say to him, so many things I had planned. In the end, though, I didn't say much. And I'm glad it was that way. Just getting to dance with Bruce was more than enough.

Try to find another 63-year-old who can swing a guitar like Bruce or do any of the acrobatics he does on stage night after night.

Here I am back in Rochester, NY, where it all began. A few original "E Streeters" were no longer with us, but there were several new additions. My excitement was almost as high as it was 32 years ago. The music was just as great, the band was just as great. This time, I sat among strangers with my friends several rows behind me, but everyone was so friendly, it didn't matter. That's what a Bruce Springsteen concert is like— you can go by yourself, but you are never alone. The music brings people together.

Thirty-two years ago, if someone told me I would be where I am today in my career, I would have laughed and said. "That will never happen." I discovered photography when I was very young, but picked up my first SLR camera when I was a teenager. Shortly after, I saw Bruce for the first time. His music brought me to another world ... actually, another planet.

Photography and Bruce Springsteen helped me through many rough times in my life—times I may not have made it through otherwise. I'd listen to his songs while dreaming about a better life and when he sang "Born to Run," I thought he knew how I was feeling. I couldn't wait to get to that place where I really wanted to be, where I felt like I belonged—and back then, it was the Jersey Shore. I never thought it would happen. I moved around a lot in my career, always trying for something better, even though I wasn't qualified for many of the staff jobs I wanted.

I always thought Bruce sang "Badlands" for me too. I had a dream, but wondered if it would it ever become real. Through many sleepless nights, I worried I was going to be stuck in towns I hated, working at newspapers where I didn't want to be. In the early days, I went to Bruce's concerts, many times alone, and saw thousands of people just like me. They got it. The music spoke to them too. And at every show, I met new friends, many who are still in my life today.

If you have a dream, follow it. If you have a passion, never quit. If it is in your heart, you will make it a reality. If people try to break you down, keep dreaming and pushing to make that dream a reality. Hold on tight to your dreams. I am living proof that dreams *do* come true.

—Debra L. Rothenberg, October 2013

ACKNOWLEDGEMENTS

Since "discovering" Bruce's music at age 16, I have met many wonderful people on this journey whom I'd like to thank: Stan Goldstein, the Springsteen historian at the NJ Shore and our driver to many shows through the sun and the snow; Billy Smith, Stephen Bumball, Jean Mikle, Bob Benjamin and Tony Pallagrosi for keeping Asbury Park alive when outsiders thought it was dead; The Stone Pony in Asbury Park, NJ—all the past and present employees; Debbie DeLisa and the Wonder Bar; Kathy Powers; Doreen Wood; Pam Ross; Bob Spadaro; Deborah Mayer; Brian Gaskill; Linda Thebold; Carol Gerber; Matt Stragazzi; Maureen Kueny; Kathryn Hanson and Janice Arlow Danckwerth for getting me to Rochester after Superstorm Sandy in 2012; Jeff Malc for cutting school with me and driving down the shore for my first visit to Asbury Park, and for being my model and posing in all the same spots I saw photos of Bruce; Mike Lipack; Jo Barefoot; Mark Bonifacio and everyone at the NY Daily News; Lori Smith; Natalie Markova; Jackie Pollack; Laura Hoey; Lynn Goldsmith; Jayne Doniger; Philip and Steven Jump; Kevin McClave; Cliff Librescu; Marty Venturo, for staying with me as I printed all night; Marti Gelfand for the 14th row ticket in 1981; Julie Dermansky (for the title) and all the Photo Women; Greg and Marilyn Weber, Amy Cavanaugh, Adam Dietz and everyone from RMAS and BruceLoops; Kenny Napalo; Michael Lentz; Robin Schaffer; Donna Marino; David Rosen; Rene Van Diemen; Rocco Coviello; Guy Aceto; Lewis Bloom; Paul Zimmerman; Piero Ribelli; John Cavanaugh; Ken Babolcsay; Larry Busacca—for noticing me behind him at a concert when I was 17 and offering to switch spots because he was taller; Gary Gershoff for making sure I got home after shooting the last show on the Rising Tour; Charles R. Cross, Erik Flanagan and Chris Phillips at Backstreets Magazine; Candy and David Cohen (thanks for the burger when I was shooting for 14 hours); Laura Hughes; my angels Maura Brown and Maxine Backus for lovingly caring for my mom in the final years before she passed away.

My writers: Gary Wien, Holly Cara Price, Kiley Armstrong, Stan Goldstein, Matty Karas, Glenn Radecki, Caryn Rose, Lisa Iannucci, Chris Rotolo, Bob Makin, Bill Daverne, Joe D'Urso, Bob Benjamin, Kathy Smith and Kelly Smith.

Mitch Wojnarowicz, for taking a chance and hiring me at my first newspaper job, and for teaching me so much about great photography.

My publisher at Turn the Page Publishing, Roseann Lentin who is more than a publisher—she is a great friend, and Robin McGeever for all the great art direction, and Trace Hull for the cover design.

Lois Brunda—my high school friend who is back in my life. Countless days when we were 16, 17, and 18, holed up in your basement listening to nothing but Bruce at a time when it seemed we were the only two in our class who "got" him.

John Heyn—the high school teacher who is now a great friend, who changed my life in the summer of 1978. If not for John, I would never have discovered Bruce's music and the New Jersey Shore—the only place I ever felt truly at home, with people just like me. I am so thankful that after many years, we have reconnected and that his family—wife Cathy and daughters Kelly and Kate, are in my life and are friends.

Bruce Springsteen and the E Street Band—for great music, the BEST live shows, and for being a great focus for my cameras for the past 30 plus years. You have helped me perfect my craft and because of you, I did learn more from a three-minute record, than I ever did in school.

My sweet, wonderful, gorgeous husband, Philip Carvalho, who has given me so much love and support in everything I do. For letting me be silly and crazy, for insisting on carrying my cameras and dragging me to shows when I thought the fire blew out, only for it to ignite again when I saw Bruce, and for naming our cat "Frankie," after one of Bruce's songs, and choosing "Happy" as our wedding song. I love you, baby.

My family—my heroes—my parents Marvin and Janet, and brothers Randy, Craig, and Stu, and sisters-in-law Susan, Diane, and Talya for enduring years of hearing about nothing else but Bruce and photography. My nieces and nephews—Elana, Dania, Jake, Dylan, Lauren, and Matthew, who have grown up on Bruce's music, and even love the old songs, and have been to his concerts.

Dedicated to my best friend—my mom, for telling me, "Never quit, never give up your dream, take it as far as you can—the sky is your limit." And for always thinking I was the one who discovered Bruce (psst...I didn't), and my dad—my heroes.

In Loving Memory of my mother, Janet D. Rothenberg- February 17, 1932—March 7, 2013. FOREVER in my heart.

A portion of the proceeds from the sale of this book will be donated to: Alzheimer's Association: www.alz.org
Parkinson's Research: www.lightofday.org
Breast Cancer Research: www.nationalbreastcancer.org